# Behavior Analysis for Lasting Change
*Fifth Edition*

# Behavior Analysis for Lasting Change
*Fifth Edition*

G. Roy Mayer
*San Diego State University*

Beth Sulzer-Azaroff
*University of Massachusetts*

Michele Wallace
*California State University, Los Angeles*

2022
Sloan Publishing
Cornwall-on-Hudson, NY 12520

Library of Congress Control Number: 2021948986

Cover photo: © Brad Holmes
Cover design: K&M Design

© 2022 by G. Roy Mayer and Beth Sulzer-Azaroff

Sloan Publishing, LLC
220 Maple Road
Cornwall-on-Hudson, NY 12520

All rights reserved. No portion of this book may be reproduced, in any form or by any means, without permission in writing from the Publisher.

Printed in the United States of America

10 9 8 7 6 5 4

ISBN 13: 978-1-59738-100-0
ISBN 10: 1-59738-100-4

# About the Authors

**G. Roy Mayer**, Ed.D., BCBA-D, is Professor Emeritus at California State University, Los Angeles, where he designed and taught a series of classes in applied behavior analysis, and obtained several grants from the United States Department of Education for training school psychologists in applied behavior analysis. He also has taught at Indiana University, where he obtained his doctorate in 1966, Southern Illinois University, and Namseoul University in South Korea. Currently he teaches part-time at San Diego State University in the Special Education Department. He is one of the founders and past president of the California Association for Behavior Analysis [who also awarded him the Outstanding Contributor to Behavior Analysis Award (1998) and Honorary Lifetime CalABA Membership (1999)], and has been a teacher, school counselor and school psychologist. His research has focused primarily on classroom management and school-wide discipline with an emphasis on prevention and reducing school vandalism, aggression, classroom disruption and issues related to school attendance. His area of professional practice has been with children having various disabilities, including autism, and in consulting with schools regarding various behavior issues. He has had numerous articles published and has written several books with Beth Sulzer-Azaroff, and four with Michele Wallace, including *Principles of Applied Behavior Analysis for Behavior Technicians and Other Practitioners* (2022), *Behavioral Consulting—Improving Client and Consultee Learning and Behavior* (2020) and *Preventing Problematic Behavior at Home, School and Work* (2022).. He also is author of *The Positive Classroom: Improving Student Learning and Behavior* (2020). In addition, he has written several practical books on behavior management in schools, including one for the California Department of Education and the Los Angeles County Schools Office.

Dr. Mayer lives in San Diego, CA. His son's family lives within ten minutes and includes three young granddaughters. All three are in college, His daughter's family are scattered in several states. She has three sons and a daughter. His granddaughter is a physical therapist. His three grandsons have all attended college. One is now in plumbing, one is a policeman, and the other is a chiropractor. He is very proud of all his children and grandchildren.

**Beth Sulzer-Azaroff**, Ph.D. Born in the midst of the great Depression, Beth Sulzer-Azaroff (ne. Beth Winer) grew up in Upper Manhattan, New York City, where she attended grade, junior high and high schools, then moved on to The City College of New York (CCNY) where she obtained bachelor's and Masters' degrees in Education. While teaching at a local elementary school and participating in the CCNY Master's program, the met Edward (Ed) Stanton Sulzer. By the time they married, Ed was enrolled in a graduate school program in psychology, at Columbia University's Teachers College, studying with Fred Keller, who schooled him in the Analysis of Behavior. The new knowledge that Ed brought home and shared seemed so promising that Beth began to apply principles of behavior analysis in her classroom teaching. The results were transformative. To the advantage of teacher and students alike, her role as teacher shifted from cajoler and disciplinarian, to shaper and dispenser of reinforcement. So, a few years later, after Ed chose to join the University of Minnesota faculty, the family (Ed, Beth, and their two young sons), Beth elected to study the analysis of behavior in greater depth, by enrolling in its doctoral program in School Psychology.

Several years later, after she completed collecting the data for her doctoral dissertation, and again was pregnant, Southern Illinois University (SIU) recruited Ed to manage its new program in "behavior modification" (i.e., behavior analysis). Shortly after their daughter was born, the SIU's Department of Educational Psychology invited her to join its faculty, which she agreed to do on a part-time basis. After accruing a series of positive student ratings and completing a number of research investigations and published reports, she agreed to undertake a full-time position in the department. That was when she and G Roy Mayer established their now-decades long professional association Meanwhile, for several years her family life continued to progress happily. In his 39th year, though, Ed was struck by and succumbed to a virulent from of cancer.

During the two-year period following Ed's death, Beth continued her successful program of teaching and research at SIU. A series of technical reports and other publications, including, the first edition of Sulzer & Mayer's *Behavior Analysis for Lasting Change* resulted. Two years later, on a Caribbean cruise, she met and just a few months later married Leonid (Lee) v. Azaroff, Professor and Director of The Institute of Materials Science at the University of Connecticut.

After the newly amalgamated family settled in Connecticut, Beth joined the Psychology Department faculty of the University of Massachusetts, Amherst. Over a 19-year period, Beth designed and taught courses in educational psychology and applied behavior analysis, conducted a series of research seminars, and obtained federal funding to support a graduate training program. Also, often in collaboration with students and colleagues, she obtained federal funding from the Office of Special Education and Rehabilitative Services (OSERS) to support programs designed to prepare doctoral candidates to participate in leadership roles in the field of developmental disabilities and management, and participated in numerous research projects (including a series of safe performance), authored and co-authored over a hundred research reports and published number of textbooks. She also assumed posts in several scientific and professional organizations, including, among others, as President of the Association for Behavior Analysis International, and of the American Psychological Association's Division 25 (Experimental Analysis of Behavior). Member and Chair of the Cambridge Center for Behavioral Studies and of the American Psychological Association's Board of Scientific Affairs; also served as Member of the National Institute of Occupational /Safety and Health research study sections. Additionally, while on sabbatical leave from the University of Massachusetts, she briefly participated as a Visiting Professor at the Western Australian Institute for Technology, in Perth, Australia.

After retiring from her full-time career, Beth and Leonid moved to Naples, Florida. Soon, she and Dwight Harshbarger partnered to form an international consulting organization, "The Browns Group." Its purpose was to teach and support organizational managers across the globe successfully to apply behavioral principles. This we accomplished in various locations including Thailand, Australia, England, Finland and Sweden. Further, Beth taught an ABA course sequence at Florida International University (where she met and admired the performance of her student, Michele Wallace (now, Dr. Michele Wallace, coauthor of this text).

From her Florida home, Beth also participated in an educational research project on distant learning. It involved comparing achievement data generated by students enrolled in on-site instruction at Florida Gulf Coast University and by a cadre of distant learners. [P.S. No differences in their superior test scores emerged.]

Meanwhile, her three offspring have grown to adulthood and established themselves in careers: David as a Professor of Neurobiology at Columbia University School of Medicine; Lenore as a Doctor or Internal Medicine, and Richard, as a packaging-design engineer at an international pharmaceutical company and father of our two bright, charming granddaughters. Also, to our delight, Leonid's niece and nephew have joined their grown daughter, her husband and grandchildren on Florida's east coast, and prior to the coved epidemic, they visited Beth regularly (and promise to do so as soon as it's again safe.)

Today, after sadly having lost her husband, Leonid, several years ago, and in her ninth decade, Beth recently elected to move to an assisted-living residence. There, she continues to read, write, exercise, and walk daily; also, to enjoy the company of many fellow seniors with fascinating stories of their own to tell.

**Michele D. Wallace**, Ph.D., BCBA-D, is a full time professor and the ABA Program Coordinator at the California State University, Los Angeles and the Research Director at the Center for Applied Behavior Analysis in California. Dr. Wallace is also Subject Matter Expert for the Behavior Analysis Certification Board and provides behavioral consultation to many agencies and school districts both within the United States and Internationally. In addition to teaching at CSULA, she has taught at the University of Nevada, Reno, The Chicago School of Psychology, and Pepperdine University. She graduated from the University of Florida in 2000 with her doctorate in the Experimental Analysis of Behavior. She has served as the Clinical Director of the Nevada Center for Severe Behavior Problems as well as the Nevada Pediatric Feeding Disorder Clinic. Dr. Wallace has served on the Board of Editors for the *Journal of Applied Behavior Analysis* and routinely serves as a reviewer for various behavioral journals. She has served on the California Association for Behavior Analysis Board in several capacities including Membership Chair 2003–2005, Newsletter Chair 2005–2007, Conference Co-chair 2001–2002 and 2006–2007, President-elect 2007, President 2008, Past-president 2009, and Professional Liaison 2012. She has been a Board Certified Behavior Analyst in the State of Florida since 1993 and a National Board Certified Behavior Analysts since 2000. Dr. Wallace has authored and co-authored books, chapters, articles and numerous presentations. Her current research interests are related to the refinement of assessment and treatment methodologies with respect to behavior problems, bridging research to practice and practice to research, and caregiver and staff training in behavior analysis.

Dr. Wallace, a breast cancer survivor, and her wife Tymerie, live in Lakewood, California with their two children (Payton and Aiden). Payton is in middle school and Aiden is in elementary school. Both are very talented and make their moms very proud.

# Brief Contents

**About the Authors**  v

**Preface**  xxv

1. Achieving Lasting Behavior Change by Applying Behavior Analysis: What Is It and How Does It Work?  1
2. Designing Effective Strategies of Change: Essential Building Blocks  21
3. Preparing a Supportive Environment for Behavior Change  34
4. Sharpening the Focus by Refining Goals and Objectives  56
5. Reinforcement: Fueling Behavior Change  83
6. Increasing Behavior by Developing and Selecting Powerful Reinforcers  102
7. Organizing for Behavior Change by Collecting Useful Data  124
8. Optimizing Client Progress by Monitoring Behavior Change: Recording, Graphing, and Analyzing Patterns of Change  151
9. Optimizing Client Progress by Analyzing the Functions of Our Interventions: Basic Experimental Designs  175
10. Setting a Foundation for Positive Change: Identifying Participant's Functional Reinforcers  201
11. Rapidly Attaining Positive Change: Implementing Reinforcement Effectively  233
12. Promoting and Supporting Group Change: Programs and Packages  261
13. Teaching New Behavior: Shaping  283
14. Teaching Complex Behaviors: Chaining, Task Analyses, and Social Skills Training  306
15. Attaining Complex Behavior by Promoting and Supporting Antecedent Control  339
16. Selecting and Applying Methods for Promoting Stimulus Control  357
17. Achieving Stimulus Control  374
18. Prompting Procedures and Instructional Programs  397
19. Teaching, Expanding and Refining Verbal Behavior  424
20. Promoting Independence: Shifting and Expanding Stimulus Control  454
21. Generalization: Expanding Stimulus Control  475
22. Maintaining Behavior: Ratio and Related Schedules of Reinforcement  502
23. Maintaining Behavior by Arranging Time Based Schedules of Reinforcement  521

24. Organizational Performance Management Systems: Supervising and Supporting Contingency Managers    546
25. Identifying Effective Interventions with Complex Research Designs    574
26. Reducing Behavior: Extinction    605
27. Preventing Challenging Behavior by Enriching the Environment    621
28. Preventing and Reducing Behavior through Differential Reinforcement    653
29. Reducing Behavior with Negative Punishment: Response Cost and Timeout    682
30. Reducing Behavior with Positive Punishment while Minimizing Coercion    709
31. Achieving Lasting Change Ethically    750

Appendix: BACB 5th Edition Task List with References to Text Pages    769
Glossary    777
References    805
Name Index    889
Subject Index    913

# Contents

About the Authors   vii
Preface   xxvii
A Note to the Reader   xxxv

**1. Achieving Lasting Behavior Change By Applying Behavior Analysis: What Is It and How Does It Work?   1**
   Introduction   2
      *The Radical Behavioral Approach*   5
   The Origin and Evolution of the Field of Applied Behavior Analysis   6
   Applied Behavior Analysis Today   8
      *Definition of ABA*   8
   The Essential Features of Applied Behavior Analysis: A Scientific, Technological and Professional Approach   9
      *ABA as a Scientific Approach*   9
      *Applied Behavior Analysis as a Technology of Behavior Change*   11
      *Applied Behavior Analysis as a Profession*   12
   Professionalism of Applied Behavior Analysis   13
   Contemporary Behavior Analytic Practice   13
   What Path Does Applied Behavior Analysis Generally Follow?   14
      *Identifying and Deciding to Address a Problem or Challenge*   17
      *Designing and Implementing an ABA Program*   17
      *Preparing an Environment Supportive of Constructive Change*   17
      *Specifying and Refining Goals and Objectives*   18
      *Identifying Current Reinforcers*   18
      *Collecting Useful Data*   18
      *Promoting Positive Change*   19
      *Implementing, Monitoring, and Experimentally Analyzing the Function of the Intervention Plan*   19
      *Getting There: Continue Monitoring Behavior and Fidelity of Intervention*   19
      *Staying There*   19
   Summary and Conclusions   20

## 2. Designing Effective Strategies of Change: Essential Building Blocks    21
    What is Behavior?    22
    What is Learning?    23
    What is Teaching?    23
    How Does Behavior Analysis Work?    23
        *Behavioral Principles and Procedures*    25
    What Does the Term Environment Mean?    26
        *Differentiating "Environment" from "Stimulus"*    25
    Respondent Behavior and Respondent Conditioning    27
    Operant Behavior and Operant Learning (Conditioning)    28
    The "C" in Operant Learning (Conditioning)    29
        *Positive and Negative Reinforcement Defined and Illustrated*    29
        *Extinction, Positive Punishment, and Negative Punishment Defined and Illustrated*    30
    The Role of Antecedents ("A"s) in Operant Learning    31
        *Antecedent Stimuli Defined and Illustrated*    31
    Motivating Operations as Antecedent Events    32
    Summary and Conclusions    32

## 3. Preparing a Supportive Environment for Behavior Change    34
    Familiarize Yourself with the Client(s) and Setting    35
        *Analyze the Current Operating System or Culture*    36
        *Involve Key People*    37
        *Determine Available Resources*    37
        *Assess Current Skill Levels*    37
        *Select Behavioral Objectives and Interventions Collaboratively*    38
        *Analyze the Function of Current Contingencies*    38
    Select and/or Design Change Methods    39
        *Select or Devise Behavioral Measures*    39
        *Analyze the Function of the Treatment*    39
        *Prepare for Constructive Behavioral Support and Change*    39
        *Organize and Manage Team Operation*    40
    Client Behavior Change: Program Development and Selection    42
        *Plan for Generalization from the Start*    42
        *Ensure Treatment Integrity*    43
        *Measuring Treatment Integrity*    44
    Assure Contextual Fit When Selecting Goals and Interventions    45
        *Select Interventions Collaboratively*    47
        *Involving Clients and Stakeholders*    48
        *Use Acceptable and Comprehensible Language to Clarify Contingency Managers' Tasks*    48
        *If Necessary, Temporarily Incorporate, then Fade Intervention Prompts within the Natural Environment*    51
    Support for the Contingency Manager(s): Performance Feedback    52
    Summary and Conclusions    54

## 4. Sharpening the Focus by Refining Goals and Objectives    56
    Getting Started    58
    Your Organization's Mission    58
    Organizational Culture    59
    WHAT IS Strategic Planning?    60
    What is Behavioral Assessment?    60
    Setting Goals    62
        *Goals Defined and Illustrated*    62

    *Factors Influencing Goal Selection*   62
    *Deciding Whether to Proceed*   63
Defining Problems and Tentative Goals Behaviorally   68
Refining Your Selection of Goals   70
General Considerations in Goal Selection   71
    *Achievable Yet Challenging*   71
    *Constructive and Functional Goals*   71
    *Direct Rather than Indirect Approach*   73
    *Foundational Skills*   73
    *Immediate and Long-Term Benefits*   74
    *Age and Developmental Level*   75
Preventing and Resolving Goal Conflicts   75
    *Participative Goal Setting*   76
    *Arranging for Advocacy*   76
    *Terminating Services*   77
    *Supporting Voluntariness over Coercion*   77
Behavioral Objectives   78
    *Defined*   78
    *Sample Behavioral Objectives*   80
Summary and Conclusions   81

**5. Reinforcement: Fueling Behavior Change   83**
Defining the Term *Reinforcement*   84
    *Natural vs. Planned Reinforcement*   84
The Reinforcement Procedure Defined and Illustrated   86
Reinforcers Defined, Illustrated, and Differentiated from *Reward*   87
Differences between Reinforcers and Reinforcement Procedures   88
Positive Reinforcers and Positive Reinforcement Procedures Defined, Illustrated, and Differentiated   89
Negative Reinforcers and Aversive Stimuli Defined and Illustrated   90
Negative Reinforcement Procedures Defined and Illustrated   91
Escape and Avoidance Defined and differentiated   91
    *Using Escape as a Negative Reinforcer*   93
Dfferentiating Positive from Negative Reinforcers   94
Are Positive and Negative Reinforcement Really Different?   95
Is Applying Negative Reinforcement Advisable?   95
Common Concerns or Disadvantages with Using Reinforcement   97
    *Use of Contrived Reinforcers*   97
    *Unwanted Side-Effects of Reinforcement*   97
    *Bribery*   98
    *Treating People Differently*   99
    *Loss of Intrinsic Motivation (The "Overjustification Effect")*   99
Summary and Conclusions   100

**6. Increasing Behavior by Developing and Selecting Powerful Reinforcers   102**
How Does a Stimulus Develop into a Reinforcer?   103
    *Primary or Unconditioned Reinforcers and Aversive Stimuli*   103
    *Secondary or Learned (Conditioned) Reinforcers*   104
    *Secondary (Conditioned) Aversive Stimuli*   105
    *Developing Secondary Reinforcers*   105
    *Generalized Reinforcers and How They Develop*   106

Classes of Reinforcers and Automatic Reinforcers   107
Selecting Reinforcers for Individual Application   108
   *Selecting Reinforcers: Surveys and Reports*   108
   *Selecting Reinforcers: Observation and Preference Assessments*   109
   *Ethical Considerations in Assessing Behavior*   117
   *Consider Motivating (Establishing) Operations and Response Deprivation in Reinforcer Selection*   117
   *Consider Individual Differences and Receptivity to Reinforcing Events: "Different Strokes for Different Folks"*   119
   *Select and Use a Variety of Reinforcers*   119
   *Novelty in Reinforcer Selection*   120
   *The Value of Reinforcer Sampling*   120
   *The Role of the Reinforcer Mediator*   122
Summary and Conclusions   122

**7. Organizing for Behavior Change by Collecting Useful Data   124**
Behavioral Assessment   125
   *Behavioral Assessment Defined and Illustrated*   128
   *Four Characteristics of a Good Measurement System*   128
   *Selecting Measures that Contribute to Treatment Outcome*   129
   *Designing or Selecting a Behavioral Measurement Method*   129
Selecting Valid Measures   130
   *Reactivity and Adaptation*   130
Selecting Reliable Measurement Systems   131
   *Calculating Interobserver Agreement*   132
Measuring Treatment Integrity   132
   *Factors Influencing Validity of Assessment*   132
   *Instructional Demand*   133
   *Measurement Complexity*   133
   *Observer Awareness of Being Assessed*   134
   *Observational Bias*   134
The Measurement Process   134
   *Measuring Behavioral Products*   134
   *Measuring Transitory Behaviors*   135
Recording and Reporting Transitory Behavior   136
   *Event (Rate) Recording*   136
   *Duration Recording*   137
   *Latency*   138
   *Interresponse Time (IRT)*   139
   *Interval Time-Sampling Systems*   139
   *Selecting a Time-Sampling Method*   141
   *Selecting Appropriate Measurements Based Upon Dimensions of Behavior*   144
   *Episodic Severity or Intensity*   144
   *Observing Behavior in Groups*   146
Methods for Calculating Interobserver Agreement   147
   *IOA for Permanent Product Measuring*   147
   *IOA for Event Measures*   147
   *Indices of Agreement (IOAs) for Duration and Interresponse Time (IRT) Measures*   148
   *IOA for Interval Time-Sampling Measures*   148
Reporting Reliability Data   149
Summary and Conclusions   149
**Summary Table: Choosing Direct Behavioral Observational Methods**   151

8. **Optimizing Client Progress by Monitoring Behavior Change: Recording, Graphing, and Analyzing Patterns of Change    151**
   Implementing Observational Systems    153
   *Behavior-Recording Staff    153*
   *Automated Recording Systems    155*
   Scheduling Behavioral Recording    156
   *Frequency of Recording    156*
   *Duration of Recording Phases    157*
   *Definitional Detail    157*
   *Unit of Analysis    157*
   Graphing Behavioral Data    158
   *Graphing Guidelines    160*
   *Standard Format for a Graph    160*
   *Steps in Graph Construction    161*
   *Graphic Variations    162*
   *Bar Graphs    162*
   *Cumulative Records    163*
   *Standard Celeration Charts    167*
   *Monitoring Changes in Behavior Patterns    167*
   Interpreting Behavioral Data    170
   *Reporting Demographic Variables    174*
   Summary and Conclusions    174

9. **Optimizing Client Progress by Analyzing the Functions of Our Interventions: Basic Experimental Designs    175**
   *Common Myths    176*
   Advantages of Single-Subject Experimental Designs    178
   *Demonstrating Functional Relations    179*
   General Requirements for Single-Subject Designs    182
   Withdrawal (Return to Baseline) Designs    182
   *Selecting and Using the Withdrawal (Return-to-Baseline) Design    184*
   *Actual Illustrations    185*
   *The (True) Reversal Design    187*
   *Additional Return–to-Baseline Design Variations    187*
   *Advantages of the Withdrawal or Return-to-Baseline Design (A-B-A-B)    189*
   *Disadvantages of the Withdrawal or Return-to-Baseline Design    189*
   Multiple-Baseline Design    190
   *Using Multiple-Baseline Designs    190*
   *Variations of the Multiple-Baseline Design    192*
   *Planning and Implementing Multiple-Baseline Designs    196*
   *Advantages and Disadvantages of Multiple-Baseline Designs    196*
   Summary and Conclusions    200

10. **Setting a Foundation for Positive Change: Identifying Participant's Functional Reinforcers    201**
    The Term "Functional"    203
    Functional Behavioral Assessment    204
    Various Functions of Behavior    205
    Approaches to Conducting FBAs    207
    *Biological & Physiological Influences    207*
    *Indirect (Anecdotal) Assessments    208*

*Descriptive Assessments* 212
*Structured ABC Assessment* 217
*Functional Analysis* 220
*Methodological Variations* 224
Telehealth Service Delivery Model and Functional Behavior Assessment 224
From FBA to Treatment Development 225
*Selection of Replacement Behavior* 225
*Selecting an Intervention* 226
Legal and Ethical Implications of Conducting Functional Behavioral Assessments in Schools 228
Summary and Conclusions 230

**11. Rapidly Attaining Positive Change: Implementing Reinforcement Effectively 233**
Informed Consent 234
Enhancing Reinforcer Effectiveness 235
*Selecting Effective Reinforcers* 235
*Timing of Reinforcer Delivery* 235
*Teaching Delay of Gratification–Improving Self-Control* 236
*Using Supplementary Reinforcers* 238
*Using Labeled Praise* 238
*Teaching Clients to Discriminate Contextual Factors* 239
*Determining the Magnitude and Quantity of Reinforcers* 240
*Incorporating Client Choice* 243
*Providing Contingent Reinforcement under Diverse Circumstances: At Different Times, in Many Places, and with Different People* 244
*Reducing, Overriding or Removing Competing Contingencies* 247
*Avoiding Reinforcing Behaviors Targeted for Reduction* 248
*Using Reinforcement Schedules to Promote and Support Lasting Change* 249
Self-Management: Its Features and Function 252
*Using Successful Self-Management Methods* 254
Summary and Conclusions 258
**Summary Table: Increasing Behavior via Reinforcement** 259
Summary Table: Nagative Reinforcement 260

**12. Promoting and Supporting Group Change: Programs and Packages 261**
What is the Value of Formally Arranging Group Contingencies? 262
Illustrative Group Contingencies 262
*Independent Group Contingencies* 262
*Interdependent Group Contingencies* 263
*Dependent Group Contingencies* 264
*Advantages and Disadvantages of Dependent and Interdependent Group Contingencies* 265
*Reducing Unwanted Behavior by Combining Group Contingencies with Extinction* 266
Defining and Applying Peer-Mediated Strategies 268
Token Systems 271
*Advantages and Disadvantages of Token Systems* 272
*Considering Whether to Implement a Token Economy* 274
*Preliminary Steps in Designing a Token Economy* 274
*Adjusting the Token System to Local Circumstances* 275
Selecting Flexible versus Fixed Earning Requirements 277
*Implementing Token Economies Effectively* 277
*Reducing Behavior within a Token Economy* 279
*Methods for Maintaining Performance Improved via Token Economies* 280
Summary and Conclusions 281

## 13. Teaching New Behavior: Shaping    283
### Shaping Defined and Illustrated    284
*Shaping Defined*    284
*Shaping Illustrated*    285
*Shaping the Performance of Adult Learners*    289
### Using Shaping Effectively    290
*Familiarize Yourself with Learners' Current Repertoires*    290
*Choose and Apply an Ongoing Measurement System*    291
*Keep Your Eye on the Goal*    291
*Find a Starting Point and Supportive Environment*    291
*Select Step Size and Duration for Remaining on a Step*    293
*Combine Shaping with Discriminative Stimuli*    294
*"Shaping" with Goal-Setting*    295
*End Every Shaping Session on a High Note*    296
*Consider Combining Physical Guidance with Shaping*    298
*Combine Fading with Shaping*    298
### Illustrative Instructional Programs that Incorporate Shaping    299
*Shaping and Programmed Instruction*    299
*Shaping and the Personalized System of Instruction (PSI)*    302
*Shaping and Computer-Assisted Instruction*    302
### Summary and Conclusions    305

## 14. Teaching Complex Behaviors: Chaining, Task Analyses, and Social Skills Training    306
### What is a Behavior Chain?    307
*Chaining Defined and Illustrated*    307
*Behavioral Links or Units*    308
*Choosing Behavioral Links*    309
*Linking Behavioral Chains*    310
*Different Classes of Chains and Their Components*    313
### Effectively Linking Behavioral Chains    314
*Analyze the Task Precisely*    315
*Develop and Validate the Task Analyses*    315
*Use Links Already in the Learner's Response Repertoire*    316
*Plan an Appropriate Starting Point*    318
*Consider Using Supplementary Reinforcers*    322
*Consider Using Supplementary Discriminative Stimuli*    322
*Combine Shaping with Chaining*    325
*Combine Chaining with Fading*    326
*Consider Instructing Students in Pairs while Using a Time-Delay Procedure*    326
### Teaching Social Skills by Means of Chaining    327
*A Special Application*    327
*Social Skills as Behavioral Chains*    328
*Identifying Social Skill Deficits*    320
*Social Skills for Academic and Job Survival*    329
*Using Chaining to Teach Social Skills*    331
### Coping With Unwanted Chains    332
*Unchaining*    334
*Reducing Behavior by Blocking Links in a Behavioral Chain*    335
### Strengthening and Expanding Newly Acquired Behavior    335
### Summary and Conclusions    336
### **Summary Table: Procedures for Teaching New Behavior**    338

## 15. Attaining Complex Behavior by Promoting and Supporting Antecedent Control    339
   The Evolution of Stimulus Control within Individuals and Groups    340
   What is Stimulus Control?    340
      *Establishing Discriminative Control*    344
      *Discriminative or Stimulus Control Illustrated*    344
      *Using Differential Reinforcement Effectively*    348
   How to Produce Complex Behavior Utilizing Stimulus Control    350
   Contextual Variables    351
      *Motivating Operations Defined and Illustrated*    351
      *Motivating Stimulus Defined and Illustrated*    353
      *Subclasses of Motivating Operations*    353
   Summary and Conclusions    355

## 16. Selecting and Applying Methods for Promoting Stimulus Control    357
   Simple Discriminations    358
   Discriminations Among Multiple Stimuli    359
      *Identifying Obscure $S^D$s*    360
      *Control by Complex Stimuli*    361
   Conditional Discriminations    363
   Stimulus Equivalence and Equivalence Classes    369
      *Stimulus Equivalence*    369
      *Equivalence Classes*    370
      *Reflexivity*    371
      *Symmetry*    371
      *Transitivity*    372
   Summary and Conclusions    373

## 17. Achieving Stimulus Control    374
   Stimulus Change    375
      *Defined and Illustrated*    375
      *Advantages of Stimulus Change*    378
      *Disadvantages of Stimulus Change*    378
      *When Stimulus Change Fails*    379
   Goal-Setting    379
      *Goal-setting Defined and Illustrated*    379
      *Goals as Motivating Operations*    380
      *Effective Goal-setting*    382
   Prompting    385
      *Prompting Defined and Illustrated*    385
      *Using Prompts Effectively*    385
   Fluency, and Supporting Stimulus Control with Precision Teaching    392
   Summary and Conclusions    394

## 18. Prompting Procedures and Instructional Programs    397
   Using Prompting Effectively    398
   Prompting by Instructing ("Telling")    398
      *Defined and Illustrated*    398
      *Using the Tell Procedure Effectively*    399
   Direct Instruction    403
   Discrete Trial Training (DTT)    404
      *DTT Differentiated from Free Operants*    405
      *Selecting Free versus Discriminated Operants*    406

Providing a Model: Imitative Prompts   406
   *Defined and Illustrated*   406
   *Developing Modeled Behavior into Imitative Prompts or Discriminative Stimuli*   408
   *Combining Modeling with Shaping*   409
   *Increasing Generalized Imitative Responding*   410
   *Video Modeling*   410
   *Using Modeling Effectively: Model Selection*   413
   *Using Modeling Effectively: Managing Contingencies*   415
Physical Guidance   419
   *Defined and Illustrated*   419
   *Using Physical Guidance Effectively*   419
Summary and Conclusions   420
**Summary Table: Procedures for Teaching and Prompting Behavior**   421

### 19. Teaching, Expanding and Refining Verbal Behavior   424
B. F. Skinner's Analysis of Verbal Behavior   426
The Duplic   428
   *The Duplic Defined*   428
   *Duplic Training*   428
   *Echoic Training*   429
The Mand   430
   *The Mand Defined*   430
   *Mand Training*   432
The Tact   436
   *The Tact Defined*   436
   *Tact Training*   437
The Intraverbal   438
   *The Intraverbal Defined*   438
   *Intraverbal Training*   440
Listener Behavior   441
Augmentative Verbal Behavioral Strategies   444
Relational Frame Theory and Derived Relational Responding   446
   *Relating as an Operant*   447
   *Relational Frame Theory in Practice*   447
   *General Recommendations*   448
   *Some Critical Communication Skills*   448
Summary and Conclusions   449
**Summary Table: Teaching Verbal Behavior**   451

### 20. Promoting Independence: Shifting and Expanding Stimulus Control   454
Reducing Prompt Dependence by Transferring Stimulus Control   454
Delayed Prompting   455
   *Defined and Illustrated*   455
   *Advantages of Delayed Prompting*   457
   *Disadvantages*   458
   *Using Delayed Prompting Effectively*   458
Graduated Prompting   458
Stimulus Fading   459
   *Defined and Illustrated*   459
   *Using Fading Effectively*   463
Errorless Learning   467
   *Defined and Illustrated*   467

  *Using Fading to Achieve Errorless Learning*  468
  *Using Response and Extra-Stimulus Prompting*  470
  *Disadvantages of Errorless Learning*  472
 Maintaining Stimulus Control  473
 Summary and Conclusions  474

## 21. Generalization: Expanding Stimulus Control  475
 Distinguishing between the Terms *Discrimination* and *Stimulus Generalization*  477
 Stimulus Generalization and Overgeneralization  477
 Distinguishing between *Stimulus Generalization* and *Response Generalization* (*Induction*)  479
 Advantages and Disadvantages of Generalization  480
  *Stimulus Generalization*  480
  *Response Generalization*  481
  *Assessing for Stimulus Generalization*  483
 Formally integrating Generalization training from the Very Start  483
  *Request Generalization*  484
  *Prompt Several People in Various Environments to Deliver Reinforcers*  485
  *Teach the Behavior in Various Environments Sequentially*  486
  *Consider Using a Generalization Map*  487
  *Incorporate Common Stimuli Across Instructional Environments*  488
  *Promote Fluency*  489
  *Apply Strategies Designed to Facilitate Carry-Over into the Natural Setting*  491
  *Pre-assess and Reduce Support for Functional Interfering, Maladaptive Behavior*  492
  *Provide Sufficient Exemplars*  492
  *Train Loosely*  495
  *Use Indiscriminable Contingencies*  496
  *Continue Training*  497
  *Teach Participants and Contingency Managers How to Promote and Support Generalization*  498
  *Record and Graph*  500
 Summary and Conclusion  501

## 22. Maintaining Behavior: Ratio and Related Schedules of Reinforcement  502
 Ratio Schedules Defined and Illustrated  504
 Characteristics of Ratio-Schedule Performance  505
  *Ratio Schedules Usually Produce Fast Responding*  506
  *Consistency of Performance*  508
  *Continued Responding During Extinction*  509
 Advantages of Ratio Schedules  510
 Using Ratio Schedules Effectively  511
  *Select Schedules to Sustain Desired Rates*  511
  *Thin Gradually*  512
  *Consider Ongoing Reinforcement Schedules Prior to Implementing Extinction to Reduce Problematic Behavior*  514
 Disadvantages of Ratio Schedules  514
  *Ratio Strain and Diminishing Performance Quality*  514
  *Interval Schedules Often are Easier to Use*  515
 Promoting High Rates  516
  *Provide Clear Instructions and Prompt Imitation of High Rates*  516
 Differentially Reinforcing Rates  516
  *Promoting More Rapid Responding*  517

    *Promoting Paced Responding with Differential Reinforcement of Paced Responding (DRP)*    517
    *Promoting Lower Rate Responding with Differential Reinforcement of Low Rates (DRL) and*
        *Diminishing Rates (DRD)*    518
    *Promoting Variability of Responding with Lag Schedules*    519
  Summary and Conclusions    519

**23. Maintaining Behavior by Arranging Time Based Schedules of Reinforcement    521**
  Interval Schedules    522
    *Defined and Illustrated*    522
    *Fixed-Interval (FI) Schedules*    523
    *Distinguishing between Fixed-Interval and Fixed-Time Schedules*    523
    *Variable-Interval (VI) Schedules*    524
  Characteristics of Interval-Schedule Performance    524
    *Rate of Responding under Interval Schedules*    525
    *Maintaining Rates Originally Established under Ratio Schedules*    527
    *Consistency of Performance*    528
    *Error Patterns*    530
    *Managing Impulsivity*    530
    *Responding During Extinction*    531
  Advantages and Disadvantages of Interval Schedules    532
  Promoting Preferred Rates of Responding under Interval Schedules    533
    *Plan Your Reinforcement Schedule with Care*    533
    *Provide a History Appropriate to Your Objective(s)*    534
    *Place a Limited Hold on Responding*    534
    *Promote Higher Responding with Differential Reinforcement of High Rates (DRH)*    536
    *Use Discriminative Stimuli*    536
    *Arrange Competition*    539
    *Capitalize on Behavioral Contrast*    539
    *Heighten Response Rates under Interval Schedules by Interspersing Easy Tasks*    540
  How Might Reinforcing One Response Affect Other Responses?    541
  Schedule Interactions    543
  Summary and Conclusions    544

**24. Organizational Performance Management Systems: Supervising and Supporting Contingency Managers    546**
  Function Matters Most    547
  Program Implementation    547
    *Be Present and Supportive*    548
    *Use Prompts Temporarily and Only as Necessary*    549
    *Provide Feedback on Program Implementation*    550
    *Maximizing the Effects of Feedback for Improving Performance*    550
    *Contingently Remove Aversive Stimuli (Negative Reinforcement)*    557
    *Addressing Program Implementation Problems*    557
  Program Maintenance    558
    *Gradually Decrease Prompts*    558
    *Set Goals Jointly*    558
    *Identify and Use Various Reinforcing Sources*    560
    *Parents*    560
    *Clients*    561
    *Peers*    561
    *Supervisors, Managers, Administrators*    561

*Others* 563
Program Generalization 563
   *Consider the Big Picture within the Organization* 563
   *Contemplate the Even Broader Picture* 563
Summary and Conclusions 564
**Summary Table: Transferring, Finding, and Maintaining Responding** 567
**Summary Table: Maintaining Behavior** 569

## 25. Identifying Effective Interventions with Complex Research Designs 574

Preliminary Considerations Prior to Adopting Programs 575
   *How Internally Valid is the Program?* 575
   *How Externally Valid is the Program?* 576
   *Will Changes in Performance Impact the Bottom Line?* 577
Functionally Analyzing Increases and Decreases in Behavior 577
Changing-Criterion Design 578
   *Changing-Criterion Designs Illustrated* 578
   *Advantages of Changing-Criterion Design* 578
   *Disadvantages of Changing-Criterion Design* 579
   *Using and Demonstrating Control via the Changing-Criterion Design* 579
   *Overall Number of Criterion Changes* 582
Multiple-Probe Design 582
   *The Multiple-Probe Design Illustrated* 583
Alternating-Treatment (Multi-Element) Designs 585
   *The Alternating-Treatment Design Illustrated* 587
   *Using the Alternating-Treatment Design* 588
   *Advantages of Alternating-Treatment Designs* 590
   *Disadvantages of Alternating Treatment Designs* 591
Conducting Component and Parametric Analyses 592
   *Component Analysis* 592
   *Parametric Analysis* 593
Selecting Appropriate Single-Subject Designs 594
Other Considerations with Single-Subject Designs 594
   *Irreversibility and Sequence Effects* 594
   *Determining the Significance of a Demonstrated Functional Relation* 598
   *Determining Experimental Significance* 599
   *Other Forms of Significance* 600
Making Decisions Applicable to Large Groups 601
Cost Effectiveness 602
Evaluating the Significance of Findings 603
Probing for Generality and Persistence of Change 603
Practicing Analytically 603
Summary and Conclusions 604

## 26. Reducing Behavior: Extinction 605

Deciding to Prevent or Reduce Behavior 606
Targeting a Behavior for Reduction 606
Nonrestrictive Procedures and the Client's Right to Effective Treatment 609
Extinction 609
   *Extinction Defined and Illustrated* 609
   *Properties of Extinction* 610
   *Using Extinction Effectively* 615

Summary and Conclusions     621

## 27. Preventing Challenging Behavior by Enriching the Environment     622
Why Choose Alternatives to Punishment?     623
Positive Behavior Interventions     623
Antecedent Control Strategies     624
Using Stimulus-Change Procedures to Prevent Problematic Behavior     626
   *Removing Impediments to Goal Behaviors*     626
Prompting Strategies for Preventing/Reducing Problem Behavior     626
   *Presenting Rules or Instructions*     626
   *Presenting Prompts*     628
   *Response Interruption and Redirection*     630
   *Using Activity Schedules: A Behavior Management Problem-Prevention Package Comprised of Several Antecedent Procedures*     632
Preventing or Reducing Problematic Behavior by Building a More Reinforcing Environment     632
   *Greeting Clients*     634
   *Distracting with Preferred Events*     634
   *Behavioral Momentum or High-Probability Request (or Instructional) Sequence*     635
   *Providing Choice*     637
   *Using Participative Goal-Setting: Promoting Success and Preventing Problem Behaviors*     638
   *Reducing Response Demand*     638
   *Promoting Academic/task Success While Preventing Problem Behavior*     639
The Importance of a Reinforcing Environment     641
Using Noncontingent Reinforcement (NCR) to Prevent Inappropriate Behavior     642
   *NCR Defined and Illustrated*     642
   *Advantages and Disadvantages of NCR*     645
   *Using NCR Effectively*     647
Other Primary Prevention Methods     648
   *Modeling*     648
   *Using Social Stories*     650
Summary and Conclusions     651

## 28. Preventing and Reducing Behavior through Differential Reinforcement     653
Differential Reinforcement     655
Differential Reinforcement of Alternative (DRA) And Incompatible (DRI) Behavior     655
   *DRA and DRI Defined, Illustrated, and Distinguished from One Another*     655
   *DRA and DRI: Group Management Programs*     657
   *Advantages of DRA*     658
   *Disadvantages of DRA*     660
   *Using DRA Effectively*     660
Differential Reinforcement of Other Behavior (DRO)     662
   *DRO Defined and Differentiated from DRA*     662
   *Whole-Interval and Momentary DRO Defined and Illustrated*     663
   *Advantages of DRO*     668
   *Disadvantages of DRO*     669
   *Using DRO Effectively*     670
Differentially Reinforciing Lower and Diminishing Rates of Behavior     673
   *DRL Defined and Illustrated*     673
Differential Reinforcement of Diminishing Rates (DRD) Defined and Illustrated     674
   *Advantages of DRL and DRD*     675
   *Disadvantages of DRL and DRD*     676
   *Effective use of DRL and DRD*     677

*The Good Behavior Game: An Illustrative DRD Behavior-Management Package*    677
Summary and Conclusions    679

## 29. Reducing Behavior with Negative Punishment: Reosponse Cost and Timeout    682
Negative Punishment Defined    683
Response Cost    684
    *Response Cost Defined*    684
    *Illustrations of Response Cost Programs*    685
    *A Variation of Response Cost: Bonus Response Cost*    686
Timeout from Reinforcement    687
    *Timeout Defined and Differentiated from Extinction and Response Cost*    687
    *Variations of Timeout*    688
Advantages and disadvantages of Response Cost and Timeout    693
    *Strong and Rapid Behavioral Reduction*    693
    *Promotes Discrimination Learning*    694
    *Potential for Long-Lasting Effects*    694
    *Convenient and Socially Acceptable*    694
    *Not Universally Effective: Misuse Decreases Effectiveness*    695
    *Punitive, Non-Constructive Contingency*    695
    *Potential for Abuse*    696
    *Suppression of Other Behaviors*    697
Additional Disadvantages of Timeout    697
    *Loss of Learning Time*    697
    *Legal and Ethical Considerations*    697
    *Public Concern with Timeout*    699
Using Response Cost and Timeout Effectively    699
    *Apply Immediately*    699
    *Combine with Other Procedures*    700
    *Create a Reinforcing Natural Environment*    699
    *Remove as Many Reinforcers as Feasible During Timeout*    699
    *Determine Magnitude Empirically*    700
    *Use the Smallest Magnitude of Aversive Conditions Found to be Effective*    703
    *Clearly Communicate Response Cost or Timeout Conditions*    703
    *Use Consistently*    704
    *Consider Delivering Response-Cost Points to a Peer*    705
    *Avoid Opportunities for Self-Injury, Self-Stimulation, and Escape during Timeout*    705
    *Monitor Implementation and Progress*    706
    *Design the Program to Minimize Emotional Outbursts*    706
Summary and Conclusions    707

## 30. Reducing Behavior with Positive Punishment while Minimizing Coercion    709
Illustrative Case    710
Positive Punishment Defined    710
Aversive Stimuli Defined and Illustrated    711
    *Unconditioned or Primary Aversive Stimuli*    712
    *Conditioned or Secondary Aversive Stimuli*    712
    *Intrinsic and Extrinsic Aversive Stimuli*    713
    *Stimuli that Signal Non-reinforcement*    713
    *Conditioning that Transforms Typically Aversive Stimuli into Reinforcers*    713
Illustrative Punishment-Based Behavioral Packages    714
    *Contingent Effort*    714
Advantages of Positive Punishment    717

  *Effectively Stopping Behavior*   717
   *Halting the Behavior Rapidly; Perhaps Lastingly*   717
   *Facilitating Adaptive Behavior*   718
  Disadvantages of Positive Punishment   719
   *Provoking Withdrawal*   720
   *Suppressing Responses*   720
   *Promoting Aggression*   721
   *Promoting Inappropriate Generalization*   721
   *Setting Conditions for Recovery or Resurgence Afterwards*   722
   *Promoting Behavioral Contrast*   722
   *Modeling Punishment*   723
   *Diminishing "Self-Esteem"*   723
   *Overusing Punishment*   724
   *Promoting Habituation to Aversive Stimuli*   724
   *Generating Public Antipathy*   725
   *Increasing Costs in the Short Term*   725
   *Review of Negative Side Effects*   725
   *Effects of Torture*   726
  Using Positive Punishment Effectively   727
   *Take Preliminary Steps Prior to Instituting a Positive Punishment Procedure*   727
   *Reinforce Acceptable Alternative Behaviors*   727
   *Select Functionally-Effective Aversive Consequences*   728
   *Vary Effective Aversive Stimuli*   730
   *Prevent Escape*   730
   *Apply Immediately and Consistently*   730
   *Select Appropriate Intensity*   732
   *Combine Positive Punishment with Extinction*   732
   *Consider and If Possible, Manage Contextual Factors*   733
   *Program for Generalization and Maintenance*   734
   *Monitor Regularly*   734
   *Teach Optimal Choice Selection Up Front*   734
   *An Illustration of Optimal Application of Punishment for Extremely Dangerous Self-Abusive*
    *Behavior: SIBIS*   734
  Applying Contingent Effort   735
   *Select Activities Relevant to the Misbehavior*   735
   *Maintain Consistency of Performance of Aversive Activities*   736
   *Extend Duration of Aversive Activities*   736
   *Consider Reinforcing Positive Practice*   736
  Right to Effective Treatment   736
  Summary and Conclusions   736
  **Summary Table: Preventing and Reducing Behavior**   738
  **Summary Table: Consequential Methods for Preventing/Reducing Behavior**   744

**31. Achieving Lasting Change Ethically**   750
  Where and With Whom May We Apply Behavioral Procedures?   751
  Human Values in Applied Behavior Analysis   752
   *Professional and Ethical Considerations*   752
   *ABA Practice within Other Areas of Specialization*   752
  Professionalizing Practice: The Behavior Analysis Certification Board®   753
  Your Legal and Ethical Responsibilities as an Applied Behavior Analyst   753
   *Guidelines and The Code for Responsible Conduct for Behavior Analysts*   754
   *Use Scientifically-Validated Assessments and Interventions*   754

       *Practice within Professional Competence*   755
       *Being Truthful and Documenting Professional Work*   756
       *Identify and Reconcile Conflicts of Interest*   757
       *Protect Clients' Dignity, Health, and Safety*   758
       *Protect Confidentiality*   759
Evaluating and Monitoring Appropriate Services   760
       *Obtain Written Service Agreement*   761
       *Continuity, Discontinuing, and Transitioning of Services*   762
       *Practicing Ethically Beyond the Client and Stakeholder*   764
Evaluate the Ethical Practices in Organizaions Prior to Your Employmet   765
Promote and Support Freedom and Dignity   766
Summary and Conclusions   766

Appendix: BACB 5th Edition Task List with References to Text Pages   769
Glossary   777
References   805
Name Index   889
Subject Index   913

# Preface

Welcome to the fascinating world of applied behavior analysis. You have elected to study this text for a reason. Perhaps you currently are, or anticipate becoming a parent, teacher, coach, manager, consultant, counselor, medical practitioner, or other behavior-change agent who hopes this new learning will help improve your own performance along with that of your clientele. Maybe you are initiating the steps toward becoming a *Board Certified Behavior Analyst®*. If so, this book probably is as good a place as any to begin. More specifically, by mastering the contents of this volume, you will become better informed about how to *responsibly* and *verifiably* teach people (and other organisms) to change their own and others' behavior in a general and lasting way. Such an ambitious goal, though, can only be attained at a price. You will need to invest considerable time and effort in the process, including reading and demonstrating your mastery of this material. But that is just the beginning, because to become a really skillful agent of behavior change you must also extend the foundational material covered in this volume to new textual material and to your own simulated and real applications, under qualified supervision.

This text actually is the product of years of effort on the part of the authors, and their colleagues, students, and clientele with whom we have worked. To provide you with a flavor of what has been invested in the process of bringing the current volume into being, allow us to share a bit of its historical background.

## THE HISTORICAL FOUNDATION OF THIS TEXT

Beginning in the late 1960's, when behavioral approaches to changing behavior were starting to establish themselves as useful and accountable, we began to prepare our first collaborative text, *Behavior Modification Procedures for School Personnel* (Sulzer & Mayer, 1972). With professional and research backgrounds in the field of education and human services, we felt that this new scientific form of practice had much to offer to students, teachers, and those professional personnel who served them. The stunning accomplishments of behavioral procedures in the fields of mental health, developmental disabilities, and related areas were beginning to show how behavior analysis could help students improve in academic achievement and "conduct" (today we would say "social skills").

That initial volume drew upon research in education and related areas, but at the time, such information was relatively sparse. Numerous fundamental principles of behavior had been identified and demonstrated through laboratory experimentation, but their application in classrooms and other group settings was limited. Much of the material in that initial text drew upon these principles, while we extrapolated speculatively about ways to apply them to help solve educational problems.

Soon afterward, behavioral research applied directly in education and other fields related to children and youth began to flourish. Major programs, many federally funded in the United States (and later elsewhere), investigated methods for preventing and ameliorating problems among youngsters with developmental disabilities and those classified as delinquent or educationally deficient in other ways. So rapidly did information start to accrue, that within a few years we included these areas in a revision and expansion of the original text, *Applying Behavior Analysis Procedures with Children and Youth* (Sulzer-Azaroff & Mayer, 1977). The availability of the ever-expanding controlled investigations enabled a more data-based and less speculative revision.

The decade following the 1977 revision witnessed an even larger expansion of behavior analytic research. Journal reports of behavioral studies grew exponentially, as did the areas of application addressed. Then, in addition to the fields of mental health, developmental disabilities and education—where the methods were continuing to be intensively tested—other applications included interventions in families, business, health, recreational, and community-service organizations. Challenges addressed moved beyond those associated with deficiency and illness, to include prevention or remediation of personal and social difficulties and ways to foster success in many realms: social skills, nervous habits, job finding, skill mastery, marital interactions, parenting, health maintenance, accident and illness prevention, energy conservation, reduced littering and other environmental concerns, productive organizational functioning, and many others.

During this time, the methodological sophistication of the field also continued to evolve. New assessment and analytic approaches eventually were subsumed under the rubric of behavioral assessment. The number of books, journals, and scholarly papers proliferated to such an extent that by the 1980s, no individual or partnership could stay abreast of the field. With educators clamoring for ways to improve the discipline, we then decided to emphasize that area for an original specialty text on the topic of behavioral education practice. *Achieving Educational Excellence Using Behavioral Strategies* (Sulzer-Azaroff & Mayer, 1986) focused on basic behavioral principles and methods and how to apply them to improve student achievement in particular skill areas such as reading, arithmetic, writing, and social conduct, along with promoting more skillful staff performance.

*Behavior Analysis for Lasting Change* (Sulzer-Azaroff & Mayer, 1991) was a response to our colleagues' clamor for an update of the then-rapidly expanding field—to cover such topics as individual and organizational clientele served, problem areas, methodological scope, approaches addressed, and new analytic technologies. At that point we did not delude ourselves into thinking that we could cover the field completely. Rather, we relied on our own knowledge and experience in the field along with numerous compendia prepared by our colleagues. With over 1300 references, we apologized to our audience for not being as inclusive as we might have been; but in the interest of our own and our audience's survival, we stopped at about that number.

They say that wisdom is a major consolation for aging. Probably we were short-changed in that area, because now, more than 45 years since the initial volume, we allowed ourselves to be seduced into preparing yet another edition of *Behavior Analysis for Lasting Change*—the present volume with over 2000 references. Fortunately, we were wise enough to invite Michele Wallace, expert in the functional assessment, research design, and the education and treatment of individuals with autism and other developmental disabilities, to join our team in preparation for the subsequent editions (2011, 2013, 2019, and 2022). Professor Wallace brings a fresh perspective to the mix, reminding us particularly to search for and remedy the factors underlying misbehavior, prior to rushing headlong into attempting its correction.

## APPLYING BEHAVIOR ANALYSIS WITHIN YOUR SPECIFIC FOCUS AREA

Prior to initiating your study and mastery of the basics of applied behavior analysis (ABA), please take a few moments to glance through this text's table of contents and its general coverage. Probably you will note the presentation of ABA's scientifically documented, well-established principles of behavior, combined with an array of examples of the successful application of those principles. Perhaps, at that point, and certainly later on, you will recognize that the majority of our illustrative references are derived from the fields of education, especially special education and clinical psychology. That is a function of the evolution of the field, which, in the 1960's initially tended to address those areas.

As time has passed, though, investigators began to recognize the general success of the application of behavior analytic principles across a wide breadth of subject areas, including regular education, families, health and medicine, safety, business, economics, industry, communities, other organizations, and even animals. You probably have your own particular current and/or area(s) of interest where these principles can be applied.

As you might imagine, offering full coverage of examples of every current area of application in one single text would be impossible. (As of this writing, Google lists over a million papers under the heading of "Behavior Analytic Application.") Should your own particular focus fall outside of those most heavily represented in this text, we invite you search the web for scientific journal articles containing illustrative examples more closely aligned with yours. Just remind yourself that while the populations and problems treated with ABA may vary, the essential basic principles serving as its foundation remain universal.

## FIFTH EDITION CHANGES

After our last revision was published, we were asked what changes we made in the new edition over the previous one. We were unable to provide a satisfactory answer. So, this time, as we made the changes we made notes to help us become aware of what change this fifth edition contains over the foutth edition:

Besides correcting typos, adding examples and moving some material around, we have:

- Increased the emphasis on lasting behavior change by elaborating and stressing the importance of fluency, timely removal of prompts, promoting generalization, thinning supplementary reinforcers, and promoting environmental support
- Increased the emphasis on problematic prevention, particularly using antecedent interventions based on motivational operations (MOs)
- Up-dated the ethics and certification sections for behavior analysts (that became effective starting January 1, 2022)
- Referenced the most current research literature and updated examples
- Increased the emphasis on personal/cultural values and beliefs
- Increased the section on Behavior Skills Training (BST)
- Incorporated using the telehealth service delivery model
- Provided a new section specifying the BCBA's supervisory responsibilities
- Included a section on reporting demographic variables
- Included a section on using the Performance Diagnostic Checklist—Human Ser vices (PPC-HS) to help address program implementation problems
- Differentiated between response prompts and stimulus prompts
- Clarified and or elaborated numerous topics and concepts, including:
  - motivating operations (MOs)
  - establishing and abolishing operations
  - modeling and imitation
  - indirect and descriptive assessments
  - criterion levels and their selection

- escape's usefulness as a negative reinforcer
- rate, celeration charting and behavior mastery
- delay of gratification
- enhancing reinforcer effectiveness
- self-recording and accurate baseline data collection
- error correction procedures
- time delay prompting (constant and progressive)
- demographic variables
- differential reinforcement
- practicality of using lag schedules of reinforcement
- influence of behavior criterion mastery on rate of responding
- frequency vs. event recording
- treatment integrity
- behavioral contrast
- greetings as an MO to promote positive behavior
- spontaneous recovery and resurgence
- Using noncontingent reinforcement (NCR) effectively
- DRA's effects on delayed reinforcement
- the Good Behavior Game
- types of inclusion timeout
- the development and importance of fluency
- behavioral contrast vs. matching law
- resurgence and spontaneous recovery
- derived stimulus relations
- stimulus equivalence

## GOALS OF THE TEXT

Our overriding goal has been to provide a text that allows students to learn the theoretical and basic concepts so that they understand where the application of behavior analysis procedures was born, as well as a resource to emulate when directly working in the field, adhering to the original characteristics set forth by Baer, Wolf, and Risley (1968): applied, behavioral, analytic, conceptually systematic, technological, effective, and generality. Our goals were for students, upon demonstrating mastery of this text, to be able to:

- read and comprehend conceptual, experimental and applied behavior analytic literature
- specify a set of core behavioral concepts and principles
- offer a range of illustrations of those concepts and principles
- be prepared conceptually to apply behavior analytic concepts and methods toward analyzing given behavioral issues and challenges
- participate in ethically and scientifically sound application of behavior analysis procedures
- develop a comprehensive understanding of why people do what they do, when they do it, and how to change it.

Moreover, given the formal oversight and requirements on the practice of behavior analysis by the Behavior Analysis Certification Board® (BACB), the Association for Behavior Analysis International (ABAI), and various state governmental agencies through state licensure, we have made sure to incorporate the knowledge requirements from these different entities (e.g., the new code of ethics and the 5th Edition task list developed by the BACB (both of which took effect January 1. 2022), content knowledge set forth by ABAI.

More specifically, goals of the text are to:

- define applied behavior analysis, its distinguishing features and, supported by our extensive glossary, to define hundreds of its technical terms
- demonstrate your familiarity with the background history of the field and its philosophical foundations

- select constructive and meaningful goals, and assisted by of a number of sets of procedural tables, design promising behavior-change intervention plans
- include generalization criteria for judging achievement of objectives
- sharpen the focus of your interventions by referring to and mastering the goals as listed at the beginning of each chapter and by preparing an environment supportive of behavior change
- describe reinforcement's central role within the behavior-change process
- articulate the utility and use of valid, reliable behavioral data-recording, graphing and functional analytic systems
- discover individually powerful reinforcers and capitalize on that information by effectively applying those stimuli to support improved performance
- expand those applications to organizational management and other methods for promoting and supporting positive group behavior change
- promote implementation fidelity
- use reinforcement selectively to teach new behaviors
- teach complex skills, including, among others, academic, personal, social, verbal, physical, vocational, professional, managerial and other skills through the application of stimulus-control strategies
- support the maintenance and expansion of recently acquired verbal and other performance skills
- substitute constructive, productive, socially valued behaviors in exchange for personally troublesome and socially destructive behaviors
- design intervention programs to prevent the occurrence of problem behavior
- assure yourself and others that your planned actions indeed are scientifically, technologically and ethically sound.

Additionally, by formally mastering the text material, you also should be well-prepared to sit for the Behavior Analysis Certification Board's® written qualifying examination toward becoming a Board Certified Behavior Analyst. (See the appendix for the BACB Fifth Edition Task List (which takes effect as of January of 2022), or go to the BACB website (http://www.bacb.com).

The ability to pass written examinations certainly indicates a readiness for sharpening one's professional skills. So that is one place to begin; but choosing correct answers does not equal performing a top-quality job. Rather, verbal rules may cue or prompt actual performance. Given our recognition that being able to recite rules and/or pass written examinations over many concepts, although crucial to gaining expertise, is not necessarily all it takes to become a highly skillful applied behavior analyst. For this reason we and several colleagues have been collaborating in the preparation a additional training resources. At this time we have assembled several useful teaching/learning packages, (*Applying Behavior Analysis Across the Autism Spectrum, Second Edition*, Sulzer-Azaroff and Associates, 2012; *Who Killed My Daddy: A Behavioral Safety Fable*, Sulzer-Azaroff, 1998, *Behavioral Consulting: Improving Client and Consultee Learning and Behavior*, Mayer & Wallace, 2020; *Principles of Applied Behavior Analysis for Behavior Technicians and Other Practitioners, Third Edition*, Wallace & Mayer, 2022; *The Positive Classroom: Improving Student Learning and Behavior*, Mayer, 2020) and, *Preventing Problematic Behavior at Home, School, and at Work*, Mayer & Wallace, 2022)..

Here we describe the teaching-learning package to accompany this latest version of *Behavior Analysis for Lasting Change*.

## THE TEACHING/LEARNING PACKAGE

### Instructor's Manual

How will you as a student know when you actually master the concepts contained in the text material? By both telling *and* showing. One typical approach asks you to demonstrate your learning by passing quizzes, examinations and acceptably performing assigned observational, analytic, problem-solving and other tasks. If you are enrolled in a formal college course, your instructor may refer to the *Instructor's Manual*, for sample quiz items and/or performance assignments (obtained, given proper bona fides, directly from the publishers of this text).

## Study Guide

If you are like many of us, prior to presenting yourself to take an examination, you want some reassurance that you have truly mastered, comprehend and are prepared, at least on a verbal level, to apply the concepts contained in each chapter. You will be assisted here by means of our *Study Guide to Behavior Analysis for Lasting Change* (2019), prepared by Cynthia A. Bolduc and freely available on-line at www.sloanpublishing.com/balc. This study guide poses questions that only can be answered satisfactorily if you have truly learned the material contained in the chapter. The question format you will encounter in the guide includes the obvious verbal/conceptual questions; but the coverage extends beyond that by asking you to use the information you have learned to analyze and discuss various sorts of problems and issues.

## Power Point Lecture Slides

A set of Power Pont Lecture Slides, developed by Ana Duenas and the authors is available by contacting the publisher at info@sloanpublishing.com.

## PREZI Lecture Slides

A set of PREZI Lecture Slides, prepared by Dr. Karen Wagner, is available at www.sloanpublishing.com/balcslides. Powerpoint adaptations are also available by contacting the publisher at bwebber@sloanpublishing.com.

## Field Manual

You only can attain true mastery of applied behavior analytic concepts, however, through high quality application. In its wisdom, The Behavior Analysis Certification Board® currently requires its candidates for certification to actually demonstrate their satisfactory practice of behavior analytic skills by participating in a series of supervised practical activities. In the event that your area of interest is educating students on the autism spectrum, you and your supervisor may find the field manual set, *Applying Behavior Analysis Across the Autism Spectrum, Second Edition* (2012; Sulzer-Azaroff & Associates; Sloan Publishing, Cornwall-on-Hudson., NY) to be a useful resource. Another set for those preparing themselves to apply these skills toward promoting safety on the job is a didactic package, consisting of a fictitious story: Sulzer-Azaroff, B. (1998), *Who Killed My Daddy? A Behavioral Safety Fable*, plus its accompanying *Activities Workbook:* Cambridge Center for Behavioral Studies: Cambridge, MA (*behavior.org*).

Otherwise, refer to or search for and identify the standards you should meet for your own area of application. Then locate sources for or design your own set of performance goals, objectives, and the methods by which those will be measured and achieved.

## Web Site

A publisher-maintained Web Site accompanies *Behavior Analysis for Lasting Change (BALC)* and is accessible at www/sloanpublishing.com/balc. This site provides additional illustrations, examples, an on-line Study Guide, PREZI Lecture Slides, and video material for selected chapters.

# BECOMING A FULL-FLEDGED APPLIED BEHAVIOR ANALYST

Demonstrating mastery of ABA concepts and skills certainly is a good beginning, but surely not the end of your journey toward becoming and remaining a skillful and demonstrably effective applied behavior analyst. Given that a dynamic field like this one undergoes continuous change, maintaining your competence requires that as a science-practitioner, you stay abreast of new discoveries and perspectives as they evolve. You must continue your education by various means, including further formal education, pre- and in-service training and auto-didactic learning, including:

- attending and perhaps presenting your work at general and specialized conferences, such as those offered by the Association for Behavior Analysis International (ABAI) and/or your own national, regional or specialty area organizations
- attending/participating in continuing education programs
- subscribing to and reading peer reviewed journal articles
- participating in scholarly, research and development activities
- reading and perhaps forming study groups to discuss texts, assessment instruments, other materials and topical and ethical issues in the ABA field in general and in your own specialty area
- preparing teaching/training materials for personnel in your organization
- developing consulting/supervision skills (Mayer & Wallace, 2020)
- training behavior technicians (Wallace & Mayer, 2022).
- and in various other ways.

ABA is such an exciting and powerful professional, scientific and technical mix that over time you may well find yourself attracted to discovering new methods and results. The data your experimental analyses produce, the feedback provided by those affected by the results, and the visibly improved performance of your clientele undoubtedly will be sufficiently reinforcing, in and of itself, to keep you going. It has done that for us!

## ACKNOWLEDGEMENTS

We would be remiss to fail to acknowledge some key "players" who have been instrumental in the evolution of this text. First, we must thank the students, instructors, and field supervisors, too numerous to mention, who have used earlier versions of this text and provided valuable feedback over the years.

As with previous editions, this text could not possibly have come to fruition were it not for Bill Webber, our publisher. His support, encouragement, fairness, and deadlines keep this book alive! Guy Ruggiero of Pristine Graphics prepared the many illustrations that grace the pages of this edition, and Caryn Sobel ably prepared the name and subject indices.

As with any large project, its completion depends on personal support and sacrifice. Each of us is thankful to those nearest and dearest to us as well as lifelong mentors.

### Roy

I thank my son Kevin and daughter Debbie for their understanding when I could not be there to support a grandchild, or to help them out due to some book-related deadline. In addition, I am extremely appreciation of Joyce Ahern who demonstrated her love, patience, support, and understanding during this project. Also, a special thanks goes to Beth Sulzer-Azaroff for the support and enlightenment she has provided throughout my professional career. And last, but not least, a special thanks to Michele Wallace for putting up with my incessant nagging. She worked on this book while working full-time, getting married, and raising two children.

### Beth

All of us are the result of a blending of heredity and environment. Once born, heredity's task is a *fait accompli*, and the power of the environment assumes control. In my own particular case, numerous individuals have played a major role in shaping my behavior. Of those who have played an especially significant role in that regard, I must begin with my mother, Celia Horwirz Golen, who was primarily responsible for setting me on a path toward independence and achievement in life, through example and direct support.

Edward Staton Sulzer, my first husband and father of our three amazingly accomplished offspring, David, Richard, and Lenore, and best friend, not only encouraged me to continue my graduate education, but also supported my professional development. He freely shared in many family-related responsibilities that, during those mid-twentieth-century days, were assumed to be the entire province of women, including shopping, household tasks and child care.

Just a couple of years following Ed's tragic, untimely demise at age 39, Lenid Azaroff, rushed in where angels usually fear to tread, assuming the role of husband and father-figure to our three youngsters. Besides welcoming our family into his beautiful home in rural Connecticut, he added his lively niece, Deanna to the tight family constellation. Despite his own responsibilities as Director of the Institute of Materials Science at the University of Connecticut, throughout most of our 42-plus years together until we lost him a while ago, he continually encouraged and supported the children's education and my ongoing professional career.

Roy Mayer and I seemed to click as colleagues during our year on the Guidance and Educational Psychology faculty at Southern University. For over half a century, we have shared our commitment to our field, especially to training those personnel who would counsel and support their clientele by applying the most promising behavior practices scientifically determined to be effective. I am so grateful for his never-ending commitment to keeping our jointly authored work up-to-date and useful.

Following our retirement from our respective professorships, Leonid and I moved to Florida. Shortly thereafter, I agreed to offer a course in applied behavior analysis at Florida International University. The thoroughly-committed students were a joy to teach. One of the class stars, Michele Wallace, stood out as especially excited with the course coverage and content. It is our good fortune that Michelle has agreed to assist us in the text revision process and especially for this particular edition, we thank her for her contributions.

**Michele**

Michele is thankful, first and for most, to Beth and Roy, for asking her to join this amazing team and mentoring her in this process along the way (it's been a great 16 years). She also wants to express her deep appreciation to her wife (Tymerie), children (Payton & Aiden), family (the Bussers, Sims, and Seymours) and friends (who she really considers family) for all their love, support, encouragement, and patience during this project. She also extends a great deal of appreciation for her longtime mentor, Dr. Brian Iwata, for without his mentoring this project would have been out of reach. Finally, she would like to thank Dr. Pat Friman for instilling the concept of being able to take technological concepts, principles, and procedures and explain them in such a way that a grandmother could understand. It is a skill that has served her well in this process.

# A Note to the Reader

## What Does ABA Have to Do with Me? My Case is Unique!

The fact that you have come to this page suggests that your curiosity has been piqued; that at various times in your life you have stopped to wonder why you and the people you contact do what you do, or fail to do, and, if called for, what you might be able to do to better the situation. Can leopards change their spots? Hardly! But their behavioral patterns can change, within the limits of their constitutions and the environments in which they live. Practically all living organisms can and must adjust to survive. But, depending on their physical attributes and learning histories, they must learn to perform particular novel acts precisely, more or less often, as environmental conditions demand or permit. As this book should convince you, the same is true of essentially all living organisms, including ourselves.

About a century ago, two luminaries, John B. Watson and B. F. Skinner, began to investigate the behavior of living organisms—primarily of small animals, but also, of young children. They sought to discover why we humans behave the way we do and what modifies those actions. Repeatedly, they found that the events closely following the act of concern influenced the future rate at which that act was expressed. When something "good" ("wanted," "needed," or "liked") followed, its rate accelerated; when nothing or something "bad" or "unwanted" happened, its rare decelerated. (Later, of course, other behavioral arrangements, including the nature of reinforcers and other classes of consequences of and antecedents to those acts, were and continue to be studied).

Over the intervening years, the scientific analysis of behavior has broadened its scope to include an extraordinary variety and number of subject participants, including those of almost microscopic size to that of elephants. Yet the fundamental laws of behavior, and the purposeful, ethically sound guidelines for applying them, continue to adhere.

Today we—yes, you and I and those we serve—are the beneficiaries of these discoveries. This volume attempts to describe and illustrate those findings and provide you with scientifically and ethically sound guidelines for applying the procedures derived from them. You may notice, though, that an outsized proportion of our examples involve people facing severe physical, intellectual, emotional, or social challenges in their lives. The reason is that the simpler, more haphazard or less organized methods (like loosely telling or showing) have failed to do the trick for them.

Just as we turn to the medical profession to ease our troubling physical concerns, we would be wise to turn to applied behavior analysis (ABA) when simpler approaches fail to produce our desired behavioral outcomes. By mastering ABA knowledge and skills of the kind included in this text, you will not only learn how to address many of the more perplexing behavioral problems facing yourself and those you serve, but you also will learn how to prevent the occurrence of many of those problems. We strongly caution you, though not to be misled into thinking that applying behavior analysis is relevant only to participants with physical and intellectual challenges due to our frequent inclusion of case examples involving those populations. Actually, formally- and informally-analyzed instances of its success reveal its universality across ages, ethnicities, cultures, tasks, intellectual, and motivational levels.

View the situation below, because it illustrates that point. Here, the challenges and objectives may seem more general, and perhaps even familiar to you. The issue was one of the financial losses a sports-shoe company was suffering due to the number of product rejects. Requested to investigate and perhaps address the situation, we (Harshbarger and Sulzer-Azaroff) were asked to visit the plant in Bangkok, Thailand. Observing the complete step-by-step operation, we noticed that each foreman supervised a small group of workers responsible for every task along the way. What we learned was that most of the foremen regularly watched the particular operation and scolded anyone whose work failed to meet quality standards. After we undertook to train foremen and their managers (right up to the owner, who functioned as translator) to regularly monitor their subordinates' performance and intermittently to compliment them when they met quality standards, rejects began to diminish and profits to increase. (The owner was wise enough to reward all the managers, and even the two of us by arranging a celebratory cruise down Bangkok's major river!)

To maximize your own personal profit from studying applied behavior analysis, we suggest that as you work your way through this text, you frequently stop to reward yourself. You can do that by reminding yourself that you are becoming increasingly more capable of responsibly applying your newly acquired knowledge and skills to promote and support your own and others' abilities and well-being. (And just for the fun of it, maybe once in a while, give yourself a healthy, delicious treat, or do something you enjoy!)

To help you keep abreast of developments in the field, a partial listing of journals that contain behavior analysis articles include:

*Analysis of Verbal Behavior*
*Autism*
*Autism Research*
*Behavior Analysis in Practice*
*Behavior Analyst/Perspective on Behavior Science*
*Behavioral Interventions*
*Behavior Therapy*
*Perspective on Behavior Science*
*Behavior Modification*
*Journal of Applied Behavior Analysis*
*Journal of Autism & Developmental Disorders*
*Journal of Behavioral Education*
*Journal of the Experimental Analysis of Behavior*
*Journal of Behavioral Therapy and Experimental Psychiatry*
*Journal of Organizational Behavior Management*
*Journal of Positive Behavior Interventions*
*Research in Autism Spectrum Disorders*
*Research in Developmental Disabilities*
*The Behavior Analyst*

Others can be found in the Reference section of this text.

# Chapter 1

# Achieving Lasting Behavior Change By Applying Behavior Analysis
## What Is It and How Does It Work?

### Goals

1. Describe how human behavior influences our welfare.
2. Describe the specific position radical behaviorists take to explain human behavior.
3. Briefly describe the evolution of behavior analysis from its early beginnings to the present.
4. Discuss the circumstances under which the behavior of organisms was found as equivalently lawful as other natural phenomenon and thereby amenable to scientific investigation.
5. List and describe the philosophical concepts on which applied behavior analysis (ABA) is based.
6. Describe the manner in which ABA consists of a (a) scientific method, (b) technology, and (c) professional approach.
7. Define *behavior*.
8. Describe ABA in simple language.
9. Say how you would justify labeling a particular intervention as being behavior-analytic in character.
10. Differentiate between *applied* and *basic* behavior analysis.
11. Specify why the BACB was developed.
12. Specify the four levels of professional ABA practitioner categories and describe their distinctive roles and functions.
13. List four current roles and functions of ABA participants of particular interest to you.
14. Specify and describe each of ABA's basic features.

15. Specify and describe each ABA practitioner category.
16. Describe *radical behaviorism*.
17. Discuss the behavioral position on assigning responsibility for an individual's particular actions.
18. Provide a general overview of the professional approach to ABA and describe and illustrate each major step or element in Figure 1.1.

**********

## INTRODUCTION

For better or worse, change is a fact of life. Change is inherent in nature and, as creatures of nature, in all of humanity's personal and social behavior. Over the millennia, familial, tribal, social, cultural, legal, educational, business, health, and numerous other organizational systems have evolved to manage behavioral change. Contemporary societies attempt to manage such change by creating laws, institutions, policies, and practices to provide a balance between personal and communal freedom, thereby enabling these societies to survive and flourish.

In the best of all possible worlds, if those systems were to function smoothly and effectively, all would be well. Alas, they often are imperfect and that is where the need for change begins. If children fail to attain appropriate verbal, social, or self-help skills, that becomes a source of distress for their families and others in the community. When members of social, service, healthcare, business, or other organizations commit mistakes or shirk their responsibilities, others within, and perhaps outside of the group pay the price. Personal and group misconduct like criminal deeds, neglectful or harmful parenting, and drug, sexual, or self-abuse certainly can take a toll on individuals and their societies. Racism and other biases toward particular groups have tremendous negative effects on society and individuals. Skinner (1945) pointed out that terms like diversity and equity should be viewed by looking at the variables and conditions under which they are used, so as to promote anti-racism

While the world's societies have made incredible progress to date, much remains to be accomplished, especially within the realm of human behavior. Probably that fact explains why so many of us are fascinated by such questions as, "Why do people (and other living organisms) do the things they do?" and "What, if necessary, can be done to produce effective and enduring learning of, or change, in a particular behavior?"

Within the past hundred years or so, a science of the behavior of living organisms has been evolving in answer to these questions. At present, thousands of scientific researchers and practitioners continue actively to pursue those questions, standing as evidence of the broad interest in humane, responsible, constructive, equitable, durable behavioral change.

Certainly most recognize just how critical a role human behavior plays in determining the future survival of humankind. Increasingly apparent is the fact that not only our own personal health and happiness, but the very continuation of we homo-sapiens as a species, heavily depend on our behavioral choices. To illustrate:

- Attaining/retaining good health by accessing, choosing, and consuming nutritious foods; exercising regularly and gaining adequate rest; having the wherewithal to function safely at work, play, and at home; and obtaining essential skilled medical assistance *versus* damaging our health by consuming excessive quantities of marginally or non-nutritious foods or of harmful substances; participating in hazardous activities; and being unable to access essential help and support.
- Optimizing our abilities to permit us to support ourselves and our dependents through education, training, and constructive planning and to detect and capitalize on available opportunities *versus* struggling just to survive.

- Saving and contributing to our own savings and the world's resources *versus* exploiting, over-expending, or wasting them.
- Cooperating and collaborating in mutually beneficial group decisions *versus* competing to the advantage of few but to the detriment of many.

The list goes on and on. As any rational person must agree, not only our present but our personal and collective future prospects depend upon how humans behave. Ergo, one of the most profound questions anyone can pose is: "What must we as individuals and as members of the human family do to advance our survival and to permit us to live longer, healthier, and more fulfilling lives?" The more we understand about human behavior and our ability to modify it humanely and effectively the closer we approach the answer to that question.

Be cautious about accepting undocumented advice, though, because, as Daniels and Lattal (2017) have pointed out, despite abundant advice available via the web, social media, and from numerous books on how to live the good life, make personal changes, and to reach one's potential, much of that material is based on outdated theories and beliefs that lack supporting data. By contrast, thanks to the science of human behavior, rigorous tools now exist for determining:

- why individuals tend behave as they do under particular circumstances and
- how effectively to:
  - promote and teach specific behaviors
  - broaden or refine the circumstances under which particular behaviors are emitted
  - reduce or eliminate inappropriate or unhealthy behavior, without necessarily having to resort to threats or punishment.

In other words, we no longer need to turn to outdated and unsupported beliefs or theories about why people (and other living organisms) behave the way they do. Rather, thanks to the findings of nearly a century of scientific study of human behavior, we now possess a set of effective tools for altering behavior for the good of the individual and of society.

Addressing people's directly observable behavioral issues goes as far back as humans have lived in social groupings. From prehistoric times onward, people have struggled to comprehend why living organisms behave the way they do, and, how to change it. This seemingly universal inclination to comprehend and change behavior has generated numerous explanations and methods. Some strategies designed to help people meet their daily challenges and gain better control over their destinies have been wise; others, though perhaps well-intended, have been fanciful or even cruel: from belief systems, folklore, social regulation and sanctions to wars, torture and various other benign or cruel strategies. Of those, the more serious-minded and systematic approaches eventually coalesced into the field of psychology.

Within the more recent past, though, many resolute philosophers and scientists began to speculate about whether the behavior of living organisms actually might obey natural laws in ways similar to those of the physical world. In keeping with that perspective, during the latter part of the nineteenth century, experimental psychology began to emerge as a scientific enterprise represented by an expanding array of methodologically-oriented investigators of the "psyche" or "mind." Some viewed behavior according to its structure. This structuralism, initially proposed by Wilhelm Wundt (1832–1920) and promoted by Edward B. Titchener (1867–1927), sought to understand the adult "mind" in terms of a set of simple, definable components. Wundt viewed the mind as being composed of the sum total of the individual's experience from birth to the present time. The structural psychologists' major tool was introspection (a careful set of self-observations made under controlled conditions by trained observers using a stringently-defined descriptive vocabulary). Using this technique, they attempted to discover how these components fit together into complex forms called hypothetical or imaginary constructs.[1] These include internal mentalistic processes like attitudes, feelings, self-concepts, or motivations, or even structures like Sigmund Freud's (1856–1939)

---

[1] See MacCorquodal & Meehl, 1948.

id, ego, and superego or Carl Jung's (1865–1961) concepts of the extroverted and introverted personality types, archetypes (differing but repeating patterns of thought and action that appear time and again across people, countries, and continents), and the collective unconscious, the repository of all the religious, spiritual, and mythological symbols and experiences.

Others, like John B. Watson (1878–1958), considered by many to be the founder of behaviorism (Malone, 2014), took an alternative, much more objective route toward exploring why people behave as they do. His methodological behaviorism emphasized directly observing human and animal action to study behavior. He assumed that, like other natural phenomena, behavior obeys certain basic laws. He particularly emphasized the interaction between maturing human beings and their environments, contending that he could guarantee to take "well-formed" healthy infants and a specifically organized world, and train those infants to become "any type of specialist... doctor, lawyer, artist, merchant-chief, and, yes, even beggerman" (Watson, 1930, p. 82). B. F. Skinner (1904–1990) assumed a similar, though more parsimonious (economical) perspective, endorsing the notion that the behavior of organisms is the subject matter of science, and considered by many to be the founder of behavior analysis.

Today, behavior analysts agree that the behavior of organisms is as subject to the laws of nature as any other natural phenomena. Like other natural scientists, radical behaviorists attribute what living organisms do and say to their **ontogeny** (*the origin and development of an individual organism from embryo to adult*) and to their **phylogeny** (*those historical patterns of relationships among their genetic endowments, past experiences, and the internal and external environmental contingencies of reinforcement currently affecting them*). Of special relevance is the way multiple events may affect one another, especially when they are contingently related to one another (i.e., preceding or following one another). Examples of contingent relations include twisting the doorknob and the door opens (positive reinforcement), touching a hot stove and getting burned and then not touching the stove when the burner is on the next time (positive punishment), inhaling pepper and sneezing, pressing the correct elevator button and arriving at the correct floor. Contingent relations of that sort are fundamental to nonhuman and human learning and behavior change. Another way of saying this is that particular patterns of behavior evolve and persist through natural selection, in much the same way that Darwinian *selectionism* (Darwin, 1872/1958) operates. Those qualities best suited to the organism's physical and its cultural environment (the local common code of systems of beliefs and attitudes about what is good and bad, right and wrong) are most readily selected for survival.

This deterministic perspective asserts that, like other natural phenomena, human behavior obeys the laws of nature—that it is causally determined—by combinations of preceding events and/or consequences. And, perhaps even more important for ourselves, as agents of behavior change, we appreciate that like physical and chemical processes, once translated into (technically, operationalized as) human actions, these behavioral phenomena lend themselves to manipulation for purposes of scientific investigation. This recognition has evoked an ever-expanding experimental analysis of behavior; one directed toward producing a body of knowledge and understanding about how contingencies of reinforcement influence what people and other living organisms say and do.

As with other scientific information (i.e. physical phenomena), many have pondered whether it would be possible to put the knowledge derived from the scientific analysis of behavior to use for the benefit of humankind. Or is it too late? The race between the forces supportive of healthy growth and of destruction is intense. The more we learn about the intricacies of the behavior of organisms, and the sooner we learn how to constructively, equitably, and compassionately apply that knowledge, the better chance humanity has to continue to survive and thrive. Bertrand Russell, the eminent philosopher, stressed this point in 1955:

Whether men will be able to survive the changes of environment that their own skill has brought about is open to question. If the answer is in the affirmative, men will have to apply scientific ways of thinking to themselves and their institutions. They cannot continue to hope, as all politicians hitherto have, that in a world where everything has changed, the political and social habits of the eighteenth century can remain inviolate. Not only will men of science have to grapple with the sciences that deal with man, but—and this is a far more difficult matter—they will have to persuade the world to listen to what they have discovered (Russell, 1955, p. 6–7).

What Russell sagely endorsed was scientifically to examine and publicly disseminate new methods for arranging and applying effective, morally and ethically justifiable behavior-change techniques, as epitomized by applied behavior analysis. This science would

- rely on an empirical approach, one based on observational and experimental practice, to seek to discover and describe as economically or parsimoniously as possible the natural laws and principles that explain and are capable of controlling human behavior.
- convince others that they should pursue such discoveries and then establish how best to apply these findings toward the betterment of both individuals and humankind in general.

## The Radical Behavioral Approach

**Radical behaviorism** *takes the perspective that feelings, sensations, ideas, thoughts and other features of mental life are subject to the same behavioral laws and principles as overt behaviors, and are influenced by one's experiences and environment.* "It simply questions the nature of the object observed and the reliability of the observations" (Skinner, 1974, pp. 16–17). So, as stressed previously, applied behavior analysts tend to focus on overt behaviors, or the products of behavior, and the environmental factors that influence them. This permits reliable observation and measurement, including what participants say and do.

Does the fact that we may find an individual's particular behavioral pattern troubling necessarily mean that the individual is flawed or at fault? Not if you take a truly radical behavioral perspective. As radical behaviorists, we recognize that the person is not to be blamed; only that the individual's pattern of behavior is unacceptable to us. Rather than faulting Dexter by saying he is lazy, we observe that he frequently fails to do his work. Nor would it be appropriate to label Paula as "a procrastinator"; despite that she regularly procrastinates. Better to comment that Bruno plays the piano with exceptional skill (something he does and that is subject to change) than simply to label him "a prodigy" (something he is.) And instead of calling Lucretia "a rotten little kid" (implying a fixed quality), a preferable description would be that of a child who frequently hits other children and grabs their toys.

By viewing people's problematic actions in terms of what they do or fail to do, rather than what they are, we are led to recognize that change is possible. We don't go about altering people; rather we attempt to change the rates with which they perform (technically "emit" particular behaviors). This is not to imply that optimally applying behavior analysis enables us to promote, or eradicate any individual's particular behavior. Successful behavior change depends on a number of factors, many of which may be well beyond the behavior analyst's control. Those include:

- Genetic endowment (i.e., the person's physical attributes and limitations) in that it can affect how rapidly and skillfully one learns to do or say or cease doing or saying particular things.
- Access to learning opportunities, material resources, medical care, and other aspects of the individual's environment.
- Prior learning, because progress may well be impeded when key pieces are missing from one's learning history.
- Historical and current antecedent and consequential stimuli, such as the reinforcers, punishers, and contextual conditions present when the individual had responded or is currently responding.

How about character? Doesn't that fit into the equation? Not really. Though a person's action patterns may be judged to be acceptable or not, the person *per se* is neither dignified nor to be condemned for committing those acts, because they were molded via interactions between the individual's physical attributes, experiences, and the conditions currently missing or in place. From the behavioral perspective, "the individual—if not his/her actions—is always right."[2]

Notice, though, we do not say that people never misbehave, (or for that matter, behave admirably,) according to particular standards or values. Rather, we do not attribute the blame (or credit) for their behavior to their ill will or malign intentions (or to their talents). Rather, blame or credit needs to be ascribed to the factors just discussed.

Given this perspective, any change procedures we choose to implement must be said to apply to behaviors, not to people. Dexter is not reinforced. His good work is. Applied behavior analysis is not in the business of changing people, only in guiding and supporting changes in their behavior.

Don't infer from this that people have no control over their own behavior, assuming they have the physical attributes and environmental histories and resources that permit them to take charge of their circumstances. As you proceed through this text, you will come to appreciate that one of the particular values of learning about behavioral principles and their optimal application is that you yourself, as a professional teacher, coach, therapist, manager, counselor, or other change agent—can use the rules to modify not only the behavior of your clientele, but also the performance patterns of your consenting loved ones as well as those of your very own self.

One more disclaimer: Whereas the behavioral approach forces us to conclude that people's actions are a function of their learning histories and any conditions currently in place, we needn't be unfeeling about what we see them say and do. The anger, frustration, or delight we experience in response to noting others' behavior is just as much a product of our own learning histories as the deeds or misdeeds of the individual generating that reaction in us. Additionally, as with our clients, you, as we, are human, with behavioral repertoires shaped by our own experiences and supported or impeded by current conditions. Nonetheless, as you master the principles governing behavior and their ethically sound application, you will begin to become increasingly more proficient in applying them not only with your clientele, but also to your own actions as a change agent. We see that particular proficiency as the major advantage you, as a student of this topic, will achieve by mastering the principles and procedures described in this text.

## THE ORIGIN AND EVOLUTION OF THE FIELD OF APPLIED BEHAVIOR ANALYSIS

By the 1940s, experimental psychology was sufficiently well established to enable Edwin G. Boring (1950) to draw upon a fairly voluminous body of work in preparing his *History of Experimental Psychology*. Among the greats contributing to the discipline was B. F. Skinner (1938), of whom you will read more in Chapter 2. Skinner undertook to experimentally analyze basic behavioral processes both within a temporal and a biological context. This endeavor was labeled "the experimental analysis of behavior." In fact, some argue that the field of the experimental analysis of behavior was formally started in 1938, with the publication of the experimental work done in Skinner's laboratory. Then, in the late 1950s and early 1960s, Skinner and several of his students and colleagues (e.g., James Holland, Sidney Bijou, Israel Goldiamond, Nathan Azrin, Fred Keller, and others) began to explore ways to extend those processes and research procedures to behavior within a social context.

With the publication of the *Journal of Applied Behavior Analysis* in 1968, and the dimensions (see Table 1.1) identified by Baer, Wolf and Risley

---

[2]B. F. Skinner contended that "the subject is always right!" in that his/her behavior was much a function of prior reinforcement history and contingencies currently operating.

**TABLE 1.1  Dimensions of ABA**

| Feature | Function |
|---|---|
| Applied | Focuses on socially significant behaviors |
| Behavioral | Focuses on observable, objective measurement of behavior |
| Analytical | Demonstrates functional relationships |
| Technological | Fully describes all procedures implemented in such detail that someone else could replicate implementation |
| Conceptually systematic | Utilizes procedures based upon principles of behavior analysis |
| Effective | Demonstrates socially significant behavior change through objective measurement |
| Generality | Produces behavior change across behaviors, people, and/or settings |

(1968), the field of **Applied Behavior Analysis (ABA**[3]**)** was born. *ABA is an evidence-based method of examining and changing what people (and other living creatures) say and do.* Practitioners of applied behavior analysis conduct their experimental investigations of behavior-environment relationships of relatively immediate individual, social, and cultural importance for the purpose of studying and successfully managing behavior in the real world.

Applications of behavior analysis soon began to expand into a variety of areas. Among others, Holland and Skinner (1961) successfully advanced college students' conceptual learning by programming instruction, that is, breaking instructional content down into small parts or "steps" and requiring the student to participate actively by answering questions on the material. Meanwhile, in the mid to late sixties, Israel Goldiamond (1968) addressed stuttering, Theodore Ayllon and Nate Azrin (1965) studied psychiatric patients' adaptive behaviors, and Sidney Bijou, Donald Baer, Jay Birnbrauer, and Montrose Wolf (see references) addressed the behavioral deficits and excesses of young children with developmental delays. The unambiguous success of those early efforts unleashed a movement toward applying behavior analysis to an array of behavioral challenges previously found quite resistant to change. Well-controlled applied experimental investigations covered the gamut from coping with communication difficulties, school learning and deportment, self-management, physical well-being, and social issues,

to an extensive list of methods for remedying other behavioral deficiencies and excesses. Not only did those investigators present compelling evidence of their participants' progress, but thanks to the tightly-controlled experimental methods of ABA, they were able to supply clear and objective evidence convincingly to support their claims.

Given that ABA was derived from the experimental analysis of behavior, it is no wonder that the philosophical concepts are indistinguishable between the two. (See Box 1.1, "Definitions of Philosophical Concepts on which ABA is Based.") As you proceed through this text, you increasingly will recognize how successfully the field of applied behavior analysis has adhered to these concepts.

Another facet of the discipline of behavioral analysis has focused primarily on the *conceptual analysis of behavior*, which verbally addresses historical, philosophical, theoretical, and methodological issues. Illustrations of the latter are found in such journals as *The Behavior Analyst, Verbal Behavior,* and numerous others, covering conceptual and professional issues.

As you will see, by referring to our list of references, the analysis of behavior—basic, applied, and conceptual—has not only survived, but continues to flourish to the extent that today literally thousands of behavior-analytic papers on the topic have been published in scientific journals. As one exemplar, ABA's effectiveness in promoting adaptive behavior among people on the autism spectrum certainly has attracted the attention of scientists, professionals, and the lay population at large. (Autism is a

---

[3]Some people called the field of ABA "Behavior Modification."

> **Box 1  Definitions of Philosophical Concepts on which ABA is Based**
>
> **Determinism:** Doctrine that acts of the will, occurrences in nature, or social or psychological phenomena are causally determined by events or natural laws.
>
> **Empiricism:** Derived from or guided by experience, objective observation, or experiment.
>
> **Parsimony:** Explaining phenomena by using the simplest theory that fits the facts of a problem.
>
> **Scientific method:** A method of inquiry based on empirical or measurable systematic observation measurement and experiment, and the formulation, testing, and modification of hypotheses or questions.
>
> **Pragmatism**: A practical approach to problems in which truth is found in the process of verification. Pragmatism and behaviorism go hand in hand (Baer, Wolf, & Risley, 1968).
>
> **Selectionism**: Behaviors evolve and persist through natural selection (based on the contingencies—antecedents, or precursors, and consequences related to the behavior's occurrence—in the environment interacting with biology) in much the same way as Darwinian selectionism in the evolution of species.

syndrome associated with communicative, emotional, social and other severe difficulties, previously highly resistant to successful treatment.) Yet the behavioral difficulties experienced by individuals with autism are only one among numerous sets of behavioral challenges addressed within ABA. Throughout this text, you will encounter extensive experimental evidence illustrating how behavior analysts have successfully applied established principles of behavior toward improving learning and performance in a myriad of specialty areas. Examples among the multitude include education, job training, developmental and rehabilitation services, parenting, personal, family and vocational counseling, sports performance, health promotion and treatment, commercial and industrial ventures, public services, public affairs, war and peace. In fact, just about any situation involving the actions of living organisms is a potential focus for ABA.

## APPLIED BEHAVIOR ANALYSIS TODAY

As our knowledge about the way organisms learn and change their behavior expands, those practicing applied behavior analysis become increasingly able to successfully and constructively guide learning and performance in specific directions. As often happens with new terms, the meaning of applied behavior analysis has been evolving over time. Essential to its definition are that ABA is a scientific method, a technology, and/or a professional approach. The *Behavior Analysis Certification Board* has provided us with the following simplified definition of ABA:

> **Definition of ABA**
>
> *ABA is the design, implementation, and evaluation of environmental modifications to produce socially significant improvement in human behavior. ABA includes the use of direct observation, measurement, and functional analysis of the relations between environment and behavior. ABA uses changes in environmental events, including antecedent stimuli and consequences, to produce practical and significant changes in behavior. These relevant environmental events are usually identified through a variety of specialized assessment methods. ABA is based on the fact that an individual's behavior is determined by past and current environmental events in conjunction with organic variables such as their genetic endowment and ongoing physiological variables. ABA focuses on treating behavioral difficulties by changing the individual's environment rather than focusing on variables that are, at least presently, beyond our direct access.*
>
> (Copyright 2012 by the Behavior Analyst Certification Board, Inc. ("BACB"). Ver. 1.1)

> **The BACB's Description of ABA**
>
> ***Behavior analysis*** *is the science of behavior, with a history extending back to the early 20th century. Its guiding philosophy is behaviorism, which is based on the premise that attempts to improve the human condition through behavior change (e.g., education, be-havioral health treatment) will be most effective if behavior itself is the primary focus.*
>
> ***Applied behavior analysis*** *(ABA) is largely based on behavior and its consequences, techniques generally involve teaching individuals more effective ways of behaving and working to change the social consequences of existing behavior. Treatment approaches based on ABA have been empirically shown to be effective in a wide variety of areas. However, because ABA was first applied to the treatment of individuals with intellectual disabilities and autism, this practice area has the largest evidence base and has received the most recognition." (Behavior Analysis Certification Board, 2021, on-line)*

## THE ESSENTIAL FEATURES OF APPLIED BEHAVIOR ANALYSIS: A SCIENTIFIC, TECHNOLOGICAL AND PROFESSIONAL APPROACH

### ABA as a Scientific Approach

When we speak of **behavior**, quite simply, we refer to *what living organisms do, including what and how they communicate*, aside from its intrinsic value or acceptability. It is a neutral term. We do not use the term to connote "good behavior" or "misbehavior," just what someone does or says. Behavior analysis is the experimental investigation of variables that influence the behavior of any living organism. From the beginning, applied behavior analysis has taken an empirical, that is, an experimental, data-based, scientific approach, drawing upon observation and experience to *describe, predict, and ethically manage ("control") behavior*. Its aim has been to identify the variables that lawfully and meaningfully influence behavior in real-world settings, such as clinics, hospitals, schools, the home, the workplace, virtual space capsules (e.g., Hienz et al., 2005), out in the community—anywhere people (and sometimes animals, like guide dogs, work horses, and others that perform service functions) participate in their daily affairs. The meaning of "applied" in "applied behavior analysis" is that the behaviors it quantitatively describes and functionally addresses are socially important. This is done by successfully teaching and supporting constructive, adaptive, healthy, safe, and satisfying learning and performance, and by reducing detrimental behavioral excesses and deficits. Baer, Wolf, and Risley (1968) originally defined and described applied behavior analyses as "experimental investigations of behavior conducted in real-world settings." In so doing, they noted that its essential dimensions specify that the behaviors to be changed are explicitly important and objectively and quantitatively measurable. Its experimental manipulations analyze with precision sufficient to "show clearly what arrangements were responsible for the change" (p. 97). That means that its descriptions of all procedures and contextual conditions contributing to that change are complete and technologically exact, while the effectiveness and magnitude of the change is of sufficient value to be meaningful and general (see Table 1.1 on page 7).

In describing the dimensions that would define the field of applied behavior analysis, Baer, et al. (1968) provided the recipe for how researchers and practitioners would apply behavior analysis. To *distinguish applied behavior analysis from the experimental analysis of behavior*, it was important to point out that the endeavors would need to focus on behaviors that are of social importance. This distinction came from the difference between *basic* and *applied* research. Both are interested in what controls behavior; but **basic research** generally addresses some phenomena for the sake of understanding those phenomena per se, and usually is conducted in laboratory settings, whereas **applied research** tends to investigate and analyze the effects of environmental changes upon socially important behavior either in a laboratory or real-life setting, to improve the behavior. In other words, in application, "the behavior, stimuli, and/or organism under study are chosen because of their importance to man and society, rather than their importance to theory" (Baer, et al., p. 92). To be clear, applied work (research or practice) needs to be pragmatic (have practical value).

By aligning with the tradition of behavior analysis in general, applied behavior analysis focuses on observable and objective behaviors (the **Behavioral** aspect). Some have mistakenly assumed this means that behavior analysts can't focus on thoughts. This is not the case, as long as thoughts can be expressed as observable and objective behaviors (*what* someone says, and perhaps, *how*—the fashion in which they say it), then addressing those behaviors falls under the cloak of applied behavior analysis.

Moreover, it is important to note that the behavior being addressed must be *the* behavior itself, not a proxy of the behavior, and special attention must be given to "which person's behavior" is changed (the individual's not the observer's behavior). In sum, the behavioral aspect also heightens the reliability of observational measurement.

Given the philosophical concepts of *determinism* and *empiricism* that guide the experimental analysis of behavior, it is no wonder that those same features would help define the application of behavior analysis. The term **analytical** means *the demonstration of a functional relationship, or in other words "a believable demonstration of the events that can be responsible for the occurrence or non-occurrence of that behavior"* (Baer, et al., p. 94). This transfer of the more basic *experimental analysis of behavior* into *applied behavior analysis* requires that we must demonstrate that the interventions (independent variables) we apply, either within a research or practical format, are responsible for the observed behavior change; and that producing that change at will (i.e., turn it off or on) is doable.

Demonstrating functional relations between the intervention or treatment and behavior change explains why, as behavior analysts, we must fully understand and master the user of single-subject or single case design. We need to demonstrate that the specific behavior change is a result of what we are doing. Demonstrating the functional relationship requires that we fully describe all the procedures implemented (its **technological features**). We can feel confident in asserting that a procedural description is sufficiently technological when someone else can directly replicate (duplicate) the implementation process solely by referring to that description.

Providing technological, or operational, descriptors of change strategies also ensures that we can assess treatment integrity to validate that what we assert is responsible for the functional relationship, truly is. It is not enough to merely label the procedure, *positive reinforcement*, but explain under what circumstances and the manner in which positive reinforcement was implemented (e.g., providing immediate attention in the form of praise contingent on the student raising their hand on a continuous reinforcement schedule, and do not provide praise if the student speaks out of turn). "The best rule of thumb for evaluating a procedure description as technological is probably to ask whether a typically trained reader could replicate that procedure well enough to produce the same results, given only a reading of the description" (Baer, et al., p. 95). Practically, when trying to decide if one's procedure is technological, give the procedure description to someone and ask them to play it out.

Besides its technological feature, the field of applied behavior analysis can only relate to basic behavioral principles (both are similarly **conceptually systematic**). Given that applied behavior analysis was born out of the experimental analysis of behavior, it readily ties back to the basic principles of behavior. No new or additional explanations are required. This parsimonious dimension is important to our field and ensures our practice is more than just a bag of tricks.

Furthermore, linking a procedure to a basic principle of behavior enables an understanding of its ins and outs. It also permits practitioners to plan when and how to optimize its application, while avoiding the temptation to become attracted to popular gimmicky therapies.

Because we are to focus on socially significant behavior change, it goes without saying that our efforts must result in significant behavior change (*effective*). This notion has developed into the concept of *evidence-based practice*, wherein we are responsible for demonstrating an outcome or effect rather than simply asserting that improvement has been achieved.

Additionally, the improvement must be shown to have practical value, not narrowly, but at a *socially significant* and *general* level: that is across behaviors, people, and/or settings (*generality*). To accomplish this important challenge, from the very beginning, "generalization should be programmed, rather than expected or lamented" (Baer, et al., p. 97).

On reviewing the history of the ABA field twenty years after publishing their initial description of applied behavior analysis, Baer, Wolf, and Risley (1987) noted that some of its elements (applied, behavioral, analytic, technological, conceptual, effective, and capable of appropriately generalized outcomes) had expanded in scope, in the sense that it was now addressing more complex problems. They also noted that, in the interim, novel (especially computerized) measurement and analytic tools and strategies had emerged, and recognized that the context in which the behavior is emitted ("expressed" or "produced") plays a more important role in determining how a person behaves at a particular time and place. Additionally, they observed that practitioners were tending to pay greater attention to the particular function of unwelcome or dangerous behavior and to the complexity of interactions between antecedent circumstances and the behavior of interest.

If, the reasoning goes, an experimenter can turn behavior on and off or up and down "at will," whether it be smiling, singing, choosing, using, solving, or whatever, the experimenter has achieved a successful behavioral analysis. Convincing parents, teachers, clients themselves, managers, and supervisors that they should be able to manage behavior similarly, however, may not be easy. But as you will discover, applied behavior analysts can also apply their methods toward teaching others how successfully to apply those behavior analytic methods (as is our purpose in preparing this text). Consequently, when describing a particular application, the behavior analyst must identify and completely specify all the actions to be taken (or perhaps to be avoided) by the change agents. To meet the technological qualification, well-prepared program implementers must be able to take that description and, assuming they apply it reliably to participants with similar behavioral repertoires, to essentially achieve or replicate (duplicate) the results.

## Applied Behavior Analysis as a Technology of Behavior Change

Behavior analysts assess behavioral challenges and design the most promising solutions by selecting methods to apply, monitor, analyze, revise and reanalyze if necessary, communicate the effects of their interventions. In general, ABA investigations involve one or more of several categories of behavior-change tactics. Among numerous examples are:

*Increasing behavior* such as:

- communicating, reading, defining words correctly
- praising, describing an accomplishment, donning safety equipment, precisely adhering to protocols
- completing assignments according to standards
- participating in decision-making and following through on agreements
- exercising more skillfully, harder, and/or longer
- creating works of art, literature, or technological solutions to problems
- adhering to health and/or self-help routines

*Teaching and maintaining behavior s*uch as satisfactorily performing:

- academic skills, including reading, writing, spelling, arithmetic operations
- technical skills, such as designing an engine, a computer program, an electromechanical device
- professional skills, like performing difficult diagnostic, surgical, or engineering routines
- self-care skills, like grooming, self-feeding, preparing meals, making beds
- self-management skills, like organizing one's time, completing assignments, controlling emotional outbursts, choosing and conforming to healthy diets and exercise
- family, organizational, and management skills such as systematizing, choosing, and monitoring individual and group goals

- job skills, as in assembling products, providing specific services, preparing reports
- social skills, such as asking and answering questions, greeting people, excusing one's inappropriate (rude) behavior, engaging in conversations, participating in community organizations
- leadership skills, as in defining an organization's mission, setting objectives, defining job requirements, assessing performance, providing feedback, reinforcing positive practices
- continuing productive, proactive practices such as those in this list
- engaging in activities of civic responsibility, like voting and caring for the environment
- detecting subtle differences in one's own or others' behavior or the products of their behavior

*Making behavior appropriately responsive to highly specific stimuli*, as in learning to label actions as correct, expert, precise, sophisticated, talented, or skillful such as:

- decoding letters and words: reading complex words and sentences in one's own or a different language
- identifying and applying the correct way to solve mathematical problems: basic or advanced operations, such as adding, subtracting, multiplying, dividing, solving a range of equations or word problems
- differentiating an actual painting by Vermeer from a forgery; a benign from a malignant tumor; a fine from an ordinary wine; a designer outfit from a knock-off; a brilliant versus an amateur musical or sports performance; a cat from a jaguar; a child with autism versus one with a hearing loss; an adult with depression from one with fatigue caused by a medical problem

*Selecting the most valid and reliable measurement or functional analytic system* suitable for a particular set of circumstances

*Generalizing* or expanding the breadth of performance to new stimuli:

- reading words written in script after seeing them in print
- using pictures to ask for food or for toys
- behaving politely with all the teachers
- using addition and subtraction with both word problems and numerals
- choosing a healthy diet at home and in a restaurant
- displaying good posture while standing as well as while sitting
- listening without interrupting to one's spouse, one's parents, and one's children

*Reducing* maladaptive, counter-productive behavior that:

- interferes with one's own or others' well-being, satisfaction, learning, or progress
- is dangerous or destructive, such as injuring others or making oneself ill
- creates an atmosphere of fear and intimidation

Beyond its thousands of success stories, including having become the standard of care for the treatment of autism spectrum disorders, ABA offers the distinct advantage of providing objective evidence of the effectiveness of its methods. To qualify as a true ABA program, every single-case application must be accompanied by graphic displays of the impact of the specific intervention. Additionally, before any treatment is deemed reliably to produce a particular result, it must duplicate that outcome in the form of multiple repetitions or replications of the treatment and effect either across different behaviors within the same individual or across different individuals or groups. Supplying evidence favoring a particular ABA intervention supports practitioners and consumers in their efforts to secure the resources essential to its implementation.

## Applied Behavior Analysis as a Profession

By its very nature, applied behavior analysis is conducted under conditions of daily living: in homes, educational and training institutions, hospitals, clinics, works settings, dormitories, out in the community—anywhere people ordinarily function. Clientele include those whose actions present both ordinary and exceptional daily challenges, such as personal problems in living, troublesome family and other social interactions, delayed developmental skills, and worrisome risks to health, safety, livelihood, and overall well-being. Because an essential feature of ABA is gathering valid evidence of behavior change over time, the method is self-correcting. By observing, recording, and graphing ongoing performance patterns, change managers can determine whether to continue with an intervention or to adjust it. Generally, they persist with those explorations until they find a mix that continues to produce solid evidence of progress. Then, to be absolutely convinced that those indications of success are indeed a function of the specific intervention and not just happenstance, they test the validity of their conclusions by using one or more experimental-analytic designs. Note that each ABA intervention is, in a sense, a single-case "experiment." This is not to say that every problem addressed by ABA is solved; just that when success is achieved, as it often is through a course of procedural adjustments, we can feel confident that the ultimate intervention, and not some other unknown factor, was responsible.

Given the confidence inspired by its precise methodology and the confirmation of its successes, numerous commercial, educational, or service organizations have adopted ABA as their key behavior change strategy and have employed trained applied behavior analysts to perform professional functions. "Behavior Analyst" increasingly is listed as a job title in educational, human service, commercial, and other enterprises.

## PROFESSIONALISM OF APPLIED BEHAVIOR ANALYSIS

Once the Association for Behavior Analysis International was formed in 1974 as a membership organization for those interested in the philosophy, science, application, and teaching of behavior analysis, the application of ABA technology began to spread worldwide. By 1998, it became apparent that standards of practice were needed to protect consumers of behavior analytic services. To that purpose, in 1998 the professional *Association for Behavior Analysis International* established the *Behavior Analysis Certification Board, Inc. (BACB)* for the purpose of establishing and maintaining professional standards of practice for behavior analysts. They accomplished this by designing and offering four levels of credentialing for Behavior Analytic practice and by establishing both educational and experience requirements for each level. The BACB also developed the current *Ethics Code for Behavior Analysts* and has specified the professional requirements for certificates (see Table 1.2 for summary of levels, requirements, and illustrative job activities). Moreover, since 2009, most states have required licensure of behavior analytic practitioners.

## CONTEMPORARY BEHAVIOR ANALYTIC PRACTICE

As you now recognize, ABA currently is practiced worldwide. If you, as a reader, have a specific behavioral interest or concern, you are reasonably certain to find a set of peer-reviewed journal publications on the topic. In the increasingly rare event that you cannot locate any, by the time you master this book and proficiently practice its methods under supervision, you may be the one to blaze a new trail in this exciting approach to evidence-based behavior change.

Probably because the field of applied behavior analysis has been associated with striking confir-

**TABLE 1.2   BACB Certification Levels**

| Title | Minimal Level of Education | Training Highlights | Pass Criminal Background Check | Illustrative Job Activities |
|---|---|---|---|---|
| Registered Behavior Technician (RBT) | High School or Above | • 40 hrs. of RBT training by BCBA<br>• Pass RBT exam<br>• Pass RBT competency assessment administered by BCBA | Yes | Provides client interventions, collects and graphs observational data under supervision of BCBA or BCaBA |
| Board Certified Assistant Behavior Analyst (BCaBA) | Bachelor's Degree from Qualifying Institution | • 225 classroom hrs. of graduate level instruction *(effective January 1, 2022)*<br>• Specified hrs. of BCBA supervised experience<br>• Pass comprehensive exam | Yes | Works with clients. Supervises RBTs. Assesses and designs intervention programs. Supervised by BCBA or BCBA-D |
| Board Certified Behavior Analyst (BCBA) | Master's Degree from accredited university | • 315 hrs. of graduate level instruction in ABA *(effective January 1, 2022)*<br>• Specified hrs. of BCBA supervised experience<br>• Pass comprehensive exam | Yes | Supervises RBTs and BCaBAs. Assesses, designs and evaluates intervention programs |
| Doctoral level BCBA (BCBA-D) | Qualifying doctoral level degree | Same as BCBA | Yes | Same as BCBA |

mation of successful management and change in socially meaningful behavior, in all walks of life, the enterprise has continued to expand rapidly. With the stated mission of its flagship organization, the Association for Behavior Analysis International, being: "… to contribute to the well-being of society by developing, enhancing and supporting the growth and vitality of the science of behavior analysis through research, education, and practice, (Marr, 2016, p. 3)" the membership, especially in its applied branch has grown from a handful of ardent, primarily United States Midwesterners, to many, many thousands worldwide. As Table 1.3 suggests, behavior analysts use their skills in the community, sports, education, and human services, as well as within clinical, health, manufacturing, commercial, financial, and numerous other institutions and organizations. Sensible behavior analysts who hope to live healthy, fulfilling lives, as we ourselves try to do, also apply that knowledge to manage their own behavior, and by mutual informed consent, that of members of their households.

As we have seen, behavior analysts may combine their expertise with other roles. Whether parents, organizational behavior or performance managers, coaches, clinicians, trainers, consultants, teachers, counselors, psychologists, psychotherapists, social workers, vocational counselors, speech and language therapists, personnel or organizational managers, or any other discipline related to analyzing

**TABLE 1.3  A Sample List of Current Roles and Functions of ABA Program Participants**

Academic task learning and engagement skills, writing
Accident prevention
Activity planning and execution
Adaptive (non-destructive, non-injurious) behavior at home, in residential placements
Aggression
Animal performance for work and entertainment
Cell-phone use, decreasing
Change at an institutional level
Choice-making
Cigarette smoking
Classroom discipline problems
Commercial and industrial ventures
Communicating skills of typically-developing children and those with delays
Community skills, functional
Conducting fire-evacuation skills
Conversing
Cooperative learning
Correct posture
Creativity
Customer friendliness
Delivering performance feedback
Dental regimens, compliance
Dental treatment, cooperation
Developmental and rehabilitation services
Direction-following
Donating food to food banks
Dropping out of school
Earplug wearing
Eating regulation; skills
Education, academic: pre-school, college, graduate, and professional
Equivalent-class formation
Fear of flying
Fire evacuation skills
Food acceptance
Frequency of recording behavioral data
Gang violence
Goal-setting
Hallucinating, exhibiting fears and phobias, obsessing
Handwriting
Health: care, promotion, treatment
Hemodialysis, cooperating during
Hyperactivity
Imitating
In-service training
Inhalation equipment, use of by asthmatics
Initiating socially
Instruction-following
Lifting, transferring patients
Manufacturing, quality, productivity
Marketing
Matching-to-sample
Mathematical problem solving
Motor performance
Nervous habits, tics
Noise, reduction in lunchroom
Organizational change
Over-selectivity
Parenting
Participation in family activities
Paying attention to work assignments
Pedestrian safety
Peer management
Peer-assisted learning, tutoring
Personal, family, and vocational counseling
Pivotal responses, learning
Preventing cumulative trauma disorders
Public affairs
Public services
Quality of manufactured goods
Quality of services
Reading
Reciprocal interactions
Recycling
Requesting skills
Residing in a virtual space capsule
Safety, on-the-job, at school, in the community
School-wide student improvement
Self-injury
Self-monitoring, recording
Separation anxiety
Service friendliness
Sick-leave, use of
Social greetings
Social skills, pro-social
Seat belt use by motorists, children in shopping carts
Self-control behavior, social interacting
Speech acquisition and other forms of communication
Speech fluency
Spelling
Staff training
Staff interactions with clients
Stair-use
Stereotypy
Student academic performance
Student deportment
Student truancy
Studying
Stuttering
Self-injury
Self-monitoring
Sports skills
Story writing
Supervisory performance
Teacher praise
Tantrumming
Task completion
Teachers greeting of students
Teaching strategies
Test performance
Tolerance for delay
Training skills, pre- and in-service skills
Transition times
Vandalism
Verbal skills
Violence
Vocational, job skills
War and peace

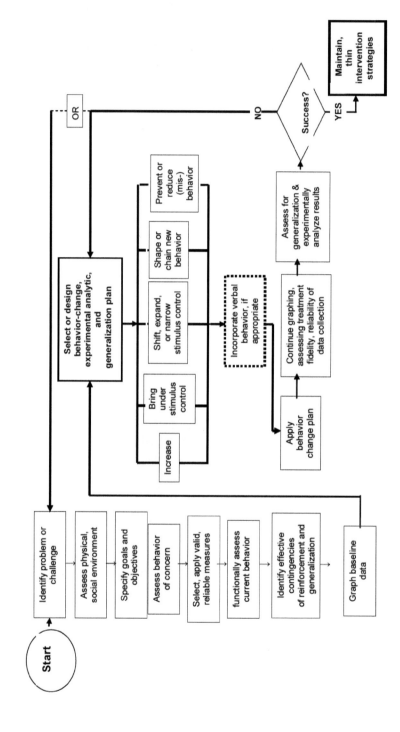

**Figure 1.1** Typical applied behavior analysis process

and improving human performance, applied behavior analysts contribute by abetting performance improvement. They accomplish this by assisting their consumers to function more effectively, efficiently, productively, maturely and constructively.

## WHAT PATH DOES APPLIED BEHAVIOR ANALYSIS GENERALLY FOLLOW?

While any *bona fide* application of behavior analysis must include the basic features described earlier and briefly summarized in Table 1.1 (Baer et al., 1968; 1987), no standard template exists for conducting ABA programs of research and intervention. Rather, the field continues to evolve scientifically and technologically. For the moment, though, Figure 1.1 typifies the steps applied behavior analysts generally follow in designing and conducting their ABA programs.

### Identifying and Deciding to Address a Problem or Challenge

Those who contemplate the need for behavior change generally are influenced by various factors. Perhaps it is one's job to manage, teach, rehabilitate, or treat people. Maybe the impetus derives from a desire to support the common good, as in protecting the environment; preserving resources; encouraging public, group, and personal health practices; promoting peace; international goodwill; or freedom from want, fear, oppression, or other threats to human well-being. Fairly often an ABA program is prompted by a presenting behavioral challenge, such as someone disrupting or failing to perform as expected within a family, organization, or out in the community. Sometimes the decision to intervene evolves from the interest or curiosity of the behavior analysts themselves or the organization employing them. Examples of the former might be searching for reasons why students cause disturbances or fail in school, while others survive and/or thrive; why a youngster regularly attacks a sibling at home; why line workers slow down production through inefficiency or unsafe work practices; why managers berate personnel to the point that their victims retaliate by vandalizing or by leaving the organization. On occasion behavior analysts may be looking for more effective methodological refinements, such as ways to collect or validly analyze complicated data or social practices. And the list goes on. Chapter 2 surveys the building blocks essential to assessing and planning behavior change programs.

### Designing and Implementing an ABA Program

No law of nature dictates a single ideal approach toward promoting enduring behavior change. Nonetheless our field of applied behavior analysis has generated various technologically sound ABA strategies that have dependably demonstrated fruitful and long-lasting outcomes. Below we present one such functionally and ethically sound system for promoting effective behavior change.

### Preparing an Environment Supportive of Constructive Change

Before initiating any action, the behavior analyst needs to know what human and material resources are readily available or attainable in the setting in which the program is to be carried out. That includes adequate funds, personnel skills, values, priorities and limitations, adequate time, space, equipment, supplies, and so on. Identifying other contenders for these and/or other resources and the strategies for adjudicating any such competition is crucial. Should adequate means be lacking in the setting, the behavior analyst must find a way to obtain or compensate for those deficiencies. Material support for many of the investigations reported in this text have included line-item budgets or special allocations, government, community, or private grants or awards, insurance reimbursements, worker organizations, client fees, and *pro bono* or volunteer contributions of time, funds, or goods.

Social and material support by family members, local supervisors, consumers, peers, subordinates, and worker organizations also can influence the success of an ABA program. When all interested parties back the aims and methods of a given program, success is likelier than when there is dissension in the ranks. Personnel can encourage or hinder progress in a myriad of ways—some obvious, such as peers voicing their approval or their condemnation; some subtle, as in their volunteering for a job like collecting data or sharing resources or "forgetting" to show up on time for a scheduled training session. This is one very important reason why wise designers and implementers of ABA programs take the time to orient those directly and indirectly affected by the proposed program, probing for any possible concerns, addressing those, and soliciting everyone's cooperation.

Suppose personnel in a work unit worry that outside observers might distract them or pose a danger due to their unfamiliarity with the area's intrinsic risks. Rather than insisting on adhering to the original plan, the behavior analyst in charge might solicit suggestions from those workers. For instance, one worker might point out potential risks (a violent client, a piece of equipment awaiting repair, a pathway that needs to be kept clear, a patient with a communicable disease, a disgruntled customer). Another might propose that outside observers team up with a member of the work unit until they become sufficiently comfortable with the setting and personnel to work alone. Fearing that the program might siphon off resources from their own units, others might take issue with the details of the intervention, such as the extra time or material resources required. In the long run, altering some aspect of the plan to gain greater support makes more sense than doggedly persisting.

Identifying the realities of existing circumstances in advance makes much more sense than prematurely initiating a program and having to terminate or delay it midway through for lack of support. The moral of the story is *"If you don't have the wherewithal to address the problem successfully and can't readily resolve it, set that challenge aside and move on to the next one."* Chapter 3 devotes itself to more thorough ways to assess and prepare the environment for successful behavior change, while Chapter 24 compliments that material by addressing broader organizational factors affecting constructive programmatic change.

## Specifying and Refining Goals and Objectives

Once sufficient evidence has been amassed to encourage initiating a particular program, the behavior analyst's next step is to sharpen the program's focus by refining its goals and objectives (see Chapter 4). Examples might be to "encourage personnel to identify additional cost-cutting methods" or "promote students' more active involvement in a new unit of study."

Those of us who espouse Goldiamond's (1974) *constructional approach* (see Chapter 4) concentrate on selecting or designing and pursuing constructive behavioral goals through positive means. An example is the *positive behavioral support* approach to working with developmentally challenged youngsters (Carr et al., 2002).[4] Rarely, if ever, is it justifiable to aim solely toward terminating an unwanted behavior without finding and substituting constructive replacement objectives designed to yield the client at least equivalent if not even more powerful reinforcers. Chapter 4, with its focus on clearly specifying goals, presents a useful technology for setting behavioral objectives springing from those goals that can be of mutual benefit to all involved.

## Identifying Current Reinforcers

Reinforcement is the fuel that drives and supports behavior change.[5] Regardless of the response on which it depends—good, bad, or indifferent—reinforcement increases the likelihood that the individual will repeat that particular behavior. Whether the focus is on increasing current, instructing new, or reducing unwelcome behavior, reinforcement is a crucial element of any teaching or behavior-management plan.

---

[4]"Positive behavior support (PBS) is an applied science that uses educational and systems change methods (environmental redesign) to enhance quality of life and minimize problem behavior." It "emerged from three major sources: applied behavior analysis, the normalization/inclusion movement, and person-centered values" (Carr et al., 2002, p. 4).

[5]Neurobiologists are homing in on the specific mechanism(s) of reinforcement within the brain. Based on extensive experimental research, current thinking is that when a behavior is reinforced, particular chemicals, such as dopamine, are released. That, in turn, strengthens the connections (synapses) between individual neurons. (See Schultz, 2000 for a layperson's explanation.)

Change agents need to explore and identify the stimuli that presently do or can be arranged effectively to provide a reinforcing function for the individual under the circumstances of concern. You will learn more about how reinforcers work in Chapter 5 and how to develop and/or select them in Chapter 6.

## Collecting Useful Data

After clearly defining the anticipated end-point of the program, the behavior analyst returns to the here and now, assessing the current status of the behavior(s) of concern to find out what conditions support it in its present form. To accomplish that, valid, reliable measures need to be identified and used to permit the collection and recording of useful data (Chapter 7). Those data then are graphed (Chapter 8) and analyzed (Chapters 9 and 25) to identify the contingencies of reinforcement currently operating on the behavior of interest or concern (Chapter 10).

## Promoting Positive Change

Once confident of having clearly specified sound, constructive objectives and reinforcers for energizing the change process, the behavior analyst selects or designs a feasible system for noting and evaluating progress and develops a sound individual (Chapter 11) or group (Chapter 12) intervention plan. If the intention is to teach a new behavior, shaping (Chapter 13) and/or chaining (Chapter 14) would be suitable. If bringing behavior under the control of simple or complex stimuli (e.g., rules, instructions) is of concern, Chapters 15 through 19 will provide the necessary guidance. When the aim is to shift or expand the breadth of responding (or of the circumstances under which the change is to occur), the relevant information can be found in Chapters 20 and 21. Training and hoping that a modified behavior will maintain happily ever after is wishful thinking, though. A better solution is to turn to Chapters 22 through 24, which provide a set of much more promising science-based maintenance strategies.

Should all the aforementioned constructive behavior-change strategies fail to prevent or remedy severely disruptive, upsetting, or dangerous behavior, in Chapters 26 through 30 we provide you with a set of options, including various primarily constructive, humane, alternative approaches to dealing with the situation. Above all, behavior analysts must operate under a strict code of conduct, ensuring thereby that their activities are and remain ethically responsible (Chapter 31).

## Implementing, Monitoring, and Experimentally Analyzing the Function of the Intervention Plan

Data are collected and graphed throughout any behavior-analytic program, under both baseline and the treatment phases during which the change strategies are implemented. These practices continue until it is determined that the change becomes meaningful and durable. Then, as mentioned, the relation of that change to the intervention(s) is experimentally analyzed (Chapters 9 and 25). Assuming the rates of improving performance reverse when the treatment is withdrawn, (for instance, are now diminishing toward the original baseline rather than continuing to increase) then the change agent becomes more confident of the efficacy of the strategy and reapplies it to the same or a new behavior. Otherwise, the behavior of concern is reassessed and a new plan designed and implemented. Alternatively, after discarding the original plan for lack of demonstrated effectiveness, the behavior analyst has the choice of trying another intervention method to address the same problem or of selecting a different challenge.

## Getting There: Continue Monitoring Behavior and Fidelity of Intervention

Data collection continues throughout all behavior analytic programs, thereby fulfilling its roles of (1) demonstrating that *the program continues faithfully to be administered according to its original design* (i.e., program fidelity), and (2) demonstrating the ongoing success or failure of the program of intervention. In the latter case, the behavior analyst and client(s) must decide whether to return to assessing the behavior anew and altering the plan of intervention accordingly, or changing the specific goals and objectives, the environment in which the intervention is being conducted, or the problem being addressed altogether.

### Staying There

When, ultimately, data convincingly demonstrate that a sought-after solution has been achieved, the behavior analyst must resist the temptation to terminate that program entirely while moving on to other pressing problems. *Getting there is not the same as staying there.* Rather, the basic change procedures need to remain in place under ongoing surveillance for quite a while longer. Only if, after reviewing the data, all key individuals have agreed that the change is well established and persisting at a steady state, is it reasonable to begin to thin the reinforcers or otherwise diminish the intensity of treatment (see Chapters 22 through 24). Eventually, control over the now-constant rate of performance may, if appropriate, be shifted to the natural environment—within the family, organization, or other social structure. Should contingency support be weak or lacking under these new circumstances, lasting change will be compromised. So, plan how to augment any necessary support to ensure change that lasts *from the very start.*

## SUMMARY AND CONCLUSIONS

After discussing the philosophical foundational underpinnings and circumstances supporting the emergence and growth of applied behavior analysis (ABA) as a science, technology, and profession, this chapter has introduced you to the key features of the field. During its evolution over the past sixty+ years, ABA has undergone a tremendous expansion. Today, this evidence-based approach to behavior change has undertaken and often successfully treated performance challenges in numerous corners of the world and across a broad range of physical, cognitive, emotional, and social behavioral challenges. Besides being adopted in various avenues or walks of life, behavior analysis based organizations also have developed significantly (see Table 1.4 for a sample of some of these organizations).

Those identifying themselves to the public as applied behavior analytic practitioners in the United States and elsewhere are responsible for incorporating all of ABA's scientific and technological features within their assessment and change methods. Actually, to ensure they include all those necessary features, both experimental and practicing ABA scientists and practitioners would be well advised to follow the same evidence-based paths. Figure 1.1 displays a template designed to guide to your own thorough and ethically sound practice in the field.

Table 1.4: Applied Behavior Analytic or Affiliate Organizations

| Applied Behavior Analytic or Affiliate Organizations | Website |
| --- | --- |
| Association for Behavior Analysis International (ABAI). | abainternational.org |
| Association for Behavioral and Cognitive Therapies (ABCT) | abct.org |
| The Association for Positive Behavior Support (APBS) | apbs.org |
| Association for Professional Behavior Analysts (APBA) | apbahome.net |
| Behavior Analysis Certification Board (BACB) | bacb.com |
| Behavior Analyst Leadership Council | balcllc.org |
| B. F. Skinner Foundation | bfskinner.org |
| Cambridge Center for Behavioral Studies | behavior.org |
| The Council of Autism Service Providers (CASP) | casproviders.org |

*Chapter 2*

# Designing Effective Strategies of Change: Essential Building Blocks

## Goals

1. Define and distinguish among *behavior*, *learning*, and *teaching*.
2. Define and illustrate *operant* or *response class* and the *three-term contingency*.
3. Define, illustrate, and differentiate *behavioral principles* and *procedures*.
4. Define and distinguish among *environment*, *stimulus*, and *stimulus class*.
5. Define and illustrate:
    a. unconditioned (or unconditional) respondent behavior
    b. conditioned (or conditional) respondent behavior
    c. unconditioned stimuli
    d. conditioned stimuli
    e. respondent or classical conditioning
6. Differentiate as to when to use the verbs *elicit* and *evoke*.
7. Define *operant behavior* and *operant learning*.[1]
8. Define and illustrate:
    a. contingencies
    b. reinforcement
    c. positive reinforcement
    d. negative reinforcement
    e. extinction
    f. punishment
    g. positive punishment
    h. negative punishment
    i. stimulus control
9. Define and illustrate three types of stimulus control stimuli.

---

[1] Some use the term *operant conditioning* instead; we prefer to avoid that usage because of the potential confusion between operant and respondent processes, which are quite different.

10. Define, illustrate, and differentiate *stimulus discrimination* from *stimulus generalization*.

11. Define, illustrate, and differentiate motivating operations and stimulus control.

*************

Mr. Straus has asked his students to read a few pages of *The Catcher in the Rye*. A star student, Ahmad, shares his especially insightful analysis of the hero's character. Mr. Straus hopes to capitalize on this teaching moment, but doesn't know how. He doesn't want to risk singling Ahmad out as someone he favors, yet would like to draw the other students' attention to the boy's excellent analysis. How should he proceed?

While visiting her mom in the hospital, Vera is dismayed to see a staff member shifting from caring for her mom's roommate, suspected of having a communicable disease, to adjusting Mom's breathing apparatus. "For heavens sake! Aren't you going to wash your hands?" What might the hospital do to prevent such risky situations?

His mom grabs Stevie's hand just as the three-year-old is about to put a ladybug in his mouth. Stevie responds by producing a major meltdown: kicking, screaming, and flailing about. What is his mother to do?

Each of the previous examples represents the kinds of behavioral challenges any of us might be called upon to address in the course of our everyday lives. Behavior analysts are trained to handle situations like these, along with a myriad of others involving what people say or do. In Chapter 1 we defined *applied behavior analysis* (ABA). In this chapter, we begin by introducing you to and illustrating a set of fundamental concepts and terms you will encounter as you explore what learning and behavior are about and how they are altered.

## WHAT IS BEHAVIOR?

*"Behavior is what an organism is doing; or more accurately what it is observed by another organism to be doing"* (Skinner, 1938, p. 6).

Given that the central theme of this text deals with changing or modifying behavior, we must first define the term. As described in Chapter 1, when we talk about **behavior**, we are referring to *what any organisms (including people) say or do*. Chirping, poking food into a nestling's mouth, writing, cursing, walking, crying, answering questions, hugging, solving math equations, spitting, smiling, reciting a poem, describing, imagining, or visualizing a picture or writing a term paper are all instances of behavior.

Behavior implies action. So labels, states, or personal characteristics like *happy, sad,* and *alert* are not included. But chirping, mating, striking someone, crying, and smiling are behaviors. Behavior analysts are not concerned with describing organisms' appearance, inner drives or personality traits. Rather, their focus is on people's (or animals') *actions (both physical and verbal)* and the *functions* of those acts. A behavior analyst would not say "Dexter is lazy;" but might comment that he frequently fails to complete his work. Calling Paula *a procrastinator* would be inappropriate, but commenting that she *regularly delays completing her assignments until the last moment* would be an acceptable way to describe her pattern of performance. We would not identify Bruno as *a prodigy*, although we might say he plays the piano extremely skillfully. We do not label Lucretia as a rotten little kid, but describe the child's *actions* as frequently hitting other children and grabbing their toys. Viewing problematic situations in terms of what people *do*, rather than what they *are*, opens the possibility of change, because while we cannot alter who people *are*, we might be able to help them change the way they act by assisting them to increase, decrease, expand, refine, or learn new or different response patterns.

## WHAT IS LEARNING?

**Learning** consists of *altering behavioral* or *response patterns, generally as a function of changes in environmental conditions*. Stated even more simply: *We only know if learning has occurred if there has been a change in behavior* (i.e., what is said or done). The way we know an organism has learned something new is by observing changes in patterns of behavior in relation to particular environmental events: While new on the job, Melba, the bank teller, generally used to open her interaction with a customer with "Yeah?" while looking off into the distance. After participating in a customer service training program and receiving intermittent supervisory feedback, now whenever a customer approaches, she regularly smiles, looks directly at, and greets the person with a phrase such as "How may I help you?" We could say that Melba has *learned* how to greet her customers in a friendly, helpful way.

## WHAT IS TEACHING?

If we accept the notion that *learning* is a relatively enduring change in behavior that occurs as a function of changes in environmental conditions, then a reasonable definition of **teaching** is *promoting learning by any or a combination of various means*: showing, telling, guiding, and most important of all for educators, differentially reinforcing or otherwise arranging matters so that reinforcers follow a reasonable portion of those efforts that are directed toward meeting particular behavioral objectives (see Chapter 4). Parent birds do that by herding their fledglings to locations where food is available.

Human parents and teachers choose a suitable environment and provide the kind of assistance that will enable the learner to succeed. Managers, trainers, supervisors, peer tutors, religious leaders, philosophers, politicians, editorial writers, lecturers, and many others may perform this intentional teaching function. Informal or even unacknowledged teaching goes on as well, as when the actions of peers, parents, family members, celebrities, and the wealthy and powerful serve as models for others to imitate, perhaps yielding comparable reinforcement to individuals in the process.

As all of us know, however, there is the *act of teaching*—playing the teaching role—and there is *effective teaching*—performance that functions to produce student learning. The act of teaching runs the gamut from being really effective to tragically inefficient or even counterproductive. Why do some students become enamored of their subjects while others consider them a nuisance? How is it that some trainees become proficient at certain skills, while others remain incapable of performing the task at hand? Certainly, native physical and intellectual attributes and deficits play a role, but the manner in which the environment supports efficient and successful behavior change matters a great deal. Here is where *applied behavior analysis* makes its entrance. ABA is designed to capitalize on the ever-growing body of knowledge about learning and behavior by effectively applying procedures based on behavioral principles for the purpose of promoting functional, ethically sound and enduring behavior change.

## HOW DOES BEHAVIOR ANALYSIS WORK?

Behavior analysis operates by breaking "…complex behavior down into its functional parts. A successful analysis should allow the behavior to be synthesized by putting the parts back together" (Catania, 2013). To accomplish such a lofty purpose, behavior analysis restricts itself to actions that can validly and reliably be observed and recorded, either by the person engaging in the behavior or by others. For example, engaging in "self-talk" would be considered behavior only if instances of "self-talk" could be validly recorded—as in using a voice recorder or a written narration to chronicle what the person is saying in the absence of any audience. (For a more detailed elaboration of the concept of behavior, refer to basic operant learning texts: Catania, 2013; Johnston & Pennypacker, 1980, and Skinner's historically important 1938 text.)

In practice, the terms *behavior* and *response* tend to be used somewhat interchangeably and are usually reserved for specific instances of activity. However, *different responses or behaviors often produce similar results under similar circumstances*. When this occurs we refer to these behaviors as belonging to an **operant class** (sometimes called **response class**): *"the composite set of behaviors that result in a single type of reinforcing event"* (Ferster & Skinner 1957). For example, when a baby cries or fusses, the crying or fussing are each specific behaviors. However, when the baby cries or fusses when hungry and then gets fed, the crying and fussing become part of the same operant class, in that they tend to produce the same reinforcer. When we talk about "going to the store," the operant class might include walking and/or bicycling or driving. If our concern is with changing Johnny's "aggressive behavior," we actually are referring to changing the operant class that includes Johnny's throwing objects, kicking, or shouting when ignored, because in the past all of these have produced his mom's attention. Unsafe responses such as failing to put on protective equipment and omitting other safety precautions when in a hurry to get home for dinner fall within the same operant class: risky behavior; but refusing to use safety goggles because they distort the worker's vision and taking shortcuts to be able to leave work earlier are members of two different operant classes, because they produce different reinforcers.

Similarly, suppose two different things are happening when we coach Mary to say "milk" and provide her with milk as a consequence, versus when we attempt to teach her to say "milk" by holding up a picture of a glass of milk and ask Mary to tell us the name of the picture. (Later you will learn that the first instance of saying "milk" is called *manding* and the second is called *tacting*; see Chapter 19.)

Generally, in ABA our goal is to change **operant** or **response classes**: *the composite set of behaviors that result in a single type of reinforcing event (saying 'please;' holding out one's hand, raising one's eyebrows while tilting one's chin)*, rather than one specific form or *topography* of a behavior. We need to remind ourselves to view both the specific set of responses that compose an operant class, along with the reinforcing *function*, or purpose, of any of the responses constituting the class. (See Figure 2.1 and Chapters 9 and 10 for more information related to function, especially the function of unwanted behavior.)

When we add the *function* of a response to the formula, we can be said to be addressing the **A-B-Cs** of behavior analysis,[1] or speaking more technically, we are referring to a *three-term contingency*. The expression **three-term contingency** connotes *the interdependency among the antecedent conditions (A), the behavior (B), and the consequences (C)*. For example: a picture of a dog, an actual dog, or the word "dog" (A) can all set the stage for the response "dog" (B), which then is followed by praise, confirmation or some other form of acceptance (C).

---

[1] We thank Aubrey Daniels for introducing the A-B-C terminology.

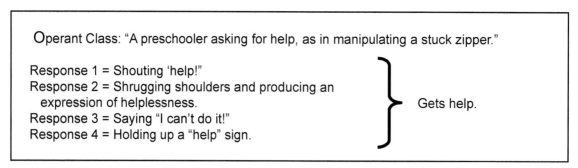

Figure 2.1   Illustrative response class

## Behavioral Principles and Procedures

Note that in many of our examples we generally refer to clusters of antecedents. These antecedent clusters set the stage for particular operant classes, which in turn may consist of a number of functionally related responses. Now, we introduce two other important concepts: 1) principles of behavior (behavioral principles) and 2) behavioral procedures. A principle of behavior is a scientifically derived rule of nature that describes the enduring and predictable relation between a biological organism's responses and given arrangements of stimuli (objects and events that can influence behavior). Principles of behavior are discovered through careful scientific investigation.[2] When we technically apply behavioral principles for the explicit purpose of changing (shaping, teaching, modifying, managing) behavior we are engaging in behavioral analytic procedures.

Behavior analysts working in applied settings, such as schools, homes, businesses, manufacturing, service, health care, or civic organizations, turn their knowledge of behavioral principles into practices. These practices are designed to influence performance in specific ethically-sound ways to teach new knowledge or skills, and/or to manage, motivate, support, sustain, or weaken particular behavior under given circumstances. To illustrate, let us look at how one practice is derived from the procedure we call "positive reinforcement." Positive reinforcement is defined by its function: that is, the operation is so labeled on the basis of evidence that it is responsible for producing an increase in the rate or probability of a behavior as a function of the frequency with which that behavior is reinforced. Recognizing the importance of the frequency of applying reinforcers enables practitioners to apply positive reinforcement more effectively to assist individuals to learn new skills such as using grammatical rules, adding columns of figures, strumming a guitar, assembling the parts of a product, saying "thank you," opening a door for someone, or (fill in the blank with respect to any given behavior you might want to change in your own life). The better informed about conditions that alter the effectiveness of positive reinforcement, the more efficiently practitioners can design successful behavioral procedures.

Consider an example: Deborah's toddler niece Fiona often refuses to share her toys with other children. Noticing that Fiona welcomes hugs and praise (choosing stimuli known to be effective under like conditions is one factor that makes reinforcement effective), Deborah hugs and praises Fiona copiously when the child shares her toys. Fiona now shares her toys with the other children more often while playing. In more technical terms, recognizing that the rate of behavior probably would increase if rapidly and frequently followed by reinforcers known to be effective under the circumstances, Deborah applied *positive reinforcement*, thereby encouraging Fiona to share her toys. Notice that Deborah didn't hug and praise Fiona every now and then, because Deborah knows that when you want to immediately increase a new behavior you need to reinforce every occurrence of the behavior until it is established. This is based on the understanding of the principles of reinforcement.

# WHAT DOES THE TERM *ENVIRONMENT* MEAN?

## Differentiating "Environment" from "Stimulus"

We label the physical and social **environment** in which a particular organism (in our case, usually a person), behaves as its *context*. Typically, the context in which an individual behaves generally is composed of multiple stimuli. Items and events abound within a classroom: desks, lights, books, other children, the teacher and their actions, and so on. Not all of those elements actually affect, or technically speaking, are *functionally related* to the *operant behavior* or *operant response class* (composite set of behaviors) of concern. For instance, the antecedent exerting the strongest influence over Mark's compliance might have been the fact that Mr. Brennan also is the football coach and Mark is

---

[2] The term *behavioral law* is occasionally applied when such relationships repeatedly occur both within and across species under all sorts of varying conditions.

eager to make the team; whether the classroom seats are wooden or plastic, even people behaving, but not noticed, are irrelevant.

A **stimulus,** by contrast, is *a specific event or combination of events (stimuli) that in some way affect(s) behavior.* For example, in Mr. Brennan's classroom (the context or environment), Mark is instructed to complete his spelling exercise (an *antecedent* stimulus, because it directly precedes that particular response; see Figure 2.2). Mark complies with Mr. Brennan's request (the *response* or *behavior*). As a result (consequence), Mr. Brennan smiles and compliments Mark (the *consequential stimuli*).

Similar to regarding a complex behavior as composed of more than one simple operant (behavior), we recognize that reinforcing consequences also may vary in their levels of complexity. Mr. Brennan may compliment Mark for completing his assignment, affix a gold star to his paper or nod cursorily when the boy hands it in.

The *antecedent or simultaneous* stimulus, or stimuli, that *set the occasion for* the behavior might be part of a broader **stimulus class:** *a group of stimuli that may vary across physical dimensions but that produce a common effect on an operant class (*to paraphrase Pierce & Cheney, 2008). The instructions for a spelling exercise could be part of a larger stimulus class that includes any of Mr. Brennan's instructions. Other stimuli, perhaps a substitute teacher lacking the same potential function of inviting Mark to join the team, are excluded. In other words, Mark tends to comply when Mr. Brennan assigns a spelling exercise, regardless of who else is there, the color of the classroom walls, the weather or lighting conditions, and so on; while in Mr. Brennan's absence, Mark may not necessarily complete his spelling exercises, even if he is capable of doing so, despite all of the other present but non-functional stimuli (children, lighting, etc.).

Johnny hits his sister when his mother is in the room. Perhaps his mother and sister are members of a stimulus class composed of people whose attention is reinforcing to Johnny. So when his mother and sister are nearby, but inattentive, the occasion is set for Johnny to hit his sister. As you might imagine, Johnny's action has a good likelihood of producing what works as a reinforcer for him: his mother's and his sister's attention.

When his supervisor Pat and co-worker Jared pass by, Ned starts complaining about the production line. It is likely that both Pat and Jared are members of a stimulus class composed of people whose attention is reinforcing to Ned. So, especially after Ned has been working alone for a while, with-

---

**An Exercise**

Serena, the physician's assistant, is especially friendly (smiles, makes good eye contact, and produces an "upbeat" vocal tone) to anyone who smiles at her and/or addresses her by name. Can you identify the stimulus and operant classes in this situation?

The stimulus class consists of being smiled at and being addressed by her name. The operant class consists of her smiling, making eye contact, and speaking in an upbeat vocal tone.

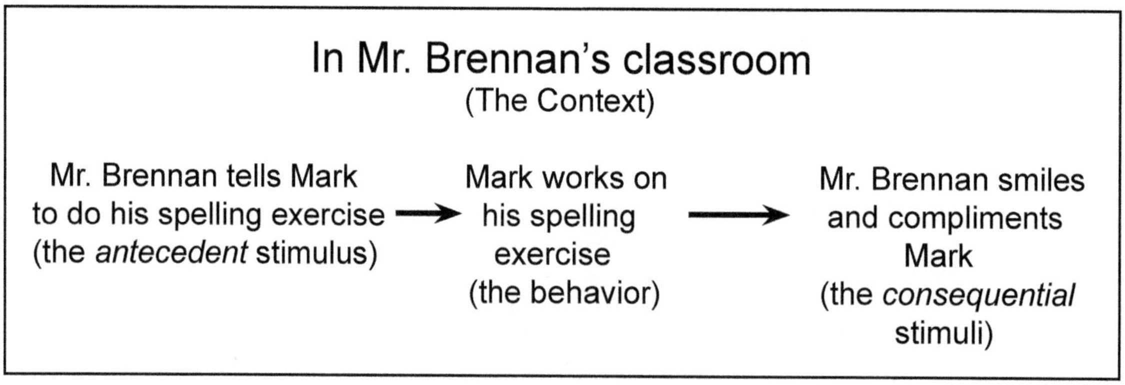

---

In Mr. Brennan's classroom
(The Context)

Mr. Brennan tells Mark to do his spelling exercise (the *antecedent* stimulus) → Mark works on his spelling exercise (the behavior) → Mr. Brennan smiles and compliments Mark (the *consequential* stimuli)

**Figure 2.2** Interrelationship of the antecedent, behavior and consequence

out any social interactions, the occasion is set for Ned to complain when Pat and Jared show up. From past experience Ned has learned that complaining is apt to produce reinforcement in the form of attention from both Pat and Jared.

When analyzing operant behavior, you might view such stimuli as analogous to antecedent or *discriminative* stimulus classes, in the sense that they generally are composed of complex units functioning within the three-term contingency. In fact, it is hard to illustrate or talk about one without the other. To avoid confusion, when considering discriminative (antecedent) and reinforcing (consequential) stimuli within any three-term contingency, think about both *operant classes* and *stimulus classes*.[3] Therefore, when you plan to analyze or modify behavior, remind yourself that applied behavior analysis is based on the assessment and modification of one *or more* components of the three-term contingency. Trusting you now recognize that *often it is not a single stimulus, but actually a collection of stimuli* that are affecting behavior, we now discuss how these stimuli exert such control or influence over behavior. Before we discuss conditioning related to the three-term contingency, we should elucidate the difference between respondent and operant conditioning.

## RESPONDENT BEHAVIOR AND RESPONDENT CONDITIONING

Unconditioned respondent behaviors are those behaviors that are reliably elicited by particular stimuli despite any prior learning. Unconditioned respondents are also known as *reflexes* and generally thought of as behaviors with which the individual was endowed at birth. Particular preceding or antecedent stimuli directly "elicit" respondent behavior. Those eliciting stimuli are referred to as *unconditioned stimuli* (*USs*) and the responses those stimuli elicit are referred to as *unconditioned responses* (*URs*). Familiar examples of USs are a bright light shined into the eyes causing the pupils to contract (UR); an object touching an infant's lips (US) pro-

ducing the response of sucking (UR); or a foreign object in throat (US) eliciting gagging (UR). The essential feature of an unconditioned reflex is that it does not depend on learning. The stimulus automatically elicits/produces the response. Many of these particular stimuli and their elicited responses have been assigned the term "reflex": the gag reflex, the salivary reflex, and so on. Although essentially all of us are born with the capability for emitting a broad set of specific unconditioned responses, we can acquire novel stimulus-response combinations through a process called *respondent conditioning*.[4]

The concept of respondent conditioning originally derived from Pavlov's work on the salivary reflex in dogs. In respondent conditioning (also referred to as *classical conditioning*), a new relation develops between a stimulus and a formerly unconditioned response. This takes place when a neutral stimulus (NS)—one that does not automatically elicit a UR—is paired with a US, thereby producing a UR. As those pairings continue, the formerly neutral stimulus gradually acquires the eliciting properties of the US, eventually changing, thereby, into a conditioned stimulus (CS) capable of eliciting a response—the *conditioned response (CR)* much the same as the UR.

Pavlov found that dogs salivated when meat powder was placed in their mouths, in the absence of any prior learning. One might describe this phenomenon as "meat powder eliciting salivation." The meat powder was the unconditioned stimulus (US) and the salivation was the unconditioned response (UR). When, initially, Pavlov rang a bell (the neutral stimulus: NS), though, the dogs did not salivate. Yet, when Pavlov regularly paired the sound of the bell with delivery of the meat powder (NS + US), the sound of the bell began to acquire *conditioned stimulus* properties. After a number of those pairings, the bell alone elicited salivation, even when the dog received no meat powder. The bell became

---

[3] Later you will discover the distinction between *operants* and *discriminated operants*.

[4] Although applied behavior analysts emphasize operant conditioning most heavily in their work, they do recognize the important role respondent conditioning can play in understanding and changing behavior.

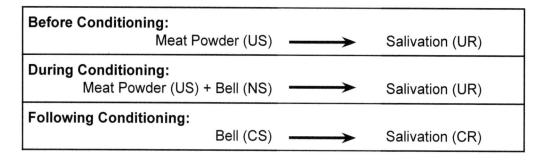

**Figure 2.3** Conditioning the sound of a bell to elicit salivation

the CS; the salivation elicited by the bell, the CR (see Figure 2.3).

Sometimes respondent conditioning has "survival value," as in the illustration above, but not always. For example, suppose as a result of an unrelated stomach virus (US), Margaret became nauseated (UR) immediately after eating spinach salad (NS). Perhaps the next time Margaret went out to lunch, just the sight of the spinach salad (CS) caused her to become nauseated (CR). Respondent conditioning may have been to blame.

It is important to note that just as a NS can become a CS, repeatedly presenting the CS in the *absence* of the US can eventually lead to the conditioned stimulus losing its eliciting effect. So with respect to Margaret becoming nauseated at the sight of spinach salad, were she determined to overcome her conditioned aversion toward the greens, she might consume tiny quantities of the salad as a first step. Assuming she continues those trials while remaining healthy, and continues to add larger and larger portions over time, eventually the spinach would no longer elicit the CR: the feelings of nausea. Actually, the acquisition of "irrational fears" of formerly neutral stimuli, [e.g., fear of spiders (arachnophobia), of large open spaces (agoraphobia) or enclosed spaces (claustrophobia), and/or various other conditioned phobias] may sometimes occur similarly. For many years *behavior therapists* have successfully used a practice called "desensitization," analogous to the method described above, to help "cure" clients' of irrational phobias by diminishing the adverse impact of the conditioned stimulus (e.g., Walker, Hedberg, Clement, & Wright, 1981). See numerous other examples in *Behavior Therapy* and other clinical psychological and psychiatric journals.).

In the case of respondent conditioning, the key focus is on antecedent stimuli functioning as "elicitors," "causes," or "producers" of behavior. (Figure 2.4 illustrates this relationship.)

In respondent behavior, responses are often said to be "involuntary" in the sense that the antecedent stimulus essentially generates or produces the response. With operant behavior, however, antecedent stimuli are *not* said to elicit a response because no particular antecedents are essential precursors to the response. Rather, the antecedent stimuli (A's) work only as a result of the individual's having experienced a history in which those stimuli immediately preceded or accompanied the reinforced or punished behavior. In such instances, the antecedents are said to *set the occasion or not for* the particular behavior, as you will learn next.

## OPERANT BEHAVIOR AND OPERANT LEARNING (CONDITIONING)[5]

Operant responses differ from reflex responses and are not said to have been elicited[6] by preceding

---

[5] You will find the term *conditioning* used sometimes in this text when we discuss operant learning because the BACB's Task List uses it. However, the term conditioning has become so closely associated with Pavlov and respondent behavior that *operant learning* is replacing the term *operant conditioning*. "The term operant conditioning is becoming obsolete" (Catania, personal communication, 2018).

[6] We use the term "evoke" or "occasion" for operant behavior, "elicit" for respondent behavior.

> **Before conditioning:**
>   Spinach salad —/→ (ill effect)
>
> **Conditioning experience:** Becomes nauseated after eating spinach salad.
>   Eats spinach salad ⟶ Stomach virus (US) ⟶ Nausea (UCR)
>
> **After conditioning experience:** Becomes nauseated by eating or maybe even seeing a spinach salad.
>
> Sees or eats spinach salad (CS) ⟶ Nausea (CR)

**Figure 2.4** Conditioning an aversion to spinach salad

stimuli. Rather, the probability of their occurrence is controlled by stimuli that follow the behavior, (often in the presence of a given stimulus or stimuli). The future rate of the behavior is a function of its previous learning history. Moreover, the way the consequence relates to the antecedent stimuli usually defines the operant. So we can analyze the three-term (A-B-C) contingency by identifying the way the antecedent(s) or "A(s)" are related to the "B," the behavior, and the "C," the consequence. Thus, contingency refers to the specified dependencies or relations between behavior and its antecedents and consequences. (As we shall see later on, contingencies may be intrinsic features of environments, or they may be deliberately arranged, as in cases of teaching, training, preaching, convincing, managing, and so on. When behavior analysts intentionally present, withdraw, or withhold stimuli for the explicit purpose of affecting behavior, they refer to such actions as procedures.) In ABA, our concern generally is with modifying operant behavior. Therefore, the remainder of this chapter is devoted to explaining the basics of operant behavior.

## THE "C" IN OPERANT LEARNING (CONDITIONING)

We begin by discussing the end of the three-term-contingency because change depends on the consequences of the behavior, including positive or negative reinforcement, extinction, or punishment. Without consequences, response patterns will not change in any lasting way. While antecedents also exert a powerful influence on behavior, first they need to gain their influence through consequences (i.e., reinforcement, extinction, or punishment). Baby cries and is fed or cuddled or changed. Baby learns to cry more often under particular circumstances, and as most new parents know, sometimes those antecedents remain a complete mystery to them.

## Positive and Negative Reinforcement Defined and Illustrated

In its broadest sense, the term *reinforcement* often is used both as a name for *how* behavior changes (e.g., "She increased the number of reports she completed on time. I suspect some kind of *reinforcement* is at work."), or as a name for the contingencies or procedures that cause an increase or persistence in the probability of occurrence of a given response (e.g., "We used a *reinforcement procedure* consisting of delivering complimentary notes when she handed in her reports on time."). The term *reinforcement* can be separated into two categories: 1) positive reinforcement and 2) negative reinforcement. In **positive reinforcement**, *the organism gains a stimulus, dependent or contingent on a response, resulting in the rate of that response increasing* or *maintaining* (e.g., praising your husband for taking out the trash, leading to an increase in how frequently he takes out the trash).

**Negative reinforcement** (read this carefully, the terminology gets tricky here) occurs when a *stimulus is subtracted contingent on a response*, also *resulting in the subsequent rate of that response* *increasing or maintaining*. (For example, you nag your husband to take out the trash and stop the nagging once he takes it out. Afterward, he starts taking the trash out more often to avoid your nagging). The important thing to remember is that regardless of whether a "reinforcing" stimulus is *presented* (praise in the above example), or an "aversive" stimulus is *removed* (nagging in the above example), reinforcement functions to increase or maintain behavior (trash gets taken out more often in the above example.) It is not the nature of the stimulus, but its effect that matters. The operation—that it is either *presented* (added, plus = positive) or *removed* (subtracted, minus = negative) earns the procedure its title. Sometimes the distinction is confusing. Does a drink of water function as a reinforcer because the water has been *presented* or because it reduces the stimulus characteristics of a dry mouth? (We provide a more detailed explanation of reinforcement in Chapter 5 and specific methods for transforming neutral stimuli into reinforcer in Chapter 6.) Moreover, if a particular operant behavior continues, we assume it is reinforced at least some of the time. Conversely, as you will learn, if you want behavior to decrease, the (conceptually) simplest way is to make sure the behavior no longer generates reinforcement.

## Extinction, Positive Punishment, and Negative Punishment Defined and Illustrated

The rate of a behavior tends to decrease when it no longer produces reinforcement (i.e., *extinction*), or when it is *punished*. Technically, the extinction operation is the discontinuation (cessation) of reinforcement as a consequence of a given behavior, leading to a *decrease* in the frequency of that behavior. (Again, the vocabulary can apply either to the change in behavior, e.g., "*her tantrums extinguished*" or to the conditions that led to the change, "*her tantrums were placed on extinction*.")

Consider an example: Logan asks for a candy bar every time he and his mother wait in the checkout line at the grocery store. When she tells him "No," he flops down on the floor, kicks his feet, and screams. His mom asks him to stop, but he doesn't.

So she gives him the candy bar. Logan stops screaming (which positively reinforces Logan's tantruming, but negatively reinforces Mom's giving him the candy bar). Subsequently, whenever in line together and Logan asks for a candy bar but his mom refuses, he immediately tantrums until he gets the candy. Thus, we can assume Logan's tantrums are being reinforced by his mom's giving him the candy bar as a consequence of his misbehavior.

Suppose Logan's mom were to ask you to help decrease Logan's tantrums. You might suggest an extinction procedure, advising her to stick to her guns and refrain from giving him the candy bar when he starts screaming and kicking. Discontinuing the reinforcer, that is, no longer giving him the candy bar during or shortly after the tantrum, eventually should result in Logan's no longer throwing tantrums under those conditions. In that case, we might conclude that the tantrums have undergone extinction. (Chapter 27 elaborates on the use of extinction as a form of behavioral intervention.)

*Punishment* is another way to reduce the rate of an unwanted behavior. Like reinforcement, punishment can be broken into two separate categories: *positive punishment* and *negative punishment*. In **positive punishment**, *the individual receives a (typically unpleasant) stimulus contingent on a response, resulting in a decrease in the future probability of that response*. By contrast, in **negative punishment**, *the individual loses a desirable stimulus contingent on a response*. In both cases the *future probability of the response decreases*. If the coach tells a member of the water polo team that he is disappointed in him for skipping class (i.e., an outcome added as a consequence of skipping the class) and the boy does not skip class any more, we would say that *positive* punishment succeeded in lowering the probability of the boy's skipping class. On the other hand, if the coach takes away the boy's playing time for the next match (a loss of a pleasant stimuli) and then the boy no longer skips class, the coach has applied *negative* punishment. (See Chapters 30 and 31 for additional details on punishment.)

Again, the important thing to remember about the concept of punishment is that it results in a decrease in the behavior of concern. The addition of the qualifiers "positive" and "negative" simply refer

|                  | **Behavior Increases**   | **Behavior Decreases** |
|------------------|--------------------------|------------------------|
| *Stimulus Added* | Positive Reinforcement   | Positive Punishment    |
| *Stimulus Removed* | Negative Reinforcement | Negative Punishment    |

**Figure 2.5** A comparison of reinforcement and punishment operations

to whether a stimulus was added/presented (positive), or subtracted/removed (negative), to produce the particular response. See Figure 2.5 for a comparison of reinforcement and punishment operations.

Beyond noting the immediate consequences of a response, we need to remember that those consequences do not occur in a vacuum. Everyone's history is unique. Different people come to a given situation with diverse histories of reinforcement and/or punishment, and these histories influence what the person will do at any particular moment. Moreover, these individual histories can also affect what functions as a reinforcer or a punisher for any given person's behavior under particular conditions. We also need to recognize that reinforcer effectiveness is relative in the sense that it is not the person but rather the relation of the reinforced response and the response allowed by the reinforcer that is crucial: you can reinforce drinking with the opportunity to eat, or reinforce eating with the opportunity to drink, depending on the relative deprivations of food and water.

## THE ROLE OF ANTECEDENTS ("A"s) IN OPERANT LEARNING

### Antecedent Stimuli Defined and Illustrated

Earlier we described how operant behavior usually is set within a three-term contingency. Generally speaking, specific antecedent events or conditions affect behavior by either signaling the nature of the consequences for responding in a given way under those current circumstances, and/or, as in the case of motivating operations (abbreviated "MOs"), by affecting the potency of the consequence. When stimulus control develops naturally, we generally refer to it as a *process*; when it is programmed intentionally we are more apt to refer to it as a *procedure*. In either case, stimulus control is demonstrated when an antecedent stimulus is shown to gain control over one or more particular behaviors. (To the outside observer, it appears as if the stimulus "causes" the response.)

Next we describe three major types of discriminative stimuli ($S^D$s):

1. *Those that often directly precede a reinforced response, and, thereby eventually come to signal the probability that a given response will be reinforced* are labeled $S^D$s Perhaps the sound of the lunch bell appears to *cause* the students to clean off their desks, but actually, having had a clean desk formerly resulted in their being allowed to go to lunch. These $S^D$s are labeled *positive discriminative stimuli* (abbreviated $S^{Dr}$s).

2. Similarly acquired through the individual's learning history, the discriminative stimulus for extinction ($S^\Delta$) *denotes an antecedent stimulus in the presence of which a particular response probably will not result in reinforcement.* Mrs. Mack places Jared's desk next to hers to ensure that he does not gain any extra attention from the other students when he acts silly. Mrs. Mack assumes her desk will become an $S^\Delta$ for acting silly, because should Jared act silly while sitting next to her desk, he gains no reinforcing attention from Mrs. Mack or the other students.

3. The $S^D$s that have been *associated with a given response having been punished are called stimuli discriminative for punishment* (abbreviated $S^{Dp}$s) or negative discriminative stimuli. The $S^{Dp}$ is a stimulus in the presence of which the individual faces an increased likelihood of receiving punishment for responding in a given fashion. Imagine Dagwood looking up from his computer

game during working hours to find his boss, Mr. Dithers standing over him and watching. You can predict what follows: undoubtedly a stream of verbal abuse of the type for which Mr. Dithers has become so notorious. Due to its association with punishment, Mr. Dithers' presence has evolved into a stimulus (an $S^{Dp}$) that inhibits or suppresses Dagwood's playing computer games. (For additional illustrations and an explanation of the differences of these terms and symbols, see Chapters 15 and 16.)

The degree of control exerted by antecedent stimuli is on a continuum, from tight to loose. In tight stimulus control, or stimulus discrimination, a given response only occurs in the presence of stimuli in which it has been reinforced in the past (i.e., the person "discriminates" the difference between stimuli). For example, you only open the door when the doorbell rings, not when the phone rings. Your door opening can be said to be under tight stimulus control. On the other hand, when you behave under loose stimulus control (referred to as stimulus generalization), responding occurs in the presence of stimuli sharing certain characteristics with those previously paired with reinforcement, as in your enthusiastically consuming just about any flavor or brand of ice cream. We might assert that when it comes to ice cream, you fail to discriminate the best ice-cream from the so-so. Technically, your responding generalizes across stimuli.

Here is another example, this time an amusing personal one, illustrating the difference between stimulus discrimination and stimulus generalization. In Latin cultures like those prevailing in locales like Miami, it is customary to greet people (social acquaintances as well as close friends and family) by kissing them on the cheek. As a native of Miami, one of the authors was accustomed to greeting just about any social acquaintance that way. (You could say kissing on the cheek was under loose stimulus control). When she entered graduate school in Gainesville, Florida (not a Latin culture) she attended a welcoming party. As she entered the house, she went around kissing everyone in attendance, most of whom were strangers. A cool reception greeted her! Needless to say, her kissing behavior quickly diminished in Gainesville and she only greeted people that way when back in Miami. You could say her kissing behavior came under tighter stimulus control. We will elaborate on variations in stimulus control later (in Chapter 16) when discussing in detail how stimulus control develops and functions. For the present, it is important for you to remember that stimulus control can vary appropriately or inappropriately and from tight to loose.

## MOTIVATING OPERATIONS AS ANTECEDENT EVENTS

Beyond stimuli that influence behavior by signaling the likely consequences in effect, another class of antecedent event exerts control by altering the potency or value of a particular consequence. We call those events *"motivating operations"* or *"MOs."* (MOs also have been labeled *establishing operations* [*EOs*], or *setting events* [*SEs*]). **Motivating operations** *modulate the reinforcing or punishing effectiveness of particular kinds of events and the control of behavior by antecedent stimuli relevant to those events* (Edwards, Lotfizadeh, & Poling, 2019b). Suppose you have not had anything to drink in the past eight hours. This deprivation makes drinking liquids more reinforcing and increases the likelihood of your seeking something to drink, say, by asking for a drink, going over to a water fountain, or using other strategies that have produced a drink in the past. Similarly, if you have just eaten a big meal and you are sated, food is less reinforcing, and behavior that has produced food in the past will decrease.

Now admit it! After all this talk about ice cream, are you tempted or did you actually go to the freezer to find some? If so, reading about or seeing this enticing picture of ice cream was a motivating operation for you! (You will learn more about MOs in subsequent chapters.)

## SUMMARY AND CONCLUSIONS

Applied behavior analysis (ABA) is designed to address essentially any behavioral challenge(s), including anything humans or animals say and do. Essentially, ABA incorporates scientifically derived principles of learning/behavior change within its practices, to effectively teach its clientele to alter their behavior in pre-determined ways.

Applied behavior analysis consists of breaking observable complex behavior down into its functional parts; then reassembling those parts differently, and presumably in pre-planned ways. Given its concern with personally and socially important (classes of) behavior, though, applied behavior analysis augments those analytic methods by adding evidence-based change—strategies of change—to increase, teach, expand, reduce, or restrict the range of and maintain new levels of socially important classes of responses.

Technically, *learning* consists of altering responses as a function of environmental conditions, while *teaching* involves the intentional promotion of change, typically in groupings or *operant classes* of behaviors. In the case of ABA, the potential for more effective teaching generally increases as the body of knowledge about principles and methods for promoting effective learning continues to evolve.

Learning takes place in particular contexts composed of a multitude of stimuli, and the learned response itself may belong to any of several members of a response class, each of which are affected similarly by a given consequence. By capitalizing on principles of behavior, change agents may apply clusters of antecedents and consequences, or *behavioral procedures*, to produce the results they are pursuing, in particular places or across a number of situations.

Behavior analysts recognize two distinct categories of behavior: *respondent* (or reflexive) and *operant*. Pavlov, who pioneered research into respondent behavior, presented the world with an analysis that permitted scientists to understand, and, by rearranging pairings of stimuli, to change respondent/physiological behavior. B. F. Skinner is credited with pioneering the analysis of operant behavior. He and his associates did this by experimentally studying particular patterns of responding implemented prior to and following given behaviors under various sets of conditions. That seminal work eventually began to evolve into systematic efforts toward addressing individuals' behavioral challenges, as in the present instance: applied behavior analysis (ABA).

A number of ABA practices have been designed, refined, and thoroughly tested. As you will learn, these include procedures designed to *increase* behavior (positive and negative reinforcement), *reduce* behavior (extinction and positive and negative punishment), *expand* (generalization), or *refine* or *narrow* (discrimination) the range of a given behavior in relation to a particular stimulus and *maintain* changed behavior over time. All of these procedures depend on carefully arranged behavioral consequences and antecedents, generally applied under particular environmental circumstances.

As time has passed, ABA practice has continued to expand widely in the challenges it addresses and to become increasingly sophisticated. In the material to follow you will learn how ABA methods are continually improving in their effectiveness, efficiency, credibility, durability, and benevolence. As you begin to master the material, surely you will find yourself contemplating ways to use your newly acquired information as a basis for bettering your own life, along with the lives of the individuals for whom you share responsibility, perhaps even those of society at large.

## Chapter 3

# Preparing a Supportive Environment for Behavior Change

### Goals

1. List the activities you can undertake to familiarize yourself with the client(s) and setting, and discuss why these are critically important.
2. Describe what actions need to be taken to prepare for behavioral support and change.
3. Differentiate between indirect and descriptive assessments.
4. What does it mean to use an evidence-based approach?
5. Describe why teamwork is helpful in addressing behavior within an organization.
6. Define and differentiate between a *Positive Behavior Support Team* (*PBST*) and a *Student Success Team* (*SST*).
7. Distinguish among *primary, secondary*, and *tertiary prevention*.
8. Provide a rationale for incorporating behavior teams within an organization.
9. Define (a) *client*, (b) *contingency manager*, and (c) *fidelity of implementation*.
10. Discuss why achieving program fidelity is important.
11. Illustrate and describe how treatment integrity can be calculated.
12. Define and illustrate treatment drift and discuss how to address its occurrence.
13. Discuss what factors should be considered when selecting an effective intervention to increase the likelihood that it will be properly implemented."
14. List and discuss the importance of including each of the following activities when selecting and developing a program:
    a. assuring contextual fit
    b. applying methods to facilitate goal and intervention selection
    c. selecting goals and interventions collaboratively
    d. addressing strategies for ensuring generalization and maintenance of change
    e. using language acceptable and comprehensible to clientele

f. incorporating and fading intervention prompts in the natural environment, as necessary

g. providing a checklist

15. Discuss why it is important to analyze the environment to determine the availability of support for the contingency manager's program implementation efforts.

16. Discuss the specific ethical codes and how they relate to preparing an environment and support behavioral change.

\*\*\*\*\*\*\*\*\*\*\*\*\*

Just as we need to prepare the soil for our garden flowers to flourish, achieving successful and lasting behavioral change in any situation also requires a supportive environment—at home, school, in health and service programs, commercial organizations, factories—just about anywhere people live, learn, work, and play. Simply entering a situation, assessing an individual's behavior, and using that assessment to design and recommend an intervention program is insufficient, especially in non-hospitable environments. As with so many other ventures, the more we invest "up front," the fewer difficulties we will encounter later on. Therefore, we advise a number of preliminary steps if constructive change is to be supported and maintained. Be patient, because careful preparation up front pays off in the long run.

## FAMILIARIZE YOURSELF WITH THE CLIENT(S) AND SETTING

Before doing anything else, we must inform ourselves about the histories of our individual **clients** (*those receiving the intervention or treatment*) and of their organizations, and identify the key sources of influence in the setting where change is to take place. Search for factors that may be affecting both adaptive and challenging behavior. As an example, consider the public school situation. There, you might look for aspects of the environment known to promote student progress, such as positive recognition, matching assignments to individual students' skill levels, and other supportive elements. On the negative side, you might observe factors detrimental to student progress, such as educators' inconsistencies in applying rules and consequences, an over-reliance on punitive methods of behavior control, a dearth of positive reinforcement, and students' histories of success or failure and associations with inappropriate peer models in the community, home, and schools (Mayer, 1995, 2001; Mayer & Ybarra 2003, 2006).

Consider the dynamics of a company eager to reduce employee absenteeism rates stemming from work-related accidental injuries, plus associated compensation costs. Before instituting a "one-size-fits-all" behavioral safety program, we behavior analysts must learn more about the organization and how it functions: its purpose or *mission*, its financial, physical, and human resources, along with who controls or manages those, and in what way. In addition, we need to determine the company's methods of operation and personnel, the various constituencies and their priorities, power struggles, concerns and gripes, and other formal and informal strengths and weaknesses. Why? Perhaps the reason is obvious: So you can build from those strengths, capitalizing on available assets while avoiding roadblocks to success. (See Chapter 4 for the importance of clarifying the key purpose(s) or "mission" of the organization or service, and the goals and objectives chosen to achieve those purposes.)

During your inquiries, you discover another dimension of this company's case. Its high rates of absenteeism and diminished rates of production appear to relate to back injuries suffered by personnel who operate particular types of equipment. Those operators appear to be eager to avoid injury, while management wants to stem the flow of cash to the company's insurance carriers. Union leaders insist that their members be protected and adequately recompensed. Worker's families also exert a certain amount of pressure to keep their loved ones safe. Your job is to (1) determine which of those or any other parties will abet or possibly impede the change process, and (2) see how currently operating contingencies of reinforcement (consequences that support and obstruct constructive change) can be adjusted to meet the common goal of injury reduction.

You inform yourself further about those elements by examining records, talking with managers, staff workers, and consumers, and above all, observing and recording behavior (Sulzer-Azaroff & Fellner, 1984). Only at this point should you choose or design and propose a preventive intervention system, which you then would circulate across the various constituencies for their comments and suggestions, and in that or modified form, gain their ultimate approval. Once those elements are in order, you are ready to move on.

Moreover, you must examine not only your own strengths, but also any of *your own* biases, cultural practices, or beliefs that could interfere with progress. Among the many characteristics of effectively-performing behavior analysts is their awareness of the influences of one's own biases and cultural diversity while planning and implementing behavior-change strategies. In fact, it is important to have cultural humility when practicing behavior analysis. Fong, et al. (2016) provided some suggestions for behavior analysts on how to apply cultural humility to their work. Basically, they pointed out how it is important to take note of one's own "cultural values, preferences, characteristics, and circumstances" (p. 84) as well as those of clients when providing behavior analytic services. One could argue that being aware could modify how one conducts behavior analysis. In fact, this permits them to adapt their change procedures to become more consonant with the contingencies of reinforcement operating in their client's lives, and in so doing, enhances the likelihood of ongoing success with a more culturally appropriate behavior change program. Ethical behavior analysts do *not* discriminate or treat others differently based on a persons' age, gender, race, culture, ethnicity, national origin, religion, sexual orientation, disability, language, or socioeconomic status. Recognize any biases you may hold and seek training to overcome those prior to engaging in any behavior-change program.

## Analyze the Current Operating System or Culture

When faced with the challenge of preventing problems or improving the performance of individuals or groups, the organization's operating system or culture needs to be analyzed, taken into consideration, and possibly adjusted to support *positive* program implementation. In the best-case scenario, the organization, group, or family is dedicated to promoting and sustaining *a constructive approach*. It recognizes that by avoiding problematic or challenging behavior in the first place, participants will be more apt to maintain their efforts. *Everyone needs to be aware of, committed to, and capable of fluently practicing skills consistent with the organization's or family's goals.* That is a tall order! Personnel, parents, or others may require further skill development if that lofty objective is to be achieved. Then those newly honed skills must be regularly supported.

Moreover, programmatic success may well depend on a consideration of cultural factors, especially during the selection of goals and treatment strategies. Teaching boys how to cook and clean, for example, is unheard of in some societies.[1] Your failure to consider a cultural perspective of that nature could well place your program in jeopardy. Concerned parties, sensing their exclusion from the process, may inadvertently or even intentionally interfere with the progress of the program rather than cooperating toward promoting a common goal.

Similarly, how the intervention is introduced can influence its effectiveness. For example, some

---

[1] For an excellent example of this consideration see Anne Fadiman's (1997) *The Spirit Catches You and You Fall Down: A Hmong Child, Her American Doctors, and the Collision of Two Cultures.* New York: Farrar, Straus, and Giroux.

parents seem to find participating in a group of one's peers more reinforcing, and perhaps less intimidating, than meeting individually with a therapist. To illustrate, a large-scale prevention study (Cunningham, Bremner, & Boyle, 1995) was conducted among families, each with a child who was highly disruptive in school. The investigators found that immigrant families, parents of children with severe behavior problems, and those whom English was a second language were all more likely to volunteer to participate in groups than in clinic-based family services.

Understanding the worldview, or cultural perspective toward how things work within the culture one is to serve, is important for effective behavior analytic practice because not everyone shares the same philosophical beliefs upon which this field is based. (See Box 1 in Chapter 1 for a review of our philosophical beliefs). It also is important to point out that it is not our job as behavior analysts, nor would it be helpful, to endorse people's world views as correct or incorrect. Rather, when faced with alternative world views, we recommend acknowledging that perspective, while explaining that your work will be conducted from within a behavioral framework. (For a more thorough discussion of this topic, see the special issue on diversity and equity in the *Journal of Behavior Analysis in Practice*, 2019, Vol 12, #4).

## Involve Key People

Those in the participants' or *clients'* natural environment must be willing to lend their support from the very beginning. So behavior analysts need to invest sufficient time and effort up front, relating to and negotiating with the people in control of the conditions—the *contingencies of reinforcement*—affecting their clientele. Consequently, we will find ourselves conferring with the participants themselves or their surrogates, along with their family members and/or significant others, administrators, teachers, managers, coworkers, parents, specialists, and so on. (One approach to gaining mutual support is to organize a team—a strategy described later in this chapter.)

## Determine Available Resources

We should familiarize ourselves early with the physical, material, and human resources in the family or organization within which the change is to occur, and learn about the values, concerns, and habit patterns of the key stakeholders. Otherwise, we may find ourselves and others working at cross-purposes, to no one's ultimate advantage. Also, look to see what adjustments might be required within the system (e.g., staffing, material, organizational, familial, or individual) to encourage, monitor, and sustain the kinds of changes being sought. We may need to obtain additional services and/or materials necessary to carry out the program as designed. Only after we are confident that all essential elements are in place should we select or devise and apply procedures known to be effective under similar circumstances.

In the event that resources cannot adequately be stretched to cover all necessary elements, we had best return to the drawing board and either adjust our objectives, our methods, or both. Any program representing itself as applied behavior analytic (ABA), must include such critical features such as *choosing and using valid, reliable measures, demonstrating treatment fidelity,* and *analyzing the function of the treatment* (described below). This means, even if our resources are strained, we must ensure that 1) our measures are reliable by assessing *interobserver agreement*, and 2) that we are implementing the treatment as designed by objectively assessing the fidelity with which we implement it. Labeling any program you design as "behavior analytic" requires that it meet the field's professional standards as described in this and other specialized texts on the subject.

## Assess Current Skill Levels

To be most helpful and efficient before embarking on a behavior change journey, we have a responsibility for assessing our clients' current behavioral repertoires. There are a number of validated indirect and descriptive assessments available for conducting these assessments (discussed in Chapter 4).

## Select Behavioral Objectives and Interventions Collaboratively

When selecting and/or defining behavioral or instructional objectives, we need to see to it that all those with a vested interest act as a team (discussed in Chapter 4). Because formal or informal organizational or family leader(s) generally control the client's most potent reinforcers and punishers, their actions can foster or impede progress. Therefore, obtaining their cooperation is essential. Senior managers, personnel directors, project managers, administrators, parents, and others must be convinced that the proposed objectives are in keeping with the organization's mission and their own professional and personal goals. So not only is it a good thing to do, it is the *right* thing to do! (Including clients and/ or their caregivers or supervisors is addressed in our Professional and Ethical Compliance Code [PECC] and ethically responsible behavior analysts will follow this suggestion.)

Ask yourself if the views of all stakeholders are represented. In a hospital, where the issue is quality of patient care, you may need to include nurses at all levels, physicians, patient representatives, dietitians, volunteers, janitorial staff, emergency teams, infection-control personnel, management, quality-of-care personnel, and so on. The point is that you need the input of such key people to determine what supports for and impediments to behavior change are in place. One strategy is to discuss with them the history of the presenting behavioral issue and to solicit the others' perspectives on the strategies under consideration.

The following episode further illustrates the value of developing objectives collaboratively: A consultant to a pre-school program advised staff to encourage a youngster to use the swings. After demonstrating by swinging the child several times, she was duly "rewarded" by becoming the recipient of the boys' motion sickness. One could overhear the teachers talking among themselves: "Teaching him how to swing himself! Now that was a really dumb objective. If she'd asked me, I could have told her the boy becomes nauseated on the swing big time! Guess she won't try that again."

Similar scenarios might follow from any other formal or informal setting: schools, homes, service agencies, sports teams, business and commercial operations, residential centers, and just about any individual or organization wherein the behavior of its membership is of interest or concern. In selecting objectives for a youngster in a pre-school for children with special needs, parents, siblings, and other close family members, the upper and middle level school administration, management, teachers, specialists in communication, art, music, and physical therapy, janitorial services, bus drivers, and kitchen and office personnel are among those you might invite, depending on the nature of the challenge. Researchers also report that parents were more in line with professionals when they were actively involved in the process of setting and implementing goals (Oien, Fallang, & Ostens, 2009). For more information on collaborative skills, see *Behavioral Consulting* (Mayer & Wallace, 2020).

## Analyze the Function of Current Contingencies

Prior to proceeding with change methods, we need to attempt to analyze the reasons for the current challenge. We do that by determining whether the contingencies of reinforcement relate to the non-occurrence or occurrence of the behavior. Discovering the explanation is critical, because depending on the answer, the change methods would differ. In the non-occurrence (omission) situation, the client(s) may simply lack the necessary skills or may be capable of performing the desired behavior but fail to do so. An inability to perform the skills indicates the need to *teach* the person those skills, while failure to practice (technically *emit*) a previously mastered skill implies a lack of adequate *reinforcement* for that behavior or even more powerful reinforcers produced by the unwanted competing behavior. (Chapters 9 and 25 focus on methods of analyzing the function of particular conditions, treatments, or interventions, while Chapter 10 is specifically devoted to assessing and analyzing the functions of challenging behaviors.) This is not something a practicing behavior analyst can overlook. Remember, behavior is complex (Skinner, 1953) and different histories have led to the current situation. Just because you have used a specific treatment with AJ to increase his sharing his toys, does not mean the same intervention will work with Kae. Rather, you need to understand the complex behavior of sharing with respect to each individual child.

## SELECT AND/OR DESIGN CHANGE METHODS

Whenever feasible, suggest change methods previously demonstrated to be effective under similar circumstances and prepare to analyze carefully the impact of procedures based on both the individual client(s)' needs and environmental considerations. For instance, to promote student success and personnel satisfaction in schools, seek, apply and evaluate the function of relevant *evidence-based practices* (e.g., Westling, Cooper-Duffy, Prohn, Ray, & Herzog, 2005). The extensive literature on applied behavior analysis now permits us to make more educated guesses about the potential of a particular set of procedures. Along with the many suggestions offered in this text and in its ancillary material, journals such as those cited in our reference list contain reports of successful behavior analytic programs in educational, clinical, institutional, work, community, home, sports, and other settings. Behavior analysts, who remain up to date with the behavior analytic literature in their areas of specialization, are more likely to make wise selections, and adhere to the ethical standards of our field. Attend particularly closely to fundamental aspects of methodology, especially descriptions of participants, settings, conditions, and staffing, as well as procedural details. Success is more likely, too, if you work under the supervision of or at least consult with experts and advisory groups before you proceed.

---

*The Evidence-Based Approach*

*Choose and use procedures scientifically found to work effectively with clients similar to yours.*

---

## Select or Devise Behavioral Measures

Assuming the environment will or can be adjusted to support behavior analytic efforts, we must consider how we are going to monitor and evaluate performance before proceeding further. We want measures that reliably and accurately reflect changes in performance. These measures will be discussed in Chapters 7 and 8.

## Analyze the Function of the Treatment

The analytic feature of ABA refers to the breaking down of our procedures and observations into their component parts, to permit us to evaluate our interventions in terms of their *functions*—the changes they directly promote. Were the original conditions and those we have changed really doing what we thought they were doing? In other words, we not only choose and use procedures, but we go further: discovering whether or not any notable change actually is related to the treatment or intervention, rather than to other events that may be happening at the same time. ABA has designed a set of strategies to suit that purpose, about which you will learn in subsequent chapters. If we are to identify ourselves as "applied behavior analysts," we *must* incorporate this analytic feature within our practice, because it permits us, convincingly, to demonstrate to ourselves and our audience the effectiveness of the behavior change programs we design and conduct.

## Prepare for Constructive Behavioral Support and Change

Once you have familiarized yourself with the setting and considered which potential interventions appear promising, determining if program mediators possess the knowledge and skills essential to adhere faithfully to the intervention protocol is crucial. If they do not, they must be prepared adequately; or, as described below, the intervention might need to be modified. Adequately preparing the program implementer may require a significant investment because bringing about lasting performance improvement is more than a "one-shot deal." Follow-up is the key! A single seminar or workshop rarely does the job.

Despite common practice, evidence repeatedly has revealed "that training, inspiration, and initial commitment, without follow-up, are usually worthless" (Malott, 2001, p. 101). Participants may display increased knowledge on pencil and paper tests, but little-to-no actual behavior change in working with their clientele.[2] In some cases, especially those in which the culture of the organization needs to be restructured, it can take up to several years of ongoing training and support to establish an ongoing effective organization-wide program (Sugai & Horner, 1999). In addition, as many have argued, further efforts are needed to sustain that program, once established:

> One reason why institutions change superficially has to do with ineffective behaviors on the part of the change agent. These proponents of change 'burn out,' or move on, before the change is fully implemented. It is necessary that a change agent possess tenacity to follow through and to return to the same tasks and the same individuals time and again. (Dustin, 1974, pp. 423–424)

As we shall emphasize in Chapter 24, *everyone involved in the change process needs to gain reinforcers for their positive contributions along the way if their considerable efforts are to be sustained.* Additionally, *problem-prevention activities need to be integrated as part of the family's or organization's day-to-day operation*, not just, as is so often the case, in emergency situations such as fatalities, injuries, loss of key personnel, financial shortfalls, low sets of scores, or poor assessments. The system must be mobilized to create an *ongoing* reinforcing mechanism to support and sustain behavior change practices, regardless of temporary crises. To mobilize the system and promote program stability, objectives also need to be linked to the organization's mission and priorities and a consensus built in support of the program. Next, we turn to using a team approach as a strategy for preventing problems and promoting progress toward achieving lasting positive behavior change and support.

## Organize and Manage Team Operation

Many business and service organizations involve *teams* as a mechanism for supporting a quality operation. (For example, see Aubrey and James Daniels' *Performance Management: Changing Behavior that Drives Organizational Effectiveness,* 2004). That can work for you, too. Effective teams remain ongoing, are integrated within the organization's program, designed to continue independent of leadership changes, and are in the best position to help establish goals and priorities. If you are thinking this concept only applies to business or educational organizations, remember, *it takes a village to raise a child.*

Personnel working within a team structure also can produce highly effective intervention plans (Goh & Bambara, 2012), especially those in which members *promote collaborative problem-solving and provide ongoing support* to those responsible for implementing the intervention. Just as a parent often needs help and encouragement from other family members and teachers, so do managers, supervisors, workers, and other organizational members require social support when initiating promising programs within their organizations. Evidence (Crone, Hawken, & Bergstrom, 2007) suggests that programs developed by teams appear to be more readily acceptable. In their situation, school personnel were found to be more accepting of interventions developed by a team that included teachers and a behavior expert than a plan developed solely by an expert.

In another example, Mayer (1995) designed and guided the organization and implementation of school-wide teams as a tactic for preventing and reducing problematic student behaviors in a number of schools in Los Angeles,. Others (e.g., Sugai & Horner, 1999), have suggested using two teams per school, what we call a *Positive Behavior Support Team* (PBST) and *a Student Success Team* (SST), dedicated to primary, secondary, and tertiary prevention, described as follows:

---

[2] It is for this very reason that we have designed a series of field activities to guide new practitioners in the autism education field. (See Sulzer-Azaroff, Dyer, Dupont & Soucy, 2012)

The **Positive Behavior Support Team (PBST)** *includes all representative stakeholders and focuses most heavily on* **primary prevention** *programs*. It is incorporated within the school site council committee, the school safety planning committee, or exists as a stand-alone special school discipline group. This team is responsible for examining and addressing *contextual* factors *including motivational operations* (e.g., histories of student failure, an over-reliance on punitive methods of control and an under-reliance on positive reinforcement by personnel) with the aim of *preventing discipline problems in the first place* (primary prevention). Well-organized and -run PBST programs have been found to eliminate about 80 to 90 percent of their students' troublesome behaviors (Sugai et al., 2000).

The **Student Success Team (SST)** has the responsibility for *identifying, addressing, and preventing problems exhibited by the ten-to-twenty percent of individual students who have not responded satisfactorily to the programs implemented by the PBST and who remain at-risk for severe academic or behavioral problems*. For example, if an at-risk student responds aggressively to peer criticism or is behind academically, that student may need some social skills training or tutoring. These **secondary prevention** activities often *involve small-group tutoring, social skills training, and so forth for such at-risk students*.

**Tertiary prevention** often *involves individualized programs (functional behavioral assessments, individual tutoring, therapy, community and other wrap-around services) designed for the few students who are at high-risk*, such as those in gangs or those who demonstrate severe behavioral and/or academic problems. Of course, school personnel working at the tertiary level require expertise in such skills as diagnosing mental health problems, conducting ongoing proactive student screening to identify those at risk for gang membership and severe academic/behavioral problems, conducting functional behavioral assessments (see Chapter 10), designing positive behavioral interventions based on the behavior's identified function, developing social skills lessons, training other staff in positive behavioral interventions and social skills, consulting with and supporting school staff, students, and families, coordinating school and community services.

(Further details, including the composition and responsibilities of these teams, can be found in Mayer & Ybarra, 2003; Mayer, 2000; and on this book's website.)

Other examples of team involvement can be identified in ABA programs within various fields. Included, among others, are those dedicated to safety and injury prevention; in research, industrial, and health-care facilities; customer satisfaction; curriculum design, evaluation, and quality assurance in educational settings; and training and consulting.

Well-constituted teams enable members to have a say in identifying their own and their group's immediate and long-term aspirations as well as highlighting the most highly valued aspects of their daily functioning. They also help to heighten participants' awareness of what features of their own performance are valued and likely to be reinforced. Of special importance is that well-conceived and -structured teams, such as those described above for schools, are designed to promote and support not only positive institution-wide change, but small group and individual behavior change as well. Such team programs are more likely to be successful if the selected procedures have demonstrated their effectiveness and have the support of those in the environment who control important contingencies for the client and the **contingency managers** (*those who implement the intervention, such as parents, teachers aides, and Registered Behavior Technicians™ [RBTs]*).

Now, before moving on, we suggest you use our examples to consider how you might organize teams in an organization (or family) of interest to you, such as to help prevent accidents, injuries, illness, dissatisfaction, non-compliance, waste, turnover, and other problems in living.

## CLIENT BEHAVIOR CHANGE: PROGRAM DEVELOPMENT AND SELECTION

Despite demonstrated effectiveness with similar clientele, sometimes the contingency managers or other stakeholders in a particular situation reject the goal or methods of intervention. Unless those consumers can be educated and/or encouraged to support that particular program, it is at risk of failure. Fortunately, as the science and technology of behavior change expands, multiple paths to the same goal often are available, especially to those who remain informed. If, for instance, a token system is unacceptable, dozens of other reinforcement packages are available, as you'll learn later on. The critical point is that you must feel confident that the program that you *do* plan will be implemented faithfully (i.e., with solid *procedural fidelity*) to accomplish its purpose. Of course, mutual support for a given approach is just the beginning. Other factors also enter in, as you will learn in the following sections.

### Plan for Generalization from the Start

Just as preparing prior to embarking on a trip to unfamiliar territory is wise, responsible behavior-change agents carefully plan what specific behaviors their clientele must be able to emit under actual environmental circumstances (i.e., people, times, places and/or situations). This is no simple task because, more often than not, practitioners of applied behavior analysis often are called upon to address rather serious clientele challenges such as major skill deficiencies, and threats to their own and others' health, safety, contentment, and well-being.

Satisfactorily accomplishing such outcomes does not come cheaply or easily, for among the many conditions that must be in place for any behavior-change program to succeed include not only clientele and families who chose this path, but also highly skilled and socially and reasonably well-supported personnel, adequate materials and supplies, and suitable physical surroundings. Sadly, all resources are finite. So, as responsible behavior analysts, we must focus on maximizing the gain our clients receive in return for the time, effort, and material they, their families, their organizations, society, and we ourselves invest in the process. Those in the business sometimes label this as "Getting the biggest bang for the buck."

*Getting the biggest bang for the buck* demands careful planning, though: Finding and securing the services of capable, eager managerial and service personnel, of affordable, safe, appropriate physical space, and sufficient funds to support and furnish them with adequate materials and supplies. Beyond that, within our field of behavior analysis, it especially means a solidly constructed program designed to enable our clientele to gain and sustain skills that will accrue to their own and their associates' present and long-term advantage.

Should you already have selected the area in which you hope to, or are applying your behavior-analytic skills, consider just how you might proceed. One trap to watch out for, though, is investing the bulk of your resources on "the quick fix": curing an employee from complaining, being lazy, or doing a shoddy job; a student from misbehaving; a family member from spending too much money on useless objects. Rather, begin by taking the long view by identifying your ultimate objective, then breaking it down into a series of more readily achievable short steps leading to it.

Of equal, or sometimes even greater, importance is selecting goals that will provide "the biggest bang for the buck." In some cases that can mean directly teaching the client "pivotal skills" (those general patterns of behavior that will open the doors to a breadth of learning: the ability to communicate, to interact socially, self-manage, acquire basic academic skills such as reading, writing, and computing; social and organizational skills such as interacting in ways compatible with their local and broader families, teams, and societies; and such personal/functional living proficiencies as meeting responsibilities, caring for one's own safety and well-being, and so on).

Because they tend to be present and concerned, often we can obtain the greatest pay-off by enabling those others within the natural living, learning or work environment to support constructive general and lasting change. For children with autism spectrum disorder, that might mean training and supporting their families' use of effective strategies to teach their youngsters functional living skills (e.g., Neely et al, 2016). For factory workers, that might involve managers (Sulzer-Azaroff & Harshbarger (1995); for students and teachers, the school principal (Gillat, & Sulzer-Azaroff, 1994); at health-care facilities, peers (Fleming & Sulzer-Azaroff, 1992) or the nurses in charge (Babcock, Sulzer-Azaroff, Sanderson, & Scibak (1992); in savings banks, tellers (Brown & Sulzer-Azaroff, 1991).

Should you, now, or in the future, be in the position of wishing to learn current best practices for promoting and supporting demonstrably *broad and lasting behavioral change*, this text should enable you to achieve that. You will discover methods for choosing behavioral goals and strategies that promise to be supported by those interacting most directly with your clients' as well as ways to apply your informed actions to your own behavior.

## Ensure Treatment Integrity

The term **treatment integrity** (also known as **procedural fidelity** or **fidelity of implementation**) refers to ensuring that *everyone involved carries out and supports the intervention as planned* (see Chapter 7 for methods of assessing treatment integrity). Procedures that veer away from their intended path pose a risk of failure. Further, Fiske (2008) points out that "a growing body of evidence suggests that treatment integrity... is related to intervention outcomes" (p. 19). Generally, the higher the treatment integrity, the more effective the intervention (e.g., Carroll, Kodak, & Fisher, 2013; Cook et al., 2010; DiGennero et al. 2007, Fryling, Wallace, & Yassine, 2012; Noell, Gresham, & Gansle, 2002; Vollmer, Roane, Ringdalh, & Marcus, 1999; Wilder, Atwell, & Wine, 2006). To take a simple case, suppose a team of workers has successfully increased its safety scores under the assumption that the reward will be an extra break on Friday. Friday arrives, but on that very day a rush order comes in. The promised break is forgotten. The next week, safety scores drop. No wonder! The fidelity of the intervention was compromised. Similarly, Donnelly and Karsten (2017) found that skill acquisition interference and performance disruption occurred when reinforcers were delivered at times other than immediately following correct completion of training steps, prompting steps were out of order, and when prompts failed to be delivered when scheduled.

Reid, Parsons, and Jensen (2017) used feedback and a collaborative team approach to increase the involvement of adolescent and adult residents with severe disabilities in functional educational tasks. The initial increases in participant involvement in functional tasks were maintained during follow-up observations spanning 30 years. Probably the team approach they employed, (described in this chapter and in Chapter 24), heavily contributed toward promoting and supporting the impressively long-term maintenance of the program.

The importance of maintaining treatment integrity also has been addressed from a legal perspective. In a review of 52 published court decisions, Etschdeit (2006) noted that the first thing hearing officers look for when making a decision is whether the *behavior intervention plan* (BIP) was implemented as planned. Case law consistently has demonstrated that failure consistently to implement the BIPs contained within a child's *individual education plan* (IEP) is tantamount to depriving the student of a *free and appropriate public education* (*FAPE*) (see Drasgow & Yell, 2001; Etschdeit, 2006).

Determining treatment integrity is no simple task without advance planning. Consider the case in which a team (Sulzer-Azaroff, Hoffman, Horton, Bondy, & Frost, 2009) surveyed the published research on an alternative or augmentative behavior-analytic-based system that enables non-speaking clients to express their desires and observations: the *Picture Exchange Communication System* (PECS; see Chapter 19). We examined investigators' descriptions of the methods they used and their results. Although all reported positive success rates, some seemed superior to others. However, trying to determine the reason why was difficult, if not impossible. The research team was not in a position to determine how stringently the contingency managers in programs reporting the effectiveness of the outcomes adhered to Frost and Bondy's (2002) thorough protocol of elements. Did some conduct more formal training, incidental teaching, and generalization trials than others or not? Did they, as advised, frequently assess for reinforcer appeal within and across trials? Were two trainers involved at the early stages and did they shift roles as recommended? And so on. We recommended that in the future researchers use and report the results of a performance (treatment integrity) checklist to permit more refined analyses of the results, because until such information is regularly published, along with descriptions of the investigative methods, we'll remain ignorant of which aspects most powerfully impact the results.

A *demonstrably* clear, accurate description of the interventions that behavior analysts apply is essential because consumers of our literature often are searching for strategies to apply within their own settings. Yet investigators (McIntire, Gresham, DiGennaro, & Reed, 2007) who examined reports of 152 school-based intervention studies contained in the *Journal of Applied Behavior Analysis* from 1991 to 2005 for data on treatment integrity found that only 30 percent reported those data. Unless authors provide convincing evidence that published descriptions actually were carried out as described, they risk leading practitioners astray by misinforming them as to how they actually achieved their treatment effectiveness.

In your own case, you will want to know if the programs you have elected to use are implemented as planned. To determine this you need to identify what stimuli are reinforcing *and* how consistently they are used, regardless of other conditions in effect. That includes the quality of assistance and support provided, the competency of those designing the program, and other features known to influence program fidelity (Cook, et al., 2010; Mihalic, 2003). Collier, Meek, Sanetti, and Fallon (2017) provide a clear rationale for and practical guide to assessing treatment integrity in educational settings, generalizable to other settings as well. Remember the basis upon which you are selecting and implementing an intervention is supported by strong evidence of treatment fidelity. Should the intervention not be implemented as planned, it cannot be considered an evidence-based intervention.

Generally, the more acceptable the intervention is the more likely it will be implemented. There are a variety of factors that influence the acceptability of an intervention. These include:

- What the treatment is called (avoid jargon)
- The severity of the client's problem (the more severe, the more willing one is to try various interventions)
- The time and effort involved
- Familiarity and knowledge with behavioral principles (the more they know about ABA the more acceptable they are likely to find the intervention)
- The more they believe the intervention will work, the more acceptable they are likely to find it
- And, positive interventions tend to be more acceptable than punitive ones.

## Measuring Treatment Integrity

Measuring treatment integrity is important because researchers have demonstrated that errors impact learning, regardless if they are errors of omission (i.e., not doing part of the procedure) or errors of commission (i.e., doing something additional to the procedure). Specifically, Bergarmann, Kodak, and LeBlanc (2017) demonstrated that both *errors of omission* and *errors of commission* within a conditional discrimination teaching program resulted in compromised learning in typical developing children. Beyond the fact that clients are less likely to benefit from programs lacking fidelity, evaluating the effectiveness of an intervention is difficult if the treatment is not accurately implemented. Thus, in addition to measuring the behavior of interest and the reliability of the measurement system itself (see Chapter 7 for measuring reliability), to truly evaluate the effectiveness of an intervention, it is essential to ensure the intervention is implemented as planned. So, you will want to *include treatment integrity as a routine part of your measurement system*. Just as you design and apply a system for measuring changes in the target behavior(s), you also will want to develop and implement a measurement system to assess the extent to which your intervention is being implemented as intended.

Here is an example: The plan is to use a three-prompt procedure consisting of verbal, model, and physical prompts to present demands followed by praise as a consequence of a youngster's complying with those demands. Treatment integrity could be assessed by scoring the trainer's correct and incorrect implementation of the procedure just prior to the third prompt. *Implementation* would be scored as follows:

Score "correct" if the trainer

- correctly implemented each step (verbal, model, physical) without providing additional prompts;
- terminated the prompting sequence contingent on child compliance; and,
- if praise was delivered following any compliance before the third prompt.

Score "*Incorrect*" if the trainer

- provided any additional prompts (error of commission);
- praised compliance after the third prompt (error of commission); *or*
- omitted any step (error of omission).

The percentage of treatment integrity could then be assessed by dividing the number of correct instances by the total number of correct and incorrect instances and multiplying the result by 100. [Total correct / (total correct and incorrect) x 100]. If a low treatment integrity score is obtained (below about 85 percent), steps would be needed to "fix" it. (Refer back to Chapter 3, where we touch on some methods for promoting program fidelity.)

To review: Make sure the procedure is completely laid out in a step-by-step fashion and that all implementers are trained until they reach the criterion set for mastery. Be especially aware of **treatment drift**, which occurs when *the application of the intervention begins to veer off course from its originally intended path.* (Instead of altering the procedure independently, ask program implementers to review their concerns with the behavior analysts, who will use the data as the main basis for deciding if and how procedural changes or more training and feedback are merited.)

The factors discussed below also influence acceptability and treatment integrity.

## ASSURE CONTEXTUAL FIT WHEN SELECTING GOALS AND INTERVENTIONS

Deciding what set of procedures to apply in any given situation is no simple matter. Time, place, human and material resources, clientele characteristics, cultural variables, and other factors may influence the outcome of any behavioral intervention. The safe way is to *begin by selecting strategies as similar as possible to ongoing practices, especially those that build on the strengths and skills the contingency manager(s) and personnel already possess.* Yes, historical evidence of effectiveness must exist, but if a new procedure is not implemented consistently because contingency managers lack proficiency in or are uncomfortable with practicing the routine, little will be accomplished. Therefore, to select the best fit between the goal, the intervention strategies, and the context into which they are to be implemented, (McLaughlin, Snyder & Welsh, 2012) behavior analysts need to familiarize themselves with ongoing practices and the contingencies currently affecting personnel within that particular context. "The goal is not to find the one true intervention, but to find an intervention that is effective and will be implemented by the people in the setting. An intervention is contextually appropriate if it fits with the skills, schedules, resources, and values of the people who must implement the plan" (Horner, 1994, p. 403). Be forewarned, though, that depending on other factors, what is contextually fitting at one point in time or in place, may not be at another (Killeen & Jacobs, 2016).

Relatedly, "The essential ingredient in our producing technology that will be useful is making sure that the technology, in addition to being effective for intended populations, will be reinforcing for all the people who will buy and use it" (Hopkins, 1987, p. 343). The goal is to maximize short- and long-term reinforcers while minimizing short- and long-term punishers, not only for our clientele, but also for the contingency managers and others who might be affected by the intervention program (Hawkins, 1986). Similarly, interventions designed "to be user friendly will be more likely to produce high fidelity, and therefore, durable intervention gains" (McConnachie & Carr, 1997, p. 123). When given a choice, then, assign high priority to interventions that not only have supportive data, but also that contingency managers can implement with relative ease, are acceptable to them, and address their concerns, while promoting improved client adjustment, adaptation, competence, or habilitation.

As an example, to help determine whether an intervention is consonant with the life of a particular family, Albin, Luchyshyn, Horner, and Flannery (1996) developed a *goodness-of-fit* assessment questionnaire. Its 12 items help implementers determine if the proposed intervention is congruent with family goals and expectations, lifestyle, implementation effort/time, and sustainability. Also, you might want to consider conducting a family ecology assessment similar to the informal interviews Binnendyk and Lucyshyn (2009) conducted to assess "family strengths, social supports and resources, stressors and goals for the child and family" (p. 52) to help them design a contextually appropriate intervention for food refusal by a six-year-old child with autism at home during snack time. The following example illustrates how features of the family's ecology contributed to the selection of support procedures:

> After years of struggling to get her son to try new foods, the mother was not confident that she would have the strength or emotional toughness needed to transform her son's eating patterns. She was also worried that starting intervention in the natural setting (i.e., kitchen) might upset her other children who were home at that time of day. The plan was therefore adjusted in response to these concerns so that initial training began with the therapist and then transferred to the mother once Karim's feeding behavior improved. In addition, training began away from the kitchen, upstairs in Karim's bedroom, with the therapist sitting next to Karim at a small table in the corner of the room (p. 53).

As with all of us, contingency managers have different training and experiential backgrounds, which, in turn, may limit their ability to implement particular programs effectively. An aide or behavior technician, unfamiliar with methods for assessing contemporary reinforcer effectiveness, is less likely to choose the most powerful reinforcers at the moment. A naïve supervisor, unskilled in delivering feedback, may misconstrue the concept of supplying powerful feedback, as in assuming his "Nice job!" is reinforcing. Should contingency managers consider a suggested intervention too difficult or otherwise unacceptable, they may shirk that task, resulting in the immediate reinforcer of escape (Alford & Lantka, 2000). Personnel who feel overextended and exhausted by their work tend to be pessimistic about the value of implementing behavioral programs (Corrigan et al., 1998). Overly complex programs not only add to the contingency manager's workload and stress, but also risk failing. Contingency managers need to be trained to a reasonable level of fluency (that is, capable of emitting the behavior smoothly, rapidly, and with little apparent effort) if they are to implement a program faithfully; and their training will need to begin at their performance and comfort levels and continue gradually until a they reach a predetermined level of proficiency (the behavioral or performance objective).

You, yourself, will want to possess sufficient basic skills to enable your own initial ABA programs to succeed, and that means choosing and using methods for teaching, motivating, and managing staff to implement programs as designed. (We return to this topic later on, especially in the chapters covering shaping and teaching complex behavior.) Among the actions you can take to increase the likelihood that personnel will adhere faithfully to the specified treatment protocol are to invite their participation in:

- selecting the goals;
- designing the procedures;
- choosing the methods for reviewing and evaluating progress;
- and seeing to it that reinforcement occurs as a result of their efforts.

Such participant involvement will tend to improve the quality of their on-the-job performance beyond that displayed when tasks or goals simply are assigned or requested (Cotton, Vollrath, Froggatt, Lengnick-Hall, & Jennings et al., 1988; Fellner & Sulzer-Azaroff, 1984; Sulzer-Azaroff, Loafman,

Merante, & Hlavacek, 1990; Binnendyk & Lucyshyn, 2009; Hieneman & Dunlap, 2001). (See Chapter 4 for a further discussion of the importance of inviting clients' and others' participation in the goal-selection process.)

Additionally, conflicts can often be avoided and cooperation facilitated when the implementer of the program is directly involved in selecting goals. To illustrate, Mr. Jones may be more willing to try to *increase his rates of commenting on his employees' specific accomplishments* (e.g., "Great! You finished this report an hour earlier than the last one.") instead of working on his rates of simply praising due to the awkwardness he feels when he praises. Or the behavioral consultant may accede to Mrs. Walker's request to provide noncontingent reinforcement to her young students every 15 minutes instead of every minute.

When selecting goals jointly, be sure those managing the contingencies are able to demonstrate their ability to implement the procedures fluently, as designed. Otherwise the program may fail. Suppose a teacher announces to his class that he prefers to have students raise their hands. Yet frequently he calls on those who shout out questions or answers. Despite his attempts and willingness to reinforce hand-raising and withhold reinforcement for shouting out, his actual "uncontrollable" responsiveness to good student contributions interferes with that goal. In such cases, the goal and/or the intervention, or both, will need to be altered, or additional coaching and support furnished. This example also reminds us that what the contingency managers *say* they can do and what they *actually* can and cannot do may be different. The best tactic is to *sample the individual's genuine level of performance over time, then and build upon that baseline.*

If they can't do it, change the behavioral objective.

## Select Interventions Collaboratively

Involving contingency managers in the process of selecting the intervention procedure allows them to air their own biases, priorities, concerns, and limitations. The selection of the goal for Karim, the 6-year-old with autism (described above), was conducted jointly by staff and family members. Managers, supervisors, teachers, coaches, aides, counselors, psychologists, parents, institutional staff members, or other "people shapers" tend to be more aware of the limitations and problems entailed in performing their jobs. Involving them in the process may enable them more sensibly to prioritize goals, assess participants' skill levels, and make judgments about whether personnel will be able to devote the time and resources required to implement the program.

As mentioned previously, you need to analyze the environment carefully to enable effective program development and selection. "Rather than entering the setting with the 'answers,' the institutional change agent should spend a period of time 'getting to know the territory.' By asking all levels of staff for their input, he will ease his acceptance by assuring them that he is, indeed, concerned with the problems as they define them" (Reppucci, 1977, p. 597). Additionally, Reppucci suggests that we "assess the existing interpersonal and organizational conflicts, the strengths and weakness of individual staff members, and formal and informal power bases" (p. 597), along with the "political reality which includes finances, bureaucracy, unions, public relations, and internal and external politics as elements of an institution's social ecology" (p. 601). Such information can be invaluable in selecting goals and reinforcers and in determining sources of support.

**Facilitating goal and intervention selection.** To work successfully with various program implementers, you not only need behavior-analytic skills but also critical interpersonal relationship-building skills (LeBlanc, Taylor, & Marchese, 2020). Several interpersonal communication skills are suggested below. However, For a more detail description of various communication skills, see *Behavioral Consulting* (Mayer & Wallace, 2020).

Useful suggestions for enabling the selection of contextually appropriate goals and interventions include these steps (Mayer, 2003):

- Develop solutions and strategies collaboratively.

- Base individual strategies on the assessment of both the problem *and* the contingency manager's skills.
- Periodically paraphrase (put into your own words) what the contingency manager is saying to convey your empathy, attention and understanding (e.g., the teacher comments, "If he doesn't start following the classroom rules soon, I'm going to talk to the principal about having him transferred out of this class." You respond, "Sounds like you're about ready the throw in the towel."
- State any points of confusion and ask for clarification. (e. g., "I'm confused—when you say that he is aggressive, do you mean he hits, bites, uses profanity, or ?"
- Summarize the contingency manager's main points within an A-B-C format: "Let's see if I understand what you have shared so far. John tends to hit (B, the behavior) when he is told he can't have something that he wants (A, the antecedent or situation), and as a result, sometimes he gets what he wants and at other times he is sent to his room (C, the consequence to the problem behavior)."
- Make frequent use of "I statements" in gathering information rather than asking too many questions: "I'm a bit confused. I understand that John hits, but I don't have a clear picture of the situation in which this behavior tends to occur. Can you help me gain a clearer picture of that situation?" This format sets a more collaborative tone and prompts a wider range of information than when the person in the role of "expert" seeks information by asking a series of specific questions.
- Check your listener's understanding of what you say by asking the individual to paraphrase what you said; then re-check and correct for any further misunderstandings.

### Involving Clients and Stakeholders

The Behavior Analyst Certification Board (2020) *ethics code for behavior analysts* states:

Behavior analysts make appropriate efforts to involve clients and relevant stakeholders throughout the service relationship, including selecting goals, selecting and designing assessments and behavior-change interventions, and conducting continual progress monitoring. (Code 2.09, p.11)

This is extremely important for successful interventions, and we hope we have given you successful guidance in implementing this code.

### Use Acceptable and Comprehensible Language to Clarify Contingency Managers' Tasks

Simply and directly clarifying the specific task to be applied, along with its rationale, is an important aspect in the preparation of contingency managers (Anderson, Crowell, Hantula, & Siroky, 1988; Squires et al., 2007; Wilson, Boni, & Hogg, 1997). Although feedback and reinforcement generally are the most powerful elements within a training program, when personnel clearly understand exactly what is expected of them and why, they usually improve their performance. In a study by Squires et al. (2007), after the owner simply defined and illustrated in everyday language how restaurant personnel were to greet customers, rates of appropriate greetings rose by ten or more percentage points. (Visual prompts and feedback heightened those improvements considerably further.)

When coaching people unfamiliar with ABA jargon, you may be wise to adjust the language you use to make it more comprehensible to them. As Carr (1996) implied, usually the decision-makers or contingency managers in our society are non-scientists. If personnel are unfamiliar with the technical language of ABA, they may find it confusing or frustrating and cause them to feel uneasy (Allen, Barone, & Kuhn, 1993). Similarly, Critchfield et al. (2017) found that there is "a tendency for behavior analysis terms to register as more unpleasant than other kinds of professional terms and also as more unpleasant than English words generally" (p. 97). "We need to recognize that people's emotional reactions are critical to successful program adoption and that behaviorally induced resistance to change can sabotage any program via vetoes or required modifications that render it virtually unrecognizable" (Foxx, 1996, p. 157). Rather, we would be wise to identify and adopt the vocabulary of the customer, be it academic, jargon, bureaucratese, or just plain English (Binder, 1994; Mayer & McGookin, 1977). In fact, using language compatible with participants' local language system and showing that their perspective is understood, has been found to heighten both the acceptability and fidelity of selected interventions (Becirevic, Critchfield, & Reed, 2016; Witt & Elliott, 1983; Witt, Moe, Gutkin, & Andrews, 1984). "Behavioral consultants need to attend to factors such as communication strategies that facilitate shared responsibility as well as to understand consultees' explanations for their problems and their treatment expectations" (Rosenfeld, 1991, p. 329). Reppucci and Saunders (1974) commented early on:

> Flexibility and sensitivity by the behavior modifier regarding the language problem could avoid difficult situations that often arise during the implementation of a behavioral program. Programs do not survive for long that do not have the support of the indigenous members of an environment.... An acceptable and comprehensible language is crucial in gaining this support. (p. 654)

The importance of using comprehensible language also is stressed in the *Behavior Analyst Certification Board (2020) ethics code for behavior analysts* that states:

> Behavior analysts use understandable language in, and ensure comprehension of, all communications with clients, stakeholders, supervisees, trainees, and research participants. Before providing services, they clearly describe the scope of services and specify the conditions under which services will end. They explain all assessment and behavior change intervention procedures before implementing them and explain assessment and intervention results when they are available. They provide an accurate and current set of their credentials and description of their area of competence upon request. (code 2.08)

For as pointed out some time ago by Lindsley (1991), "A technology has only technical jargon… a profession has both a technical jargon and a set of plain English equivalents… (p. 450).

A guideline of effective teaching is to *begin at the learners' level of skill or expertise, not where you would like them to be*. Research findings on the subject of modeling (e. g., Bandura, 1965c) suggest that we avoid modeling behaviors that are too complex; rather we should stress similarity between our terms with those use by the audience. Caution suggests that at least initially we identify and use program implementers' common parlance or terminology (e.g., "motivated," "self-worth," "self-concept," "strokes," etc.). Also, substitute lay terminology like "individualized instruction" for such technical terms as "shaping and chaining," or "fostering independent learning" instead of "fading," and "learning from consequences" in place of "operant conditioning." Using the everyday language of your program implementers may increase their comfort with the behavioral approach because it is more familiar. Also, as you will learn when you study the concept of *shaping*, it is wise to begin at the learner's current performance level. And, as with the *modeling* procedure, your suggestions will seem simpler when you connect with implementers' communicative repertoires. In short, *success demands we choose language* that matches the repertoire of our audience. As Bailey (1991) has suggested, we should be wise to conduct a front-end analysis to determine what those consumers who are to apply the contingencies are looking for, what form the procedures should take, and how they should be packaged and delivered.

Similarly, when communicating with non-behavior analysts we should use the language of ethics rather than that of technology (Carr, 1996). We need to emphasize how the proposed intervention strategies can help promote personal responsibility, freedom, dignity, equality, and justice. "What is required is that we see beyond our intimidating jargon to discover our link with higher values and the necessity of communicating technological achievement to society in a language that reflects those values" (Carr, 1996, p. 269). We can also stress the humaneness of the approach (Foxx, 1996). Regardless, the key is to communicate in a language that is not off-putting and that the implementers of our programs will understand and accept.

Selecting the appropriate language, terminology, or words to use is similar to selecting reinforcers (see chapter 6 for reinforcer selection); their impact is largely dependent on the individual's previous learning history. Thus, select those that have the most desirable effect on the listener (Lindsley, 1991; Becirevic et al., 2016). Table 3.1 suggests some alternative non-technical words you might consider using in your interactions with those such as parents, supervisors, managers, teachers and other contingency mangers cooperating in the venture (based on Mayer & McGookin, 1977). Also, Critchfield (2017) points out that "Visuwords® offers one means of vetting substitute expressions that non experts might find more palatable than jargon" (p. 319). "Applied behavior analysts will find Visuwords® simple to use, intuitively understandable, and at least broadly applicable to the goal of preventing audience-insensitive verbal behavior from turning them into "Attila the Hun" in the eyes (or ears) of those who can profit from their expertise" (p. 321).

**TABLE 3.1  Everyday Terms for Technical ABA Terminology[3]**

| Technical Term | Alternative Term | Plain English |
|---|---|---|
| Reinforcement | Rewarding, giving incentives | Increasing the behavior by praising, attending to, or recognizing accomplishment and effort; providing special rewards, events, and activities; removing nagging or criticism |
| Stimulus generalization | Transfer | Teaching clients who have learned skills under one condition to apply them under conditions sharing similar qualities |
| Stimulus change | Environmental change | Teaching clients to act differently under different conditions by changing the environment |
| Modeling | Demonstrating, showing | Teaching by setting an example; demonstrating a new task or behavior |
| Shaping and Chaining | Individualized instruction, coaching | Teaching clients by beginning at their current level of performance and breaking down complicated learning tasks or behaviors into smaller parts that they can learn one portion at a time |
| Fading | Fostering independent learning | Enabling the client to assume increasing independence by helping, reminding, and suggesting less and less often |
| Scheduling | Developing intrinsic motivation | Assisting the client to increasingly perform the behavior in the absence of rewards, which, in turn, promotes the client's personal satisfaction with accomplishments and achievements |
| Extinction | Appropriate withholding of reinforcement | Reducing an unwanted behavior by withholding attention or other rewards from behaviors that interfere with constructive learning or performance |
| Timeout | Temporary separation from the group | Reducing an unwanted behavior to maintain a supportive or safe learning environment by temporarily separating the person from the group to allow him or her to regain self-control and composure, or to protect others from harm |
| Response cost | Penalties | Reducing an unwanted behavior by subtracting points, losing yardage, fining |
| Satiation | Excessive use, consumption, or repetition of a behavior | Reducing an unwanted behavior by providing excessive amounts of rewards or activities, which brings about a reduction in the activity, e.g., eating, shouting, lifting weights. |

[3]The lay language is only illustrative and not representative of all possible types of applications of the term.

## If Necessary, Temporarily Incorporate, then Fade Intervention Prompts within the Natural Environment

*Should program implementers require some initial encouragement when operating within the natural environment, temporarily incorporate, then fade intervention prompts.* Concrete items like certificates, tokens (i.e., points, chips, etc. exchangeable for various backup reinforcers), positive notes, or other readily obtainable and noticeable items can serve to prompt contingency managers to deliver praise or other reinforcing consequences, or otherwise implement the program according to plan. For example, you might set a timer to sound, or a light to flash, at particular times of day to remind staff to perform a particular task, like scanning for opportunities to deliver praise. Display an attention-commanding change in the surroundings like tilting a picture hanging on the wall (Latham, 1994). A supervisor might switch her wristwatch to her other wrist, so whenever she checks the time, the altered location reminds her to monitor her employees. Posting a note to oneself on the wall or refrigerator are other possibilities. The cue commands attention, thereby reminding the implementer to scan the client's behavior and, if merited, to praise it. Consider, as well, programming your cell phone to emit soft tones or vibrating signals to prompt yourself to implement your planned action.

Communicating intervention requirements very precisely tends to add to the comfort with which contingency managers function. Early on we (Farber & Mayer, 1972) encountered a high school teacher who reported that he felt awkward praising his students' appropriate behavior. We suggested that he try: (1) praising at least one student for starting class work during the first minute of class; and (2) spending two five-minute periods, while the students were working, circulating about the room complimenting those engaged in completing their assignments. This detailed structure eventually encouraged his use of praise. Later, as he began to dispense praise in his classes more regularly, he commented on how much his classroom had improved. In a different instance—this time a program serving people with developmental disabilities—all it took to encourage home supervisors to increase the timeliness of their report submissions was to announce specific target dates (Cronin, 1982). More recently (Cohrs, Shriver, Burke, & Allen, 2016), teachers in two different schools failed to meet their goals of using specific praise under particular circumstances. After the frequency and conditions under which they were to use specific praise were included in their objectives, most teachers satisfactorily increased their levels of specific praise. So, to promote greater cooperation and program implementation, clearly specify the results you are seeking. (You will learn how to specify objectives in the next chapter, and how to fade out prompts like these over time in Chapter 20.)

**Promote self-monitoring.** Don't overlook self-monitoring, which can heighten your client's awareness of what they are doing or failing to do. Cook et al. (2016) asked teachers to self-monitor their ratios of positive-to-negative interactions with their students. This simple strategy resulted in fewer classroom disruptions and increased academic engagement. (We return to self-monitoring and recording in Chapter 8.)

**Provide a checklist.** You can design a checklist similar to the ones many of us use when we shop or to remind ourselves to address a particular chore; that is, by itemizing the item or event, then asking the program implementer, or someone else (and/or even yourself), to check off each as it is accomplished. Suppose you and your staff have identified a set of essential skills to perform in the classroom: complimenting students when they enter in an orderly fashion, when they get down to work quickly, periodically as they continue working during the period, and as they wrap-up in an orderly fashion. Goings et al. (2019) used a checklist with feedback to assist teachers to improve their classroom appearance and organization, which included items such as putting away toys and electronic devices and placing chairs under tables. As a result, the classrooms improved their appearance and organization. Such checklists simplify self-recording, improve performance, and serve as an effective prompt to engage in the desired behavior (Bacon, Fulton, & Malott, 1982; Burg, Reid, & Lattimore, 1979; Mouzakitis, Codding, &

Tryon, 2015). Additionally, as Cook et al. (2016) found, this strategy *can support treatment integrity.* Such checklists actually have been found to improve the performance quality of personnel from assembly workers (Sulzer-Azaroff & Harshbarger, 1995) to that of personnel working in intensive care units (Pronovost, Wu, & Sexton, 2004).

## SUPPORT FOR THE CONTINGENCY MANAGER(S): PERFORMANCE FEEDBACK

As you now are aware, simply explaining how to implement the intervention or providing written instructions often is insufficient to promote high-quality program implementation. Further actions usually are required prior to, during, and following training to enable personnel to master the particular skills. Those may include modeling, role-playing, or directed rehearsal, along with supportive performance feedback and reinforcement during both preliminary training and initial program implementation (e.g., Adams, Tallon, & Rimell, 1980; Flanagan, Adams, & Forehand, 1979; Krumhus & Malott, 1980; Rose & Church, 1998; Sterling-Turner, Watson, Wildmon, Watkins, & Little, 2001; Ward, Johnson, & Konukman, 1998). As many have learned the hard way, however, such training often is insufficient to *sustain* program implementation (among others, Fleming & Sulzer-Azaroff, 1988; Fox & Sulzer-Azaroff, 1983; Gillat, & Sulzer-Azaroff, 1994; Montegar, Reid, Madsen, & Ewell, 1977; Gable, Park, & Scott, 2014; Mortenson & Witt, 1998; Mozingo, Smith, Riodan, Reiss, & Bailey, 2006; Noell, et al., 2000; Petscher & Bailey, 2006; Pollack, Fleming, & Sulzer-Azaroff, 1994; Sulzer-Azaroff, Pollack, Hamad, & Howley, 1998). For example, Petscher and Bailey observed that instructional assistants were not accurately implementing a token economy for which they had received routine training from their school system. A brief follow-up in-service training by the investigators brought about no further improvement. Only after the assistants were provided with ongoing prompting, self-monitoring, and accuracy feedback did the implementation rate improve. Similarly, DiGennaro, Martens, and Kleinmann (2007) used a more complex in-service training design that involved the consultant meeting with teachers to review the function-based intervention plan, model the intervention steps, answer questions, and obtain an agreement to implement the plan. The consultant also continued to coach and provide immediate corrective feedback until the teachers implemented the plan with 100 percent fidelity on two consecutive occasions. Ongoing support and feedback however, were required to assure maintenance of the program. Indeed, in a meta-analysis on ABA and intervention within autism populations, Virues-Ortega (2010) concluded that the degree of treatment integrity (in this case the suggested "dose," (i.e., hours of treatment) certainly was related to the size of the effect of that treatment.

Fortunately, once a new behavior is well established, feedback and reinforcement can be thinned gradually to weekly (Mortenson & Witt, 1998), bi-weekly (Codding, Feinberg, Dunn, & Pace, 2005), or even less frequently as features of the natural environment begin to assume contingency control. Such a strategy helps to maintain the behavior (see Chapters 22 through 24 for maintaining behavior).

When faced with the challenge of changing well-established staff performance patterns, follow-up support and feedback from significant others such as supervisors, managers, or peers is *crucial* for maintaining high-quality program implementation. Therefore, as we will emphasize further in Chapter 24, if you cannot make contact with the contingency managers regularly (say, about twice a week) to provide them with ongoing reinforcement for implementing novel or complicated procedures, we advise you to postpone the intervention. Without ongoing support, the program is apt to fail as contingency managers revert back to reactive strategies like punishment (McIntosh, Brown, & Borgmeier, 2008), or at best plateau where you ended your direct involvement. For instance, when Howlin et al. (2007) discontinued consulting with school personnel previously trained to use the Picture Exchange Communication System, (a method of communicating based on exchanging pictorial images rather than spoken words, Bondy & Frost, 1994) children's progress rates flattened out. Similarly, Dengerink and Mayer (2018) reported little to no change in parent rates of approval/disapproval following two, two-hour in-service workshops. When the workshops were followed by in-home coaching or collaborating, parents significantly increased their approving statements and decreased their disapproving comments or actions. Those changes, in turn, were shown to relate to significant increases in child compliance. Investigators (Lequia, Machalicek, & Lyons, 2013) provided parents of children with autism and/or ADHD with four 45-minute weekly behavioral training sessions plus an average of six individual coaching sessions. This combination of parental training and coaching resulted in decreases in their children's challenging behavior and increases in their task engagement. As we shall see throughout this text, promoting long-term change depends upon high-quality follow-up support![1]

Also you will encounter other examples of identifying and applying meaningful reinforcers to accomplish a myriad of goal accomplishments. The true boxed story in Box 3.1 illustrates why assessing and tapping the sources of reinforcement within an organization can pay off handsomely in the long run. (Turn to Figure 17.2, page 368, if you are curious to see the impact that the program had on the production of shoes that met quality standards and on those that were defective.)

---

[1] Further examples of similar outcomes are distributed throughout this text.

---

**Box 3.1**
**Assessing and Tapping Sources of Reinforcement Can Really Pay Off: An Example**

We had been invited to Thailand to address a sports shoe manufacturer's concern with product quality. Reject rates were costing the company major losses.

As an initial step, we toured the factory to learn about the manufacturing operation. As we stood behind a worker watching her performing her task, she suddenly noticed that we were present. Her face tensed in apprehension.

"Why is she so frightened?" we asked.

"She thinks she will be punished," replied our guide.

That incident spoke volumes.

To address the quality problem, we investigated the entire process, starting with whether personnel were aware of the quality standards for their particular jobs. For instance, were seams straight or edges smooth? ("What is a good job?") Then we questioned if each employee was capable of performing the job to standard ("Can I do a good job?"). If not, their supervisors would provide them with further training by showing, telling, and guiding (i.e., shaping) their performance. On our next visit, samples of acceptable and unacceptable product parts were posted everywhere and supervisors now spent a much larger portion of their time observing and constructively coaching their personnel.

Meanwhile, during intensive training sessions, which included demonstrations, practice, feedback, and reinforcement, we taught the quality staff, supervisors, and managers how to give positive, specific, constructive feedback to inform workers about the quality of their performance. Workers now knew the answer to "Am I doing a good job?" Of course, to crown the entire process, we taught all the managers and supervisors about choosing and using effective reinforcers ("What happens when I do a good job?"). By our next visit, charts and graphs containing goal lines and performance accomplishments were displayed everywhere. On Friday afternoon, we watched as supervisors gathered their teams to celebrate progress and goal achievements with congratulations, and sometimes refreshments were served. It did not take long for product quality to conform increasingly to standards and for defects to diminish (see Figure 17.2, page 368). Needless to say, the owners were delighted. To celebrate, having learned their lesson well, senior management invited us and the entire quality and management staff to a never-to-be-forgotten river-barge party cruise at the end of our stay.

By our last visit through the plant, the mood appeared to have changed entirely, from one of worker apprehension to one of satisfaction. Now workers and managers greeted us everywhere, not with frowns or fearful faces, but with the smiles for which the Thai people are so famous! Fear was put to flight!

Sulzer-Azaroff, B. & Harshbarger, D. (1995) Putting fear to flight: While enhancing quality of performance. *Quality Progress*, 28(12), 61–65.

Note that while past evidence of program effectiveness is an important ingredient for future success, that is no guarantee *your* program will maintain. Achieving lasting change requires that each particular environmental setting be *examined for sources of confirmed support and availability of materials prior to selecting or designing the program*. When all involved stand to gain reinforcing consequences and avoid aversive ones by adhering to the behavior-change protocol, the program has a better chance of succeeding. (In Chapter 24, we return to the topic of the necessity of organizational support if constructive change is to succeed.)

## SUMMARY AND CONCLUSIONS

To bring about effective change, it is important to ensure that interventions for behavior change are being implemented properly. A variety of factors were presented that can influence treatment integrity, or the accuracy in which interventions are implemented. Each need to be carefully considered before and during program implementation to help promote effective behavior change.

In this chapter we have focused on the necessity of the behavior analyst to become familiar with and to alter the environment as necessary. As B. F. Skin-

**Checklist 3.1: How Well Have You Prepared the Environment to Permit Behavior Analysis to be Applied Productively?**

| Did you familiarize yourself with the setting by finding out if those requesting your services and program participants: | |
|---|---|
| • are dedicated toward a constructive approach? | Y/N |
| • can practice skills that are in keeping with collective goals? | Y/N |
| • are supportive? | Y/N |
| • can provide adequate resources? | Y/N |
| • are or will be involved in setting objectives? | Y/N |
| Are objectives reasonable and achievable? | Y/N |
| Are the procedures under consideration evidence-based? | Y/N |
| Are the intended measures accurate (valid) and reliable? | Y/N |
| Have you identified the material and human resources essential to meeting the objective(s)? | Y/N |
| Have you assessed conditions currently supporting desired and undesired behaviors? | Y/N |
| Have you obtained the support of those who control the client's contingencies? | Y/N |
| Have you obtained the support of those who control the program implementers' contingencies? | Y/N |
| Are you prepared to analyze the function of the intervention? | Y/N |
| Have relevant problem-solving and support teams been organized and are they operating? | Y/N |
| Have you arranged for essential staff preparation? | Y/N |
| Have you arranged for ongoing reinforcement of correct practice while the program is in place? | Y/N |
| Can selected intervention programs be conducted faithfully? | Y/N |
| Have contextually appropriate goals and interventions been selected jointly? | Y/N |
| Do program participants have a clear understanding of the actions they are and are not to take and the reasons underlying those responsibilities? | Y/N |
| Are essential prompting strategies in place to support the intervention? | Y/N |
| Are contingencies in place to support the ongoing participation of personnel according to plan? | Y/N |

ner (1971) advised, rather than placing the focus on changing the behavior of individuals, the emphasis should be on changing the world in which they live.

Successful interventions are contextually appropriate, composed of demonstrably effective change programs, faithfully implemented as planned, and include ongoing feedback and follow-up support. In your own programs, you will want to select contextually appropriate interventions and prompt and reinforce their application. Training alone is *not* sufficient. If the initiated change is to persist, follow-up support is a *must*.

Affected individuals need to participate in problem-solving teams and otherwise join in the *planning process* if they are to be expected to continue supporting a program. Wisdom and data also suggest that it pays to involve team members in developing and selecting intervention methods, in assuring that those are faithfully implemented over time, and in applying practices helpful in promoting short- and long-term maintenance. When contingency managers are encouraged and their performance reinforced, overall morale improves, resulting in the use of less punitive, more positive behavior intervention strategies. If both novel as well as established programs are to be sustained and skilled staff retained, supporting both their initial *and* their ongoing efforts is essential. This text emphasizes procedures and strategies designed to work successfully not only with clients or students, but also with those who manage contingencies of reinforcement.[2]

A range of solid ongoing support-system options is available to those organizations or families fully committed to and supportive of the selected programs or routines. Only under such circumstances will it be feasible to sustain essential *long-term effort,* despite any key or systemic changes. In your own particular case you might refer to Checklist 3.1 to assess your organization's or family's readiness to embark on a promising ABA program of intervention.

---

[2]For additional information on how to promote program fidelity and client behavior change in consulting with change agents (e.g., parents, RBTs, supervisors, teachers and peers) see: *Behavioral Consulting: Improving Client and Consultee Learning and Behavior* by Mayer & Wallace (2020).

# Chapter 4

# Sharpening the Focus by Refining Goals and Objectives

## Goals

1. Describe what is meant by the *mission* of an organization and why it is important for behavior analysts to be familiar with their own organization's mission.
2. Define and illustrate *strategic planning*,
3. Define and differentiate among the three levels of assessment (indirect, descriptive and functional).
4. Define, illustrate and differentiate among *goals*, and *behavioral goals/ behavioral objectives*.
5. Specify at lest two components deemed essential to the successful implementation of school-wide positive behavior support systems.
6. Specify and describe the three levels of assessment.
7. Discuss what factors should be considered prior to selecting a goal for a formal behavior analysis program.
8. Define, illustrate and discuss the relevance of each of the following to goal selection:
   a. behavioral cusp
   b. pivotal behavior
   c. target behavior
   d. operational definition
   e. short- and long-term benefits
9. Discuss the relation between the behavior analyst's competencies and ethical practice considerations.
10. Describe one of the first tasks of a behavior analyst.
11. Discuss how test scores, records, and other materials are used and the purposes they serve in goal selection.

12. Discuss how each of the following general considerations enter into goal selection:
    a. goals achievable yet challenging
    b. goals constructive and functional
    c. interventions direct or indirect
    d. skills foundational or enabling
    e. short- and long-term benefits
    f. client's age and/or developmental level
    g. mission of the organization
13. Define the *constructional* approach.
14. Define and differentiate between *functional* and *alternative* goals.
15. Discuss which goals are best defended on ethical grounds.
16. Discuss some ways to avoid and resolve goal conflicts.
17. Define *advocate*.
18. Define and discuss the usefulness of behavioral contracts.
19. Discuss and illustrate the differences between *voluntariness* and *coercion*.
20. Define and illustrate the components of behavioral objectives, including specifying the:
    a. context
    b. behavioral dimensions
        i. rate
        ii. latency
        iii. intensity
        iv. topography
        v. criterion level
        vi. accuracy
21. Define and illustrate a FERG.
22. Develop and specify two behavioral objectives for a client or yourself, following the format provided in this chapter. One must include a FERG and the other an alternative non-FERG behavior.

\*\*\*\*\*\*\*\*\*\*\*\*

## GETTING STARTED

"Okay folks. Let's pile on board. The bus is ready to leave."

"I'm ready. Got my suitcase full of ABA principles and procedures. What's my first stop?"

"You're the expert! You decide."

"All right. Let's take a look at the map!"

A map is a good idea (see Figure 4.1), because lacking a good plan, you could meander about pointlessly and waste your own and your clients' resources. A far better approach is to spend the time up front to maximize your contributions toward the best possible outcomes for everyone concerned. Find out what the family or organization and its constituents value (more technically, "their reinforcers"); what they see as their *mission* (what success would look like), and what specific steps they are hoping to take (their *strategic plan*) toward meeting that mission. Discover what human and material resources are available. Identify major challenges (maybe the basis for your services being sought) but, of crucial importance, discover current programmatic strengths in the form of recent achievements and current progress.

## YOUR ORGANIZATION'S MISSION

Schools, institutions, agencies, and other service and business organizations exist for its particular **mission,** or *fundamental purpose for existing*. An illustrative example of a school's mission may be to *enable students to gain the knowledge and skills necessary for functioning independently in society*. For a business organization, it might be *increasing or maintaining profitability by providing high-quality goods or services at competitive prices*. At the public service level, the mission usually articulates the nature of the assistance it hopes to provide for its clientele. Similarly, sub-units within organizations have their own key reasons for being: e.g., "Our social studies department is directed toward preparing students to *participate as responsible members of our democratic society*"; that of the claims department of an insurance company, "to *process claims fairly and expediently*"; a factory's safety department, "to *promote the health and well-being of workers*"; its quality-control division, "to *increase profits by reducing rejects*."

While families may not formalize missions for themselves, their members undoubtedly share a number of short- and long-range hopes and dreams. Articulating, negotiating and prioritizing those can

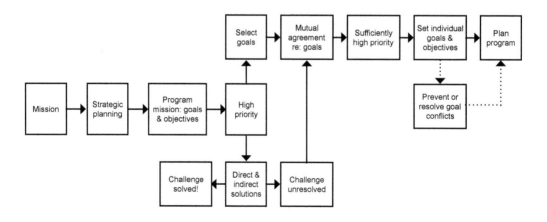

**Figure 4.1** A road map to mutually agreeable objective selection.

## Box 4.1

In the past, the Psychological Services Division of the Deep Valley School District has concentrated primarily on assessing students for special education placement. Mr. Ernest ("Ernie"), new on board, is more interested in preventing student problems from arising in the first place. To this end, he has designed an in-service consultation program for the teaching staff, emphasizing direct consultation with teachers, and before Ernie initiates those services, he presents his plan to his supervisor. Together they review the mission of their unit: "To prevent or, if necessary, remedy students' social, emotional, and academic difficulties." Ernie convinces his supervisor to allow him to demonstrate that providing consultation to teachers will be more efficient and cost effective in the long run. The program succeeds and the supervisor becomes Ernie's strongest supporter.

provide a function similar to that of an organizational mission.

To operate productively within an organization or family, everyone involved (or their surrogates) must agree to pursue a precisely articulated set of common goals. Identify and clarify any that appear confusing. Then mutually negotiate a series of steps to be undertaken in pursuit of those goals. You will then be able to see whether all concerned seem to be working together toward that common goal rather than at cross-purposes. Now you will be better informed as to how closely your own efforts link up with those of your colleagues and supervisors, and how much organizational support you might reasonably anticipate.

## ORGANIZATIONAL CULTURE

"Behavior comes to conform to the standards of a given community when certain responses are reinforced and others are allowed to go unreinforced or are punished" (Skinner, 1953, p. 415). Skinner uses the term *culture* to define such environments and elaborates on how local and broader cultures influence the group practices that generate patterns of behavior, manners, and customs. Within business organizations in the United States, for example, the overarching power for executing its goals often is vested in a single individual, the Chief Executive Officer. Yet, that is not always the case. For instance, in various Native American tribes, power is shared far more broadly (Lowery & Mattaini, 1999). That may be the case, too, in particular families and business, educational, and service organizations.

Yet, just as cultures vary across and within nations, so they do at the local level. The ethos within one family or subculture may reflect a value for (and therefore reinforce) conformity and docility, punishing assertiveness; another might tend to reward individual self-expression and deliberately teach assertiveness skills. Similarly, local standards of what constitutes reinforcement, extinction, and punishment prevail wherever behavior analysts apply their skills, whether with individuals from various ethnic cultures or within families, community, educational, social, business, commercial, or other organizational settings. Before involving yourself as an external or internal consultant, you are well advised to determine not only local legal statues that apply, but also how closely your own ethical and cultural values mesh with theirs.[1] For one typical example, personnel in some programs serving persons on the autism spectrum feel it appropriate routinely to treat maladaptive behavior with punishment, never stopping to investigate *why* the behavior is happening in the first place. Others refuse to apply any form of aversive management (positive or negative punishment), despite clear threats of endangerment to themselves or others. Today, many, appropriately, base their intervention practices on the results of formal functional behavior assessments (see Chapter 10).

So, to succeed and gain satisfaction from your own involvement, examine your own ethical values and consider how those mesh with the program's, or group's policies and practices before committing your affiliation. As a case in point, the key goal of

---

[1] The analysis of behavior concerns itself with scientific methods and the results of those investigations. Behavior analysts, both experimental and applied, also must concern themselves with humane and ethical methods. Watch for the image of the scales of justice when material related to ethics or legal issues is discussed.

the *School Wide Positive Behavior Support program* (Sailor, Dunlap, Sugai, & Horner, 2009) is to: *develop a culture that focuses on safe and effective learning environments for all students.* Were you to productively contribute to that purpose in your role as behavior analyst, you would be best advised not only verbally to endorse that goal, but, especially, to demonstrate your support for it through your actions.

## WHAT IS STRATEGIC PLANNING?

"Simply put, **strategic planning** *determines where an organization is going over the next year or more, how it's going to get there, and how it'll know if it got there or not*" (McNamara, 2008). An example we have selected because the plan incorporates evidence based on applied behavior analytic research is the Virginia Strategic Plan for Pedestrian Safety (2005–2010) (Porter, Anderson, Martinez, & Anderson, 2005). That particular program's planned strategies for the five-year period included:

- evaluating long-term use of programs
- focusing on crash, injury, and fatality changes
- obtaining funding for long-term evaluations of programs showing one- to two-year effectiveness
- changing public perceptions with enforcement and/or fear appeals

During the first two years their actions included documenting risk and exposure, educating children, preparing crosswalk signal technologies, implementing law enforcement for pedestrians and driver non-yielders, and assessing attitudes.

Notice how this kind of planning permits groups to operate accountably by mutually stipulating *where, when,* and *how* they hope to accomplish their purposes. Although a strategic plan usually is focused on the entire organization, members of progressive personnel teams or groups also are well-advised to collaborate in laying out their intended goals for the year and describing how they plan to get there.

Returning to our earlier example, the *School Wide Positive Behavior Support* (SW-PBS) program uses a strategic plan to help ensure its widespread adoption of the system by all individual stakeholders. The five components that have been deemed necessary to successfully implement a SW-PBS include:

- Developing a schoolwide leadership team
- Identifying schoolwide agreements and resource management
- Developing and implementing a data-based action plan
- Implementing supports
- Ongoing evaluation

The goal of using strategic planning in SW-PBS is to ensure widespread adoption, accurate and maintainable implementation, and to ensure a cultural fit (Sailor et al., 2009).

## WHAT IS BEHAVIORAL ASSESSMENT?

As behavior analysts, we often rely on assessment findings to select the behavior(s) to target for change. The information gleaned by taking this step can enable us to focus on the most relevant and cost-efficient change strategies. Before identifying and defining goals and objectives, allow us to explain what is meant by *assessment* and its three levels: *indirect, descriptive, and functional*.

**Indirect assessment** refers to those strategies that rely on learning about behavioral needs without directly observing them. This might include interviewing the clients themselves, supervisors, peers, parents, or caregivers or reviewing previous records and reports. As an example, *The Vineland Adaptive Behavior Scales: Third Edition* (Sparrow, Cicchetti, & Saulnier, 2016) uses a semi-structured interview to measure adaptive behavior by asking parents about their child's abilities. It is an instrument used to identify various concerns parents have with their child's self-help skills and behavioral concerns.

When clients are incapable of communicating clearly and adequately about their own concerns, needs, and desires, we can turn to their caregivers, to discuss those issues and the environmental factors that appear to influence them. For example, suppose you have been considering teaching a young boy with developmental delays to label colors. A reasonable approach would be to ask his parents if color labeling would be a useful skill for their son to acquire, and if so, to explore whether he possesses such necessary prerequisite skills as being able to match colors. Should all agree about the value of pursuing that goal, you also would want to explore, by watching and asking, the conditions most supportive of the youngster's cooperation in the process. (Such strategies will be presented in detail in Chapters 7 & 10).

A number of indirect assessments are available to assess social skill development. For example, Fahmie and Luczynski (2018) have developed an assessment instrument that identifies skills for school readiness, such as responding appropriately to name, complying with instructions, requesting assistance, and sharing. McGinnis and Goldstein (1997) have developed social skill inventories that elementary school age children can fill out themselves, or adults can use to assess the child's social skills, such as: "Is it easy for me to start a conversation with someone?" Others (Goldstein, Sprafkin, Gershaw & Klein, 1980) have published a structured learning approach to teaching prosocial skills to adolescents, though many apply to young children as well, such as listening, introducing self and others, giving a compliment, asking for help, apologizing, paying attention, saying thank-you, asking permission, goal setting, persisting with a task, and many others. Caregivers who know your client well can fill out the questions on such social skill inventories. Many of these skills, though, can be easily discovered by using descriptive assessments: Look to see if your client pays attention, persists on task, etc. See Chapter 14 for more detailed information on assessing and teaching social skills.

Many indirect assessment instruments are available for the purpose of assessing people's academic skill levels, such as the *Iowa Test of Basic Skills* or the *Wide Range Achievement Test*, or their "personality traits," like the *Minnesota Multiphasic Personality Inventory* and numerous others. The results from such tests, though, are not designed to provide information sufficient to permit us to design an intervention based upon what the client tends to do, or fails to do, how frequently, intensively, according to what pattern, and so on. Rather, as behavior analysts, we focus on assessing an individual's overt behaviors: what they actually say and do, where, when, how proficiently, how often, perhaps with what intensity or other physical properties, because those are the features that guide the selection of individually tailored behavioral goals and intervention procedures. For example, if conducting a curriculum-based assessment, you assess what skills in the curriculum that the client needs to learn and which have been mastered. For example, testing for addition facts the child might be asked, "What is 2+3 and 2+5; 3+3 and 3+5; etc." to determine what addition facts the child can perform and cannot perform. Once this information is obtained, it can be useful in identifying what addition facts to use in a fluency-based program.

The next level, **descriptive assessment,** is based on objective observation. That is, we watch the client to determine the circumstances under which s/he does and does not emit the behavior. For example, in the above example, you might ask the child to perform those skills prerequisite to the goal behavior of color labeling, such as being able to pick up an item and hand it to you. Some common examples of descriptive assessments protocols for verbal behavior are the *Verbal Behavior Milestones and Placement Program (*VB-MAPP) and the *Picture Exchange Communication System* (PECS). The VB-MAPP is an instrument that addresses various classes of verbal behavior and identifies those upon which one should focus. (We elaborate further on verbal behavior and the instruments used to assess it in Chapter 19). For problem behavior, the ABC, or contingency analysis, assessment is often used (see Chapters 2 & 10).

A **functional behavior assessment** (FBA), appropriate to use with a wide range of unacceptable behaviors, is a tool designed for the purpose of guiding the development of promising behavior intervention plans (Alter, Conroy, Mancil, & Haydon, 2008). It accomplishes this by determining what particular conditions and/or events contribute to the emission and/or maintenance of a given client's (usually unwanted/maladaptive) behavior. The FBA involves objectively observing and recording valid measurements of the individual's reaction patterns during systematic presentations of particular antecedents to and consequences of a given behavior. (See Chapter 10 for a more thorough description of this methodology.) The results facilitate the identification of those conditions (e.g., a skill deficit, a discrimination issue, a compliance issue; an aversive stimulus or the absence or withdrawal of reinforcers) that tend to evoke and/or maintain the behavior of concern. As you will learn in greater detail later on, by enabling practitioners to select target skills and interventions best suited to the client's behavioral repertoire, functional behavior assessments play an especially crucial role in the teaching and management of individuals exhibiting a wide range of maladaptive behavior patterns (e.g., Lerman, Vorndran, Addison, and Khun, 2004).

## SETTING GOALS

Once behavior analysts begin operating within a system, an overabundance of concerns may be brought to their attention. If no strategic plan is in place or no one else is there to help set priorities, you, in your behavior analyst role, would need to do that yourself. Because time, energy, material, and other resources always are finite, they need to be distributed carefully. You also would need to decide whether a particular intervention is warranted and, if so, obtain the consent with those concerned (or their advocates) to pursue the program's goals, specific objectives and intervention methods. Next we offer some suggestions to help guide you through this difficult decision-making process.

### Goals Defined and Illustrated

In contrast to the more specific *behavioral objectives* (about which you will read later in this chapter), **behavioral goals** indicate *the general nature of the behavioral change we are seeking: to see it emerge; its rate increase, maintain, or decrease; to watch the circumstances under which it is emitted become broader or narrower; or to note its complete disappearance.* Goals generally are formulated in broad-brush terms like hoping to enable a person to *increase* a behavior (e.g., compliment more often), *learn* a new behavior (e.g., master operating a new piece of equipment), *transfer* it to a new context (e.g., use math skills at the grocery store), *maintain* it over time (e.g., regularly compliment merited staff performance), or to *diminish* or *cease* doing it (e.g., stop hitting himself). Goals, then, are not vague or contradictory, such as a professor telling their psychology class: "For the final exam, you need to study Post-Freud, Neo-Freud and Pre-Freud..., however, you will not be held responsible for Freud." In this chapter, we begin by discussing goal and objective-selection in general. (Later, in Chapter 24, we return to that topic to discuss the how supervisors or managers might incorporate the concept of goal levels within organizational goal-setting.)

### Factors Influencing Goal Selection

Many factors need to be considered when deciding whether pursuing a goal, a detailed behavioral objective, and/or an intervention to address that objective is warranted. Besides its consonance with the mission and goals of the organization or family, these include: legal mandates, determining how much their achievement will contribute to the organization's mission, the severity of the problem, how realistic the goals are, the availability of human and material resources, the particular nature of the challenges, and the specific roles and functions of those to be involved.

**Organizational purpose.** We have emphasized already the value of becoming familiar with the mission of your organization. So one of the very first issues to address in setting goals is: How would accomplishing the goal support that mission? In our example of Ernie, the behavior analyst working in the schools (Box 4.1), we saw how the change in focus from exclusively testing to consulting with teachers turned out to be better suited to the program's mission.

If your organization spends many of its resources on superficial aspects, such as the aesthetics of its workspace, ask how important that is, in contrast with providing adequate personnel or materials to support its mission.

**Legal mandates.**  Public organizations generally are designed to serve communal needs. In the United States, for instance, all special education programs are required to generate clearly specified goals.[3,4] According to the *Individuals with Disabilities Education Act Amendments of 1997* (IDEA) and the *Individuals with Disabilities Education Improvement Act* (IDEIA, 2004), strategies to address behavior problems for youngsters in special education are to be considered by the IEP (Individual Education Plan) team when the student's behavior impedes his or her learning or the learning of others. Those strategies must include (a) *writing goals and objectives* to address the problem behavior and (b) developing *measurable evaluation criteria to assess progress toward those goals.* (Soon we describe the technique many behavior analysts have grown accustomed to using to achieve those dual purposes.)

**Real challenges and specific goals.** Being realistic about what constitutes a concern or challenge is important. A person may label a pattern of responding "a problem," when in fact the difficulty exists only in the eyes (or ears) of the beholder. For instance: a worker who hums slightly off key while working bothers the shift supervisor but no one else; you view yourself a failure because you have not yet become a celebrated concert pianist, Olympic champion, or author of a bestselling novel. Similarly, supervisors, parents, and teachers may set unreasonable goals for themselves, their employees, children, and pupils. When those goals fail to be attained, participants may be seen as owning the problem. For example, a straight-A student who can't sit still but doesn't bother other peers, does not have a problem that needs to be addressed. Perhaps it's the teacher who needs to learn to handle her own reaction.

Sometimes particular behaviors are designated as problematic on the basis of *hearsay evidence* or a lack of familiarity with common norms. Timmy's previous teacher may have warned his new teacher to watch out for Timmy, especially during recess. The mere fact that Timmy is now under closer scrutiny may cause the new teacher to overreact to Timmy's normal horse-play. In an actual example experienced by one of the authors, a particular student had been classified as "aggressive" because he indulged in a behavior actually regularly displayed by a majority of his fellow students: throwing his backpack in the air at the end of the lunch period.

Also, irrelevant factors can distort people's perceptions, as in the case of Joyce, who may appear unusually boisterous to the members of the community board simply because she has a particularly loud, deep voice. Or the significance of particular data may be magnified: Sue is convinced that she is fat because she weighs two pounds above her self-designated ideal weight; Mario that he isn't smart enough because he missed two items on an especially challenging intelligence test.

## Deciding Whether to Proceed

How do we decide when a behavioral issue is serious enough to justify applying behavior analysis? Here are several factors you might consider while pondering your decision:

**Several independent requests for assistance with the same individual.** Do multiple parties request assistance in handling the behavior of the same individual or group? Here are a few examples:

Lucretia frequently has been sent home by neighbors for fighting. Her parents observe that other children avoid Lucretia, while her parents freely admit to the behavior analyst that they have no control over her. She bullies her younger siblings and others in the neighborhood. It is reasonably safe to conclude that the time has come to address Lucretia's behaviors.

---

[2]This symbol of justice scales will appear throughout this text when ethical or legal issues are discussed.

[3]Simply because other publicly or privately supported programs do not necessarily mandate specific behavioral objectives at this time does not mean they aren't warranted or won't be mandated in the future.

[4]See U.S. Department of Education, Office of Special Education and Rehabilitation Services "Celebrating Thirty-five years of Access, Accountability, Achievement. (2010)

Paula, who labels herself "a procrastinator," also has received feedback on her yearly supervisory evaluations indicating that she has a severe problem with meeting deadlines. In fact, her coworkers also share their concerns about Paula's procrastination. Because that habit prevents Paula from gaining the promotion she seeks, the behavior probably is sufficiently serious to deserve being addressed.

By contrast, Sue's concern about her minor weight fluctuations is not corroborated by her physician, husband, or friends. Eventually, they convince Sue that this is not a problem serious enough to merit an intensive intervention.

**Functional skills radically different from those of typical group members.** Standardized test scores and the results of other formal evaluations reveal how the person has performed in comparison with group norms. The more evidence that can be gathered from various independent sources, the more probable it would be to conclude that a problem probably exists:

Charlie scores three years below his grade level on a standardized achievement test, lower than 85 percent of his peers on a mental-maturity test, and several years below his chronological age level on a developmental inventory. Formal and informal observations provide useful data as well. The number of reading tasks he completes compared to others in his class, his poor physical performance in tasks such as throwing a ball, and his erratic social behavior suggest that Charlie is need of some help.

Kaxdin (2011) applied this kind of **social comparison** strategy in an investigation designed to determine whether the conversational behavior of two 22-year old male head-trauma patients matched the norms derived from an earlier social comparison group (Gajar, Schloss, Schloss, & Thompson, 1984). Later, he used those results to develop goals for the two participants.

**Dramatic changes in an individual's behavior.** Again, information from a number of sources helps to confirm the existence of a concern, especially when an individual's behavior apparently has recently undergone a striking change.

**Have direct and informal solutions been attempted?** Is the behavior of concern related to a *physical* problem? For example, Marsha might be ill; perhaps she has a vision problem causing headaches or something more serious. Suppose a child has recurring toileting issues. Whenever a client's troubling bodily issues, such as frequent regurgitation or falling, tend to persist, the change agent should refer the individual to a physician for diagnosis or treatment prior to considering any behavioral intervention.

Sometimes promising *logistical changes* (that is, simple alterations in the ways of managing the flow of services efficiently and effectively) may be revealed by simply examining and analyzing the sequence of interactions between the individual and the physical environment (described more fully in Chapter 10). For example, Charlie appears easily distracted by other students' fidgeting. Placing a partition between him and the others may encourage him to complete more assignments.

*Changes in the physical environment*, such as in lighting, furnishings, equipment, room, or seating arrangements also may quickly solve the problem at hand. Only when each of the children in a preschool class had access to necessary materials did everyone participate in activities (Doke & Risley, 1972). Similarly, the stereotypic and self-abusive behavior of a group of children with autism lessened after their environment was enriched with a high density of preferred events (Van Camp, Lerman, Kelley, Contrucci, & Vorndran, 2000). Numerous studies also have shown that environmental modifications, such as clearly designated pedestrian crossing lanes, can contribute toward the prevention of accidents and injuries (Van Houten, 1988; Van Houten, & Malenfant, 1992).

Sometimes even minor alterations in staff assignments or job descriptions can result in major improvements. Todd, Haugen, Anderson, and Spriggs (2002) simply requested that staff increase their specific feedback to regular education students to a ratio of 4:1 positive to corrective comments. This both reduced problem behavior and increased staff satisfaction. One student in a study reported by Wilczenski, Sulzer-Azaroff, Feldman, and Fajardo (1987) increased his level of participation simply by being assigned to a different work group; another improved when his seat was reassigned.

Checklists, as described in Chapter 3, can serve to prompt personnel thoroughly to engage in the desired behavior (Bacon, Fulton, & Malott, 1982). Instances include improvement of the performance of those laboring on an assembly line (Sulzer-Azaroff & Harshbarger, 1995) and of personnel working in intensive care units (Pronovost, Wu, & Sexton, 2004).

The *nature* of the demands made of people matter, too. *Challenging but achievable* tasks work best, whereas those that are either too demanding or too easy tend to create problems (Carr & Newsom, 1985; Iwata, Pace, Kalsher, Cowdery, & Cataldo, 1990; Lee, Sugai, & Horner, 1999; Umbreit, Lane, & Dejud, 2004). When 3-year-old Marsha is told to remain at the table until she consumes a whole plate of non-preferred foods (think liver, spinach, and beets), she "shuts down" altogether and refuses to eat.

Other solutions may seem so obvious to be hardly worth mentioning; but sometimes we overlook them. One is to *ask people to change their behavior*. In some situations, the offender may be unaware that what he is doing is unwelcome, as in the instance of Joyce, who repeatedly sings off-key to herself while working on the assembly line. Maybe Joyce is unaware that her voice carries as far as it does. Perhaps just taking her aside and asking her to restrict her singing to outside the workplace will solve the problem.

Undertaking a formal behavior analysis program often entails investing considerable resources (time, materials/equipment, skilled personnel, etc.) If simple solutions fail to remedy a concern, though, we suggest you consider a few additional factors prior to committing to an ABA intervention:

**Is the challenge serious enough to justify proceeding?** In responding to this question, you may find it useful to consider the following factors:

- whether the occurrence of the behavior is dangerous: Dealing with emergencies and critical events
- whether changing the behavior is in keeping with the mission and/or long-range objectives of the organization, family, or individual
- the clients' willingness to participate and assent
- the likelihood of success
- if *behavioral cusps* and *pivotal behaviors* (defined below) are involved
- the predictable degree of public and supervisory support
- the source(s) of control over goals and interventions
- the behavior analyst's competence
- the availability of alternative services
- practical considerations such as funds and personnel

**Dealing with emergencies and critical events.** Critical events or emergencies, such as imminent danger to clients, personnel or others must be assigned a very high priority for treatment. Problems such as extremely aggressive or self-abusive behavior, serious addiction, criminal acts, and exposure to an environmental catastrophe fall into this category. As always, assuming these issues are in keeping with the organization's mission and priorities, major life decisions such as dropping out of school, transferring to different training programs, marrying, undergoing an abortion, and so on, may also be addressed.

**The clients' eagerness and/or willingness to participate.** The highest priority status should be accorded to those requesting help. Here are some examples:

- Paula, hoping eventually to attain a job promotion, seeks assistance in overcoming her tendency to procrastinate that interferes with her gaining a job promotion.

- Pearl's parents are desperate to obtain guidance for their daughter who seems to be friendless.
- Vinny requires clarification about the routines he needs to follow to reduce the frequency and severity of his asthma attacks that cause him such discomfort.
- When resources are limited, though, perhaps it would be justifiable to postpone addressing Harry's failure to admit, no less to deal with, his childish whining when things go wrong on the job.

**The likelihood of success.** The thousands of published research reports on applied behavior analysis now provide us with abundant information to guide us in choosing from the most promising programs available. Journals like the *Journal of Applied Behavior Analysis* and others cited in our reference list contain reports of behavior analytic programs that have yielded successful results in educational, clinical, institutional, medical, vocational, community, home, and other settings. (In fact, in its first issue, the *Journal of Applied Behavior Analysis* [1968] heralded the substantial beginning of the movement toward scientifically addressing behavioral issues arising within applied settings.) Behavior analysts who stay informed[5] about procedures consistently found to be effective as well as about new and promising techniques are more likely to make wise selections. In fact, the behavior analyst is ethically responsible for remaining informed about promising new findings and incorporating those, as appropriate, within their interventions. (See Chapter 31 and the Behavior Analyst Certification Board (BCBA) (2020) *ethics code for behavior analysts*.)

**Behavioral cusps and pivotal behaviors.** Behavioral cusps and pivotal behaviors often are assigned priority status because they are *behavior upon which other behavior can be built.* They are basic building blocks that can facilitate the acquisition of complex behavioral repertoires. Consider such examples as being able to *match* a sample image or object to another containing the same essential features ("match-to-sample"): Think one breed of *dog* (terrier) to another (shepherd); one type of *flower* (daisy) to another (tulip); one *emotional expression* (sad face) to another (excited face). In each case, learning additional cases sharing the same basic features with other members of those categories tends to happen more rapidly.

Bosch and Fuqua (2001) state that a behavior is likely a cusp if it meets one or more of the following five criteria: "(a) access to new reinforcers, contingencies, and environments; (b) social validity; (c) generativeness (the potential for recombination of minimal repertoires into more complex response classes); (d) competition with inappropriate responses; and (e) number and the relative importance of people affected" (p. 123). The more of these criteria the behavior meets, the more appropriate it is to say the behavior is on a cusp; and, from a pragmatic perspective, the more appropriate it is to focus on teaching those cusps. Consider being able to adhere to a musical score or to follow assembly diagrams.

Similarly, **pivotal behavior**, once learned, *produces changes in other adaptive untrained behavior* (Koegel & Koegel, 1988; 2006). For example, "self-initiations" such as requesting help and initiating play are likely to function as pivotal behaviors in that they "appear to result in widespread positive changes in a number of areas"; these self-initiations help clients to interact more effectively with others in their environment (Koegel, Carter, & Koegel, 2003, p. 134). Staying at one's work area longer, and recording one's own behavior also appear to be cusps or pivotal behaviors (Ainsman & Mayer, 2018).

Note the correspondence between the two concepts: *behavioral cusps* stress greater access to new contingencies and environments while *pivotal behaviors* stress associated changes in other untrained behaviors. As greater access to additional environments and contingencies often leads to changes in other behaviors, these terms often are used interchangeably. The advantage of selecting and teaching behavioral cusps and pivotal behaviors is that once learned, besides expanding their reper-

---

[5]Readers who master this book will have the necessary knowledge and vocabulary to read and comprehend much of the professional literature.

toires and helping them learn more rapidly,[6] they can enable your clients to heighten their access to other contingencies of reinforcement.

**Public and supervisory support.** Parent groups, boards, committees, and other public groups often are major determiners of organizational priorities. They may, for example, urge that primary emphasis be placed on quality assurance, reading achievement, citizen responsibility, or preventing sexually communicated diseases, drug abuse, or some other high priority issue. Because continued support is so important to the success of any program—particularly one that departs from traditional custom—this consideration is not trivial. Those served by schools and other community agencies deserve a major say about the nature of those practices. Establishing priorities that reflect members' concerns and involving their representatives in program planning heighten the likelihood of ongoing support.

Just the backing of their spouses, relatives, and/or friends encourage parents to sustain their adherence to a program intervention. Job supervisors can strongly influence the long-term effectiveness of programs within their organizations. Because supervisors manage powerful personnel contingencies like job retention, salaries, promotions, assignments, approval, and privileges, their support usually is essential to the continued cooperation among those involved in a behavior analysis program. As with other affiliated groups, their ongoing supervisory support and encouragement is more predictable when they are involved in setting priorities and procedures.

**Source(s) of control over goals.** With supportive factors in place, we may feel confident that our goals are about to be achieved. Yet sometimes progress bogs down: Why does production at Purple Triangle remain stagnant, despite our consultation? We need to ask ourselves "Are those goals beyond our control? Do we have access to the way the important antecedents and consequences of the behavior are managed or not?"

Perhaps the union at a manufacturing facility considers the proposed rates of increase in production to be exploitive of labor and therefore unacceptable. When change agents recognize or strongly suspect that a behavioral goal will not be supported because outside forces hold greater power than they themselves do, they would be well-advised to seek the cooperation of that person or group in refining the goal (or, as we discuss in Chapter 6, identify contingencies of sufficient power to override those impediments). By, for instance, collaborating more sensitively with union representatives at your manufacturing facility, you may better succeed in identifying mutually satisfactory, acceptable, and realistic production goals. The same sort of sensitivity during decision-making may well apply within families, schools, clinics, or other settings in which performance matters.

**The behavior analyst's competence.** Along with our fellow professional practitioners—physicians, lawyers, teachers, social workers, counselors, psychologists, and others—applied behavior analysts must limit their practice to those programs they are competent to conduct. In fact, we are ethically responsible for having mastered those skills through supervised training prior to implementing them. Besides mastering a skill, however, we also need to understand the special qualities inherent in the organization or agency with which we intend to involve ourselves. Approaches to applying behavioral skills in schools are different from practicing ABA in hospitals, factories, banks, clinics, insurance companies, sports teams, the military, with families in the home, and so on. Missions, goals, priorities, and specific objectives differ from one context to the next, as do the key contingencies of reinforcement. So, any analysts considering affiliating themselves with an organization whose purpose, structure, operation and/or function is unfamiliar to them are best advised to dedicate themselves to learning in depth about those elements, under supervision, before embarking on any ambitious undertakings. Otherwise, they should limit their activities to those areas of application for which they possess the requisite skills and with which they are thoroughly

---

[6]A responsive teaching curriculum has been developed for teachers and parents that focuses on pivotal developmental behaviors (e.g., attention, persistence on task) for children with autism, Down syndrome, and other developmental disabilities (Mahoney & MacDonald, 2007).

familiar. (We elaborate further on these ethical considerations in Chapter 32.)

**Availability of alternative programs.** Suppose you are employed by a school system located in a community with an effective drug-treatment program, and that is not your specialty area or in line with the system's highest priorities. Referring drug-abuse cases to that program would be reasonable. If a problem seems to arise from family difficulties, local family clinics might be appropriate referral agencies. A personnel manager probably should refer employees experiencing serious adjustment problems to reputable mental health clinics. As a behavior analyst, you would want thoroughly to acquaint yourself with, and, as appropriate, communicate and/or collaborate with personnel in community and school programs to which you may make referrals.

**Practical considerations such as funds and personnel.** When establishing priorities for behavior analysis programs, consider the availability of skilled personnel plus auxiliary funds for special services, facilities, equipment, and materials. For example, suppose you were planning a pre-school program, you probably would anticipate requiring a playroom, observational facilities, observers and aides, individualized instructional materials, video equipment and other costly items. If sufficient funds to fulfill the requirement are unavailable, attempting the program makes little sense. Before rejecting the notion altogether, though, recognize that you as an imaginative and persistent behavior analyst often can tap resources (in the form of donations, grants, contracts) not immediately apparent. (Suggestions for free and inexpensive materials and support services are scattered throughout this book and across the web.)

Before investing your efforts and resources into designing a systematic behavior analysis program to treat a troubling behavior, review the checklist in Figure 4.2 related to setting priorities. Affirmative responses to most of the items on the checklist suggest that you have identified a major area of concern. In that case, the appropriate decision is to proceed. However, some behavioral goals lend themselves to simpler direct or informal solutions and will not require the same level of detailed assessment or monitoring as the more challenging ones.

## DEFINING PROBLEMS AND TENTATIVE GOALS BEHAVIORALLY

As we have seen, organizational or individual goals often are expressed in broad strokes; but to work effectively with those challenges, we must translate them into a sequence or set of operant behaviors (behaviors for which "…no correlated stimulus can be detected upon occasions when it [the behavior] is observed to occur"; Skinner, 1938, p. 21). That is, we must express them behaviorally. (See below). Within applied behavior analysis, we refer to this particular class of operant behaviors as **target behaviors**: i.e., *the behaviors to be addressed systematically.*

> "Ramon is lazy; he should realize his potential and stop goofing off."
>
> "Paula procrastinates; she hopes to rid herself of that nasty habit."
>
> "Lucretia is hostile; she should learn to get along better with her playmates."
>
> "Henrietta is a hypochondriac; she should not be so obsessed with her bodily ills."

Obviously these labels need to be defined as specific actions. Why is that? Daniels and Lattal (2017) point out:

> Labeling causes us to miss seeing what the person is actually doing that is contrary to these stereotypes or that has its own value. We limit the human potential of another through labeling; an unwise choice for many reasons (p. 48).

We already know that the behavioral approach limits itself to the things people (and other living organisms) do and "say"—actions that are objectively observable and measurable.[7] Restating actions behaviorally permits us to program and monitor

---

[7]This does not eliminate behavior such as thinking, because thinking is something that we do and can be measured by verbal reports. However, we have elected to consider them only minimally in this book. If this area is of special interest to you, we suggest you consult texts on cognitive behavior therapy.

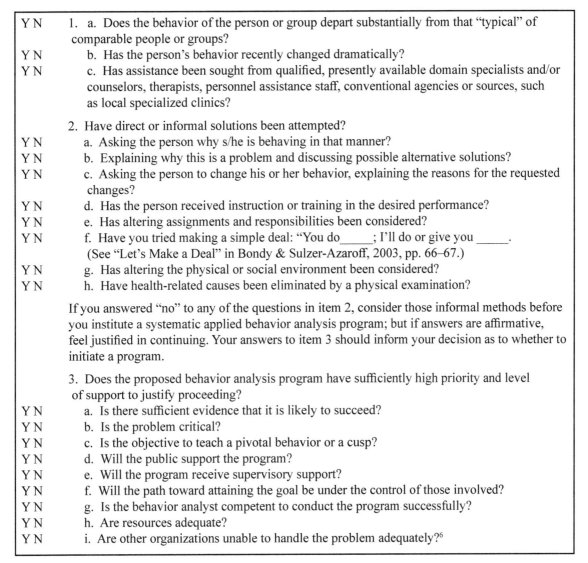

**Figure 4.2** An informal checklist for deciding whether a problematic behavior warrants implementing a formal functional assessment and/or intervention program

change more effectively and convey our purposes, methods, and results more clearly.[8] So when we rephrase terms like *lazy, cooperative, lovable, hostile,* and *hypochondriacal* into precise observable actions or operations, by altering the events that precede, accompany, or follow those actions, we find ourselves in a better position to design and monitor programs of change *precisely.*

A good way to approach the task is to ask, "What would each of the individuals *be doing* (remember the *action* orientation of behavior analysis) if each one were to be coming closer to "realizing their potential?" Complete more assignments accurately, offer more correct answers, ask to assist others in group activities, read and report on more books, obtain a work-study job and receive satisfactory performance ratings, win a Nobel Prize? When those concerned with Ramon's behavior are con-

---
[8]See "Let's Make a Deal" in Bondy & Sulzer-Azaroff, 2003, pp. 66–67.

vinced that they are all referring to the same action, outcome monitoring is easier because **operationally defined behavior** *can be observed and measured objectively* (e.g., assignments completed, accuracy levels achieved, instances of volunteering answers).

An **operation** is *an act that affects the environment*. When *terms are broken down into objectively observable and measurable components, they are said to be* **operationally defined**. Writing is an operation because it produces measurable changes on paper. Hitting is an operation because it is a quantifiable force that comes in contact with an organism or object. Screaming is an operation because it raises the level of ambient decibels of noise. "Intelligence," "anxiety," and "hostility" are *not* operations. They are inferred internal states. But answering questions correctly, tensing one's muscles, or hitting and kicking others are operations. One of the behavior analyst's first tasks is to help program implementers and clients translate vague terms and problems into specific, quantifiable operant behaviors. (We shall return to this point in our discussion of *behavioral objectives*.)

A further caution: While what people *report* they do often matches their actual performances, it doesn't always match precisely. Saying and doing are two *different* behaviors. Baer, Wolf, and Risley (1968) noted that, in specifying goals, the issue is what individuals do, not what they say they do, because ABA:

> ... usually studies what subjects can be brought to do rather than what they can be brought to say; unless of course, a *verbal response* is the behavior of interest. Accordingly, a subject's description of his own nonverbal behavior usually would not be accepted as a measure of his actual behavior unless it were independently substantiated. Hence, there is little applied value in the demonstration that an impotent man can be made to say that he no longer is impotent. The relevant question is not what he can say but what he can do. (p. 93; italics added)[9]

---

[9]D. M. Baer, M. M. Wolf, & T. R. Risley. "Some current dimensions of applied behavior analysis." *Journal of Applied Behavior Analysis*, 1968, 1, 91–97. Copyright 1968 by the Society for the Experimental Analysis of Behavior, Inc.

## REFINING YOUR SELECTION OF GOALS

Once the behavior of concern and *tentative* goals have been operationally defined, you will want to do some homework to determine how reasonable and realistic those goals may be. Review relevant documents such as test scores, records, and other materials, and then analyze the current situation.

**Test scores, records, and other materials.** Standardized test results, sales and reject figures, records in personnel files, a teacher's grade book, production or safety reports, assignment folders, library records, behavior assessment systems, and other documents may provide valuable information relevant to both general program goals and specific objectives, as well as for the selection of promising procedures for given clients.[10] Ramon's school records may show that his intelligence and reading test scores are above average but that he completes very few reading assignments. His library card may indicate that he has checked out two books on dinosaurs and that the results of an interest inventory peak in the natural sciences area. This suggests a reasonable starting place, a set of assigned tasks and accompanying materials for Ramon.

Be cautious about interpreting the results of standardized tests, though. Scores derived from even the most carefully conceived tests can be influenced by factors stemming from the respondent's history, culture, or ethnicity and current circumstances. Think illness, lack of sleep, stress, noise, temperature variations etc. (For other examples, see Ayllon & Kelly, 1972; Bradley-Johnson, Graham, & Johnson, 1986).

Clients' case records often contain useful information. Data on physical condition, social and emotional development, and academic or vocational progress may inform decisions about goals and procedures. Ramon's records might indicate reasonable

---

[10]For specific client challenges, see the journal *Behavioral Assessment* and behavioral checklists, such as the Functional Assessment Checklist for Teachers and Staff (March et al., 2000), the Adaptive Behavior Scale for schools (ABS-S) (Lambert, Nihira, & Leland, 1993), and the Adaptive Behavior Scale for community and residential settings (ABS-RC) (Nihira, Leland, & Lambert, 1993).

progress until ninth grade. Perhaps something mysterious about the class, the teacher, the materials, friends, or other events may have affected his performance. The fact that Ramon has progressed satisfactorily in the past, however, does say something about his capabilities: Planning a program to help bring his performance up to the level of his classmates would not be totally unreasonable. Yet this sort of information must be augmented with more current and objective evidence. Directly observing and recording the behavior of the person in the natural setting can be especially valuable in the goal-setting process.

## GENERAL CONSIDERATIONS IN GOAL SELECTION

When selecting goals we must take into account ethical, practical, and scientific factors. It used to be said that "the behavioral approach is a headless technology, having no built-in goals about what should be taught or accomplished.... As an applied science, behavior *therapy*[11] is simply a collection of principles and techniques about how to change behavior; it says nothing about who should modify what behavior, why, or when..." (Wilson & O'Leary, 1980, p. 258). That orientation began to change in the mid 1980s, when, for example, Hawkins (1985) pointed out that goal selection "is as much a scientific question as is the question of effective technique; it is simply a question that behavior therapy and behavior analysis have neglected" (p. 1138). In this text, we consider such general ethical, practical, and scientific factors (among others) as supporting constructive over suppressive goals; direct rather than indirect approaches; foundational or enabling skills; age and/or developmentally-appropriate objectives; benefit to the client, significant others, peers, staff, and society.

We also offer a broadened perspective, by suggesting that behavior analysts examine the relation of intended behavioral *outcomes* to the individual's, organization's, community's, and/or family's priorities. Additionally, you will see why focusing not only on short-term but also on long-term *outcomes* is important.

## Achievable Yet Challenging

Every single one of Paula's reports has been late over the past year. She is determined to stop procrastinating immediately. Yet is her goal achievable? How about Lucretia's mom's requests that her daughter never hit another child or grab another toy? If goals are too far out of reach, everyone involved suffers. Progress disintegrates and all efforts are fruitless. Think about fitness goals. Currently recording the number of steps one takes is all the rage. Some experts have suggested ten-thousand steps per day as the desired criterion. Well, if on some days you fail even to break 1,000, setting the goal at 10,000 probably is neither going to be achievable nor result in lasting behavior change. Rather, it probably would be advisable for you to set a starting goal of 1,000, then work your way up slowly until eventually you do complete the 10,000.

The achievability feature applies to us as behavior analysts, as well. Resist the temptation to collaborate with clients in setting goals that require you to manage conditions beyond your control. Frustration and failure will result. Do not expect to sustain a program directed toward employee satisfaction if an organization is in the process of scaling down and would welcome reductions in its workforce. Recognize the futility of independently competing with teenage peer pressure or the inherent pleasures of such temptations as substance abuse and sexual activity. After all, you cannot jump into others' skin and act for them.

## Constructive and Functional Goals

Fortunately, alternative approaches may prove feasible. Perhaps, you might be able to harness some of the contingencies ordinarily beyond your control by collaborating with others. By conferring with organizational managers and labor representatives, for instance, you might be able to influence worker-goals or job-safety guidelines. Through clever

---

[11]In the early years, the terms behavior modification, behavior therapy, and applied behavior analysis were used interchangeably. However, applied behavior analysis is reserved for the demonstration of functional relationships, whereas the other two are not necessarily so.

reinforcement tactics, you may induce siblings to support change within a family or members within a peer group.

Avoid goals that are too easy, though. They may prove punishing to clients who see themselves as progressing too slowly or who feel insulted by being asked to achieve something they see as trivial. Rather, challenging them to succeed by suggesting difficult but not impossible goals and setting up the conditions supportive of their doing so may prove a great source of satisfaction for all (Latham & Baldes, 1975; Umbreit, Lane, & Dejud, 2004). Actually, *reasonably challenging* goals stand a better chance of being achieved than those that are patently simple or overly ambitious. Paula might reject a too-easy five percent or a too-difficult 100 percent completion target, aiming instead for handing in one-fourth of her reports on time for several weeks. Then after that target is accomplished, she could raise the standard for success by another one-fourth of the original target, and so on until she approaches perfection, at which point the requirements might be lowered. (Perfection is hard to come by for any of us.) Initially, Lucretia might be more likely to succeed in making it through a five-minute play session without hitting; later, six minutes, etc. Success is much more likely under such circumstances. So choose goals you have good, preferably data-based, reasons to believe your clients will need to strive for but that you feel confident they are capable of achieving.

**Use a constructional approach.** You can see why, whenever possible, those goals that serve to construct repertoires and increase options are preferable to those directed toward eliminating or reducing performance. Try to *state goals in terms of what the person is to **do**, rather than is **not** to do*: "Be on time" rather than "Don't be late"; "Complete tasks" instead of "Don't waste time"; "Bring work materials"; versus "Don't forget your materials." Goals are *not* to be selected for the primary benefit of caregivers (e.g., "Be quiet, be still, be docile"), but for that of the client (Winett & Winkler, 1972). A **constructional approach**, which we advocate, *teaches or builds rather than reduces or eliminates behavior* (Goldiamond, 1974, 2002; Hawkins, 1986). Specifically, the constructional approach (Goldiamond, 1974, 2002) involves:

- Observing or interviewing to determine the desirable outcome or the repertoire to be established.
- Identifying the current effective repertoires upon which to build.
- Selecting change procedures that will build on the current effective repertoires in steps that can be accomplished successfully.
- Selecting and using reinforcers that will maintain the goal behavior throughout the duration of the program and thereafter.

The constructional approach also emphasizes using natural reinforcers such as those that previously reinforced the problem behavior. A study by Carr and Durand (1985) illustrates this aspect: Some of their students with autism were being disruptive while working on assigned tasks. The investigators wondered whether the disruption continued as a function of the attention the students gained or of the difficulty of the task. Reversing the order of treatment between groups, the researchers taught one group of these students to say, "How do you like my work?" (which was followed by adult attention and approval); and then later to say, "This is too hard" (which was followed by adult assistance). Some of the students (presumably those seeking attention by disrupting) who were taught to say "How do you like my work?" disrupted less often while learning the other (help) phrase hardly impacted the frequency of their disruption. Similarly, when the other students (seemingly those who were disrupting as a way of seeking relief from a task too difficult for them) were taught to obtain attention by saying "How do you like my work?" their rates of disruption continued. Only after learning to say, "This is too hard" did they disrupt less frequently.

Note that rather than arbitrarily punishing the disruptive behavior, Carr and Durand first identified the students' functional reinforcers (i.e., attention and relief; see Chapter 10 for means of identifying these functional reinforcers) and then taught them sound constructive alternatives that would generate reinforcers identified as effective for them in that setting. By teaching their students how to achieve functional goals, "… these researchers circumvented the disruptive behaviors that were immediately costly to the teacher and ultimately costly to the child" (Hawkins, 1986, p. 358).

**Incorporate functional and alternative goals.** Functional goals *produce functional reinforcers* by focusing on teaching clients how to obtain their reinforcers in socially acceptable ways (e.g., appropriate ways of gaining attention; escaping from a punitive situation; gaining access to items, activities, or sensations; etc.). Selecting goals that expand clients' functional repertoires and yield them reinforcement is critically important. Nevertheless, when Green et al. (1987) observed 43 classrooms of students with severe handicaps, they found that about two-thirds of all tasks were nonfunctional; the skills being taught would not result in reinforcement from the natural environment, as would proper eating, toilet training, or requesting rather than demanding. The situation was remedied when Reid et al. (1985) used in-service training to teach these teachers how to alter their curricula to favor teaching functional tasks.

When the concern is with diminishing or eliminating an unwanted behavior, *replacement goals* also need to pass the test of functionality for clients; that is, new goals must be designed constructively as adequate substitutes for obtaining the reinforcers the aberrant behaviors formerly provided. That point is critical! Nonetheless, though, the scope of applied behavior analysis reaches far beyond that sort of management to increasing, hastening or slowing, shaping, refining, transferring, and otherwise abetting performance improvement. Most program goals will tend to fall within the latter categories and will be pursued by identifying individually-effective reinforcement strategies.

Beyond those concerns, we also need to be sensitive to the perspectives of others intimately involved (parents, teachers, supervisors, managers, peers, subordinates, and so on). For example, a boy may swear and refuse to perform a difficult task. The *functional goal* (behavior that gets him what he wants in a socially acceptable manner) might be to teach him to say that the task is too difficult or to request breaks. However, his workshop supervisor may wish to pursue additional **alternative goals** not necessarily designed to serve the same function for the client as his misbehavior did, but teach him alternative ways to behave. These might include him also (1) completing his work, and (2) ceasing his refusing and swearing. There is no reason why such goals may not be added to the mix, provided the emphasis is on teaching the client constructive behaviors. In fact, you probably will include multiple goals in many of your behavior-change programs.

## Direct Rather than Indirect Approach

In a direct approach we target the behavior of concern, whereas with an indirect approach we try to accomplish our purpose by addressing some other behavior that we presume will influence the target. In the past, analysts assumed that if we could just get students to stop disrupting and misbehaving they would automatically learn more; just by persuading workers to stop being off-task, they would produce more. Now we recognize that these assumptions were naive (Ferritor, Buckhold, Hamblin, & Smith, 1972; Scheirer & Kraut, 1979). If what we are hoping to see is Ramon performing better in school, our best strategy would be to select as primary goals those directly related to improved school performance, rather than diminished disruptiveness.

Along those same lines, concentrating all one's efforts on reducing the aberrant acts of individuals with personal, social, or developmental dysfunctions does not necessarily produce success. We are better advised to teach new skills (in preference or in addition to working on reducing interfering behaviors). If readying Helen for community employment is the long-range goal, we would want to be sure to teach her to do her job well, rather than concentrating on eliminating her occasional conversations with imaginary friends. Whenever possible, take the direct path.

## Foundational Skills

When higher-level skills *clearly* depend upon more basic ones ("behavioral cusps," "keystone," "pivotal," "foundational," or "enabling" skills, the value of some of which we have mentioned earlier)—we must first assess for, and if necessary, teach those fundamental proficiencies. Holding the pencil properly, positioning the angle of the paper correctly, and drawing freehand lines and various shapes are enabling skills for handwriting; explaining the functions of each lever and button on the console is designed to promote enabling skills for operating a cutting machine. So, as necessary, remember to begin by teaching missing *foundational skills*.

## Immediate and Long-Term Benefits

Surely most specialists who prepare personnel and serve clients assume their efforts are worthy. The responsible application of behavior analysis, however, requires something beyond good faith. Beside possessing competence in ABA methodology, especially in their area of application, they also share a deep responsibility for otherwise practicing ethically. Among other fundamental ethical practices (see Chapter 32), for current purposes, we also explicitly negotiate with our clientele about the intended outcomes of the program, including anticipated long- and short-term benefits, while continuing to monitor and analyze progress along the way.

Educators, clinicians, healthcare professionals, managers, direct-service personnel, and other such service providers must be able not only to defend the client *goals* they plan to encourage, but also to justify the *actions* they intend to undertake. Clearly-explained goals simplify this process by highlighting the relation between the methods and anticipated outcomes. In addition to defending the value of helping Ramon improve his academic performance, his teachers (or counselor or school psychologist) would need to describe how his future instructional environment would successfully support the attainment of that goal.

When benefits are stated ambiguously ("She will be a better person for it!"), controversy may arise because concerned parties may fail to see the value of the activity. Rather, consumers tend to find precisely described performance goals (e.g., properly grasping a pencil, tracing, and writing; setting up, analyzing, and solving an equation; or performing a specific job skill) much easier to understand and to accept. In modern society, acquiring such skills is valued, and schools and training programs have been established to further those purposes. How important are some of the subtler classes of behavior—paying attention, appreciating the value of a task, displaying social skills—work habits that may promote or impede productive or healthy change, and so on? How important are staying on a task for long periods of time, independently seeking more information, following directions, cooperating, organizing activities, and refraining from aggressing or inciting others to engage in disorderly acts? It is our job to clarify and defend the value of those goals that enable the development of other beneficial behaviors, as in explaining that paying attention is necessary for learning.

Long-term goals often can be accomplished by mastering a succession of readily acquired short-term aims. If, when change agents initiate any complex program of behavior change, they first select rapidly achievable goals, not only the client but also others directly affected (parents, teachers, supervisors, etc.) will gain immediate reinforcement.

The most ethically supportable goals are those selected to promote improved adjustment, adaptation, competence, or habilitation; that support the development of a "repertoire that maximizes short- and long-term reinforcers, for the person and for others, and minimizes short- and long-term punishers" (Hawkins, 1986, p. 351). How adaptive the quality of any particular response to the environment may be is *"the degree to which it maximizes the benefits and minimizes the cost"* (Hawkins, 1986, p. 351). Notice how flexible and general, yet economical, this rule is. Goals selected according to those features are measurable, broadly applicable, individually and culturally adaptable, and consonant with the perspective that "adjustment" is a continuous (a question of degree) rather than a dichotomous (either/or) variable. Credit and blame for problematic behavior are avoided, yet the impact of the goal achievement is assessed in terms of its effect on the client, and also on the significant others in the client's immediate and broader environment. As Hawkins (1985) has further pointed out:

> The scientific question, then, in terms of setting goals for individuals is "what will reduce the costs and/or increase the benefits to this person and/or others?" For an unhappy freshman who is facing vague, existential problems and is questioning the meaning or value of his or

her life—a type of problem for which behavior therapists and behavior analysts are least prepared, because no behavior is referred to by the client—one might hypothesize that one or more of several goals is relevant: greater skill at studying or at making new friends, becoming active in an activist organization, setting more realistic academic goals, coming to a decision about tentative career objectives, and so forth. If one or more of those goals is then achieved and it is scientifically demonstrated, by methods such as those suggested by Barlow, Hayes, and Nelson (1984), that the person is no longer unhappy or questioning the value of his or her life, the conclusion suggested is that the goals selected were, indeed, functional for that individual. Similarly, if a clinician teaches a delinquent youth to, for example, carry on conversations effectively with middle-class nondelinquents, to read as well as age peers, and to "read" people's positive and negative social reactions; and if that youth no longer engages in delinquent behaviors (which primarily cost others, at least in the short run), the conclusion suggested is that these "target behaviors" were functional for this individual and relevant to his other problem. (p. 1138)

Above all, the behavior analyst should be guided by concern for the client and by evidence that the natural environment will support the goal. Teaching Lucretia socially constructive alternatives, such as speaking in a firm voice or displaying other non-aggressive forms of assertiveness, probably would require considerable time and effort. Yet she only will benefit if those in her environment adequately reinforce that assertiveness. One of our jobs then, would be to assess her social environment by observing her teachers, family members, and playmates to determine if appropriately contingent reinforcement is likely to be forthcoming or can be trained and managed.

## Age and Developmental Level

*Goals* that are mission oriented, functional in terms of short- and long-term payoff, and serve as founda-

> **Consider Developmental Factors when Setting Goals**
>
> Watch children pretending. As Lifter and Bloom (1989) have suggested, pretend play is not only reinforcing in its own right, but also serves as a vehicle for learning verbal and other skills that typify the performance of most children of those ages. You can see why knowing the ways young people's behavior typically evolves is essential for practitioners participating in goal selection.

tions for more advanced performance, are apt to be (but not necessarily) well suited to the client's developmental level. As Dyer, Santarcangelo, and Luce (1987) have shown, selecting communicative goals for individuals with developmental delays according to the sequence in which typical children tend to acquire language skills did allow the students to progress more rapidly and accurately than when the goals were too advanced. But that does not necessarily mean that we should provide instructional materials suitable for much younger children to older clients with severe developmental delays. Rather, we need to make every effort to adjust learning tools and materials to be challenging but achievable, yet as age-appropriate as feasible. Many actual jobs, for instance packing, labeling, and so on, require the kind of eye-hand coordination that can be trained in much the same way that younger folks learn to sort and match toys or geometric forms.

Don't forget about clients with advanced capabilities either. Above all, be certain to shape and reinforce the efforts of every one of your typically developing, advanced or delayed progeny, students, subordinates, or clientele by rigorously applying the procedures that you are about to master.

## PREVENTING AND RESOLVING GOAL CONFLICTS

Unfortunately, sometimes program personnel and/or family members disagree about the priorities they assign to particular goals. One supervisor may prefer quiet; another may have no objection to "normal hustle and bustle." Pop may want to train his son to take on the neighborhood bullies, while Mom is intent upon having her son avoid any form of physical violence. Similar sorts of conflicts can arise from many sources: managers, parents, therapists, workers and/or their representatives, and so on. To avoid working at cross purposes, we must find ways to avoid and resolve such disputes. While reviewing the suggestions below, recognize that no simple one-size-fits-all solution to goal conflicts exists, but some mechanisms can function to prevent or limit their escalation. These include participation by clients, parents, and other concerned individuals (worker organizations, supervisors, individual staff, community members); also advocacy and behavioral contracting strategies.

## Participative Goal Setting

Sometimes *goal setting* (Chapter 3, and further elaborated upon in Chapter 21) is legally required to be participative; other times, a case must be made based on evidence that it reflects "good practice." Be aware that in some jurisdictions, key participants, including parents, and when possible, students, are required by law to be involved in the selection of short- and long-term goals and treatment procedures during the special educational planning process (e.g., *The Individuals with Disabilities Education Improvement Act of 2004, as amended 2017*). Plus, as previously discussed, consumers' participation can aid the selection of more rapidly achievable goals; those apt to be achieved more rapidly and supported by the natural environment. Also, be aware of the ethical consideration involving client participation. (See Chapter 32).

## Arranging for Advocacy

Public policy, internationally and locally, recently has trended toward ensuring equal rights for everyone, regardless of disability or group affiliation. Similarly, representatives of previously powerless groups, like children or people with severe emotional or developmental disabilities, have become increasingly insistent that the perspectives of those so affected be considered when decisions are made affecting them. This can mean that in addition to their traditional supporters (parents, relatives, or guardians), severely disabled, abused, or very immature clients also may be represented by outside advocates.

When a client clearly does not have the capacity to participate in setting goals or endorsing methods—for example, a child who lacks speech or an adult fails to communicate clearly in any form—an **advocate** should be appointed to represent his or her interests. The appointee may be a community representative, (e.g., a clergyman, law student, or even a panel of interested citizens), who undertakes to consider the goal from the point of view of the client. The advocate serves as *the client's agent*, not the agent of an organization or institution. Advocates *put themselves in the place of their clients and argue on their behalf,* an arrangement more likely to serve the client's best interests.

Conflicts can arise during goal selection when benefits and costs affect different members of the group unequally. By negotiating a *behavioral contract* stipulating mutually acceptable *responsibilities* and *anticipated outcomes*, each of the parties stands a better chance of receiving fair treatment insofar as program goals and procedural details are concerned. The negotiation should consist of a discussion, as many short- and long-term benefits and costs as can be anticipated along with a statement of how their accomplishment might affect each of the participants for better or worse. Benefits might include enhanced personal, social, academic, or job skills, or diminished rates of responses that interfere with other desired outcomes. Costs could involve increased expenditures of material and human resources (skilled performance, time, effort); loss of control or power; loss of other social rewards; or increases in unpleasant events, such as delays until clients are dressed, amplified noise levels, the need to wait patiently, and so on.

**Behavioral** or **contingency contracts**, sometimes referred to as "therapeutic contracts" (Sulzer, 1962), detail *the behavior analysis program goals and procedures that clients or their representatives, the change agent and others involved, or affected, jointly negotiate.* Because those goals and procedures are set in advance by all concerned parties, conflicts are minimized. (For a more in-depth discussion of this topic, see Chapter 11.)

## Terminating Services

The BCBA (2020) *ethics code for behavior analysts* addresses service termination as follows:

> Behavior analysts include the circumstances for discontinuing services in their service agreement. They consider discontinuing services when: (1) the client has met all behavior-change goals, (2) the client is not benefiting from the service, (3) the behavior analyst and/or their supervises or trainees are exposed to potentially harmful conditions that cannot be reasonably resolved, (4) the client and/or relevant stakeholder requests discontinuation, (5) the relevant stakeholders are not complying with the behavior-change intervention despite appropriate efforts to address barriers, or (6) services are no longer funded. Behavior analysts provide the client and/or relevant stakeholders with a written plan for discontinuing series, document acknowledgment of the plan, review the plan throughout the discharge process, and document all steps taken. (p. 14, code 3.15)

No responsible independent adult should be forced to undergo behavior analytic services. The freedom of clients (or their surrogates) to terminate behavior analytic services has been incorporated into the BCBA's ethics code for behavior analysts, as can be seen above. In such cases it would seem prudent to consider alternative strategies, which might include identifying different program placements or any other educational or psychological change techniques scientifically demonstrated to effectively remedy the presenting problem.

## Supporting Voluntariness over Coercion

*Voluntariness* is an important element of a behavioral contract, but the term voluntariness invites ambiguity. A dictionary defines *voluntary* as (1) proceeding from the *internal will* or from one's own choice or full consent; (2) unconstrained, self-impelled, freely given, done, etc. Definitions of words like *intent* and *will* unfortunately are non-operational beyond the behavioral realm because as you progress through this text you will see that essentially everything we do is controlled in some way. Some sources are obvious, others subtle: salaries, material gifts, awards, bonuses, eye contact, nods of approval, others' agreement or disagreement, privileges, particular activities, observing other people being rewarded, relief from discomfort, and an endless array of others. Well informed behavior analysts recognize that even very occasional reinforcement can promote the repetition of particular words or deeds.

Similarly, stimuli in the form of threats and unpleasant consequences also continually operate on behavior. Obvious examples include: drivers foolish enough to speed along at over 90 miles an hour probably watch out closely or worry about being stopped by the police or having an accident; failing to fulfill job responsibilities which can result in job dismissal; non-completion of assignments, resulting in poor grades. Other consequences are far more subtle: inattention to uninteresting conversation; a slight shoulder shrug or no response to a stated opinion. How long would any of us continue studying if we were not rewarded with grades, enhanced job opportunities, salary increments, approval from important people in our lives, or at least by encountering interesting, engaging, or potentially useful material? Don't we avoid negative consequences—censure, poverty, loss of prestige — by remaining in a job, attending school, maintaining a household, and so on? Numerous reinforcers and punishers operate in the daily lives of us all. From the behavior analytic point of view, the concept of total voluntariness is a myth, because reinforcers and punishers are ever present in our lives. So when behavior analysts, use the term **"voluntarily,"** they might define it as *the client's consenting to participate in the program in the absence of coercion.*

What is **coercion**? Its defining aspects include: *oppressive or aversive force* and/or *disproportionately powerful incentives*. In other words, the more intense the aversive or reinforcing stimuli used to cajole or suppress the act of concern, the more coercive we might deem it to be. Let us consider a couple of examples.

Willie comes to class, rapidly organizes his material, and promptly begins to produce excellent quality work. When the teacher requests assistance with an exhibit, Willie offers to participate. First, consider some aspects of Willie's reinforcement history: Willie has received top grades for good performance in the past. His girlfriend admires his seriousness. Willie's teacher, Mr. Mulligan, smiles and nods from time to time while the Willie is completing his assignment. Willie recognizes he has learned to solve a challenging problem: "That was a tough one, but I did it!"

Was Willie's performance voluntary? Maybe his dad had promised him a motorcycle, a car, or a trip to Europe if he did well in his studies? Would we still consider it voluntary?

Suppose that on the other hand, Willie previously suffered frowns, poor grades, and ridicule from his teacher and friends for poor performance. Maybe his dad threatened to deny him the use of the car for the remainder of the year if his grades failed to improve. Would any of those actual or threatened negative consequences imply that Willie's classroom performance is coerced?

The concepts *volunteered* and *coerced* form two ends of a continuum, the former expressed absent any threats or promises; the latter emitted solely for the purpose of avoiding threats or seeing promises fulfilled. Therefore, to meet the ethical features of "voluntariness," a reasonable approach might be to identify the contingencies commonly functioning in the setting and, if indicated, to match the conditions a prudent person would consider to fall within similar bounds.

## BEHAVIORAL OBJECTIVES

After all affected participants have mutually agreed upon the general goals of the anticipated program, the next step is precisely to formulate your behavioral objectives. These should be prepared in writing and approved by the client or surrogate—someone empowered to make decisions for him or her. (See Chapter 32 for more detailed caveats.).

### Defined

A **behavioral objective** *consists of: (1) a goal behavior; (2) clear specifications of the conditions or context within which the behavior is to occur; and, (3) the criteria, or standards for determining when the objective has been accomplished* (Mager, 1962, 1972, 1997b). Having previously discussed goal selection, we next address *context* and a variety of behavioral dimensions used to set the *criteria* by which a client's success would be judged.

**Specify the context.** The **context** *includes the surrounding conditions under which the desired response is to occur, including the setting, furnishings, materials, personnel, and so on.* If Ramon is to write more reports, is he to do all his preparation during social studies class, or whenever he wishes? To what materials can he have access? If Lucretia is to play cooperatively with other children, sharing materials and not hitting, pushing, or grabbing, how many children is she to play with, where, and with what toys? Obviously, it would not be appropriate for her to share toys during her nap or at mealtimes. Is Bill's workspace open or enclosed? Where is his supervisor located?

The description of the context must specify any givens or restrictions to be placed on the response: how, where, with what, with whom, and when it is or is not to occur. Because it is essential to consider *generalization* and *discrimination* from the beginning, at the outset we must specify each setting, including across times and people, in which the behavior will or will not be supported at the outset. (See Chapter 21 for methods designed to promote generalization of the behavior across different conditions and discrimination between one setting and another.)

**Specify the criteria.** The **criteria** constitute the part of the objective that states the s*tandards used to determine whether or not the objective has been achieved.* Criteria are expressed as measurable **behavioral dimensions** (such as frequency, rate, acceleration, quantity, and so on) that *characterize particular aspects of the performance.* (See Table 4.1 for examples.)

What would convince us that the behavior of concern was *firmly* established or *fully* extinguished? Adding another behavioral dimension, the **rate of criterion level**, (*the rate at which the criterion level maintains*) then may come into play. In such a case, prior to shifting over to a mainte-

**TABLE 4.1  Measure of Proficiency Levels**

| Dimension | Measure | Definition | Examples |
|---|---|---|---|
| Level of Proficiency | frequency | The number of times a response occurs | Paula will complete 4 reports.<br>Shakisha will provide at least one answer and one question when conversing with peers.<br>The team will accumulate 20 days without a lost-time injury. |
| | percentage | Proportion or number of times achieved or correct, divided by total possible times multiplied by 100 | Ramon will complete 90 percent of his assignments each week.<br>80 percent of the work teams will have a quality assurance plan in place by the end of the fiscal year. |
| | duration | The length of time that passes from the onset to the offset of a behavior | Shakisha will converse audibly for at least 30 seconds.<br>Henri will brush his teeth for a full two minutes.<br>Betsy will exercise for a full hour. |
| | rate | The number of times a response occurs within a given period of time or per opportunity | Bruno will practice an hour a day.<br>Betsy will exercise five days per week.<br>Betsy will do 25 push-ups within three minutes.<br>The team will assemble 30 engines per day. |

nance mode by thinning the schedule with which reinforcers are delivered, we must ask ourselves, "With what *consistency, frequency, and/or over what duration should the criterion level be matched before we will confidently conclude the behavior is sufficiently established in (or obliterated from) the person's repertoire?*" For example, our goal might state: "Bruno will practice an hour a day *five times per week*, over a period of three months"; or "Shakisha will provide one answer and one question *three times a week*, for ten weeks in a row." After our clients meet those goals, then it might well be appropriate to shift over to a maintenance mode by adjusting the requirements accordingly (See Chapters 22 and 23).

Also, the criterion level that you set also can influence maintenance of the behavior. For example, investigators (Fuller & Fienup, 2018) found that, higher mastery levels (e.g., they compared 50 percent, 80 percent, and 90 percent), such as 90 percent per unit of time, produce higher levels of maintenance responding. In addition, higher rate levels help to produce greater fluency, which also has been shown to facilitate maintenance.

To summarize, *the final criterion level should be set functionally to represent mastery or fluency* (i.e., indicating a level in which the behavior occurs smoothly, rapidly, with little or no effort, or at a high rate). By doing so, the occurrence of *maintenance and generalization* will likely be facilitated.

When developing your own objectives, unless clearly apparent to all concerned (e.g., "Never set another fire in the stairwell"), you also will need to indicate the *conditions*: all the various circumstances or settings in which the behavior is (*generalization*) or is *not* to take place (*discrimination*). You will also need to consider the length of time the behavior is to continue or remain absent; that is, how long *the change is to last!*

**Specify other relevant behavioral dimensions.** Depending upon the goal and the circumstances, your objective may include additional behavioral dimensions, including accuracy, latency, intensity, and topography. See Table 4.2 for descriptors and examples of these terms.

Above all, the key standard for determining whether a significant behavioral change has

**TABLE 4.2** Additional Dimensions of Behavior

| Dimension | Descriptor | Examples |
|---|---|---|
| Topography | The form, appearance, or shape of the behavior; its physical or natural features | Lea is to sit with all 4 legs of the chair on the floor, facing forward, her buttocks on the seat, with her feet on the floor. |
| Accuracy | The extent or degree to which the response meets standards | Ramon will score 90% or above on his completed assignments. |
| Latency | The time that elapses between an antecedent (cue, prompt, signal) and a response | Lucretia will begin to pick up her toys within 2 minutes of her mother saying, "Time to clean up." |
| Intensity | Strength or force with which a behavior is expressed | Shakisha will speak loudly enough for all her friends to hear.<br>Joe Duffer will hit the golf ball hard enough for it to reach the 100-yard mark. |

occurred is its *practical importance* (Baer, Wolf, & Risley, 1968). Participants should mutually agree upon the *minimum* (not necessarily the ideal) *acceptable standard* or *criterion for success* at the outset of the behavior-change program. To avoid subsequent indecision, disagreement, or bias in determining if and when the goal has been achieved. Naturally, this choice does not place a cap on even better levels of performance; it simply serves as a standard against which to assess progress. If the behavior of concern has been altered sufficiently enough to satisfy those affected by the change, including, as appropriate, the clients themselves, significant others, supervisors, managers, teachers, parents, students, and/or staff, the goal can be said to have been achieved.

## Sample Behavioral Objectives

The following illustrate a useful format for writing behavioral objectives:

***Behavior of Concern:*** Vinh, an asthmatic, fails to follow her physician's instructions.
  *Goal:* Comply with instructions for using inhaler.
  *Topography:* Inhale twice deeply as demonstrated and practiced.
  *Context/Conditions:* Wherever an asthma attack occurs (home, work, community).

***Criterion Level:***
  *Rate of Behavior:* Use 4 times a day and whenever an attack occurs.
  *Rate of Criterion:* Specified rate of behavior is to occur for 5 consecutive days.
  *Latency:* The inhaler will be used within 2 minutes of the start of an attack.
  *Intensity:* N/A; Accuracy: N/A

***Behavioral Objective:*** As demonstrated, Vinh will inhale twice deeply 4 times a day as well as within 2 minutes of the onset of an attack, for 5 consecutive days.

******

***Behavior of Concern:*** Lucretia does not share with other children, but instead hits and pushes them and grabs their toys.
  *Goal:* Lucretia will hand toys to another child on request.
  *Topography:* Toy handed (not thrown) to playmate.
  *Context/Conditions:* 1 or more other children, array of toys.

***Criterion Level:***
  *Rate of Behavior:* At least once, conditions appropriate, in each of 3 out of 4 half-hour blocks of time.
  *Rate of Criterion:* 3 consecutive days.
  *Latency:* Within 1 minute of request.
  *Intensity:* N/A; Accuracy: N/A

*Behavioral Objective:* In the presence of 1 or more other children, upon request, Lucretia will hand toys to another child within 1 minute, at least once in each of 3 of 4 half-hour blocks of time for 3 consecutive days.

\*\*\*\*\*\*

*Behavior of Concern:* Shakisha does not converse with her peers.
   *Goal:* Shakisha will ask questions and respond to her peers' questions.
   *Topography:* Requests and responses will be in complete sentences.
   *Context/Conditions:* Recreation room, break time.

**Criterion Level:**
   *Rate of Behavior:* At least 1 answer and 1 question per day.
   *Rate of Criterion:* 3 consecutive days.
   *Latency:* Responses to questions will occur within 30 seconds.
   *Intensity:* Loudly enough to be clearly heard by the listener.
   *Accuracy:* N/A

*Behavioral Objective:* In the recreation room during break, Shakisha will ask and answer questions within 30 seconds, in complete sentences loud enough to be heard by the listener, at least once daily for 3 consecutive days.

Here is an example that incorporates the findings of a functional assessment:

*Behavior of Concern:* Nakita throws work material to the floor to escape from long, difficult tasks.
   *Functionally Equivalent Replacement Goal (FERG):* Request breaks or assistance from supervisor, as appropriate.
   *Topography:* In a normal speaking tone and in a complete sentence.
   *Context/Conditions:* When given long, difficult tasks at a sheltered workshop and in a residential center.

**Criterion Level:**
   *Rate of Behavior:* at least 2 requests for breaks and/or for assistance per 45-minute period, while working on a long, difficult task.
   *Rate of Criterion:* 4 of 5 days
   *Latency:* N/A
   *Intensity:* Loud enough to be heard by supervisor.
   *Accuracy:* N/A

(Note how it is helpful to include the purpose or function of the replacement behavior when preparing a functional objective. This way you are in a better position to select the FERG.)

*Behavioral Objective:* In complete sentences and loud enough to be heard by the supervisor, Nakita will request breaks and/or assistance at least twice per 45-minute period while working on long, difficult tasks during 4 out of 5 days.[12]

## SUMMARY AND CONCLUSIONS

While they are not behavior analytic procedures *per se*, goals and objectives guide our design of behavior analytic intervention plans. Assuming precisely articulated, constructive criteria are incorporated within our objectives and intervention strategies, we should readily be able to determine when and under what conditions our goals have been achieved and maintained. Constructively, precisely stated goals and objectives are essential to the design and implementation of ethically defensible, successful behavior intervention programs.

In setting goals and objectives, we must take into account a number of practical considerations; above all, whether a behavioral goal and intervention is justified. These points are summarized in Figure 4.2.

Once we determine that a behavioral goal is warranted, it must be operationalized to permit reliable observation and progress monitoring. Therefore, a common early task for the behavior analyst is to assist program implementers and clients to specify problems and goals in behavioral terms. However, the selected goal(s) and objective(s) must also be appropriate to the client and situation. Therefore, other ethical, practical, and scientific factors that may influence goal selection must be considered

---
[12]Additional behavioral objectives can be found on the text Web page, including those that target the problem behavior (reducing the behavior).

to ensure that the selected goals and objectives are reasonable and realistic. These include: reviewing test scores, records, and other materials; ensuring that the goal is achievable yet challenging; selecting constructive, functional, and alternative goals; taking a direct rather than indirect approach; assigning priority to foundational behaviors; considering immediate and long-term benefits for the client and important others; ensuring that the goal is as appropriate as possible to the clients' age and developmental level; and assuring that the goal compliments the organization's, parents', and/or society's mission. We also supplied several suggestions to help prevent and/or resolve goal conflicts, including participative goal setting, advocacy, and behavioral contracting. Finally, we illustrated several different kinds of behavioral objectives and described their components.

As you continue to read this text, you will discover that a behavior is not well established until: (a) it is fluent (Chapter 17), (b) occurs across situations, people and times of day (generalization has occurred—Chapter 21), (c) is no longer prompt dependent (stimulus control has been transferred from prompts to natural $S^D$s in the environment, and (d) reinforcers are no longer intrusive, have been thinned, and come from sources in the natural environment (Chapters 22 through 24). Establishing your objective is just a step toward achieving the goal of behavior change. In the next chapter, we look at how reinforcement functions to encourage the client to achieve the objective.

*Chapter 5*

# Reinforcement: Fueling Behavior Change

## Goals

1. Describe and illustrate the following terms:
    a. *reinforcement*
    b. *reinforcement procedure*
    c. *emit*
    d. *behavioral repertoire*
    e. *aversive stimuli*
    f. *negative reinforcement procedures*
2. Describe three distinctive applications of the term *reinforcement*
3. Define, illustrate and distinguish between:
    a. *reinforcers* and *reinforcement procedures*
    b. *reinforcer* and *reward*
    c. *positive reinforcer* and *positive reinforcement*
    d. *escape* and *avoidance*
    e. *reinforcement* and *punishment*
4. Discuss and illustrate the functional similarities and differences between positive and negative reinforcement
5. Outline the grounds on which you would decide whether or not to apply negative reinforcement and explain how you would justify your actions.
6. List and respond to common concerns about using reinforcement.
7. Discuss the "*overjustification effect*" and the scientific evidence related to its possible influence on "*intrinsic motivation.*"
8. Offer a plan for explaining to potential consumers how reinforcement operates and for addressing any concerns they might express regarding its application.

\*\*\*\*\*\*\*\*\*\*\*\*

Precisely articulating our behavioral objectives sets the direction for our behavior analytic program by specifying exactly where we are headed and how all concerned will recognize when those objectives have been achieved. But now we face the big challenge: "How on earth will we get there?"

Our answer: Turn to the evidence derived from the scientific study of the behavior of organisms and to the demonstrably effective, ethically sound, change technologies derived from that knowledge.

In this chapter we focus on *reinforcement*, the fundamental biological *process* that drives and supports behavior (Skinner, 1953), and the behavior-change *procedure* derived from our knowledge of how that process operates. Reinforcement occurs naturally during the course of the lives of all complex organisms and is responsible in large part for what, specifically, we learn, how we learn, and for how long that learning lasts. It promotes our current behavior repertoires, or in simpler terms, what we *say* (both overtly and covertly—i.e., "think") and *do*. As you learn about reinforcement, you will begin to see how your own and others' behavioral patterns develop over time. But even more important for our mutual purposes, you will become empowered by mastering the most promising procedures for altering those patterns. Soon, by mastering the fundamental knowledge produced by the experimental analysis of behavior and the demonstratively effective technologies derived from that knowledge you should be in a position competently and responsibly to modify behavior. In this chapter, we explain what reinforcement is and does, illustrate the various subcategories of reinforcement, and begin to explain how effectively to implement this foundational building block of applied behavior analysis. In subsequent chapters, we shall detail some of the finer points of developing and identifying reinforcers and of applying them effectively.

## DEFINING THE TERM *REINFORCEMENT*

The terms **reinforcer** and **reinforcement** are defined in various ways: One is to *describe the natural process and/or observable event* responsible for a change in behavior (e.g., "She continued to practice the piano because she gained so much reinforcement from hearing the music she produced"). Or, said more simply, "Hearing the music was so reinforcing." Another, especially in our field of applied behavior analysis, is to describe reinforcement as a **behavioral procedure** (e.g., "applying positive reinforcement") by specifying the contingencies to be in effect (the *arrangements* between the response we hope to increase and the consequential reinforcing stimuli.). We may infer that reinforcement has taken place when we observe a feature of an individual's behavior (its frequency, rate, duration, intensity, and/or other dimension) increasing or stabilizing following the presentation of the stimulus in question.

Or, we may infer that the reinforcement was responsible when we observe a person or non-human animal repeating a particular behavior more often, faster, longer, or with greater intensity or stability as a consequence of what s/he has experienced *contingent* (or *dependent*) on that behavior.

## Natural vs. Planned Reinforcement

We use the term *reinforcement* to describe either

1. a process inferred by observing an increase in or maintenance of an individual's rate of emitting a specific behavior after that behavior has been followed by a particular consequence

*or*

2. a procedure designed to increase the rate of an individual's particular behavior by presenting a particular desired (positive reinforcement) or withdrawing a particular unwanted (negative reinforcement) stimulus as a consequence of that behavior.

*Example:* Jonathan continues to place the paper napkins just so after his Mom has smiled and remarked "Good boy, Jonathan, you're placing the napkins so neatly." Mom has reinforced Jonathan's napkin placement. (Table 5.1 lists some other familiar examples of reinforcement from everyday life.)

A **reinforcement** *procedure* is related, but consists of *a clearly planned sequence of actions that change agents use to promote or sustain the rate of a given behavior.* We might say that the agent arranges a *behavior-reinforcer contingency*, as in the following case:

In an attempt to increase Candace's on-task behavior, the teacher affixes a gold star to the girl's paper (a well-established high-preference reinforcer for that student) commenting "You finished your arithmetic assignment and got everything right, Candice. You really deserve this gold star."

*That reinforcement contingency may be represented symbolically as follows*:

**Behavior (B)** ⟶ **Reinforcer (S$^r$)**
finishes assignment         gold star

To enable their individual and collective survival, all societies adopt methods for managing the performance of their members. Typically included are strategies for encouraging behaviors like gathering, hunting, producing, or purchasing food, caring for their young, providing essential services, and cooperating in various ways. Formally and/or informally, the survival of the group depends on enabling their members to acquire numerous skills, ways to avoid danger and become increasingly independent, and much, much more. Sometimes they incorporate tangible or social "rewards" (prizes, ceremonies, etc.) to encourage progress. Regardless of whether managers or participants are able to *articulate* a set of guidelines for effective behavior change (of the kind we offer in this text), those societies that do survive probably apply those guidelines reasonably well.

Advanced societies, though, do design and execute their practices far more intentionally, by carefully organizing their members and designing management systems, articulating who is responsible for accomplishing what, to what level of performance, and with what ultimate results. The same is true at regional, local, and perhaps even familial levels. (Table 5.2 displays familiar instances of the *intentional* or *planned* application of reinforcement methods in our ordinary daily lives.)

Recognize that whether impromptu or planned, reinforcement can operate to the detriment or advantage of an individual or group. A prime example is the "spoiled" child who whines or throws tantrums until he gets his way. Why does he continue to do that? Because his tantrums often have yielded him what he wanted. That arrangement constitutes reinforcement. From his parents' perspective, giving in to the child's demands is reinforcing for them too, because letting the child have his way terminates or removes the tantrum that so upsets them. (Guess what happens in the future!)

**TABLE 5.1   Everyday Examples of Natural Reinforcement**

- An infant turning his face toward the bottle because he has received milk by turning in that direction in the past.
- A person wearing gloves on a cold day because gloves previously avoided cold fingers.
- An addict sniffing cocaine as a function of earlier effects it produced.
- A teenager complying with her friends' dares because accepting such challenges permitted her to be included in their activities and avoid their ridicule.
- A man's leaving his papers strewn about, because his house-mate has usually picked them up in the past.
- A woman learning that it is easier to "just do it herself" than to argue and have a scene with her family.

**TABLE 5.2  Examples of *Planned Reinforcement***

- A teacher giving a student a coveted gold star or an A for reciting his multiplication tables correctly
- As promised, a boy's mother delivers the controls to his computerized game program after his chores are completed.
- A salesperson receiving a bonus for closing a large number of sales.
- A mother exclaiming "How great! I see you have assembled the ingredients for dinner," when her daughter has done at least a portion of her assigned chores.
- A teacher allowing students to have extra time at the computer or activity table upon completing their work.

Sometimes, as discussed earlier, powerful positive reinforcers inspire people to behave in curious ways. High salaries may encourage workers to execute unpleasant or possibly harmful tasks, like working in unsafe mines or oil rigs. And all of us are familiar with cases in which consequences like access to power, wealth, and approval from esteemed peers have reinforced bullying, stealing, cheating, and even violence.

You might ask, "if reinforcement is a natural aspect of daily life, why bother studying it?" Because those charged with protecting, assisting, supporting, guiding, counseling, managing, and educating others have a duty to provide their clientele with the best services available. True, most of us have encountered intuitive "people experts," who have accomplished striking successes despite never having heard of principles of behavior. But even *they* are unwise to remain uninformed, because when faced with unfamiliar challenges, they too may not know where to turn. Rather than comfortably relying on their past successes, generosity, and good intentions, all behavior managers hold a responsibility for continuously improving their own skills. Our present concern, then, is to enable our readers consistently to apply state-of-the-art reinforcement and other behavior change procedures in as effective and ethically responsible manner as possible.

## THE REINFORCEMENT PROCEDURE DEFINED AND ILLUSTRATED

As mentioned earlier, a reinforcement *procedure,* consists of deliberately and systematically applying reinforcing stimuli for the purpose of increasing or maintaining particular behaviors, as in teaching, training, managing, treating, counseling, or otherwise modifying those behaviors. For many years, scientists have been intensively studying a large number of measurable behavior quantities or parameters. **Parameters** *are physical properties, such as timing, frequency, intensity, and others whose values influence the effectiveness of any reinforcement procedure.* Their discoveries have permitted practitioners to hone their skills as teachers and behavior-change agents by intentionally incorporating those findings within their strategies for increasing and maintaining behavior. Anyone who masters principles and effective practices of reinforcement (see Chapter 11) and of applied behavior analysis in general should better be able to understand, and more effectively and efficiently manage his or her own behavior as well as that of others. Of course our affiliated Association for Behavior Analysis International (ABAI) profession insists we do this humanely—for the betterment of program participants and of society in general.[1]

Behavior analysts apply reinforcement procedures for varied purposes: as *strengthening behavior* that individuals are capable of performing that already is part of the person's **behavioral reper-**

---

[1] Scientific facts are natural truths and cannot be judged in the abstract as either good or evil. It is the way humans make use of that information that imbues them with value. As a socially-responsible group, professional applied behavior analysts have produced an ethical compliance code to which its members are required to adhere. We refer to that code in various places in this text, while the complete *Professional and Ethical Compliance Code for Behavior Analysts* can be located on the Behavior Analysis Certification Board website: http://www.bacb.com.

toire—what the person has **emitted**[2] (i.e., said or done) in the past. They also judiciously present and withhold consequences to teach new behaviors, strengthen others that will replace unwanted ones, and teach subtle distinctions between stimuli (i.e., discriminations).

This section focuses on the simplest case of applying reinforcement: strengthening behavior already established in the individual's behavioral repertoire. Initially we discuss reinforcement in detail to explain how it operates. You will learn how to support and maintain behaviors already established in the person's repertoire and how best to arrange reinforcers to achieve given objectives. Later you will see the function reinforcement performs within more complex situations, including teaching novel behaviors.

## REINFORCERS DEFINED, ILLUSTRATED, AND DIFFERENTIATED FROM *REWARD*

A **reinforcer** is a *stimulus*—an object or event—that when gained or lost as a consequence of a behavior, *increases or maintains the likelihood that the behavior will be repeated*. Note that stimuli that increase or maintain the behavior are called "reinforcers," regardless of whether the individual obtains the particular stimulus (*positive reinforcer*), as in the case of *positive reinforcement*, or is relieved of an *aversive stimulus*, as in *negative reinforcement*, as a function of the behavior. Beware of a common error: identifying a given stimulus as a *reinforcer* based simply on how it strikes the observer. ("Anyone would love an outfit, a meal, an award, a ticket to a rock concert...") Rather, before we can appropriately call a stimulus "a reinforcer," we have to show that either gaining that object or access to that event (the positive reinforcer) or being relieved of the object or event (the aversive stimulus) leads to *an increase* in the rate of the behavior associated with it.

Notice that, although similar, the terms *reinforcer* and *reward* are not identical. A **reward** is *an arbitrarily selected item or event chosen under the (sometimes misguided) assumption that it will encourage an individual to repeat a given behavior.* By contrast, to be identified correctly as a *reinforcer*, the stimulus the individual has gained or experienced as a consequence of a particular response must have demonstrated its function by its having promoted an increase in or by maintaining the rate of *emission* (occurrence) of that behavior, at least under given conditions. While conventional *rewards* (medals, trophies, cash prizes, products etc.) often do function as reinforcers, depending on the recipients' histories and conditions in effect, they might not. Most of us are acquainted with people about whom it can be said that, "Rewards just don't work for him/her." In fact, if a certain reward lacks reinforcing properties for an individual under the circumstances in effect, it probably will not change his or her behavior. In applying behavior analysis, you need to be confident any rewards you select actually promise to serve a reinforcing function for that individual at that time and place. For example, consuming a hot dog, fries, and a soft drink might be reinforcing for a hungry child at breakfast time, but not for his mother. Similarly, a teacher may assume that a gold star is a reinforcer. But simply because she has announced that it is good to earn gold stars, she should not necessarily conclude that it actually serves a reinforcing function. Only after she has been able to demonstrate that the rate of the behavior that has produced the star has increased or persisted over time can her assumption be justified.

**Primary reinforcers**[3] such as food for the hungry, fluids for the thirsty, sexual engagement for the sexually aroused, and rest for the weary, function as reinforcers in the absence of any prior learning history. But *beware* of assuming that the particular

---

[2] The verb *to emit* is a technical term used in connection with a category of behavior called *operant behavior*, behavior that is modified by its consequences to emphasize that the behavior occurs because of its consequences and not because it has been produced by some stimulus. (An analogy is the spontaneous emission of a particle from the nucleus of an atom of a radioactive element.) With respondent behavior, stimuli are said to *elicit* behavior. Because this text is largely limited to operant behavior, you generally will see the term *emit*; not the term *elicit*.

[3] Some prefer the term *unconditioned reinforcers*.

events, activities, or objects *you* might especially appreciate (public recognition, particular foods, music, books, certificates, jewelry, participating in or watching certain sports or other forms of entertainment) are equally powerful for others. Frequently we have been told "reinforcement does not work with that person!" This makes no sense because, by definition, if the behavior upon which it is contingent does not increase, then the stimulus was not a reinforcer. To identify reinforcers for the given individual, you need to identify the *stimuli that operate to increase the rates of the behaviors they regularly follow,* at least under particular sets of circumstances. Results (the effect of the consequence) are what count; not the delivery agent's intent.

> When Kevin misbehaves, he successfully avoids having to do his math work. After his teacher first referred Kevin to the school psychologist for an assessment, the psychologist asked his teacher if she had tried to use reinforcement to encourage Kevin to do his work. His teacher insisted that reinforcement just didn't work with Kevin; that she had tried to give him snacks, extra computer time, and classroom privileges for doing assignments—all to no avail. His teacher assumed incorrectly that these items (snacks, extra computer time and classroom privileges) would be powerful reinforcers for Kevin, when in actuality, under those circumstances at least, they were not. Avoiding math took precedence.

Applied behavior analysts generally use the term *reinforcement* to describe either *a natural event* (an increase in the rate of a given behavior as a result of an experience in which that behavior was followed by a reinforcing stimulus) or a *planned procedure* in which known reinforcing consequences are arranged to follow a response for the purpose of increasing the rate of that response. When applying reinforcement intentionally to increase responding, they systematically follow particular guidelines (described in further detail in Chapter 11).

Behavior ⟶ Something changed ⟶
Increase in the rate of that behavior

## DIFFERENCES BETWEEN REINFORCERS AND REINFORCEMENT PROCEDURES

To summarize, for our purposes, a **reinforcer** is *a specific stimulus, either the addition of which (positive reinforcer) or withdrawal of which (aversive stimulus) functions to increase or maintain the behavior upon which it is dependent.* A **reinforcement procedure** is *the change agent's planned presentation of positive reinforcers, or removal of aversive stimuli, as a consequence of a given response, for the explicit purpose of increasing or maintaining the rate of that response under similar circumstances.* Those applying reinforcement to achieve lasting change are wise to incorporate within their procedures a number of features known to influence the outcome. These include:

**Quality:** Selecting an array of stimuli that actually can be counted on to function as reinforcers under the present circumstances (Chapters 6, 9, and 10).

**Quantity:** Presenting an optimal quantity and/or intensity of those stimuli (not too much nor too little; Chapters 11 and 12).

**Immediacy:** Presenting the reinforcing stimuli right after the response (Chapters 11 and 12).

**Schedule:** Precisely scheduling how and when to present the stimuli (Chapters 22 and 23).

If you are explicitly planning to arrange reinforcers to the individual student's or client's advantage, you also need to understand how stimuli gain their reinforcing properties and to master particular methods for converting given stimuli into powerful reinforcers for them (see Chapter 6). But for now, let us more clearly differentiate between different types of reinforcers and reinforcement procedures.

>
> **Angela's Reinforcement Plan**
> Angela has decided to institute a family cooperation program. Three people, 7-year-old Jonathan, his 14-year-old sister, Heather, and Angela herself, are to be involved in changing their well-established but unacceptable behavior patterns. Angela realizes that she will need to identify stimuli (objects or events) that will function as reinforcers for each of them (including herself), especially when they are tired or hungry, or when they are tempted to do something else. Then she will need to design and follow through with a plan to see to it that those reinforcers are applied as intended.

## POSITIVE REINFORCERS AND POSITIVE REINFORCEMENT PROCEDURES DEFINED, ILLUSTRATED, AND DIFFERENTIATED

Earlier we mentioned that reinforcement includes two different types of consequences. One class consists of those that the individual *gains* as a consequence of emitting a behavior. They serve to increase or maintain the rate of that behavior. Technically speaking, we call *a stimulus a* **positive reinforcer** *if its contingent presentation increases responding.* Food, praise, monetary incentives, or symbolic items are typical examples. When incorporated within a positive reinforcement procedure, positive reinforcers are presented as a *consequence* of a response for the purpose of strengthening that response. As Daniels and Lattal (2017) point out, "positive reinforcement is to behavior as rocket fuel is to a rocket" (p. 58).

Notice how positive reinforcement is applied in a few illustrative studies: To reduce adolescents' smoking rates, Roll (2005) distributed vouchers, redeemable at a local department store, to those participants whose carbon monoxide levels met the criterion of < 6 ppm (indicating no recent cigarette smoking). Also, he awarded bonus vouchers of increasing value as a function of the number of days each abstained from smoking. 83 percent of the participants in that group continued to attend sessions. At one month post-intervention, 66 percent remained smoking abstinent. Apparently the vouchers were powerful reinforcers in that the number of days that the youths' carbon monoxide levels indicated continued abstention from smoking increased. (Later you will recognize this as a *differential reinforcement of other behavior*, or DRO procedure.)

Ortega and Fienup (2015) reported that a mother's verbal attention (e.g., praise) during *tummy time* (i.e., when the child is placed on his or her tummy to help develop muscle tone) improved her infant's behavior (e.g., less fussing and more head-raising) than when such attention was not provided. This strategy consisted not only of contingent but also non-contingent reinforcement (NCR). (See Chapter 27 to learn in more detail how NCR can be used to prevent and reduce unwanted behavior.)

In a study by Nuzzolo-Gomez et al. (2002), when teachers provided praise and edibles like pretzels and crackers to pre-school children with autism contingent on their engaging with books, the children increased the amount of time they spent with books and became less passive. Apparently attention, candy, pretzels, or popcorn also served as powerful reinforcers for play, in that the children spent more time playing with toys and less engaging in **stereotypy** (*the persistent and inappropriate repetitions of phrases, gestures, or acts*).

To support the training and exemplary performance of paraprofessionals in schools, Feldman and Matos (2012) used positive feedback to teach them to implement social facilitation procedures with children with autism. In a different application area, Grindle, Dickinson, and Boettcher (2000) reported how using incentives and/or feedback enhanced safe performance and/or reduced accidents in numerous work settings. Zerger, Miller, Valbuena, and Miltenberger, (2017) used a very simple reinforcing strategy to increase the physical activity levels of children, ages 9 to 12. After pairing students with high step counts (as recorded by a pedometer) with those with low step counts during recesses, they then encouraged the pairs to compete each day for the highest step count. As a result, the students increased their step counts considerably.

## NEGATIVE REINFORCERS AND AVERSIVE STIMULI DEFINED AND ILLUSTRATED

The second class consists of aversive stimuli. These are stimuli that an individual acts to remove as a consequence of behaving. **Aversive stimuli** are *those that people and other organisms attempt to avoid or from which to escape*; typically those associated with discomfort, pain, or unpleasantness: a frown, a noxious taste, a reprimand, and so on. *When a response increases or maintains its rate as a function of the termination, removal, reduction, or postponement of aversive stimuli,* we label the process **negative reinforcement**. Behaviors that stop, eliminate, or reduce such unpleasant stimuli as teasing, headaches, temper tantrums, criticism, or a literal or figurative itch are likely to be repeated under similar circumstance because they bring relief from those aversive stimuli.

The *negative reinforcement procedure* consists of the contingent removal of aversive teasing, ridiculing, headaches, criticism (etc.), because being relieved of those unpleasant conditions leads to an increase or maintenance in the rate of the response. (Note that in applied behavior analysis, the term "positive" means to *add* or *present* a stimulus, not necessarily a desirable or worthy consequence; the term "negative" refers to *subtracting*, *removing*, or *reducing*, in this case *diminishing* the intensity of an aversive stimulus. In negative reinforcement procedure, the manager removes aversive stimuli, like teasing, criticizing, or ridiculing, as a consequence of the target behavior, for the purpose of accelerating the rate of the target behavior. Although negative reinforce*ment* may involve an aversive stimulus, it is *not* defined as presenting an unwanted, or aversive stimulus as a consequence; that latter arrangement is called *punishment*.)

Experience teaches people to use aversive stimuli with or without being aware of doing so (in popular jargon, "consciously" or "unconsciously") as a tool for influencing others' behavior. After her boss, Eduardo, reprimands Kim's poor quality work, he observes that Kim's next few products conform more closely to quality standards. Because the reprimand worked successfully, Eduardo, subsequently tends to rebuke any of Kim's low quality work. Similarly, when physical abuse brings the abuser temporary relief from irritation the abusive behaviors are reinforced. Under such circumstances, the rate of abusing often escalates (unless the abuser's acts are immediately, consistently, and powerfully punished, as you will learn in Chapter 30).

Numerous instances of negative reinforcement can be seen in the research literature, particularly in reports of studies among populations of children who frequently display dangerous behavioral deficits or aberrations. Several investigators (e.g., Carr & Durand, 1985a; Weeks & Gaylord-Ross, 1981) found that some children increased their rates of self-abuse and aggression when assigned difficult tasks; Carr, Newsom, and Binkoff (1980) report that by resorting to aggression, boys successfully reduced or eliminated the demands placed upon them. In both cases, when task demands were removed, the rates of self-abuse and aggression diminished. Apparently ridding themselves of the annoying demands (the aversive stimuli) served to maintain or reinforce the abusive behaviors.

Koegel, Dyer, and Bell (1987) also suggested that negative reinforcement is responsible for many of the social-avoidance behaviors exhibited by learning-handicapped people. Examples are gaze aversion, head-banging, turning or moving away and blank expressions. Presumably, individuals whose repeated failure has been paired with a history of non-reinforcement learn that those acts of avoidance successfully terminate demanding social situations, thereby gaining them negative reinforcement. After Koegel et al. modified their teaching activities to permit youngsters with autism to share operational control, the youngsters began more often to engage successful social and learning situations.

Iwata et al. (1982) posited that sometimes self-injurious behavior (SIB) results from a history of positive reinforcement in the form of adult attention; at other times from reinforcement in the form of escape from adult demands or some other aversive stimulation. Kodak, Miltenberger, and Romaniuk (2003) demonstrated how escape from an aversive instructional task can be used successfully as a negative reinforcer for the absence of problem behavior. Whenever two four-year-old boys with autism did not engage in a problem behavior for gradually increasing time periods, they received a ten-second break. As a result, problem behaviors such as grabbing, throwing, pushing, scribbling on materials, and hitting were reduced substantially. Similarly, Voulgarakis, and Forte (2015) addressed the food refusal issues presented by an 8-year-old male with cerebral palsy. The child was allowed to exit the treatment area contingent upon the acceptance and ingestion of a pre-set number of bites. The requisite bite number gradually increased under this negative reinforcement contingency.

We caution you to resist the temptation to apply negative reinforcement as the sole intervention when attempting to reduce a problematic behavior. Rather, we encourage you to emphasize increasing productive behaviors that cannot co-exist with the unwanted behavior. Nonetheless, sometimes, lacking any viable constructive alternative methods, you may need to turn to negative reinforcement as a teaching device, as in a case in which Groskreutz, Groskreutz, Bloom, and Slocum (2014) taught children with autism to say "stop" to permit them to escape stimuli they found aversive (e.g., sound of a vacuum; crying, someone singing "Happy Birthday," a peer yelling, the sound of hair clippers, and an alarm clock).

## NEGATIVE REINFORCEMENT PROCEDURES DEFINED AND ILLUSTRATED

Whether occurring naturally or by design, negative reinforcement can be a powerful motivator. When the weather is cold, we run back inside or add extra clothing to escape our discomfort. Teachers might offer to reduce the length of a homework assignment contingent on the occurrence of a particular target such as the class achieving a certain average grade on a test. Consultants may establish themselves as sources of reinforcement for a teacher by removing or reducing disruptive behavior in a classroom.

Most organisms will work to escape unpleasant or painful (i.e., "aversive") stimuli. We can capitalize on that propensity by intentionally applying a **negative reinforcement procedure**; that is, one in which *the change agent arranges intentionally to remove or reduce ongoing aversive stimulation, as a consequence of a particular desired response, for the purpose of strengthening that response.*

Note the application of the negative reinforcement procedure in the following examples: Jorge has been working diligently on a set of problems he finds unpleasant. After he completes ten of the difficult problems correctly, his teacher allows him a short break from doing the problems. After his break Jorge returns and rapidly resumes the work once again. Billy used to cover his ears and scream when recorded music was played, but rarely did that at other times. Apparently he found music aversive. Later, he was taught to work while music played by means of negative reinforcement in that his teachers terminated the music contingent to his working for gradually increasing periods of time during which he did not disrupt (Buckley & Newchok, 2006).

Table 5.3 summarizes, illustrates, and contrasts positive and negative reinforcement.[4]

## ESCAPE AND AVOIDANCE DEFINED AND DIFFERENTIATED

Taking action to avoid or escape from aversive stimuli like frowns, bitter tastes, extra assignments, or temper tantrums is natural. No one needs to teach us to do that. We cover our ears when assaulted by a painfully loud sound; pull our hand away from a hot stove; come in from the freezing cold or searing heat. The employee who quits his job because his boss is "constantly on his case" or the student who hangs back from the group to stop their teasing is

---

[4]To help you determine how well you understand these two procedures, review the examples on the web page associated with this text and decide whether positive or negative reinforcement is operating.

**TABLE 5.3  Positive and Negative Reinforcement Defined and Illustrated**

| Term | Operation Producing Rate Increase | Function/Effect | Example |
|---|---|---|---|
| Positive Reinforcement | The individual gains a positive reinforcer (something s/he "wants" to have or do at the time) as a consequence or function of the behavior.<br><br>Behavior →Reinforcer may be abbreviated like this:<br>**R**(esponse)→**S**$^r$<br>Some use the following abbreviations:<br>**B**(ehavior)→**S**$^r$<br>or (**R**$^+$) | ***Increases* or *maintains*** the rate of the behavior on which the reinforcer is contingent (or dependent). | When Francisco brings flowers to Joanna, she hugs and kisses him. Francisco brings Joanna flowers more and more frequently.<br><br>Kim learns to give her kitty expensive canned food because when the cat receives that kind of food, she runs to her bowl and quickly gobbles it up, which pleases Kim. Kim now gives her kitty that brand almost all the time. |
| Negative Reinforcement | A stimulus that the individual finds aversive or unpleasant (that s/he does "not want" to have or do) is withdrawn as a function of the behavior. Behavior→Aversive stimulus removed. May be abbreviated like this:<br>Behavior→(**S**$^{r-}$ **removed** )<br>Or<br>**B**(ehavior)→**S**$^{r-}$ (or **R-removed**)<br>Response (behavior) leads to removal of the aversive stimulus. | ***Increases* or *maintains*** the rate of the behavior on which the removal of the aversive stimulus is contingent. | When Francisco says cajolingly "Aw honey, don't look at me that way," Joanna stops scowling at him. Francisco learns to sweet-talk Joanna out of her scowls.<br><br>When kitty meows pitifully, Kim rushes to feed her to stop the meows. Kitty does stop meowing once fed (and begins to purr). Kim learns to feed kitty more and more rapidly once she returns home. |

engaging in **escape behavior** (*actions that reduce or remove aversive stimulation*). Eventually, experience may teach them other more efficient and effective ways to prevent or avoid those sorts of noxious stimuli.

We learn to dress in accordance with weather conditions, wear oven mitts when handling hot pans, or wear ear plugs along to a KoRn rock concert to avoid aversive stimuli. Avoidance behavior is similar, but not identical to escape behavior. **Avoidance** describes a class of behavior that succeeds in *postponing* or *circumventing* an aversive stimulus. Unlike *punishment,* which subjects recipients to aversive stimuli from which they try to escape, as Hineline (1984, p. 204) clarifies, *avoidance* permits them, to "prevent or postpone aversive stimulation rather than to remove it" in the first place. Avoiding a nagging spouse by working late at the office, taking a dare to shun ridicule from one's peers, or cutting class to avoid taking an exam illustrate that subtle but important difference. Another example of differentiating escape behavior from avoidance can be seen in Figure 5.1.

Often the puzzling behaviors our children, clients, students, employees, friends, and relatives *emit,* or express, permit them to avoid or terminate events aversive for them. Considering whether any particular actions enable people (or other organisms)

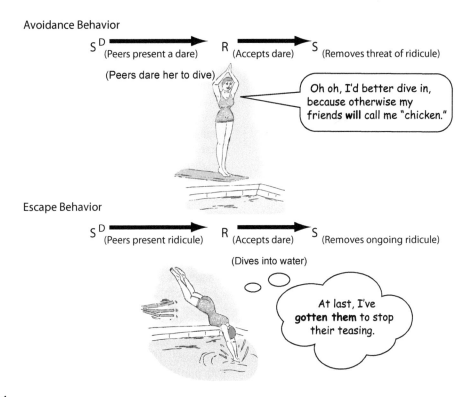

**Figure 5.1**

to avoid or escape some sort of aversive situation may help us understand why those behaviors are continuing and what actions we can take to avoid that trap. For instance, individuals often acquire annoying habits that eliminate the discomfort stemming from others' unrealistic or unwanted demands of them. Generally they develop those habits through negative reinforcement. Perhaps Oscar has learned to hide from his boss to avoid extra assignments. Angela may find herself agreeing to prepare dinner for Heather and Jonathan, because it frees her from their complaints. What, however, does Mom's capitulation teach Heather and Jonathan? If they sulk or complain they will still get dinner—a positive reinforcer for them. And the pattern can transfer or *generalize* to other situations. While shopping with her mom, Heather sees a pair of shoes she really covets. She sulks until her mom buys them for her. Their mutual histories of negative reinforcement have taught Heather to sulk and Angela to indulge her daughter. Some have suggested that substance abuse may be maintained by the individual avoiding the symptoms accompanying withdrawal (Blume, 2001).

## Using Escape as a Negative Reinforcer

Permitting escape from aversive conditions often serves a reinforcing function. For example, you can take a break as soon as you finish X amount of the assignment. Similarly, investigators (Rogalski, Roscoe, Fredericks, & Mezhoudi, 2020) achieved compliance with children 5 to 13 with autism. Along with positive reinforcement for compliance, success was achieved by using a larger escape magnitude for compliance relative to their problem behaviors (e.g., 240-second escape for compliance and only 10-secs of escape for problem behaviors). By combining larger escape periods than those achieved by the problem behavior along with positive reinforcement for compliance, success was achieved. A shorter magnitude of escape (10 seconds vs. 90) was not effective. Thus, as Rogalski, et al. point out, "Providing larger escape magnitudes for compliance relative to problem behavior may facilitate treatment involving concurrent-reinforcement schedules for escape-maintained problem behavior" (p. 1514).

## DIFFERENTIATING POSITIVE FROM NEGATIVE REINFORCERS

Despite our subjective impressions that a stimulus must be pleasant or unpleasant, we only can accurately label a stimulus as a reinforcer or a punisher after monitoring its influence on the behavior upon which it has been contingent. If the subsequent rate of the behavior has *increased* as a function of experiencing a particular consequence (the rate of the behavior increases when a stimulus is either added [positive reinforcement] or subtracted [negative reinforcement]) then that stimulus is a reinforcer. If the *rate has decreased as a function of experiencing the consequence* (either a stimulus is added or removed), it is a **punisher** (also called "aversive stimulus"). (These conditions are analogous to those we have discussed earlier; that is, how *presenting* praise, attention, smiles, recognition, or other positive reinforcers, or *removing* aversive stimuli, such as frowns or reprimands, dependent or contingent on a behavior, and that typically result in an increase or maintenance of the rate of the behavior, are instances of *reinforcement*.)

In the language of the layperson, *negative reinforcement* often is confused with *punishment*. Permit us to alert you to some of the essential differences between those two. By definition, in *reinforcement*, whether positive or negative, the organism experiences consequences contingent on a behavior that generate an *increase* in the subsequent rate of the behavior, while in **punishment**, as described in Chapter 2 (also see Chapters 30 & 31), the organism's behavioral rate *decreases* as a function *of the consequences it has experienced contingent on that behavior*. Remember, then, that *punishment decreases behavior*, while *reinforcement*, (whether gaining individuals positive reinforcement or permitting them to escape from negative consequences) *increases behavior*.

Recognize, though, by contrast, that both negative reinforcement and punishment involve aversive events like scolding, complaining, disrupting, crying, or other painful or uncomfortable irritants. When, for example, a nurse discovered her aide reading a magazine instead of tending to the patients, the nurse reprimanded the aide, who then returned to her assigned task. The nurse's reprimand terminated the aide's magazine reading, qualifying it to be labeled an *aversive stimulus* or *punisher*. When a behavior *weakens* (stops or diminishes) as a function of its having experienced an aversive stimulus, we say that the behavior was *punished*. (Remember, though, that what one person finds aversive actually may appeal to another and vice versa.)

By contrast, as discussed earlier, when a behavior *strengthens* (accelerates or continues) as a function of the *subtraction* or *removal* of an aversive stimulus, we say the behavior was *negatively reinforced*. (*Reminder*: Don't confuse this term with punishment! Negative reinforcement promotes *increases* in behavioral rates, while punishment promotes *decreases* in behavioral rates.) How was the *nurse* affected by censuring the aide? The irritation of seeing the aide "goofing off" disappeared. In other words, chiding the aide *worked* (at least for the moment). Despite resolving to handle her staff amicably, the nurse may be more likely to scold the aide next time should she encounters a similar situation, because her reprimand was negatively reinforced. To recapitulate: *negative reinforcement* involves the contingent **removal** *of an aversive stimulus*, while *punishment* involves the *contingent* **presentation** *of the aversive stimulus*. Should the woman preparing to dive depicted below actually follow through but land in a painful belly-flop, she might very well refuse to try again. We would say that her diving had been punished.

Consider the following illustration to heighten your confidence in your ability to differentiate among negative reinforcement, punishment, and positive reinforcement:

- Every time Sue passes Harry's desk, he pats her on the rear. Sue's protests seem only to encourage him further. So one day just as he reaches up to pat her, Sue "accidentally" spills her coffee all over Harry's paperwork. Harry withdraws his hand and the next time Sue walks by with her coffee, he resists the temptation to pat her.

- ° Why is Sue likely to carry a cup of coffee with her the next time she has to pass Harry's desk? Because spilling coffee terminated the aversive pats.
- ° What stopped Harry's unwanted touching? Punishment! In the future he resists patting Sue.

Notice that instead of *trusting* that a given method will work, we need carefully to observe the actual effects our intervention may be having. Sometimes an attempt backfires, the way Sue's protests did. The same sort of thing can happen with intended punishment—reprimanding, for instance. Sometimes a public reprimand can have a reinforcing effect, while a private one can have a punishing influence. To illustrate, O'Leary, Kaufman, Kass, and Drabman (1970) observed students disrupting in five classes. They found that when reprimands were loud enough for other students to hear, the rate of disruption *increased*. When reprimands were audible only to the students to whom they were directed, the rate *diminished*. We surmise that quiet reprimands served as punishers, whereas public reprimands gained students sufficiently reinforcing peer attention to override the reprimand's punishing aspects.

## ARE POSITIVE AND NEGATIVE REINFORCEMENT REALLY DIFFERENT?

Though Skinner (1953) and his colleagues made a distinction between negative and positive reinforcement, some professionals question whether or not those terms should be preserved (Baron & Galizio, 2005; Michael, 1975). Occasionally people experience difficulty discriminating between the two. Suppose a person is cold and requests and receives a warm coat: is this positively reinforcing because warmth was added, or negatively reinforcing because feeling cold was alleviated, or is it both? Is a sexual orgasm positively reinforcing because it adds a pleasurable sensation, or is it negatively reinforcing because it reduces tension, or a combination of the two? Is eating positively reinforcing because it tastes good, or negatively reinforcing because it reduces a hunger, or is it the two combined? Is attention reinforcing, or is it relief from feeling ignored? Is it escape from an aversive assignment, or the access to an alternative activity that reinforces a client's aggression? Is watching television a (positively) reinforcing event or is it negative reinforcement derived by escaping from boredom, housework, or other responsibilities? Baron and Galizio (2005) and Chase (2006) have contended that positive reinforcement and negative reinforcement essentially are two sides of the same coin. Others argue that the two are not always combined, and when they are, one facet takes precedence over the other (Iwata, 2006; Sidman, 2006). Because more recently, the field of neurobiology has discovered that neural pathways are distinctively different under each set of conditions (i.e., Egervari, 2016) we tend to align with those considering the two as separate.

Beyond the ambiguity of whether positive and negative reinforcement are functionally the same or different, other issues remain unresolved. Does reinforcement tend to be more effective when negative and positive reinforcement are combined? Is arranging deprivation a way of combining negative reinforcement with positive reinforcement, rather than an operation that establishes a particular stimulus as a reinforcer?

The authors of this text also agree with Baron and Galizio (2005, p. 96) who conclude: "the distinction is so well embedded within discussions of operant behavior that one cannot navigate the literature without being familiar with it" (i.e., the two reinforcement procedures). In addition, as opposed to fundamental processes, the procedures involved in the two operations are different because one—negative reinforcement—would involve identifying and/or arranging for an ongoing aversive condition, avoidance or escape from which would be reinforcing, while the other—positive reinforcement—only depends on adding a positive or "desired" stimulus or event.

## IS APPLYING NEGATIVE REINFORCEMENT ADVISABLE?

If negative reinforcement is an effective method for increasing behavior, how justified are change agents in using it as a tool? To answer this question, let us first review the procedure. For negative reinforcement to work, aversive stimulation must be ongoing or noticeably imminent. In this case, reinforcement consists of removing or preventing the aversive stimulus contingent on the emission of the desired behavior. As we show in more detail in Chapters 30 and 31 on punishment, however, aversive stimuli tend to promote undesirable behavioral side effects like escape, avoidance, and aggression (Adrian & Holz, 1966). Jim skips school, thereby avoiding assignments he finds too daunting. Fred tunes out his father's scolding by thinking about other things; Myrna punches the girl next to her when the teacher doesn't permit her to join the others at recess until she completes her assignment; Bob scratches a nasty message on the bathroom door after his boss chewed him out. That kind of aggressive reaction to aversive conditions happens fairly frequently, not only on an interpersonal but also on a group and even the world level, as in cases in which heads of state lob angry threats at one another.

The ongoing aversive stimuli essential to negative reinforcement also can promote new forms of unwanted behavior. Staff working in disagreeable surroundings may begin to increase their number of sick days, during which they become addicted to computer games; students to use their time away from school to experiment with drugs or other antisocial activities.

Recognize, nevertheless, that negative reinforcement can be a powerful motivator, as when people accept challenges to avoid or escape peer derision: learning new skills like skiing, diving into a pool from the high-diving board, riding a bicycle, driving a car, or initiating bad habits or destructive acts like smoking, abusing drugs, and stealing. (Of course, many bad habits probably continue as a function of both negative and positive reinforcement.) Under rare circumstances, perhaps in health-related and life-threatening situations, you may need to tap this source, as when the most powerful positive reinforcers you can arrange are insufficient to produce a crucial change.

Allen and Stokes (1987) found that "simply providing a prize contingent on cooperative behavior during [dental] treatment was insufficient to reduce the disruptive behavior of children" (p. 388). They then taught the children to lie still and be quiet by using frequent, brief rest periods (escape), plus attention, contingent on cooperative behavior. Those interruptions were reduced gradually until the children ultimately experienced the natural escape of the end of the session. In a related study with five children in a dental office, simply allowing them a brief escape periodically, not necessarily contingent on their behavior, substantially reduced disruptions. In addition, the dental staff's use of physical restraint was reduced to near zero across all five children (O'Callaghan, Allen, Powell, & Salama, 2006). Comparable results were achieved with several youngsters on the autism spectrum when brief opportunities to play were interspersed along with the escape contingencies in a related case (Soucy, Pardi, Kay & Sulzer-Azaroff, unpublished).

Negative reinforcement often functions as a natural motivator, accounting for such behaviors as receiving immunizations or taking medicine (to avoid or recover from an illness), using air conditioning (to escape from oppressive heat), using birth control (to prevent unwanted pregnancy), and numerous others. In addition, both forms of reinforcement sometimes can be used in combination to accelerate change. Consider this case: A junior high school teacher found student tardiness during first period a cause for concern. On inquiry, he discovered that instead of arriving on time, students wandered the halls "looking for action" before coming to class. According to school rules, tardy marks were noted on report cards and students receiving five such marks would be expelled. When the teacher realized that many had earned three or four marks within the first quarter of the school year, he adjusted the program to one incorporating negative reinforcement, in the form of removing one tardy mark from his record book for each week during which a student was punctual every day. He combined this with positive reinforcement: complimenting timely arrivals: "I sure am glad to see you made it here on time today."

"You are becoming a responsible class." "Joe, you *really* have improved. Let's cross off another of these checks. Soon you won't have any." "You are doing so well as a class, let's have ten minutes of free time." The program worked successfully. After all the checks had been removed, the students continued to come to class on time. Punctuality apparently was strengthened initially by the combination of negative and positive reinforcement but eventually maintained by social and natural (non-contrived) reinforcers.

*Note:* In most cases, effectively applying positive reinforcement (as described in detail in Chapters 6 and 11) will be sufficient to promote the behavioral changes you seek. Consequently hereafter, when we use the terms *reinforcer* and *reinforcement,* unless we refer specifically *to negative reinforcement*, you should assume we are referring to *positive reinforcement.*

## COMMON CONCERNS OR DISADVANTAGES WITH USING REINFORCEMENT

In our experience, sometimes change agents unfamiliar with the field of applied behavior analysis raise concerns about the purposeful use of reinforcement. Addressing such issues as they arise is important. Otherwise those agents may fail to apply the procedures correctly, if at all. Below, we list and analyze some of the more common concerns.

### Use of Contrived Reinforcers

What does distributing a cookie or a trinket have to do with improving performance on the job or in the classroom? Maybe very little. Actually, whenever possible, we try to use reinforcers that are a behavior's inherent function, because those conditions tend to support its maintenance. Supplying entertaining reading material provides skilled readers the natural consequences of reading. Obtaining a desired object by describing or asking for it by name is a natural consequence of increased language proficiency. A warm, comfortable shelter is the reinforcer for building a cabin in the woods; a well-manicured landscape the reward for mowing the lawn. If natural reinforcers control their related performances, does introducing contrived extrinsic reinforcers into the system makes sense? Maybe once in a while, to sustain worthy actions, but, in general, not a whole lot. We suggest you reserve using *contrived reinforcers when natural consequences fail sufficiently to reinforce specifically targeted actions.* Greene and Lepper have stated, "Many important and potentially interesting activities, including for example, reading, may seem like drudgery rather than fun until one has acquired a few rudimentary skills. There is no question, therefore, that extrinsic motivation is often needed to get people to do things they wouldn't do without it" (1974, p. 50). But after reaching a sufficiently high level of proficiency as readers, interesting contents alone can be sufficient to keep us going.

Krumboltz and Krumboltz made a similar point: "For many types of behavior which ultimately bring their own reward, the initial reinforcer is merely a temporary expedient to get the behavior started. Sometimes a shift from a concrete reward to a less tangible one is a step toward gradually helping the child become independent of external rewards" (1972, pp. 111–112). According to Mayer, "The goal of any reinforcement program should be to help individuals become less and less dependent on material or other contrived reinforcers. However, programs must start where individuals are and gradually help them move up the developmental ladder" (2000, p. 14).

Seeman (1994) has defended using extrinsic rewards because "developmentally (and over simplifying), children are first motivated by extrinsic rewards (food, toys), then emotional rewards (approval, grades), and finally, if they attain this, intrinsic rewards (a feeling of pride, self-satisfaction, enjoying it for its own sake)." At times, then, when access to other social or activity stimuli fail sufficiently to motivate the behaviors you are seeking, you may find that dispensing edibles or trinkets contingent on progressive steps toward the desired response promotes success for some students.

## Unwanted Side-Effects of Reinforcement

Is reinforcement in and of itself good, bad, or indifferent? Probably your immediate response is to say "Good, of course." We know that reinforcement supports learning and as a *process* also produces good feelings (which neurobiologists now tell us are evoked by the release of various chemicals in the brain; see Bamford et al, 2004). But producing good feelings is only a portion of our concerns as behavior-change agents. Rather, we had best view the big picture.

What reinforcement does is to *condition*—that is, to promote and maintain (or in the language of evolutionary biology, *select*) particular classes of behavior. Values such as *good* (*wanted*) or *bad* (*unwanted*) are irrelevant to the reinforcement *process*. Where issues of value do arise is when we intentionally harness the power of reinforcement by designing and implementing reward procedures to achieve particular purposes. Then we had better be careful, because we may get more or less than we bargained for.

As a case in point, Balsam and Bondy (1983) have discussed research findings warning us that delivery of rewards may promote a variety of stereotypic and addictive behaviors. Additionally, presenting reinforcing stimuli may elicit responses that compete with that (or those) targeted for the client or student, as in the case of displaying a coveted toy or food item which, in turn, evokes staring at or reaching for the item, or even continuously tracking the dispenser of those reinforcers. Those authors also have reminded us that in situations in which certain responses are very heavily reinforced, other desired responses may begin to dissipate locally or generally. Consequently, they wisely advise that we monitor other desirable but non-targeted responses along with those responses that interfere with therapeutic goals (as they later clarify in Balsam & Bondy, 1985), and that we adjust reinforcement schedules accordingly. They also suggest we design our interventions to include *all the circumstances* under which each of the desired responses are to occur, lest they become limited to when the change program is in effect.

As you will learn later, all other factors being equal, punishment often produces a more rapid behavioral change than positive reinforcement, but its own side effects may be especially detrimental. Nonetheless, as just indicated, positive reinforcement is not without its ethical drawbacks, as in a given case in which its relatively slower impact fails to delay or remedy dangerous situations. These aspects must be carefully considered when planning behavioral-change strategies.

## Bribery

Isn't using reinforcers a form of bribery? *No!* Bribery has no place in managing the behaviors of others, because by definition, bribery often is used to corrupt conduct, pervert judgment, and to promote dishonest or immoral behavior. It also serves primarily to benefit the person offering the bribe, not the recipient, and usually involves artificial or contrived rewards that bear little relation to the act. Additionally, bribes are tendered before the act, whereas reinforcement occurs afterward. Further, functionally, when children are bribed, they often learn subsequently to comply only when a bribe has been offered.

By contrast, applied behavior analysts attempt to use reinforcers in as natural a form as feasible. We see these strategies as benefiting the individuals whom we serve. Also, we reinforce actions the community supports, with the kinds of events that we experience in our own everyday lives: praise, recognition, and material rewards. How long would you continue working at your job if you received no consequences, such as recognition or remuneration, for your actions? Why should the individuals we treat be expected to be any different? Reinforcement helps improve people's view of their own worth and makes learning enjoyable. Punitive or non-reinforcing environments, on the other hand, do the opposite: promote negative self-attributions and encourage escape and aggression. What kind of environment do you want to provide for those whose performance you are responsible?

We must concern ourselves more with *what is* rather than what *should be*, within, of course, ethical and humanitarian constraints. Arranging formal reinforcing events is unnecessary if, for example, our clients or subordinates are performing satisfactorily and their progress seems to be supported adequately by the natural consequences. Instead, we would continue to praise and recognize their accomplishments intermittently, as merited. If, rather, they are not performing satisfactorily, then implementing a reinforcement program to teach or improve that performance might be advisable.

## Treating People Differently

Given that each person's learning history is unique, may it be necessary to treat some differently from others? Certainly it will, especially if you are unable to identify a sufficiently potent reinforcer common among all members of the group. Realize, though, that we already do treat people differently when we attend to troublesome behavior. Some gain more attention than their peers; others are granted allowance for their different skill levels. Would seating a member of the audience with a vision or hearing problem in the front of the auditorium, in essence granting that privilege, be fair to the others? Because everyone possesses unique genetic, learning, and experiential histories, individuals may respond distinctively to particular circumstances. What do you think? Is treating individuals differently always unfair? We think *not*. Are we responsible for acting identically toward everyone? If we were to treat each person the same, wouldn't we be denying the reality of individual differences? Accepting the distinct uniqueness of each person underscores the postulate that: "nothing is more inequitable than the equal treatment of un-equals."

Still, many remain concerned about jealousy, especially when group members see others receive special reinforcers. That is a reasonable issue; but, because each group is different, we have no simple answer. Yet, ponder the following:

1. Often the peers of a misbehaving individual share a sense of relief when help is finally on the way. The peers may have been victims of the person's difficulties and recognize that they stand to benefit from the special intervention. Sometimes it helps to identify this benefit to the members of the group and reinforce their supportive efforts, as Christy (1975) discovered when working with two classes of children, ages three-and-a-half to six years.

2. By explaining that each person is unique and that each of us has special interests, skills, and areas of weakness (yourself included), often peers will understand that it makes sense to focus on changing different behaviors by using different methods. ("*Different strokes for different folks*.")

3. Use special reinforcers for *progress* so that everyone stands to improve in some way. If a few complain that someone is getting special privileges, consider broadening your reinforcement program to include the others by finding and addressing their particular areas of strength and weakness. Or ask those others to identify some skills they feel they would like to sharpen, and initiate a similar program for them. In fact, why not, at least intermittently reinforce all behaviors we want to increase, especially when the reinforcer is free?

4. Sometimes, too, the individual currently involved in the program can earn the special activity or item(s) not only for him or herself, but for the group as a whole, as in a *dependent group contingency* (about which you will learn more in Chapter 12).

## Loss of Intrinsic Motivation (The "Overjustification Effect")

As you can imagine, anyone whose main concern is to enable people to accomplish their own constructive aims and those of their families, communities, workplaces, and broader societies certainly would want to avoid recommending procedures counter to those aims. Rather, they would want to defend what they teach by facing and successfully refuting unjustified criticism. This was the perspective taken by applied behavior analysts and others implementing scientifically and ethically sound approaches to promoting effective behavior-change strategies when their methods came under attack. The story goes back to the early 1970s, when Lepper, Greene, and Nisbett (1973) used a pre-test/

post-test design to evaluate the effects of extrinsic rewards on the "intrinsic motivation" of preschool children. The youngsters were divided into three groups: an unexpected reward condition; an expected reward condition; and a control condition. During the pre-test, participants were observed drawing with markers. Those who colored at relatively high rates were selected to participate in the experiment. During the experimental condition, participants in the *unexpected reward* group simply were given a "good player" award at the end of the session, while the *expected reward* group was told ahead of time that if the members drew the whole time they would earn a "good player" award, and the *control* group earned nothing. During the post-test, the experimenter made drawing materials available and measured the rate at which the children elected to draw. Results indicated that children in the expected reward group spent less time drawing during the post-test condition compared to the other two groups. Lepper et al. (1973) coined this phenomenon as the "**overjustification effect**."

Seizing upon this finding, in 1993 Kohn published a book entitled *Punished by Rewards*, in which he argued that rewards were destroying the overall motivation of society. The basic premise behind his assertion was that receiving expected, extrinsic, tangible rewards reduces intrinsic motivation. He called for the elimination of any type of artificial reward in such settings as schools, work environments, and homes. However, research has failed to support this position. Since then, over 100 published empirical investigations have been conducted and published on the overjustification effect. True, "negative effects are found on high-interest tasks when the rewards are tangible, expected (offered beforehand), and loosely tied to level of performance" (Cameron, Banko, & Pierce, 2001, p. 1). (Who, though, we wonder, would offer extra rewards to people for engaging in tasks they already perform at high rates under naturally ongoing contingencies?) Rather, in ABA, when conditions call for the use of extrinsic reinforcers to shape and increase behavior, such detrimental effects have not been detected (Cameron, 2001; Cameron et al., 2001; Cameron & Pierce, 1994; Levy, et al., 2017). *In fact*, researchers have concluded that "*reward contingencies do not have pervasive negative effects on intrinsic motivation*" (Cameron et al., 2001, p. 1).

Research on this topic has highlighted how procedural or methodological differences play a role in the use of reinforcement and its long-term effects. When appropriate reinforcers are provided contingent on either low- or high-interest tasks, they generally produce positive effects on free choice and motivation. We suggest that critics of the use of reinforcement examine the science-based guidelines for its application (see Chapter 11) and the thousands of positive and benign research-based results they have produced.

## SUMMARY AND CONCLUSIONS

In this chapter we have acquainted you with the terms *positive reinforcers, positive reinforcement, aversive stimuli* and *negative reinforcement* and explained how they function and resemble and differ from one another and other classes of stimuli. You also learned that both positive and negative reinforcement can occur simultaneously, and that determining which one is responsible for promoting the more powerful effect can be unclear. In general, though, when positive reinforcers are added and aversive stimuli subtracted, dependent upon a particular behavior, that behavior tends to increase. On the whole, positive reinforcement is preferable to negative, because, beyond its main influence—strengthening behavior—it often promotes desirable side effects. Nonetheless, positive reinforcement is no panacea. We need to monitor and intervene should we note any accompanying increases in competing, stereotypic, and addictive behaviors, or decreases in the individual's rates of appropriate responding.

A thorough knowledge of what reinforcement is and how it works is fundamental to understanding the behavior people (and other organisms) emit and to becoming competent in changing it. In this chapter, you were introduced to the concept of reinforcement, to common concerns[5] about its use and to reasonable responses to its critics' and skeptics' concerns. Anyone applying behavior analytic procedures must be prepared to alleviate the

---

[5] See our web page for additional discussions of other common concerns

apprehensions of parents, colleagues, supervisors, other professionals, and members of the community. Your ability to do so may thwart opposition to or interference with the execution and maintenance of the program as designed.

In this chapter you learned that reinforcement is the fuel for operant (learned) behavior. In the next chapter you will learn how reinforcers evolve naturally, how to identify them, how intentionally to support their development, and how to tailor those reinforcers to the needs and circumstances facing the particular individuals involved. After that, in Chapters 7 through 10, you will discover how to identify, record, and analyze the impact of elusive reinforcers currently in operation. Chapter 11 then presents key rules for implementing reinforcement procedures effectively to promote particular behaviors, while Chapter 12 discusses various methods for implementing reinforcement-based procedures designed to address challenges facing people operating within groups.

*Chapter 6*

# Increasing Behavior by Developing and Selecting Powerful Reinforcers

## Goals

1. Define and illustrate *primary (unconditioned or unconditional) reinforcers* and *primary (unconditioned or unconditional) aversive stimuli*.
2. Define and illustrate *secondary* or *learned reinforcers* and *aversive stimuli*.
3. Define and illustrate how to develop *secondary* or *learned reinforcers*.
4. Define *generalized reinforcers* and illustrate how they are developed.
5. Identify and illustrate each of the *four major classes* of reinforcers.
6. Identify and illustrate *automatic reinforcers*.
7. Differentiate between *functional* and *arbitrary reinforcers*.
8. Illustrate and be prepared to use reinforcer surveys and reports.
9. Describe and illustrate the similarities and differences between observation-based versus selection-based assessments.
10. Illustrate and be prepared to conduct *reinforcer-preference* or *choice assessments* (RPAs) including duration based, single-stimulus, paired-stimulus, and multiple-stimulus assessments.
11. Define and discuss how *motivating* or *establishing operations* and *response deprivation* influence reinforcer selection.
12. Discuss what may influence an individual's unique preferences for particular stimuli besides prior learning histories.

13. Define and illustrate the meaning of *deprivation* and the *response deprivation hypothesis*.
14. Define and illustrate the *Premack principle*.
15. Illustrate and discuss the importance of:
    a. selecting a *variety* of reinforcers
    b. incorporating *novelty* into reinforcer selection
    c. using *reinforcer sampling* in reinforcer selection
    d. selecting *effective sources* of reinforcer delivery

\*\*\*\*\*\*\*\*\*\*\*\*\*

You have just given a presentation to the members of your team describing your success with a particularly challenging case. Your teammates applaud and your supervisor flashes you a thumbs up. Later, when you return to your office, you discover a couple of notes pinned to your bulletin board: "Excellent!" "Great Job!"

You are floating on air. Why do those extrinsic consequences make you feel so good? Apparently, they have reinforcing value for your behavior. But are such events universally reinforcing? Would they work as well with people who don't speak our language or know our culture? How about little babies, strangers, or the chairman of the board?

In this chapter, you will learn how stimuli such as applause, a thumbs-up, or another gesture, or a congratulatory note that in and of themselves were originally neutral, gain their reinforcing properties. Additionally, we will teach you about particular tactics you can use to transform neutral stimuli into powerful reinforcers for your associates and clientele or students. You also will learn how to select highly effective reinforcers for individuals in general, because what is reinforcing to one person may not be reinforcing to another. This will enable you to arrange reinforcers explicitly to the advantage of your client(s).

## HOW DOES A STIMULUS DEVELOP INTO A REINFORCER?

### Primary or Unconditioned Reinforcers and Aversive Stimuli

Previously, we talked about reinforcers and reinforcement, the essential ingredients of applied behavior analysis. Reinforcement is essential to the survival of most living organisms, enabling them to learn and change in ways essential to maintaining their existence, thriving, and reproducing. Yet, as we have mentioned, what is reinforcing for one individual's behavior at one time and place may not be for the behavior of a different person, or even for the same person under different conditions. For example, Mary may find praise delivered in private quite reinforcing but aversive in public. Perhaps you are curious about how such differences come to pass. The answer is through learning: both natural and planned.

From the very beginning, new organisms, human or otherwise, are born hardwired, in a sense, to respond to particular stimuli in predictable ways. You learned in Chapter 2 that some responses (reflexes) may occur independent of reinforcement. For example, when a human's patellar tendon is tapped, the leg kicks forward. Even without guidance or experience, infants orient toward or grasp those humans connected with food and physical comfort, and often loudly and forcefully reject or attempt to escape from others connected with pain and discomfort. If they didn't, their chances of survival would be lower. In fact, babies only minutes old when placed upon their mother's abdomen will crawl unassisted and root until they reach their mother's nipple to nurse. But other responses continue only as a function of the reinforcers they provide. These are the behaviors we call "learned." New forms of responding—those that produce reinforcing consequences (e.g., comfort or escape), are likely to be repeated under similar conditions. This second type of behavior is termed *operant*, because it works or operates on the environment. (Refer back to Chapter 2 to refresh yourself about the distinction between respondent and operant behavior).

Some consequences, termed **primary** (or **unconditioned**) **positive reinforcers** *function as reinforcers the very first time they occur*. That is, the first time the consequence occurs contingent on a given response, the rate of that response increases or is maintained at some higher level. This concept resembles the term "peak performance." Examples are: nourishment for a food-deprived individual, liquids for the fluid-deprived, warmth for one who is chilled, and so on. Physical discomfort, hunger pangs, and unpleasant noises exemplify **primary** (or **unconditioned**) **aversive stimuli**, *the cessation or prevention of which is reinforcing, regardless of prior learning (i.e., negative reinforcement)*. Primary reinforcers probably hold survival value for individuals and their species. Organisms who fail to find nourishment or avoid harmful events will perish. If acts of procreation were not reinforcing, the species would become extinct. In other words, *primary reinforcers function to promote and sustain the life/evolution of the individual*. So to endure, organisms must have the capacity to obtain reinforcers from key sources, and this propensity probably, at least in part, is inherited.

## Secondary or Learned (Conditioned[1]) Reinforcers

Stimuli that *acquire their reinforcing properties only as a function of events in the individual's life* are called **secondary** or **learned** (conditioned) **reinforcers**. Yes, a secondary reinforcer is *an initially neutral stimulus which has acquired reinforcing properties for the individual's behavior because of its relation to, or association with, strong primary or secondary reinforcers*. Secondary reinforcers develop as a result of the individual's particular learning history. Once secondary reinforcers become solidly established, they gain the capacity to strengthen the behavior on which they are contingent. For example, pairing, or contiguously presenting, praise (a mom saying "You're such a good girl") with primary reinforcers (while stroking her baby's cheek when she nurses) can transform the praise into a secondary reinforcer for that individual's behavior.

For these reliably to influence behavior, specific conditions and events must have been appropriately related in the person's history. Without that learning history, such stimuli exert little influence on what the person does. For example, a teacher telling a child she is a good girl for doing her class work will not be likely to act as a reinforcer if the child has never learned that the words "good girl" accompany good things (such as food and comfort). Likewise, receiving a winning lottery ticket or a traffic ticket in the mail will have little effect if a person has neither seen nor heard of such objects. Soon you will learn why.

People's (and other animals') learning histories are critically important to their individual behavioral repertoires, because each one's history is unique. A given consequence can affect the behavior of each in a distinctly different way. Newborn Tina's parents feed, hold, and cuddle her, using certain gestures and vocal tones. When pleased with her actions they praise her, "Good girl." Over time, the gestures, tones, words, and other events or stimuli that have frequently accompanied food, comfort, or other strong reinforcers are transformed into secondary reinforcers for Tina. Greg's family may be too occupied with other matters to spend much time talking to him and may rarely use the phrase "Good boy," so "Good boy" never develops into a reinforcer for Greg, and the words have little impact when his teachers say it.

How do tangible items evolve into secondary reinforcers for an individual? Consider the way pennies, gift certificates, or coupons become sec-

---

[1] As we mentioned in Chapter 2, the term *Conditioned* is being becoming obsolete in operant behavior terminology and is being replaced with the term *Learned.*.

ondary reinforcers because that is easy to understand: they are linked with highly valued items. But what happens if the objects or events that usually become learned reinforcers fail to be related to primary reinforcers or effective learned reinforcers? Gift certificates (or dollar bills or checks) would not affect the behavior of people who had no way to exchange those objects for items of value for them. How rewarding would you find a lottery ticket if you already knew that the winner, someone other than yourself, had already been selected? Growing up without experiencing typical combinations of primary and learned reinforcers, like contiguously presenting food or other powerful reinforcers with verbal praise, may explain why some people are less easily influenced by familiar secondary reinforcers such as approval and good grades.

## Secondary (Conditioned) Aversive Stimuli

Of course the same is true of *learned aversive stimuli, the removal or prevention of which also becomes a reinforcing event*. Neutral stimuli become *aversive* by virtue of their contiguous relations to primary or other strong secondary aversive stimuli. To illustrate, reprimands often are followed by primary aversive stimuli: "No, no, Tina, don't touch the stove. It will hurt you." But it is too late and Tina gets hurt. After frequently experiencing the "No, no" in combination with unpleasant consequences, Tina begins to arrest her actions when she hears "No!" The stimulus "No!" has now become an aversive event in its own right. Finally, successfully evading or escaping from that aversive event strengthens Tina's rate of complying through *negative reinforcement*. Tina will learn that there are things she had better do to avoid nasty consequences (technically *avoidance behaviors*); others she should not do or stop doing to steer clear of the "No, no's."

The abusive alcoholic parent, who regularly arrives home and physically abuses members of his family, is another example. The parent's arrival home may have started out as neutral, but over time it has become aversive. When pairings like those occur rapidly and often enough, people (and non-human organisms) learn particular behaviors that gain various reinforcing stimuli or permit them to avoid aversive ones.

## Developing Secondary Reinforcers

While all of us undergo the general kind of learning experiences we have been describing, the particular stimuli that have become reinforcing or aversive depend on the individual's unique learning history. A "high five" may have no value for someone from a culture in which no one uses such signals, or it may be *aversive* to others who might view such touching as a sign of disrespect. So before using any presumed reinforcing stimulus for teaching purposes, you need to determine if it actually reinforces the behavior of the individuals involved. Otherwise, you may first need to turn to primary reinforcers or more powerful secondary reinforcers before you make general use of that particular stimulus in your setting.

If you wish to transform a neutral stimulus into a learned reinforcer, you would need to *contiguously present the neutral or weak stimulus with primary and/or other learned reinforcers* known to have a powerful effect on the behavior of that person. In other words, they need to occur together. Over time, the previously neutral stimulus acquires reinforcing properties for him or her. For example, in Greg's case, we could combine the expression "Good boy" with a sincere tone of voice, eye contact, a hug, and pats on the back or, if necessary, preferred items or foods that he apparently enjoys.[2] By doing so, the expression "Good boy" would likely become a learned reinforcer for Greg, just as "Good girl" did for Tina. Similarly, Mr. Grump learns to accept compliments graciously only after they have been linked repeatedly with supplementary reinforcers, such as preferred assignments and good merit ratings: "Wonderful job, Grumpy. Let me take over while you go on break."

Another example, from one of the authors' clinical case files, describes how a five-year-old girl was taught to respond to learned reinforcers in her natu-

---

[2]The functional assessment methods, about which you will read in Chapter 10, were designed for the explicit purpose of identifying powerful reinforcers for individuals incapable of accurately communicating their wants and needs.

ral environment. When brought to the clinic, she rarely looked at the clinician or responded to her gestures or verbal directions. On those rare occasions when her behavior approximated a desired action, the behavior analyst said "Good" or smiled. As this approach had no apparent effect, more effective reinforcers—her preferred foods—were used to teach the child to follow directions. Lunch was brought to the clinic, and the child was given small bites whenever she followed such directions as "Come here," Sit down," and "Look at me." Within a few months the youngster was complying with a wide range of instructions. However, following the youngster around with lunch and a spoon would be impractical for a classroom teacher, so a program was instituted for developing secondary reinforcers. Each time the therapist gave the child food she accompanied it with a word or phrase like "Good," "Fine," "Yes," and "You're doing so well," and with an action like a smile, a hug, or a nod. *Gradually*, as the child began to master given skills, the food reinforcers were eliminated. Soon the child was practicing those skills despite receiving only a word like "Yes," a nod, or a smile. Eventually, she progressed to the point that the learned, or conditioned, reinforcers were sufficient to support the therapist's efforts.

On pausing to consider, you will realize that many instructional programs are designed to enable trainees to eventually attain objectives that become reinforcing in their own right (i.e., learned secondary reinforcers). Becoming able to read, play a musical instrument, analyze a story, poem, or problem situation, or craft an exquisite object (even write a book) are wonderful accomplishments. But of what use are they if the learner fails to derive sufficient reinforcement from exercising the skill? That skill will go unpracticed and probably deteriorate once external contingency control is discontinued. For this reason, *practicing the skill needs to become as reinforcing as possible*. Use multiple contingencies regularly to strengthen the ties between the new proficiency and other powerful reinforcers. In plain language: *Bombard learners with currently powerful reinforcers (as natural to the circumstances as possible) contingent on progress and achievement!*

Perhaps by taking a page from the Madison Avenue advertising culture, behavioral practitioners have devised numerous clever techniques to increase the rate with which formerly neutral objects or events can be transformed into reinforcers. These include: displaying live or video-recordings of models obviously enjoying the reinforcer; providing free samples; "talking-up" the reinforcer and/or having the person's friends and idols do the same; displaying reinforcers as prompts or cues; and, of course, continuing to reinforce as many instances of progress as feasible. In fact, Singer-Dudek, Oblak, and Greer (2011) did just that when they conditioned children's books from a neutral stimulus to a conditioned reinforcer by having participants observe peers gaining access to these books contingent on correct responses.

Now you should be able to explain how learning histories affect the way previously neutral stimuli acquire their reinforcing (or, as you will learn later, their aversive) properties. This understanding should heighten your ability to become a much more effective agent of behavioral change. To illustrate how others have profited from this knowledge, you have but to research the behavior analytic literature. In one case, for instance, Hanley, Iwata, Roscoe, Thompson, and Lindberg (2003) demonstrated how they were able to transform seven people's non-preferred vocational activities into more highly preferred vocational activities. Among the set of procedures they used were high frequency or preferred contingencies, supplemental reinforcement for engagement in the non-preferred activities as well as others. Ultimately all seven individuals increased their involvement in previously non-preferred vocational activities.

To summarize, while primary reinforcers are nearly universally effective under given circumstances, the strength of a learned or secondary reinforcer depends on the individual's *learning history*. Though learned reinforcers are not universally functional, when a person's experiences solidly establish the connections, they may well become as capable of operating as effectively as primary reinforcers.

## Generalized Reinforcers and How They Develop

When it comes to teaching, training, managing, and consulting, being proficient in using reinforcing stimuli to increase or shape a wide range of behaviors to be emitted under many circumstances is a major benefit. That is the advantage *generalized reinforcer*s bestow. A **generalized reinforcer** is *a learned reinforcer that has become effective for a wide range of behaviors under a variety of circumstances or settings*. Generalized reinforcers gain their strength through a history of having been frequently coupled with an assortment of previously established, powerful reinforcers—primary and/or learned. As a result, generalized reinforcers tend to be effective longer and in more situations than more restricted primary reinforcers. The effectiveness of a generalized reinforcer does not depend on any single state of deprivation. For example, gaining social recognition is a fairly common generalized reinforcer among many, though not all, people. The same is true of money or certain kinds of tokens. For example, you don't need to be hungry, have a sweet tooth or not eaten sweets in a while for money to be reinforcing. Because generalized reinforcers do not depend on a specific motivation (e.g., deprivation state), they tend to be more effective under multiple circumstances. Russell, et al. (2018) illustrated this fact by comparing two participants' break-points in responding to both edible and token reinforcers after providing presession access to edibles. Results demonstrated that presession access to edibles only affected the break-points for edibles, in that children stopped working for the edible reinforcer (i.e., break-points decreased for the edible reinforcer but not for the token reinforcer). (**Tokens** are *items exchangeable for reinforcing objects and events*, and are described and discussed in detail in Chapter 12.)

## CLASSES OF REINFORCERS AND AUTOMATIC REINFORCERS

Now that we have explained how reinforcers develop, we assume you recognize why a particular stimulus may fail to function universally as a reinforcer. That being the case, if you are to develop a program designed to teach clients to learn new ways of behaving (academically, socially, on the job, etc.) you need to learn how to identify what stimuli are capable of reinforcing each individual's behavior under the circumstances to be in effect. But before we discuss how to identify functional reinforcers, allow us first to provide you with an overview of the four key categories of reinforcers.

For convenience, behavior analysts have devised different terms to categorize reinforcers. The term **social reinforcer** describes *any reinforcing event*, such as recognition, compliments ("What a good boy!"), or peer approval that are *mediated by other people*. **Edible reinforcers** are *consumable items*, like milk and snacks; **tangible reinforcers** are *objects* such as toys, gold stars, bonuses, and trophies; while **activity reinforcers** are *individuals' preferred pastimes*, such as working at the computer, spending time at the activity table, or baking bread.[3]

Moreover, beyond the actual *class* of reinforcers, noting the medium of reinforcer delivery also is important. Reinforcers can be *delivered by another person* (**socially-mediated**), as in family members paying attention to a child sucking his thumb, or they can be *produced directly by the response itself* (**automatic reinforcers**). We can infer that an activity is serving as an automatic reinforcer for a young girl when, despite no other apparent consequences (e.g., no one reacting to her), she continuously sucks her thumb, repeatedly sings the same song to herself, twirls her hair, or rocks back and forth. Eating food then would be an automatic reinforcer unless the food was being dispensed by someone else. Masturbation would be an automatic reinforcer, but sexual intercourse would not in that it is socially mediated. Identifying and using reinforcers directly produced by the response itself rather than those that are mediated socially can be more advantageous to the individual, because response-produced reinforcers are immediate. Finding more socially acceptable ways (providing a rocking chair or hairbrush, or teaching where and where not to engage in the behavior) to allow the person to manage and enjoy the same reinforcer is often a good place to begin! Recognize, though, that because the behaviors of that sort produce their own reinforcing func-

---

[3]For a sample listing of consequences often found to operate effectively as reinforcers, see the page labeled "Illustrative Reinforcers" on this book's Web site.

tion, troublesome behavior maintained by automatic reinforcement can be especially resistant to change (more on this later).

## SELECTING REINFORCERS FOR INDIVIDUAL APPLICATION

We now have discussed how reinforcers develop and the different classes of reinforcers you can use to change behavior. You also need to understand, however, how to select reinforcers that actually are functional for your client's behavior; not stimuli that would affect *you or others*, but those that show promise for the individual whose behavior you are responsible for changing. Consequently, in a behavioral program, before you choose to have any stimulus serve as a reinforcer, you need to demonstrate that it possesses reinforcing properties for the behavior of the individual under the circumstances in which it is to be applied. Resist the temptation to pick reinforcers because they appeal to you or to many of your clientele or have been reported to be successful for others. Select them *only if you have evidence that they maintain or increase the behavior of the specific individual(s) involved*. Also, remember that teachers, parents, managers, peers, and others can unintentionally reinforce misbehavior because they fail to recognize the reinforcing functions of their own actions. Therefore, knowing how to determine what objects and events actually function as specific reinforcers for an individual in given situations is very important. For example, investigators (Conine, Vollmer, & Bolivar, 2020) found that young children (ages three to eight) with autism responded better when offered tangible reinforcers than simply contingent praise when being taught to respond to their names. Dyer (1987) found that to compete successfully with and suppress stereotypy (i.e., persistent and inappropriate repetition of phrases, acts, or gestures), external reinforcers must be very strong. Below we provide some strategies you might try as you search for truly functional reinforcers in your own situation.

Before we embark on identifying reinforcers, we should also describe the difference between functional versus arbitrary reinforcers. The term **functional reinforcer** means that *the reinforcer is currently maintaining or reinforcing a behavior* (you will learn about functional reinforcers for problem behavior in Chapter 10). On the other hand, **arbitrary reinforcers** *are reinforcers or preferred stimuli that can function as reinforcers but may not be currently functioning in that way*. Generally speaking, when we are trying to identify items or events to serve as reinforcers that are not already doing so, we are identifying arbitrary reinforcers.

### Selecting Reinforcers: Surveys and Reports

One fairly obvious way to narrow down the search for effective reinforcers is to *ask* people to select their own, but they must know themselves very well and not be influenced by what they assume the inquirer wants to hear. People with reasonable verbal repertoires and capable of viewing their own behavior and the conditions that influence it generally should be able to respond to a reinforcer survey with a reasonable degree of accuracy. Actual questions would depend upon the client's developmental level and social-cultural environment. However, reinforcer surveys typically include questions such as:

What are your favorite foods?

If you had _____ dollars to purchase whatever you wanted, what would you buy?

If you had 30 minutes of free time at (school, work, home), what would you really like to do?

What are three of your favorite things to do (at work, at home, at school, with friends)?

Who are the people you prefer doing things with at (home, school, work)?

These types of assessments are deemed indirect in that you are not directly observing the effects of stimuli but trying to garner information from asking the person or someone in that person's life. Numerous adult-mediated reinforcer surveys exist for preschool children and individuals with various handicapping conditions, (e.g., *Reinforcer Assessment for Individuals with Severe Disabilities*, RAISD: Fisher, Piazza, Bowman, & Amari, 1996). Most of these can be located by searching "reinforcer survey" in a library or on the Web. One user-friendly, clinically relevant reinforcer survey for adults (Clement, 1999) contains a wide array of possible reinforcers (Lecomte, Liberman, & Wallace, 2000). When using the survey, the respondent is asked to identify the people, places, things (hobbies and items), and activities that he/she prefers and/or performs most often. If the client is unable or unwilling to offer reliable responses, their **significant others,** such as family members, teachers, or close friends *with substantial knowledge of, contact with, and/or control over many of the client's contingencies*, can complete the survey.

As a starting point, significant others also might be asked to complete the survey, as an additional source of information. Once their reports have been obtained, look for a general consensus before moving on to functionally assessing the accuracy of the information more formally (see Chapter 10). It is of utmost importance that the suggestions obtained from significant others be validated by checking them out; that is, by doing a preference assessment or by functionally assessing them, because some research (e.g., Cote, Thompson, Hanley, & McKerchar, 2007; Fisher et al., 1996; Northup, 2000) has demonstrated that even with the sincerest intentions, the information that clients themselves or others supply is not necessarily totally accurate. Thus, it is important to conduct a direct assessment of items identified within an indirect assessment before programming to use those items to reinforce behavior. Similar to other assessment strategies, when trying to identify reinforcers it is important to conduct direct observation and to "test" if an item is indeed a reinforcer via a preference or reinforcer assessment before utilizing it in a behavior change program. Below are some procedures for doing just that.

## Selecting Reinforcers: Observation and Preference Assessments

No matter how earnest or sincere people's words may seem to be, when choosing reinforcers, *don't rely exclusively on those identified by the client or others*. One method to identify potential reinforcers is to observe what the individual gravitates toward or identify how specific stimuli affect the individual's performance. Objectively demonstrate the effectiveness of suspected reinforcers instead! Little Elroy's teacher discovered how important hugs and pats were for him by first counting for several days the number of directions he followed without any hugging or patting after he complied. Then for another few days she hugged or patted Elroy each time he followed a direction, and his rate of compliance increased. To fully establish the extent to which compliance was dependent on those consequences, she discontinued them for a few days, during which time she noted a drop in Elroy's compliance rate. Only when hugs and pats were reintroduced did he again begin to follow directions. Having demonstrated the reinforcing properties of her hugs and pats for Elroy, the teacher could now use them to promote other behaviors and eventually to develop other learned reinforcers: gestures like smiles or "high fives," and words like "Good job!" "Nice going!" (See Figure 6.1 for a graphic representation of Elroy's behavior.)

Although it may not always be necessary to follow such an elaborate routine to demonstrate the effectiveness of reinforcers, developing a successful program requires that individuals and reinforcers be matched on the basis of objective observation. If the rate of a behavior does not increase or continue when a particular stimulus is delivered contingent on that behavior, one possible explanation is that the stimulus is not sufficiently reinforcing for the client, or at least for this client under these circumstances. Other reinforcers should be attempted until a set or at least one is found to be effective under the conditions expected to be in place during the intervention.

Several alternative methods are available to help you to identify reinforcers *objectively* and *with reasonable confidence*. These include:

- Systematically observe the effect of a set of different *suspected* reinforcers to determine which consequence(s) produce increases in the behavior. If the client smiles, and works harder, and especially, increases or maintains performance, you have evidence that the consequence is functioning as a reinforcer.

- Withhold free access to potential reinforcers and make them available only contingent

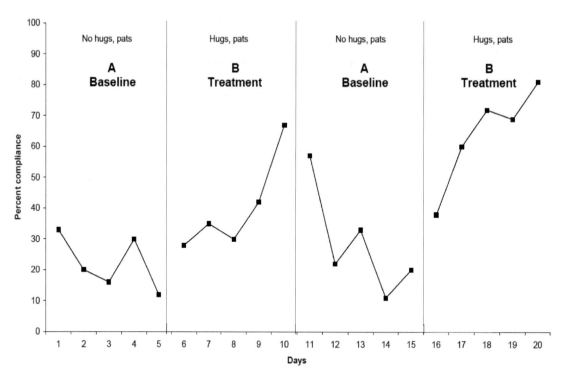

**Figure 6.1** Elroy's compliance rates (fictitious data)

upon the target behavior. Observe to determine what behaviors the client chooses to engage in; look for high-frequency or at least moderately-occurring behaviors. Then make access to the potential reinforcers available only after the target behavior occurs. If, for instance, time on the computer is an activity that the client chooses, set up the contingency so that the client earns access to the computer only after completing a particular section of an assignment or making progress on some other target behavior. Again, if this strengthens the behavior, you have evidence of reinforcer effectiveness.

- Withdraw or withhold access to suspected reinforcers as a consequence of a behavior, and determine whether the behavior decreases in that situation. If so, you have gathered some evidence of reinforcer effectiveness within that context, because you demonstrated that those reinforcers maintained behavior by showing that the behavior decreased in the absence of the reinforcers.
- Provide opportunities for reinforcer selection. (People respond at higher rates when those responses produce high-preference rather than low-preference items) (Graff, Gibson, & Galiatsatos, 2006; Flood & Wilder, 2004).
- Use a **reinforcer menu** consisting of *an array of possible reinforcers*. Identify which stimuli the client repeatedly select.
- Present several objects or activities and determine which one(s) the individual *selects or approaches repeatedly*.

**Reinforcer preference assessments.** More formal, validated applications of this fourth approach have been packaged under the heading of **reinforcer preference assessments** (RPAs) (e.g., Pace, Ivancic, Edwards, Iwata, & Page, 1985; DeLeon, Iwata,

Conners, & Wallace, 1999; Hagopian, Rush, Lewin, & Long, 2001; Roscoe, Fisher, Glover, & Volkert, 2006; Worsdell, Iwata, & Wallace, 2002). These *choice approaches* are geared at demonstrating a "reinforcer effect" by demonstrating an increase in a selection response to obtain a specific stimulus. A number of RPAs have been developed over the last 35 years, which are designed to not only identify a reinforcing stimulus but to demonstrate that the specific stimulus is a reinforcer because it maintains a selection response. With RPAs, usually *several items are repeatedly presented and the individual is observed to determine which items s/he repeatedly (1) approaches, (2) chooses, (3) with which s/he spends the most time and/or (4) consumes*. These items or activities then are selected as reinforcers for the intervention program.

One approach, the **duration-based assessment,** *an observation approach to determine how long the client spends with each item,* is used most often with individuals who have severe and profound developmental disabilities, especially when results of the selection methods (discussed below) are ambiguous. To illustrate, different items are placed on a table or desk. The individual is observed each time for two minutes, to determine how long s/he spends with each item. The therapist records the duration the individual spends with each stimulus and compares the total durations (see Roane, Vollmer, Ringdahl, & Marcus, 1998 for an example). Those items with which the person spends the most time are then selected as the reinforcers. Examine Figure 6.2 and choose Carson's top three reinforcers for today. Also, see the section on Bar Graphs in Chapter 8 for another illustration of conducting and graphing a preference assessment.

It should be noted, however, that selection- or choice-based assessments (describe below) have been demonstrated to produce more valid results (Kodak, Fisher, Kelley, Kisamore, 2009) compared to other observation based methods.

One choice-based assessment is the **Single-Stimulus Assessment** (Pace, et al., 1985). In this assessment *one single item at a time is presented to individuals and you record whether or not they select the item* (e.g., consume item by eating, drinking, or interacting with it). You *then summarize the results with respect to which items were selected*

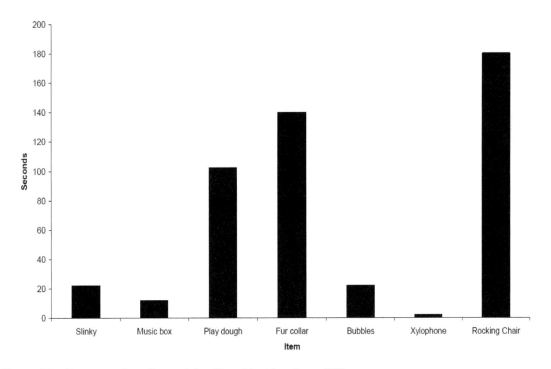

**Figure 6.2** Carson: number of seconds handling object (maximum 180)

*vs. which items were not.* Subsequently, the items that were selected would be utilized within programming as reinforcers. As you can imagine, one problem with the single-stimulus assessment is that you do not know how the items compare to each other. For example, if you were conducting a single-stimulus assessment with one of the authors and presented: chocolate, wine, beer, and sugar cookies. They would select all of them when presented; however, when used as a reinforcer in a behavior change program one of those items might work better than another.

The **Paired-Stimulus Assessment** was designed to overcome the potential limitation of the single-stimulus assessment (Fisher, et al., 1992). In this assessment, *pairs of stimuli are presented to individuals and you record which stimulus the individual selects. Each stimulus is paired with every other stimulus on separate trials.* By comparing each stimulus to one another, you can determine how each stimulus ranks compared to every other stimulus (or how "reinforcing" each item is to the other). When items are presented, the therapist records which item was selected. After all items have been presented with every other item, summarize the rank (number of times selected divided by the number of times presented multiplied by 100 percent).

This assessment will give you the relative percentage selected when compared to other stimuli. Going back to conducting this type of assessment with one of the authors, the results would suggest that the chocolate will work better as a reinforcer because when presented against the other items, it was selected 100 percent of the opportunities. Although this assessment method ranks each item against every other item, it can be time consuming.

The **Multiple-Stimulus Assessment**, was designed to overcome the potential limitation and time constraints of both the single-stimulus and paired stimulus assessment (DeLeon, et al. 1999). There are two variations of this assessment: **Multiple-Stimulus Assessment with Replacement and without Replacement**. In this assessment, *an array of items is presented to the individual and s/he is asked to pick one. In the one with replacement, you would replace the item chosen in the array on the next trial.* This one with replacement (also known as the *free operant assessment)* may be more appropriate than the other preference assessments to use for individuals who engage in problem behavior maintained by access to tangibles (Tung, Donaldson, & Kahng, 2017). *In the one without replacement, you do not replace the item and present the remaining items on the next trial.* In the end, after you have presented all the trials (which should be equal to the number of items being tested), you calculate preference in two ways: (1) by dividing 1 by the trial number it was chosen for without replacement, or (2) the number of times chosen by the number of trials for each item for with replacement. This method, like the paired-stimulus assessment, ranks the items within a percentage selected. Also, a video modeling with voice-over instruction has been developed to teach staff how to conduct a multiple stimulus without replacement preference assessment (Bovi, Valadescu, DeBar, Carroll, & Sarokoff, 2017).

Preference assessments need not be limited to clients with special needs. Given that higher rates of undesired behaviors are more likely when students are assigned less-preferred activities (Dyer, 1987; Heal & Hanley, 2007), these tools are being used increasingly among typically-developing students as a means of avoiding their misbehaving. In their study, Heal and Hanley compared (1) children's behavior within an unstructured play-oriented activity, to (2) that within a context in which highly preferred teaching materials were embedded, to (3) a sequential context that included highly preferred edible items, and to (4) a control condition that did not include highly preferred activities or items. As expected, the preschool children selected the unstructured play activity over all the teacher-led activities. However, when that play context was not available, all the children preferred the sequential context. The control was the least desired and rates of undesirable behavior were highest in that condition. The authors concluded that: "A child's preference may be an important factor to consider when adopting teaching strategies because children may be more inclined to seek out and less likely to actively avoid learning opportunities provided under highly preferred and properly motivating conditions" (p. 259).

Children's (and presumably adult's) preferences for particular items or activities vary as a function of how long they are available. Steinhilber and John-

CHAPTER 6  INCREASING BEHAVIOR BY DEVELOPING AND SELECTING POWERFUL REINFORCERS • 113

## Paired Stimulus Assessment Form

Name: _____   Date: _____

I. Identify 7 items that you would like to test and list below:

   Item 1: _____ Item 2: _____

   Item 3: _____ Item 4: _____

   Item 5: _____ Item 6: _____

   Item 7: _____

II. After you have gathered the items, pair each item with every other item and circle the item they select. When you present the items, state "pick the one you want." If they attempt to grab both, block and represent the command to pick one. After they have selected one, allow them a brief time to consume the item (e.g., 30s to 1 min for leisure items and a small piece or amount if it is a food or drink) and then present the next pair.

Item Pairing:

| 1 X 7 | 6 X 3 | 4 X 5 | 1 X 5 | 2 X 7 |
| --- | --- | --- | --- | --- |
| 4 X 6 | 5 X 2 | 6 X 7 | 2 X 1 | 5 X 3 |
| 7 X 4 | 3 X 1 | 5 X 7 | 7 X 3 | 4 X 1 |
| 3 X 4 | 6 X 2 | 1 X 6 | 2 X 3 | 6 X 5 |
| 4 X 2 |  |  |  |  |

III. Calculating Percentage Selected

   Item 1: # Selected/ 6 = _____

   Item 2: # Selected/ 6 = _____

   Item 3: # Selected/ 6 = _____

   Item 4: # Selected/ 6 = _____

   Item 5: # Selected/ 6 = _____

   Item 6: # Selected/ 6 = _____

   Item 7: # Selected/ 6 = _____

# Multiple-Stimulus Without Replacement Assessment Form

Name: _____     Date: _____

I. Identify 7 items that you would like to test and list below:

   Item 1: _____ Item 2: _____

   Item 3: _____ Item 4: _____

   Item 5: _____ Item 6: _____

   Item 7: _____

II. After you have gathered the items, present the items according to the trials below and state "pick the one you want." If they attempt to grab more than one item, block and represent the command to pick one. After they have selected one, allow them a brief time to consume the item (e.g., 30s to 1 min for leisure items and a small piece or amount if it is a food or drink), circle the item selected AND block that item number out of remaining trials, and then move to the next trial.

TRIAL 1: 1 X 2 X 3 X 4 X 5 X 6 X 7

TRIAL 2: 1 X 2 X 3 X 4 X 5 X 6 X 7

TRIAL 3: 1 X 2 X 3 X 4 X 5 X 6 X 7

TRIAL 4: 1 X 2 X 3 X 4 X 5 X 6 X 7

TRIAL 5: 1 X 2 X 3 X 4 X 5 X 6 X 7

TRIAL 6: 1 X 2 X 3 X 4 X 5 X 6 X 7

TRIAL 7: 1 X 2 X 3 X 4 X 5 X 6 X 7

III. Calculating Percentage Selected

Item 1: 1/ Trial Selected = _____     Item 2: 1/ Trial Selected = _____

Item 3: 1/ Trial Selected = _____     Item 4: 1/ Trial Selected = _____

Item 5: 1/ Trial Selected = _____     Item 6: 1/ Trial Selected = _____

Item 7: 1/ Trial Selected = _____

Note: Because you are not replacing the item, cross off the number of the item chosen for remaining trials. For example, if client selects item 2 on first trial, cross off #2 on remaining trials.

# Multiple-Stimulus With Replacement Assessment Form

Name: _____    Date: _____

I.  Identify 7 items that you would like to test and list below:

   Item 1: _____ Item 2: _____

   Item 3: _____ Item 4: _____

   Item 5: _____ Item 6: _____

   Item 7: _____

II.  After you have gathered the items, present the items according to the trials below and state "pick the one you want." If they attempt to grab more than one item, block and represent the command to pick one. After they have selected one, allow them a brief time to consume the item (e.g., 30s to 1 min for leisure items and a small piece or amount if it is a food or drink), circle the item selected AND block that item number out of remaining trials, and then move to the next trial.

TRIAL 1: 1 X 2 X 3 X 4 X 5 X 6 X 7

TRIAL 2: 1 X 2 X 3 X 4 X 5 X 6 X 7

TRIAL 3: 1 X 2 X 3 X 4 X 5 X 6 X 7

TRIAL 4: 1 X 2 X 3 X 4 X 5 X 6 X 7

TRIAL 5: 1 X 2 X 3 X 4 X 5 X 6 X 7

TRIAL 6: 1 X 2 X 3 X 4 X 5 X 6 X 7

TRIAL 7: 1 X 2 X 3 X 4 X 5 X 6 X 7

III.  Calculating Percentage Selected

Item 1: 1/ Trial Selected = _____    Item 2: 1/ Trial Selected = _____

Item 3: 1/ Trial Selected = _____    Item 4: 1/ Trial Selected = _____

Item 5: 1/ Trial Selected = _____    Item 6: 1/ Trial Selected = _____

Item 7: 1/ Trial Selected = _____

son (2007) found that "the duration of availability may function as a motivating operation that affects the momentary preference for a stimulus. That is, we may determine stimulus preference, in part, by the duration for which that item is available.... From a practical perspective, the current results suggest that the duration of post-selection access may influence an item's ranking in a preference assessment" (p. 770). Consequently, during a preference assessment, the time allowed for access to the reinforcers should resemble that allowed in the natural environment. Just as you might pass on an offer of a fourth banana split, the extent to which others value any particular reinforcer can change over time, even within a session or moment to moment (Mason, McGee, Farmer-Dougan, & Risley, 1989).

Bruzek and Thompson (2007) found that preference for activities or items often increases when individuals observe peers engaging with them. This supports the strategy of conducting RPAs periodically to ensure continued reinforcer effectiveness, because an individual's reinforcer preferences differ as a function of various circumstances and over time (Butler & Graff, 2021). Be especially vigilant when using primary reinforcers, especially if the rate of the behavior you are attempting to promote begins to decline.[4]

As each of these four methods is based on observation rather than simply someone's guesses or estimates, you can feel reasonably confident about using the reinforcers again under similar circumstances. Refer to Box 6.1 for an example of how this strategy might play out in a classroom situation. However, research (Johnson, Vladescu, Kodak, & Sidener, 2017) indicates that not only must the selection and application of reinforcers be tailored to different individuals, but also to the different types of skills that are requested of the individual. In other words, some skills may require that more powerful reinforcers be used to bring about learning than other skills. This is another reason why multiple preference assessments need to be administered. Not only do reinforcers vary among individuals, but also change over time and with what task the individual is being asked to perform. For example, Daniels and Lattal (2017) share an example in which textile mill workers rejected money as a bonus reinforcer for good work because in the past such events had been followed by negative experiences, such as being asked to work overtime, on weekends, or to perform undesirable tasks. Thus, bonus money did not function as a reinforcer for doing work in this textile mill.

Generally, RPAs are conducted by evaluating the actual stimulus; however, the efficacy of using alternate (presumably more efficient) forms of stimuli (pictorial, verbal, video) within these various assessment formats has been investigated. Although some of those alternative forms of stimuli have been shown to be effective, others may require particular prerequisite skills (e.g., the ability to match picture-to-object and object-to-picture with pictorial assessments). In a review of the literature on this topic, Heinicke, Carr, and Copsey (2019) found that the RPAs accurately identified reinforcers. After checking the validity of several types of assessments, they found accurate reinforcer identification in 61 percent of the cases for pictorial assessments, 37 percent of the cases for verbal assessments (i.e., asking if the participant wanted an item or to choose between

---

[4]Examples of RPAs and how to use them as a tool for dealing with problems can be found on this text's Web page under "Reinforcer Preference Assessment." Also, there are on-line training programs for teaching you how to do preference assessments (e.g., see Higgins, et al., 2017).

| Box 6.1 |
|---|
| A Functional Behavioral Assessment based on direct observations of Kevin's performance, has informed us that he finds breaks from work reinforcing. Therefore, if we want to increase some behavior (say, work completion), one way to do that would be to provide breaks from work contingent on completing particular assignments or minutes working. Additionally, we could ask Kevin, his teacher, and his parents what kinds of objects or activities Kevin likes. We then would test to determine if providing those presumed reinforcers contingent on staying on task increases his work-completion rate. If, and only if, Kevin actually completes more work than he did during baseline, would we be able to assert that those items are actual reinforcers for Kevin. |

which items are their favorite), and 75 percent of the cases for video assessments among individuals with developmental disabilities.

## Ethical Considerations in Assessing Behavior

The Behavior Analysis Certification Board™ (BACB, 2020) reminds us that when assessing, recommending, reporting, and making evaluative statements, we need adequately to substantiate our findings as experienced, qualified professionals. We must use our techniques as intended; that is, we must assess and implement our intervention programs, reporting results and interpretations validly and reliably. We also must resist any temptation to overstate our case.

Clients or their legally empowered surrogates must supply written approval before behavioral assessments are implemented. A functional assessment (described in Chapter 10) is essential to designing an effective behavior-change program, and must be suited to systematically gathering information about the antecedents, consequences, setting events, and/or motivating operations.

According to the *ethics code for behavior analysts* (BACB, 2020):

> Before selecting or designing behavior change interventions behavior analysts select and design assessments that are conceptually consistent with behavioral principles, that are based on scientific evidence; and that best meet the diverse needs context, and resources of the client and stakeholders. They select, design, and implement assessments with a focus on maximizing benefits and minimizing risk of harm to the client and stakeholders. They summarize the procedures and results in writing. (section 2.13, p. 12)

> Behavior analysts select, design, and implement behavior change interventions that… (3) are based on assessment results; (4) prioritize positive reinforcement procedures; and (5) best meet the diverse needs, context, and resources of the client and stakeholders. Behavior analysts also consider relevant factors (e.g., risks, benefits, and side effects; client and stakeholder preferences, implementation efficiency; cost effectiveness).… (section 2.14, p. 12).

## Consider Motivating (Establishing) Operations and Response Deprivation in Reinforcer Selection

Recall that a **motivating operation (MO),** or **establishing operation (EO),** is *an event that alters the reinforcing or punishing value of a stimulus and increases or decreases the rates of behaviors that produce that consequence.* Familiarize yourself with relevant recent events in the client's life, such as how long it has been since the person has eaten, had something to drink, or been physically active, for these events will affect the reinforcing value of food, liquids, or exercise for a while. Remember that conditions like those may explain why stimuli found to be effective under some circumstances may not be under others. For practical reasons, you will want to select those stimuli demonstrated to be effective under circumstances currently in effect.

Of course, motivating operations often are easily manageable. You could withhold reinforcers for a while (i.e., set up deprivation conditions) to make them more powerful, or alter conditions to heighten the probability that particular behaviors will be emitted. Recognize, however, that depriving a person of food far beyond regular mealtimes is ethically questionable and in some cases illegal. To take advantage of the establishing operation of food deprivation, plan instead to conduct your teaching sessions just prior to the client's next meal, perhaps dispensing portions of that meal (or, as Azrin and Armstrong [1973] referred to them, "mini-meals"). Once your instructional session is over, you can permit free access to the remainder of the meal. Or withhold a specific preferred edible reinforcer (e.g., raisins) rather than all food, and then incorporate the withheld food item within your reinforcement program. Also, be cautious when incorporating deprivation within your intervention program in that it can lead to problem behavior, as Mueller, et al. (2001) found: restriction of high-preference toys produced higher rates of aggression than restriction of less preferred toys. Now let us look at specific instances of motivating operations.

**Deprivation and the response deprivation hypothesis.** **Deprivation** is *the absence or reduction of a reinforcer's availability for a period of time.* The **response deprivation hypothesis (RDH)** is a special instance of motivating operations, and is defined as follows: "*...if access to one of a pair of events is restricted below free operant levels (baseline of naturally ongoing behavior), an organism will work to regain access to that activity*" (Redmon & Farris, 1987, p. 327). In other words, if access to a reinforcing activity is restricted, admission to it becomes more reinforcing as a function of the deprivation conditions in effect. Consider this example: When one of four items shown to be preferred by a child, either a leisure item (e.g., playing cards, coloring book, Barbie book) or a toy (e.g., Lincoln Logs, dump truck, paddle ball), was withheld from 12- to 18-year-old youths with developmental disabilities, or from typically-developing preschool children, for 24 to 144 hours, the individuals tended to choose that item more frequently once it was again made available (McAdams et al., 2005). Those results support the response deprivation hypothesis (Timberlake & Allison, 1974), thereby providing us with a useful tool for maximizing the reinforcing effect of a given stimulus by limiting the person's access to one activity (e.g., using his iPod) to below its baseline level. The individual then needs to engage in the targeted activity (e.g., doing chores) at a level exceeding baseline rates to gain access to the deprived activity.

**The Premack principle.** The **Premack principle** (Premack, 1959) states that *contingent access to higher-probability behavior ("preferred activities") reinforces lower-probability behavior.* To illustrate, in a study by Hanley, Iwata, Thompson, and Lindberg (2000), adults living in a state residential facility for people with developmental disabilities were allowed contingent access to high-frequency stereotypic movements as reinforcement for alternative behavior such as manipulating a string of beads, a rubber snake, a textured rubber ball, or other leisure materials. According to Redmon and Farris (1987, p. 328), an activity is made effective as a reinforcer not because of its higher probability (as previously contended by Premack), "but because when one arranges a contingency, access to one of the events is deprived below its usual level." "The reinforcement effect will occur only when the condition of response deprivation is present in the contingency" (Konarski, Johnson, Crowell, & Whitman, 1981, p. 660).

To further demonstrate the effectiveness of response deprivation in applying the Premack principle, Konarski, Johnson, Crowell, and Whitman (1980) showed that math could act as a reinforcer for coloring for first-grade children in a special education class, only "when the conditions of response deprivation were present, even though it was clearly shown in the baseline to be a lower-probability response" (p. 600). They further concluded that, "These results support the predictions of the Response Deprivation Hypothesis, while being contrary to the notion of probability differential as the critical condition for reinforcement" (p. 606). Similarly, Konarski, Crowell, and Duggan (1985) showed that feedback, with or without the added element of being allowed to do math, had no positive effects on the cursive writing of 7- to 11-year-old students with mildly handicapping conditions, but adding the combination of corrective feedback and the response deprivation contingency for math (i.e., access to math was restricted) "resulted in significant increases in the percentage of words written correctly for all of the children" (p. 21). "It appears that the task of establishing effective reinforcement schedules is not limited to finding already potent reinforcers but may be one of *simply establishing schedules that induce response deprivation by drawing upon behaviors already in the student's repertoire*" (Konarski et al., 1985, p. 29; italics added).

Arranging for response deprivation may enable reinforcers to be established that meet "a person's changing behavioral needs" (Konarski et al., 1985, p. 29), expanding our ability to identify and develop reinforcers within the context of the Premack principle. Almost any behavior in which the individual engages is a potentially effective reinforcer, provided access to that response can be restricted. For example, knowing the baseline levels of two important job performances, a manager can establish one as a reinforcer by restricting access to that response for a while, then using it to reinforce the rate of the other. We would suspect that most practitioners will continue to elect to use behaviors that occur frequently or at least at a moderate rate, so that deprivation conditions can be established more quickly and reinforcers applied more frequently. Still, as Podsakoff (1982) has noted:

> almost any response which occurs in an organizational setting may serve to reinforce another response as long as the operant level of the two behaviors exceeds zero and a schedule is imposed which produces a greater disparity from the baseline than is already in effect. If this is a reliable finding, it may eliminate many of the problems managers have in identifying effective reinforcers. (p. 346)

From an ethical perspective, though, we encourage you to emphasize choosing and using those reinforcers the person would freely select, not simply the lesser of two "evils," as might happen when restricting access to all but one of two non-preferred activities. (As one of the authors commented, "If my only choices were sewing buttons or ironing, both of which I actively avoid—'loathe' might be a better descriptor—I'd probably be a very unhappy person!")

## Consider Individual Differences and Receptivity to Reinforcing Events: "Different Strokes for Different Folks"

Are there individual biological differences in sensitivity to positive feedback? Probably "yes." We are sure that you have noticed that particular individuals seem to respond differently to specific presumed reinforcing events. Although prior learning histories surely heavily account for much of these differences, research with vervet monkeys (Groman, et al., 2014; Isquierdo, Brigham, Radke, Rudebeck, & Holmes, 2017) suggests that, as elsewhere, the biological structure of the individual's brain probably plays a very important role. Those investigators found that each individual participant's performance and sensitivity to positive feedback was associated with *in vitro* (i.e., test-tube) estimates of the density of the individual's distinctive dopamine receptors. Interestingly, the investigators also found that these differences could be linked behaviorally to eye blink rate. These findings may help explain individuals' unique preferences for particular stimuli. The bottom line for applied behavior analytic practitioners is that we share a responsibility for behaviorally assessing for the efficacy of a reinforcement protocol (quality, quantity, schedule, etc.) at the individual level to determine which stimuli are true reinforcers for each individual.

## Select and Use a Variety of Reinforcers

When selecting reinforcers, select a variety; do not depend on just one or two. Varying reinforcers not only *introduces novelty*, a factor we shall consider soon, but also *decreases* the likelihood that reinforcers will lose their effectiveness due to *satiation* or other processes. Additionally, establishing operations, along with the specific nature of the reinforcing item or event, whether *primary* (your favorite ice cream), which leads to rapid satiation, or *generalized* (smiles and nods), which are less susceptible to satiation, as well as other factors, can influence the effectiveness of any reinforcer at a given time. To illustrate, Vollmer and Iwata (1991) showed that extended access to social and food reinforcers decreased the subsequent rate of responses maintained by these reinforcers. For these reasons, Hanley, Iwata, and Roscoe (2006) recommended assessing preferences frequently to detect changes as a function of exposure, or, alternatively, providing a variety of reinforcers from which the client makes a selection. If one reinforcer doesn't work at that moment, another might.

Rather than just one, Tiny Tina's mom feeds her little one a variety of her favorite foods: carrots, applesauce, and pudding, to encourage the child to feed herself. To minimize adaptation, Angela, the supervisor, changes her praise statements from one time to the next: "Nice going. You really succeeded in encouraging your staff to work harder." "Good job!

Look at 'em go!" "All right. That really did it!"—instead of sounding like a broken record: "Good job!" "Good job!" "Good job!" Yes, to heighten the effectiveness of your program, vary your reinforcers. Moreover, reinforcer variety also has been shown to increase the potency of lesser-preferred items. For example, Najdowski, Wallace, Penrod, and Cleveland (2005) compared the amount of work children engaged in when presented with a single high-preferred item, a single low-preferred item, or one of a variety of low-preferred items. When low-preferred items were presented in a single format (the same low-preferred reinforcer throughout the duration of the session), participants did not engage in as much work as when low-preferred items were presented in a varied format (one of three items rotated throughout the session). Moreover, using several different low-preferred items worked as well as a single high-preferred item (see Figure 6.3). Similarly, Egel (1981) "showed declining trends in both correct responding and on-task behavior when the same reinforcer was consistently presented, whereas varying the reinforcers produced significantly improved and stable responding" (p. 345). So, *to hasten increasing the rate of a behavior, vary the reinforcers*. This appears to be important even when the reinforcer you are using is a high preference reinforcer (Becraft & Rolider, 2015).

## Novelty in Reinforcer Selection

"Other things being equal, organisms will often prefer to put themselves in novel situations" (Millenson, 1967, p. 397). This conclusion, supported by the results of several studies, is one that contingency managers should find especially appealing. Capitalizing on this principle frequently pays in that novel situations often present a wider variety of potential reinforcers. Varying reinforcers allows you to capitalize on the feature of novelty, especially when a single reinforcer has been presented over and over. However, too much or too little novelty may reduce responding. For example, in designing educational games, researchers (Lomas, et al., 2017) found, with 5,065 subjects, that moderate novelty was optimal, while too much or too little reduced responding. Some illustrations follow:

A teacher we know prepared a surprise box containing slips of paper containing all sorts of different directions: Draw a picture of a cow; wash the blackboard; get a drink of water; write a paragraph describing your pet; take five minutes of free time; tutor a friend in reading; and so on. Students drew slips from the box after completing their assignments. Their lack of familiarity with what the slips contained added considerable excitement.

The "job jar" is a closely related tool: Coveted assignments are listed on slips of paper, placed in a jar, and drawn at random following the desired behavior. Similarly, variable prizes at carnival booths and many computer games capitalize on novelty. Sometimes organizational performance managers distribute surprise treats or gifts, like donuts and coffee, or tangible rewards (which often, but not always, function as reinforcers) when their subordinates have met their goals several times in a row. Those are other ways of taking advantage of the reinforcing quality of novelty. The most successful teachers continually seek new activities to stimulate and excite their students (as well as themselves and their associates). Parents can recharge a child's preference for a toy by simply rotating toys systematically (e.g., limiting accessibility to the particular toys on a weekly basis). Think how reinforcing it is to hear a favored song or symphony you haven't heard for a while, versus hearing it broadcast repeatedly within a brief time period.

## The Value of Reinforcer Sampling

Although variety and novelty may heighten the reinforcing features of a stimulus, some of our clientele may be hesitant to try something new. They don't know what they're missing until they try. For example, Shirley was generally timid in the beginning, hesitant to try water skiing, ride a roller coaster, or contribute to the class discussion; but afterward she really began to enjoy these activities. Before a person has had experience with a potentially reinforcing stimulus, its appeal may be minimal. Holz, Azrin, and Ayllon (1963) found that after psychiatric patients were persuaded to try new things, like certain foods, the patients subsequently worked to acquire them. Consequently, Ayllon and Azrin (1968) suggested a reinforcer-sampling rule: Before

CHAPTER 6  INCREASING BEHAVIOR BY DEVELOPING AND SELECTING POWERFUL REINFORCERS  •  121

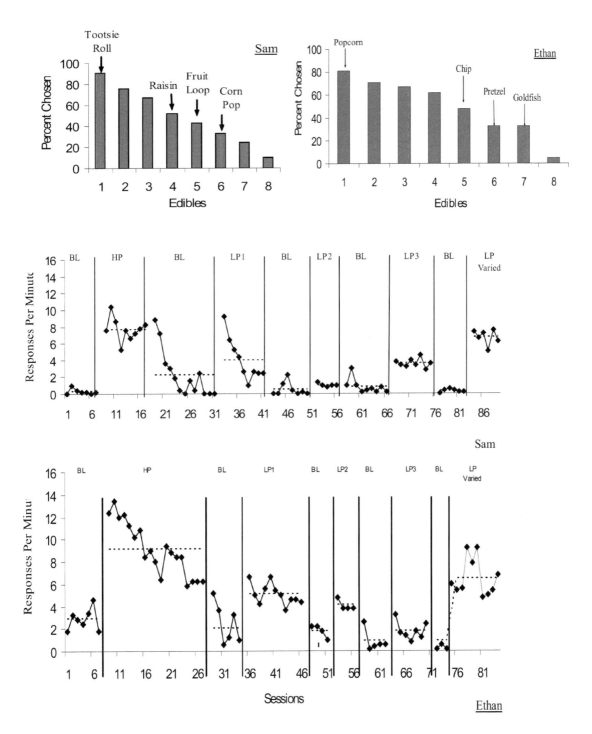

**Figure 6.3** Preference assessment. From Najdowski, Wallace, Penrod, & Cleveland (2005). Used with permission from John Wiley & Sons, Inc.

using a new stimulus as a reinforcer (in a behavior-change program), arrange for potential consumers to sample it in the situation in which it will be used.

Examples of reinforcer sampling in society are numerous: Cable TV companies allow viewers to watch programs for several days at no charge. Teachers display new books, read the beginnings of fascinating stories, teach new games, organize new projects, and otherwise expose youngsters to novel events or objects. Once the students begin to enjoy an experience, it is transformed into a reinforcer that can then be presented contingent on completing a targeted task: "As soon as we finish our reading, we will use the remainder of the period to play the new game we learned yesterday;" or vice- versa: "As soon as recess is over we can return to reading the story we began yesterday." Companies distribute free samples of new products, anticipating that if potential customers try out and enjoy them, they will purchase them in the future. The Internet is replete with examples of the use of reinforcer sampling: displaying a few intriguing images so viewers will pay for others; presenting segments of or whole musical selections or video clips, and even entire chapters of new books.

## The Role of the Reinforcer Mediator

A final factor we suggest you consider before selecting your reinforcers is, "Who is going to be delivering them?" It is important to determine which, if any, of the identified reinforcers the contingency manager is most and least likely to administer consistently. Then you should select those most apt to be implemented; those that best suit the situation. Fairbank and Prue (1982) also suggested that we consider how the role of those who dispense reinforcers may influence the success of an intervention program. This point has been supported by Boyce and Geller (2001), who reviewed a number of occupational safety studies and concluded: "A noteworthy difference between successful and unsuccessful maintenance-producing programs is that the *researchers* delivered the consequences in the unsuccessful maintenance interventions, whereas in the successful programs *on-site workers* [italics added] delivered the prize or drew the winning tickets in the prize or cash lotteries" (p. 44). Gloria may well find receiving a compliment from the big boss or one of her respected coworkers more reinforcing than one from an outside researcher. Additionally, when those in the natural environment deliver reinforcers, the change tends to maintain longer. After all, those agents are the people who remain in contact with the contingency manager or client and continue to be available to dispense reinforcers. Therefore, when feasible, people from the natural environment should be the ones dispensing the reinforcers.

The specific person serving as the reinforcement agent sometimes matters, too. We may feel devastated when certain people (your mother, your life partner) are critical of our actions ("Aren't your clothes getting a little tight on you?"), whereas when others (e.g., the obnoxious shipping clerk) offer the same criticism, it might bounce off us. Although relatively little research has been done on the impact of the *source* of reinforcers, in one case, Fox and Sulzer-Azaroff (1989) compared feedback from either direct line supervisors or from safety specialists. Neither proved more powerful in general, but some individual employees responded differentially to one versus the other. In other studies (e.g., Broussard & Northup, 1997; Lewis & Sugai, 1996), however, attention from peers but not from adults was shown to maintain problem behavior at school.

To varying extents, people occupying different roles within organizations have served as effective agents of reinforcer and feedback delivery: parents, managers, teachers, supervisors, consultants, peers, subordinates, and others. We suspect that people who are in control of many powerful social or material reinforcers (the rich, famous, powerful, alluring, charming, lovable, and/or entertaining) would be good choices. So would close friends, popular peers, doting and generous grandparents, supervisors responsible for making personnel decisions, and clients (whose improvement or satisfaction mean so much to us). Occasionally, though, relying on others to furnish reinforcers has its limitations. When no other more powerful alternatives are available, people may arrange consequences for their own behavior, especially if they can obtain the support of others.

## SUMMARY AND CONCLUSIONS

This chapter acquainted you with a variety of key behavior analytic concepts and terms related to reinforcement. You have become more familiar with *primary* (unconditioned or unconditional) and *secondary* (conditioned) *positive reinforcers* and *aversive stimuli*, found out how each might have evolved to function at the individual level, and how each stimulus category may intentionally be incorporated within behavior-change programs. You learned to distinguish positive from negative reinforcement, as well as how to differentiate these from other types of contingencies. You have learned of the importance of choosing and using effective reinforcers to suit each individual's preferences at the moment. You will find that each of these features is fundamental to understanding people's behavior and to successfully to changing it.

Primary reinforcers are universally influential because their reinforcing attributes usually come "pre-packaged" within each human individual as mechanisms of survival. The potency of primary reinforcers depends on conditions such as deprivation and satiation. By being repeatedly associated with currently effective primary and/or learned reinforcers, neutral stimuli can develop into effective reinforcers. Nonetheless, the strength of any given learned reinforcer varies as a function of the individual's history of learning and current circumstances.

Discovering, selecting, and applying reinforcing stimuli currently potent for a particular individual (whether based on biology and/or previous learning) can be a challenge, but are essential to the success of any behavior-change program. We have discussed various promising reinforcer selection strategies, including the following steps:

- Begin by gathering information about those stimuli the person is known to prefer, by means of such tools as reinforcer surveys.
- Use a reinforcer preference assessment (RPA), either a single-stimulus, paired-stimulus or a multiple-stimulus assessment. Use this list of items and events to assemble a pool of potential reinforcers.
- Put each of those to the test by observing and recording whether each of those consequences actually influences the person's ongoing behavior.
- Consider the effects of establishing operations and deprivation conditions.
- Select a variety of high preference reinforcers (not just one or two).
- Incorporate novel reinforcers.
- Allow the person to sample reinforcers freely before introducing them into the paired-comparison assessments. When choosing reinforcers, bear in mind that contingency managers need to feel comfortable in applying them. A powerful reinforcer that change-managers avoid using is worthless.

Later on, in Chapter 10 we return to identifying elusive reinforcers for seriously problematic behaviors, while in Chapter 11 we present a set of key rules for applying reinforcers effectively. By the time you master the particulars of effective reinforcement, you will be able to design procedures not only to increase, but also to reduce and teach specific behaviors. However, before we move on to these topics, you will need to acquire some additional skills. For example, you will need to be able to observe and measure behavior validly to select effective reinforcing contingencies and to determine their effect on behavior, the main topic of our next chapter.

## Chapter 7

# Organizing for Behavior Change by Collecting Useful Data

### Goals

1. Define *behavioral assessment* and discuss why it is important.
2. Define and illustrate four characteristics of a good measurement system:
   a. sensitive
   b. objective versus subjective
   c. reliable
   d. valid
3. Define *treatment utility of assessment*.
4. Define and illustrate *reactivity* and *adaptation*, and discuss what might indicate reactive effects and how to minimize their occurrence.
5. List two major sources of error contributing to low interobserver reliability.
6. Describe how reliability data influences validity and what can be done to obtain believable, high interobserver reliability data.
7. Define, illustrate, and describe how to minimize the effect of each on lowering validity:
   a. instructional demand
   b. measurement complexity
   c. observer's awareness of being assessed
   d. observational bias
8. Define, illustrate, and differentiate, pointing out the advantages of the following observation methods:
   a. recording products of behavior
   b. recording transitory behavior, including *event, duration, latency, inter-response time (IRT)*, and the three *interval time-sampling* recording systems.

9. Define and illustrate (a) *trials to criterion*, (b) *rate of behavior*, and (c) *percentage of opportunities*. Also, discuss when it is appropriate to use each.
10. Define and differentiate among *behavioral products*, *transitory behavior*, *discrete behavior*, and *continuous behavior*.
11. Define and illustrate assessing for *episodic severity*.
12. Discuss the importance of collecting episodic severity data.
13. Define and illustrate a *behaviorally-anchored rating scale* (BARS).
14. Define and give original illustrations of the *zone system* and *PLA-Check*.
15. Define, illustrate, and differentiate among methods for determining IOA (interobserver agreement) for the following observational measures:
    a. permanent product
    b. event or frequency
    c. duration and IRT
    d. interval time sampling
16. Describe how to report reliability data.
17. Define *observer drift* and *recalibration*.
18. Differentiate observer drift (See Chapter 3) from treatment drift.
19. Illustrate with a unique example and justify the selection of each observation method.

*************

## BEHAVIORAL ASSESSMENT

Whether at a global, national, local, or personal level, human society is beset with an infinite number of challenges: from issues of life and death, war and peace, to economic, social, and personal problems, along with a myriad of others. Unfortunately, no group or individual can fix everything, especially given how limited our natural and human resources are. The obvious approach is to choose the strategies that most rapidly produce the best results.

Things are not quite so simple, of course, because people often disagree as to the best approach to take. No matter the concern—issues of health, our children's or students' learning and deportment, our own bad habits, our employee's job performance, our supervisor's management tactics, etc.—solutions seem to abound. Daily, the popular media are filled with the latest panacea for controlling weight, exercising, turning children into angels, ridding ourselves of nasty habits like nail-biting, increasing production and quality, and so on. Because it sounds so simple and relatively inexpensive, our natural tendency is to rush out and try the "quick fix."

But how do we *really* know whether our efforts are paying off? Not by confidence alone, but by using some sort of reproducible measure: pounds lost, blood-pressure readings lowered, level and amount of student work completed, length of fingernails grown, production rate or product quality increased.

For an example close to home, over the years Heather has tried to improve her posture at the computer keyboard, where she spends a good part of her time writing, preparing, and managing data. As part of her job, she has read and studied about good posture while stroking the keys, so she should be able to position herself perfectly. She is well aware of the risks posed by poorly positioning her feet and legs, back, hands and arms, neck and shoulders: repetitive strain injuries, bad posture, and various other aches and pains; and she knows exactly what proper positioning should look like. Like everyone else she has attempted various "quick fixes," such as posting signs, placing the message "sit straight" on her screensaver, asking her co-workers to compliment her for good posture, and just *trying* to remember. But she wonders if any of that helped over time. How could she really find out?

She rejects using her own personal ratings because typically she is so immersed in her work that she fails to notice her body positioning. Asking others for their impressions is hardly more useful because they could be biased or misinformed. Having them fill out questionnaires might be an improvement, but, then again, faulty recall might affect the ratings. What she concludes she really needs is to monitor her posture by using an objective and valid measurement system.

When it comes to making important decisions about how to address behavioral challenges, most of us are tempted to choose the easiest path. We often accept our own impressions of performance and progress, which, as we have seen, are easily tainted: "Heather's posture has to be great, given her expertise in the area." "Why would she do it any other way?" Yet take a look at her supervisor's assessments in Figure 7.1 (based on very precisely defined measures) for just one brief observational session. That should give you some hint as to how well Heather is doing.

Posture at the Computer
(y = yes, correct; p = partial; n = incorrect)

| \multicolumn{7}{c}{**Posture at the Computer** (y = yes, correct; p = partial; n = incorrect)} |
|---|---|---|---|---|---|---|
| Date | Time | Feet | Shoulders | Back | Hands | Head |
| 03/15/09 | 4:25 | y | p | n | n | n |
| | 4:32 | y | p | y | p | n |
| | 4:41 | y | y | y | p | n |
| | 4:48 | y | p | n | n | n |
| | 4:56 | y | p | n | n | n |
| | 5:23 | p | n | n | n | n |
| | 5:30 | y | n | n | p | n |
| | 5:38 | y | n | y | n | n |
| | 5:46 | y | n | n | n | n |
| | 6:00 | y | p | n | n | n |
| Total yes | | 9/10 | 1/10 | 3/10 | 0/10 | 0/10 |

**Figure 7.1** Heather's supervisor's assessment of her posture over a 95-minute period

Heather has discussed the issue with her supervisor and co-workers, all of whom agree that this is an important goal, especially because "baseline" data reflecting Heather's and her colleagues' performance collected over several days were persuasive. If they hoped to avoid the types of injuries associated with poor body positioning at the keyboard, they would need to participate in a posture-improvement program. That would entail ongoing observation and measurement of Heather's and her co-workers' postures. Then, depending on the data, that phase might well be followed by a feedback and a reinforcement intervention program.

How did the appreciation for rigorous measurement of behavior come about? In the mid-twentieth century, professionals affiliating with the branch of laboratory psychology calling itself the **experimental analysis of behavior** (*a scientific method designed to discover the functional relation between behavior and the variables that control it*) began to share the same concerns as other sciences regarding the accuracy (*validity*) of their findings. They rejected data based on hunches, guesses, impressions, or even structured interviews and questionnaires as potentially biased or possibly even misleading. Consequently, following in the footsteps of B. F. Skinner (1938) and others, these *behavior analysts* gravitated toward using *valid, direct, useful,* and *sensitive* measures to assess behavior directly in context. Fortunately, since that time this approach has begun to reward society by allowing scientists and practitioners to depend on the information they gather to discover, choose, and use powerful, ethically acceptable methods to promote effective, rapid, and enduring behavioral changes.[1]

Today, savvy individuals, families, and organizational personnel across the globe are turning to applied behavior analysis to address their daily challenges at work, play, home, and in the community.[2] Why? Because, as you will witness repeatedly throughout this text, one of ABA's features is that it promotes success by using *objective measures* (defined below) to guide the design, implementation, and evaluation of behavior-change programs. (See Figure 7.2)

---

[1] Along with any license based on standardized tests (what they *say*), only practitioners who consistently apply their interventions as designed (what they *do*) merit the title of "applied behavior analyst."

[2] The Association for Behavior Analysis International currently boasts membership in the many thousands from among roughly two hundred countries around the world.

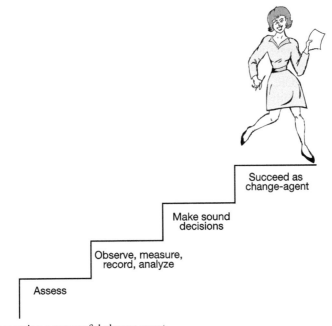

**Figure 7.2** Steps to becoming a successful change agent

## Behavioral Assessment Defined and Illustrated

Within the field of applied behavior analysis, we use the term **behavioral assessment** to describe our approach to *validly observing, measuring, and recording behavior*. Thus, the purpose of this chapter is to (1) teach you how to assess behavior to *develop and use rigorous observational, measurement, and recording systems*; (2) enable you, thereby, to *use that information to make scientifically and ethically sound decisions*, which, in turn will (3) *contribute toward your becoming a successful, effective, and efficient agent of behavior change*.

## Four Characteristics of a Good Measurement System

In their assessments, evaluations, and reports, ethically responsible behavior analysts rely on information and techniques sufficient to substantiate the results of their assessments and the recommendations based upon them.[3]

A first-rate measurement system is characterized by the use of *sensitive, objective, reliable,* and *valid* measures. A **sensitive measure** is one that *reflects subtle changes in the target response* (the response of interest). For example, suppose that to measure how rapidly someone ran the 50-yard dash, you used a watch that only measured time in minutes. That method would be less sensitive than if you had used a stopwatch that displayed time in *tenths* of a second.

An **objective measure** is *publicly verifiable*. Personal feelings or interpretations do not affect the scoring, and the definitions of the behavior are *observable, free of inferences, and unambiguous*. Generally, clear operational definitions of the behavior (i.e., behavior that is observable and measurable) are a part of objective data collection. (In contrast, a **subjective measure** i*s not publicly verifiable and does not readily permit others to reliably repeat or 'replicate" it.*)[4]

A **reliable measure** is one that is repeatable, i.e., *remains standard, or consistent, regardless of who does the measuring, on what occasions*. The measurement instrument produces consistent (repeatable) findings. Suppose two students, Ashely and Jorden, and a few of their friends used the same rubber ruler and concluded that a particular sheet of paper was 12 inches in length. We would say that the instrument was *reliable*. Suppose, instead, Ashley measured the length of that same piece of paper with a standard 12-inch wooden ruler and recorded 11 inches, then Jordan and several others independently measured the same piece of paper with the same ruler and also recorded 11 inches; we then would conclude that the instrument—the ruler—and the findings were reliable. But, if Ashley had measured the same paper with the rubber ruler and Jordan had measured it with the wooden ruler their results would differ. In that instance, they would know that their measurement methods were not reliable. When it comes to measuring *behavior*, you can only obtain reliable measures if the single measurement instrument includes objective behavioral definitions and precise instructions for use, so that regardless of who does the measuring the results will be essentially identical.

A **valid measure** is one that gauges *what it claims to measure*.[5] A scale measures weight, not height; a ruler measures dimensions of an object. We just saw, though, that if a measure is unreliable, it *cannot* be valid. Yet even if measures are found to be reliable they may *not necessarily* be valid. Probably the rubber ruler in our example above was not valid, because it had stretched over time. In another actual instance, one that happened in a case in one of

---

[3]We suggest you review the latest "Professional and Ethical Compliance Code for Behavior Analysts" endorsed by the Behavior Analysis Certification Board™ (2016).

[4]"One's judgment is subjective when it is based on something that cannot be shared with or repeated by others—the relevant events in such cases are usually called private. (By the way, that does not mean they are mental—they are events just like any others, but not as accessible—what's done behind a curtain is private just as what one does inside the skin when thinking is private—both are behavior, but it's easier to pull the curtain on the former than the latter.)" (Personal communication by A. Charles Catania, 8/24/10.)

[5]For those interested in the historical precursors of the concept of validity in testing/assessment, refer to Cronbach & Meehl (1955).

our space expeditions, while using a metric ruler to measure feet and inches did produce reliable results, they were invalid. Why? In that situation, a set of numbers based on imperial measurements—our feet and inches—was confused with those based on metric measurements. We could conclude that metric (wooden) rulers are reliable instruments because one would repeatedly obtain the same measurement results, but if inches are needed, the metric ruler clearly will not be a valid measure. Such questions about whether instruments really measure what they are supposed to measure are especially important in social assessments such as political polls, as well as in cases of human behavior.

We must use sensitive, objective, reliable, and valid measures to reveal clear patterns of performance prior to, during, and following a behavioral intervention. To illustrate, suppose our computer operators organize a team to research contemporary wisdom on the elements of safe posture (e.g., Alvero, Struss, & Rappaport, 2007; Burch, Clegg, & Bailey, 1987; McCann & Sulzer-Azaroff, 1996). We define each aspect in detail. All concur that the measures meet requirements for sensitivity, objectivity, reliability, and validity.

Now we should be just about ready to assess performance. But first, we pause to reassure ourselves that our plans are just, by reviewing our professional organization's ethical compliance code requiring that the assessments will be conducted and supervised by qualified persons and that appropriate steps will be taken to avoid their own or other's misuse of their intended ABA assessment or intervention methods. We must do our best to recognize the limitations of our chosen methods and avoid misinterpreting or misusing any findings we generate.

## Selecting Measures that Contribute to Treatment Outcome

Prior to initiating any action, especially before moving on to collecting baseline data, though, another issue also is worth considering. We need to reassure ourselves that our *measures are likely to "contribute to the outcome of treatment"* (Nelson, 1983). Hayes, Nelson, and Jarrett, (1987) use the phrase **treatment utility of assessment** to describe this general feature. In other words, the assessment must be able to contribute to the treatment's effectiveness. For example, in the previous chapter assessment data helped determine reinforcer effectiveness. Similarly, if assessment data show that the behavior is not improving as anticipated, you may need to modify the intervention. If your data show excellent progress in the target behavior, you would want to continue the intervention until the behavior has met your objective's criterion and is ready for you to implement maintenance strategies. What we do as behavior analysts is data based. In the case of the computer operators, the behavior analyst has studied ergonomic literature about the safe operation of computers, and the critical features of that operation are included in the set of measurements. Accordingly, as the measures of each element improve, so should the ultimate well-being of the operators. Lower incidence rates of repetitive strain injuries should result.

Here is another example: Suppose a classroom student is disruptive about 80 to 90 percent of the time. After the first week of intervention, the boy's disruption has been reduced by 10 to 20 percent. In the absence of plotted data, the gradual reduction may go unnoticed. The youngster might be seen as continuing to remain quite disruptive, so a promising program may risk being abandoned. However, after viewing a graph displaying the rate reduction, the contingency manager would be more likely to persist with the program, with a reasonable likelihood that the boy's conduct will continue to improve over time. The measures permitted continuation of a useful treatment.

## Designing or Selecting a Behavioral Measurement Method

As you become more familiar with the concepts of validity and reliability in behavioral measurement, you will begin to understand how the method used to record particular behaviors can influence those critical features. Some categories (or *classes*) of behavior lend themselves to one system of recording; others to another. For example, when behavior results in a tangible product, like the number of shoes assembled according to quality standards, simply *counting* is sufficient. When the behavior is fleeting or "transitory," another, such as *event* or *time sampling* (see below), may be preferable. The main consideration when selecting or designing a measurement method is that it should accurately or *validly* measure what it is supposed to measure. (To qualify as valid, measures also must be sensitive, reliable and objective.)

## SELECTING VALID MEASURES

As explained above, a *valid* measure is one that *assesses what it is supposed to measure*. According to Webster, *validity* implies that the measure is "… supported by objective truth or generally accepted authority." Valid measures must be appropriate to the variable they are to assess. You would not use a bathroom scale to measure shoe size or a ruler to determine the weight of a barbell. Recognize, though, that besides making sure you are using appropriate measurement systems, other factors, such as *reactivity* and *adaptation*, can influence the validity of the observation.

### Reactivity and Adaptation

**Reactivity** describes *the way the assessment procedures themselves* (not any intervention) *influence the client's behavior*, compromising, thereby, the validity of the data. For example, when the presence of live observers or recording equipment alters the environment, separating the effect of those on the client's behavior from those produced by the behavior-change program itself may be difficult. Because reactivity is a possible threat, when conducting live observation it is important to allow for *adaptation* prior to collecting baseline and intervention data. **Adaptation** refers to *a period of time that allows reactivity to subside*. When performance is relatively stable (say, no new highs or lows for three to five days in a row), you should feel confident in concluding that reactivity has diminished sufficiently for typical behavioral patterns to emerge.

Remember, *reactivity* is the individual's temporary, initial reaction to being observed; adaptation is the return to typical performance despite the ongoing observation, that is, the participant "gets used to being observed." Once adaptation has taken place, reactivity is less of a threat to the validity of the data. Let's look at an example. Professor Adams has presented his multimedia training workshop to impress institutional personnel with the importance of making frequent contacts with clients. The next day the professor visits his trainee's work sites, takes video records of interactions between the supervisor and clients, and later counts the number of times the staff has made contact with the clients. He returns on two other occasions, each time a month apart. How confident would you be that Adams' data validly represent what is happening in the worksite during his absence? The supervisors could have been reacting (atypically) to Professors Adams' presence, recalling his suggestion that they increase the number of times they make contact with their clients. Reactivity effects intrude when "observing a subject or subjects alters, either permanently or temporarily, their behavior" (Haynes & Horn, 1982, p. 370).

According to Haynes and Horn (1982), we may suspect reactive effects in observational data when there is:

- Systematic change in behavior rates, such as increases and decreases in behavior while an observer is present (e.g., a second observer finds that the number of contacts is much lower when Professor Adams is not present than when he is).
- Increased variability (the data jump around depending upon who is conducting the observation).
- Subjects' self-report of reactive effects. ("When I saw him come in, that reminded me that I needed to increase my contact with clients.")
- Any discrepancy among measures of the same behavior (Adams' observations and the client's reports of contacts by supervisors bear little relation to one another).

Such reactive effects appear to increase as the observation environment becomes increasingly more novel or different from the natural environment (e.g., Lipinski & Nelson, 1974). The degree, direction, or rate of occurrence of reactive effects also may vary among subjects as well as behaviors (Haynes, 1978; Haynes & Wilson, 1979). Here, based on suggestions by Haynes and Horn (1982), and on our own and others' experiences, we offer methods designed to minimize reactive effect:

- Minimize the obtrusiveness of the observers and observational process. For example, observers should sit in an inconspicuous location. Also, keep environmental change to a minimum.
- Minimize interactions between the subjects and observers as well as other discriminative (i.e., readily noticeable) properties of the observers.
- Instruct subjects to "act natural."
- Allow sufficient time for signs of reactivity in observational data to dissipate, signifying that subjects have adapted to the measurement system.
- Use a number of observers or observational procedures to cancel out the unintended bias (over- or underestimating; see below) that any single observer's recordings or observational procedures might unintentionally contribute.
- Involve participant observers or different or supplementary measures (e.g., products or results of behavior).
- Observe covertly, if necessary, especially if your presence is apt to bias the data. You can record through one-way mirrors, aluminum shade-screens like the inexpensive aluminum shade-screen box used by Brechner, Linder, Meyerson, and Hays (1974), or use wall-mounted cameras. For example, if observing using a telehealth service delivery model via video conferencing, turn off your video (i.e., the video that displays you) so your involvement is not obvious to the client.
- Use telemetry, video cameras, tape recorders, iPods, mobile phones containing video cameras, or other miniaturized systems directly within the setting, provided performers (or their guardians or advocates) agree to the monitoring of their behavior. Video-recordings have the advantage of preserving both motor and verbal behavior and can be replayed at regular, slow, or rapid speed as necessary for scoring purposes.

Contemporary video equipment also permits numerical counts to be superimposed upon the image, easing determining the rate of response. Live observers need not be involved to collect reliable data. Tape recorders and cameras can be programmed to sample behavior at pre-selected times.

## SELECTING RELIABLE MEASUREMENT SYSTEMS

Aunt Minerva has an erratic bathroom scale. Sometimes when she weighs herself the scale reads 150 pounds. In that case, she steps off and immediately steps back on, repeating the process until the scale reads 145 pounds. At this point she walks away, smiling and telling herself, "The diet is working!" Of course, Minerva's conclusion probably is flawed. The scale is unreliable, and she really has no way of knowing whether the diet is effective or not. A reliable scale—one that measures consistently—would provide Minerva with more convincing evidence of how well her diet is actually working. Probably you can see that reliability also influences the validity of the measurement system. Although high reliability is no assurance of high validity, high validity scores cannot be obtained if reliability is poor. For example, suppose Aunt Minerva gets on the scale and it is reliable in that it consistently reads 90 pounds, although her true weight is 150 pounds. Even though it is reliable, her scale does not provide a valid measurement.

Behavioral measurement requires consistency. If the observation system is not reliable, data may reflect a change in our own observing and recording response patterns, rather than in the behavior of interest itself (Baer et al., 1968). Consequently, to avoid inadvertently introducing error into the measurement system, prior to collecting formal data we must ensure that observations can be recorded *reliably—that more than one independent observer obtains essentially identical results.*

Two related major sources of error contributing to low interobserver reliability result from: (1)

not precisely specifying all the acts included in the target behavior, and (2) not providing a clear topographical description of what the behavior looks like. When broad or general evaluative categories such as *positive, negative,* or *neutral* are used, low interobserver agreement tends to result (Stouthamer-Loeber & Peters, 1984).

## Calculating Interobserver Agreement

We can best avoid introducing error into the measurement system by providing precise operational definitions of target behaviors, and training, supervising, and, if necessary, retraining the observers in their recording skills. Involving two (or more) observers, one who is naïve as to the purpose of the data collection and who simultaneously but independently records identical episodes, can also contribute to the reliability of the observation. Data become much more believable when at least one regular observer remains totally uninformed about the intervention procedures and expected outcomes. *By comparing the recordings of the two observers from episode to episode, we can determine how often their recordings match.* This comparison is known as **interobserver agreement (IOA)**. (You will learn an array of methods for calculating IOA later on in this chapter.)

The purpose of assessing IOA is to determine the consistency with which the target behavior is being recorded. We obtain IOA by having two independent observers (e.g., a teacher and an assistant, a mother and grandmother, or a staff manager and a floor manager) record the same target behaviors of the same individual during the same observation period. Afterward, we compare the two records and calculate the percentage of agreement. The higher the percentage, the more consistent the recording is, which, in turn, increases the reliability of the results. Although some might argue that achieving an IOA of at least 80 percent is necessary, there is no exact set standard. In fact, striving for as close to 100 percent as possible is best. Moreover, the *range* of IOA scores may prove to be more valuable than just the mean across a condition. For example, an IOA of 80 percent with a range from 10 to 95 percent is less reliable than an IOA of 75 percent with a range from 70 to 90 percent, even though it shows a higher average percentage agreement. Assessing IOA during each condition and phase, on multiple occasions, across days, times, settings, and observers is also important. Many recommend that at least a quarter to a third of all observation sessions include an assessment of IOA, so that the reliability data will more likely represent the individual's performance within that context (Kennedy, 2005; Poling, Methot, & LeSage, 1995).

## MEASURING TREATMENT INTEGRITY

**Treatment integrity**, also called **fidelity of implementation** or **program integrity**, refers to the *accuracy with which the intervention or treatment is implemented* (as described in Chapter 3). In other words, program fidelity exists if *the intervention was conducted as planned*. Measuring treatment integrity is important because researchers have demonstrated that errors impact learning, regardless if they are errors of omission (i.e., not doing part of the procedure) or errors of commission (i.e., doing something additional to the procedure). Specifically, Bergarmann, Kodak, and LeBlanc (2017) demonstrated that both errors of omission and errors of commission within a conditional discrimination teaching program resulted in compromised learning in typical developing children. Beyond the fact that clients are less likely to benefit from programs lacking fidelity, evaluating the effectiveness of an intervention is difficult if the treatment is not accurately implemented. Thus, in addition to measuring the behavior of interest and the reliability of the measurement system itself, to truly evaluate the effectiveness of an intervention, it is essential to ensure the intervention is implemented as planned. So, you will want to *include treatment integrity as a routine part of your measurement system*. Just as you design and apply a system for measuring changes in the target behavior(s), you also will want to develop and implement a measurement system to assess the extent to which your intervention is being implemented as intended.

Here is an example: The plan is to use a three-prompt procedure consisting of verbal, model, and physical prompts to present demands followed by praise as a consequence of a youngster's complying with those demands. Treatment integrity could be assessed by scoring the trainer's correct and incorrect implementation of the procedure just prior to the third prompt. *Implementation* would be scored as follows:

Score "correct" if the trainer

- correctly implemented each step (verbal, model, physical) without providing additional prompts;
- terminated the prompting sequence contingent on child compliance; and,
- if praise was delivered following any compliance before the third prompt.

Score "*Incorrect*" if the trainer

- provided any additional prompts (error of commission);
- praised compliance after the third prompt (error of commission); *or*
- omitted any step (error of omission).

The percentage of treatment integrity could then be assessed by dividing the number of correct instances by the total number of correct and incorrect instances and multiplying the result by 100. [Total correct / (total correct and incorrect) x 100]. If a low treatment integrity score is obtained (below about 85 percent), steps would be needed to "fix" it. (Refer back to Chapter 3, where we touch on some methods for promoting program fidelity.)

To review: Make sure the procedure is completely laid out in a step-by-step fashion and that all implementers are trained until they reach the criterion set for mastery. Be especially aware of **treatment drift**, which occurs when *the application of the intervention begins to veer off course from its originally intended path.* (Instead of altering the procedure independently, ask program implementers to review their concerns with the behavior analysts, who will use the data as the main basis for deciding if and how procedural changes or more training and feedback are merited.)

## Factors Influencing Reliability and Validity of Assessment

Factors that can raise validity issues include *instructional demand, measurement complexity, observers' awareness of being assessed,* and *observational bias.*

### Instructional Demand

**Instructional demand** refers to the effect on behavior produced by *variations in the manner in which instructions are presented to clients.* For example, Frisch and Higgins (1986) found that discrepancies in instructions influenced participants (i.e., instructional demand) by altering their performance during role-playing of social skills. Further, the investigators suggested that by varying instructions, an analyst might be able to optimize the validity of role-play assessments or identify the individual's response limits or capabilities. This sounds like a good suggestion, provided the object is to determine the limits of the individual's performance capabilities (what s/he *can* do); not to assess for *typical* ongoing behavior (what s/he typically *does* do). In the former case, the behavior analyst would need to standardize instructions so any observed changes in the client's behavior could then be attributed to the altered instructions. In other words, *standardizing and monitoring instructions are critical to ensuring that changes in client behavior are due to the procedure in place and not to changes in the way instructions are presented.*

### Measurement Complexity

**Measurement complexity** refers to t*he number and intricacy of the behaviors you are targeting.* Observers tend to collect more accurate data when the behaviors to be observed are not overly complex and they are limited in number (Dorsey, Nelson, & Hayes, 1986; Mash & McElwee, 1974). Remember, *an observer is more likely to accurately assess three or four behaviors than eight or nine.* If it is absolutely necessary to record information on many behaviors, we suggest you use several instruments and multiple observers. In this way, each observer can track a smaller, less complex set of behaviors.

### Observer Awareness of Being Assessed

Just as our clients' performance patterns may change as a function of being observed (reactivity), the same can be true of observers (**observer awareness of being assessed**). In fact, *when observers are conscious that their own scoring is being monitored,* observers' data have been found to be more accurate (Reid, 1970; Kent, Kanowitz, O'Leary, & Cheiken, 1977; Romanczyk, Kent, Diament, & O'Leary, 1973). Given this effect, when attempting to increase accuracy of measurement, you should frequently score and report the reliability of their measures back to the observers.

### Observational Bias

**Observational bias**, the *observer(s)' expectation that change will follow a particular direction,* can also influence data recording. Consequently, observers should avoid becoming vested in, or having a *bias,* toward particular behavioral outcomes. As mentioned, when feasible, it is best to keep at least one of the observers "blind" to the intervention procedures and desired outcomes or goals of the program.

## THE MEASUREMENT PROCESS

If you are to have confidence in the data you collect, you certainly will need to assure yourself and others that they truly represent the behaviors of interest. So, of course, you will do your best to ensure that your data measurement systems are valid, objective, reliable, and sensitive. Because no single data recording method serves all needs, researchers and practitioners in the field have designed a useful array of techniques suited to those requirements. We begin with simple counting and then move to more complex measures.

### Measuring Behavioral Products

Some behavior, like answering quiz questions or cleaning tables, leaves physical evidence in the form of a product that endures more or less permanently after the performance. The number of words or sentences written, accident reports turned in, clean table-tops, beds made, items below quality standards, woodworking projects completed, windows broken, and graphs drawn (each according to a preset standard) can be directly counted, either right away or perhaps later. Assessing **permanent products of behavior** for reliability should be fairly straightforward, because *the evidence remains intact.*

Most organizations use ongoing data systems such as rates of attendance, punctuality, records of injuries, production, quality, waste, unit costs, profits and losses, and other sorts of results. Schools gather standardized test scores, attendance, and other data from their students and staff. Health and service institutions document statistics on job and residential placements of clients, while advertisers calculate data about patronage of restaurants, hotels, and television broadcasting stations. Service, businesses, and political organizations survey the public to determine opinions and satisfaction with the concepts they are trying to promote. Sometimes these ongoing data systems can be used directly as primary measures of behavioral patterns, especially when they closely mirror the performance of concern. When attendance or punctuality is targeted for improvement, using attendance and time clock records would be suitable. **Permanent product recording**, then, is *an observational method based on assessing durable products of behavior.*

**Permanent products** are *outcomes of the behavior of interest;* therefore this method sometimes is referred to as **outcome recording**. Just about any tangible item directly tied to human performance illustrates a *permanent product*: a manufactured item, such as the quality of an athletic shoe (Sulzer-Azaroff & Harshbarger, 1995), a test paper, or the number of protective gloves used and disposed of by healthcare personnel (Babcock, Sulzer-Azaroff, Sanderson, & Scibak, 1992). Glenn and Dallery (2007) used permanent product recording to compare the effectiveness of two interventions designed to reduce cigarette smoking (transdermal nicotine patch versus a voucher-based reinforcement system): Participants were asked to breathe into an apparatus designed to measure and provide a *printout* of carbon monoxide readings. (Incidentally, they found that the voucher-based reinforcement system was more effective than transdermal nicotine patches.) In another illustration, Sulzer-Azaroff and Austin (2000) reviewed *published reports* of recorded data on *injury rates* before and after the implementation of behavioral safety programs in various work settings. (Results heavily favored the behavioral safety programs.)

Permanent product recording has several advantages. Most notably, it is convenient, especially because it does not require an observer at the exact moment the behavior occurs. This feature has the added advantage of reducing any potential *reactivity* (participants' temporary adjustment away from typical performance in response to observers). A classroom teacher does not have to sit and watch a student take a math test, but simply notes the number of math problems completed correctly.

Although outcome recording is convenient, some disadvantages are worth noting. One concern is that the responses accountable for producing a particular outcome may vary. For instance, it would be a mistake to assume that a student who scored 100 percent on a math test studied for any fixed time period. For example, Jack may have studied for 25 hours to get the 100 percent, while Aiden only studied for five hours to get the same result. Additionally, some outcomes can be influenced by factors other than the target response. Consider this example: Susan is quite overweight and hopes to become slimmer. She and the behavior analyst decide the best approach would be for Susan to change her habits, that is, to eat a healthier diet and to exercise. You measure her compliance with the suggested habit changes by recording Susan's weight each week. Suppose the numbers actually did diminish from one week to the next. Although that is what you want, you would really have no idea whether Susan actually lost weight as a function of exercising and adhering to a healthy diet, or in some other way (e.g., taking diuretics or purging). Thus, when deciding on a measurement system, you need to ask yourself if you are interested in just the outcomes or the mediating behavior(s) responsible for those outcomes as well.

Another potential issue with outcome measures is that sometimes it is impossible to know who was responsible for the outcome. For example, imagine you enter into a cafeteria and there is food and trash all over the floor. You could measure the number of items on the floor by simply counting each individual piece of trash, but still would have no idea who was responsible for putting the trash on the floor.

## Measuring Transitory Behaviors

Many kinds of behavior with which behavior analysts, teachers, and parents are concerned are **transitory behaviors**; that is, *they can be observed and counted as they come and go, but do not produce tangible, quantifiable outcomes or products.* Measuring such fleeting responses is more difficult. Hitting oneself, fighting, smiling, disrupting, consuming a healthy diet, working out, completing all steps in proper order in a training trial, sitting quietly and attending to a task, praising staff members, and the like are not permanent and cannot be assessed accurately after the fact. Quantifying such behavior requires that a live observer record the action while it is ongoing or else some other method needs to be chosen to preserve the performance, such as a video and/or audio recording. The latter methods, for example, can be both cost effective and at least as reliable as directly observing particular behaviors, such as the details of parent-child verbal interactions (Hansen, Tisdelle, & O'Dell, 1985).

Transitory measurement methods are flexible and can accommodate a wide range of behavioral dimensions. These include **topography**, *the form of the response* (which was elaborated upon in Chapter 4), its **magnitude size** or **intensity**, as in *the forcefulness of the response* (also described in Chapter 4, and later in this chapter under "episodic severity"); **frequency/event**, *the number of times the response occurs (when the number of times is measured over some constant time unit, as in responses per minute, the measure is often called a rate rather than a frequency)*; **duration**, *how long the response persists*; **latency**, *the time elapsed from some starting point to the onset of the response*; and **interresponse time (IRT)**, *the time between instances of the response (elapsed time from the end of one response to the beginning of the next).*

## RECORDING AND REPORTING TRANSITORY BEHAVIOR

### Event (Rate) Recording

Among the most common techniques for recording transitory behavior involve one or more of the following: frequency, event recording, duration (timing), and time sampling. Frequency recording involves simply counting the occurrences of a behavior, such as number of interruptions without regard to time (Carr, Nosik & Luke, 2018; Merbitz, Merbitz, & Pennypacker, 2016). Event recording, one of the more frequently used observational methods, involves counting how often a specific behavior occurs within an interval, session, class period, day, week, month, or observation period. Event and frequency recordings are particularly appropriate for measuring discrete behaviors: behaviors that have both a clear beginning and end. The number of pages read, days present, answers correct, paper airplanes thrown, sibling bites, or tasks completed are all discrete events. However, the behavior must not occur so rapidly that the observer loses count, as in pencil tapping or blinking. Furthermore, occurrences should be roughly equivalent in duration, or the data could be misleading. For example, suppose you decide to measure the number of times a child cries. The first day the child cries three times throughout the day and each time cries for only two minutes. The next day the child only cries once throughout the day, but it lasts for ten minutes. Has crying decreased or increased? Were it based on event recording, your data would erroneously suggest it decreased, because the number of episodes of crying dropped from three to one. Based on the total amount of *time* spent crying, however, the behavior actually increased from six minutes to ten minutes. Here you can see why event recording would not be valid unless the instances were roughly equivalent in duration. For such reasons, event recording is *not* appropriate for (1) behavior occurring at such a high frequency that an accurate count is not possible, or (2) behavior that tends to vary in duration.

> *Event recording (rate) = number of times behavior repeated per specific period of time*

Event recording has been used for a range of classes of discrete behaviors, such as the number of tics exhibited by children (Himle et al., 2006), words read correctly and incorrectly (Gorthmaker, Dally, McCurdy, Persampieri, & Hergenrada, 2007), times an individual asks for a preferred item (Wallace, Iwata, & Hanley, 2006), donations made to a supermarket food bank (Farrimond & Leland, 2006), repetitive behavior exhibited by a child (Wetterneck & Woods, 2006), instances in which an individual engages in self-injury (Worsdell, Iwata, Hanley, Thompson, & Kahng, 2000), or aggresses (Johnson, McComas, Thompson, & Symons, 2004), to name a few.

A variety of instruments have been used to record such discrete events:

- checklists
- pencil and paper notations
- wrist counters (Lindsley, 1968; Landry & McGreevy, 1984)
- hand or golf counters (such as those used to count the number of people entering public events)
- electromechanical counters/micro-switches, some of which may be connected to a computer for subsequent analysis
- smart phones equipped with observation software that can be taken along with you

Another simple way to count events is to transfer paper clips, beans, pennies, or some other type of small object from one pocket to another each time the behavior occurs, or simply to make a tally mark on a piece of paper.

Once you have documented behavior using event recording, there are a few ways you can summarize, report, and graph the data. At the simplest level, you can indicate *frequency of occurrence* (e.g., Marty swore nine times on Monday and ten times on Tuesday). You also can use frequency to report **trials to criterion**: *the number of responses it takes for someone to meet the standard set for success.* You also can report **rate** of behavior, *expressed as the number of occurrences divided by a standard period of time.* When the observational time is consistent from observation to observation, you can report the event with the understanding that it is for a specific amount of time. However, reporting *average rate* is preferable when the time during which observations are conducted varies from one session to the next. For example, suppose you observed for one hour, from 9:00 a.m. until 10:00 a.m. on Monday, and recorded that Marty swore nine times; then observed for two hours, from 9:00 a.m. until 11:00 a.m. on Tuesday and recorded that Marty swore ten times. You would, appropriately, report the data as *rate per hour*: nine per hour on Monday (rate = 9/1) and five per hour on Tuesday (rate = 10/2).

> Rate =
> number of responses (divided by) standard time period and expressed as "per _____ (the time period)"

Sometimes, neither event nor rate are appropriate measures to report, particularly when the occurrence of interest depends on when available opportunities are limited (i.e., restricted) or time blocks vary. In such cases, you must report **percentage of opportunities** (occurrences/opportunities x 100) or percentage of time blocks (occurrence of days a behavior occurs/number of days sessions took place that week X 100). Suppose, for instance, I wanted to report the number of times Mrs. Kettler called on Ryan when the boy raised his hand. Given that Mrs. Kettler's behavior depends on Ryan's behavior, the appropriate approach would be to record the number of times Mrs. Kettler called on Ryan and divide it by the number of times Ryan raised his hand. If Mrs. Kettler called on Ryan 10 times and Ryan raised his hand 20 times we would report that Mrs. Kettler called on Ryan 50 percent of the opportunities. Using percentage data is similarly appropriate when conducting *discrete trial training programs* (in which the student is to follow a specific series of instructions). *Whenever the rate of response is limited or restricted, you must report the number of response opportunities and the percentage responded to correctly.* (Note: when recording the number of opportunities and the number of occurrences of a behavior, it is important to calculate IOA for both the number of opportunities AND the number of occurrences. More on this topic later in this chapter). This point becomes extremely important if the number of opportunities varies from one observation to the next. To illustrate further, suppose you were recording a bank teller's courteousness (e.g., defined as looking at, smiling, and greeting customers by name). Simply listing the number of times the teller engaged in those skills would be meaningless unless you also counted the number of customers the teller served per hour. (See Brown & Sulzer-Azaroff, 1994, for a related study.)

> Duration =
> time elapsed from the beginning to the end of responding

## Duration Recording

**Duration recording** measures *the total time elapsed between the start of the behavior and its completion.* Duration recording is especially useful when the time the individual engages in the behavior is of particular concern or when the occurrences of a class of behavior varies in duration, as with the earlier crying illustration. You can use a wall clock, stopwatch, kitchen timer, or wristwatch to measure the duration of behavior. Most cell phones are equipped with clocks that permit users to record the onset and offset of an event with relative ease.

Suppose Mr. Taylor is worried about how much time his employee, Karen, seems to be spending on her breaks. Mr. Taylor could activate a stopwatch whenever Karen leaves her work station and stop it when she returns. After observing for, say, five days, he could then determine Karen's average break time by combining the durations of all breaks and dividing it by the number of breaks she took during the week. Duration measures also have been used to help guide treatment selection for problem behavior maintained by automatic reinforcement. In a concurrent assessment (noncontingent vs. differential reinforcement arrangement), Berg, et al., (2016) utilized duration not only to measure how long individual clients manipulated objects and engaged in problem behavior, but also to measure the client's relative preference for social reinforcement. They subsequently utilized this information to heighten the effectiveness of developing and implementing interventions to eliminate problem behavior.

The duration of the time people spend on-task (*engaged time*), such as in learning or job activities, often is quite important. As Gettinger (1986, p. 14) has reminded us, "academic engaged time is related to student achievement." The same is true, of course, of remaining involved in job tasks, sports and other recreational activities, and so on. For instance, duration has been the primary measure of academic task engagement (Athens, Vollmer, & Pipkin, 2007), preference for vocational tasks (Worsdell, Iwata, & Wallace, 2002), and free-time social interactions for students with autism and their typical peers (Kamps, Barbetta, Leonard, & Delquadri, 1994), among others.

## Latency

We often take a rapid response to a signal as a sign that the individual is eager to get going (i.e., "likes the activity"), as when children scurry off to hunt for Easter eggs as soon as the starting signal sounds. One indicator of runners' skills is how rapidly they dart from the starting block. Conversely, beginning slowly hints at a lack of enthusiasm, as in procrastinating before starting work on a term paper or attacking a pile of ironing or old photographs that need sorting. In these instances, latency would be a measure to consider. **Latency** *is measured by recording the amount of time elapsed between the onset of when a signal is provided until the response occurs* (see Figure 7.3). For example, in a race we might measure the time elapsed from the starting gunshot

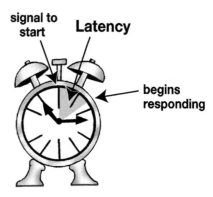

**Figure 7.3** Latency is measured by recording the time that elapses from the signal to begin until the response occurs.

to the runner's darting forward (the onset of the behavior). Sometimes we wish to combine measurement systems. For example, Wehby and Hollahan (2000) wanted to measure not only task engagement (a duration measure), but also to evaluate the effects of a high-probability request procedure on the time it took an elementary school student to initiate an academic task, math work (a latency measure). Suppose Paula is interested in reducing the time it takes her to begin preparing her reports. She can start a stopwatch at the moment that she notes she has collected her last necessary piece of information and stop it when she strikes the first key on her computer, recording the elapsed time, or her latency, of responding.

*Latency* has been used as a measure of treatment effectiveness in a number of clinical cases. One tested a method designed to increase food consumption and reduce food-packing (collecting food inside the mouth) by four children with severe feeding disorders (Gulotta, Piazza, Patel, & Layer, 2005). The method consisted of redistributing the food with a bristled massaging toothbrush while personnel assessed the time it took for food to be absent from the client's mouth. While all the children reduced their food-packing, two also shortened their *latencies* to attaining a clean mouth.

*Latency = time elapsed from signal until initiation of response*

## Interresponse Time (IRT)

Still another important measure is the time between two like responses—their **interresponse time (IRT)**. IRT is measured by recording *the time from the offset of one response (R1) to the onset of the next (R2), or the time between instances of the response.* (When response duration is brief, the time from the beginning to the end of the response can usually be ignored.) IRT measures have been used to program various treatment schedules (Kahng, Iwata, DeLeon, & Wallace, 2000) as well as to synchronize model IRT rhythmic beats to treat stuttering (Azrin, Jones, & Flye, 1968). In a recent study, Page, Griffity, and Penrod (2017) used interresponse time (IRT) to measure and help manage the rapid eating of a young lady with autism; that is, when a given (increasing) time interval elapsed, they used a vibrating pager to signal that it would now be appropriate for her to take a bite. As a result, the IRT between bites increased.

> *Interresponse time = time elapsed from R1 to R2*

As in event recording, several methods may be used to record duration, latency, and interresponse times (IRT): activating a stopwatch to measure *duration*; recording starting and ending times and subtracting the former from the latter; using a paper and pencil to record onset and offset times on a data sheet. Alternatively, you can mount a computer program on a laptop or a personal data assistant (PDA) (see Kahng & Iwata, 1998, for a review of computerized observational programs).

## Interval Time-Sampling Systems

When instances of behavior have no clear onset and offset, counting episodes is not feasible. Just as measuring the quality of every drop of water in a reservoir, or the quality of every cubic foot of the air above a city would not be feasible, the same is true of many kinds of continuous behaviors: remaining on-task, playing cooperatively with other children, operating a computer keyboard safely, rocking, chewing gum, and so on. An alternative approach is to use *sampling* to estimate how often the behavior occurs over time by periodically probing events or continuing actions (Arrington, 1943).

Lucretia's parents have decided to observe her closely to determine how cooperatively she is playing with other children. They consider counting the frequency of cooperative play episodes. It soon becomes apparent, however, that cooperative play does not lend itself to counting because the durations of play vary so much. Additionally, Lucretia's mom really prefers not to have to spend all her time recording because she needs to take care of other chores. The behavior analyst explains that their problem is not unique and that systems of measurement have been devised to solve this challenge. These are called *interval time-sampling systems*.

Many kinds of behavior are not clearly discrete but rather are **continuous**: *they do not have a clear beginning or ending.* For example, deciding exactly when each response begins and ends is difficult when it comes to behavior such as talking to peers, thumb-sucking, engaging in stereotypy, humming, etc. Or suppose a client makes many loud and disruptive noises, screeching, shouting, hitting furniture, and rattling his chair. Counting each response or measuring its duration would be difficult. When does one episode of chair rattling end and another begin? In such instances, interval time-sample recording provides the most reliable data.

With a stop-action camera or video player, assessing such responses within brief time frames is possible. Those data may then be used as samples of the client's behavior. This is the process involved in **interval time-sampling** recording systems: *The simple presence or absence of the responses of interest within an interval is scored. The interval time-sampling method requires that the observer divide the observation session into time intervals of equal lengths, and record behavior as occurring or not occurring within each interval.* Later the measure is converted into a *percentage of intervals* during which the behavior occurred. Although in the simplest case, the intervals are of equal durations, you may use *preset* varying intervals. However, for the time being, we limit ourselves to describing and illustrating the simpler recording methods (those with constant intervals) to illustrate time-sampling methods.

Three popular interval time-sampling methods are used to estimate the rate of a response. In **whole-interval time sampling**, *the response must be emitted throughout the entire interval* if it is to be scored as occurring. In **partial-interval time sampling**, *the response must occur at least once during any part of the interval, even if only briefly,* for it to be scored. In **momentary time sampling**, *the response must occur at the moment the interval ends* for it to be scored. Let us see the various ways one could score Jared's annoyingly loud humming, using these three different time sampling methods:

Look at the data sheet displayed in Figure 7.4. Do you notice that although the humming was present identically in all three cases, the results changed as a result of the sampling system used? As a basis for recording, suppose someone activated a stopwatch to accumulate all moments when humming was ongoing. Results may have been more accurate (valid), but that would have been very labor intensive. Time sampling generally turns out to be more practical. Time-sampling methods have been used to measure a wide range of behaviors such as disruption (O'Callaghan et al., 2006), children's tics (Himle et al., 2006), on-task behavior (Allday & Pakurar, 2007), and social interactions (Petursdottir, McComas, McMaster, & Horner, 2007), to name but a few. We need to choose our method and the size of sampling intervals with care if our measures are to be valid.

**Summary of Jared's behavior.** According to whole-interval time sampling we would say that Jared engaged in humming during 25 percent of the intervals. However, if we used partial-interval time sampling we would say that Jared engaged in humming during 95 percent of the intervals. Finally, if we used momentary time sampling we would say

Name: Jarred; Behavior: Humming – depicted by continuous production of sound. (Appropriate for any other form of behavior lacking clear-cut beginnings or endings, such as smiling, frowning, playing, sitting straight, spinning around, making eye contact of just about any of that nature). Which appears to be more conservative, liberal, valid in this case?

**Step 1:** Break observation period into equal intervals. (Here we have 20 thirty second intervals.)

| 1 | 2 | 3 | 4 | 5 | 6 | 7 | 8 | 9 | 10 | 11 | 12 | 13 | 14 | 15 | 16 | 17 | 18 | 19 | 20 |

**Step 2:** Record occurrence of response during intervals.

**Whole interval time sampling:** Record response only if it occurs throughout the interval.

Ummm......mmmmm......mmmmmm........m...mmmmm..m.........m.............m..........mm.........mmm

|   |   |   | + |   | + | + |   | + |   |   |   |   |   |   |   |   |   |   |   |

**Partial-interval time sampling:** Record response if it occurs at any time during the interval.

Ummm......mmmmm......mmmmmm........m...mmmmm..m.........m.............m..........mm.........mmm

| + | + | + | + | + | + | + | + | + | + | + | + |   | + | + | + | + | + | + | + |

**Momentary time-sampling:** Record response only if it is occurring at the very moment when the interval ends.

Ummm......mmmmm......mmmmmm........m...mmmmm..m.........m.............m..........mm.........mmm

| + |   | + | + |   | + | + |   | + |   | + |   | + |   | + |   | + |   |   |   |

**Step 3.** Convert into percentage of occurrence.
**Whole-interval** time-sampling: 5/20 = 25%
**Partial interval** time-sampling: 19/20 = 95%
**Momentary time-sampling**: 10/20 = 50%

**Figure 7.4** Illustration of a time sampling recording form

that Jared engaged in humming during 50 percent of the observed instances. (Momentary time sampling does not involve collecting data in intervals, but only at the moment the behavior is observed. Certain intervals may have passed, but unlike partial- or whole-time sampling, the data are not collected in intervals.) You simply record if the behavior is occurring or not, each time at the moment you observe the client's behavior.

## Selecting a Time-Sampling Method

We always want to be conservative when measuring behavior; that is, we want to avoid claiming that an intervention was more or less successful than it actually was (accepting a false or rejecting a true conclusion). Now that we see how the three time-sampling methods are used, let us discuss the characteristics inherent in each and when selecting each method is most appropriate.

Usually, when you want to measure a non-discrete or continuous behavior with the goal of increasing it, select the more conservative whole-interval time sampling. For behaviors that have been targeted for reduction, again to remain conservative, select partial-interval time sampling. When you hope to promote the total presence (e.g., attending to work) rather than the absence (as in our humming instance) of a behavior, choosing whole-interval scoring is most appropriate. Heather hopes to maintain correct posture at the computer at all times, so finding a way to continuously assess that set of behaviors, such as recording and scoring a video taped while she worked at the keyboard, would yield the most useful or valid results. She or someone else then could score whether her body positioning completely matched the standards for proper posture, or not, throughout each interval.

Because we only count intervals during which the behavior (e.g., sitting properly) persists *throughout*, whole-interval time sampling tends to be a conservative measure for sitting properly (see Alvero et al., 2007). In fact, it *underestimates* the rate of sitting properly (since Heather may have been sitting properly for portions of some of the intervals); thus any results we report would conservatively estimate the treatment's effectiveness. Had Heather rounded her back for even a second, the entire interval would lose its opportunity to be scored. We could say that the momentary slouch "spoiled" the interval. (It is for reasons like this that some use the term "interval spoilage" in whole-interval sampling systems.) Therefore, *using a whole-interval method is the more conservative time-sampling measure to use when your goal is to increase, not to decrease, behavior.*

For another example of what we mean by a "conservative estimate," notice that if the whole-interval system were used for the humming example, only time blocks 1, 4, 6, 7, and 11 would be scored as containing the behavior. Yet Jared certainly was humming during portions of other intervals. Such a measure would not provide a conservative, but actually an inflated, measure of progress toward the goal of reducing the behavior (his humming), as discussed below.

Partial-interval time sampling *overestimates* behavior, because emitting the behavior during even a small fraction of the time within the interval results in the entire interval being scored for the behavior. Therefore, in the case of Jared's humming, partial-interval time sampling is appropriately conservative, because the goal of intervention is to *decrease* behavior. Recognize that if the observer detected the slightest hum, the entire interval would be credited with containing the hum, thereby making things appear worse than they actually were. On the other hand, were the interval scored with a minus, we would be quite confident that the hum was entirely absent for that time period. When intervals scored for any behavior diminish over time, we, as viewers of the data, would be able to conclude with a fair degree of confidence that it *really* was diminishing.

"Whoa!" we can hear you saying. "Yes, I do want to use data as a basis for determining the effectiveness of the procedure I'm trying, but where am I to get the resources to have my students (or clients, personnel, customers, patients, members…) observed continuously? Even recording and scoring videotapes consumes more time than I can possibly muster."

That's right! Whole- and partial-interval time samplings require that the individual's behavior be observed and recorded continuously. Therefore, for his teacher to teach a class while recording her student Marty's on-task behavior (or for a person to conduct a therapy session, serve clientele, address administrative tasks, and so on) would be difficult if not impossible. The teacher could never turn her back on Marty. What *would* be feasible, however, is for her to obtain an estimate of how much time Marty remains on-task by using momentary time sampling recording. (See Repp, Roberts, Slack, Repp, & Berkler, 1976, for a more detailed explanation of errors produced by time sampling methods.)

Momentary time sampling permits the recording of the behavior during *preset fleeting points in time*, say when cued by a random-time generator, kitchen timer, audio or vibrating (a preferred choice, because the timer sound may cue the individual) timer signal, or other method. (Can you guess why the observation times must be *predetermined*? If you answered that you minimize biasing the data, you are on the right track.) The distortions this method may produce tend to be randomly distributed, leading sometimes to over-estimating and sometimes to underestimating the actual occurrence of the behavior of interest. When using momentary time sampling, the way to remain conservative is to keep the intervals as short as feasible and to adhere to a schedule of frequent preset observations. In fact, Sharp, Mudford and Elliffee (2015) provide an equation to utilize to determine how often one should record behavior using momentary-time sampling for it to be both accurate and efficient. If you are unable to do one or the other, you risk producing error patterns in your observational data. Remember, though, that because time sampling is a form of estimating, the method can pose risks to validity. Even when you keep the intervals short and observe frequently, you cannot fully predict or control the errors. Consequently, we suggest you limit sampling to situations when the behavior of concern is not dangerous and/or when you involve data collectors who are assigned to record ongoing behavior as one of their main job functions.

"But," you might protest, "momentary time sampling makes little sense in some of the cases you described"; and you are right. We probably wouldn't want our supervisors to compliment their employees so often that they would risk being labeled "gushy." Depending on the employee's long-term and recent history of reinforcement (Berg et al., 2000), a minimum of, say, once every fifteen minutes might be sufficient. In that case, we would be better served by using a partial-time interval (or "interval spoilage") system. A reasonable recording interval here could be fifteen minutes; the first time the supervisor delivered a compliment within the interval, we would score the interval a plus, and then be able to turn to our other duties.

To obtain reasonably valid results when using partial-interval scoring, Powell, Martindale, and Kulp (1975) have suggested using intervals of 80 seconds or shorter; Jacobsen (1982), less than five minutes. Of course, one must balance this time consideration against available resources, including personnel, other problems needing to be addressed at the same time, the skill of the observer, and so on.

Here is a semi-fictitious example of how the above considerations might fit into the larger scheme of things: Consider, once again, the risk of poor body positioning while operating a computer keyboard for long time periods. As mentioned, one approach to dealing with those challenges has been to observe the operators' positions while typing, and to provide them with feedback on their levels of safe posture. In a case of this nature, one would record (1) the operator's safety performance and (2) the supervisor's regularity in providing feedback. In this situation, the observer would watch and record each worker's posture in sequences of six one-minute intervals, using a whole-interval recording system. Whichever positions—feet, hands, shoulders, or head—remained correct, according to pre-designed and trained standards, throughout the interval (a whole-interval method) would be circled.

Simultaneously, the observer would record *any instance* of a supervisor providing feedback during that interval (partial-interval) and whether it was negative or positive. (See Figure 7.5 for a sample scoring sheet.)

Another consideration when designing observational systems is whether or not reserving a time interval for recording the data is necessary (e.g., ten seconds to *observe*; five seconds to *record*). When trying to capture a single response pattern, such as the presence or absence of hitting or remaining on-task, all an observer needs to do is make a single mark, so setting aside an interval for recording probably wouldn't be necessary. In situations like in Figure 7.4, allowing a specific minimal length of time to record seems reasonable, so the observer can return to paying attention to the behavior of interest. Recognize, however, that some portions of the ongoing behavior will be missed during the scoring interval; therefore, keep the gap allowed for recording just brief enough to optimize validity. The longer that recording interval, the more data will be lost during that interim.

To summarize, paper-and-pencil as well as computerized methods are acceptable ways of collecting time-sampling data.[6] While time sampling is an acceptable alternative to measuring every instance of a behavior, it does carry a certain amount of risk with it, because, depending upon the factors just discussed, the results can be biased to some extent. Be careful, then, when selecting a time-sampling system. (Refer to Table 7.1)

**Contra-indications for using time sampling.** Besides the estimation errors inherent in time-sampling methods, time-sampling recording is not practical for observing certain important but fairly infrequent behaviors. Two boys, for example, may fight no more than once a week. Because no one is observing them continuously, those infrequent events may not be recorded. Nevertheless, given the seriousness of the situation, it probably would need to be addressed. Arrington (1943) suggested that, as a general rule, if the dependent variable (the behavior of interest) occurs less than once in 15 minutes on an average, some other method of recording needs to be chosen. Moreover, Sharp et al. (2015) demonstrated that using momentary time sampling with behavior with low durations produced inaccurate results as compared to behavior that occurred with intermediate or high durations.

---

[6]See the text's Web page for examples of partial-interval, whole-interval, and momentary time sampling data sheets

---

Observation Form

Scoring abbreviations:
Worker Performance: Feet & Legs (F); Hands (Ha); Shoulders (S); Head (Hd).
Supervisor Performance: Ignore (I); Positive feedback (P); Negative feedback (N)

Interval 1 2 3 4 5 6
Worker [F Ha S Hd] [F Ha S Hd] [F Ha S Hd] [F Ha S Hd] [F Ha S Hd] [F Ha S Hd]
Supervisor [ P N I ] [ P N I ] [ P N I ] [ P N I ] [ P N I ] [ P N I ]
Interval 1 2 3 4 5 6
Worker [F Ha S Hd] [F Ha S Hd] [F Ha S Hd] [F Ha S Hd] [F Ha S Hd] [F Ha S Hd]
Supervisor [ P N I ] [ P N I ] [ P N I ] [ P N I ] [ P N I ] [ P N I ]
Interval 1 2 3 4 5 6
Worker [F Ha S Hd] [F Ha S Hd] [F Ha S Hd] [F Ha S Hd] [F Ha S Hd] [F Ha S Hd]
Supervisor [ P N I ] [ P N I ] [ P N I ] [ P N I ] [ P N I ] [ P N I ]
Interval 1 2 3 4 5 6
Worker [F Ha S Hd] [F Ha S Hd] [F Ha S Hd] [F Ha S Hd] [F Ha S Hd] [F Ha S Hd]
Supervisor [ P N I ] [ P N I ] [ P N I ] [ P N I ] [ P N I ] [ P N I ]
Interval 1 2 3 4 5 6
Worker [F Ha S Hd] [F Ha S Hd] [F Ha S Hd] [F Ha S Hd] [F Ha S Hd] [F Ha S Hd]
Supervisor [ P N I ] [ P N I ] [ P N I ] [ P N I ] [ P N I ] [ P N I ]

**Figure 7.5** A portion of an observation form for monitoring posture and supervisor feedback.

**TABLE 7.1 Choosing a Time-Sampling Method**

| Method | Errors | Use Especially When |
|---|---|---|
| Whole | Underestimates | Increasing Behavior |
| Partial | Overestimates | Decreasing Behavior |
| Momentary | Random | Observational Constraints |

## Selecting Appropriate Measurements Based Upon Dimensions of Behavior

Knowing the specifics of each measurement system is a good place to start when trying to select how you will record data on the behavior identified for change. However, most behaviors do not necessarily lend themselves to just one measurement system. Thus, selecting the appropriate measurement system is a process. One way to ensure that you have selected an appropriate measurement system is to record data and see if you get the information you need regarding that specific behavior. Another way of selecting the measurement system is to determine the dimension of the behavior you are interested in and then pairing it up with a specific procedure. In fact, one of the authors teaches her students how to select the appropriate measurement system by taking all of the systems and asking can the behavior be recorded based upon each system (if not, scratch that system off the list). Then after identifying the ones that can work, go through the benefits and disadvantages of each to decided which system to utilize. LeBlanc, Raetz, Sellers, and Carr (2016) proposed a decision-making model for selecting a measure system to record problem behavior.

## Episodic Severity or Intensity

When dealing with challenging behavior, the severity of an episode may be especially relevant. Consider the distinction between gently patting someone on his head versus delivering a crushing blow to his skull. This particularly relevant feature often has been overlooked in situations in which simple frequency measures were used to assess classes of behavior of that nature. A more sensitive metric can be added to the assessment: **episodic severity (ES)** or *"the measure of intensity or gravity of a behavioral incident"* (LaVigna & Willis, 2005, p. 47). This more refined method offers some simple suggestions for obtaining sensitive and valid measures of challenging behavior, based on the justification that:

- "the social validity of a behavioral support plan can be enhanced by measuring and reducing the ES of challenging behavior, in addition to improving quality of life, to reducing the rate and severity of the behavior over time, and to ensuring the durability and generalization of results." (p. 48)
- Assessing and validating ES may lead to "a validated technology for crisis management." (p. 49)

**Assessing episodic severity.** LaVigna and Willis suggested a number of ways for assessing ES, depending on the problem behavior. One is a rating scale for behaviors such as self-injury, aggression, and temper tantrums. For example, a 5-point rating scale could be used for self-injury, with a rating of 5 indicating a need to go to the hospital for medical treatment; 4 representing an injury that could be treated in the facility; 3, an injury that left marks but required no treatment; 2, self-abusive behavior that did not leave any markings; and 1, attempted physical self-abuse that was stopped before it occurred (e.g., an attempt at self-hitting was blocked, or the client's behavior was redirected before the arm or hand made contact with his body). The ES for temper tantrums might also be measured by the *duration* of the episode. The severity of property destruction might be measured by the cost to repair or replace the damaged property. Once such additional data have been collected, "these results could be reported in terms of the mean severity rating of behavioral incidents during baseline and subsequent treatment phases and the range of those severity ratings" (p. 48). It is impor-

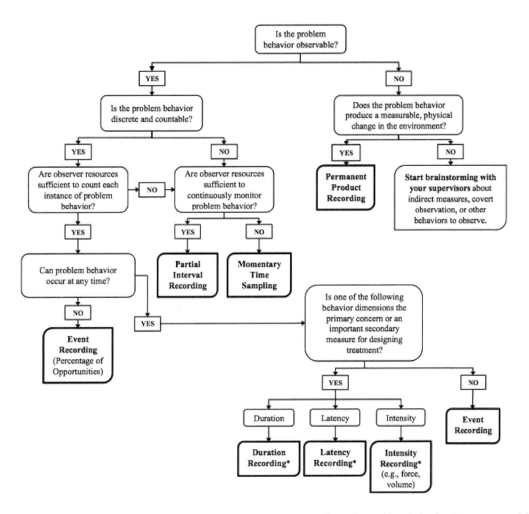

**Figure 7.6** A decision-making model for selecting measurement procedures for problem behavior. Note; an asterisk also generates a frequency count.

tant to note that these scales must be completely objective and that each unit of the scale must be fully operationally defined.

Consider a similar approach in other situations in which intensity, quantity, or quality of a particular behavior may produce a socially meaningful difference (intensity of acts of kindness, strength or power of a physical activity like pitching a ball, degree of gentleness in caring for a younger sibling, and so on). If you do decide to use a qualitative rating of this nature, though, be certain to define each score precisely, train your observers thoroughly, and maintain quality assurance by regularly assessing scorer reliability. Some will recognize this sort of rating scale as a BARS or **behaviorally-anchored rating scale**, *a method of assessing performance by assigning a numerical value to one's judgments. Each number on the scale represents a specific set of observable behaviors, such as steps, tasks, or skills involved in a complex task. These numbers and their corresponding behaviors are located on a rating scale.*

## Observing Behavior in Groups

Sometimes our concern is with changing the performance of groups of individuals. Fortunately, a variety of observation systems have been developed for special situations like this, specifically the *zone* system, *PLA-Check*, and *ecobehavioral assessment*[7] that lend themselves to observing the behavior of group members.

**The zone system.** Observational recording of behaviors with no clear beginning and end, like engaging in social play (continuous); or of behaviors with clear on- and off-sets, such as moving to a new specific location (discrete); or their results can prove difficult in large settings, especially when individuals tend to move from one area to another. The **zone system** was developed for these circumstances and is used not only in our own field of human and animal analysis and intervention, but also by animal ecologists to track the behavior of nonhuman animals (e.g., white-tailed deer, Jacobsen, 1982). The method is analogous to the time-sampling system, except rather than, or in addition to, dividing up time into small intervals, you divide up *space*. Using whatever observational method is appropriate for the behavior being observed, *the observer sequentially observes within one particular area or zone at a time, regardless of how many are present.* To illustrate, this system might be appropriate to record social cooperation (as defined) in areas of the school cafeteria or playground, or the level of safe performance of a set of factory workers (Sulzer-Azaroff & Fellner, 1984).

You may want to test the extent to which particular behavior occurs within a given activity area. You can do that by (1) choosing that zone, (2) dividing it up into sub-zones if necessary, (3) specifying a time limit for observing within each of those sub-zones, and (4) totaling the number of individuals engaged and not engaged with that time period (LeLaurin & Risley, 1972). Alternatively or in addition, you can count (1) *the number of individuals* actively occupying and performing in the zone as intended (or not), and/or (2) the total number of *instances* of a particular discrete behavior (e.g., offering assistance), (3) the number of *individuals* engaged in any of a variety of *other* behaviors, or even (4) the *results* of particular behaviors (e.g., toys put away) when those occur during the observational time period within that particular zone or area.

To obtain as representative a picture as possible of what actually is happening:

- Keep each zone relatively small.
- Spend equivalent amounts of time observing in each zone.
- Repeat the observations at given time intervals such as every three minutes for however long it is appropriate to continue (e.g., during "free-play" sessions) (Jacobsen, 1982).
- Provide similar opportunities for the target behaviors to be emitted within each zone.
- It may help to sketch a map onto the recording sheet to remind observers of the location of each area (Sulzer-Azaroff & Mayer, 1986, p. 29).

**PLA-Check.** Used widely in educational, day care, rest home, and other human-service settings to estimate the extent to which participants are engaged in planned activities, **Planned Activity Check (PLA-Check)** is a variant of momentary time sampling (Risley & Cataldo, 1973). *The observer simply counts the number of individuals who are actually engaged in the assigned activity at a particular moment. The sum is divided by the total number of individuals assigned to the activity.* Observations are conducted frequently over several days. In one study, the object was to determine how best to organize the educational environment to promote high levels of productive student engagement (Wilczenski et al., 1987). Teachers used PLA-Check to assess patterns of performance by mainstreamed special education students and their peers. PLA-Check also was used to describe preschoolers' preference for various classroom activities, advocating using such data to design effective free-play contexts (Hanley, Cammilleri, Tiger, & Ingvarrson, 2007). Thus, PLA-Check can be used to help determine how best to alter an environment to promote high levels of productive engagement. Similarly, managers and administrators could use PLA-Check to determine how effectively different leaders, supervisors, or teachers promote rates of productive engagement.

---
[7]See Chapter 10 for a more thorough description of ecobehavioral assessment.

## METHODS FOR CALCULATING INTEROBSERVER AGREEMENT

Earlier in this chapter, we discussed how important it is for our data to be reliable, because unreliable data cannot be valid. Now that you have become familiar with an array of observational recording systems, you will want to become skilled in assessing *interobserver agreement (IOA)*, especially so the data you use to support your recommended strategies are really convincing. Here we offer an array of methods suited to that purpose.

### IOA for Permanent Product Measuring

As several methods are available to calculate IOA, the technique you use should depend on the selected recording method. The formula for calculating percentage IOA for permanent product recording is: *# of agreements (A) / # of agreements (A) + # of disagreements (D) x 100*. Consider an example: Suppose Marty tours the packaging area at the end of his shift and counts the number of aisles leading to the fire exits that are free of packing cases and other obstacles. He reports that aisles 2, 4, 5, 7, and 9 are clear. Gary tours the packaging area independently and reports aisles 2, 3, 4, 5, and 7 are clear. The IOA = 67%. In this example, Marty and Gary agreed 4 times and disagreed twice, thus 4 / 4+2 x 100 = 66.7%. Now it is your turn.

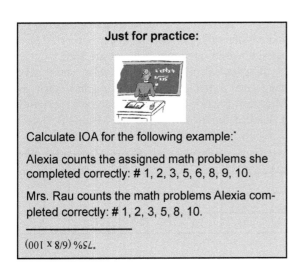

**Just for practice:**

Calculate IOA for the following example:*

Alexia counts the assigned math problems she completed correctly: # 1, 2, 3, 5, 6, 8, 9, 10.

Mrs. Rau counts the math problems Alexia completed correctly: # 1, 2, 3, 5, 8, 10.

---

*75% (8/9 x 100).

### IOA for Event Measures

Two methods are commonly used to calculate percentage of IOA, for both event and frequency measures: (1) total and (2) block-by-block (Page & Iwata, 1986)—block-by-block being the more accurate of the two. With the *total* method (in practice the same as the method for calculating IOA for permanent product recording), the total count recorded by each observer is compared using the following formula: *smaller total / larger total. You multiply the above by 100 if you wish to report your results as a percentage.* For example, suppose Observer 1 recorded that Lucretia hit Tracy with her plastic sand-spade 15 times, and Observer 2 recorded 22 times; then the IOA would equal 68.2%.

In the *block-by-block* method, *the observation session is broken further into intervals, and events or occurrences are recorded per interval. Next, each interval is compared to obtain an IOA score.* Intervals in which both observers agree exactly receive a score of 1, while intervals in which the observers do not agree are assigned a zero. Then a coefficient of agreement is calculated by dividing the smaller total by the larger. After that, the coefficients for each interval are added together and divided by the total number of intervals. Let us calculate *total* and *block-by-block* IOAs for the example in Figure 7.7:

| Observer 1 | Observer 2 | Block-byBlock Coefficients |
|---|---|---|
| 4 | 5 | .8 |
| 5 | 5 | 1.0 |
| 6 | 4 | .7 |
| 3 | 3 | 1.0 |
| 7 | 5 | .7 |
| 6 | 8 | .75 |
| 8 | 4 | .5 |
| 6 | 6 | 1.0 |
| 3 | 6 | .5 |
| 6 | 5 | .8 |
| 53 | 51 | 7.75 |

**Figure 7.7** Calculating an Index of Agreement

To calculate *total* IOA we add up the totals for both observers (53 and 51, respectively) and then divide the smaller by the larger (51/53) and multiply by 100 to obtain 96%. To calculate *block-by-block IOA*, we calculate the coefficients for each interval, sum the intervals (7.75), and divide by the number of intervals (10) to obtain (78%). You can see that *the block-by-block IOA is a more conservative measure than the total method.* In fact, technically, with total IOA, the observers might not agree on any one instance and could still obtain an IOA score of 100%. For example, had Observer 1 scored the behavior as occurring in the first five intervals and Observer 2 scored the behavior as occurring in the second five intervals, they actually never really agreed on any one instance of behavior. Yet, if Observer 1 had simply recorded the behavior as occurring 10 times and Observer 2 recorded the behavior as occurring 10 times, the deceptive IOA would be 100%.

## Indices of Agreement (IOAs) for Duration and Interresponse Time (IRT) Measures

If you are recording a duration measure, then you calculate IOA according to the following formula: *shorter duration / longer duration x 100.* For example, if Billy's mom recorded that his tantrum lasted 25 minutes and his grandmother recorded 23 minutes, IOA would equal 92%. You can use the same formula to calculate agreement indices for latency and interresponse (IRT) measures. For example, if the production manager recorded the time it took workers to hit the emergency *stop* button after the machine jammed (an IRT measure) as 16 seconds, and the floor manager recorded it as 12 seconds, IOA would equal 75%.

## IOA for Interval Time-Sampling Measures

When using time-sampling methods (*whole-interval*, *partial-interval*, or *momentary*) the *interval-by-interval* method applies when calculating IOA: *# of intervals agreed / # of intervals agreed + # of interval disagreed x 100.* Let us calculate IOA for the example in Figure 7.8.

If the interval-by-interval IOA method were used, then 6/6+4 = 60% for the above example. Because the interval-by-interval method is likely to *overestimate* agreement between observers measuring behaviors occurring at very low or high rates, two additional techniques, called *scored-interval* and *unscored-interval*, are suggested when one uses whole-, partial-, or momentary time sampling (Hawkins & Dotson, 1975). In *scored-interval, only those intervals in which the behavior was scored as occurring are included in the analysis.* In the above example, intervals 2, 4, 6, 7, and 10 would be scored as agreements and intervals 1, 3, 8, and 9 as disagreements. When using scored-interval, IOA = 5/5+4 = 56%. In the *unscored-interval* calculation, *only those intervals in which behavior was not scored as occurring are included in the analysis.* In the above example, interval 5 would be scored as one agreement while intervals 1, 3, 8, and 9 would be scored as disagreements. According to this method of calculating, the IOA for unscored-intervals would be 1/1+4 = 20%. Note, then, that when behavior occurs at *low* rates, the more conservative measure of IOA bases its calculation on scored-intervals. For behavior that occurs at *high* rates, however, unscored-intervals are used.

Besides calculating IOA by *hand*, some have suggested utilizing computer programs such as Microsoft Excel®. Reed and Azulay (2011) provide a detailed report on how to use Microsoft Excel®

|  | 1 | 2 | 3 | 4 | 5 | 6 | 7 | 8 | 9 | 10 |
|---|---|---|---|---|---|---|---|---|---|---|
| Obs 1 | X | X |  | X |  | X | X |  | X | X |
| Obs2 |  | X | X | X |  | X | X | X |  | X |
| A/D | D | A | D | A | A | A | A | D | D | A |

**Figure 7.8** The interval by interval method for IOA

to calculate IOA using total, block-by-block (i.e., partial-agreement within intervals), exact, trial-by-trial, and interval agreement. When calculating and reporting IOA for a number of sessions (e.g., 33% of 100 sessions), it might be better to rely on inputting the data into a spread sheet like the ones presented by Reed and Azulay.

## REPORTING RELIABILITY DATA

Those reviewing IOA data generally are interested in the *mean* (arithmetic average) IOA across each condition for each participant and/or behavior as well as the *range* of IOA scores. For example, suppose IOA were calculated for sessions 1 (IOA = 90%), 3 (IOA = 98%), and 5 (IOA = 97%) during baseline and sessions 6 (IOA = 99%), 7 (IOA = 96%), 10 (IOA = 98%), 12 (IOA = 100%), and 15 (IOA = 100%) during intervention. One could report the following: IOA was assessed on 60% of the baseline sessions and 50% of the intervention sessions. The average agreement score was 95% (R or reliability = 90%–98%) during baseline and 98.6% (R = 96%–100%) during intervention. In addition to reporting IOA scores, Morris and Rosen (1982) have recommended other methods including: noting on a graph days on which reliability was assessed, reporting the reliability data directly on the graph itself, and/or presenting the range across which reliability scores are distributed (reliability bands)[8] (see Chapter 8 on graphing). The responsibility for maintaining reliable observation does not end by recording and reporting IOA. If IOA is low, steps must be taken to repair the problem. In addition to ensuring that behavioral definitions are clear and complete, that observers are trained prior to scoring behavior, and that they are supervised periodically while scoring, one more feature we need to be aware of **observer drift**—*observers slowly shifting or adjusting their focus, resulting in an increasing divergence between the scoring of one versus that of the other(s)*. Should poor IOA scores suggest observer drift of that nature, it is time to **recalibrate** by *retraining observers as previously*.

## SUMMARY AND CONCLUSIONS

Observing and recording behavior is fundamental to conducting a behavior-analytic change program. Without solid behavioral measures, there is no way to monitor and assess the effect of a program on the behavior(s) of concern. Similarly, a failure to measure treatment integrity prevents us from determining how faithfully and accurately the selected intervention was implemented.

The specific measurement system one uses depends on the target behavior. Table 7.2 summarizes various measurement techniques along with a brief description of what is recorded, *when* the technique should be used, *how* to report the data, and *how* to conduct interobserver agreement indices (IOA). In addition, assessing episodic severity was addressed; systems for recording behavior in group settings described; factors influencing the reliability and validity of collecting observational data provided; and methods of calculating interobserver reliability presented as a basis for conducting valid behavioral assessments. Regardless, though, of which assessment procedures are selected, before you use them, they must be explained to the client and/or caregiver, including how the resulting information will be used. In addition, the client's or caregiver's written approval of the assessment procedures must be obtained (BACB's Professional and Ethical Compliance Code for Behavior Analysts, 2016).

---

[8] For interested readers, see Morris & Rosen, 1982, who detailed these procedures further.

**SUMMARY TABLE 7.2  Choosing Direct Behavioral Observational Methods**

| Observation Method | Records the: | Used When | Example: Use to Record | Use to Report | IOA Method; % coefficient |
|---|---|---|---|---|---|
| Permanent product | Outcome of the behavior | Behavior has enduring effects | The number of math problems completed | Total amount of behavior | Total agreement smaller/larger x 100 |
| Event | The number of times the behavior occurs within a unit of time | Behavior is transitory, discrete, with durations roughly equivalent in length | The number of times a child is aggressive | Total number, rate (when time varies), or % opportunities (when target is restricted) | Total, or block-by-block smaller/larger x 100 |
| Duration | The time from onset to offset of a behavior | Behavior is transitory, discrete, and time the person engages in the behavior is important | The duration of a tantrum | Total, mean, or proportion of time | Total smaller/larger x 100 |
| Latency | The time from a stimulus to the onset of a response | Behavior is transitory, discrete, and the time it takes to respond to a stimulus is important | How rapidly a person stops a machine after it begins to malfunction | Total, mean | Total smaller/larger x 100 |
| IRT | The time from offset of a response to onset of the next response | Behavior is transitory, discrete, when interested in the time between responses | How much time passes between a basketball player's three-point shots in a given game | Total, mean | Total smaller/larger x 100 |
| Whole-interval time sampling | Response if it occurs throughout the interval | Behavior is transitory, continuous, and goal is to increase behavior | The total time devoted to remaining on-task | % intervals | Interval Agreements/Agreements plus disagreements x 100 |
| Partial-interval time sampling | Response if it occurs at any time in the interval | Behavior is transitory, continuous, and goal is to decrease behavior | The presence or absence of thumb-sucking within a series of time blocks | % intervals | Interval Agreements/Agreements plus disagreements x 100 |
| Momentary time sampling | Response if it occurs at the end of the interval | Behavior is transitory, continuous, and there are observation issues | The presence or absence of an autistic child's stereotypic behavior at the moment the teacher observes | % intervals | Interval Agreements/Agreements plus disagreements x 100 |

## Chapter 8

# Optimizing Client Progress by Monitoring Behavior Change: Recording, Graphing, and Analyzing Patterns of Change

## Goals

1. List at least three reasons why graphing behavior is important.
2. Define and illustrate the following:
   a. baseline
   b. datum
   c. behavioral technician
   d. operational definition
   e. line graph
   f. y-axis
   g. ordinate
   h. x-axis
   i. abscissa
   j. vertical phase change lines
   k. phase label
   l. bar graph
   m. cumulative records
   n. standard celeration chart
   o. change in level
   p. trend
   q. variability
   r. equal-interval graphs (and differentiate them from standard celeration charts)
   s. trendline

3. List and discuss who besides behavioral technicians might observe and record behavior.
4. Discuss the issue(s) involved in using self-recording during baseline and during intervention.
5. Discuss the relevance and provide an example of automatic data collection.
6. Describe a rule of thumb for determining when *reactivity* has subsided.
7. Explain why it is important to precisely define your measures.
8. Explain the importance of the schedule that you use in your behavioral-recording session and how it influences the validity of your measure.
9. Discuss how long data should be collected during each baseline and intervention phase.
10. Illustrate how to plot multiple sets of different kinds of data that are apt to co-vary.
11. Differentiate among *line*, *bar*, and *cumulative* graphs and specify when to use each.
12. Describe when a (a) *change in level* and (b) *trend* become apparent.
13. Describe why examining the nature and sources of variability is so important.

*************

Do you wonder if you are eating too much junk food? Are you convinced you get plenty of exercise? Maybe a child's parents and teachers believe that his behavior is totally out of control; the situation hopeless. Is Jaime's supervisor correct in concluding that the boy wastes too much time surfing the Web during working hours? How do you determine the accuracy of what actually is happening? Graphic displays of the **baseline**—*repeated measures of the ongoing behavior, designed to represent its typical pattern of occurrence prior to any intervention*—enable you to view the situation more realistically.

Beyond giving a realistic picture of ongoing behavior, graphs also provide the basis for designing sensible and realistic **interventions,** or *behavior-change programs,* and for monitoring their effectiveness. They objectively inform behavior analysts about whether behavior is improving, worsening, or remaining stagnant.

Another important reason for using precise behavioral measurement is that it helps to reveal subtle changes, especially during the initial stages of an intervention. This is especially valuable because, not uncommonly, parents, teachers, managers and/or others are tempted to conclude that a problematic behavior has failed to improve, despite slight though potentially significant rates of change. They fail to realize that behavior change often progresses gradually. Yet, when presented with graphic representations of changes in frequency, trend, and/or variability of the behavior(s) of interest, prior to, during, and after a program has ceased, you and they are better able to detect any improvements that have taken place. As a behavior analyst, you must be certain to base your decisions on objective evidence—what the **data**, *the numerical results of measuring some quantifiable aspect of behavior*, tell you, rather than your "gut feelings."

The singular form of *data* is *datum.*

Graphing is essential to your practice as an applied behavior analyst because it serves as one of your most useful diagnostic, monitoring, and analytic tools. For these reasons, once you have selected appropriate measures, the next steps in a behavior-change plan are to actually record behavior, graph the results, and analyze the data under baseline and then intervention conditions. Here we describe the steps you generally will follow when recording and graphing, and make you familiar with a few basic steps in analyzing graphic data. Before beginning, though, you will need to refine your definitions of the behaviors of interest and identify the individual(s) who will conduct the observations.

## IMPLEMENTING OBSERVATIONAL SYSTEMS

Before starting a behavior-change program, you must make the sometimes difficult decision about who actually will record the behavior. Will the behavior analyst or the behavior-change agent also be responsible for recording data? Do you have the luxury of staff assigned to that task? Will the client record his or her own behavior?

### Behavior-Recording Staff

Identifying the behavior-recording staff depends in part on the type of organization with which you are working. In large enterprises, data recording may be a specialized task assigned to employees as an aspect of their jobs. In our own experience, depending on the nature of the organization and its resources, various individuals in various settings, besides researchers and their technical staff members, have fulfilled this function:

*Factories and offices*: supervisors, safety staff, or peer worker-volunteers.

*Business and service organizations:* quality-assurance staff, volunteers, supervisors, clients.

*Healthcare delivery settings*: volunteers or middle management personnel.

*Schools and human service agencies:* either full or part-time **registered behavioral technicians**™ **(RBT)**[1] who *implement treatment, design and implement observational recording systems, and who are under the supervision of a BCBA. The BCBA supervises the data collection and graphing schemes for continual monitoring* (Sulzer-Azaroff, Thaw, & Thomas, 1975). Additionally, teachers, advanced students, teacher aides, school psychologists or counselors, parents, college students or parent volunteers are sometimes assigned as data recorders.

*Homes*: RBTs, parents, caregivers, or sometimes the clients themselves, often paired for reliability purposes, with RBTs, colleagues or significant others.

*Working in varied locations*: technicians who video-record, collect products, or otherwise preserve evidence for later scoring of the behavior of concern over time

Increasingly, many educational and human service agencies assign data collection responsibilities to RBTs and sometimes to Board Certified Assistant Behavior Analysts™ (BCaBAs).[2] Occasionally, state civil-service departments have built those responsibilities into their human-services career ladders.

When behavioral technicians are unavailable, you must explore alternatives. For example, parents, senior citizens, individuals with developmental disabilities (Craighead, Mercatoris, & Bellack, 1974), college students on practicum or internship assignments, older children (McLaughlin & Malaby, 1975a), peers, or even clients themselves (see below) may serve as observers. In an electronics plant to which one of us consulted, a retired manager was rehired on a part-time basis to audit plant safety targets. In another situation, monitoring and recording quality measures were included in quality-control inspectors' job descriptions (Sulzer-Azaroff & Harshbarger, 1995). Hiring people who "know the business" can be especially beneficial because

---

[1] For information and training regarding RBTs, see Wallace and Mayer, 2020. Also see the BACB's website (BACB.net)

[2] See the BACB® website, http//:BACB.net for a description of the responsibilities of RBTs and BCaBAs.

they understand the nature of the behavior they are going to observe and record.

Some programs require monitoring in many settings and/or around the clock, which may pose a particularly difficult challenge. Then, either the contingency managers or the clients themselves may have to serve as behavior recorders. However, technological advances have made it possible to video-record the session and subsequently chronicle behavioral data by watching the video clips. It should be noted, though, that doing so takes more time. Also, sometimes video recording can present an ethical dilemma, as in the case of inadvertently filming footage of people who have not given their informed consent to be taped (for example, the other children in a client's classroom). Sometimes there are privacy issues that make it difficult to have others record or to video tape for later scoring. For example, if you are taking data on a client appropriately completing showering steps. In these situations, it might be the best alternative to have the caretaker collect data, or have the client take data on themselves.

**Clients as behavioral self-recorders.** Engaging clients in observing and recording their own behavior has become increasingly popular. In addition to the advantage of decreasing workloads for registered behavioral technicians or contingency managers, *self-recording frequently results in desired behavior change* (e.g., Nagatomi & Wemura, 2017; Edwards, 1995; Fujita & Hasegawa, 2003; Harmon, Nelson, & Hayes, 1980; Kazdin, 1974a; Kern, Childs, Dunlap, Clarke & Falk, 1994; Ninness, Fuerst, Rutherford, & Glenn, 1991; Trammel, Schloss & Alper, 1994; Willis & Nelson, 1982). This happens especially in self-management programs (Mace & Kratochwill, 1985), and when, due to current contingencies, the client has a vested interest in changing his or her own behavior (Komaki & Dore-Boyce, 1978). Thus, self-recording can be viewed not only as a means of data collection, but also as a possible intervention. Furthermore, as we shall show later on, self-recording is an integral part of self-management or self-control programs.

Self-recording systems may take various forms. To illustrate, people can use a system as simple as transferring objects from one pocket to another,

> What do we mean by an *operational definition* in applied behavior analysis?
>
> An **operational definition** is a *clear, precise description of how the properties of events or items are measured*. Operational definitions are essential to the dependable and reliable measurement and implementation of behavioral procedures (as in assessing procedural reliability or treatment integrity) and/or the collection of behavioral data. For a behavior to be operational, it must be observable and measurable.

score the frequency of a particular behavior on a card or piece of paper, or use a smart phone. In fact, one of us kept a record of the number of pages she wrote each day when composing her dissertation (and is convinced that were it not for the reinforcement yielded by the self-recorded data, she would never have finished). Videotapes and other automated recording systems also have been used to provide observational feedback to students, teachers, counselors, and others (Delano, 2007; Hosford, Moss, & Morrell, 1976; Kagan, 1972; Phaneuf & McIntyre, 2007; Walz & Johnson, 1963).

Even young clients—some as young as six years old—have used self-recording (Ballard & Glynn, 1975; Fixsen, Phillips, & Wolf, 1972; Kazdin, 1974a; Thoresen & Mahoney, 1974, Blick & Test, 1987). Self-recording is not, however, as simple as it may first appear. Thomas (1976) found that second-grade students varied in accuracy of recording from 56 to 95 percent. Should your clients self-record inaccurately or unreliably, the best way to deal with that is to reinforce accuracy and reliability *per se*. That usually solves the problem (Broden, Hall, & Mitts, 1971; Fixsen et al., 1972; Kazdin, 1974a).

Variability in recording also may occur because, while some target behaviors permit simple and precise recording (e.g., answers to multiple-choice questions, number of buttons buttoned, pages written, problems correctly solved, products completed), others are more ambiguous. Compare the latter with such personal qualities as "shy," "cooperative," "neat," and other subjective descriptors. Such terms need first to be described in operational language. Then candidates for participating in self-monitoring need to be carefully trained, supervised, and their scoring carefully calibrated, a point underscored by Thoresen and Mahoney:

> Training in the discrimination and recording of a behavior is essential. Such training may be enhanced by modeling, immediate accuracy feedback, systematic reinforcement, and graduated transfer of recording responsibilities (external to self).... Discrete behaviors and simple recording systems appear to enhance self-monitoring accuracy. (1974, p. 63)

Several researchers have successfully trained individuals to self-record such behaviors as remaining on-task (Kern et al, 1994), motor tics (Woods, Miltenberger, & Lumley, 1996), skin picking (Twohig & Woods, 2001a), increasing reinforcer delivery (Cook et al. 2016), and stuttering (Wagaman, Miltenberger, & Arndorfer, 1993). Not only did their clients learn reliably to record these behaviors, but when the self-recording was combined with other reinforcement-based procedures, the problematic behaviors were successfully reduced or eliminated. Knowing, as we do now, that participants' behavior often improves as their self-recording becomes more reliable, we can see why one must be cautious about assuming that self-recorded data accurately represent baseline performance patterns. Unless a co-observer were surreptitiously to record baseline data prior to involving the client in self-recording, *depending on self-recorded data alone for establishing a true baseline may be futile*. Other factors may influence the validity of self-recording as well, including having a vested interest in the progress of the program (Komaki & Dore-Boyce, 1978). Richards (1981) concluded that with individuals "motivated to self-monitor and change their behavior... self-reinforcement may occur naturally" (p. 163), so separating self-monitoring from self-reinforcement may not be possible.

**Contingency managers as data recorders.** Special arrangements are necessary when contingency managers are not only responsible for implementing the program but for also recording behavioral data. Kubany and Sloggett (1973) noted that classroom teachers are sometimes so involved in instructional activities that they sometimes forget to record, and as a result their composite data may be unreliable. You can imagine the same could happen with other contingency managers. For instance, it might not be realistic to expect sheltered-workshop staff to implement individual behavior-intervention plans across six individuals with developmental disabilities while accurately recording data on the correctness of each one's assembly of goodie bags and also ensuring each participant's safety.

Should you be faced with this predicament, some solutions are possible. One alternative is to observe and record intermittently at predetermined, random times throughout the day. That permits the observer/contingency manager to return to the regular task until the next preset time after the brief observation period.

Regardless of who is recording data (self-recording or other's recording), it is important to make sure the person recording is sufficiently trained. Moreover, it is important to utilize what we know about training when teaching individuals how to record behavior. Matthews and Hagopian (2014) compared using didactic training versus a training based upon behavioral skills training (BST—i.e., instruct, model, practice, and provide feedback) to train paraprofessionals how to collect data and demonstrated that the paraprofessionals took more reliable and valid data when they were trained via BST. With that said, it is important to incorporate systematic training procedures when you train your observers.

## Automated Recording Systems

Often our access to staff whose sole or major task is to observe and record ongoing behavior on-site is limited. In such instances, an alternative to turn to is Internet-based video- or audio-recordings that can be scored (i.e., treated as permanent product data) and analyzed subsequently, locally or from a distance. Such recordings also have the advantage of permitting replaying, stopping, slowing, or speeding up action, enabling the superimposition of time indicators and other features. We have used video recordings to measure children's social interactions, teachers' applications of particular instructional skills, child meal-time behavior, and many other purposes. One consideration, though, is the time it takes to review the recordings and score and record the data.

Fortunately, computerized recording systems may come to the rescue. Early on, Bernal, Gibson, Williams, and Pesses (1971) developed a device for automatically activating an audio recorder at various times in the daily routine of a family. In a recent study, Edmunds, et al. (2017) used a point-of-view camera to measure eye gazing in young children with autism.

Advances in computer technology have led to the development of various other systems for recording data, including using desktop computers, laptop computers, and pocket PCs. Kahng and Iwata (1998) provided a critical and informative review of a number of software programs available for data collection purposes. Since then, this technology has continued to develop. For example, for those more technologically inclined (or at least not technologically challenged), Jackson and Dixon (2007) have provided a task analysis for developing a computerized data collection system for a pocket PC. Edwards (2000); Sidener, Shabani, and Carr (2004) also have described their computer-assisted observational software; and Noldus, Spink, and Tegelenbosch (2001) their design for collecting, managing, and presenting time-structured data from videotapes and digital media files. Analyses of website visits and of the contents of email correspondence (with appropriate permissions of course) are broadening opportunities for conducting reliable measurement of various behavioral classes. In just one of many examples, Danaher, Boles, Akers, Gordon and Severson (2006) used visits to a Web site to assess participants' exposure to information about a smoke-free substitute for smoking. In one of our own field studies (Weissman, Sulzer-Azaroff, Fleming, Hamad, & Crockett, 2004), we collected video recordings of parents or teachers to monitor, from a distance, the performance of parents and teachers as they progressed through an Internet training course, and today real-time visual communication systems like Skype™ are being added to the ABA observational repertoire. In a recent study, Martner and Dallery (2019) recorded smoking by having participants blow into an electronic device attached to an internet-based platform that measured carbon monoxide levels. (Later we return to a few other historically important and user-friendly methods for both recording and analyzing data.)

Regardless of the observational system you choose, though, watch out for participant *reactivity*, the atypical behavior pattern that occurs as a function of the participant's being observed. Reactivity also may be a problem with intrusive forms of automated recording, such as using handheld cameras or recording data via video-conferencing. If less intrusive observational systems are unavailable, be sure to allow sufficient time for *adaptation* (for reactivity to the recording device to subside) before officially recording and graphing baseline data. A rule of thumb for assuming that behavior has become reasonably stable and no longer reactive to the observational conditions is to examine the data points and wait for a series containing no new high or low points for several (at least three or more) sessions in a row.

## SCHEDULING BEHAVIORAL RECORDING

Always keeping the concept of *validity* (that the method measures what it is supposed to measure) in mind, you need to schedule your behavioral recording sessions in such a way that the data you collect truly measure what they are supposed to measure. If times of day, days of the week, weather conditions, task assignments, physical or social surroundings, personnel, the status of the participants in terms of satiation or deprivation regarding food, fluids, ambient weather or temperature conditions, and a myriad of other variables threaten to influence the data, you need to make certain these are evenly distributed throughout baseline, intervention, and follow-up phases. For, obviously, if they are not so controlled, you will not know which one or combination was responsible for any changes taking place during your behavioral intervention phase.

### Frequency of Recording

Other questions arise at this point: How *frequently* should we measure, under what condition(s)? As you will see later on, we must review our objective once again. If we are concerned simply with increasing or decreasing the rate of a behavior, as in number of products meeting or not meeting standards, or correct and/or incorrect answers on a test over given periods of times, then all we need to do is to use our validly-defined objectives across standard time periods. If, instead, our aim is to shape new behavior or teach our clientele to differentiate one stimulus from another, we may need to observe and record as often as moment-to-moment or trial-by-trial results.

## Duration of Recording Phases

How long (*duration*) we maintain baseline or each intervention phase depends on the data themselves. One of several rules of thumb, depending on other factors such as urgency to implement intervention, practical considerations, and so on, is to *continue to assess performance until the data become stable according to your pre-specified definition of stability. An example of such a definition is that data reveal no new highs or lows for five (or some larger number) sessions in a row.* Stable baselines provide a standard against which to evaluate subsequent changes in levels, trends, or variability. You want to be able to view a series of data points to see whether, and if so how, there has been a discernible change. For instance, you may want to compare the data revealed under baseline versus those within one treatment condition, or those generated in other treatment(s) versus still others, and so on).

## Definitional Detail

How detailed do you want your performance measures to be? Of course, that depends on the aim of your program. If it is simply to increase the *rate* of an already operationally-defined and validated measured performance, such as number of items produced to standard, numerical problems solved correctly, or safety precautions practiced, all you need do is to decide *yes* or *no*. Counting, summing, and graphing the data probably would be sufficient. In other circumstances you may need to return to and revise your objective until anyone with the appropriate training and supervision can reliably assess the performance.

## Unit of Analysis

What size should you elect to choose as the unit to be analyzed? The "unit of analysis" for assessing and examining performance variability might be large for a total production task. Take the example of Fern, who packs "goodie bags" in a sheltered workshop. In her case, you might decide to observe closely and record the time it took her to fill each bag over time, because that would permit you to detect and reinforce sequences of responses occurring at higher rates than usual.

Also ask yourself and your associates how *refined* you want your analysis to be; to what extent you want to combine data for purposes of graphing and analyzing. You may decide that graphing every single response, as in *cumulative* recording, will provide you with the information you need. Or perhaps you are considering combining your data by intervals of time or groups of responses. An example of the former would be merging sets of items assembled on the basis of day of the week (see Figure 8.1). Notice that our participant, Fern, assembled between 482 and 583 goodie bags per day. Examine those data more closely. Do you notice anything special about them? If you said that Fern's productivity was generally lower on Fridays, and almost as poor on Mondays, you would be correct. If you were her supervisor, what further information might you seek? What changes, if any, would you consider making in her weekly schedule? Or, these data might impress you with the potential value of investigating what happens to influence Monday's and Friday's lower scores. (For instance, does she get to bed too late on Sundays? Is she tired by Fridays, or is she distracted by weekend plans?)

Suppose instead, you were to combine the data into weekly data or the number of hours it takes to assemble a given number of items. You then could examine the graphic representation of the data, as in Figure 8.2, to see if any particular response configurations emerge that you then could productively analyze, interpret, and subject to various interventions until you found one that was most effective. Alternatively, you may determine that graphing each response, as is done in *event* or *cumulative* recording (described below) will provide you with the information you need.

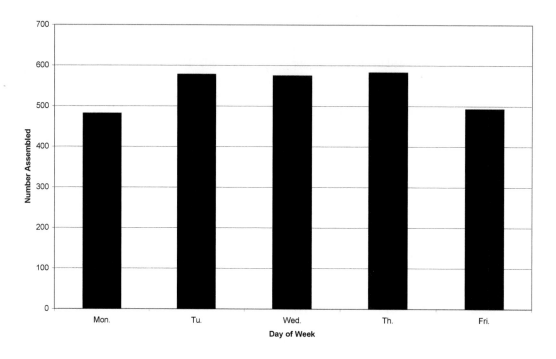

**Figure 8.1**  Bags Fern assembled by day of the week

The various ways of plotting and analyzing data that we have just presented provide us with some interesting hypotheses about factors that influence Fern's productivity. Yet there are many other levels of data analysis. For instance, you could examine the numbers on the basis of hours of the day or minutes within the hour. Or you could look at weather conditions, or day of the month, or Fern's physical condition.

Suppose you wanted instead to examine Fern's weekly productivity more closely, as in Figure 8.3. Notice the big surprise during week seven—Fern's productivity was atypically high on Monday and Thursday of that week. This information might send you off on a mission to discover what special events may have occurred during that week, either within or outside of the workshop. Maybe you would learn that on those two days Fern could use her earnings to play bingo, so now you will have found a potentially valuable reinforcer for Fern.

Maybe, instead, you decided to combine the data into bi-weekly data or the number of hours it takes to assemble a given number of items. You then could examine the graphic representation of those data to see if any particular response patterns emerge; patterns you could then analyze, interpret, and productively subject the program to various interventions until you found the one that was most effective.

> **Ethical Code 217**: Behavior analysts actively ensure the appropriate selection and correct implementation of data collection procedures. They graphically display, summarize, and use the data to make decisions about continuing, modifying or terminating services. (p. 12)

## GRAPHING BEHAVIORAL DATA

As you already recognize, a behavioral graph provides a visual representation of behavior over time. By plotting and connecting data points, we begin to notice performance patterns emerging. The configurations formed by repeated measures of the behavior as it typically occurs, that is, taken before any

CHAPTER 8 OPTIMIZING CLIENT PROGRESS BY MONITORING BEHAVIOR CHANGE • 159

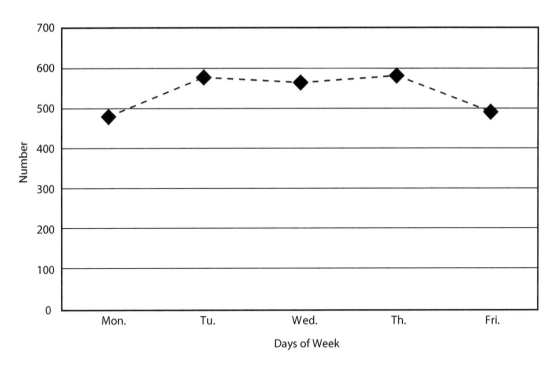

**Figure 8.2** Combining Fern's data by day-of-the-week, across a seven-week period

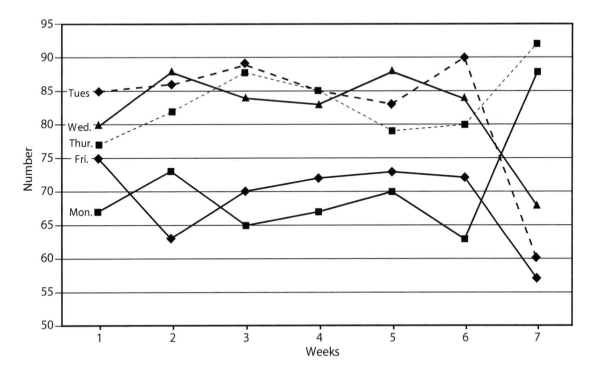

**Figure 8.3** Fern's weekly production

intervention, maybe used as a standard or *baseline* against which to assess any subsequent changes that take place, either as time passes and/or as new conditions are introduced. A number of graphing conventions have come to be accepted during the evolution of the field of applied behavior analysis.

## Graphing Guidelines

After behavior is recorded, as we have seen, the resulting information must be graphed immediately to permit change patterns to be observed and documented. Graphic representations of data are the primary bases for monitoring whether systematic alterations in the behavior(s) of concern co-vary with given behavior-change programs (i.e., whether, when the behavior-change program is implemented, the behavior changes correspondingly) and for deciding whether any procedural changes are indicated. By visually inspecting the graph we can determine whether the performance measure, and/or its trend and/or its degree of variability, systematically are changing while the intervention is in place. If so, we then determine if any changes are in the anticipated or the opposite direction; whether alterations in trend are accelerating or decelerating; or whether the behavioral pattern is becoming more variable or consistent.

By convention, ABA practitioners and researchers tend to use a standard graphic format. Becoming skillful at viewing and interpreting a graph requires a bit of readily-gained technical skill. Here we guide you through the process by reviewing the components of an ABA graph.

## Standard Format for a Graph

We use Figure 8.4 to illustrate, in simplified form, several features of a fairly standard ABA line graph. A **line graph**, the type of graph described below and used most frequently in this field, usually *displays data that can be scaled along some dimension, such as time or the order of responses in a sequence*. The graph in Figure 8.4 displays how the self-injurious behavior (SIB) of a child named Joy changed over successive conditions: During baseline (BL), SIB occurred relatively often, but decreased to very low levels during an intervention procedure called NCR (noncontingent reinforcement). Examine the details of constructing a graph of this type:

First are the vertical and horizontal lines: The *vertical* line is called the **y-axis**. The **ordinate** is the y value. The y axis *usually provides a standard for measuring the dependent variable (the behavior)* such as "Frequency," "Time," "Number," "Percentage," etc., and contains *axis scales* or *numerals*. In Figure 8.4, the numerals on the ordinate (representing the y-value) begin at zero and progress in units of five. (If a data set contains many zero points, say three or more, for the sake of clarity the y-axis can start a little below zero rather than at zero, as in this example.) The horizontal **x-axis**, *displays the label for the observational sessions*. These may be composed of specific observational sessions (usually described in more detail in the accompanying narrative) or standard units of time, such as hours, days (as in this example), weeks, or months. The first data point graphed on Figure 8.4, then, has an *ordinate* value of 20 (occurrences of self-injurious behavior) on day one, noted on the **abscissa** (the x-value).

Next, after allowing for adaptation, we add the *data points* as they are collected. Usually the first several data points constitute the *baseline*(s). After sufficient baseline data have been collected, labeled, and plotted on the graph, some sort of change strategy (the *intervention* or *treatment*) usually is introduced. To indicate when that happens, we add and label vertical lines, and label each phase (e.g., BL, NCR) between the last observational sessions and those generated under the new conditions. As you will learn in more detail shortly, assuming performance patterns have changed in the anticipated direction, we then either withdraw those conditions to see if behavior returns to its former patterns (in the A-B-A-B design), apply the change strategy to a new behavior, person, or location (in the multiple-baseline design), or follow a different experimental design path (some of which will be covered in Chapter 25. Here, then, is a review of the steps you follow

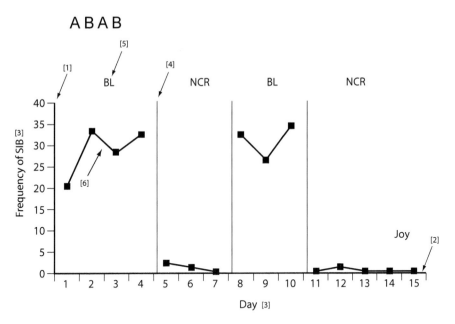

**Figure 8.4** Typical withdrawal[4] (A-B-A-B) graph

## Steps in Graph Construction

in constructing an ABA graph using Figure 8.4 as an example:[3]

- Draw the vertical (y-axis) line (1).
- Draw the horizontal (x-axis) line (2).
- Indicate the labels and units of measurement on the axes (3).
- Add the data points (x and y plots) *representing the responses across time* (6). Note that you connect data points *within* a phase and *disconnect* them *between* each phase.
- Add **vertical phase-change lines** (4). Phase lines can be solid, as in Figure 8.4, or broken, as in Figure 8.12. These *indicate that a new condition is in effect; usually a different "treatment" or independent variable is being implemented.* For example, a phase-change line would be inserted *between* the last baseline session and the first treatment session (e.g., between baseline and NCR—noncontingent reinforcement).
- Add a **phase label** (5). The phase label *uses a simple descriptor of the condition(s) in place* (e.g., baseline, treatment, follow-up, etc.).
- Omit large areas of dead space by using a break in the axis. Take care, though, not to distort the magnitudes of effect when you do this. (Notice on Figure 8.5 below that the change from day 4 to day 10 is actually only about 15 percent. Note that the numerals on the vertical axis [y-axis] jump from 0 to 50, then continue in increments of 10.)
- If needed for clarity, should many (three or more) data points fall on the zero line, extend the ordinate to below zero.
- If the variations in the data plot seem to obscure a socially important change, expand the ordinate.
- Usually only one data set is plotted on a graph. However, should you decide to plot more than one data set, be sure to use dif-

---

[3]Sometimes the term "reversal" is used to describe this design. Technically, though, as you will see in Chapter 10, "reversal" refers to switching the contingencies, so consequences now are the opposite from what they had been previously. In the present case, that would mean shifting to providing reinforcement contingent on the response.

ferent symbols and/or connecting lines for each (see Figures 8.3 and 8.6).
- Give the graph a brief descriptive label. The labels should make it possible for another person to examine the graph and understand what happened when and under what conditions.

For a step by step example of graphing utilizing Microsoft Excel, see Wallace & Mayer, 2019 or search on YouTube for a video tutorial.

## Graphic Variations

Typically we plot only one set of data on a graph. However, plotting both data sets on the same graph can be especially informative, particularly when multiple sets of different kinds of data are expected to relate to one another in some way, as in the case of remaining on- and off-task and number of problems completed. Should you decide to do something similar, you can use both the left and right y-axes. The left might represent off-task; the right, problems completed. As the graph begins to extend in time, you can see if, and how, the changes relate to one another. If you decide to plot multiple data sets on a single graph, use distinct symbols and associated connecting lines for each. In Figure 8.6, closed squares represent off-task behavior, while closed triangles represent math problems completed.

## Bar Graphs

Unlike line graphs, **bar graphs** *do not represent response sequences. Rather, they are used to compare discrete sets of data that may be, but are not necessarily related to one another; or to summarize performance within a condition or group of individuals.* Typically such information is based on data combined across sessions, hours, or even days or weeks.

Figure 8.7 displays Jerry's choices when, during the first trial, he is permitted to select one item

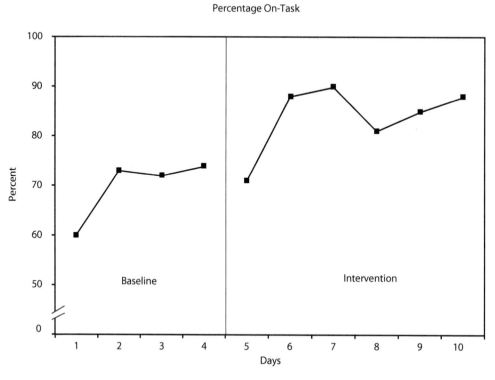

**Figure 8.5** Breaking the ordinate when no data appear in a range (Notice the break on the ordinate between zero and fifty.)

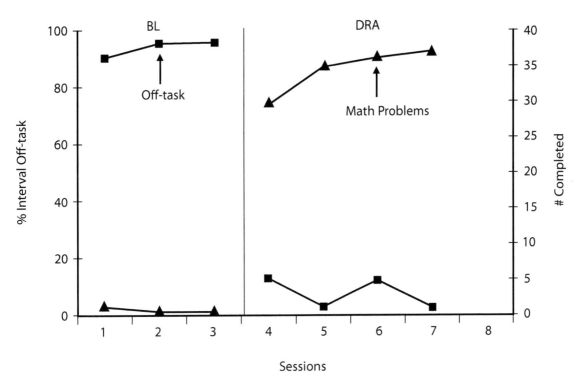

**Figure 8.6** Multiple data-set plot (double Y graph)

from a tray containing the full array of the foods he is reported to like, including a cookie, a chip, a piece of candy, a slice of an apple or a pear. The cookie wins, hands down. During the second set of choices, the cookie has been removed from the array and he chooses chips six times, candy twice, and the other two once each. By the time the assessment is completed we know that Jerry likes all the chosen items, but when we really hope to "motivate" him, it would be wise to have a goodly supply of his favorite cookies and chips on hand.

## Cumulative Records

Like the ebb and flow of the waves and the tide, behavior shifts over time. The contingent relations in effect at one point may change at another. Think of your own swings in attention, depending on sequences of internal and external events. While watching television, your stomach growls and you imagine the contents of your refrigerator. Your cell phone rings, immediately commanding your attention while distracting you from your reading. Your close companion looks angry; you interrupt your meal preparation to try to find the cause. While in everyday life, these temporary shifts usually aren't troublesome, but sometimes they can be. Temporarily withdrawing attention from a job operation or from the road while driving to answer the cell phone may lead to an injurious accident. A child's throwing a tantrum in the midst of a normally calm visit to the supermarket or a restaurant may be extremely disturbing to you and others. In such cases, you may want to inspect behavioral patterns more closely, from moment to moment, rather than from session to session or day to day.

Instead of inspecting data combined within and/or across sessions, then, we recognize that there are times when it is helpful to be able to examine stimulus-response relations more closely. Early on in the ABA field, investigators appreciated this fact, finding various tools for such purposes. These included the multiple-event recorder, which permitted several variables to be measured simultaneously (response rates, presentations of discriminative and reinforc-

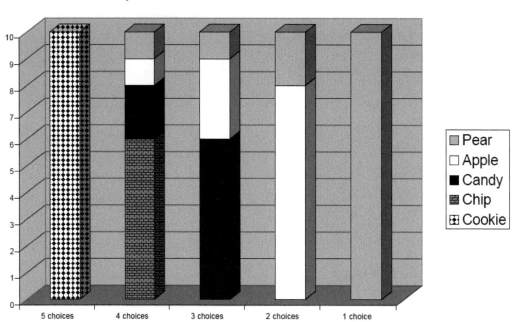

**Figure 8.7** Preference assessment graph (bar graph) (Percentage selected within trials with that item)
Notice also the reduction in variability of the data. Distance probes were taken from another vantage point; morning probes at a different time of day.

ing stimuli, and so on), the cumulative recorder, and the logarithmic chart. We describe those next.

B. F. Skinner (1957) invented a device called the *cumulative recorder* that produced cumulative data plots. These plots permitted investigators to inspect moment-to-moment changes in rate directly, an extremely useful metric. In the cumulative recorder's original laboratory application, each of the organism's rapidly repeated responses deflected a pen upward by a fixed amount as the recording paper moved at a steady speed. This produced an overall slope or curve, similar to the idealized image illustrated in Figure 8.8. (In actual use, the height of the pen deflection is much smaller, allowing for many, many more responses before the pen reaches the top of the paper, then dropping back to the bottom to again begin its upward climb.)

The paper rolls and each time a response occurs, the response pen moves upward until it reaches a particular height. At that point, the pen drops back to its lowest point and again begins its journey upward once again. Delivery of reinforcers is indicated by the small hatch marks. Hatch marks on the lower pen indicate some particular event, such as a change in illumination.

*The cumulative record* has the advantage of *revealing, at a glance, the frequency of responses over time, or rate.* The researcher can examine the record to note places where the rate slows, quickens, or becomes especially variable, and match those changes with other events. Did the rate diminish gradually over time? Perhaps the subject (or participant) was becoming sated with the reinforcer. If the rate varied, was that because other response options and/or reinforcers became available or because consuming food changed the probability of the other behavior, such as drinking? Maybe the ambience of the laboratory altered, as in a nearby female of the same species in heat, or the lights turned off, or someone slamming the door? Many a new experimental direction has been the outgrowth of unex-

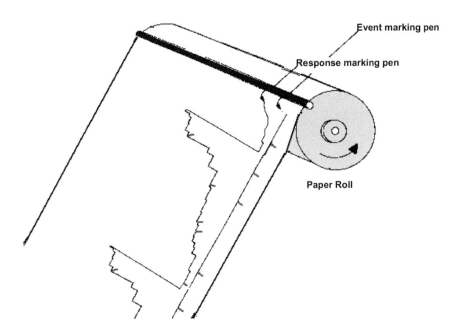

**Figure 8.8** A simplified description of the way a cumulative recorder operates. From the Fly Fishing Devon website, © Dr. C.A.P. Kenyon.
The paper rolls and each time a response occurs, the response pen moves upward until it reaches a particular height. At that point, the pen drops back to its lowest point and again begins its journey upward once again. Delivery of reinforcers is indicated by the small hatch marks. Hatch marks on the lower pen indicate some particular event, such as a change in illumination.

pected events, because their effect was reflected on the cumulative record.

**Cumulative records** *display rates of some event (usually a response), in the form of changes in the slope or curve of the record* (e.g., number of responses / a specific time period) as a function of conditions in effect. The record shows how rapidly or slowly the responses are repeated. When you view a cumulative graph, you should recognize that the steeper the slope, the more rapid the response being recorded. When the data line goes sideways, or straight across, it means that no occurrence of the behavior was recorded. Additionally, the cumulative record permits one to view at a glance the total number of responses emitted (accumulated) during the recording period.

In her doctoral dissertation research, one of the authors[4] used a cumulative recorder to assess the reinforcing function of different classes of poten-tially reinforcing stimuli, (candy, displays of colorful images, sequential numerals, and so on) on the match-to-sample behavior of typically-functioning children and those with developmental delays. Besides displaying the total response frequency at a glance, the cumulative records permitted us to see changes in rate from one experimental condition to another. The steeper the angle described on the cumulative record, the more rapidly the child was responding. Today, applied behavior analysts use more advanced instrumentation to produce cumulative records, but under many circumstances, the utility of the cumulative record remains.

Because they display both the rate of responding and total number of responses, low-tech cumulative records also can be useful for applied behavior analysts working in the field, as illustrated in Figure 8.9. Suppose, on Day 1, Margaret ran 3 miles, and on Day 2 she ran 4 miles. The first data point is plotted at 1–3 (X-Y intersection); the second data point at the 2–7 intersection (because four miles were added to the three of the first day). On some days

---

[4]Sulzer, B. (1966). "Match-to-sample behavior by normal and retarded children under different reinforcing conditions." Unpublished doctoral dissertation, University of Minnesota.

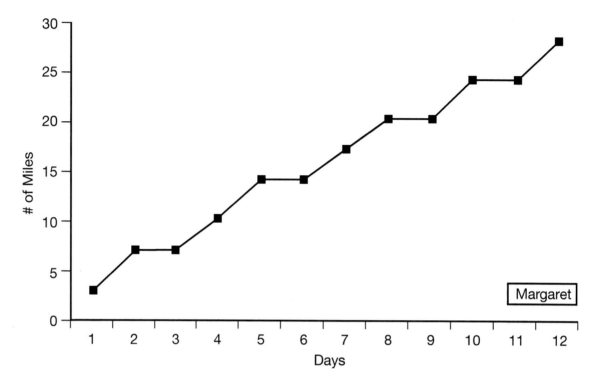

**Figure 8.9** Cumulative graph of the miles Margaret ran per day (fictitious data)

(e.g., between Day 2 and 3 and Day 5 and 6) the line remains flat, because Margaret did not run on those days. A useful feature is that by looking at the last data point we can see immediately that Margaret ran a total of 29 miles over the twelve-day period.

Recognize, then, that cumulative records allow us to demonstrate local as well as overall response rates. Penrod, Wallace, and Dyer (2008) first used simple line graphs to examine differences in levels of performance under two conditions (high-preferred [HP] and low-preferred [LP] reinforcers) under a *progressive ratio (PR) schedule* (in a PR, *the ratio of required responses to reinforcers continues to increase*). At first glance, both the HP and LP reinforcers produced similar responding in that both resulted in similar breaking points under the progressive ratio schedule. However, differences were not obviously apparent in a simple line graph. Cumulative records subsequently were used to demonstrate distinctive within-session patterns of responding (see Figure 8.10). For example, Sam's (participant 1) cumulative-record data revealed that he consistently responded during the PR-HP condition (a steep slope), but he took more breaks during the PR-LP condition (the slope was flatter), even though he worked at about roughly the same rate for both reinforcers under a pure fixed-ratio schedule.

Cumulative recordings also permit us to view the point at which responding ceases (the "break point,") as the schedule requirement increases, demanding more and more responses or faster and faster response rates. Such information informs us about how to select reinforcers and schedule requirements (the higher the break point, the more potent we assume the reinforcer to be), especially if the goal is for the participant to sustain responding at a reasonable and consistent rate. So, when Serge's beloved maestro gradually increases the time he asks Serge to practice the viola, to receive reinforcement in the form of praise Serge continues to expand his practice schedule until he "reaches his limit of five hours per day" (the break point), because he must begin writing a term paper for his zoology course. That resistance to change informs us that the reinforcer is powerful indeed (Grace & Nevin, 1997).

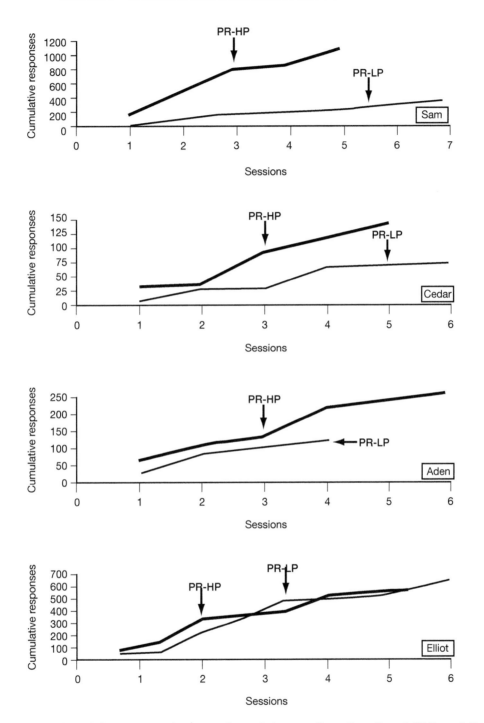

**Figure 8.10** Assessing reinforcer potency by means of cumulative recordings. From Penrod, Wallace, & Dyer (2008), Figure 3. © 2008 by the Society for the Experimental Analysis of Behavior, Inc.

## Standard Celeration Charts

Another way to show number or frequency of responses over time is to use a standard celeration chart (Figure 8.11). Even children can learn to use this graphing technique, but it takes a few training sessions. The **standard celeration chart** is *a variation of a semi-logarithmic chart, which shows proportional or relative instead of absolute changes in behavior*. Stated simply, unlike the **equal-interval** (all intervals are the same size) line, bar, cumulative, and other **graphs**, the semi-logarithmic scale allows data to be squeezed into progressively tighter and tighter bundles. In a standard celeration chart, changes of equal proportions are shown by equal distances on the vertical axes, using a semi-logarithmic axes scale with 6 to 10 cycles on that y-axis. The major y-axis divisions in Figure 8.11 all show changes by a factor of 10: from .1 to 1, from 1 to 10, from 10 to 100, and so on. The elegant feature of such a graph is that whenever behavior changes by some factor (e.g., a doubling) within a given time period, the slope of the change looks the same whether you start with a very high or a very low level of behavior. Imagine increasing one child's accurate responding from 2 to 4 correct answers per day, and another from 10 to 20. If you plotted these on standard linear graphs, the first child's improve-

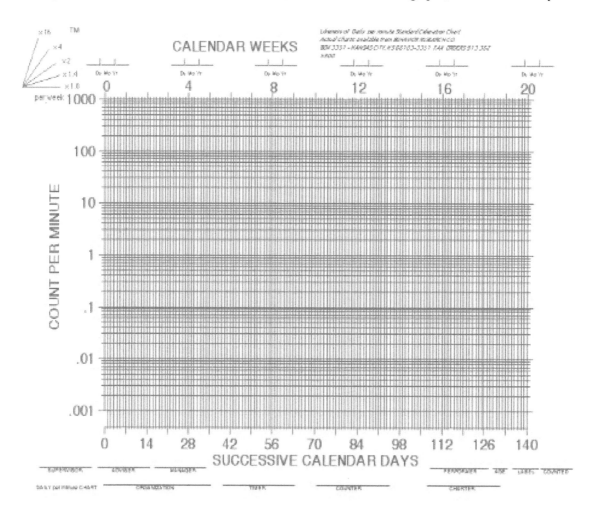

**Figure 8.11** Standard celeration chart

ment of only 2 correct answers that day would seem small compared the second child's improvement of 10. But in terms of percentages, both children improved by 100 percent as a result of your teaching. Their equality in terms of percentage change would show as equal progress if plotted on a standard celeration chart.

One application of behavior analysis that relies heavily on using standard celeration charts is precision teaching,[5] an individualized instructional method that emphasizes rate building and charting of performance (Lindsley, 1991). Notice on Figure 8.11 how the graph accommodates response rates of 001. per minute (about a single response in a day) to 1 per minute and so on to 1000 per minute. Lindsley used a semi-logarithmic scale for the y-axis, so that particular behaviors that occurred over very different time scales could efficiently be compared to one another. The chart included frequencies ranging as widely as from 1 per day to 1,000 per minute on a single graph covering 140 successive calendar days (about one school semester). That made it possible to plot both frequent and infrequent behaviors on the same graph over four months or more.

When might you find it practical to use a semi-logarithmic graph? Primarily when your concern is promoting rate of responding—something you will want to concern yourself with because it is a fact that the more rapid and fluent the rate of correct responding, the more durable the learning (Johnson & Layng, 1994). For example, two students each score 100 percent on an exam. However, one student took only 15 minutes to complete the exam, the other took 30 minutes. Their scores reported in percent do not indicate who might have mastered the material more thoroughly. However, because celeration charting graphs rate performance, it would show the difference between the two students. Semi-log graphs, then, accommodate the kinds of major changes we hope to see in fluency building (i.e., speeding up rates of answering math problems, writing spelling words, answering questions correctly, inputting keyboard entries, and so on). Additionally, the standard celeration chart lends itself to comparisons across many kinds of behavior within varied contexts. For example, if student academic progress were recorded individually on standard celeration charts in different schools or school systems, it would be very easy to see which ones were generating the most progress in terms of percent improvement. But such records cannot be produced unless adequate resources are devoted not only to the record keeping, but also to maintaining adequate measurement criteria. But, as Johnson and Layng (1994) have reported regarding their Morningside Model of Generative Instruction, following brief training, students can learn to assess, graph, and input data on their own performance quite accurately.

## Monitoring Changes in Behavior Patterns

Sometimes, even when we do not detect a change in level or a trend, we may observe an important change in variability. Consider the value of attempting to increase the *level* of a response such as promoting children's rates of wearing safety helmets and doing so more consistently (less *variably*) while biking. Van Houten, Van Houten, and Malenfant (2007) accomplished that by using peer goal-setting, public posting of the percentage of correct helmet use, and shared reinforcers. View Figure 8.12 and notice how successful they were in achieving both purposes.

In and of themselves, variable data are not necessarily problematic. Nevertheless, assuming your objective is to promote behavioral *increases*, you can monitor, catch, and reinforce the behaviors or sequences of behaviors producing the highest points. When *lower* rates are what you are after, just do the opposite: Reserve reinforcement for those sequences of responses that are seen to fall at the lower ranges.

As Fahmie and Hanley (2008) acknowledge, combined data often are easier to graph, examine, and analyze for purposes of detecting change in relation to the condition(s) in effect. They permit us to uncover adjustments in response patterns over time, including **change in level** (*is the rate or frequency or accuracy of the behavior increasing, decreasing or remaining the same?*), **trend** (*is the rate changing in any particular direction—slowing down or speeding up—over time?*), and **variability**

---

[5]See Chapter 17 for a more detailed description of precision teaching.

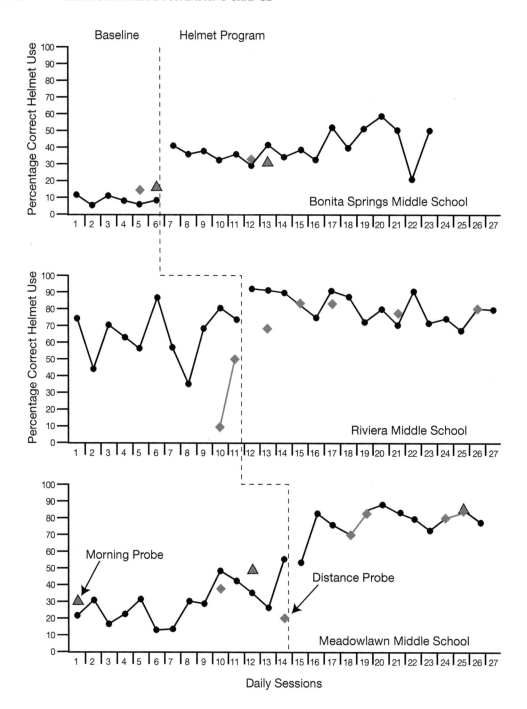

**Figure 8.12** An illustration of changes in percentage of correct helmet use. From Van Houten & Malenfant, (2007). © 2007 by the Society for the Experimental Analysis of Behavior, Inc.
Notice also the reduction in variability of the data. Distance probes were taken from another vantage point; morning probes at a different time of day.)

(*does the rate of the behavior fluctuate a lot, a little or hardly ever?*). These three terms are discussed in more detail below.

Yet the benefits of seeing the image from afar exact a cost, in that we may risk overlooking essential details—those subtle but critical factors that may be influencing moment-to-moment behavior. So, when the inexplicable happens and you want to unravel the mysterious "cause" (functionally related factor[s]), you will need to investigate the situation more closely and look at individual and smaller aggregates of stimulus and response relations to discover what is influencing the outcome immediately following, during, and/or prior to each single repetition of the response(s) of interest. Fahmie and Hanley (2008, pp. 327–328) have listed and illustrated such circumstances. We combine those items with some of our own. Examine circumstances more closely to:

- Describe naturally occurring behavioral relations: whether a particular event (thunder, phone ringing, a parental tone) occurs prior to a response, or after (a smile, loss of an object or attention).
- Determine behavioral function(s) via direct assessment, as in specifically presenting or withdrawing attention following crying.
- Detect within-session trends: rate of key entry during a daily observation.
- Safeguard clients: such as noting instances of the client's ingesting cigarette butts.
- Create sufficient data for analysis: assessing an operator's posture while working at the computer minute by minute rather than sampling by days.
- Determine observation-session duration: the behavior, such as slouching, tongue thrusting, or sideburn tugging happens so often that a brief sample is adequately representative.
- Clarify counterintuitive response patterns: Who would expect a client to become increasingly aggressive after receiving her typically favored reinforcer—a magazine? In that case, you could examine the moment-to-moment data to try to detect the increase in the client's rate and intensity of aggression *and* search for other conditions that may have intruded at those times to set her off (e.g., she lacked her glasses or the light level changed).
- Understand behavioral processes: determining whether the change was a function of satiation (many, many reinforcers, over and beyond the historical number for that participant) or deprivation, because reinforcers sufficient to maintain the behavior were unavailable.

## INTERPRETING BEHAVIORAL DATA

Remember that in and of themselves, data or graphic representations of behavior are but a shorthand means for conveying information. They gain their value according to how useful they are in helping us to make sound, meaningful decisions, as in whether or when to institute a particular program of teaching or management, and if or when to change it. In other words, as pointed out in the previous chapter, graphic representations need to contribute to the treatment's effectiveness (the treatment utility of assessment).

To make the *most* of our data, we need first to examine them closely to detect what they are, or are not, telling us. Armed with that information, we then can feel more confident about continuing or altering our practices, provided we keep monitoring the data patterns after any procedural changes.

To interpret the data you must ask:

- *How much* has the behavior changed? We discover this by looking at *level changes*.
- *In what direction* (for better or worse) is the change headed? We can determine this by looking at *trend*.
- How *consistent* (regularly or irregularly) is the change that is taking place? In this case, we examine *variability*.

A *change in level* is demonstrated when the data's average value changes (*mean*, or sum of the values divided by the total number of occurrences of a set of data; or *mode*, the value of the data point most heavily represented; or *median*, the value of the score in the middle of the array of scores arranged from lowest to highest). Level changes are easily documented by taking the average value of each condition and comparing them. (Refer back to Figure 8.6. Note the change in level demonstrated between the baseline and the DRA (differential reinforcement of alternative behavior) condition in both the number of math problems completed (from an average or *mean* ($M$) = 1.33 to an $M$ = 34.5, while the percentage of intervals off-task diminished from an $M$ = 93.3% to an $M$ = 3%).

A *trend* becomes apparent when data points seem to be producing patterns that either rise or fall over time. Figure 8.13 displays actual equal-interval data showing the increasing attendance trend at the annual meeting of the *Berkshire Association for Behavior Analysis and Therapy* over the ten years from 1998 to 2008. Viewers readily can see the trend; that the number of people attending has been increasing steadily from year to year.

When data are more variable, an easy way to describe a trend is to use your computer's data management program to produce a simple **trendline**.[6] The trendline can tell you whether the data generated are increasing or decreasing over time, and can give you *a standard of reference for determining if the rate of change is accelerating or decelerating over time*. Look at Figure 8.14 (Northup, Vollmer, & Serrett, 1993, p. 533) and you can see several trend categories of publication topics from the *Journal of Applied Behavior Analysis*. Note, for example, that the number of papers on skill acquisition and on behavioral excesses among people with developmental disabilities increased over the first 24 years, while other classes of topics showed declining trends.[7]

*Variability* refers to the extent to which data "bounce around" on the graph. In applied behavior analysis, of course, that refers to measures of an individual's ongoing performance during baseline and/or during one or more intervention or follow-up periods. When we inquire about variability, we ask

---

[6]See http://office.microsoft.com/en=us/help

[7]Fitting lines to an array of data points on semi-logarithmic paper works similarly, although because the scale changes from one level to the next, the lines that would best fit the distribution of data points are more apt to form curves. Various statistical tests have been designed to enable consumers of the information to determine the significance of the results obtained.

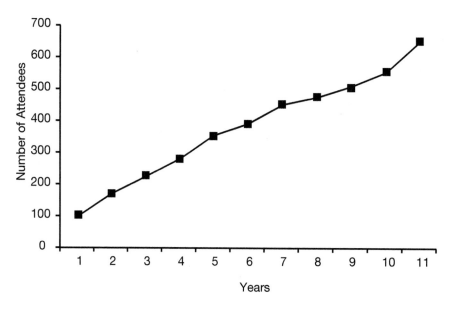

**Figure 8.13** An example of an increasing attendance trend at the meeting of The Berkshire Association for Behavior Analysis and Therapy, from 1998 to 2008.

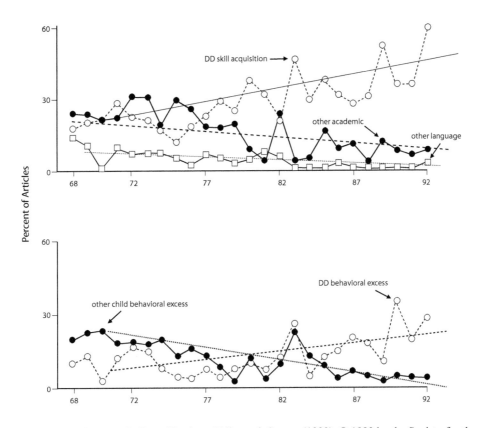

**Figure 8.14** Illustrative data trends. From Northup, Vollmer, & Serrett (1993). © 1993 by the Society for the Experimental Analysis of Behavior, Inc.

if the behavior of interest is being emitted fairly consistently (*homogeneously*) or jumping around from one data point to the next (*heterogeneously*). Why is information on variability so important? That depends on your purpose in recording in the first place—how it serves your achieving the objective of the program. To illustrate, sometimes variability can be problematic, as in the case of maintaining safe conditions. At other times it can be an advantage. As a case in point, suppose you are attempting to *shape* a new behavior by reinforcing only those responses that more and more closely approach a goal ("successively approximate" is the technical term; see Chapter 13). You would want to record responding very often, say, every 15 seconds, to allow you to detect and treat the slightest behavioral variation in the preferred direction. Ponder how closely you may wish to examine your series of data points for indications of variability, or to detect, measure, and treat (reinforce) those responses that indicate changes in given directions.

In maintaining safety, variations in responding can become matters of life and death, as in the case of children using helmets when riding bicycles discussed earlier (Figure 8.12; Van Houten et al., 2007). Those investigators scheduled their measurement intervals to permit detecting such variations and also to differentially reinforce improvements in performance. Notice, for instance, that the data show not only an improvement in helmet use, but also in consistency.

However, sometimes behavior is just highly variable. One such behavior is physical activity. In a recent study, Valbuena, Miller, Samaha, and Miltenberger (2017) present seven strategies to utilize when behavior is variable and include: phase mean and medial lines, daily average per week, weekly cumulative, proportion of baseline, 7-day moving average, change point detection, and confidence intervals.

They apply these strategies in this particular study to looking at step-count data, while highlighting the advantages and disadvantages of each strategy.

Level, trend, and variability are further illustrated in the sections in Chapter 9 on Demonstrating Functional Relations and General Requirements for Single-Subject Designs.

## Reporting Demographic Variables

It is important to describe demographic variables when reporting your data. These include (Jones, St. Peter, & Ruckle, 2020) the client's:

- age, or age range if working with a group
- educational or current grade level and/or degrees
- sex/gender
- diagnoses, including medical and/or educational or labels
- race/ethnicity or group identity
- socioeconomic status (SES)
- level of functioning
- test scores (if any)
- language spoken in school and at home

Reporting such information helps identify relations between these variables and the effectiveness of various behavioral interventions. As Jones, et al. contend, demographic variables are "often underreported, which may limit the broader dissemination of these behavior-analytic studies and the development of culturally responsive modifications to behavioral interventions" (p. 1304).

> **Ethical Code 2.18**: Behavior analysts engage in continual monitoring and evaluation of behavior-change interventions. If data indicate that desired outcomes are not being realized, they actively assess the situation and take appropriate corrective action. When a behavior analyst is concerned that services concurrently delivered by another professional are negatively impacting the behavior-change interventions the behavior analyst takes appropriate steps to review and address the issue with the other professional. (p. 12)

## SUMMARY AND CONCLUSIONS

Understanding and interpreting graphs and appropriately recording, graphing, and interpreting data are essential elements of applied behavior analysis. Validly and reliably observing and recording data permits us to accomplish a number of purposes: to determine objectively what an individual's or group's performance looks like prior to any intervention—that is, during baseline—as well as during and following the treatment or intervention.

In this chapter we have described several of a number of choices available to you when you design your graphing methods: *who* to involve in the process, and *how* you might prepare them skillfully and objectively to display and analyze behavioral data. You have viewed simple line graphs that permit viewers to detect changes in the level, trend, and variability of the data they have collected, and have seen some examples of different methods for describing and interpreting response patterns.

As a behavior analyst you have a responsibility to collect and graphically display data using the methods described in this chapter. You will use these graphic displays for decisions and recommendations for behavior change program development. You also will use your graphic displays to explain in understandable language to your clients and caretakers their progress and results. In addition, before any intervention or assessment is conducted, you must have your client's and/or caretaker's written consent (the Behavior Analyst Certification Board (BCBA) (2020) *ethics code for behavior analysts*).

Description alone, though, is insufficient. To convince ourselves and our clientele that the implemented intervention was responsible for the alteration in the targeted behavior, we must take another step—the step inherent in the term analysis in "applied behavior analysis"—by employing an experimental design. Yes, learning what experimental designs are and how they do their job are essential skills for every behavior analyst. That is the subject of our next chapter.

*Chapter 9*

# Optimizing Client Progress by Analyzing the Functions of Our Interventions: Basic Experimental Designs

### Goals

1. Define and illustrate:
   a. single-subject experimental design
   b. functional relationship
   c. confounding variables
   d. ipsative data
   e. evidence-based practices
   f. dependent variable
   g. independent variable
   h. POV
   i. return-to-baseline (ABAB) or (withdrawal) design
   j. reversal design, and specify how it differs from the withdrawal design
   k. multiple probes
   l. multiple-baseline design
2. Explain why each of the three identified myths are not true.
3. Describe the purpose of experimental designs.
4. Describe how prediction and obtained performance are utilized to determine if experimental control has been achieved.
5. Discuss how to determine if you have collected sufficient baseline data.
6. Discuss the advantages of single-subject experimental designs.
7. Identify purposes that baselines can serve when evaluating experimental data.
8. List general requirements for single-subject designs.
9. Describe the purpose of using repeated withdrawal (return-to-baseline) probes.
10. Provide the logic underlying the withdrawal design.

11. Describe the withdrawal design's variations.
12. Discuss the advantages and disadvantages of the withdrawal design.
13. Describe how POVs are achieved in the ABAB design to demonstrate experimental control.
14. Provide the logic underlying the multiple-baseline design.
15. List essential requirements for multiple-baseline designs.
16. Describe the multiple-baseline design's variations.
17. Discuss what factors (e.g., independence; multiple behaviors, environments, or subjects; tolerance for delay of treatment; and/or availability of subjects for concurrent baseline data collection) must be taken into consideration before each of the four multiple-baseline variations are selected.
18. Discuss the advantages and disadvantages of the multiple baseline-design; include in your discussion how to minimize various disadvantages.
19. Describe how POVs are achieved in the multiple baseline design to demonstrate experimental control.
20. Describe the added demonstration needed beyond POVs in the multiple baseline design before one can state experimental control has been achieved.

*************

Concerned about her recent weight gain and loss of energy, Jocelyn consulted her physician, Dejuana Hunter. The good doctor prescribed a particular routine of self-managed exercise, diet, and medication.

On her return visit several weeks later, Dr. Hunter was quite impressed to see that Jocelyn's condition had improved. She considered assigning that program to all her patients. But after further thought, a gnawing doubt seized her: "Perhaps Jocelyn's improvement is just a happy coincidence, and the procedure had nothing to do with it." What would she need to do to allay those suspicions? One choice would be to tell Jocelyn to stop the program temporarily and see if she continues to lose weight, or to have other patients try the program and watch them carefully. Maybe the doctor would find that the program's seeming effectiveness was just a chance event, influenced by unidentified factors.

Along with all responsible applied scientists and practitioners, behavior analysts must adopt a similar air of skepticism. The approach we take is to demonstrate the effects of our efforts by incorporating experimental designs into our programs of change. Our goal is to draw scientifically valid inferences (i.e., conclusions about relations among variables that can be duplicated or replicated). In behavior analysis, it is not good enough to find a demonstration of said program in the literature; we must demonstrate a functional relationship (i.e., a cause and effect relationship) with our clients to state that an intervention is effective. If this sounds too technical or impersonal, allow us to start by dispelling some common myths on the subject.

## Common Myths

**Myth 1:** *I don't need to understand experimental designs unless I intend to conduct research.*

Remember, as indicated in Chapter 1, *experimental analysis* is an essential feature of applied behavior analysis. If practitioners are to provide convincing evidence of a procedure's effectiveness, they need to analyze exactly how their procedures operate to produce the outcomes they do. This is done by demonstrating that (1) *the behavior of inter-*

*est* (i.e., the *dependent variable or the target behavior*) changed, and (2) that the behavior change was "a function" of *the intervention* (i.e., the *independent variable or what you implemented*). So, if you are to perform responsibly as an applied behavior analyst, you must ask yourself: "Is the particular procedure I'm implementing responsible for the change(s) I observe, or might some other conditions or variables help account for the outcome?" To answer these questions, you employ a **single-subject experimental design** *to demonstrate the relation between what you did (that is, the experimental manipulation of a specific independent variable, such as implementing a reinforcement program) and the outcome, in this case, the nature of the behavioral change (e.g., the result) and that the change was due to the manipulation and not some other confounding variable.* Fortunately, this requirement corresponds with the public's demand that medical and other human service practitioners choose, use, and demonstrate the efficacy of their best contemporary *practices*. These practices include best skills, processes, and solutions supported by the most appropriate resources, and continuous improvement. Beyond that, increasingly the public poses even tougher questions of practitioners, such as: "What are we getting for our money?" "Are these interventions data-based, and do they make a difference?" "What are the current effects of the intervention?" This contemporary trend favoring *evidence-based practice* actually requires that we objectively evaluate the effectiveness of services such as healthcare, education, and organization management. Consequently, if you hope to survive and thrive as a practitioner in this consumer-skeptical world you must understand, be thoroughly capable of, and routinely implement experimental designs because they are the vehicles that permit you to demonstrate, beyond a reasonable doubt, the effectiveness of the interventions you implement.

In the human arena, that requirement is easier said than done. As Baer, Wolf, and Risley recognized in 1968, attempting to alter behavior under real-world conditions and demonstrate the relation between what one reports having done and the outcomes of those interventions can be daunting. As they commented within their initial description of the field of behavior analysis:

The analysis of a behavior, as the term is used here, requires a believable demonstration of the events that can be responsible for the occurrence or non-occurrence of that behavior. An experimenter has achieved an analysis of a behavior when he can exercise control over it. By common laboratory standards, that has meant an ability of the experimenter to turn the behavior on and off, or up and down, at will. Laboratory standards have usually made this control clear by demonstrating it repeatedly, even redundantly, over time. Applied research, as noted before, cannot often approach this arrogantly frequent clarity of being in control of important behaviors. Consequently, application, to be analytic, demonstrates control when it can, and thereby presents its audience with a problem of judgment. The problem, of course, is whether the experimenter has shown enough control, and often enough, for believability. (pp. 93–94)

Fortunately for practitioners and their clientele, though, behavior analysts continue to make progress toward the overall goal of increasing the believability with which they demonstrate that specific behavioral changes are indeed a direct function of their particular change procedures. Single-subject research designs are used to demonstrate this on-and-off effect. We describe many of these analytic methods in the present chapter and in Chapter 25.

**Myth 2:** *I can wait to apply an experimental design until after I change behavior.*

Finding the "best fit" *after* you have implemented an intervention does not demonstrate experimental control. Experimental control is using the "best" or most appropriate design to demonstrate the functional relation between the behavior changes and what you did (the intervention or independent variable). Moreover, addressing the questions "Is the procedure producing the desired change?" and "Are my efforts responsible for this change?" while you are implementing a behavior-change program ensures that you do not waste your own, your client's, and perhaps the public's time and resources. In fact, one of the chief benefits of ABA is that the analysis is ongoing, thereby revealing the impact of any changes occurring as a function of systematic interventions *while the program is in progress*. This ongoing data monitoring also provides you with a basis for modifying or terminating an ineffective or counterproductive intervention.

**Myth 3:** *Because the intervention I am implementing is evidence-based I do not have to demonstrate experimental control for my best practice interventions on my clients' behavior.*

Remember, you are not practicing behavior analysis nor are you behaving according to the ethical guidelines if you do not demonstrate that the behavior change you obtained was due to the intervention you implemented and not some other confounding variables. Moreover, by demonstrating the control over the behavior change you are also ensuring that you are making decisions on program or intervention effectiveness based upon data.

The purpose of an experimental design, then, is to demonstrate a **functional (or experimental) relation** between the behavior change and the intervention; that is, to reveal (a) *whether the observed behavior change(s) are a direct function of the intervention* and if so, (b) *to what extent they are related.* Experimental research designs also prevent people from attributing the behavior change to non-related or extraneous causes. Depending on the situation, though, some experimental designs are better suited than others to demonstrating those functional relations. You will learn more about these alternatives later in this chapter and in Chapter 25.

To summarize, ABA uses **single-subject experimental designs** (variously called *intensive, within-subject, single case, repeated measures,* and *time-series experimental designs*) *to demonstrate a functional relation between the behavior change and the intervention.* We do this to convince ourselves and our audience that our programming and management of the behavior of concern was in fact a result of our efforts. Moreover, those designs permit us to rule out the likelihood that *unrelated variables* (e.g., **extraneous** or **confounding variables**) are responsible for the behavior change. In this chapter we provide a general overview of single-subject experimental designs as used within applied behavior analysis and introduce you to the two particular designs you probably will encounter most frequently in ABA research and practice: the *return-to-baseline* (also called by many "reversal" or "withdrawal") design and the *multiple-baseline* design. Later, in Chapter 25, we describe several other designs better suited to more complex circumstances. (For a more in-depth coverage of the topic of experimental design in ABA, see Kazdin, 2010; Johnston & Pennypacker, 2020).

## ADVANTAGES OF SINGLE-SUBJECT EXPERIMENTAL DESIGNS

The main advantage of using single-subject over group-experimental designs is their ability to go beyond providing probability statements or drawing conclusions about group characteristics based on normative data. Within behavior analysis, we base our demonstrations of functional relations on **ipsative data,** that is, *data based on each individual's behavior,* not on group averages. These single-subject designs are based on each individual's performance rather than on the data derived from sample groups' norms and distributions. Consequently, data can be used to investigate what methods succeed with an individual, rather than for a group in general (but not for any particular individual). Moreover, this demonstration of functional relations serves as a source of accountability for the outcome of an intervention with an individual client. Indeed, this single-subject approach qualifies ABA as an **accountable** or *evidence-based* scientific approach.

Consumer confidence in applied behavior analysis is further strengthened by the fact that ABA uses objective data to demonstrate those functional relations. Today's savvy consumers are no longer content to accept methods simply because practitioners are trained to use them, or because they "intuitively feel" or believe that they will work, or because they worked with other people or under other situations, or because former clients or onlookers have attested to their success. ABA methods ideally meet the increasing public demand for policies and practices to be *based on clear evidence of procedural effectiveness*, often referred to as **evidence-based practices**. An example is the provision requiring such evidence contained within United States Department of Education, Public Law 107–110, January 8, 2002 ("No Child Left Behind"): that *practices be limited to those demonstrated to be effective with like populations.*

As Horner et al., (2005) have asserted,

> single-subject research has proven particularly relevant for defining educational practices at the level of the individual learner.... Of special value has been the ability of single-subject research methods to provide a level of experimental rigor beyond that found in traditional case studies. Because single-subject research documents experimental control, it is an approach, like randomized control-group designs (Shavelson & Towne, 2002) that may be used to establish evidence-based practices. (pp. 165–167)

## Demonstrating Functional Relations

We determine the effectiveness of a particular intervention by demonstrating *functional relations* between the measures of the **dependent variable**, *the behavior of concern* (e.g., health status, rate of language acquisition, rate of sales, etc.), and the **independent variables**, commonly *the components of the intervention or the behavior-change procedure* (e.g., differential reinforcement, extinction, or any among the numerous other procedures found in this book). To establish a functional relation, we manage particular independent variables and demonstrate convincingly that a given behavior or dependent variable changed accordingly. Once we amass evidence sufficient to support the conclusion that the behavior change was a function or result of the newly arranged contingencies, we insist on confirmation by *showing that the dependent variables change reliably* **when and only when** *the intervention or treatment is in place and not when it is absent.* Said using the more technological jargon of the field, we demonstrate experimental control via **predication (P)**, which is *what would happen if nothing changed;* **obtain data (O)** or results, which is *what happens to the dependent variable when we implement the independent variable;* and we **verify (V)** *when the P and O don't overlap (the O increases or decreases compared to baseline).* Finally, we get *replication* by demonstrating at least three POVs[1]. Phases prior to treatment (*baseline*), during treatment (*intervention*), and after treatment (*follow-up*) are designed to permit sufficient sets of repeated measures to demonstrate validly that the behavior of concern (i.e., the targeted behavior) occurs as a function of the intervention. For example, we predict ensuring performances by extrapolating from prior (baseline) performance patterns—our best guess being that absent any intervention, future performance will persist unchanged at baseline. Just as we might want to determine which of three wall switches controls a particular light, we flick the switch up and down and watch to see if the bulb illuminates and darkens correspondingly. Once we have introduced and sustained the independent variable (often referred to as "treatment" or "change procedure[s]") and discover that only following that point does performance change reliably, we are on our way toward amassing evidence favoring the existence of a functional relation between the two. To increase our confidence, we seek to duplicate the outcome by then replicating the process of *prediction, obtained,* and *verification* (POV) at least three times.

More specifically, recall that we assess the extent of the change by plotting the results on a graph and noting any marked changes over time in the *level* of the data (how high the data have climbed or low they have dropped); the *trend* or the inclination of the change rate (whether the rate is speeding up or slowing down within a given time); and the *variability* of the data (the extent to which the data points have bounced about). (See Chapter 8.)

To illustrate what we mean by *level*, refer to Figure 9.1, a fictitious graph. The story goes like this: Lenny, a senior honors student, was eager to maintain a firm, healthy body, especially since he met Olga, the adorable exchange student in his history class. One part of the plan was to walk briskly before dinner every day. "To stay motivated, I'm going to use my new Fitbit to keep track of the number of steps I take. Then I'll graph the

---
[1] The usage of the term POV is not an "official term" but one that has been used by one of the authors to help students understand and evaluate research."

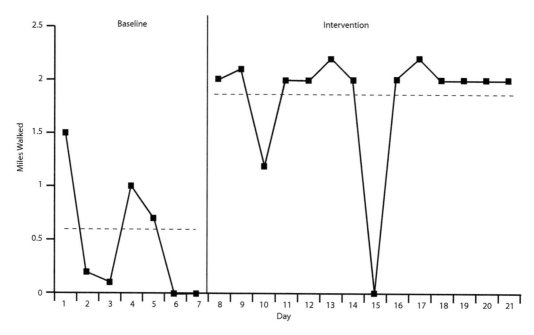

**Figure 9.1** Changes in level from baseline to intervention (fictitious data)

results daily." So, Lenny hung a graph on the wall and every evening he recorded the distance he had walked. He succeeded in walking a mile and a half the first day, but dropped down to covering only about three blocks on the second. On Day 3 it was drizzling and Lenny was tired, but he did take the short walk back to his dorm rather than taking the bus. The next two days, he made a half-hearted effort. Then he found excuses for not walking at all the next two days. Discouraged, Lenny decided to design a more stringent plan. He asked Olga if she would be willing to help by checking with him daily about whether, and if so, how far he had walked that day. Olga agreed to pay special note to his walking at least two miles before dinner, rain or shine, and to attend a concert with him three weeks later if he met this goal at least 80 percent of the time until then. Glance at Figure 9.1 and see what happened. His plan did work pretty well. He only confessed to failing to meet his schedule twice—once (Day 10), when he received an email from an old friend asking him how things were going at school. He just *had* to read and answer it right away, so he started walking later than planned and needed to return after covering only 1.2 miles, to avoid missing dinner. "Olga won't think any the less of me," he consoled himself, "At least I hope not." But just to be on the safe side, from then on, he resolved not to check for messages until he returned. The other time was on Day 15, when there was a terrific downpour.

Now take a look at the graph of Lenny's walking, first from the perspective of changes in *level* (Figure 9.1). We can calculate the average for the phase to determine the general performance level. Probably you are most familiar with computing averages by adding all the measures and dividing by the number of measures taken. The technical label for that kind of an average is the *arithmetic mean*. Lenny's baseline mean was about 0.5 miles walked, while during the intervention (Olga's positive feedback and promise to join him at a concert), he averaged about 1.9 per day.

Review the graph once again and perhaps you will notice something important about the data. In what direction do they appear to be headed—up, down or relatively flat? In Figure 9.2 we have superimposed a *best-fit* or *trendline* on the two sets of data—prior to and then during the "reporting to

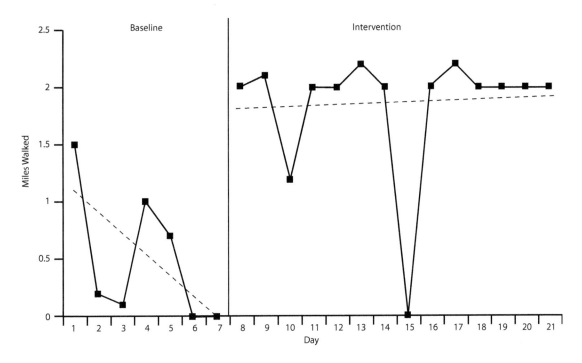

**Figure 9.2** Changes in trend from baseline to intervention (fictitious data)

Olga" contingency. Notice the line during the first week indicates a downward direction, while after the *if-then contingency* (if I walk, then Olga will be impressed) was placed in effect, the trend shifted to a slightly upward direction (see Deochand, Costello, & Fuqua, 2015 for a tutorial on adding trend lines using Excel).

The other important feature of a distribution of data is how much it bounces around—its *variability*. Although you might decide to assess the variability of a data set by using statistical tests such as *analyses of variance*, in applied behavior analysis that is generally not necessary because the graphs show you how much the data points vary from one time to the next. In the graph of Lenny's walking data, the data are much more variable in baseline than during the treatment, a sign that walking is under much tighter control during that second phase. Behavior analysts generally attempt find ways to support steady behavioral progress, especially because very high and very low rates sometimes can be dangerous or otherwise undesirable.

(Think about extremely high or low rates of eating, drinking, or going without sleep). We in the field tend to continue trying different contingency arrangements until progress toward the sought-after change moves steadily toward attaining goal levels, stability, and durability.

Notice that in the circumstances just described, we are able to see what typical performance looked like and how it changed under new contingency arrangements. Yet in Lenny's case, could we be certain that Olga's feedback and willingness to go out with him was responsible? Maybe the quality of the dorm food improved or Lenny was feeling especially peppy, or his best buddy joined him during his walk, or the weather was especially lovely during every day but one of the second and third weeks. How could we find out that any contingency arrangement, such as the ones just described, was responsible? In fact, how can we examine whether any behavioral change has been brought about as a *function* of new contingency arrangements and not of some other factor(s)? Read on and find out!

## GENERAL REQUIREMENTS FOR SINGLE-SUBJECT DESIGNS

Before we explain how one might use a specific experimental design to decide whether a particular intervention was a function of the altered behavioral contingencies, we should go over some preliminary requirements that pertain to all of the various designs classified as *single-subject* (or *within-subject or single-case*): First and foremost, single-subject research is based upon repeated assessment. Repeated measures are essential because the evaluation relies on the analyst's ability to project future performance (i.e., prediction) on the basis of current performance and to demonstrate that the intervention changed the behavior measure's previous path (i.e., data obtained) to verify the functional relationship. (Said another way, baseline data patterns serve as the standard against which intervention data are compared.) In the typical situation, first we generate a baseline consisting of repeated patterns of behavior. We then predict the pattern of behavior from the baseline if we were not to do anything (this is our prediction line). Next we add the intervention over repeated sessions. Then we review the pattern generated during that new intervention phase to determine whether the obtained performance *level* has moved higher, lower or stayed the same (if prediction line and the obtained data are different we have a verification). Additionally we consider *trend* and *variability*. Are the data points forming an upward or downward path, or are they remaining fairly flat? Do the data points vary widely or within a narrow band? Generally, we answer those questions to our satisfaction by visually inspecting the data. (Peek ahead at Figure 9.3 for one example of a patently obvious level change.) Sometimes, especially when the data points are so scattered that they obscure change patterns, yet *any* behavioral improvement is deemed crucially important, we may elect to apply statistical tools (such as *analyses of variance* or *t-tests*). Finally, as described below, we then choose one of several possible design arrangements to enable the analyst to rule out the possibility that unrelated variables actually may have been responsible for the behavior change by replicating or reproducing the effect.

## WITHDRAWAL (RETURN TO BASELINE) DESIGNS[2]

Recall that the term *functional relation* means that changes in the independent variable reliably relate to corresponding changes in the dependent variable(s). If a given treatment or *independent variable* (e.g., approval from Olga) functionally relates to an individual's behavior (e.g., Lenny's rate of taking long walks), then contingently presenting that treatment (Olga's approval) should systematically affect that behavior (Lenny's rate of walking should increase). If Olga's attention is indeed a reinforcer, *withholding* it following his walks should sooner or later lead to a decrease in Lenny's exercise routine. (If instead, Lenny's despised enemy, and competitor for Olga's attention, delivers praise, that praise will instead function as an aversive stimulus and would produce a decrease in the rate of the behavior.) So, *systematic changes in the dependent variable that are a function of the presentation of the independent variable serve to increase our confidence in the functionality of the relation*. We conclude that our procedure, rather than some extraneous variable, such as what someone else might be doing nearby or the fact that the individual has been maturing, accounts for the changes in behavior. This is the logical foundation of the *withdrawal or* **return-to-baseline** design.

### Selecting and Using the Withdrawal (Return-to-Baseline) Design

The withdrawal design consists of several phases: First we repeatedly observe, measure, record, and graph the behavior of interest (the dependent vari-

[2]In applied behavior analysis, we have elected to use the term withdrawal design instead of the often-used term reversal design, because the label for the latter design can be ambiguous, in the sense that the reversal technically requires an intervention crafted for the purpose of supporting the obverse of the change accomplished in the $B_1$ condition. Examples might include supporting indolence instead of exercise, or fighting instead of cooperating, not just, as in the popular understanding, temporarily withholding or withdrawing the condition to reveal temporary alterations in the change patterns. Practitioners need to seriously consider the risks of even temporarily reversing contingencies to the extent that they support deleterious behavior.

able), under *typical* ongoing conditions (which means that adaptation has taken place previous to baseline data collection) to establish a *baseline*. We continue these observational measurement sessions until we see that the graphed data are emitting a convincingly stable pattern of behavior with *no new highs or lows over several sessions in a row*, which lets us predict performance if nothing were to change. That *baseline* ($A_1$) allows us to predict future behavior by serving as the standard (i.e., prediction line) against which the effects of applying the independent variable (the *intervention/treatment* or $B_1$ phase; obtained performance) are compared. After response patterns show obvious progress in the anticipated direction, within that initial $B_1$ phase compared to baseline performance (obtained for our first verification of effectiveness), we temporarily withdraw the intervention, labeling that phase the **withdrawal of treatment** condition ($A_2$) In this situation, performance during $B_1$ becomes the new basis for predicting new performance patterns. So, if during $A_2$, behavioral patterns tend to return to those noted earlier ($A_1$) and are different from performance predicted by $B_1$ phase, we begin to conclude that the behavior is functionally related to the conditions in effect (We have our 2$^{nd}$ POV. (In some cases, when a simple withdrawal doesn't work to demonstrate experimental control, we actually *reverse* the treatment, as in now delivering the reinforcers for the undesired instead of desired behavior. In that case, the label "reversal design" would be most apt.)

Next, during $A_2$ should the data pattern reveal a clear return toward the original baseline performance patterns (this becomes the new prediction line), we re-introduce the *treatment* (the second B condition or $B_2$). Presuming the prediction based on $A_2$ is verified using $B_2$ conditions in the form of reliably recovering and sustaining change, this is our third POV and we have experimental control, we then usually add a *maintenance* phase, during which the treatment conditions may gradually be diminished or thinned.

Of course, our main interest in any behavior analytic investigation is to change the level, trend, and/or variability of a given response pattern by applying procedures based on behavioral principles (many of which you are learning about in this text). Why is it important to resist the temptation simply to implement a promising procedure and hope for the best rather than bothering with baselines and experimental designs?

The baseline phase serves a number of distinct purposes: It (1) displays actual current performance patterns or features, (2) serves as a basis for predicting future levels of and variability in performance were no intervention implemented, (3) enables us to assess the durability of change in response patterns after the intervention has been implemented and then discontinued, and, depending on those results, (4) provides us with evidence for deciding whether to reinstate, and perhaps permanently establish or eventually slowly phase out the intervention. You can see, then, that the withdrawal design demonstrates experimental control by showing that:

- once the intervention is solidly in place, behavioral measures change from those recorded during baseline. (This permits one to predict and demonstrate how patterns actually have changed in contrast with those predicted solely on the basis of baseline performance.);
- after the intervention is removed, they then begin to return toward former baseline rates (prediction and obtained data again for a second POV); and
- when the intervention is re-implemented, the pattern of change repeats itself (verifications are further supported).

Just as the position of a light switch affects whether a light is on or off, if presenting or withdrawing the independent variable reliably affects the trend, level, and/or variability of the behavior measures, we can assert that the intervention is *functional* or *functionally related* to the measured behavior. Another way of looking at the situation is to recognize that it is appropriate to conclude that the behavioral change is functionally related to the intervention *when and only when* the level, trend, and/or variability of performance obtained during the intervention (B phase) no longer matches that predicted or extrapolated from that of baseline.

Beyond demonstrating the functionality of the intervention, *repeated returns to baseline condi-*

*tions* allow us to predict how durable the change might be should the intervention be removed altogether. If after several withdrawal (baseline-condition) sessions, the behavior drops back completely to its former baseline levels, we know we had best reintroduce the intervention. Later on, when the presumably satisfactory pattern of behavior recovers and smooths off at an acceptably steady rate under the treatment (B), we can return to baseline conditions (A) once more, to determine how durable that recent change has been. We can continue to apply these periodic probes until such time as performance persists steadily at the desired level. "Probing" with these return-to-baseline phases is far safer than leaving matters to chance, under the assumption that change will continue indefinitely.

Like most of us, you may find yourself becoming impatient, wanting to terminate baseline and attempt your intervention. Uh, uh—don't end the baseline prematurely. "Okay," you may say, "but how shall I know when I have collected sufficient baseline data to validly represent the individual's current behavioral pattern?" Unfortunately, no hard and fast rules exist. Certainly, though, you will want to feel confident that your data-display accurately represents those ongoing patterns. In case you never have informally observed the individual engaging in the behavior of interest and you note over three or four sessions that none of the data points fall above zero, you are fairly safe in concluding that the response probably is missing, at least under those particular circumstances. Baseline can stop there. Otherwise, a convenient rule-of-thumb for concluding that you have collected and displayed sufficient data during any particular phase, including baseline, is to specify in advance, "No new highs or new lows for X (say, five) days in a row." You should also ensure that if there is a trend it is occurring in the opposite direction than the hypothesized behavior pattern. For example, if you have an increasing trend and you hypothesize that your independent variable will increase behavior, then you should not end baseline. However, if you have an increasing trend and your independent variable is expected to decrease behavior, then you should stop baseline. (This same logic should be used when stopping one condition and starting another.)

To provide you with sense of the logic and utility of the return-to-baseline treatment design, permit us to walk you through Figure 9.3, the self-injury (SIB) graph for Joy from the previous chapter (represented here with projected levels of performance (dashed lines) and the actual obtained levels (ovals surround behavioral measures). Notice that during baseline (BL), Joy engaged in high levels of self-injury. Based on this information, we would predict that Joy would continue her high levels of SIB. Draw a dotted line from baseline performance into the next condition (at around 30, the approximate baseline average; dashed line). During the intervention phase, notice that upon the implementation of the treatment (providing reinforcement non-contingently, or NCR), Joy's level of self-injury practically disappeared and did *not* match the projected performance from baseline (see encircled data points). This is our initial source of supportive evidence (i.e., our first POV). Given this new level of performance, we might predict that Joy would desist from engaging in self-injury. Now draw a horizontal dotted line at Frequency 1, from the NCR condition into the second baseline condition (the withdrawal of treatment). Again, note, in our second replication, that the obtained performance does not match the prediction (compare the dashed line with the circled performance). Joy's self-injury reverted back to high levels (i.e., second POV). Finally, based on this new level, we would predict that Joy's level of SIB would remain high (draw a dotted line at around 30 into the next condition) (prediction). Once again, we see that after NCR was re-implemented (the second phase B), Joy essentially ceased engaging in self-injury (supportive evidence and third replication). The obtained level of performance did not match the level predicted on the basis of how she behaved during the return-to-baseline phase (i.e., third POV). When the actual levels of performance fail to match the levels predicted by those displayed during the previous condition, but do change (presumably improve) systematically, *experimental control is demonstrated.* In other words, we may conclude that the implementation of the independent variable was "responsible for," or to use our technically correct terminology, *functionally related* to the behavior change (i.e., the data support the functional relation).

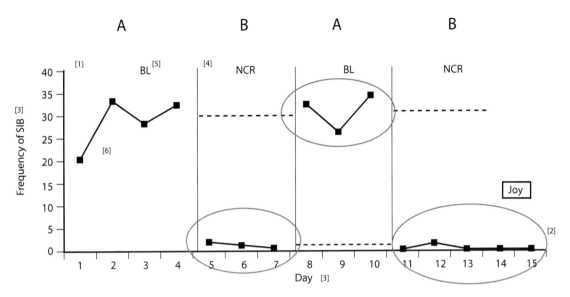

**Figure 9.3** Joy's level of self-injurious behaviors (SIBs): A fictitious return-to-baseline design demonstration of a functional relation.

Let's look at Figure 9.3, a fictitious graph utilizing an ABAB design that does not demonstrate experimental control. In this graph you will notice that if you draw your prediction from $A_1$ (based on its average trend) and compare it with your obtained data in $B_1$ you have your first POV (Although notice the increasing trend in baseline in the direction of the desired change. If you had similar data it would be wise to continue baseline until either data are stable or the trend is in the opposite direction of desired change). The next step would be to extend your $B_1$ prediction line into $A_2$ and for it to be obtained in $A_2$. Oh no, they overlap, thus there is not a POV. After extending the $A_2$ into $B_2$ and comparing it to the data obtained you have a second POV. However, remember to demonstrate experimental control you must have at least three POVs. Thus, because we only have two POVs and not three we do not have experimental control.

## Actual Illustrations

An excellent actual example from the literature illustrates experimental control by means of a withdrawal (return-to-baseline) treatment design for three of four participants (see Figure 9.5) (Ahearn, Clark, MacDonald, & Chung, 2007). The investigators sought to examine the effects of response interruption and redirection (the treatment in B) on the vocal stereotypy (meaningless repetitions of vocal sounds) of four children with autism. The design demonstrated that the intervention was successful for three of the children, although not for Peter. Notice that during baseline all the participants engaged in high levels of stereotypy; but each time the intervention phase was implemented, that level diminished substantially for Mitch, Alice, and Nicki, and partially for Peter. When baseline conditions were reinstated, three of the participants' levels of stereotypy recovered; then subsequently diminished when the intervention was re-implemented. By contrast, although Peter's level of stereotypy lessened during the first implementation of the intervention, after the second baseline was implemented, his stereotypy levels did not return to their previous highs. That being the case, the analyst was prevented from being able to conclude with confidence that the intervention was *solely* responsible for Peter's diminished rates. Perhaps other events contributed to that encouraging outcome. In Nicki's case, notice that it took until the latter part of the second A condition for the data to reverse direction. Sometimes the effects of an intervention or of a "treatment return to baseline (or reversal)" condition are rapid; some-

186 • BEHAVIOR ANALYSIS FOR LASTING CHANGE

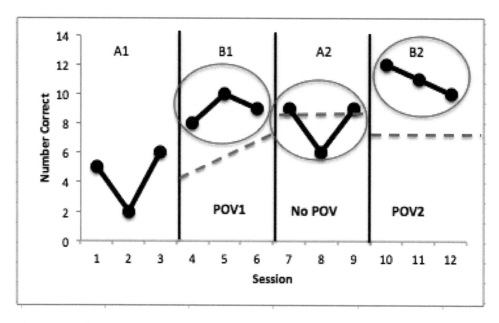

**Figure 9.4** Number of correct problems completed: A fictitious return-to-baseline design demonstration without experimental control.

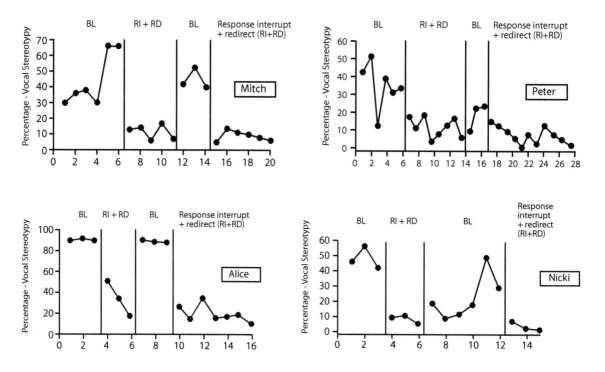

**Figure 9.5** An illustrative ABAB assessment design. The figure clearly demonstrates the effect of the response interruption and redirection for three of the four participants. Selected from a figure displayed by Ahearn, Clark, MacDonald, & Chung (2007). © 2007 by the Society for the Experimental Analysis of Behavior, Inc.

times they take time. In applying behavior analysis, patience is a must.

## The (True) Reversal Design

Although, as we have indicated, many behavior analysts interchange the terms withdrawal (*return-to-baseline design*) *with the term reversal design*, the ("true") reversal design is a *variation* of the return-to-baseline design. In reversal designs, the effects of the treatment are tested by introducing a *differential reinforcement of alternative behavior* (**DRA**) or a *differential reinforcement of other behavior* (**DRO**) condition (see Chapter 28) during the second A phase. The purpose is to determine whether the direction of the recently accomplished change data in the $B_1$ condition reverses or shifts in a direction away from that observed during the B condition. (For example, in the second A, or baseline condition, being out-of-seat is reinforced instead of remaining in-seat). *A* **reversal design**, then, *requires an intervention phase crafted for the purpose of reversing the target behavior (turning it around in the direction opposite from that intended to prevail during treatment), as in intervening during the $A_2$ (second) condition to promote the unwanted behavior.* This design may seem foolish, in that it intentionally reverses the positive effects accomplished during the first treatment condition ($B_1$). And, who wants to provide a history of intermittent reinforcement for undesired behavior? Yet, if the effect of condition $B_1$ is powerful, the reversal generally takes place even for difficult-to-reverse behaviors (e.g., behaviors that begin to receive reinforcement from their natural environment). The change also occurs much more rapidly than it would under the ($A_2$) phase of the more conventional A-B-A-B design. As a result, the functional relation between the treatment and the behavior can be determined more rapidly, thereby enabling the behavior analyst to resume the effective intervention much sooner.

To illustrate, sometimes conditions warrant rapidly demonstrating the power of a set of contingencies, as in conditions of risk to the client or others. Suppose, for example, you are looking hurriedly for really powerful reinforcers to support the healthy eating choices made by a youth with diabetes. While the boy is in your direct care, you are unwilling to provide any sort of a "typical condition" baseline. You might select a different behavior altogether, say exercising, and, following a baseline (A), apply your stimulus (points toward a ticket to an athletic event, B), as a consequence of his running a treadmill. Assuming the rate of the former does increase, you could *reverse* conditions, now applying the points for the opposite—for *not* using the treadmill. Assuming the rate of the treadmill running diminishes, you have rapidly accumulated evidence favoring the efficacy of your selected reinforcing contingency. Switching back to the previous condition and seeing the earlier effect reproduced (treadmill use again increasing) should nail down the value of your reinforcing stimulus. Now you can feel more optimistic about continuing the point contingency for other classes of behavior, such as reinforcing healthy food choices.

 When faced with clear and present danger, consider maintaining a consistent level of reinforcement throughout. During the A condition, though, you would deliver reinforcers on a *time*, rather than a *response*-based schedule; that is, non-contingently (NCR) or according to some other differential reinforcement schedule (e.g., DRO, DRA, or DRD, about which you will read in Chapter 28). Then you would apply the reinforcer directly as a consequence of, or contingent on, the desired response. Thompson, Iwata, Hanley, Dozier, and Samaha (2003) used a similar, though more complex, reversal approach to examine the utility of extinction, noncontingent reinforcement (NCR), and differential reinforcement of other behaviors (DRO) as control procedures. Results suggested that extinction produced the most consistent and rapid reversal with the fewest observed negative side effects.

## Additional Return–to-Baseline Design Variations

Return to baseline designs lends themselves to a number of variations, depending on your aim. For example, you might wish to:

- evaluate multiple interventions (e.g., ABA-BACAC) in which C is yet a different condition
- omit or minimize the initial baseline, particularly when measuring it is patently inappropriate. (You know that the individual either *always* engages in the behavior or it needs to be treated immediately, as in a client hitting his head non-stop; or the behavior is something he has *never* been seen to do as in riding a two-wheeled bicycle or operating a new, complicated piece of equipment; or the treatment is already in place and cannot be removed temporarily, like the physical surroundings or a cochlear implant), or to evaluate order of conditions [e.g., BABA versus ABAB] wherein you are attempting to discover if one of those conditions has an effect on the subsequent one.)
- vary the number of treatment return to baselines, especially after planning and failing with the initial (B) intervention. To illustrate, Tarbox, Tarbox, Ghezzi, Wallace, and Yoo (2007) used an ABACACAB design to evaluate the effects of adding a blocking phase (C) to manage mouthing of leisure items, while Gouboth, Wilder, and Bocher (2007) added and tested a C phase (a signaling stimulus consisting of an informative statement and a timer), within an ABA-CABAC arrangement, to supplement the noncontingent reinforcement (NCR) present during the B phase. Figure 9.6 displays the data for each of those three phases for one of the students, Sam.

Note that in the latter cases, the investigators began by planning to use a simple return-to-baseline design, not intending to evaluate multiple interventions at all. They proceeded to add the C phases after the B conditions proved ineffectual. In fact, given the time demands and the potential for unintended sequence effects (the earlier intervention affects responding in the subsequent intervention), a return-to-baseline design may not be the most efficient way to compare multiple interventions from the outset. Later, in Chapter 25, we provide you with a couple of viable options for conducting such comparisons, including the *alternating treatment* or the *multi-element design*.

*How do you know when to terminate the baseline* and move on to the intervention or treatment? Generally, as performance stabilizes; that is, when you *observe no new highs nor lows for three to five sessions in a row*. As mentioned above, though, when extended or repeated baseline measurements would be patently absurd, as in cases of danger to the person or those in the vicinity, or when no one has ever seen the individual emitting the target behavior, numerous baseline measurements makes

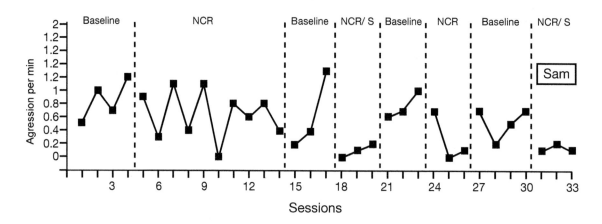

**Figure 9.6** An example of an A-B-C design. A simplified version based on Gouboth, Wilder, & Bocher (2007). © 2007 by the Society for the Experimental Analysis of Behavior, Inc.

little sense. In such situations, you can justify a brief initial baseline phase, say of two or three data points.

## Advantages of the Withdrawal or Return-to-Baseline Design (A-B-A-B)

The return-to-baseline design's main advantage is its ability to provide accountability by simply and convincingly demonstrating a functional relation between the behavior (dependent variable) and the intervention (independent variable). Also, it is one of the few designs capable of demonstrating the effects of one, or sometimes more, interventions on the behavior of a single individual, without specifying particular behavior change criteria in advance. Moreover, this design can educate contingency managers and consumers by demonstrating the efficacy of the new procedures and the value of continuing them rather than returning to former, less constructive, approaches to handling the behavior that were used during baseline. For example, yelling when the child engages in an inappropriate behavior during baseline, compared to not responding to the inappropriate behavior but reinforcing acceptable, alternative behaviors during intervention. Once the contingency managers see the contrasting effects during the ABAB design, it helps to reinforce their continuation of the intervention strategy, rather than continuing with using yelling during baseline. In other words, it might help promote continued treatment integrity.

## Disadvantages of the Withdrawal or Return-to-Baseline Design

Before starting a return-to-baseline design (or any other intervention or design procedure) consider the plan from an ethical perspective. You would not want to risk running a lengthy baseline under dangerous circumstances. For example, to delay treating seriously aggressive, self-abusive, or risky behavior merely to collect extensive baseline data to obtain stability would be ethically questionable. Similarly, you must very carefully consider the perils of reinstating baseline conditions after successfully eliminating a serious behavior problem, such as head banging, substance abuse, or other hazardous behaviors. In such cases, choosing an alternative design or conducting very brief baseline probes—e.g., only momentarily removing restraints from the wrists of a client with a history of gouging her eyes—would be preferable.

A-B-A-B designs require reasonable baseline stability. When baselines are highly variable and/or trending toward the anticipated change, they threaten to obscure the influence of the experimental variable (i.e., the intervention). If, in fact, you actually observe a general trend in the desired direction, you should consider a different design. Or, if that trend is sufficiently robust, leave well enough alone. You may not need to intervene at all.

Another disadvantage is that this design interrupts progress, thereby delaying achievement of the objective. Additionally, practitioners may express their concern that the modified behavior may not recover after returning to baseline conditions. Your rejoinder is to cite the well-established fact that once behavior has been acquired initially, it generally is reacquired more rapidly (Keller & Schoenfeld, 1950). You might also reassure contingency managers by explaining that the target behavior need not necessarily return completely to its baseline level during the return- to-baseline phase. An unambiguous shift back in the direction of baseline generally is sufficient to convince most skeptics.

Some may even question **multiple probes** (Horner & Baer, 1978)—*withdrawing the intervention briefly*—on ethical grounds. A reasonable rejoinder is that those *probes provide a basis for predicting how the participant is apt to function without the program, a necessary step assuming the intention is ultimately to eliminate the program altogether*. A good strategy for avoiding such objections is to negotiate in advance, with participants or their advocates, the plans for assessing the persistence of change. (In Chapter 25, we discuss multiple probes as a technique for functionally analyzing the relation between an intervention and the acquisition of untreated responses.)

Recovering former baseline performance during the return-to-baseline conditions may be impossible, especially when natural reinforcing contingencies gain control. For example, suppose during baseline Pirsha did not initiate interactions with her peers on the playground. Subsequently, a prompting and reinforcement program was implemented to teach her how to approach and talk to the other children. Once she mastered that skill, natural reinforcers in the form of gaining the other children's attention and joining in their games took over. Now, regularly enjoying the new contingencies, even if the intervention were withdrawn, Pirsha would be unlikely to revert to her earlier baseline patterns. From the outset, consider the possibility of circumstances like these and whether you would be better advised to choose an alternative experimental design, such as the multiple-baseline.

## MULTIPLE-BASELINE DESIGN

The *multiple-baseline* design is an excellent alternative to a design requiring a return to baseline conditions. In a **multiple-baseline design**, we *implement the intervention sequentially across several baselines, each of differing lengths,* to control for *such time-dependent extraneous variables as history, maturation, reaction to being measured for longer or shorter periods, seasonal influences, and so on* (one of the authors likes to call this ruling out the **earthquake effect**). In so doing, should we find (as with the A-B-A-B design) that the *level, trend,* and/or *variability* change substantially *when and only when* the independent variable is applied and that said change doesn't occur at the same time across baselines, then we may conclude that the independent (intervention or treatment) and the dependent variables are *functionally related.*

Like return-to-baseline designs, multiple-baselines initially represent the ongoing (baseline) levels of one or more behaviors (and/or possibly trends and variability). To design a multiple-baseline design, we collect pre-intervention response measures of the same dependent variable (e.g., behaviors, situations/settings, or individual participants or "subjects") across more than one baseline. It is better to include three or more baselines. Assuming we note desirable change in the treated but not in the untreated performance, we then apply the independent variable to the next baselines, in a staggered sequence. If the level, trend, and/or variability of the treated behavior changes, yet the others—those continuing under baseline conditions—remain steady, we begin to suspect that the intervention is responsible. If we begin to observe changes similar to those seen with the first *when and only when* the treatment is instituted, we become more confident that the intervention is responsible. Then, as the effect reproduces itself across additional baselines, we become increasingly convinced of the functionality of the relation. In other words, in replicating the procedure and reproducing the results we have completed the prediction-verification cycle across multiple situations.

### Using Multiple-Baseline Designs

To achieve a clean comparison, each among the set of baselines *must be independent* of the others and must end at a different point in time. Otherwise, in the first instance, we will not have ruled out the possibility that applying change procedures in one circumstance affects behavior in the others, due to the possibility that the results of the investigation may have been tainted. In the second—varying baseline lengths—we rule out the possibility that simple passage of time is responsible for the change. (Remember, the logic of the design demands that the behavior changes *when and only when* the independent variable is applied. Otherwise the circumstances responsible for the change remain obscure.)

Figure 9.7 is a hypothetical graph demonstrating the use of single-subject research logic to determine if indeed the treatment is responsible for the behavior change. Notice that the projected levels of performance (dashed lines) do not match either of the obtained levels of performance across both participants and, more importantly, the desired behavior change occurs at different times across the two participants (noted by the arrows) supporting the validity and predictability of the data. In this hypothetical example, to demonstrate experimental control, there would need to be a third baseline and IV demonstration to obtain a third POV.

Now, let us consider an actual example: A multiple-baseline design across participants was used (see Figure 9.8) to demonstrate the effectiveness of a system of training three cocktail servers (who

CHAPTER 9 OPTIMIZING CLIENT PROGRESS BY ANALYZING THE FUNCTIONS OF OUR INTERVENTIONS • 191

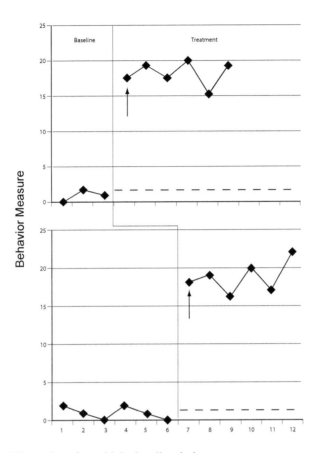

**Figure 9.7** A hypothetical illustration of a multiple- baseline design.

generally worked on separate days) to carry trays safely on the job (Scherrer & Wilder, 2008). During baseline, Sara performed fewer than 60 percent of the behaviors safely, while after training (session 4) her score was above 80 percent correct. Although Sara now carried her tray more safely, the other two participants still did not. Mike, the second participant, achieved the safer, above 80 percent, level only following his training, after session 13. Yet, despite the improvements in both Sara and Mike's performance, Tanya's remained at an unsafe level until she too received the training—prior to session 19. Note how clearly this multiple-baseline design demonstrates experimental control over an intervention. Yes, it did comply with the requirements essential to a multiple-baseline design: the baseline lengths varied (3, 12, 18 sessions), the participants acted independently of one another, and each server's behavior changed *when and only when* she or he received the intervention (sessions 4, 13, and 19). Notice in this example that treatment effects were immediate across all three participants; however, had they not been you would have to ensure that there was no earthquake effect by indicating at what session stable treatment effects were obtained and that they did not occur in the same session number across participants.

 *Warning!* When considering using a multiple-baseline design, be sure the behaviors you select are independent of one another, so they are unlikely to covary. Suppose the behavior analyst targeted *talking to peers* and *turning around* as the two dependent variables in a classroom intervention. If the first were changed, the second probably would change as well, making it impossible to demonstrate a functional relation. Rather, one should be able reasonably to evaluate the effects of the intervention across inde-

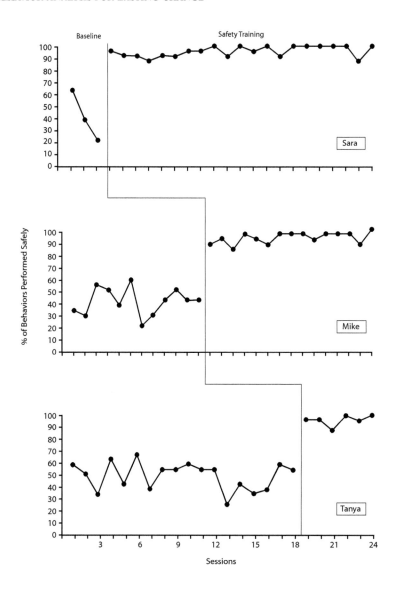

**Figure 9.8** An illustration of a multiple-baseline design: Percentage of behaviors performed safely during baseline and after training across the three participants. From Scherrer & Wilder (2008), Figure 1. © 2008 by the Society for the Experimental Analysis of Behavior, Inc.

pendent problematic behaviors, such as hitting other students, gouging out designs on the desk, or shouting. To summarize, the multiple-baseline across-behaviors design can be a practical and useful design, but if the measured behaviors (dependent variables) tend to co-vary—that is, to change in tandem with one another—choose an alternative design.

## Variations of the Multiple-Baseline Design

There are several formats of the multiple-baseline design, including staggering the intervention across *individuals, behaviors,* and/or *settings*. Here, we elaborate on those variations.

**Across-individuals (subjects) multiple-baseline design.** In Figure 9.8, we already have displayed one form of the multiple-baseline design: *across subjects*. If you are considering using this control strategy, though, be certain the participants behave independently of one another. You do not want the behavior change of one influencing the behavior of the others. Suppose, for instance, you were designing and testing an effective strategy for teaching office workers to position themselves safely at the computer, and hope to use a multiple-baseline design as your analytic strategy. You would want to train and treat each participant separately. Otherwise, the second participant might observe the training protocol and begin to alter her posture accordingly; then you will lose the opportunity to rule out such possible *confounding variables* (the ones that muddy the waters) as being caused by passage of time alone.

**Across-behaviors multiple-baseline design.** A second variation of the multiple-baseline design is implementing the intervention *across different behaviors within the same individual*. You begin by taking a baseline on two, or preferably, more behaviors that are *not* expected to co-vary. Then you apply the intervention to only one of the baselines while you continue measuring the others. Take, for instance, very distinct sports skills. In baseball, you might choose batting, pitching, and catching as the three skills to functionally analyze. You would not choose throwing to first base, throwing to the outfield, and throwing the ball to home plate. Why? Because you want to avoid interdependent behaviors, those that will tend to co-vary, or you will have lost experimental control over your training intervention. Similarly, be extremely cautious about using this design when working with behavioral cusps or pivotal behaviors (recall that cusps or pivotal behaviors once learned result in changes in other behaviors. For example, Ainsman and Mayer (2018) used self-recording matched to teacher recordings as an intervention, and targeted time at their work tables in a pre-school. The other behaviors being evaluated included sharing and appropriate classroom voice. All behaviors changed once the students learned to self-record their staying in their work areas. Thus, experimental control was not demonstrated.

In an effort to improve the soccer skills of three female high school players, two promising techniques, public posting and goal-setting, were used (Brobst & Ward, 2002). The experimenters conducted training across three skills not expected to co-vary: movement with ball, movement during restarts, and movement during passing. They carried out the intervention during practice scrimmages while recording data both during practice as well as during actual games. Figure 9.9 displays the results for one of the young women. Note that her performance improved in both situations *only* when the intervention was applied on movement with the ball, not during restarts or after passing. Then later, after the intervention was implemented for restarts, it too improved consistently, the data matching that of movement with the ball. Movements after passing only improved after the intervention was put in place for that skill. Notice, too, that the player improved her skills not only while practicing but also during games.

In a second illustration of an across-behaviors multiple-baseline design (Figure 9.10), notice how Marckel, Neef, and Ferreri (2006) used a prompt-fading procedure to test whether children on the autism spectrum could learn to improvise by combining multiple images they had previously mastered via the Picture Exchange Communication System© (PECS) (Bondy & Frost 1994, 1998), a method of communicating by means of exchanging pictures rather than through the spoken word. (See Chapter 19 for a more elaborate description of PECS.) The experimenters used a multiple-baseline across (use of) descriptors (functions, colors, shapes) design—analogous to an across-behaviors multiple-baseline design—to examine the effects of training on the number of requests made independently by correctly improvising from training and generalization stimuli. An example: the child picks out the pictures corresponding to "I want eat white circle" and hands it to his teacher to request a marshmallow. Notice how rapidly the children learned to combine descriptors after those combinations permitted them access to their preferred reinforcers.

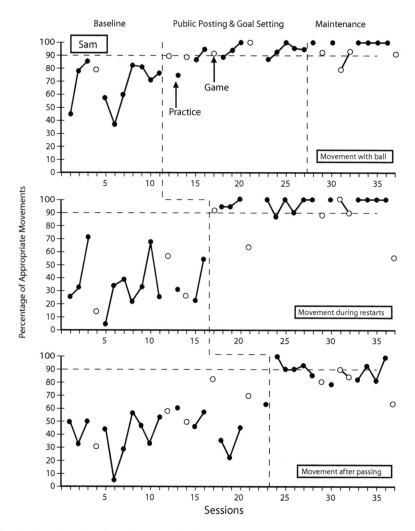

**Figure 9.9** Feedback and goal-setting: An example of an across-behaviors multiple-baseline design. From Brobst & Ward (2002). © 2002 by the Society for the Experimental Analysis of Behavior, Inc.

Open data points represent untrained requests during baseline and generalization probes. (Marckel, Neef, & Ferreri, 2006)

**Across-settings multiple-baseline design.** The **across-settings multiple-baseline** design is a third variation of the multiple-baseline design. Here, we implement an intervention in *several distinctly different settings* (say, at school, at home, and at work). We want to assure that distinctiveness because the more features the settings share, the greater the likelihood that the newly acquired behavior will generalize from one to the next; then we would have lost the opportunity to determine whether the success in each of the settings resulted from their shared features rather than from the intervention per se. Rather, in terms of the *power of the experimental design* (but not in regard to the economy of training effort, as you will learn when you study chapter 21 on generalization), the more *dissimilar* the settings, the better, because if the intervention is effective in one place and is shown to be successful in a very different place *when and only when* the intervention is implemented there, then the consumer's confidence in the power of the intervention grows. Additionally, when the locations are quite dissimi-

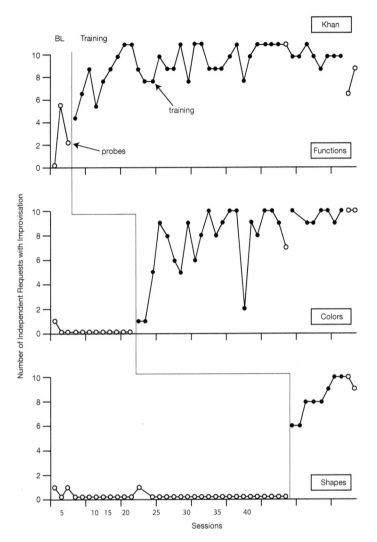

**Figure 9.10** Across-behaviors multiple-baseline design. Open circles indicate baseline conditions. From Marckel, Neef, & Ferreri (2006). © 2006 by the Society for the Experimental Analysis of Behavior, Inc.

lar from one another, and the behavior changes only when treatment begins, even the skeptic would realize that the behavior change is likely due to a function of the intervention rather than generalization. For example, this design might be used on a high school student's saying "hi" in response to another greeting him across English, math, and P.E. settings (all three settings have different teachers and groups of students). The design could be illustrated similar to Figure 9.7, except different settings would replace the names (e.g., in place of Sara, place math; in place of Mike put English; and in place of Tanya place P.E., and you see an across-settings multiple baseline design).

**Concurrent versus nonconcurrent multiple-baseline designs.** In a concurrent multiple baseline design, baselines are initiated across all three behaviors, situations, or persons at the same time (i.e., concurrently), and the IV is sequentially introduced to $BL_1$, then $BL_2$, then $BL_3$. In a nonconcurrent multiple baseline design, either baseline and/or intervention (AB) is collected with the first person, setting, or behavior prior to collecting the second and third baseline, or the start of baseline collection does not occur at the same time across the baselines (i.e., nonconcurrently). Using nonconcurrent baselines is basically doing a data based, single subject case study with replications across subjects, settings, or behaviors. The more replications, the more evidence (POVs) you collect as to your program's effectiveness.

The analysis of a concurrent or nonconcurrent multiple baseline designs usually are exactly the same; ensure you have three POVs and no earthquake effect (i.e., extraneous variables influencing the outcome). For an example of the use of a nonconcurrent multiple baseline design in a school setting, see Winn, Skinner, Allin, and Hawkins (2004). They demonstrated the use of a multiple baseline design across participants when referrals to the school psychologists were made at different times throughout the school year.

## Planning and Implementing Multiple-Baseline Designs

When you decide to use a multiple-baseline design, you will want to consider several factors, including the number of baselines and of intervention phases to include. As you will see, this design is quite flexible, lending itself to a variety of experimental questions.

**Choosing the number of baselines.** Your job in designing any behavioral analysis is to produce credible and convincing results. The more often you reproduce an outcome, the more firmly you will persuade your audience that a functional relation exists between behavior and the intervention. Customarily, ensure that you have three POVs regardless of the single-subject design utilized. Thus, generally speaking it is necessary to have at least three baselines (either participants, behaviors, or settings) when utilizing a multiple baseline design to demonstrate experimental control. However, it is possible to link up multiple pairs of multiple baselines to obtain the minimum of three POVs. For example, Alnemary et al., (2017) paired two participants in a multiple baseline design and included four different pairs. Thus demonstrating eight POVs (see Figure 9.11).

**Selecting the number of interventions.** Generally in a multiple-baseline design, we assess the function of just a single intervention. Yet, sometimes we investigate several. This is what Waters, Lerman and Hovanetz (2009) found (see Figure 9.12). They implemented a visual schedule, but it alone did little until it was combined with a *differential reinforcement of other behavior* procedure; then the effect was quite convincing. When this happens, insert a vertical phase-change line after the original intervention and before the added intervention to clearly depict the effect of the added intervention.

**Using a multiple-baseline design as a method for probing and analyzing progress.** Suppose you are conducting a program consisting of very dense, rapid-fire presentations of stimuli, a useful technique for promoting fluency and retention. Scoring and recording every single response may not be feasible or advisable. Instead, consider *sampling* rates of progress by conducting periodic multiple-baseline *probes,* perhaps at the beginning and end of a session or according to a daily or weekly schedule. Such samples will suggest whether change is taking place, and if so, how rapidly. Figure 9.13 illustrates this design approach; one in which students were being taught the concepts of "more than" and "less than" (Berens & Hayes, 2007).

**Graphing Multiple Baseline Data.** Some people prefer to develop hand-drawn graphs. Many have been using the graphing software by Excel 2016. Graphing using Excel 2016 helps to communicate client progress much more clearly. However, others have found Excel 2016 confusing to use effectively. More recently Watts and Stenhoff (2021) have described, in a step by step tutorial, how to create multiple baseline graphs with phase change lines using Microsoft Excel for Windows and macOS. If you find the excel 2016 a bit confusing, as we have, we recommend you review Watts' and Stenhoff's tutorial for graphing multiple baseline graphs.

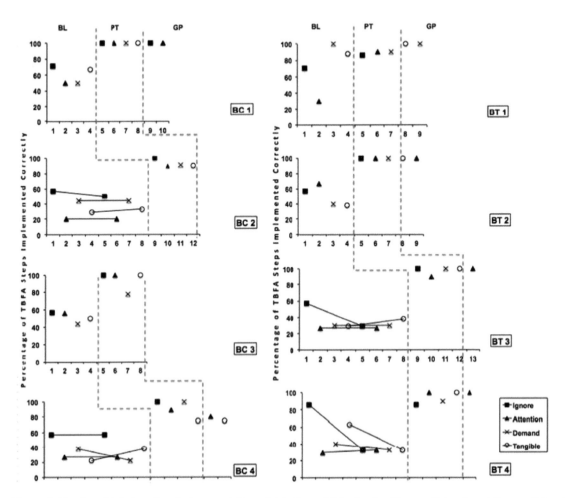

**Figure 9.11** A multiple-baseline design consisting of data for multiple dyads of two participants and four participants with two different baseline lengths. From Alnemary, Wallace, Alnemary, Gharapetian, & Yassine (2017).

## Advantages and Disadvantages of Multiple-Baseline Designs

**Advantages.** A major advantage of a multiple-baseline design is that it does not require returning to non-treatment conditions; that is, you do not need to stop implementing a promising treatment to demonstrate the functional relation between the intervention and the effect. This feature makes it especially useful in many educational, medical, industrial, and other organizational settings in which any, even temporary, setbacks may be dangerous or particularly disruptive. Moreover, because the intervention lags across time, these designs are especially handy across multiple settings. Change agents are not required to intervene everywhere simultaneously. Instead, while some individuals are treated, others are waiting in the wings as their baseline performance continues to be assessed. Additionally, because multiple-baseline designs introduce interventions sequentially, rather than all at once, each new intervention becomes less demanding for the client (as in across-behavior multiple-baseline design) and behavior-change agent (as in across-subject, -behavior, or -setting multiple-baseline design).

**Disadvantages.** The multiple-baseline design has several notable disadvantages: A major pit-

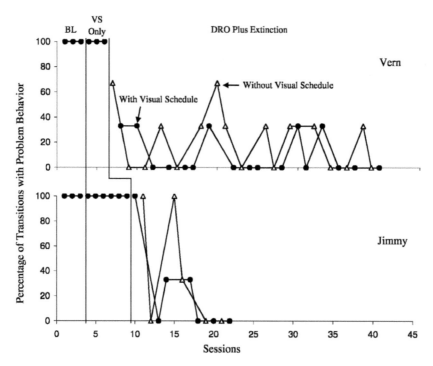

**Figure 9.12** Percentage of transitions with problem behavior for Vern and Jimmy during the brief functional analysis (top) and during the treatment evaluation (bottom). VS = visual schedual. DRO = differential reinforcement of other behavior.

fall, especially with replications across individuals within the same setting, is that those receiving treatment might influence the relevant behavior of the other intended participants whose treatment is to be delayed. We must be careful not to place participants in situations in which the behavior of interest of one affects that of the others.

Some also might reasonably argue that a multiple-baseline design is a weaker form of replication in that the procedure is not necessarily reproduced across the same exact dependent variables. Features of the participant's behavioral repertoire or of the setting could and probably do vary to some extent. That is why *reproducing the effect across three or more baselines*, preferably in different locations, generally is preferred.

Another concern related to using the multiple-baseline design is that one must see to it in advance that the *dependent variables are not interdependent or highly interrelated*, as happens when the behaviors are members of the same *response class*. (Malott, 2008, defines response classes as "*Those responses occasioned by physically similar stimuli, that co-vary when reinforced or punished or that produce the same outcome,* p. 129)." Although such ripple effects can be welcome because you have gotten something for nothing, the demonstration of experimental control will be weaker because significant change has not coincided with the implementation of the intervention. If smiles are associated with eye contact and answering questions, then an increase in any one of these target behaviors probably will be associated with corresponding increases in the others. So be cautious. Before you use multiple-baseline designs, try to foresee whether the effects are apt to transfer from one baseline to the other(s). Also, to minimize the unplanned transfer of the behavior across baselines, if feasible, select sufficiently dissimilar contexts for each subsequent baseline. Should unplanned generalization occur with any of the multiple-baseline arrangements, all is not necessarily lost, because you always have the option of nesting the multiple-baseline within a different experimental design. In the case of smiles

CHAPTER 9 OPTIMIZING CLIENT PROGRESS BY ANALYZING THE FUNCTIONS OF OUR INTERVENTIONS • 199

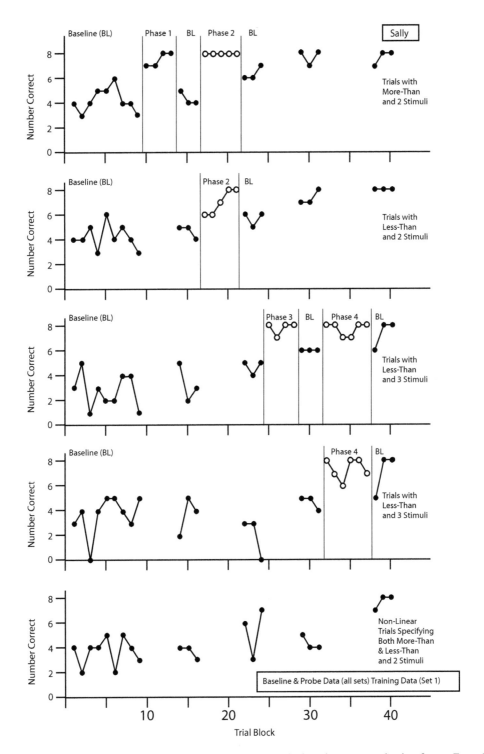

**Figure 9.13** Using a multiple-baseline design to probe progress in learning communicative forms. From Berens & Hayes (2007), Figure 4. © 2007 by the Society for the Experimental Analysis of Behavior, Inc.

co-varying with eye contact, then, you might temporarily interpose a return-to-baseline (no-treatment) phase, during which you should notice both behaviors beginning to decline more or less simultaneously. Both would then recover once again when the intervention is reapplied. You have saved the day!

A third noteworthy disadvantage of the multiple-baseline design is the requirement that each intervention must be put off in time, some for extended durations. Notice that when implementing the intervention sequentially across baselines, we must wait for reasonable stability before applying it to each subsequent baseline. That delay might entail deferring treatment of several days or weeks, thereby raising a clinical and/or ethical obstacle, especially when your concern is alleviating serious behavior problems. In cases like these, you are advised to keep baselines brief, conduct intermittent baseline probes, or choose a different design (see Chapter 25).

## SUMMARY AND CONCLUSIONS

Many in the helping and managerial professions are tempted to dismiss experimental rigor and just move on by applying the techniques that appear most promising. Yet, if their aim is to design, develop, and apply the most effective and efficient methods available, they must base their strategic decisions on objective evidence of effectiveness at the individual level. In so doing, they need to plan and monitor the results of their experimental-design methods well before instituting any change program. Then they can follow through, perhaps revising systematically, until they demonstrate a clear functional relation between the intervention and the changes in level, trend, and/or variability that they have been seeking.

The *return-to-baseline (withdrawal,* or *ABAB) design* involves precisely and validly discovering the ongoing patterns of the behavior of concern, which then serve as a baseline (A) against which any change during the treatment phase can be compared. After that baseline is established, you implement the most promising intervention (based on the literature or your own pilot work). Sometimes, though, informed by principles of behavior of the kind detailed later in this text, you may design and analyze a novel intervention. Assuming you obtain evidence of change in the intended direction to reassure yourself and your audience that the intervention was responsible, you temporarily remove it, in a second A phase. Then, following convincing evidence that the behavior is beginning to revert to its prior unacceptable pattern, you reinstate the procedure once again. Sometimes, when your initial effort fails (and yes, that certainly can happen), you might attach a different intervention onto the first, without necessarily establishing a new baseline.

Some object to using return-to-baseline designs because the return to the no-treatment phase can delay progress. Your rejoinder: Better to slow down a bit to gather evidence that the current procedure is effective than to continue with a program that may have not actually relate to any actual improvements.

The *multiple-baseline design*, another widely-used analytic method, does avoid the issue of withdrawing treatment and thereby possibly interfering with progress. It accomplishes this by replicating the intervention across behaviors, people, or settings. To control for passage of time, we implement pre-intervention baselines of varying lengths. Especially convincing are data demonstrating that change has taken place *when and only when* the intervention has been applied. In using a multiple-baseline design, we must be careful, though, not to select behaviors that may co-vary with one another, because then determining whether the change was due to the intervention or to the change in the related behavior is not possible. In multiple-baseline designs, delaying some participants' access to a promising treatment for a time period, for other behaviors, or in other settings may pose a problem. Fortunately, alternatives are available in the form of other experimental designs (see Chapter 25).

Having read and mastered this chapter, you should now be capable of implementing some basic strategies for determining whether, and, if so, how effectively and efficiently your change program is progressing.

## Chapter 10

# Setting a Foundation for Positive Change: Identifying Participant's Functional Reinforcers

## Goals

1. Define the terms *function* and *functional behavior* as used in applied behavior analysis.
2. Define and illustrate (a) *functional consequences* and (b) *functional assessment*.
3. Describe the purposes of conducting a functional behavioral assessment (FBA).
4. List and describe the various categories of *behavioral functions.*
5. Describe how biological or physiological variables can influence behavior.
6. List the three approaches to conducting a functional behavior assessment.
7. Define, illustrate and list advantages and disadvantages of *indirect* (anecdotal) *assessments.*
8. Define, illustrate, and provide advantages and disadvantages of *descriptive assessments.*
9. Define, illustrate, and provide advantages and disadvantages of *functional analysis.*
10. Describe the "standard" methodology for identifying behavior function.
11. Provide a summary of the methodological variations and when you would use them instead of the "standard" methodology.
12. Describe the Telehealth Service Delivery Model.
13. Describe and differentiate between store-and-forward and video conferencing telehealth service delivery models' approaches.
14. Discuss some possible considerations and how you would address them when conducting a functional analysis utilizing a telehealth service delivery model.
15. Describe and illustrate how an FBA leads to treatment development.
16. List minimum guidelines for behavior improvement plans (BIPs).
17. Describe what must be done prior to developing a behavior-reduction program.

> **Box 1 Case Example**
>
>
> Mrs. Mack, a fifth-grade teacher, is at a loss as how to deal with Kevin's misbehavior in class. She has requested a meeting with school personnel to re-evaluate the boy's placement, proposing he be removed and placed in a self-contained classroom for children with special needs. Mrs. Mack believes that Kevin's Asperger's syndrome accounts for his hitting, kicking, and disrupting, in the form of shouting out quotations from TV shows and threatening to kill people. Mrs. Mack, who has not yet implemented an individual behavior plan with Kevin, tends to use such classroom management techniques as detention, sending him to the principal's office, taking away privileges, timeout, and so on. Apparently, those have not been successful. Nevertheless, prior to removing Kevin from the class, the behavior analyst suggests conducting an assessment to try to determine the function(s) of his aggressive and disruptive behavior and to identify preferable alternative behaviors to enable him to gain the same reinforcers.

Professionals and members of the public often are puzzled about what makes some people behave well under certain circumstances, yet become extremely disruptive, aggressive, non-compliant, or otherwise behave unacceptably within other situations. In their effort to understand, they may rely on faulty or misleading explanations: "The student's ADHD (attention-deficit hyperactivity disorder) causes his disruption." "John refuses to complete his work because he is developmentally disabled." "Mary aggresses because her parents physically abused her." "Mark yells at his employees because he is mean." "Sue misses a lot of work because she is depressed." Their logic often is circular: "He acts out because he has ADHD." "How do you know he has ADHD?" "Because I see him acting out." Beyond the circularity of the logic, given that the underlying condition, ADHD, presumably, is immutable, they fail to specify what could be done to change the behavior.

Furthermore, after unsuccessfully using such standard techniques as reprimands, timeouts, suspensions, or loss of privileges, others may conclude the individual is "uncontrollable." Situations like this beg for the implementation of a **functional behavioral assessment** (FBA): *a method of inquiring into why a person repeats particular behaviors, or why the behavior occurs.* In Chapter 7 you learned how to measure or assess behavior targeted for change; in Chapter 9, some methods for experimentally analyzing the relation between behaviors of interest and the conditions that might be influencing their function. In the present chapter we build upon that material by offering a number of assessment methods for identifying the factors that might explain *why* troublesome behavior occurs: its function (purpose) and what events might be evoking (triggering) or abating (inhibiting) it.

Electing to conduct an FBA is especially wise because we know that functional behavioral assessments permit us to approach problematic behaviors constructively. In so doing, we may avoid having to resort to punishment, thereby avoiding the recipient's engaging in aggressive or escape responses, the predictably counter-productive side effects (Durand, 1999; Iwata, Dorsey, Slifer, Bauman, & Richman, 1994). Additionally, programs featuring FBAs have been found to reduce behavior problems more successfully than others (Horner, Carr, Strain, Todd, & Reed, 2002). Moreover, FBAs are essential to the design of effective intervention plans, and thereby more consonant with our emphasis on promoting pro-social behavior change in favor of simply trying to eradicate noxious behaviors (Pelios, Morren, Tesch, & Axelrod, 1999). In fact, this constructive perspective is supported by U.S. public policy, and actually is *mandated* by U.S. Federal (e.g., IDEA, 1997; IDEIA, 2004) and state regulations. Moreover, the United States National Institutes of Health (1989) and the National Research Council (2001), among others, have recommended that treatment for severe behavior problems be based on the results of an FBA. Moreover, as behavior analysts, it is our ethical duty to conduct a functional assessment prior to developing and implementing a behavioral reduction program (interventions are based on assessment results—ethical code 2.14).

Although FBA methodology typically has been used to develop interventions to change problematic behaviors within school, home, and mental health settings, its relevance for treating problems within commercial, business, health, and other organizational settings should not be overlooked. For example, suppose you had a highly skilled but chronically argumentative employee. You could conduct a functional behavioral assessment to try to discover what contingencies were supporting his quarrelsome behavior. Does it gain him attention, allow him to avoid or escape from assignments, and/or make him "feel superior" (i.e., he thinks he is shrewder and better)? Furthermore, we would hope to discover if his behavior is a long-practiced habit that has yet to undergo extinction or be supplanted by a more acceptable style of interacting.

## THE TERM "FUNCTIONAL"

We often encounter the words **functional**, or **function**, in the field of applied behavior analysis. In your various readings, you may see that term incorporated within phrases such as: "functional analysis of behavior," "functional consequences," or "functional behavioral assessment." Technically, the term *functional* implies *the lawful manner in which the rate, form, or other pattern with which the behavior is repeated relates to how the antecedents and consequences of that behavior have influenced it previously.*

Consider the following true story:

A laboratory technician wanted to expose a specific polymeric material to a very high oven temperature to analyze its performance qualities. Safety protocol required that any time people used the oven they were required to use safety glasses. In fact, the glasses were kept on a shelf just to the side of the oven. Because the technician had often conducted similar heat analyses without any untoward effects, he elected to shortcut by not putting on the glasses. Unfortunately, this one time, as he was removing the material, it exploded into many pieces, some of which lodged in his eye. Were it not for the care of a skilled surgeon, the technician might have lost the sight in that eye altogether.

Our assessment of the situation suggested that natural contingencies of reinforcement controlled the technician's failure to take proper precautions. Taking shortcuts was reinforcing, in that it had previously allowed him to complete the job faster and more comfortably.

Interestingly, that episode led to the development of a whole new safety initiative within the organization. All laboratories in the facility were inventoried for essential safe practices. The personnel then were taught those practices. Regularly thereafter, those performances were measured, with results of those measures immediately reported back to laboratory personnel in the form of posted memoranda. Additionally, every few months, personnel in the laboratories with ongoing acceptable scores were invited to a celebration—a pizza party. Safety scores improved substantially and remained high. By implementing the intervention in different sets of laboratories on different dates, in multiple-baseline fashion, we were able to demonstrate that the workers' safer performance was indeed a function of the formal procedure we had put into effect (Sulzer-Azaroff, 1978). (You will recognize that method as a multiple-baseline experimental analysis.) The system remained in place for nearly thirty years with injuries at the facility remaining extremely rare.

Fortunately, one need not always go quite so far as to conduct a full-fledged, long-term experiment to analyze the relations between particular behaviors and their consequences. Instead, we can use methods of the sort presented in the previous chapter to examine how the behavior is systematically influenced by given consequences. When we successfully identify the **functional consequences**, *those providing our clientele with currently effective positive reinforcers or ridding them of current aversive stimuli*, we are then in a more promising position to intervene successfully. To illustrate, suppose you are in a foreign country and feel thirsty. No one speaks your language. You need to find a way to ask for something to drink. You can do that by saying or reading a phrase from a dictionary, gesturing that you are drinking, pointing to a picture or a word on the menu, pointing to someone else drinking what you want, nodding when the server points to a drink on a tray, and so forth. As long as you receive the drink, your response was functional; it produced the reinforcing consequence that you sought. When perceptive and eager parents, teachers, managers, colleagues, friends, and lovers learn to identify and promptly deliver reinforcers currently functional for the person whose particular behavior they hope to increase or preserve, the relationship begins to improve.

We use the term *functional behavioral assessment* to describe a method of inquiring about why a person repeats particular behaviors, both adaptive and maladaptive. The mystery to be solved is what the person gets or gets rid of by performing those behavior(s). Historically, these methods have been utilized for especially puzzling, dangerous, or serious disruptive behaviors, specifically because the answer(s) enables the person to take a substitute route, one that is safer, healthier, or more socially acceptable, toward gaining consequences of equal or better value. The methods actually are much the same as any other informal or formal *functional* or *experimental* analysis of the relation between any good, bad, or indifferent class of behavior and the environmental events controlling it. This particular chapter, though, focuses specifically on the analysis of single individuals' troublesome behaviors. (See Table 10.1 for precise definitions of these terms.)

# FUNCTIONAL BEHAVIORAL ASSESSMENT

*Functional behavioral assessment* (FBA) is based on a set of core assumptions: (1) regardless of whether the behavior of concern is considered appropriate or inappropriate, the likelihood of its being repeated depends on its history of success under similar internal and external environmental conditions, and (2) when the behavior is socially unacceptable, it can be eliminated by isolating the function of the behavior and identifying one or more socially acceptable alternative ways for the person to attain that same function. Because FBAs help explain maladaptive

**TABLE 10.1   Functional Assessment Terminology**

| Term | Aim | Methods | Example |
|---|---|---|---|
| *Functional behavioral assessment* or *Functional assessment* | Any of several methods used to explain why a particular behavior is or is not occurring, under specific or general circumstances | • Interviews<br>• Informal observations<br>• Formal observations<br>• Functional analyses | Mom and teachers report that Jaime flaps his arms and hands when he is "frustrated" by his inability to follow an instruction. |
| *Functional analysis* or *"Functional analysis assessment"* | A specific behavior-analytic strategy used within a functional behavioral assessment to demonstrate the lawful relation between particular behaviors and the antecedents and/or consequences of those behaviors | Explicitly and systematically manipulating antecedents and/or consequences to demonstrate their lawful effect on the behavior of interest | Flapping is defined; its rate is recorded and graphed under a sequence of two distinct sets of conditions, as in, recording rates of flapping are when Jaime is instructed, in random order, (1) to perform a set of activities he has difficulty doing (tying his shoes and so on), and (2) when he is allowed to play with his favorite toys. |

behaviors *and* yield potential constructive solutions to the challenges those behaviors raise, the United States Department of Education mandates the use of FBAs to analyze what particular reinforcer(s) challenging behaviors provide to individuals with special educational needs; also that the information be used to tailor socially acceptable solutions for the individual (IDEA, 2006).

The kinds of environmental events frequently suspect in cases of harmful or noxious behaviors include social, ecological, health, and medical factors that function in advance of the maladaptive behavior (labeled variously *antecedent events, discriminative stimuli, setting events,* or *motivating operations*) and, especially, those that support or reinforce the behavior(s) of concern (including social positive, social negative, or automatic reinforcers). Identifying those conditions permits us to design an intervention to address such problematic behaviors by eliminating the antecedents and/or consequences associated with them. Meanwhile we teach appropriate replacement behavior(s) designed to produce the same or superior consequences. FBAs also yield information about what specific conditions can be added to activate and support appropriate alternative or replacement behaviors and they inform us about what reinforcers to withhold if and when the problematic behavior occurs. For example, if an FBA reveals that 18-month-old Mary tantrums to get her mom to give her milk and cookies, we might instruct Mary's mom to prompt the child to say "cookie." We could then teach Mary's mom to give her daughter milk and cookies only after saying "milk" or "cookies" or close approximations thereto. Additionally, we would want to make sure that Mary's mom does not give the child cookies when she tantrums (or prompt her). Along similar lines, suppose Kristen tends to protest and call her husband, Jim, names because she wants to encourage him to stay home and pay attention to her instead of going out with his friends. Their marriage counselor might instruct Jim to remind Kristen that if she wants him to stay home with her all she has to do is ask in calm, loving voice. The counselor could then support Kristen's practice of the behaviors that successfully encourage Jim to stay home with her and give her the kind of attention she desires.

In sum, the *purposes of a functional behavioral assessment* (FBA) are twofold: (1) *to determine the probable function the behavior serves the individual (usually problematic, but possibly also for preferred behavior)*, and (2) *to develop a behavioral-intervention plan.*

Although, in practice, functional behavioral assessments have tended to emphasize examining what the disturbing behavior gains the client, *we encourage you also to explore the circumstances under which the same person behaves acceptably.* Observing people in context doing what is expected of them can be especially informative. Watch Mary when she sits quietly awaiting her milk and cookies. Is it the presence of the other children serving as positive models that makes the difference? Is it the fact that the teacher is singing a "milk and cookies" song? That Mary had a snack just two hours earlier, or that the aide is rubbing her back and telling her how nicely she is sitting?

---

**Box 10.2  An Exercise**

Now refer back to the opening episode in this chapter. Note how a functional behavioral assessment may not only help Mrs. Mack identify what circumstances might be promoting and supporting Kevin's aggression and disruption, but also what she can do to encourage the boy to do his schoolwork rather than to behave inappropriately.

---

## VARIOUS FUNCTIONS OF BEHAVIOR

As indicated, *the very same types of analytic methods can be used to explain why the particular behavior of an individual improves as those that explain why they act inappropriately.* Specifically, a person repeats a behavior because it has previously been reinforced. Problematic, as well as appropriate action, produce such common reinforcers as coveted items, comfort, or attention (in the absence of anything better, possibly even attention in the form of reprimands or attempts to redirect the individual to alternative activities). While contingency managers may view their efforts as attempts to cope with the situation, from the responders' perspective, they may have gained someone's undivided attention or access to preferred activities or objects (e.g., the computer, a particular toy, or a candy bar). Any of those may well function as reinforcers for that individual's behavior at the moment.

Attention is not only often a reinforcer for humans, but also for other animals. For example, Mclain (2011) pointed out that dogs who demonstrate "amorous" behavior to a person's leg or object, such as a teddy bear, may do so for the attention it provides:

> Some dogs' mounting behavior is attention seeking. Just think —when your dog rubs on the teddy bear in front of dinner guests, what's your response? If the dog gets attention like someone laughs or calls his name, that person, just positively rewarded the dog for the behavior. Even negative attention, such as yelling, is still attention and may encourage the behavior. (p. 28)

One way to determine if the behavior occurs to gain attention is to set up a video camera and record the behavior when no one is at home. If no mounting occurs, you have evidence that the behavior is probably attention seeking.

Problematic behavior may also terminate an ongoing unpleasant activity or task by allowing the offender to be excused from completing assigned work, sent out of class, or even suspended from school (*instances of social-negative reinforcement*). Again, it is important to view these consequences from the vantage point of the individual engaging in the problem behavior, not that of the person providing the consequences. While the behavior manager may deem a particular consequence punishing, the student, employee, or client actually may have found escaping from the aversive condition (i.e., the work task) to be quite rewarding. (Review Chapter 5 for a more detailed discussion of positive and negative reinforcement).

Identifying the *source* of *reinforcement*, that is, whether mediated by another person (i.e., *socially mediated*) or *produced automatically by the behavior itself*, also is crucial in determining the behavior's function and designing an appropriate intervention. *Automatic reinforcement* may involve either positive (producing a pleasing sensation) or negative (removing an unpleasant sensation) reinforcement (Review Chapter 6). As with other classes of reinforcers, we may view the reinforcing event from both sides because one or both may be operating. Giving a hungry person access to food is positively reinforcing; eating also is negatively reinforcing in that it relieves sensations from being hungry (hunger pains). In practice, when searching unsuccessfully for elusive reinforcers, we usually classify an event as automatic reinforcement after any social mediation is ruled out. In essence "automatic reinforcement" serves as a "default" function (Vollmer, Marcus, Ringdahl, & Roane, 1995).

Generally, behavior that serves an automatic function either *produces or regulates sensory stimulation*. Like socially mediated problem behavior, some behaviors that others find irritating might permit the person to obtain sensory stimulation. An example is a child's attaining pleasurable sensations through rocking in a chair or repeatedly flapping his hands. Likewise, people also can engage in behaviors that successfully regulate or terminate sensory stimulation. A child might cover her ears to reduce or escape from the disturbing ambient noise level, or repeatedly injure herself (engage in *self-injurious behavior* or *SIB*), thereby releasing endorphins which mask the pain associated with her ear infection. On the other hand, it is unlikely that Kevin hits the other children or otherwise disrupts the class to produce or regulate sensory stimulation (automatic reinforcement). Kevin's aggression toward his classmates gains him something quite different: his teacher's undivided attention (social-positive reinforcement), or, if he is sent to the principal's office for such offenses, avoiding having to do his class work (social-negative reinforcement).

Occasionally, the identical class of behavior can serve more than one purpose. Lang et al. (2009) demonstrated distinctly different functional assessment results for their participant, depending upon the setting. It is not unusual to find a student using aggression as a way of *avoiding* completing a math assignment in class or to *obtain access* to a basketball during recess. At home, Kristen might shout at

Jim to get his *attention*; while at work she might shout at a coworker to stop the person from annoying her. While the form or *topography* of the behavior is the same in both settings, the two outcomes or functions differ. In fact, this is why it is so important for us to remember that the form of behavior alone cannot reveal its function. For that, we need to know how the behavior affects the environment.

Beyond circumstantial changes, the function of behavior also can shift over time. If Kevin's teacher adjusts her management methods, he might find other (better or worse) ways to obtain reinforcers. And, as we are well aware, deprivation and satiation influence how appealing or aversive a particular stimulus is at the moment. Given this tendency for the reinforcing value to shift as a function of various circumstances, we need to conduct assessments *routinely, not as single events and within specific contexts*. Regular assessments not only help behavior analysts to monitor the ongoing effectiveness of an intervention, but also to determine when to modify the intervention.

## APPROACHES TO CONDUCTING FBAS

To determine the reinforcement contingencies currently maintaining particular problematic behaviors or those usually failing to reinforce appropriate behaviors, we need to assess the antecedents (A) (discriminative stimuli, setting events, or other "activators"[1]), the behavior (B), and the consequences (C) (reinforcing events or "supports"). In general, three distinct approaches have been devised to assess the function of behavior of the troublesome variety: *indirect (anecdotal) assessments, descriptive assessments, and functional analyses*. Note, though, how essential it is that we rule out any suspected biological or physiological factors that may relate to the problem behavior prior to conducting these assessments, or that we address them during the assessment and intervention.

### Biological & Physiological Influences

Although concluding that individuals engage in problem behavior (e.g., aggression) *because* they are diagnosed with a disorder (e.g., autism) is circular and therefore inappropriate, biological or physiological variables certainly may be related to problematic behavior, or to conditions that interfere with adaptive behavior. Consequently, identifying any such influences prior to conducting a functional behavioral assessment and developing an intervention is essential. To illustrate, when addressing pediatric feeding disorders, prior to conducting a functional behavioral assessment and implementing an intervention it is customary to conduct a nutrition analysis, a swallow test, and to assess oral motor skills. These assessments not only rule out possible treatment obstacles, but also allow for the evaluation and incorporation of physical, oral, and psychological influences during treatment development (Piazza & Roane, 2009). (As you will note in Chapter 32, considering biological variables affecting the client is an important aspect of ethical practice.)

You may be asking yourself, "If biological and physiological variables are not *causes* of behavior, then why is assessing them important?" It is true that these variables do not control behavior; however, those conditions can serve as antecedent influences of behavior. For example, O'Reilly (1997) demonstrated that an individual's SIB *only* occurred during periods of *otitis media* (ear infection). A functional analysis demonstrated that *otitis media* was the likely motivational operation related to escape from ambient noise and that it was responsible for maintaining the problem behavior. Others have demonstrated that sleep deprivation and allergies influence problem behavior of school-aged children (Kennedy & Meyer, 1996). And, we all know that visual and/or hearing acuity may influence behavior. Moreover, understanding how someone's current medication might affect his or her behavior is important. When Zarcone, Napolitano, and Valdovinos (2008) reviewed the state-of-the-art methodology used to evaluate the behavioral effects of medication as it pertains to individuals with developmental disabilities, they concluded that, at a minimum, it is important to record changes in medication that do or may correspond to observed behavioral changes.

---

[1] Notice the array of terms that you, as an applied behavior analyst, may elect to use, depending on the repertoire of your audience.

Symptoms of psychiatric disorders (e.g., manic behaviors) also have been shown to influence the results of functional analyses and demonstrate the importance of taking them into account prior to and during assessments. Allen, Baker, Nurnberger, and Vargo (2013) demonstrated that the presence of manic behaviors was correlated with the function of episodic problem behavior (attention). Specifically, results showed that when manic behaviors were absent, functional analysis results were inconclusive, but when manic behaviors were present, the functional analysis elucidated the function of the problem behavior. In sum, assuming we are attempting to understand the indirect influences of behavior as well as its current functional causes, we must be certain to leave no stones, including biological ones, unturned.

## Indirect (Anecdotal) Assessments

Although behavior analysts may use indirect assessments initially to gather background information about the conduct of interest, technically they are not applying behavior analytic methods. Nevertheless, those assessments can provide a useful starting point when the situation is so fraught with confusion that one needs guidance in focusing on which behavioral contingencies to analyze. The clinician may use **indirect assessments** to take the first step toward attempting to identify the troubling behavior's antecedent stimuli and supports. Moreover, indirect assessment can assist caretakers to view behavior as serving the purpose of gaining the client social-positive reinforcement, social-negative reinforcement, or automatic reinforcement (i.e., it models the FBA approach). *Tools include client self-reports and anecdotes supplied by significant others in the person's life* (e.g., parents, teachers, spouses, co-workers). Generally, *information is obtained about the circumstances under which the behavior does and does not occur, with an emphasis on ecological variables*. Often interviews, along with instruments like checklists, rating scales, and client records (e.g., previous incident reports, individual education plans (IEPs), psychological evaluations, medical reports, and so on) are *used to help provide a more detailed picture of the client's behavioral patterns and the stimuli that appear to relate to them.*

Indirect assessments can be useful, whether you are assessing either problematic or appropriate behavior. Probably because troublesome behaviors are so annoying to the people around them, formal indirect assessments have been developed to assess challenging behavior. These formal assessments have been developed over the years for particular

---

**Box 10.3**
**Further Discussion of Example of Indirect Assessment**

Let us further investigate the indirect assessment started for Kevin in Figure 10.1 (next page). Mrs. Mack reviewed the boy's school records and noted evidence of behavior problems since first grade. He has been suspended repeatedly from school as well as sent to the school counselor's office to discuss the inappropriateness of his behaviors. Currently, he performs below grade level in mathematics. Now Mrs. Mack has completed the Indirect Functional Assessment Questionnaire (IFAQ) according to the format described by Christensen et al. (2002). (See Table 10.2.)

When adhering to this particular format of the IFAQ, all the points for questions 2, 5, and 10 (attention), 4, 8, and 11 (tangible), 1, 6, and 9 (escape), and 3, 7, and 12 (automatic) that are addressed in the Christensen et al. questionnaire, cited in Table 10.2, are added. According to Mrs. Mack's answers, social-positive in the form of attention scored a 3, social-positive in the form of tangible scored a 1, social-negative in the form of escape from demands scored a 4, and automatic scored a 2. Thus, based on analyzing the IFAQ results from Mrs. Mack, the counselor developed a working hypothesis that Kevin's aggression serves to gain him escape from demands. However, actually observing it will be important to see what those specific antecedents and consequences are that actually occur in the classroom surrounding his aggression. Such observation is essential prior to developing a hypothesis related to their possible grading function.

# Indirect Functional Assessment (IFA)

Client's Name: <u>Kevin</u>  Interviewee: <u>Mrs. Mack</u>

Definition of target behavior: <u>Aggression including hitting and kicking and disruption</u>

Instructions: Read the following questions to the interviewee inserting the clients name in the blank labeled name and the target behavior in the blank labeled TB. The interviewee must respond no/never, maybe/sometime, or yes/always. Do not interpret the question or explain the question. Insert the score according to the point system below in the box next to the question. After completing all of the questions, add up the number of points in each column. Graph points for each function on bar graph at bottom of page. The column with the highest score indicates the hypothesized function for the target behavior.

Scoring System:   0=No/Never   1=Maybe/ Sometimes   2=Yes/Always

|  | Attn | Tang | Escape | Auto |
|---|---|---|---|---|
| 1) Does *(name)* refuse to do work or task when asked? |  |  | 1 |  |
| 2) When *(TB)* occurs do others console or ask *(name)* to stop engaging in the behavior? | 1 |  |  |  |
| 3) Do you ignore *(name)* when he/she engages in *(TB)*? |  |  |  | 1 |
| 4) Do you try to make *(name)* stop doing *(TB)* by giving hem/her their favorite things/objects? |  | 0 |  |  |
| 5) If you are busy and *(name)* engages in *(TB)* do you stop what you are doing and respond to him/her? | 1 |  |  |  |
| 6) When asked to do some form of work or task does *(name)* engage in *(TB)*? |  |  | 2 |  |
| 7) *(Name)* will engage in *(TB)* throughout the day, regardless of your reaction. |  |  |  | 1 |
| 8) Does *(name)* engage in *(TB)* when things that he/she likes are taken away from him/her? |  | 1 |  |  |
| 9) When you have asked *(name)* to do a task and he/she engages in *(TB)* do you do the task for him/her? |  |  | 1 |  |
| 10) When you are on the phone or talking to someone, will *(name)* engage in *(TB)* to get your attention? | 1 |  |  |  |
| 11) Could you stop *(name)* from engaging in *(TB)* by giving him/her something/an object? |  | 0 |  |  |
| 12) If someone is talking to *(name)*, he/she is playing with preferred things, and is not being asked to do any thing, they engage in *(TB)*? |  |  |  | 0 |
| **TOTAL SCORE** | 3 | 1 | 4 | 2 |
|  | Attn | Tang | Escape | Auto |

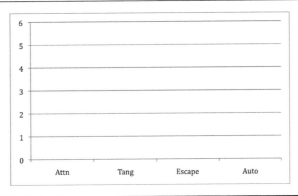

**Figure 10.1**   Indirect functional assessment (IFA)

**TABLE 10.2  Indirect (Anecdotal) Functional Assessments (IFAs)**

| Name | Authors | Description |
|---|---|---|
| Motivation Analysis Rating Scale (MARS) | Wieseler, Hanson, Chamberlain, & Thompson (1985) | 6-item questionnaire, Likert scale |
| Motivation Assessment Scale (MAS) | Durand & Crimmins (1988) | 16-item questionnaire, Likert scale |
| Behavioral Diagnosis and Treatment Information Form (BDTFI) | Bailey & Pyles (1989) | Open ended questionnaire, includes questions regarding physiological variables |
| Functional Analysis Interview Form (FAIF) | O'Neill, Horner, Albin, Storey, & Sprague (1990) | 11-part clinical interview, containing sections on topography, general factors, antecedents and consequences, communication skills, reinforcers, history of treatment |
| Stimulus – Response Questionnaire | Lauterback et al. (1990) | Child-directed interview, hypothetical situations presented |
| Stimulus Control Checklist (SCC) | Rolider & Van Houten (1993) | Open-ended questionnaire, includes questions regarding physiological variables |
| Student-Assisted Functional Assessment Interview | Kern, Dunlap, Clark, & Childs (1994) | Student-directed questionnaire |
| Problem Behavior Questionnaire | Lewis, Scott, & Sugai (1994) | Teacher-based instrument, inclusion of peer-attention function |
| Questions About Behavioral Function (QABF) | Matson & Vollmer (1995) | 25-item checklist |
| Functional Analysis Screening Tool (FAST) | Iwata (1995) | 18-item questionnaire, yes or no |
| Functional Assessment Checklist for Teachers and Staff (FACTS) | March et al. (2000) | Teacher-based instrument |
| Indirect Functional Assessment Staff (IFA) | Christensen et al. (2002) | 13-item questionnaire |
| Functional Assessment Informant Record for Teachers Preschool Version (Fair-TP) | Dufrene, Doggett, Henington, & Watson (2007) | Semi-structured interview format |
| Teacher Functional Behavioral Assessment Checklist (TFBAC) | Stage, Cheney, Walker, & LaRocque et al. (2002) | Checklist |
| Open-Ended Functional Assessment Interview | Hanley (2012) | 4 open-ended questions pertaining to background information and 16 open-ended questions to inform the design of a functional analysis |

categories of behavior problems, populations, and/or settings (see Table 10.2).

Regardless of the actual formal procedure, an indirect assessment should include some common questions, such as:

- What is the topography of the behavior (i.e., what form does it take; how does it look)?
- What immediate antecedents (e.g., stimuli, motivating conditions) precede the display of the behavior?
- What motivational operations (i.e., antecedents, conditions, or events usually occurring more distant in time) are correlated with the display of the behavior?
- Under what conditions/settings is the behavior most likely to occur?
- What consequences typically follow the behavior?
- What does the individual engaging in the behavior obtain, escape from, or avoid by engaging in the behavior?
- What unsuccessful interventions have been conducted in the past?

**Advantages.** A number of advantages have been associated with indirect assessment approaches. When compared with the other methods, this approach is:

- simpler to implement (i.e., it requires little expertise to administer and does not demand a large time commitment).
- less risky for the client or other individuals present.
- useful for providing preliminary information about the circumstances maintaining the behavior, identifying potential variables to evaluate in a functional analysis, along with some potential directions a behavioral intervention might take.

**Disadvantages.** Despite these advantages, indirect assessment methods have some serious limitations. Information based on these tends to be subjective and unreliable, and therefore questionable as a sole source of input (e.g., Conroy, Fox, Bucklin, & Good, 1996; Paclawskyj, Matson, Rush, Smalls, & Vollmer, 2001; Zarcone, Rodgers, Iwata, Rourke, & Dorsey, 1991). In general, you should view indirect assessment approaches as only an initial step in the FBA process, particularly for serious behavior. Although additional direct observational assessments are preferable for all classes of behavior, in the case of non-serious behaviors when data gathered from questionnaires, interviews, self-reports, and review of records all point to the same probable function, some practitioners develop an intervention based on that hypothesized function. We strongly encourage you, though, to collect some supportive A-B-C observational data (as described in the section on descriptive assessments below), and, especially in the case of dangerous or seriously troublesome behavior, to conduct a full functional analysis (Pence, Roscoe, Bourret, & Ahearn, 2009) before you select and implement a formal intervention. Those findings may save you time in the long run, by pointing you in the right direction.

**Developing a hypothesis concerning function.** After an indirect assessment is conducted, the challenge is to summarize and interpret its results. Behavior analysts need to remind themselves that the purpose of the indirect assessment is to focus on the function of the target behavior. Positing the function helps us generate a tentative hypothesis about the contingencies that contribute to the behavior, such as those involving social-positive consequences in the form of access to attention or tangible items, social-negative consequences in the form of permitting escape or avoidance of an unpleasant situation, or automatic reinforcers. These assessments should permit us to focus on identifying its purpose, rather than simply to describe the form of the behavior, its intensity, or the environment in which it occurs.

Specifically, when interpreting scores from indirect assessments, it is important to remember that the scores represent a *vaganotic measurement system* (i.e., the scale or units are *not* equal; Johnston & Pennypacker, 2020). Thus, the difference between scores is not relative, and one can only state which function was identified as having the greatest impact, or scoring the highest. In other words, *the highest score wins!* Or at least wins that round. *It is imperative to conduct additional assessments* before developing a tenable or valid hypothesis regarding the function of problem behavior.

## Descriptive Assessments

**Descriptive assessments** similarly are aimed at zeroing in on the function the behavior of interest serves under natural conditions. But *conclusions are based on observational data rather than the verbal reports of concerned individuals. Observers directly monitor and record the motivational operations (MOs), direct antecedents, and the consequences that appear to correlate with the behavior and analyze the influence of those contingencies.* The basic assumption is that descriptive assessments may indicate which factors to analyze when we are seeking to identify a true functional (i.e., a cause and effect) relation between the behavior of concern and the events controlling its occurrence. The more closely the antecedents, behaviors, and consequences are correlated, the more likely a functional relation exists (Bijou, Peterson, & Ault, 1968). In descriptive assessments, observers record information in the form of narratives[2] or frequency counts (see Kevin's A-B-C analysis in Figure 10.2). Those, in turn, are inspected to determine how closely the given environmental events and the behavior(s) of

---

[2] A narrative recording is a written description of behavior in progress that can be organized later into an A-B-C format as in Figure 10.2.

| Dates: 9/13/04; 9/14/04; 9/17/04 | Student: Kevin | | Obs: Mrs. Mack |
|---|---|---|---|
| **A** **Antecedent** | **B** **Behavior** | **C** **Consequence** | **Possible Functions** |
| Late to school; missed math lesson; given math assignment | Yells "butter toast" | Prompted to get started on work and to stop yelling | Attention & Escape |
| Told to get started on work and to stop yelling | Throws book | Sent to office | Escape |
| Doing independent seat work | Pulls his shirt over his head | Told to stop pulling his shirt over his head and to get busy on his work | Attention & Escape |
| Told to stop pulling his shirt over his head and to get busy on his work | Tells aide to leave him alone | Sent to timeout | Escape |
| Told to go back to his desk and work | Hits another student | Sent to office and suspended | Escape |
| Math test | Throws pieces of his eraser at other students | Aide starting to tell him to get to work | Escape |
| Aide walking over to Kevin to tell him to get to work | Pushes desk into aide | Sent out of class to "think" about his behavior and told he failed the test | Escape |

**Figure 10.2** Kevin's A-B-C analysis

concern coincide with one another (see Figure 10.3 for additional examples of analyzing ABC data). Note that in the A-B-C analysis, Kevin's problem behavior appears to have provided him with attention twice and escape seven times. When the results are not patently obvious, many make use of conditional probability statistics (Bakeman & Gottman, 1986; Sackett, 1979) or correlations (e.g., Vyse & Mulick, 1990) to determine how likely it is that the results happened by chance alone. Lerman and Iwata (1993) have offered a set of four basic conditional probability equations suitable for analyzing descriptive data. These are used to help determine the degree of relationship between contingencies and include:

*Antecedent Correlations:*
a) Intervals containing problem behavior that followed an antecedent event
    Intervals scored with problem behavior

b) Intervals containing an antecedent event that preceded problem behavior
    Intervals scored with that event

*and Consequence Correlations:*
a) Intervals containing problem behavior that preceded a consequence event
    Intervals scored with problem behavior

b) Intervals containing a consequence event that followed problem behavior
    Intervals scored with the event

To illustrate, suppose your record shows that Kevin engaged in aggression during 20 observation intervals and that of those 20 intervals, 15 occurred when the antecedent event consisted of someone walking away from him (thereby ceasing to pay attention to him). Then the first antecedent correlation would be $15/20 = 0.75$. For that observational session, the probability of Kevin's engaging in aggression following the removal of attention was 75 percent. So far, loss of attention seems to correlate highly with his aggression. (Recognize though, that we should not base our hypotheses of function on single observational sessions or on antecedent probabilities alone.) Moreover, when analyzing A-B-C data it is important to address the complete set of contingencies operating, not just the obvious antecedents or consequences.

Beyond the A-B-C analysis, numerous other descriptive assessment formats have been designed to evaluate a broad array of challenging behaviors within a variety of settings, including homes, schools, or institutions (see Table 10.3 for a few examples). Some, such as the Scatter Plot analysis (Touchette, MacDonald, & Langer, 1985; see Chapter 16 for an illustration), are better suited to obtaining global rather than the specific information sought in an A-B-C assessment. Rather than recording information about explicit antecedents and consequences correlated with a particular instance of behavior, the Scatter Plot is designed to record the extent to which behavior occurs (none, a few occurrences, or many occurrences) during specified (usually half-hour) intervals throughout the day and across successive

| Antecedent | Behavior | Consequence | Possible Function |
|---|---|---|---|
| Mom is on the phone and child is watching T.V. | Kid hits sister and she starts to cry | Mom yells at kid for hitting his sister | Social Positive—Attn |
| Teacher tells class to get out their math book | Johnny throws his math book across the room | Teacher tells Johnny his behavior is not ok | Social Positive—Attn AND Social Negative—Escape |
| Mary is out at recess | Mary starts jumping and flapping her arms | Kids walk away from her | Social Negative—Peer avoidance AND Automatic |
| Dad tells Mark to wash the dishes | Mark tells his dad off | Dad tells him to finish washing the dishes | Social Positive—Attn |

**Figure 10.3** Additional examples of analyzing ABC data

**TABLE 10.3  Descriptive Assessments**

| Name | Authors | Description |
|---|---|---|
| A-B-C | Bijou, Peterson, & Ault (1968) | Notes the antecedents, the behavior, and consequences as well as date and time with respect to the behavioral event |
| Interval Recording[2] | Wahler (1975) | Identifies environmental events occurring in home and school setting |
| Time Sampling | Epstein, Parker, McCoy, & McGee (1976) | Demonstrates behavioral patterns with respect to the likely presence of specific antecedents and consequences |
| Frequency-of-Occurrence and Conditional Probabilities | Mace & Belfiore (1990) | Uses conditional probabilities to indicate the likelihood of a behavior given a specific antecedent and/or consequence |
| The Scatter Plot | Touchette, MacDonald, & Langer (1985) | Records behaviors with respect to time of occurrence throughout the day (provides temporal patterns) |
| Structured Descriptive Assessment | Freeman, Anderson, & Scotti (2000) | Manipulates antecedents prior to collecting data in an effort to occasion problem behavior, rather than waiting for the triggers to occur naturally |
| Ecobehavioral Assessment | Rogers-Warren (1984) | Analyzes standing patterns and episodes, at discrete and exchange levels, across behavior-behavior, behavior-environment, and environment-environment relations |
| Contingency Space Analysis | Martens, DiGennaro, Reed, Szczech, & Rosenthal (2008) | Graphs two conditional probabilities to evaluate contiguity, conditional probability or schedule, and degree of contingency |

days and conditions. Although the Scatter Plot may provide global information on the relation between stimulus conditions and behavioral patterns, it is important to note that sometimes visually identifying those patterns may be difficult (Kahng et al., 1998). Moreover, recall the importance of using a procedure that attempts to obtain information not only on the behavior itself, but also its antecedents *and* its consequences across successive days and conditions.

**Ecobehavioral assessment.** **Ecobehavioral assessment**, a specific form of descriptive assessment, is potentially a very useful treatment development tool. It hybridizes applied behavior analysis and

> **Box 10.4 Does a Correlation Equal a Functional Relation?**
>
> ***Question:*** Does the fact that the sun comes up when the rooster cock-a-doodle-doos mean that the rooster causes the sun to come up?
>
>
>
> ***Answer:*** No, even though two events may be correlated, that does not mean that the change in one is a function of (or that one "causes") the other. The relation may be due to happenstance—two events occurring more or less simultaneously—as often is the case in superstitious learning.

ecological psychology (Rogers-Warren, 1984). Basically, ecobehavioral assessment *broadens the definition of behavior and environment by considering the circumstances beyond those directly contiguous with the behavior, along with clients' histories of reinforcement.* Within ecobehavioral assessment, a given behavior is examined not only in relation to the social events immediately preceding and following it, but also in terms of its general context of ongoing and prior events, plus particular features of the physical environment. So, when assessing Kevin's difficulties, we might consider not only what his teachers said and did immediately prior to and following his unwanted behavior, but also such other factors as how the work was introduced to Kevin, whether he was rested and well fed, and so on. Also a *review of his records* may shed light on any earlier difficulties he may have had and how those were treated, as well as factors that might be contributing to his current behavior.

At this point, we recognize that beyond the assessment of the behavior's immediate function, ecobehavioral assessments can yield valuable information about the contextual variables that control a person's behavior. Indeed, researchers have demonstrated that escape behavior can be correlated with such factors as sleep deprivation or allergy symptoms (O'Reilly, 1995; Kennedy & Meyer, 1996; O'Reilly & Lancioni, 2000). Basically, you are searching for motivational operations (MOs).

**Advantages.** A number of advantages are associated with descriptive assessments. They can:

- yield objective and quantitative information.

- be conducted under naturalistic conditions.
- serve to identify correlated relationships that might reflect causal relationships.
- provide information of relevance to the design and implementation of further, more refined assessments and treatment.
- Model for caregivers how to analyze the environment for causes versus relying on faulty explanations

**Disadvantages.** Descriptive assessments also have their limitations. Given that correlations are identified by examining the temporal relationship between or frequency of two or more events, they may fail to detect intermittent response-consequence relationships. For example, David's father does not typically give him attention when he screams; but while on the phone with a business associate, he finds the boy's screaming intolerable. At that point, he tells David to be quiet, thereby furnishing him with attention (and that single episode may have made a lasting impression!), but this crucial relationship may well have been overlooked.

Remember, too, that correlations between events are *not* the same as functional or causal relationships (see Box 10.4). Mark is continually late to basketball practice. Coach Johnson lectures him about why commitment to the team is important and how being late is unacceptable. Meanwhile, the other team members have already run their sprints for the day. While both events (attention and escape from running sprints) happened simultaneously, perhaps only one of the contingencies is truly functional (say, getting out of running sprints). In fact, when Pence et al. (2009) compared three descriptive methods (the A-B-C, the conditional probability, and the conditional and background probability) to the functional analysis method, they found that though the descriptive assessments results were similar, they differed substantially from the functional analysis outcome. Given these limitations, you should view descriptive assessments only as the second step in a three-step approach to functional behavioral assessment. The third step needs to be an actual functional analysis. The main value of descriptive analyses is in the way it may guide behavior analysts toward making their best guesses as to what circumstances (including direct and indirect motivating operations) functionally control which behavior patterns. They have demonstrated their utility in helping us hone in on which specific MOs are in operation. We then can use that information as the basis for conducting plausible analyses of functional relations. In one illustrative instance, Kennedy and Meyer (1996) first noted, and then systematically demonstrated, that sleep deprivation and allergy symptoms functionally influenced their client's escape-maintained behavior.

**Developing a hypothesis about the function a given behavior serves.** As with the indirect assessment, the summary of results of the ecobehavioral assessment may guide us toward designing a full functional analysis of the behavior. That, in turn should explain why it is occurring as it is, what reinforcement contingencies probably are maintaining it, and what situations are likely to evoke it. The final payoff should be our ability to design and implement an effective intervention plan.

Parents, teachers, and managers often conclude that a combination of A-B-C observational assessments and indirect assessments are sufficient to explain why certain individuals misbehave. However, as discussed earlier, and substantiated experimentally (Pence et al., 2009), only a complete functional analysis of the unwanted behavior optimizes the accuracy of the findings. As you will discover in later chapters, due to their insufficient training in behavior analysis, many parents, teachers, or other behavior managers inadvertently reinforce the very misbehavior they find troublesome (even experienced behavior analysts may find themselves mismanaging contingencies and reinforcing their own children's and spouse's problematic behavior). A young boy throws a temper tantrum when refused a requested item, or doesn't want to perform a particular task. If the parent or teacher then provides the item or excuses him from having to complete the requested task, he learns to engage in such tantrums. The tantrum "worked," in the sense that the child got what he wanted. A worker scowls when his supervisor asks him to remain after hours to complete an important job. The supervisor relents and agrees to finish the job himself. The A-B-C analysis would help identify why such behavior is occurring.

## Box 10.5
## Narrative Summary of Episodes of Concern in Kevin's Day

***Monday:*** *Kevin's mom drops him off late to school today because he has missed the bus. Mrs. Mack has scheduled a math assignment right after morning announcements. When Kevin arrives at class, having missed the lecture explaining the assignment and helpful hints for completing the math problems, Mrs. Mack gives him an abridged version of the material. Afterwards, Mrs. Mack tells Kevin to do the odd-numbered problems in the book. Kevin starts yelling "butter toast" over and over again. When Mrs. Mack goes over to Kevin's desk to ask him to get started on his work and to stop yelling, Kevin throws his book at her. Frustrated, Mrs. Mack tells Kevin to go to the principal's office.*

***Tuesday:*** *Kevin is doing an independent science worksheet. One problem on the worksheet requires Kevin to compute velocities. Kevin starts to pull his shirt over his head. The teaching assistant asks Kevin to stop pulling his shirt over his head and finish his work. Kevin tells the aide to leave him alone. Mrs. Mack then goes over to Kevin's desk and tells him he needs to get busy on his work right away or he will have to go to the timeout area. Kevin starts singing aloud. Mrs. Mack sends him to timeout and tells him when he is ready to do his work he may rejoin the class. After about 10 minutes, Mrs. Mack goes over to Kevin in timeout and tells him to go back to his desk and start his math assignment. On the way back to his desk, Kevin hits another child on the head. Mrs. Mack tells Kevin to go to the office and he is suspended for a day.*

***Friday:*** *Kevin is supposed to be taking his math test, but instead of working on the test he is throwing pieces of his eraser at other students. The teacher's aide goes over to Kevin to prompt him to get back to work and Kevin gets up and pushes his desk into the aide. Mrs. Mack sends Kevin out of the class to "think" about how he could have hurt the aide and tells him that he failed the test.*

It also may provide useful information about ways to reduce the unpleasant reaction and to teach the offending individual alternative acceptable behaviors. It may also possibly explain why an appropriate behavior is *not* occurring, such as an absence of appropriate antecedents or supports in that specific context. However, it is important to remember that a complete functional analysis is essential to yield the likeliest explanation for the occurrence of the problematic behavior.

Figure 10.2 depicted how the events recorded in a narrative recording were observed in relation to Kevin and the antecedents and consequences of his misbehaviors (compare the narrative in Box 10.5 below with Figure 10.2). We noted that Kevin escaped from having to do his work seven times and received attention twice for engaging in problem behavior. Therefore, we might hypothesize that the function of Kevin's problem behavior is to get out of doing work, more specifically math-related work.

Remember, however, that thus far the identified relationship between Kevin's misbehavior and various environmental events is only correlational (not functional). To support our sense that math assignments produce Kevin's misconduct, and that escape from the assignments reinforces his misbehavior, our last responsibility is to conduct a functional analysis (i.e., the third step in a functional behavioral assessment).

## Structured ABC Assessment

Obtaining objective information may be challenging when we request others fill in the antecedents and consequence sections of an Open-ABC assessment. Moreover, in particular, behavior analysts sometimes find analyzing data from an Open-ABC assessment difficult. Brian Iwata developed a Structured ABC Assessment that provides objective antecedents and consequences to check off and

218 • BEHAVIOR ANALYSIS FOR LASTING CHANGE

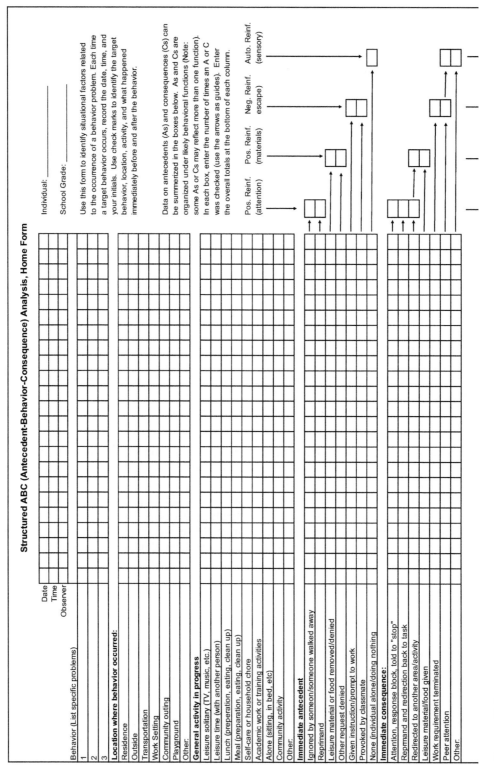

Figure 10.4

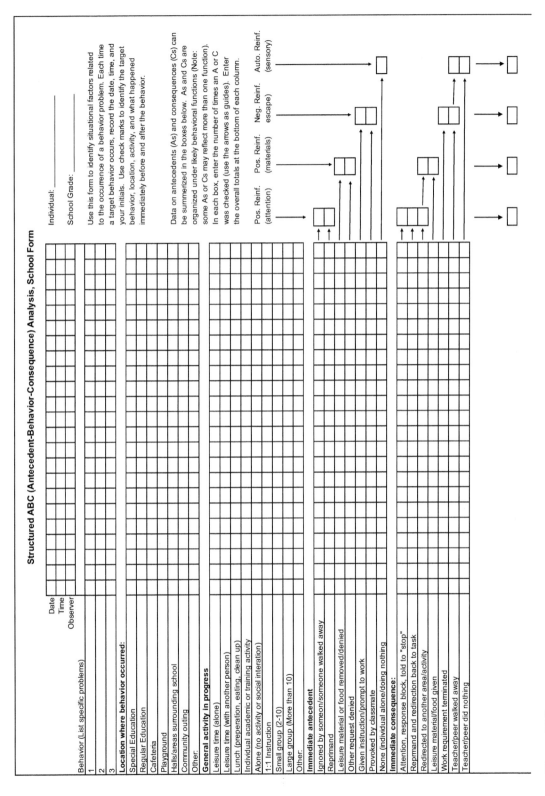

**Figure 10.5**

has a built-in analysis of function (be it correlational). Specifically, the *Structured ABC Assessment Home* form includes common antecedent and consequence events that occur in homes, while the *Structured ABC Assessment School* form includes antecedent and consequence events relevant to an educational setting (see Figures 10.4 and 10.5, respectively).

Were one to use the *Structured ABC Assessment School* form to analyze the data presented in Figure 10.2, the score for the possible maintaining functions would be: 3 for *positive reinforcement in the form of attention*, 0 for *positive reinforcement in the form of materials*, 11 for *negative reinforcement in the form of escape from demands*, and 0 for *automatic reinforcement in the form of sensory stimulation*. As a practitioner, one could either use these forms to collect ABC data, or as a means for assisting in the analysis of ABC data.

## Functional Analysis

A functional analysis is the most complete form of evidence-based assessment. As you learned in the previous chapter, **functional analyses** involve *manipulating* (i.e., turning on and off) the *suspected maintaining variables* (positive and negative reinforcers). They also *control for motivational operations (MOs), including setting events or establishing operations*. In essence, we conduct a functional analysis to demonstrate a cause-and-effect relationship. We accomplish this by repeatedly comparing at least two conditions to show their lawful influence(s) on behavior (i.e., a causal relationship between particular external and internal environmental events and particular behaviors): In condition A, we systematically set the occasion for (activate) the behavior of concern; then, in turn, we arrange for it to be reinforced (supported). We then compare the results to those in condition B, circumstances that remove the suspected activators (or antecedents) and reinforcers (consequences). For example, suppose you are trying to determine if someone's (operant) coughing is maintained by attention: many people ask, "Are you okay?" You would set up a condition (say, for 10 minutes) during which every cough produces attention and compare it with another 10-minute condition in which attention is delivered noncontingently and coughing produces no attention. After repeating both sets of conditions, you would compare how often the person coughs under each of the two conditions. If coughing occurs more frequently in the condition in which attention is provided contingent on coughing, you would conclude that the person's coughing probably is maintained by positive social reinforcement in the form of attention. On the other hand, if coughing remains roughly equivalent across both conditions, you would conclude that attention probably does not affect coughing nor induce the behavior. (Notice how this method follows logic analogous to the withdrawal design described in Chapter 9.)

**Advantages.** Among the many advantages of conducting a functional analysis when attempting to address challenging behaviors are that:

- it provides a clear demonstration of a functional relation between the behavior of concern and its consequences, possibly along with possible other environmental circumstances.
- by controlling the environment, it can isolate intermittent, subtle, and/or idiosyncratic variables functioning to maintain the behavior.
- it suggests short-term strategies for managing the behavior (i.e., informs you how to turn it off).
- it provides a clear basis for developing a treatment protocol.

Suppose, in the above example of coughing, the individual only coughs when attention is provided; then your functional analysis will inform your subsequent actions. To eliminate the "operant coughing" you would arrange for everyone with whom the individual comes in contact to ignore the coughing and attend to appropriate attention-seeking behavior.

**Disadvantages.** Because when conducting a functional analysis you intentionally attempt to provoke the behavior of concern, the method could pose a risk to the individual. Suppose Johnny's self-injurious behavior (SIB) actually were maintained by attention. Then, during the attention phase of the functional analysis, his rate of self-injury probably would maintain. However, this risk also is present in the absence of a functional analysis, given the fact that the behavior is currently occurring at a high rate in the natural environment. Furthermore, because conducting a functional analysis requires that those involved manipulate variables systematically, they must understand fundamental principles of learning and behavior, as well as being able to control the assessment context. In this example, had we been unaware of the importance of testing for an *attention* function or if we could not manage other people's responses, we would be unable to conduct a valid functional analysis. Moreover, it is likely that in the natural environment the behavior is reinforced on an intermittent schedule, while in the functional analysis, an FR1, or a continuous schedule of reinforcement, is used. Remember, intermittent schedules are more likely to produce higher rates than continuous schedules.

The greatest potential risk posed by functional analyses, though, is the possibility of establishing a new dysfunctional relation, as when novel consequences provided following the problem behavior begin to reinforce that problem behavior (Shirley, Iwata, & Kahng, 1999). To illustrate, suppose that during a functional analysis a teacher gave a youngster access to the computer every time he shouted profanities. Suppose, further, that access to the computer functioned as a strong reinforcer for him, the youngster might start shouting profanities not just to get out of work (the original maintaining reinforcer) but also to obtain access to the computer. To avoid this possibility, we recommend limiting conducting functional analyses only to those relations previously noted via indirect and/or descriptive assessments (specifically descriptive assessments, because delivery of the potential reinforcer actually was observed, unlike in the indirect assessment). In the example above, unless the computer was actually delivered contingent on the student yelling profanities, we would be wise to avoid a condition during which computer time is provided contingent on problem behavior.

**Determining function.** Although numerous functional analytic strategies have been conducted over the years, Iwata et al. (1982/1994) have developed a "standard" methodology shown to be quite successful in identifying the function of obnoxious, puzzling, dangerous, or destructive behavior, regardless of its topography or the setting in which the analysis is conducted. The array of potential reinforcers assessed in the "standard" functional analysis includes *social-positive reinforcement*, in the form of attention; *social-negative reinforcement*, as in permitting escape from demands; and automatic reinforcement in the form of sensory stimulation (Iwata et al., 1982/1994). In another variation we also assess not only attention but access to tangible items (activities, preferred items, or food) as well. This latter condition, however, should be limited to situations in which the descriptive assessments revealed that access to tangibles was provided contingent on problem behavior. This, then, suggested that access to tangibles might be responsible for maintaining the problem behavior. Otherwise, those should be avoided because artificial tangible reinforcing functions can be established rapidly (Shirley et al., 1999). In the "standard" functional analysis, the three, or possibly four, *test conditions* are conducted along with a *control condition*. Each test condition contains: (a) an antecedent that prompts or occasions the behavior (see Chapter 2); (b) a *motivating operation* or condition (e.g., an antecedent such as deprivation or a task that the individual finds aversive) that influences the effectiveness of the reinforcer (see Chapter 2); and, (c) a *source* of the contingent *social reinforcer* (i.e., social positive in the form of attention, social negative in the form of escape from demands, social positive in the form of access to tangible items) or absence of *social reinforcer* (i.e., alone/ignore condition). During the **control condition** *alternative explanations for the behavior can be eliminated by observing the effect of withholding the antecedent stimuli or conditions, as well as socially-delivered reinforcers and any tangible items suspected of functioning as reinforcers*. Because each condition is associated with a specific motivating operation, we suggest you order the conditions as follows: alone, attention, control, and demand. (See Table 10.4 for a description of each condition.)

Data collection procedures can be as simple and direct as the systems described in Chapter 8 (e.g., recording the frequency or duration of the behavior(s) of interest during each condition), or as complex as

**TABLE 10.4  Description of "Standard" Functional Assessment Conditions**

**General Procedures:**
Sessions should be:
- at least 10 minutes in length.
- conducted in the following order: Alone, Attention, Play, Demand.
- Collect data on the frequency of occurrence of the target behavior.
- Compare the frequency of the target behavior per unit of time under each test condition and the control condition (Play) (e.g., Alone vs. Play, Attention vs. Play, and Demand vs. Play).
- If other assessments (i.e., indirect or descriptive analyses) have indicated that the target behavior enables the individual to obtain a desired object or activity, conduct a Tangible condition at the end of the series (e.g., Alone, Attention, Play, Demand, Tangible).

**Alone Condition (To set the occasion for testing for Automatic Reinforcement):**
- Individual is alone and does not have access to leisure items. If it is not possible to leave the person alone, then make sure you ignore the individual throughout the session.
- Observe and record occurrences of problem behavior.
- Do not provide social consequences following the target behavior.

**Attention Condition (To promote testing for Positive Reinforcement in the form of access to attention):**
- Instruct individual that they can play with some toys and that you have some work to do. Then ignore.
- Individual emits appropriate behavior (asks you for attention: Ignore, do not respond.
- Individual emits problem behavior: Express concern paired with brief physical contact.

**Play Condition (To eliminate MO for social and automatic reinforcement; control):**
- Direct individual toward favorite activity.
- Deliver attention at least once every 30 seconds.
- If individual initiates appropriate social interaction, deliver attention.
- If individual emits problem behavior, ignore unless you are about to deliver attention; then wait until the behavior has stopped for 5 seconds and deliver attention.

**Demand Condition (To promote testing for Negative Reinforcement in the form of escape from demands):**
- Assemble material for at least 10 demand episodes (e.g. "Work on ..." or "Do ...") and begin trials using the following prompting procedure:
    - First instruction (prompt): Instruct individual to do task. Then, if...
        - Individual complies: Deliver praise.
        - Individual emits problem behavior: Withdraw materials and turn away for 30 seconds.
        - Individual emits any other behavior: Continue demand sequence.
        - Individual emits no response: Continue demand sequence.
    - Second prompt: Repeat instruction and demonstrate.
        - Individual complies: Deliver praise.
        - Individual emits problem behavior: Withdraw materials and turn away for 30 seconds.
        - Individual emits any other behavior: Continue demand sequence.
        - Individual emits no response: Continue demand sequence.
    - Third prompt: Repeat instruction and physically guide. Do not deliver praise.
        - Individual emits problem behavior: Withdraw materials and turn away for 30 seconds.
        - Individual emits any other behavior: Continue Demand sequence.
        - Begin a new trial after the completion of the demand (regardless of whether physical guidance was necessary or not) or at the end of the 30-second break.

*Continued...*

### TABLE 10.4 (continued)

**Tangible Condition (To promote testing for Positive Reinforcement in the form of access to items, activities, or food):**
    Provide a small amount of the tangible item prior to starting the session (e.g., 2 minutes access to item or a small bite of food).
    After client has had access to the item, remove item and start session, or if food, start session when client is finished consuming the piece of food.
    Individual emits appropriate behavior: Ignore
    Individual emits problem behavior: Give tangible item to client and allow client to either consume a small piece of the food or play with the item for a short amount of time (e.g., 30 seconds) and then remove item again.

---

**Box 10.6**
**Standard Functional Assessment for Kevin**

Let us return to the case study to see how we would functionally analyze Kevin's problematic behavior. Based on the indirect and descriptive assessments, we hypothesized that Kevin engages in problem behavior to avoid or escape math work, and to a lesser extent, to obtain attention. Consequently, to completely analyze these two different behavioral functions (negative and positive social attention), we decided we would need to conduct three conditions: one to test for negative reinforcement in the form of escape from math work; a second to test for positive reinforcement in the form of attention; and a third, a control condition to compare the rates of problematic behavior during typical circumstances.

We then conducted a standard functional assessment, in which we compared Attention, Demand, and Control conditions. During the assessment, Kevin was aggressive and/or disrupted 10 times under the Demand condition, 0 times in the Attention condition, and 0 times in the Control condition. On the basis of those data, we then concluded that Kevin engages in aggression and disruption to avoid or escape from math work. Furthermore, given that the assessment determined the function of Kevin's problematic behavior, we decided to design and implement an individual intervention targeting these unwanted behaviors along with a set of replacement behaviors.

---

recording their frequency and their relation to specific antecedent and consequent manipulations. (Table 10.4 also provides more detailed suggestions for conducting a "standard" functional analysis. Also, see Chapter 7 to review behavioral observation.)

As with any other assessment techniques, the value of the functional assessment method depends upon the accuracy of the data and the validity of the interpretation. So, first you need to be certain your data are reliable and accurate. That means (1) training observers and examining the fidelity with which they conduct the observational protocol, and (2) the reliability of their recordings. You then examine the results of the functional analysis by comparing the rates (frequency/time) of problematic behaviors under the test conditions against those recorded in the control condition. If you find the problem behaviors are dependably more frequent under any specific test than under the control condition, you will have identified a behavioral function. For example, suppose in a functional analysis you obtain the mean number of responses per minute (number of times the behavior of concern occurs, divided by the length of the session in minutes) as follows: Alone = 0, Attention = 4, Control (Play) = 0, and Demand = 1; you would conclude that the individual's behavior at the time is maintained by access to attention (social positive reinforcement). It is important to point out that although only one series was utilized in this example, normally a minimum of three series should be conducted so that the rules of visual inspection can be utilized (i.e., the analysis of level, trend, and variability).

The major advantage of a functional analysis is that it helps you determine why the targeted behaviors are or are not occurring. That information then allows you to develop a treatment intervention protocol based on the function served by the unwanted behaviors. In fact, once you have completed an FBA and identified the function(s) of the unwanted behavior, you have all the essential information for developing an effective intervention that focuses on the relevant antecedents and consequences.

## Methodological Variations

It is beyond the scope of this text to cover all of the methodological and procedural variations that have been developed and examined in the literature; however, it would be remiss of us not to mention the most common and recent variations that are now being adopted in clinical practice. Some of the methodological variations are minor in nature, such as which behavior the contingencies are applied to, when to conduct a session, and how to measure problem behavior. For example, in the Precursor Functional Analysis (e.g., Smith & Churchill, 2002), instead of applying the contingencies associated with each "standard" condition to the problem behavior, the contingency is applied to an identified precursor behavior (i.e., a behavior that reliably precedes the problem behavior). Some researchers have altered the antecedent variables within specific conditions, such as the divided attention condition (e.g., wherein therapists divert their attention to another adult in the beginning of the session vs pretending to be busy; Fahmie, et al., 2013) or devised a screening phase for automatic versus social reinforcers (Querim, et al., 2013). For example, if a client always yells before engaging in aggression, then instead of doing the functional analysis on aggression you would do it on yelling. In the Low-Rate Functional Analysis (e.g., Tarbox, et al. 2004), the "standard" conditions are conducted and you apply the contingencies to the problem behavior, but the session is initiated contingent on problem behavior. In other words, the alone, attention, play, demand, or tangible condition is not initiated until the target behavior occurs. Then you stop whatever is going on in the natural environment and start the FA condition session. Another variation of the "standard" FA is the Latency FA (Thomason-Sassi, et al., 2011). In the Latency FA, you record the latency from the start of the session till the individual engages in the problem behavior, at which time you deliver the contingency and end the session. Subsequently, instead of comparing rate in each test condition to that of the control condition, you compare the latency to the first response in each test condition to the control condition.

Some methodological modifications are more significant, such as the Trial-based FA (Bloom et al., 2011), the Transition FA (McCord, Thomson, and Iwata, 2001), and the Synthesized FA (Hanley, et al. 2014). For a detailed understanding of these variations and when to utilize them, we suggest that you review the growing literature covering these advances in functional analysis methodology.

## TELEHEALTH SERVICE DELIVERY MODEL AND FUNCTIONAL BEHAVIOR ASSESSMENT

One of the most significant advancements in the practice of functional behavior assessment pertains to the possible modes of implementation. Many health care service providers have made use of Telehealth service delivery (TSD) models, thereby expanding the promise of extending the possible reach of providing behavior analytic services beyond geographical barriers, especially in the area of functional assessment. TSD is a mode of delivering services via information and communication technologies. To illustrate, behavior analytic practitioners have demonstrated two main ways of utilizing TSD in the functional assessment literature: a) store-and forward approach (e.g., Najdowski. et al., 2008); and b) video conferencing approach (Barretto, et al., 2006). In the store-and-forward approach, both clinicians and caregivers utilize video recordings as a basis to discuss information pertaining to how to conduct assessment sessions as well as the results of those assessment sessions. In the video conferencing approach, clinicians (located in the main clinic) are connected with caregivers and clients (in remote sites) via telecommunication systems, and as needed, a consultative approach is used to complete assessments (i.e., the clinician's coach caregiver is assisted in implementing the assessment conditions as needed). In a recent review, Schieltz and Wacker (2020) summarized the results of 18 studies illustrating the effectiveness and utility of the TSD model within the assessment and subsequent treatment of problem behavior. Other researchers (Neely, MacNaul, Gregori, & Cantrell, 2021), after reviewing a number of studies, also concluded that "the literature supports the use of telehealth to conduct behavior assessments and provide interventions designed to establish or strengthen behavior." However, they contend that more research is needed to establish if telehealth is useful with interventions designed to reduce behavior. Videoconferencing also has been found to be more effective than email feedback in promoting treatment integrity. Investigators (Zhu, Bruhn, Yuan, & Wang, 2021) report that "videoconference feedback produced faster mastery and better sustained integrity after the removal of the intervention" (p. 618) than did email feedback.

Using a TSD model demands that a number of steps be taken when conducting functional behavior assessments. First and foremost, decide whether the videos will be stored and discussed at a later time, or will a video conferencing approach be used? Next, after selecting which TSD model will be used, it is important to determine which specific assessments will be utilized (i.e., which indirect assessments, open or structured descriptive assessments, and what kind of functional analytic instrument or strategies) and how data will be collected. Similar to conducting face-to-face functional assessments, it is important to ensure all relevant materials are available. However, the material must be available at the remote site in addition to the main site when conducting a functional assessment via a TSD model. Similarly, it is especially important to ensure that both the essential hardware (e.g., computers) and software (video conferencing platforms) are available at both sites.

One unique concern that must be addressed with respect to material when utilizing a TSD model is to ensure the caregiver has access to protective equipment. As behavior analytic professionals who regularly serve this population, we understand the risk associated with conducting a functional analysis of a client's aggression and have been prepared accordingly on how to reduce the risk of injury. This, however, is generally not necessarily the case with caregivers. For this reason, you might consider assembling packets of protective equipment, such as shin guards or other protective gear along with the other material necessary to conduct sessions if the client's problem behavior is, for example, kicking. The fourth step in conducting functional assessments via TSD is to train the caregiver in the assessment procedures. It is important to remember that you are not trying to teach them how to be behavior analysts, you are trying to train them to implement very specific assessment conditions and interventions. Behavior skills training (i.e., use of instructions, modeling, practice and feedback) has been utilized in numerous studies to teach caregivers how to run specific functional analysis conditions and as such, is recommended here. After training the caregiver on what and how to conduct assessment conditions, it is time to begin the assessment. With respect to conducting all three assessments in the functional behavior assessment, it is recommended that sessions are scheduled without the client for the indirect assessment to reduce caregiver distractions.

There are a number of considerations that should be addressed when utilizing a TSD mode when conducting a functional assessment. Ethical and confidentiality safeguards must be adopted within this process. For example, the videoconferencing platform should be Health Insurance Portability and Accountability Act (HIPAA) compliant. Additional considerations include access difficulties with respect to both hardware and software as well as connectivity issues. It is important to have a plan for what will happen, for example, if connectivity is lost in the middle of an assessment. Given the lack of professional personnel present at the remote site if occurring in the home, additional safety measures must be taken and an emergency plan must be developed. It is also a good idea to utilize one of the functional analysis modifications developed to address safety concerns (e.g., precursor functional analysis or latency functional analysis).

# FROM FBA TO TREATMENT DEVELOPMENT

## Selection of Replacement Behavior

Problem behavior occurs because it serves one or more functions. Simply designing a program to eliminate the problem behavior is insufficient. Ethics require that we address the behavior's function, because otherwise we are depriving the person of any opportunity to obtain his or her morally acceptable wants or needs, as in supplying food to a hungry child. Rather, we must select and teach **replacement behaviors** that yield functions equivalent to that which the problem behavior(s) previously provided the client. Replacement behaviors need to be acceptable within the context and permit clients to get at least a reasonable amount of the reinforcers they prefer. To paraphrase Carr et al. (2002), our task is to help our clientele to achieve their goals in a socially acceptable manner, by rendering problem behavior irrelevant, ineffective, and inefficient. For example, we determined that the function of Kevin's problematic behavior was escape. As replacement behaviors, we could teach him acceptable alternative behaviors to achieve escape, such as displaying a card requesting a break. To reduce the aversiveness of a specific task, we also might elect to include a higher proportion of already-mastered skills among his assignments, as well as to teach him to request assistance politely. His motivation to escape would thereby be lessened.

Similarly, if the function of an individual's problem behavior is gaining attention and various other reinforcers, then we would want to select socially-acceptable alternative replacement behaviors that would yield equivalent reinforcers. For example, we could teach Kristen to engage in appropriate attention-seeking behavior, such as suggesting to Jim that they plan time to discuss their weekend schedule and, by encouraging Jim to give her lots of attention and to take a break, to spend time with her on those occasions. Alternatively or additionally, she could be coached to ask him in a calm voice, instead of nagging or whining, to stay home with her instead of going out with his friends; he could be advised to do so under those circumstances. If José calls out in class to obtain his teacher's attention, he could be taught to raise his hand to obtain her attention instead. Were the function of an action to permit the person to obtain or reduce sensory input, we could teach replacement behaviors that would be similarly reinforced. For example, we might teach Ty to request time to swing in the playground, in place of rocking, or Mike to chew gum, instead of biting his nails.

## Selecting an Intervention

Once we have identified a behavioral function, we then can apply a behavioral intervention that focuses on altering the antecedents and/or the consequences maintaining the problematic behavior. Specific methods are discussed in detail throughout this text.

**Modifying antecedents.** Often a simple change in antecedent conditions can alter behavior. For example, in Kevin's case, we should check to be certain that his assigned material matches his functional level, and if not, adjust it accordingly. Also, by removing or reducing his task demands, we could reduce his troublesome behaviors. Eventually, of course, after he has learned the replacement behaviors, we would gradually increase the task demands. Similarly, when the function of an unacceptable behavior is sensory, we would want to increase the person's access to alternative, acceptable sources of stimulation. If the function of a form of misbehavior has been to produce reinforcers, we would clearly indicate the new conditions under which reinforcers would be attained. That helps the client recognize what is required for reinforcers to be forthcoming. Also, although we want to avoid prompting unnecessarily, we might initially opt to use some minimal prompts, such as gestures, requests, and modeling. Those may help occasion the replacement behavior, thereby enabling the individual to connect the new actions to an increased frequency of reinforcer attainment (remember, though, it is important to not prompt the individual immediately after they engage in the problem behavior so as to avoid teaching an inappropriate behavior chain).

The presence of a peer receiving the same consequences also can influence the outcome. For example, Singer-Dudek and Oblak (2013) found that if the pre-school client observes a peer, known or not known to the client, receiving the same consequence for the same targeted behavior, the value of the consequence appears to be enhanced. Including a peer model, then, who can be seen receiving the same reinforcer may serve as a motivational operation for some children.

When conducting functional behavioral assessments, look carefully at the features of the antecedents that may be setting the occasion for the wanted or unwanted behavior. For example, within a given escape situation, the person might be attempting to flee from an especially difficult task; in another, perhaps the length of the assignment (Smith et al., 1995). Therefore, we suggest you analyze the range of variants within each function to effectively modify the appropriate antecedents.

**Selecting consequences.** Functional behavioral assessments can guide us toward especially powerful individual reinforcer choices to deliver contingent upon selected replacement behaviors. In Kevin's case, we now know that his aberrant behaviors serve an escape function. So, at this point we might decide to provide him the opportunity to escape, say in the form of acceding to his request for a short break, following his emitting the replacement behavior—doing a portion of his work. We probably should supplement these newly identified functional reinforcers with others, selected according to the procedures described in Chapter 6. Then we can provide those, contingent on the occurrence of: (1) reduced rates of the problem behavior, (2) periods of time during which the problem behavior has not occurred, and/or (3) for various other acceptable behaviors. Additionally, to the extent possible, we must eliminate any reinforcement for the problem behavior; that is, extinguish it.

One important caveat: Remember that reinforcers can and do change across time and circumstances. Our chef loves garlic in her sauce, but on recalling the date she has later on with the love of her life, she decides to avoid garlic! Let us assume, then, that our functional behavioral assessment revealed that a given problem behavior initially permitted the person to escape from a difficult task. We set up an escape intervention that successfully reduces the behavior. Yet, at a later time, we note the behavior beginning to increase again, even though we have continued consistently to apply the "effective" program. An additional functional behavioral assessment might reveal that the problem behavior now allows the individual to gain access to preferred items. Thus, "When relapse occurs following successful treatment to reduce problem behavior, it is often attributed to inconsistent implementation of maintenance programs. Although less likely, another potential  cause for relapse is a change in the behavior's maintaining contingency over time" (Lerman, Iwata, Smith, Zarcone, & Vollmer, 1994, p. 357). In the event your data reveal a relapse despite the chosen intervention being implemented consistently, you should conduct a new functional behavioral assessment to determine if different treatment components are required. This is another reason for conducting functional behavioral assessments periodically, rather than viewing them as singular events. You need to plan periodic functional behavioral assessments within programs focusing on seriously troublesome behaviors to better understand changes in the behavior and to fine-tune the intervention.

**Using functional behavioral assessments to identify which procedures to avoid.** Plan in advance which specific consequences you will not apply in the event the problem behavior reoccurs. Functional behavioral assessments help you to do that. Suppose, for instance, we determined that the person's problematic behavior previously allowed him to escape having to work on some task. We had best avoid a timeout consequence, because that actually would reinforce the problem behavior by permitting the person to escape from the task. Nor would ignoring the misbehavior work, because the individual could just continue to escape the task while being ignored.

> **Box 10.7  Exercise in Intervention Development**
>
> Let us turn to the case of Kevin and develop an intervention to help Mrs. Mack eliminate Kevin's problem behavior.
>
> Based on the functional behavioral assessment we now know that Kevin engages in problem behavior to escape from having to complete certain assignments, so first we determine whether Kevin has any socially acceptable means of gaining respite from a task under either current or different conditions. Perhaps we find that Kevin already asks appropriately for a break by raising his hand and making the request in a polite tone during Mr. Caine's Spanish class. This information would be helpful when choosing the replacement behavior, in that teaching him to use a behavior he already knows (raising his hand) would be easier than some new one. Identifying the antecedents and supports for hand-raising in Spanish class, such as the teacher delaying recognizing Kevin until he quietly raises his hand and waits patiently for the teacher's response, certainly would be helpful. Another tactic might be to manipulate the antecedents that occasion the behavior by decreasing the aversiveness of the demand. That might be accomplished by interspersing less difficult tasks among the more challenging ones. Or, we might decrease the total number of tasks Kevin is required to complete. We also would want to stop reinforcing his current obnoxious avoidance behaviors by not allowing him to escape the situation (e.g., avoid sending him to timeout). Were it necessary to remove him from class we would make sure his work requirement accompanied him. As to replacement behaviors, certainly we could teach Kevin to display a card requesting a five-minute break from work and/or a "help" card to request assistance.

When the goal or function underlying a form of misbehavior is gaining attention, avoid using verbal reprimands, interrupting, or redirecting the individual, because those forms of attention can worsen the behavior. Along the same lines, deny contingent access to items if the function of the individual's problem behavior is to gain an item, food, or activity. Should a child kick and scream for a particular package of cookies, withhold her access to that item at the moment. Wait to provide it until after the replacement behavior occurs. Or suppose the function of the misbehavior has been found to be sensory or automatic reinforcement. Withholding attention or placing the individual in timeout is not likely to work. Such situations readily allow the individual to continue the self-stimulation. Now try the exercise in Box 10.7.

## LEGAL AND ETHICAL IMPLICATIONS OF CONDUCTING FUNCTIONAL BEHAVIORAL ASSESSMENTS IN SCHOOLS

As we have illustrated, analyzing the function of a behavior is relevant to any challenging human situation, and functional behavioral assessments are especially useful for designing ethically and legally sound educational programs for people with  developmental disabilities. In the United States, the reauthorized Individuals with Disabilities Education Improvement Act (IDEIA, 2006) and its predecessor, the Individuals with Disabilities Education Act (IDEA, 1997), require individualized education program (IEP) teams to develop behavioral improvement plans (BIPs). For those students whose behavior impedes their own or others' performance, BIPs are to be based on functional behavioral assessments. However, neither statute provides guidance concerning the substantive components of these plans. At the time of this writing, though, we have found it feasible to glean some guidelines based on judicial interpretations and the professional literature.

In 2006, Etschdeit reviewed 52 published judicial decisions from predominantly state-level administrative hearings involving appeals of behavior improvement plans (BIPs). Based on these decisions, she identified five features defining acceptable BIPs (see Table 10.5). Were any of those missing, the school district tended to lose the appeal. (Note our commentary on each.) Several of the legal decisions reviewed by Etschdeit (2006) required the school districts to hire outside experts, including certified behavior analysts, to conduct the FBAs and BIPs. To obtain skillful behavior-improvement

**TABLE 10.5  Discussion of Features of an Acceptable Behavior Improvement Plans**

| Feature | Description |
|---|---|
| A BIP must be developed when a behavior interferes with student learning. | Many of the strategies contained in this book can be used to develop a BIP as well as other behavioral interventions. In one legal decision (Wachusett Regional School District, 2002) it was concluded that absent a BIP, placement in a less restrictive placement would be impossible and FAPE (free, appropriate public education) would be denied. |
| The BIP must be based on the functional behavior assessment (FBA). | This chapter has shown you how to conduct an FBA and relate the proposed intervention to the FBA's findings. |
| The BIP must be individualized or based on the student's needs. | Throughout this text we teach you how to individualize any behavioral intervention plan. |
| The BIP must include and emphasize positive behavior interventions and supports. | Many chapters in this text emphasize positive behavior interventions and supports. |
| The BIP must be implemented as it specifies and its effects monitored. | You have already learned how to observe, monitor, and evaluate the effects of interventions and how to determine program fidelity. |

plans, many districts now hire Board Certified Behavior Analysts to conduct and supervise behavioral assessments within their district.

In another case (http://www.documents.dgs.ca.gov/oah/seho_decisions/2006100159-2007031009.pdf) it was found that evidence of the fidelity of implementation of the BIP was not recorded, nor did the student's behavior improve. Yet the plan had not been rewritten. Also, the quality of the plan was questionable. The hearing officer ruled that the lack of an effective behavior plan violated the free and appropriate public education (FAPE) mandate, warranting compensatory education findings. (Lack of effective behavior support is not always a FAPE violation, but this decision is worthy of note.)

A Pennsylvania district failed to include a behavioral management plan in a tenth-grader's IEP (Lauren P., by David and Ann Marie P. [parents] vs. Wissahickon Sch. List. 48 IDELR 99, E. D. pa 2007). Rather than developing a BIP for the student, the district asked the student to become more responsible, apply strategies learned in mainstream courses, and learn to concentrate on the task at hand. The United States District Judge stated that, "These statements demonstrate the district's failure to respond to deficiencies in previous IEPs and thus meet its responsibility to provide [FAPE]. As a result, the district was ordered to provide compensatory education to the then-19-year-old student, and to repay the student's parents for private school expenses. The judge also noted that the 10th- and 11th-grade IEPs marked a continuation of the existing behavioral strategies that had failed the student in the past. Thus, do not place the responsibility on the student to change his other behavior without an appropriate intervention plan (BIP).

Beyond the themes just highlighted, researchers have elucidated six substantive components of a legally defensible and educationally appropriate BIP (see Browning-Wright, et al., 2007):

- Behavior serves a particular purpose or function for individuals (e.g., positive or negative reinforcement). Therefore, the BIP must be based on the functional behavioral assessment (FBA).
- Behavior is related to the context/environment in which it occurs.
- "Changing behavior involves addressing both the environmental features AND teach-

ing a functionally-equivalent behavior that the client can use to satisfy the function of the behavior in an acceptable way" (p. 95).

- Acceptable replacement behaviors must be effectively reinforced to result in behavioral increases as well as generalized performance and maintenance.
- Implementers need to know how to handle the problem behavior if it reoccurs; therefore this topic must be addressed in the BIP.

For optimal team performance, indicating the roles and responsibilities for carrying out each element is crucial. All important stakeholders need to communicate with one another frequently enough to produce regular monitoring of program fidelity and client behavior change.

These guidelines have been incorporated into a tool, the Behavior Support Plan–Quality Evaluation Guide (BSP-QE), designed to assess the quality of the developed BIP (Browning-Wright et al., 2007). Cook et al. (2007) and Browning-Wright et al. (2007) have evaluated the reliability and validity of this instrument. They found interrater reliability estimates exceeding 0.80—a promising level. Interestingly, though, Cook et al. (2007) found that only 11 percent (8 out of 76) of the BIPs developed in typical schools were rated as "adequate," while 65 percent of the plans achieved that designation when teams included a more experienced and skilled member. Similarly, the majority of BIPs developed in today's schools are inadequate and potentially legally invalid due to substantive and procedural violations (Van Acker, Boreson, Gable, & Potterton, 2005). However, there is hope. School professionals were four times more likely to develop BIPs rated as adequate after they received training on using the BSP-QE to evaluate and rate the quality of their BIPs (Browning-Wright et al., 2007). Similarly, autism educators in a graduate-level university program significantly improved positive behavior support (PBS) plans after brief training on the BSP-QE (Kraemer, Cook, Browning-Wright, Mayer, & Wallace, 2008).

Why is the quality of the BIP so important? Because the higher the quality, the more likely it is to result in positive student outcomes (Cook et al., 2010), including reductions in problem and increases in positive and replacement behaviors; also in improved academic performance. In addition, BIP quality was positively related to treatment integrity, including the extent to which the intervention was implemented as written and the degree of adult behavior change.

Clearly, functional behavioral assessments are improving the quality of behavioral services provided in the fields of special education and special adult services. Along with the other relevant concepts and methods supplied in this text, when designing a BIP, professionals certainly should include the features described above within their plan. In addition, expanding ongoing research continues to enhance our knowledge and skills in this field. Behavior analysts who (among their other areas of focus) develop and supervise the implementation of BIPs need regularly to maintain their familiarity with progress in the field by attending professional meetings, reading scientific and professional journals, and otherwise continuing their educations.

Table 10.6 offers several possible interventions dependent on the behavior's function. Once you have studied various interventions, you might want to refer back to this table.

## SUMMARY AND CONCLUSIONS

Functional behavioral assessment methodology enables teachers, family members, managers and other change agents more effectively to meet the needs of people with simple as well as puzzling and troublesome behaviors. These methods help explain why an individual engages in a particular challenging behavior or why s/he fails to act appropriately under given circumstances. They also discourage people from misusing behavior management techniques. To identify the internal and/or external environmental factors contributing to a particular behavior problem, functional behavioral assessments make use of three general procedures: Indirect (anecdotal) Assessments, Descriptive Assessments, and Functional Analyses. Results from a complete functional behavioral assessment (including an indirect assessment, a descriptive assessment AND a functional analysis) have the advantage of clearly explaining what the behavior

## Table 10.6
### Matching Interventions to Functions of Behavior

| Function of behavior | Some potential interventions |
|---|---|
| Social negative reinforcement in the form of escape/avoidance from demands | **For Task Avoidance:**<br>• Reinforce compliance<br>• Teach how to seek a break<br>• Reinforce absence of problem behavior<br>• Initially remove/reduce task demands and then gradually introduce/increase demands<br>• Change difficulty level and/or length of task<br>• Use behavioral momentum (Hp–Lp Task Presentation)<br>• Follow through with demand task (guide to task completion if necessary)<br><br>**For Social Avoidance:**<br>• Pair social attention with strong reinforcers<br>• Reinforce compliance<br>• Reinforce absence of problem behavior<br><br>**Avoid:**<br>• Timeout |
| Social positive reinforcement in the form of attention | **For Attention:**<br>• Increase attention for appropriate behaviors<br>• Use extinction (do not give attention for problem behavior)<br>• Teach socially acceptable ways to gain attention (including FCT)<br>• Provide noncontingent attention<br>• Use timeout as last resort<br><br>**Avoid:**<br>• Verbal reprimands<br>• Response interruption/redirection<br>• Attention in the form of prompting to use communication (speak, select or point to word or image) contingent on problem behavior (simply wait until communication skill or approximation of communication skill is emitted,, or reinforce another's modeled behavior) |
| Social positive reinforcement in the form of access (To materials, activities, persons, or food) | **For Access:**<br>• Withhold access (Extinction) contingent on problem behavior<br>• Teach socially acceptable alternatives to obtain access<br>• Provide frequent non-contingent access<br>• Use response cost or timeout as last resort<br><br>**Avoid:**<br>• Allowing access to materials, activities, persons or food following problem behavior.<br>• Prompting to use communication contingent on problem behavior |

*Continued on next page...*

| Table 10.6 (cont.) | |
|---|---|
| *Function of behavior* | *Some potential interventions* |
| Automatic reinforcement in the form of sensory stimulation or pain relief | **For Automatic Reinforcement**<br>• Increase access to alternative sources of stimulation<br>• Interrupt/redirect behavior<br>• Sensory extinction<br>• Use differential reinforcement strategies (including access to automatically maintained behavior contingent on engaging in appropriate behavior)<br>**Avoid:**<br>• Withholding attention<br>• Timeout |

yields the person, while providing a set of concrete strategies for eliminating maladaptive behavior and teaching appropriate replacement behavior(s). Functional behavioral assessments enable behavior analysts, parents, teachers, and caregivers both to determine the function of a behavior, and, by manipulating the antecedents that set the occasion for the behavior and the consequences supporting the behavior, to design and conduct constructive change strategies. A TSD mode of conducing functional behavior assessment can help bridge geographical and other barriers to assessment. Overall, ongoing functional behavioral assessments guide practitioners toward designing and implementing effective behavioral interventions in support of more constructive and socially acceptable repertoires among their clientele.

Before conducting functional assessments, as with most any assessment, be sure to obtain the client's (or caretakers) informed consent. Also, according to our code of ethics, you MUST do a functional assessment before you develop a behavior-reduction program (BACB's Professional and Ethical Compliance Code for Behavior Analysts, 2016).

**An Invitation to Behavior Analysts Working with Clients with Challenging Behaviors**

Try using functional assessments to analyze the conditions under which clients are observed to behave optimally. You may be able successfully to identify and incorporate the conditions that heighten and support those pro-social behaviors within their Behavior Intervention Plans.

*Chapter 11*

# Rapidly Attaining Positive Change: Implementing Reinforcement Effectively

## Goals

1. Specify what obtaining informed consent for program implementation entails.
2. Discuss the importance of reinforcer timing or delay to reinforcer effectiveness.
3. Discuss how to teach people to delay gratification, and explain how those methods relate to reinforcer timing. Define and illustrate when to use *labeled or specific* praise.
4. Discuss when and how to use *supplementary reinforcers* and their relation to reinforcer timing.
5. Define and illustrate when to use *labeled or specific* praise.
6. Discuss how to teach *discrimination* of contextual factors.
7. Discuss the importance of the magnitude or quantity of reinforcers on reinforcer effectiveness.
8. Define and differentiate between *satiation, adaptation,* and *habituation* and discuss how reinforcer type, satiation, adaptation, and habituation relate to the amount of reinforcers provided and to responding.
9. Discuss the influence of *response cost, quantity,* or *effort* on the quantity or density of reinforcers provided.
10. Discuss the importance of client choice on reinforcement effectiveness.
11. Describe the use of the Treasure Box activity.
12. Illustrate and discuss the usefulness of *behavioral contracts*.
13. Define and describe the use of the daily report card system.
14. Discuss the value of applying *contingent reinforcement* in a variety of situations (times, places, and people) in promoting program effectiveness.
15. Discuss the importance of and illustrate how to reduce, remove, or override competing contingencies.
16. Discuss how to avoid reinforcing behaviors targeted for reduction.

17. Define and illustrate how to use reinforcement schedules to provide a supportive environment to promote maintenance.
18. Define, illustrate, and specify when to use *continuous* and *intermittent reinforcement* to maximize reinforcement effectiveness.
19. Specify why using *self-management* is important.
20. Specify the component skills involved in self-management.
21. Specify methods likely to make self-management successful and describe in what ways they can help maximize reinforcement effectiveness.

*************

> **Case Analysis**
>
> Mark, a supervisor at a local medical billing company, has a number of personnel employed on his team. All are required to download their work for the week by 5 P.M. Friday. Beth, one of Mark's employees, rarely adheres to that schedule, sometimes delaying the task until the following Monday. Mark feels he has really tried to use "reinforcement" with Beth, but that it just doesn't work. How would you respond to Mark?

*The only way people will ever reach their potential is through the effective use of positive reinforcement"* (Daniels & Lattal, 2017, p. 110).

In this Chapter we detail how to implement reinforcement *effectively*. In Chapter 6, we discussed ways to identify powerful reinforcers. In this chapter, we address additional factors that may influence the effectiveness of a given reinforcement program, regardless of the individual(s) whose behavior is the subject of modification. We especially emphasize ways for applying these elements to our own behavior, because instituting any novel program begins with the change-managers themselves doing something differently.

However, before implementing an effective reinforcement program, or any planed intervention, it is important to obtain informed consent.

## INFORMED CONSENT

The ethics code for behavior analysts (provided by the Behavior Analysis Certification Board—BACB) has defined *informed consent* in two major sections. The first section, service and research, is usually communicated to clients (or their advocates) and/or parents and caretakers. It states:

> Providing the opportunity for an individual to give informed consent for services or research involves communicating about and taking appropriate steps to confirm understanding of: 1) the purpose of the services or research; 2) the expected time commitment and procedures involved; 3) the right to decline to participate or withdraw at any time without adverse consequences, 4) potential benefits, risks, discomfort, or adverse effects; 5) any limits to confidentiality or privacy; 6) any incentives for research participation; 7) whom to contact for questions or concerns at any time; and 8) the opportunity to ask questions and receive answers. (p. 7)

The second part of the code addresses sharing information, and is called *information use/sharing*. It states:

> Providing the opportunity for an individual to give informed consent to share or use their information involves communicating about: 1) the purpose and intended use; 2) the audience; 3) the expected duration; 4) the right to decline or withdraw consent at any time; 5) potential risks or benefits; 6) any limitations to confidentiality or privacy; 7) whom to contact for questions or concerns at any time; and 8) the opportunity to ask questions and receive answers. (p. 7)

In other words, before implementing an intervention program you will need to specify its purpose, the time commitments required of the various parties, the procedures that will be implemented, the right to decline to participate or withdraw at any time without adverse consequences, potential benefits, risks, discomfort, or adverse effects that may occur, any limits to confidentiality or privacy, whom to contact for questions or concerns at any time, and the on-going opportunities to ask questions and receive answers. All this must be done in language that is comprehensible to the parties involved, as described in Chapter 3. However, before you can explain the intervention you plan to implement you will need to know how to implement it effectively. So, let us continue with our discussion of how to implement reinforcement effectively.

## ENHANCING REINFORCER EFFECTIVENESS

Have you heard the statement, "I've tried using reinforcement and it didn't work?" If so, your questions about reinforcement as *a procedure* should be: "What do you mean by *trying* reinforcement? What were your exact actions? Under what conditions were they taken?" By definition, reinforcement works because it is defined by its function as a procedure that strengthens behavior (i.e., the behavior's frequency, rate, duration, intensity, or other dimensions increase or persist) by arranging stimuli that *are consequences of,* or **contingent**[1] on, some response. We would explain that practices based on reinforcement can vary in effectiveness, from none to optimal, depending on the care with which they are implemented. Nevertheless, the effectiveness and efficiency of a given reinforcement procedure depends on numerous factors. If any given reinforcement practice has failed to work, one or more features were probably lacking. And the more those elements have been overlooked, the less likely it is that the given reinforcement procedure will prove successful. By contrast, the more these factors are considered and incorporated within the system, the

more likely the approach is to succeed. This chapter, then, focuses on selecting and using especially promising reinforcement methods.

### Selecting Effective Reinforcers

Selecting an appropriate variety of reinforcers based on the client's learning history, as described in Chapter 6, is only one aspect of ensuring that a given reinforcement strategy will work. Once we have chosen effective consequences, we need to remind ourselves of a number of other key features that have been found to influence how rapidly, generally, and durably a given strategy works. Beyond the *quality* of any reinforcing stimulus, other elements of any reinforcement program, such as *timing* (how soon), *quantity, density* or *intensity* (how much and/or how powerful), *frequency* (how often), *schedule* (according to what pattern), *antecedents* and motivational operations (MOs) with which they are paired, and perhaps others can profoundly influence the effectiveness of any given reinforcement procedure.

### Timing of Reinforcer Delivery

> *One basic principle of behavior is that immediate reinforcement is more effective than delayed reinforcement (Skinner, 1938).*

Charlie's supervisor has decided to give Charlie a report at the end of the day with a positive rating when he performs well in his vocational training program. But suppose Charlie is misbehaving later on, just as the rating forms are delivered. The positive rating may well reinforce that misbehavior. Immediate reinforcement, in the form of the supervisor delivering his positive comments while catching Charlie in the act of performing well, could have avoided possible reinforcement of the misbehavior.

So, whenever possible, try to provide immediate, contingent reinforcement. Immediate reinforcement can help clients discriminate the saliency, or conspicuousness, of the behavior-consequence relation. Greater saliency of the relation appears to promote more correct responding (Fisher, Pawich, Dickes, Paden, & Toussaint,

---

[1] The word "contingent" implies *a dependent relation between the behavior and its consequences and/or antecedents.*

2014). Unless specific alternative steps are taken to teach waiting, young children and those with weak verbal comprehension skills have an especially difficult time with delayed reinforcement. But as verbal competence increases, people are better able to bridge the delay" (Catania, 2017, Chapters 14 & 26)). Delayed reinforcement also influences discrimination acquisitions. For example, Sy and Vollmer (2012) report that delayed reinforcement slowed down or prevented discriminations (e.g., discriminations among words, colors, pictures of objects or animals, number of items) in some children with developmental disabilities.

Sometimes delays are unavoidable. Here is one example of how to approach this challenge: Schweitzer and Sulzer-Azaroff (1988) assessed six preschoolers whose teacher identified them as being impulsive. A pre-assessment found that all consistently selected a box containing a smaller amount of immediate reinforcers (food and/or stickers, according to their preferences) over larger, more delayed ones. By gradually increasing the durations of the delay interval, the experimenters were able to teach five of the children to select the box containing a larger amount of more delayed reinforcers, rather than the one containing the smaller amount of immediately attainable items. Results demonstrated the feasibility of teaching young children to make more advantageous choices as well as how one could incorporate delays into a reinforcement procedure.

Apparently, though, because their own verbal behavior may help them to bridge the gap between the response and reinforcement, people with reasonable verbal comprehension skills can often still progress despite delayed outcomes: "Charlie, you will get a high mark at the end of the month if you learn to put the new kits together well."

In another actual situation (Brown & Sulzer-Azaroff, 1991), bank tellers apparently were capable of bridging a time gap of several hours prior to receiving feedback. In the interim, tellers made an effort to be pleasant, in the form of greeting customers by name and smiling. At the end of each interaction, the teller gave the customer a color-coded chip to insert in one of several slots in a box in the lobby. Each slot designated the level of the customer's rating of the teller's friendliness, which they could review at the end of the work shift. Performance improved accordingly, even though the delays between their pleasant behavior and the feedback they received for it were substantial.

However, just having verbal comprehension skills is no guarantee that it will help people to accept large delays between the response and reinforcement. If you are considering delaying reinforcement, first make certain that the individual has already demonstrated the ability to tolerate delays of that nature, or else conduct training to ensure the time-bridging skill will be used regularly and fluently.

## Teaching Delay of Gratification— Improving Self-Control

What is clever about the fact that doctors and dentists often supply an array of magazines in their waiting rooms?

While catching people in the act of being good is the best approach, circumstances often conspire against that. Additionally, everyone needs to be able to wait calmly for reinforcers (a characteristic of self-control) while studying, learning, and in general, to function successfully in society. As soon as we can, then, we must systematically teach our clientele to remain calm during delays of *increasing* duration until their reinforcers are delivered. We do that by *gradually programming delay into the routine.* When Charlie persists in pestering his supervisor to look at his work or constantly asks to have his accomplishments praised, we might reasonably assume he has not learned this type of patience. The supervisor then may set up a program with Charlie to help him bridge the time gap. For a while, the supervisor may try to check the work upon request. Little by little, he can begin to delay those consequences for a moment or two, simultaneously using verbal prompts: "I'll be over to check your work in a couple of minutes." After many instances of successfully using brief delays, he can gradually lengthen the delay between the time that Charlie finishes his work and when the teacher checks it.

Recognize that people generally attempt to maximize reinforcers (King & Logue, 1987; Logue, Pena-Correal, Rodríguez, & Kabela, 1986).

Therefore, try to *boost the quantity and/or quality of your delayed reinforcers above that of the more immediate ones*, as mentioned earlier. For example, Neef and colleagues (Neef, Bicard, & Endo, 2001; Neef et al., 2005) showed that the behavior of individuals with ADHD was heavily influenced by reinforcer immediacy. However, reinforcer delay could be increased by introducing more highly-preferred stimuli. This can be accomplished in several ways. We saw how, by increasing the length of the delay periods very gradually, Schweitzer and Sulzer-Azaroff (1988) taught five preschoolers to select larger, delayed reinforcers over smaller, immediate reinforcers. Similarly, this *progressive delay of reinforcer* method was used with adults with developmental disabilities (Dixon et al., 1998) and with children with ADHD (Binder, Dixon, & Ghezzi, 2000) to teach greater self-control, or tolerating delay of the reinforcer. The participants initially selected only smaller reinforcers that were immediately available, not larger, delayed reinforcers. Therefore, initially both smaller and larger reinforcers were made immediately available. Then, delays were progressively increased for the larger reinforcers only. The participants learned to select the larger, delayed reinforcers. Also, investigators (Juanico, Dozier, Payne, Brandt, & Hirst, 2016) reported success in achieving 3-minute delays for typically developing preschool children (3.5 to 5-years-old) when only high preference toys (and sometimes moderate-preference toys) were available, and only for delayed choices. Other investigators (Dunkel-Jackson, Dixon, & Szekely, 2016) working with 3 adults with autism were able to increase the delay period 10-fold by gradually increasing the delay period to obtain the larger reinforcers.

In discussing laboratory research on interventions that may involve delayed reinforcers, Stromer, McComas, and Rehfeldt (2000) offered the following suggestions:

- Make the reinforcer(s) visible during the delay (the visual display can serve as a reminder).
- Gradually increase the delay or gradually increase the time engaged in the task to receive the reinforcer.
- Provide learned or conditioned reinforcers during the delay, such as tokens, points, gold stars, praise, and/or verbal reminders of the reinforcers to come. In fact, Austin and Tiger (2015) reported that problem behaviors were less likely when alternative reinforcers were available during delays. Thus, if problem behavior is an issue during delay, try using alternative reinforcers during the delay.
- Teach clients to engage in providing themselves with self-instructions or self-prompts (e.g., "When I finish this I will be able to ____"). (Self-management techniques are discussed in more detail later in this chapter.)

Just gradually increasing delay, (the time required to remain engaged in the task) before reinforcement delivery is not always sufficient. Staubitz, Lloyd, and Reed (2020) found that progressive delay training, alone, did not improve the self-control of elementary-level students with emotional and behavioral disorders (EBD), and who also tended toward impulsivity. However, when these students were treated to progressive delay training, combined with a rationale and a rule for selecting the delayed reward, the self-control of three of six did improve.

Investigators (Drifke, Tiger, & Lillie, 2020) also have reported that to promote improved tolerance to delayed reinforcement, it is helpful to reinforce the occurrence of acceptable alternative behaviors as they occur during the delay between the target behavior, and reinforcer delivery. This strategy was found to be more effective than awaiting the passage of time without reinforcement, or reinforcing the absence of the problem behavior while time passed. Further teaching, strengthening and establishing other appropriate behaviors also contribute to the success of the intervention.

Another method used to support patient waiting for reinforcers is to *introduce distracting stimuli during the waiting period*. For example, Volpe, King, and Logue (1988) found that radio music decreased impulsiveness in situations in which adults were otherwise found to act quickly rather than making the most advantageous choices. Adding distracting stimuli can diminish the aversive properties of having to wait. Other investigators have suggested

While shopping with his mom, Morty tends to run up and down the aisles knocking things off the shelf. To cope with this problem, his mother promises to give Morty a candy bar when they reach the cash register for "being good in the store." What would you suggest Morty's mother do to help Morty behave himself during the reinforcer delay period? One possibility would be for his mother to ask Morty to "help" put things in the basket. What other ideas can you suggest?

teaching people coping strategies for managing waiting or introducing an alternative task during the delay period (Dixon & Cummings, 2001): singing songs, counting, practicing relaxation exercises, playing games, and so on. Such activities can support waiting patiently in the sense that they will reduce the likelihood that problem behaviors may emerge. Therefore, consider combining strategies like these while you gradually lengthen the delays between behavior and its contingent reinforcers.

## Using Supplementary Reinforcers

Sometimes factors beyond our control make it difficult or impossible to reinforce immediately. Using supplementary, learned reinforcers is another way to cope with necessary delay. In such circumstances, signaling precisely what is being done correctly at the moment becomes particularly crucial. Nods, winks, smiles, a "V for victory" sign, and enthusiastic "okays" and "all rights" suit that purpose well. These signals can function just as well with other clients whose skills are advanced, including able adults, as we have found in teaching nursing staff to lift safely (Alavosius & Sulzer-Azaroff, 1986, 1990).

Attempting to apply reinforcers immediately also may prove unwieldy for managers who supervise large groups of people, as when a group is striving to earn a powerful incentive that entails a necessary delay. Ms. Feeney has decided to take her class on a field trip to reinforce the students' correct completion of the week's assignments. Naturally, delivering the trip to each student immediately, contingent on the completion of an assignment, would be impossible. Ms. Feeney could use **supplementary reinforcers** as *a signal to indicate that a stronger reinforcer will be forthcoming*: "Good, I see you are getting your work finished. You certainly have earned the opportunity to go on the trip on Friday." If a verbal statement is not effective, a token system might be. (See Chapter 12 on using tokens to bridge delays.) Perhaps, then, to become eligible to go on the trip, each student would be required to complete a set of assignments to earn a given number of tokens.

## Using Labeled Praise

**Labeled** or **specific praise** involves *specifying the target behavior, providing the reason or rationale for its delivery* (why that behavior is being praised), and should be paired with *eye contact, and a sincere, enthusiastic tone of voice*. Bernhardt and Forehand (1975) suggested that specific praise is a particularly effective way to convey approval and provide a person with rules to guide subsequent responding (which is an important antecedent control, as we shall see). Examples of specific praise include: "How wonderful! You remembered to take your medicine without being reminded!" "Congratulations! Your personal examples are directly relevant to the concept we've been discussing." "Thank you for waiting for me to get off the phone before asking for a glass of milk." "I notice how well you've matched the color of your shirt with your sweater!" "Gosh, it makes me feel so good when you tell me how much you enjoy my cooking!" Specific praise provides contingent reinforcement that places the emphasis on the behavior, rather than on the person. As a result, it facilitates discrimination as to which behavior is effective or functional. When praise is withheld after inappropriate behavior, people may recognize that it is not themselves but their actions that are deficient. Specific praise increases the likelihood that the correlated behaviors will be repeated in the future.

While providing specific praise contingent on a response, do your best to maintain eye contact with your client. Children were found more likely to comply with parental requests if the parents maintained eye contact, and even *more* likely to do so if compliance with the parental requests was followed by both eye contact *and* contingent reinforcement (Everett, Olmi, Edwards, & Tingstrom, 2005). In a recent study, Adamo, et al. (2015) utilized specific praise as an intervention component to increase the physical activity of young children with down syndrome.

In a recent review of the past 50 years of research into educational practices, Ennis et al., (2020).emphasized the value of behavior-specific praise, a cornerstone classroom management procedure, as an effective and efficient low-intensity procedure. "The way you made a good straight line to the left and below the circle on the "P" makes it clear that the word is "pay," rather than "day.""

Also, to reemphasize, praise needs to be delivered enthusiastically. Research indicates that clients are likely to acquire responses more rapidly when praise is delivered enthusiastically than in a more neutral tone (Weyman & Sy, 2018). Similarly, according to a recent review of the last 50 years of research in educational practices, Ennis et al., (2020). emphasized the value of behavior-specific praise, as a low-intensity effective and efficient cornerstone classroom management procedure.

## Teaching Clients to Discriminate Contextual Factors

One way to facilitate **discriminative learning**—*knowing which behavior leads to reinforcement under specific conditions and which does not*—is to clearly indicate the context or stimulus conditions under which a given response will be reinforced.

If Travis must complete all his chores before 9:00 A.M. to receive his allowance, his parents should stipulate those conditions. If you were a teacher, you would specify the circumstances under which hand-raising is to be acknowledged (i.e., reinforced), such as during study time, but not during recess or discussion time when spontaneous participation is acceptable. Tell your employees where, when, and how they must perform their jobs if they are to earn bonuses or positive evaluations. Prepare precise job descriptions. Clearly specifying a behavior's context and/or the qualities it should possess for it to merit reinforcement should heighten the probability that your expectations will be met. This is one reason why educators in effective schools clearly specify classroom and school disciplinary rules, and successful organizations prepare precise policies and procedures (Dyer & Osher, 2000; Mayer, 2002; Mayer & Ybarra, 2003; Sugai et al., 2000).

Many successful behavioral programs clearly communicate the conditions for obtaining reinforcement when effective verbal repertoires are present, because that tends to result in more rapid behavior change. The conditions signaling the probability of attaining reinforcement for a specific response can be communicated in different ways. In addition to instructions, objectives, promises, rules, guidelines, policies, and so on, clients may observe others receiving reinforcers following the targeted response (i.e., *modeling*), or their performance can be prompted or guided. Or, as Fisher et al. (2014) did, you can make the accumulation and loss of reinforcers visible by placing them in front of the client. They placed an edible in clear containers in front of the clients for correct responding and removed an edible for incorrect responding. This helped to highlight the saliency of the behavior-consequence relations that resulted in improved correct responding by children with ASD who had exhibited persistent errors. Once their consecutive correct responses occurred, the client received the three edibles.

Verbal prompts often are used to cue a verbal response: "If you want to properly distinguish between the terms *ordinate* and *abscissa* (the vertical and horizontal axes of a graph, respectively), remember that the word 'ordinate' has an 'o' for 'on top.'" This sort of a prompt will help you to respond *ordinate* next time someone asks you about labeling the vertical line sitting on top of the abscissa. A gesture or verbal reminder from another also can help us to perform a nonverbal response correctly—like demonstrating (*showing*) the motions to be imitated or *telling* the person how to do it (e.g., "Keep your eye on the ball!").

*Physically guiding* a movement, such as a tennis swing or soccer kick, helps communicate how a particular body movement should be executed if reinforcement is to result. **Self-monitoring**, *observing and recording one's own behavior* (described below) and behavioral contracting (discussed later in this chapter) also can facilitate the if-then relation (if I finish five problems, then I can work on my shop project).

These examples demonstrate how important it is to clearly specify the conditions under which reinforcement will occur, and to follow through accordingly. What you are trying to accomplish is to teach the learner to identify the contingencies under which a particular behavior will be reinforced.

## Determining the Magnitude and Quantity of Reinforcers

Generally, access to activity reinforcers for longer durations are more effective than shorter durations (Hoffmann, Samaha, Bloom, & Boyle, 2017). However, the decision about the *quantity or reinforcer magnitude*—how *much* of a reinforcer(s) to deliver following the target behavior—depends on a number of factors: (1) the class or type of reinforcer used; (2) the level of deprivation from or satiation to the stimulus; and (3) the cost (time, effort, and additional resources required to make the response). We discuss each of these factors below.

**Reinforcer class or type.** As described in Chapter 6, *generalized reinforcers* are *those that can be exchanged for a variety of other reinforcers and are only minimally affected by adaptation or satiation*. Tokens, money, coupons, trading stamps, or credits are examples. Because they are minimally affected by satiation, generalized reinforcers can be delivered frequently without compromising the potency of the stimulus as a reinforcer. Even individuals with large bank accounts usually continue to strive to increase their funds. The same is true of events that signal forthcoming reinforcers, like a smile or a promise.

Some reinforcers involve a greater variety of activities, or stimuli, than others. For example, a study by Hoffmann et al. (2017) found that clients will work for longer periods of time for longer periods of access to high-preference, high-tech items, such as "a tablet computer, MP3 device, personal video player, personal gaming devise, mini tablet computer, or e-reader device," than for high-preference low-tech items, such as "cars, dolls, blocks, or books" (p. 226). They compared 30-second to 600-second durations with four females in a sheltered workshop day program with intellectual and developmental disabilities, ages 21 to 33. Short duration access to the low-tech items was found to be more effective in promoting production than the long duration access. But, the reverse was true with the high-tech items. Thus, item type and magnitude appear to interact to influence preference and reinforcer efficacy. Perhaps the clients satiate more quickly with the low-tech items.

**Habituation, adaptation, and satiation.** Sometimes we don't know what to do when a particular reinforcing contingency arrangement appears to stop working. In those instances, *habituation, adaptation,* or *satiation* may be the culprits. **Habituation** refers to *reductions in the respondent (reflexive) responding* **elicited** *by a stimulus over repeated presentations* (as when the startle response to a loud noise diminishes with repeated presentations), whereas **adaptation** refers to *reductions in the responding* **evoked** *by an antecedent stimulus over repeated or prolonged presentations* (as when the client no longer reacts to the presence of the observer). *Habituation*, then, is a term primarily used in respondent or classical conditioning while *adaptation* is the term used in operant learning. **Satiation** refers to *the reduction in the effectiveness of a reinforcer with repeated presentations or with consumption during continued availability* (as, in the most familiar case, with continued consumption of food).

Notice the term "elicited" in the definition of *habituation*. That cues us to look for unconditioned (UCS) or conditioned (CS) *antecedent stimuli* of the type encountered in *classical conditioning*: Lightning flashes, followed immediately by a painfully loud thunderclap. Baby Judy jumps, her heart races and she screams loudly. The next time lightning flashes, her heart begins to race in advance of the thunderclap. But throughout the storm's long hours, even though the lightning and thunder persist, Judy's screams and her increased heart rate begin to diminish. We might say that Judy has begun to *habituate* to the sound produced by the thunder.

Behavior analysts sometimes use the term *habituation* more broadly to refer to the temporary change in the rate of both respondent and operant behavior patterns as a function of repeated presentations of an aversive or novel antecedent stimulus. Here, though, as mentioned, we have elected to use the term *adaptation* to describe that sort of temporary change in the rate of operant behavior. What often makes a joke funny, a work of art seem so original, a certain passage in a piece of music so exciting? The unexpected! It grabs our attention and we laugh or perhaps enjoy what we hear or see. But after many repetitions of those same arrangements of sight or sound we begin to tune out, or adapt, to the previously novel stimulus. It no longer serves a reinforcing function. So, if you choose to use a novel stimulus to evoke a behavior, be sure to monitor its effect over time, because there is a good likelihood that the recipient may "adapt" to the stimulus and begin reacting minimally or perhaps not at all. For example, if giving praise as a reinforcer, to avoid adaptation to the comment, you might vary the actual statement. Rather than repeating "good job," ad nauseam, substitute more descriptive praise: "Wow! Your letter 'O' is so nice and round!" "Your analysis of the hero's character helps us to understand why he made that key decision!"

*Satiation* is very different. The term focuses on the consequence side: Although an individual

---

**Habituation**

Unconditioned stimulus (UCS, loud noise) ➔ Unconditioned response (UCR, startle response) occurs *every time*.

After many repetitions of the UCS, presenting the UCS ➔ UCR occurring *less and less frequently*.

---

**Adaptation**

Discriminative stimulus ($S^D$ = Tells joke) ➔ Laughter the first time or two

Repeatedly presenting the $S^D$ ➔ Laughter diminishes

---

**Satiation**

Response ➔ Reinforcement (on a very dense schedule).

After many repetitions of the same response/reinforcer combination ➔ the rate of the response begins to diminish or cease.

may have repeated at a very high rate a behavior that previously has produced a given (*reinforcing*) consequence, that high rate appears to be falling off. The soccer coach shouts "Good play!" whenever he notices any of the members of the team making an obvious attempt to perform well. After weeks of hearing the same phrase repeated for about the thousandth time, "Good play" seems to be losing its reinforcing effect, as evidenced by the fact that the players appear not to be trying quite so hard, nor do they smile and raise their heads and shoulders higher following his repetitive praise. Here, of course, is *operant learning*. All things being held constant, sooner or later the response rate begins to diminish.

Similarly, intervention reinforcers appear to function more effectively following a period of time in which those reinforcers are not available. When working with six children with autism, Center and Fienup (2020) found that the majority of their students, learned better following a 15-minute period of access to high preference toys absent frequent social reinforcers than when they did receive frequent social reinforcers during the pre-session. It took five of the six youngsters fewer sessions to meet mastery criterion and they required less time for training with attention following the 15 minutes of no pre-session attention. All acquired the target skills, while only four of the six acquired them under the pre-session attention condition. So, consider withholding those reinforcers used during intervention for a brief time interval, prior to introducing a challenging new reinforcement-rich lesson along with social reinforcement.

The *rate* of habituation seems to relate to the degree to which the recipient experiences the particular stimulus as aversive or positive. Those aspects, in turn, probably depend on the recipients' sensory functioning and learning histories. A person with a hearing impairment might habituate (tune out the stimulus) more rapidly to a pleasant or unpleasant sound than someone with acute auditory functioning. Similarly, a person who has experienced that crunchy food textures are pleasant would satiate less rapidly on foods with lots of crunch than might her buddy who only finds smooth textures reinforcing.

In general, response rates are less likely to decline when the stimuli are generalized reinforcers than when they are primary or secondary. Additionally, *the more deprived of the reinforcer the client is, the more likely it will function as a reinforcer*. It is best then, to limit the client's access to reinforcers. For example, Hoffmann et al. (2017) made sure that the reinforcing items were available only during their study's sessions.

Taking an empirical approach is the best way to discover what circumstances are responsible for a curious change in rate despite all other factors being held constant. That requires monitoring conditions along with moment-to-moment changes in patterns of behaving. For instance, when you would like to determine why a given "highly preferred" food appears to have lost its potency as a reinforcer (as reflected by a reduction in the rate of responding over time despite the reinforcing stimulus remaining intact), record the number of hours since the client has eaten that as well as any other food.

**The required "cost" of the response (quantity or effort).** All other factors being equal, *responses requiring measurably more effort or cost require stronger and/or more frequent reinforcers* than easier or less costly tasks and/or than those that are "intrinsically" reinforcing (i.e., "maintained by consequences that are natural and automatic results of responding," Dickinson, 1989, p. 2). Assume two college courses enabled you to gain the same objectives and provided you with the same number of credits. Ask yourself, in which course would you choose to enroll: one that required a reasonable amount of work, or one requiring twice as much effort because it entailed lots of busy work?

Research by Tustin (1994) and DeLeon, Neidert, Anders, and Rodriguez-Catter (2001) support the position that responses requiring more effort or cost demand more reinforcement. When work requirements were increased, the concurrently available reinforcers led to a decrease in response rate. For example, "Samantha displayed a strong preference for positive reinforcement when few completed tasks were required but displayed unstable preferences when ten tasks were required" (DeLeon et al., 2001, p. 524).

In treating food refusal, by promoting a child's consumption of non-preferred foods, Cooper et al. (1999) reported that increasing the amount of reinforcers provided (i.e., bites of potato chips or number of sips of a soft drink) resulted in the client (a typically developing child) increasing his rate of food acceptance. So it seems that *the less preferred the activity, the more reinforcers will be needed to effect change.*

When an activity requires additional work or effort, or is consistently rejected in a choice situation, it is often necessary to identify especially highly preferred reinforcers to support its continuation or acceptance. For example, behaviors that produced more (a higher rate of) *low* preference reinforcers were less likely to improve than when they produced fewer (a lower rate of) *high* preference reinforcers (Neef, Mace, Shea, & Shade, 1992). Consider offering high preference reinforcers, then, to help support behavior change when responses require extra effort.

We might look at our own behavior as parents, teachers, employers, and managers as a case in point. Attempting to alter our patterns of interacting socially to reinforce good performance—a more effortful response pattern—instead of criticizing poor performance is a difficult blueprint to follow. To more effectively teach ourselves (or one another) to increase our rates of reinforcement, we may need to supplement reinforcement with additional preferred incentives (for example, seeking positive feedback from others about client success, praise from peers or supervisors, release from duties, extra free time, and easier assignments). By now, it should be apparent that no simple formula exists for determining what quantity of reinforcers to deliver. The final judgment must be made empirically, on the basis of observed performance patterns.

Similarly, intervention reinforcers appear to function more effectively following a period of time in which those reinforcers are not available. When working with six children with autism, Center and Fienup (2020) found that the majority of their students, learned better following a 15-minute period of access to high preference toys absent frequent social reinforcers than when they did receive frequent social reinforcers during the pre-session. It took five of the six youngsters fewer sessions to meet mastery criterion and they required less time for training following the 15 minutes of no pre-session attention. All acquired the target skills, while only four of the six acquired them under the pre-session attention condition. So, consider withholding those reinforcers used during intervention for a brief time interval, prior to introducing a challenging new reinforcement-rich lesson.

It is also important to remember that as effort for one response is increased or decreased, it might shift responding to another behavior not just make a reinforcer more or less valuable. This can be a good thing or a bad thing. In a recent example, Cagliani, et al. (2017) manipulated the delay and effort associated with a PECS response and a vocal response and were able to get children to vocalize more when the PECS response was associated with a longer delay and when it was associated with an increase in effort (the book was moved across the room).

## Incorporating Client Choice

When selecting reinforcers, *it is important to offer clients the opportunity to choose among a variety of reinforcers.* Providing such choice is thought to increase the reinforcing value of the stimulus (Michael, 1982; 1993; Romaniuk et al., 2002; Tiger, Hanley, & Hernandez, 2006). This in turn lessens the time it takes for the participant to adapt to the reinforcing stimulus or to become satiated with the particular stimulus. Consequently, providing people with an array of reinforcers from which to choose enhances both the effectiveness of the intervention (Tiger et al., 2006) and lowers the likelihood that disruptions and other problem behaviors will emerge (Carter, 2001).

The disruptive behavior of students with autism or severe learning disabilities decreased more rapidly when they could choose their vocational tasks and edible reinforcers than when teachers assigned the same activities and reinforcing stimuli (Dyer, Dunlap, & Winterling, 1990). Similarly, rates of disruptive behavior were lower when students could choose their academic assignments than when those were assigned by their teachers (Dunlap et al., 1994; Powell & Nelson, 1997). Providing academic-choice opportunities for students with emotional and behavioral disorders positively affected two of three students' academic and social behaviors (Jolivette, Wehby, Canale, & Massey, 2001). Further, embedding choice-making opportunities

> **Box 11.1**
> **Providing Choice: The Treasure Box**
>
> Teachers, parents, counselors, pediatricians, dentists, and others who work with children can use a clever device called the "Treasure Box" for delivering reinforcers following a challenging, yet productive, session.
>
> • Survey your population's parents, friends, and/or the children themselves to identify safe, inexpensive, popular toys and/or materials.
> • Place them in a box decorated to look like a treasure chest.
> • Prepare a pictorial and/or written set of simple rules.
> • Post the rules.
> • Review the rules with the client(s).
> • Choose a few times when the client is following the rules to compliment and remind him or her of the waiting surprise.
> • On completion of the session, or when the criterion is met, compliment the child and allow him/her to choose a surprise from the treasure box.

within routines reduces protests and increases task initiations (Dibley & Lim, 1999). After reviewing 14 studies on choice-making from 1975 to 1996, Kern et al. (1998) concluded that choice-making in (a) vocational or domestic activities, (b) academic activities, and (c) leisure, recreational, or social activities "resulted in behavioral improvements with some, if not all of the participants" (p. 151). Others (Toussaint, Kodak, & Viadescu, 2016) also report that clients prefer choice-making opportunities and that they often result in increased treatment efficacy. Thus when feasible, *provide your clients with a variety of high preference reinforcer-choice opportunities*. Choice, paired with variety and novelty, are all incorporated in the **Treasure Box**, *a motivational tool commonly used in homes and classrooms*. (See Box 11.1) Also, see Chapter 27 as to how choice can be used to help prevent the occurrence of problem behaviors.

## Providing Contingent Reinforcement under Diverse Circumstances: At Different Times, in Many Places, and with Different People

As pointed out in Chapter 4 on objectives, *generalization must be considered from the start*. That requires various people to deliver reinforcers whenever the target behavior occurs in appropriate situations throughout the day, particularly under those circumstances specified in the objective. Otherwise, the behavior is likely to be restricted to those limited situations in which they receive reinforcers, or to the people who deliver them. When teaching students who are unable to use functional speech to choose and exchange pictures to express their wants, needs, and bids for social attention, Bondy and Frost (2002) recommend supporting generalization of communication skills across objects and events, people and places. (You will read more about this *Picture Exchange Communication System [PECS©]* in Chapter 19.)

**Daily Report Cards.** A *daily report card* system (also sometimes called *daily behavior report card, home school note*, or *good behavior note*) is a clever mechanism for supporting contingent, specific, positive, frequent feedback and reinforcement across both the students' classroom routine *and* their home.

Chafouleas, Riley-Tillman, Sassu, LaFrance, and Patwa (2007) described a daily report card as a daily rating of one or more specific behaviors that is shared with someone other than the rater. A typical daily report card might contain items such as com-

| Name Joey Adams Date March 12 Daily Report Card |||||
|---|---|---|---|---|
| Today, Joey | Always | Sometimes | Once in a While | Never |
| Sat down quickly | | √ | | |
| Got his things ready | | √ | | |
| Went over the job he needed to do | √ | | | |
| Raised his hand for help | √ | | | |
| Did all his work | √ | | | |
| Finished his work on time | | √ | | |
| | | √ | | |
| **Comments**: Joey is doing better. Once or twice he was slow to get down to and finish his work, but he is being more careful and remembers to raise his hand for help. Please compliment him for his improvement and put his "good work" magnet on the refrigerator. | | | | |

**Figure 11.1** An illustrative daily report card

pleting assignments, following directions, helping when asked, and/or making progress toward other behavior-change objectives. See the illustrative daily report card on the next page (Figure 11.1). Usually, a teacher rates the behavior and shares the information with the parents, who reinforce improvements or positive ratings. Teachers of students with special needs often find the "daily report card" to be particularly helpful (Chafouleas, Riley-Tillman, & Sassu, 2006). The daily report card system has been "widely accepted and used across a variety of situations to intervene with challenging behaviors and to document change in those behaviors" (Chafouleas et al., 2007, p. 30), including effectively decreasing problem behaviors in preschool settings (LeBel, Chafouleas, Britner & Simonsen, 2013). They also have been used effectively with six- to seven-year-old students with intellectual and developmental disabilities, as well as behavior challenges, who were receiving extended school year services as mandated by their respective Individualized Education Plans (Taylor & Hill, 2017). Teacher ratings on the cards appear to be similar to those collected by external observers using systematic direct observation or a daily report card form. Perhaps some day you might consider using daily report cards as a convenient way to estimate the quality of a student's performance and/or as a compliment to a more complete behavioral assessment (Chafouleas et al., 2007).

**Behavioral contracts.** *Behavioral contracts* (first introduced in Chapter 4) also can be used across a range of clientele as a mechanism for ensuring that behavior-change methods are conducted in a fair, ethically responsible manner (Brooks, 1974; Luiselli, Putnam, & Sunderland, 2002; Robinson & Rapport, 2002; Sulzer-Azaroff & Reese, 1982). They also may serve to reinforce progress, minimize goal conflicts, and to support unified team efforts. Some contracts are designed very simply: to communicate *who* is to do *what* with or to *whom,* by *when,* with what *anticipated outcomes* (e.g., an agreement between a client and care provider, supervisor and employee, parent and child, teacher and student). Others are much more formal and detailed, perhaps legally binding. See Figures 11.2 and 11.3.[2] Behavioral contracts have several advantages, including

---
[2] See the text Web page (www.sloanpublishing.com/balc) for additional examples of behavioral contracts.

> Monday, October 3, 20____
>
> If Harold completes reviewing the Arnold contract before the end of the workday on Friday, then, at 5 P.M., Arthur will take him to Fiorno's and treat him to a pizza dinner!
>
> _____
> (Harold Procrastinator)
>
> _____
> (Arthur Eager)

**Figure 11.2** An informal behavioral contract

---

Client: David Jones      Mother: Mrs. Jones
Counselor: Mrs. Deneau   Math Teacher: Mr. Callaway
Effective Date: Feb. 21 to Feb. 28.

**Goals**
Long-term: David will graduate from high school.
Short-term: David will complete his homework assignments in math and earn a grade of C (or better) on his homework.

**Responsibility**
(Who, What, When, How well)

1. David will turn in his completed math assignment to Mr. Callaway at the beginning of class
2. Mr. Callaway will correct David's Homework and inform Mrs. Deneau of his grade by 1 p.m. each day.
3. (If the homework does not earn a grade Of at least a C, this contract will be revised next week.

**Privileges**
(Who, What, When, How much)

David will be excused from the last period of the day (study hall) so he can go to work 1 hour early.

Mrs. Deneau will thank Mr. Callaway and she will keep all graphs of David's progress.

David will be excused from the last period of the day (study hall) so he can go to work 1 hour early.

**Bonus**
If all assignments are turned in for the week, and all are graded C or better, David can leave for work 2 hours early on Friday.

**Penalty**
None

Who will monitor the behavior? Mr. Callaway and Mrs. Deneau

What records will be kept? Homework assignments; number turned in and grade.

Who will be responsible for the delivery of reinforcers, privileges? Mrs. Deneau

Signed  David Jones   Date: Feb. 17   Thomas W. Callaway   Date: Feb. 17
            Client                     Teacher  Janice C. Deneau  Date: Feb. 17

        Marilyn S. Hancock  Date: Feb. 18   _____
            Counselor                              Mother

This contract will be reviewed (date) Feb. 28

**Figure 11.3** Contract with a high school student [Based on Sulzer-Azaroff & Reese (1982, p. 22)].

keeping goal conflicts to a minimum, delineating the roles of participants in the change process, and specifying individual and mutual outcomes.

Participants should be able to enter into the agreement free from coercion. This can be accomplished by obtaining their voluntary informed consent. This information must be communicated at a level that will be understood by the client or advocate if consent or rejection is to be considered "informed." In a formal legal document that involves minors or dependent people, consent will need to be obtained from parents, legally-designated guardians, or advocates. Attorneys representing organizations serving children or dependent people should know the age of consent in their jurisdictions. For instance, currently the age of consent is 16 in Canada and 18 in the United States.

Therefore, the negotiation of behavioral contracts should consist of discussing the various goals and methods, as well as how the participants might be affected for better or worse. This includes as many short- and long-term benefits and costs as can be anticipated. Benefits may include enhanced personal, social, academic, or job skills, or diminished rates of particular responses that interfere with desired outcomes. Costs could entail increased expenditures of resources (materials, time, and effort); loss of control or power or of other social rewards; increases in unpleasant events, such as delays until clients are dressed, amplified noise levels, being required to wait patiently, and so on.

Another feature of contract negotiation is the participants' *freedom to terminate the contract*, and the conditions under which termination is acceptable. For example, if Ramon decides to change his vocational objectives, he may renegotiate his contract. All parties to the contract have a right to be informed and consulted about any participant's wish to terminate. Terms, of course, depend on a number of factors, yet spelling everything out in advance should minimize misunderstandings. Maya has a tendency to lose her temper at the slightest provocation. In a moment of fury, she might decide she wants to leave the program immediately. For someone like Maya, stipulating a 48-hour cooling-off period prior to withdrawal would be reasonable. Other contracts might stipulate participating in a meeting with a human rights advocate prior to withdrawal. Though it may not be legally binding, a behavioral contract freely negotiated by concerned parties provides evidence that care has been taken to incorporate voluntary informed consent into the program.

Behavioral contracting is a tool that can serve a valuable function within the behavior-change operation. (The importance of therapeutic behavioral contracts was first noted by Ed Sulzer in 1962), Now, developing and implementing behavioral contracts for supervisory purposes has not only been recommended as an effective supervisory training practice in the field of applied behavior analysis (Sellers, et al., 2019), but also is one of the standards of professional practice endorsed by the Behavior Analysis Certification Board (BACB).

## Reducing, Overriding or Removing Competing Contingencies

Behavior does not occur in a vacuum. Human environments are filled with a complexity of competing contingencies. Think about those operating on your behavior at any one time:

- Reinforcement for your performance of assigned educational or job tasks; punishment for nonperformance.
- Attention from friends—or perhaps inattention in social settings.
- Consequences from parents, spouses, or roommates for the chores you do or don't do.

Sometimes, the contingencies directly oppose one another. For example:

- Reinforcement in the form of getting good grades by staying home on the weekends and studying versus social reinforcers provided by friends when you join them on the weekend.
- Parents teaching a child she can't get what she wants by throwing a tantrum versus giving the child a candy bar at the checkout line to stop her from crying and embarrassing them.

Contextual stimuli guide your choice of activities outside the home—shopping, recreation, traveling, and just about all of your other actions. The path people follow depends in good measure on which particular contingencies are, or have been, most powerful. Alone with his teacher, Elmer's completion of his tasks might be sustained just by her approval. But as one of 28 children in her class, Elmer is rarely alone with his teacher. Instead, his environment consists of a network of contingencies. For instance, Elmer may find Jane's giggling at his grimaces far more reinforcing than the teacher's approving his academic performance; or avoiding his buddies' ridicule more reinforcing for misbehaving than avoiding a scolding by conforming to school rules. From his teacher's perspective, in a one-to-one setting, any slight improvement in Elmer's performance could be reinforcing; but in the class setting, the relief she experiences by ejecting Elmer from the room and no longer having to contend with his antics might be even more reinforcing.

You can see why successful programs depend on using A-B-C analyses, scatter plots, and so on to assess the contingencies currently in operation in the person's life. *When natural contingencies support competing behavior, managed contingencies must be powerful enough to override, reduce, or eliminate them, or the entire effort will be to no avail.* For example, Elmer's teacher would need to heavily reinforce both Elmer's remaining on-task and the other students ignoring his disruptive behavior (a strategy described in the next chapter on group contingencies).

When we have noted conflicting external contingencies operating, we have addressed this issue by identifying all family and personnel (e.g., school psychologists, clinical psychologists, psychiatrists, occupational therapists, speech/language specialists, and medical doctors in the case of students with language delays and/or social issues, or personnel managers, supervisors, worker representatives and concerned others in a manufacturing enterprise). Then we organize a strategic planning session, during which we discuss common goals, illustrate promising contingencies and organize, implement, and monitor systems in support of those goals. (See Chapter 24 and the Mayer and Wallace (2020) consultation text for further suggestions along these lines.)

The teacher who finds removing Elmer from the room more reinforcing than witnessing his marginal progress might be furnished with supplementary reinforcers for keeping him in class and coping with the problem. Approval from supervisors and consultants, changes in responsibilities more to the teacher's liking, and encouragement from peers might combine to shift the balance.

Some reinforcers happen automatically (i.e., those directly produced by the response) and may not be amenable to manipulation. Therefore, changing the behavior may depend upon *overriding* those current reinforcers with even more powerful ones. For example, Mary likes sucking her thumb. Regardless of what you do, you can't change the fact that sucking her thumb reinforces Mary's thumb-sucking. Thus, to change her behavior, you might have to provide an even "stronger" reinforcer to encourage her to keep her thumb out of her mouth, perhaps by rewarding her for blocks of time when her hands are occupied in productive activities incompatible with thumb-sucking (playing, doing crafts projects, squeezing a ball, and so on). Thumb-sucking typically stops when children reach a certain age, perhaps in part because social consequences become relatively more important as children interact more and more with peers.

Sometimes, rather than overriding them, you can *remove* competing contingencies to assist you in attaining your goal. Suppose you are on a weight-loss diet. Think how clever you would be to remove your favorite high calorie desserts from the refrigerator so they don't "call your name" and instead you see and choose to eat a carrot.

## Avoiding Reinforcing Behaviors Targeted for Reduction

Iwata (1987) has urged us to "identify how environments that we create may provide negative reinforcement for undesirable behaviors" (p. 365). Despite our best intentions, parents, teachers, managers, and others inadvertently may be teaching the very behaviors they are trying to eliminate. By failing to address the negatively reinforcing function that particular forms of misbehavior serve the individual, we actually may be promoting the very behavior we are hoping to eradicate. A student is being naughty.

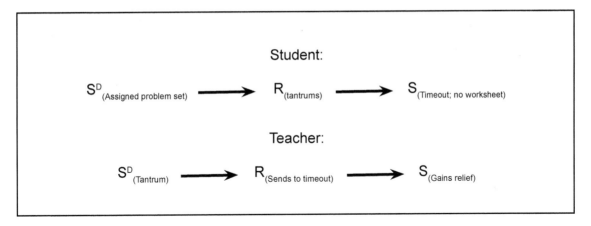

**Figure 11.4** One person's intended timeout may turn out to be negatively reinforcing for either one or both. Better watch the data carefully!

The teacher assigns him to timeout (to sit in an isolated area). This arrangement allows him to escape or avoid some unwanted task, demand, assignment, or person.

Let us look at another example: Jim screams at the top of his lungs when his teacher asks him to complete a difficult assignment. The teacher takes the materials away and places him in a distant area of the room, away from the other children. He has successfully escaped from, or at least temporarily avoided, the task. (Simultaneously, the behavior manager's actions have been negatively reinforced, in that placing the individual in timeout removes the disruption.) We can see an unhealthy cycle evolving in Figure 11.4.

In technical language, we could say that both the student and the teacher *escaped* from aversive situations, or that the behavior of both was negatively reinforced.

Avoiding negatively reinforcing undesirable behaviors is not the only issue. For example, if you want to develop independent responding it might be best to not reinforce responding that requires you to provide additional prompts to evoke the desired response. Investigators (Hausman, Ingvarsson, & Kahn, 2014) reported that independent responding is likely to occur at higher rates for some children when correct responses that follow additional verbal prompts (given due to an incorrect response or no response) were not reinforced than when they were. In other words, they found it best only to reinforce the correct responding that occurred following the initial response (e.g., "match coins"; "spell words"—by inserting correct missing letters), and to not reinforce when additional prompting was necessary to obtain the correct response.

People also sometimes positively reinforce problem behavior unintentionally. For example, when an individual does something annoying, the manager might try to redirect the individual to another activity, thereby providing the attention he or she seeks. Teachers may attend to students who call out answers rather than raising their hands. Parents often are seen giving a child a toy or candy to terminate a temper tantrum, thereby positively reinforcing the tantrum.

Such inappropriate uses of reinforcement can be avoided by: (1) having a clear understanding of how positive and negative reinforcement work, (2) carefully observing the effects of given consequences (that is, determining whether contingent consequences maintain or increase the behavior), and (3) by using functional assessments to determine the function of the targeted behavior.

## Using Reinforcement Schedules to Promote and Support Lasting Change

A **reinforcement schedule** is defined as *the "rule followed by the environment in determining which among the many occurrences of a response will be* *reinforced"* (Reynolds, 1968, p. 60). If his supervisor praises him every time Oscar follows safe weight-lifting practices, this is **continuous reinforcement (CRF)**—*a schedule of reinforcement in which each occurrence of a response is reinforced.* More typical, though, is the situation in which workers are only occasionally complimented for lifting safely: **intermittent reinforcement**—*a schedule of reinforcement in which some, but not all, of the occurrences of a response are reinforced.*

**Continuous reinforcement (CRF).** Many different schedules of reinforcement have been identified. Each has its distinctive properties and produces reasonably predictable effects. We know that *when the goal of an intervention is to increase or stabilize behavior, using a very dense or even a continuous schedule of reinforcement is best.* As Daniels and Lattal (2017) point out: "A common failure of people who are trying to teach or change behavior is to reinforce too little in the early stages" (p. 60). If parents are trying to teach their children a new routine, the more often they reinforce implementation of that routine, the better. The Hendricks decide that the time has come for Amber and her brothers to put their dirty dishes in the sink. Every time the children comply, their parents should pour on the praise. After the behavior has become fairly well established (is occurring very consistently, at a high and steady rate), they can reduce the frequency and regularity of reinforcer delivery. Generally it is not possible for a parent, teacher, employer, or anyone else to reinforce every occurrence of all desired behavior indefinitely. That is actually a good thing because, as shown in the chapters on maintaining behavior, established behaviors will withstand conditions of non-reinforcement (extinction) better after the individual has been exposed to non-continuous reinforcement. *Use CRF for increasing and stabilizing a behavior,* but not for maintaining it over the long haul.

To change our own well-established behaviors, most of us initially require frequent reinforcers. If you are a trainer, supervisor, or consultant to employees, management, or staff, your success will depend in large measure on the extent to which your trainees receive regular and frequent reinforcers. Indeed, the use of consistent reinforcers may well prevent staff burnout. The value of frequently delivering reinforcing feedback has been shown in many studies. In one study, Balcazar, Hopkins, and Suarez (1985–1986) examined 126 reports of the use of feedback as a management tool. They noted that the strongest improvement in participants' performance included use of regular feedback, especially when paired with other reinforcers and/or goal-setting. In another example, Austin, Weatherly, and Gravina (2005) combined periodic verbal feedback with task clarification and posted graphic feedback weekly to increase the dishwashers' and servers' completion of closing tasks in a privately-owned restaurant. Results showed a 15 and 38 percent increase in task completion for the two work shifts.

While you may dismiss the notion of continuously reinforcing a set of behaviors as being totally impractical, don't be so fast! You may be able to succeed if you plan your solutions creatively. Though contingency managers' personally-mediated reinforcing feedback can be especially powerful,[3] other potential vehicles exist: charts, graphs, telephone calls, and notes of the type illustrated in Chapter 6, and these can be mediated by peers and even by the performers themselves. In any case, dense reinforcement must continue until desired performances are repeated at high, steady rates over time.

**Intermittent reinforcement.** Once change is reasonably well established, reinforcement can be scheduled to occur more intermittently. You might gradually begin to reduce the frequency of such reinforcers as praise, phone calls, charts, and graphs to a comfortable, workable level. Along with ongoing social support, such intermittent reinforcement should enable you to diminish the amount of time you need to devote to the program, and, of greater convenience, is the fact that you need not repeat the exact same schedule of reinforcement each time. Fortunately, intermittent reinforcement has been shown to be especially well-suited to maintain-

---

[3] Elsewhere you will learn that feedback in and of itself is not necessarily reinforcing, as when it is used to correct unwanted behavior.

ing behavior change. And interestingly, laboratory research results have suggested that, under some conditions non-human subjects have been observed to choose unreliable (variable) reinforcer schedules, over dependable ones (Lalli & Mauro, 1995). In the latter case, the researchers posited that other factors such as signaling, the duration of the reinforcement schedules in effect, the context in which the signaling occurs, and the effects of secondary reinforcement may influence the behavior of organisms, including humans.

Interestingly, most youngsters appear to prefer to delay reinforcement if it is of sufficient magnitude. For example, adolescents appear to prefer to complete a larger set of responses if it is followed by a longer duration of access to the reinforcer (Bukala, Hu, Lee, Ward-Horner, & Fiend, 2015; DeLeon, et al., 2014; Fienup Ahlers, & Pace, 2011). However, younger children (e.g., pre-school) may prefer several smaller sets of responses followed by brief reinforcer access that result in the same overall amount of work and reinforcement (Ward-Horner, Muehlberger, Vedora, & Ross, 2017). As pointed out by Ward-Horner et al., the younger children may be more impulsive and need a richer (i.e., more frequent) schedule of reinforcement. Or, perhaps they have not been taught delay of gratification. It would appear, then, that before an initial schedule is selected, ask your clients what they prefer, or observe what schedule they appear to perform best under. And, as emphasized earlier, reinforce alternative behaviors while gradually thinning the reinforcers contingent on the target behavior (Drifke et al., 2020).

Supporting the extra effort involved in delivering reinforcers can be daunting. Yet, in their study on school principals as agents of change for teacher performance, Cossairt, Hall, and Hopkins (1973) found that teachers maintained and even increased their praise of student work when they (the teachers) were praised intermittently for doing so. Usually when combined with other antecedent control strategies such as instructions, modeling, rehearsal, and/or goal-setting, intermittent feedback also has improved a broad array of skills: employee cleaning performance (Austin et al., 2005), teachers' implementation of discrete-trail teaching (Sarokoff & Sturmey, 2004), skill practice by female soccer players (Brobst & Ward, 2002), and supervisor performance (Green, Rollyson, & Passante, 2002). Consequently, as elaborated in Chapters 3 and 24, you will want to ensure that staff members are *trained* to an acceptable level of competence and

---

**Box 11.2**
**Selecting Effective Reinforcers**

Beth continually failed to download her work on time. Mark thought he had been using reinforcement properly, but Beth's tardiness in downloading continued. He asked for our advice.

We asked Mark to describe how he used "reinforcement." Mark mentioned that he promised Beth that if she downloaded her work on time for the next six months, he would give her a $25 gift certificate to a local department store. He explained that his choice of the gift certificate was based on an employee-wide survey.

Take a moment to note how Mark used reinforcement to try to change Beth's behavior. Describe a different and more promising way that he might adjust the above strategies to improve the way he implements reinforcement.

*****

Now for our analysis: First and foremost, the reinforcement was not immediate, in that even if Beth downloaded her work as planned on any given Friday, it could take up to six months until she earned her reinforcer. Consequently, assuming Beth met the download schedule on time on Friday, we would suggest that Mark provide her with a "reinforcer" at 5:01 P.M.

Because it would be impractical for Mark to distribute a $25 gift certificate to Beth every Friday (plus, just because it may work for most employees, we do not know if it will work for Beth), we explained to him how each Friday he might instead distribute tokens to her, as merited, and allow her to use her tokens to earn a gift certificate to a store of her choosing after a month or two. This new arrangement would permit Beth to choose from among multiple items available at her preferred store. The tokens would also prevent Beth from satiating on any particular reinforcer, in that she could select from a variety of available of items.

regularly *supervised* in using reinforcement along with other procedures or skills they are expected to apply. (Specific strategies or schedules for thinning reinforcers are discussed in Chapters 22 and 23.) (See Box 11.2 for an integrative example of selecting effective reinforcers.)

## SELF-MANAGEMENT: ITS FEATURES AND FUNCTION

Self-management can be an effective, time-saving method of behavior change. Although some may choose to share a few of these responsibilities with others, capable self-managers should be able to perform all the following five skills fluently before they can be said to be capable of total **self-management**:

- *Selecting their own goals*
- *Self-monitoring*, or observing and recording their own behavior (usually using permanent product, event, or duration observational recording systems)
- *Selecting procedures* for changing their own behavior
- *Implementing the procedures*, including reinforcing their own behavior
- *Self-evaluating*, including monitoring and determining how effectively the procedures enabled the targeted behavior to match an external standard or criterion

Using even a few of these self-management components, such as self-monitoring, can lead to impressive results.

When designed and implemented with care, self-management permits people to provide their own reinforcers and/or to supplement those delivered by other change agents, while in the process augmenting the *choice, variety, frequency,* and *immediacy* of reinforcer delivery. In other words, self-management can serve to maximize the effectiveness of reinforcers. It minimizes the client's risk of becoming a victim of coercion, can help reduce behavior problems (McDougall, 1998; Reid, 1996), and often is preferred by participants over standard instruction (Wolko, Hrycaiko, & Martin, 1993).

Most importantly, *it frees the client from having to depend on others for their reinforcers*.

Many illustrations of populations who have used self-management successfully have been reported in the behavioral literature:

- Those with severely handicapping and other disabling conditions (e.g., Fowler, Baer, & Stolz, 1984; Graham & Harris, 2003; Reid, 1996; Shapiro & Klein, 1980)
- Children with emotional and behavioral disorders (Hansen, Wells, & Kamps, 2014: and Smith & Sugai, 2000)
- Children with moderate learning disabilities (Boyle & Hughes, 1994)
- Youngsters with ADHD self-regulating, maintaining attention, sustaining effort, modulating motor activity, and organizing and finishing tasks (Reid, Trout, & Schartz, 2005)
- Children with autism who frequently engaged in stereotypic behavior (Koegel & Koegel, 1990), and for engaging in reciprocal social conversation (Koegel, Park, & Koegel, 2014)
- Four-year-old pre-school children with various handicapping conditions (Ainsman, Mayer, Jogoleff-Olstad, & Brown, 2018; Briesch & Briech, 2016; Kartal & Ozkan, 2015)
- Elementary, middle school, and secondary students with learning disabilities with a history of frequently staying off-task (Dalton, Martella, & Marchand-Martella, 1999; Shimabukuro, Prater, Jenkins, & Edelen-Smith, 1999; Wolfe, Heron, & Goddard, 2000)
- Children and youth at-risk for school maladjustment and academic failure (Hughes & Hendrickson, 1987 Peterson, Young, Salzberg, West, & Hill, 2006; Wood, Murdock, Cronin, Dawson, & Kirby, 1989)
- Low-achieving Korean elementary school students (Lee & Tindal, 1994

- Low-performing regular high-school students (Moore, Anderson, Glassenbury, Lang, & Diddan, 2014)
- A post-institutionalized 13-year-old striving to improve on-task behavior within a regular classroom (O'Reilly et al., 2002)
- Young gymnasts working on the balance beam (Wolko et al., 1993)
- People of all ages with nervous habits such as nail-biting, finger sucking, hair twirling, tics, and so on (Miltenberger, Fuqua, & Woods, 1998)
- Employees needing to improve work engagement (Breeevaartt, Bakker, & Demerouti, 2014)
- Teachers learning to use specific praise (Simonsen, MacSuga, Fallon, & Sugar, 2013)
- Vocabulary acquisition (Hogan & Prater 1993)
- Reading comprehension (Edwards, Salant, Howard, Brougher, & McLaughlin, 1995; Shimabukuro et al., 1999)
- Math productivity (Brown & Frank, 1990; Lee & Tindal, 1994; Prater, Hogan, & Miller, 1992; Shimabukuro et al., 1999)
- Written expression (Shimabukuro et al., 1999)
- Responsiveness to verbal initiations and reductions in disruptive behavior in children with autism who displayed severe deficits in social skills (Koegel, Koegel, Hurley, & Frea, 1992)
- Reduction of disruptive behaviors and increases in on-task behaviors (Reid et al., 2005; Shimabukuro et al., 1999; Wood et al., 1998)
- Drug dependency (Higgins & Budney, 1993)
- Parental skills in modifying their children's anti-social behavior (Serketich & Dumas, 1996)

After reviewing 24 studies wherein workers self-monitored productivity or safety behaviors, Olsen and Winchester (2008) concluded that behavioral self-monitoring was effective across a variety of workplace settings and behaviors, including direct care and teaching behaviors, ergonomic postures, sales of services, safe driving, and wearing personal protective equipment. Several colleagues of our acquaintance have taught high-school-age youngsters behavior principles and supervised them as they modified their own behavior. Similarly, we ourselves have taught college and graduate students self-management skills (Sulzer-Azaroff & Reese, 1982).

The efficacy of self-administered reinforcers was demonstrated years ago (e.g., Perri, Richards, & Schultheis, 1977). Those authors discovered a major difference between college students who were successful in reducing their smoking rates and those who were not; the former group reported that they delivered more earned reinforcers to themselves. Similarly, Heffernan and Richards (1981) found that college students who monitored their own behavior and administered the reinforcers had better study habits and grades.

Through role playing, an aide taught a fifth grader to practice managing his own behavior in math class, earning praise as a result (Stevenson & Fantuzzo, 1984). In addition to an environment that apparently initiated and/or supported interventions of this nature, steps included:

1. Setting a goal for the number of problems to be completed accurately.
2. Counting and recording on a chart the number of problems correctly completed.
3. Comparing the number with the predetermined daily goal.
4. Awarding himself a gold star if he achieved his goal.
5. Exchanging the gold stars for various items from a self-determined menu of reinforcers.

Weekly meetings with the aide, who provided intermittent reinforcers, prevented his self-management skills from deteriorating. Not only did the boy perform better in math, but so did the boy next to him, who was not trained in self-management (this carryover was probably due to modeling effects and fewer distractions). Also, the deportment of both students improved in school and at home.

Peterson et al. (2006) taught five inner-city seventh- and eighth-grade general education students, at risk for school failure, five basic social skills: staying on-task, following instructions, accepting "No" for an answer, accepting teacher feedback, and appropriately obtaining teacher attention. They were also taught how to observe and record their own behavior. If on Friday their personal self-monitoring matched their teachers' ratings across the five different classes, they were awarded points exchangeable for back-up reinforcers, such as school materials (e.g., pencils, writing tablets, paperback novels), game time (e.g., chess, Connect Four, checkers), computer time, and snacks (e.g., chips, candy, soda). As a result, all five students improved their social skills across all class periods. Similarly, by 1) providing a form to elementary students with moderate learning disabilities; 2) modeling how to self-monitor each time a tone sounded, and; 3) by praising correct use and correcting misuse of the technique, Boyle and Hughes (1994) taught students how accurately to discriminate and record whether they were on-task or not. Eventually, reinforcers provided by the teacher were terminated and the frequency of the tone gradually diminished, requiring the students to record less and less frequently. Ultimately, the form also was removed and the students were requested to periodically silently ask themselves if they were working. This training resulted in substantial increases in both time on-task and task productivity.

In the study by Reid et al. (2005) listed earlier, the authors reported the results of a meta-analysis of the literature on various self-management programs for children with ADHD: "self-regulation interventions can produce meaningful improvements in student on-task behavior, academic productivity and accuracy, and reduction of inappropriate or disruptive behaviors" (p. 373). Also, investigators (Schonwetter, Miltenberger, & Oliver, 2014) were able to increase the number of laps that high school swim team members performed once self-monitoring began. When feedback was added, an additional increase in the percentage of assigned laps were accomplished as was the accuracy of the self-recording.

## Using Successful Self-Management Methods

What methods make self-monitoring and self-management successful? Jones, Nelson, and Kazdin (1977) and Sulzer-Azaroff and Mayer (1986) have speculated, and recent research has supported, the notion that a number of external variables can be especially influential in producing effective self-management systems: Linking self-management procedures to functional analysis results, the individual's history as related to self-management, criteria setting, self-monitoring, surveillance, and external consequences for self-reinforcing and as a consequence of the emission of the target behavior. Here we elaborate on these:

**Link self-management procedures to functional analysis results.** Individual self-management programs designed to diminish maladaptive behaviors have been found to work best when procedures are selected on the basis of a functional behavioral assessment (see Chapter 10). For example, to guide their design of a self-management program, Kern, Ringdahl, Hilt, and Sterling-Turner (2001) used a functional assessment to select replacement behaviors functionally equivalent to the undesirable target behavior. Each participant of a group of 4- to 8-years-olds was taught to self-manage appropriate behavior as well as appropriate requests for reinforcers (i.e., escape, attention, materials). Each was taught to self-record one of the following: "I played by myself or asked appropriately for attention"; "I worked or asked for a break appropriately"; and, "I asked for the toy nicely or waited my turn." Smith and Sugai (2000) also based their self-management program on the results of a functional assessment on the problem behavior of a seventh-grade boy with emotional and behavior problems. After determining that the function of the boy's inappropriate comments to peers and teachers and talking to peers during work-alone time was to gain teacher and peer attention, the behavior analyst taught him to record his own work completion, raise his hand appropriately, instruct himself to "keep cool," and to recruit adult attention in more socially-acceptable ways. Accurate self-recording was also reinforced with adult attention. As a result, he completed more work, spent more time on-task, and decreased his rates of talk-outs. Similarly, working with three school children with emotional and behavior issues, Hansen et al. (2014) determined the function of their behaviors, and not only did the students' various behaviors improve when those reinforcers were self-delivered, but they also found the intervention more effective than consequences delivered by teachers.

An advantage of this approach is that individuals learn not only to reduce problem behaviors, but also learn socially appropriate and functional replacement behaviors. For instance, in the Kern et al. (2001) study, individuals not only lessened their rates of throwing objects, kicking, cursing, hitting, hair-pulling, pinching, biting, and destroying materials, but they were also taught socially appropriate and functional replacement behaviors.

**Determine the individual's history as related to self-management.** Both the individual's prior involvement in a program of training to learn self-administration of reinforcers as well as the length of time the target behavior has been treated by external contingencies can be influential, because they help determine the nature of the change process. When implementing self-management strategies you will first need to provide an intensive program of *training*. Here you will need to teach your participants to compliment themselves, take breaks, and/or engage in a preferred activity immediately contingent on meeting criteria for improvements, such as amount of progress and/or accomplishments. Prior to gradually shifting primary control over to the individual, continue to apply external contingencies intermittently to establish a history sufficient to support the behavioral change and the person's continued production of appropriate self-management sequences.

**Set criteria.** Criteria for assessing success can be imposed externally, set by those involved, or be the result of a collaborative process. Different outcomes may be achieved, depending on whether goals are lenient or stringent. The results of several goal-setting studies suggest that the most promising approach is to have individuals set fairly challenging, though achievable, criterion levels. (See Chapter 4 on goal setting.)

**Incorporate self-monitoring, as appropriate.** Systems that incorporate self-administration of reinforcers typically include *self-monitoring*— observing and recording one's own behavior. As we learned previously, the very act of observing and recording has been found to influence performance. Separating self-monitoring from self-reinforcement is not always possible, so the degree to which the two factors interact remains unclear. Richards (1981) concluded that with individuals "motivated to self-monitor and change their behavior self-reinforcement may occur naturally" (p. 163). The amount of effort or the time individuals invest in the process, though, depends upon the extent to which their environment supports the change. To illustrate, the productivity rates of adults with developmental disabilities employed in a sheltered workshop increased only when self-monitoring was combined with reinforcement from others (Mace, Page, Ivancic, & O'Brien, 1986). External reinforcement alone was less effective than external reinforcement combined with self-monitoring. Similarly, Petscher and Bailey (2006) used a combination of self-monitoring, prompting, and feedback on accuracy to successfully help instructional assistants to accurately implement a token economy. Agran et al. (2005) taught general education seventh- and eighth-grade students with moderate to severe disabilities to self-record their frequency of (1) acknowledging a given direction, (2) beginning the activity, and (3) completing the task, and calculated the percent of completed steps in the task sequence. Verbal feedback and praise were provided contingent on the students' responding. "All students learned the strategy and maintained their performance at mastery levels for the duration of the maintenance condition. Social validation from participating general and special educators supported these findings" (p. 3). Teaching such skills, and supporting the change with self-recording, improved the students' performance in general education, thereby increasing their opportunity to become mainstreamed. Similar studies of self-recording among at-risk elementary- and middle-school students, with and without disabilities, who were assigned to inclusive classrooms also demonstrated meaningful academic improvements (Rock, 2005; Wood, Murdock, & Cronin, 2002).

Ballard and Glynn found that third-graders' self-recording of writing "did not increase the number of sentences, number of different action words, or number of different describing words, or improve the quality of the stories" (1975, p. 387). Only after self-selected and self-administered reinforcers were added did their response rates and story-quality ratings increase substantially. Martella et al. (1993) decreased the negative statements of a middle-school student with mild learning disabilities ("I'm going to kill you," "I hate this f---ing calculator") by teaching him to self-record whenever he made such a comment. He then received reinforcers, in the form of being allowed to select from posted reinforcer menus, for correctly discriminating between positive and negative statements, as well as for self-recording accurately. If his recordings agreed with those of the trainer at least 80 percent of the time and the number of negative statements was at or below a set criterion level, he could choose a small reinforcer. If he achieved the criterion for four consecutive sessions, he could choose a larger reinforcer. As a result, his negative statements decreased while his positive statements collaterally increased. Likewise, Hayes et al. (1988) demonstrated that external feedback needed to be combined with self-administration of reinforcers for the study skills of college students to improve. Hence, the effectiveness of self-monitoring and self-administration of reinforcers appear to be dependent, at least to some extent, on supportive conditions. We suggest that you combine self-reinforcing and self-monitoring procedures, particularly when natural reinforcers are delayed or obtained infrequently.

Another factor that can affect the value of self-monitoring is the impact of the particular self-monitoring procedure on the behavior. In a study in which pre-teen-aged boys self-monitored their swimming rates, if the self-monitoring interrupted the behavior, as it did when swimmers needed to pause to mark laps completed, the rate of the behavior decreased to a level *lower* than when no self-monitoring was employed (Critchfield, 1999). Critchfield aptly recognized that "Characteristics of self-monitoring procedures must be selected to fit the situation of interest" (p. 391).

Spieler and Miltenberger (2017) used self-monitoring without self-recording. They taught college students to become more aware of and reduce their use of nervous habits during public speaking by teaching them to monitor their behavior. Three habits were targeted for reduction: pauses filled with sounds such as "um" and "uh," tongue clicks' and the inappropriate use of the word "like." Participants were first shown a video in which they identified instances of their using these habits. Then during speech delivery each participant was asked to raise their hand each time a target behavior occurred. The instructor (investigator) also raised her hand each time a target behavior occurred during the early phases of the speech. After the occurrence of the first five target behaviors, the investigator only raised her hand to prompt the participant when he or she failed to detect the occurrence of a target behavior within two seconds. After several such sessions, each participant reduced their nervous habits and improved their overall public speaking ability.

Note, helping the client to obtain greater awareness by self-monitoring the target behavior can help increase or decrease its occurrence depending upon the goal of the client. This is probably one reason why specific praise or punishment works: It helps the client to become more aware of the target behavior like self-monitoring does.

**A caution in using self-monitoring.** We have found that several of our students were having their clients collect baseline data for them. As a result, we have added this paragraph in our book: Because self-monitoring has been shown to change behavior, it actually can function as an intervention. Consequently, if you seek an accurate assessment of the behavior as it typically occurs prior to the intervention, *avoid using self-monitoring as a means of collecting baseline data.* Self-recording itself, as you now know, can promote client behavior change, thereby resulting in an inaccurate assessment of the true baseline.

**Reinforce the accuracy of self-monitoring and self-delivery of reinforcers (surveillance).** Epstein and Goss (1978) involved a 10-year-old, highly disruptive boy in a self-management program because it appeared that a positive reinforcement program would be too "burdensome for the teacher to maintain" (p. 111). After training the child in self-evaluation, they asked him to score his own behavior. If the teacher agreed with the score the boy had given himself for the day, they doubled his points. This aspect was important, for *youngsters' and adults' self-reporting is more likely to be accurate when accuracy is reinforced.* (See Ainsman & Mayer, 2018; Boyle & Hughes, 1994; Broden, Hall, & Mitts, 1971; Fixsen, Phillips, & Wolf, 1973; Kazdin, 1974a; Kern et al., 2001; and Petscher & Bailey, 2006, for examples of the value of *accurate* self-recording). The boy could exchange the points for time playing games and extra recess for the entire class. The student maintained his improved behavior by enthusiastically adhering to this program throughout the rest of the school year.

The presence of an external agent, such as a teacher, employer, peer, consultant, or someone else who monitors how accurately people self-reinforce tends to encourage them to be more scrupulous in conducting their programs. McCann and Sulzer-Azaroff (1996) found that keyboard operators worked more safely when they monitored their own hand/wrist positions; but they improved their performance levels even further when they set their own improvement goals and when, along with reinforcement for evidence of improvement, external agents also presented their own scores as feedback. Even if the external agent is not intentionally monitoring the self-administration of reinforcers, individuals may be influenced by the person's presence. Whether to arrange for surveillance will depend on your own circumstances, but the data you collect will indicate which kind of surveillance works best.

You also may need to reinforce accurate reporting or penalize inaccurate reporting, as Speidel and Tharp (1980) discovered when they saw participants award themselves undeserved reinforcers. *From the very beginning, plan to use a system to reinforce accurate self-administration of reinforcers and to withhold reinforcers from inaccurate use of self-reinforcement methods. Do not wait until difficulties arise.* We have found that if we enthusiastically praise honesty during initial phases of a program, accuracy is more apt to persist.

**Use supplemental (external) consequences.** As mentioned earlier, *a supportive or socially-reinforcing environment is essential for achieving effective behavior change.* For example, sometimes (though not always) publicly announcing the number of reinforcers certain individuals earn can backfire, in the form of negative peer reactions. (Other times the method is quite successful.) If a target behavior readily improves and remains satisfactorily over time, avoiding highly-contrived external reinforcing methods is probably best, because the environment apparently is sufficiently supportive. But if arranging self-reinforcing strategies in isolation is insufficient, temporarily adding supplemental reinforcing contingencies may have merit. Eventually, you could try gradually to remove the external reinforcers to see if the self-administered reinforcers adequately support continuing improvement.

Another option is to have the participants recruit their own reinforcement, a strategy used by Todd, Horner, and Sugai (1999). Within a general education classroom, they trained Kyle, a fourth-grade student with learning disabilities and problem behaviors, to self-monitor and to self-recruit teacher praise. Kyle awarded himself a "plus" if he remained on-task during the preceding three-to-five-minute variable interval schedule. After Kyle gave himself three pluses for being on-task during instruction, he would raise his hand or, during group project time, walk up to the teacher and request feedback on his performance. The teacher then acknowledged and praised his good work. Over time, the time intervals were increased to every four to six minutes. This combination of self-monitoring and self-recruited feedback resulted in a "decrease in the frequency of problem behaviors, an increase in on-task behavior, and an increase in task completion." In addition, "the intervention was associated with increased positive teacher perceptions of student performance" (p. 66).

We repeatedly have stressed the importance of reinforcing environments, and will continue to do so throughout this text. However, should you wish to investigate this area in more detail, we call your attention to the following sources that elaborate on promoting reinforcing environments. One, a book by Tony Biglan (2015), *The nurture effect: How the science of human behavior can improve our lives and our world*, focuses on the importance of cultivating compassionate, positive, nurturing environments in all aspects of society. Another, authored by G. Roy Mayer (2020) is, *The positive classroom: Improving student learning and behavior*. It describes how to employ reinforcement as a tool to improve student learning and deportment.

## SUMMARY AND CONCLUSIONS

Several guidelines for optimizing the impact of reinforcement procedures have been presented in Chapter 6 and here in Chapter 11. When a reinforcement plan does not succeed, one or more of those guidelines may have been overlooked. To guard against this, when designing a reinforcement program, arrange to:

- Select reinforcers appropriate to the individual, using those as natural to the situation as possible.
- Reinforce immediately, if possible via specific praise alone; or, if necessary, augment with other identified reinforcing stimuli and/or add other promising strategies, until the behavior is occurring at a high and steady rate. Then gradually introduce a period of delay between the response and the reinforcer(s).
- Specify the conditions under which reinforcers will be delivered and provide other promising antecedent conditions.
- Use labeled or specific praise.
- Deliver reinforcement sincerely and enthusiastically
- Consider whether and, if so, which motivational operations may currently be operating.
- Deliver reinforcers in quantities sufficient to maintain the behavior without producing rapid satiation.
- Use a variety of currently effective reinforcers.
- Permit choice.
- Try to include both novel and general reinforcers.
- Provide opportunities for reinforcer sampling.
- Teach the behavior in a variety of situations.
- Consider the source of reinforcer delivery.
- Eliminate, reduce, or override competing contingencies.
- Avoid reinforcing behavior that interferes with acceptable conduct or is targeted for reduction.
- Initially reinforce very densely, until the behavior is well established; then gradually introduce intermittent reinforcement.
- Incorporate self-management into the program as feasible.
- Finally, and most importantly, do your best to *raise the general level of reinforcement in your setting*, because high levels of reinforcement promote positive behavior change.

Because self-management can function so effectively in support of behavior change, we described programs consisting of clients' self-selection of goals, observing and recording their own behavior, selecting and applying reinforcers for changing their own behavior, and determining the effectiveness of their self-management programs. Self-management programs bolster reinforcement programs by promoting discrimination and generalization, permitting more choice and frequent and immediate self-administration of reinforcers following the proper occurrence of each target behavior. Those programs also allow participants greater independence from external sources of influence. However, recall that self-management is a skill that needs to be taught and that involves various strategies, including following the same guidelines that make reinforcement work effectively under other circumstances. Also, we do not recommend that you depend on the data gleaned from self-recording when your aim is to collect highly precise, accurate baseline data, or for purposes of research.

# Summary Table: Increasing Behavior via Reinforcement

| Procedural Label/ Operation | Maximizing Effectiveness | Temporal Properties | Durability of Effect | Other Features |
|---|---|---|---|---|
| **Positive reinforcement:** Present positive reinforcer contingent on target response | 1. Clearly specify features of behavior to be reinforced<br>2. Plan for generalization (where, when, how, with whom or with what behavior should occur)<br>3. Identify pool of stimuli and assess for reinforcer effectiveness<br>4. Identify conditions under which reinforcers will be most effective<br>5. Specify conditions under which reinforcers will be delivered<br>6. Reinforce immediately<br>7. Use specific, sincere praise in an enthusiastic tone of voice<br>8. Deliver in quantity sufficient to maintain behavior without promoting rapid satiation<br>9. Select reinforcers appropriate to individual in that context<br>10. Consider or manage motivational operations<br>11. Vary reinforcing stimuli and situations<br>12. Incorporate novelty<br>13. Provide periodic opportunities for reinforcer sampling<br>14. Periodically review client's reinforcer choices to help avoid satiation<br>15. Select as reinforcers highly preferred stimuli as natural to the environment as feasible<br>16. Highlight saliency of the behavior-consequence relationship<br>17. Arrange for supportive sources of reinforcer delivery<br>18. Eliminate or minimize competing contingencies<br>19. Initially reinforce densely<br>20. Gradually thin reinforcement density<br>21. Combine with modeling or other prompts, if necessary and/or appropriate<br>22. Combine reinforcement with positive social events (praise, smiles, etc.)<br>23. Within group setting, provide feedback and reinforcement both individually and collectively<br>24. Once behavior high and steady, continue supporting generalization and maintenance by planning and introducing<br>• intermittent delivery<br>• delay<br>• reduction in the nature, size or value of reinforcer(s)<br>• fading of prompts | Gradual | Long-lasting | 1. Positive<br>2. Constructive<br>3. May occasion positive self-statements |

## Negative Reinforcement

| Procedural Label/ Operation | Maximizing Effectiveness | Temporal Properties | Durability of Effect | Other Features |
|---|---|---|---|---|
| **Negative reinforcement:** Remove aversive stimulus contingent on response | 1. Specify act to be reinforced<br>2. Identify ongoing aversive stimulation<br>3. Remove aversive stimulation *immediately* contingent on preferred act<br>4. Remove aversive stimulus *consistently* contingent on preferred act<br>5. Combine with positive reinforcement of desired alternative act(s), adhering to relevant guidelines listed above | Gradual | Maybe long lasting, especially in presence of stimuli discriminative for aversive events | 1. Aversive stimulation may evoke avoidance, escape, aggression<br>2. Behavioral increase may be restricted to teaching context |

*Chapter 12*

# Promoting and Supporting Group Change: Programs and Packages

## Goals

1. Define *group contingencies*.
2. Define, illustrate and differentiate among the use of three popular group contingencies.
3. Discuss the major advantages and disadvantages of *dependent* and *interdependent group contingencies*.
4. Define *extinction* and describe how to use group contingencies to achieve extinction conditions.
5. Define and discuss how to use *peer-mediated strategies*.
6. Justify involving peers as contingency managers and tutors.
7. Explain the reasons for the success of *peer tutoring* and *peer contingency management*.
8. Describe the circumstances under which to consider implementing a token economy.
9. Define and illustrate *token* and a *token economy*.
10. Define and illustrate *backup reinforcers* and differentiate them from tokens.
11. Differentiate between *natural* and *artificial reinforcers*.
12. List and describe the preliminary steps in setting up a token economy.
13. Describe how to maintain behavior while phasing out token economies.
14. Describe *tiered* or *level* token economy systems and discuss how they can be used to promote maintenance.

\*\*\*\*\*\*\*\*\*\*\*\*

Our living, working, and learning contexts influence the way we interact with and feel about ourselves and others. We enjoy reinforcing environments, but not punitive ones. In fact, the latter evoke escape, aggression, and emotional reactions—reactions that impede learning, productive performance, and individual or social harmony (see Chapters 29 & 30).

Within groups, the behavior of peers can have an enormous impact on the social environment. Peers control many positive stimuli: attention, approval, praise, and other forms of support along with many that are aversive: threats, coercion, criticism, and put-downs. In group settings, peer reactions may prompt and/or reinforce such desirable behaviors as becoming more *socially effective* (e.g., Robertson, Green, Alper, Schloss, & Kohler, 2003; Strain, Cooke, & Apolloni, 1976), remaining *on-task* (e.g., Payne, Dozier, Briggs, Newquist, 2017) and performing better academically (e.g., Egel, Richman, & Koegel, 1981; Heering & Wilder, 2006; McDonnell, Thorson, Allen, & Mathot-Buckner, 2000), becoming *more skillful* (Fleming & Sulzer-Azaroff, 1992), *safer* (Sulzer-Azaroff & Austin, 2000) and *productive* (Honeywell, Dickinson, & Poling, 1997). On the other hand, they may reinforce such unwanted acts as *disruption* (e.g., Flood, Wilder, Flood, & Masuda, 2002; Solomon & Wahler, 1973), *noncompliance*, *complaining*, and *fighting* (e.g., Christensen, Young, & Marchant, 2004; Christy, 1975).

## WHAT IS THE VALUE OF FORMALLY ARRANGING GROUP CONTINGENCIES?

Surely by this point we agree that our best hope as parents, teachers, consultants, or managers is to learn how to apply the rules for using reinforcement effectively. However, favoring a perspective is one thing; following through is something else entirely. With the best of intentions, any of us may falter occasionally because our learning histories and current circumstances often interfere.

Lurking in ambush, ready to sabotage our noble intentions, are the demands of daily life. As with so many of our best-laid plans, competing pressures seem continually to command center stage. One natural reaction is to give up in despair. Be hopeful, though; rescue is at hand in the form of "contingency packages": easily applied ABA procedural combinations, containing all the essential pieces. In this chapter we illustrate a few of the numerous possibilities available to you: a trio of group contingency arrangements, peer-mediated strategies, and token economies. Inventive contingency managers everywhere have designed other packages, and your mastery of behavioral principles and procedures may enable you to do so one day as well.

## ILLUSTRATIVE GROUP CONTINGENCIES

**Group contingencies** are *arrangements in which consequences are delivered to some or all members of a group as a function of the performance of one, several, or all of its members*. Among the various ways of organizing group contingencies, we describe three that many of our colleagues have found especially promising. Included are: distributing reinforcers to (1) individuals working *independently*, (2) those operating *interdependently*, and (3) those operating *dependently* (Litow & Pumroy, 1975). Here we define these, examine the nature of the peer reactions each tends to evoke, and discuss ways to apply each most effectively.

### Independent Group Contingencies

**Independent group contingencies** are fairly common group arrangements, often involving *setting the*

> Let's see... Besides all my other responsibilities, all I have to do is to remember to **reinforce** their performance by frequently providing them with *something they are eager to receive at that moment*, as soon as they make a move in the right direction.
> Piece of cake!

*same response requirements for all group members, but applying the reinforcers to performance individually.* The criterion level can be the same for each member, as when each participant earns reinforcers as a consequence of reaching a particular level. To illustrate: "Each assembly-line worker who meets the production quota will earn a bonus"; "Each student must have 9 out of 10 math problems correct to earn two tokens" (described below); "Every employee who meets his or her sales quota by the end of the month receives a $50 bonus." "Any student who obtains 90 percent or more on the exam receives an 'A.'" Alternatively, the criterion can vary to allow for individual differences, as when one child is required to complete 10 arithmetic problems and another child, 20; or when a more skillful worker receives a higher pay rate than her peers who are performing the same job, but more slowly. Because any person failing to achieve the standard loses access to the reinforcer, one member's reinforcer does not depend on the performances of others in the group. Independent group contingencies permit each individual to profit regardless of the performance of other members in the group, so peers have no incentive to try supportive (e.g., tutoring) or coercive (e.g., bullying) tactics to influence one another. Ennis, Blair, and George (2016) were able to decrease classroom disruptions and increase appropriate behavior with an independent group contingency. Moreover, the authors compared the effects of four types of group contingencies (independent, interdependent, dependent, and random), and all were demonstrated to be equally effective. However, teachers indicated their preference for the independent and dependent group contingencies.

## Interdependent Group Contingencies

**Interdependent group contingencies** involve *treating the members of a group* (class, row of students, sales division, personnel in a particular production or surgical unit, and so on) *as if they were a single behaving entity. The behavior of the group is reinforced contingent on the collective achievement of its members.* In an occupational example, after the team of workers in each section of the assembly line met the weekly quality-level standard goal (e.g., percentage of non-defective shoes), the group foreman assembled the group, showed them the graph displaying their accomplishment, congratulated them, and distributed refreshments (Sulzer-Azaroff & Harshbarger, 1995). In a recent study, Hawkins, Haydon, Denune, Larkin, and Fite (2015) demonstrated the use of an interdependent group contingency to improve the transition between lunch and class in high school students with emotional behavioral disorders. Besides utilizing an interdependent contingency related to students receiving reinforcement contingent on a group of students transitioning appropriately, they incorporated a random criterion related to the number of students in the group who had to transition appropriately for the group to receive reinforcement.

---

**Interdependent Group Contingency**

**Collective performance of all group members achieves criterion ⟶ reinforcer (S$^r$)**

---

An interdependent group contingency was used that required residential treatment workers to meet two-week attendance criteria to participate in a subsequent drawing for prizes (Brown & Redmon, 1989). Staff members were eligible for a bimonthly lottery contingent upon cottage staff attendance totals. If the unscheduled cottage sick leave totaled between 7 and 16 hours for two consecutive weeks, the staff of that cottage could select one worker to participate in the lottery. If the total for a cottage was 0 to 6 hours, two workers were eligible to participate. Employees who won the lottery were allowed to choose one of the following rewards: (1) four hours of paid time off; (2) twenty dollars; (3) four movie passes; or, (4) a paid lunch and "feedback" session with a supervisor. "Significant reductions in unscheduled sick leave in each work unit" (p. 13) were obtained during this five-month study.

An interdependent group contingency successfully diminished the noise in a public school classroom with the help of a decibel meter to monitor sound level (Schmidt & Ulrich, 1969). Any noise, regardless of source, was registered, and everyone had to cooperate to keep the noise level below a preset criterion for the class to earn extra gym time. A similar procedure was effectively applied in a school cafeteria (Michelson, Dilorenzo, Calpin, & Williamson, 1981). Other investigators (DePaolo, Gravina, & Harvey, 2019) used a combination of negative reinforcement with an interdependent group contingency to improve the performance of 12 collegiate women's lacrosse players. The negative reinforcement involved removing sprints at the end of practice for desired group performance.

Costello and Smyth (2017) used interdependent combined with an independent group contingencies to help improve attendance for at-risk adolescents (13 to 17 years of age). They identified ten at-risk male adolescents, each who served as a captain of a fantasy football team. Each selected four other students to serve on the team. Points were earned for the team attendance, completion of projects, completed work sessions, each half hour of good behavior, while misbehavior during the half-hour resulted in the loss of a point. Ten points were lost if a player appeared in court, was arrested, or violated his bail conditions. Any points earned or lost by the team captain were doubled in value. A weekly ranking for each team, as well as each player, was publicly posted. Prizes were given each week to the wining team, or the team could build up their weekly prize money. "A significant increase in school and project attendance was noted from baseline to intervention" (p. 379).

In another case, second- and third-grade students at risk for severe behavior disorders participated in both an independent and an interdependent group contingency (Thorne & Kamps, 2008). The *independent* procedure consisted of distributing lottery tickets to individual students for appropriate behavior. Four or five of those lottery tickets were drawn twice a day and winners won small rewards (e.g., pencils, stickers). For the *interdependent* aspect of the program, after every student in the class recorded having earned 27 lottery tickets, the class earned a pizza. Not only did the groups earn pizza parties about once a month, but their academic engaged time increased and inappropriate behavior decreased within each class as a whole.

Unlike individual and competitive contingencies, interdependent group contingencies may promote relatively higher rates of academic achievement and cooperation in regular classrooms (Hamblin, Hathaway, & Wodarski, 1974; Popkin, 2003; Slavin, 1983), and in classes for adolescents with emotional problems (Popkin, 2003; Salend & Sonnenschein, 1989). Those in the interdependent group arrangement achieved the greatest academic productivity when the performance of each group member was clearly visible, quantifiable, and accountable to the other group members (Slavin, 1983). Building on this knowledge, Skinner, Cashwell, and Skinner (2000) paired interdependent group contingencies with public posting, with the result that fourth-grade students' reports of peers' prosocial behavior increased. Too often, peers tend to report on antisocial behavior (tattling), but this study demonstrated that peers can learn to focus instead on reporting prosocial behavior, helping to make the school environment become more positively reinforcing (a very important goal, see Mayer, 2020).

## Dependent Group Contingencies

Under **dependent group contingencies**, *group members attain reinforcers contingent on the behavior of a selected group or subgroup of members, or of a specific individual (e.g., supervisor, manager).* Reinforcers for dependent group contingencies do not, as with interdependent group contingencies, depend on the entire group's performance. For example, a retail sales organization could announce that all the clerks in a large department store will receive a bonus dependent on the three lowest performing clerks collectively meeting a certain sales target.

Sometimes the whole group shares an individual's earned reinforcers (Walker & Buckley, 1972) as in the case of one of the authors who played high-school basketball. It was not uncommon for the coach to pick one player to shoot a three-point shot. If the player made the shot, then the whole team got to leave practice 10 minutes early (a really powerful reinforcer since the last 10 minutes of practice entailed running drills). In the Hamblin et al. (1974) program, the class received reinforcers dependent on improvement in the level of the lowest three scores in the class. This arrangement encouraged the more able students to tutor the less advanced, thereby raising the achievement level for the group as a whole. Another study compared a dependent group contingency in one school (grades 2 through

---

**Dependent Group Contingency**

If performance of one or more group members achieves criterion, then $S^r$ (for all group members)

---

5) to an independent group contingency in a second school (Williamson, Williamson, Watkins, & Hughes, 1992). The dependent group contingency (if someone in the class guessed correctly, the whole class received a prize) resulted in superior estimation accuracy (guessing the number of objects in a container) and cooperation among students. Heering and Wilder (2006) used a dependent group contingency to increase the rates of third- and fourth-grade students' remaining on-task. They randomly chose a row to observe and determine the degree to which the students in that row were on task. Observers used momentary-time sampling to record either a *yes* or a *no* as the basis for determining whether all students in the row were on task. During baseline, on-task behavior was 35 and 50 percent in the third- and fourth-grade classrooms, respectively. During intervention, if students in the observed row were on-task for 75 percent or more of the observed intervals, the class was given access to previously identified preferred items or activities. Both classroom means rose above 80 percent during intervention. Similarly, a teacher designed a "work-meter," onto which she added five points when a target child in her class completed his assignment. When the meter reached a certain level, the whole class received a treat. The child's assignment completion increased.

Another study (Cariveau & Kodak, 2017) used the following dependent group contingency to increase academic engagement during small group reading and writing instruction. Second grade students were told: "I will randomly pick someone in our group. If I see the student following the rules I will choose an item out of this bag and all of you will get to play with it. You won't know who has to follow the rules, to earn the reward, so you should all try your best" (p. 125). Items in the bag were selected using a preference assessment based on a predetermined list of tangible items. Academic engagement improved for a number of students and continued at high levels after the dependent contingency was withdrawn.

## Advantages and Disadvantages of Dependent and Interdependent Group Contingencies

**Advantages.** In contrast to independent group contingencies, when interdependent and dependent group contingency arrangements are in place and the group members work to achieve a common goal or reinforcer, peers have often been noted to attempt to influence the performance of other group members by telling or showing the others what to do and how to do it (Frankowsky & Sulzer-Azaroff, 1975; Heering & Wilder, 2006; Speltz, Shimamura, & McReynolds, 1982; Van Houten & Van Houten, 1977). Cooperative learning or cooperative reward approaches (Axelrod & Greer, 1994; Johnson, Maruyama, Johnson, Nelson, & Skon, 1981; Slavin, 1991) frequently rely on dependent and interdependent group contingencies. In the cooperative learning approach, students working in small groups give one another help and suggestions to produce a single final product. This product is graded and each member receives the composite grade. When reinforcers are shared or depend on the accomplishments of others, people often try to boost one another's performance by prompting, reminding, encouraging, and helping one another. When used in schools, academic performance tends to improve (Hamblin et al., 1974; Speltz et al., 1982), as do peer interactions (Eisner Hirsch, Healy, Judge, & Lloyd, 2016).

**Disadvantages.** A potential drawback to such group contingencies, however, is that, in the absence of further rules, there is no guarantee that the pressure exerted on group members will be positive or supportive. Instead, participants may resort to threatening or punishing the performance of the peers upon whom their own reinforcers may depend (Axelrod, 1973; Romeo, 1998; Skinner, Cashwell, & Dunn, 1996). Although, as we have seen, positive interactions often do increase, to avoid coercion and its negative side effects. Should you contemplate using group contingencies, *be sure that all members can perform the task as required, and that criteria for reinforce-*

*ment are set at achievable levels.* As Axelrod and Greer (1994) have pointed out, it's fine to use group contingencies when the problem is motivational, but "it's another matter to apply group contingencies to academic behaviors where students lack the skills to perform the necessary behaviors" (p. 44).

Similarly, Van Houten and Van Houten (1977) demonstrated that while interdependent group contingencies heightened lesson-completion rates and peer comments favoring their team, supportive peer comment rates increased even further after members were taught how to remark positively on achievement. In a related case, an interdependent group contingency increased social interactions between children with autism and socially competent peers (Kohler et al., 1995). The interdependent group contingency increased sharing, assistance, and play organizing. Nevertheless, few or no correlated supportive exchanges occurred until the children were taught exactly how to provide direct supportive comments and how to prompt their playgroup members.

Sometimes other contingencies may be at work. For example, Stoneman and Dickinson (1989) found no differences between interdependent group contingencies and individual contingencies on assembly-line task production. They reported a "leveling effect" in which participants' productivity *within* a group did not differ much from one member to another, regardless of the type (i.e., group or individual) of small monetary contingency used. However, productivity *between* groups did vary, indicating that "an individual's performance was greatly affected by the performance of the other group members" (p. 146).

Although some studies have shown the negative side effects of peer interactions, others have shown no differences in negative side effects (Payne, et al., 2017). With that said, it would be remiss not to mention that if it is suspected that some members of a group lack the essential skills requisite for either performing the task at hand or providing supportive coaching to other members, group contingencies may not be appropriate. To be on the safe side, you would be wise to teach and rehearse skills such as coaching, prompting, and praising with participants who may need to assist their peers, and be certain to monitor peer interactions throughout. (See *peer-mediated strategies* below.) See Box 12.1 in which the three group contingencies are illustrated.

Given the advantages and disadvantages associated with each specific type of group contingency, it is no wonder that practitioners ask, which type of group contingency they should implement. Although each has been demonstrated to be effective, it wasn't until recently that their actual effects were compared. Vargo and Becknell (2019) compared the effectiveness of three group contingencies on reducing the disruptive behavior of typically developing eight-graders. Interestingly, even though all were equally effective, most students preferred the independent group contingency.

## Reducing Unwanted Behavior by Combining Group Contingencies with Extinction

In Chapter 6 we indicated that one way to identify a reinforcer is to withhold the suspected reinforcing stimulus and see if the behavior upon which it is contingent subsequently decreases. When operant behavior no longer produces any discernible reinforcers at all, the behavior probably will decrease. As we know, an *extinction* procedure consists of withholding *all* sources of reinforcement contingent on a behavior. But, achieving total extinction conditions can be difficult when peers are the source of many reinforcers.

Ramon frequently made noises and jokes that disturbed his coworkers and attracted the attention of his manager and peers. The manager decided to implement a dependent group contingency by allowing him to earn points exchangeable for an extended lunch break for the whole group. The points were contingent upon gradually longer periods of time during which Ramon did not disturb others and continued work at his station. However, to avoid the possibility of Ramon's peers becoming angry with him while he was distracting them from their tasks, and to help extinguish the disruptive behavior, the manager also implemented an interdependent group contingency. That is, if his coworkers ignored Ramon's antics instead of telling him to "shut-up," laughing, and so on, they still earned points toward the extended lunch break. While ignoring Ramon's antics, the manager also quietly acknowl-

> **Box 12.1    Applying Various Group Contingencies**
>
> **Case Example: Using Group Contingencies**
>
> Mr. Macky, an elementary-school principal, believes that in-service instruction is one of the most important components of staff development and effectiveness. Whenever such training sessions are offered, though, only about half of the teachers at his school attend. Mr. Macky hopes to increase attendance by offering an end-of-year Gala Dinner as the reinforcer. What are some group arrangements he might plan to increase the effectiveness of that reinforcer?
>
> Here we offer one possible response for each type of group contingency:
>
> **Independent** (remember to apply the contingency to each teacher's performance separately):
> *Mr. Macky could give each teacher a ticket to the Gala Dinner contingent on attending the in-service session.*
>
> **Interdependent** (remember to make the reinforcer contingent on the whole group's performance):
> *Mr. Macky could inform the teachers that if everyone (all 20 teachers) attends the next in-service session he will arrange a Gala Dinner for them.*
>
> **Dependent** (remember to either have the group receive reinforcement contingent on one person's or a sub-group's behavior): *Mr. Macky could select the teachers who normally don't attend the in-service sessions and make the Gala Dinner contingent on at least 75 percent of those teachers attending the session.*
>
> Now propose your own, different example of how Mr. Macky could use each of the three categories of group contingencies to increase the number of teachers attending the training sessions.

edged Ramon's coworkers for their restraint, and of course complimented Ramon whenever he earned a point. Coworkers quickly learned not to respond to Ramon's antics, and Ramon learned to work quietly. (You can use a similar strategy, of course, in various situations. For example, replace "manager" with "teacher," "extended lunch break" with "special class activity," and "coworkers" with "class" and you have a school example.)

Numerous examples of group contingencies operating to reduce unwanted behavior have appeared in the research literature over the last 60 years. For example, Patterson (1965) described an approach in which the classmates of Earl, a hyperactive 9-year-old boy, were rewarded for withholding their attention during his antics. Earl and his classmates also could obtain candy or pennies from a "magic teaching machine" whenever Earl was on-task for a short period of time. Extinction conditions were rapidly achieved, resulting in a decrease in Earl's antics, and the teacher himself appreciated the more favorable classroom environment. In a similar study by Broussard and Northup (1997), the class earned access to preferred items and activities for not attending to their peers' disruptive classroom behavior.

Flood et al. (2002) approached the problem of removing peer attention to disruptive behavior more systematically. They taught peers in a simulated math classroom environment to differentially reinforce and prompt on-task behavior and extinguish off-task behavior among children with attention-deficit hyperactivity disorder (ADHD). All participants reduced their rates of off-task behavior and completed more math problems. Adding permitting access to preferred items contingent on math completion further improved the behaviors. (The method of training and supervising peers in the present example is actually a *peer-mediated strategy*, a topic we address shortly.)

Group contingency arrangements have been studied extensively within organizational behavior management (e.g., Wageman, 1995). As research on this topic continues, it becomes increasingly clear that beyond the particular *class* of contingency (e.g., independent vs. interdependent vs. dependent), variations *within* the class can powerfully influence the ultimate outcome. Measurable factors (or *parame-*

*ters*) such as task requirements, group size, characteristics and skill level of members, the nature of the reinforcing and/or discriminative stimuli, the rules governing the delivery of reinforcers, and many others can affect which group arrangement might be ideal in a given situation.

Notice that although extinction is part of all of the previous illustrations, it is always combined with group contingencies that make the continued delivery of reinforcers likely. By doing so, the undesirable side effects of taking away reinforcers are less likely to be seen, and the likelihood is increased that alternative (presumably more acceptable) behaviors will be strengthened.

## DEFINING AND APPLYING PEER-MEDIATED STRATEGIES

Some group arrangements of the kind described above serve indirectly to promote peer cooperation and assistance. Directly planning and implementing **peer-mediated strategies** can be even more powerful and have been applied successfully by behavior analysts working in a breadth of organizational areas, including in the rapidly growing area of behavioral safety.[1] Such tactics involve *directly training, supervising and monitoring peers as "co-therapists," coaches, or tutors* (Greenwood et al., 1988). To illustrate, in a series of investigations sponsored by the U.S. Occupational Safety and Health Administration (OSHA), Sulzer-Azaroff and colleagues demonstrated that following training and support, peers working in a paper mill could independently function as peer safety monitors and coaches, which resulted in increases in safe behavior and reductions in accidents.[2] Within educational settings, illustrations include *classwide peer tutoring* (Jones, Ostojic, Menard, Picard, & Miller, 2017;

Bowman-Perrott, Greenwood, & Tapia, 2007; Delquadri, Greenwood, Whorton, Carta, & Hall, 1986) and *partner learning* (McNeil, 1994; McDonnell et al., 2000). In these studies, peer contingency managers, from preschool children to adults, were trained, supervised, and monitored by a teacher, counselor, psychologist, consultant, supervisor, behavior analyst, or employer to serve in co-therapist or tutor roles. Peers were taught to deliver reinforcers or other elements of a planned behavior-change program. In comparing group contingencies to peer–mediated strategies, Axelrod and Greer (1994) asserted that a peer-mediated strategy is a *more powerful, stronger data-based approach* to teaching individuals than just the use of group contingencies. Thus, "wise teachers would probably opt for trained tutoring" (p. 44) over simply arranging group contingencies.

Involving peers as job coaches, trainers, tutors, or in other teaching capacities is broadly practiced in job and educational settings. One survey found that peer training is the most frequent method used to orient coworkers to new job functions. Moreover, peers have effectively implemented interventions for decreasing problematic behavior exhibited by others (Flood et al., 2002; Jones et al., 2000; Northup et al., 1995). Peers from the preschool to university level, as well as within job settings, also act as tutors. Peer contingency managers may, for example, help teach successful participation in routine preschool activities, including circle/story time, on-task behavior, interactive play (Robertson et al., 2003), incidental teaching (McGee, Almeida, Sulzer-Azaroff, & Feldman, 1992), or some other social interaction (James & Egel, 1986). They may deliver points within a token economy (Greenwood, Baskin, & Sloane, 1974), contingently withhold attention (Fowler, Dougherty, Kirby, & Kohler, 1986; Goldstein & Wickstrom, 1986), or provide reinforcing feedback (Bowman-Perrott et al., 2007; Fleming & Sulzer-Azaroff, 1992). Similarly, peer tutors present learning tasks, monitoring and responding contingently to the performance of their tutees (Greenwood, Delquadri, & Carta, 1997; Yurick, Robinson, Cartledge, Lo, & Evans, 2006). In one study, peer-mediated intervention was found to be more effective than using the traditional teacher-mediated method of teaching elementary students with developmental

---

[1]See the Web sites for organizations with a special focus on behavioral safety, including the Special Interest Group on Behavior Safety affiliated with the Association for Behavior Analysis International (http://www.abainternational.org) and the informational material the lay audience posted by the Cambridge Center for Behavioral Studies at http://www.behavior.org.

[2]Grant from National Institute of Occupational Safety and Health, 1983–1985.

disabilities health and safety facts such as body parts, drugs and their effects, poisons, and dangerous situations (Utley et al., 2001). It has also been shown that peer-mediated Check-In/Check-out can be effectively used to improve the social skills of neglected students (Collins, Gresham, & Dart, 2016).

Peer-mediated interventions also are effective with children with autism. Kamps, Dugan, Potucek, and Collins (1999) used fourth graders to tutor first graders with autism to recognize sight words. They found that not only was the peer tutoring more effective than traditional instruction, but that the process increased the first graders' time and social engagement with typical peers. Kamps et al. (2002) concluded that "peer training formats that have included the use of modeling, prompting, and reinforcement strategies within the context of activities, and those that included multiple peers over time, have shown notable changes in interaction skills for students with autism" (p. 183). Peer mediated interventions also have been found effective in promoting generalization of various social skills among adolescents with autism (MacFarland & Fisher, 2020). Similarly, investigators (Bass & Mulick, 2007; McConnell, 2002; Odom et al., 2003; Strain & Schwartz, 2001) have reviewed a number of studies using peer-mediated approaches with children with autism. Typical conclusions are that peer-mediated strategies are an "emerging and effective practice" (Odom et al., 2003), and that such approaches "represent the largest and most empirically supported type of social intervention for children with autism" (Bass & Mulick, 2007, p. 727).

Peer-mediated strategies have been used across other child populations. Christensen et al. (2004) used same-age peers as change agents in helping to implement positive behavior support plans of two male third-grade students who were at risk for social and academic failure. Both students showed immediate, marked improvement in their socially appropriate classroom behavior and their gains maintained as reinforcement was thinned. Similarly, McDonnell et al. (2000) examined a partner-learning process with fourth- and fifth-grade students: One student with severe disabilities and two peers without disabilities provided one another with spelling practice and review. The results obtained from weekly spelling tests "indicated that partner learning led to improved spelling accuracy for the student with severe disabilities and did not negatively affect the spelling accuracy of their peers" (p. 107). It also led to improved rates of academic responding and reduced rates of competing behavior for five of six students. Older students participated in a study by Harris, Marchand-Martella, and Martella (2000), in which it was found that partner learning increased at-risk high-school students' reading fluency and reading performance scores on standardized tests. Yurick et al. (2006) examined the effects of peer-mediated repeated reading on students' reading skills, in which the students read in pairs, each alternating paragraphs every 10 minutes. The students, regular third and fourth graders, followed a scripted correction procedure when errors occurred. This peer-mediated procedure resulted in improved oral reading rate, reading accuracy, and comprehension.

Using effective prompting and reinforcement techniques does not necessarily come naturally to peer-coaches, tutors, or trainers. Despite the fact that approval, recognition of accomplishments, and statements of caring are among the most commonly powerful reinforcers known, learning to apply these reinforcers optimally is a skill requiring reinforced practice. A number of schemes have been devised to promote competence in those skills. Informal methods are designed to heighten the level of social reinforcement in general,[3] while next we examine a few more systematic approaches.

**Systematically involving peers as contingency managers.** As emphasized earlier, peers may have a powerful influence on group members' performance, especially when they are proficient at applying social reinforcement. Considering why and how peers should be more formally involved in behavioral programs, therefore, should prove of value to you:

- Given their frequent, daily contact, peers are usually in an excellent position to continuously *monitor and respond regularly and rapidly* when target behaviors occur (Bowman-Perrott et al., 2007; Strain et al., 1976).

---
[3]See "informal methods for training peers to be socially reinforcing" on the text Web site.

- Peers provide a *natural context* for teaching social skills.
- Peer-managed intervention is often *preferred by the clients* (Phillips, Phillips, Wolf, & Fixsen, 1973).
- Peer tutoring promotes effective improvements in academic areas: *reading* (e.g, Fischer, 1999–2000; Fuchs, Fuchs, & Kazdan, 1999; Greenwood, 2001; Veerkamp, Kamps, & Cooper, 2007), *math* (e.g., Allsopp, 1997; Fuchs & Fuchs, 2001; Mayfield & Vollmer, 2007), *spelling* (e.g., Bowman-Perrott et al., 2007; Cheung & Winter, 1999), *computer literacy* (e.g., Newell, 1996), *biology* (e.g., Bowman-Perrott et al., 2007) and *prevention of school failure in general* (e.g., Greenwood & Delquadri, 1995). A systemic review of peer-mediated interventions (Dunn, Shelnut, Ryan, & Katsiyannis, 2017) reported that the most consistent gains have been observed in spelling, math, reading, and English.
- Peer involvement more readily promotes targeted behavior occurring in the natural environment, across new settings, times of day, and under conditions that follow program termination than when others manage the contingencies (Kohler & Greenwood, 1986; Smith & Fowler, 1984; Strain, 1981).
- A peer who has served as a contingency manager is likely to *cue* the client to engage in the desired behavior following program termination (Robertson et al., 2003; Smith & Fowler, 1984).
- "Peer-mediated intervention programs present clear benefits both for the children receiving intervention and the children providing intervention" (Smith & Fowler, 1984, p. 214). Not only do the clients benefit from learning the social, work, or academic skills being taught, but the peer managers also often learn the skills better, sometimes improving almost as much as the client does because of the augmented opportunities for practice (Dineen, Clark, & Risley, 1977; Flood et al., 2002; Harris et al., 2000; Jones et al., 2000; Mayfield & Vollmer, 2007; Yurick et al., 2006).
- Peer mediated interventions can help promote maintenance. For example, investigators (Beaulieu, Hanley, & Roberson, 2013) taught four typically developing preschoolers to attend to their teacher when she called their name individually, or as part of a group. However, these skills did not maintain until peer mediation was introduced consisting of peer reminders and/or praise for responding to the teacher's request for attention.
- Individuals "retain more of what they learn and make greater advances in social competence ... compared to traditional teacher-led instruction" (Bowman-Perrott et al., 2007, p. 67).
- Peer tutoring has been demonstrated to be more cost effective than reducing class size, computer-assisted instruction, or increasing learning time (Levin, Glass, & Meister, 1984).
- Peer tutoring has been found to be more effective than conventional instruction (Bloom, 1984; Bowman-Perrott et al., 2007; Utley et al., 2001; Veerkamp et al., 2007).
- Students participating in peer-tutoring programs for at least one academic year perform considerably better than the peers who have not participated (Whorton, Walker, Locke, Delquadri, & Hall, 1987).

Peer-mediated strategies help overcome logistical difficulties that change agents often face in attempting to reinforce frequently, consistently, and immediately. In an after school program, Grauvogel-MacAleese and Wallace (2010) were able to use peers to manage problem behavior and help academically during a study hall. Peer tutoring among school children has been shown to be beneficial in the following ways:

- Reducing classroom behavior problems (Greenwood et al., 1989; Flood et al., 2002; Jones et al., 2000; Kohler, 1986; Wolfe, Fantuzzo, & Wolter, 1984).

- Increasing social interactions between children with autism and typical children within a play and other contexts (Kamps et al., 2002; McGee et al., 1992).
- Improving interpersonal relations between racially or ethnically different students (Johnson & Johnson, 1983; Sharan, 1980) and persons with and without disabilities (Anderson, 1985; Johnson, Johnson, Warring, & Maruyama, 1986; Kamps et al., 1999; McDonnell et al., 2000; Wilcox, Sbardellati, & Nevin, 1987).
- Improving peer affiliation, self-concepts, and attitudes toward school (Maheady & Sainato, 1985; Pigott, Fantuzzo, & Clement, 1986; Roswal & Mims, 1995).
- Improving academic performance indicated previously and below.

**Why are peers successful as contingency managers and tutors?** We have provided various reasons why peers can serve as effective contingency managers (e.g., control of multiple contingencies, frequent contact, promoting generalization, etc.). Peer tutoring increases student engaged time (Bloom, 1980) along with providing participants the opportunity to respond to academic material orally and in writing (Greenwood et al., 1997; Hall, Delquadri, Greenwood, & Thurston, 1982). Each is necessary for academic achievement (Delquadri et al., 1986). Without a doubt, peer tutoring can produce "powerful and practically important academic and social effects" (Greenwood et al., 1988, p. 262). Further, it appears that meaningful gains can be obtained regardless of what role students play: tutor, tutee, or alternating between roles (Dunn et al., 2017).

Successful peer management programs depend upon peer tutors or contingency managers being carefully trained, supervised, and gaining reinforcement for carrying out their roles as designed. A motivational plan for the tutors is essential. To illustrate, Veerkamp et al. (2007) found that results on weekly tests improved under class-wide peer tutoring (CWPT) as compared with teacher-led instruction. In addition, they found that CWPT plus peer-tutor eligibility to participate in a lottery resulted in even further improvements. Similarly, Bowman-Perrott et al. (2007) found that class-wide peer tutoring among high-school students with emotional and behavioral disorders was more effective when combined with a class-wide self-management program in which students were awarded citizenship points by their peers based on how well they worked with and followed tutoring procedures with their partner.[4]

## TOKEN SYSTEMS

Our next topic is one of the most elegant methods for conveniently optimizing contingencies of reinforcement: the token system. Simply stated, in a **token system** (also referred to as a **token economy**) the *contingency manager contingently delivers a learned (conditioned) reinforcer* (the **token** or **exchangeable** or **artificial reinforcer**) *in the form of a ticket, voucher, checkmark, or other symbolic item, which is exchangeable at a later time for a coveted reinforcing item or event* (the **back-up reinforcer**). (See illustration below.) The token gains its reinforcing qualities by being correlated with (first immediately; then later after a gradually extended time period) the delivery of a powerful "backup" reinforcer. Once those reinforcing attributes of the token have been demonstrated, the token-exchange requirement can be adjusted by changing the required number of tokens.

---

[4]If you plan to use peer tutoring, we urge you to include a motivational program and carefully review this text's Web site sections on *organizing a peer tutoring program* and *selecting and training tutors*.

---

**A Token System**
*Given appropriate motivational operations*

Antecedent stimuli ⟶ Response ⟶ $S^r$ (Token) ⟶ $R$ (Exchange of token) ⟶ $S^R$ (Backup reinforcer)

Token economies are hardly new and have been traced as far back as the fourth millennium B.C. Actually, money is a form of a token. Today, all of us are familiar with the coins, paper bills, tickets, checks, cash credits, and numerous other items we can exchange for goods, services, or rebates. But it took creative pioneers like Ayllon and Azrin (1968) and Wolf, Giles, and Hall (1968) to design methods that incorporate all the essential features of powerful reinforcement within token systems, and to test their efficacy, respectively, among in-patient psychiatric populations and delinquent youth. (See also Risley, 1997, 2005; Rodriguez, Montesinos, & Preciado, 2005; Schmandt-Besserat, 1979).

Numerous reports of the utility and efficacy of token systems have appeared and continue to appear, including as a feature of social-skills training programs for young, high-functioning children with autism (Chung et al., 2006), adherence to treatment in pediatric chronic or life-threatening health conditions (Carton & Schweitzer, 1996; Kahana, Frazier, & Drotar, 2008), increasing physical activity among chronically ill adults (Conn, Hafdahl, Brown, & Brown, 2008), increasing distance walked by adults with mild to moderate intellectual disabilities (Krentz, Miltenberger, & Valbuena, 2016), and increasing attentiveness and reducing disruptiveness among youngsters with attention-deficit hyperactivity disorder (Reitman, Hupp, O'Callaghan, Gulley, & Northup, 2001; see Figure 12.1 from Carton and Schweitzer, 1996), which illustrates the impact of a token system on a youngster's "willingness to cooperate" in a hemodialysis procedure (i.e., to remove waste products from the blood.) Student teachers

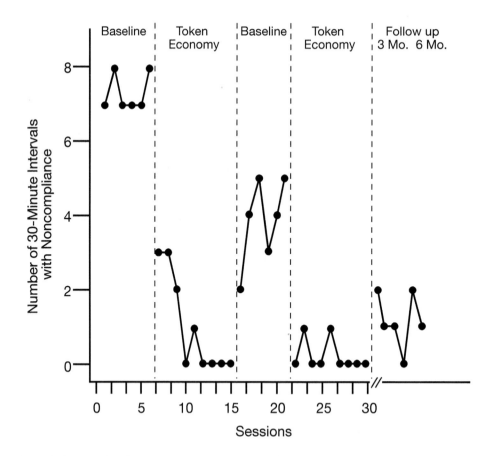

**Figure 12.1** The impact of a token system on a youngster's "willingness to cooperate" in a hemodialysis procedure. From Carton & Schweitzer (1996). © 1996 by the Society for the Experimental Analysis of Behavior, Inc.

also have used token systems to promote improvements in pupil learning and deportment (Fergusen & Brink, 2004).

## Advantages and Disadvantages of Token Systems

Presenting tokens is a much more practical and manageable practice than supplying reinforcers immediately contingent on target behavior every time it occurs. Permitting an assembly-line worker who meets a goal an extra break while the line is moving would interfere with production. Allowing Dexter to leave the room to shoot baskets as a reward for writing legibly during a spelling test would be disruptive. Awarding Marci access to her favorite leisure item for two minutes each time she completes a step on a stair climber would certainly be counter to the spirit of her exercise management program. But delivering a token exchangeable for access to the reinforcing activity at some future time could work just fine in each of those cases.

Other advantages of token systems are that they can be used with both individuals and groups under interdependent and dependent group arrangements. For instance, a teacher can stipulate that whoever hands in completed homework earns three tokens or that ten tokens can be used to purchase the first position on the lunch line. In these instances, common criteria apply to all members of the group.

Perhaps you fear, as others have, that "using a token economy in one classroom might harm pupil performance in situations wherein those contingencies do not operate" (Kistner, Hammer, Wolfe, Rothblum, & Drabman, 1982, p. 85). However, their study found no consistent effects in other classrooms as a result of the implementation of a token economy in one classroom. Furthermore, the token system did not appear to influence the children's attitudes toward teachers who did not implement a token system. "The token economy manipulation appeared to have a specific, desirable effect on the targeted behavior (i.e., work rate) and had minimal negative or positive 'side effects' on teacher popularity" (p. 85).

We have seen some teachers use play money exchangeable for items of varying costs within a token economy as a means of teaching the distinctive value of different bills, addition and subtraction skills, money management, and economic factors (e.g, how and why prices varying in relation to supply and demand.

Token systems also share some advantageous properties of tangible and other more natural reinforcers. When earned as an immediate consequence of a target behavior, they can acquire learned reinforcing properties (think money!), as well as signaling that other more powerful reinforcers will be forthcoming. In essence, tokens bridge the time gap between the behavior and the delivery of the reinforcer.

Informal token systems are fairly common, as when a teacher awards students points toward grades for assignments or a supervisor distributes lottery tickets to personnel who follow time-consuming safety precautions. A mother who dispenses checkmarks or gold stars that can be turned in later for money or special privileges is using a token system. And, of course, as mentioned, paychecks, script, vouchers, and money itself are all forms of tokens. (In 2008 it was reported that a number of schools in New York City rewarded teachers and students with money as a consequence of the students' improving their performance on standardized tests.[5])

Like coins and dollar bills, tokens possess little *intrinsic* worth. For example, if I handed you a piece of colored cardboard each time you said, "Thank you" and "You're welcome," your rate of uttering those phrases might not alter at all. However, if I invited you to exchange those pieces for a dollar each at the end of the day, they probably would begin to acquire reinforcing properties. The backup items or events for which tokens can be exchanged are what count. Haphazardly organized token systems, as in failing to follow tokens with backup reinforcers, are of limited benefit. But token systems that incorporate principles of effective behavior change have demonstrated their value across numerous populations, cultures, age groups, and behavioral targets.

Though token systems have a number of advantages, sometimes offering direct access to the back-up reinforcer works even more effectively. Investigators (Bonfonte, Bourret & Lloveras, 2020) compa-

---

[5] Medina, J. (2008, March 5) Next question: Can students be paid to excel? *The New York Times*, pp. A1, A19.

red the reinforcing efficacy of tokens versus primary reinforcers (edibles) with two adolescent males with autism. They reported that the "high-preference primary reinforcers maintained higher response frequencies than did tokens" (p. 1593). However, as we know, clients can satiate rather quickly on edibles.

To avoid recipients' satiating on any particular backup reinforcer, well-designed token systems also include an assortment of client-tailored items and privileges as backup rewards. Of course, timing, scheduling, managing the quality and amount (i.e., to prevent deprivation or satiation), and relating token delivery to social reinforcers are also important, as illustrated below.

## Considering Whether to Implement a Token Economy

Because token economies are artificial and require an investment of time and effort, reconsider for a moment before launching such a program, as it may contribute little beyond what simpler methods can achieve (Howie & Woods, 1982; Manos, 1983). For motivated clients, such as adults desiring to rid themselves of troublesome habits like stuttering, slouching, or interrupting, a simpler or more direct procedure can serve the purpose just as well. Developing an elaborate token economy would be like trying to kill a fly with an elephant gun.

When *should* you consider instituting a token economy? After:

- other more natural good teaching, management, and training methods prove unsatisfactory.
- tasks and materials have been matched to the interests and skill repertoires of the people involved.
- scheduling, group arrangements/contingencies, interesting activities, and other less complex but optimally arranged contingencies have not worked.
- resolving to avoid applying aversive contingencies.

- determining that the gap needs to be bridged between when the behavior occurs and the time when reinforcers can be consumed.
- teaching money management and economic considerations.

Preliminary planning is crucial because token economies can be intrusive and extra precautions need to be taken, including some related to legal and ethical considerations. Additionally, tokens may need to be eventually phased out and supplanted by reinforcers more intrinsic to the natural environment.

## Preliminary Steps in Designing a Token Economy

Before implementing a token economy, you need to take several steps. These may include obtaining approval and informed consent, familiarizing yourself with potential legal issues, developing a record-keeping system, and training and supervising staff.

**Obtain consent.** Token economies are relatively intrusive because they introduce many novel and artificial stimuli into a situation. Consequently, obtaining approval before implementing the program is a wise move. Describe the exciting data on token economies and the promise the system holds for enabling the program's participants to improve their learning and heighten their pleasure. Be prepared to respond to questions and concerns as you obtain the approval and informed consent from those who will be directly and indirectly involved: administrators, supervisors, and/or employers, union representatives, if applicable, and naturally the participating clients or their parents or other agents. It may be necessary to negotiate terms, for example, coming to consensus about a set of mutually agreeable backup reinforcers.

**Review the law.** If you are in a situation involving dependent clients (such as those residing in institutions or supervised residences), become familiar with laws delineating fundamental privileges to which they must have noncontingent access. In the United States, the outcome of the landmark Wyatt vs. Stickney case (1972, pp. 379–386, 395–407) led to a set of benign, protective legal provisions and protections for those clients, including those related to communication (mail and some telephone privileges); meals, including access to nutritionally adequate food in the dining room; the privilege of wearing their own clean clothing; space in specified areas; heating, air conditioning, ventilation, and hot water; specified furnishings for the residence unit and day room; bathrooms with clean, safe equipment and supplies; housekeeping and maintenance by the staff; and various clearly specified privileges connected with religion, exercise, medical care, grooming, education, and interaction. (Budd & Baer, 1976, have discussed this list in greater detail.) Education and mental health law at national and regional levels also has evolved, with an increasing focus on objective evidence of learning and/or behavior change. Naturally, laws adjust and differ between communities, states, and nations, so you must keep current with those affecting your clientele. If you have any question about the legality of withholding or using a particular reward or privilege in your setting, obtain legal advice.

**Develop a record-keeping system.** Besides the usual records you keep on changes in target responses, also plan to record token exchanges to determine high- and low-preference items to inform token price-setting. Record, as well, numbers of tokens earned and conditions under which they have been delivered. The conventional measures of the key dependent variables—the subject(s) of the intervention—inform us about how effectively the system is working, while the other records provide useful information for staff on how closely procedures are adhered to and signal when to alter the price of a backup reinforcer, vary response requirements, begin to phase out the economy, and so forth. Viewing data indicating improvement in targeted responses also can prove reinforcing to the staff and participants who are able to comprehend the results.

**Train and supervise staff.** The success or failure of a token program rests upon the precision with which it is implemented (including the care with which it is monitored), the way tokens are delivered, and how consistently other logistical aspects are implemented. Success is best accomplished by training participating personnel via video or live demonstrations, oral or written instructions, and group discussions, along with some direct practice. As in any effort to teach or alter behavior, instruction alone often is insufficient. Intermittently reinforced on-the-job practice, sometimes paired with self-monitoring and self-reinforcement (Watson & Tharp, 2007), is essential if newly acquired skills are to persist over time. Like everyone else, *staff members tend to keep a response going only as long as contingencies continue to support it.*

## Adjusting the Token System to Local Circumstances

Given their flexibility, token systems can and do tend to vary among clientele and across sites. Choice of backup reinforcers, tokens, delivery methods, and other features depend upon the population served, skill of participating personnel, economic, and various other considerations.

**Selecting backup reinforcers.** Central to the success of a token system are the material and activity (backup) reinforcers for which the tokens are to be exchanged. Usually these are of the kind not readily dispensed immediately contingent on the behavior of interest. Rather, they are items or activities whose delivery must be postponed for purposes of convenience or practicality. To illustrate, depending upon the recipients' developmental level, learning history, and contingencies currently in effect in the situation, you might include access to the items and activities which, given free reign, the person would readily choose: recreational activities like listening to music, reading, attending or participating in sports; tickets to films or theatrical events; privileges such as assignment to preferred jobs or work spaces, work or vacation schedules; access to computer games; specialized instruction; bonuses or salary increases; consumable treats; luxury activities (massages, manicures, etc.); lottery tickets; and others of the kind many of us long for. One big advantage of

> **Box 12.2  Using Readily Available Tokens:
> The Case of the Reluctant Fitness Participant**
>
> One of us (Wallace) supervised the exercise routine of a young woman with Prader Willi syndrome. (Prader Willi syndrome is a rare genetic condition characterized by cognitive impairment, lack of muscle tone, and insatiable hunger, leading to obesity.) To avoid interrupting the cardio aspect of the session, we instituted a token economy using a ticket, of the type found at carnivals, to be placed in a fanny bag worn around her waist. At the end of the session, she counted her earned tokens and redeemed them for access to preferred activities. Although we thought the tokens were not easily accessible outside of the training session, we were wrong. In fact, the clever young lady fooled us by locating a roll of tickets at her vocational setting and slipping them into her fanny pack prior to a session.

a token system is that it permits backup items and events to be changed along with shifting preferences at the time. However, even when using current high-preference reinforcers, be sure to use a variety from which the client can select. *Depending on one or two high preference reinforcers tends to be less effective in promoting behavior change than having a variety of backup preferred reinforcers from which to select among* (Becraft & Rolider, 2015).

**Selecting tokens.**  What kinds of tokens should be used? Among those familiar to us are plastic chips, "bankbooks" (Bucher & Reaume, 1979), trading stamps (Fox, Hopkins, & Anger, 1987), poker chips, points, stars (Claerhout & Lutzker, 1981; McGinnis, Friman, & Carlyon, 1999), tickets, stickers, letters (Campbell & Skinner, 2004), foreign coins, play money, beads, points, washers, coupons, holes punched in cards, beans or marbles in a jar, happy faces, and other similar objects. Robinson, Newby, and Ganzell (1981) used metal tokens that could be used to operate video and pinball games. Ask your clientele and staff for suggestions, but be certain your selections are not readily available outside the system (i.e., you do not want participants showing up with large numbers of unearned tokens), are safe (e.g., they should not be non-edible objects readily swallowed or capable of causing injury or harm), and are relatively indestructible for the population for which they are to be used. See Box 12.2 for an example of mistakenly using readily available tokens.

Another way to meet both logistical and instructional purposes with tokens is to try the method that Kincaid and Weisberg (1978) used to teach preschoolers to discriminate and name the letters of the alphabet. Tokens were chips on which letters were superimposed. Before being allowed to exchange a token for a backup reinforcer, the children were

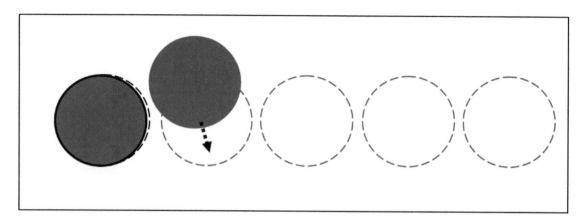

**Figure 12.2**  A simple token board

required to name the letter written on the token. No wonder the children rapidly learned the letters of the alphabet!

So, you can see that the form of a token may range from points in a grade book, on a chart, or on a blackboard to much more elaborate objects like play money, puzzle pieces, trading stamps, or instructional materials. Try simple systems first, such as using geometric shapes that can be placed individually into in a wooden, styrofoam, or rubberized form-board (Figure 12.2), using more elaborate methods only if they better suit your purposes. Other alternatives may consist of any items your clients are able to handle safely and that cannot be easily forged: trading stamps, stickers, beads, plastic forms, jigsaw-puzzle pieces, and many other items.

## SELECTING FLEXIBLE VERSUS FIXED EARNING REQUIREMENTS

Typically, token system are assigned a predetermined fixed value in advance of their being exchanged for back-up reinforcers. Flexible earning requirements, though, also may be effective. When investigators (Cihon et al., 2019) used a flexible token system with three four- to six-year-old children with autism, it increased their rates cumulative number of novel comments. The children were told:

> Today we are going to work on talking. Each time you talk, I will give you a mark (interventionist put a mark on the dry-erase board). If you have enough marks to meet or beat my magic number (interventionist drew a circle on the dry-erase board), you can take something home from the treasure chest (interventionist pointed to the treasure chest). (p. 551)

After three minutes passed during snack time, the children were told: "Let's see if you met or beat my magic number." Those who did were given access to the treasure chest to pick an item to take home. Those who did not, continued with the session.

## Implementing Token Economies Effectively

Assuming, as with any intrusive program, that you have obtained the necessary approvals, and that you have selected the form of tokens to use, developed a record-keeping system, and trained and supervised your staff, you are ready to review the factors that influence the effectiveness of a token economy.

To help establish the tokens as reinforcers, begin by allowing the token exchange to take place immediately. Once the tokens are established as reinforcers, then you can deliver them contingently on the target behavior(s), and gradually increase the delay or delivery and/or cost of the back-up reinforcers.

Here is an example of a token economy used with preschool children to increase their physical activity. Investigators (Patel, Normand & Kohn, 2019) provided tokens that resembled smiley faces contingent on increased physical activity. The tokens could be exchanged for high preference tangible items immediately following each session. Before beginning the token intervention, the participants were taught how it worked using the following three steps:

1. Tokens and rules for earning and exchanging the tokens were described and defined.
2. The procedure for token delivery was modeled and each participant was encouraged to engage in the physical activity required to receive tokens.
3. The procedure for token exchange was modeled and participants exchanged the tokens they received during step 2 for a preferred tangible item.

The authors concluded "that token economies can be used to increase MVPA" (moderate-to-vigorous physical activity).

**Deliver tokens immediately, often, and in sufficient quantity to permit frequent exchange.** One of the token system's major advantages is that tokens of particular values can be dispensed as soon as the target response is emitted and exchanged later for items chosen from an array of backup reinforcers of varying costs. Notice how these characteristics lend themselves to incorporating the key features of effective reinforcement strategies: immediacy, frequency, quality, quantity, and schedule. For instance, the number of tokens you dispense at any one time should be sufficient to maintain performance, yet sparse enough to prevent satiation.

As in all other aspects of applied behavior analytic practice, in data-based decision making, choosing an optimal quantity of reinforcers to deliver is crucial. If clients are responding at an acceptable rate, you can assume the arrangement is appropriate. If the rate begins to diminish, question whether the number of tokens and backup reinforcers you have dispensed is sufficient (to avoid extinction) or excessive (to avoid satiation). You may need to adjust prices so participants can afford their backup reinforcers and still have some tokens or points left over. Otherwise, develop some sort of insured-savings system and/or pay interest on savings to prevent bankruptcy and its unwanted consequences—cessation of responding or misbehavior (Hogan & Johnson, 1985). Chapters 6 and 11 pointed out the importance of *clearly specifying the condition for reinforcer delivery* and *individualizing reinforcer selection*. When the rules of the game are clear, participants are more likely to follow them. This applies to token economies as well. Pictorial pricing charts, for instance, are useful with young or non-literate populations (see Figure 12.3). An underlying assumption of a token system is that reinforcer *quality* should match participants' preferences. So, if feasible, involving participants in the selection of backup reinforcers is a good idea, because it heightens their awareness of and may increase the value of the backup reinforcers. Also, include a breadth of both **natural** (*reinforcers indigenous to the natural environment*) and **artificial** (*reinforcers not usually present in the natural setting or not a natural consequence of the behavior*) backup material and activity reinforcers. To illustrate, in exchange for tokens received for appropriate cleaning activities by housekeepers at a large, urban hotel, artificial reinforcers consist-

ing of commercial trading stamps (the functional equivalent of tokens), time off with pay, dinner for two at the hotel's finest restaurant, and/or a two-week lunch pass to the employees' cafeteria were provided. Once the behaviors were well estab-

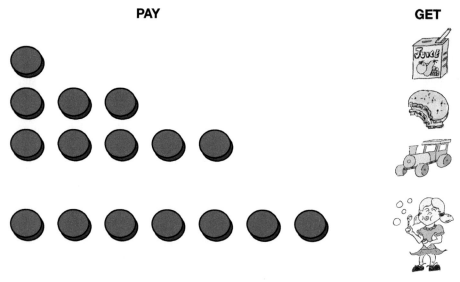

**Figure 12.3** Simple pictorial price chart

lished, the backup reinforcers and token system were eventually thinned to management feedback alone (the natural reinforcers) (Anderson, Crowell, Sponsel, Clarke, & Brence, 1983).

**Consistently relate positive social feedback to token delivery.** If providing simple positive feedback, such as praise or approval, has functioned adequately to reinforce a given response, there is little need for a token economy. *Only when such feedback is insufficiently reinforcing do token systems make sense.* Nonetheless, transforming praise into a learned reinforcer may, depending on the situation, be a key long-term aim of many token economies. The way to accomplish this is for the contingency manager to precede token delivery by positive social feedback: Not wishing to interrupt a client living in a group home, the supervisor pats him on the shoulder, smiles, and places a token on the client's token board. "How terrific! You've done a beautiful job of making your bed. Here's your token." (Perhaps it has occurred to you that, beyond the other advantages of using a token economy, the tokens themselves may prompt the contingency manager to deliver social feedback more frequently (Breyer & Allen, 1975; Mandelker, Brigham, & Bushell, 1970).

**Consider combining your token system with interdependent and dependent group contingencies.** Beyond "rewarding" independent performance, tokens may be shared, divided, or exchanged. Assume that group cooperation is a goal. Under an interdependent group contingency, all members can work toward a common award, such as a party, trip, dance, game, sporting event, musical program, puppet show, or play, or talks on interesting topics like politics, ecology, natural foods, adventure, sexual practices, child rearing, auto repairs, or whatever is intriguing to members. For example, in the Campbell and Skinner (2004) study, once the class of sixth-grade students earned all five letters in the word MUSIC, they could exchange the finished word for the opportunity to hear music during independent seat work.

Alternatively, as in the Broussard and Northup (1997) program, the class could earn points exchangeable for preferred items and activities contingent on their ignoring their fellow students' disruptive behavior. When access to special activities depends on the performance of each individual, group members often help and encourage one another (Speltz et al., 1982). If one or two members fail to earn the requisite number, it is possible to adopt a *collective* system (Ulman & Sulzer-Azaroff, 1975), in which all tokens are pooled until the required total is earned. If necessary, the non-cooperating members may be assigned to a separate activity elsewhere while the rest of the group enjoys its reward. Assuming your clientele tend to support one another, you can use the group arrangement as a vehicle for inducing constructive peer feedback. If you have reason to expect that, rather than support and encouragement, your group members will turn to coercion, model (Chapter 18) and shape (Chapter 13) the former.

**Capitalize on effective economic principles and practices.** Kagel and Winkler (1972) compared the token economy to a "closed economic system," contending that the fields of economics and of applied behavior analysis have much to learn from each other. Ayllon and Azrin (1968) and others who have conducted token economies have profited by heeding well-tested practices and principles from the business and economic community. One illustration is the law of supply and demand, with high-demand items priced higher than low-demand items. When preferences change, prices can be adjusted accordingly (Ruskin & Maley, 1972). Additionally, as marketing experts have long known, novelty and change (e.g., fresh displays of merchandise) play a great part in the desirability of an object of merchandise. In the token economies we have designed, we adjusted the backup reinforcers, adding novel backup items from time to time. Also, just as bonuses seem to promote good personnel performance in business situations, bonus tokens also may heighten productivity elsewhere. For instance, students in a summer-camp remedial program increased their academic productivity after they were given *bonus tokens* contingent on increases over their best previous three-day records (Rickard, Melvin, Creel, & Creel, 1973).

As with monetary economies, "A robust token economy is one in which savings are low or nonexistent; this promotes the high rates of token earning and spending critical to overall success of the program" (Hackenberg, p. 428). Two key ways are especially helpful when you hope to encourage spending:

1. Include a wider range of preferred reinforcers; and
2. Have mandatory exchange periods in which all participants must empty their bank accounts.

## Reducing Behavior within a Token Economy

Within token economies, various procedures (see Chapters 26–31) can be used to reduce inappropriate behavior, including providing tokens for the absence of specific problem behavior (Carton & Schweitzer, 1996; Higgins, Williams, & McLaughlin, 2001), punitive interventions like penalties (LeBlanc, Hagopian, & Maglieri, 2000) and timeout (Chapter 29) from spending. However, we recommend that the more punitive reductive procedures (e.g., penalties, timeout from spending) be avoided unless absolutely necessary (see Chapters 29–30). Usually, a combination of the more positive behavioral interventions will work satisfactorily (in addition to this chapter see Chapters 26–28). For example, investigators (Taylor & Mudford, 2012) used a token economy in a residential therapeutic community for drug and alcohol rehabilitation for youngsters 14 to 17 years of age. The youngsters were able to negotiate target behaviors that would receive tokens and choose backup reinforcers. The results included not only decreases in messy rooms but increases in positive verbal statements across settings and improved leadership responsibilities.

## Methods for Maintaining Performance Improved via Token Economies

Technically, just as most adults' compensation systems remain in effect throughout their employment, contingency managers should be willing to maintain token economies over time. Nonetheless, phasing the tokens out in favor of more naturally reinforcing contingencies may make sense in given situations. Token systems take time, require additional resources, and they also require careful planning and monitoring.

Sometimes natural contingencies take over to support ongoing performance, even after the token economy has been discontinued. In an industrial situation involving use of tokens to support use of ear protectors, Zohar and Fussfeld (1981) temporarily instituted a token economy to encourage that practice. No decline in ear protection was noted three months after the token economy was withdrawn, and only the new managerial standard remained in effect. Similarly, Anderson et al. (1983) used management feedback on randomly selected hotel rooms to maintain specific cleaning activities of various housekeeping personnel in a large, urban hotel. (Note that these studies again stress the importance of environmental support if behavior is to be maintained; see Chapters 3 & 24.)

A commonly used maintenance strategy is to increase the delay between token delivery and token exchange. You might accomplish this by increasing the work requirement, or the number of tokens needed to purchase a backup reinforcer, rather than increasing the number of responses required to earn a token (Hackenberg, 2018). We suggest that you prepare your clientele by explaining that the increase is due to inflation. Or, Tarbox, Ghezzi, and Wilson (2006) increased the magnitude of the backup reinforcers as their cost went up. For example, if the price for three minutes of toy access was ten tokens, and you increase the cost to 15 tokens, then you might reasonably increase the time for toy access to 4.5 minutes.

Be aware, too, that token economies may not be included in new settings, so participants may need to be weaned from their current token arrangement for their behavior to be maintained in different settings. Several more formal methods are available for achieving this end.

**Using tiered or level systems to promote maintenance.** Tiered or **level token economies** *are economies in which participants can move up or down a hierarchy of levels, contingent upon their improved behavior or number of accumulated tokens (e.g., meeting set criteria).* The higher the level, the more privileges the participants have and the more independent their behavior is from the rigid structure of the token system. These tiered token economies incorporate increasingly more natural conditions, including gradually delayed reinforcement. Smith and Farrell (1993) contend that tiered economies enhance both self-management skills and personal responsibility for social, emotional, and academic performance. In an example from the Achievement Place tiered program (Phillips, Phillips, Fixsen, & Wolf, 1972), when youths began the program, they entered a very highly structured "earn and lose" exchange system: earning or losing points almost on a moment-to-moment basis, with exchanges permitted every couple of hours.[6] As the individuals progressed toward developing acceptable social, academic, and maintenance behaviors, they moved up tiers or levels: first into a daily, then a weekly, then a merit, then a homebound system. In this way, while the youths remained at Achievement Place they acquired increasingly more refined repertoires and privileges while token use and value were thinned.

Sometimes, though, well-structured token systems may need to remain in place more or less permanently. The early hope had been that once the youths of Achievement Place were weaned off the system they would be able to return home, yet sustain their improved performance. But after the youths went home, old contingencies resurfaced along with their former maladaptive behavior (Wolf, Braukmann, & Ramp, 1987). Noting this unfortunate outcome, those authors argued in favor of publicly funded long-term ongoing support systems for troubled youth in lieu of returning them to their original living environments.

**Other methods for maintaining performance improved via token economies.** In general, once tokens have been phased out, you can use the methods you will read about in Chapters 22 and 23 of this book to maintain the improved behavior. To provide you with a flavor of those maintenance techniques, we describe a system we used in a classroom years ago to gradually remove artificial reinforcers and replace them with more natural ones (Sulzer, Hunt, Ashby, Koniarski, & Krams, 1971):

1. Back-up reinforcers were replaced periodically.
2. As responding reached and maintained its intended rate and tempo, we continued *praising* and giving other forms of recognition, but began to substitute available activities and privileges for the tangible rewards.
3. Next, we shifted to certificates, transferable for time to be spent at high-interest educational or otherwise relevant activities. Little by little, phasing out the tangible and artificial activity reinforcers became possible.

The scheme for moving from the tokens to more natural reinforcers (e.g., praise or feedback) is also discussed in Chapters 22–23, along with various methods for maintaining behavior in general. Chapter 21 discusses expanding the behavior to other settings.

## SUMMARY AND CONCLUSIONS

Much of our work in the ABA field is set within a group context. This presents many opportunities for heightening the effectiveness of our interventions, because we can capitalize on the presence and influence of peers. When operating within group arrangements, members can wield considerable influence over the actions of one another and also serve as readily available sources of immediate and frequent feedback and reinforcement. Harnessing peer power may prove invaluable when attempting to promote and sustain change in academic, social, or work behavior. One natural though indirect way to accomplish this is by arranging interdependent or dependent group contingencies. These are particularly well suited to evoking peer support, because under those conditions the performance of individual members impacts the reinforcers received by

---

[6]Today we are convinced that the "lose" part of the original tiered system need only be used in exceptional cases. A carefully crafted token system should be able to incorporate positive behavioral interventions to prevent/reduce problem behavior; see Chapters 26–28.

other group participants. Consequently, peers are energized to encourage and assist one another.

Group arrangements alone do not necessarily ensure that peers function as agents of change. A more straightforward approach is to teach, monitor, and supervise peer tutors and contingency managers within interdependent groups. They are then more likely to succeed and benefit by gaining enhanced leadership skills and status, additional fluency with the skills they are promoting, and a heightened sense of themselves.

Massive numbers of consumers have found token economies effective and acceptable. Nevertheless, developing these systems requires considerable planning and careful execution. Designers of token systems are well advised to incorporate all the features of an effective reinforcement program, including immediate and consistent delivery of stimuli identified as functionally effective among group participants.

Probably, because they require a considerable investment of time and other resources, you would be wise to reserve designing and implementing token economies for situations in which less-intrusive contingency arrangements have been found or promise to be unsatisfactory. Should you decide to proceed, you should implement a token system only after obtaining proper clearance and carefully planning your methods. You will need to consider logistic, economic, legal, and other issues, and when appropriate, devise plans for eventually phasing out the system. You accomplish this by shifting from artificial to natural backup reinforcers, by programming delays of token delivery and backups, by gradually reducing token deliveries in amount or frequency, and by gradually switching from tokens to contingencies more natural to the context. If you are fairly certain that returning to natural contingencies will undermine the gains achieved, you may need to retain the system indefinitely, though perhaps in some less intrusive form.

*Chapter 13*

# Teaching New Behavior: Shaping

## Goals

1. Define, recognize, and give original illustrations of each of the following terms:
    a. shaping
    b. successive approximations
    c. contact desensitization
    d. programmed instruction
    e. programmed instructional frames
    f. generative learning
    g. personalized system of instruction (PSI)
    h. computer-assisted instruction
2. List and illustrate the major variables that promote the effective use of shaping.
3. Give an example of combining (a) instructions, (b) physical guidance, and (c) fading with shaping.
4. Describe how the personalized system of instruction (PSI) incorporates principles of effective shaping.
5. List the advantages of teaching by means of computer-assisted instruction (CAI) and describe how shaping can be incorporated within CAI programs to heighten their effectiveness.
6. Design a shaping program for a particular student, trainee, or client, and provide the details of its implementation.

************

Penny, a four-and-a-half-year-old with cerebral palsy, had only been walking since she was three and needed to learn many more motor skills: step walking, sliding, rolling, and so on (Hardiman, Goetz, Reuter, & LeBlanc, 1975). In contrast to our examples in earlier chapters, in which simple or differential reinforcement were sufficient to increase behavior, those contingencies were insufficient here. Those motor skills were not part of her repertoire. First, she would need to acquire the component skills, through *shaping*. Then, these would be *chained* together to form the more complex behaviors. Of course, reinforcement would be integral to the whole process, including strengthening the component responses along the way as well as in their ultimate form. In this chapter we focus upon shaping; in the next, chaining. Both procedures are suitable for teaching new motor, verbal, social, personal, and other classes of behavior.

If learning new behaviors by means of natural response "selection" through reinforcement of increasingly more productive responding seems familiar to you, it should. After all, how do many organisms learn the skills required for them to thrive, reproduce, and survive? A young bear, owl, or trout, for instance, must learn how efficiently to capture its prey if it is to remain alive long enough to reproduce. As Skinner pointed out in *Science and Human Behavior* (1953), humans, too, need to learn ways to obtain sustenance sufficient for them to survive and multiply.

Simply reinforcing the missing behavior or prompting it is unreasonable because it has been emitted rarely or never. Reinforcing an infant's language is impossible if the infant has never said a comprehensible word. Nor will young children write numbers or letters if those behaviors or their components are absent from their repertoires. Expecting Mr. Grump to accept a compliment graciously is unreasonable, as he has never been seen to display any but the slightest bit of geniality. Becoming skillful at promoting learning by reinforcing responses progressively approximating important functional behaviors (i.e., shaping) provides parents, teachers, and other managers of human behavior with an extraordinarily useful tool. That capability permits us to shape behaviors that are weak or missing altogether from the individual's repertoire. "Learning how to shape correctly is the most important behavior-change skill you can have as a parent, teacher, coach, manager, executive—anyone who has this skill has the potential to influence the behavior of others" (Daniels & Lattal, 2017, pp. 68-69).

## SHAPING DEFINED AND ILLUSTRATED

### Shaping Defined

**Shaping** consists of *teaching new behavior by differentially reinforcing successive approximations toward the behavioral objective.* The procedure change agents use for shaping a new behavioral form, for example, begins with a response as it currently exists in the individual's repertoire. Then they reinforce slight changes, in the form or *topography* of the behavior, as they gradually approach or *approximate* the target behavior. Said another way, we differentially reinforce those elements or subsets of behavior increasingly resembling or *approximating* the target behavior, while placing those of lesser or poorer quality on extinction. Behavior analysts use the term **successive approximation** to describe *a particular response that has shifted along some dimension, such as quality, rate or intensity as it more closely approaches its target criterion.* This process of reinforcing closer approximations and putting previous mastered approximations on extinction continues until the target behavior is reached. Both differential reinforcement and extinction are cogent processes at work during shaping.

Leroy has never made a mark that approximates a straight line, but the teacher plans to teach him how to write the number 1. On occasion, Leroy has drawn a slightly less squiggly line. If the teacher selectively reinforces the production of lines more closely approximating a straight line, Leroy probably will produce straighter lines increasingly more often. This continues until Leroy consistently produces an acceptable numeral 1. Simultaneously, old or inappropriate responses (curvier lines) will not be reinforced; technically, the drawing of curvier lines will extinguish. Similar processes also could be applied to the shaping of firmer lines, or of those drawn at a given rate, and so on.

In this chapter we describe many applications of shaping. But, from whence did this brilliant shaping- technology derive? Thanks to Gail Petersen (2004), the history of its origin has been brought to our attention in the form of a quotation from an article by B. F. Skinner (see Box 13.1).

## Shaping Illustrated

To broaden your familiarity with the shaping procedure, permit us to share a few additional illustrations. Suppose the goal were to teach Pearl to pay attention to the therapist on request. At first, in response to "Look at me," any attending in the direction of the therapist (for instance a body angle no more than 45 degrees away from the therapist) would be accepted (reinforced). Once such orienting became well established (say for 25 of 30 requests over 3 days), the next step could be to make reinforcement contingent on narrowing the angle to no more than 25 degrees for x trials over y days. After that, the criterion for acceptance could be restricted gradually until Pearl consistently turned her body toward the therapist when asked to look at her. Next, the focus could shift to Pearl's orienting her head so she would be apt to see the therapist's face, an essential requirement if Pearl were to acquire a number of functional skills. Shaping has been used in this way to teach many youngsters deficient in attending to a teacher or therapist to acquire this essential prerequisite to learning many other behaviors.[1] In fact, Fonger and Malott (2019) used shaping to teach eye contact to children diagnosed with ASD as a prerequisite to other learning programs.

One of the common characteristics of autism is the individual's failure to make and sustain eye contact, which in turn interferes with the learner's ability to attend to relevant instructional stimuli. To remedy this barrier to learning, special educators have turned to shaping, an invaluable tool in such situations. Consider the approach taken by Fonger

---

[1] In situations like this, varying helpers and therapists is a good idea, so the student's responding is not restricted to only one adult. (See related suggestions in the *Picture Exchange Communication System*© teaching guidelines, Bondy & Frost, 2001a.)

---

**Box 13.1**
**The Origins of Shaping**

"In 1943 Keller Breland, Norman Guttman, and I were working on a war-time project sponsored by General Mills, Inc. Our laboratory was the top floor of a flour mill in Minneapolis, where we spent a good deal of time waiting for decisions to be made in Washington. All day long, around the mill, wheeled great flocks of pigeons. They were easily snared on the window sills and proved to be an irresistible supply of experimental subjects.

"This was serious research, but we had our lighter moments. One day we decided to teach a pigeon to bowl. The pigeon was to send a wooden ball down a miniature alley toward a set of toy pins by swiping the ball with a sharp sideward movement of the beak. To condition the response, we put the ball on the floor of an experimental box and prepared to operate the food-magazine as soon as the first swipe occurred. But nothing happened. Though we had all the time in the world, we grew tired of waiting. We decided to reinforce any response which had the slightest resemblance to a swipe—perhaps, at first, merely the behavior of looking at the ball—and then to select responses which more closely approximated the final form. The result amazed us. In a few minutes, the ball was caroming off the walls of the box as if the pigeon had been a champion squash player. The spectacle so impressed Keller Breland that he gave up a promising career in psychology and went into the commercial production of behavior." (Skinner, 1958b, p. 94).

and Malott (2019) who used shaping with several pre-school children with autism who did not exhibit eye contact. This skill was taught as a prerequisite to discrete trial training. The shaping procedure consisted of first reinforcing orientation to the instructor's body.

> At the beginning of each trial, the instructor removed a preferred item and waited until the child made the appropriate orienting response before returning it. If the orienting response occurred within 5-s of the removal of the item we provided an edible reinforcer and 15-s access to the preferred item and the trial was recorded as correct. A latency longer than 5-s resulted in 5-s access to the preferred item and the trial was recorded as incorrect (p. 217).

Next, they reinforced orientation to the instructor's face. All sessions during intervention ranged from three to 20 trials and required a performance of at least 80 percent or greater for two consecutive trials before moving on to the next step. The third step involved shaping the duration of eye contact starting with any instance of eye contact; then at least one second of eye contact; then at least two seconds; followed by at least three seconds of sustained eye contact. Each of these steps required meeting the time requirement at least 90 percent of the time for two consecutive sessions. This successful shaping intervention was reported to be a "practical technique for gaining attention before delivering an instructional demand" (p. 216).

On the rare occasions when anyone complimented Mr. Grump, he responded with a harrumph and a dismissive wave of his hand. Now suppose one day you decided to try to teach Mr. Grump to politely accept a favorable comment. So, whenever Mr. Grump acknowledged a compliment, whether graciously or not, you would smile at him or pat him on the shoulder (reinforcers you know to work with him). After he began responding consistently with the slightest hint of a smile or a more pleasant word, you would deliver the reinforcers contingent on improvements in the way he acknowledged a compliment. Eventually, you might work up to a point where you sincerely could comment, "You know, Mr. Grump, your saying you appreciate my remarks really makes me feel good!"

Writers of most textbooks, workbooks, teacher's guides, and training manuals assume that to acquire new skills, readers must gradually move from previously acquired abilities toward more advanced instructional objectives. One set of responses is acceptable at a given level, different ones at more sophisticated levels—a strategy similar to shaping. A handwriting workbook, for instance, could be designed along such lines. At first, letters assigned to be reproduced are simple and reasonably distinct from any others (e.g., an O or an X). Then the student is guided through a series of steps in which more and more precision is required. Meanwhile, the teacher praises the student for producing letters increasingly matching the samples printed in the book.

An excellent illustration of shaping is illustrated in a study early in the evolution of ABA (Harris, Wolf, & Baer, 1967). A little boy spent almost no time on the climbing frame while he was on the school playground. His teachers decided that climbing on the frame was the sort of vigorous activity that could further his physical development. The contingent reinforcer was their attention: "The teachers attended at first to the child's proximity to the frame. As he came closer, they progressed to attending only to his touching it, climbing up a little, and finally to extensive climbing. Technically, this was reinforcement of successive approximations to climbing behavior" (p. 154). The boy ultimately came to spend more than half of each recess on the climbing frame.

In a related study, investigators (Cameron & Cappello, 1993) hoped to encourage a 21-year-old man with Down syndrome and developmental delay to exercise more frequently by teaching him how to leap over hurdles. First, they reinforced jumping over hurdles laid flat on the floor. They then raised the hurdles to 4 inches, then to 8, and then 12 inches. Also, they increased the number of hurdles from two, then later, after the client had achieved success with the two, to four at each height. In another study, Scott et al. (1997) successfully used prompts and shaping to improve pole vaulting. The intervention "consisted of breaking a photoelectric beam with the hands at the moment of take-off. The height of the beam was gradually increased until the vaulter reached maximum arm extension at take-off" (p. 573). Both arm extension and bar height clearance increased.

Shaping also has been found to effectively reduce social and personal problem behaviors, as reported by Carr, Newsom, and Binkoff (1980), who shaped adaptive behaviors as substitutes for problematic ones. Similarly, college students rated high in performance anxiety (Kirsch, Wolpin, & Knutson, 1975) successfully overcame their stage fright by proceeding through a series of graded tasks. The tasks progressed from reading lists of unrelated words through reading another student's speech, writing an original speech, delivering the speech from notes, to delivering the speech from note cards. We also have learned of shaping used to teach young people how to behave during job interviews, on dates, and while proctoring peers. Shaping may even be used to manage unhealthy or perilous behaviors, as in the following instance:

Karim was a six-year-old child with autism, who refused to accept many of the food items his parents presented (Binnendyk & Lucyshyn, 2009). Shaping was selected as the teaching method; presentation of preferred foods, such as cookies or crackers, or brief access to a preferred toy, were the reinforcers for successive steps toward food acceptance. Successive approximations consisted of the following steps: tolerating the therapist's first depositing a pea-sized drop of food, the amount of which increased over time, on or inside his bottom lip; opening his mouth to accept the spoon, even if he spit it out. (In the latter case the parent was instructed to present another spoonful of the same food until Karim accepted and consumed it.) Gradually, the amount of food presented on the spoon was increased to a spoonful. Finally, reinforcement was delivered when the child opened his mouth, and accepted and swallowed the food within 30 seconds.

Parents and society in general often practice shaping without being aware they're doing it. Language development is a case in point. Although humans acquire verbal behavior by means of imitative, occasionally chained (complex combinations of simple responses, described in Chapter 14), differentiated, and generalized responses, shaping is a critical aspect of the process: The child produces those sounds that more and more closely approximate the ones s/he hears from caregivers. The closer and closer they get to those "models," the more powerful the reinforcement. But it does not end there, because generally parents and/or other communicative partners contribute to the mix of reinforcers with their own verbal and other socially reinforcing responses.

Occasionally, though, that natural process is insufficient. In some instances the learner has failed to imitate verbal samples adequately, or has some well-practiced but poorly enunciated speech patterns. Then, proper enunciation may have to be shaped. An illustration is the way infants acquire some of their earliest verbalizations. When an infant babbles, parents tend to reinforce any similarities between the baby's speech and acceptable words by smiling, mimicking the baby's sounds, and *oohing* and *ahing*. At first, they reinforce distant approximations to real words, like "Mmm" or "Ma" for *Mom* or "Ba," "Da," or "Pa" for *Dad* or *Pop*; "ook" or "kuk" for *cookie*. Later, closer approximations are demanded if the response is to qualify for reinforcement. As the child grows older, others also differentially reinforce improved speech patterns and extinguish poorer ones. Non-family members also contribute by differentially reinforcing comprehensibly communicated statements and requests over poorly and inappropriately enunciated sound combinations.

Behavior analysts, as well as effective teachers and speech professionals, regularly apply shaping to aid youngsters with poor communicative repertoires to refine or broaden their verbal skills.[2] For example, as described later in Chapter 19, Bourret et al. (2004) combined shaping and modeling (i.e., demonstrating the behavior) to teach clients diag-

---

[2]Be careful, though, to recognize that, as opposed to challenges in enunciating clearly or having a sparse vocabulary due to insufficient stimulation (Hart & Risley, 1995), a major delay in learning to communicate physical wants and needs and bids for social attention is a totally different matter. That calls for much more sophisticated teaching protocols about which you will read later on.

nosed with autism or mental retardation to produce clear verbal requests (i.e., *mands*; see Chapter 19). Similarly, Howie and Woods (1982) used shaping to promote fluent speech, beginning with a very slow pace and then differentially reinforcing increasingly more rapid rates of speaking. As you might imagine, shaping some complex responses requires considerable attentiveness and diligence. Fortunately though, the process can be made more manageable because the successive approximations can be incorporated directly within group, textbook, and computerized instruction—approaches described below.

**Contact desensitization** uses shaping in a particular way: by *differentially reinforcing closer and closer approximations (approaches) to an object or activity that the client fears or avoids*.[3] Investigators (Ricciardi et al., 2006) used this technique with Rich, an eight-year-old boy with autism who demonstrated an intense fear of electronic animated figures, such as a dancing Elmo doll, blinking Halloween decorations, life-size replicas of Santa Claus, and so on. Rich would scream, flee, and hit any person attempting to block his escape. The intervention consisted of providing access to preferred objects. These were initially placed 6 meters (m) from the animated figures. "Starting with the third session, the distance criterion was advanced in a five-step graduated sequence that required Rich to remain 5 m (Step 1), 4 m (Step 2), 3 m (Step 3), 2 m (Step 4), and 1 m (Step 5; terminal criterion) from the figures" (p. 446). The criterion for advancing a step was that Rich had remained at the specified distance criterion for 90 percent or more of the recording intervals for two consecutive sessions. As long as Rich remained within the specified distance, the preferred objects were available to him. During the final session, he approached and touched the figures every time he was requested to do so. Parents also reported that results were maintained in the natural environment.

Similar methods have been used to reduce all sorts of phobias, such as avoidance reactions to getting in a swimming pool (fear of deep water) (Chan et al., 2016), and among snake-phobics (Barlow et al., 1970). In the Barlow et al. study, the client's actions of approaching the snake increasingly closer were socially reinforced. When the therapist modeled the successive approximations, the client's approach rate increased even more rapidly. Similarly, investigators (Buckley, Luiselli, Harper, & Shlesinger, 2020) described two adolescent males with autism, resistant to haircutting, who gradually were exposed first to the hair clippers and then to a gradual increase in the of duration of the hair clippers against their scalp and hair. They then received edible reinforcers contingent on completion of a step lacking interfering behavior. Both students learned to tolerate complete haircuts. The senior author of the current text (Mayer) used a similar approach with a youngster who refused to allow anyone to touch his head, making it almost impossible to wash his hair. First, a high-preference interactive toy was presented, then while he was interacting with the toy, we gradually moved our hands closer and closer to his head, until we could touch it without him producing any objections. Next, he allowed his hair to be washed without emitting any interfering behavior. This type of an approach also can be used with fears related to dental and medical challenges.

Let us examine what is happening in the above contact desensitization process: Reinforcers are repeatedly offered in the presence of the feared object, and because the demands are gradual, the client is not forced immediately to confront strong fear-inducing stimuli. Due to its frequent relation to strong reinforcers and to the initially wide spatial separation from the primary aversive stimulus, the client begins to remain calm in the presence of the previously feared object. Gradually he begins to discriminate the stimulus as cuing the presence of positive reinforcers rather than aversive stimuli.

**Animal training.** Fittingly, because shaping was discovered in research with nonhumans, it also has become a favorite method for *humane animal training*. Shaping has been used with tigers at the San Diego Zoo to help avoid tranquilizing them and making unnecessary trips to the veterinary hospital (Carmignani, 2010). The tigers are trained to: (1) rise up on their hind legs so that their bellies and paws can be inspected; (2) open their mouths so their teeth can be checked; (3) allow their ears

---

[3] Many illustrations of this form of desensitization may be found in various behavior therapy journals (e.g., *Behavior Therapy, Behavior Therapy and Experimental Psychiatry*, and other clinical psychology and psychiatry journals.)

to be touched; (4) sit; (5) go and stay in their "station"; and, 6) allow blood to be drawn from the base of their tails for laboratory analysis. To get a tiger eventually to allow blood to be drawn from its tail, "baby steps," or successive approximations, are reinforced by first providing a short tweet from a whistle to bridge the time between the behavior and the delivery of a meatball, which serves as a reinforcer. The tweet eventually becomes a learned reinforcer because it is immediately followed by the delivery of the meatball. When the cat appears relaxed, the reinforcer is delivered (i.e., a tweet, then a meatball, are provided), then the tail is touched by a hook at the end of a pole. Once the cat accepts that approximation and receives reinforcement, the tail is drawn towards the barrier, and eventually through the barrier to the keeper. Again, approximations are reinforced. Initially, the cat will jerk its tail back, but over time it allows its tail to be drawn through the barrier and blood to be drawn. Similarly, to get a cat to open its mouth, the first approximation might be the cat sticking its tongue out. The next would be the mouth slightly open, and so on. All training sessions are kept brief and enjoyable in that "there is nothing to gain by frustrating a 400-pound tiger" (p. 29). (See Box 13.2 and Karen Pryor's *Don't Shoot the Dog*, 1999, for further illustrations.)

## Shaping the Performance of Adult Learners

Those involved in the teaching or training of adults may capitalize on the features of effective shaping to promote verbal-conceptual, motor, or just about any other class of learning or performance skills. With or without awareness, successful teachers or trainers routinely integrate the rules of effective shaping within their instructional activities. Here we elaborate on this point via a quote from a paper written by Sulzer-Azaroff (2004), describing how Skinner's (1958a) paper on teaching machines profoundly influenced her own efforts as an instructor to encourage class participation:

> One tactic I've used is to pose a question and ask the group to write down a brief reply. Then we go around the room, asking each person to read his or her written statement.

---

### Box 13.2

Ferguson and Rosales-Ruiz (2001) used shaping to train five pedigree quarter horse mares, previously forced into trailers through the use of whips and ropes, to enter horse trailers peacefully. First, they paired the sound of a clicker* with the presentation of food, to transform it into a secondary reinforcer. Next, they taught each horse to touch a target, shaping by first placing the target near the horse's nose and when the horse touched the target, by providing one of a variety of different foods as a reinforcer. They gradually moved the target further and further away, eventually placing it in the field in various locations near the horse. Each time the horse touched the target, a reinforcer was delivered. Once the horse was following the target to various locations, they added the word "touch"; then once the horse touched the target, a reinforcer was provided. Once each horse reached a criterion of 90 percent correct within five seconds over five sessions, trailer training was instituted. Trailer training consisted of placing the target a short distance in the trailer in front of the horse and requesting the horse to "touch" it. Each touch was followed by the clicker and a food item. As long as the horse responded to the prompt, "touch," the trainers moved the target forward to the next approximation. If the horse did not move forward, she was led away from the trailer and another trial began, with the target located in the same position. All horses successfully completed the shaping sequence, although one required the presence of a companion horse to facilitate training (i.e., this companion horse may have served as a model, and/or its presence may have reduced competing emotional behavior). Their trailer loading also generalized to different trainers and trailers.

---
* Karen Pryor (1999) describes the use of clicker training; initially used to shape dolphin behavior (Pryor & Norris, 1991).

Of course I attend closely to and compliment the praiseworthy parts of each contribution, especially the spontaneous (unscripted) ones. Before long the other students begin to follow that lead. Other short written assignments, such as filling out forms, writing abstracts and so on, gradually become longer and more complex, as participants continue to share what they have with one another. By the end of the program, each learner generally gives a fairly sophisticated oral presentation before the class. Many eventually present posters and papers at meetings, conferences and conventions. Practically all are able to state and defend their points of view, an ability essential to effective participation in just about any skilled job performance. (p. 132)

## USING SHAPING EFFECTIVELY

Watching a skillful shaper at work can be as impressive as observing a talented stage director or sports coach. The shaper's actions are adept, fluid, and sensitively attuned to the learner's moment-to-moment patterns of behavior. The learner remains attentive and engaged as s/he smoothly and gradually progresses from one level of proficiency to the next. Reaching the goal is a source of pleasure for everyone—learner, shaper, peers, and those with ultimate responsibility for the outcome (employers, teachers, team owners, parents, leaders, and so on). By adhering to the suggestions offered below, you will gradually enhance your own proficiency as a behavior shaper. How will you know? You and your clientele will learn better, faster, and more durably and display your mutual pleasure and satisfaction.

### Familiarize Yourself with Learners' Current Repertoires

"That's okay. You don't need to tell me. I've got it." As a student of a fairly sophisticated subject matter like *applied behavior analysis*, undoubtedly you know the feeling. We'd wager you probably are a facile conceptual/verbal learner. Undoubtedly, more than once in your student career, you've had the sense that you were being provided with more prompting and guidance than you felt you really needed; or that you were burdened down by having to wait for your peers to catch up. But then, maybe your skills in other areas, such as within the motor, social, or emotional realm, are not as advanced as they might be. Every individual possesses a distinctive repertoire of skills, along with a unique capability for learning new ones at a particular pace, as a function of their physical attributes and learning histories.

Applied behavior analysts need to learn as much as they can about their clientele, especially in relation to their current repertoires of learning (what they have already mastered in the areas of current concern), as well as their learning skills and styles. In the case of a mainstream student experiencing difficulties in school, that might mean finding out about his academic achievement levels—so you can identify an appropriate starting point; his personal and social adjustment history—so you can discover possible personal-interpersonal barriers to his progress; any physical challenges such as perceptual, motor, or other deficits—so you can adjust your teaching to his individual strengths and weaknesses; his family support system—so you can select or design achievable change strategies; his generally preferred reinforcers, for reasons by now well known to you, and so on. Educational systems in modern societies usually provide specialized assessment and/or psychological services to help supply such information.

In the world of work, personnel specialists usually undertake similar responsibilities for employees. Often they assess people's special skills, preferences (e.g., reinforcers), and learning styles. Clinicians serving individual clientele experiencing problems in living look for strengths, weaknesses, excesses and deficits, functional reinforcers and aversive stimuli, and other sources of influence on the person's ongoing performance.

In fact, the field of *behavioral assessment* is vast.[4] Acquainting yourself with its content and methods, especially functional behavioral assessment, will serve you well. Many in our field find functional behavioral assessment essential to prac-

---

[4] See the journal *Behavioral Assessment* and also refer to research and development in behavioral assessment in our own area of application.

tice in their specialized areas of application. Behavioral assessment will assist you to identify the most promising place to begin to teach/train and/or modify the behavior of an individual, but also to select particular instructional and reinforcing stimuli, plan the size of the steps to take, and the standards for deciding when to move on to the next level.

## Choose and Apply an Ongoing Measurement System

As always, whenever applying behavior analysis, you select a reliable, valid measurement system to assess progress. Because shaping advances gradually, a simple method is to identify the phase or step on which you are currently concentrating plus those previously taught, as well as those you still are planning on teaching. Then, often enough to provide a fair (i.e., reliable, valid) account of performance, you probe progress according to a predetermined schedule.

Sometimes it is possible to break up a task into its smaller components, that is, to use a *task analysis* (described and illustrated in more detail in Chapter 14) to *identify each of the steps in the sequence of successive approximations toward the terminal instructional goal*, as was done in the program represented in Figure 13.1. In such cases, you can order the steps within a checklist. Then, use the checklist as the basis for deciding, according to a predetermined criterion (e.g., three-correct-in-a-row on each of two separate days) of when the learner has mastered a step.

At other times, you will need to plan the size of the next step(s) *during* the shaping process because you find it necessary to expand or contract your step sizes. Nevertheless, adding those sequentially to a checklist still will make your assessment task easier. It also will behoove you to spend some time on determining steps, or closer approximation, to the terminal behavior. It is far too easy to erroneously reinforce a behavior that, in the moment, you think is getting you closer to the terminal behavior, to later determine that you have to go back because the behavior is far from a closer approximation to the terminal behavior. For example, if you want to shape hopping on one foot, but along the way you reinforce jumping off the ground with both feet, it will be more difficult to get hopping on one foot. A better way would be to reinforce picking up one foot off the ground versus reinforcing jumping in the first place.

## Keep Your Eye on the Goal

As with other behavior analytic procedures, the first step in shaping is clearly to specify (or "pinpoint") the instructional goals and objectives (see Chapter 4). Other requirements for applying behavior analytic procedures, such as selecting and testing reliable and valid performance measures, also should be met (see Chapters 7 and 8). Additionally, you will want to identify criteria for any sub-goals or approximations, including such dimensions as the number, topography, intensity, or other performance features upon which reinforcer delivery is to be based along the way. Precise pinpointing minimizes the risk of strengthening irrelevant responses, while increasing the likelihood that appropriate approximations will be reinforced.

Although she speaks aloud at home, suppose Violet has hardly ever responded to a question in an audible voice when any adults, other than her parents, were present. If the terminal and sub-goals were vaguely stated (e.g., "decreasing Violet's elective mutism"), contingency managers might overlook and thereby fail to reinforce some approximations to the desired objective. For instance, Violet may speak loudly and shout when playing with her friends. In the absence of an objective such as, "speaking without the listener needing to say 'What?' at least once a day for 5 days," any approximations such as her speaking audibly to peers may well be missed or possibly even punished. With the specific objective in mind, however, the adult is more likely to reinforce any audible vocalizations, no matter where emitted, as the first step toward the terminal goal.

## Find a Starting Point and Supportive Environment

Just as a ceramic vase must be molded from a lump of clay, new behavior must be shaped from existing

behavior, through reinforcement of successive approximations toward the final objective. But, first you need to know where to begin. As mentioned, acquainting yourself with the learner's current behavioral repertoire with respect to the objective is crucial. Besides informing your choice of goals and reinforcers, becoming well acquainted with your learners or clients better enables you to identify the most promising starting point, that is, to identify whatever behavior appears most closely to resemble the final performance. In addition to determining what the learner already does, you also would be well advised to find how often it is done and how much that varies. The latter is especially important when you begin shaping, because the range of variations will determine which responses you might initially select for reinforcement. A good rule of thumb is that the more variable the range of the behavior you start with, the easier shaping will be and the more quickly you will be able to move the behavior toward the target. For this reason, observing the person over time in the natural setting is very important, allowing you to identify the array of behaviors that bear at least some resemblance to the final objective and that the client emits at a reasonably high rate.

Choosing a starting point depends on a number of factors: practical considerations, like access to materials; the time available for preparing new individualized assignments; and/or the similarity between the initial and the terminal behavior. A key consideration here is evidence that the client is physically capable of performing the next step or successive approximation toward the final or terminal behavior. Practically speaking, preparing Helena, who at age 21 is 4 feet 10 inches tall, to compete in the Olympics high hurdles event probably would be foolish, although training her for other gymnastic events might be reasonable. Nonetheless, don't dismiss an objective that on first viewing seems outlandish. Shaping can move behavior a lot, even when it proceeds in very small steps. (Think of the amazing feats accomplished by contestants in the Special Olympics.) You may be surprised at how far you can take it. For that reason, you should not in principle rule out the possibility of desirable target responses, even though they may seem hard to achieve.

Your best bet in identifying the starting point and teaching location is to observe the client's ongoing pattern of responding in relation to the ultimate objective. That requires some careful sleuthing on your part. Observe the individual in action at various times of the day, under all sorts of conditions, and at as many locations as you can. We have been told, for example, that Violet speaks aloud in the presence of her parents. How about with her playmates out in the playground? While jumping rope or when her group is singing a popular song?

Suppose that, for practical reasons, we have decided to invite Violet's mom to participate in the early phases of teaching, because we have heard the child speak aloud in her mother's presence.

Mother and teacher will jump rope with Violet, each of them taking turns jumping and turning the rope, singing familiar jump-rope songs together. Of course, Violet will receive reinforcers, perhaps in the form of extra turns, for singing more loudly than before.

As an alternative, Violet could be seated close to an adult who will read her a story and ask questions or play a game that Violet seems to enjoy. If she has ever been overheard talking to another child, that child might be invited to join the activity. The adult should be prepared to reinforce any approximations to speech: facial expressions, gestures, sighs, grunts, whispered words, and other rudimentary behaviors resembling attempts to communicate. Reinforcing the entire range of such behaviors over many trials should increase their frequency. Then, if Violet's whispering could be heard fairly consistently, it would be chosen to be selectively reinforced, whereas gestures and other forms of nonverbal communication would not. A starting point for shaping audible speech would have been established.

In an actual case, Van Der Kooy and Webster (1975) taught an "electively mute" six-year-old child who did not speak at all outside the home. After unsuccessfully trying various positive approaches to helping him talk, they selected an avoidance response: splashing him during swimming period. They stopped the splashing when the child said "No" or "Go away." Once this approximation to conversational speech was regularly uttered and negatively reinforced, prompting and positively reinforcing other similar approximations became possible.

When Ferguson and Rosales-Ruiz (2001) needed to determine the starting point for shaping the trailer loading of horses (Box 13.2), they selected the point in the trailer where most of the horses began to emit maladaptive responses (e.g., turning the body, freezing, head tossing, and rearing).

## Select Step Size and Duration for Remaining on a Step

We already have discussed shaping's progression and recognize that the responses between the starting point and the terminal goal must be broken down into a sequence of successive approximations. Now, let us consider a few important nuances in the process:

- The *size* of each step (approximation/subgoal)
    - should be large enough to permit reasonable rates of progress
- How *long* a client needs to remain at each step before proceeding to the next
    - long enough to establish the advancing behavior reasonably well at that level
    - but not so long that repetitions of the behavior become fixed at that level
- What to do if the client's behavior begins to disintegrate? Unfortunately, no hard and fast rules exist, so we extrapolate from what we know about training and instruction in general:
    - First, observe the individual's behavior closely. If progress is consistent and satisfactory, assume the reinforcers,

step size, and duration of remaining at that level have been selected appropriately.
- If progress begins to level off or deteriorate, then reexamine those choices.

Essentially, those same guidelines are applicable to progressive goal-setting approaches. If you stretch the goal levels too far or adjust them upward too often, participants' efforts will begin to extinguish (and may start to produce "extinction-induced aggression," about which you will read in Chapter 27). The preferred alternative is to watch as you arrange those features to discover when participants seem to be progressing at a realistic pace without becoming overwhelmed or exhausted. They should be able to succeed much more often than not at a particular goal level before the requirement is elevated.

**Sequence of steps.** Suppose the behavior analyst and teachers have suggested a starting point to address Violet's elective mutism: When she whispers within one foot from one of several coaches[5]—older students and adults. The next concern is the sequence of steps to be followed. Violet is to be seated a few inches farther away from the coach, who reads a story and asks questions about its contents, until Violet whispers loudly enough to be clearly understood for five consecutive statements. Naturally, she receives reinforcers for these utterances (some reinforcers more potent than others, to induce the variability upon which shaping depends). The coach may say, "Violet, you've made an interesting point" and repeat it to others; she may agree, smile, and allow Violet access to a favorite activity; or she may use any of the other reinforcers that have been determined to be effective for Violet. Once the criteria for success in the first step have been documented, the second step can be taken: Violet's chair is moved back about a foot, and the same criteria and procedures used in step

---

[5]In working with animals, Pryor (1999) suggests one trick—one shaper, which differs from our advice. Probably progress is more rapid when a single individual trains a specific skill, but to suit human societies in which people encounter and must accommodate to numerous others, we feel our suggestions about involving several teachers (coaches) in shaping the same components are more promising in the long run.

1 are employed again. The process continues little by little until Violet is seated across the room from any one of her coaches. Again, her behavior must be carefully observed. If the new behavior progresses consistently, it can be safely assumed that appropriate criteria have been selected for practice and success at each level. Remember, any disintegration of the behavior suggests the need to lower the requirements by contracting the step size and/or planning additional practice of mastered steps. The main point is that the individual must obtain reinforcers for *accomplishing the step correctly several times in a row before being challenged further.* To illustrate, Ricciardi et al. (2006) arranged for Rich, the boy with autism who feared animated figures, to remain at the specified distance criterion for 90 percent or more of the recording intervals for two consecutive sessions before being introduced to the next approximation toward the feared object.

In educational and training settings, because groups of learners usually include many members, teachers or coaches often select steps to accommodate the requirements of the majority. Both those unable to keep up the pace, and those capable of acquiring new behaviors in larger units and/or with less practice, may become inattentive or turn to unrelated activities. As an alternative, forming subgroups of members with roughly equivalent repertoires or substituting different materials for those participants is advisable. Eliminating some of the steps or practice items, and either replacing them with more challenging assignments or encouraging participants to engage in peer tutoring, are also good possibilities.

**Addressing plateaus.** Occasionally, just as things seem to be progressing smoothly, movement seems to stall, or "plateau." Maybe you delivered too many reinforcers at a particular level of responding, so that variability diminished. If that happens, you should still be able to take advantage of those smaller variations to keep the behavior moving in the appropriate direction. Reinstate progress by permitting a very easy next approximation and allow a few trials of several small steps. Suppose, for example, that the coach provided Violet with too many reinforced opportunities to whisper at one particular location, thereby firmly establishing whispering from that distance. In so doing, she may inadvertently have interfered with Violet's acceleration toward talking louder. An appropriate modification might be to move her several inches back every few days, rather than a foot at a time. Under such circumstances, she might be forced to whisper just a little more loudly and ultimately to combine more audible sounds with the whispers.

Sometimes altering reinforcers increases behavioral variability. If the individual fails to produce varied responses, try substituting some weak reinforcing stimuli or even withhold reinforcers altogether. Predictably, you should begin to notice changes in the client's response patterns, with some lesser and some more preferred approximations emitted. Now, assuming you remain extremely vigilant, you should have the opportunity to pounce upon the latter by providing more powerful reinforcers.

## Combine Shaping with Discriminative Stimuli

If the individual has not yet learned an important element of the behavior, prompting it by demonstrating or *modeling*, or by providing instructions, or gestures will be unlikely to evoke it in its entirety. Such prompting, however, sometimes will produce a bit of appropriate behavior, and thereby speed up shaping beyond what might have happened if you simply waited. But you must not take this so far that the learner gets to the point of always waiting for a prompt before doing anything. Referring back to Violet, who failed to speak aloud, consider this: Assuming she has begun to whisper to the adult next to her, the teacher could prompt repetitions of that response. For instance, she could say, "Good; I like the point you made" (reinforcement) and then, "Would you please say it again?" Other whispering responses could be occasioned by asking Violet other questions, nodding expectantly toward her, or gesturing. Van Der Kooy and Webster (1975) used prompts like those to teach their "electively mute" client to speak. As discussed earlier, the adapted physical education teacher in the study by Cameron and Cappello (1993) taught their client to leap over hurdles by reinforcing leaping over gradually higher hurdles. Shaping was combined with prompts consisting of holding the client's hand and instructing him to leap over the hurdle. Next, instructions were provided and the appropriate behavior modeled. Finally, only instructions were provided. This maximum-to-minimum sequence of prompts occurred at each hurdle height until the skill was mastered. Similarly, Harrison and Pyles (2013) combined instructions and shaping to improve tackling by high school football linebackers.

## "Shaping" with Goal-Setting

You have read in detail about goal-setting in Chapter 4. When goals are set in advance, participants have a clearer vision of where they are headed; what new levels will result in reinforcers. Notice in Figure 13.1 the broad goals that *Headsprout Reading Basics*™ (Layng, Twyman, and Strikeleather, 2004) uses within its reading curriculum. Although technically this does not illustrate shaping in its purest sense, the practice of setting gradual step-wise goals in educational, service, occupational, and other settings is analogous, and similar guidelines apply. Performers in programs of this sort are taking giant steps, but success depends on reinforcement along the way. In the case illustrated here, students record their accomplishments and receive merited praise from staff and fellow students along the way. While a major portion of the reinforcers (as in bonuses, celebrations, increases in grades or hourly pay) in goal-setting derives from achieving a goal, wise behavior managers take a page from the shaping literature and make certain to reinforce achievement of smaller-sized progressive steps along with the bigger ones.

Chan et al. (2016) helped three children, ages three, four, and seven, decrease their phobic reactions to approaching a swimming pool, and increased their water approach skills by jointly selecting three goals with each child during each session. The first goal selected was the most advanced skill in the baseline period or previous intervention session. The ten water approach goals started with refusing to approach the pool and then beginning to approach the water without entering the pool to entering the pool independently and standing on the bottom of the pool, or holding onto the side if too short, and submerging the head in the water. To teach each goal, the investigators instructed each child how to perform the skill mentioned in the goal, modeled

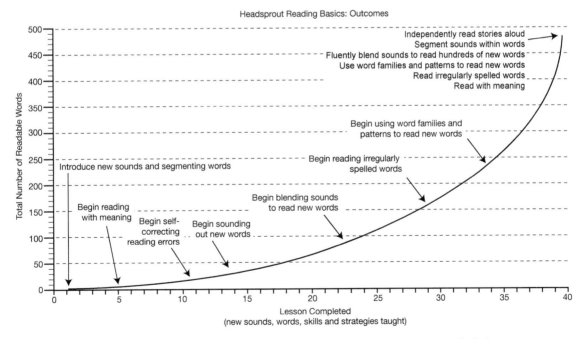

**Figure 13.1** An example of reading goals (Llayng, Twyman, & Strikeleather, 2004 with permission)

the skill, had the child rehearse the skills, provided feedback, and then the child was asked to practice the water approach skill again.

## End Every Shaping Session on a High Note

As a method for teaching *new* behaviors or skills, by its nature, shaping must face the learner with new and difficult challenges. To permit the learner to experience reinforcement sufficient to encourage his willing return to the instructional environment, try to end your sessions on a high note; that is, with some guaranteed-to-be-reinforcing trials. If participants show signs of frustration as the time for session-termination approaches, drop back a step or two and offer the opportunity to experience several successful trials.

Perhaps it has occurred to you that goal-setting may prove useful as a shaping tool. Yes, adding progressively more challenging goal-levels corresponds to progressively changing the levels you aim for as you engage in shaping. To illustrate, in our quality enhancement work within the manufacturing sector (Sulzer-Azaroff & Harshbarger, 1995), managers, unit supervisors, and quality assurance personnel were trained how to set challenging yet achievable goals. We suggested that they do this by examining their work teams' performance over the recent past and identifying the four or five highest data points achieved during that time. That information served as the basis for setting a new goal level. Based on that hard evidence, associates recognized that although the new goal level was challenging, it certainly was achievable. By adhering to those simple guidelines, within several months worker performance was shaped to more and more closely approach perfection, resulting in considerable savings to the company and an obvious increase in participants' pride of workmanship. (See Figure 13.2.)

In a case set in a human service organization, managers used goal-setting successfully to promote the integrity with which staff implemented their treatment programs (DiGennaro, Martens, & Kleinmann, 2007). Look at Figure 13.3., a graph describing the performance of teachers who had been participating in a program designed to support their improved instructional skills. Notice that when teachers participated in directed rehearsal (DR), received performance feedback (PF) about

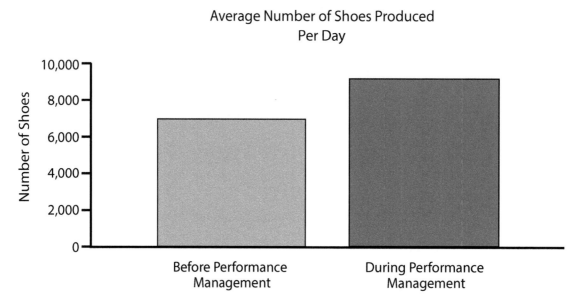

**Figure 13.2**   Goals setting, feedback and reinforcement to promote conformance to standards in a shoe-manufacturing plant (Based on a study by Sulzer-Azaroff & Harshbarger, 1995)

CHAPTER 13   TEACHING NEW BEHAVIOR: SHAPING   •   297

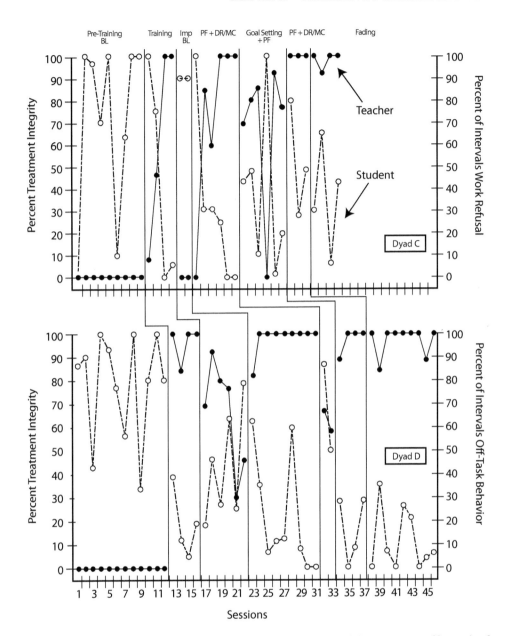

**Figure 13.3** Percentage of treatment steps implemented by two teachers and the percentage of intervals of target problem behavior by students C and D across all phases of the study (DiGennaro et al., *Journal of Applied Behavior Analysis* (2007). *40*(3), p. 456. Copyright Society for the Experimental Analysis of Behavior, Inc.).

their own accuracy in implementing their function-based treatment packages, set *treatment-integrity goals* for their own performance, and were excused from directed rehearsal meetings as a consequence of meeting their goals (meeting cancellation, MC), their treatment integrity improved substantially as did their students' participation in their school work.

## Consider Combining Physical Guidance with Shaping

Physical guidance often is used to prompt approximations of motor skills. Suppose you had unsuccessfully attempted to use modeling or imitative prompts (to be discussed later in more detail) to teach a youngster on the autism spectrum to smile. You might try prompting the response as DeQuinzio et al. (2007) did successfully by using two fingers to turn up the corners of the child's mouth. Successful responses were reinforced. Similarly, young community-bound, developmentally disabled women were helped to acquire housekeeping skills—folding clothes, mopping floors, and washing tables—by guiding and then reinforcing approximations of the skills (Thomas, Sulzer-Azaroff, Lukeris, & Palmer, 1977). Fitterling and Ayllon (1983) also used physical guidance as an aspect of training programs in football and ballet. Physical guidance is frequently used when prompts or other methods have failed repeatedly to evoke the desired response. For example, in preparation for the child's first birthday, one of the authors decided to teach her daughter to be able to hold up one finger when asked "How old are you?" When no appropriate behavior occurred in response to the question, "How old are you?" and when modeling by showing a raised finger failed, she used physical guidance to teach the child to hold up one finger while her mom held down the remaining four. Afterward, even if the finger was curved or not displayed completely independently, her mom heaped on the praise and kissed her when she held up one finger. Subsequently, the physical guidance was faded, while approximations to an increasingly straighter finger were reinforced. By the time her birthday arrived, to her grandmother's and uncle's amazement, she successfully held up one finger when asked "How old are you?"

In some cases, physical guidance is necessary from the beginning. For example, Penny's successive approximations were physically guided as she learned to climb, reinforcing her progress along the way: "Good Penny, you put a different foot on each step" (Hardiman et al., 1975, p. 405). Similarly, physical assistance enabled clients to learn how to leap over hurdles in preparation for competitive races (Cameron & Cappello, 1993).

## Combine Fading with Shaping

We have discussed how shaping can be expedited by using instructions, prompts, and physical guidance to prompt approximations. Those supports eventually will need to be removed if the terminal goal, *responding independently*, is to be firmly established within the learner's repertoire. As Bruno acquires virtuosity in the performance of the scherzo movement of the sonata he is studying, he must become less dependent on his teacher's coaching and the notations in the score; gradually that support must be faded. While we consider fading in more detail later in Chapter 20, for our *present* purposes be aware that fading as used here involves *gradually removing antecedent stimuli that might be supporting the behavior* in its present form.

In one inventive application of fading, graduated guidance reduced developmentally disabled children's dependence on physical assistance while they learned to walk independently (O'Brien et al., 1972). As a substitute for an adult's hand, a thick, taut rope with a pulley was attached to the ceiling. Gradually the rope was loosened and ultimately detached from the ceiling. Next, portions of the rope gradually were removed, until its length became very short. Eventually, now able to walk independently, the children discarded the rope altogether. In each instance, cues and prompts to approximations were faded. Again, one of the authors used a similar procedure to encourage her daughter to walk independently (e.g., not holding onto objects or hands).

Recall the Binnendyk and Lucyshyn (2009) food-acceptance program (p. 249). Before concluding the intervention, the implementers faded prompts from physical (e.g., to block resistive behavior), to partial physical prompts, to gestural prompts (e.g., prompting mouth opening), to specific verbal prompts, to nonspecific verbal prompts.

Fading and shaping procedures frequently are combined in the development of instructional materials. Fading reduces errors. For an example, see *Handwriting Without Tears,* which incorporates fading and shaping (info@LWTears.com) to help teach writing skills.

## ILLUSTRATIVE INSTRUCTIONAL PROGRAMS THAT INCORPORATE SHAPING

As mentioned above, shaping is often combined with other procedures to develop various instructional programs. Below, we briefly introduce an assortment of several such successful programs.

### Shaping and Programmed Instruction

**Programmed instruction (PI)** epitomizes a creative and especially successful educational application of the shaping procedure. *PI is an instructional application of shaping characterized by contingencies managed in such a way that the student progresses successfully in steps from one level of difficulty to the next. Reinforcement derives primarily through confirmation of correct responses.* In 1958, B. F. Skinner described the teaching machine—a device for delivering programmed instruction directly from methods developed in the laboratory, while later on, among many others, his daughter, Julie Skinner Vargas and son-in-law and Ernest Vargas (1991), then professors at West Virginia University, further elaborated upon and illustrated the method. All recognize the value of incorporating shaping within programs designed teach academic skills. Generally any discussion of that nature includes an emphasis on the importance of shaping and reinforcement, primarily in the form of confirmation of correct responses, as the student progresses in steps from one academic level to the next. PI programs usually begin with questions the student can answer very easily. The difficulty level advances in gradual increments, or *successive approximations*, with various prompting and fading strategies to maximize success throughout. Being correct serves as a powerful reinforcer for many students, so the reinforcement schedule is quite dense and students continue to progress at a fairly constant rate. Vargas and Vargas properly suggest a bit of caution, though, because:

> This presupposes both that the student will be right most of the time and that being right will be enough of a positive consequence to keep the student working. As with any "reinforcer," such an outcome is not inevitable, and the program designer should be prepared to design other kinds of reinforcers into an instructional system if being "right" is not sufficient. (pp. 240–241)

Actually, in one of our own early studies (Sulzer et al., 1971), we did put that question to the test by interposing a phase during which students could earn points paired with a bit of positive social attention in addition to gaining confirmation that they had produced correct responses in programmed instructional reading and spelling assignments. While that "points-only" condition was paired with substantial increases in both number of frames completed, performance was somewhat variable and began to deteriorate over time. After a return to a no-points or attention baseline, which produced a drop in rate and more variability, we introduced a new phase in which students could earn points exchangeable for small trinkets. The students substantially increased the number of correct responses, catapulting the group to a high, steady class average in the high nineties. (See Figure 13.4.)

Today, instructional programs assume many forms: books, tapes, strips of paper, computer programs delivered via personal computer or over the Internet, CDs, Microsoft PowerPoint slides, or various other online programs. Teaching segments generally consist of *a series of finely graded steps in a programmed instruction program* called **frames**. *The learner responds to each frame, and usually*

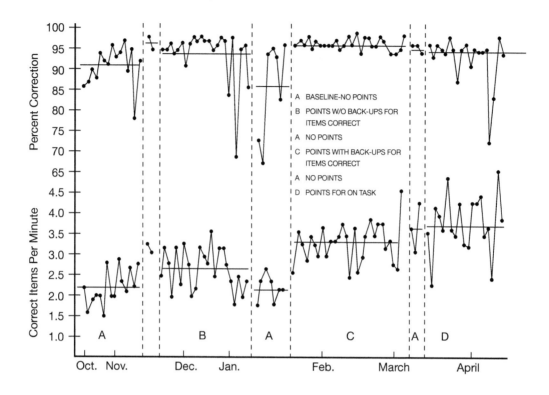

**Figure 13.4** Reading performance among students working independently on programmed instructional material: Class mean. Horizontal line signifies the mean for the phase (Sulzer et al., 1971).

*must get it correct before progressing to the next frame.* The content of the frames proceeds in graduated steps from the simple to the more complex. This gradual, cumulative progression helps the student to be correct and receive confirmation as often as possible. For example, here is a frame that entails active responding, similar to what is in the classic book, *Families* (Patterson, 1971):

> Whatever action turns off something painful is strengthened. When the TV set is turned up too high and your yelling leads someone to turn it down, then _____ is reinforced.[6]

*The Headsprout Reading Basics Program*™ (Layng, Twyman, & Strikeleather, 2003; Layng et al., 2004) exemplifies a more contemporary, sophisticated form of programmed instruction, based on a combination of controlled investigation of the subject-matter specialty plus principles derived from the experimental and applied analysis of behavior. The program uses shaping within a computerized set of programs capable of being deployed over the Internet to teach children consistently, quickly, and accurately to identify and combine letter-sound combinations with other letter-sound combinations. The developers have found that training to *fluency* (a high, steady pace) "improves the retention of new skills, enhances the comprehension of new material, and facilitates the recognition of new words. This builds confidence and accelerates reading as a whole" (2004, p. 173). By teaching to fluency and teaching behavioral cusps (see Chapter 4), **generative learning** occurs that *facilitates comprehension of new material as a result of previous learning. Individuals are more likely to engage in (learn) new behaviors on their own without training.* One advantage of the Internet distribution system is that the program can adapt to each learner's

---

[6]The answer is "yelling."

behavior because all data are uploaded and analyzed on Headsprout servers.

Among the numerous advantages of shaping concepts through programmed instruction are:

- The material is organized and presented in a logical sequence.
- Frequent and active responding is required of the student, which, in turn, expedites learning.
- The student receives immediate feedback.
- Students can begin at their own levels, move at their own rates, and not be held up or forced ahead by classmates.
- Students frequently master material more rapidly than through traditional lecture-based instruction (Fernald & Jordan, 1991; Ingvarsson & Hanley, 2006).

Effective programs are based on empirical evidence. Students work on an initial draft, and their performance is evaluated for each frame. If a student fails to learn, it is the fault of the program, not of the student. Items or frames may be revised, reorganized, expanded, or reduced until most students progress without error. Sometimes, as mentioned previously, providing tangible, edible, attention, or activity reinforcers adds to the excitement and fun of the learning task.

In one study (Davis, Bostow, & Heimisson (2007), three variations of computer-assisted programmed instructional formats were compared. To analyze those elements, the investigators developed a programmed-instructional tutorial about how ABA addresses feelings. This tutorial

> was programmed into programmed instruction (frames) and also into prose in a scrolling Web page format. It covered contrasts between respondent and operant conditioning, setting conditions, public and private behavior, and the difference between feelings and practical behavior. It explained emotions as by-products of contingencies rather than causes, and how feelings can be modified by context management.... No more than two or three sentences appeared in one frame. Typically, frames contained one blank to which the user responded by typing a word or phrase.... Frame step size was refined through reiterative field testing, such that the probability of answering correctly was maintained at better than .70 per frame and generalization responses were intermittently required. (p. 180)

In the *progressive prompting* programmed instruction condition, college students were presented one frame at a time. Initially, the frame appeared without prompts (i.e., letters of the answer). If the student filled in the blank correctly, the next frame was presented. If the answer was incorrect, a letter contained in the answer appeared next to the blank in the re-presented frame. If the student continued to get the answer wrong, an additional letter continued to be provided until the answer was complete. Whenever the student supplied a correct answer, the next frame was presented. The second condition was the *traditional* programmed instruction, permitting only one attempt. That is, if the student supplied an incorrect answer, the correct answer was provided and the program progressed on to the next frame. The third condition, the *scrolling prose* condition, presented the same frame content in paragraphs on one scrolling Web page without blanks to fill in an answer.

What was the outcome of the Davis et al. study? The two forms of programmed instruction produced no statistically significant differences, although the progressive prompting intervention promoted slightly better scores. However, posttests demonstrated that both of the programmed instructional programs resulted in significantly better use of behavioral terminology and understanding of the ABA material in contrast with the scrolling prose condition. Those behavioral gains also generalized to different settings. The authors concluded that, as demonstrated in previous studies (e.g., Kritch & Bostow, 1998), when compared to prose reading alone, programmed instruction produced superior gains. Additionally, as previously noted by previous studies (e.g., Kritch & Bostow, 1998; Miller & Malott, 1997; Tudor, 1995), results also confirmed the importance of overt interactions combined with feedback. In a more recent example, Storey, McDowell, and Leslie (2017) were able to improve the oral reading and word recognition of children using the Headsprout™ reading program who were in foster care by having them do one lesson *four* times a week. *It does appear that the more frequently the student actively responds and gains contingent feedback, the better the performance.*

## Shaping and the Personalized System of Instruction (PSI)

Box 13.3 describes a **personalized system of instruction (PSI)** course in operation. Notice how closely PSI resembles programmed instruction, in the sense that goals are clearly defined, step sizes are relatively small, correct responses are prompted via study questions, and feedback and reinforcement are delivered consistently and with minimal delay. PSI is *characterized by self-pacing, use of proctors, unit mastery, emphasis on the written word, and lectures and demonstrations used primarily for motivational purposes* (Buskist, Cush, & DeGrandpre, 1991).

Because PSI is directed toward a population of students who are more advanced and mature, it permits the students to work more independently and progress in larger steps than they would with programmed instruction. In his classic article "Goodbye Teacher," Keller (1968), who developed PSI, used an illustration similar to that in Box 13.3 to introduce the system. PSI has been used in thousands of classes and training groups at all levels to teach many subjects: basic and applied sciences, humanities, and many other disciplines. PSI promotes student learning and retention of material better than conventional instruction and has many other advantages (Johnson & Ruskin, 1977). One key reason that PSI is so effective is because it incorporates the principles of effective shaping. Approximations consist of mastering the concepts included in short prose passages. Achievement is reinforced consistently and with minimal delay.

## Shaping and Computer-Assisted Instruction

PSI now is also being packaged as computer-aided PSI (CAPSI). Based on student performance and ratings, the technique appears to be "a viable on-

---

### Box 13.3 PSI in Action

Lee approaches a more advanced student, Karim, the Course Manager.

"Hi, Karim, I'm ready for the study questions for Chapter 13 on shaping."

Karim rummages through the files and locates a set of pages, entitled "Chapter 13, Shaping." It contains the reading assignment and approximately 40 "study questions," each of which provides sufficient empty space to accommodate a written response.

"Thanks, Karim. See you on Tuesday, when I plan to take the Chapter Mastery Quiz."

Lee returns to his room and reads the assigned pages through once. Then he takes the study questions and, rereading the material, writes his answers. After a few hours of reading, answering, checking, and studying, he feels that he has mastered the chapter. On Tuesday he goes to a separate study area near the quiz room to review his material briefly one more time.

"Here you are, Chapter 13, Form B."

Lee signs for the quiz form and proceeds to respond on a separate answer sheet. The quiz contains a series of questions requiring short answers and/or brief essays based upon the study questions. All essential points of the chapter are probed, with some questions requiring integration of several concepts. When Lee completes the quiz to his satisfaction, he returns the quiz form and gives his answer sheet to a proctor. Virgil, his proctor, a more advanced student, takes his answer sheet and checks it against his key.

"Questions 1–7 and 9–12 are fine, but number 8 is unclear. Could you say more about why you think this illustrates the concept of reinforcing successive approximations?" Lee responds, apparently to Virgil's satisfaction. He asks him to write down his clarification.

"Fine. You've mastered this chapter." Virgil records Lee's "pass" on his folder, and Lee returns to Karim for the next set of study questions.

line educational method" (Pear & Crone-Todd, 1999, p. 205). CAPSI is a self-paced instructional program (Springer & Pear, 2008). It shares many features (Martin, Pear, & Martin, 2002a) of PSI: (1) It provides clear study questions for each unit based on written material, not on lectures. In fact, there are no class meetings (Pear & Crone-Todd, 1999). (2) Students must pass a short-essay test on each unit before progressing on to the next unit. (3) Tests are attempted when the student indicates his or her readiness to take the exam. If the student fails the first attempt at the test, other forms covering the same unit are available. (4) These tests are scored and feedback is provided by proctors (advanced students who had taken the class previously). Moreover, "the advanced students learn from the answers of the less advanced students" (Pear & Crone-Todd, 2002, p. 221). However, the proctors tended to mark incorrect test items correct about 67 percent of the time (Martin et al., 2002a). Thus, it is of utmost importance that proctors are provided with a key and trained in scoring whatever items are being used. Periodic reliability checks with feedback to each proctor would also be helpful. Martin, Pear, and Martin (2002b) also reported that only 61 percent of the instances of feedback provided by the proctors were used, at least partially, for items that were repeated. This indicates to us that long-term retention was minimal, which is further verified by an earlier study (Pear & Crone-Todd, 1999) which reported that students obtained a class average of only 71 percent on their final exam.

In a similar computerized application of PSI, we presented a series of courses in applied behavior analysis via the Internet (See Sulzer-Azaroff, Fleming, Tupa, Bass, & Hamad, 2008). Along with required participation in discussions and regular sets of field and laboratory activity assignments, students received study questions as an aid to preparing for their weekly quizzes. When they felt prepared, they took a multiple-choice quiz on that unit. Questions covered an array of course objectives chosen on the basis of a survey of experts in the field. (See Sulzer-Azaroff et al., 2008.[7]) Students received results on their performance along with relevant feedback as soon as they submitted their quiz. Required to attain over 80 percent before being permitted to continue on to the next assignment, they could retake as many forms of the quiz as necessary. Compared to a pre-test score of just below 60 percent, the post-test (final) class average on comparable items was well above 80 percent, and all but two of the 16 students scored above 80 percent.

**Computer-assisted instruction (CAI)**, *instruction aided by computer technology*, has a number of advantages (Ingvarsson & Hanley, 2006):

- The presence of an expert or supervisor is not required.
- It "can potentially survive staff and supervisor turnover to a greater extent than supervisor-mediated training programs" (p. 204).
- It is self-paced and therefore the clients can determine when and how long to interact with the program.
- Due to its self-paced nature, assignments can be completed at various times.
- Computers can be programmed as to when to prompt, fade the prompts, and to allow the presentation of new material only after the previous material has been taught.
- "Computer programs can automatically collect and analyze training data with great accuracy and reliability" (p. 204).

Computer assisted instruction also permits branching into remedial or advanced instruction where appropriate, and, of course, as we have seen, can be delivered in a laboratory setting or online.

Many computer-assisted or aided instructional (CAI) programs are available to teach people of all ages and ability levels. You have already become acquainted with the computer-assisted program *Headsprout*™, which obviously qualifies as another example of a program that teaches beginning reading to children via CAI. *The Competent Learner Model* (CLM) (Tucci, Hursh, & Laitinen, 2004;

---

[7]A revised form of this program has been offered by the Department of Psychology at the University of Massachusetts, Lowell. In 2008 it was recognized by the Sloan Consortium as the winner of the Most Outstanding Online Teaching and Learning Program in the nation.

Tucci, Hursh, Laitinen, & Lambe, 2005), another highly regarded computer-assisted instructional program, "is a mastery-based, self-paced program with a variety of ways for individuals to learn and practice the formulation, delivery, and monitoring of effective instruction" (Warash, Curtis, Hursh, & Tucci, 2008, p. 448) and includes coaching to assure accuracy of implementation. The program teaches teachers how to improve the behavior and learning of their students via a *CLM Course of Study* available on CDs or through online instruction, along with ongoing collaborative consultations. Using many illustrative examples, the *CLM* program is designed to shape and chain together new teacher behavior. The teachers also are coached through the "course of study that prepares them to strengthen desirable repertoires and weaken undesirable repertoires" (Warash et al., 2008, p. 447). For example, after experiencing two years of CLM, 79 people with autism, ages 4 to 22, achieved significant improvements in a variety of adaptive behaviors, as well as decreases in stereotyped behaviors and the overall autism index (Cihelkova, et al., 2012). The focus is on helping students learn to become effective talkers, participators, observers, listeners, readers, writers, and problem solvers, to enable them, in turn, to take full advantage of developmentally appropriate curricula.

The CLM model also has recently developed a contingency management system. It is a cloud-based application for selecting and designing effective contingencies for learners (personal communication with Tucci, Feb., 2021).

In an especially interesting study on the performance of 53 children with autism (Bisen-Hersh et al., 2010), CLM was compared with two other commonly-used teaching methods (*discrete trail training*, see Chapter 18, and *applied verbal behavior*). While student performance improved in all three of the approaches, students in the CLM classrooms had significantly higher rates of learning academic and language skills than students exposed to the others. As a result, the investigators concluded that the CLM approach to instruction appears to be an effective program for treating autism. Although the results of this pilot study are colored by many of the problems associated with any pilot study, should the results be duplicated within a carefully controlled experimental study using random assignment and different and similar assessment instruments, the findings would be of considerable importance. We suspect that the superiority of the CLM model can be attributed to the fact that, in contrast with the other two approaches, CLM included focusing on (1) achieving fluency and (2) training and supporting coaches who provided ongoing assistance, feedback, and reinforcement for program implementation. These two factors, fluency and supervisory intensity, may prove critical to the success of such intervention programs.

Many other programmed or computerized instructional programs have been designed to diagnose and teach conceptual skills such as math, reading, writing, foreign language, and identifying or defining terms to a variety of students. For example, Connell and Witt (2004) developed specialized software to aid teachers and parents "in developing individualized programs to address deficits in prereading skills" (p. 71). Youngsters using the program are taught to match lower- and uppercase printed letters to the auditory name of the letter. Next, they are taught to match the letters to one another, and then to letter sounds. After they have acquired those skills, they are taught to match printed to spoken words.

Software capabilities also allow the teaching of many other classes of skills, including studying (e.g., Grabe, 1988), promoting accurate and frequent use of parents' names by teachers (Ingvarsson & Hanley, 2006), differential dental and medical diagnoses (e.g., Watt & Watt, 1987), and so on. Programs have even been developed for teaching students how to shape behavior (Shimoff & Catania, 1995) and use computer software (Karlson & Chase, 1996) and computer programming commands (Kritch & Bostow, 1998).

Computer-assisted instruction is a rapidly growing field of specialization. Be aware, though, that just because instructional or training programs are attractively or impressively packaged, that is no guarantee that they will teach effectively. They must incorporate rules for effective shaping if they are to succeed in producing the intended results and should provide data on the program's success to date and, specifically, its utility for the students for whom it was developed. Only then should teachers or trainers feel reasonably confident about trying out the material with their own similar populations.

When contemplating using any particular instructional program, educators need to attend to both group and individual performance data. Assuming that treatment fidelity was maintained (that the program was conducted exactly as specified), should students commit too many errors or appear to become bored and distracted, you may conclude that the program is not performing its intended function. Perhaps it needs to be limited to that subpopulation of students for whom it does operate effectively, and/or to be revised further, or replaced. Few specific programs are universally successful. So, you need to monitor and supervise individual and group performance carefully to identify the subpopulation for which the material is best suited.

Should you be in the situation of selecting software for instructional purposes, consider Shimoff and Catania's (1995) guidelines for selecting effective computerized instructional software:

> Effective software necessarily provides effective contingencies of the behavior of students: The programs are typically easy to use, instructions are clear and simple, and students learn what the program was designed to teach. (p. 307)

The program also needs to take into account the student's preexisting behavioral repertoires: "Lecturers who misjudge their audience's skills and abilities can backtrack and elaborate; software must have such elaborations built in" (p. 308).

> "Even programs that are intrinsically interesting must compete with other activities, so assigning computer activities with no contingencies for completion is not likely to maintain much student behavior. Effective academic software should make it easy for the instructor to impose contingencies for completing the programs." (p. 308)

In other words, the software shaping program must incorporate the same procedural elements that heighten the effectiveness of any shaping procedure.

## SUMMARY AND CONCLUSIONS

Shaping, a very important behavior change skill, is used to move existing behavior to some new target. Shaping is conducted by reinforcing successively closer approximations to the desired target behavior, which, in turn, requires that objectives be clearly specified. While shaping is being conducted, learner performance must be carefully monitored to determine the appropriateness of the size of each step, the length of time the learner remains at each of those steps or successive approximations, and any variations in the direction of the instructional goal monitored for and reinforced. Well-designed training and teaching methods, including programmed, computer-assisted, and personalized systems of instruction, combine the features of effective shaping and chaining (see next chapter for chaining).

Combining shaping with other procedures, such as setting goals, giving instructions, demonstrating ("showing," or "modeling"), and physically guiding can expedite the process. Naturally, any artificial or intrusive prompts must be faded before the objective can be said to have been achieved, because you do not want the shaped behavior to depend on those supports. Only when the response of interest depends strongly on the contingencies intrinsic to the setting, and not on extraneous stimuli or conditions, can the results of a given shaping program be considered complete. *The child who does something because it works is empowered; the child who does it only because someone has prompted, guided, or modeled it remains dependent on that other individual to initiate the appropriate behavior.*

*Verbal behavior* can be an especially useful adjunct to shaping. In Chapter 19 we discuss the methods for and advantages of shaping verbal skills.

*Chapter 14*

# Teaching Complex Behaviors: Chaining, Task Analyses, and Social Skills Training

## Goals

1. Define, recognize, and give original illustrations of each of the following terms:
   a. chain
   b. links
   c. task analysis
   d. chaining procedure
   e. forward chaining
   f. backward chaining
   g. concurrent (total or whole-task) chaining
2. Describe and illustrate the dual-stimulus function played by each behavior (link) in a chain.
3. List seven dimensions of a chain and discuss how each can influence how rapidly and accurately the complex behavior is learned and retained.
4. List what can be done to enhance the effectiveness of forging behavioral chains and describe why each task is important.
5. Discuss and illustrate how chaining incorporates a task analysis.
6. Describe three methods of developing and validating a task analysis.
7. Differentiate by discussion and illustration between serial (forward or backward) and simultaneous (concurrent, whole, or total-task) methods of chaining.
8. Describe how and why backward chaining works.

9. Discuss why and how reinforcement is arranged during the development of a chain, and explain why interim reinforcement shouldn't be overdone.
10. Give an example of combining chaining with stimuli, fading, and shaping.
11. Describe how chaining is used in social skills training.
12. Discuss and describe the importance of the two major social skill areas.
13. Describe how to identify social skill deficits.
14. List and briefly describe the behavioral procedures commonly used to teach social skills.
15. Describe how unchaining and blocking works to prevent problem behavior.
16. Define and illustrate precursors to problem behavior.
17. Describe how to strengthen a chain once it occurs.

*********************

Probably now, or in the future, you anticipate being involved in some capacity as a behavior change agent: perhaps as a teacher, manager, leader, counselor, consultant, psychotherapist, supervisor, communication specialist, advisor, behavior analyst, or in some other related capacity. Those who operate in such roles often are concerned with matters beyond supporting the development of simple unitary acts like arriving at work on time, asking for a cookie, or answering a question. Rather, much of their focus is on attempting to teach composite behaviors consisting of sequences of similar and/or different components like organizing one's day, designing an intricate computer program, mastering a complicated basketball maneuver, or writing a client or research report.

In the last chapter you learned how to use *shaping* to fashion *new* behavior. Yet, even though you or your client may have mastered separate components (e.g., putting tooth paste on a toothbrush, brushing bottom teeth, and brushing top teeth) of a complicated activity (e.g., brushing teeth), fitting them together into a unitary whole is a different story. This chapter on teaching complex behaviors will inform you about how people master behavioral sequences composed of many parts, and how you can establish and support such sequences or disassemble those you deem inappropriate. We begin by elaborating on the concept of a *behavior chain*, and then offer you some guidelines for selecting the size of the behavioral unit you hope to teach. We follow with a useful array of data-based ideas for linking established behaviors together to form behavior composites, such as complex social skills, and discuss how disassembling or blocking links in chains can minimize troublesome behavior.

## WHAT IS A BEHAVIOR CHAIN?

### Chaining Defined and Illustrated

A **behavior chain** can be formally defined as "*a sequence of responses that are functionally linked to the same terminal reinforcer*" (Kuhn, Lerman, Vorndran, & Addison, 2006, p. 263).

Behavioral or response chains are composed of elements or **links** (responses or **R**s) each of which has dual functions: 1) reinforcing ($S^r$) the previous link and 2) setting the occasion ($S^D$) for the next link. Generally, the component responses in a behavior chain are *already included within the repertoire of the individual*. To teach Charlie to brush his teeth, his parents may be able to help him combine several instances of behavior that he has already demonstrated (how to put paste on a brush, place the brush against his teeth, move the brush up and down, and so forth) into a more complex chain. Charlie combines these separate components (**R**s for responses or **"links,"**) in proper order, to constitute the chain, as displayed in Box 14.1. Once Char-

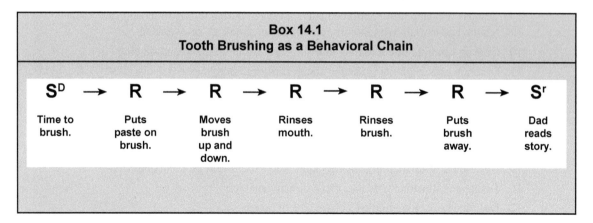

Box 14.1
Tooth Brushing as a Behavioral Chain

$S^D$ → R → R → R → R → R → $S^r$

Time to brush. | Puts paste on brush. | Moves brush up and down. | Rinses mouth. | Rinses brush. | Puts brush away. | Dad reads story.

lie has completed the total sequence in the proper order, his dad praises his tooth-brushing skill (the whole chain) and reads him a story as his reward (the conditioned reinforcer or $S^r$). Now, the complex behavior of tooth brushing is on its way to becoming well established.

Sometimes we select chaining procedures to teach a substitute for an inaccurate or undesirable behavior. If Charlie had rinsed his mouth without first moving the brush up and down, the appropriate chain would not have been emitted. Or, if after rinsing his brush, he threw it at another person instead of putting it away, the chain would have been inaccurate. To conclude that a target chain is emitted correctly, *each link must occur in succession, with no links omitted and none added.* Sometimes clients engage in completely inappropriate behavior chains. For example, some behavior chains that have been associated with Obsessive-Compulsive Disorder (OCD), such as opening and closing the front door 12 times before leaving the house, are inappropriate behavior chains. Disassembling or blocking the links in the chain can eliminate this inappropriate behavior.

In chaining, you need to describe the task completely, with the elements in proper sequence, because omitting or inadequately describing its elements can prove disastrous. You know what happens when a chain has a weak link! In a bow-tying **task analysis**, if we neglected to include *tightening the bow* after the bow was formed, that would increase the risk of it falling apart. As a demonstration, try to do a *rational* or "armchair" analysis of a task very familiar to you, like washing dishes, putting on an article of clothing, or boarding a public bus. To conduct a **task analysis**, *you study the subject matter and specify the process or procedure you presume to be involved in performing the task;* that is, you list the tasks based on your own experience or what you believe the tasks should be. Then, to see whether you have actually included all the links in the chain, ask a cooperative friend to follow the sequence *exactly as written—neither adding nor subtracting any elements*. Not long ago, a student-instructor needed to add about a dozen steps to his task analysis before his professor (one of us) successfully performed what appeared to be an extremely simple magic trick.

## Behavioral Links or Units

When we talk about the response elements incorporated within a chain, we must carefully define their parameters—those physical properties whose values determine their characteristics. That is easier said than done. Think of your own daily activities, or those of your family members, or of your clients. If you were to attempt to record those, you would be faced by an immediate dilemma. What do you mean by an "activity"? Would you list events like "wake up," "shower," "get dressed," "eat breakfast," "tidy up," and so on? Or do you mean something larger: "get ready for work," "go to work," "come home," "have dinner," "relax," and "turn in"? Or smaller: "set out cereal, juice, and coffee," "drink juice," "eat cereal," and "drink coffee"? Or smaller still: "go to the refrigerator," "open the door," "take out juice container," "bring it to the counter," "pour the juice"....?

 You get the picture. Like Russian nesting dolls, practically every behavior with which we might concern ourselves generally consists of smaller, and still smaller, units. So, when we involve ourselves with teaching and behavior change, how do we choose the size of the behavior unit to address? Does this raise a familiar concern? Perhaps you began to ask the same question while reading Chapter 4 on objectives. A good rule of thumb is to analyze the aggregate performance and continue breaking it down until each of its components appear to be sufficiently challenging, yet reasonably attainable by your student or client.

The key to forging a behavior chain is to *teach each link in its specific or proper order*. If, for instance, you know how to toss a basketball into a hoop and how to run, you can combine these into a play sequence by following specific steps. Or, in the case of a musical performance, you must play the notes in their proper sequence, without adding extra or wrong notes. Similarly, to teach a child to come in quietly from recess and take his seat, you want a chain consisting of: (1) walking to the classroom from the playground, (2) walking into the classroom, (3) walking to the desk, (4) sitting down, (5) quietly taking out materials, and (6) starting the assignment on the board, to occur without other behaviors interfering, such as walking to a friend's desk or turning around and talking to a neighbor after sitting down. If extra links are added or critical ones are missing, the objective has not yet been mastered.

## Choosing Behavioral Links

Consider the case of young children risking severe malnutrition, or worse, because they refuse to consume food. Investigators analyzed an eating sequence that included: (1) accepting, (2) chewing, (3) swallowing, and (4) retaining the food (Patel, Piazza, Martinez, Volkert, & Santana, 2002).[1] In preparing to use chaining to teach a composite behavior like this, the first question is whether the learner is capable of performing each behavior component

---
[1] Further details of Patel et al. (2002) study appear in Chapter 26.

(*teachable unit* or link) or not. If not, then each missing or flawed link must be taught or refined by means of shaping or differential reinforcement. Eventually, as the student masters each link, the set can be connected into a behavior chain.

A formal method for identifying the specific links composing a behavioral chain is to conduct a task analysis, in much the same way you learned to construct a task analysis for purposes of shaping. With chaining, though, you begin by *identifying each among a series of **sequentially ordered responses (links)** that compose the more complex behavior. Each small teachable unit, step, or element of the task analysis represents a **link**.* Remember it is important to assess if the client has these individual links in their repertoire. This is a good time to check to see if the client can perform the individual links in the behavior chain (i.e., the steps in the task analysis). These links then are to be connected into a *chain*, by fusing several links in sequence (ensuring each link is reinforced by the next link and that each link serves as a discriminative stimulus for that next link). Eventually more links are combined until reinforcing the complete series as a unitary behavior becomes possible. Examine the task of *frying an egg* and notice that placing the frying pan on the stove reinforces taking the pan out and also "prompts" taking out the egg.

---

**Box 14.2**
**Task Analysis of Frying an Egg**

Take out the frying pan→Place it on the stove→ Take out the egg→Place it on the counter→Take out the butter→Place it on the counter→Take out the salt→Place it on the counter→Take out a bowl R, R, R →…. etc., until ultimately you place your fried egg on a plate, set it on the table and—the terminal, reinforcing link: ***Eat it***!

---

Box 14.3 presents another example. Because Mary Jane seemed unable to learn to emit her tennis serve as one cohesive unit, the instructor analyzed the serve, *breaking it down into its component tasks*. Technically speaking, the instructor was using the process we refer to as a task analysis. Afterward, when Mary Jane could perform each of the subtasks

> **Box 14.3**
> **The Tennis-Serve Club**
>
>
>
> Mary Jane's instructor told and showed her the steps in serving:
>
> 1. Place your feet at a 45-degree angle to the net.
> 2. Hold the racket down over your shoulder.
> 3. Grasp the ball toward the tips of your fingers.
> 4. Position your hand over the foot closest to the net.
> 5. Gently toss the ball upwards.
> 6. Swing the racket over your shoulder.
> 7. Strike the ball with the racket.

separately, the coach taught her to follow each element in sequence. Then Mary Jane was able to serve the ball properly, and seeing it land in the proper place reinforced her serve.

For another illustration, consider an infant going to sleep. According to Blampied and France (1993), this "…begins with a sequence" (or chain) of "bed-preparation behaviors and ends in a period of behavioral quietude just before sleep begins. This period of behavioral quietude is the consummatory response for sleep" (p. 478). Seeing infant sleep disturbances in this light opens the opportunity to train parents to reconnect the chain of behaviors constituting preparing their infant for sleep. In actuality, just about any reasonably complex behavior can be conceived of as, and divided into, a chain of component responses. Viewing performance from this perspective offers exciting options for embellishing, refining, or modifying challenging (complex) behavioral chains. Table 14.1 lists additional examples of actions addressed in that manner.

## Linking Behavioral Chains

How is it possible for a series of previously learned responses to be combined and strengthened when the reinforcer appears to occur only at the end of the chain? Charlie's dad reads him a story only after he has completed all the links integral to brushing his teeth. The instructor praises Mary Jane when she places her tennis serve well. Paula is complimented for finishing her report only after she has engaged in a long sequence of behavior. The whole sequence of tasks that Santiago must perform to produce a new program for his organization's personnel department is reinforced only when he implements the finished plan and produces evidence of success. Solving a challenging arithmetic problem will be reinforced only after the student has obtained a solution. Asthmatic children only achieve relief from their symptoms after they properly follow the prescribed sequence for using bronchodilator medication (Renne & Creer, 1976).

Did you notice the delay between the early links in a chain and the reinforcer? Recalling the earlier discussion of how critical immediacy of reinforcement is to learning, this essential delay might give you cause for concern. How do chains become established naturally, despite the delay factor? The answer lies in *secondary reinforcement*. If, as you learned earlier in Chapter 6, a stimulus or event directly precedes the major reinforcer (e.g., scoring a point), eventually it will begin to acquire reinforcing properties of its own. Those acquired reinforcers serve to forge earlier links into a complex chain that ultimately is strengthened or maintained by a single reinforcing event. This is why it is so important to make sure there is a strong reinforcer that occurs after the completion of the behavior chain.

Permit a few illustrations: Notice how the skillfully placed final serve in a game of tennis or the last expert roll of a bowling ball each produce a better score for the player. The sensation of the racket making perfect contact with the ball acquires its own reinforcing properties. Such stimuli reinforce prior responses such as the player's bearing or posture. Or, if you have ever enjoyed the pleasure of baking bread, you know that the dough must rise to a certain level, then be placed in the oven at a particular temperature, then removed at a given time and set to cool, before you get to eat it. The appearances of the risen dough, plus the other visual and olfactory cues, contain reinforcing properties. Each of those serve to support the preceding elements of

**TABLE 14.1    Illustrative Applications of Linking and Disrupting Behavioral Chains**

| Composite Behavior(s) | Author(s) |
|---|---|
| *Linking Chains* | |
| Choice and play skills | Barry & Burlew (2004) |
| Dancing | Quinn, Miltenberger, Abreu, & Narozanick (2017) |
| Internet skills among adults with developmental disabilities | Jerome, Frantino, & Sturmey (2007) |
| Personal hygiene skills | Stokes, Cameron, Dorsey, & Fleming (2004) |
| Recovery of upper-body dressing ability following a stroke | Suzuki et al. (1987) |
| Requesting in special education classrooms | Sigafoos, Kerr, Roberts, & Couzens (1994) |
| Social skills in the form of social stories (in school) | Kuttler, Smith-Myles, & Carlson (1998) |
| Social skills in the form of social stories (in home) | Lorimer, Simpson, Myles, & Ganz (2002) |
| *Unchaining or Disrupting Chains* | |
| Bedtime problems and night wakings in infants and young children | Morgenthaler et al. (2006); Blampied & France (1993) |
| Chain of behaviors leading to eye-poking | Hagopian, Paclawskyj, & Kuhn (2005) |
| Chain interruption in criminal behavior | Berzins & Trestman (2004) |
| Chain interruption in self-injury | Hagopian et al. (2005) |
| Chain interruption to teach communication skills | Carter & Grunsell (2002 |
| Consuming inappropriate foods or excessive calories | Wadden, Butryn, & Byrne (2004) |
| Disruptive outbursts during athletic performance | Allen (1998) |
| Reversal of habits such as nervous habits, tics, stuttering, alcohol abuse, enuresis, aggressive and disruptive behaviors | Miltenberger, Fuqua, & Woods (1998) |
| Rock Climbing | Walker, Mattson, & Sellers (2020) |

the response chain (that is, assuming you get to eat the bread fairly soon!)[2]

Are you starting to recognize the way the components of a complex behavioral chain may operate in dual fashion; that each link may operate both as a discriminative (occasions the next behavior) and a reinforcing stimulus (reinforcing the previous link)? In our technical language, we call a stimulus that sets the occasion for—*occasions*, for short—a response that is likely to be reinforced, a *discriminative stimulus*. Discriminative stimuli ($S^D$s) are events (sometimes called "antecedent events"), that precede a particular behavior and tend to evoke (occasion) or inhibit (abate) it—see Chapter 15). Suppose you have an appointment for an important meeting on the twenty-second floor. Seeing the

---

[2]Now be good! Restrain yourself from running to the kitchen to bake a loaf of bread right now. Finish studying the chapter first! ☺

elevator button occasions pressing it; the reinforcer is the elevator doors opening; open doors then set the occasion for entering the elevator; the discriminative stimulus is the array of floor buttons; those occasion pressing your floor button; the doors open on the twenty-second floor; which occasions your getting out of elevator and reaching your terminal reinforcer: arriving at your destination. Through further associations with reinforcement ($S^r$)[3], the discriminative stimuli ($S^D$s) themselves (putting the brush and paste away; arriving at the twenty-second floor) may begin to function as reinforcers ($S^r$s) of the previous links in the chain (rinsing the brush; pressing *22*). Following a similar process, rinsing the brush or pressing *22* may become both a discriminative stimulus ($S^D$) that sets the occasion for putting the brush and paste away or exiting on *22*, and also a learned reinforcer ($S^r$) for the prior link in the chain, rinsing the mouth or surveying the array of elevator buttons. This sequence is illustrated in Figure 14.1, an elaboration of Box 14.1. *Each link in an established chain, then, serves a dual function: it reinforces the behavior that produced it, and it sets the occasion for the behavior that comes next.*

Early in the process of learning the sequence of responses within a complex behavior, each element can stand alone, as in each of the examples presented so far. Assuming the total sequence continues to be supported by sufficient reinforcement, given reinforced practice, over time the intermediate discriminative function of the links begins to fade and those components begin to coalesce into larger segments. Most of us have long ago dismissed any intermediate prompts integral to our own toothbrushing practices, while the experienced baker or pro tennis player have discarded intermediary discriminative stimuli as their skill becomes one fluent complex chain. We simply brush our teeth; they just bake a loaf of bread or serve the ball. At that point the behavior is no longer a behavioral chain, but a single complex response.

On the other hand, many complex behaviors are constrained by the environment, and as a consequence must remain as chains. For example, although grocery shopping is becoming more automated, generally making a purchase in a store depends on the availability and accessibility of the merchandise and a clerk to negotiate the sale. Operating an elevator depends on your choosing from an array of buttons to summon the elevator and to select the floor. Behavior managers and educators need to recognize the difference between chains of behavior that depend on the external environment for their completion and those that do not. Fluency must always be constrained to some extent in the first situation, but need not be in the second. One example from the training world is lock-step instruction in which assignments and materials are distributed on a week-by-week basis. Contrast that with self-managed instruction, in which on day one students receive the full set of assignments, materials, and other resources required to complete the entire course sequence independently. Which of the two do you think has the greater potential for promoting students' ability to learn autonomously, as a unitary complex response, and that for which studying must remain a behavioral chain?

---

[3]As will be explained in more detail in the next chapter, $S^r$ is the notation for *reinforcer* and $S^D$ is the notation for *discriminative stimulus*.

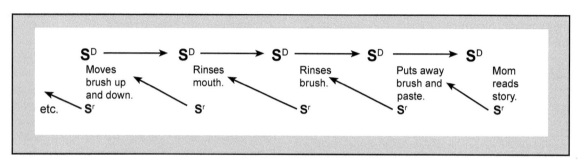

**Figure 14.1** The dual function of stimuli in a behavioral chain

## Different Classes of Chains and Their Components

As you consider the sequences of responses that are joined into a cohesive complex behavior, you also will notice that chains can vary on numerous *dimensions*, such as length, complexity, difficulty, interdependence, task organization, discriminative features, intrinsic reinforcers, and the various ways in which the elements are organized. Those features may influence how rapidly and accurately the composite behavior is learned and retained (see Table 14.1 for some examples in the literature).

**Length.** Some chains are relatively short: opening a door with a key. Others are longer, like doing the laundry; or much longer: designing a complicated computer program. Naturally, other factors being equal, short chains are easier to master than longer ones. As you add segments to a chain, errors might crop up, although this effect may be moderated by providing feedback on accuracy (Richardson & Warzak, 1981). Another choice is to break the task into clusters representing natural breaks, as Snell (1982) did when teaching bed-making by instructing and reinforcing the accomplishment of each cluster, in sequence.

**Complexity.** A chain can be *homogeneous*, in the sense that each component essentially is identical to the next, as in hammering a nail or doing a set of knee-bends, or it can be *heterogeneous*, with component responses differing from one another, as in playing a football game or assembling a wheelbarrow or barbecue grill. Notice that in the heterogeneous chain of dance steps described by Vintere, Hemmes, Brown, and Poulson (2004) (Box 14.4),[4] the tarantella contains fewer links and is somewhat more homogeneous than the butterfly dance. Presumably, it is easier to acquire a string of responses consisting of similar than of varied links.

**Difficulty.** Wexley and Yukl (1984) contend that not only complexity but also difficulty needs to be taken into consideration when deciding what to teach if personnel are to perform their jobs correctly and efficiently. A long ground ball requires a more powerful swing than a bunt; lifting a heavy object demands much more exertion than lifting a light one. The extra effort required may impair

---
[4]Description altered slightly.

---

### Box 14.4
### Dance Steps Composed of Heterogeneous Chains

#### Tarantella
Alternating gait of 8 steps

Step 1: forward step on the right foot
Step 2: hop with the left leg in front with the knee bent while right arm moves up over the head
Step 3: forward step on the left foot
Step 4: hop with the right leg in front with the knee bent while the left arm moves up over the head
Steps 5–8: steps 1–4 repeated once

#### Butterfly Dance
Alternating gait of 18 steps

Step 1: sliding step forward on the right foot
Step 2: jump on the right foot while bringing the left leg up in the back
Step 3: sliding step forward on the left foot
Step 4: jump on the left foot while bringing the right leg up in the back
Step 5: run forward on the balls of the feet (tiptoe)
Step 6: stop
Steps 7–18: steps 1–6 repeated twice

the robustness of the sequence. How well established the link is in the person's repertoire also influences its level of difficulty. Chains containing weak, non-fluent links risk breaking apart (*unlinking or unchaining*). Of course, weak links probably reflect the presence of difficult components, which in turn are less likely to be reinforced. The best way to avoid chains becoming broken due to weak linkages is to give special consideration to those difficult links. Follow-through when driving a golf ball is an example. An option would be to use *graduated guidance*, the combined use of physical guidance and fading: i.e., the pro uses hand-over-hand guidance to essentially guarantee an excellent swing each time, only very gradually shifting control back to the player (see Chapter 20 for a more complete discussion of graduated guidance).

**Interrelation among links.** Lifting the tennis racket clearly is a prerequisite for hitting the ball, whereas setting a screw does not necessarily depend on the prior installation of a washer. In cases in which one link is not necessarily dependent on the prior one, you will have to be careful to include each essential part of the chain as you train.

The degree of interrelation among the parts of the complex task is an important descriptor of the chain (Wexley & Yukl, 1984). All the aspects of a tennis serve are closely interrelated because it would be physically impossible to dispense with any of the links and complete an acceptable serve. Yet each separate subtask involved in assembling a barbecue grill is not essentially tied to every one of the others. Whether the links are closely interrelated or not, though, they all functionally relate to the same terminal reinforcer (Kuhn et al., 2006). How closely interrelated the tasks are may determine the best approach to teaching the chain. For example, Wexley and Yukl (1984) conclude that highly organized tasks are best taught by the "whole method" (to be discussed later).

**Discriminative features.** Some links of a chain are paired with readily noticeable or discriminable properties, like the different sizes and shapes in an assembly kit or the diverse responses in completing a gymnastics routine. Others bear a closer resemblance to one another, such as the seemingly minor (but important) variations between one kind of baseball pitch and another. Keeping grossly different links in proper sequence generally is easier than those difficult to distinguish or discriminate from one another (just think about how frustrating it is when you are on the last step of putting together a piece of furniture and then to realize you used the wrong screw on step 2).

Driving home from work consists of taking particular turns in the road. Each landmark not only signals increasing proximity to the final destination, but each junction also signals what the appropriate next turn should be. The importance of these discriminative features pertaining to driving home from work became very cogent for one of the authors after Hurricane Andrew in Miami, the landmarks and street signs were no longer present and made finding her way home very difficult, even though she had "mastered" the skill of driving home from work.

**Intrinsic or automatic reinforcers.** Just as the crowd roars its approval for a well-placed ball in a tennis match, or the scoreboard displays two additional points for a ball sunk in a basketball game, responses in some complex chains produce secondary reinforcers supplemental to the ultimate reinforcer, like winning the game. Some responses in a chain make you feel good: tasting your favorite flavor of ice cream combines with satisfying your hunger. Other responses contain few supportive auxiliary reinforcers: buttoning one's shirt or making the bed. Chains incorporating intrinsic or automatic reinforcers will probably be acquired more readily than those lacking those reinforcers.

As well, other topographical and functional features of the complex behavior and its components impact upon the rate and accuracy with which a given complex behavior is mastered and maintained. In planning to implement a chaining procedure, you should examine such factors carefully to determine how to proceed.

# EFFECTIVELY LINKING BEHAVIORAL CHAINS

You now know that *simple responses are capable of being connected together into chains*, often as independent links, and that you need carefully to examine the features of the task and the capabilities of the person who is to perform it. Accordingly, you surely will want to conduct a complete and precise task analysis and assessment of the client's repertoire when planning any chaining procedures. : Matching the two, tasks steps and client's repertoire, should enable you to progress more rapidly.

## Analyze the Task Precisely

Very precisely analyzing a complex task can be a challenging activity. Fortunately, because conducting *task analyses* has gained popularity as a method for describing, training and, evaluating optimal job performance, many examples are publicly available across specialty areas. Examples follow in Table 14.2. A thorough library search may enable you to identify studies for which data of effectiveness are available and/or that you might adjust to suit your particular clientele.

## Develop and Validate the Task Analyses

Armchair task analyses (or task analyses found on the internet) have their shortcomings, the most serious of which is that they might compromise the validity of the description. Imagine, for a moment, how you might feel about your surgeon practicing on you a technique erroneously detailed by her colleague during a flight to a conference! What other methods are available to ensure that a task analysis is complete, with each component in the proper sequence? Besides just engaging in trial and error or googling to find a task analysis on the internet, there are three major ways to develop and validate a task analysis:

1. *Observe a competent individual performing the task.* One of the most straightforward ways of developing and validating a task analysis is to observe someone who is competent in actually performing the task, and record the steps as they are performed. Subsequently, it would be important to test the validity of the task analysis by having another person follow the task analysis step-by-step to see if indeed it leads to accurate performance of the complex behavior. This process was utilized by Horner and Keiltiz (1975) to develop a tooth brushing task analysis and by Creer, Kotses, and Wigal (1992) to develop a task analysis for a child with asthma on how to use their inhalation equipment. Sometimes it might be helpful to observe a number of competent individuals performing the same task and developing a synthesized

TABLE 14.2  Examples of Chaining Studies Based on Precise Task Analyses

| *Participant(s)* | *Elements of Chain* | *Source* |
|---|---|---|
| Anesthetists | Steps to follow in conducting job | Weinger et al., 1994 |
| Entire schooling process | Steps constituting the elements | Selinski, Greer, & Lodhi, 1991 |
| Six primary-school children with moderate to severe mental retardation | Components of hand-washing | Parrott, Schuster, Collins, & Gassaway, 2000 |
| Mildly developmentally-delayed clients | Steps in effecting shopping | Taylor & O'Reilly, 1997 |
| Mildly developmentally-delayed clients | Steps in making choices | Shevin & Klein, 2004 |
| Eight-year-old girl with mild mental retardation | 60-step task analysis as a chain for hygiene routines | Piazza, Contrucci, Hanley, & Fisher, 1997 |

task analysis.

2. *Consult with experts.* This procedure involves consulting with experts regarding how to perform specific complex behaviors. In Walker, Mattson, and Sellers (2020), they consulted a rock-climbing manual that was written by experts to develop the task analysis of three specific rock-climbing behaviors that they later taught using expert video modeling. The task analysis for the positioning of wheelchair-bound patients, shown in Figure 14.2 (Alavosius and Sulzer-Azaroff, 1986), was based on input from ergonomists, physical therapists, and other specialists in preventing back injury. Again, it is important that, once a task analysis is developed based upon the expert consultation, it is validated by having someone follow the task analysis.

3. *Perform the task yourself.* As the old saying goes, sometimes the proof is in the pudding and it might be speeder to engage in the task oneself while recording the steps taken to accomplish it. After developing the task analysis from one's own performance, it is important to make sure it works by having someone else, besides one's client, follow the task analysis.

It should be noted that regardless of the method utilized to develop the task analysis (observing a competent person performing the task, consulting with an expert, or performing the task oneself), any task analysis must be validated prior to utilizing it with a client. To validate the task analysis, you along with your colleagues should follow the task analysis step-by-step and see if indeed the complex behavior is performed by doing so. If following the task analysis does not lead to accurate performance, the task analysis must be modified and re-tested until a valid task analysis is developed.

Behavior analyst Anthony Cuvo and his collaborators have developed and experimentally analyzed numerous task analyses to assist disabled clients to function more successfully in the community. Cuvo (1978) recommended that tasks be validated by using skill and subject (area of disability) experts. Social, developmental, and educational validity might be added to this list (Voeltz & Evans, 1983), along with cost effectiveness and other considerations mentioned earlier in this text.

Before assuming that any given task analysis is suitable to your population, validate it by testing it out with a few representative participants. When scoring each element in the sequence of behaviors, be sure it occurs in the specified order to judge it to be correct. Suppose step 8 in Box 14.5, rinsing hands thoroughly, was omitted? The client would hardly have clean hands. If you repeatedly encounter troublesome steps, consider whether to break those down further into their sub-elements, rearrange, add new, or subtract current links.

## Use Links Already in the Learner's Response Repertoire

A fairly basic guideline for establishing chains efficiently—one that should be obvious by now—is, when feasible, to form the chain from behavior already well established in the individual's repertoire. Teaching children to write their names if they can already write each of the component letters is simpler than teaching the student to write each letter during the same lesson. Training a clerk to file is easier if he already is familiar with the various classification schemes important to the operation of the office. When standing up and speaking before a large audience for the first time, the young professional who has already mastered a set of component skills such as organizing materials, speaking distinctly and loudly enough to be heard at a distance, using appropriate gestures, and looking directly at the audience, probably will perform much more fluently than someone lacking those skills.

Investigators (e.g., Kelso, Miltenberger, Waters, Egemo-Helm, & Bagne, 2007) recognize the value of prior mastery of components of longer chains when teaching firearm injury prevention skills to second- and third-grade children. In that particular case, they began training by using skills already within the youngsters' repertoires and then combining instructions ("Stop," "Don't touch," "Leave the area," "Tell an adult," p. 29) with demonstrations (modeling), rehearsal, and corrective feedback.

Employee_____     Unit/Ward_____
Date/Time_____    Location_____
Observer_____    Purpose of Lift_____

| Check | | | Task component |
|---|---|---|---|
| YES | NO | N/A | One Person Transfer (Total Lift) |
| ___ | ___ | ___ | 1. Positions wheelchair near goal (transfer across shortest distance). A 90-degree angle is best. |
| ___ | ___ | ___ | 2. Explains to client what they are to do (words or gestures). |
| ___ | ___ | ___ | 3. Locks wheelchair brakes. |
| | | | 4. Removes adaptive devices: |
| ___ | ___ | ___ | a. tray. |
| ___ | ___ | ___ | b. arm rests (if possible) |
| ___ | ___ | ___ | c. seatbelts(s). Other adaptive equipment. |
| | | | 5. Positions for lift by: |
| ___ | ___ | ___ | a. Standing at side of chair, at client's hip angle |
| ___ | ___ | ___ | b. with feet apart (width of hips, at least) |
| ___ | ___ | ___ | c. Bending posture, knees bent, and spine straight, may be slight bend forward at waist. |
| ___ | ___ | ___ | 6. Slides client forward on seat, to permit adequate room for step 7. |
| | | | 7. Supports client for lift: |
| ___ | ___ | ___ | a. One arm beneath client's arms and shoulders to support head, neck and upper torso. |
| ___ | ___ | ___ | b. Other arm beneath client's thighs to support pelvis. |
| ___ | ___ | ___ | 8. Hugs client (reduces distance between client and staff). |
| ___ | ___ | ___ | 9. Lifts straight up by unbending knees (back remains straight and erect) *Smooth movement.* |
| ___ | ___ | ___ | 10. Pivots (turns on balls of feet, or short steps without twisting torso) and aligns client with new surface. |
| ___ | ___ | ___ | 11. Bends knees, lowers client to new surface. Back straight. |
| ___ | ___ | ___ | 12. Securely positions client on new surface, then releases. |
| ___ | ___ | ___ | 13. Fastens seatbelts, where appropriate. |
| ___ | ___ | ___ | Total |

Describe unsafe components, if any:_____
_____
_____

How long did it take to complete this observation?_____

**Figure 14.2**  Positioning a patient in a wheelchair  (Permission obtained from Alavosius & Sulzer-Azaroff, 1986.)

## Box 14.5
## Hand-Washing Task Analysis

| Step | Instructive Feedback Stimuli |
|---|---|
| 1. Walk to sink. | |
| 2. Turn on water. | While pointing, "This is the cold water, and this is the hot water." |
| 3. Put hand under soap dispenser. | |
| 4. Push soap dispenser 1 time. | |
| 5. Put hands under running water. | While pointing, "You wet your right hand and your left hand." |
| 6. Rub hands together to form a lather. | While pointing, "You have soap on your right hand and your left hand." |
| 7. Spread soap on back and front of hands and fingers. | While pointing, "You have soap on your right hand and your left hand." |
| 8. Rub hands to rinse soap. | While pointing to each, "You rinsed your right hand and your left hand." |
| 9. Turn water off. | While pointing, "This is the cold water and this is the hot water." |
| 10. Walk to towel dispenser. | |
| 11. Turn handle 3 times. | "You count 1-2-3." |
| 12. Pull off towel. | |
| 13. Wipe palms of hands. | "This is the palm of your hand." |
| 14. Wipe back of hands. | "This is the back of your hand." |
| 15. Locate garbage can. | |
| 16. Put towel in garbage. | |

Often diverse paths may lead to the same end performance, as in teaching someone to wash her hair in the shower rather than at the sink. Or, we may adjust our presentation styles depending on the audience, using an informal, conversational style rather than a formal one, showing slides instead of using gestures, and so on.

When two acceptable complex terminal behaviors resemble one another, the alternative that includes components well established in the person's repertoire will probably be acquired more easily. Fern can use snaps but cannot tie a bow. In teaching her to dress herself, if possible, her caregiver should provide clothing with snaps and not ribbons or strings.

## Plan an Appropriate Starting Point

Given the intricacy of most complex skills, instructors need to decide where to begin. Should teaching be initiated with the first link, with the last, or with the whole task? Should simple discrete responses be joined one at a time or as groupings of subtasks? Finally, consider the value of combining multiple procedures, as in adding various types of discriminative stimuli, fading, and/or shaping, as illustrated later.

To begin to address these questions, first we need to distinguish between three chaining methods: *forward, total task*, and *backward chaining*.

Let us use coaching a tennis serve to illustrate **forward chaining**: *developing a chain of responses by training the first response or link in the chain initially, then joining the second link next, and so on; until the entire chain is **emitted** or "expressed" as a unitary complex behavior.* Training begins with the link occurring first in the sequence: positioning the feet. This link then is joined with holding the racket over the shoulder (the second link), and so on (as you saw in Box 14.3). Remember to provide reinforcement after completion of the link(s) currently being addressed because the end reinforcer will not be achieved naturally (e.g., in this case scoring points off the perfect serve). With forward chaining, the complex behavior is not completed by the client during initial step during training and will only be completed by the client when the last step is addressed. In the tennis serve example, the client will not actually "serve" or strike the ball until step 7 is addressed. Given that the complete task is not completed when teaching earlier steps, forward chaining relies heavily on supplemental reinforcers.

The forward chaining method was used in teaching family-style dining skills to a group of clients with severe developmental delays. Instruction began with gathering eating utensils and progressed until the clients had served themselves appropriately and were ready to eat their meal (Wilson, Reid, Phillips, & Burgio, 1984). Snell (1982) used the same sort of approach to teach adults with developmental delays to make their beds.

The **concurrent**, **total**, or **whole-task method** *involves training all sub-skills at the same time, or jointly, rather than adding one link at a time* as with forward and backward chaining. An example of the total-task method would be demonstrating the entire chain of hammering a nail. Walls, Zane, and Ellis (1981) combined all three techniques to teach assembly tasks like putting together a circuit board or bicycle brake. Investigators (Quinn et al., 2017) used to whole-task method to teach adolescent dancers how to turn, kick, and leap. Each skill was broken down into a 14- to 16-tip task analysis. The dance movement was scored as the percentage correct of the dance movement tasks. Public posting and feedback were used to help teach each skill. Each dance movement improved as a result of the intervention package. Usually, when the whole-task method is used, it is combined with modeling, differential reinforcement, public posting, and/or feedback.

**Backward chaining**, like forward chaining, focuses on one link at a time, *but progresses in the opposite direction, starting with the last link*. Generally, the therapist will perform all of the previous steps before the step that is being addressed. For example, if using backward chaining to make a bed, the therapist would perform all the steps of making the bed before the last step of putting the pillow on the bed. The therapist would then use a teaching method (e.g., prompting) to get the client to engage in the last step and then provide reinforcement. Subsequently, the therapist would leave the last two steps (e.g., pulling the cover up to the top and putting the pillow on the bed) and prompt the client to engage in those two steps. This process of linking additional steps would occur until the client is expected to perform the entire chain from the beginning of the task analysis to the end.

Backward chaining was used to help students with severe developmental delays learn to walk from their residences to school without assistance (Gruber, Reeser, & Reid, 1979). Training began close to school and progressed in stages from locations farther and farther away. Backward chaining also has been used to help five students with autism, ages 3 to 9, learn to communicate by handing a card with the picture of the item that they want (Fritz, Jackson, Stiefler, Wimberly, & Richardson, 2017). The chain consisted of three steps: 1) moving the participant's hand toward the card, 2) picking the card up, and 3) handing the card to the therapist. Minimal physical guidance was used as necessary to prompt each child during each step, starting with handing the card to the therapist.

Notice an important advantage of backward chaining, in contrast to the forward training method, is the congruency of the response and the reinforcer. In other words, because the client always completes the last step of the chain and then receives reinforcement, the contingency is maintained. However, in the forward training method, the client does not engage in the last step of the chain and thus does not come into contact with the terminal reinforcer until later. That it is why it is necessary to include arbitrary reinforcement after the completion of steps during forward training. Moreover, given the potential length and response effort involved with the total task method, supplemental reinforcement may be necessary initially in between steps: "Good. You remembered to lock the wheels of the chair!"

**How and why backward chaining works.** In Chapter 6 we discussed the way stimuli evolve into secondary reinforcers. You saw that stimuli may take on learned, or secondary, reinforcing properties as a result of being repeatedly coupled with either primary or other powerful secondary reinforcers. In the tooth-brushing example discussed earlier, which link in the chain was coupled most frequently with father's reading a story (the functional reinforcer)? The behavior of putting the brush and paste away, because it is the behavior emitted with the closest proximity to and the shortest delay before the reinforcer: the story. Putting the brush and paste away under these circumstances should, in time, come to operate as a reinforcing event in itself. It will be a stronger reinforcer than the previous link in the chain: rinsing the brush. The shorter the delay between the response and the reinforcer, the more effective the reinforcer is. Note that from the point of view of immediate reinforcement, training with the final, as in backward chaining, instead of the initial link, works best.

First, father could read his son the story after the brush and paste were put away. Next, the reinforcer would be made contingent on rinsing the brush and putting it and the paste away. Once this chain had occurred fairly frequently, the reinforcer could be made contingent on rinsing the mouth, and so on, until the entire chain solidified into a unified complex behavior.

Notice how Gruber et al. (1979) applied this strategy to teach independent walking skills: Once the students experienced an overview of the course they would need to travel, they received intensive training. Their initial trials began very close to the school, with later trials beginning farther and farther away, until ultimately the students completed the entire route autonomously. Backward chaining succeeded in that particular instance.

Jerome et al. (2007) combined most-to-least prompting and backward chaining to teach three male adults with disabilities (autism and mental retardation) Internet skills. The chain consisted of the 13 steps found in Box 14.6.

Prior to each day's session, a preference assessment was conducted to determine which edibles were to be used as reinforcers (e.g., jelly beans). Also, because program staff had access to the clients' Web sites, staff members were asked to identify the site the client visited for the longest time. Those were the sites to which clients would learn to gain access. Teaching progressed as follows: Staff completed the first 12 steps for each participant, so the only step remaining was for the client to click on the Web site of choice. If the participant correctly completed this step, he was allowed five minutes at the site. If the client did not click the mouse after five seconds, a most-to-least intrusive prompting procedure was implemented. "The prompting procedure continued until the participant independently

---

**Box 14.6
Using the Internet**

1. Press the computer power button.
2. Press the monitor power button.
3. Place hand on the mouse.
4. Move the cursor with the mouse until it points to the Internet Explorer® icon.
5. Double click the Internet Explorer® icon.
6. Move the cursor with the mouse to the Google® search box.
7. Left click in the box.
8. Type in the search topic of interest.
9. Place hand back on mouse.
10. Move cursor to the box labeled "search."
11. Single click the box.
12. Move the cursor with the mouse down to the Web site of choice.
13. Single click the Web site of choice.

completed each of the 13 task-analysis steps two times consecutively. After mastery of each step, training on the previous step was added" (p. 187).

In another illustration, a teacher had been using forward chaining to teach computation skills unsuccessfully for months and so decided to try backward chaining instead (Benoit, 1972).

The major steps for multiplying 2-digit numbers by 2-digit numbers were outlined:

1. Multiply the 1's times the 1's.
2. Multiply the 1's times the 10's.
3. Leave a place for the zero.
4. Multiply the 10's times the 1's.
5. Multiply the 10's times the 10's.
6. Add partial products.

The last step produced the correct answer and social reinforcers from the teacher. Figure 14.3 illustrates the actual backward chaining steps taken. Several practice trials were given at each step. Within 30 minutes, the student was multiplying appropriately.

One reasonably may ask, "What evidence have we that this approach is any better than teaching by adding components from the beginning of the chain?" The answer remains ambiguous. In one comparison study (Walls et al., 1981), it was shown that when vocational assembly tasks were taught, both forward and backward chaining resulted in far fewer errors than a whole-task method. Conversely, others (Spooner, Weber, & Spooner, 1983) discovered that a total-task method required fewer trials to criterion and was associated with fewer errors than backward chaining. After reviewing studies on forward chaining, backward chaining and total-task chaining from 1980 to 2001, Kazdin (2001) concluded: "Direct comparisons have not established that one is consistently more effective than the other" (p. 49). If your standard approach to teaching a chained sequence of responses seems ineffective, then we advise you to try the other.

What accounts for the ambiguity? Perhaps backward chaining operates more effectively with some complex sequences than others. Maybe the opportunity for an interim reinforcer or the size or difficulty of the task makes a difference. In most of the studies of whole-task and forward chaining, opportunity existed to reinforce links of the chain externally while they were being emitted.

Sometimes external reinforcement is not feasible, as in situations demanding independence. The trainer can't readily provide a sky diver with supplemental reinforcers for pulling his rip cord at the right moment. The only reinforcer is the ultimate one—a safe landing. Additionally, backward chaining might be the only option when clients with no receptive language are involved, because the prompts that usually accompany forward chain-

---

**Bold** = steps by teacher
*Italics* = steps completed by student

```
                1.   94                           2.   73
                   x 57                              x 67
                    658                               511
                   4700                              4380
     (Step 6)     5358             (Steps 4–6)      4891

                3.   40                           4.   23
                   x 19                              x 43
                    360                                69
                    400                               920
     (Steps 3–6)   760             (Steps 1–6)       989
```

**Figure 14.3** Backward chaining in teaching multiplication

ing procedures would not be functional for them. Another possibility is that backward chaining is most successful when the completion of the chain entails a reinforcer the individual finds especially powerful: reaching a destination, obtaining a tasty meal, or constructing a useful object. Only future research will permit this problem to be solved. In the meantime, you might test various approaches. If you want to use the total-task method with an especially long or complex sequence, though, try using small groupings of responses first; then combine them.

## Consider Using Supplementary Reinforcers

Although the ultimate reinforcer for learning a complex behavior is supposed to be completing it independently, thereby gaining access to the terminal reinforcer (e.g., meeting the challenge or completing the task or assignment correctly), you may be able to speed up the process by reinforcing the correct components as they are expressed along the way. For example, Snell (1982) combined continuous praise with pennies for clusters of correctly completed bed-making skills, and Parrott et al. (2000) continuously praised and allowed clients to choose a small piece of candy or a sticker for good performance until they reached at least 80 percent accuracy for two sessions. Investigators also used praise or other strong reinforcers in many of the programs already cited. They also used instructive feedback for many of the tasks in the hand-washing chain (see Box 14.5); once the criterion was met, the reinforcers added at intermediate points in the chain were gradually thinned out, while praise eventually was delivered only when the chain was completed.

Be especially careful not to overdo reinforcement within a chaining procedure. Rather, try to save the most powerful reinforcers until the end. Evidence from a study of responses by pigeons, at least, suggests that the reinforcement of some responses might interfere with the maintenance of others, and that the same might happen across the different reinforcers arranged within various components of chains (Catania, Sagvolden, & Keller, 1988). Diminish your supplementary reinforcers as quickly as feasible to allow the subsequent link in the chain to assume secondary reinforcing properties.

## Consider Using Supplementary Discriminative Stimuli

In addition to the stimuli inherent in the response chain, supplementary prompts often support the connecting of specific links in the chain. Both "prompts and reinforcement are used to teach each response in the chain in a manner that ensures that the sequence of behaviors operates as a functional unit" (Kuhn et al., 2006, p. 263). Verbal directions, gestures, written instructions, demonstrations, physical guidance, and similar prompts may effectively shorten the time needed to establish a behavior chain. To illustrate, asthmatic children were taught to use an intermittent positive-pressure breathing (IPPB) device by prompting the links *eye fixation*, *facial posturing* (keeping the mouth firmly around the mouthpiece while not puffing the cheeks and while breathing through the nose), and *diaphragmatic breathing* (Renne & Creer, 1976). Prompting of the last link consisted of "pushing in on the abdomen of the subjects while, at the same time, instructing them to breathe out as fully as possible from their mouths. They were then told to use their stomachs to push the experimenter's hand away while breathing in as deeply as possible through their mouths" (1976, p. 4). Proper responses were praised and rewarded with tickets that the children could later exchange for surprise gifts. In another example, components of words were modeled (e.g., for Monday, "Say 'mon'") for three children, ages three through seven, two with autism and one with developmental delays (Tarbox, Madrid, Aguilar, Jacobo, & Schiff, 2009). Once one component of the word was learned, the next component was taught (e.g., "Say 'day'"). Once all components of a word were learned, the child was helped to chain them together (e.g., "Say 'Monday'"). This procedure was effective for all three children.

In an interesting conjunction of video modeling and forward chaining, Shrestha, Anderson, and Moore (2013) were able to effectively use a procedure coined point-of-view video modeling (POVM).

In POVM, each link in the chain has a corresponding video-model taped from the perspective of the client and the video-models are presented as individual links of the chain. For example, Shrestha et al. taught a four-year-old child to independently serve himself cereal and clean up once done. A 13-step task analysis as well as separate videos modeling each step was created. During training, the therapist gave the instruction to make a snack. Initially, the therapist would show the video-model of the first step and then have the client complete the step. Once the client performed the first step consistently, the therapist would show the first step video, wait for the child to respond, then show the second link video. They continued this procedure until all 13 steps were shown and subsequently removed the video models and the child independently engaged in the chain of making himself a snack and cleaning up.

Shipley-Benamou, Lutzker, and Taubman (2002) used whole-chain video demonstrations (i.e., total-task chaining) to teach functional living skills to three five-year-old children with autism: how to make orange juice, put a letter in the mailbox, clean a fish bowl, and set the table. They carefully programmed tasks to assure proper video modeling by the primary researcher. During baseline, the child was told, "[name], here is everything you need to [task]. When I say 'go' I want you to [task]. Do the best you can" (p. 168). During the viewing of the video, the instructions provided at the beginning of each task on the videotape were: "Here is everything your friend needs to [task]. When I say 'go' I want you to watch your friend [task]. Ready, go" (p. 168). As reinforcers, two of the children earned candy, while the third was provided with a favorite battery-operated toy after successfully completing the chain. According to a one-month follow-up, not only did all three children succeed in learning the skills, but retained them as well for at least that month. Similarly, by using a total-task chaining procedure, peer models taught three children with disabilities mainstreamed in elementary-level general education classrooms to sharpen a pencil, operate an audiotape, and use a calculator (Werts, Caldwell, & Wolery, 1996).

To minimize errors, Parrott et al. (2000) immediately followed directions for each task (e.g., "Walk to the sink and wash your hands") with physical guidance. They then conducted daily probes following the session to determine if such prompts were no longer needed. Probing was stopped either after the learner failed to respond or after they mastered the chain.

Similarly, in our tooth-brushing illustration, if Charlie's father had said (and later faded), "Remember to rinse your brush and to put the toothbrush and toothpaste away" and had consistently reinforced the emission of those links, Charlie might have acquired them more rapidly than if he had simply waited for him to emit them spontaneously.

By teaching four low-functioning boys with autism (ages 9, 9, 11, and 14) to use photographic activity schedules, the investigators (MacDuff, Krantz, & McClannahan, 1993) found the boys became capable of displaying lengthy and complex chains of leisure and homework activities. In addition, the boys' on-task and on-schedule activities improved and occurred independently, and "their schedule-following generalized to new sequences of activities and to novel photographs and materials with no additional training" (p. 96). Further, the investigators anecdotally reported fewer aberrant behaviors.

In a study mentioned earlier (review Box 14.4), Vintere et al. (2004) compared the effects of demonstrations and praise versus demonstrations, praise, plus self-instructions (getting the children to repeat the instructions they'd been given) on preschool dance-class students' learning a gross-motor chain of dance steps. Both teaching methods succeeded in teaching the chains, but the addition of self-instructions often caused participants to acquire the chain more rapidly. Therefore, when teaching a chain, consider adding self-instructions to prompt the desired sequence of behaviors.

When you teach staff a new, complex procedure, consider breaking the terminal goal into a set of sub-goals or sub-tasks. Then use the operational description of each sub-task to encourage that particular approximation. Suppose, for instance, your objective is to teach an employee a particular set of instructional skills. You might first hand the trainee a checklist containing the steps: readying materials, attaining eye contact, orally instructing the client, waiting for, and, if necessary, prompting or guiding the response, then reinforcing that response. If necessary, you might demonstrate each of those skills, and then reinforce its satisfactory imitation. (See Fleming & Sulzer-Azaroff, 1989, for an example.) Later on, to maximize long-term success, you and your staff-trainees might use the checklist as both a reminder and as a recording instrument. You might also use the checklist as a tool for prompting and reinforcing performance of the correct step. A pictorial schedule of each step of the chain also may serve as a useful adjunct to the procedure. See Figure 14.4 for an example.

As long as the demonstrated or modeled behavior is not too complicated and learners are capable of performing its components, observers may attempt to imitate novel complex behaviors: mastering a new assembly task, repeating lines of poetry, doing homework and craft projects, and so forth. Many of the studies cited in this chapter have included modeling as an adjunct to formal chaining procedures. (See Chapter 18 for effective application of modeling and model selection.)

With more intricate behavior, however, simply providing imitative prompts may be insufficient, especially if a complex response sequence is presented in its entirety. We might request an older brother to demonstrate the full tooth-brushing sequence for his little sister. That might be sufficient to occasion the chain. The whole process would be less likely to work with longer or more complex

| Pictorial Cue | Event (S$^D$) | Action |
|---|---|---|
|  | Timer signal operating | Check time |
|  | Time to record | Obtain recording sheet |
|  | Ready to record | Observe and record staff action |
|  | Assess staff action | Provide feedback to staff |
|  | Reorganize materials | Return to ongoing activity |

**Figure 14.4** A sample pictorial schedule for observing and recording staff performance

chains, such as organizing and conducting a debate or installing and using an intricate new computer program. Instead, the chain might be broken down into shorter sequences, each one demonstrated and the learner then asked to imitate each separate link. Afterward, the chain could be connected gradually, as previously described, and the segment prompts phased out. That is exactly how Gustafson, Hotte, and Carsky (1976) taught hair-washing and other everyday living skills to their community-bound clients. When necessary, a tell, show, or guide prompt was used to occasion individual links in the chain.

When teaching motor responses, if all else fails, physical guidance usually will work. Cronin and Cuvo (1979) physically guided mending of clothing, while Snell (1982) and Tarbox, Wallace, Penrod, and Tarbox (2007) did the same, respectively, with bed-making and compliance. Tarbox, et al. used a three-step minimum-to-maximum prompting procedure (described in Chapter 17). If the client failed initially to respond to a verbal prompt, the instructor demonstrated the behavior. If that did not work, physical guidance followed.

At this point you may ask, "Why not limit ourselves to prompting or demonstrating whenever we teach complex chains?" The answer lies partially in the fact that showing (providing imitative prompts) and telling (giving directions) often are insufficient to extract the desired response. Similarly, locating effective models for the person who fails to follow directions may be difficult, if not impossible. Additionally, many instructional and behavioral goals are much more intricate than those we have illustrated, and the learner may lack the essential components of the particular chain in his response repertoire. Those first must be shaped. Furthermore, as you know, too much prompting may cause learners to become overly dependent on those artificial supports. Fading prompts as rapidly as possible, then, becomes critically important.

Hold on for a moment, though. Ask yourself if any of these prompting strategies are really necessary. If your concern is that the behavior of interest be expressed independently, eventually you will need to *discard any artificial prompts and cues you added during training*. So, now that we have suggested a variety of useful prompts and cues for your consideration, before rushing headlong into using them, we suggest you think the matter over once again. Moreover, research has demonstrated that if one includes prompts and makes errors associated with the prompting or when reinforcement is delivered, skill acquisition will be interfered with as well as disruption in performance of mastered skills (Donnelly & Karsten, 2017).

## Combine Shaping with Chaining

If the learner has already mastered all the component links, surely s/he will master the chain more rapidly. Occasionally, the person may have failed to master one or two of the essential links. Perhaps Fern has a difficult time rinsing the shampoo out of her hair, or a student in the college personalized system of instruction (PSI) course, is unable to fill out her study guide in sufficient detail. Shaping and then reinforcing each missing or weak link would permit them to acquire the chain more readily.

Consider how backward chaining plus shaping were used successfully to teach Josh, a 12-year-old boy with autism and moderate retardation, to drink water. Due to his complete refusal of food and liquids, Josh was dependent on a nasogastric tube (a tube that ran from his nose to his stomach) for survival (Hagopian, Farrell, & Amari, 1996). The chain of drinking water from a cup was specified as (1) bringing a cup of water to his mouth, (2) accepting water into his mouth (the missing link), and (3) swallowing the water (swallowing was present). A 100 percent criterion level for two consecutive sessions was set for moving to the next phase in the study. To shape swallowing water, the first approximation was to prompt Josh to swallow (in the absence of the water). Next, he was required to swallow after an empty syringe was depressed onto his tongue. Once that approximation was established, a small amount of water was added to the syringe and swallowing the water from the syringe was reinforced. Then, the amount of water from the syringe was gradually increased from 0.2 cc to 3 cc. Then, Josh was required to bring a cup with 3 cc of water to his mouth, and presumably to avoid the (aversive) presence of liquid in his mouth, to accept, and swallow it. Finally, the amount of water in the cup was gradually increased from 3 cc to 30 cc. Later, water gradually was faded to juice by gradually adding more and more juice, or less and less water. As the authors pointed out, "this study… provides an illustration of how a chain of responses that is totally absent (drinking) can be shaped by first targeting a simple preexisting response in the chain (swallowing)" (p. 575).

The combination of chaining, shaping, and prompting also has been used to improve articulation. For example, Eikeseth and Nesset (2003) first presented parts of a word separately,

> and then closer and closer together in time across successive trials until the child could articulate the word as a whole (e.g., /c/ and /up/ were first presented separately and then closer and closer together in time until the child articulated /cup/ when presented as a whole). Difficult sounds were prompted by exaggerating loudness or clarity, for example, by modeling the correct mouth, lip, and teeth position or by repeating sounds (that had been substituted or omitted) several times on consecutive trials before presenting the whole target word (e.g., the therapist would have the child imitate the sound /c/ six times quickly before presenting the whole word /cup/). (p. 330)

If your own client's particular chain of responses is missing several links, however, seriously reconsider teaching the selected target behavior. In all likelihood it is overly ambitious for that particular learner. Rather, think about seeking a more basic behavioral objective.

## Combine Chaining with Fading

Before concluding that you have finished your teaching or training job, you must remove within-chain prompts. In the solution of long-division problems, for instance, the ultimate goal would be for the students to carry out the entire process without any external prompts. Otherwise, few would agree that the terminal behavior (being able to solve long-division problems) had been mastered. A better criterion for success would be *correctly solving a number of long-division problems independently*.

As with shaping, if the complex skill is to be judged accurate and fluent (the behavior occurs smoothly, rapidly, and with little apparent effort), it must be emitted without supplementary and/or intermediate prompts. Removing these prompts too abruptly might cause the chain to become unlinked. Prompts for the asthmatic clients (Renne & Creer, 1976) were faded first by gradually eliminating the "hand-against-the-abdomen" prompt; then, as appropriate responding was seen to increase, by diminishing verbal instructions. Similarly, guidance, demonstrations, or verbal cues for each link in the hair-washing chain were faded gradually as instruction shifted from the highly intrusive to the most natural cues.

"Where (at which link) should we begin to fade prompts?" Again, this is an empirical question still awaiting a decisive answer. Your best bet is to begin with the most well-established link. Unless some other link was very well-established before you began to teach the complex behavior, the last one is probably the strongest, because, in backward chaining especially, it has been practiced most frequently and reinforced most immediately. So remove your prompt for that one first. In the long-division example, the instruction to reduce the fraction to the smallest common denominator should be the first one eliminated. As that final link and the one immediately before it become fairly tightly connected, the cue for the preceding link (the instruction to place the remainder over the divisor) may then be eliminated, and so on, until the entire chain is performed with perhaps only the single, and now natural, cue at the beginning ("Divide 987 by 31").

## Consider Instructing Students in Pairs while Using a Time-Delay Procedure

Sometimes you can successfully remove *all prompts or other supports at once* using a time-delay procedure. If you are wary of doing that, to be on the safe side, choose a progressive or constant time-delay method. Snell (1982) instituted time delays that progressed from 0 to 8 seconds (graduated delayed prompting) while teaching bed-making, and Schus-

ter et al. (1988) introduced a constant time delay of five seconds during instruction in food preparation. When teaching three boys with autism social play skills such as requesting peer assistance, Liber, Frea, and Symon (2007) gradually delayed prompting. Besides all three acquiring the play skills, one increased his pretend play and two generalized the social play skills.

Perhaps you are teaching a vocational or other complex skill to students with developmental delays. Think about using a constant time-delay procedure—say of 10 seconds—to instruct pairs of students who take turns observing and practicing skills. You may discover, as Wall and Gast (1999) did, that along with the student-participant, the student-observer might acquire considerable incidental information simply by listening to the instructions or watching the other participant engage in the learning task.

## TEACHING SOCIAL SKILLS BY MEANS OF CHAINING

### A Special Application

Social skills are vital to people's success in school and society in general (Hinshaw, 1992; Moffitt, Caspi, Harrington, & Milne, 2002; Newman et al., 1996; Patterson, Reid, & Dishion, 1992). Deficient social skills are a root cause of many adjustment problems, including a lower probability of graduating from high school and a higher probability of victimization (Caprara, Barbranelli, Pastorelli, Bandura, & Zimbardo, 2000; Chandler, Lubeck, & Fowler, 1992; Hinshaw, 1992; Lopez & DuBois, 2005). Further, adequate social skills protect people from dropping out of school, becoming delinquent, depressed, and/or from engaging in a variety of antisocial behaviors (Lane, Gresham, MacMillan, & Bocian, 2001; Luczynski & Hanley, 2013; Smokowski, Mann, Reynolds, & Fraser, 2004). Given your recent familiarity with chaining techniques, allow us to illustrate further by describing their utility as a tool for teaching social skills.

Before we proceed, perhaps you are wondering what accounts for individual social skill differences. Habitual family patterns may be one source: Some families encourage activities or provide materials like puzzles or games that inspire *persistence*; others may not. If no one reads to the children or encourages their participation in family discussions or other social events, they miss out on opportunities to learn to *pay attention*, *take turns*, *wait patiently*, and so on. Instead, they may become inattentive, impulsive, impatient, or engage in other inappropriate behavior.

When youngsters fail to pay attention, persist with a task, comply with requests, invite others to participate, assist peers requesting help, or other socially appropriate acts, parents, teachers, or employers often turn to punishment rather than teaching the deficient social skill. The situation then worsens, because, as you will learn in Chapters 30 and 31, punishment tends to provoke problematic behavior. Punishment teaches one *how not to behave*; it does not teach *how to behave*. So when young children's social skill deficits are not addressed by teaching them acceptable replacement behaviors, those problematic acts are at risk for continuing into adolescence and adulthood (Sheridan, 1995). Conversely, when compared to control populations, roughly two-thirds of students with emotional and/or behavioral disorders subsequently become successful after they learn productive social skills (Gresham, Cook, Crews, & Kern, 2004). Similarly, preschoolers, who were taught by instruction, modeling, role play, and differential reinforcement to appropriately request teacher attention, teacher help, preferred materials, and to tolerate delays and denials of those events, not only engaged in the skills but also engaged in less problem behaviors than those in a control group (Suczynski & Hanely, 2013).

The goal of social skills training is to teach socially acceptable behaviors that will be naturally recognized and accepted (reinforced) by high status, productive peers and significant others. How, then, is social skills training conducted? The majority of social skills training programs consist of chains of given responses, typically derived from an analysis of the tasks constituting the particular social skill to be taught. To illustrate, we present two skill sets that most of us would agree are critical to social success: academic or job survival skills and peer relationship skills.[5]

## Social Skills as Behavioral Chains

We suspect you are familiar with the pejorative terms people often use to describe those lacking particular social skills: "What a nerd, geek, pest, or bully...."

---

[5]Social skills such as these often are related to an individual's popularity (Blom & Zimmerman, 1981; Gresham & Nagle, 1980).

Those aren't especially helpful. Instead, what you need to do when constructing a task analysis to manage the challenge is to operationally define any such labels and break them down into their components or sub-skills. For example, instructions for *paying attention* might be specified as:

1. Look at the face of the person who is talking.
2. Nod once in a while to show you are listening.
3. Wait until the person stops talking before you talk.
4. Be ready to answer, to ask a question, or to react to what the person said.

Before concluding that your social-skills task analysis is complete, though, test it out to determine if any more links in the chain are needed (e.g., request the skill, demonstrate the skill, and so on). Breaking the skill down into its components allows you to (1) teach each part more easily, and (2) use each description as a discriminative stimulus or prompt to remind clients of the specific behaviors they need to practice.

A number of social skills training programs are commercially available. For example, McGinnis and Goldstein (1997) and colleagues have developed several manuals containing numerous **skill cards**, *task analyses of social skills often printed on 3 x 5 cards* to serve as a prompt to help preschool children, elementary-school children, adolescents, and adults know what to do (Goldstein, Sprafkin, Gershaw, & Klein, 1980).

## Identifying Social Skill Deficits

A number of critical social skills have been identified. Some are prerequisites for doing well in school or on the job (see Social Skills for Academic and Job Survival in Box 14.7), and several peer relationship skills identified below tend to help youngsters be more popular among their peer group.

Also, important preschool life skills have been identified that when taught can help prevent prob-

> **Box 14.7**
> **Two Social Skill Sets**
>
> **Social Skills for Academic and Job Survival**
> Many agree that behaviors such as these constitute *academic or job survival skills*:
>
> - Persisting with a task
> - Paying attention
> - Complying with requests and directions
> - Requesting help when needed
> - Requesting feedback
> - Nodding to communicate understanding
> - Providing appreciative feedback
> - Greeting the teacher or supervisor
>
> **Peer Relationship Skills**
> Critical peer relationship skills generally include the following:
>
> - Saying "Hi" or "Hello"
> - Introducing self by name
> - Asking questions about the other person (name, likes, and so forth)
> - Identifying and discussing common interests
> - Sharing something about oneself
> - Delivering specific compliments
> - Asking permission
> - Sharing materials/objects with others
> - Assisting others who want assistance
> - Introducing others
> - Inviting others to participate
> - Smiling
> - Caring for physical appearance or grooming
> - Taking turns with preferred items/activities

Table 14.3  Preschool Life Skills*

| Skill # | Skill Description | Skill # | Skill Description |
|---|---|---|---|
| **Unit 1** | **Instruction Following** | **Unit 3** | **Tolerance for Delay** |
| 1 | Responding appropriately to name | 8 | Tolerating delays imposed by adults |
| 2 | Complying with simple instructions | 9 | Tolerating delays imposed by peers |
| 3 | Complying with multi-step instructions | | |
| **Unit 2** | **Functional Communication** | **Unit 4** | **Friendship Skills** |
| 4 | Requesting assistance | 10 | Saying "thank you" |
| 5 | Requesting attention | 11 | Acknowledging or complimenting others |
| 6 | Framed requesting to adults | 12 | Offering or sharing |
| 7 | Framed requesting to peer | 13 | Comforting others in distress |

* Table developed by Fahmie and Lucznski (2018), p. 184. Reprinted with permission

lem behavior and increase school readiness (Fahmie & Luczynski, 2018). (See Table 14.3) In addition, there is an *Autism Social Skills Profile* (ASSP) (Bellini & Hopf, 2007) that is used to help identify target behaviors and behaviors that may interfere with social interactions.

Observation and rating scales are two tools designed to identify people's specific social skill deficits.

**Observation.** We often can identify the social skills people lack by observing them in action. Sometimes those are particularly obvious, as when a student consistently fails to "pay attention" by failing to look at the teacher during instruction, posing questions or answers not relevant to the lesson, and so on. You also will find from observations that some children are more honest than may be socially desirable. That is why investigators (Bergstom,

Najdowski, Alvarado, & Tarbox, 2016) taught (by using rules, role-play and feedback) three children with autism to tell socially appropriate lies when they received an undesired gift or when someone's appearance changed in the wrong direction. Similarly, children with autism often have trouble showing empathy to others. Investigators have shown that the 10 to 12-year-olds in their study were able to learn empathetic responses after social skills training (Argott, Trownsend, & Pouolson, 2017). Similarly, investigators (Najdowski et al., 2018) taught children with autism to identify play partners' toy preferences and to make appropriate toy offers to their play partners.

To choose which behavior is desirable in the setting, you also can observe the behavior of others who impress you with their effective social skills. Reviewing a social-skills inventory or rating scale may sensitize you to the specific behavior to observe when pinpointing elusive deficits. If you are unable to identify a very subtle social deficit by observation alone, you might consider using a social-skills rating scale to lead you toward the behavior to identify and measure.

**Rating scales.** Of the various types of social-skills inventories available, we include portions of two for illustrative purposes. The first is a rating scale developed by McGinnis and Goldstein (1997) for students to fill out (see Figure 14.5). The second, developed by Sulzer-Azaroff and Mayer (1994) is an informal scale for the teacher and the student's parents to complete (Figure 14.6 displays a number of sample items). Another option, when you are attempting to pinpoint the components of a specific social skills area, is for you to prepare your own questionnaire. For example, you may wish to focus primarily on the peer relationships or academic and job survival skills listed above.[6]

Once you select the instrument, you can ask anyone who knows the individual to complete it. Also, if they are old enough or functionally able, it is best to have the clients fill out the inventory themselves; if they recognize a need to learn new behavior, they will be more likely to use it in new situations (McGinnis & Goldstein, 1997). Additionally, selecting and teaching that behavior is

---

[6]See http://www.sloanpublishing.com/balc4/ss_inventory for the complete social skills inventory

---

INSTRUCTIONS: Each of the questions will ask you about how well you do something. Next to each question is a number.

Circle number 1 if you *almost never* do what the question asks.

Circle number 2 if you *seldom* do it.

Circle number 3 if you *sometimes* do it.

Circle number 4 if you do it *often*.

Circle number 5 if you *almost always* do it.

There are no right or wrong answers to these questions. Answer as you really feel about each question.

1. Is it easy for me to listen to someone who is talking to me?  1 2 3 4 5
2. Do I tell people "thank you" for something they have done for me?  1 2 3 4 5
3. Do I have the materials I need for my classes (like books, pencils, paper)?  1 2 3 4 5
4. Do I finish my schoolwork?  1 2 3 4 5
5. Is it easy for me to start a conversation with someone?  1 2 3 4 5

**Figure 14.5** Illustrative social-skills inventory items for client

| When in situations in which the following would be desired, the individual— | Never | Seldom | About half the time | More often than not | Always |
|---|---|---|---|---|---|
| **B. Initiates social contact** as evidenced by: | | | | | |
| 2. Introducing self by name. | 1 | 2 | 3 | 4 | 5 |
| 4. Asking questions about other person (name, likes, etc.). | 1 | 2 | 3 | 4 | 5 |
| **H. Handles teasing** as evidenced by: | | | | | |
| 1. Ignoring it. | 1 | 2 | 3 | 4 | 5 |
| 2. Making a joke of it. | 1 | 2 | 3 | 4 | 5 |
| **K. Responds positively to teacher** as evidenced by: | | | | | |
| 2. Providing verbal feedback that is appreciative or approving (e.g., "thank you," "Oh, now I understand," etc.). | 1 | 2 | 3 | 4 | 5 |
| 9. Complying with the teacher's requests. | 1 | 2 | 3 | 4 | 5 |

**Figure 14.6** Illustrative social-skills inventory items for raters
See the Web for the complete social skills inventory. http://www.sloanpublishing.com/balc

further justified when the client and others agree on the identification of a particular social deficit or excess.

## Using Chaining to Teach Social Skills

We teach social skills the same way as other behavior. Most social skills training techniques rely on chaining, prompting (or other support such as instructions, modeling or demonstrations), and differential reinforcement of alternative behaviors (DRA). For example: If a student is off-task, you would reinforce instances of on-task behavior. Rather than remaining silent when another is introduced, saying "hello" would be reinforced. (See Chapter 28 for additional examples of DRA.) When training is individually matched to each client's deficit(s), the outcome is more promising. For example, as a result of such training, four elementary-school students' positive social skills increased substantially while their competing problem behaviors decreased, and these positive changes were maintained over two months (Gresham, Van, and Cook, 2006). Similar results were reported with ten adolescents who also generalized their social skills to various school settings and to their homes (Barreras, 2009). Investigators (Naylor, Kamps, & Wills, 2018) also used an interdependent group contingency and differential reinforcement to help teach social skills to all the students in a first grade classroom. The social skills of gaining the teacher's attention appropriately, following direction and ignoring inappropriate peer behavior were taught. The class was divided into teams of three to four students each. If all the students within the group displayed the skills that were taught at the end of every few minutes, the team earned points toward a daily goal. Each group that met the point goal by the end of the class period would receive a reward. As a result, on-task behavior increased for the class and for target students who were disruptive. The target students' disruptive behavior also reduced. By mastering the strategies in this book, rather than depending on prepackaged materials which may or may not address your client's critical needs, you should be able to apply behavior analytic methods effectively to teach social skills.

**Social stories: Applying chaining methods to promote deficient social skills.** Some typically developing individuals, as well as those with specific challenges, appear quite insensitive to the social cues that control the behavior of most people. An example is the person who approaches a group of adults at a gathering, fails to notice that someone else is speaking and barges into the conversation with an irrelevant topic. Although most of us probably have encountered such individuals, many on the autism spectrum seem to have a particularly difficult time "reading" subtle social cues.

Among many successful examples, Kuttler, et al. (1998) enabled a student with autism to use social stories to support a new, much more adaptive behavioral chain as a substitute for inappropriate vocalizations and dropping to the floor, that had served as precursors to tantrum behavior (see Figure 14.7. Also see Chapter 27 for further discussion of social stories.) Remember, though the task-analyzed social story is not the key to success, one must ensure that engaging in the appropriate social skill results in reinforcement for social stories to actually work.

**Using generative learning procedures to teach social skills.** Generative learning (see Ch. 13) strategies are used to get additional responses beyond the specific responses taught. One method that has been used to get generative responding is stimulus equivalence (see Chapter 16) and Relational Frame Theory (see Chapter 19). Recently researchers have utilized matrix training to teach social play skills to facilitate generative repertoire of two-component solitary and social play skills in a child diagnosed with autism (Wilson, Wine, & Fitlerer, 2017). Prior to the intervention the child rarely engaged in toy play according to manufacturer directions or in a manner of typically developing peers. In addition, the child did not engage in prosocial play with his sibling. The researchers used a matrix, divided into sub-matrices to teach two-action-item combinations (e.g., "roll the police van" and "jump the police car") across the following categories (toy: police van, police car, Mack truck, fire truck, snowplow, lifeguard pickup, and jeep) with the following skills (roll, jump, drop, crash, give, trade, and ask for). After the child was taught a specific skill, the researcher probed the untrained skills (e.g., if taught "roll police van" but not taught "roll snowplow") to see if recombinative generation occurred. Results demonstrated that recombinative generation accounted for 86 percent of the acquired responses. Moreover, the child engaged in social play with his sibling without direct training.

**Using the teaching interaction procedure.** The teaching interaction procedure consists of labeling or specifying the target skill, providing a rationale for its importance, describing the steps or links in the target skill, modeling the skill, and providing feedback throughout the training interaction. This strategy has been shown to be effective in teaching various clients social skills and for teaching training in using the teaching interaction procedure (Green et al., 2020). If using this approach, be sure to use its various components effectively (e.g., for the feedback, be sure to select high preference reinforcers and use them effectively, and for the other components, use them effectively too—see summary tables throughout this book for using procedures effectively).

# COPING WITH UNWANTED CHAINS

Flora describes her "addiction" to donuts: "I am determined to avoid high-calorie foods. So every time I pass the bakery department, I escape as quickly as I can, usually passing through to the frozen foods section. Then I wander into the produce department; but inevitably I end up back at the baked goods. I watch as the newly fried doughnuts slide off their trays into the display case. "Yum!" I tell myself, "They smell so good. Chocolate icing. My favorite. I think I'll just buy one and have a bite or two tonight and save the rest for tomorrow…. On the other hand, maybe two would be better; one for me; the other just in case Wayne drops over …"

See what we're getting at? Yes. Flora's well-established chain of behaviors leading to her consuming a doughnut or two looks like Figure 14.8.

What Flora would like to accomplish is to break or *unchain* the chain, so she will not return to the bak-

We eat lunch at school every day.

When we go to the lunchroom,
I pick up my tray and sit at the table.

I eat slowly, using a fork and spoon.
(fork icon; spoon icon)

When I finish, I take my tray and sit at the table.
(finished icon; clear table icon)

I wait with my friends until the teacher
tells me to go to class.
(wait icon)

My teacher says "good job" and
gives me a sticker when I come back to class.
(classroom icon, sticker icon)

I like to earn stickers. If I earn stickers,
I can pick a prize.
(sticker icon, prize bag icon.)

**Figure 14.7** An illustrative social story. From Kuttler, Myles, & Carlson (1998), The use of social stories to reduce tantrum behavior in a student with autism. *Focus on Autism and Other Developmental Disabilities 13*, 176–182. Reprinted with permission from Sage Publications.

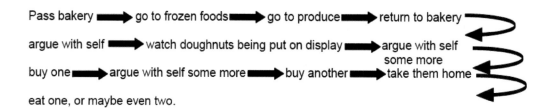

**Figure 14.8**

ery after going to the produce department. Perhaps, she reasons, if, when she enters the produce department, she buys a carton of the sweetest smelling, juiciest field-ripened strawberries, that might disrupt the last part of the chain—returning to the bakery.

## Unchaining

Think about the important people in your family, social, and working life. Given sufficient determination, you probably can identify numerous useful and benign routine behavior chains: daily practices, productive work and study habits, leisure and recreational activities, and so on. Unfortunately, perhaps there are some chains you would be delighted to see reduced or eliminated: The way a client, co-worker, employee, or even you yourself respond to correction; how you dawdle or become distracted when deadlines loom; your repeatedly displaying a "nervous habit," such as humming off-key, drumming fingers on the desk, or grimacing whenever some of your less favored colleagues or clients pass by. Now, like Flora, wouldn't you be delighted to see some of your own or others' undesirable behavior chains break apart? Flora would be pleased if she successfully avoided her final return to the bakery department.

**Unchaining** *(sometimes called "disrupting" or "unlinking" a chain) is a method designed to lessen behavior by unlinking one element of the chain from the next so that one link no longer serves as a discriminative stimulus for the next link, nor as the reinforcer for the prior link.* This may be accomplished by reinforcing the last response in a chain even if it occurs in the absence of the other responses in the chain (Kuhn et al., 2006). Suppose, in a two-segment chain, the last part of a response (R2) continues to produce the reinforcer, regardless of whether the earlier link is emitted or not:

> Junior: "Pick me up. Pick me up."
> Dad: "Say '*Please* pick me up.'"
> Junior: "Please pick me up."
> Dad picks Junior up.
> Later, Junior emits the complete chain, "Please pick me up."
> Dad picks Junior up.
> Next day, Dad is distracted:
> Junior: "Pick me up."
> Dad picks Junior up.

Guess what happens to the first link in the chain—the "Please"? Presumably, as Jack Michael (1982, 2000) found with his laboratory animals, R2 will remain unchanged because it continues to produce the terminal reinforcer, but R1 (the first part of the response, e.g., "Please") will diminish. So, if you are determined to see a chain persist with its entire series of links remaining intact, be very cautious in avoiding reinforcing the last link unless it has been preceded by each of the others.

Kuhn et al. (2006) tested this concept when they taught children with autism to chain together a couple of sign language requests—to ask for a box to be opened, then to ask to gain access to the food contained therein. After that, the investigators provided the youngsters with the food when the last link of the chain, signing for the food, occurred, even if the youngsters omitted the initial link, "open." Under those conditions, the early response, but not the second response in the chain, diminished in rate. The chain was broken.

In the above examples, unchaining resulted in the elimination of *desirable* links or behaviors. *Unwanted* links in a chain can also be eliminated through unchaining. Suppose Junior screams to be picked up and his dad frequently complies. Eliminating the screaming by breaking the chain would call for Dad to pick Junior up *consistently* whenever (and *only* whenever) the child asks to be picked up without screaming first. That would be difficult for Dad to do, because it might require many days of his interrupting his work or other activities until screaming no longer is linked to asking to be picked up. Later on, of course, were Dad to adhere to good behavioral practices, say, by complimenting and otherwise reinforcing Junior's polite requesting, he eventually could shape Junior's waiting to be picked up for increasingly longer time periods.

We will see later that it is not enough for a reinforcer to follow behavior. Suppose an undesired behavior, like tantruming, has been maintained by some reinforcer delivered by a parent. If the reinforcer is delivered whether or not the behavior occurs, over time that reinforcer will maintain the behavior less and less strongly and it will be easier to shape different alternatives to the problem behavior.

## Reducing Behavior by Blocking Links in a Behavioral Chain

Blocking a chain's progress can also interfere with unwanted behavior, as investigators have reported when attempting to prevent self-injurious behavior maintained by *automatic reinforcement* (i.e., when the reinforcement is produced directly by the response itself, as with thumb sucking, hair twirling, and masturbation) (LeBlanc, Piazza, & Krug, 1997; Lerman & Iwata, 1996; McCord, Grosser, Iwata, & Powers, 2005; Smith, Russo, & Le, 1999). However, the effect of blocking is not universal and sometimes it produces undesired side effects such as aggression (Murphy, MacDonald, Hall, & Oliver, 2000; Rapp, Dozier, & Carr, 2001). Suppose Wayne joined Flora on her shopping trip and tried to bar her from approaching the bakery counter; she might become very angry with him, telling him off in no uncertain terms.

Research indicates that blocking is only likely to be effective in preventing self-injurious behavior, such as pica (eating non-nutritive items such as cigarette butts, bits of glass, string, etc.), if any initial touching of the non-nutritive item is *consistently* blocked early in its response chain (McCord et al., 2005). This also was found by investigators (Wunderlich, Vollmer, & Zabala, 2017) to be true of self-induced vomiting (putting fingers down throat). McCord et al. found, in addition, that sometimes supplemental interventions (e.g., noncontingent reinforcement, redirection; see Chapters 26 and 27) are required to eliminate the behavior completely.

In your own situation, watch your clientele vigilantly for the particular steps in a chain that terminate in aggression. Initially an individual may sigh, place his head down on a desk or table, and then break his pencil. The chain may continue, with defiance, criticizing others, arguing, yelling, or swearing, eventually leading to physical aggression. Redirection (see Chapter 26) or blocking an early link in the chain that generally leads up to physical aggression can often prevent such acts (Mayer, 2000; Redford & Ervin, 2002; Walker, Ramsey, & Gresham, 2004). Other examples of possible precursors leading to problem behavior include negative vocalizing, feet stamping, standing, and hand flapping (Borlase, Vladesu, Kisamore, Reeve, & Fetzer, 2017). Such **precursors** have been defined as *behaviors "that reliably occur prior to, and are functionally related to, target problem behavior"* (p. 668). By initially functionally analyzing and treating precursor behaviors of problematic behavior chains, behavior analysts can help eliminate those chains altogether (Najdowski et al., 2008).

## STRENGTHENING AND EXPANDING NEWLY ACQUIRED BEHAVIOR

Reaching the goal does not end the story. Simply using shaping or chaining to construct new behavior does not guarantee that it will become permanent. The newly achieved performance must be strengthened, primarily by using effective reinforcement practices. Violet quickly will revert to whispering if her audible talking is not immediately and consistently reinforced. The first time that Charlie brushes his teeth or that Haruka completes her study guide in sufficient detail, the response is still rather weak. The same would be true of Flora bypassing the bakery counter. Unless strengthened, the chain can easily break apart; components omitted, their order confused, or inappropriate components added. Charlie may take his brush, wet it, and replace it on its rack; Haruka may again answer her study-guide questions too sketchily or after altering her route through the supermarket, Flora may return to her earlier "habitual route." If a newly established complex chain is to persist intact, you must see to it that the *fully correct* chain is reinforced as often as possible, with minimal delay, and with adequate amounts of reinforcers known to be effective for the individual.

Before immediately reading him his favorite story, Charlie's father will have to observe his son brushing his teeth, to be certain he carried it out correctly. Haruka's instructor will want to check her study guide several times and comment positively when it has been completed in sufficient detail. In this latter instance, after that practice becomes better established, a slightly more delayed but especially powerful reinforcer—demonstrating mastery of the material by passing the unit quiz—will begin to support the behavior more naturally. You also will want to be certain that you have seen to it that appropriate supports are already in place, but only as long as they are needed. Then, as in all instances in which newly mastered behavior is at low strength, you will want to use whatever means it takes to promote and support the fluency of the new behavior.

Simply because a particular complex behavior has been established in one context, there is no guarantee that it or a closely related behavior will be emitted under other circumstances. The bad news is that in many cases you must intentionally program for generalization, rather than leaving that to chance. Choose the times, places and other conditions under which you hope to see the new behavior(s) occur and be prepared to implement your effective reinforcement strategies under those circumstances. In Chapter 21, you will learn a good deal more about promoting desired generalization.

## SUMMARY AND CONCLUSIONS

In the chaining procedure, we take behavior links, such as those developed by shaping, demonstrations (modeling), and other support methods, and weld them into a sequence to form a more complex behavior. Combining chaining with supports such as instructions and demonstrations can expedite the process. Afterward, any artificial or intrusive supports need to be faded before the objective can be said to have been achieved. So, if you don't really need a prompt, omit it, because in the long run you'll save the time and effort it took to put it in. What is essential, though, is that while or after the chain is being formed, as always, you apply principles for effectively strengthening, maintaining and, promoting generalization (Chapter 21). As with shaping, only at that point would we consider a chaining program complete.

The chaining procedure was devised to produce cohesive, complex behavior from components the performer is already able to produce. Chains of behavior derive their ability to aggregate from the fact that links begin to acquire dual functions: each link of the chain reinforces the behavior in the link that came before, and signals the behavior in the link that comes next. Chains vary from one another in terms of their length, complexity, and difficulty for the learner; the interdependence among links; the organization of task elements; discriminative features; the reinforcers intrinsic to their expression; and perhaps in other ways.

Effectively linking the components of a behavior chain depends on a precise task analysis, validated as accurate through observation by competent individuals, consultation with experts, performing the task oneself, and careful planning of the temporal order of the links. Chains can be forged by joining one link to the next in a forward or backward direction or by presenting the whole task and prompting and reinforcing correctly performed links. Although not always practical or feasible, the backward chaining method has the advantage of capitalizing on the reinforcing properties inherent in completing the chain. Forward and whole-task chaining must depend on external prompting and reinforcement. Occasionally, a weak link may require additional shaping. Regardless of the direction taken, any

**TABLE 14.4  Review of Chaining Practices**

| Purpose | Practice |
|---|---|
| Promote a desired chain | After occasioning or teaching each link separately, gradually reserve reinforcers for increasing combinations of those links in the proper order. |
| Maintain an intact chain | Reinforce densely at first, then once well established, gradually less often following the last link in the sequentially correct complete chain. |
| Eliminate an unwanted chain | Withhold reinforcers following the last link in a chain. |
| Eliminate unwanted links in a chain | Reinforce following the desired sequence of links but discontinue reinforcers if sequence contains unwanted links or essential links are missing. |
| Unchain | Reinforce last but not other links of chain. |
| Reduce complex behavior | Block link, especially early in chain. |

interim prompts need to be faded and supplemental reinforcers thinned out completely before the behavior can be said to have been fully mastered.

Also be certain that supports are already in place. Then, as in all instances in which a newly mastered behavior is at low strength, you will want to use whatever means it takes to promote and support the fluency of the new behavior (Chapter 11).

Along with the additional procedures for preventing and modifying problematic behaviors, (see Chapters 26–30), chaining also is integral to effective social skills training, especially when a particular complex behavior is troublesome for individuals and/or those around them. As people become increasingly socially skillful, group and individual difficulties lessen. Blocking the early links in such chains, and arranging to substitute those with more effective practices can aid in the prevention of unwanted behavior in the first place.

Table 14.4 presents a summary of the various aims that can be accomplished by means of chaining practices.

See below for the *Summary Table for Teaching New Behavior.*

# SUMMARY TABLE
# PROCEDURES FOR TEACHING NEW BEHAVIOR

## Teaching New Behavior with Shaping and Chaining

| Procedure/ Operation | Maximizing Effectiveness | Temporal Properties | Durability of Effect | Other Features |
|---|---|---|---|---|
| **Shaping:** Reinforce successive approximations to goal | 1. Start with behaviors in individual's repertoire<br>2. Select and apply ongoing measurement system<br>3. Keep your eye on goal<br>4. Begin with behaviors that most closely resemble goal behavior<br>5. Promote supportive environment<br>6. Select challenging but achievable step size<br>7. Remain at a given step only long enough to establish it within individual's repertoire<br>8. Watch for behavioral disintegration; if it appears imminent, drop back a step or two<br>9. Combine temporally with prompts; then fade them<br>10. End every session on a high-note—with a successful trial<br>11. Use effective reinforcement procedures throughout<br>12. Strengthen newly acquired complex behavior | Gradual, depending on number and complexity of successive approximations | Long-lasting, assuming strengthened and supported by natural environment | Positive, constructive approach; requires careful planning |
| **Chaining:** Reinforce combinations of two or more response links (behavioral components) to form a complex behavior | 1. Do careful task analysis<br>2. Validate task analysis<br>3. If possible select components or links in individual's repertoire<br>4. Plan appropriate starting point<br>5. Consider starting with final link<br>6. Consider use of supplementary reinforcers<br>7. If necessary, occasion response combinations with prompts; then fade prompts<br>8. Shape individual components if necessary<br>9. Use effective reinforcement during teaching and to consolidate ultimate complex behavior | Gradual. If links already in repertoire; may be accomplished more rapidly than shaping | Long-lasting if optimally reinforced during and after complex behavior mastered | Positive, constructive approach |

*Chapter 15*

# Attaining Complex Behavior by Promoting and Supporting Antecedent Control

## Goals

1. Recognize, define, and give original illustrations of each of the following:
   a. stimulus control
   b. discriminated operant
   c. the different categories of discriminative stimuli ($S^D$, $S^\Delta$ or $S^{De}$, $S^{Dr}$, and $S^{Dp}$)
   d. $S^+$, $S^-$, and $S^0$
   e. three-term contingency
   f. differential reinforcement (DR)
   g. motivating operation (MO)
   h. establishing operations
   i. abolishing operations
   j. unconditioned motivating operation (UMO)
   k. conditioned motivating operation (CMO)
   l. $S^M$ (motivating stimulus)
   m. transitive motivating operations
   n. reflexive motivating operations
   o. surrogate motivating operations
2. Name the procedure that establishes stimulus control and describe how it operates.
3. Describe several factors that can weaken the $S^D$ response connection.
4. List four features that must be present for stimulus control to occur.
5. Describe and illustrate the dual function of an $S^D$.
6. Describe and illustrate how to make the color blue a discriminative stimulus for saying "blue" and not for saying "yellow."
7. Describe and illustrate how to use differential reinforcement effectively to support the development of stimulus control.

339

8. Provide examples of at least three behaviors under complex stimulus control.
9. Differentiate between motivational operations (MOs), discriminative stimuli ($S^D$s), and other antecedents.

*************

Dr. Patel is highly admired by her colleagues and the community at large for her finely honed diagnostic skills. Like most other experts, she accurately responds to the presence or absence of particular stimuli. Can such proficiency be trained by applying behavioral procedures? Indeed. In an actual case, specialists in pediatrics, internal medicine, family practice, orthopedics, and neurosurgery at the Fargo Clinic improved the accuracy of their diagnoses plus other important skills when they participated in a behavioral training program (Snyder, 1989). A major aspect of that program involved methods designed to promote stimulus control.

We suspect you already have begun to recognize the crucial role *stimulus control* (when antecedent stimuli control or influence behavior) plays in everyday life, including what you have been and will be learning while mastering the content in this text. As you read on, your perspective on the topic should broaden. Yes, stimulus control lies at the foundation of just about all actions we call informed, skilled, logical, rational, cognitive, conceptual, civilized, and creative ("thinking," "reasoning," "remembering," "classifying," "identifying," and so on). Our health and well-being—yes, our very survival as individuals and groups—depend on stimulus control, because it permits us to adjust to static and changing internal and environmental conditions. Were organisms and species unable to distinguish between edible and poisonous plants or animals, to locate food and water, to identify and seek protectors or mates, to distinguish and avoid predators, enemies, or hostile environments, their days would be numbered. Beyond simple survival, stimulus control is essential to all organisms and societies. It supports people's acquisition and refinement of knowledge and skills. Where would technology, science, and health be without stimulus control? From what source would the tools essential for advanced learning and understanding and enhanced life quality derive, were it not for stimulus control?

# THE EVOLUTION OF STIMULUS CONTROL WITHIN INDIVIDUALS AND GROUPS

All creatures, large and small, rapidly learn to provide cues and to respond to evident signs that nurturance, comfort, and danger are present or on their way. They notice and adapt to internal and external environmental changes. The basic ingredient of stimulus control is that something detectable—a stimulus (loosely, some event or something present in the environment)—is correlated with the consequences of responding.

Stimulus control is essential to learning, progress, protection, and appreciation within groups. Just about all forms of basic and advanced information and skill dissemination related to technology, science, health, commerce, and so on depend on this natural feature of operant learning. And, of course, so do formal civil structures—educational and training institutions, businesses, governments, social organizations of all kinds and their yield: skilled people, products and profits, societal order, well-being, comfort, and satisfaction.

Of special concern to us here, though, is how the science of behavior in general and its analysis of stimulus control in particular have aided and continue to aid individually and socially valued behavior change.

# WHAT IS STIMULUS CONTROL?

The term **stimulus control** is used to label *the relation between a stimulus and a response when the stimulus (formally labeled* **discriminative stimulus** *and often abbreviated as* $S^D$*) sets the occasion on which the response will likely have a consequence.* See the examples in Table 15.1.

> **Box 15.1**
>
>
>
> Why do you think this seagull in the upper image leaves his flock (lower image)? When a response is often reinforced (in this case coming to the area where the umbrella is and arriving at a good place to snatch food), in the presence of a stimulus (here the umbrella), the stimulus(i) begin(s) to set the occasion for, or "to occasion" (for short) or to "evoke" the response. His learning history has taught him that reinforcement is highly probable when the umbrellas appear. Stimuli correlated with the presence of people, such as the umbrella, have come to signal or have become discriminative for easy pickings, because the people who come with the umbrellas feed him or leave their food unguarded. So as soon as he sees the first open umbrella of the day he peels off from his fellows, lands on the umbrella and, although beach attendants try to shoo him off, he stays there for the rest of the day except when filching a tasty morsel.

A discriminative stimulus occasions or sets the occasion for responding when the stimulus has been correlated with a contingency in which the responding has some consequence (see examples of such $S^D$s in Table 15.1). The responding may then be called a *discriminated operant*. In other words the **discriminated operant** *is operant, or learned, behavior under stimulus control.* Behavior that is occasioned by a discriminative stimulus, or $S^D$, is sometimes said to be evoked by the $S^D$ in that it signals the likelihood of reinforcement. For example, first the seagull comes to the umbrella, but once the seagull is there, it is not the umbrella but rather people with food that sets the occasion for stealing the food. You may recognize this as an example of chaining that we discuss in Chapter 14. We have so far discussed the discriminative stimulus as producing responding, but under some circumstances it also may reduce responding, such as when it signals extinction or punishment instead of reinforcement.

**TABLE 15.1  Examples of Behavior under Stimulus Control**

| Discriminative Stimuli that Set the Occasion for | Behavior | Consequence |
|---|---|---|
| Instructions from air traffic controller | Pilot comes in for a landing | Safe landing |
| Telephone rings | Penny picks it up and says, "Hello." | Caller answers, "Hello." |
| A defective sample of floor covering | Quality-assurance technician rejects the whole lot as substandard | Company loses money but does not disappoint customers |
| The computer screen flashes "5 × 4" | The student answers "20" | The computer flashes "good" |
| Study question asking for definition and example of *stimulus* | Kennie provides acceptable definition and illustration | Kennie gets good feedback |
| A particular musical selection | Paula and Sandy get up and dance | Pleasure of rhythm and movement |
| Consultant suggests supervisors use labeled praise | Supervisor compliments Paula for reporting on all the essential points in her memo | Supervisor is pleased that Paula's memos are complete more often |

We have listed only a few possible reinforcers in the examples above, and you may be able to supply others. With regard to Kennie in Table 15.1, for example, just checking his answer against a textbook and finding it is correct might be reinforcing. If he does this consistently, his judgment of the accuracy of his answers will improve. That is an important skill, because he will then be able better to allocate his study to things he realizes he needs to work on rather than to things he already knows well.

For present purposes, we focus on contingencies that involve responses likely followed by reinforcers. Later we will see that discriminative stimuli can also signal that particular responses are likely to be followed by aversive events. As you know, continuing on your way ordinarily will be reinforced when the traffic light is green (you safely get closer to your destination), but that same behavior may be punished if the traffic light is red (you may have an accident or get a traffic ticket).

The **discriminative stimulus for reinforcement** ($S^{Dr}$) *signals that in its presence, a given response is apt to be reinforced if it occurs.* Conversely, a stimulus is called an **S-delta** or $S^\Delta$ *when it signals that the response is not likely to produce a reinforcer* (or, in other words, the response will undergo extinction conditions). However, we prefer the symbol $S^{De}$ as the $S^\Delta$ has some communication issues. In addition, the $S^{De}$ is more similar and consonant to the other stimulus control symbols ($S^{Dr}$ and $S^{Dp}$).[1] We will use this symbol throughout this text, but you will still need to know the $S^\Delta$ symbol because it is still being used in the ABA literature. (Also, you will sometimes find that the terms $S^D$ and $S^\Delta$ appear together in literature that you read, with the first applied to the stimulus that signals a reinforcement contingency and the other applied to the absence of that stimulus, as in our example above of the umbrella and its absence.) We use the term $S^{Dr}$ to refer to an antecedent that signals a behavior will likely receive reinforcement if it occurs, and $S^D$ to refer to any type of discriminative stimulus.

Think of the seagull when no umbrellas appear on the beach. The absence of the umbrellas (the $S^{De}$) signals that people are not likely to show up with food, so the seagull does not fly over to that area. When stimulus control contingencies have generated effective $S^{Dr}$s and $S^{De}$s, the particular response is maintained in the presence of the $S^{Dr}$ and decreases and perhaps even disappears in the presence of the $S^{De}$.

---
[1] See the paper on "Communication Issues with the $S^\Delta$" on this book's web page under Chapter 15.

As you've probably guessed already, responding in the presence of a stimulus can be reduced not only by having it signal extinction but also by having it signal punishment. Many use the label $S^{Dp}$ (O'Donnell, 2001; O'Donnell, Crosbie, Williams, & Saunders, 2000) to designate that in the presence of that *particular stimulus, a given response is likely to be punished*. For example, a child might learn the hard way that if a neighbor's dog is wagging its tail ($S^{Dr}$) it can be safely petted, whereas if it is growling ($S^{Dp}$), then reaching toward it poses the risk of getting bitten. The growling, then, qualifies it as an $S^{Dp}$. It signals that reaching and petting are likely to be punished by a dog bite. Children who have been bitten by a growling dog learn such lessons quickly (once bitten, twice shy) and stop trying to pet growling dogs. In fact, getting bitten is so aversive that we sometimes worry that dogs in general, and not just growling ones, will become $S^{Dp}$s for this child. We'll discuss such issues when we get to the topic of generalization in a later chapter.

Experiencing the relations among those particular accompanying or antecedent stimuli, responses, and consequences brings our behavior under *stimulus control*. **Stimulus control**,[2] then, is demonstrated when *a given response dependably becomes either more or less probable in the presence of specific antecedent or accompanying stimuli*. (Occasionally you will encounter the term *abates*, which some use as a synonym for *reduces* or *decreases*: e.g., Laraway, Snycerski, Michael, & Poling, 2001).

To review, there are three major classifications of $S^D$s: 1) The stimulus discriminative for reinforcement, ($S^{Dr}$), which signals that in its presence, a given response is apt to be reinforced, (2) the stimulus discriminative for extinction ($S^{De}$)[3], which signals that in its presence, a response probably will *not* be reinforced, and (3) the stimulus discriminative for punishment ($S^{Dp}$), which signals that in its presence, a response probably will be punished. In common parlance in the field of applied behavior analysis, we often say that stimuli discriminative for reinforcement "occasion," "signal," or "evoke" behavior and attribute that function to the organism's prior history with the three-term contingency (antecedents; behavior; consequences). The same is true of $S^{De}$s and their relation to extinction and $S^{Dp}$s and their relation to punishment. Later in this and subsequent chapters, we elaborate on these various $S^D$s. (See Figure 15.1 to see how the symbols depicting these discriminative stimuli are related.)

*Behavior, then, is influenced by the interrelation of the behavior to its consequences and antecedent stimuli.* The phone ringing evokes answering it, which usually results in hearing someone's voice (see Table 15.2). The ring is essential. If we pick

---

[2]Recognize that the word *control* has many meanings. In this instance it simply describes a highly predictable relation between an antecedent stimulus and a response. The term does not imply exploitive or coercive control.

[3]Please see the web page for Chapter 15 for a justification for using this symbol.

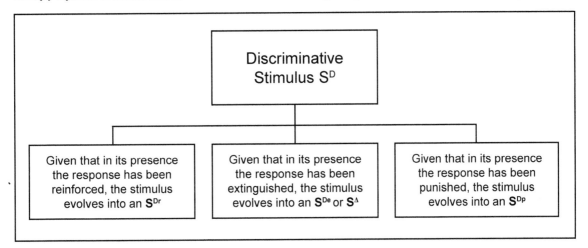

**Figure 15.1** Various classes of discriminative stimuli

**TABLE 15.2 Components of a Three-term Contingency in the Development of Stimulus Control**

| Antecedent Stimulus Condition (A) | Response (B) | Consequence (C) |
|---|---|---|
| Telephone rings ($S^+$ will become $S^D$) | Picks up telephone; says "Hello." | Other person says, "Hello." |
| In the absence of a ring ($S^0$ will become $S^{De}$) | Picks up telephone; says "Hello." | Dial tone: no one answers. |

up the phone when it hasn't rung, we would not hear a voice. Jumping into the ocean may have been reinforced during hot weather but not during cold, and we learn to check the temperature of the water before plunging in. Saying "Four" may be reinforced when the teacher asks "Two plus two equals?" but not when the teacher asks "Two plus three?" As Green (2001) pointed out: "Because the aim of virtually all instruction is to get specific responses to occur reliably under particular antecedent stimulus conditions, but not under other conditions, all instructional techniques involve manipulations of antecedent stimuli, *along with manipulations of consequent stimuli*" (p. 74). Then, she added "virtually all skills involve discriminating among, or responding differentially to, environmental events—sounds, colors, shapes, letters, numbers, words, foods, clothing items, people, responses, locations, and the like" (p. 74).

Table 15.2 summarizes the various terms and abbreviations behavior analysts sometimes use to label particular stimuli.

In the section to follow, we focus on (1) how people (and other organisms) learn to discriminate particular stimuli from one another; (2) how a particular behavior becomes more probable in the presence of that particular $S^+$ (*the stimulus designated ultimately to become the $S^{Dr}$*) because the individual learns that the $S^+$ sets the occasion for behavior or, in other words, signals that it is likely that the behavior will be reinforced; and, (3) how that $S^+$ eventually begins reliably to evoke certain responses and not others. Once that happens, we refer to the $S^+$ as an $S^{Dr}$.

### Establishing Discriminative Control

In the simplest instance of the development of stimulus control, suppose an infant emits a given response **R** (e.g., the sound "ma"). At first "ma" may be emitted at any time, but if the infant utters "ma" in the presence of the mother, powerful reinforcing consequences ($S^r$s) follow (e.g., mom says "yes, that right I'm mommy you are so cute" and kisses the baby). In the absence of the mother, these consequences are weak or absent altogether. Once the child utters "ma" more in the mother's presence than in her absence, we can say the mother has become a discriminative stimulus ($S^D$). This stimulus control came about because a three-term contingency existed in which discriminative stimuli ($S^{Dr}$s and $S^{De}$s, the presence versus absence of the mother) signaled whether the response (R, "ma") was likely to have reinforcing consequences ($S^r$, the mother's attention to the infant).

As you probably have realized, a good part of our discrimination learning occurs as a matter of course in natural environments. No specific training is necessary. Young children don't require formal instruction to reach for the presents Santa distributes or to cover their ears as they watch a firecracker being ignited. One or two experiences do the trick. The same basic operations enable individuals to respond dependably in the presence of many varied important stimuli. For the sake of clarity, however, we begin the discussion with a few examples of the kind illustrated in Table 15.2.

### Discriminative or Stimulus Control Illustrated

When we see an individual respond consistently in the presence of a particular antecedent stimulus, we say the response is *under the control of* that stimulus. These sorts of contingencies are learned. After noting that the stimulus reliably evokes the person's response, we say that the response is under *stimulus control*. Now, for that person, the antecedent stimulus fits within the category of being discriminative for that particular response. This control may evolve naturally (as when, having seen what happens when

**TABLE 15.3  Summary of Terms and Abbreviations**

| Abbr. | Term Denoted | Definition | Example |
|---|---|---|---|
| S | Stimulus | An object or event that may influence behavior | An illuminated bulb; a smile |
| **Consequential Stimuli** | | | |
| $S^R$ | Primary reinforcing stimulus | Reinforcing in absence of a prior learning history | Fluids, when deprived of them |
| $S^P$ | Primary aversive stimulus | Aversive in absence of a prior learning history | The surface of a very hot stove |
| $S^r$ | Secondary reinforcing stimulus | Initially had no reinforcing properties but now does through its earlier relation to other reinforcers | Money |
| $S^p$ | Secondary aversive stimulus | Initially had no aversive properties but now does through its earlier relation to other aversive stimuli | "No. Bad boy!" |
| **Antecedent Stimuli*** | | | |
| $S^+$ | Neutral stimulus | A stimulus that has not yet acquired controlling properties but for which reinforcing contingencies have been arranged to make it a discriminative stimulus ($S^{Dr}$) | The written word "water" before the child learns to read it |
| $S^-$ | Neutral stimulus | A stimulus that has not yet acquired controlling properties but for which punishing contingencies have been arranged to make it a discriminative stimulus ($S^{Dp}$) | The spoken word "don't" before it affects the youngster's behavior |
| $S^0$ | Neutral stimulus | A stimulus that has not yet acquired controlling properties but for which the withholding of reinforcing contingencies have been arranged to make it a discriminative stimulus ($S^\Delta$). | The problem 3 x 3 is to become an $S^\Delta$ for the answer 6. |
| $S^D$ | Discriminative stimulus | A general term referring to any or all of the next three discriminative stimuli below: | |
| $S^{Dr}$ | Stimulus that signals reinforcement | • A stimulus in the presence of which a given response is likely to be reinforced | The green light sets the occasion for stepping on the gas and continuing on your way |
| $S^{De}$ or $S^\Delta$ | Stimulus that signals extinction | • A stimulus in the presence of which a given response does not produce reinforcers | The gas gauge shows your tank is empty, so stepping on the gas has no effect |
| $S^{Dp}$ | Stimulus that signals punishment | • A stimulus in the presence of which a given response is likely to be punished | The red light signals that stepping on the gas may get you into an accident or earn you a traffic ticket |
| MO | Motivating operation | An event or experience that influences the strength of the signaled consequences | The time since the person last ate can influence the reinforcing value of food items. |
| $S^M$ | Motivating stimulus | A stimulus that makes some other stimulus a reinforcer | Missing the keys to a car's ignition evokes seeking the keys, because you cannot start the car without them |

*Michael (1982) initially distinguished between a direct discriminative stimulus (the $S^D$) and another form of stimulus change, without which the response of interest could not be executed. He and his colleagues labeled that other form the "establishing operation (EO)." The EO, or motivating operation (MO), enabled the $S^D$ to occasion or abate the response, while the "establishing stimulus" signaled the need for that operation. We tend to use the more conventional designation, "motivating stimulus" (i.e., Kellogg, 1941). O'Donnell (2001) further distinguished such enabling antecedent stimuli according to whether they signaled reinforcement ($S^{Dr}$), punishment ($S^{Dp}$), or extinction ($S^\Delta$).

a match is touched to the fuse of the firecracker we *learned* to cover our ears) or through the mediation of others (e. g., the teacher says, "What is 3 + 2?" "Five." "YES!" or "Name the person in the picture." "Benjamin Franklin." "You got it."; "What is the mascot name for the University of Connecticut basketball team?" "The Huskies." "YES!" As mentioned, we use the abbreviation S$^D$ to designate *discriminative stimuli*—those antecedent stimuli that reliably set the occasion for a response.

As a response is repeatedly reinforced in the presence of stimuli (e.g., the response "5" is reinforced given stimuli "3 + 2" or "2 + 3"), those stimuli begin to assume control over the response. Eventually, "5" is reliably evoked in the presence of "3 + 2" or "2 + 3" but not by other stimulus sums except 4+1. These discriminative stimuli, 3+2, 2+3, and 4+1 are referred to as a **stimulus class** *in the they all produce the same response: 5*. Fundamental to the development of stimulus control, this **differential reinforcement (DR)** *is composed of two basic components: (1) reinforcing the appropriate response in the presence of some stimuli, and (2) not reinforcing it (i.e., extinguishing and/or punishing it) in the presence of others*. But if these differential contingencies are not maintained, stimulus control may weaken or disappear. For example, if a child learning an arithmetic fact, as in the above example, practices with a friend whose arithmetic skills are weak and gets lots of incorrect feedback as reinforcers, this discriminated operant class may be seriously disrupted; in other words, the child will begin to make many errors.

While applying differential reinforcement may seem conceptually simple, producing powerful stimulus control sometimes can prove especially challenging. Consider:

- Those attempting to teach languages, science, or any academic subject matter.
- The behavior analyst assisting a teacher or parent to use effective but unfamiliar behavior-management techniques in appropriate settings.
- Manufacturers training employees to high standards of quality control in an assembly line.
- Physicians struggling to achieve correct diagnoses when faced with confusing arrays of symptoms.
- A manager concerned with workplace safety trying to alert workers to warning signs of potentially dangerous conditions that may come up on the job.
- Essentially everyone concerned with changing performance in specific settings.

Differential reinforcement sometimes can be difficult because:

1. The appropriate response must first be emitted; and for this to happen, the response or its component elements must already be in the learner's repertoire.
2. The learner must be able to detect the antecedent stimuli.
3. Behavior must be reinforced adequately enough to firmly establish the three-term contingency.
4. Inappropriate responses must not be reinforced in the presence of the essential discriminative stimuli.

Note how those four features for establishing stimulus control are represented in the following example:

A tape-recorded click sounded every 20 seconds to prompt a class of 14 preschool children to pick up 50 large hollow blocks quickly at the end of free play (Goetz, Ayala, Hatfield, Marshall, & Etzel, 1983). The click and the request occurred simultaneously: "It's time to pick up the blocks." Only after teachers began to praise compliance and withhold reinforcement for non-compliance did pick-up time decrease substantially. Further, once the click and the praise had occurred together, pick-up times became shorter, even after the click alone. Initially, teacher praise was necessary to get the click to function as an S$^{Dr}$ for picking up the blocks efficiently. Once the click functioned reliably to signal the children

**TABLE 15.4 Developing Saying "I" Reliably in the Presence of the Stimulus "i"**

| A | B | C | Result |
|---|---|---|---|
| Shown letter "i" → | Client says "i" → | Reinforcement ($S^r$) | After presentation of the letter "i" and saying "i" has been repeatedly reinforced in its presence, the letter "i" reliably sets the occasion for saying "i." The letter "i" now functions as an $S^D$ for saying "i." |
| Shown letter "i" → | Client says "j" → | Punishment ($S^p$) | After repeatedly receiving punishment for saying "j" [or some other letter] in the presence of the letter "i," the letter "i" functions as an $S^{Dp}$ for saying "j" (or any other letter name). |
| Shown letter "j" → | Client says "i" → | Extinction (no stimulus) | After consistent non-reinforcement for saying "i" in the presence of the letter "j" [or some other letter], the letter "j" functions as an $S^{De}$ for saying "i." |

to pick up the blocks, however, intermittent praise became sufficient to maintain stimulus control.

Table 15.4 illustrates how to develop the letter "i" into an $S^{Dr}$ for saying "i" by using differential reinforcement.

Just about any stimuli that are within the sensory capacities of an organism can serve a controlling function once they reliably signal the consequences of responding. These consequences may involve reinforcement, extinction, punishment, or even combinations of reinforcement and punishment (no pain, no gain). To review, an $S^\Delta/S^{De}$ is *a stimulus that signals that a response in its presence will be extinguished,* while an $S^{Dp}$ is *a stimulus that signals that a response in its presence will be punished.* According to O'Donnell (2001, p. 262), an $S^{Dp}$ is "a stimulus condition in the presence of which a response has a lower probability of occurrence than it does in its absence, as a result of response-contingent punisher delivery in the presence of the stimulus." Consequently, *any discriminative stimulus may have multiple functions.* The math-fact stimulus "3 + 2" is an $S^{Dr}$ for the response "5" if the teacher usually reinforces correct answers, but it is also an $S^\Delta/S^{De}$ for any other answer in a classroom provided the teacher ignores errors. Or, it could be an $S^{Dp}$ for errors in a classroom in which the teacher punishes errors.

Consider another example: You are teaching a child color names. When the child says "red" in the presence of the color red, you deliver a reinforcer (for naming, just confirming that the answer is right is often reinforcer enough: Horne & Lowe, 1996). If in the presence of red, the child says anything other than "red," you do not reinforce. You also do not reinforce if the child sees yellow and says "red." In fact, you negate the answer and pair it with a look of disapproval. The youngster learns that saying "red" given red is apt to be reinforced while calling other colors "red" is not.

Another illustration may be drawn from a study by Kazdin and Erickson (1975). A group of children with severe mental handicaps failed to follow instructions like "Sit down"; "Catch the ball"; "Roll it to me." During training, each time a child followed an instruction correctly, he or she received food and praise. Initially, if the child failed to follow the instruction correctly, s/he was physically guided to produce the suitable response, which then was followed by food and praise. Later, the reinforcers were given only for unguided correct responses while incorrect responses were extinguished. Eventually the children attended to instructions in the absence of guidance. Their behavior had come under the control of the verbal stimuli.

In a recent example, Catagnus, Hineline, and Brown (2020) taught a student to respond to group attending calls (e.g., "everyone") from the teacher by first teaching the student to attend to the teacher when the bell rang and reinforcing that. Subsequently, they paired the bell with the group calls and again reinforced attending to the teacher. Once the student began attending when the teacher rang the bell and called the group for attention, the sound of the bell was faded. Attending to the teacher's call for group attention maintained during follow-up.

## Using Differential Reinforcement Effectively

Discrimination learning is fundamental to practically all but the most basic knowledge and skills that parents, teachers, managers, trainers, spiritual leaders, coaches, and anyone else concerned with changing behavior might hope to teach[4]. When using differential reinforcement for the purpose of bringing particular behavior under the control of certain stimuli, you will find that you need to consider a number of factors to be successful.

**Clearly identify relevant stimulus properties.** When promoting stimulus control, we must either deliver or withhold reinforcement contingent on specific behavior in the presence of specific stimuli, so the contingency manager must be clear about the exact features of those stimuli. Instructors, for example, should specify such $S^D$ properties as their function, form, position, or size, plus any other relevant dimensions. The program designer must ask, "Under what very specific circumstances should the target response be reinforced or not reinforced?" Clyde's father clearly classifies *all* instances of taking property belonging to others without permission as "stealing." That allows him to be consistent in differentially reinforcing his son's judgments. The professor of neurobiology describes the features and functions of glial cells (i.e., that, among others, they serve to physically support neurons and regulate and nourish the internal environment of the brain, including the fluid surrounding neurons and their synapses) and shows slides illustrating their defining features and how their appearance differs from that of a generic neuron.

At a much more rudimentary level, Fisher, Kuhn, and Thompson (1998) used differential reinforcement to help reduce the destructive behavior of two clients: a 13-year-old girl with mild mental retardation, and a nine-year-old boy with autism, Attention Deficit Hyperactivity Disorder (ADHD), and moderate mental delay. Either verbally requesting ("Excuse me, please" or "I want my toys, please") or signing for identified functional reinforcers, such as attention, toys, hugs, or games, was differentially reinforced. Attention was available when a photo of two people (the $S^D$ correlated with attention) was present, and toys were available when a drawing of toys (the $S^D$ correlated with toys) was present. They found that destructive behavior rapidly diminished. Combining differential reinforcement with the discriminative stimuli that signaled the availability of the reinforcers reduced the unwanted behavior "to low levels regardless of whether the functional reinforcer or an alternative reinforcer was available" (p. 543). Notice how the procedure entailed caretakers determining what reinforcers would be available and using the appropriate discriminative stimuli to communicate that information, thereby enabling the client to recognize "when and how often those consequences are delivered" (p. 558).

Ponder such instances for a moment. Yes, it is at this point that the subject-matter expert or specialist comes into the picture. The master wine expert is able to differentiate between examples of excellent and of reasonably tasty wine. The proficient coach discriminates between acceptable and unacceptable movements or team plays. The respected critic distinguishes among poor, average, and great productions. The master teacher is able to judge exactly whether a student is improving or not and adjust her strategies accordingly. So if you, as a teacher, trainer, or consultant, are naïve about the particular concepts or skills to be taught, you will need to acquire the essential information or expertise yourself or collaborate with someone else. Only then will you be able to program your differential reinforcement of a learner's progression toward mastery of given objectives.

---

[4]For an excellent example of the value of mastering the ability to make very subtle, but potentially life-saving discriminations, see http:www.mammotech.com. Hank Pennypacker, the originator of the Mammoth program, has made optical use of behaviors analytic strategies for teaching women to discriminate between healthy and unsafe breast tissue, a possible life-saver for the two female authors of this text.

As we continue talking about methods of instructing complex behavior, from time to time we refer to examples such as those just mentioned. Remember, though, that regardless of the intricacy of the relevant stimulus properties, differential reinforcement remains fundamental to the technique. Beyond that, program designers need to be adept at defining or discriminating the stimuli that are to serve a discriminative function, so they can distinguish relevant from non-relevant or inappropriate stimuli. Otherwise, or additionally, they must broaden their own expertise by studying and/or by consulting experts.

When, for example, Alavosius and Sulzer-Azaroff (1985) wanted to develop a program to prevent back injuries among nursing staff, they called upon the expertise of ergonomic and orthopedic specialists, who told them exactly which rules to apply to safely lift and transfer patients. They then translated that information into behavioral terms, so staff managers would know under what antecedent conditions they should reinforce particular actions. Glover and Gary (1976) did essentially the same thing while attempting to promote creativity. They studied the topic, found that it consisted of a set of particular qualities (fluency, flexibility, originality), and learned what people *do* when they are being fluent, flexible, original, and so on. With the answer rephrased as a set of response definitions, they then prepared and presented instructional stimuli to teach each of the creative responses.

Specifying the discriminative stimuli that define a concept, a stimulus class, or a response class is not always easy, though, especially when differences between acceptable and unacceptable behavior are slight. One approach to handling such situations—successfully identifying the antecedent stimuli that should be used to signal reinforcement ($S^{Dr}$s) from those that should be used to signal extinction ($S^{\Delta/}$ $S^{De}$s), or under some circumstances perhaps punishment ($S^{Dp}$s)—requires careful live observation of ongoing responding, or intensive study of audio or video recordings of acceptable and unacceptable performance. For instance, a speech and language professional could tape and listen to brief samples of the extra sounds made by a stutterer during a conversation. Then she could decide which speech portions should be reinforced. Or a youth counselor and client could view a tape containing a demonstration of an episode in which a young man retained his composure in a situation generally apt to provoke anger. During the observation, they could isolate key features of the interaction:[5]

"See, when George annoys Charlie, Charlie seems as if he will begin to lose it. But he remains cool. Does that kind of pestering bother you too? How can you learn to be more sensitive to cues that you are becoming irritated? Let's play that sequence again. When you notice that Charlie is about to become angry, watch what he does. Yes. He takes a deep breath and relaxes. Now let's you and I stop to consider what sets you off and talk about alternative ways of handling the situation."

**Present specific instructions.** As with specific reinforcement and punishment, *the more specific your instructions, the more rapidly you will achieve the desired behavior.* Additionally, research has demonstrated that the more precise the discriminative stimuli, the more closely the desired behavior begins to correspond to the intended outcome. When, for instance, Bouxsein, Tiger, and Fisher (2008) heightened the precision of their instructions, "Billy, answer your math questions," they found that student performance was superior to that achieved with more general instructions (i.e., "You need to do this").

**Emphasize or boost relevant antecedent stimulus properties.** Simply identifying for your learners the relevant properties of the $S^+$ (*the neutral stimulus designated to serve later as a functional discriminative stimulus*) is no guarantee that everyone's behavior will come under the control of exactly those features. You may need to take further steps. Consider the case of five minimally literate juvenile offenders (Murph & McCormick, 1985) who were learning to read road signs. The instructors showed the boys each sign, discussed its function (e.g., warning, yield, road construction, pedestrian crossing, bike crossing, and merge left), and pointed out each crucial feature and its specific meaning (e.g., shape, color, location, and what to do). After discovering that the students were still unable to correctly iden-

---
[5]Refer to the earlier material on behavioral objectives in Chapter 4, and note how clearly-stated objectives serve this purpose.

tify and say in their own words the type of sign, its meaning, and what it was telling them to do, they taught the youngsters individually to discriminate each sign, following correct answers with checks, stars, and praise and incorrect ones with minus signs and no praise. Differential reinforcement made the difference. Within one to eight months, all five boys correctly identified the signs in the driver's license manual.

Let us consider a few additional examples that emphasize the importance of specificity in teaching people to detect subtle discriminations. A teacher of art appreciation wants to illustrate how particular characteristics of a painting can convey distinctive sensations. First, she displays Duchamp's abstract *Nude Descending a Staircase*. Then a student comments that it conveys a sense of "movement." Then she shows a reproduction of Monet's *Water Lilies* and asks the class members to describe the feeling the painting projects. One student mentions "peaceful"; another "serene." The teacher and some of the other students agree. Most of the students however, apparently are reticent about offering their impressions, and appear to be at a loss. At this point, the teacher decides to help them by focusing on the distinguishing aspects of the two works and by generating some rules.

> "What are some of the distinctive qualities of each?"
>
> "In the *Water Lilies,* the edges are blurred," says one student.
>
> "The pastel colors—especially the soft blues and greens—blend into one another, whereas in the Duchamp painting, the sharp parallel lines vividly contrast with the light areas. The diagonal angles are conspicuous," comments another.

Now, when the teacher displays other examples, the students focus their attention on the relevant properties and are able to express themselves more knowledgeably and confidently. Their responses are reinforced by the agreement of their peers and the teacher.

A father complains to the therapist that his teenage son is rude and leaves a mess in his wake wherever he goes. An in-home observation suggests that the parents focus most of their attention on the behavior that irks them while ignoring acceptable behavior. The therapist asks the family to audio-tape dinner-time conversations for a few days. To help them detect their son's cooperative behaviors, they identify instances of politeness or cooperation. Having found sufficient examples, the parents are now better prepared to reinforce those. They decide to select at least one worthy behavior to recognize and approve during each course in the meal—salad, main dish, and dessert.

**Apply rules for effective reinforcement**. Surely by now you are well aware of effective reinforcement practices. Naturally, you should address the essential parameters (e.g., quality, quantity, frequency, ratio, immediacy, schedule) within your plan to bring someone's behavior under the control of particular stimuli. (Review Chapters 6 and 11 for methods to select and enhance reinforcer effectiveness.) In just one example, Dube and McIlvane (1997) differentially applied a rich, as opposed to a thin schedule of reinforcement and found that the more frequently the responding was differentially reinforced, the more robust the stimulus control became.

# HOW TO PRODUCE COMPLEX BEHAVIOR UTILIZING STIMULUS CONTROL

Now that we have discussed the various types of discriminative stimuli and illustrated the areas that you have to think about to obtain or develop stimulus control, let's look at some examples of developing stimulus control to achieve complex behavior. Shillingsburg, Cariveau, Talmadge, and Frampton (2017) utilized prompting (see Chapter 17) and fading (see Chapter 20) plus differential reinforcement to train children with autism how to accurately report past behavior or improve their "memory" regarding describing what happened during their day. Still another area in which stimulus control has been demonstrated to be useful is in producing response variability that is necessary for creativity and problem solving. In a recent study, Dracobly, Dozier, Briggs, and Jucanic (2017) were able to not only teach response variability with the use of lag schedules (in which reinforcement is dependent on a variable response; see Chapter 22) but were able to further develop stimulus control and produce repetitive responses under certain stimulus conditions and varied responses under other stimulus conditions in children with autism—basically having them engage in stable responding when that is the desired outcome and variable responding when that is the desired outcome. Other researchers have developed stimulus control to reduce complex behaviors.

Tiger, Wierzba, Fisher, and Benitez (2017) were able to successfully control the "car hoarding" of a teenager with autism. Prior to intervention he would grab toy cars and put them in his pocket, regardless of who the toy cars belong to or where they were (e.g., store), and if interrupted he would engage in self-injurious behavior and tantrum. The authors were able to develop stimulus control so that when they gave him a specific toy car, it signaled that the therapist would block access to other toy cars. This reduced his attempts at hoarding. They were then able to generalize this control to multiple environments (e.g., playroom, playground, and classroom).

Others have developed both $S^{Dr}$ and $S^{\Delta}/S^{De}$ to control classroom behavior. Torelli, Lloyd, Diekman, and Wehby (2017) were able to use a multiple schedule where one stimulus signals that responses will be reinforced and a different stimulus signals a response will not be reinforced to control the classroom behavior of elementary students. Initially students randomly recruited teacher attention during inappropriate and appropriate times. But by developing stimulus control, the researchers were able to reduce disruptive bids for attention when attention was not available. They demonstrated an effective classroom management strategy that could be used by teachers classwide.

## CONTEXTUAL VARIABLES

### Motivating Operations Defined and Illustrated

Recall how in Chapters 2, 3, and 10 we mentioned another class of antecedent events that exerts control.

They supplement the signaling of consequences by discriminative stimuli by altering the potency of the consequences arranged within stimulus-control contingencies. We call these **motivating operations** or **events,**[6] sometimes abbreviated as MOs (Laraway, Snycerski, Michael, & Poling, 2003). Motivating operations are *antecedents that (a) alter the value or strength of the $S^D$s and consequences, and that may (b) alter the behavior as a result*. The value-altering effect may be an increase or a decrease in the reinforcing or punishing effectiveness of some stimulus. MOs that increase reinforcer effectiveness relative to baseline are referred to as **establishing operations (EOs)** and those that reduce reinforcer effectiveness are referred to as **abolishing operations (AOs)** (Poling, Lotfizadeh & Edwards, 2020). For example, food deprivation makes food more potent as a reinforcer, so responding reinforced with food is likely to increase, whereas food satiation makes food less potent as a reinforcer, so responding reinforced with food may decrease. Inversely, increasing the intensity of an electric shock makes the shock more potent as a punisher, so responding punished by shock is likely to decrease, whereas decreasing its intensity makes the shock less potent, so responding punished by shock may increase.

As you can see, the effects of motivating operations on behavior can include either *increases in behavior* (called by some an *evocative effect*), or *decreases in behavior* (labeled by some an *abative effect*; e.g., Laraway et al., 2001). Suppose you have not had anything to eat in the last eight hours. Your time without food is an antecedent event that makes the presence of food a more powerful reinforcer, and therefore makes eating more reinforcing. This food deprivation is called an **unconditioned**

---

[6]Motivating operations have also been called establishing operations—EOs, or setting events—SEs. Setting events were originally defined as altering the function of the $S^D$ (Wahler & Fox, 1981), and establishing operations were defined as altering the value of the consequence (Michael, 1993). However as Mayer (1995) pointed out, these two terms in all likelihood are one in the same, in that if the reinforcer effectiveness is altered, the $S^D$, or stimulus-response relation, also is altered. Similarly, if the stimulus-response or $S^D$ function is changed, the reinforcer effectiveness probably is also altered. Because of the confusion with these terms, we now restrict the use of EOs to those MOs that influence the reinforcing effectiveness of the consequence (Poling et al., 2020) and no longer use SEs (setting events).

"Look, off to the southwest, a tornado! Quick. Let's go to the storm cellar!" This *motivating operation* is an antecedent produced by a natural environment. Heading for the storm cellar is an avoidance response, an example of negative reinforcement in which the crucial consequence is that in the storm cellar you are likely to be safe from the consequences of the twister's passage overhead. Notice also that the twister functions both as a *motivator* (you wouldn't need to go to the cellar if there were no tornado threat) and as a *discriminative stimulus* (you wouldn't give the warning if the sky was clear). Try to describe these contingencies and some of the possible sequences of events using the languages of stimulus control and motivational antecedents.

**motivating operation (UMO)** because *the effect of the reinforcer does not depend on learning history.* Your responding in the presence of food or engaging in food-seeking activities that have led to food in the past (e.g., asking for something to eat, going to cupboard or refrigerator) increases. On the other hand, if you have just eaten an especially filling meal, that eating, in producing satiation, is a UMO that decreases the reinforcing potency of food, and you will be less likely to seek food or to eat. Note also that, to the extent that the presence of food may also set the occasion on which you may eat, it can also function as a discriminative stimulus ($S^{Dr}$), the potency of which may also be affected by deprivation or satiation. Other examples of UMOs can be changes in temperature, illnesses and drug use.

When asked ($S^D$) to perform a given task, a person with a history of repeated failure with that task is less likely to comply and instead may be more apt to emit overt (hit, kick) or subtle (sneer, raised eyebrow) aggressive responses as a means of escaping the situation (e.g., Munk & Repp, 1994). This is an example of a learned **conditioned motivating operation** or **CMO**, wherein *the effect of an antecedent depends on learning history*—the person has *learned* that certain tasks result in failure. Actually, as you will discover later on, when circumstances demand that the individual perform a particular activity, a history of failure with respect to that activity (e.g., the individual is requested to do the activity—the $S^D$), can establish aggression or escape as a response. We might say that such a history transforms the activity into a motivating antecedent for aggression or escape. To illustrate, Durand (1985) found that overly-large sized job assignments influenced employee absenteeism. By remaining absent, personnel no longer needed to address the formidable tasks but escaped from them instead. Why? Because the employees' histories of failure or difficulty with the task made escape from the situation reinforcing.

Although both discriminative stimuli and motivating operations are antecedent events, you should be able clearly to differentiate them. *Discriminative stimuli* evoke, maintain, increase, or decrease responding, depending upon the consequences for responding that they signal (based on the person's learning history). *Motivating operations,* however, maintain, increase, or decrease the effectiveness of the consequences as reinforcers or punishers. Changes in behavior, then, are determined both by particular combinations of discriminative stimuli and by motivating operations. As Michael (1993) pointed out, discriminative stimuli are related to the differential *availability* of reinforcement, while motivational variables "are related to the differential reinforcing *effectiveness* of environmental events" (p. 19; italics added). Therefore, to understand what is influencing behavior, you need to analyze the contributions of both discriminative stimuli and motivational antecedents. *You cannot have effective reinforcers or punishers without having motivational antecedents that make them effective*, so you always need to think about both kinds of antecedent, and not just one or the other. Seeing antecedent events in this light will enable you more successfully to manage your target behavior by manipulating stimuli and/or events in advance.

## Motivating Stimulus Defined and Illustrated

Michael (1982) described one set of contingencies that produces an evocative relation similar to that of an MO: when a response becomes important but it cannot occur unless some stimulus change enables it. For example, you cannot drive your car unless you have the key, but you have misplaced it. So, you look in all the familiar places until you find it. Once you wanted to drive, the key became a reinforcer—hunting for it was *evoked* by those particular circumstances. Michael (2007) would label this particular stimulus situation a *motivating stimulus ($S^M$), or transitive conditioned motivating operation (CMO-T)*. We can apply that term to an antecedent-response relation of the type encountered between the time when you find yourself "desperately seeking" or "needing" an item, event, person, tool, or different environment to engage in the behavior, and when you respond according to your prior experiences (i.e., your learning history).[7] Another example would be a situation in which hunger is the MO and a bowl of hot soup is served minus a spoon (the $S^M$). The individual must then request or locate a spoon to eat. Or, suppose a person is putting a puzzle together and discovers a piece (the $S^M$) is missing. He must request or locate the missing piece before being able to complete the puzzle. In other words, a **motivating stimulus ($S^M$)** *is a stimulus that must be present to allow the individual to engage in the behavior that is primed for reinforcement. Its absence evokes seeking out that stimulus.*

## Subclasses of Motivating Operations

Michael (2007) has suggested some subclasses of motivational operations. Since they have not come into general use in the literature of applied behavior analysis and because their utility is questionable (Poling et al., 2020), we only briefly summarize them here.

**Transitive Conditioned Motivating Operation (CMO-T).** Briefly, "an environmental variable that establishes (or abolishes) the reinforcing effectiveness of another stimulus and thereby evokes (or abates) the behavior that has been reinforced by that other stimulus is a labeled a transitive CMO" (Michael, 2007, p. 391), or *motivating stimulus ($S^M$)* (the term we prefer). For example, food deprivation not only makes food a more potent reinforcer; other stimuli involved with food, such as eating utensils, also become reinforcers. Michael argues that unconditional motivating effects (UMOs), such as those of food deprivation, transfer to the conditional reinforcers, such as eating utensils, and when they do so he calls them *transitive conditional motivating operations (i.e., motivating stimuli or $S^M$s)*.

A **reflexive MO** also depends on conditional relations among reinforcers and other stimuli. Such operations *acquire their effectiveness as motivating operations by preceding a situation that either is worsening or is improving* (Michael, 2007). For example, a sequence of failures (perhaps increasing unpleasant emotional reactions) has been shown to set the occasion for escape (say in the form of aggression, self-injury, leaving the situation, and so on). A history of failure, then, becomes a reflexive MO, discouraging continued effort. Alternatively, getting closer and closer to one's goal may function as a reflexive MO that encourages continued performance. Because of the intrinsic ties between the behavior and its success or failure, it is difficult and perhaps impossible to separate their functions so as to assess their roles experimentally.

A **surrogate MO** is *a stimulus that has acquired its effectiveness by accompanying some other MO, and has come to have the same value-altering and*

---
[7]Earlier, Michael (1982) proposed the term *establishing stimulus* ($S^E$). We prefer to use the term *motivating stimulus* ($S^M$) because it more closely resembles the term it replaces (establishing stimulus; $S^E$) and also because of its relative simplicity compared to "transitive conditioned motivating operation" (CMO-T).

*behavior-altering effects as the MO that it has accompanied* (Michael, 2007). Imagine a picture of your favorite coffee cake (the surrogate) versus seeing an actual cake in the bakery window. Both make your mouth water. The functions of surrogate MOs have not yet been extensively studied within applied behavior analysis (McGill, 1999), although it has been argued that their effects may be quite powerful (Michael, 2007). Often it does pay to advertise!

**MOs that evoke antisocial behavior.** Over time, behavior analysts have identified a number of different classes of motivating operations that appear reliably to evoke an array of antisocial behaviors among children and youth. These include, among others: being regularly exposed to punitive behavior-management practices or to authorities' inconsistencies in setting and enforcing rules; experiencing sexual or physical abuse (e.g., Dishion, 1992; Loeber & Dishion, 1983; Mayer, 1995; Patterson, DeBaryshe, & Ramsey, 1989; Tolan & Guerra, 1992); viewing media displays of aggression (Mestel, 2002); access to antisocial networks (Dishion, 1992; Tolan and Guera, 1992); high rates of disapproval or reprimands (Van Acker, Grant, & Henry, 1996); and non-reinforcing environments (Wehby, Symons, & Shores, 1995). On the other hand, when those conditions are replaced by more positively reinforcing environments, antisocial behavior diminishes and prosocial behavior increases. In one specific case (Mayer, 1995), when teachers' levels of approval increased and levels of disapproval diminished, their students attended school and remained on-task more regularly, while students' rates of disruption and vandalism dropped. Similarly, Todd et al. (2002) found that, after teachers progressively increased the density of specific feedback to students until it reached a ratio of four positive for each corrective comment, problem behavior decreased and staff satisfaction increased. Others have reported that when they are permitted to make choices, students are less disruptive (disruptions decrease) and their positive interactions increase (positive behaviors are evoked) (Carter, 2001, Romaniuk & Miltenberger, 2001). Even simple greetings appear to promote increased worker productivity and customer satisfaction (Allday & Pakurar, 2007; Brown & Sulzer-Azaroff, 1994). MOs, then, can be used to promote a variety of positive behaviors, and for preventing those that are contextually inappropriate. Numerous MOs are described and used to help prevent the occurrence of behaviors often targeted for reduction in Chapter 27 and in a small paper back, Preventing Problematic Behavior (Mayer & Wallace, 2022). Clearly, comprehending the function of motivational antecedent events and how to apply them effectively is crucial to becoming an effective behavior change agent.

The sorts of antecedents listed in the lower half of Figure 15.2 combine with learning history to play

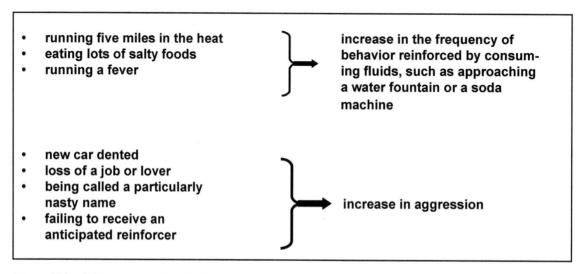

**Figure 15.2** Other examples of motivating operators

an important role in cases of spouse and child abuse, especially when there has been a heavy reliance on punitive disciplinary techniques (Mayer, Butterworth, Nafpaktitis, & Sulzer-Azaroff, 1983a).

The potency of some stimuli as reinforcers can be enhanced or diminished either by endogenous chemicals (produced naturally within the body) or by exogenous ones. An example of the latter is Ritalin (methylphenidate or MPH), a pharmaceutical used to decrease hyperactive behavior (Rapport, Murphy, & Bailey, 1982; Farone, Spencer, Aleardi, Pagano, & Biederman, 2004). Perhaps MPH reduces or blocks the reinforcing value of excessive movement or enhances the reinforcing value of certain environmental stimuli; or maybe the excessive movements now require so much additional effort that they begin to become aversive (e.g., Sagvolden, Johansen, Aase, & Russell, 2005; Catania, 2005).

Regardless, ADHD medication has been found to influence rates of responding, certainly among laboratory animals. It does this in distinctively different ways, depending on the schedules of food reinforcement in effect as well on the dose level of MPH (Heyman, 1992). Low drug dosages increased responding maintained by the leanest reinforcement schedule but had little effect on responding being maintained by denser reinforcement schedules, while high doses of the drug decreased responding maintained by the leaner schedules and also increased responding maintained by the denser schedules.

In an investigation with humans, Northup, Fusilier, Swanson, Roane, and Borrero (1997) examined the effects of MPH on reinforcer assessment outcomes for children diagnosed with ADHD. They found that when receiving a placebo (an inert or innocuous substance), participants generally worked for coupons exchangeable for food and tangible items. When receiving MPH, although food remained the preferred reinforcer for one participant, the value of the food coupon decreased for the other two, who now favored activities instead. In addition, two of the three participants completed more math problems when they received MPH than when they received the placebo. Moreover, Wallace, Stevenson, Ellsworth, and MacAleese (2007) demonstrated that the predictive validity of preference assessments depended on the time of the day when the assessment was conducted, and whether the participants were fully or partially medicated. Preference assessments conducted during full medication status validly predicted reinforcer strength, but those conducted during partial status did not validly predict reinforcer value for three children receiving medication for their ADHD.

The effects of motivational antecedents need not depend on histories of discrimination learning. After the first time a baby is nauseated, he or she will refuse food. The baby didn't need experience with the various consequences of eating. Similarly, regardless of whether injuring an adversary has been differentially reinforced, when injured, an animal will attack any creature nearby (Ulrich & Azrin, 1962). Again we see that motivating antecedents have functions different from those of discriminative stimuli, and they obtain their functional properties in a different way.

Motivational antecedents may influence many other discriminated operants, often in rather dramatic ways. In fact, such circumstances affect challenging behaviors as well as the results of assessments conducted to evaluate them. For instance, O'Reilly (1995) demonstrated that sleep deprivation was correlated with escape-maintained aggression, while Kennedy and Meyer (1996) found that sleep deprivation and allergy symptoms influenced rates of negatively reinforced problem behaviors. For this reason, parents, care-givers, human service personnel, managers, and others need to consider these antecedents when analyzing perplexing behavior. Most parents and teachers recognize that if a child is acting way out of character, they should try first to find out whether some physical condition or other overarching event, such as a family crisis, has altered the youngster's typical behavioral patterns.

## SUMMARY AND CONCLUSIONS

In this chapter we have introduced, defined, illustrated, and discussed how stimulus control develops. This is information that behavior analysts must master if they are to promote effective behavior change. Stimulus control is said to exist when specific antecedent events signal the consequences of responding or, in other words, indicate the contingency relation between responses and their consequences. If the reinforcement of a response is indicated, responding will be maintained or will increase in the presence of that stimulus. When extinction is signaled, responding will not be maintained and will decrease in the presence of that stimulus. Responding also will decrease in the presence of a stimulus that signals that the response will be punished. When antecedent stimuli have such effects, they are called discriminative stimuli ($S^D$s). The relation among the three terms, discriminative stimulus (antecedent), behavior, and consequences, is referred to as the *three-term contingency*. This contingency relation cannot be reduced to the pair-wise relation between any two of the three terms: the three-term contingency creates functional units called *discriminated operants*.

There is also another class of antecedents called *motivational events* or *operations (MOs)*. These affect the potency of the stimuli that serve as reinforcers or punishers within discriminated operant classes and therefore can determine how easily discriminations can be taught and how effectively they can be maintained.

These concepts are fundamental to our ability to analyze and manage learning and teaching more successfully, and to change human performance in general.

*Chapter 16*

# Selecting and Applying Methods for Promoting Stimulus Control

## Goals

1. Recognize, define, and give original illustrations of each of the following terms:
   a. simple stimulus control
   b. simple discrimination contingency
   c. concept
   d. conditional discriminations
   e. four-term contingency
   f. matching-to-sample
   g. simultaneous matching-to-sample
   h. delayed matching-to-sample
   i. stimulus or functional equivalence
   j. equivalence classes
2. Describe and discuss the purpose of:
   a. scatter plots
   b. sequence methods
3. Describe and illustrate with an example the importance of stimulus control in concept formation.
4. Describe how to teach conditional discriminations.
5. List the advantages of using stimulus equivalence teaching procedures.

\*\*\*\*\*\*\*\*\*\*\*\*

Now, equipped with a general perspective of stimulus control and a number of terms, you should be ready to examine at closer range several methods you can use to promote stimulus control in your daily activities. In the pages to come, watch for guidelines and examples of strategies for promoting higher-order skills among your clientele. You can do this by simultaneously or sequentially combining the stimuli they experience before, during, and after the responses of interest. We begin by describing how simple discriminations are acquired.

## SIMPLE DISCRIMINATIONS

Recall how the sound of the click we mentioned in the last chapter was used to signal "clean-up time." Technically, listeners were *discriminating* (detecting) the presence of a stimulus from its absence and behaving according to their experience. Often, though, what we discriminate is not presence versus absence of a stimulus, but instead two or more different stimuli or classes of stimuli, like red, yellow and green traffic lights, or cats versus dogs, or between men and women. A myriad of examples abound in our daily lives, beyond the realm of research. Here are just a few illustrative discriminations that most of us have learned very well:

- hearing your wake-up alarm ring versus a telephone ring
- hearing your telephone ring versus your doorbell ring
- hearing a friend's voice when you answer the phone versus a stranger's voice
- seeing your car versus other cars when you look for where you parked it
- seeing the book from which you need to study for an exam versus other books
- seeing a clear path versus a muddy path as you take a walk after the rain
- hearing a report that the weather will be sunny versus a report that it will snow
- reading that your flight will be on time versus that it will be delayed
- seeing various products you can select while shopping online
- finding the shortest line in a fast food restaurant
- seeing that some items are left on your list versus that you've gotten to the last one (and this one is it!)

Ludwig, Gray, and Rowell (1998) reported that locating recycling receptacles primarily where beverages were consumed, rather than in central locations, led to an increase in the percentage of cans recycled. The receptacles were discriminative stimuli that occasioned proper recycling more readily than if they had been placed at a distance. (Of course, the receptacles did not serve as reinforcers for recycling. That behavior previously had been strengthened.)

Simply because a stimulus is present, and even relevant, does not necessarily mean it will set the occasion for a particular behavior (i.e., function as a discriminative stimulus). For example, although instructions can serve as important antecedents by encouraging appropriate behavior, the presence of the instructions does not necessarily change the contingencies acting on the instructed behavior. Using small dashboard stickers displaying a message such as "Safety Belt Use Required of All Vehicle Occupants" often occasioned fastening seat belts (Rogers, Rogers, Bailey, Runkle, & Moore, 1988; Thyer & Geller, 1987; Weinstein, Grubb, & Vautier, 1986). Similarly, placing a sign that said "Please Buckle Up, I Care" near the exit of a university parking lot cued adults to buckle up while driving (Simpson, 2006). (But notice that in both cases the fastened seatbelt will do its job whether or not an instruction is present.)

Sometimes, the actions intended to assist a client can serve inadvertently as antecedent stimuli that promote the very behavior the contingency manager is trying to reduce. To illustrate, Tarbox, Williams, and Friman (2004) discovered that compared to periods with no diapers, diapering an adult with developmental delays increased urinary accidents. Once the adult discriminated between wearing and not wearing a diaper, he realized that with a diaper he could comfortably urinate in his pants. That led him to use the toilet less often. Perhaps, based on similar contingencies, the efficient absorption of urine by contemporary diapers may well contribute to more extended periods of toilet training for small children than may have been the case with earlier, less absorbent diapers. Note, then, the importance of observing and identifying the effects of particular stimuli on the behavior of your clients. Despite your best intentions, the management methods you use can promote undesired behavior.

Generally, though, if you are well acquainted with your clientele and their highly preferred reinforcers, you can enhance or diminish target responses by systematically using differential reinforcement to promote **simple stimulus control.** That is, *you can present a single discriminative stimulus ($S^D$) to evoke or reduce particular behavior*, as described previously. When you do so, you must also decide which consequences to arrange and when, by setting up a **simple discrimination contingency.** *A simple discrimination contingency consists of the antecedent stimulus, A (or $S^D$), the behavior, B (or response, R), and the consequence, C (or reinforcer, $S^r$)* (Green, 2001). The child who is developing social skills must discriminate relatives from strangers. Hugging relatives is reinforced, hugging strangers is not. (In fact, that may be punished.) Bonnie must not call strange men "Daddy." Running around naked is acceptable only at home, while running and screaming (clothed) is permissible in the gymnasium or playground, but not in the library or during a chamber-music concert. From an array of flasks, Dexter must select the one containing ammonia. Of a variety of social events, Clyde learns about those during which swearing will not be condoned.

Just as we don't expect written instructions to work with illiterates, particular antecedents will only evoke specific responses if some learning history has made them effective. So signs, instructions, modeled performances, signals, directives, assistance, goals, guidelines and policies also exemplify this category. To be convinced that a given response is under proper stimulus control, it must occur under specific circumstances but *not* under irrelevant stimulus conditions. Ms. Chung wants to know whether Fern can distinguish boxes of particular sizes, so she asks Fern to get the largest box. Fern complies (the response). Does this guarantee that Fern is discriminating that box from the others? It does only if she consistently demonstrates the behavior in the presence of boxes of other dimensions.

## DISCRIMINATIONS AMONG MULTIPLE STIMULI

Many of our examples have involved the presence versus the absence of stimuli, but that actually is not the most general case. Our day-to-day discriminations more typically involve two or more stimuli, each of which signals a different reinforcer. If we open the refrigerator and see a container of milk and another of juice, reaching for either one may be reinforced, but the reinforcers, milk or juice, will be different (unless you happen to relish both juice and milk on your cereal!). You could say that the $S^{Dr}$ *for one response often is the $S^{De}$ for the other*, but in such cases, it is far simpler to talk just about the two different discriminative stimuli, $S^{Dr}$ and $S^{De}$.

Learning to read is an example of this sort of stimulus control. When presented with *p*, the student must discriminate it from other letters and say "p"; when presented with *q*, the student must say "q"; and so on for all of the letters of the alphabet. Similarly, a *2* occasions "two," a *7* occasions "seven," and so on for other numbers. You can see how tedious it would be not only to call each letter an $S^{Dr}$ in its turn, but also for each to list at the same time the 25 other letters as $S^{De}$s. In most cases involving two or more discriminative stimuli, it will be pretty obvious whether it is important to mention $S^{De}$s, so expect that very often you will see stimulus control procedures described just in terms of $S^{Dr}$s.

Almost imperceptible cues like turned-down lips and knitted eyebrows generally become discriminative for non-reinforcement, whereas turned-up lips and eyes crinkled at the corners generally herald reinforcers. What accounts for the acquisition of those discriminations? In each of these instances, differential reinforcement has occurred: One particular response, but not others, was reinforced in the presence of a specific stimulus. Other responses are reinforced only in the presence of their own corresponding antecedent stimuli. Bonnie learns only to approach Dad for a hug when he smiles. To summarize, to teach an important distinction:

- the response must have been established in the person's behavioral repertoire.
- the person must attend to the relevant antecedent stimulus.
- the response must have had a sufficient history of reinforcement with regard to the requirements of the three-term or the antecedent-stimulus (S)-response (R) contingency (as in, for example, $S^D$ - R - $S^R$).
- the person's behavior must either produce different reinforcers, in the case of the discrimination between two stimuli, or result in no reinforcers, in the case of a reinforcement versus extinction discrimination.
- other circumstances, such as different or unintended contextual variables or motivating operations, must not interfere with the response.

When attempting to comprehend why a given procedure has failed, one needs to examine how faithfully the users have adhered to the format rules for applying that particular procedure. This "rule of thumb" can allow us to begin to understand the mixed results produced by that particular procedure. So, by examining the way given instances of using Social Stories failed to produce the desired results may reveal the misuse and misunderstanding of implementing or inserting stimuli that led to the ineffective behavior change (Leaf, et al., 2020). However, sometimes the explanation as to why a particular behavior occurs remains mystifying. Fortunately, some clever behavior analysts have developed various tools for identifying those.

## Identifying Obscure $S^D$s

**Scatter plot.** Determining what stimuli may be evoking or reducing behavior is not always easy. Sometimes, as discussed in Chapter 10, a scatter plot can assist. To prepare a **scatter plot** for this purpose, *one variable, usually time of day, is plotted on the ordinate (y-axis), and a second variable, usually days, is plotted on the abscissa (x-axis).*

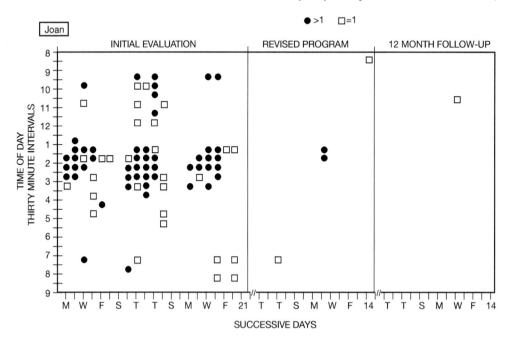

**Figure 16.1** Scatter plot of a patient's aggression. From Touchette, MacDonald, & Langer (1985). © 1985 by the Society for the Experimental Analysis of Behavior, Inc.

*Groupings of those data points may help to identify elusive environmental stimuli.* In Figure 16.1 (Touchette et al., 1985), note how the behavior (aggression in this case) tended to occur at certain times and on certain days and not others. With such information, the behavior analyst can zero in on which stimuli are present or absent at the times when episodes of aggression or non-aggression usually are observed.

**Sequencing method.** Another way to assess for the antecedent stimuli controlling a response is to use a **sequencing method**, *trying first one, then combining two, three, (and so on) potential $S^D$s,* as Halle and Holt (1991) did. The developers suggested the method because "when a learner is taught a new response, the stimuli that influence its display are often unknown" (p. 579). Working with four young adults with moderate developmental delays, the investigators attempted to teach them to add "please" to requests for particular items. To determine the controlling $S^D$s, Halle and Holt specified four elements present during training: the requester, the item to retrieve, the receiver, and the setting. First they presented each stimulus alone to determine if it would evoke the word "please." Only one learner responded to a single stimulus by saying "please." The investigators then combined stimuli to determine which combinations evoked "please." Two of the other young adults responded with "please." They did not continue with other combinations for the fourth young adult because he started saying please as part of his requests during the baseline condition. You too can use this method of combining stimuli such as particular people, places, material, and so on, to determine which, if any, set the occasion for the desired response.

A therapist we know used this method with his client with autism to discover the controlling $S^D$s. She taught a child to touch his nose, mouth, head, etc., when requested to do so. She then informed the child's teacher of what the child could now do. The teacher requested him to touch his nose, etc. and got no response. The therapist then tried being present to see if that would evoke the behavior. Again, when the teacher requested the responses, they did not occur. The therapist then made the requests in the presence of the teacher. Again, no correct response.

Next the therapist asked her client to engage in the behaviors in her office, and the client did so. Finally, after trying various combinations to discover what $S^D$ or combination of $S^D$s controlled the behavior, the therapist discovered if the table and chair from the therapy room were present when the request was made, the child would engage in the requested behavior, regardless of where the request occurred and who made the request. (This illustration is an example of a client engaging in *stimulus overselectivity,* a type of responding often observed with children with autism, that we will discuss in the next chapter.)

Once you find those effective $S^D$s, you can take steps to appropriately expand their range or teach the client generalization and discrimination skills. For instance, you can extend the training to other necessary stimulus conditions or you can try some of the other methods we cover later, in Chapter 21, on the topic of generalization.

## Control by Complex Stimuli

Many kinds of behavior are controlled by multiple discriminative stimuli, not just one. Consider the ability to sort, or *classify.* Items with an exclusive property are placed in one group; those with another into a different one; and soon: "Acceptable products go in this box; defective ones in that." Or "distinguish epic from romantic poems." Actually, the procedures by which we teach such complex discriminations are essentially the same as those for simpler stimuli, but with complex stimuli it may be more difficult for the teacher to maintain appropriate contingencies. Defective boxes may be defective in many ways, and it may be difficult to draw a line between the acceptability of one with a very minor blemish and another with a more serious flaw. Some epic poems may include romantic passages and some romantic poems may include epic ones, but how can a teacher decide the proportions that separate these different classes of poetry if some cases seem marginal? In other words, in teaching fine discriminations, the teacher must already have appropriate discriminative skills, or the teacher will be unable to differentially reinforce the learner's behavior.

The teacher's discriminations need not be identical to the learner's, though. For example, sighted teachers can teach the names of geometric solids, such as cubes and spheres, to blind children, even though the children give the names based on what they feel as they handle the solids, and the teachers reinforce the children's correct naming based on what they see the children handling.

Complex stimulus control is usually involved in what we call *comprehension*, which may be assessed by presenting several different instructions and evaluating the responses. Translating a series of phrases written in a foreign language is an obvious example. Suppose the person is able to take a set of instructions, such as a recipe or a list of steps to follow in assembling a tool or implementing a given behavioral procedure, and follow through successfully. Apparently an adequate history of differential reinforcement has been at work.

A marvelous aspect of stimulus control is that it serves as the foundation of all sorts of complex human behavior—solving problems, understanding concepts, behaving differently as a function of time, place, or circumstances (e.g., in private versus in public)—indeed the wide array of behaviors involved in most instances of covert and overt responding. Understand how stimulus control operates, and you will begin to realize its role in the most subtle and sophisticated nuances of your own behavior. At the core is just one key element: the array of stimulus features that reliably set the occasion for reinforcement, extinction, or punishment.

Identifying simple concepts like *immediate family members* or complicated ones such as *beauty* or *gracefulness* happens in exactly the same way. You isolate admissible stimulus features (e.g., in the case of *immediate family*, a parent, sibling, or offspring; in the case of *beauty*, maybe "attracting viewers to view the item; prolonged attending, producing a positive emotional reaction"; and so on). Reinforcers are delivered when the individual assigns a particular label in the presence of those features. Stimulus control functions similarly, to guide "rational thought," as in using covert cues to set the occasion for sequences of self-statements ("Now if I activate the GPS, and tell it where I want to go, it will lead me there") or to guide complex sequences of overt responding, as in reciting to oneself the rules for performing a particular surgical procedure or for flying a plane under adverse weather conditions. Stimulus control is responsible for enabling people to learn to distinguish right from wrong, to solve problems on the job, at home, in the community or school, or even to resolve moral dilemmas. It even applies to your learning behavioral concepts. For example, to be able to identify a positive reinforcer, you must recognize three critical aspects or discriminative stimuli: (a) the presence of a *consequence*, (b) that is contingently *added*, (c) resulting in the response *increasing or maintaining*. If any critical aspect is changed, for example—the (c) behavior decreases—you have a different concept (positive punishment).

Concepts are classes of stimuli that fit a particular category: redness, persuasiveness, elegance, honesty, and so on. Technically, a **concept** is *a set of critical properties shared, perhaps only in part, among a number of stimuli*, much the same as the features that permit one to set up classifications. Consider the concept of "dog." Among the features common to most dogs are that they are of a certain shape and size range, have hair, tails, and four legs; they bark; and they are readily domesticated—i.e., relate well to humans who care for them. That leaves out many creatures including rodents, raccoons, and cats, who don't bark; seals, who don't have four legs; turtles, who don't have hair; and wolves, not easily domesticated. (Of course there are exceptions, as in the case of a hairless cartoon dog like Snoopy, who shares very *few* of those features. Nonetheless, children easily learn to call it a dog, perhaps by the way it relates to other humans or animals.) Similarly, the written *A* and the spoken "a" share a common function but do not share any stimulus properties (they cannot, because one is a shape and the other is a sound). Nor can we identify physical properties common to the sharpness of a knife and the sharpness of an image and the sharpness of a pain. Many classes called *concepts* come together not because of any identifiable common stimulus property, but rather because their members share *functions* in their reinforcement histories or in the contingencies that helped to create them. However particular concepts originated, as Keller and Schoenfeld (1950) pointed out, ultimately they are learned on the basis of discriminations between concept classes and generalization within each class.

Again, the basis for teaching this form of stimulus control remains the same: differential reinforcement. In this instance, however, the response is reinforced in the presence of any of a variety of antecedent stimuli possessing the appropriate properties; the response is not reinforced in the presence of stimuli that do not contain some appropriate combination of those properties. If Bonnie called a seal a dog, her parents would not reinforce that response. In English-speaking cultures, her parents will reinforce "blue" spoken in the presence of blue things and "green" spoken in the presence of green things. In some cultures, the language does not include separate words for blue and green, and so parents in that culture will reinforce different ways of naming colors. Does that mean those children cannot discriminate those colors? Of course not, but they might run into problems in a conversation with an English-speaking child. As another example, in our culture those who deal professionally with fabrics or home decor or visual arts usually have very sophisticated color vocabularies compared with the vocabulary of the average person. The point is that these color concepts were created by appropriate contingencies and can vary tremendously across individuals, so we must look at those contingencies when we need to make decisions about control by complex stimuli.

## CONDITIONAL DISCRIMINATIONS

While the simpler forms of discrimination learning just discussed probably account for a large proportion of human and other learning, a goodly amount of what all of us hope to learn, teach, and manage is more complex. Think about your own current learning, teaching, training, and managing—as in the subject at hand, or in the other subjects you are studying or promoting. Much requires going beyond rights or wrongs, goods or bads. Among others, subtler forms of labeling, classifying, analyzing, grouping, or separating various stimuli are central to much advanced learning and performance. Some of these impress us mainly because they involve fine discriminations. Think about the ability to distinguish between one kind of pain versus another, as a physician must; or the chemist's skill at separating different chemical compounds; or the musical director's judgment in detecting and coaching his choral group's tonal clarity. Consider your own activities and those of people whose daily occupations are familiar to you, and you will see how often making fine discriminations of a conditional nature are involved.

In other cases, though, what is important is not the fineness of the discrimination but the circumstances under which it is appropriate. For example, it may be realistic for a youth in an inner city to discriminate among other youths in his neighborhood on the basis of their race or ethnicity, but once he gets to college he will find that the racial or ethnic discriminations are regarded as inappropriate and that other discriminations based on academic achievements have become far more important. He may still continue to discriminate based on racial or ethnic characteristics when he goes back to his old neighborhood; maybe in his neighborhood that will be critical to staying out of fights and avoiding other kinds of trouble. But now his racial and ethnic discriminations are conditional; they remain important when he visits his old neighborhood, but he discovers that they begin to drop away while he is on campus. Of course, we know that discriminations may persist, and they will do so as long as they are sustained by real contingencies, as exist in many social settings, not just in urban environments but also in suburban and rural ones. But the possibility of changing them through conditional discriminations gives us hope that they can eventually be replaced by discriminations based on other dimensions such as social skills, academic competence, and so on. Now and in the future, you will find that learning methods to support the acquisition of conditional discriminations will be advantageous to you as a student and as a behavior manager.

Sidman and Tailby (1982) have defined **conditional discrimination** procedures in terms of a **four-term contingency**, where *conditional stimuli provide the new fourth term*:

> *Given conditional stimulus S1, one three-term contingency operates:*

*A1 signals that a contingency relating B1 to C1 is operating*

*Given conditional stimulus S2, a different three-term contingency operates:*

*A2 signals that a contingency relating B2 to C2 is operating*

Suppose S1 is the presence of a light in the ceiling of a pigeon chamber and S2 is its absence. The pigeon faces a green key on the left and a red key on the right, with a feeder below them. During S1, its pecks on the green key (A1) produce food but its pecks on the red key do not produce food. On the other hand, during S2 its pecks on the green key do not produce food and its pecks on the red one (A2) do. Whether pecks on green produce food or pecks on red produce food depends on, or is conditional on, whether the chamber light is on. The pigeon will quickly learn this conditional discrimination, in that it will learn to peck green when the ceiling light is on (S1) and to peck red when it is off (S2).

This particular arrangement is called a conditional reversal, because the contingencies for the two keys are switched or reversed depending on which conditional stimulus, S1 or S2, is present. But the conditionality can involve any forms of discriminations, not just reversals. For instance, in our earlier example, very different discriminations were occasioned for the youth depending on the conditional stimuli defined by whether he was in his neighborhood or on campus.

Notice that the terms of the **four-term contingency** *include the following elements*: *(1) conditional stimuli, (2) antecedent stimuli, (3) responses (behaviors), and (4) consequences.* As Green (2001) has pointed out:

> Conditional discriminations are established by reinforcing responses to particular antecedent stimuli *if and only if* they are preceded or accompanied by particular additional stimuli.... In contrast with simple discriminations, here each antecedent stimulus is discriminative for reinforcement or not, depending on (conditional on) the presence of another particular antecedent (Sidman, 1986; Sidman et al., 1982; Sidman & Tailby, 1982). (p. 75)

**Matching-to-sample.** As children develop, much of their learning depends not on single properties of stimuli such as size or color. Instead, they learn about stimulus relations, such as something being to the left of or something being on top of something else. A particularly interesting case is the relation of matching, as in selecting color-coordinated components of an outfit. Children fairly readily learn to match, but it can be relatively difficult to train nonhumans or nonverbal humans to do so. Consider the special case called **matching-to-sample**, *a task in which an individual selects from two or more alternatives (e.g., objects, figures, letters, or sounds — the antecedent stimuli, of which the one that matches the conditional stimulus will become the $S^D$) the stimulus that matches or corresponds to a standard or sample (the conditional stimulus).* Infants may be taught to match the objects they see to others of the same kind: items like blocks to similarly shaped or colored blocks, or other items such as toys, facial expressions, sounds, pictures, and many more. School children learn to match the shape of a state or country to its representation on the globe; numerals or letters to quantities or pictures. Whenever you use an instructional manual containing pictures or diagrams, you are matching to sample, and when the picture on your driver's license is checked, the official matches the picture to your actual appearance. Our economic survival demands that we learn to match the proper array of coins to a bill, while test-taking as a student requires that we choose the correct answer from an array of multiple-choices.

Notice that some matches can be based on identity, as when reds are matched with reds and greens with greens. But other kinds of matches, such as those of objects with their names in different languages, may be totally arbitrary. Saying "red" when you see something that is red is a kind of matching, but is specific only to English-speaking communities.

Matching is a form of conditional discrimination: If *this* is the case, then *that* goes with it; if *something else* is the case, a *certain other item* goes with it. For instance, given a set of picture cards of different auto parts, the task is to take the single sample (the conditional stimulus), such as a card with a picture of a fan part, and to see if the responder can match it against the same fan part in the array (of

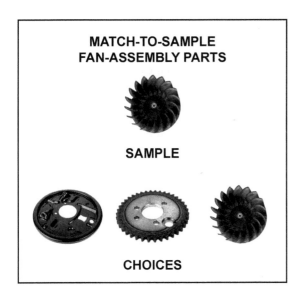

**Figure 16.2** Simultaneous match-to-sample

which the part that matches the conditional stimulus will become an $S^D$ to the response) (see Figure 16.2).

In **simultaneous matching-to-sample**, *the sample item*, often a picture, though sometimes a three-dimensional object, *is presented while the choices remain exposed*, as in Figure 16.2. To illustrate further, suppose Fern's job coach has prepared a sample display of items to be packed in a goodie-bag. The coach holds up the display and says, "Pack a bag like this." The sample goodie-bag items remain displayed while Fern chooses the matching items. If her choices are correct, her coach praises her. Otherwise, the coach withholds praise. Had the sample display been shown, then removed in advance of Fern's selections, the task would have been an instance of **delayed matching-to-sample**, *a type of matching in which the sample item is removed before the choices are presented*. Of course, during training, the coach could increase the delay by gradually extending the time between removing the sample display and allowing Fern to choose.

In an actual study, Melchiori, De Souza, and De Rose (2000) taught beginning reading skills to preschoolers, first graders, special-education students, and adults. The learner first matched printed with dictated words, by pointing to one of two printed words presented on a piece of paper. Participants then were asked to arrange individual letter tiles to match the word selected from the preceding matching trail. Not only did the students learn to match but they also learned to read the words. "In addition, most of the students learned to read new words that involved re-combinations of the syllables of the training words" (p. 97).

Notice that the previous example involved combining what was learned in different tasks. When different stimuli participate in common matches, the learner sometimes begins spontaneously to *treat all members of the class as interchangeable. They all evoke the same response*. When that happens, all of the interchangeable antecedent stimuli are called a **stimulus class**. For example, if a child learns to match written *A* to written *a*, and written *A* to spoken "a," and spoken "a" to written *a*, etc., all three, *A*, *a*, and "a" are members of the stimulus class that we sometimes label as the letter A. Each of these members has different stimulus properties and those properties are not necessarily shared: the sound "a" has no shape. We will see further extensions of these procedures later, when we discuss *equivalence classes*.

Lane and Critchfield (1998) used delayed matching-to-sample to teach vowel and consonant stimulus classes to two adolescent females with moderate mental retardation. On one computer screen, assume the vowels *A* and *O* were shown. This screen was then removed. On the next screen a *D* and *A* appeared. The subject would be asked to select the vowel.

> The correct comparison stimulus matched only one of the letters in the compound sample.... Both participants acquired five-member classes of vowel and consonant stimuli, which subsequently generalized to vocal classification and to identification in the context of four-letter words. Follow-up tests showed that the generalized performances remained intact after 6 weeks. (p. 21)

Hanna, De Souza, De Rose, and Fonseca (2004) also used delayed matching-to-sample to teach spelling to six first graders, aged 8 to 10, with histories of school failure. Their training procedure consisted of presenting:

a card with a printed-word sample for 10 s [seconds] or until the child said "pronto" (ready), whichever came first. The experimenter then removed the sample and asked the child to construct the word with movable letters. Afterwards, the card was placed beside the constructed word and the child was required to say whether the construction was correct. Correct constructions were followed by praise and tokens, and the child named the word aloud. After incorrect constructions, the card remained beside the constructed word while the child corrected its spelling. (p. 224)

If the child continued to make errors on a word, s/he was prompted to compare each of the letters in the word with the sample and to make the appropriate corrections. Not only did this procedure increase correctly spelled words, as evidenced by all participants improving significantly over their baseline levels, with five receiving 80 percent or more on subsequent tests, but the correct spelling also generalized to their cursive writing.

The matching-to-sample technique has been used to support bringing complex skills—(verbal, visual, or other sensory-based skills such as sound, taste, and touch) under stimulus control, across a range of human participants (e.g., Sidman, 1969, 1977; Sidman & Cresson, 1973; and many others, some mentioned previously) and non-humans (i.e., Kasdak & Schusterman, 1994). The contingency manager uses stimuli with which the individual is familiar and teaches the person to match or pair those with stimuli the learner is to group together as functionally equivalent, i.e., as members of the same stimulus class. Suppose a student can identify a picture of a doctor but does not know how to read the word "doctor." The learner may be capable of identifying an egg beater but not know its function. The matching-to-sample method can be used to teach the student to match the picture with its corresponding word and not some other word, and/or the word with a picture (e.g., of the doctor) and not with an inappropriate picture (e.g., of a plumber, carpenter, or astronaut), or even an actual 3-D object with its equivalent. Rehfeldt and Root (2005) have used matching-to-sample methods to establish requesting skills in adults with severe developmental disabilities. Also, picture to object matching-to-sample is a key feature of the *Picture Exchange Communication System—PECS©* (Bondy & Frost, 2001). Current research has utilized matching to sample to teach reading Braille (Lillie & Tiger, 2019); visual analysis of graphs (Blair, et al., 2019), reading emotional faces in deaf and hard of hearing and typical children (Tsou, et al., 2020), among others.

Akin to matching the picture of the doctor to its corresponding printed word, Sidman (1977) used the match-to-sample method to teach developmentally-delayed students words like *car* or *boy*. The samples were three-letter words projected onto a center window, surrounded by nine windows upon which different pictures were projected. If the student touched the picture matching the central word, a reinforcer was delivered. Otherwise, nothing happened. Naturally the student continued trying until the reinforcer was received. To test whether the student actually had learned appropriate matching, the instructor dictated the word, and had the student select the printed word from several available choices. Remarkably, many students were successful in learning the spoken and printed words along with pictures as a *class* of functionally equivalent stimuli. They could select any one of the three correctly when either of the other two was presented. Sidman called these stimulus classes "equivalence classes." We will consider them further below.

The technique also can be used to teach uses or meanings, such as the purpose of an eggbeater or a carving knife. Instead of printed words as the set of choices, it might include pictures of the tools being *used*, such as an eggbeater whipping eggs, a hammer hitting a nail, a spatula spreading frosting, or a knife slicing a turkey. Other arrays might include similar pictures, including perhaps a knife carving a roast, and so on, so sufficient exemplars of the functions of a carving knife could be displayed while the student correctly matched the tool to pictures of many of its applications.

The match-to-sample method also lends itself nicely to teaching *errorless* discriminations. That is especially advantageous for people who, despite considerable effort, have failed previously to acquire such discriminations. The basic approach is to ensure correct choices all along the way by beginning with very easy tasks, such as touching the only window or picture displayed before the choices are displayed. Other (incorrect) choices are progressively introduced, while correct matches continue to be reinforced.

If your client can match dictated name samples to pictures, do not assume that s/he can match visual stimuli (pictures, letters, or numbers) to themselves. For example, Kelly, Green, and Sidman (1998) found that their five-year-old client with autism could match dictated name samples to pictures, but did not perform well in matching identical visual stimuli to one another. Additionally, the way the matching task is organized can influence performance. The client performed poorly on identity-matching tests conducted on the table top, failing to improve "...until the stimulus array was made to resemble the stimulus arrangement on the computer" (p. 237) that he had experienced during his preliminary training.

Evidently, many adjuncts for producing suitable stimulus control stand ready. In deciding which to choose, you first determine which stimuli currently are functional—that is, which antecedent stimuli currently control the behavior. Then, from among those, you select the one(s) that function to direct the learner's attention to the critical features of the natural and *relevant* stimuli. Your objective is to gradually wean the learner away from prompts or other contrived or artificial cues and toward those inherent in the stimulus situation. (See Figure 16.3 for an illustration of a problem of this nature: shifting from pictorial to written words, as in reading the word *fruit*.) In Chapter 17 we discuss systematic prompting strategies designed to minimize errors during the learning process in greater detail. For present purposes, though, always ensure that the learner can discriminate the features that distinguish one antecedent stimulus from another.

**Teaching matching-to-sample.** After reviewing about twenty years of research on teaching matching-to-sample (or *conditional discrimination* skills) Green (2001) recommended the following:

Objective: Say the word "fruit" when you see the word "fruit."
(Learn to read the word *fruit*)

What works now:
Sees fruit ➜ says "fruit."

What you *want* to work:
Sees pictures of fruit; chooses written word "fruit."

What you instruct:
"See the pictures. Choose the word that matches."

FRUIT　　　　　　　　　　　　　　　　　FLAT

**Figure 16.3** The Challenge: Shifting stimulus control from pictures to a written word

- *Teach learners how to perform matching-to-sample (MTS) tasks before teaching them discriminations.* Those include orienting toward stimuli, scanning multiple comparisons, pointing to (or selecting) single comparisons, and sitting quietly between trials. She emphasized:

  If the learner lacks one or more of these skills, she or he is likely to make errors on MTS tasks that might be erroneously interpreted to reflect deficient conditional discrimination skills (Johnson et al., 2000). Similarly, auditory-visual matching and visual-visual matching procedures differ somewhat. If the learner does not know how to do tasks that employ both types of procedures, his or her performance on one or the other may lead to erroneous conclusions about discrimination skills deficiencies (Kelly, Green, & Sidman, 1998, p. 78).

- When presenting the sample (i.e., the item to be matched), present it in an unsystematic order within a block of trials, though equally as often as the other samples. Avoid presenting the same sample more than twice in a row.
- Generally, provide at least three comparisons for each trial. "Because each comparison is designated correct with one sample, the number of different sample stimuli presented in a session or block of trials should equal the number of comparison stimuli presented on each trial" (p. 76).
- Unsystematically (randomly) vary the positions of the comparison stimuli from one trial to the next, to prevent the learner from attending to position instead of the sample stimulus that is to be matched by the comparison.
- Avoid introducing novel incorrect comparisons because the learner may choose or reject that new stimulus simply based on its novelty.
- If your sample is spoken, present it clearly, emphasizing the word to be matched. Then repeat it again every two seconds or so "until the learner responds to a comparison or to some maximum number of repetitions" (p. 77). You want to reduce the risk "that (a) they will not hear it, (b) they will hear it but not discriminate it from samples presented on other trials, or (c) they will hear it but not remember it throughout the interval that elapses while they examine the comparison array" (p. 77).
- Differentially reinforce the learner's pointing to the correct comparison stimulus.
- Between trials, rearrange the comparison stimuli out of the learner's sight, to help prevent the learner's responding to extraneous cues such as the first or last thing the instructor touched.
- Use errorless teaching methods (described in Chapter 17) to reduce the additional errors and emotional responses that can interfere with learning and generalization (Heckamon, Alber, Hooper, & Heward, 1998; MacDuff, Krantz, & McClannahan, 2001).

When using matching to sample to teach receptive labeling to children with autism spectrum disorders, it appears to be more effective to use conditional discriminations, as suggested above (Green, 2001). That is, start with a multiple stimulus array (e.g., a field of 3 or 4) rather than using the single-conditional method, or progressively incorporating more stimuli into the field (Grow, Carr, Kodak, Jostad, & Kisamore, 2011; Grow Kodak & Carr, 2014).

Written lists also appear to help promote effective matching-to-sample performances. Also, a list "may serve important functions in facilitating or even enabling later behavior" (Stromer, Mackay, McVay, & Fowler, 1998). For example, a grocery list requires simultaneous matching that can increase the likelihood that the needed items on the list are obtained. Because currently available lists support remembering, they have been shown to enhance instruction-following tasks and matching-to-sample performance (Stromer et al., 1998). More recently, Cummings and Saunders (2019) provide explanations on how to teach matching to sample using PowerPoint on laptops with touch screens, and Cariveau, Hunt, and McCord (2021) describe how to individualize PowerPoints (2016/2020) for teaching matching to sample on the iPad.

Take note: Using a match-to-sample procedure is a cogent way to teach clients how to complete their grocery shopping independently. Give a bit of thought as to how you might incorporate such a strategy within a program to teach a concept or skill of interest to you.

What might you consider doing if a client has difficulty matching words containing a number of letters in common (e.g., *car*, *can*, *cat*)? Walpole, Roscoe, and Dube (2007) suggest conducting lessons during which the learner spends some time matching the distinguishing letters of the overlapping words (e.g., *r*, *n*, and *t*, respectively). When those investigators asked a 16-year-old young woman with autism and cognitive delay to match the distinguishing letters, her accuracy scores for words containing letters in common improved and remained high, even after the matching of distinguishing letters was discontinued.

## STIMULUS EQUIVALENCE AND EQUIVALENCE CLASSES

### Stimulus Equivalence

Must contingencies be arranged for every possible combination of antecedent stimuli for the behavior to become part of a discriminated operant? Fortunately not, thanks to a phenomenon called *stimulus equivalence* or, sometimes, *functional equivalence.* When humans are taught a series of distinctive discriminations, the stimuli inherent in these discriminations may begin to function in ways not explicitly taught. "*Physically dissimilar stimuli come to be treated as equivalent to, or substitutable for, one another in certain contexts*" (Green, 2001, p. 79). Managers, trainers, parents, or caregivers often take advantage of **stimulus** (or **functional**) **equivalence**, typically investigating it experimentally within a matching-to-sample format.

Permit us to explain: X, Y and Z might consist of varieties of the same tool, such as a wrench, or of diverse ways of representing the same number, or different examples of the same concept. Suppose a child learns "given the word THREE (X), pick the number 3 (Y)." The child is then taught to pick an unfamiliar visual form from another array in response to one of the previously learned stimuli. For example, "Given THREE (X), pick ☺☺☺ (Z)." With this kind of training, there is a good chance that many children will spontaneously select THREE from an array of comparisons when given 3 or ☺☺☺ as samples, without additional instruction and even though they had never seen this problem before. They are also likely to select Y given Z as a sample, and Z given Y as a sample (e.g., Sidman, 1971; Sidman, Cresson, & Willson-Morris, 1974). Stated another way, if a child is taught matches of THREE to 3 and of 3 to ☺☺☺, then the child is likely to match THREE to ☺☺☺ without any additional instruction. These relations also are reversible. The child may also respond: 3 = THREE; ☺☺☺ = 3 or THREE (see Figure 16.4). Sidman, Wynne, Maguire, and Barnes (1989) defined **functional equivalence** as "*when changes in the contingencies controlled by one pair of stimuli are sufficient to change the subject's behavior with respect to other pairs*" (p. 272).

In a similar case, say that through differential reinforcement, one stimulus, the spoken word *cat,* becomes discriminative for choosing the picture of a cat from an array of pictures of other animals. That is, when the responder hears the word *cat* he selects the picture of the cat. Additionally, he learns to select the written word C-A-T from an array of cards on which other words are written, such as C-O-T, C-O-A-T, or B-A-T. Now the responder is given the two assortments of cards: the written words and the pictures. Lo and behold, he matches the written word C-A-T with the picture, despite a lack of direct differential reinforcement for doing so! Each of the stimuli is discriminative for each of the others, so all fuse together into a class of equivalent stimuli.

---

If (word) THREE occasions (numeral) 3

and (word) THREE occasions (3 objects) ♥ ♥ ♥

then (numeral 3 occasions (3 objects) ♥ ♥ ♥

and (3 objects) ♥ ♥ ♥ occasions (numeral) 3

(word) THREE and (numeral) 3 and (3 objects) ♥ ♥ ♥

have become the members of an equivalence class

---

**Figure 16.4** An example of matching results that demonstrate functional equivalence

As Green (2001, has pointed out,

> stimulus equivalence methods can provide a lot of 'bang for the buck,' because after just a few conditional discriminations are established through direct training, many others typically emerge 'for free,' without any additional instruction whatsoever. Additionally, *generative* (untrained) performances... occur quite reliably when stimulus equivalence procedures are used. (p. 80)

## Equivalence Classes

You have learned that *when stimuli assume equivalent functions, they can be grouped together into sets called* **equivalence classes**. In fact, "equivalence relations always give rise to stimulus classes as products" (Hayes & Barnes, 1997, p. 235). Calling the set an *equivalence class* depends on being able to demonstrate three defining relations. We will illustrate them here using just two stimulus classes as examples: class 1, which consists of A1, B1, and C1, and class 2, which consists of A2, B2, and C2. We could of course expand things to include more classes and more stimuli within each class, but it will be convenient to keep our classes small and simple.

1. *reflexivity, sometimes called identity matching*—The individual will be able to match items to themselves regardless of size, color, etc.: given X1 as a sample, choosing X1 from an array of comparisons, and given X2, choosing X2 from the array;
2. *symmetry*—The individual will be able to reverse the direction of matching: if the individual has learned to choose Y1 given X1, the individual also chooses X1 given Y1; and,
3. *transitivity*—The individual will be able to choose appropriately given ordered matches that share a common member: if the individual has learned to choose Y1 given X1 and Z1 given Y1, the individual also chooses Z1 given X1.

You could now plug in the stimuli 1 and ONE and * for X1, Y1, and Z1, and the stimuli 2 and TWO and **, and you can see how useful these classes might be for teaching numbers to children.

The point is that after just a few relations have been taught, others that can be derived from those few can emerge without having to be taught. These relations that occur without being taught are called **derived stimulus relations**: *A relation between two or more stimuli that is not directly trained and not based on physical properties of the stimuli.* For example, if 3 = *** and *** = three, then 3 = three; (the derived stimulus relation); or if X1 = Y1 and Y1 = Z1, then X1 = Z1) (Sidman, 1994; Sidman & Tailby, 1982; Sidman et al., 1989). Such equivalences are among the simplest examples of derived stimulus relations (Barnes-Holmes et al., 2005).

Stimulus equivalence probably is at play when people learn to "decode" or give the "meaning" of new words as in reading, language comprehension, and other conceptual and language skills. When given a particular written word, a child is taught to point to a particular object, and given the object the child may then point to the word without specific additional training. Many investigators have used naming tasks to study language (e.g., Green, 1992; McIlvane, Dube, Green, & Serna, 1993; Horne & Lowe, 1996; Rosales & Rehfeldt, 2007; Sidman & Tailby, 1982; Sidman, Kirk, & Willson-Morris, 1985; Spradlin & Dixon, 1976). In particular, they have used stimulus equivalence procedures with individuals with learning difficulties to assist them to develop math, reading, spelling, and augmentative or alternative communication skills (for reviews, see Remington, 1994; Sidman, 1994; Stromer, Mackay, & Stoddard, 1992). To illustrate, Connell and Witt (2004) developed special computer software to teach five-year-old kindergarten students, who were unable to identify any letters in the alphabet successfully, to recognize letter-names and letter-sounds. The children were taught to match: (1) uppercase and lowercase printed letters to the corresponding letter names; (2) lower- and uppercase letters to one another; (3) upper- and lowercase letters to sounds; and (4) printed to spoken words. The investigators concluded that such programs "can aid teachers and others (e.g., parents) in developing individualized programs to address deficits in prereading skills" (p. 71). Children lacking stimulus equivalence skills have much

## Box 16.1

Let's look at another example of what it would look like to train for stimulus equivalence as well as how you would graphically represent the trained and untrained relations (responding).

Stimulus A: a picture of a cat

Stimulus B: the word "cat" written on a card

Stimulus C: the spoken word "cat"

Test for equivalence by giving A, a picture of a cat, and asking participant "what is it?" Also test for equivalence by asking the participant to point to a "cat" among other distractor pictures. If the participant cannot do this correctly then following the training protocol.
  *see first panel in graph

## Reflexivity

**Step 1:**
Present a picture of a cat and ask participant to match while presenting a picture of a cat and a distractor. [A=A]

**Step 2:**
Present the word "cat" written on a card and have the participant match to a card with the word "cat" written on it instead of a distractor card. [B=B]

**Step 3:**
Say "cat" and participant says "cat". [C=C]
  *See second panel in graph

## Symmetry

**Step 1:**
Present a picture of a cat, ask participant to match with the word, use MTL prompting until participant matches the picture of the cat with the written word "cat". [A=B]

**Step 2:**
Test for Symmetry: Ask participant to match the written word "cat" on the card with the correct picture of a cat among distractors. [B=A; untrained relation]

**Step 3:**
Ask participant to point to the word "cat" written on a card among distractor cards, use MTL prompting until participant points to the card with the word "cat" written on it when asked to do so. [B=C]

**Step 4:**
Test for Symmetry: Ask the participant "what does this say" while holding up the card with the work "cat" written on it. [C=B; untrained relation]
  *See third panel in graph

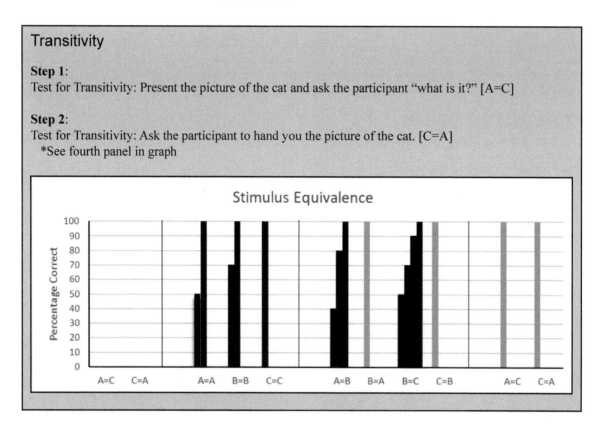

more difficulty not only learning to read, but also to communicate in general. For example, severely handicapped children lacking spontaneous productive use of signs or speech generally fail to show equivalence (Devany, Hayes, & Nelson, 1986). Consequently, they often need to be trained systematically to master general skills before being able to acquire higher-level expressive verbal skills.

Skill in stimuli equivalence and recognizing equivalence classes are foundational to reading comprehension skills. A child needs to understand that the printed word house is the same as the spoken word house, an actual house, and a picture of a house. That is, they are all called a house and are considered a stimuli class. Similarly, the number 4 is the same as the word four, and 4 items. If:

four = 4, and
four = ****, then
**** = 4

because the stimuli are equivalent to one another. *Such skills are foundational to developing reading comprehension and math skills.*

Rosales and Rehfeldt (2007) taught two adults with severe developmental disabilities and language deficits to match dictated names to pictures and to printed words. Afterward, maintenance test probes revealed that the learners were able to spontaneously vocally request (i.e., mand; see Chapter 19) needed items. Their conclusion: "a history of reinforced relational responding may facilitate the expansion of a number of verbal skills" (p. 105).

Several experimenters have shown the utility of teaching functional equivalence by using many stimulus materials across an array of human populations (Dixon, 1976; Gast, Van Biervliet, & Spradlin, 1979; Green, 2001; Hayes, Tilley, & Hayes, 1988; Mackay & Sidman, 1984; Remington, 1994; Sidman, 1994; Spradlin & Dixon, 1976; Wulfert & Hayes, 1988). Even children as young as two years old have displayed such effects (Devany et al., 1986). Especially appealing to many parents, teachers, and caregivers is the fact that clients can be taught functionally equivalent behaviors like different ways of asking for help instead of becoming violent. Sprague and Horner (1992) successfully reduced one of their participant's misbehaviors by teaching him to request instead of lashing out.

Notice how all this distills down to various ways of combining stimulus-control contingencies, and how these approaches form the foundations of various classes of orderly human performance. Behavior ranging from moving when the light turns green to interpreting poetry, diagnosing illnesses, and safely flying airplanes under adverse circumstances all arise from stimulus control. In the next chapter you will learn how you can use more specific stimulus-control procedures to promote discrimination learning.

## SUMMARY AND CONCLUSIONS

We discussed A-B-C or contingency analyses as part of conducting functional assessments in Chapter 10. These assessments help us to identify $S^D$s and various reinforcers of problem behavior. In this chapter we described two additional methods that can help you identify obscure or complex $S^D$s: scatter plots and sequencing methods. We also discussed various discriminations.

Discriminations vary in complexity depending in large measure on the relations between antecedent stimuli and responses. In three-term contingencies, responses are evoked, or the occasion is set for them to occur, as a result of the consequences signaled by discriminative stimuli. In conditional discriminations, a fourth stimulus, the conditional stimulus, signals whether one or another three-term contingency will be operating, as when the particular correct matching response is determined by (is conditional on) the features of the sample stimulus. For example, the identical set of three different geometric figures may all be available, say a circle and a square and a triangle. But which selection of a given form will be reinforced depends on whether the child is asked to match to a circle or a square or a triangle as the sample stimulus. Similarly, the child's choice of form may depend on a verbal stimulus, such as asking the child to point to the circle or the square or the triangle. If the child learns various conditional discriminations involving these forms and their written and spoken names, separate equivalence classes for each of these shapes may be formed. In this chapter, we have offered various guidelines for teaching such matching-to-sample skills.

Developing stimulus control by complex stimuli, sometimes referred to as *conceptual learning*, involves classes that include various features that have come to be significant because of the contingencies that have created them. Familiar examples include: learning the letters of the alphabet, where different forms of spoken and written letters cannot have common physical features; or learning numbers, where spoken and written numerals do not share common physical features, nor do these verbal forms share common properties with the groups that may be identified by the number of objects they contain. These kinds of equivalence classes are established through teaching rather than through exposure to natural contingencies. So if we wish to teach those classes, it is especially important for us to understand how we can use three-term and four-term stimulus-control contingencies to create them.

# Chapter 17

# Achieving Stimulus Control

## Goals

1. Define and illustrate:
   a. stimulus change
   b. strong stimulus control
   c. weak stimulus control
   d. habituate
   e. goal-setting
   f. sub-goal
   g. prompting
   h. response and stimulus prompts
   i. minimum-to-maximum prompting
   j. maximum-to-minimum prompting
   k. stimulus overdependence or prompt dependence
   l. stimulus overselectivity
   m. the differential observing responses (DOR) technique
2. Differentiate between habituation and adaptation.
3. Describe the advantages and disadvantages of stimulus control.
4. Discuss the use of the terms: (a) *set the occasion* for a response, and (b) *elicit* response.
5. Give five reasons why stimulus control might fail and an illustration of each.
6. Discuss why goals tend to function as MOs.
7. Describe how to use goal-setting effectively.
8. Describe how to use prompts effectively.
9. Illustrate how stimulus overdependence and stimulus overselectivity can be corrected.
10. Describe how to develop fluency.
11. Describe *precision teaching* and how it relates to response fluency.
12. Explain why rate is a better indicator of mastery than percent correct.

If the consequences of a response matter as much as we now recognize, does that mean that all those orders, directives, lectures, demonstrations, explanations, sermons, pep talks, instructional guides, laws, warnings, threats, hints, promises, and other events that precede a behavior are useless? Hardly. As the power of an engine energizes the motion of a train, contingencies of reinforcement boost performance. Yet, like the tracks of a railroad, the stimuli operating in advance of or during the behavior guide, alter, narrow, or expand its potential directions. To produce meaningful behavior change, then, contingency managers must be capable of analyzing and/or arranging antecedent conditions by properly setting the stage for and supporting *when*, *where*, and *under what conditions* the behavior is to be emitted.

Within the realm of learning and behavior change, stimulus control provides an especially useful function in that it directs and focuses clients' behavior. Research suggests that *assistance before, rather than correction after the response accelerates acquisition of skills* (Walls, Zane, & Thvedt, 1980; Zane, Walls, & Thvedt, 1981)" (Schoen, 1986, p. 62). Likewise, LeBlanc and Ruggles (1982) have pointed out that from the outset, stimulus control may reduce or prevent errors during the learning process. Errors committed during learning produce extinction and punishment "which in turn could lead to response reduction and possible resistance to future responding…." (p. 130).

In this chapter we present various methods for using and promoting stimulus control. Initially we concentrate on stimulus change; subsequently, we address specific ways of arranging antecedent events, such as providing discriminative stimuli ($S^D$s) and motivational operations (MOs).

## STIMULUS CHANGE

### Defined and Illustrated

**Stimulus change** *involves either presenting or removing antecedent stimuli such as discriminative stimuli ($S^D$s) or some types of motivating operations (MOs).* When a response is under the tight control of given antecedent stimuli, presenting or withdrawing those stimuli readily increases or decreases the response's probability of occurrence. We use terms like **strong**, **tight**, **powerful**, or **complete stimulus control** *when a given response reliably occurs at a much higher or a much lower frequency in the presence of the relevant stimulus than in its absence*; **weak** or **incomplete stimulus control** *when the behavior occurs inconsistently in the presence of the relevant stimulus*. In other words, the term "strong stimulus control" denotes a strong relationship between the discriminative stimulus ($S^D$) and the response. Weak stimulus control represents a fragile relationship between the $S^D$ and the response.

By first analyzing stimulus control functions, then using that information to promote strong stimulus control, we can become much more effective while teaching, parenting, training, coaching, and consulting (e.g., see Smith & Iwata, 1997). Managers' instructions exemplify stimulus-change procedures. So does this textbook, because it combines antecedent stimuli that we trust will function as $S^D$s for you; that is, if you learn the rules for analyzing and applying behavioral procedures, you will be more likely to use them successfully to guide your own practice. (Readers of previous versions of this text have often mentioned that they frequently refer to the text when designing and implementing particular behavioral procedures or when trying to pass the "big" exam.) Rules for successfully obtaining your objectives may be symbolized as follows:

A ⟶ R ⟶ $S^r$

Illustrative rules — Conducts program — Achieves objectives

*Any time we present or withdraw an antecedent stimulus for the purpose of changing a behavioral pattern, we are using a stimulus-change procedure.* The antecedents may include physical, social, verbal, gestural, textual, pictorial, or other classes of stimuli. Altering the physical environment is a familiar example of stimulus change, as when we paint our living room a soft color or play soothing background music to induce relaxation.

The research literature contains numerous examples of the value of using stimulus change in the form of presenting discriminative ($S^D$) and/or motivating ($S^M$) stimuli or arranging other antecedents such as instructions:

- After furniture was rearranged (Melin & Gotestam, 1981) so they could see one another, patients diagnosed with senile dementia conversed and ate more frequently. Perhaps facing one another eased conversation, because they could hear better, see their companions' reactions, and, as a consequence, gain more reinforcers.
- Similarly, when elderly residents were notified of availability of free coffee and cookies in a lounge area of a nursing home, they spent more time in the lounge and interacted more with others. They also decreased the amount of their television watching (Quattrochi-Tubin & Jason, 1980). Those kinds of minor changes in elderly patients' physical surroundings helped to "promote therapeutic changes" (Melin & Gotestam, 1981, p. 47).

To reduce the problematic behaviors of three students with severe disabilities, Kennedy (1994) used a stimulus change strategy. A preliminary descriptive analysis suggested that task demands evoked problem behavior, while social comments (e.g., the instructor's remarks about previous events or some aspect of the current environment—"I think the Dodgers will win the World Series this year," p. 163) were associated with positive social affect. After the instructor began to heighten the frequency of social comments and gradually to fade the task demands across sessions, problem behavior diminished and sustained at near zero levels. Afterwards, the task demands were gradually reintroduced, yet students' problem behavior did not recover. For two of the students, task demands were found to no longer serve as $S^D$s for problem behavior.

Self-injury is another class of behavior often found to be sensitive to changes in the physical environment. Investigators (Favell et al., 1982; Mulick, Hoyt, Rojahn, & Schroeder, 1978; Van Camp et al., 2000) have found that, in contrast with sterile or non-reinforcing surroundings, making particular reinforcing items available to clients reduced the extent to which clients injured themselves. Sometimes self-injurious clients managed their own antecedents to keep from hurting themselves, using objects like rigid tubes to constrain their arm movements or putting their hands in their pockets (Pace, Iwata, Edwards, & McCosh, 1986).

As discussed further in Chapter 24, providing social comments (Kennedy, 1994), friendly greetings (Allday & Pakurar, 2007; Brown & Sulzer-Azaroff, 1994; Edwards & Johnston, 1977) and choice-making opportunities (Stenhoff, Davey, & Lignugaris/Kraft, 2008) heightens prosocial behavior. Providing distractions with preferred events also can enhance compliance (Davis, Reichle, & Southard, 2000; Vaughn, Wilson, & Dunlap, 2002), while interspersing easier among more challenging tasks has been noted to promote superior task engagement, success, retention, and fluency levels (e.g., Johns, Skinner, & Nail, 2000).

Numerous other conditions of the physical and social context can set the occasion for different classes of behavior. Along with the abundant instances described in the behavior analytic literature, look to social psychology and human ecology to identify other circumstances that correlate with favored and unwanted behaviors: size of groups, crowding, furnishings, noise level, exposure to aggression on television, and so on. Take crowding, for instance. Turley and Millman (2000) reported how crowded conditions restrict shopping behavior, while Paulus and Matthews (1980) demonstrated that such conditions negatively impact task performance, and Evans (1979) discovered that such conditions are paired with increased heart rate and blood pressure. A number of investigators have noted the relation between aggression and antecedent events like viewing television violence (e.g., Anderson & Bushman, 2002), heat (Anderson & Anderson, 1984), and noise (Donnerstein & Wilson, 1976).

Responses elicited by unconditioned stimuli do often weaken or **habituate**. This phenomenon has been described as "...the weakening of an *unlearned* environment-behavior relation when the environmental event is repeatedly presented without consequence" (Donahoe & Palmer, 1994, p. 358). That is, the *relation between the eliciting stimulus and the* *respondent reaction weakens.* For example, a loud noise elicits a startle response, but after repeatedly being exposed to the loud noise, the startle response decreases—the individual has habituated to the noise. Similarly, habituation to odors occurs as a result of repeated exposure to those odors (Pellegerino, Sinding, de Wijk, & Hummer, 2017). So, what happens when new stimuli are introduced during the habituation process? When the aim is to *prolong* the effect of an eliciting event, stimulus change, such as introducing novel stimuli, can promote dishabituation, i.e., it can reverse the effect of habituation and responding to the stimulus returns (McSweeney, Kowal, Murphy, & Wiediger, 2005). To illustrate, McSweeney et al. found that when flashing lights were introduced during habituation, laboratory rats' elicited responses returned, rather than continuing to decrease.

How does habituation differ from adaptation? *Habituation is a term we use with respondent, or automatic responding.* We use the term adaptation for operant (learned) responding. We adapt to the presence of an observer. We habituate to a loud sound. In some reflex relations, elicited responding is highly reliable. For example, except under unusual circumstances (e.g., eye drops in preparation for an eye exam) a bright light will always *elicit* a pupillary contraction. But discriminated operants are not so rigidly determined. Depending on the learning history of the individual, $S^D$s simply *set the occasion for* certain responses. The antecedent stimulus derives its strength from a prior history of reinforcement, extinction, or punishment of the responses emitted in its presence. (It might be helpful to re-read the section of the text on respondent versus operant behavior and then re-read this section to ensure a complete understanding of this distinction).

 Antecedent stimuli also may be used to *discourage* behavior. Remember that people who have learned that given responses are not likely to be reinforced in the presence of particular antecedents are less likely to emit those behaviors within that context. Having experienced the lovely fragrance of a rose and the lack of aroma of a buttercup, we are much more likely to sniff roses than buttercups. Buttercups are an $S^{De}$ for sniffing.

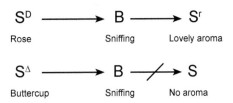

Just as well-established $S^{Dr}$s can promote behavior, discriminative stimuli ($S^{De}$s) can reduce responding. Paula's boyfriend Sandy hardly ever continues the conversation when Paula calls during work time. In other words, Paula's calls to Sandy have not been reinforced. So work time becomes an $S^{De}$ for calling Sandy. Another variation is the $S^{Dp}$, the antecedent discriminative for punishment. If sniffing ragweed resulted in sneezing (an $S^P$—punisher) you would stop sniffing ragweed, because the pollen that you sniffed made you sneeze—in other words, sniffing of ragweed has been punished. However, probably you will continue to sniff roses because that sniffing was reinforced. Those experiences teach you to reliably discriminate roses from buttercups and ragweed (or as in the case of one of the authors who has learned that sniffing any flower or weed is a bad idea; in other words, natural foliage has become a strong $S^{Dp}$ for her sniffing).

In another instance, usually when Bruno plays the piano in the Campus Center lounge, his friends gather around and smile admiringly. Yet, when Bruno begins to play while their favorite TV sitcom is being broadcast, they punish his playing by shouting "Not now, Bruno" or other more colorful epithets. Now, when that TV program is on, Bruno no longer plays the piano.

Notice that as long as behavior is tightly controlled by discriminative and motivational antecedents, whether an $S^{Dr}$, an $S^M$, an $S^{De}$, or an $S^{Dp}$, presenting these classes of stimuli can affect the behavior. They might function by increasing it, by decreasing it, or possibly by simply supporting its continuation when it might otherwise have ceased.

*The effects of discriminative stimuli on behavior can be modified by different contexts.* We refer to those behaviors as *conditional discriminations.* If bad weather causes a school closing, then the student may ignore the due date for a term paper and immerse himself in his favorite video game. If Bruno sees that the lounge TV is broken, he might play the piano during the time when the favorite sitcom typically has occurred, even though his friends are still present.

## Advantages of Stimulus Change

The most obvious advantage of establishing and using stimulus control to manage particular behaviors is that you can influence the frequency of those behaviors simply by presenting or withdrawing the controlling $S^D$s. That generally is the easiest way to accomplish your purpose.

Whereas other methods presented in this text aim toward producing more lasting effects, stimulus change has the advantage of being able to evoke or suppress behavior temporarily. That feature makes stimulus change an especially useful adjunct to other procedures. Earlier, you saw how reinforcement can be combined with stimulus-control procedures. Similarly, you may use stimulus-control strategies to heighten the effectiveness of many of the other behavioral procedures discussed in this text, including shaping, chaining, and others designed to reduce, extend, and maintain behavior change.

## Disadvantages of Stimulus Change

The main problem with depending on stimulus change is that it may prove unreliable on any particular occasion because other factors readily alter its effects. Even when stimulus control over a given response is well established, presenting or withdrawing the antecedent stimulus will not necessarily turn the behavior on or off every single time. One would be mistaken in assuming with certainty that the antecedent stimulus will guarantee the behavior (sometimes the intrigue of touching and smelling a new flower overcomes the $S^{Dp}$ effects of nature). Remember, *we are describing a probabilistic, not a one-to-one relation as in respondent conditioning, between the antecedent stimulus and the response that follows it.* For example, being exposed to crowding, viewing (actual or televised) acts of aggression, and hot weather are correlated with violence. These "motivational conditions" (fortunately) do not guarantee eruptions of violence as they might in respondent conditioning (another difference between respondent and operant behavior). So, whereas a bright light always *elicits* a pupillary contraction, discriminative stimuli such as ringing telephones do not necessarily produce a learned reaction every time. Just as Desmond may continue working during a fire drill, the ringing telephone may go unanswered while the individual is in the shower, bathing the baby, or making love. Although our supervisees have shown their ability to adhere to policies and procedures, they may fail to do so on any particular occasion.

The form of response can vary also, as in the commission of errors and mistakes: Clyde confuses the definition of stimulus control with that of respondent conditioning. The sports announcer identifies a football player incorrectly; Ivana twirls instead of leaping, as directed during the third scene of the ballet. In those instances, stimulus control is incomplete or weak or possibly the behavior is under the influence of unusual contextual variables.

Another disadvantage of depending exclusively on stimulus control is that contingency managers are not always in the position to arrange each and every stimulus that may set the occasion for a desired response. Powerful competing stimuli beyond their control may nullify any procedural impact. If the essential materials have not been delivered, no amount of encouraging production workers to meet their quotas will succeed. Despite parental threats and promises, the conflicting urgings of their adolescent peers often take precedence over the contingencies that parents arrange.

Our ability to take charge of antecedents over our own behavior may be limited, even when we are highly determined to control what we do. Physiological events, such as hunger, sleepiness, illness, or tension may evoke crabbiness or depression. So may covertly and obsessively repeating negative self-statements and distressing behaviors of a similar vein. If you suspect those sorts of stimuli are at work, you probably should refer your client or take yourself to a relevant professional like a physician and/or a behavior therapist. The latter profession focuses most heavily on managing antecedents and consequences at an individual level, enabling their clientele to take greater charge of their bodies and behavior.

### When Stimulus Change Fails

Several circumstances may explain why stimulus change fails in any given situation. Among those are: the behavior's absence from the client's repertoire, weak or deficient stimulus control, interfering stimuli, absence of reinforcement or a history of punishment.

**Behavior is absent.** Stimulus change is bound to fail if the person has yet to learn the *behavior* you are trying to evoke; it is missing from his or her repertoire. For example, placing a "break card" on Johnny's desk will not evoke the behavior of him asking for a break, because the card does not yet serve a function for his taking a break. To investigate if the behavior is in his repertoire, use strong reinforcers, instructions, prompts, or demonstrations to see if those will occasion the behavior. If the response is clearly absent, then before stimulus change can be successful, the behavior will have to be taught, perhaps by demonstrating (modeling) it or by shaping, or chaining.

**Stimulus control is weak or absent.** Stimulus change risks failure when stimulus control is too weak (incomplete) or absent. If stimulus control is weak (i.e., *the response occurs only some of the time in the presence of the $S^D$*), then we might try strengthening it systematically through differential reinforcement (that is, making sure to reinforce the response only in the presence of the stimulus every time it occurs). If control is absent, it will need to be developed as described in the previous chapter, or possibly by using several of the methods we describe later in this chapter.

**Interfering stimuli.** Distractions or various contextual factors may intrude, such as being under the influence of drugs or alcohol, undergoing a serious illness or that of a close friend or relative, failing to hear or see because other stimuli get in the way or due to sensory deficits and so on. Such variables may need to be investigated and, if necessary, modified, before successful control can be achieved.

**Absence of reinforcement.** Often, however, a breakdown in stimulus control is traceable to deteriorating contingencies within that context. Again, to correct this situation, differential reinforcement needs to be systematically and optimally reinstituted.

**History of punishment.** A failure to respond to a stimulus that you believe should have discriminative function also could be traceable to a history of punishment produced by responding in its presence. Perhaps once upon a time, Desmond was severely rebuked for getting out of his seat while he was supposed to be working on an assigned task. So this time, he remains seated when the fire bell sounds. If you suspect a history of punishment might be responsible when an antecedent fails to induce a person to respond, you may have to override that effect by finding an effective supplementary prompt, such as gentle guidance, or by reinforcing an approximation toward the behavior with especially powerful consequences. If those methods prove ineffective, you will need either to employ more systematic prompting and fading strategies or shape the response anew in the context, as described in Chapter 13. Regardless of how you initiate your attempts to establish stimulus control, though, remember that differential reinforcement is essential to success.

Now we turn to a set of systematic stimulus-change procedures, starting with introducing goals as motivational operations, followed by prompting.

## GOAL-SETTING

### Goal-setting Defined and Illustrated

As described in Chapter 4, **goal-setting** refers to *specifying a performance quality and/or level to be attained*. Goals are stated in the form of verbal descriptions or numerical values. Notice that goals are antecedents, but they sometimes may fail to function as discriminative stimuli. First of all, they may be absent in any form, either written or spoken, at the time the relevant behavior is supposed to occur. A supervisor may tell her workers in a briefing room about an assembly-line goal, but what she said will no longer be present once they are at work on the shop floor. Second, if the task is the same whether or not the goals have been stated, then the same contingencies may operate whether the goals are stated or not. For example, a supervisor may arrange reinforcers for workers on an assembly line depending on how much they produce, but the contingencies will be the same whether she tells them about the target they must meet or she just keeps track of that goal herself. For convenience, we may occasionally speak loosely about stimuli and consequences here, but remembering that complex verbal contingencies may contribute to behavior such as setting goals or following instructions.

Goals may refer to:

- *Ultimate long-range outcomes*, such as those contained in the organization's mission statement (e.g., to enhance the quality of life of people with developmental disabilities in the state).
- *Bottom-line results* (e.g., increasing yearly profits by a certain percentage).
- *Sets of intermediate or enabling goals* that permit the bottom-line results to be achieved, including such behaviors or results as Y amount of profits each month.
- **Sub-goals**, *usually numerical quantities designating the daily levels to be accomplished* (X rate of delivering praise) that contribute toward achieving the broader goals listed above. These generally are the goals we set on a daily basis.

In the section to follow, we focus on the latter: setting sub-goals.

Here is an illustrative case (Sulzer-Azaroff et al., 1990): The well-being of employees was included in the mission statement of a large service company. To enable that mission to be achieved, accidents on the job needed to be reduced. To that end, an assessment was conducted and acts that had contributed to accidents in the past were identified for each of several departments. Safe alternatives were specified, and tasks were analyzed and placed on a checklist for measurement purposes.

Next, safety personnel set a *logistical objective* of "100 percent safe performance for at least three weeks in a row on each of the safe alternatives." Meeting those criteria would be the occasion for a major departmental celebration. Achieving that objective rapidly, however, was judged overly ambitious, so they specified *sub-goals*. They selected these by examining prior performance patterns and choosing a level toward the upper portion of the existing distribution. In Figure 17.1, the horizontal lines depict each sub-goal level to be achieved. When workers achieved a new sub-goal a few times in a row they were presented with a small item, such as a tape measure or a pen.

What happened? In contrast to one work unit's total of 13 lost-time injuries plus "recordable accidents" during the previous six-month *pre-intervention period*, the number dropped to only one during the six-month intervention period (see Figure17.1).[1]

Goal-setting strategies like these can be used for any performance: reports, projects, to-do items completed on time, percentages of top-quality products, number of interactions with clients, and so on. As graduate advisers we have used goal-setting to encourage our students to progress toward completion of their major tasks, such as writing review papers and conducting and reporting the results of their theses or dissertations. (Former graduates of the University of Massachusetts Developmental Disabilities Program who were guided in such a way assure us today that they never will forget the pairs of feet stamped on a wall chart in their adviser's office and, also, if they wished—and most did—on the back of their hands, each time they achieved a milestone toward their degrees.) We also set goals with clients who provide services to organizations, with our own employees, and for ourselves as we write. Numerous organizations have discovered the value of including goal-setting within their management systems, because, as Balcazar et al. (1985–1986) have discovered, goals may combine well with feedback and/or other reinforcers to improve personnel performance.

## Goals as Motivating Operations

The purpose of any goal is to govern the quality, quantity, and/or direction of performance to be

---

[1] A survey of recordable accident rates based on "behavior-based" safety studies (Sulzer-Azaroff, 1998, Behavioral safety programs reduce workplace injuries. *Safety First.* Greater New York Safety Council, 2, 1).

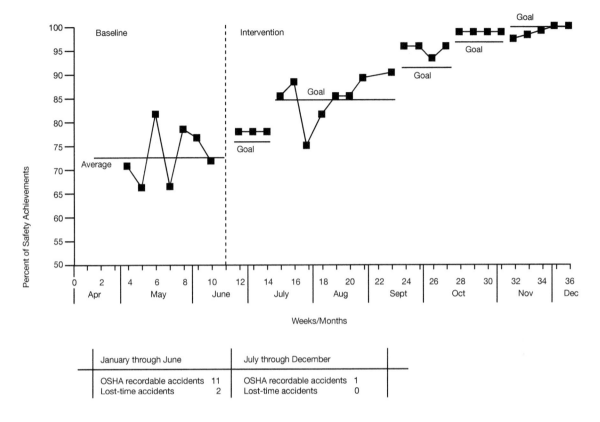

**Figure 17.1** Safety performance as a function of levels of sub-goals
*Source*: Sulzer-Azaroff, Loafman, Merante, & Hlavacek (1990), p. 12. Permission to reprint from *The Journal of Organizational Behavior Management* and the authors.

accomplished. The lines displayed on the posted chart in Figure 17.1 were intended to encourage or motivate participants to strive to reach those new levels. Often, but not always, goals of that nature possess motivational functions. It seems that when participants establish goals jointly, and realize that attaining those goals may lead to reinforcers, they are more apt to strive for them. Perhaps this is why investigators (Rowe, Mazzotti, Ingram, & Lee, 2017) found that teaching goal-setting to middle school students at risk for academic failure resulted in greater academic engagement. Suppose, for instance, in your efforts to heighten job satisfaction among your staff, one of your aims is to encourage members to compliment one another whenever they witness a coworker doing something especially noteworthy.[2] You describe the method:

- Set aside a bulletin board for posting complimentary messages.
- Supply participants with packets of adhesive-backed note papers.
- Explain the system:

    "Whenever you observe one of your coworkers doing something especially admirable, such as offering to assist or other simple acts of kindness, creating solutions to common problems or clever ways to accomplish tasks, and so on, jot down the person's name and what he or she did and post the note."

---

[2] This method, furnished originally by Aubrey Daniels' organization (Aubrey Daniels and Associates), is one currently used with great success in an educational program known to us that serves young children with autism.

- Set goals for the number of such notes to be posted.
- When that number is reached, celebrate with a break, refreshments, or other events known to be appreciated by everyone.
- Then meet to jointly set a new goal level.

Beware of the risks in using goal-setting, though. The system may fail, when goals or sub-goals are too *challenging* or too *easy*. In the first case, participants may be unsuccessful in achieving overly-difficult goals and their associated reinforcers. Think about the number of times you have set the goal of running three miles each day, when you haven't run one mile in over a month... you run the first three miles then are sore and stop running again. It would be better to set a realistic sub-goal and move toward a bigger goal (take it from someone who runs). In the second, they may find the acknowledgment of accomplishing such simple challenges insulting (punishing), or become satiated with the related "reinforcers." (How many ballpoint pens, picture frames, or personalized address labels can we appreciate?)

## Effective Goal-setting

**Develop behavioral objectives.** Goals need to be stated as full behavioral objectives, including the acts to be performed, under what conditions, along with the standards or levels of accomplishment (see Chapter 4). Such specificity makes the critical aspects of the antecedent conditions clear to everyone—those striving to achieve the goal and those who are to deliver consequences contingent on its accomplishment.

**Use participative goal-setting.** As discussed in Chapter 4, one possible way to make the most of goal-setting is to invite the people concerned to participate in the process themselves. Of course, you may need to provide some guidelines to prevent them from choosing outlandishly easy or difficult sub-goals. Guidelines may be based on prior performance patterns, as when goals are numerical assessments of given categories like "increasing delivery of specific feedback," "conducting X performance or functional assessments," "preparing X reports," "submitting X performance plans," or "achieving at or above X level on quality measures." (Refer back to Figure 17.1, for an example.) Consider posting large display graphs (e.g. 3' x 5') in the work area depicting ongoing performance and drawing horizontal goal lines based on the three highest data points achieved during the previous phase. When the work team meets, you can point out and compliment progress, inviting the team to use that information as a basis for choosing the next goal level.

Sometimes goals consist of discrete performances of the type you may already be keeping in your own date book—number of "interviews conducted," "reports completed," "parents contacted," "charts posted," "medications ordered," "exercise" or continuing education unit (CEU) sessions attended," and so on. Here you might post or list the tasks on individual forms, along with a column for "date due" and "date completed." For the participative aspect, supervisor and employee(s) might meet individually or as a group to report their previous accomplishments and announce their intentions for the next time block.

**Develop goals for specific units within the organization.** If you are working in a large organization, individual members' contributions may become lost (a speculation posited by Wallach, Kogan, & Burt, 1967). We suggest that you break the groups down into smaller-sized units. Then, even if you wish to mask individuals' contributions, everyone still can discern the impact of their own participation. From a behavioral viewpoint, the issue becomes how group size might influence the extent to which each individual's efforts are reinforced as a function of the size of the group. An example follows:

> While attempting to improve product quality in a factory employing hundreds of operators working simultaneously, Sulzer-Azaroff and Harshbarger (1995) suggested dividing the workforce into production teams consisting of about twenty or fewer people. Worker performance was observed, recorded, and provided with positive feedback. Also, if necessary, suggestions were offered periodi-

cally throughout the day. Data were graphed daily and the work teams gathered to review their performances at the end of that week. Based on those data, the team set challenging yet achievable goals for the following week. When goals were met, workers were congratulated and their accomplishments occasionally celebrated with refreshments. As you will note by reviewing Figure 17.2 (actual composite data), products conforming to quality standards increased and defects diminished. Apparently, once managers and supervisors learned the value and methods of feedback, differential reinforcement, and shaping, this organization increased its standing from quite low in quality performance to the highest position in production quality among the nearly dozen such factories in the city. What's more, the company gained large savings, and judging from the demeanor of the workforce, more pleasant working conditions.

**Set challenging but achievable goals.** As mentioned, overly-ambitious goals may seem insurmountable to team members, while especially easy ones may come across as insulting (i.e., punishing). What you may need to do is to select goals (or, if those goals are too challenging, use sub-goals) that set the stage for participants to make an extra effort; that when accomplished all involved feel as if they have achieved something really meaningful. In the program just described, we trained supervisors to observe, record, graph, and post their work-teams' daily quality scores. Following a celebration based on attaining prior goals, the team reviewed the performance data and identified the three highest points for that period. Then they drew a new sub-goal line beneath the lowest of the three. That served as the

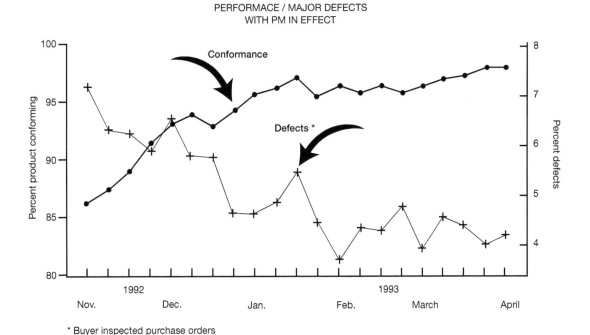

**Figure 17.2** Bottom-line results of a performance-management program involving small work teams. From Sulzer-Azaroff & Harshbarger (1995), p.63.

new goal level. Having already reached that level several times, team members recognized that the goal was indeed achievable, but they also realized that it would take a concerted effort by their cohort to climb to that new step. (See Figure 17.3 for an example of the way we trained supervisors to set new goals.) Similarly, investigators helped a normally developing 10-year-old boy to improve his spelling with a combination of goal setting and contingent reinforcement (Hansen & Wills, 2014), and helped healthy adults to increase their running distance with goal setting (long-term and weekly short-term goals) and performance feedback (Wack, Crosland, & Miltenberger, 2014).

Think for a moment how *you* might make use of this goal-setting and reinforcer combination. Try it first with your own personal goals; then in your professional activities. Assuming you follow all the other rules for effective reinforcement and goal-setting, you will be pleased and delighted with the results.

**Use differential reinforcement.** Naturally, *differential reinforcement* is the foundation of a successful goal-setting program. Achieving a goal or sub-goal should always be reinforced. The reinforcer need not be extremely costly. Often, especially with typical adults, feedback plus a bit of approval will be sufficient, as long as the accomplishment is clearly recognized as being valued. Intermittently, though, particularly when an especially challenging goal has been met, or when improved performance has persisted for several occasions in a row, you might surprise participants with more powerful reinforcers (such as letters of commendation from the boss, a gift certificate, or whatever item or event excites them). For major goal achievements, seize the opportunity to mount a big celebration, such as by highlighting the group's accomplishments in a feature article in the organizational newsletter, or provide some other highly visible and valued object or event. The accomplishment will be reinforced and perhaps serve as an incentive to others in

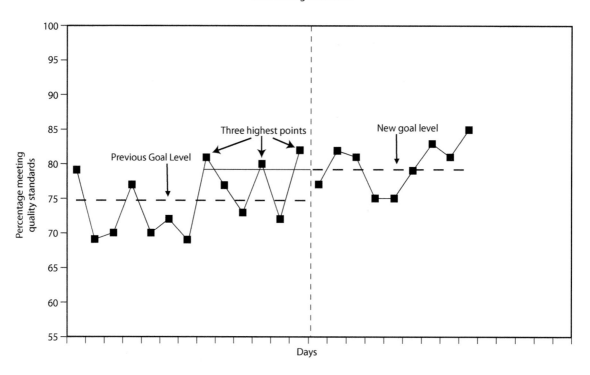

**Figure 17.3** A promising method for setting challenging but achievable goals

similar circumstances to continue pressing forward. The participants in the safety program cited earlier were delighted by the elaborate luncheon given in their honor for achieving such an outstanding safety record. So were their supervisors, who stood to earn bonuses for improved safety, and top managers, who recognized the enormous value of preventing the human suffering and financial expenditures entailed by accidents.

**Set mastery level of goals to promote maintenance.** As mentioned in Chapter 4, investigators (Fuller & Fienup, 2018) found that higher mastery levels, such as 90 percent per unit of time (e.g., they compared 50%, 80% and 90%), produce higher levels of maintenance responding. In addition, higher rate levels help to produce greater fluency, which also has been shown to facilitate maintenance.

# PROMPTING

## Prompting Defined and Illustrated

We use the term **prompting** to denote *applying a functional but irrelevant or contrived discriminative stimulus that evokes the desired response.* According to Touchette and Howard (1984, p. 175), "*Prompts are stimuli that control the desired behavior but that are not functionally related to the task.*" Think, "hints," "reminders," or "showing!" Prompts can be in the form of either response prompts or stimulus prompts. **Response prompts** *act directly on the response and include behavior from a therapist (e.g., verbal instructions, modeling, and physical guidance).* By contrast, **stimulus prompts** *act directly on the stimuli that cue the response, as either within stimulus prompts (e.g., magnifying critical features, changing the color or size of the cue*—see Chapter 20) *or are extra stimulus prompts (e.g., adding a picture to the original cue: changing the letter b to resemble a bird by adding a beak, eye, and tail feathers when teaching what sound it makes).* Everyone resorts to using prompts sometimes; usually when they are eager to see a given response happen right then and there, "Don't tell me. Just give me the first letter." When Sue is trying to achieve the goal of driving a car without an automatic transmission, her father prompts her with the comment, "Remember what you do with the clutch." Other prompting examples include: "Say 'pl____' if you want your juice." "Don't forget to turn in your paper before you leave." Generally when other antecedents fail, we use prompts "… to get the response going" (Green, 2001, p. 73). In their work, applied behavior analysts often use prompts such as physical guidance and modeling (described in Chapter 18), moving or still pictures, tactile and auditory stimuli, and written text. Formal prompting strategies of this type are used in management, training, therapy, counseling, and instruction for the very same purpose—to encourage people to match their behavior to a standard of performance.

## Using Prompts Effectively

As Tarbox et al. (2007) and Miltenberger (2001) have indicated, three key guidelines that allow us to use prompting effectively include: (1) present the antecedent stimulus, (2) prompt the correct behavior, and (3) reinforce the correct behavior whether prompted or not. Let us begin by looking at how to select effective prompts.

**Identify effective prompts.** Any antecedent that evokes the wanted behavior—instructions, rules, demonstrations, gestures, pictures, simulations, goals, physical guidance, and so on—can work. But, how do you decide which prompts to start with? To answer this question, first assess the person's behavioral repertoire to determine which antecedent stimuli ($S^D$s) currently control the wanted response. To facilitate learning and eventual transfer to natural $S^D$s, order each stimulus from this array into a hierarchy from the most natural (the one most closely resembling the relevant $S^D$), to the *most artificial* or *least natural* (the one that bears the least resemblance to the $S^D$). Then proceed slowly, beginning with the one that works and working backward, gradually fading out the artificial and fading in the natural cues.

A variety of $S^D$s can be used as temporary or sometimes permanent prompts to evoke responses not yet under the control of antecedents. Bruno uses a musical score while memorizing a concerto, or the coach diagrams football plays in advance. A sign posted at the exit of the university parking lot says "Please Buckle Up." (The sign resulted in higher rates of seatbelt use (Clayton, Helms, & Simpson, 2006). Clayton et al. also used a similar prompting strategy to reduce cell-phone usage while driving.) Similarly, Farrimond and Leland (2006) posted signs in a supermarket that said "HOW ABOUT BUYING ONE FOR THE FOOD BANK BIN," followed by "THANK YOU," and another on the food-bank bin that said, "FOOD BANK BIN." These prompts increased food-bank donations. Others (Bennett, Mand, & Van Houtem, 2014) investigated which type of prompt would increase pedestrian safety by prompting drivers to yield to pedestrians at crosswalks. They found that if signs were posted in the middle of the crosswalk, or street, and at both ends of the cross walk, very high levels of driver yielding were obtained; and this approach was more effective than other more expensive treatments.

Many of us are able to imagine pictures, graphs, models, and so on as memory aids (mnemonics) to help us recall verbal concepts of the kind you see scattered throughout this text. Instructional manuals and operating guides use sketches, and pictures can be especially helpful for nonreaders or for those who have difficulty following written instructions. In one example, adolescents with severely impaired development were provided pictorial steps to follow in performing daily living tasks such as dusting tables, folding laundry, and stuffing envelopes (Wacker, Berg, Perrie, & Swatta, 1985). Pictures also helped developmentally delayed adults to prepare complicated meals (Martin, Rusch, James, Decker, & Trtol, 1982). And, printed words or pictures were arranged in notebooks to form activity schedules to guide individuals with autism to complete extended sequences of behavior (Krantz, MacDuff, & McClannahan, 1993; McClannahan & Krantz, 1999). Similarly, research indicates that using a highlighting tool to emphasize critical content may increase math computation accuracy and reduce off-task behavior for students with attention problems (i.e., Kercood & Grskovic, 2009).

We need to be careful, though, about presuming that what works for one will work for all. Singh and Solman (1990) pointed out that using pictures can "inhibit some students' learning of new words." Their conclusion was based on the fact that all eight seven- to nine-year-olds with cognitive delays who served as participants performed poorly when the picture of the word was presented alone and then followed by the presentation of the picture and the written word. Six of the eight subjects achieved their highest percentage of words read correctly when the written words were presented without the pictures. The other two did best when an enhanced written word was presented alone, followed by the word and picture of the word. Be sure, then, to not let the client's response become dependent upon the picture. Fading might assist in such a situation (see Chapter 20).

Tactile prompts (e.g., sandpaper-covered numerals) aided a deaf and blind student to learn how to package and to stuff envelopes (Berg & Wacker, 1989), while Charlop, Malmberg, and Berquist (2008) designed a Braille-modified *Picture Exchange Communication System* (PECS) to allow a visually impaired therapist to communicate with three children with autism. Taylor and Levin (1998) made use of another tactile prompt, a vibrating beeper, to prompt learners with autism to initiate conversations with adults and peers.

Miniaturized electronic prompts may be used to encourage desired behavior. For example, Kheterpal et al. (2007) sent an automated alphanumeric pager and email reminder to the medical resident or Certified Registered Nurse Anesthetist to improve the compliance rate for the documentation of arterial catheterization in the perioperative setting. Such inexpensive automated reminders significantly improved compliance without the need for negative or positive feedback, and was projected to have produced an increase in professional fee reimbursement of $40,500 per year. Similarly, Lopez and Wiskow (2020) implemented combined tactile and textual prompts that were delivered via a text message sent to an Apple Watch to prompt social initiations with peers during free play by two six-year-old boys with ASD. As a result, both boys increased the number of times they independently initiated socially, and a month later, one of the boys continued independently to engage in high levels of unprompted social initiations. Similarly, prompts via mobile phones were used effectively to promote self-monitoring and reporting of daily exercise as part of a diabetes prevention program (MacPherson, Merry, Locke, & Jung, 2019).

Sometimes color prompts can be especially beneficial instructional aids. Four girls and two boys with severe mental handicaps, who ranged in age from six to 18, matched colors correctly but did not climb stairs one foot at a time (Fowler, Rowbury, Nordyke, & Baer, 1976). They learned the skill via temporary color prompts: red or yellow tape was affixed to alternating steps and also to the youngsters' shoes. Except for one student who needed physical guidance, all that was required of the youngsters was that they place their shoes sequentially on the steps containing their corresponding colors. After considerable reinforced practice, it was possible gradually to remove the tape from either stairs or shoes and for the teacher to begin to distance herself, while the students continued to climb the steps in the newly acquired alternating pattern.

**Consider the complexity of the intended prompt.** One of the most critical challenges to bringing behavior under the control of antecedent stimuli is the subtlety and *complexity* of those antecedent stimuli. Identifying and distinguishing a glass of milk from a glass of orange juice is rather straightforward (unless the responder is an infant, speaks a different language, or is hampered by a disability). However, distinguishing the health of a bodily organ by its color, size, shape, or other vague features; or a slight deflection on a dial among an array of many dials; or the significance of a metaphor in a line of a Shakespearean drama, would be a major obstacle for many people. Generally, to create such expertise, the critical differentiating features of those stimuli and features must be indicated, and when accurately discriminated, must be differentially reinforced.

Avoid assuming that a stimulus that appears simple to you is also simple to others. Suppose, for instance, you are trying to teach a student to identify the first letter in the Hebrew alphabet, *aleph*. Various alternative prompting strategies are available to simplify the learning task for the student. You might focus the learner's attention on the inherent characteristics of the stimulus, for instance, by enlarging the size and/or elaborating on the configuration of the *aleph* (see Figure 17.4). These are *within-stimulus prompts*. Otherwise, you can use a prompt external to the stimulus—an *extra-stimulus prompt*: you

**Figure 17.4** Elaborating on the configuration of the *aleph*

can embellish it with a pattern, a focus a light on it, or fashion it in sandpaper to provide its own unique texture, and so on. Of all the possible alternatives, probably a prompt that draws the attention to the configuration of the letter by magnifying its critical features is best, whereas a prompt that distracts the learner from attending to the letter's configuration is counter-productive. So, to design an appropriate prompt, *emphasize its critical features*, as in the simplified letter to the right.

Dutch students with developmental disabilities bettered their performance in arithmetic (Lancioni, Smeets, & Oliva, 1987) after the appropriate arithmetic operational symbol, i.e., a multiplication sign, was embedded in a picture depicting multiple quantities of objects. Pictorial prompts also enabled Hoogeveen, Smeets, and Lancioni (1989) to teach four children to match the shape of a letter (grapheme) with the sound the letter made (phoneme) by embedding it in a picture of an object beginning with the sound of the letter.

But be careful. For example, block capital letters include no left-right or up-down reversals, but reversals do appear in lowercase letters (p, b, q, d). If you use prompting to teach block capitals, take care also to teach left-right and up-down discriminations before moving on, because the child will not have learned to attend to these simple discriminations while learning the block letters and they might give the child trouble when you are ready to move on to lowercase letters. (See Figure 17.6 below for one possible way to approach this issue.) Left-right is irrelevant for block capital letters, but becomes highly relevant for lower case letters.

Numerous other methods have been developed to emphasize the relevant properties of an antecedent stimulus. When acquiring *form discriminations*—

numbers, letters, shapes, and the like—students may be asked to trace the distinctive parts of each stimulus with their fingers. Yarn, clay, and other textures may be added temporarily to magnify the critical features (see, for example, Fauke, Burnett, Powers, & Sulzer, 1973).

Consider minimum-to-maximum (least-to-most) prompting for training. In many situations, you will want to train by using the fewest artificial prompts necessary. If so, consider a **minimum-to-maximum, or least-to-most, prompting** strategy, *beginning with minimal prompting, then gradually moving to more intrusive prompts, while taking care to supply no more support than necessary.* This prompting strategy is the one used "most commonly by special education teachers" (Fisher, Kodak, & More, 2007, p. 490), and is considered "an evidenced based procedure for teaching chained responses related to community, self-care, and vocational skills to individuals with moderate intellectual disability who are 13 years of age or older" (Shapley, Lane, & Ault, 2019, p. 313). In the case of skill instruction, the hierarchy usually (though not always) progresses from instructions or simple communicative gestures to imitative to physical prompts. For example, Tarbox, et al. (2007) implemented a commonly used three-step prompting procedure that consisted of (1) a verbal prompt; (2) then, if that did not evoke the behavior, an imitative (modeled) prompt; (3) then, if the latter still did not evoke the behavior, physical guidance. The investigators trained caregivers how to apply this three-step procedure with three noncompliant children with autism. The caregivers' application of the procedure resulted in decreases in the number of prompts they delivered and increases in all three children's levels of compliance. It may be best to start by combining such prompts with modeling. For example, when working with two boys, ages 8 and 9 who were diagnosed with autism, investigators (Murzynski & Bourret, 2007) reported that when teaching response chains, video modeling plus least-to-most prompting resulted in fewer trials and fewer prompts than skills taught with least-to-most prompting alone.

Sometimes, minimum-to-maximum prompting is reserved just for verbal behavior. Here, the prompt level generally progresses from minimally informative instructional prompts through the array of artificial or intrusive prompts that culminate in a "giveaway" prompt. The idea is to try to keep the prompting as minimal and natural as possible, *moving to more intrusive verbal prompts only as necessary.* Should contrived prompts be required, teaching begins at that level, with those supportive prompts gradually replaced until the critical features of the stimulus alone are sufficient to prompt the correct response.

Consider **maximum-to-minimum** (most-to-least) **prompting for training**. There are times when you may want to take the opposite approach, however, moving from the **maximum-to-minimum prompting** level. Here, *begin with a prompt known reliably to evoke the behavior and gradually move to less intrusive, more natural prompts.* Although this approach may involve unnecessary training steps, it virtually guarantees success, as Luyben, Funk, Morgan, Clark, and Delulio (1986) found. Their students—three male adults with developmental delays—were taught a nine-component soccer pass via a hierarchy beginning with instructions combined with a strong physical prompt, then continuing on to a mild physical prompt, an imitative prompt, and then a gestural and verbal cue. Balance prompts also were provided and gradually withdrawn, such as a walker, to a quad cane, to a standard cane, to no support. (Later, in Chapter 20, you will recognize this method as a standard "fading" procedure.) The main advantage seen by the researchers was that the players were successful almost every time (96.7 percent), a reinforcing event they rarely had experienced in the past.

**Deciding which prompting strategy to use.** Information on the relative effectiveness of most-to-least (MTL or maximum) versus least-to-most (LTM or minimum) prompting is sparse. Nonetheless, Libby, Weiss, Bancroft, and Ahearn (2008) did compare the two prompting strategies with five boys in a residential school for autism and related disabilities (ages 9 to 15). In their first study, MTL was found to be effective for teaching all the youngsters how to build play structures; LTM was effective for only three. Those three nonetheless learned more quickly with LTM than MTL. In their second study, the researchers compared LTM to MTL with and without a delay (a two-second delay prior to using manual guidance). "MTLD [MTL with delay] provided an opportunity for the child to initiate responding independently, but still minimized the likelihood of errors. Results showed that acquisition was nearly as rapid when the teacher used MTLD as LTM, but it produced fewer errors than LTM" (p. 37). Thus, as the investigators conclude: "MTLD is likely the best default response prompting technique when a child's learning history is unknown" (p. 42). Also, another more recent study (Cengher, et al., 2016) did find MTL prompting to be more effective than LTM, but only when prompts were used with each client that were determined to have demonstrated effectiveness. So, at this time we would agree with Libby et al. (2008) — *use MTL as the default when you are not sure which would be most effective with your client.*

In another study (Leaf, Sheldon, & Sherman, 2010), the behavior analysts compared maximal prompting to *no-no prompting* for the purpose of teaching rote math skills, receptive labels, and answers to "wh" questions to three children with autism, ages three, four, and five. Maximal prompting, also known as *simultaneous prompting*, involves using "a prompt that results in the learner making a correct response 100% of the time" (p. 215). The no-no prompting consisted of providing "reinforcers following correct responses and corrective feedback (e.g., "no" or "try again") for incorrect or no responses, and then repeating the trial. After two consecutive errors, teachers deliver a controlling prompt with the instructions" (p. 216). (The controlling prompt was the least intrusive prompt type resulting in 100 percent accuracy, such as the correct answer.) Both interventions increased correct responding. However, "no-no prompting was generally more effective and efficient, allowing participants to reach mastery criterion more quickly" (p. 225). So here was an intervention that began with no initial prompting (other than the presentation of the task). In the first instance an error was followed by corrective feedback; in the second, by a maximal prompt. That combined strategy worked more effectively than using maximal prompting alone.

**Avoid encouraging stimulus overselectivity (or restrictive stimulus control) and stimulus overdependence.** At one time or another all of us have experienced **stimulus overselectivity** by *responding to one or more non-relevant stimuli among the full array of stimuli*. Often people with developmental disabilities tend to engage in stimulus overselectivity, especially when stimuli are presented fleetingly (2s & 5s) rather than for longer durations (10s) (Reynolds & Reed, 2018). It also occurs in most people, regardless of intellectual status, but less frequently. Maybe you saw someone off in the distance wearing a particular item of clothing or moving in a particular way. "Oh look! There's ...." But under closer scrutiny, you realized the person was a total stranger. For the moment, you were responding "overselectively" to a single, though inappropriate, feature in the person's appearance. When this kind of overselectivity becomes an established pattern, then we have a problem.

While reading aloud, Melanie sees a picture of Dick playing with his dog, Spot. The passage says "Dick and Sally want to play." Melanie substitutes the word "Spot" for "Sally." Why? Because, once she has noted the initial S, Melanie analyzes the word no further. She has become overly dependent on the pictorial and the initial letter cues.

Archie, the foreman of the electrical shop, is responsible for maintaining a safe environment. He asks Kaisha if all the tools are in proper working order. "Absolutely," Kaisha firmly reassures him. What both have failed to notice is an active soldering tool beginning to overheat on the wooden workbench. Archie has become over-dependent on Kaisha's tone of certitude, rather than on what he would have seen by doing a thorough inspection on his own. Because dependence on irrelevant cues of this nature (i.e., overselectivity) may seriously impede learning and performance, and sometimes even be dangerous, we need to know how to avoid or minimize this pitfall.

**Stimulus overdependence**, or **prompt dependence**, is most likely to result from either least-to-most prompting (Fisher et al., 2007) or because a contrived cue is kept in place too long. Instead of the response being controlled by the critical features of the stimulus (the person's face, body, and movements; the full complement of letters in a word; the actual status of electrical equipment) the response has been "over-prompted." *When a response becomes dependent on an artificial prompt*, we need to take action (Clark & Green, 2004), especially when attempts to fade out the prompt results in little or no progress (Brown & Miranda, 2006; Oppenheimer, Saunders, & Spradlin, 1993). Fisher, Kodak, and Moore (2007) suggest *you minimize overdependence on a prompt by avoiding over-prompting or prompting for too long during training.* It is important when you make the decision to insert a prompt to obtain desired behavior that you immediately have a plan to fade the prompt (see Chapter 20) so as to avoid overdependence.

Least-to-most promoting can contribute to both overdependence and overselection. "The individual may learn to imitate the modeled prompt (e.g., simply pointing to the option the therapist pointed to rather than learning to point to the picture of Alex after the word 'Alex' is spoken" (Fisher et al., 2007, p. 490). The learner may just point because she or he had received reinforcers for imitating a model in the past and has become dependent on such prompts (Fisher et al., 2007). In such situations, the prompts being used are not cueing the client to attend to the relevant stimulus dimensions. Alternatively, Fisher et al., (2007) suggest you try promoting *a differential observing response.*

Figure 17.5 shows another example: "Underline the Greek letter *delta.*" You probably correctly selected the second character from the left. But the basis for your selection may well have been an irrelevant cue: the indicator arrows or the distinctive size or shading of the letter. To test yourself, don't study the shape of the letter and in an hour or so, turn to your dictionary's Greek alphabet. Cover up the transliterations (the phonetic names written in Latin letters) and try to locate the *delta.*" Were you able to?

Now consider this example:

Roses are red, violets are blue,
*Twenty-one and one are twenty-* ____?

Probably you supplied the correct word *two*, but, again, the response was occasioned by an irrelevant feature. The rhyming properties of *blue* and *two* probably acted as more effective antecedents than the appropriate, "Twenty-one and one equal what?"

From the above discussion, it probably is apparent to you that the overselectivity, characterizing the responding of some people with autism—about one out of five (Rieth, Stahmer, Suhrheinrich, & Schreibman, 2015)—is a result of their dependency on one or a few cues instead of the full complement of distinctive features of the stimulus; for example, responding, as illustrated above, to the texture or color rather than the shape of a symbol. Familiar instances of overselectivity among people on the autism spectrum are giving an answer based on the placement of an object, its color, or the people doing the teaching instead of on their critical features (Lovaas, Schreibman, Koegel, & Rehm, 1971). The *placement* of the object (or the size or texture of the Greek letter, as in Figure 17.5), not the object itself, might cue the student to label it correctly. Naturally, generalization of correct responding to other situations is compromised.

Some professionals maintain that overselectivity and overdependence are roughly equivalent (Fisher, et al., 2007). We agree that the terms do overlap, as you can see by the above discussion, but we maintain that they are different enough from one another to maintain both terms. Overdependence is a result of using a prompt too often, or for too long a period of time, like constantly showing clients what to do so that their behavior becomes dependent on the instructional method used (i.e., showing), while stimulus overselectivity involves the client focusing on non-relevant stimuli, which may or may not be dependent upon excessive previous prompting. Also, the intervention for overdependence—of avoiding using a prompt too often, or over too long a period of time—is not used for most situations of overselectivity.

Here is another example of stimulus overselectivity, not overdependence: A therapist known to one of the authors mentioned to a child's teacher that he had taught her student with autism to point to various parts of his body when requested (e.g., "Touch your nose, touch your eyes," etc.). The teacher requested the child to do so and had no success. The therapist then said, "Perhaps I need to be present." The teacher made the requests in the

**Figure 17.5**   Irrelevant cueing

presence of the therapist, but again there was no success. Nor was the therapist successful when she requested the behavior in the classroom. Finally, after a number of attempts in using the sequencing method to identify obscure or complex S^Ds as described in Chapter 16, they discovered that the child would touch or point to the requested body part only if the table and chair from the therapy room were present. Along with the requests, the youngster had focused on the non-relevant stimuli, the presence of the table and chair, while the requests were made. Another example that will be familiar to teachers is the way some instructors can only recall their students' names by the location of the seats in which they sit and not by recognizing their faces. When passing the same students on campus, these instructors are in trouble.

In either case, we think you would agree that you need to be careful with using prompts to evoke behavior, and make sure you have a plan for fading out prompts (see Chapter 20) to avoid overdependence. Also, try to make the prompt highlight the stimulus that you want to control behavior rather than leaving it up to the client to "select" the stimuli (e.g., overselectivity).

**Correct for stimulus overselectivity.** Constantine and Sidman (1975) and Geren, Stromer, and Mackay (1997) enabled their clients to improve their accuracy on delayed matching-to-sample tasks by instructing their clients to name (rather than point to, as in the Fisher et al. study described below) the sample stimulus prior to presenting the comparison stimuli (i.e., an observing response). Naming helped to ensure that the clients discriminated the critical elements of each sample stimulus.

Sometimes it is helpful to *magnify the critical features of the stimuli*—a strategy we now know to be more effective because it focuses the learner's attention on the *relevant* properties, such as with the numerals 2 and 7 (see Figure 17.6). Note that the distinctive stimulus properties are highlighted: the horizontal line on the bottom of the 2 and the "pointy nose" on the 7. Or, you could also emphasize the curved line of the 2 versus two straight lines of the 7 coming together to form a point. In other words, as suggested by Fisher et al. (2007), "arrange prompts that ensure that the participant looks at and

**Figure 17.6** Magnifying critical features

discriminates the distinguishing visual characteristics of the comparison stimuli" (p. 491).

Walpole, Roscoe, and Dube (2007) developed a technique for correcting overselectivity, called the **differential observing responses (DOR)** method. The purpose of DOR is to *gain the client's attention and to teach him or her to discriminate the defining characteristics, or critical features, of each sample stimulus prior to the matching-to-sample task* (Fisher et al., 2007). Walpole et al. taught a 16-year-old client with autism and cognitive delays who generated high accuracy scores in a matching-to-sample task when words had no common letters (e.g., lid, bug, cat). But the young man committed many errors when words had two letters in common (e.g., can, cat, car). The DOR strategy required the client to distinguish the distinctive letters (e.g., n, t, r) of the words immediately prior to having him match the whole words. Even following the withdrawal of the DOR phase, they found that the reader's accuracy improved and remained high with words containing two common letters.

Fisher et al. (2007) combined an identity-matching, or DOR condition, with a traditional least-to-most prompting hierarchy with two clients, ages 10 and 12, who were diagnosed with autism and communicated primarily with gestures. In the least-to-most matching condition, the client was asked to point to one requested object (e.g., a cup) or a person (e.g., "point to a picture of Kim") from among four objects or persons. Correct responding to the verbal request resulted in brief access to a preferred item or one small food item. If the client did not correctly respond, rather than demonstrating the correct response, the instructor implemented a DOR condition by holding a picture identical to the correct comparison stimulus before the client's face and saying, "This is ___," while pointing to the correct stimulus. The client then was told to "point to ___" while the therapist gestured to the comparison stimuli. If the client then correctly pointed to the matching item, the next trial began. If the client responded incorrectly, the therapist again requested the client to point to the object or person and physically guided the correct response. Fisher et al. found this combined strategy to be more effective than either the least-to-most or a control condition. "Results for both participants indicated that mastery-level acquisition of spoken-word-to-picture relations occurred only…" (p. 489) when the identity-matching condition was combined with, or embedded in, the least-to-most prompting method.

Correcting or preventing overselectivity requires reasonable technical skill, because control must be transferred to the critical aspects of the stimuli. Several additional tactics seem to be useful in this regard. Alternating trials involving single components of the complex stimulus with trials containing the intact complex stimulus can be helpful as well (Schreibman, Koegel, & Craig, 1977). One method is to *train the behavior* (e.g., to point to various body parts) *under a variety of conditions (time, places, trainers, and so on)*. If this were done when teaching the child with autism to touch his nose, etc. in the above example, stimulus overselectivity probably would not have occurred. This enables the client to learn to focus on the relevant stimuli. Another is to use intermittent reinforcement schedules. As an example, Koegel, Schreibman, Britten, and Laitinen (1979) taught 12 children with autism to choose correctly from pairs of cards on which multiple stimuli were displayed. After reaching a criterion of correct responses 10 times in a row, they received 100 additional trials, with reinforcers either occurring every correct response for one set, or for an average of every third correct response for the other set. Surprisingly, the intermittent reinforcement condition produced much lower rates of overselectivity. Perhaps, as the investigators posited, the absence of reinforced trials inherent in the intermittent schedule caused the learners to suspect they may have committed an error, prompting the children to attend more closely to the subsequent stimuli. (We return to the topic of transferring stimulus control in Chapter 20.)

## FLUENCY, AND SUPPORTING STIMULUS CONTROL WITH PRECISION TEACHING

In academic and vocational education, the heaviest emphasis is placed on the content of the curriculum. As we have seen, though, behavioral educators strongly emphasize the learner's responding. We are not satisfied simply to dish out pearls of wisdom, but instead look to our students for evidence that their own behavioral repertoires have expanded to include mastery of new sets of verbal and motor learning objectives. And we look to ourselves as teachers and trainers to see how effectively we have arranged the learning environment to support the acquisition, retention, and transfer of our selected instructional objects.

An especially important aspect of newly acquired learning is the fluency with which the newly learned behavior is performed. When someone is said to be "fluent" in a language, it indicates that s/he speaks and comprehends that language easily, at a high rate, while rarely hesitating or committing errors. In ABA, we use the term **response fluency** similarly to describe *correct sequences of responses emitted smoothly and without hesitation. Fluency is developed through frequent practice of the behavior, or response, and modeling the fluent behavior, as in modeling fluent reading* (Melekoglu, 2019). When providing practice, it is best not to use traditional drill. Traditional drill can be punitive and not as effective as other practice strategies. We recommend practice interventions such as **incremental practice** (e.g., you add an unknown word or math fact to a group of words or facts that the youngster knows. Once it is mastered, add another unknown in place of one that is fluent. This process is repeated.) Incremental practice has been shown to produce high retention and fluency (Burns, et al., 2019). Another practice strategy shown to be helpful in promoting reading fluency is **varied practice**, in which different passages are read that contain the same words rather than reading the same passage over again several times (Reed, Zimmermann, Reeger, & Aloe, 2019).

The advantages of fluency are that when occasions arise in which it is appropriate to combine two responses, fluent learners are much more likely to do so than those who are not. For example, suppose a child has learned basic multiplication facts, such as 3 x 5 = 15. Suppose the child has also learned to translate sentences about quantities, such as saying "Three times five" when asked "How much money would you need to buy three toys costing five dollars each?" The child who has mastered these skills fluently will be likely to quickly give the correct answer, "Fifteen dollars," whereas the child who has barely mastered them may well produce this answer slowly if at all.

Recently, *fluency* flashcards, part of the competent learner model (see Chapter 13), have been developed to allow users to "practice learning information to fluency, beyond accuracy—guaranteeing retention, endurance and application of their performance" (Tucci & Johnson, 2017). Learners can build their own flash card decks. These decks are shuffled automatically, and latency data are tracked. "Cards whose performance latencies are below the average latency required for a deck continue to appear in timings, giving a learner an opportunity to practice beyond accuracy to fluency." Fluency has been an important component of *precision teaching*, which we consider next, as well as other innovative teaching systems (e.g., Binder, 1996; Johnson & Layng, 1992).

In Chapter 8 we introduced you to the standard celeration charting used in **precision teaching**— *the individualized instructional method designed to build and support enduring response fluency.* Here we return to the topic to elaborate on the system as a highly successful application of stimulus-control strategies. Precision teaching's curricula are designed to permit each specific behavior to be taught, reinforced, and mastered under all the conditions in which it is expected to occur and are intended to accelerate *correct, rapid, fluent, and enduring responding* (Lindsley, 1991; Johnson, & Layng, 1992; Fox & Ghezzi, 2003; Twyman, Layng, Stikeleather, & Hobbins, 2005). As Lindsley (1991) and Johnson and Layng (1992) have demonstrated, focusing on rate-of-responding, rather than percentage correct, as the main metric enables students to learn better, faster, and more enduringly. Many who use precision teaching have demonstrated a doubling or even tripling of rates of learning over those achieved in instructional programs in which percentage correct is the main basis for assessing performance.

The foundational assumptions underlying precision teaching (Greer, 1985) include that:

- Behavior change is not additive but multiplicative. Students participating in precision teaching often double their output weekly as they work toward their goals.
- Behavior is unique within and between individuals as are their reactions to the learning environment. Therefore, each student needs individual attention.
- Learned behavior may be limited to the circumstances in which it has been taught. To avoid such narrowness, it must be taught within an array of settings, times, and conditions.
- Each behavior is independent of the others. Changing one behavior will not necessarily produce change in the next.
- Behavior is shaped by its consequences.

Within *precision teaching*, students keep data on their own performances by marking a graph that displays the number of items (e.g., words read, problems solved, and so on) they performed correctly and the number of errors they made within fixed periods of time (e.g., one minute timings) distributed across the day or week. The goal is to increase the number of correct answers and decrease the number wrong within the set time period. *The focus is not on percentage correct, which places a fixed limit on the number of the assigned tasks, but on how rapidly learners perform correctly, for which there is no ceiling.* **Rate** (frequency per unit of time) *reflects mastery of the behavior much better than per-cent correct or accuracy. When the frequency increases per a unit of time, or the time decreases for the same frequency, rate improves as does fluency, retention and ease of generalization.*

Celeration charting illustrates that when two students score 100 percent correct, they might not know the material equally. For example, student A and B both score 100 percent, but A completes the task in 15 minutes while B takes 30 minutes to complete the task. It illustrates, which student has achieved greater fluency, or knows the material better. Percentage scores by themselves do not provide this information. Students are eager to see their "rights" go up and their "wrongs" go down, as depicted in figure 17.7. The wider the angle between "rights" and "wrongs" and the faster they perform, the greater the student's achievement. You probably now recognize precision teaching as a rate-building measure analogous to differential reinforcement of high rates of correct responding (DRH) while inaccurate responses are extinguished. Children seem to enjoy seeing the shark's jaw widening as the rate of their correct responses increases, as during weeks 11 through 15 on the standard celeration chart (Figure 17.8).

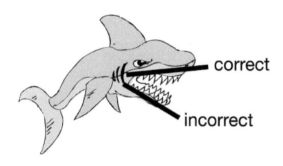

**Figure 17.7**

Recall that a key feature of the standard celeration chart is that the y-axis is scaled so that equal spacing shows equal multiples rather than equal intervals. Thus, instead of going up by steps of 10, as in 0, 10, 20, 30, 40, etc., the scales go up by multiples, as in 2, 4, 8, 16, 32, etc., or as in 10, 100, 1000, 10000, etc. The latter, in factors of 10, is useful because a doubling looks the same no matter where the starting point of a doubling is. A doubling from 1 to 2 correct responses on a given day by a child on the autism spectrum is as worthy of recognition as a doubling from 100 to 200 correct responses on a given day by a child who is already proficient in a reading or math task. The logarithmic scale is widely used in science, in such realms as the decibel scale for sounds or when scaling the intensities of earthquakes or hurricanes.

Should you be curious about the impact of the Morningside Academy Model of Generative Instruction on student performance in reading, note the progress from the baseline (90–96) to the first, then second year of implementation of the program across all schools depicted in Figure 17.9[3]. Also, the Morningside Academy, a private school in Seattle, Washington that works primarily with "average students," who have fallen behind in school in various subjects, has for the last 30 years increased learning by two to three grades a year per student (Snyder, 2013).

The Morningside Model of Generative Instruction is now described in a recent book (Johnson, Street, Kieta, & Robbins, 2021). In it:

> The authors describe a technology of instruction based on scientific research that has improved the academic performance of children at schools and agencies throughout the world. *The Morningside Model of Generative Instruction* combines curated curriculum, formal instruction, practice to fluency, and a focus on directly teaching function thinking repertoires for generative responding. The result is expert and confident learners who apply skills and strategies to think about the world around them, continue to learn on their own, and solve problems of daily living (Personal communication from Kent Johnson, January, 18, 2021).

## SUMMARY AND CONCLUSIONS

Now you have learned that you can use stimulus change when antecedents strongly control behavior. You also have become acquainted with various ways to strengthen weak stimulus control by using prompts to evoke the wanted response under particular circumstances. In the event that a given behavior did not occur in the absence of the prompt, you need to know why. Is the response absent from the person's repertoire or is stimulus control weak? In this chapter we

---

[3]For further information, go to: http://www.morningsideteachers.org/documents/MTA_Empirical_Data.pdf.

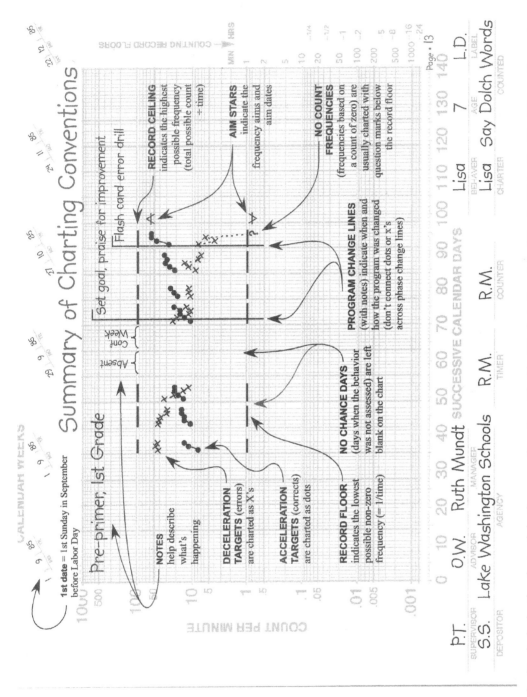

**Figure 17.8** Standard celeration chart and charting conventions. From *The Chart Book: An Overview of Standard Celeration Chart Conventions and Practices*,' an on-line tutorial prepared by Owen R. White and Malcolm D. Neely (2004). Used with permission.

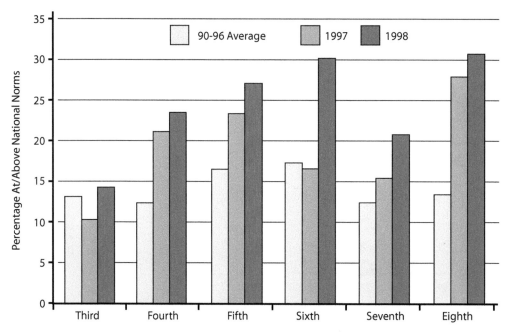

**Figure 17.9** Morningside student reading progress during two years compared to national norms

have discussed approaches to answering those questions, along with methods of prompting responses. These include using minimum-to-maximum or maximum-to-minimum prompting. If the relatively direct prompting strategies suggested here fail, you can turn to one of two general strategies: (1) using more systematic prompting methods, such as instructions, modeling, and/or guidance (Chapter 18), or (2) teaching the behavior as a new skill or concept by using shaping (Chapter 13) or chaining (Chapter 14).

In either case, before the newly acquired stimulus-control relation can be said to be occurring independently, any artificial or contrived prompts must be removed, preferably by fading (Chapter 20), thereby allowing the behavior to come under the control of the natural critical stimuli. Goals and objectives are classes of antecedents readily available to almost everyone. When those goals or objectives are overly challenging, though, they can be broken down into sub-goals or objectives, the achievement of which can be reinforced. Each time a new level is reasonably well established, natural variation permits new performance levels to be identified and selected for reinforcement in a series of steps.

The way instruction is organized and managed can influence the speed and precision with which students and trainees master, retain, and apply their newly acquired verbal and performance skills. When stimulus control methods are combined with rate-building techniques, as in *Precision Teaching* and *Generative Instruction*, results can be most impressive. In this chapter, we have discussed a range of strategies especially well-suited to heightening accurate, rapid, and fluent learning and retention of such skills. Try applying them to your own studying, or with your students or clientele and you may be happily surprised by the results.

Hopefully it is now apparent that "the potential to achieve is limited mostly by our own failure to arrange conditions that help... [people] thrive" (Daniels & Lattal, 2017, p. 98).

## Chapter 18

# Prompting Procedures and Instructional Programs

## Goals

1. Define and illustrate:
    a. telling/instructions
    b. rule-governed or verbally-controlled behavior
    c. contingency-shaped behavior, and differentiate it from rule-governed or verbally-controlled behavior
    d. instructional demand
    e. free operants
    f. modeling
    g. imitation and differentiate imitation from modeling
    h. generalized imitation
    i. video modeling
    j. en-vivo contact desensitization
    k. self-modeling, and differentiate it from self-observation
    l. coping models
    m. Behavioral skills training (BST)
    n. physical guidance
    o. proprioceptive cues
2. Describe how to use the *tell* procedure effectively.
3. Describe *direct instruction* (DI).
4. Describe *discrete trial training* (DTT).
5. Illustrate illustrate the use of an effective error correction procedure.

6. Differentiate between a *free operant* and *DTT*.
7. Differentiate between a *free operant* and a *discriminated operant.*
8. Describe how to develop a modeled behavior into a discriminated stimulus ($S^D$).
9. Describe an example of modeling combined with shaping.
10. Describe a promising plan for teaching a child to imitate the actions of others
11. Describe how to promote generalized imitation and how to discriminate what to imitate.
12. Describe how to use modeling effectively, addressing both model selection and how to manage the contingencies and how to teach your client to discriminate the particular behaviors they should imitate.
13. Describe how to use physical guidance effectively.

*************

As you learned in Chapter 17, prompting can be a valuable aide to teaching and training. Indeed, initial learning and performance are heavily dependent on prompts. Do you remember the first time you tried to swim, ride a bicycle, or scramble eggs? In all probability, someone was there to support or coach you along the way until you could do so independently. Only after *artificial supports were removed* did you know deep down that you *really* knew how to perform the task. So, when you teach, train, or coach, prompt judiciously—only when the situation really demands it, and fade prompts as rapidly as possible. Nonetheless, when guidance is demanded, the ability to prompt effectively is a major asset for any applied behavior analyst. In this chapter we elaborate on three commonly-used prompting strategies: instructing, modeling, and physical guidance.

## USING PROMPTING EFFECTIVELY

By their very nature, prompts are artificial devices that usually must eventually be removed if a behavior is to come under the control of natural cues. Regardless of which one or combination of strategies they use to bring about that eventual result, those who capitalize upon artificial prompting strategies are advised to interpose the natural $S^D$ just prior to the desired response. Then they should be able eventually to proceed to fade out the artificial prompts, beginning with the most intrusive (usually physically guiding), next the demonstrations, and next the spoken instructions, while always allowing the natural $S^D$ to remain. An example would be a coach telling, showing, and physically guiding a novice football passer how to toss the ball. He might first diminish his physical guidance; then his demonstrations; then his instructions, while the learner continues to assume increasing responsibility over the form he will eventually depend upon while actually participating in the game.

> *Most added prompts eventually must be subtracted.*

## PROMPTING BY INSTRUCTING ("TELLING")

### Defined and Illustrated

In addition to setting goals, instructions are generally among the least intrusive and most efficient kinds of prompts you can use. All you have to do is *say, sign, or otherwise signal what to do*. "Aim to the left rear of the court; keep the ball low," coaches the tennis instructor. "Remember the sign for the interrogative that precedes a question in Spanish" reminds the Spanish language teacher. "See," guides the consultant, "this is the moment to catch the child being good." "Now check the pressure and temperature so the mixture doesn't thicken too much," drills the production supervisor.

Just about everyone who works in a teaching, training, or supervisory position uses instructions to prompt particular behaviors. Coaches, consultants, clinicians, teachers, and parents use instructions freely—and for good reason. When natural antecedents fail to set the occasion, instructions may readily generate the desired response. Eventually, of course, the instructions may be eliminated, but they can be extremely helpful as temporary stopgaps. Illustrations abound in the research literature, as you will see in the illustrative situations described below.

## Using the Tell Procedure Effectively

Managers, teachers, parents, and consultants have used the *tell* procedure from time immemorial. Why, then, does this topic need to be considered at all? Because a number of variables have been identified that might influence the procedure's success. Earlier, you became familiar with several of those, such as being certain the response is in the person's repertoire, that optimal reinforcement methods are being employed, and that the context is supportive. Others include determining:

- whether the person's responding generally is *rule-* or *verbally-governed* (controlled by verbal antecedents), or whether verbal governance needs to be developed.[1]
- whether the verbal stimuli are artificial prompts or are the actual critical variables of concern—the $S^+$s intrinsic to the task.
- when and how often the instructions are presented.
- whether instructions should be combined with modeling (described later in this chapter).

**Ensure that instructions govern the individual's behavior in general.** Instructions (or rules) begin to exert control early in people's lives. Infants rapidly learn to look, wave "bye-bye," lie down, and play "peek-a-boo" in response to cues from their parents. Later on, phrases like "Come here," "Give me," "Pick up," and so on begin reliably to evoke the appropriate responses. Ultimately, verbal instructions alone start to control broad classes of the child's behavior. How is this *generalized verbal control of behavior* (**verbally-controlled** or **rule-governed behavior**) achieved? You guessed it. First, by repeatedly obtaining responses by whatever it takes—guidance, demonstrations, or any discriminative stimuli that work—and then *consistently* differentially reinforcing the appropriate behavior when the rule is provided.. Mom picks up Baby Bonnie's hand and helps her wave it back and forth, or assists the infant to play "peek-a-boo," cooing her approval and hugging the little one all the while. When Bonnie responds to Mom's and Dad's demonstrated prompts and instructions: "Wave goodbye to Daddy," or "Peek-a-boo," good things happen. Her parents laugh, hug her, and make pleasant sounds. So she learns to comply to their verbal prompts in general. Too often people make the mistake and just think that a person or a child should follow rules; however, if rule following or verbally-controlled behavior has not been developed, rule following will not occur.

Anne was a 16-year-old with moderate intellectual disability who frequently engaged in inappropriate touching in a community based vocation training setting: touching herself in the genital region of her body. A brief functional assessment determined that the inappropriate touching was maintained primarily by escape from demands. The investigators (Cihak, Alberto, & Fredrick, 2007) first taught her to use an MP3 player and headphones with prerecorded two-step instructions. She was taught to turn on the player, listen to the auditory recordings when played, verbally repeat what was heard, and then engage in the prompted behavior. She had to reach 100 percent criterion for two consecutive sessions. The following instructions and information was then recorded on her MP3 player: "It's time to start your work" (they were told in advance that if they were already working and heard this request, to just keep working); "When you finish you will get a break"; "You'll be on break soon"; "It's almost break time"; and, "Anne,

---

[1] Because it covers a broader array of verbal stimuli, the term "rule-governed behavior" generally has been replaced by the term "verbally-controlled behavior."

keep using your hands to arrange the cookies." This set of auditory prompts was delivered at least four times per a 10-minute session. Inappropriate behaviors were not responded to. In additions, if Anne was on-task at the end of each 30-second period, she received specific praise and a token exchangeable for preferred items (e.g., snack, drinks). If not, no praise was given at the end of that interval, and the next 30-second interval began. Anne typically followed the instructions and inappropriate touching decreased to zero.

The behavior of people with inconsistent differential reinforcement histories may be *more susceptible to generally prevailing contingencies than to verbal stimuli such as instructions*; that is, much of their behavior can be said to be **contingency-shaped** rather than verbally-governed. For example, if parents reinforce compliance at some times but not at others, their children may learn to comply irregularly, except when stimuli (e.g., parental expression, tone of voice, etc.) indicate highly probable consequences for compliance or non-compliance. Consider a school example: The teacher states the rule that students are to raise their hands and wait quietly to be called upon when they have a question. Nevertheless, when a youngster calls out a question, the teacher typically responds. Children whose behavior is strongly governed by instructions are more apt to obey the rule, but those whose behavior in class has been more effectively determined by contingencies will be more likely to call out, because this teacher is likely to reinforce that behavior.

How precisely a given set of rules governs someone's behavior depends upon that person's learning histories (e.g., consistency of differential reinforcement within particular contexts), physical status, and other current circumstances (contingencies), just like all other forms of stimulus control. So, you cannot take for granted that just because you tell people to do something, they will comply. Although instructions may predictably govern or control behavior under some conditions, they may not under others. Notice in the cartoon (below) how one might conclude the child's behavior was differentially reinforced after the third time he was called. Instead, both of his parents should have consistently provided consequences for compliance and non-compliance after calling him the first time.

"But you only called me once, Dad! Mom calls me three times before she gets mad!"

Some people have extremely low rates of complying with particular categories of rules. Consider a rebellious adolescent who consistently fails to fulfill his parents', teachers', or supervisors' requests, even when the operative contingencies are clearly described: "If you pick up your clothes before five o'clock, I'll let you use the car." But junior keeps playing his computer games and does not put his clothing away by the deadline.

At one extreme, people for whom verbal antecedents exert little or no control often are labeled as highly independent, creative, or self-reliant, especially when their actions are socially valued. At the other extreme, especially when their actions are aversive to others, they may be perceived as immature, foolish, delayed, psychopathic, delinquent, or emotionally disturbed. *The issue, however, is not what they are, or how we label these individuals, but what they do or fail to do under what conditions—and what can be done to rectify the situation.*

Something as simple as the wording of instructions may influence the way an individual responds: Northup, Kodak, Lee, and Coyne (2004) worked with a five-year-old girl diagnosed with ADHD.

She was told to stay in her seat and work quietly. If she did not, she was told that the consequence would be having to "take a break," which consisted of "the therapist turning Marie's chair away from the desk, removing the task, and turning away from the student for 30 s" (p. 510). At other times, she was told that the consequence would be "timeout," which consisted of the same consequence as "taking a break." The results showed that the child's rate of problem behavior was high when the contingency was described as *taking a break*, but almost zero when it was described as *timeout*. Probably the difference was due to her learning history. This is example of **instructional demand**, which is *an alteration in behavior as a function of variations in the way instructions are delivered*. In other words, the manner in which instructions are given can produce different categories of verbal governance, and therefore different types of behavior. Here is another example we encountered with a client. The goal was for the client to point to a picture of her father from an array of several pictures. The behavioral technician (BT) first asked her to point to her father. The client did not respond. The BT then told her to point to her dad. Again, the client did not respond. Finally, after discovering the phrase used in the home for the father, the BT said, "Point to your dada." The client pointed to the picture of her father. In a related case, a client was asked to solve a series of division problems. But she only responded to those division problems that were presented within the following format: 4/2=? She had not learned the sign for division.

Sometimes, as we know, a skill deficit may explain the particular response. Due to their deficiencies, people with severely delayed receptive language frequently fail to profit from spoken instructional prompts. So, before instructions will exert control, one must teach the "meaning" of the instructions by correlating them with clear antecedents and consequences; that given certain verbal stimuli, particular participant actions are reinforced, while others are extinguished or punished. Alternatively, when people are known to be capable of following instructions and yet fail to respond appropriately, contingencies may need to be carefully rearranged, as described elsewhere in the text. Instruction following also can be related to the relevance of the requested task. For example, investigators (Sy, Donaldson, Vollmer, & Pizarro, 2014) found that 5-year-old children with intellectual disabilities were much more likely to follow instruction that required object manipulations that were relevant, or familiar, to them. Thus, as the authors state: Findings highlight the need to train instruction following under different conditions to ensure that responding comes under stimulus control of the instructions" (p, 101).

When done properly, specifying that a given response is likely to be reinforced should permit the words to exert their intended function.[2] (But be careful. The parent who makes deals such as "You can have some computer time when you finish cleaning up your room," may find that the child cleans up only if the deal has been offered. Those who complain that reward amounts to bribery are probably thinking about the effects of such arrangements, and they are right to think that handling things in this manner sometimes can be problematic. If used at all, the child's fulfillment of responsibilities should not permanently depend on such verbal stimuli. That is why the verbal deals must be faded out as quickly as possible.) A more preferable approach is to ensure that the individual receives special approval, positive attention of even occasional rewards as a result of unprompted responsible behavior.

**Higher-order classes.** Notice that some of our examples include contingencies nested within other contingencies. One set of contingencies in our last example involves the reinforcement of cleaning up one's room (a lower order class), and another is following instructions (the higher order class). (Cleaning one's room when requested is nested within the higher order responding of following directions.) Sometimes these can support one another, but sometimes they conflict. Soldiers learn the instructional control that we call "following orders," which is created and maintained by complex social contingencies. But if they are commanded to do something highly dangerous, like attacking an enemy position over open ground, the contingencies for obeying commands in general may be pitted against

---

[2]Instead of labeling the instructions as discriminative stimuli, some, for instance Blakely and Schlinger (1987), prefer to use the term "function-altering contingency specifying stimuli" because these stimuli are not typically present when eventually they have their effects.

the contingencies of following that particular dangerous command. Their behavior, then, depends on two different sets of contingencies: a higher-order class we might call obedience in general, and the many lower-order classes based upon the separate contingencies for each individual subclass, as in our military example.

**Develop instructions as discriminative stimuli.** As with other antecedents, when instructions do serve as discriminative functions for the individual, they can become effective and expedient behavioral prompts. That is why books, lectures, seminars, discussions, and workshops are so heavily relied on to teach and promote appropriate behavior. Barker, Bailey and Lee (2004) used a simple verbal instruction, "Have a nice day and don't forget to buckle up" (p. 528), with the result that the use of child safety-belts on shopping carts in two different stores increased substantially. A group of 24 chronic insomniacs met weekly with medical practitioners for a sequence of sessions. They were taught rules to strengthen the tie between the bed as an occasion for sleep, and were instructed not to use the bed as an occasion for activities that might interfere with sleep: Use the bed for sleeping and sex only; do not engage in strenuous intellectual or physical activity for at least one hour before bedtime; do not take naps; and so on (Baillargeon, Demers, & Ladouceur, 1998). Patients were encouraged to follow the regimen during subsequent sessions. Fifteen patients completed the program, with 80 percent of them reducing their latency of sleep onset. Six of seven who had been using sleep medication were able to diminish or terminate it altogether.

**Use stimuli known to be in the repertoire of the learner.** When Clarke, Remington, and Light (1986) taught words to educationally handicapped children in *total communication* format, the youngsters more rapidly acquired the words with which they already were familiar than those unfamiliar to them. One reason the chapter goals in this text suggest you define terms is to permit you to use those terms appropriately. Analogously, before you attempt teaching a complicated discrimination, be sure the stimuli are detectable to the student. If you are studying at the graduate level, perhaps you recall that section of the Graduate Record Examination (GRE), or a similar exam, with which you encountered problems. Could the source of your difficulty have been that you were unfamiliar with the definitions of words for which you were to choose synonyms? Similarly, if people find instructions difficult to read, they are less likely to engage in the desired behavior. For example, Song and Schwarz (2008) found that instructions presented in difficult-to-read font (e.g., Brush 12-point or Mistral 12-point) resulted in people experiencing more difficulty with tasks, such as following a recipe or exercise routine, and were less willing to perform the behavior, than when instructions were presented in easy-to-read font (e.g., Arial 12-point). These examples indicate why becoming well acquainted with your clientele's current behavioral repertoires is so important.

**Present instructions rapidly** (i.e., maintain brief intervals between trails). Rapidly paced instructions have been associated with lower rates of student disruption and superior comprehension (Carnine, 1976; West & Sloane, 1986). When you are teaching a skill (e.g., to discriminate, label, sequence, or imitate), then, see to it that the elapsed time between the delivery of the reinforcer for success in one trial and the initiation of the next trial is brief. In a specific case, Koegel, Dunlap, and Dyer (1980) found that when the stimulus for each trial was presented about one second after the end of the previous trial, their students with autism answered more accurately and learned more rapidly than when those time periods were four seconds or longer. As the investigators noted, "… it seems increasingly important to examine characteristics of the learning situation which occur between trials. The present results show that such variables can have a relatively large influence on teaching these children" (p. 98). In a more recent study, Cariveau, Kodak, and Campbell (2016) were able to replicate these findings and suggested that instructors use short intervals (2 s) between trials with varied-trial format (i.e., presenting three target stimuli in a pseudorandom order) versus longer intervals (20 s) between trails with massed-trial (i.e., presenting the same target stimulus during all trails) formats.

**Instructional modality.** Instructional format also can affect the outcomes. To illustrate, investigators (Funk, Kosch, & Schmidt, 2016) compared different systems, including using in-situ projection, table instructions, head mounted displays, and paper instructions to guide the assembly process. They found that assembling parts was significantly faster using in-situ projection and "participants made less errors and have less perceived cognitive load using in-situ instruction" (p. 934). Consequently, try to identify the instructional modalities best suited to your student's or client's learning repertoire. We present many throughout this text.

**Combine instructions with goal-setting and modeling.** Sometimes, despite the best efforts of the contingency manager, verbal instructions fail to accomplish their purpose. The responder appears unable to act according to a particular set of verbal guidelines and no amount of telling, training, or consulting bears fruit: "Clean up your room, Joey." But on inspection, Joey's room remains like the aftermath of a hurricane. "I shall munch on carrots, not on potato chips, for the rest of the year," says Dottie the Dieter, whereas Mr. Garcia vows he will scold less and praise more. Yet neither follow through on their resolutions. The teacher announces, "Look, more new books for you to read!" and only two of eight children respond by reading (Haskett & Lenfestey, 1974). Obviously, the instructions fail to govern the desired responses.

Attempts to use verbal or instructional stimuli to govern behavior often fail because the participant finds responding to those stimuli too difficult or time consuming. One solution is to support instructions with goal-setting and/or modeling (the *show* procedure) or to use physical guidance, to be described shortly.

VanWormer (2004) counseled three self-referred, overweight adults. He combined instructions for increasing walking and using pedometers with scheduled weekly email conversations during which progress was reviewed, goals were set, and praise provided. This combined strategy resulted in two of the participants nearly doubling their daily total steps and losing a modest amount of weight.

Adding modeling to instructions may produce results superior to those gained by using instructions alone (LeBlanc & Ruggles, 1982). This tactic is especially useful when attempting to promote mastery of a complex skill, such as replacing a garbage disposal, donning a life jacket, or operating a piece of equipment. In fact, a quick search on YouTube will probably offer a vast array of appropriate models of complex behaviors. Of course, to promote independence after the response is well established, you would want gradually to remove the *show* prompt, while retaining the instructions for a bit longer before fading them out as well. In the sections to follow, we survey several of many procedural packages that illustrate methods for combining a number of the instructional guidelines just reviewed.[3]

## DIRECT INSTRUCTION

Direct instruction is a system of teaching a number of academic subjects. (For a more detailed description of the components of direct instruction, see Watkins and Slocum, 2003). *A teaching method that involves using a prepared curriculum,* **Direct Instruction (DI)** *relies on stimulus control interventions to help teach general concepts, principles, and problem-solving strategies* (Becker & Carnine, 1981; Becker, Engelmann, Carnine, & Maggs, 1982; Kinder & Carnine, 1991). Specifically, teachers who implement DI:

1. follow a very carefully organized and detailed sequence of instruction. They follow scripts to ensure that material is presented properly and followed with appropriate consequences. This minimizes problems related to *instructional demand* and supports delivery of merited reinforcement.
2. teach in small groups as appropriate.
3. prompt unison group responding (choral responding).
4. use signals to encourage all students to participate at specific times during a lesson.
5. use rapid pacing during presentation.

---

[3] In Chapter 13, we discussed another of the many such programs that capitalize on behavior analytic principles, the highly-successful computer-assisted instructional program for challenged students, the "Competent Learner Model (CLM)."

6. apply specific techniques for minimizing and correcting errors, including graphing errors, supplying the correct answer in discrimination tasks, prompting students to use a multi-step strategy, and others.

7. use praise as merited.

Slocum (2003) has pointed out that: "Direct Instruction is about producing measurable improvements in student performance" (p. 111), and is based on "research-validated instructional practices" (p. 112). Broad-scale standardized test scores and other measures have shown that this program effectively enhances the specific reading skills of normally-developing preschool and older children, as well as those with various challenges including developmental delays, autism, inability to speak English, bilingualism, deafness, and economic disadvantages (Becker & Gersten, 1982; Becker et al., 1982; Weisberg, 1983–1984; Kinder & Carnine, 1991). DI material has also been found to significantly improve mathematical problem-solving and spelling and to accelerate the learning of students in reading (Schaefer, 1979; Sexton, 1989), spelling (Robinson & Hesse, 1981), and science (Romance & Vitale, 1992). In other words, as stated by Frampton, Shillingsburg and Simeone (2020), DI "is an evidence-based approach to education that has been shown to be effective across a wide variety of student populations" (p. 648).

DI has branched out to include computer-assisted instruction (Collins, Carnine, & Gersten, 1987; Woodward, Carnine, & Gersten, 1988), low-cost networking (Hayden, Wheeler, & Carnine, 1989; Woodward, Carnine, Gersten, Moore, & Golden, 1987) and videodisc courseware (Hofmeister, Engelmann, & Carnine, 1989; Moore & Carnine, 1989; Niedelman, 1991; Woodward & Noell, 1991). It has also been applied to critical reading, social studies, literature, and higher math skills (Kinder & Carnine, 1991) and continues to grow and expand its applications, as noted below. Similarly, Frampton et al. (2020) utilized speech-generating devices with three students with ASD while teaching the Language for Learning Curriculum, Lessons 1–10, enabling all three students to participate and complete their assigned exercises. They also "demonstrated improved performance, positive affect, and overall timely completion of exercises" (p. 648).

Direct Instruction also has helped to narrow Wisconsin's achievement gap (Parnell, 2005). "Low-income students with five years of DI tracked between third and fourth grades increased their reading and math scores more than higher-income students did" (p. 1). DI "shows great promise for closing the 'achievement gap' between low-income and minority students and their peers" (p. 2).

Klahr and Nigam (2004) and Strand-Cary and Klahr (2008) compared *Direct Instruction* with *Discovery Learning* (a method of instruction, based on the assumption that allowing learners to discover facts and relationships for themselves is best). Their purpose was to determine which did a superior job of teaching students the conceptual basis for designing simple, tightly-controlled experiments capable of enabling causal inferences. The investigators found that not only did more students acquire the information from DI than from discovery learning, but the results served as a better predictor of transfer in the form of enabling them to make broader, richer scientific judgments. (For additional summaries of research on DI with a wide range of learners, see Adams and Engelmann, 1996; also Binder and Watkins, 2010, Kameenui, Simmons, Chard, and Dickson, 1997, and MacIver and Kemper, 2002. Also refer to the *Journal of Direct Instruction*, that publishes current research and evaluation of DI.)

# DISCRETE TRIAL TRAINING (DTT)

*Discrete trial training* has been used frequently as a method for teaching communicative skills to children with autism. Within **discrete trial training (DTT)**, *tasks are broken down into short, simple trials*. A **discrete trial** *is a single cycle of behaviorally-based instructional routine consisting of four or five parts*: (1) Presenting, if necessary, the appropriate antecedent stimuli—e.g., a short, clear instruction or a cue to which the client can respond. (2) Providing a *temporary* prompt (if necessary), such as *showing* (or *verbally instructing* or *guiding*) the client's correct responding. (As you will learn in Chapter 20, when prompts are used, they eventually need to be faded out.) (3) Waiting for the learner to emit the skill or behavior that is the target of the instruction. (4) Providing the reinforcer, such as praise or a high-preference item designed to motivate the client to continue responding correctly contingent on the behavior. (5) Ending with an inter-trial interval consisting of a brief pause between consecutive trials. We call the trial discrete because it has a definite beginning and end.

To illustrate:

The teacher holds up a cup and says, "What is this?" (the antecedent).

The student says, "Cup" (the response or behavior).

The teacher says, "Good. Here is some chocolate milk" (or other favored reinforcer).

Had the student failed to respond correctly, the teacher would apply an **error correction procedure**. The teacher might present a prompt, perhaps by saying the whole word: "It's a cup" or part of the word ("It's a cu_"). Research findings (Kodak et al., 2016; McGhan & Lerman, 2013) suggest that an error correction procedure that includes modeling and/or demonstrating the correct response appears to generate the best participant outcomes. (See the following section on using modeling effectively.) Also, be sure to have your clients imitate or echo the correct response and be sure to reinforce their correct responding (Carroll, Owsiany, & Cheatham, 2018; Kodak et al., 2016). Repeat the trial following the error correction procedure, until your client consistently emits the correct response, absent any prompting for a few days.

This method was first demonstrated by Wolf, Risley, and Mees (1964) and Wolf, Risley, Johnston, Harris, and Allen (1967), who worked under the direction of Sidney Bijou. Lovaas, Koegel, Simmons, and Long (1973) presented one of the first extensive evaluative reports of a program incorporating the discrete training strategy. They found that the inappropriate behavior (e.g., self-stimulation and echolalia) of all twenty clients with autism decreased, while their appropriate behavior (e.g., speech, play) increased. So did their IQ scores. Also, those children whose parents were trained to carry out the interventions kept improving, while institutionalized children lacking such treatment continued to regress. From the 1960s to the 1990s, additional findings by Lovaas and his colleagues (e.g., Lovaas, 1977) contributed to the general acceptance of applied behavior analysis as the treatment of choice for children with autism who sometimes progressed to the point of "recovery" (i.e., the child was no longer labeled "autistic").[4] DDT training also is having an international impact (e.g., Eid, Aljaser, AlSaud, et al., 2017).

## DTT Differentiated from Free Operants

A **free operant** is *a response class unlimited by constraints or prompts from others, so that it may be freely and repeatedly emitted* (Skinner, 1938). Within an instructional or training situation, the participant's behavior does not depend on an instruction, prompt, or any supportive discriminative stimulus provided *by another individual*. Whatever discriminative control is present is natural to the environment.

Watch a group of preschoolers out in the park running and screaming just for the sheer joy of it. Their running and screaming could be termed *free operants*. Teach the children through differential reinforcement that they may only run and scream (gain reinforcers) when instructed to do so. Assuming they comply, their running and screaming then would be labeled **discriminated operants:** *a response under stimulus control, with the initial $S^D$s usually provided by others* (also see Ch. 15). *The response occurs more frequently under specific antecedent conditions than under other antecedent conditions. In other words, a discriminated operant is a behavior, or operant, under stimulus control wherein the response is more likely to occur with a discriminative stimulus present than when it is not.* DTT uses discriminated operants. Observe a friend lifting heavy objects. Does she follow the rules for safe lifting (verbally-governed—under stimulus control) or just reach, grab hold, and position the objects arbitrarily (free operant). Other common examples of free operants include laboratory animals' independent and unconstrained bar pressing

---

[4]Read *Let me hear your voice* (Maurice, 1993) for an inspiring glimpse of this method's potential.

or key pecking or students preparing for an exam haphazardly (free operant) versus following a particular sequence of steps, including reading, answering study questions, checking answers, and so forth.

Note that with free operants, the participant does not, as with DTT, wait for an instruction or another prompt for the next response. *Free operants are those whose repetitions are not constrained.* Free operants, then, are measured by *rate* (occurrences per unit of time) while DTT responses are measured as the number of correct responses and the number of trials and reported as percentage correct.

## Selecting Free versus Discriminated Operants

In and of themselves, free and discriminated operants are neither good nor bad. Rather, the issue is whether the purpose of the intervention is to promote independence and generality (as with free operants) or to promote tightly controlled performance (as with discriminated operants). In the working world of most adults, certain performances must be under precise discriminative control. Only when the dentist notes that a tooth is beyond repair will (should) she extract it. The oil-rig operator must lock down the system if a particular meter reading extends beyond a given safety zone.

Applied behavior analysts may promote either free or discriminated operants, depending on the long-range goals for the participants. Discrete trail training is one of the most familiar methods for teaching discriminated operants to students on the autism spectrum (the response is correct when and only when a particular stimulus is present). However, DTT sometimes results in over-dependence on prompts.

**Avoiding prompt dependency.** If during DTT, learners appear to be dependent on the instructor's cuing (perhaps due to their being encouraged to wait passively for a prompt rather than independently initiating the communicative or other responses), training must be adjusted to gradually fade any extra prompts. This can be rather costly in terms of time and effort. To avoid this pitfall, various behavior analytic-based methods have been devised to minimize prompting to its barest and most essential levels right from the start. Examples include, *incidental teaching* (see Chapter 21), and some aspects of *Picture Exchange Communication System* (PECS)© (see Chapter 19). In the former case, children's preferred objects are displayed beyond reach. Those objects serve naturally to prompt the child to initiate a request. The trainer provides the barest cue to encourage the child to initiate requesting the object. In the latter case, the trainer guides the child toward the preferred object (displayed by another instructor) physically cueing at the most minimal level; and then prompts the child to exchange a picture for the object, via prompt fading (see Chapter 20). As Smith (2001) has pointed out, while most programs designed to teach children with autism incorporate DTT, combining that with other interventions, such as incidental teaching, tends to promote even more productive learning and generalization. In support of this assertion, Delprato (2001), for example, found that incidental language training demonstrated greater functionality and generality than discrete trial training. Similarly, when children were taught by incidental teaching rather than discrete trial training, their speech was more intelligible (Koegel, Camarata, Koegel, Ben-Tall, & Smith, 1998). Sundberg and Partington (1996) have advised that both discrete trial training and natural environmental teaching can be combined successfully. (For reviews of discrete trial training, see Eikeseth [2009], Ghezzi [2007], and Tarbox and Najdowski [2008]).

## PROVIDING A MODEL: IMITATIVE PROMPTS

Teach a child with developmental disabilities generalized imitation, and future expansion of the child's repertoire can suddenly and systematically be as explosive as the social environment cares to make it, simply by modeling new skills. (Rosales-Ruiz & Baer, 1997, p. 535)

### Defined and Illustrated

**Modeling** *is a stimulus-control procedure based on demonstrations, or "showing," to prompt an* *imitative response*. Imitation depends on modeled behavior. The two terms are distinctly different. The *antecedent of showing how to perform a behavior, or skill, is the model or prompt to be imitated. The observer's behavior that reproduces the modeled behavior is called* **imitation** *(or an imitative response)*.

Often, just seeing someone performing, demonstrating, or *modeling* behavior is sufficient to prompt its imitation. To whit, when, despite encouragement, the students in the Haskett and Lenfestey (1974) study failed to read their new books, tutors began to pick up the books and read aloud. The students soon began following suit, substantially increasing their reading and related responses. Similarly, modeling was more effective in rapidly changing parental behavior than direct instructions or group discussions (Johnson & Brown, 1969). Modeling and role playing also were superior to written instructions or lectures in teaching parents to use timeout appropriately (Flanagan, Adams, & Forehand, 1979), perhaps because the procedures both promote discriminating between more and less optimal performance and increase the likelihood that matching the behavior will be reinforced.

Modeling has been shown to facilitate the acquisition of a variety of responses, both simple and complex, such as socially-appropriate conduct (Bandura, 1969, 1977, 1986), cooperative behavior during dental treatment (Stokes & Kennedy, 1980), preschool life skills (Hanley, Heal, Tiger, & Ingvarsson, 2007), athletic skills (Shapiro & Shapiro, 1985), preschoolers' dance skills (Vintere et al., 2004), and language skills (Brody & Brody, 1976; Brody, Lahey, & Combs, 1978; Goldstein & Brown, 1989; Heward & Eachus, 1979). It also has been shown to be more effective than instructions in teaching typically-developing children and those with ADHD how to distribute their responding to obtain the most reinforcers (Neef et al., 2004):

> During the instruction condition students were told how to distribute responding to earn the most reinforcers. During the modeling condition, students observed the experimenter performing the task while describing her distribution of responding to obtain the most reinforcers…. Both instruction and modeling interventions quickly produced patterns of response allocation that approximated obtained rates of reinforcement, but responding established with modeling was more sensitive to subsequent changes in reinforcement schedules than responding established with instructions. (p. 267)

Modeling along with explanations were used to teach young adults with mild intellectual disabilities to respond appropriately to lures from strangers (Fisher, Burke & Griffin, 2013). First the trainer began by describing what a stranger is, which was followed by a description of the most common type of lures: "your mom asked to pick you up"; "Please come with m"; "I will buy you a ____ if you come with me": and, "Can you help me carry this to my car?" Or, "Can you help me find my ____ (dog, daughter, turtle, etc.)?" Next, the three-step safety response was described and the participant orally repeated it. This consisted of (1) saying "no" within three seconds, (2) moving away within three seconds of the requests, and (3) reporting the event to a trusted adult. Next, four examples and two counter-examples of appropriate responding were modeled and discussed. Finally, the participant practiced appropriate responding in five role plays. Behavior-specific praise was provided for appropriate responding during each role-play. This was followed by generalization training and feedback across situations. All participants were reported to have learned the skills, but did not consistently report the lure. Similarly, Bergstrom, Najdowski and Tarbox (2014) taught children (10 to 12 years of age) with autism to respond appropriately to lures from strangers; and, Vanselow and Hanley (2014) report successfully using computerized training, which incorporates video modeling to teach safety skills to young children, including abduction prevention, poison and lighter safety. Also, investigators (Ledbetter-Cho, et al., 2016) using explanations and video modeling taught four children with autism how to respond to simple requests, appeals to authority, incentives, and assistance request made by strangers. All four left with the confederate strangers during baseline. After being taught to refuse, move away, and report, their abduction-prevention skills improved considerably. Modeling also has been very successful in teaching acceptable alternatives to behavioral problems, described in Chapter 26.

Perhaps modeling operates so effectively because words cannot adequately describe the nuances of certain responses. Try instructing a child to tie shoelaces just by telling the child how to do it. Sometimes demonstrating is much more efficient, especially when learners are incapable of comprehending verbal descriptions of the response. No mother would teach her infant to play "peek-a-boo" by words alone. Nor do successful physical education, art, or music teachers rely entirely on rules or instructions, instead amplifying those by demonstrating and reinforcing ever closer matches to the modeled response: "Serve the ball like this." "Listen to the melody while Bruno plays it." Ultimately, the demonstration can be eliminated, controlled either by generic instructions ("Remember how I showed how you throw the ball") or the critical antecedent stimuli (the musical score) and their natural reinforcing consequences. As with instructions, the instructor needs to sequence the demonstration carefully and, when necessary, apply effective techniques for transferring stimulus control (discussed in Chapter 20).

Modeling also seems to operate more effectively after the learner has failed on a prior task (Gelfand, 1962; Mausner, 1954). Perhaps more eager to perform successfully following failure, learners are more likely to focus on a model's demonstration. There are limits, though. While modeling can be an effective teaching device with children with autism, many appear deficient in reproducing certain of the subtleties of the model's behavior, such as their "style," mannerisms, facial expressions, or affective qualities (Hobson & Lee, 2003: Rogers, Hepburn, Stackhouse, & Wehner, 2003; Stone, Ousley, & Littleford, 1997). Children with autism also appear to be more capable of imitating concrete play with objects than pretend play (Dawson & Adams, 1984; Roeyers, Van Oost, & Bothyune, 1998). Nonetheless, through careful modeling and shaping, Lifter and colleagues were able to teach several preschool children with autism to engage in a series of pretend-play activities (Lifter, Sulzer-Azaroff, Anderson, & Cowdery, 1993). Notice also that modeling can be thought of as a *higher-order class*, based on the correspondence between what the modeler does and what the learner does, whereas the lower-order classes are all the specific individual cases (e.g., imitation in general versus imitation of hopping, imitation of skipping, and imitation of jumping).

## Developing Modeled Behavior into Imitative Prompts or Discriminative Stimuli

From the earliest months, infants generally learn *imitative behavior through differential reinforcement*. "Peek-a-boo" says Mama, covering her eyes, smiling, and laughing. If baby doesn't initially duplicate Mama's behavior by bringing his hands to his eyes, Mama assists by guiding them. When baby responds to "peek-a-boo" with an approximation of his own, bells ring, fireworks explode, and trumpets blare: "Look! He's playing peek-a-boo!" Baby's imitation of Mama's behavior is reinforced heavily. Junior rubs cream over his face, pretending to shave. Daddy says, "You're a big man, just like me!" Imitative responses are prompted and socially reinforced similarly throughout childhood: "See, Penny's doll is in the kitchen. Can you put yours there too?" The observing child is being taught that if she imitates her playmate's behavior (the imitative prompt), her imitation is likely to be reinforced by approval.

Differential reinforcement also is integral to many children's games, like "Simon Says" and "Follow the Leader." Research with laboratory animals (Epstein, Lanza, & Skinner, 1980; Hake, Donaldson, & Hyten, 1983) has shown that under some special circumstances differential reinforcement can be used to teach animals to imitate one another.[5]

Children with various handicapping conditions sometimes need to be helped to develop imitation skills. For example, Garfinkle and Schwartz (2002) intervened with four preschool children in an integrated classroom during a regular activity. Three of the children were diagnosed with autism and one with developmental delays. The children

---
[5]The ability to imitate varies across species. Some, like parrots and domesticated dogs, do so readily (Kubivi, Topal, Miklosi, & Csanvi, 2003).

were asked to imitate the peer group leader, who volunteered or was chosen by the teacher. Acts of imitation were reinforced by the teacher. If a participant did not imitate, the children were verbally prompted to watch the leader and do the same. If the verbal prompts were ineffective, physical guidance was used to assist the participant to imitate actions to objects, such as placing his or her hand on supplies. As a result, peer imitation, proximity to peers, and the number of social interactions with peers all increased. Similarly, Ganz, Bourgeois, Flores, and Campos (2008) worked with four eight- to 13-year-old boys with autism who failed to imitate peers during classroom activities. To teach imitation, they used a simple teacher-friendly strategy during small group activities. The group consisted of three children with autism, plus a peer leader. The youngsters were supplied with the appropriate materials, including "…dough, cookie cutters, Popsicle sticks, and wooden dowels; magnetic drawing boards, with magnetic pens and three magnetic stamps; and construction paper with craft supplies, including glue, crayons, cotton puffs, confetti, and foam shapes. These materials were chosen because the participants enjoyed and could use them independently" (p. 59). The children then were instructed to "Do the same as the leader." If a child did not imitate after five seconds, (1) he was first told: "Look at what the leader is doing," and the trainer took the child's hand to help him point to the picture, supplemented with text, saying, "Do the same as the leader." (2) If the child failed to imitate, he was told what the leader was doing and asked to do the same. (3) Failure to imitate resulted in the child's hand being placed on the materials. (4) Continued failure cued the trainer to physically guide the child to imitate the leader. As a result, the participants' imitation skills increased and their reliance on physical prompts decreased.

If the client has not learned to attend to the model's behavior, it best to first teach your client to attend before teaching imitation. This is what MacDonald and Ahern (2015) did. They first taught attending to 6 children with autism, ages 8 to 21 years of age, using instructions and physical guidance (described later in this chapter). Once attending to modeled behavior was taught, they were then able to teach their clients to imitate.

Eventually, after numerous instances of imitation are reinforced within varied contexts, children begin to acquire **generalized imitation** as a response class (a higher-order class), *using the imitative skill not only in response to familiar examples, but in novel contexts as well.* Although usually adaptive, generalized imitation sometimes leads to trouble. Observe children engrossed in fantasy play to see what we mean. Junior picks up Dad's briefcase, pretends to head out the door, and in a deep voice, just like Daddy's says, "Bye, Honey, see you tonight." His adoring parents beam and congratulate their son's cleverness. But when junior makes believe he is yelling at the television—"How could you have dropped that pass, you #!*#!," his accurate portrayal lands him a scolding. Junior must learn to discriminate who can be safely imitated and when imitating is appropriate.

Some children need to be taught not only to imitate but also to discriminate what to imitate; or, to imitate behavior that receives reinforcement in their environment and to not imitate behavior not receiving reinforcement. For example, in teaching observational learning to children with autism, investigators (DeQuinzio & Taylor, 2015; MacDonald & Ahearn, 2015)) taught the children to discriminate the consequences applied to an adult's modeled behavior, and to imitate only the behaviors that received reinforcement when modeled.

## Combining Modeling with Shaping

Modeling may occasion imitation, especially if skills in the client's repertoire approximate the demonstrated behavior and if the client has received reinforcers previously for emitting responses resembling those of the model. Just as other antecedents may occasion some variations in behavior, modeling may prompt an approximation to a response that would otherwise be too complex to be imitated in its entirety. Rather than simply awaiting the emission of the desired form, the change agent can demonstrate it to the client.

Speech therapists often use this procedure when attempting to shape the proper enunciation of a word. Suppose a client is able to enunciate only one or two components of a complex word, as in the case of being presented with a picture of a ball of string. He pronounces the word "fing," because the *str* combination missing from his repertoire. The components of *str* are presented as models for the client to imitate. First the *s* sound is modeled, and the client asked to repeat it a number of times; then the *t* sound is presented repeatedly, and then the *st* sound. The procedure continues until the correct response is shaped.

Surely you are familiar with how teachers and parents use similar methods to shape the components of various academic tasks (e.g., handwriting, computation, and reading), or self-help skills (e.g., dressing, washing, and eating); or how supervisors use modeling in on-the-job training. In fact, show-and-tell methods like those probably are the most prevalent job training strategies used, even in executive-skill preparation (Dingman, 1978).

Individuals with autism frequently display inappropriate affect (emotional behavior). DeQuinzio et al. (2007) attempted to remedy that deficiency with three male three- to six-year-old children with autism. Before the study, these children would cry or display sad facial expressions when others smiled at them, or laugh when others cried. Nor did they imitate displays of appropriate facial affective responses (e.g., smiling, frowning, showing surprise, or anger) in response to verbal prompts. Again, if they failed to imitate, they were verbally prompted again (i.e., "do this") and two facial motor movements topographically related to the target response were modeled. If they responded by successfully imitating the approximations, then the target facial model was immediately re-presented. All three children increased their levels of correctly imitating during training and two of the three generalized that responding across stimuli.

## Increasing Generalized Imitative Responding

Although most people acquire generalized imitation in their early years, some remain deficient in this skill. Because well-established imitative responding is essential to the rapid acquisition of many types of behavior, generalized mimicry skills may need to be trained intentionally. Imagine trying to teach someone incapable of imitating to knit; solder; slam a Ping-Pong ball; pronounce a word in a foreign language; shuffle cards; or stop, look, and listen. Actually, the person lacking the latter skill is in serious jeopardy. So much behavior depends on being able to imitate: learning to speak, socialize, or acquire complicated physical or cognitive skills—like orienting toward instructional materials—would be compromised.

Generalized imitation is taught by *heavily reinforcing members of the imitative response class as often and under as many circumstances as possible.* For example, in a study by Neef et al. (2004), clients generalized the skills they had learned via modeling to other situations, thereby maximizing their reinforcers. Several investigators (e.g., Baer, Peterson, & Sherman, 1967; Lovaas, Berberich, Perloff, & Schaeffer, 1966) taught initially non-responsive individuals with autism and severe retardation to imitate by pairing instructions, for example, "Touch your head," with a demonstration of the act. Any imitative reaction then was reinforced with praise, small bits of food, and so on. Ultimately, the demonstrations were faded, as verbal instructions began to serve as adequate prompts. (See the section on fading prompts in Chapter 20.) These same techniques also have been used to teach sign language to people lacking or deficient in language due to hearing impairments, developmental delays, and socio-emotional difficulties, enabling them, thereby, to communicate at last (e.g., Barrera, Lobato-Barrera, & Sulzer-Azaroff, 1980).

## Video Modeling

Using video demonstrations is an excellent way to facilitate the acquisition of a range of skills. For example, Haring, Kennedy, Adams, and Pitts-Conway (1987) attempted to teach purchasing skills to three young adults with autism both in their classrooms and either in their cafeteria or a nearby convenience store. Very little skill generalization took place, however, until their instructor showed the youths videotapes of non-handicapped peers of similar age making purchases in various community settings, followed by questions about what they were viewing. Similarly, Charlop-Christy and Milstein (1989) reported how three young children with autism acquired and generalized conversational speech after they viewed videotapes of familiar adults engaging in such conversations and practiced the conversations with a therapist. Also, Charlop-Christy and Daneshvar (2003) taught children with autism perspective-taking ("the ability to determine mental states of others in order to explain or predict behavior," p. 12) by showing videos of adults modeling the requisite behaviors, and then reviewing what was on the video. The strategy resulted in the children rapidly acquiring and broadly generalizing perspective-taking. Investigators also taught social perception skills to five adolescents with ASD and/or intellectual disabilities (Stauch, Plavnick, Sankar, & Gallagher, 2018). Shipley-Benamou et al. (2002) used video modeling to teach children with autism daily living skills such as making orange juice, cleaning the fishbowl, and table setting. Assessments revealed that all subjects learned and maintained the skills for at least a month. Similarly, Reeve, Reeve, Townsend, and Poulson (2007) were able to establish a generalized repertoire of helping behavior among children with autism by using a multi-component teaching package composed of video modeling, prompting, and reinforcement. Green et al. (2017) used individualized video modeling to help preschool children (three four-year olds, none diagnosed with a disability) to improve their social interaction skills (e.g., sharing, turn-taking). Two were described as reticent and internalizing with their peers, the third as aggressive and externalizing. Two of the three children, those who were reticent, improved their social interactions, the one described as aggressive did not. After reviewing 16 studies on the subject, Baker, Lang, and O'Reilly (2009) concluded that video modeling is an effective intervention for increasing peer interaction and on-task behavior, as well as for decreasing inappropriate behavior.

Video modeling has been found to be more effective and efficient in the acquisition of meal preparation skills and produced fewer errors than the use of video prompting that depicted each step in preparing the meal (Thomas, DeBar, Viadescu, & Townsend, 2020). The success of video modeling has been demonstrated across broad populations. To illustrate, Moore and Fischer (2007) found that while neither lectures nor partial video modeling resulted in significant improvements, after the video had provided a wide range of exemplars, video modeling was found to be an effective training strategy for teaching professionals functional analysis methodology. Similarly, Collins, Higbee, and Salzberg, (2009) used video modeling to teach staff in a group home for adults with developmental disabilities to implement a problem-solving intervention correctly. They taught clients to identify problems, solutions, and consequences to each possible solution, and to choose the best solution. Previously, staff had access to a written description of the intervention and had role-played situations. These interventions were continued, but when video modeling was added, the "percentage of correctly implemented problem-solving steps increased for all participants, and the effect was maintained over time, generalized to novel problems, and generalized from role play with a researcher to actual clients" (p. 849). Video modeling also was found to be effective in teaching seven- to ten-year-old female competitive gymnasts (Boyer, Miltenberger, Batsche, & Fogel, 2009). They showed the children a video of an expert performing a specific gymnastics skill and compared it to the video of their performance. All improved on the skills taught using this video modeling comparison intervention. Investigators (Deliperi, Vladescu, Reeve, Reeve, & DeBar, 2015) also used video modeling with voiceover instructions to teach staff, such as behavior technicians, to implement a paired-stimulus preference assessment for discovering client reinforcers. In a recent study, Taber, Lambright, and Luiselli were able to change the type of attention that teachers delivered to students by using video modeling. Not only did the teachers start delivering the attention that was modeled in the video, their behavior generalized to delivering other appropriate forms of attention to students.

Video modeling has also been used as a vehicle for providing feedback. For example, Phaneuf and McIntyre (2007) added individualized video feedback to a parent training program serving four parents. The mother and experimenter viewed video tapes of the mother interacting with her developmentally-delayed preschool child during playtime. The therapist stopped the video and praised the mother's behavior every two minutes, provided the mother had not done anything inappropriate during the previous interval. If inappropriate behavior occurred, the video was stopped and the mother was asked to identify preferable alternatives. The therapist then praised and modeled those suggestions and then asked the parent to role-play the skills. Praise or corrective feedback followed as merited. As a result, the parents improved their parenting skills. Investigators also successfully used video feedback to improve horseback-riding skills (Kelley & Miltenberger, 2016) and martial arts performance (BenitezSantiago & Miltenberger, 2016). However it is our opinion that a combination of video feedback with a video or model demonstrating the correct skill would be more effective than just video feedback. Investigators (Carlile, DeBar, Reeve, & Reeve, 2018) also have taught children with autism help-seeking skills to use when lost, with the assistance of video modeling: making FaceTime® calls and displaying an identification card.

Behavior therapists often use video examples as a tool to help dispel individuals' fears and phobias.[6] However, the technique may prove inadequate when used in isolation, especially under especially challenging situations such as when clients are to undergo a dental procedure. For example, Conyers et al. (2004) found that only one of three adults with severe to profound mental retardation was seen to profit from video modeling, as contrasted with **in-vivo contact desensitization**.[7] The latter, *a system based on shaping in which the phobic stimulus is gradually introduced while the participant relaxes*, worked successfully to increase five participants' compliance with dental procedures. When it was effective, though, the video modeling did work rapidly, while desensitization took some time. Consequently, you might want to try video modeling first, in that in vivo desensitization may be considerably more time-consuming.

In a similar vein, in the absence of additional reinforcing consequences, video modeling of perspective-taking (described above) may sometimes fail to *generalize* to untrained tasks (LeBlanc et al., 2003). As we have noted repeatedly, change wrought by altering antecedent stimuli is unlikely to persist without at least some ongoing reinforcing consequences.

Also, video-modeling is not likely to result in learning unless the client has the prerequisite skill of delayed imitation of actions with objects. Investigators (MacDonald, Dickson, Martineau, & Ahearn, 2015) found that individuals who did imitate after a short delay were more likely to learn from video modeling than those who did not. For example, they requested the individual to "Do this" and modeled a one-step action with an object. The modeling materials were then removed for three seconds by holding them under the table. After the three seconds, the materials were given to the individual to see if he or she could imitate the action with the object. All those who performed well with video modeling also scored high (above 75 percent) in this delayed imitation of actions with objects. Fourteen of the 18 who scored low on video modeling also scored low on delayed imitation. Thus, we recommend that *before you take the time and trouble to set up and use video modeling as a training tool, check to see if the client can attend to the model's behavior and perform well on delayed imitation of actions with objects, or short term recall.*

When televisions and computers are not accessible for video modeling, consider using handheld devices. To illustrate, Cihak, Fahrenkrog, Ayres, and Smith (2010) delivered video modeling via iPods along with a system of least prompts. They found that this intervention worked to assist elementary students with autism spectrum disorders to improve their transitional behaviors from one general education area to another (e.g., bus, classroom gymnasium, bathroom, cafeteria, and playground). Also, when working with a single client, you can consider using your phone to video the behavior you want your client to imitate.

**Video self-modeling** *is a special application of video modeling in which recordings of the clients' optimal behavior are extracted and used as the model to be imitated.*

Self-modeling works like this: the student is videotaped while performing a particular skill. The tape then is edited to remove weak performance and external prompts. Only the

---

[6]Especially encouraging are technologies of "virtual reality exposure therapy," which make the phobic stimuli seem even more realistic. (See, for instance Rothbaum, Hodge, Smith, Lee, & Price, 2000.)

[7]See texts on behavior therapy (e.g., Guevremont, D., Woonsocket, D., & Spiegler, M.D., 2002, *Contemporary behavior therapy*, Cengage Publishing.)

exemplary performance is retained. (This differentiates *self-modeling* from *self-observation*.) The taped performance then is shown to the student to prompt imitation (Sulzer-Azaroff & Mayer, 1986, p. 118).

Self-modeling procedures have been used to teach a variety of professional, academic, social, conversational, play, and physical skills (e.g., Boudreaux & Harvey, 2013; Buggey, 2007; Buggey, Toombs, Gardner, & Cerveti, 1999; Delano, 2007; Dowrick & Dove, 1980; Hosford, 1980; Moore & Fisher, 2007). To illustrate, Delano (2007) used the procedure with three adolescent students with Asperger's syndrome to increase number of words written and functional essay elements included. We have used self-modeling to train teachers to apply particular instructional strategies and child-safety skills. Also, Marcus and Wilder (2009) found that self-modeling was more effective than the use of peer modeling in teaching three children with autism to identify and label novel letters. The three children were two males, ages four and nine, and one nine-year-old female. All spoke in multiple-word sentences and could imitate others. Investigators (King, Radley, Jenson, Clark, & O'Neill, 2014) also have used a combination of peer videos and self-modeling videos to teach on-task behavior during independent seat-work time in math for four second and third grade students (ages seven to nine). Each of the four students displayed high rates of off-task behavior. Results showed immediate, large and durable changes in on-task behavior for each of the students. So consider using a playback of the client's own exemplary performance as the imitative prompt and maybe combine it with effective peer models. (See Buggey, 2007, for specific tips on creating effective self-modeling stimuli.)

## Using Modeling Effectively: Model Selection

Beyond generalized imitative ability, skill at attending to models' behavior, successfully imitating following a delay, and individuals' specific learning histories, other variables have been seen frequently to influence the probability of a given imitative response.[8] The people who serve as models matter, along with whether other strategies are applied during training. Based on that information, you are well advised to choose multiple models who:

- share common characteristics with the observer.
- are competent in the skill to be imitated.
- have initially experienced difficulty learning the skill.
- have had previous positive interactions with the observer.
- are prestigious.

**Select models similar to the observer.** *Similarity* refers to characteristics shared commonly by the models and the individuals who observe them (e.g., socio-cultural background, job roles, age, grade, interests, physical appearance, and experiences). People are more likely to imitate someone they recognize as sharing attributes, talents, or deficiencies with themselves (Bandura, 1968; Byrne, 1969; Byrne & Griffitt, 1969; Kazdin, 1974b; Kornhaber & Schroeder, 1975; Statland, Zander, & Natsoulas, 1961). Kevin is likely to mimic people who resemble himself physically, so Pete, who is shorter and heavier, would not be the best choice as a model. (Both gender and body weight can influence peer selection choices; Souza, et al. 2020.)

Of course, no one is more similar than the individual clients themselves, which probably is one of the reasons why self-modeling can be so effective. However, the particular types of similar model attributes that may occasion imitation can vary among individuals.

As children mature and begin to move into adolescence, they more readily imitate their peers, particularly their friends (Barry & Overman, 1977; Hicks, 1965; Kazdin, 1974b; Kornhaber & Schroeder, 1975). Adults' friends may serve as especially effective models for one another because such friendships are often based on shared skills and interests. That could be one reason why friends tend to mimic one another's dress, social deportment, and

---

[8] Refer to the extensive work of Albert Bandura and colleagues for sources on the topic of modeling (e.g., Bandura, 1989).

activities. When searching for a model, say for on-the-job or other essential skill-training, try to choose a friend or co-worker competent in the behavior to be performed (Jones, Fremouw, & Carples, 1977).

*Similar* is not to be confused with *identical*. Unavoidable differences actually may be helpful, because too homogeneous a group can impede improvement. If all group members engage in the same problem behavior (stealing, classroom disruption, drugs, etc.), they are likely to reinforce each other's troublesome behavior. Just as variability of responding is essential to shaping, performance diversity among group members is necessary if you are to have a range of appropriate responses from which to select, reinforce, and otherwise set the stage for others to imitate.

**Select competent models.** Competence of the model is another valuable model characteristic. People who are seen to accomplish what they set about to do are the most apt to be imitated (Croner & Willis, 1961; Kanareff & Lanzetta, 1960; Rosenbaum, Chalmers, & Horne, 1962; Thomas, Due, & Wigger, 1987). In fact, the *functional value* of the modeled behavior (i.e., its proficiency in producing consequences, Bandura, 1986) outweighs age and other characteristics of the model (Schunk, 1987). Model similarity suggests an answer to the question, "Can I do it?" while model competence addresses the question, "Will it get me what I want?" (i.e., the reinforcer). Of course, if the act doesn't lead to reinforcers, the peer observer may ask himself, "Why should I bother doing it even if I can?"

The importance of exposing learners to peers with more advanced competence in the task of interest has been used as an argument favoring "mainstreaming" youngsters with special educational needs by integrating them among their contemporaries (Mann, 1975). That learning is enhanced by the availability of peers competent in the behavior to be modeled is well substantiated. Several studies support this conclusion. For example, Egel et al. (1981) found that youngsters on the autism spectrum, with IQs ranging from 50 to 87, evidenced very low levels of correct responding when prompted by the therapist, but when "normal peers" modeled correct responses, the ASD children's correct responding increased dramatically" (p. 9), and these increases were maintained after the peer models were removed. Similarly, Garfinkle and Schwartz (2002) used typically-developing peers to teach preschool children with autism to imitate a variety of skills. Similarly, due to the demonstrated effectiveness of peer tutoring, investigators (Haas, Vannest, & Smith, 2019) used a hypothetical classroom peer to demonstrate how to implement two common peer-tutoring strategies (Classwide Peer Tutoring and Peer-Assisted Learning Strategies) within general education classrooms that included children with autism spectrum disorder (ASD). Also, investigators (Cardon, Wangsgard, & Dobson, 2019) discovered that by using typically developing preschool-age peers as models in videos for children with ASD in an integrated pubic preschool setting, they obtained an increased attention to the videos. And, the children with ASD not only imitated the video-modeled social communication skills, but imitation generalized to other social communication behaviors. Typical peer models also have had similar effects on the performance of children with various severe cognitive handicaps (e.g., Apolloni, Cooke, & Cooke, 1976; Barry & Overman, 1977; Rauer, Cooke, & Apolloni, 1978).

**Select coping models.** A third factor is to select coping models. Generally, **coping models**, *those who now have the skill to be demonstrated but are known to have experienced difficulty with the behavior to be imitated in the past*, have proven more effective than "mastery models," those who portray complete competence from the onset (Bandura, 1986; Rosenthal & Bandura, 1978). Many modeling programs capitalize on this by selecting those who have experienced the same type of problems. Learners' growth in this area demonstrates approximations to the desired behavior that are neither too complex nor unrealistic for the others to imitate. For example, in one study (Jones et al., 1977), not only did teachers successfully instruct their colleagues in strategies of classroom management, but maybe because their own skills continued to improve correspondingly, disruptions decreased even further than previously in their own classrooms as well.

**Select models who have shared previous cooperative experience with the learner** (Mausner & Block, 1957). Perhaps a history of prior positive interactions between the model and the learner may help explain why live participant modeling generally is more effective than filmed anonymous models—(Bandura, 1986; Downs, Rosenthal, & Lichstein, 1988). Another explanation might be that live participant modeling offers more multi-sensory input than that based on films (Rosenthal & Downs, 1985). Therefore, when feasible, select live models who have shared previous cooperative experiences with the observer.

**Select prestigious models.** A prestigious individual is one who receives an above-average portion of reinforcers from peers and supervisors, as is the case with natural group leaders. Thomas et al. (1987) found that the model's prior success influenced the degree to which the less-competent observer subsequently imitated the model. Ernie's friendliness, athletic prowess, handsome appearance, and cheerfulness have gained him lots of attention, particularly from attractive women. Observing this, other youths would be more likely to imitate Ernie's behavior, rather than that of someone who is ignored (Bandura, Ross, & Ross, 1963b; Mayer, Rohen, & Whitley, 1969; Thomas et al., 1987). Remember, though, to hedge your bets by ensuring that the models share sufficient attributes with the observers.

As prestigious models, stage, screen, video, and advertising personalities tend to occupy especially influential roles in society, and their ability to influence behavior is well established. In the previous chapter we pointed out the relation between youth aggression and their frequency of viewing television violence (e.g., Anderson & Bushman, 2002). Similarly, Heatherton and Sargent (2009) found:

> Compared to adolescents with low exposure to smoking in movies, those with high exposure are about three times as likely to try smoking or become smokers.... This effect remains statistically significant after controlling for numerous other traditional risk factors, such as personality, parenting style, and sociodemographics. Indeed, the movie-smoking exposure effect on adolescent smoking initiation is greatest among... those low in sensation seeking and those whose parents do not smoke. (p. 63)

**Select multiple models.** Select multiple models because several models exert more influence than a single one (Barton & Bevirt, 1981; DeRicco & Niemann, 1980). The advertising media also take this advice to heart because multiple models tend to exert such a heavy influence on behavior. Additionally, you are well advised to vary the models you select in schools or organizations, because choosing the same classmates or associates too often may cause them to become ostracized by the group, labeled as "teacher's pets," or given some other colorful label.

## Using Modeling Effectively: Managing Contingencies

Beyond care in selecting their models, change agents can profit by engaging in several other factors that influence modeling, described next.

**Highlight similarities between models and observers.** You now know the importance of models and observers resembling one another, but those similarities may not always be obvious to the observer. In such cases, highlight them for the observer (Bandura, 1968; Byrne, 1969; Byrne & Griffitt, 1969; McCullagh, 1987). You might stress how they enjoy the same activities, or share common histories, or prior experiences. Have you noticed how commercial advertisements often emphasize the qualities common among their models and their intended consumers? "Mrs. Blue, a cat lover like you, uses Farfel Cat Food."

**Encourage behavioral rehearsal.** Imitation does not necessarily occur spontaneously. Despite modeling to facilitate sharing, Rogers-Warren, Warren, and Baer (1977) found that preschool children did not share, while Barton (1981) found that children needed to be shown and told how to share and then requested to rehearse or practice the skills to accomplish the goal. After the children began to increase their rates, prompting and praising of sharing in the natural group setting accomplished even more. Along similar lines, by combining instructions, modeling, role play, and feedback to teach their whole preschool class instruction-following, functional communication, delay of gratification, and friendship skills, Hanley et al. (2007) were able to promote a 74 percent decrease in problem behavior and a more than four-fold increase in preschool life skills. Also, Blew, Schwartz, and Luce (1985) found that involving normal peers as models of functional skills for children with autism was not successful until the models tutored and helped (modeled and instructed) the children with autism to practice those skills in the community. Similarly, investigators (Dukes, Brady, Scott, & Wilson, 2016) found that their intervention consisting of modeling, rehearsal, and praise was effective in teaching fire safety, to four- to five-year-old children with autism. The children were taught six skills to engage in once a fire alarm sounded using this modeling strategy:

1. Walk or run to the exit door.
2. Go outside.
3. Walk at least 20 steps from the building.
4. Face an adult and say "fire" or "fire alarm."
5. Remain at least 20 steps from the building until told to go else-where by an adult.
6. Complete these steps within three minutes following sounding of the alarm.

**Provide instructions, rules, and rationales.** Verbal instructions and rules can strengthen the effectiveness of modeling as in the Blew et al. (1985) study. Similarly, Zimmerman and Rosenthal (1974) found that novel and relatively stable abstract performances, like the Piagetian concept of "conservation," can be taught by combining modeling with verbal instructions and rules to guide the model's behavior. Also, recall how to assist youngsters to distribute their responding to optimize the number of reinforcers they received. Neef et al. (2004) combined modeling with a rationale, or the "thought process" that the successful model used.

Not only imitation, but also generalization and retention may increase when you explain in the observer's presence why a model's particular action is appropriate (Braukmann, Maloney, Fixsen, Phillips, & Wolf, 1974; Poche, Brouwer, & Swearingen, 1981; Zimmerman & Rosenthal, 1974). Have you seen this rule applied throughout this book? Note how in this section we have provided lists of rules and reasons for practicing specific methods to promote imitation, such as why you should use multiple models. Now is a good time for you to recite to yourself a rule like "I will maximize the positives and minimize the negatives for myself if I imitate the exemplary performances of those about whom I've been reading."

**Ensure simplicity of imitative prompt.** Avoid modeling behavior too complex for the observer to imitate. To give you a flavor of the significance of  this rule, watch and try to imitate someone operating a complicated instrument, or star dancers or athletic performers in action, and attempt to mimic them. You will see what we mean. According to Bandura (1965c), imitative behavior is likely to be acquired more rapidly if it includes some components that the individual previously has learned, and if the complexity of the stimulus is neither too great nor presented too rapidly. When behavior is too complex to be mimicked successfully, break it down into its components, explain the value of each, then arrange for each to be demonstrated and role-played.

Suppose Ms. Hau had been orienting Fern to her new work assignment: wrapping individual gift items. She selects another worker to demonstrate the novel job skill to Fern. Success would be more likely if Fern has had prior experience wrapping items. But suppose she hadn't? The complex behavioral sequence might be too much for her. In that case, Fern may first have to practice imitating each step separately before attempting the complete task. Once she masters the component steps, they can be connected with the others, one or two at a time, until she can execute the full pattern. (See Chapter 14 for guidelines in breaking down complex behavior for more effective instruction.)

Imagine you are a counselor or psychologist trying to teach a student how to firmly but politely refuse an offer of illicit drugs? How might you use modeling if the fully competent response failed to evoke the desired reaction? Yes, break the response down into its parts: effective use of eye contact, gestures, tone of voice, verbal statements, and so on. Video recordings can be especially helpful here as they permit replay as often as necessary, possibly even in slow motion.

**Reinforce the modeled performance.** Reinforcing the model's performance has been found to increase imitation (Bandura & Kupers, 1964; Bandura et al., 1963a, 1963b). As mentioned earlier, this technique may heighten the "prestige" of the model. Children who watched a model choose and receive reinforcers for picking one particular picture from a pair were more likely to imitate that choice than if the model's choice had been punished or ignored (Levy, McClinton, Rabinowitz, & Wolkin, 1974). In a related investigation, high-school juniors deciding on their careers listened to the audiotapes of other high-school students receiving reinforcers from peers and a counselor for such information-seeking behaviors as talking, reading, listening, writing, visiting, and observing (Stewart, 1969; see also Krumboltz & Thoresen, 1964; Lafleur & Johnson, 1972, for similar examples.)

The following episode illustrates alternative ways in which imitative antecedent stimuli may be used in the classroom: One day Dexter correctly describes the series of steps to follow in solving an algebraic equation. Yet the next day he omits a crucial element. The teacher can handle such a situation either by modeling the appropriate solution or can call on another child, Tim, to model it. Assuming Tim supplies the appropriate response, reinforcers would follow. Then, Dexter might be asked to try to solve the problem again. Having heard Tim praised for producing the correct answer, Dexter would be more likely to be correct, and earn some reinforcers for himself as well. Dexter then may more successfully solve that form of equation correctly in the future. Procedures like these can be used to increase all sorts of performances: from hanging up one's coat, to paying attention, to doing a competent job, or even to presenting flowers to one's lady love (see the cartoon below). Yes, reinforcing the model's behavior can be an especially effective good instructional strategy.

**Reinforce imitating.** Reinforcing the particular act of imitating a model would seem obvious, particularly in light of the message throughout this book: If you want behavior to increase, greet it with positive consequences! While this guideline is conceptually simple, we have found that reinforcing imitation in general may be easier said than done. Having seen the client misbehave recently, for instance, the managers may find it difficult to present reinforcers when the former miscreant imitates desired behavior. However, *if the imitative act is not reinforced, imitation is less likely to continue.* Barton (1981) found that when children who shared well were praised, the others in the group did not necessarily copy them. Later on, though, when those others did imitate and gain approbation for sharing, their rates increased. Ollendick, Dailey, and Shapiro (1983) made a similar discovery. Some children were praised while working on puzzles; others were not. For a while the "observing" children increased their performance just as the models did. But after a time, the number of puzzles the observers correctly completed began to drop off. When observers received intermittent praise for puzzle placement, though, they performed as well as the models. In other words, differential reinforcement can create classes restricted to specific categories, such as those that have been recognized as acceptable within a particular school setting, but are generalized across all of those acceptable instances. Remember the child who learned that he could safely imitate only some of Daddy's behavior, and even then, only some of the time.

As always, you need to examine the environment to assess whether the natural milieu will provide sufficient reinforcers for the behavior. If not, you need to provide supportive contingencies. Observers first must obtain frequent positive feedback for practicing and/or role-playing the modeled skill until a mastery criterion is achieved, after which reinforcers can be gradually thinned (Rickert et al., 1988).

Be careful, though, about which imitative acts you reinforce, because *saying* and *doing* are not the same. In one case (Rogers-Warren et al., 1977), preschoolers shared more only after reinforcers were limited to *accurate*, not fabricated reports of their sharing. So be certain that what the individual reporting says corresponds to what s/he *does*. If you lack accurate information on the correspondence between the person's saying and doing, we suggest you restrict your reinforcers to deeds rather than words.

**Combine with other procedures.** Modeling is commonly used as part of what is called **behavioral skills training (BST)**, which *consists of instructing, modeling, practicing, and providing feedback* (Miltenberger, 2008; 2012). For example, to improve interviewing skills of college students, investigators (Stocco, Thompson, Hart, & Soriano, 2017) used BST to teach skills such as answering typical questions they were likely to encounter, smiling, posture, and asking appropriate questions. As a result, the majority of participants improved their interviewing skills. Similarly, instructors used BST to teach restaurant-job skills to an 18-year-old student (Morgan & Wine, 2018). The skills included: setting up and running a commercial dishwasher, folding a napkin into a triangle, cleaning silverware, placing a knife and fork on a napkin and rolling the napkin around the utensils, busing a table, and cleaning the bathroom. They task analyzed the various skills and used BST to teach each sequence of steps for the various skills. Also, they combined BST with prompts during conversations to teach adolescents and young adults with developmental disabilities how to accept and give complements related to performance (activities or products), possessions (e.g., "I like your model airplane") and appearance (Hood, Olsen, Luczynski, & Randle, 2020). Within a single training session, Vladescu, Day-Watkins, Schnell, and Carrow (2020) also were successful in using a mannequin and common infant items to teach caregivers in various community-based agencies to avoid sudden unexpected infant deaths by arranging safe infant sleep environments. BST also was used to teach caregivers of children who engaged in aggression to position their bodies safely and how to prevent access to dangerous items (Metoyer, Fritz, Hunt, & Fletcher, 2020).

BST has been successfully used to teach parents of children with autism to become social skills trainers (Dogan, et al., 2017); to teach safe tackling skills to youth on a Pop Warner football team (Tai

& Miltenberger, 2017); and to teach a stepwise agility program to female soccer athletes to help prevent anterior cruciate ligament injuries (Harris et al., 2020). It also has been used to teach safe responding in the presence of potential poisons (e.g., Summers et al., 2011), firearms (Jostad, Miltenberger, Kelso, & Knudson, 2008), fire starting materials (Houvouras & Harvey, 2014), a variety of dangerous stimuli (Rossi, Vladescu, Reeve, & Gross, 2017), and abduction lures from strangers (e.g., Summers et al., 2011).

The BST intervention is not complete until the behavior you have taught is generalized (Chapter 21) and fluent (Chapter 17). Behaviors are more likely to last when both generalization and fluency have been incorporated into the intervention.

## PHYSICAL GUIDANCE

### Defined and Illustrated

Goal-setting, instructions, modeling, or a combination of these often succeed in prompting a desired response. Yet sometimes, as described earlier, none of these approaches suffice. At that point consider adding to the mix **physical guidance**, *in which the appropriate body part or parts are physically guided through the proper motion by another person.* "When you hit the ball, you must follow through, like this" instructs the golf pro, who then demonstrates. Despite watching closely and hearing and reading the instructions, the duffer fails to follow through appropriately. The pro then may physically guide the observer to follow through as he swings until he eventually "gets the feel" of the motion. If the duffer is coached properly, the physical prompting eventually can be faded.

Physical guidance can be a particularly useful way to teach young, inexperienced, or developmentally-delayed people new skills as well as to correct bad habits. By using a "putting through" or physical guidance procedure, Striefel and Wetherby (1973) taught a nonverbal boy with severe cognitive delays to follow instructions, such as "nod your head yes (or no)," "drink from the glass," and other such useful skills. Physical guidance was paired initially with the verbal instructions in a series of steps, eventually terminating in the appropriate responses occurring independent of any physical guidance. Barrera and Sulzer-Azaroff (1983), and Clarke, Remington, and Light (1986) used physical guidance to help severely handicapped youngsters learn to communicate by signing. Parents use similar methods to teach youngsters everyday skills like learning to dress, as in helping them to grab hold of the essential portion of the sweater and pull it over their heads, or pull their pants up. To permit imitative and instructional prompts to gain stimulus control, conscientious teachers correct mistakes, such as inappropriate pencil holding, by guiding the correct grasp, just as the sailing instructor guides the novice sailor's steering before gradually lessening his assistance.

### Using Physical Guidance Effectively

When using physical guidance to prompt a response, you need to follow several guidelines:

**Secure the client's cooperation and keep guidance to a minimum.** Relaxed learners can focus on the way their performance looks and feels while being guided through a motion, so they need to be comfortable with the contingency manager's touch. Tension or resistance will cause them to miss those essential cues. Resist the temptation to use force, because that could incite the individual to become agitated, evoking interfering reactions like struggling to escape, fighting, or crying. Besides being a motivating operation for competing emotional behaviors, using undue pressure is ethically questionable, while excessive force is dangerous! This general admonition is especially important during physical guidance, because the ultimate objective is for individuals eventually to respond independently.

The setting should be pleasant and comfortable and the contingency manager must speak calmly. Providing a few noncontingent reinforcers at the beginning of a training session and/or interspersing easier tasks throughout the session can be helpful too. Typical mature learners should adapt rapidly, permitting training to progress with ease.

**Help learners attend as well to *proprioceptive* cues**—*the stimuli or sensations that arise from* *within their own bodies*. Ask what they feel (tension, pain, comfort, calmness) and allow their answers to guide your own coaching.

**Transfer stimulus control.** Gradually transfer stimulus control (elaborated upon in Chapter 20) from the physical prompt to other discriminative stimuli to permit the learner eventually to follow instructions, the driver to respond to road conditions, and the writer to see and feel how to position the pencil properly.

**Tips for using physical guidance with tense or resistant special-needs clients.** If people with special needs resist or appear anxious or fearful, you should proceed cautiously and try the following techniques:

- Wait patiently for them to calm down before you take each new step.
- Maintain physical contact and move passively with the client if necessary until the struggling ceases and you are able to guide the movements gently.
- Keep the amount of pressure exerted to the minimum required to guide the movement properly.

Consider providing preliminary relaxation training (see Cautela & Groden, 1978, for a relaxation training manual for adults and children, and children with special needs; also Fisher & Laschinger, 2001; Fricchione, 2004; Lohaus & Klein-Hessling, 2003; and other sources on relaxation therapy).

Sometimes, physical guidance is necessary and/or more effective than the use of the *tell* and *show* prompts. For example, Sasaki et al. (2016) demonstrated that a patient with severe hemiplegia and cognitive disorder after having a stroke only successfully drove his wheelchair after the use of physical guidance. During baseline, instructions and modeling were used; however, the individual did not successfully drive the wheelchair until physical guidance was utilized and faded.

## SUMMARY AND CONCLUSIONS

Several specific prompting techniques were presented in this chapter: the *tell*, *show*, and *guide* procedures. Before you select any, be sure a prompt actually is necessary. Then decide which one or what combination to use. Your best bet is to begin by interposing the natural $S^D$ just prior to when you anticipate the response. If the response is not emitted, use instructions, modeling, and/or physical guidance, whichever is most relevant and least contrived or intrusive.

If prompting is not effective, perhaps the participant must first be trained in the skills of following instructions, imitating, or moving under guidance. If imitative cues fail, perhaps you need a more appropriate model to perform and receive reinforcers for the behavior. Or, as pointed out earlier, you may need to teach your client to look for behavior that receives reinforcement and imitate it. Whichever single or combination of procedures you select, always consider the factors that influence its effectiveness. Once the response does occur reliably, then you can begin to transfer or fade control from one of the auxiliary, or artificial, $S^D$s—the *guide*, *show*, or *tell* prompts—to the appropriate $S^D$, a topic we return to in Chapter 20. As always, providing reinforcers according to the appropriate three-term contingency should continue until the behavior is established firmly. Afterward, you will want to deliver reinforcers less and less frequently, but always contingent on evidence of continued stimulus control.

See the *Summary Table for Teaching and Prompting Behavior* starting on the next page.

# SUMMARY TABLE
# PROCEDURES FOR TEACHING AND PROMPTING BEHAVIOR

## Promoting Stimulus Control via Differential Reinforcement

| Operation/Procedure | Maximizing Effectiveness | Temporal Properties | Durability of Effect | Other Features |
|---|---|---|---|---|
| **Differentially Reinforcing:** Reinforce responses only in presence of $S^D$s; withhold reinforcers in presence of $S^A$s and $S^{D_p}$s | 1. Identify relevant stimulus properties<br>2. Emphasize relevant stimulus properties<br>3. Use differential reinforcement consistently<br>4. Apply, then fade prompts<br>5. Identify & manage $S^D$s for interfering behaviors | Gradual | Temporary until stimulus control firmly established; then, given intermittent differential reinforcement, long-lasting | Risk of over-dependence on supplemental prompts or over-selectivity unless supplemental prompts faded |
| **Matching to Sample:** Prompt individual to select the stimulus from two or more alternatives, one (or sometimes more) of which match or correspond to a standard sample | 1. Teach identity matching via matching-to-sample before teaching discriminations<br>2. Present sample in unsystematic order and not more than twice in a row<br>3. Usually provide at least three alternatives for each trail<br>4. Randomly vary position of alternative<br>5. Avoid novel incorrect alternatives (may be rejected by learner based on novelty)<br>6. Differentially reinforce correct pointing or selecting<br>7. Arrange comparison stimuli between trails out of learner's sight to avoid providing extraneous cures (e.g., may select last item you touch)<br>8. Use errorless teaching methods | Gradual | Long-lasting once stimulus control firmly established | -- |

## Prompting Behavior via Stimulus Change

| Operation/Procedure | Maximizing Effectiveness | Temporal Properties | Durability of Effect | Other Features |
|---|---|---|---|---|
| **Stimulus Change:** Present or remove discriminative stimulus | 1. $S^D$s manageable<br>2. Stimulus control well established<br>3. Select most powerful $S^D$s<br>4. Combine with other procedures, especially differential reinforcement | Rapid change | Continues as long as $S^D$(s) present | May be affected by ongoing competing or supportive contingencies |

## Goal Setting

| Operation/Procedure | Maximizing Effectiveness | Temporal Properties | Durability of Effect | Other Features |
|---|---|---|---|---|
| Goal setting: Specify performance level or quality to be achieved | 1. Select challenging but achievable objectives<br>2. Use participative goal setting<br>3. Develop specific goals for specific individuals, groups or units within organization<br>4. Select challenging but attainable sub-goals and goals<br>5. Intermittently reinforce goal attainment to maintain performance at criterion level | Depends on history of reinforce-ment for achieving goals | Lasts as long as achieving goal level reinforced intermittently | (May function as an MO) |

## Prompting and Behavioral Skills Training (BST)

| Operation | Maximizing Effectiveness | Temporal Properties | Durability of Effect | Other Characteristics |
|---|---|---|---|---|
| **Prompting:** Temporarily apply a contrived but effective discriminative stimulus ($S^D$) in place of (or in addition to) stimulus designated ultimately to become functional $S^D$ | 1. Identify effective prompts<br>2. Minimize complexity of prompt<br>3. Assess for and select most promising prompting strategy<br>4. Avoid conditions for promoting stimulus overselectivity, overdependence or dependence on contrived or irrelevant cues<br>5. Correct for overdependence and stimulus overselectivity<br>6. Fade prompts as rapidly as possible without compromising the behavior of concern | Rapid | Lasts as long as prompt present | If not faded appropriately, may create overdependence on prompts |

## Prompting and BST (cont.)

| | | | | |
|---|---|---|---|---|
| **Instructions:** Tell, say, sign, demonstrate, display pictorial image or guide the behavior | 1. Ensure verbal control exists or teach it<br>2. Use $S^D$s familiar to learner or teach effective $S^D$s<br>3. Present rapidly<br>4. Combine with differential reinforcement, goal setting, and modeling if needed<br>5. Fade supplementary instructions | Rapid unless need first to develop $S^D$s | Lasts as long as functional $S^D$s are present | May create overdependence if supplementary instructions not faded |
| **Modeling:** Demonstrate or "show" to prompt imitative response | 1. Teach generalized imitation, if absent from repertoire<br>2. Be sure model attends to modeled behavior and displays delayed imitation<br>3. Select models who<br>   • are competent in the skill of interest<br>   • are similar to client,<br>   • may have been seen experiencing difficulty initially learning skill of interest<br>   • share positive prior experiences with client<br>   • are prestigious<br>4. Select multiple models<br>5. Highlight similarities between client and models<br>6. Encourage rehearsal of modeled behavior<br>7. Provide instructions, rules &/or rationale for behavior<br>8. Keep behavior simple<br>9. Reinforce model's behavior<br>10. Reinforce act of imitation<br>11. Fade out the modeling | Rapid, assuming behavior in response repertoire and under imitative control | Long lasting if imitative response intermittently reinforced sufficiently often | Positive |
| **Behavioral Skills Training (BST)** | 1. Use instructions with maximal effectiveness as specified above<br>2. Use modeling with maximal effectiveness<br>3. Provide lots of role playing and/or practice until fluency is achieved<br>4. Provide effective reinforcement | Moderate to rapid | Can be long lasting | |
| **Physical Guidance:** Physically guide the performance | 5. Secure client's cooperation<br>6. Guide minimally<br>7. Avoid forcing<br>8. Help learner attend to *proprioceptive* cues<br>9. Gradually fade out physical guidance (i.e., use *graduated guidance*) | Moderate to rapid | Long lasting if artificial prompts faded and independent response reinforced | |

*Chapter 19*

# Teaching, Expanding and Refining Verbal Behavior

## Goals

1. Define and illustrate *verbal behavior* and *verbal operant*.
2. List the four controlling antecedent variables and the two consequential conditions essential for acquiring verbal behavior.
3. Describe the value of a functional approach to communication and what that involves.
4. Define and describe the functional value of *duplic behavior, echoics*, and *imitative responding*.
5. Describe at least two echoic training methods.
6. Define, illustrate, and discuss the importance of *mands*.
7. Identify and describe at least three methods of training people to mand.
8. Describe *functional communication training* (FCT).
9. Define, illustrate, and discuss the importance of *tacts*.
10. Discuss and illustrate the difference between *tacting* and *naming*.
11. Identify and describe at least two methods of training people to tact.
12. Define, illustrate, and discuss the importance of *intraverbals*.
13. Describe at least two intraverbal training methods.
14. Differentiate among and exemplify *echoic, intraverbal, tact*, and *mand responding*.
15. Describe how to teach listener behavior.
16. Briefly describe the PEAK or the VB-MAPP
17. Briefly describe and illustrate *augmentative verbal communication systems* such as the *Picture Exchange Communication System*© (PECS) and others.

18. Define Relational Frame Theory and how it differs from a Skinnarian approach to verbal behavior.
19. Define and provide an example of *verbal relating*.
20. Define Acceptance and Commitment Training or Therapy.

\*\*\*\*\*\*\*\*\*\*\*

A pair of cave-dwellers ambled along the edge of a wooded area. Hanging down from a tree was a luscious pear. The male reached up, grabbed it, and gobbled it down. The female, who hadn't eaten for quite a while, felt her stomach grumbling. Inspecting the branches of the tree, she saw several shimmering yellow pears. She stretched and stood on her toes, but couldn't quite reach them. She even rolled a rock beneath the branch, but that didn't extend her reach sufficiently. "Ugh, ugh," she pointed. Finally, her companion "got it." Scaling the tree, he picked several juicy pears and presented them to her.

What is wrong with that picture?

Probably your first reaction was: "Why didn't her companion (that clod!), help her in the first place? Couldn't he see her attempts to reach the pear? That she was hungry? Why didn't she say something? And if she couldn't talk, surely, she must have grunted, rubbed her stomach, or conveyed her hunger some other way."

Of course, you are right! We agree he was a clod. His companion used a variety of methods to try and get him to respond (i.e., she tried to communicate), even if she was not able to speak in words: facial expressions, reaching, climbing, maybe even the rumbling of her innards spoke for her. But to be of assistance, her companion would have had to be capable of understanding her communicative efforts. How would he know to get her a pear?

No doubt the ability to change what someone else does by making sounds or gestures was available to our prehistoric ancestors, because other species are able to communicate in a multitude of ways. (See Maeterlinck's 1901 classic, *The Life of the Bee*, to learn of the extensive repertoires bees apply to manage the performances of their fellow hive dwellers; for instance, which ones are to head in what direction to gather nectar.) If you have a pet, you know what we mean. Perhaps your dog brings you the leash or scratches at the door to let you know when he wants to go out. Does your cat follow you, meowing all the while to tell you it is supper time? Because the behavior of the female in our story eventually did serve to gain her a reinforcer via the mediation of the "clod," she was behaving *verbally*. We define **verbal behavior** as *behavior reinforced through the mediation of other persons. It includes any spoken or non-spoken form of communication that helps people to get what they want and avoid what they don't want.*

Probably we all agree that the ability to produce and respond to verbal stimuli is one of the most important skill sets we humans possess. Yet verbal behavior is also one of the most challenging behaviors to study and analyze. Complex behaviors such as interacting socially, solving problems, thinking (covertly speaking and forming images), and detecting and understanding simple and complex topics such as history, politics, religion and pop culture are all heavily dependent on verbal skills. Yes, everyone behaves verbally with some degree of facility, and usually we recognize when others are doing it. More challenging, though, is providing a clear operational definition of verbal behavior, particularly in its troublesome forms. Consider the various approaches to this dilemma.

Some have addressed verbal problems *topographically*—in terms of their shape or form, as in poor word choices or enunciation or disfluent speech. Indeed, applied behavior analysts have applied many of the teaching/training methods previously mentioned in this text to address those sorts of problems. Examples include the shaping methods Guess (1969) used to teach students with developmental delays to distinguish and correctly use the plural form, and that Wheeler and Sulzer (1970) applied to guide a youngster with autism to use the present participle form in a sentence. Additional instances include Bailey, Timbers, Phillips and Wolf's (1971) use of a combination of peer modeling, shaping, approval, contingent points, and feedback as a function of progressively clearer articulation of /l/, /r/, /th/, and /ting/, while Mirenda and Donnellan (1986) applied similar tactics to promote improvement in conversational skills. More recently, though, addressing verbal problems from a *functional* perspective has shown itself to be even more successful, and as a consequence, has become more prevalent. This perspective is founded in Skinner's analysis of the *functional* role verbal behavior plays in our lives.

## B.F. SKINNER'S ANALYSIS OF VERBAL BEHAVIOR

In his text on the topic, *Verbal Behavior*, Skinner (1957) suggested two general functional classes of behaviors that lead to reinforcers: One consists of *acting directly on the environment* (the male gathering fruit for himself) and the other is that *mediated by the behavior of others*—**verbal behavior** (the male detecting the woman's food-seeking behaviors and then interceding on her behalf).[1] Moreover, Skinner proposed that *verbal behavior is learned, increases in quantity and breadth, and is maintained in the same way as nonverbal behavior* (that is via specific relations to contingencies of reinforcement). *Verbal behavior is composed of one or more verbal operants.* A **verbal operant**, then, *is a single learned instance of verbal behavior, such as saying Hi" or "How are you?"* Skinner also distinguished between *speaker* and *listener* verbal operants. He contended that natural contingencies produce verbal behavior as children interact within their own verbal communities. He also pointed out that in those cases in which their verbal behavior fails to develop at a reasonable rate, it is important to instruct those people to behave verbally as speakers and also to react appropriately to the verbal stimuli provided by speakers (i.e., to be a listener). Moreover, Skinner stated that although, in some cases, learning one type of behavior facilitates learning another, *speaker and listener behaviors are quite separate and represent different functional response classes.*

Skinner avoided using the common terms *expressive language* and *receptive language*. Rather than seeing them as merely different manifestations of the same "underlying cognitive processes," he viewed them in terms of the functional relations between behaviors and their controlling stimulus events (or antecedents and consequences). In the process, he rejected the notion that individuals first must learn the "meaning" of words as listeners and then use the words as speakers. Instead, Skinner explained that, "The behaviors of the speaker and listener taken together compose what may be called the total verbal episode" (p. 2). Furthermore, your own recognition that the listener serves multiple functions within the verbal episode (e.g., as when a spoken word—e.g., "good," "right"— serves both as a discriminative stimulus and as a reinforcer) should heighten your ability to apply behavior procedures to promote language development.

Skinner also saw verbal behavior as *behavior that is reinforced via the mediation of others, not as* "communication," because while communication implies transmission of information, it may be unidirectional. And moreover, that term omits the essential critical function—*that the behavior (verbal behavior) is reinforced via the mediation of others.* Our esteemed colleague, Fred Keller, transmitted information as a telegrapher (Keller, 2009), but if he did not decode and find the message interesting nor receive any response (gain reinforcing stimuli), he was engaging in motor but not verbal behavior. Were you to read *The Life of the Bee* to me in French, unless I simply enjoyed hearing the cadence or sounds, that would fail to serve as a reinforcer; and it would not fall under the category of verbal behavior. Were you to read it to me in English, and I were to listen and find the information fascinating, what you were doing would qualify as verbal behavior. So, would any further discussion of the contents of the book, because we probably would be swapping reinforcing information along with paying rapt attention to one another.

---

[1]The verbal response also may be self-mediated, as when one takes on different roles such as talking overtly or covertly to oneself—reviewing, preparing a speech, solving a problem, etc. (e.g., playing the part of both speaker and listener).

Given verbal behavior's critical impact on people's lives, it should come as no surprise to you that we are devoting a chapter to the topic. This includes methods for teaching or promoting or overcoming difficulties related to verbal behavior. Let us hasten to confess, though, that, as with many of the other chapters in this book, this one only touches lightly on the topic by illustrating and explaining a few fundamental points and by briefly describing strategies behavior analysts have used successfully to address verbal behavioral challenges. You should be able to expand and enrich your own mastery of the subject by studying Skinner's 1957 text, other texts that address verbal behavior, and articles from the journals *The Analysis of Verbal Behavior, Behavior Analysis in Practice,* and *Journal of Applied Behavior Analysis* (to name a few), and attending educational events offered by behavior analytic specialists in the area of verbal behavior.

Skinner (1957) hardly has been alone in his attempts to explain verbal behavior in all its richness. Others concerned with communication have attempted to study, describe, and/or clarify its evolution and function. In fact, outside of the behavior analytic field, linguists (e.g., Chomsky, 1959) have taken issue with Skinner's formulation of language, usually because many linguists give priority to structural considerations, such as what makes a sentence grammatical, over functional ones, like how to teach advanced students like you to distinguish form from function. (Among others, Palmer [2006] has offered a convincing behavioral rebuttal to Chomsky's position.) The topic of verbal behavior even has sparked a healthy discussion within our own field of behavior analysis (see, for example, Chase & Danforth, 1991; Hayes & Hayes.1989; Hayes,1994; Leigland 1997, 2007; Barnes-Holmes, Barnes-Holmes, McHugh, & Hayes, 2004; Fienup, 2019; Barnes-Holmes, Barnes-Holmes, & Cullinan, 2000b). For instance, those along with other scholars and practitioners have exchanged perspectives on the pros and cons and utility of the concept of *derived relational responding* to describe the development of language skills. More about this later in the chapter, but for now, we proceed by emphasizing particular approaches that have contributed demonstrably to successfully solving the actual verbal-behavioral challenges currently facing many people in current society based upon Skinner's analysis of verbal behavior.

Rather than simply describing (spoken and non-spoken) language topographically (based on its shape or form), Skinner's framework has provided us with a useful way to *functionally analyze* verbal behavior, and as a consequence, to be able to do something about it when that class of behavior is aberrant and/or deficient. For that purpose, he focused on the relation between the behavior of the speaker and that of the listener, including the self as listener. This perspective has enabled practitioners to treat an array of communicative disorders, as well as to devise ways to promote effective communicative functioning.

> Skinner identified *four controlling antecedent* (italics added) variables of verbal behavior: 1) some *state of deprivation* or *aversive stimulation*, 2) some aspect of the environment, 3) other verbal behavior, and 4) one's own verbal behavior. He also identified two *consequence conditions*: 1) something related to the state of deprivation/aversive stimulation or 2) social (what Skinner referred to as "educational") consequences. His analysis was based on these variables as they occur in isolation or in combination. In describing these operants, he developed new terminology to describe these functional relations to minimize confusion with lay terminology or vocabulary from other professions. (Frost & Bondy, 2006, p. 105)

As a reader, your ability to analyze the utility of a particular verbal behavior should guide you to design more effective interventions, especially formal instructional strategies. Grasping the function of each class of behavior (what it gains the "speaker") will better prepare you to manage antecedents and consequences to produce more optimal learner performance; and you will be less likely to omit crucial skills, as in teaching students to memorize addition facts without also instructing them about how to apply those facts under various circumstances.

Considering the breadth and complexity of function that verbal behavior serves in modern society, probably you will agree that any attempt to cover the subject thoroughly would not be feasible in a text of this nature. Nonetheless, the topic of verbal behavior has been the subject of considerable recent behavior-analytic investigations, especially among the many millions of children world-wide with various sorts of language deficits, (e.g., nearly eight percent of children ages three to 17 in the United States display some form of communicative disorder(s) (Black, Vahratian, & Hoffman, 2015). So, instead of attempting to completely cover the subject in all its basic and sophisticated forms, here we emphasize those aspects about which society currently seems to have its greatest concern: promoting the more fundamental verbal operants, including *mands*, *tacts*, *echoics*, and *intraverbals*, among those who have failed to acquire such behavior in natural environments. Remember, that as we initiate this discussion, you should recognize that we treat words in terms of their *functions*, not their *topographies* (form or shape). Saying a particular word, like "water," (one topography—form or shape) can serve multiple functions, assuming that appropriate reinforcement contingencies are in place:

- requesting a drink of water (a *mand*)
- responding to someone pointing to water on the floor (a *tact*)
- describing the action of someone watering a plant (a *tact*)
- repeating "water" when Mom asks "Do you want water?" (an *echoic*)
- answering "What is 'agua' in English?" (an *intraverbal*)

As you will learn, identifying the *function* of particular verbal operants is far more important than simply being able to label them or translate their definitions. To fulfill this aim, we turn to a description of the classes of verbal behavior that Skinner and his followers have adopted.

# THE DUPLIC

## The Duplic Defined

The ability to duplicate a spoken or gestural model often serves learners well. The teacher of Spanish pronounces the phrase "Buenos dias" at the start of class. Her students imitate her so often in their reply, that eventually saying "Buenos dias" becomes second nature. Jack Michael (1982) used the term **duplic** to describe "… a situation in which the response form is controlled by a verbal stimulus and the response product has formal similarity to the controlling stimulus (p. 3). The duplicated stimulus can be a spoken word, a sign, a gesture or a written stimulus.

Both **echoic** (*repeating or vocally imitating the verbal behavior of another person*, as in parroting what another has said) and **imitative responding** (*duplicating with point-to-point correspondence the physical action of another*, such as producing a gestural sign) fall under the category of *duplics*. When I say "stickie," and my one-year-old daughter then says "stickie," that is an example of an *echoic*. An illustration of an *imitative response* is a person signing "peace" (e.g., the sign for peace) by mimicking precisely the physical movement of a model. As we saw in Chapter 18, imitating precisely often is critical to learning many complex tasks.

## Duplic Training

Training people to echo is a fairly universal effort because echoics serve various extremely important functions. Consider how children typically learn to communicate, and you immediately will see the importance of echoics. From early on, babies attempt to master echoic repertoires. Despite not anticipating any particular response, parents of infants and young children often speak to their babies: "I love you." "Hi Bubba, you're such a good girl." They sing songs and recite nursery rhymes. In return, their babies babble and slowly begin to approximate those same sounds "ba," "d," "ma," etc. When they do, the parent or caregiver responds with powerful reinforcers: "Wow! You said 'Ma'," along with lots of smiles, hugs, and kisses. Young children's growing skillfulness in repeating basic sounds impacts on their ability to repeat words. That, in turn, promotes their acquisition of other spoken verbal operants. In fact, in-depth research has revealed that the relation between the extent to which parents talk to their children is directly tied to the children's subsequent linguistic ability and cognitive development

(Hart & Risley, 1995; see review by Sulzer-Azaroff, 1997). Moreover, echoic prompts are the most common form of prompt used by teachers and parents to teach other verbal operants such as mands, tacts, and intraverbals, as you will soon read.

## Echoic Training

Although the goal of echoic training is to enable the speaker to repeat the trainer's sounds, words, or phrases, generally the end goal is to transfer the response form to other, generally more advanced, verbal operants. Shaping probably is the most commonly used form of echoic training: The teacher presents a vocal verbal (spoken) stimulus and reinforces the student's successive approximations toward the sample. For example, the trainer says "car" and differentially reinforces sounds that progressively match that sample presentation: "c-," "c-a," until "c-a-r" is achieved. Adults, older siblings or peers use that technique quite naturally. However, if opportunities to provide such guidance don't occur often enough, it would be advisable to engineer them, as is done in *incidental teaching* (discussed below). Also, during training, skillful speech therapists may use mirrors to point out or physically prompt children's correct lip or tongue positions.

In a fairly standard echoic training situation for people with delayed communicative repertoires, the therapist presents a vocal model "car" and provides reinforcers contingent on the student's successive approximation to an acceptable echoic response. Another echoic training procedure incorporates joint presentation of stimuli and automatic reinforcement: The therapist follows her vocal model (e.g., "ba") with the delivery of a preferred item, such as a toy. This practice is based on the rationale that after the sound is combined with an already-established reinforcer, the sound itself will become a learned reinforcer, so the child's vocalizations are automatically strengthened by the sounds they produce (this process probably also shapes the vocalizations of typically-developing children, where they hear themselves making sounds that more and more closely resemble the reinforcing sounds they hear their caregivers producing).

Among others, Miguel, Carr, and Michael (2002), Sundberg, Michael, Partington, and Sundberg (1996), Smith, Michael, and Sundberg (1996), and Yoon and Bennett (2000) conducted a series of studies of such procedures, which they call stimulus-stimulus pairing.[2] Results revealed increases in children's rates of vocal behavior. After Carroll and Klatt (2008) used this procedure to increase vocalizations, they were able to subsequently bring vocalizations under echoic control by using direct reinforcement. In other words, stimulus-stimulus pairing promoted an increase in the client's vocalization rate, which, in turn, served as an approximation that could successively be shaped into a recognizable word. It can be argued that because typically-developing newborns have a preference for their mom's voice (DeCasper & Fifer, 1980) or their native language (Jusczyk, 1993), their acquisition of verbal behavior is already influenced by a "natural" stimulus-stimulus pairing. Thus, verbal play itself can be reinforcing and can serve as building blocks for future verbal operants. Moreover, it is important to have a baseline of behavior to reinforce because some children with disabilities vocalize at very low rates. In such cases stimulus-stimulus pairing can be an important first step in a language program designed to increase verbal play as reinforcing, and to serve as a building block for future operants. It should be pointed out, though, that although stimulus-stimulus pairing has been successfully taught, the results may be fleeting and inconsistent (e.g., Esch, Carr, & Michael, 2005; Normand & Knoll, 2006; Yoon & Feliciano, 2007).

With that said, Lepper and Petursdottir (2017) sought to evaluate if the stimulus-stimulus pairing procedure was more effective if it was presented contingent on a response rather than on a time-based procedure (which was generally how this procedure has been applied). The two stimulus-stimulus pairing procedures that were compared were: 1) Response-contingent pairing (RCP), where a presentation of a neutral stimulus paired with a reinforcer was contingent on an observing response (touching a button); and 2) Response-independent

---

[2]Note that pairing does not necessarily imply that one stimulus predicts that another will occur; if S1 and S2 often occur together but S1 and S2 also often occur by themselves, S1 may not become a good predictor of S2. Procedures defined in terms of pairing will work most reliably if the paired stimuli rarely occur separately.

pairing (RIP), where the presentation of the neutral stimulus paired with a reinforcer was presented on a time-based procedure that was yoked (meaning the schedule was the same so as to remove that as a potential reason for the results) to the presentation in the RCP condition. Results demonstrated that the RCP procedure was more effective compared to the RIP procedure. Clinically, these results suggest that it may be beneficial to present the stimulus-stimulus pairing procedure contingent on a simple response rather than on a time-based schedule. For example, a therapist could say "look at me" and when the child looks, present the stimulus-stimulus pairing (i.e., presenting a vocal stimulus with another stimulus) plus reinforcement for looking. More research, however, is needed to elucidate the variance in when this procedure is and is not effective at increasing vocalization in individuals who are non-verbal.

Stimulus-stimulus pairing has been successfully utilized by parents of children with Autism Spectrum Disorder to increase the vocal production of targeted and non-targeted echoic sounds by addressing their child's low levels of babbling/verbal behavior (Barry, Holloway, & Gunning, 2018). After initial increases in echoic sounds, parents were taught how to use direct reinforcement to further their child's babbling/verbal behavior. The authors assessed social validity of the procedure by asking the parents to rate their experience with the intervention regarding: 1) How confident they felt about implementing the procedure; 2) if it was difficult to find time to conduct the intervention; 3) if they noticed an increase in their child's babbling/verbal behavior; 4) if they felt the intervention provided them with meaningful one-on-one time with their child; and 5) if their child was less likely to engage in problematic behaviors during the intervention. Parents reported positive results across all questions (e.g., they were confident, it was not difficult to find time, they noticed an increase in the child's babbling, they felt the intervention provided meaningful one-on-one time, and that their child seemed to enjoy the sessions).

A related method for increasing echoic behavior is to directly reinforce increases in rates of vocalizations. The trainer sets up an echoic situation and reinforces the echoic response. For example, if a child is saying "ba-ba-ba," the behavior analyst says "ba-ba-ba." After the child repeats "ba-ba-ba" once again, that presumably echoic response is reinforced. This interaction sets up the conditions for promoting echoic behavior, which in turn may serve as the basis for further shaping of communicative skills (Lovaas, Berberich, Perloff, & Schaeffer, 1991). Again, when implementing verbal behavior programs, it is important to remember that one must have behavior to reinforce, thus increased vocalizations of any kind can lead to future success.

## THE MAND

Human verbal-skills repertoires vary greatly. Included in those repertoires are, among others, the *range* of their vocabularies from quite limited to the extraordinary; the *complexity* of what they say overtly (aloud) or covertly (i.e., by "thinking"); the *fluency* or smoothness, and especially for present purposes, the *functional utility* of their communications.

What do we mean by *functional utility*? As in all other forms of operant behavior, in plain language, **functional utility** *gets you what you want.* Skinner (1957) extended to *speaking* (overtly or covertly—aloud or as "thinking") and *listening* the perspectives he had presented earlier to describe and interpret other classes of operant behavior. "If the listener's behavior is reinforcing for the speaker in his current state of deprivation or aversive stimulation, the speaker's behavior will be affected" (p. 151). He then proceeded to identify various classes of verbal behavior in terms of how useful they are for the individual.

### The Mand Defined

Skinner defined the **mand** as "*a verbal operant in which the response is reinforced by a characteristic consequence and is therefore under the functional control of relevant conditions of deprivation or aversive stimulation and...the response has no specified relations to a prior stimulus*" (1957, pp. 35–36). Notice, the specific form is not limited to speaking aloud in this definition. It can and does include gestures such as pointing; facial expressions like displaying eager anticipation; formal sign languages; picture exchanges; activation of communication devices; and even dangerous or irritating actions, as long as they work to reinforce the behavior of the "speaker" often enough to maintain it. Earlier, especially in the sections on *functional assessment*, you encountered many examples of the problems that may arise as a result of people's restricted ability to mand, *to get what they want, when they want it*, in ways acceptable to their listeners. Clearly, the mand

has to be one of the most essential classes of communicative behavior.

In an attempt to refine Skinner's definition, Jack Michael (1988) proposed to define the **mand** as "*a type of verbal operant in which a particular response form is reinforced by a characteristic consequence and is therefore under the functional control of the establishing (i.e., motivating) operation relevant to that consequence.*" As such, it "has no specified relation to a prior *discriminative stimulus*" (pp. 7). Said a bit differently, *a mand describes a verbal response in which a person "requests" something* (i.e., a specific reinforcer) *and the "request-ing*" (or *demand*ing) *is controlled by* a specific relation between the motivating antecedent and the reinforcer. *The individual uses the mand to request a reinforcing object or event.* It is important to note that a mand only becomes a mand once it has been reinforced. Examples include: When deprived of food for a time, the (hungry—the MO) child "asks" for a cookie and her mom gives it to her, because when she was hungry yesterday she asked for a cookie and received a cookie. After tasting her dinner, your houseguest detects its blandness and asks you to pass the salt, because formerly under similar stimulus conditions she has asked for and received salt. An employee who is uncomfortable wearing a suit comments, "Gosh, it sure would be nice to have casual Fridays" and the boss announces that henceforth everyone can wear jeans to work on Fridays. Again, this mand is based on the employee's past history—that when he has asked for something he has received it as well as the fact that he has been more comfortable wearing jeans than a suit. A husband asks his wife where the keys to the car are and his wife tells him they are hanging by the door. In this last case, although posed as a question, the stimulus functions as a mand. (Can you identify the specific motivating antecedent–reinforcer relation in the above examples?) See Table 19.1 for a simple analysis of those examples.

Understanding why the mand is so important should not be difficult for you. Mands tend to get people what they desire. But if you would rather not take our word for how important mands are, just keep track of and analyze all the verbal interactions you produce every day. Actually, it has been suggested that half of an adult's daily verbal interactions consist of mands, including for objects

**TABLE 19.1   Examples of Mands**

| Motivating Operation or Antecedent | Mands | Reinforcing Consequences |
|---|---|---|
| Child is hungry, wants cookie. | *"Cookie"* | Mom gives child cookie |
| Bland food | *"Pass the salt"* | Gets salt and sprinkles on food before eating |
| Uncomfortable in suit | *"Gosh, it would be nice to have casual Fridays."* | Gets to wear jeans |
| Needs to go to work; keys missing. | *"Where are my keys?"* | *"Keys are hanging by the door"*; finds keys and leaves for work |

and actions as well as for information (Michael, 1988). Yet, many people with language delays simply do not have the verbal skills to produce mands in socially appropriate ways when they need help, directions, water, food, bathroom facilities and other such valuable reinforcers. Sundberg (1983) pointed out that "Manding is often quite weak for a language-delayed person because the majority of traditional language instruction mainly involves receptive language and procedures for teaching the names of objects and actions" (p. 296). Given the importance of manding, the question is not "*should* we train mands?" but rather, how best to do it.

## Mand Training

First things first. Before a mand is to be taught, a motivating operation (MO) needs to be in effect at the time of training. *This is arranged by either capturing a naturally occurring motivating event or by contriving one* (Sundberg, 1993a). Remember, the mand is controlled by the mere existence of a motivating antecedent. In fact, this is true for any reinforced behavior. Without motivating operations, there are no reinforcers. Similarly, without motivating antecedents, there are no mands.

One way to ensure an MO is to capitalize on one that occurs naturally. For example, a parent may take advantage of the fact that a child has not had anything to eat or drink in a while. At that time, either food or a drink would function as an effective form of reinforcer for the mand "eat, please" or "drink, please." But suppose the child just returned from Grandma's house where he received a big serving of ice cream and cake? The parent would need to set up situations that establish events as motivating antecedents for manding (e.g., withhold cookies for a couple of hours to set the stage for cookies to be reinforcing; provide salty foods to enhance the reinforcing value of fluids, and so on).

Contriving MOs sometimes can be complicated. For example, how would you set the occasion for a toddler's "asking" for information (e.g., to teach the child to ask where his "blanky" is, so he will then go readily to bed)? When manding for information (i.e., asking questions), the relevant motivator sets the occasion for the individual behaving to gain access to the reinforcer. The value of the motivating antecedent is the extent to which it increases the likelihood that other antecedents will enable the individual to obtain the reinforcer. Suppose a child doesn't know where her "blanky" is. She might ask her mother "Where's blanky?" because at that precise moment the information is especially valuable. Sundberg, Loeb, Hale, and Eigenheer (2002) contrived motivating antecedents to teach three children with autism to mand information by removing the toy from its typical location, then instructing them to get the toy. Teaching consisted of shaping the child's asking *where* a toy was (experiment 1); then, by answering "I gave it to a teacher," they set the stage for the child's asking *who* had the toy (experiment 2).

In a recent example, Landa, Frampton, and Shillingsburg (2020) successfully taught four children with Autism Spectrum Disorder to mand for (request) information from their social partners. Specifically, participants were asked questions about their social partners (e.g., what was the social partner's age, how many sisters did the social partner have, what was the social partner's favorite movie). If the child answered without manding for the information from their social partner, it was considered "guessing" and was not reinforced. Initially, they prompted the child to request the information from their social partner, then faded the prompts later on. Only responses about their social partners following manding for information were considered correct (i.e., the information was only considered to be not guessing if they asked the social partner for the information) and were followed by praise and tokens. In another example, Kahlow, et al. (2019) taught children with Autism Spectrum Disorder to mand for information with respect to "when" something would be available. Specifically, they used an audio model prompt to teach the three participants to ask "when do I get it, or when can I have it?" in response to being told a preferred item was not available. Researchers demonstrated that the participants were able to maintain and generalize the skill (i.e., asking "when").

*A related intervention for teaching manding is to contrive motivating stimuli ($S^M$s).* You will recall from Chapter 15 that motivating stimuli are those antecedents that heighten or lessen the reinforcing value of a stimulus, and that increase or reduce the likelihood that particular learned actions permit the individual access to those stimuli. Be careful about simply *assuming* that a motivating antecedent, whether natural or contrived, is in place in any given situation. We are responsible for *ensuring* that it is. In fact, several studies have illustrated that functional mands can only be established when *currently relevant* MOs are incorporated into the training situation (Bowman, Fisher, Thompson, & Piazza, 1997; Sundberg et al., 2002). Moreover, *presuming* that a motivator is operating is not the equivalent of *ensuring* that several current functionally-reinforcing objects are available for consumption. Wallace et al. (2006) demonstrated that unless an item currently has a reinforcing function, manding will not occur. (And don't forget that people rapidly satiate on many items and events. The fifteenth time in a row you receive praise for an accomplishment or a serving of your most favorite chocolate candy, they will have lost their reinforcing qualities.)

Given that manding is such a powerful verbal tool, it is small wonder that many programs serving clients with communicative disorders begin by teaching people with severely limited verbal skills how to mand. Certainly the most sensible approach is to use items and activities the learner prefers at the time, and to incorporate those within the instructional protocol. (Refer back to Chapter 6 for methods of assessing reinforcer preferences.) Also, "for mand training to be most effective, caregivers must implement mand training with high levels of integrity" (Pence & St. Peter, 2015, p. 575). (See Chapter 3 for a discussion on treatment integrity.)

*Incidental teaching* (Hart & Risley, 1975), sometimes referred to as *in situ* training, *naturalistic* teaching, or *non-intensive* teaching) is an ideal way to incorporate MOs into the protocol for teaching verbal skills. We apply **incidental teaching for manding** directly within the environment in which the learner would be expected to use the particular verbal skill naturally: *prompt and request the child to mand in the natural environment (e.g., home, school, community) for any item or activity that he or she wants throughout most of the day*. For example, analogous to the primitive woman in the opening scenario of this chapter, a child reaches for a banana (or a toy or a tool or a piece of a puzzle essential for completing the picture), but can't quite grasp it. The parent might prompt "What do you want?" and then pause and model the word "banana." Hart and Risley (1975) described incidental teaching at work as follows:

> Children in a preschool serving lower-income families were observed to speak and use elaborate language markedly less often than their more privileged peers. Time in school, intermittent teacher praise, and social and intellectual stimulation were insufficient to remedy the problem. Although formal group instruction effectively increased the children's rates of using color-noun and number-noun combinations within that context, they did not spontaneously initiate such behavior elsewhere.
>
> Incidental teaching then was employed during free-play activities. Whenever the children seemed to want to play with a particular item (toy, game, and so on), they were prompted and required to ask for it (mand). This procedure was not only effective in increasing the number of mands the children emitted, it was also responsible for increasing more complex language use (mand + intraverbal[3] = compound sentences including adjective-noun combinations). By the end of the preschool year, the rate of speaking and degree of elaboration of the children's unprompted words equaled that of other more affluent preschool children, regardless of whether the response had been specifically trained or not. (Hayes, Aguiar, & Hayes, 1991; pp. 361–362)

In 1980, Hart and Risley described the cogent features of incidental teaching as follows:

---

[3] Skinner used the term *intraverbal relation* to describe communicative behavior lacking point-to-point correspondence with an antecedent verbal stimulus, as in answering questions or reciprocally interacting verbally.

First, incidental teaching is conducted within the very setting conditions that naturally maintain language use. That is, incidental teaching is conducted in a richly varied stimulus environment, full of people, things, and activities to be accessed and manipulated through language use...

Second, incidental teaching is conducted casually throughout the child's day, at various times, in various contexts, in relation to whatever aspect of a varied stimulus environment the child selects as a momentarily prepotent reinforcer. As the child initiates with language related to many different aspects of his environment, many different elaborations are requested...

Third, incidental teaching is by its nature "loose training" (Stokes & Baer, 1977). Adults arrange the context for incidental teaching, but they have little control over the particular stimulus a child will select to initiate about at any given moment. The child in fact controls the incidental teaching interaction because he or she initiates it, specifying a reinforcer an adult can deliver.... Therefore, the adult must focus on keeping the child initiating rather than on a criterion for a specific response topography. This means keeping the incidental teaching interaction brief, positive, and focused on the child-selected reinforcer.

Fourth, the conditions of incidental teaching are such that the actual contingencies of reinforcement are likely to be much less discriminable than those in a one-to-one training situation. The adult conducts incidental teaching only when he or she has both the time and an appropriate, reinforcer-related prompt for elaboration. Therefore, the adult sometimes delivers a child-requested reinforcer without asking for language elaborations; sometimes he or she prompts once, sometimes more than once. Over time, merely the focus of close adult attention when the child initiates is likely to become a discriminative stimulus for elaboration, such that the adult does not have to prompt at all.

Perhaps most importantly, incidental teaching establishes a class of behavior, language use, which is likely to be generalized by stimulus similarity across settings and occasions. Not only does language function differentially to gain access to reinforcers, but language initiation is followed, on an intermittent schedule, by close, receptive adult attention; focus on the reinforcer the child has selected; and often a request for more of the behavior, language. A response class, language *use*, is reinforced in a wide variety of stimulus conditions. (pp. 409–410)

Another, more focused, way to build on motivating operations is to tempt the learner more directly, while keeping prompts to the barest minimum. In the *Picture Exchange Communication System*© (Bondy & Frost, 2001), instructors learn in advance about their student's preferences. After teaching the individual to choose and exchange a picture with each of several adults, and then to approach one of those adults from a distance, they are taught next to discriminate one picture from another. This is accomplished by providing the learner with access to a picture of a preferred object (let's say a sweet, juicy seedless grape) and of a non-preferred item (a shoe lace). The child receives the item represented on the card s/he has given to the teacher. Eventually the child learns the value of examining each picture and selecting the one that matches the preferred item. PECS has also been used to teach peers how to interact with children with developmental delays. Thiemann-Bourque et al. (2016) taught seven students without disabilities how to use PECS. These children not only learned how to use PECS when communicating with their disabled peers, they actually became more responsive listeners when the child with disabilities used PECS to communicate. Another growing area of the use of PECS is with the use of tablets with applications that produce speech (see Kagohara et al., 2013 for a review).

It is important for children to learn that statements like "not now'" or "you can have that later" do not mean "no." That they mean at another time. Once that is learned, it appears easier to teach them to mand, or to ask, "when?" In other words, statements like "not right now" acquire MO properties for the child saying "when." Landa, Hansen, and Shillingsburg (2017) taught three six- to seven-year-old children with autism to ask "when" by alternating statements like "not right now, after you wash your hands," with statements like, "not now." By so doing, and by providing the child with the answer to "when" if asked within five seconds, the children learned to ask "when" after being told "not now," "later," etc.

> **Box 19.1**
>
> He: Watching the football game.
> She: Arrives, displaying her new outfit. "So, what do you think?"
> He: (Riveted to the TV screen, ignores her.)
> She: "Got it on sale. Amazing bargain."
> He: "Shh. I want to hear the yardage."
> She: Goes over and turns off the TV.
>
> He: Looking up at her at last, "Why'd you do that?"
> She, angrily: "Well, at *least* I've got your attention!"

Can misbehavior serve a manding function? Indeed, yes! After all, manding is just our name for a particular variety of the reinforcement of verbal behavior. Although behavioral problems and verbal behavior may differ in topography (form), assuming that either one gets people what they want at the time, their functions are equivalent. How did "she" succeed in gaining "his" attention in Box 19.1?

The more often you reinforce people's prosocial actions, the less apt they will be to shift over to less acceptable forms. Carr and Durand (1985a) developed a procedure to rectify maladaptive behavior, labeling their method **functional communication training (FCT)**. FCT can be viewed as an application of mand training (see Mancil, 2006 for a review of FCT). FCT *involves using differential reinforcement to teach people to mand in a socially acceptable way for the same reinforcer that historically served to maintain the problem behavior* (see Chapter 28 for more details on the use of differential reinforcement of alternative behavior). Carr and Durand documented and evaluated this method of using differential reinforcement of communication in a number of studies (e.g., Carr & Durand, 1985; Durand & Carr, 1987, 1992). First, they reported conducting an assessment to determine the function of the problematic behaviors of four children with developmental disabilities, concluding that the children emitted the problem behavior either to gain attention or when faced with difficult task demands. Subsequently, they demonstrated that when they taught those children whose problem behavior was identified as gaining the reinforcer of attention how to solicit attention (in a more acceptable way), they were able successfully to reduce problem behavior and increase manding. Those whose problem behavior was identified as relating to difficult task demands were taught to solicit assistance. As in teaching other mands, when teaching individuals to mand for specific reinforcers, ensuring that the mand is functional (i.e., serves the same purpose as the problematic behavior) is essential. To emphasize the point, when Carr and Durand (1985b) taught participants to ask for attention when their problem behavior was maintained by escape from demands, the students did not mand and their problem behavior persisted. Only after the children were taught to mand for the functional reinforcer (i.e., to seek help) did their problem behavior diminish.

More recently, in a review of functional communication training (FCT) (Ghaemmagharni, Hanley, & Jessel, 2021), the authors conclude that teaching functionally appropriate alternative behavior has resulted in "substantial reductions of a variety of topographically and functionally different types of problem behavior in children and adults.... Our review finds overwhelming evidence in support of FCT as an efficacious treatment" (p. 122).

Communication of wants and needs does not necessarily depend upon the person's ability to speak. When Charlop-Christy, Carpenter, Le, LeBlanc, and Kellet (2002) taught students with autism to use pictures to ask for what they wanted, within the format of the *Picture Exchange Communication System*©, the participants' problem behavior diminished. Regardless of its form, the ability to mand is by far one of the most important classes of behavior we humans learn. So, by teaching manding skills, we enable people to gain valuable control over their environments. In other words, we empower them. That, in turn, increases the value of language for them. So, if you want to teach individuals to behave verbally, start out by teaching them how to mand. That is one of the fastest ways to demonstrate what language can do for them. (Table 19.1 contains additional suggestions for promoting manding.)

One criticism related to utilizing behavioral interventions to teach manding is that the individual can become robotic. In a recent study aimed at addressing this issue (Brodhead et al. 2016) used discrimination training and lag schedules (discussed in Chapter 22) to increase mand variability in young children with autism during snack time. They demonstrated that behavioral interventions do not necessarily lend themselves to producing robotic responders, but lack of knowledge on how to produce variability does.

# THE TACT

In our own social environments, the ability to precisely express the names of people, items, or events can earn people—you, me, as well as those with limited repertoires—lots of positive consequences, too. We turn our attention to that end now.

## The Tact Defined

Skinner defined the **tact** as "*a verbal operant in which the response is reinforced by generalized conditioned reinforcement and is under the functional control of a nonverbal discriminative stimulus*" (1957, p. 52–55). *Tacting* designates saying a word in the presence of *an object, an event, or a feature of an abstract stimulus class*. In simple English, *tacting involves naming or labeling an object, action, abstraction, or private event that is currently present or being experienced.* You probably recognize that much (though not all) of your learning of applied behavior analysis so far has emphasized tacting, as in discussing objects, actions, relations, and properties. But notice that we cannot tact things that are not present, so if we see that someone used a particular method in an experiment and we name the method, that is not tacting; the method is not there as a stimulus if we have only read about it.

Examples of tacts are a little girl saying "dog" in the presence of a dog and saying "tree" in the presence of a tree. Her mom reinforces that tacting by saying, "Yes, sweetie, that is a dog/tree," and gives her daughter a big hug. In another case, Mom confirms a boy's observation: "Yes, Donnie, that big yellow car is going fast." Just providing confirmation can be reinforcing, and much verbal behavior in natural environments is shaped by such casual interactions when children talk. That is why typical children ordinarily learn thousands of words in their early years, even though only a small fraction of those words were explicitly taught.

Although teaching someone how to tact can be important in its own right, you would be mistaken were you to conclude that by teaching people the name of an item they will automatically become capable of requesting the item. But notice that *naming is not tacting*. You can name something that is not present, but *you can only tact something when it is present*. You must be able to tact something to name it, but naming is more than tacting. In fact, if naming and tacting were the same, we would not have needed a different word for each. Tacting often is the focus of successful communication-development programs (Petursdottir et al., 2005), because a child who has learned to tact can more easily be taught to mand. Plus, tact training can be used to help improve listening and categorization by children with autism (Miguel & Koibari-Wright, 2013).

Why is it important to tact things? Besides serving a basic social function, just think for a moment of how important it is for a child to be able to name internal states such as "I'm hungry," "I'm sad," "I'm tired," or "My tummy hurts." Those *verbal* operants fall under the category of *tacting*. But teaching children to tact private events is tricky. Mommy can see the colors the child sees while the child is tacting reds, greens, or blues, but Mommy cannot feel the child's tummy ache. Mommy can only reinforce tacts of private events by way of public events that accompany it (e.g., the child's crying and touching his tummy while doing so). Because it is difficult for verbal communities consistently to reinforce tacts of private events, many tacts of private events are less reliable than tacts of public ones. Can you really be sure why someone said, "Sorry, but I've got a headache?" But by now it should be obvious to you that *the ability to tact objects, actions, properties of objects and actions, relations, and abstractions, as well as private events, is essential to living and thriving in society.*

## Tact Training

Because the goal in tact training is to bring the verbal response under the control of a nonverbal stimulus (e.g., saying "car" in the presence of a toy car), one of the easiest ways to train a tact is to take advantage of other verbal repertoires. If, for instance, a child has a strong echoic repertoire, then transferring control from a verbal model "car," to control by a toy car may be relatively simple: The trainer presents the nonverbal stimulus (toy car) along with an echoic prompt ("car") and differentially reinforces when the child repeats "car." Meanwhile the echoic prompt is faded. Barbera and Kubina (2005) evaluated a combination of commonly-used transfer procedures to teach tacts to a child with autism. It included a match-to-sample method (displaying a sample of the item and requesting the responder to match it by choosing the same item from an array of varied choices), to an echoic, to a tact transfer. Prior to the intervention, the child had not acquired any of the target tacts; afterwards he had mastered over thirty.

A different strategy for teaching tacting consists of prompting "What is it/that?" and then modeling, then fading the prompt. To illustrate, Wallace et al. (2006) taught three individuals with developmental disabilities to use sign language to tact particular objects. The therapist would hold up an item (e.g., a toy instrument) while asking, "What is it?" Then she would prompt by modeling or, if necessary, physically guiding the individual to produce the proper sign and then differentially reinforce any approximations the individual made toward correctly signing the word "music." Slowly she would begin to diminish, or fade, the amount of prompting until the individual independently tacted the word "music" correctly. Note that modeling or instructional demonstrations were combined to obtain the study's results. Typically, when teaching children to name items, combining instructional demonstrations with reinforcement is more efficient than supplying consequences alone (Hranchuk, Greer, & Longano, 2019).

Support systems such as vocal simulators or lower-tech tools like the *Picture Exchange Communication System*© (PECS) also can be used to promote appropriate tacting. Within the latter program, after students have reliably demonstrated their ability to initiate exchanging a picture (e.g., of juice) for a reinforcer (the actual juice), teachers begin to interpose a delay between their receipt of the picture from the communicator, saying "Oh, you want (pause) juice" and then delivering a small amount of juice. As time passes, they begin to extend the length of the delay between the child's request and its fulfillment. Eventually many learners begin to anticipate the teacher by initiating the spoken word or an approximation to it. To illustrate, in their case report of their application of PECS with 85 children, Bondy and Frost (1994) reported that of those previously non-verbal students who completed *all phases* of the program, 29 percent combined speech and pictures; 48 percent used speech alone; while 23 percent employed pictures without any vocal speech. In a full experimental analysis, Charlop-Christy et al. (2002) found that their three participants learned to communicate and expanded their mean lengths of utterances. As a bonus, presumably because now they were able to use functional communication to obtain their reinforcers, participants' rates of inappropriate behavior also diminished. (See Hart & Banda, 2009 and Sulzer-Azaroff et al., 2009 for reviews of PECS investigations.)

If a verbal response is controlled by an artificial prompt, such as "Say *cookie*," you will want to fade it as rapidly as possible, so eventually the response is brought under the control of natural stimuli (from "Say *cookie*" to displaying the cookie jar which is located out of reach). Carroll and Hesse (1987) used a *tact frame*, a standard phrase with the key word omitted ("This is a ____") to establish tacting, while Sundberg, Endicott, and Eigenheer (2000) used intraverbal (defined below) prompts (e.g., "sign bed") to establish tacting by two non-vocal children with autism. During the

intraverbal prompt condition, the therapist said, for example, "bed," while displaying the object. Then, omitting the verbal prompt, the trainer praised correct responses to the question ("What is that?"). It is especially important in any communication-training program to eliminate any unnatural prompts, to ensure that control eventually transfers completely to the natural stimulus (e.g., the presence of an unattainable object or the setting event). Also, remember to use incidental teaching whenever possible, because the more you incorporate language training into the natural course of the learner's day, the more promising the outcome. (Refer to Table 20.1 for a summary of suggestions for promoting tacting.).

iPads are being used more and more to help teach verbal behavior. For example, investigators (Rivera, Hudson, Weiss, & Zambone, 2017) used a multicomponent multimedia shared story as an intervention to teach science vocabulary to elementary school students, ages six to eight, with developmental or intellectual disabilities. The stories, shared over an iPad, consisted of photographs, text, and videos to support generalization of the vocabulary (e.g., including different situations and colors of objects — red flower, yellow flower). The students not only learned to identify pictures verbally, but they also generalized their vocabulary to other stimuli.

It is important to note that these procedures can be used to teach more than just the "name" of objects. For example, Majdalany et al. (2014) were able to teach students to tact the shapes of countries. More importantly they evaluated which teaching presentation method: massed-trial, distributed-trial, or task interspersal prompted acquisition the fastest. For five out of the six participants, massed-trial presentation led to acquisition of targets quicker than the other two procedures.

Recall that a functional tacting repertoire can be broad in scope, in fact, individuals are taught to report current internal states as well as to describe their past behavior (e.g., "How do you feel," "Did you do your homework," "Did you make your bed"). Rajagopal et al. (2021) successfully taught children with Autism Spectrum Disorder to tact tactile stimulation when applied to various parts of their body (e.g., "prickly" when a hairbrush was applied). In another study, Shillingsburg et al. (2019) taught children with Autism Spectrum Disorder to report past behavior via a speech-generating device. Specifically, they were taught how to tact the location of where they performed a specific activity (e.g., Participant colored on the carpet. Therapist asked "where did you color?" Participant responded "carpet." Skinner (1957) coined reporting past behavior as self-tacting. (Some have argued that, depending on the stimulus controlling the reporting of past behavior, the verbal operant is either self-tacting or might actually be an intraverbal (see following section). Palmer suggested that if the response is controlled by private or public antecedent stimuli, the reporting of past behavior is self-tacting; however, if the behavior is under verbal antecedent control, then the behavior is actually an interverbal. However, the argument is beyond the scope of the current text.)

## THE INTRAVERBAL

### The Intraverbal Defined

An **intraverbal** *is controlled by a verbal antecedent stimulus without point-to-point correspondence or formal similarity and is reinforced by nonspecific reinforcers* (Skinner, 1957). In effect, some verbal stimuli occasion other verbal responses, as when you learn math facts ("2 + 3 equals?" The response "5" is an intraverbal). Intraverbal behavior can assume many forms, such as social interchanges (e.g., "You're welcome" after someone says "Thank you"); word associations (e.g., "black" when someone says "white"); translations from one language to another; answering questions such as "What is a tact?" with a set response ("A tact is a verbal operant under the functional control of a nonverbal discriminative stimulus and is reinforced by generalized secondary reinforcers"). Repeating verbal behavioral chains such as one's address or phone number also suit the definition. The *functional component* of an intraverbal consists of the fact that the behavior is controlled by the preceding verbal stimulus and produces nonspecific reinforcement. Generally speaking, *what is described as conversational language, question answering, and reciprocal language often incorporates intraverbal behavior within it*; from a behavior-analytic perspective, however, their components only fall under the intraverbal umbrella if they meet the criteria that a particular verbal stimulus occasions *a particular verbal response that produces some generalized reinforcer as a consequence*. Say "ABC" and not only your listener but probably you yourself will be inclined to continue with "DEF." Said another way, an intraverbal acquires its strength by being reinforced in the presence of the verbal antecedent. It is not enough that a response follows a verbal antecedent.[4] We teach children many of the intraverbals fundamental to social and communicative ability, such as reciting the alphabet or the sounds an animal makes: "What does the dog say?" followed by "woof, woof." After a few repetitions of "What does the dog say?" the child responds "woof, woof," and we praise her. Or, we teach children categories, such as *a cat is an animal* or that *red is a color*. The very same response, saying "cat," may not be an intraverbal under other circumstances. "Cat" would be classified as an *echoic* response if the child said "cat" after hearing someone else say "cat," a *tact* if she said "cat" when seeing a cat, and a *mand* to request a stuffed cat. Notice that it is not the form of the response "cat" that matters. We call it one or another type of verbal response depending upon its function.

Of what value is an intraverbal repertoire? It facilitates other verbal as well as nonverbal behavior. Sundberg and Michael (2001) have stated it plainly:

> It prepares a speaker to behave rapidly and accurately with respect to further stimulation and, at a more advanced level, plays an important role in continuing a conversation. For example, a child hears an adult speaker say "animal" in some context. If this stimulus functions to evoke several relevant intraverbal responses, such as "elephant," "lion," "camel," "bear," and so on, the child is then better able to react to other parts of the adult's verbal stimulus that may be related to a recent trip to a zoo. One might say that the child is now thinking about animals and now has relevant verbal responses at strength for further responses to the adult's verbal behavior. (pp. 713)

Thus, the animals in this example are intraverbals to the adult's response "animal."

Recall that a functional tacting repertoire can be broad in scope, in fact, individuals are taught to report current internal states as well as to describe their past behavior (e.g., "How do you feel," "Did you do your homework," "Did you make your bed"). Rajagopal et al. (2021) successfully taught children with Autism Spectrum Disorder to tact tactile stimulation when applied to to various parts of their body

(e.g., "prickly" when a hairbrush was applied). In another study, Shillingsburg et al. (2019) taught children with Autism Spectrum Disorder to report past behavior via a speech-generating device. Specifically, they were taught how to tact the location of where they performed a specific activity (e.g., Participant colored on the carpet. Therapist asked "where did you color?" Participant responded "carpet." Skinner (1957) coined reporting past behavior as self-tacting. (Some have argued that depending on the stimulus controlling the reporting of past behavior that the verbal operant is either self-tacting or might actually be an intraverbal (see following section). Palmer suggested that if the response is controlled by private or public antecedent stimuli the reporting of past behavior is self-tacting; however, if the behavior is under verbal antecedent control then the behavior is actually an interverbal. However, the argument is beyond the scope of the current text.)

Recognize that while a tact repertoire allows a speaker to talk about an object or event that is actually at hand, *an intraverbal repertoire allows*

---
[4]Palmer (2010), personal communication.

*a speaker to talk about objects and events that are absent*. With intraverbal behavior, we actually can go beyond just discussing particular events, to thinking about (covertly or imagining) them as well. That distinction highlights the special value of training and promoting intraverbal repertoires. But we must remind you that this is just a small piece of the story. A lot more goes on in verbal behavior, and the classes we have discussed so far are not adequate to deal with complex adult verbal behavior. Skinner's (1957) book introduces other verbal classes, such as the **autoclitic**, (*a form of verbal behavior that modifies other forms of verbal behavior*, as in "Don't look now, but I think I see Grant with a new girlfriend.") The autoclitic involves verbal responses for which the functional properties of the speaker's ongoing verbal behavior provide the discriminative stimulus; one such as: "Who is she?" In another example, suppose you are about to say something. If you are going to precede your statement appropriately either with "I'm really certain...," versus "I'm not really sure..," you need to know about the conditions under which you will say it. Skinner's treatment of such complex behavior in terms of stimulus control and basic operant contingencies makes for fascinating reading. But we must now return to our concerns with (verbal) behavior change per se.

## Intraverbal Training

The intraverbal repertoires of people with learning and developmental disabilities, including those on the autism spectrum, tend to be limited or even nonexistent. Some may explain this as the individual's "inability to process the auditory stimulus." We should point out, however, that verbal stimulus control is not the same as nonverbal stimulus control, and that a successful tact is not the same as an appropriate intraverbal (e.g., Braam & Poling, 1983; Partington & Bailey, 1993). In fact, Sundberg and Partington (1998) have advised delaying intraverbal training until the learner has well-established mand, tact, echoic, imitation, receptive, and matching-to-sample repertoires (Sundberg & Partington, 1998). Verbal stimulus control is thought by some to be more difficult to train than nonverbal stimulus control.

Sundberg and Michael (2001) advise that it is best to avoid teaching new topographical responses when conducting intraverbal training, especially to those whose communicative skills are delayed. Learning appears to progress more smoothly when the student already has mastered the vocal response within some other class of verbal skill. For example, if teaching the song "twinkle, twinkle little ____," the individual should already have the vocal response "star" as a tact, mand, or echoic response.

One way to teach intraverbals is to use a *mand frame*. Begin with a motivational antecedent (colloquially, something the learner will want), a non-spoken prompt (item), and a verbal stimulus. Subsequently fade out the motivational antecedent, and the nonverbal prompt. For example, you want a child to say "apple" in response to "You eat an ___." You would start off with the motivational antecedent (the child hasn't eaten an apple in a while and prefers to eat apples), the apple (the non-verbal prompt), and the verbal stimulus ("You eat an ___"), and when the child says "apple," you give him a piece of apple. Subsequently, you fade out the motivational antecedent or motivator, and when the child says "apple" you provide generalized reinforcers (e.g., praise, "That's right. You eat an apple"). The last phase would be to fade out the nonverbal prompt and to make sure to praise when the child says "apple" in response to "You eat an ___." The goal is to bring the vocal response under the control of a new stimulus. If you initially use mand frames to control behavior, recognize the need to fade out the motivator, because you want the stimulus control to transfer from specific to generalized learned reinforcer(s). Unfortunately, this procedure is less effective when teaching many important intraverbals such as the ability to recite your home address, in that setting up a motivating operation for the mand component may be difficult or impossible.

The bulk of the studies designed to analyze the transfer of stimulus control from echoic or tact prompts to intraverbal control have involved delayed prompting or errorless learning (Braam & Poling, 1983; Luciano, 1986; Partington & Bailey, 1993; Sundberg, San Juan, Dawdy, & Arguelles, 1990; Watkins, Pack-Teixterira, & Howard, 1989). An alternative approach is to transfer stimulus control from tacts to intraverbals by combining *both* echoic prompts and errorless learning, in the form of delayed prompting. Goldsmith, LeBlanc, and Sautter (2007) taught three children with autism to name items associated with pre-selected categories (e.g., "What are some things you wear?"). Although the intervention successfully taught the targeted intraverbals, generalization to a non-targeted category was limited.

Miguel, Petursdottir, and Carr (2005) also examined the effects of multiple tact training (both item name and class; "carrot," "vegetable") and found little generalization. Taking the next step, they decided to conduct intraverbal training directly. They used the following procedure to teach the children to directly identify the category to which an item belonged in the following way:

A trial began with the experimenter asking, "What are some [category]? Tell me as many as you can." All correct responses were immediately praised. If additional responses did not occur within 10 s, the experimenter provided a tact prompt by showing the child one of the pictures from the training set. If the child did not respond to the tact prompt, an echoic prompt was provided. A correct response following a prompt was praised, but the trial was scored as prompted. If the child made an incorrect response, the experimenter said "A [name] is not a [category]" (e.g., "a flute is not a tool") and then implemented the same prompting procedure. If the child repeated a previous correct response, the experimenter said, "Yes, you already said [name]" and waited 10 s for another response. If the child made a response that was considered correct by the experimenter but was not included in the training set (a novel response), the response was praised and counted among the total number of unprompted responses. A trial was terminated when the participant had emitted all 10 responses in the training set (with or without prompts) and 10 s had elapsed without further responding. Intraverbal training was conducted until participants had made 10 or more unprompted responses on three consecutive training trials. These responses did not have to be part of the training set, as long as they were considered members of the category. (pp. 31–33)

Note the results of that strategy with two of their students, Sarah and Martha. The multiple baseline demonstrated that neither multiple-tact nor receptive-discrimination training were sufficient to promote transfer of stimulus control, whereas the intraverbal training, described above, did produce successful results. (See Figure 19.1.)

Other research has specifically investigated the effects of these interventions on generalization. Partington and Bailey (1993) demonstrated only limited generalization for half of their participants. Of interest, though, is that in the Goldsmith et al. (2007) study, the students' rates of acquiring subsequently trained targets accelerated over those required for them to master the first target. This result speaks to the efficiency of multiple target training.

Although a number of procedural variations (e.g., mand, tact, echoic, textual i.e., written word/picture) designed to promote transfer to intraverbal control have been conducted, given the limited comparative research, no single approach stands out as superior. In one instance, though, Finkel and Williams (2001) compared written word/picture and echoic prompts for teaching intraverbals to a child with autism. Although they found that both were effective, written word/picture prompts produced a more immediate and robust effect. Becoming informed about the child's learning history by, for example, finding out if s/he tends to respond better to pictorial or visual, as opposed to auditory or gestural cues, may inform practitioners as to the most promising starting point for a given individual.

It is important once again to remember that you do not necessarily want rote responding, but varied intraverbal behavior. Dickes and Kodak (2015) were able to provide instructive feedback on the variability of intraverbal responses for two children with autism successfully. For example, when asking for the child to say some shapes, after the child said the three shapes, the therapist said the name of three additional shapes and said they were shapes too. Moreover, some intraverbals we desire to teach are controlled by multiple stimuli (e.g., "Name a red vehicle") evoking a conditional discriminated response "fire truck" if both the "red" stimulus and

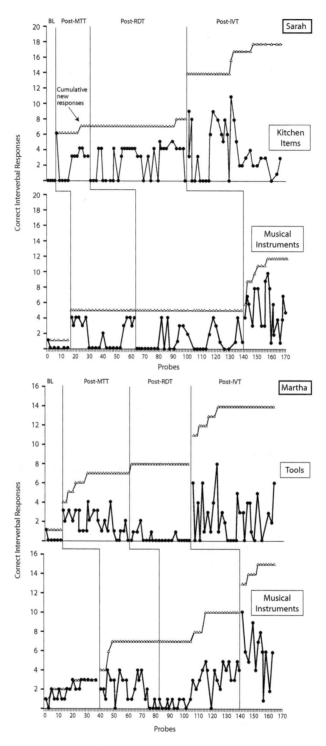

**Figure 19.1** The number of intraverbal responses per probe (filled circles) and the cumulative number of intraverbal responses (open triangles) for Sarah (upper panels) and Martha (lower panels). From Miguel, Petursdottir, & Carr (2005). Used with permission from the authors and ABAI.

the "vehicle" stimulus is controlling the response. However, if both stimuli are not controlling the response the child might respond "apple" for the "red" stimulus or "car" for the "vehicle" stimulus, thus not engaging in a conditional discrimination form of an intraverbal. Kisamore et al. (2016) noted that the use of a five-second prompt delay, error correction, and differential reinforcement was successful in teaching these more complex intraverbals. Based upon their results, they recommended that, if this procedure does not work, adding a prompted differential observation response (such as "say *stimulus 1* and *stimulus 2*") prior to the individual needing to respond. Or, the implementation of the error correction procedure can help with acquisition of these types of intraverbals.

## LISTENER BEHAVIOR

Although Skinner (1957) distinguished between verbal behavior related to the behavior of the speaker and behavior of the listener, most of his analyses focused on behavior of the speaker (e.g., mands, tacts, intraverbals, etc.). Given that both repertoires are important for effective communication, it is important to touch on both the behavior of the speaker and that of the listener. In fact, to understand, predict, and control verbal interchanges (i.e., between those of the speaker and of the listener), we must account for the whole episode. Why? Because as Skinner emphasized, the listener plays an essential role in mediating reinforcement for the speaker. Consequently, understanding those contingencies that first establish, *and* those that maintain listener behavior, are equivalently important.

Most would argue that listener behavior probably is maintained by some form of generalized conditioned reinforcement, such as attention, provided by the speaker (Greer & Speckman, 2009). Skinner pointed out, however, that the listener gains additional benefits from the verbal stimuli produced by the speaker. Consider the reinforcer the listener gains when the speaker informs him that a particular herb is poisonous.

Generally, listener behavior is established early in humans' lives. Research suggests that a mother's voice becomes a conditioned reinforcer and infants respond differentially to the voices of their own mothers (DeCasper & Spence, 1987). Moreover, this conditioning continues throughout infancy, and at some point parents begin prompting children to respond to verbal stimuli (i.e., instructions) by differentially reinforcing correct responding via some form of generalized conditioned reinforcement. Such interactions commonly are sufficient to promote listener repertoires (Sundberg & Partington, 1998). However, just as promoting speaker behavior sometimes is necessary, specifically targeting listener behavior as an instructional objective may be critical under some circumstances. Here again, applied behavior analysis can play a vital role.

Discrete Trial Teaching (DTT), incidental teaching, and natural environment training (NET) are among those methods commonly used to teach listener behavior (Sundberg & Partington, 1998). During the early education of students on the autism spectrum, such listener stimulus-selection task-assignments as receptive labeling (Leaf & McEachin, 1999; Lovaas, 2003; Maurice, Green, & Luce, 1996) are frequently employed. To illustrate, given an array of blocks of different colors, the instructor says, "Give me the green block." In such cases, instructors often have used such procedures as simple discrimination training (i.e., they ask the student to select a stimulus in the absence of distracters) before instruction progresses to a conditional discrimination training phase (i.e., in the presence of distracters). In other situations, instruction begins at the conditional discrimination level (with distracters present). To review: during simple-conditional training, when presented with a single item or picture, participants are taught to emit a single verbal response, while during conditional discrimination training, they are taught to respond to a verbal stimulus by selecting a particular picture or item from an array of stimuli. Should you wonder which of the two approaches to try, consider some recent evidence (Grow et al., 2011) that using conditional discrimination training from the beginning may be more efficient than starting with a simple discrimination and progressing to conditional discrimination training. So, try that first.

*Incidental teaching (IT)* can be an especially effective method for promoting listener selection. McGee, Krantz, Mason, and McClannahan (1983) used an incidental teaching procedure to instruct listeners to discriminate items in the context of an ongoing preferred activity (e.g., making lunch). During that study, the participants were trained to select four different sets of materials from an array of five items when instructed "give me __." Following correct responses, the participants were allowed access to the objects needed to continue making lunch. It should be pointed out, though, that in this study, the learners' behavior may well have been controlled by both the verbal stimuli and by the display of the objects. To be certain that modeled spoken labels eventually are replaced by the objects themselves, instructors need to apply procedures clearly designed to transfer stimulus control. For example, to transfer from modeling to spoken instruction, one could begin by using delayed prompting, starting out by modeling a motor movement, and then shifting over to the verbal stimulus (i.e., verbal instruction; e.g., Striefel, Bryan, & Aikins, 1974). As originally conceived, IT included only a single trial within a teaching episode. Implementers of IT, however, may achieve improved outcomes if they augment the number of incidental teaching opportunities they provide, as Charlop-Christy and Carpenter (2000) demonstrated by using a strategy called *Modified Incidental Teaching Sessions (MITS)*. In contrast with simple IT or discrete trial instruction alone, when they tripled the number of practice trials they were able to promote acquisition and generalization outcomes superior to those produced via discrete trial instruction alone.

Listener behavior goes beyond responding to specific mands. In fact, Najdowski et al. (2017) were able to teach children with autism how to respond to disguised mands (i.e., a mand in which the speaker does not describe the MO or the reinforce). Basically, they used a multiple exemplar training package consisting of rules, role play, and feedback to teach three boys with autism how to respond to the mand "That looks really good" by giving the therapist the food, "this is really heavy" with the person giving them a chair, and "that looks like fun" with access to the activity. In fact, some would argue that they taught these kids some perspective taking.

Thus far two great articles have reviewed the contributions of Skinner's analysis of verbal behavior and how it can help the development of treatment strategies to overcome communication delays especially in children with autism, and we encourage readers to take a look at them to further develop treatment strategies with respect to overcoming verbal delays (see Sundberg & Michael, 2001 and DeSouza, Akers, & Fisher, 2017) beyond the examples provided in this chapter. Moreover, researchers and practitioners have started to develop and improve on assessment procedures to identify skill deficits in the area of verbal behavior. For example, Esch et al. (2010) have developed an assessment tool called the *Early Echoic Skills Assessment* to determine the level of skills a student has with respect to echoing single vs. multiple words that can be used to establish a starting point for teaching verbal behavior (for example if the student cannot engage in multiple word echoics, then teaching them to mand "Can I have strawberries, please" may not be the best starting point. Another assessment tool that has been developed is the *Verbal Behavior Milestones Assessment and Placement Program* (*VB-MAPP*; Sundberg, 2008). The VB-MAPP is a criterion-references assessment and curriculum guide for verbal behavior programming. The assessment targets mand, tact, echoic, intraverbal, listener, motor imitation, independent and social play, visual perceptual and matching-to-sample, linguistic structure, group and classroom skills, and early academic skills. It also provides guidance on curriculum development to address the identified skill deficits. The VB-MAPP has both validity and reliability (Barnes, Mellor, & Rehfeldt, 2014). A third assessment tool is the PEAK (*Promoting the Emergence of Advanced Knowledge) Rational Training System*. It may "provide a more robust measure of advanced language skills in individuals with autism," (Dixon et al. 2015, p. 223) even though the VB-MAPP and the PEAK are highly correlated.

In this chapter, we have provided you with the basic understanding of Skinner's (1957) analysis of verbal behavior. The next step is to become competent in the implementation of assessments to identify the targeted skill(s) deficit and in the development and implementation of a comprehensive program to address such skills. It is beyond the scope of this text to teach you how to utilize the VB-MAPP, or the PEAK, but we encourage you to seek out training on these tools if you are going to focus on verbal behavior in practice. If you work at a company that provides services for children with autism, it will probably have a copy of one or both of these assessment tools that you can look over. If you work in a school, the psychologist or speech therapist may have a copy.

## AUGMENTATIVE VERBAL BEHAVIORAL STRATEGIES

The vast majority of people use vocal speech as their primary verbal medium, as in manding a desired item ("Salt, please") or tacting an event ("See Daddy") because it gains them reinforcers or rids them of stimuli they find aversive, sometimes even including unwanted objects or attention. Gestures, like wrapping one's hands tightly around oneself and shivering to designate "cold" or smiling and waving often lead to a reinforcing response from the audience (a blanket, a return smile), even often across different cultures. But gestures or facial expressions only take one so far. All of us require a more functional and flexible mode of communication if we are to achieve and maintain a reasonable quality of life.

Whether as a result of sensory, motor, or developmental disorders, though, many individuals experience difficulty in communicating via the common modes of speaking, writing, or keying into a computer. Such deficits place them at a severe disadvantage, limiting their success in attaining reinforcers and gaining relief from discomfort. Fortunately, beyond speaking and writing, an array of alternative or **augmentative/alternative verbal communication (AAC)** methods exist, including *signing, touching,* or *exchanging an image*. Given that to date no specific augmentative communicative method has been shown conclusively to be more effective or easier to teach than any other, we briefly mention the more popular augmentative/alternative communication (AAC) methods.

That said, there are other practical factors that one should take into account when choosing to teach a given verbal response topography. First, prior to selecting the particular medium, we must consider the "speaker's" current repertoire of verbal skills, along with those of his audience. Teaching an individual to communicate by means of International Sign Language has been found to be an effective way to promote successful expressive communication, sometimes eventually even leading to speech (e.g., Horne, Lowe, & Harris, 2007, among others). But using sign language requires that the audience is capable of decoding the signs. So, as a means to an end (i.e., spoken communication), sign language can work effectively; but unless the "speaker" can shift his or her medium over to oral or written speech or has access to a community of other signers, the person's opportunities remain limited.

Another possibility is a *computerized voice-operated communication device*. (See, for instance, Olive et al., 2007). In that particular study, three children were successfully taught to use a communication output tool to request items while at play. Of course, such devices are somewhat costly, and, as with other augmentative communication media, the potential vocabulary is limited to those items contained within its program.

**The Picture Exchange Communication System**© or **PECS**, (Bondy & Frost, 2001), mentioned earlier, *uses pictorial images rather than spoken or written words as the communicative medium.* Within PECS©, students learn to mand by exchanging pictorial images for reinforcers. Supported by two or more trainers (one to display a pre-identified reinforcer, the other to physically guide them), participants are taught to select and discriminate pictures from one another; to persist in approaching communicative partners across increasing distances, to expand the pool of pictures of items for which they can mand, and of events they can tact, and to broaden their repertoires of relevant descriptive attributes. They also learn to use images to comment on items and events around them; and often, by means of an interposed time-delay procedure, to speak and/or further elaborate on their pictorial-based communications. Numerous studies have demonstrated that when applied according to the standard protocol, PECS frequently has been shown to promote increasingly complex pictorial-based, if not spoken verbal skills, and to reduce misconduct among many of its users (See Sulzer-Azaroff et al., 2009). Despite cultural and linguistic differences, the audience can grasp and respond rapidly to the purpose of the communication. PECS's reasonably powerful success rates, low cost and flexibility probably explains its expanding worldwide acceptance

As previously mentioned, no single augmentative communication method has been shown to be superior. Recently, Winborn-Kemmerer, Ringdahl, Wacker, and Kitsukawa (2009) demonstrated that an individual's proficiency with a specific topography could affect the outcomes of a functional communication training (FCT) intervention. They conducted a mand-topography assessment and identified the proficiency with which three individuals used several different mand topographies, including microswitch activation, picture-card touch, manual sign, and DynaWrite (an augmentative communication device) use. Subsequently, two mand topographies (high- and low-proficiency mands) were then compared during an FCT intervention. Results demonstrated that the FCT intervention incorporating the high-proficiency response was more effective in terms of teaching use of mands as well as promoting decreases in problem behavior.

Beyond the individual's skills, the environment must support the topography of the communicative medium. As suggested earlier, if the audience doesn't know any sign language, teaching a child only to use sign language would hardly be functional. Therefore, if you are considering using an AAC method, ensure that the communicative environment will support the particular response topography. Additionally, consider the effort required. Horner and Day (1991) demonstrated that an FCT involving less-effortful responses (e.g., signing "break") was more successful than the more effortful signing "I want to go please." Subsequently, Bailey, McComas, Benavidas, and Lovascz (2002) and Buckley and Newchok (2005) obtained similar results. Some researchers have supported using a topography-based modality (e.g., sign language) over a selection-based program, stating that it is easier to learn and has far fewer disadvantages (see Shafer, 1993 and Sundberg, 1993b for a review of communication modalities). A drawback of sign language, though, is that the audience must be restricted to those who have large receptive-signing vocabularies. By contrast, pictorial media have been shown to function effectively across a broad range of audiences, many of which lack any training in augmentative communication methods (Tincani, Crozier, & Alazetta, 2006). Nonetheless, large-scale comparison studies of this point remain to be conducted.

When selecting an AAC be sure to consider the client's sensory and motor abilities in that individuals with complex communication needs often have concomitant sensory and physical disabilities that may have a bearing on which AAC program might be the best to use. Seek out AAC vendors, connect with veteran practitioners and review the AAC research, such as the *Augmentative and Alternative Communication* journal, before selecting an AAC program, because specific apps keep changing. It is best to leave the selection of an app to a professional Speech-Language Pathologist unless you have had supervised training in their selection and use.

## RELATIONAL FRAME THEORY AND DERIVED RELATIONAL RESPONDING

In addition to viewing verbal behavior through a Skinnerian lens, another approach has taken off within the last 15 years: *Relational Frame Theory (RFT;* see Hayes, Barnes-Holmes, & Roche, 2001). **Relational Frame Theory** is a behavioral psychology of language and cognition. It basically seeks to understand and explain how individuals relate concepts together that have not been directly taught. This approach is deeply seeded in Sidman's stimulus equivalence (Sidman, 1971, 1977; Sidman & Cression, 1973). Sidman demonstrated that *through specific training, relations that had not been directly instructed would emerge (i.e., equivalence relations, such as verbal relating [defined below] and stimulus equivalence)*. These untrained skills were later explained by RFT folks as symbolic or referential behavior. For example, if a child is taught a word-object relation ("book"–a book), a parent might ask the child "where is the book" and the child will point to it, which will be followed by praise from the parent (maybe even the parent reading the book to the child). Likewise, the object-word relation (the actual book–the word "book") would be established by the parent holding up the book and asking the child "what is it?" followed by the child saying "book" and the parent praising the child.

Based on these learned relations, others might emerge. For example, now the parent asks "where is the cat?" and the child points to the cat (word–object relation) and without further training now if the parent holds up the cat and asks "what is it?" the child will say "cat" (object–word emerged relation).

Since Sidman's pioneering work, a number of conditions have been elucidated regarding stimulus equivalence, multiple stimulus relations, as well as derived or untrained stimulus relations (which is at the heart of RFT). Some would argue that this approach goes beyond teaching the basic relations (e.g., tacting, manding, and responding to intraverbals) and teaches functional language skills. Proponents of RFT explain that stimulus equivalence is "an empirical phenomena; RFT is a behavioral theory about how the phenomenon (and other phenomena) comes about" (Fox, n. d.).

The approach based upon RFT has been successful in establishing a history of reinforced relational responding that is an effective means for developing such skills as reading and spelling (Hanna, de Souza, de Rose, & Fonseca, 2004), requesting preferred items (Rosales, & Rehfeldt, 2007), and understanding basic mathematical concepts (Lynch & Cuvo, 1995) The idea behind this approach is to teach the learner how to relate, rather than focus on what they are relating (thus relating becomes the operant response).

The explosion of such research and application can be seen in the number of articles published on the use of RFT in educational practices as well as a recent practitioners guide on the use of procedures based on RFT for learners with autism and other development disabilities (Rehfeldt & Barnes-Holmes, 2009). For example, Dixon et al. (2017) utilized the PEAK-E curriculum (Dixion, 2015) to establish derived categorical (i.e., intraverbal) responding in children with disabilities. In this study, they evaluated a procedure to promote the emergence of untrained intraverbal categorical responses. Specially, three four-member equivalence classes including three stimuli (A, B, and C; e.g., A = triangle; B = square; and C = circle) and a category name (D; e.g., D = shape) for each class were trained using a match-to-sample procedure: First A–B training took place and the selection of B in the presence of A was tested (i.e., selecting square when presented with a triangle); then B–C training took place and the selection of C in the presence of B was tested (i.e., selecting circle in the presences of square), then D–C training took place and the selection of C in the presence of D was tested (i.e., selecting circle in the presences of shape). Subsequently, probes were conducted for two derived relations (D–B; selecting shape in the presences of square, D–C; selecting shape in the presences of circle) as well as intraverbal categorization (D–A/B/C; selecting shape to describe the category of triangle, square, and circle). Results demonstrated that these procedures were successful in producing the derived relations.

Most proponents of RFT would agree that targeting early relational operants such as coordination (i.e., bidirectional sameness), distinction, opposition, comparison, and hierarchy would be a great start to language training programs. Before looking at how one would program to target these operants, we should define what is meant by deriving stimulus relations as it pertains to verbal behavior. **Verbal relating** *is responding to one event in terms of another that is controlled by contextual cues beyond the nonarbitrary stimulus properties.* For example, a traveler can be taught that a Canadian quarter is less than an American quarter and can automatically derive that an American quarter is worth more than a Canadian quarter. Moreover, this relational responding is not based on the fact that one quarter is smaller or larger than the other. With respect to early language learners, the goal is to teach them how to discriminate between the relevant and irrelevant features of a task (i.e., get them to respond relationally to the contextual cues rather than the physical stimulus properties or nonarbitrary stimulus properties).

## Relating as an Operant

Teaching the Relational Frame of Coordination ($C_{rel}$) is generally considered the most basic relational activity. It is basically teaching the "is same" or "goes with" relations. For example, A is the same as B, thus B is the same as A. If B is the same as C, C is the same as B, and thus A is the same as C and C is the same as A. By using multiple exemplar training with nonarbitary stimuli as well as testing with arbitrary stimuli, and promoting fluency and flexibility (across stimuli, contexts, functions, training/testing formats, etc.) one should get the application of $C_{rel}$. For example, after a learning multiple exemplar training on the above relations, then if A is deemed dangerous, without training B and C will be dangerous (transformation of functions). With the relational frame of opposition, the same schematic is used but instead of "is" or "same as" you would teach "is the opposite of." In this case the result would be that if A is *blank* then B is the opposite of *blank* and C is *blank*. The relational frame of comparison is based upon "is more/less than" resulting in the following transformation of function: A is more than B, B is more than C; A is hot, then B is less hot than A, and C is less hot than B. Hence C is less hot than A. For a more detailed understanding of how to utilize these frames when training, we highly suggest the book *Derived Relational Responding: Applications for Learners with Autism and Other Developmental Disabilities* (Rehfeldt & Barnes-Holmes, 2009).

## Relational Frame Theory in Practice

A common criticism of incorporating derived responding in practice was that the original research was mainly conducted with typically developing adults (see Dymond, et al., 2010 for a review); A recent review, however, illustrates that the RFT approach is being used for the purpose of ameliorating communication deficits and addressing children's particularly troublesome behavioral repertoires (Belisle, et al., 2020). Specially, following the authors' analysis of the current literature on the topic, they found that 123 studies have involved the use of an RFT approach with children, with and without disabilities. In fact, ABA service providers have begun to include RFT procedures based upon the empirical research found in the literature (e.g., Belisle, et al., 2020; Zagrabska-Swiatkowska, et al., 2020) when teaching children with Autism Spectrum Disorder. However, RFT has led to a third-wave behavior therapy approach; Acceptance and Commitment Training or Therapy (ACT; Hayes, Strosahl, & Wilson, 2012) that has begun to emerge as an area of practice for behavior analysts.

In a recent paper, Dixon, et al. (2020) examine whether ACT is an appropriate practice for behavior analysts. "ACT is an approach to behavior change that uses verbal interventions to alter the functions of private events, to increase the flexibility of perspective-taking and contact with the internal and external environment (p. 561)." The authors discuss how ACT meets the seven dimensions put forth by Baer, Wolf, and Risley (1968) and can fall under a behavior analysts scope of practice. Moreover, the authors provide a questionnaire to engage in a self-assessment prior to implementing an ACT intervention that addresses scope of behavior analysis, scope of practice, and scope of competence. In summary, the research literature has secured RFT as having a place within applied behavior analysis. It will be interesting to see the evolution of RFT practices in applied behavior analysis over the next decade and the development of evidence-based practices based upon this approach.

## General Recommendations

Given the complexity of the behavior(s) being taught it is no wonder that there are some specific recommendations prior to initiating such a language development program. First and foremost, it is beyond the scope of this textbook to teach you how to develop and implement a specific program based upon RFT. Thus, it is important that before embarking on such a task that you are familiar with some of the basic training procedures utilized in such a program, including: errorless learning (Chapter 20), within and extra stimulus prompting (Chapters 17 and 20), fading (Chapter 20), schedule thinning (Chapters 22 and 23), and match-to-sample procedures in that you will be teaching simple and conditional discriminations. Moreover, specific discrimination procedures to teach particular relational frames have been established and should be followed (see Rehfeldt & Barnes-Homes, 2009 for procedural models). It is important when developing such a language-training program to understand that you will focus on teaching both speaker and listener responding throughout the intervention. It also is important to incorporate multiple-presentation formats, multiple contexts, as well as multiple-exemplar training to promote derived relational responding.

Given that the goal is to teach relational responding, it is important to determine the specific words or phrases you will use to teach. For example, it might be important to utilize the phrase "same as" during training for coordination. Because we are trying to teach the relation, research has suggested utilizing nonarbitrary stimuli prior to arbitrary stimuli (Barnes-Homes, et al. 2004; Berens & Hayes, 2007) is most effective. Finally, don't forget that if we want behavior to occur, in this case relating, we must reinforce the behavior of relating.

## Some Critical Communication Skills

Now that we have introduced the topic of verbal behavior, you may wish to focus more closely on which specific verbal class promises to be the most functional for your client at the moment. Below we list nine critical communication skills, identified by Bondy, Horton and Frost (2020), that probably will promote your client's learning and satisfaction:

1. Requesting reinforcers
2. Requesting assistance
3. Requesting a break
4. Rejecting offers
5. Accepting, or when to nod or say "yes"
6. Responding appropriately to "wait" or "no"
7. Following directions
8. Following a schedule
9. Dealing with transitions from high preference to lower preference activities (see Chapter 27)

In addition, a number of critical social skills are listed in Chapter 14 that can help your client function more effectively in various environments (e.g., saying "Hi" or "Hello," introducing self by name, requesting help and feedback, saying "thank you," delivering compliments, etc.

## SUMMARY AND CONCLUSIONS

*Verbal behavior* is a behavioral class that is reinforced through the mediation of others, yet is acquired and maintained in the same way as other behavioral classes. Those whose verbal repertoires are lacking or deficient are at a distinct disadvantage because their repertoire of behavior for producing the reinforcers they seek is restricted. In general, individuals acquire *manding* skills at a very early age because those are linked to their physical survival, as in communicating a need for nourishment and relief from discomfort (these are motivational antecedents). As social attention becomes more reinforcing, youngsters' *tacting* repertoires (e.g., as components of naming or labeling or describing) tend to expand as well. Humans' manding skills generally follow a path from babbling and crying to gesturing and uttering simple and then complex sounds functional in their local societies. For various reasons, though, some fail to progress along those lines. Instead of speaking, these individuals do whatever it takes (whether acceptable or bothersome or both) to get the message across. Many behavior analysts have addressed the difficulties linked to delayed manding skills by teaching useful alternatives to speaking. A number have designed programs, taught specific skills, experimentally analyzed and implemented such functional communication techniques as picture exchanges, picture pointing, sign language, computer-assisted devices, and others. *Incidental teaching* arranges to make objects and events inaccessible within the natural environment to set the occasion for non-speakers to make an extra effort to broaden the scope of their verbal manding and tacting skills.

Training *duplic* or *echoic* skills enables learners to replicate others' verbal behaviors, a useful tool for teaching and expanding people's verbal repertoires. Tools include activities like matching spoken responses to samples or to imitative prompts. *Intraverbal* skills are maintained by generalized reinforcers like attention, conversational responses, information, and so on. The *mand frame* can be a useful tool for teaching these skills, provided that a sufficiently powerful motivating operation is in place. Otherwise, one can promote intraverbal skills by teaching them directly.

When a particular verbal stimulus occasions a particular verbal response, and that, in turn, produces a generalized reinforcer, we refer to the verbal class as an intraverbal. Just for fun, think about the nature of your interaction with this book. Describe several instances of your having emitted intraverbal responses. See how far you have progressed!

When people experience difficulty in speaking, various *augmentative/alternative communication* methods are available to enable them to successfully emit verbal behavior. The list includes pictorial programs, such as the *Picture Exchange Communication System©*, the use of hand-signs and gestures, and computer-generated and other mechanical or electronic devices. As technology expands, additional possibilities may come to the fore to enrich the lives of people whose verbal repertoires are limited. The selection of the AAC must be done carefully, with input from other professionals as well as parents. (Some apps cost around $300.)

In the times of getting more than you paid for or asked for, the use of derived relational responding seems timely, especially in teaching complex verbal behavior. Although only briefly touched on in this chapter, it would be wise to look at more extensive explanations of this "new" behavioral procedure to build verbal skills in individuals with language deficits.

See the *Summary Table for Teaching Verbal Behavior* starting on the next page.

# Summary Table
# Teaching Verbal Behavior

| Operation/ Procedure | Maximizing Effectiveness/Intervention | Additional Features/Comments |
|---|---|---|
| Assessing client's current verbal repertoire; identify powerful reinforcers | • Conduct and review results of speech and language assessments; case history and other information relevant to verbal skill performance<br>• Assess reinforcer choices periodically | Refer to and select validated verbal behavioral assessment tools, including case histories |
| Assessing for and establishing motivating operations or conditions | • Emit, present or display known reinforcers, the attainment of which requires the mediation of others.<br>• Periodically assess for currently effective reinforcers<br>• If necessary, design and implement motivating conditions (i.e., establish MO's) | Conduct reinforcer assessments (e.g., requesting, taking, choosing, pointing, displaying etc.) |
| Promoting Echoic (duplic) behavior: Duplicating with point-to-point correspondence the verbal behavior of another | • Vary communicative partners<br>• Model or demonstrate verbal (communicative) stimulus to be imitated: spoken word, gesture, sign; displaying exchanging symbol or picture, operating electronic communicative device<br>• Differentially reinforce student's successive approximations toward matching sample demonstration<br>• Differentially reinforce echoic responses or approximations thereto within natural environment<br>• Gradually fade out prompting echoics<br>• Gradually thin and delay delivery of reinforcers by pausing or distancing communicative partner or "listener" (audience) | Consider "marketing" reinforcers by displaying, describing and/or demonstrating their function; provide reinforcer sampling;<br>Forms a foundation for learning other verbal skills.<br>Use in promoting spoken, sign, and picture communication. Also refer to and apply suggestions in summary table for prompting and fading exchange behaviors |
| Promoting Manding: Requesting a reinforcing object or event. | • Ensure motivating stimulus visible but unattainable<br>• Prompt as minimally feasible to occasion response<br>• If no response after many repeated efforts consider using augmentative communication system.<br>• Conduct training in environment in which skill is functional (i.e., use incidental teaching)<br>• Gradually expand distance between communicative partner and learner | Manding evoked by motivating conditions; VB evolves into mand after it has been reinforced sufficiently often. |

## Summary Table
## Teaching Verbal Behavior

| Operation/ Procedure | Maximizing Effectiveness/Intervention | Additional Features/Comments |
|---|---|---|
| Promoting Manding: (cont.). | • Teach to mand in a socially accepted ways using reinforcer(s) same or similar to those that historically served to maintain problem behavior (i.e., use functional communication training)<br>• Differentially reinforce mand or approximations thereto<br>• Gradually fade prompts (see Chapter 20) and thin artificial reinforcers as mand becomes functional<br>• Promote generalization by varying operations for establishing different reinforcers, by involving multiple communicative partners and varying settings and other conditions | Use augmentative communicative systems, if necessary |
| Promoting Tacting: Saying word in the presence of an object, event, or a feature of an abstract stimulus class. | • Once echoic or matching repertoire developed, present object or event (e.g., a toy car; boy swinging) along with an echoic prompt ("car" "boy swinging") if necessary. Differentially reinforce client's use of tact (e.g., saying "car" "boy swinging") with social or other reinforcing events. Gradually fade echoic prompt and thin reinforcers<br>• Teach and test for correspondence between stimulus and response, e.g., match-to-sample; delayed match-to-sample. Ask "What is that?" Differentially reinforce correct choosing; labeling.<br>• Prompt, if necessary, then gradually fade verbal prompt and thin reinforcers. | |

## Summary Table
## Teaching Verbal Behavior

| Operation/Procedure | Maximizing Effectiveness/Intervention | Additional Features/Comments |
|---|---|---|
| Promoting use of Intraverbals: Controlled by a verbal stimulus without point-to-point correspondence or formal similarity and reinforced by nonspecific reinforcers. Verbal stimuli that occasion other verbal responses | • Prompt and differentially reinforce use; gradually fade and thin supplementary reinforcers<br>• Use words learner has already mastered (e.g., the vocal response sought should already exist as a tact, mand or echoic response)<br>• Consider using an established mand frame to supplement training: Child has not eaten for a while (MO); likes apples; apples are present; you say: "You eat an ___." When child says "apple," you provide a piece of the apple. You gradually fade out the motivational antecedent, then the apple, and then provide a generalized reinforcer such as praise for correct responding | Facilitates other verbal as well as non-verbal behavior. An intraverbal repertoire allows speaker to talk about absent objects and events |
| Promoting more generalized communication | • Involve many communicative partners; prepare and organize establishing operations, setting events, materials, reinforcers<br>• Teach and promote array of verbal behaviors (matches, choices, gestures, signs, exchange items), to label objects, actions, qualifiers | |

*Chapter 20*

# Promoting Independence: Shifting and Expanding Stimulus Control

## Goals

1. Define and illustrate each of the following terms:
    a. delayed prompting (and list the other names that this procedure is called)
    b. progressive (or graduated) delayed prompting (or progressive time delay), and differentiate it from constant delayed prompting (or constant time delayed prompting)
    c. moment of transfer
    d. graduated prompting, increasing assistance, or minimum-to-maximum prompting
    e. fading
    f. graduated guidance
    g. errorless learning
    h. within-stimulus prompts
    i. stimulus equalization
    j. extra-stimulus prompts
    k. response delay

2. List the advantages and disadvantages of delayed prompting.
3. List and describe what can be done to help enhance the effectiveness of delayed prompting.
4. Differentiate between *progressive delayed prompting* and *graduated prompting*.
5. Compare the use of graduated prompting to maximum-to-minimum prompt reduction. Describe a context for each prompting style in which it might be the best procedure to use.

6. List and give illustrations of the major variables that facilitate fading.
7. Describe within-stimulus prompting methods that can be used to help achieve fading for errorless learning. Point out the advantages and disadvantages of using within-stimulus prompting.
8. Differentiate between *within-* and *extra-stimulus prompting*.
9. Discuss the advantages and disadvantages of errorless learning.
10. Discuss and compare how fading, response delay, and delayed prompting can be used to minimize errors.

\*\*\*\*\*\*\*\*\*\*\*\*

"Hey, man, not like that," shouts Mr. Walker, head of the truck pool. "You can't try to zip a cement truck around the way you do your own car. With all that weight, the momentum is terrific. Just think what would happen if you needed to make a sudden stop. Suppose a kid or a dog ran in front of you. I can't be around you every minute. You have to learn to tell the difference. If I see you speeding like that again...."

Of course, in cases of this sort, the supervisor can't be everywhere at once, so the behavior of concern in this instance, driving more cautiously, needs to be self-regulated. Yet, unless responses of this sort occur "automatically," as needed, *independent* of artificial supports like prompting and correcting on the spot, your job is not done. In this chapter we address techniques for shifting antecedent control from artificial to natural supports, circumstances essential to teaching your clientele to perform independently and with precision under the conditions in effect.

## REDUCING PROMPT DEPENDENCE BY TRANSFERRING STIMULUS CONTROL

Because unprompted performance tends to be more efficient, society tends to reinforce behavior that is independent of contrived supplementary cues. Those considered to be self-sufficient or expert require few prompts. A highly skilled surgeon hardly needs to refer to directions, reminders, or flow diagrams while performing a difficult operation. Nor does the master photographer need to refer continuously to her camera's operating manual; or the star quarterback to remind himself how to position his body while running with the ball. *Only when artificial or supplemental prompts are completely eliminated and only natural discriminative stimuli remain to set the occasion for a response can we say that a person is functioning independently* (Schoen, 1986).

Beyond efficiency and independence, prompting can be punishing. How would you feel, as an adult, if your parent or partner frequently reminded you how you should be driving, or to button your coat, to wear your overshoes, or to call home? What is your reaction when someone gives you detailed directions for carrying out a task you feel you have mastered, such as playing a bridge hand or the best way to study for an examination?

As Krumboltz and Krumboltz recognized some time ago:

[M]ost people do not like to depend on others to give them cues. They want to be independent and will readily interpret someone else's deliberate cue as an effort to control. Adolescents, in their strenuous effort to achieve an independent identity, are particularly sensitive to cues which they may perceive as a challenge to their own good judgment. (1972, p. 76)

Unnecessary prompting also can inadvertently cause responders to make subsequent errors, as shown in teaching college students to use spreadsheets (Karlsson & Chase, 1996). As opposed to progressive delayed prompting (described later), students trained with continuous prompting made twice as many errors on post-tests.

Having mastered a new skill is no guarantee that the learner will spontaneously transfer it to those stimuli that are supposed to control it naturally. Sometimes the person becomes totally dependent on prompts. Although an adult, Mel still counts on his fingers. The only time Dexter opens a book is when his teacher instructs him to, and Leroy only stops hitting his head briefly when told to stop. This dependency may exist because the change agent fostered overdependence on prompts, or because other circumstances impeded the shift from artificial to natural stimulus control. This sort of over-reliance on artificial supports compromises performance. In this chapter you will learn a set of instructional strategies designed to prevent or repair such difficulties. First, we will define, illustrate, and discuss *delayed prompting,* a method for removing prompts by interposing time delays. Next, we present *graduated prompting,* a technique that usually involves shifting from a class of less intrusive prompts to a class of more intrusive prompts, as in moving from subtle gestures (because they do not prompt the behavior) to elaborate verbal instructions. Third, we describe *fading,* a procedure for shifting control, often within a given prompt category, such as from one visual or tactile stimulus to another. Finally, we discuss instructional methods designed to prevent errors altogether: *errorless learning* instruction.

## DELAYED PROMPTING

### Defined and Illustrated

**Delayed prompting** (also called **time delay** or sometimes **delayed cuing**) is a tool designed to *transfer stimulus control from an artificial or unnecessary prompt to the natural stimulus. The agent first presents the natural stimulus and then introduces either a constant* (**constant time-delayed prompting**) *or a graduated* (**graduated time-delayed prompting**) *time delay before a prompt is provided.* This helps separate the prompt from the natural discriminative stimulus. **Constant delayed prompting** (sometimes called **constant time delayed prompting**) often *consists of initially presenting the prompt immediately after the instruction for several trials (a 0-second delay). Next, the agent introduces a delay, generally about a 3-second delay between the natural stimulus ($S^+$) and the prompt. This 3-second delay remains constant until the target response occurs prior to the prompt, and the prompt is no longer needed* (Caldwell, Wolery, Werts, & Caldwell, 1996; Schuster, Griggen, & Wolery, 1992).

**Progressive** (or *graduated*) **delayed prompting**, (also called **progressive time delay**), is designed to shift the stimuli, or prompts, currently controlling the response (the $S^D$s) to the stimulus designated to evoke the behavior ($S^+$) by *interposing gradually increasing period of time between the discriminative stimulus and the (artificial) prompt. Ultimately the learner begins to respond before the prompt is provided, thereby allowing the prompt to be discarded altogether.*

To use *progressive delayed prompting*, first present the request, or the stimulus you intend to make functional as a discriminative stimulus. As necessary, follow this with as minimally obtrusive a prompt as possible; yet one that reliably occasions the response. "It's five minutes until recess. Please put away your projects." The prompt might consist of gentle guidance or a demonstration, gesture, verbal cue, or a correct answer. After it is evident that the group is responding correctly (e.g., after two consecutive correct trials they have put away their projects), present the stimulus (e.g., your request to put away their materials) but include a brief delay before you present the prompt, or request, again. Delay the prompt a bit longer after you've seen several correct responses (e.g., cleaning off their desks starting at five minutes before recess) in a row, and use a shorter delay after incorrect responses (Note: although we are not being systematic in this example, it is important that you have rules that you adhere to while delaying the delivery of prompts.) Eventually, the group members begin to "anticipate," or respond *before* the delayed prompt. *The point at which each individual anticipates* (responds before the prompt) is called the **moment of transfer**. Now all are starting to clean off their desks without having to be asked.

Several reviews of the literature on delayed prompting (Handen & Zane, 1987; Kennedy, 1992; Walker, 2008) have concluded that the method may be used successfully to teach an array of tasks to people ranging in age from three to 60, including subjects of normal intelligence and those with developmental or sensory disabilities. Illustrative task performances have included learning to:

- apply purchasing skills (McDonnell, 1987).
- distinguish difficult numerals, letters, and words (Bradley-Johnson et al., 1983; Touchette & Howard, 1984).
- use sign language (Browder et al, 1981; Thompson, Cotnoir-Bichelman, McKerchar, Tate, & Dancho, 2007; Thompson, McKerchar, & Dancho, 2004).
- perform practical assembly tasks (Walls, Haught, & Dowler, 1982).
- make beds (Snell, 1982).
- acquire social play skills (Liber, Frea, & Symon, 2007)
- read English sight words (Rohena, Jitendra, & Browder, 2002)
- travel independently (Masataka, 2002)
- point to items missing in pictures (Sigafoos, Couzens, Pennell, Shaw, & Dudfield, (1995)
- teaching sight words (Swain, Lane, & Gast, 2015)
- promoting peer imitation (Sweeney, Barton, & Ledford, 2018)

Box 20.1 illustrates progressive delayed prompting for teaching a numeral in Spanish.

After a peer modeling procedure was found to be unsuccessful, Charlop and Walsh (1986) used a progressive delayed prompting strategy to teach four boys with autism to verbalize affection spontaneously while being hugged; to say things like "I like you" or "I love you." Whether prompted or not, whenever the child uttered those words of affection, he was praised and given a preferred food. After the child correctly imitated the phrases twice in a row, the experimenter added a two-second delay between the discriminative stimulus, the hug, and the modeled phrases. Eventually, after further training by peers and parents in the home, modeling and reinforcing the words became unnecessary. As a result of the treatment, parents and siblings reported that

> **Box 20.1**
>
>
>
> Teacher: "What is the word for the numeral two in Spanish?" Pause. "Uno, (pause—no answer) dos."
> Student: "Dos."
> Teacher: "Muy bien!"
> Teacher: "What is the word for the numeral two in Spanish?" (Pause—no answer). "Uno," (pause) "do——"
> Student: "Dos."
> Teacher: "Muy bien!"
> Teacher: "Numeral two?"
> (Pause, but student murmurs numerals in Spanish); then says "Dos."
> Teacher: "Dos. Muy bien. So how many fingers am I showing you?"
> Student: "Dos."
> Teacher: "Muy, muy bien. Dos."

the boys were more socially responsive, loved them more, and that they themselves had begun to spend more time interacting with the children. Similarly, Liber et al. (2007) used graduated delayed prompting to teach three boys with autism a form of social play that required making requests for peer assistance. All three acquired the play skills, one increased his pretend play, and two demonstrated generalization of the social skills. Figure 20.1 illustrates the delayed prompting process. In another similar study (Lane, Gast, Ledford & Shepley, 2017), four to five-year olds with significant developmental delays and ASD were taught to share and to name each peer's preferences (reinforcers). Progressive time delay started with 0-seconds and gradually increased by a second up to 4 seconds.

Thompson et al. (2004) and Thompson et al. (2007) have used delayed prompting to teach sign language to infants. In the 2007 study, the investigators used modeling in an initial attempt to teach each of four infants a single sign. If the modeling did not evoke imitation or an approximation thereto after five seconds, they followed the imitative prompt with physical guidance. They then delivered a designated reinforcer following all signs, whether prompting had been necessary or not. They gradually increased the delay to the modeled prompt from zero to 80 seconds, usually in five-second increments, "until high levels of independent signing occurred for several sessions" (p. 17). They

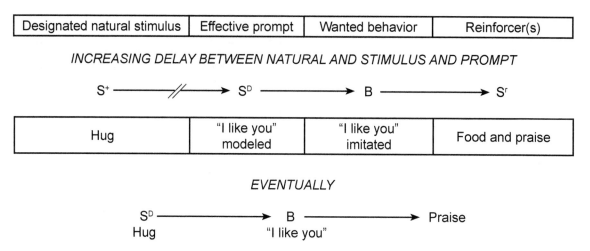

Figure 20.1 Using progressive delayed prompting

used this method to teach Heather, a ten-month-old infant with Down syndrome, to mand, or request, an assortment of toys (e. g., musical toys, balls) and Betty, a six-month-old typically-developing infant, to mand for a bite of baby food and brief attention. Geoffrey, also a typically-developing ten-month-old, frequently cried when not receiving attention. While Geoffrey's crying was placed on extinction, he was taught to sign for attention and an assortment of toys. Lyle, nine-months of age, frequently cried when not being held. As a result, he often had been picked up. Lyle was taught to sign "up," while his crying also was placed on extinction. All children learned the sign that was taught to them and "readily performed the target signs under a variety of relevant stimulus conditions" (p. 21). Also, the last two infants decreased their rates of crying and whining.

Rohena et al. (2002) used a fixed two-second time delay to teach English sight words of the kind displayed at local grocery and department stores to four Puerto Rican middle-school students with intellectual disabilities. Not only was the procedure effective in teaching the children the sight words, but they also generalized their reading from the classroom to stores in the community.

## Advantages of Delayed Prompting

Delayed prompting increases learners' opportunities to respond independently, perhaps because the best way to obtain the reinforcer rapidly is to respond in advance of (or to *anticipate*) the prompt. Perhaps the delay works because it allows the learners extra time to respond. Investigators (Heckaman, Alber, Hooper & Heward, 1998) found that progressive time delay prompting generated fewer errors and less disruptive behavior than least to most prompting when used on the disruptive behavior of students with autism who had been assigned difficult tasks. Several investigators (Bradley-Johnson, Sunderman, & Johnson, 1983) compared the use of delayed prompting to stimulus fading (described later) in teaching pre-schoolers easily confused letters and numbers. They reported that the group of children that received delayed prompting showed greater progress and made fewer errors than the fading group during a follow-up a week later. When carefully programmed, the method can enable students to discriminate while committing few or essentially no errors (Touchette & Howard, 1984; see the section on *errorless learning* below). These same authors (Bradley-Johnson, et al.) also have suggested other advantages:

- The individual is less likely to attend to an irrelevant prompt.
- Training stimuli need not be modified, as required in stimulus fading (discussed later).
- The trainer will know the exact moment of transfer—the moment when the $S^D$ takes

over control—thereby allowing the trainer to avoid presenting unnecessary training trials or unnecessary prompts.

## Disadvantages

Striefel and Owens (1980) noted several disadvantages of the delayed prompting method:
- The response must already be in the person's repertoire; otherwise, it must be taught.
- Some individuals may never emit the response unassisted, regardless of the length of the interposed delay.
- Others may produce incorrect responses during the pause between the relevant stimulus and the prompt.

## Using Delayed Prompting Effectively

No single variation appears best for everyone, for as Handen and Zane (1987) commented, "variables that proved to be advantageous within one category of comparison were often found to be a hindrance in another" (p. 321). However, Walker (2008) and O'Neill, McDowell, and Leslie (2018; 2020) did address whether the delay should be lengthened gradually or remain constant. Based on a review of 22 empirical studies, Walker (2008) found both constant and progressive delay methods were successful, though the constant delays resulted in more errors, more procedural modifications, and in a belated moment of transfer of stimulus control, as compared with the progressive delay methods. O'Neill, et al. (2018; 2020) also found the progressive prompt delay strategy reduced learner errors more effectively and efficiently during instruction (2018).

They (O'Neill, et al., 2020) concluded that clinicians would be wise to select progressive prompt delay initially, because constant delay prompting's higher error rates tend to impede later learning. Also, it seems likely that people with long histories of failure and dependence on others would profit most from a progressive increase in the delay, beginning with short intervals of a second or less. Consequently, assuming that no strong counterargument surfaces, *we continue to recommend* (Mayer et al., 2012) *that you choose progressive over constant delayed prompting.*

Regardless of which method you might be using, though, suppose your student responds incorrectly during the delay. What might you do? Several corrective methods have been used: prompting the correct response, removing your attention (as in turning away briefly), or, in the case of a matching (pointing) task:

- removing the client's hand from the stimulus
- presenting the next trial
- modeling the response
- physically guiding the response
- repeating or terminating the trial

Again, the method you select will depend on the specific task at hand and the client's behavioral repertoire.

Delayed prompting, then, can be an effective strategy for teaching independence from supplementary prompts. If people are capable of performing the instructed behavior, the delay seems to set the occasion for the desired performance (Halle, Baer, & Spradlin, 1981). Should the method fail to evoke the desired response, you always can attempt to teach it, perhaps by substituting a different and progressively more natural series of prompting categories, as in moving from modeled to guided prompts.

## GRADUATED PROMPTING

A method variously called **graduated prompting** (Correa, Poulson, & Salzberg, 1984), **increasing assistance** (Gaul, Nietupski, & Cerro, 1985; Schoen, 1986), or **minimum-to-maximum prompting** (as described in Chapter 17) *begins with the natural, non-intrusive discriminative stimulus, and progresses by interposing increasingly intrusive prompts until one of those succeeds in evoking the wanted response.* An example would be shifting from gestural to spoken to physically guided prompts. The rationale for following this sequence is similar to that for delayed prompting, in that it offers the learner the opportunity to *anticipate* or to respond in advance of the successively more intrusive prompts. The intention, as you would expect, is for the learner to begin to respond to the least intrusive, and then, eventually to *anticipate* or respond in advance of the prompt, at which point he would no longer need to depend on it at all.

Yang, Chu, and Chiang (2018) used graduated prompting (gradually increasing levels of hints) to teach second graders to complete mathematical tasks and achieve learning goals. They reported that graduated prompting enhanced the learning of those who received the intervention as compared to the control group. Additionally, correctly guiding the youngsters to answer questions enabled them to "step up their thinking, and understand the learning content in the learning process" (p. 322). Should you consider using this technique, you may find it useful to check out Zhang, Lai, Cheng, and Chen (2017). They recommend using computer-based graduated prompting assessments when designing specific prompting strategies to promote students' academic performance. Another study, Drifke, Tiger and Wierzba (2017) taught parents who were applying behavioral skills training to use graduated prompting as a tool for teaching their children buttoning, zipping, and snapping clothing; tracing letters; putting on shoes; sorting silverware; placing toys in a basket; and, pointing to body parts as directed by their parent. However, to minimize client errors, we would recommend graduated guidance (see below) for many of these behaviors, rather than graduated prompting.

A study by Steege, Wacker, and McMahon (1987) illustrates the relative effectiveness of "least-to-most" graduated prompting, compared to a variation that had been used as an assessment tool. Under this variation, the trainer sequentially initiated increasingly restrictive levels of prompting until the functional prompt was identified. Then, rather than sequentially initiating the much more restrictive levels each time the student failed to respond to the natural prompt, as with traditional graduated prompting, the trainer provided a prompt within the category just below (less restrictive than) the functional one. So, for example, if the student reliably responded to partial guidance, training trials began with a gesture plus a verbal prompt. The functional prompt (e.g., partial guidance) was provided only if the student was not successful at this level. Both graduated prompting and the variation of graduated prompting were successful in teaching the skill. However, the variation accelerated the learning. The authors pointed out that the greater efficiency was probably due to the fact that the graduated prompting variation provided for a more precise selection of prompts, thereby reducing unnecessary errors. (For additional illustrations, refer back to the section in Chapter 17 on using prompts effectively.)

So, to summarize this variation of graduated prompting, first determine the functional prompt. Then, rather than starting each time with the least intrusive prompt, start with the prompt within the category just below (less restrictive than) the functional one, and provide the functional prompt only if the client is not successful at this level. Once the individual succeeds for several consecutive sessions at the less restrictive level, move to the next less restrictive level until the desired discriminative stimulus eventually is achieved.

Sometimes, instructors combine delayed prompting and graduated prompting to facilitate the transfer of stimulus control from a prompt to the natural $S^D$. Say you are using least to most prompting with a 5-s delay, the prompting pattern might look like:

SD (verbal prompt)→wait 5 s→

model prompt→wait 5 s→physical prompt.

The delay interval allows the individual potentially to respond before the next more intrusive prompt.

Presuming individuals ultimately begin to respond in advance of progressively more intrusive prompt levels, eventually natural or minimally intrusive circumstances should assume stimulus control. Suppose, however, a person remains overly dependent on a given prompt. What methods might we use to overcome that barrier? *Fading* may be the answer.

## STIMULUS FADING

### Defined and Illustrated

In **stimulus fading** *artificial or intrusive prompts are gradually and systematically removed for the purpose of enabling control to transfer to the ante-*

cedent stimuli ($S^+$s) that are supposed naturally to evoke the response. A systematic review of stimulus' or prompt-fading procedures (Cengher, Budd, Farrell, & Fienup, 2018) found that "all prompt-fading procedures were generally effective in promoting acquisition of behavior" (p. 155).

Fading begins by providing whatever prompts the person needs to succeed, but you gradually remove those prompts while gradually introducing the designated antecedent stimuli. (In the language of fading, some stimuli can be *faded in* at the same time as others are *faded out*; see Becker, Engelmann, & Thomas, 1975; Deitz & Malone, 1985; Freeman & Piazza, 1998; Hively, 1962; Rilling, 1977.) Often the shift occurs *within* a prompt category, as in substituting one visual (or auditory or tactile) stimulus for another. At other times, control transfers *from* one prompt modality to another, as from physical guidance to instructions. Either way, *prompts are reduced by moving from maximal to minimal assistance* until control transfers to the more natural or appropriate stimulus. To summarize, "In fading, a property of a stimulus is gradually changed on successive trials to transfer control of responding from one property of a stimulus to another" (Rilling, 1977, p. 466) or, we might add, eventually from one stimulus—the prompt—to another—the natural antecedent.

During *fading*, the response and reinforcers usually remain constant, while the prompts, those discriminative stimuli that have temporarily served to occasion these behaviors, are slowly and progressively removed or replaced by stimuli that are natural (e.g., in Figure 20.2 the picture of the cat, or prompt, is gradually replaced by what will become the natural $S^D$, or the word "gato"). Fading does not necessarily involve interposing delays between the prompt and the relevant antecedent stimuli (although such a method also may be used as an adjunct to the procedure). Rather, the prompt is changed across sessions or trials. Similar to the other procedures used to transfer stimulus control, *fading is designed to result in the desired stimulus evoking a given behavior reliably, independent of other supportive prompts.*

As you saw illustrated in Chapter 17 in the section on shifting stimulus control, fading is a useful instructional tool suitable for just about everyone—adult or child, developmentally-challenged or not.

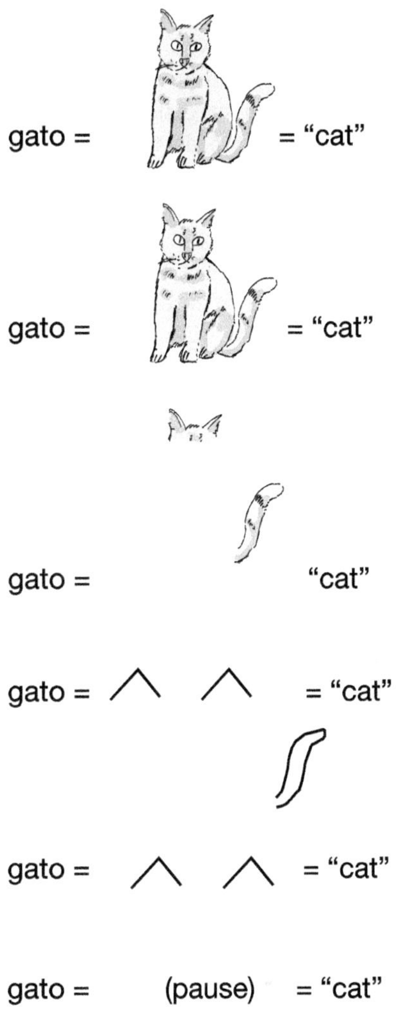

**Figure 20.2** Fading of pictorial cues

It is applicable to diverse classes of responding, including language, motor, social, and other skills. Suppose a teacher is instructing a student to translate the Spanish word *gato* into the English word *cat*. She could use numerous prompts to evoke the English translation (a picture of a cat, the sound "meow," a purring sound, the initial "ka" sound, pictorial representations of cats' ears and whiskers, and so on) to occasion the right answer. But to obtain a fully independent response, she would have to fade those prompts, perhaps by saying them more softly or gradually removing aspects of the extra-stimulus pictorial cue (e.g., by making it darker and darker) until all prompt elements vanished (see Figure

20.2). However, you need carefully to evaluate this technique's effectiveness with individual students, especially those with autism spectrum disorders, because some research suggests the graphics may distract or otherwise impede their learning (Dittlinger & Lerman, 2011).

Similarly, suppose a teacher or parent is trying to teach a child to recognize color names. The child can recognize the colors, just not the names, so the word *red* could be printed in red (a within-stimulus prompt). Over successive trials, we gradually could fade out the color and fade in the intensity of the lines while reinforcing the child's continuing to say "red" in the presence of the word *red*. Eventually, the color is no longer present, yet the child still reads the word "red."

Properly cleaning oneself following a bowel movement is a common issue among many children with autism and other disabilities. Fading was used as an important element of a program to teach two boys, almost six and seven years of age with autism spectrum disorder (ASD), *how to clean themselves after a bowel movement* (Byra, White, Temple, & Cameron, 2018). Some pieces of paper were smeared with a small amount of SunButter, others were not. The experimenters asked, while holding out a piece of paper, "Is this clean or dirty?" Initially, they verbally modeled the correct answer (e.g., It is clean"). Eventually, they faded out part of the answer until it was no longer provided, and the child could repeatedly provide the correct answer. Next, a doll was prepared with the SunButter and each child had to indicate if the toilet paper used to clean the doll was clean or dirty. Once they met mastery, they then asked the parents to score whether their child correctly identified if their child's used toilet paper was clean or dirty after wiping himself. The skill successfully generalized to the home to the delight of the parents.

While teaching her students to assemble equipment, the shop instructor might describe each step as the trainees progress through the task. After performing the job successfully several times with the aid of the verbal guidance, the instructor can then gradually fade out the supplementary verbal prompts while acceptable performance continues to earn reinforcers. Parallels to these examples can also be found in physical education, language, and music training (Carlson & Mayer, 1971; Greer, 1980, 1981), as well as elsewhere.

Here we provide several illustrative studies to demonstrate the versatility of this procedure.

- In one case, an enuresis-control device was deactivated after a boy with a history of bed-wetting achieved 30 consecutive dry nights. First one pad, then another, then the control device was gradually faded. Yet the boy remained continent (Hansen, 1979).
- In another illustration, McNeill, Lizotte, Krajcik, and Marx (2006) sought to determine whether continuing to provide written instructional guidance or gradually fading the guidance better prepared 331 seventh-grade students to write scientific explanations for a chemistry unit. On posttest items, the group for which the detailed instructions and explanations were faded gave more convincing reasons than the group that received continuous instructional guidance.
- McDougall and Brady (1998) found that by fading components of a self-management program (see Chapter 11), both math fluency and engaged time improved. Also, fluency generalized to answering math word problems.
- Atkinson, Renkl, and Merrill (2003) noted that incrementally fading worked-out solution steps promoted independent problem solving on similar tasks, but this was not reliable with tasks that were not very similar ("far-transfer tasks," p. 774). Consequently, they first added prompts and then faded those prompts to encourage learners to identify the underlying principles in each step of their worked-out solutions. For example, they asked their college-student participants to select which principle of probability each partial solution exemplified. This component was gradually faded. The strategy fostered greater generalization among college students learning statistics, as well as among high-school students learning advanced algebra.

- In another study (Banda, McAfee, & Hart, 2012) worked with a 14-year-old student with autism and Tourette Syndrome who engaged in severe self-injurious behavior (SIB). A behavioral assessment determined that less SIB occurred when the student wrapped his hands tightly in a large blanket. The blanket was used by the investigators to keep the rate of the SIB down, and the blanket was gradually faded by gradually reducing its size. Also, the student was provided with attention every ten seconds that he did not hit himself. The student remained at near-zero rate of SIB six months after the blanket was eliminated.

- Krantz and McClannahan (1998) used fading to help teach social-interaction skills to three boys with autism (ages four, four, and five with IQs of 36, 42 and 62 respectively). The boys spoke only when answering questions or requesting an item. The intervention consisted of a script-fading procedure placed within a photographic activity schedule currently in use in the classroom. The script "Watch me" was placed above photographs of activities; the prompt "Look" below pictures in the schedule. Initially, each child was manually guided to point to the script. If he did not say the script, a verbal model was provided (e.g., "Watch me").

  The child was then manually guided to obtain the relevant materials (e.g., a hat or basketball), approach the recipient and say the script, and then perform the target task (e.g., wearing the hat or throwing the ball).... Prompts for pointing to and saying the scripts and approaching the familiar adult were faded as quickly as the boy's performance permitted, and manual guidance was replaced by spatial fading, shadowing, and decreases in teacher proximity.... Scripts were faded... by successively cutting away portions of the cards on which they appeared.... The teaching condition ended after each participant reliably said the scripts without prompts and after two consecutive sessions during which the teacher stood near the wall opposite the boy's desk and delivered no prompts of any kind, either for following the activity schedule or for saying the scripts. (p. 195)

  The method enabled the children to converse with adults, to benefit from adults' language models, and to engage in the sort of language practice that contributes to fluency.... After scripts were faded, unscripted interactions not only continued but also generalized to different activities that had not been the topic of teaching. (p. 191)

Other investigators (e.g., Freeman & Piazza, 1998; Mueller, Piazza, Patel, Kelley, & Pruett, 2004; Patel, Piazza, Kelly, Ochsner, & Santana, 2001; Shore, Babbitt, Williams, Coe, & Snyder, 1998) have used fading to assist children with *feeding disorders*. Freeman et al. pointed out that: "Children with feeding disorders often display severe food selectivity. For many of these children, consuming highly-textured foods may be aversive or potentially dangerous because of frequent gagging" (p. 621). Their intervention with four two- to five-year-olds consisted of gradually *fading* from smooth to rougher textures (e.g., the amount of junior food was gradually increased in the pureed food, then ground food was gradually increased in the junior food, and then finely chopped was gradually increased in the ground food). In addition, food acceptance and swallowing were reinforced, and food refusal and expulsion were extinguished. "All participants successfully advanced to consumption of age-appropriate texture and volume" (p. 621). Similarly, Mueller et al. were able to increase the variety of foods that two young children ate by gradually blending in non-preferred with the preferred foods. And, Patel et al. progressively added Carnation Instant Breakfast© and then milk to water (a liquid that the child would drink) to increase the consumption of calorie-dense fluids.

*Compliance training* also has been achieved through fading (e.g., Ardoin, Martens, & Wolfe, 1999; Ducharme & Worling, 1994; Stuesser & Roscoe, 2020). Stuesser and Roscoe promoted compliance by children with autism during medical exams by gradually introducing small components of problematic exam steps. Ardoin et al. used fading in a regular second-grade classroom to help promote compliance during transitions, while Ducharme and Worling used the procedure to maintain high levels of compliance that originally had been obtained by requesting high-probability responses (a procedure called *behavioral momentum*; see Chapter 27). Initially a series of requests were made to which compliance was especially likely (for example, we would expect a child to comply with requests such as "Would you like some ice cream?" and "Do you want to play with your favorite toy?"), immediately prior to low-probability requests ("Time to clean up," "Say 'thank-you' to Julio for helping you"). After compliance with the low-probability requests stabilized, the investigators gradually reduced the frequency of the high-probability requests and gradually increased the time between the high- and low-probability requests. This method produced and maintained compliance by two children with developmental disabilities: a five-year-old's compliance with "do's" and "don'ts" and a 15-year-old girl's compliance with "do's," but not with "don'ts." However, compliance was achieved when the "don't" requests were re-phrased as "do" requests. This result should come as no surprise, in that evidence and experience (Hagopian & Adelinis, 2001; Mayer, 2000; Walker et al., 2004) suggests that *noncompliance is more probable following "...a terminating than an initiating request"* (Mayer, p. 79). For example, rather than telling children to "stop playing," they would be more likely to comply if they were told, "Come now, we are going to eat." Or, "Now we get to go and do ___."

## Using Fading Effectively

The above examples probably have supplied you with a reasonable understanding of how fading is designed and executed, but you might find some additional suggestions useful. For instance, you can more smoothly and effectively shift from supplementary prompts to natural antecedent stimuli with minimal disruption if you remove prompts gradually first from more to less, and then ultimately, to no intrusive prompts. Depending on the class of current supports, you might arrange to shift control from physically guided to self-guided motor behavior or from demonstrations to instructions; and/or from irrelevant prompts to relevant antecedent stimuli. Next, we detail some of those techniques, including several methods for preventing or minimizing errors.

**Remove prompts gradually.** As illustrated in the studies cited above, once prompts have begun to reliably occasion the desired response, those prompts should be removed slowly. To illustrate, Haupt, Van Kirk, and Terraciano (1975) taught nine- and ten-year-old children addition, subtraction, and multiplication number facts by gradually covering the answer to the number fact with increasing layers of cellophane or tracing paper, so the answer eventually became invisible. This fading procedure enabled students with long histories of unsuccessful experience with typical instructional procedures to produce fewer errors and to retain the facts longer.

**Remove antecedents that may occasion unwanted responses.** You also can use fading to reduce control by natural, but undesired, stimuli and thereby inhibit unwanted responses. Begin by preventing the unwanted response and then gradually remove the impediments until you have returned to the natural stimuli. For example, suppose a child's thumb sucking has reached the point where a dentist is concerned that it will affect his teeth. The thumb is always there as a natural stimulus, so to prevent nocturnal thumb-sucking, Van Houten and Rolider (1984) began by placing a boxing glove on a child's hand when he went to bed. Later, they progressively faded the impediment to sucking by progressively replacing the glove with absorbent cotton over the thumb, then with a fingertip bandage over the thumb, and finally with no obstacles at all. To optimize the outcome, they combined the fading with daily feedback and other reinforcers for non-thumb-sucking, resulting in the successful elimination of the habit.

**Prevent overdependence on prompts.** Fade *physical* as well as other prompts as systematically and rapidly as possible to prevent overdependence on those prompts. One often overlooked physical prompt is the presence of the therapist (Athens, Vollmer, Sloman, & Pipkin, 2008). An 11-year-old boy with Down syndrome and autism diminished his vocal stereotypy when the therapist was present, but not when she was away. By very gradually fading the therapist's presence in the room, the investigators successfully managed to maintain the youngster's low level of vocal stereotypy.

Fading is an especially useful teaching and training tool. Several more examples follow: if Dad insists on grasping the wheel whenever he takes his son out to practice driving, the boy might never learn to drive independently. What he should do instead is to combine physical guidance with demonstrations, instructions, or both. Then he needs to remove his physical guidance gradually, while continuing to demonstrate and/or provide instructions. Little by little, instructions alone should suffice. Ultimately, he can fade instructions until the critical features—visual stimuli, the feedback from the car's movement, the positions of the feet and hands on the steering wheel and pedals—assume full control over his son's driving.

Singh and Solman (1990) found that failing to fade *pictures* while teaching word recognition (e.g., the word apple with a picture of an apple) resulted in some students failing to learn the new words. Instead, the children became dependent on the pictures, not the written words (i.e., the pictures, not the written words, became the $S^D$s for saying the word). If that has been your experience, plan to fade such prompts as rapidly as feasible (see Figure 20.3).

As should by now be apparent to you, fading is designed to promote independence from artificial or intrusive prompts. This conclusion was supported when Schunk and Rice (1993) compared their standard teaching practices to those augmented by fading and feedback. In that study, forty-four fifth-grade remedial reading students reported that the latter conditions made them feel more capable ("self-efficacious"). The students also comprehended the material better and teachers continued to use the strategy.

**Consider using graduated guidance to fade physical assistance.** Sometimes simply reinforcing a few physically guided trials is sufficient as learners begin to assume control of the movements on their own. When that fails, consider trying **graduated guidance** (Foxx & Azrin, 1972). In graduated guidance, the therapist physically prompts the particular movement, over time gradually lessening the

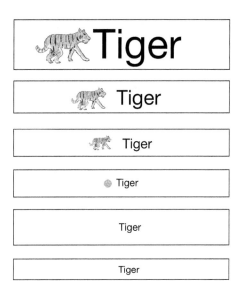

**Figure 20.3** Possible flashcard steps in stimulus fading of pictorial, color, and size prompts

locus and amount of the control s/he provides. Azrin and Foxx (1972) suggested that you *begin while the client is being cooperative, using the minimal amount of physical guidance necessary to evoke the correct response, and then gradually fade out the physical guidance*. (Note: Do not confuse this procedure with graduated prompting, in which prompts are gradually *faded in* or *added* rather than faded out. Also, avoid using graduated guidance with highly resistant or uncooperative clients. To do so is ethically questionable and usually counterproductive, in that agitated clients are not likely to learn from this procedure.)

As a trainer, you first focus guidance on the body part that is the locus of action. For example, the hand in spoon feeding; the arm while teaching swinging a baseball bat or a hatchet. Little by little, reduce the pressure you exert and shift away from the point of guidance, making it increasingly remote.

Here is an example: Young Joey Jordan fails to follow through when batting the ball. Instructions, modeling, and even some forms of physical guidance have failed to prompt the appropriate motions. So, at this point the coach places one hand directly on Joey's arm and the other on the bat, exerting enough pressure to promote the follow-through. As the coach begins to feel Joey responding appropriately, he gradually diminishes his pressure on the boy's arm. As Joey's movements gradually approximate the proper follow-through, the coach continues to reduce the pressure, moves the locus of the contact to Joey's shoulder, then his outer shoulder; then just shadows his movements—ultimately moving away altogether. Control has shifted over to Joey slowly enough so that errors have not emerged. Similarly, with spoon feeding, you might start by holding the child's entire hand, but then you can move gradually to a very gentle grip on the child's wrist or lower arm.

Combined with verbal and/or gestural prompts, graduated guidance is an effective method for teaching many complex responses, including, among others:

- *Self-care and vocational skills* to developmentally-delayed women (Thomas et al., 1977) and adults with autism and profound intellectual disabilities (Lattimore, Parsons, & Reid, 2008)
- *Independent play skills* to adults with profound mental retardation (Singh & Millichamp, 1987) and to children (Morrison, Sainato, Benchaaban, & Endo, 2002)
- *Self-dressing* to a variety of individuals (e.g., Azrin, Shaeffer, & Wesolowski, 1976; Hughs, Schuster, & Nelson, 1993; McKelvey, 1992; Sewell, Collins, Hemmeter, & Schuster, 1998; Young, West, Howard, & Whitney, 1986)
- *Toileting* (Cicero & Pfadt, 2002)
- Parents teaching yoga to children with developmental delays (Gruber & Poulson, 2016)
- *On-task and on-schedule behavior* among young children with autism (Bryan & Gast, 2000)
- *Expressive sign language* (Dalrymple & Feldman, 1992)
- *Functional use of voice-output communication devices* (Schepis, Reid, & Behrman, 1996)
- *Completion of vocational tasks* by an adult with developmental disabilities (Steed & Lutzker, 1997)
- Clients with autism *initiating social contact with peers* (Krantz & McClannahan, 1993)

Graduated guidance also has been used as an error correction procedure. For example, Gardner and Wolfe (2019) used video priming and prompting, followed by graduated guidance for errors, to teach adolescents with autism appropriate dishwashing skills. This graduated guidance strategy is also a feature of the most to least (MTL) prompting strategy. Fading MTL prompting might look like Figure 20.4. It is important to remember when planning to use graduated guidance to determine the fading criteria you will use before you start fading (example: two independent consecutive trials at 100 percent will not work; you might need to use two trials of

---

| |
|---|
| Trial 1: present S$^D$→physically guide response→deliver reinforcer |
| Trial 2: present S$^D$→physically guide response→deliver reinforcer |
| Trial 3: present S$^D$→model response→client performs response→deliver reinforcer |
| Trial 4: present S$^D$→model response→client performs response→deliver reinforcer |
| Trial 5: present S$^D$→provide verbal prompt→client performs response→deliver reinforcer |
| Trial 6: present S$^D$→provide verbal prompt→client performs response→deliver reinforcer; |
| Trial 7: present S$^D$→client performs response→deliver reinforcer. |

**Figure 20.4**

most intrusive prompt, then fade just one level at a time).

**Fade modeling and instructional prompts.** The basic system just described for fading physical prompts is analogous to the methods you would use with modeled and instructional prompts. You continue to fade prompts until your trainee begins to respond correctly without those prompts. One way to accomplish this is, after fully modeling the target behavior, to reduce those prompts to increasingly more subtle gestures and then eventually to eliminate them altogether. Tina's mom prompts her to wave "bye-bye" by modeling the response herself. As Tina becomes progressively more adept at waving "bye-bye," her mom will not fully model the behavior. Eventually, Tina will wave "bye-bye" when verbally prompted. Ultimately, the stimulus that should naturally occasion her response, the words "Bye-bye Tina," will assume control. Again we must urge you to have a systematic plan for fading prompts. For example, Tina's mom tells her to "wave bye-bye" while modeling the response until Tina starts to make a similar motion with her hand and does so five times. Next instead of completely modeling waving, Tina's mom just raises her hand when she says "wave bye-bye." When Tina is now waving bye-bye for five more times, Tina's mom stops raising her hand and just states "wave bye-bye." Then after Tina is waving bye-bye for five times, Tina's mom stops saying "wave bye-bye" when people leave and say "bye-bye Tina." It is important not to just *wing* it when fading prompts. In our experience without a fading plan, prompts tend to not be faded and prompt dependency takes over.

## ERRORLESS LEARNING

### Defined and Illustrated

**Errorless learning** is accomplished when *instructional methods specifically designed to prevent or substantially minimize any learner errors are used to teach particular discriminations*. As pointed out by Green (2001), most-to-least prompting and fading methods are especially suitable for teaching new skills errorlessly, especially when making fine discriminations is required.

> The learner is given the most assistance necessary on initial trials to ensure that the target response occurs so that it can be reinforced frequently, and to minimize errors; the amount of assistance is then systematically decreased as long as the learner continues to respond correctly. If an error occurs, there is typically a provision for "backing up" to the preceding prompt level on the very next trial to reduce the likelihood that another error will occur. Following a correct response, the systematic fading process resumes. (Green, p. 78)

Methods of teaching students to learn without producing errors are especially applicable to young students (e.g., first-graders, Robinson & Storm, 1978) as well as to clientele faced with special challenges, such as developmental disabilities (Markham, Giles, Roderique-Davies, Adshead, Tamiaki, & May, 2020; Repp, Karsh, Johnson, & VanLaarhoven, 1996), "severe disabilities" (Dube, Iennaco, Rocco, Klenderas, & McIlvane, 1992), those with acquired brain injury (Lloyd, Riley, & Powell, 2009), psychoses including schizophrenia (Kern, Wallace, Hellman, Womack, & Green, 1996; Kern, Green, Mintz, & Liberman, 2003; O'Carroll, Russell, Lawrie, & Johnstone, 1999), those with everyday memory problems of the Alzheimer type (Clare et al., 2000), and those with severe memory impairment (Tailby & Haslam, 2003). The method seems to operate effectively with a range of task requirements including, among others, arithmetic operations (Robinson & Storm, 1978), card-sorting (Kern et al., 1996), job skills (Kern et al., 2003), or learning routes through a city such as Nice, France (Lloyd et al., 2009). Though highly effective in a most situations, errorless learning may not be best suited for teaching virtual reality games to bright adults. For example, investigators (Ma, Wang, & Fuminami, 2020) compared teaching bright young adults Pokemon characters under errorless and errorful learning conditions. The participants learned more quickly under the errorless learning condition, but found the errorful condition more fun. Perhaps under the former condition they missed the negative reinforcement they received by avoiding punishing traps. In most (though not all) of the circumstances under which behavior analysis works, punishment is plentiful in the natural environment. Surely, we want to avoid pairing punishment (errors and their aversive consequences) with learning new skills; plus, because many clients have received too much punishment already in their lives, it is important to become familiar and comfortable with the various methods that are available for promoting errorless learning. We detail an array of these next.

## Using Fading to Achieve Errorless Learning

The primary problem with errors is that once they have occurred, they are much more likely to recur (McCandless, 1967; Sidman & Stoddard, 1967; Sidman, 1989; Terrace, 1963, 1966). Suppose the objective was for the student to point to five specific body parts, three times in a row, when so instructed. Having pointed to the wrong body part even once, the client would be more likely to repeat the error (perhaps because a similar response was reinforced a long time ago or more recently in some other setting). To avoid that situation, consider turning to any of the methods for minimizing errors already presented. Otherwise try *fading for errorless learning*, a technique consisting of removing prompts so gradually that the likelihood of any failure to conform to the specifications of the behavioral objective falls essentially to zero. In the present instance, you would maintain prompts long enough to support correct responding and prevent errors, only gradually removing the prompts after the desired response begins to occur reliably. (For a review of errorless learning applications specifically designed for children with pervasive developmental disorders, see Mueller, Palkovic, & Maynard, 2007).

**Begin by highlighting the differences between critical discriminative stimuli.** As mentioned, regardless of how carefully instruction is programmed, errors are bound to occur from time to time. Maybe an inappropriate stimulus occasions the desired response, or else the appropriate stimulus might occasion an inappropriate response. So be aware of techniques enabling you, first, to avoid situations that promote errors and, second, to reduce the probability that an error will reoccur. To avoid the pitfall of your student committing an error because the differences between your discriminative stimuli are too subtle, *alter "the physical characteristics of the stimuli to be discriminated to increase the likelihood that correct responses will occur early in training"* (Green, 2001, p. 78). Such **within-stimulus prompts** facilitate errorless learning. A systematic review of the literature (Markham, et al., 2020) revealed that within-stimulus errorless learning methods, including the fading of within-stimulus prompts, can be very effective for teaching discrimination skills to individuals with intellectual and developmental disabilities.

As illustrated in the video *Training for the Special Child* (1971)[1], Ellen P. Reese and her students developed one of the earliest behavioral teaching programs to demonstrate within-stimulus prompting. They used size fading to help the children with various disabilities to discriminate one numeral from another. In one portion, for example, they showed children five sets of objects differing in number and asked each child to select the set corresponding to a particular numeral (see Figure 20.5). Before the program, most children could recognize some numerals and some could recite the words "one," "two," "three," in order, but none matched either numerals or names with actual numbers of objects nor could they match sets of objects on the basis of number. If they were shown a set containing three objects, they did not select from five alternatives another set that contained three objects.

The initial training program was designed to teach matching sets of objects based on number. Because the children had no difficulty discriminating differences in size, the objects in the sample set and in the correct alternative were very large, whereas the objects in all the incorrect alternatives were very small. So, initially, the children choose the correct set on the basis of size alone. As the program progressed, though, the size of the incorrect

---
[1]Reese's videos may be found on the Cambridge Center for Behavioral Studies Web site: http://behavior.org/

**Figure 20.5** Matching a numeral with corresponding number of items, assisted by size prompts.

objects was gradually increased. By the end of the program, all objects were of uniform dimension, and the correct choice depended on number alone.

In approximately three-and-a-half hours (spread over several weeks), all the children learned to match as many as four objects. After that, they were taught to match numbers of objects to numerals. This second fading program took approximately two hours, even less time than the first program. Training transferred from these two matching tasks to seven other tasks, including two that did not involve matching: counting a given number of objects when they were handed to the child and counting out a requested number of objects from a set of 30 and handing them to the experimenter. Reese later reported that these gains were maintained a year later and that most of the children had acquired further skills with numbers. Most could tell time on the hour and some could exchange five pennies for a nickel (Reese, Howard, & Reese, 1977).

When incorporating matching-to-sample methods within errorless instruction, designers systematically program stimuli to promote shifts of control from irrelevant to relevant stimuli, in much the same way as described earlier in Chapter 16: when a sample stimulus is presented, the student's task is to select the matching stimulus from an array of several alternatives (often, as in Figure 20.6, just two). As instructors, we also can arrange stimuli to maximize chances that each time learners respond they are almost certain to make a correct match.

For instance, early on we can make the matching stimulus very large and distinct and the non-matchings stimulus very small and faint (within-stimulus prompts). Then gradually, we can fade the differences in size and intensity in or out so that ultimately the matching and non-matching stimuli are presented at the same size and intensity. Alternatively, we might use different irrelevant stimulus properties, such as color, pictorial, texture, visual, audio, tactile, or others, all now readily feasible due to advances in micro-computing. (Refer back to Figure 20.3.) Notice the dimensions on which fading have been programmed. Also, the relevant stimulus features can be introduced gradually, and/or the irrelevant ones can be faded. For a related example, see Figure 20.6, which displays selected steps in a program designed to teach the learner to match the numeral 2 with an array of two objects.

The major advantage of initially presenting non-matching stimuli that are quite different from the matching ones is that the learner is much more likely to respond correctly. Consequently, the ratio of reinforced to non-reinforced responses is going to be much greater. Later, non-matching stimuli that are more and more similar to matching stimuli can be introduced, but during initial instruction this sort of procedure minimizes the negative side effects that frequently accompany extinction.

**Highlight critical elements of the positive stimuli.** In Chapter 17, we presented a similar within-stimulus prompting procedure as a tool for preventing overdependence or overselectivity (see Figure 17.6). That method appears to be among the more effective methods for teaching discriminations (see Demchak, 1990; MacDuff et al., 2001 for reviews). Following their review of a number of studies on within-stimulus errorless learning, the authors (Markham, Giles, Roderique-Davies, Adshead, Tamiaki, & May, 2020) reported that a melding of the within-stimulus and fading strategies proved to be a very effective tool for teaching various discriminations to clients with intellectual and developmental disabilities.

You must take special precautions, though, when using errorless methods to promote discriminations because the individual ultimately will need to respond one way in the presence of one stimulus

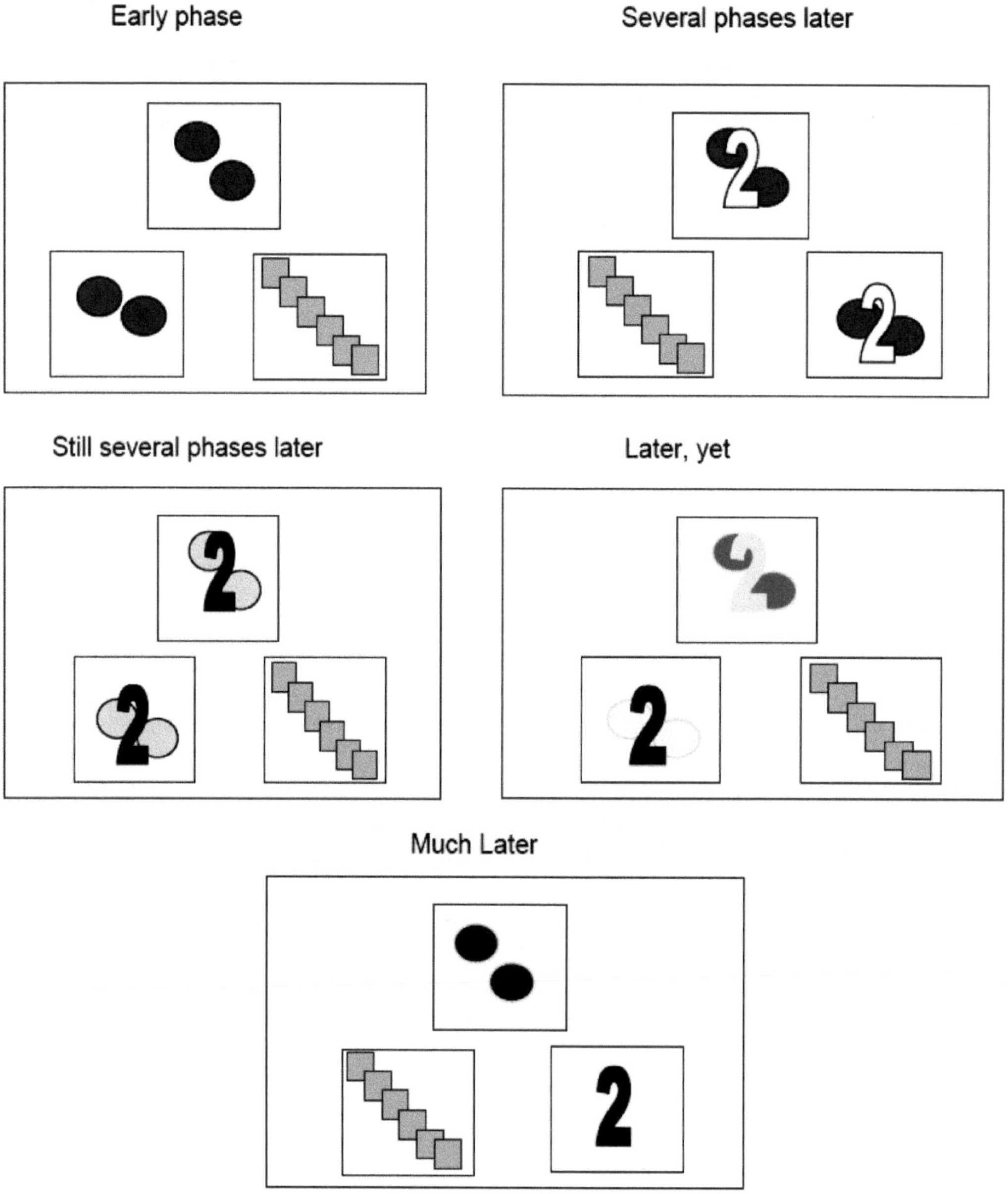

**Figure 20.6** Objective: To teach matching two circles to the numeral *2*

and differently in the presence of an often subtly different one. Think of your own difficulty in naming each of a pair of identical twins! Other examples are distinguishing and/or correctly labeling stimuli such as letters, words, pictures, tastes, and sounds, not to speak of the different features of safe adults (e.g., parents, family members, policemen, including those who may be unfamiliar) and those who may be unsafe. Unless the prompt relates to the critical or relevant property of the stimulus during training (as pointed out in the previous chapters), superimposing other cues on the stimuli may, as

Koegel and Rincover (1976) and Schilmoeller and Etzel (1977) discovered, impede transfer of control. For example, one of the authors used to differentiate between two twin students by one who wore glasses and the other didn't. Then one day in research lab, the one that wore glasses started wearing contacts. The result, you guessed it, couldn't tell them apart. The irrelevant stimulus must not distract the individuals' attention from the critical properties of the relevant stimuli. Such an untoward result could occur if you were presenting non-vocal sounds ("f," "s") along with words appearing on a panel. The student might attend to the sound source rather than to the panel on which the word appears. If the student does not attend to the critical feature, the word itself, responding to the relevant stimulus may decrease (Anderson, 1967; Terrace, 1966). The task here, as pointed out by Green (2001), is to alter *"the appearance of only those features of the stimuli that differentiate them from one another.* An example is exaggerating the vertical parts of the lowercase letters b and p on early training trials and gradually making them appear more and more alike over succeeding trials" (p. 78).

**Remove irrelevant stimuli.** Irrelevant stimuli sometimes can interfere with people's discriminative abilities. To illustrate, Dixon (1981) found that severely handicapped, nonverbal adolescents were unable to pair a photo of an object with the original until the figures in the photos were cut out. Apparently the photo and its facsimile resembled one another more closely after the irrelevant background of the photo was removed.

Similarly, Hoko and LeBlanc (1988) used a procedure they called **stimulus equalization** to *eliminate differences in the irrelevant dimensions of stimuli.* They temporarily reduced the complexity of the stimulus by eliminating irrelevant dimensions. *Only the critical dimensions were left.* To illustrate, consider the case of a student experiencing difficulty selecting snapping turtles from a varied array of harmless mud turtles. First, present all the figures the same size and color with the same size feet, and so on, so that they differ only in the slope of their heads. Once the student begins responding correctly, gradually reinstate other differences. Correct responding probably will continue after differences

**Figure 20.7**

in size, color, and shape of the harmless turtles are reintroduced. (See Figure 20.7 for examples of early, middle, and later discrimination training sequences.)

Take care not to inadvertently miscue your student by using one distinctive reinforcer to teach one component of a conditional discrimination and another to teach a different component. For example, if the reinforcer for identifying a snapping turtle correctly is a gingersnap cookie and that for choosing a mud turtle correctly is an oatmeal cookie, the match may be disrupted if the effectiveness of one of these reinforcers changes under natural circumstances (e.g., the child becomes allergic to oats) (Dube et al., 1987). Therefore, unless the reinforcer has a truly natural or intrinsic tie to the stimulus ("Yes, it's okay for you to approach that rabbit," where the opportunity to pet the rabbit is the reinforcer) you should consider varying the reinforcers when you teach these sorts of discriminations.

As a fading tactic, you may increase the delay between the sample stimulus and the choice stimuli (the array of those from which the participant is to select the correct match). Be sure to proceed slowly as you add to the delay, though, because as Sidman (1969) found with his neurologically impaired patient-subjects, the longer the delay, the fewer the correct matches.

## Using Response and Extra-Stimulus Prompting

Besides using within-stimulus prompts, such as the critical properties of the stimulus, to minimize errors, consider using extra prompts such as modeling, response delay (described below), and/or gestures (e.g., pointing to the correct comparison stimulus), and graduated guidance. Such prompts initially need to be provided with the $S^+$ or $S^D$ without delay. Then, as the target behavior becomes established, gradually remove those through delayed prompting and/or fading. As a case in point, Jerome et al. (2007) used backward chaining (see Chapter 14) and most-to-least prompting to help teach computer usage to three male adults. Two of the learners, ages 32 and 24, were diagnosed with autism and mild intellectual disability. The third was 25 years old and was diagnosed with mild intellectual disability and deafness. Thirteen steps were identified for using the computer, starting with pressing the computer power button and ending with single-clicking on the icon of the Web site of choice. To begin, the experimenter completed each of the first 12 steps and the students were only to click on the Web site of choice. Once they mastered that step, they had to complete the last two steps, then the last three steps, and so on. The graduated guidance aspect of the procedure consisted of "hand-over-hand guidance, followed by hand-over-wrist guidance, then hand-over-elbow guidance, and finally hand-over-shoulder guidance" (p. 187). This continued until all prompts were faded and the participant independently clicked on the Web site of choice or the links not already completed by the experimenter. "The prompting procedure continued until the participant independently completed each of the 13 task-analysis steps two times consecutively. After mastery of each step, training on the previous step was added" (p. 187). All three subjects learned how to use the computer as a leisure skill, and these skills generalized to a novel computer.

**Response delay** entails *preventing the client from responding too quickly ("impulsively") by requiring a preset delay between the discriminative stimulus and the response* (Dyer, Christian, & Luce, 1982). The technique was used to teach receptive and expressive language to three residents of a facility for children with autism. In two of the cases, the child was to point to an object according to its proper pronoun reference or to its function. In the third case, the child was to follow a motor instruction, such as "Raise your right hand." The response delay aspect was managed by holding the child's hand for a three- to five-second interval before permitting the response. The delay procedure appeared to evoke better performance than the no-delay condition for these three children, at least. The authors suggested that because having their hands held seemed aversive to the children, others might introduce the delay by removing the stimuli to be touched beyond the child's reach for a set interval.

Inserting a response delay also can promote an individual's physical skill performance. Bradshaw, Watt, Elliott, and Riddell (2004) investigated 25 five- to 11-year-old children's grasping and reaching for two different-sized objects thrown from two different distances. Following a two-second delay, the children's reaches were longer in duration, had lower peak velocities, and larger peak grip apertures than when they were asked to perform the reach immediately. Thus, the transport and grasp components were improved by response delay. Additionally, response delay has been found to improve inhibitory control in both high- and low-impulsive adolescents (Vazquez-Moreno, Gonzalez-Garrido, & Ramon-Loyo, 2019).

Response delay is what we do when we stop and wait for a few moments to remind ourselves of the bidding in a hand of bridge or covertly rehearse the sequence of steps we should follow in preparing to taxi our plane down the runway or to execute a complex dance routine. (Some of our best friends call those behaviors "thinking"; a few of our professional colleagues would label them "cognitive processing.") Thus, the procedure is worth applying when your students or trainees tend to commit errors by responding too rapidly.

However, *the way individuals covertly respond during the delay may affect their post-delay overt (observable) responding*. To illustrate, De Castro, Bosch, Veerman, and Koops (2003) pointed out that "boys with aggressive behavior problems are frequently taught to 'stop and think' before they act" (p. 153). To investigate the legitimacy of this assumption they compared asking 32 boys from special-education classes who had been identified as aggressive and 31 typically-developing boys to (a) monitor and regulate their own emotions, (b) consider the provocateur's emotions and intentions, or (c) wait ten seconds before responding. The covert responding differentially affected aggressiveness: When the aggressive group monitored and regulated their own emotions they became less hostile. On the other hand, those told only to wait ten seconds or only to consider their peer's emotions and intentions before responding *actually became more aggressive*. So, let's suppose you want to teach your students or clients to become less aggressive. For response delay to work effectively, try teaching them what they should say or do; then to picture themselves saying or doing that during the delay. In addition, if they seem capable, have them monitor and regulate their own emotions.

## Disadvantages of Errorless Learning

Although keeping errors to a minimum has obvious advantages, the question of whether consistent, error-free responding is desirable has yet to be resolved. During the early development of this practice, Terrace (1966) questioned whether a lack of frustration tolerance might "...result from a steady diet of errorless discrimination learning" (p. 335), while Krumboltz and Krumboltz (1972) echoed that concern.

The precise and detailed errorless instructional programming we have been describing probably would be offered primarily to those facing specific learning challenges and not to the broader population, because this programming is costly in terms of time, effort, and money. Additionally, we presume that no one can avoid all mistakes completely. Despite the best of planning, failure is bound to occur often enough in many other environments in which the clients interact. Such experiences should teach people receiving these interventions to persist in the face of failure. Additionally, behavior analysts should be equipped to teach persistence in the face of failure. So, frustration tolerance should be a lesser concern when it comes to errorless learning.

Programming for errorless learning requires a considerable time investment. However, the effort involved in programming stimuli is more than compensated for when students with long histories of failure do finally succeed. Nonetheless, you certainly would want to avoid programming for errorless learning with students who make few errors and find the slow pace distasteful. The frequency of mistakes is one way to tell whether a curriculum has been over- or under-programmed. Before concluding that errors mandate errorless instruction, be sure those errors are not a function of inattentiveness because the task is too simple or unchallenging. To decide which direction to take, vary the task difficulty and observe how that impacts performance.

Promoting errorless learning may be an effective approach when teaching many of the kinds of discriminations clients need to acquire, but the method need not necessarily be applied in every situation. True, "errorless learning has been shown to be very successful in the rehabilitation of memory problems, particularly in patients with severe forms of memory impairment" (Hasiam, Gilroy, Black, & Beesley, 2006, p. 505). And yes, when Hunkin, Squires, Parkin, and Tidy (1998) used an error-prevention method to teach a group of memory-impaired individuals lists of single words, it produced higher levels of prompted recall performance than trial-and-error learning. Again, we stress the importance of remaining currently informed about research discoveries when choosing which specific interventions might be most appropriate for particular classes of behavior, clientele, and circumstances.

# MAINTAINING STIMULUS CONTROL

Various methods for developing and transferring stimulus control have been designed to bring behavior under the control of appropriate antecedents. Once accomplished, the control needs to be firmly established. Accordingly, the *response* evoked by the relevant antecedent stimulus must continue to be reinforced at least occasionally. The optimal approach is to reduce the quantity of reinforcers gradually, to shift their quality to more natural ones, and gradually to introduce a delay before delivering a reinforcer. Chapters 22, 23 and 24 will discuss guidelines for maintaining behavioral change. Here, suffice it to say that the reinforcer should be delivered less and less frequently until the behavior continues to occur reliably in the presence of the stimulus, with only an occasional reinforcer.

To illustrate, suppose the primary-school child continued correctly to label 2's and 7's. You would occasionally dispense more natural, such as "Uh huh" and/or a nod, rather than less contrived reinforcers. The youth counselor might arrange meetings with his formerly misbehaving client, during which he supplied congratulatory feedback about the apparent self-control the boy had demonstrated earlier that day or week, rather than presenting reinforcers immediately. The crucial point to remember in initiating such a change in quantity or density, immediacy, and quality of reinforcement is that if stimulus control appears to be disintegrating, the shift has been too abrupt. At that point, back up to a more optimal reinforcement strategy to reestablish the *relevant contingencies*, and then begin once again to thin out the reinforcers, but at a slower pace. And, of course, you want to help the natural environment assume contingency control in your absence.

## SUMMARY AND CONCLUSIONS

Shifting and expanding stimulus control is about transferring the evocative and inhibiting functions of discriminative stimuli from prompts to more natural stimuli. Several procedures can be used to achieve this transfer of control from prompts to relevant antecedent stimuli. These include delayed prompting, graduated prompting, and fading. *Delayed prompting* interposes a time—constant or graduated—between the antecedent or discriminative stimulus and the prompt. *Graduated prompting* begins with the natural antecedents and progresses to more intrusive prompts until the person exhibits the desired behavior. This latter method, though, does not prevent all possible errors, because sufficient prompts will not be presented until less-restrictive prompts have failed. The maximum-to-minimum prompt reduction procedure does a better job of preventing errors, but risks over-prompting, which can be aversive for the client and delay progress unnecessarily. When possible, it is best to start with the currently functional prompt and gradually transfer stimulus control to the natural discriminative stimulus.

*Fading* is the gradual removal of a prompt combined with, when appropriate, the gradual introduction of the antecedent discriminative stimuli, as illustrated by the *errorless learning* method. Although often used in conjunction with other methods of transferring stimulus control, fading does not necessarily require interposing a delay between the antecedents and the prompt.

Which procedure you select to transfer stimulus control is best based on the individual. No one strategy appears "superior" to another, but may be more effective on one person's behavior compared to another (Lerman, Vorndran, Addison, & Kuhn, 2004; Libby et al., 2008; Seaver & Bourret, 2014; Wall Ellis Zane, & VanderPoel, 1979). However, as we discussed in Chapter 17, most to least prompting was found to be more effective than least to most when previously demonstrated effective prompts are used (Cengher, et al., 2016). It remains to be seen, though, if this finding will be replicated across a variety of clients and situations. In the meantime, we continue to agree with Libby et al (2008) who suggested that we use most to least prompting as the default when you are not sure which would be most effective with your client.

Regardless of the approach taken to promote transfer of stimulus control, however, the behavior taught (discriminated operant) needs to be strengthened and maintained by at least occasional reinforcers. (See Chapters 22, 23 and 24 for discussions of ways to maintain behavioral change.) Prompting and fading are methods for bringing behavior under appropriate stimulus control. But if a response is to be prompted, it must already be available within the person's repertoire. Otherwise, it will have to be taught.

Always realize that a behavior is not well established until (a) it is fluent (Chapter 17), (b) occurs across situations, people, and times of day (generalization has occurred; Chapter 21), (c) is no longer prompt dependent (stimulus control has been transferred from prompts to natural $S^D$s in the environment, and (d) reinforcers are no longer intrusive, have been thinned, and come from sources in the natural environment (Chapters 22–24).

*Chapter 21*

# Generalization: Expanding Stimulus Control

## Goals

1. Define and illustrate each of the following terms:
   a. discrimination
   b. generalization
   c. stimulus generalization
   d. overgeneralization
   e. response generalization or induction
   f. correspondence training
   g. exemplars
2. Compare and contrast *stimulus generalization* and *response generalization* or *response induction*.
3. Discuss when and why programing for generalization is necessary.
4. List several strategies designed to promote generalization and discuss the values and costs of applying each.
5. Describe what factors need to be considered before asking others to implement specific intervention programs, shown to be effective with the client, in their settings.
6. Describe several training loosely methods.
7. Describe how self-management methods can help promote stimulus generalization.
8. Describe using generalization training to occasion a behavior in more than one setting, across behaviors, and/or with other people.
9. Discuss why recording and graphing generalization data are important.

\*\*\*\*\*\*\*\*\*\*\*

"I just don't get it," Florence's academic advisor, Martha, wonders to her colleague. "Florence's examination grades were outstanding. Yet her clinical supervisor tells me that when an emergency arises out on the floor Florence becomes flustered and confused. And she caught the woman just about to give the wrong pill to a seriously ill patient!" smacking her hand against her forehead. "Heaven help us!"

"I've had similar experiences with my students," remarks Martha's colleague, Sandra. "They are able to say what they should do, but then they do something else. I remember when I used to teach grade school, I'd assign arithmetic problems and the kids would be able to solve them; but then when I'd ask them to use the same operation to figure out how much money they'd need to bring for their school tee-shirts, they'd be lost. Now, with my student teaching advisees here at the U, despite their having learned to list the negative side-effects of aversive control, who'd imagine that when I visit them at their practicum placements, more often than I care to admit, I, uh...."

"OMG, Martha! Something just occurred to me. I just remembered what B.F. Skinner used to say about 'misbehavior?' I hate to admit it, but maybe I'm at least partially responsible, because I haven't paid enough attention to generalization in my teaching. I wonder if we need to build more closely supervised laboratory and practicum training within our nurse-preparation curriculum. What do you think?"

"Interesting idea, Sandy. Let's think about it. In the meantime, okay, I accept that 'the student is always right,' but I refuse to assume the total responsibility for my students' failure to transfer the skills I taught them into the real world. They tell me that the principal at our chief school placement is a real bear and frightens both the kids and teachers. Maybe Florence's supervisor also intimidates and bewilders her. Or perhaps the girl is distracted about something in her private life."

"Yes, but let's be honest with ourselves. Do we really do everything feasible in our teacher-training curriculum, to enable our own students to generalize effectively? Do they get a chance to bridge the gap between lecture courses and student teaching; to test and get feedback on their teaching and management skills before they step into the student-teaching role? Anything like video recorded tutoring assignments or other observation and supervision of their practice?"

"Hmm—you're hinting that we might need to look for better ways to prepare our students if we are hoping to see them practicing what we teach out in the field?"

"Something like that. Despite who, or what else out there might be partly to blame, I suspect there are at least probably a few things I can do to improve the situation. You know, this is weird, but suddenly I'm excited about creating new ways to promote my students' ability to generalize the concepts and skills they learn in our class to the real world."

Perhaps talk of generalization sounds familiar to you, and it should, because this is not the first time we have discussed the topic. In the present chapter we remind you of this absolutely essential aspect of effective teaching, management, and other behavior change stratagems, and offer you a set of systematic guidelines for promoting the kind of spread of effect you hope to achieve.

First, though, allow us to review the purpose and meaning of the way we use the terms *stimulus generalization* and *discrimination* in this text.

## DISTINGUISHING BETWEEN THE TERMS *DISCRIMINATION* AND *STIMULUS GENERALIZATION*

Technically speaking, the aim of transferring stimulus control is to shift the functions of stimuli that currently evoke or inhibit given responses over to more natural evocative or inhibiting stimuli. With both generalization and discrimination training, the focus is upon what settings, or in the presence of what stimuli, the behavior should and should not occur. That being the case, you must plan your generalization and discrimination training strategies accordingly, *from the very start*, beginning by selecting your objective and proceeding to incorporate those features within your intervention design.

As you learned earlier, **discrimination** training involves *restricting the range of stimuli that are designated to "set the occasion for" or "evoke" a given behavior*, as in the case of teaching Baby Bonnie to distinguish, or, technically, to discriminate her dad from other people (or, as described in Chapter 16, for a client to learn where and when growling is and is not acceptable,) Discrimination training's main purpose is coaching our clientele to recognize the critical stimulus features that differentiate the $S^{Dr}$s from the $S^{De}$s. Consider this example: One of our clients, "Mat," had a habit of growling like an angry dog. We reasoned that the growling *per se* was not a problem; only that it should be restricted to his room, or the bathroom; not emitted out in public. As his public growling diminished, Mat began to call his bedroom the "growling room." We might say that Mat learned *to discriminate* the context in which the behavior was acceptable from that in which it was not. (We have designed similarly successful programs for masturbation.)

Think about it—many behaviors are acceptable only under particular conditions, but not under others. We accept boxing, or hitting in the ring, but not in the home or classroom. Running is okay outside, but not in the house, classroom, church, etc. Saying "O" when seeing O is fine, but not in the presence of "Q." In and of themselves, most behaviors are neither good nor bad *per se*. Rather the extent to which they are considered "appropriate" depends upon the circumstances (that is, the *stimulus conditions*) currently in effect.

By contrast, the **stimulus generalization** process *broadens the range of stimuli or, abbreviated, $S^D$s* (objects, sounds, times, places, other people, and so on,) sharing common properties, that function to *"set the occasion for"* or evoke particular behaviors. Were it not for stimulus generalization, most living organisms, including humans, would have a hard time surviving. They would have to learn each and every particular stimulus-response relation anew: e.g., whether approaching, touching, or consuming any specific plant, animal, location, object, and so on, is safe or unsafe. So the ability to generalize on the basis of common stimulus features plays a crucial role in the lives of all organisms. Fortunately, as humans, we also make use of our abilities to acquire and employ complex verbal repertoires to train our students and clientele to *generalize* or expand the range of circumstances under which emitting a given behavior is acceptable—as when we want children to generalize the physical behavior evoked by the words "stop" to red lights and "go" to green lights. Note that while spoken words and colored lights do not possess common *physical features,* the contingencies they share in common permit them to serve equivalent *functions.*

Those of us who serve as teachers, trainers, or in any managerial capacity, certainly intend that our consumers will transfer (i.e., *generalize*) to all the environments in which those are to be practiced, the information and skills they read about or hear from us in the classroom, during training sessions, or directly on the job. To illustrate the point, a cohort of experts in the field of behavior analysis in autism education cited *the ability to promote generalization* as **the** *most crucial concept and skill* for ABA practitioners-in-training for them to master (Sulzer-Azaroff et al., 2008).

## STIMULUS GENERALIZATION AND OVERGENERALIZATION

In stimulus generalization "the individual responds in the presence of a new stimulus in the same way as to a previously taught stimulus having some of the same characteristics" (Becker, Engelmann, &

Thomas, 1975, p. 145). Baby Bonnie's parents have shown and labeled an apple, a strawberry, and her brother's wagon "red"; then asked her to repeat the name of the color after them. When she complies, they lavish her with praise. Later on, she sees a red fire engine and says "red." Bonnie's answer, "red," has generalized to the new stimulus. During training, Dr. Garcia accurately discriminates various symptoms to diagnose a difficult case, thereby promoting her patient's recovery and receiving the congratulations of her supervising physician. Now in practice, when she sees other patients with similar symptoms, she makes the same correct diagnosis.

In Figure 21.1, you see two plants. Their similar appearance (common stimuli: green, small, pointed, shiny-leaved climbers) suggests that both are ivy (generalization), but we had better learn to discriminate between the two and avoid the one on the left containing three leaves on the stem—because, as you probably recognize, it is poison ivy.

**Figure 21.1** Discriminating poison ivy from other ivy.

So we see that certain generalizations may be appropriate; others not. In some cases, they depend on natural circumstances, such as the common properties shared among them—e.g., labeling both the benign, decorative specimen as well as the poison variety as "ivies." Others are a function of social convention, as in stopping on red or going on green and not because of any physical properties of those colors.

Notice that while some particular generalizations may be spot on, others may miss the mark completely: At one point, Baby Bonnie calls her pink dress "blue"—an inappropriate generalization. Besides imitating his expert moves on the ice, Jerome's ice hockey teammates also mimic his penchant for using his stick as a weapon for attacking members of the opposing team, a different class of inappropriate generalization. Baby Bonnie points to and calls every man she sees "Dada." Racial or gender biases also are instances. In the latter case, the person might respond to an irrelevant stimulus, such as a person's skin color or gender, as if it were an aversive stimulus. We use the term *overgeneralization* to describe such inappropriate generalizations. Discriminating among stimuli appropriately is the opposite of overgeneralizing: After Bonnie's parents teach her to label pink correctly, and she no longer confuses it with blue, one then can say she *discriminates* between pink and blue. Dr. Garcia bases her diagnoses and treatment recommendations on subtle differences in her patient's symptoms. It would be proper to say that she has *discriminated* the relevant symptoms. To remain eligible to participate in a race, contestants must await the starting signal, "Go." Those who wait for the signal are *discriminating* the critical stimulus "Go!" from other instructions. In less technical language we might say that the starter's stimulus, "Go!" prompts running because it signals that running will no longer produce a false start penalty and now the contestants are eligible to win the race.

As you now recognize, discriminative stimuli, abbreviated $S^D$s, are said to *occasion* (or *set the occasion for*) responses because they signal that particular reinforcement contingencies currently are operating. Those stimuli have gained their influence for individuals as a result of a history in which a particular response of theirs has frequently been reinforced in the presence of specific stimuli. So, eventually those stimuli begin to *set the occasion for* (or in non-technical language *prompt*) the response.

Sometimes, though, the aim is to promote responding the same way in the presence of similar but not identical stimuli (i.e., *stimulus generalization*): A student is taught that the symbol "R" is pronounced "rrr." So responding with that sound to variations of written or printed R's (R, r, *R*, **r**) is appropriate. A counselor teaches a shy woman to look at him while they converse as a way to encourage her to generalize her response by looking at other people while conversing.

As we learned in earlier chapters, though, we need to beware of overgeneralizing, which then would call for discrimination training. Consider an example: Ingvarsson, Tiger, Hanley, and Stephenson (2007) taught four preschool children with and without disabilities to respond to questions to which they did not know the answer by saying "I don't know" or "I don't know, please tell me." Three of the children overgeneralized these responses to some of the questions to which they actually did know the answers. To correct for the overgeneralization, these students were only allowed access to toys for correct responding. The experimenters concluded that "the addition of a restricted reinforcement contingency was sufficient to establish correct answers to a portion of previously unknown questions" (p. 411). Some recent evidence suggests that dopamine influences stimulus generalization by reducing activity in the region of the brain called the hippocampus (Kahnt & Tobler, 2016). The investigators posit that dopaminergic activity in the hippocampus may relate to the degree of generalization, thereby suggesting some cases might be potential targets for neuropsychiatric treatment.

## DISTINGUISHING BETWEEN *STIMULUS GENERALIZATION* AND *RESPONSE GENERALIZATION (INDUCTION)*

**Response generalization** (Skinner 1953), sometimes called **response induction** (Catania, 2007), is different from *stimulus generalization*. Response generalization may be defined as "*a spread of an intervention effect from a targeted behavior to a similar non-targeted behavior*" (Geller, 2001, p. 65). (See slight definitional variations among Catania, 2007; Daniels, 2001; Kazdin, 2001; Staddon, 2001; and others.) With response generalization, the act of interest does not remain intact, as with stimulus generalization, but it begins to shift its form or topography. (Hint: the word that proceeds the word generalization tells you what is different. In response generalization the responses are different but the $S^D$ that evokes the response is the same, whereas in stimulus generalization, the stimuli that evoke the response are different but the response is the same. See Table 21.1). Consider these examples:

- After reading his book on winning golfing techniques, Joe Duffer tries out his new swing. The first time his club connects beautifully with the ball, but afterward he misses more often than he connects. The form of his response has varied from an initially successful to a less successful swing.
- Sometimes Mr. Busser praises his employees with moderate enthusiasm, sometimes with a flat tone, and once in a while quite heartily.
- Willie has been taught to follow a given strategy for solving scientific dilemmas. On occasion, he modifies the strategy by eliminating or adding steps.
- When you drive a different car, you adjust the way you shift gears to match its own particular system of operation.
- When asked, "Is it OK?" Jim responds, "Yes," "Sure," or "It's OK."
- When a child is asked to draw a straight line, some are straighter than others.

When our interest is in changing behavior, shifts in the desired direction provide contingency managers with the opportunity to reinforce successively closer approximations to a goal, or to shape the goal behavior. Suppose you want to teach a child to draw a straight line. You reinforce initial attempts even though the lines are not very straight. Soon you see the child drawing some lines that are straighter as

Table 21.1: Illustration of what is the same or different across discrimination, stimulus generalization, and response generalization.

|  | *Stimulus* | *Response* |
|---|---|---|
| *Discrimination* | Same | Same |
| *Stimulus Generalization* | Different | Same |
| *Response Generalization* | Same | Different |

well as some that are wavier. You now know the child's capabilities, so you limit your reinforcement to the straightest of the successive approximations. You continue shaping until your criterion for reinforcement becomes a line you consider acceptably straight.

Notice that although response induction (also labeled by some as "response generalization") is essential to our ability to shape new behavior, professionals may disagree as to how different the behavior must be for a single instance to be labeled a case of response induction (generalization). Geller (2001) has pointed out that some (e.g., Houchins & Boyce, 2001) claim that the "target and non-target behaviors must reach a certain level of dissimilarity before a spread of effect from one response to the other can be considered response generalization" (p. 66). Others (e.g., Austin & Wilson, 2001) have maintained that the behaviors must be topographically similar. But "similar" and "different" are hard to define. To what extent must the response vary to allow us to label a response as *different*? What is the range of variability we would accept as *same*? From our behavior-change perspective, we need to decide in advance what would constitute an appropriate or inappropriate response variation on a case-by-case basis: giant steps for some response classes or for some clients; baby steps for others. Despite whether we label such response variation "response generalization" or "induction" or something else, the important point is that shaping would be impossible without it. They are essential to planning specific shaping strategies.

## ADVANTAGES AND DISADVANTAGES OF GENERALIZATION

Depending on circumstances, whether of the stimulus or the response variety, generalization may promote or impede desired behavior change.

### Stimulus Generalization

Sometimes un-programmed generalizing across varied stimulus conditions can prove to be a great asset, as when an instructed response, such as a child's making eye contact, spreads beyond the teaching situation, or when you successfully support a teacher's increasing distribution of merited descriptive praise or an engineer applies a particular problem-solving strategy to address a novel design challenge. Using new vocabulary taught in school is useful there as well as at home, on the job, and in the community. So is a teacher's or supervisor's use of praise. Whether planned or not, by fostering achievement of aims by "lesser means" (Stokes & Baer, 1977), generalization can conserve time, effort, and material resources—big economic advantages. Initially, teaching service personnel to smile, to greet people by name, and to look at customers directly (e.g., Brown & Sulzer-Azaroff, 1991) may require that trainers invest considerable time in the initial setting. After that, if only occasional prompts promote smiling under new conditions, the cost will be far less than were new training required each time circumstances changed. Although generalization may not necessarily provide it for nothing, it may offer the product at bargain prices.

There is some evidence (Mace & Nevin, 2017) that generalization training also can help prevent resurgence, or spontaneous recovery, of the problem behavior from occurring. It may be that if the problem behavior continues to receive reinforcement in other situations, resurgence is more likely to occur in the training environment.

In an actual case, Miles and Wilder (2009), used a package consisting of modeling, rehearsal and feedback to support three staff members' implementation of a behavioral skills training package with children who tended to be non-compliant. As figure 21.2 shows, not only did all three staff substantially increase their rates of implementation of the package, but their responding generalized to other situations as well. Those efforts, in turn, resulted in two of the three children's increasing their compliance rates.

On the *downside*, unintended stimulus generalization can be awkward, as when we attempt to use our native language in a country in which a different tongue is spoken. Baby Bonnie's mom blushes with embarrassment whenever her little one calls a bearded stranger "Da-da." Making eye contact and smiling serve us well in many social circumstances, but can you think of cases where they might be

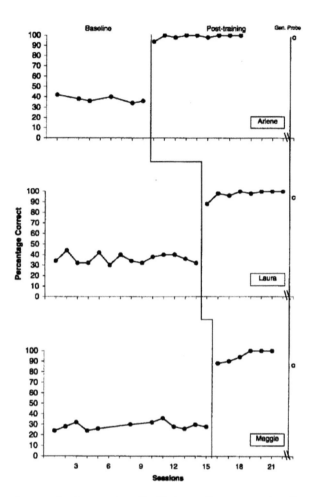

**Figure 21.2** The percentage of correct implementation of guided compliance across baseline, post-training and a generalization probe for Arlene, Laura and Maggie.

harmful? How about smiling at a stranger lurking in a dark alley? Or looking directly in the eye of an adult authority figure? (In Japan, a child who does that is considered rude.) We know of an instance in which a group of developmentally-delayed youngsters were taken on a field trip to a department store. Seeing a display toilet, one of the boys began to lower his pants. A lesson in discrimination training had to be conducted on the spot.

Remember, when the objective is for behavior to occur under only some circumstances and not others, we must differentially reinforce with care. Remedying unwanted generalization after the fact adds to the cost of changing behavior, because then we are required to take a step back to teach new discriminations. A preferred alternative is to teach the trainee to discriminate all the key features of the situation in advance. (Recall how in Chapter 16 you learned how to train individuals to discriminate between one stimulus and the next.) Nonetheless, when one hopes to expand the scope of the behavior beyond a particular instance, knowing how to foster generalization is essential.

## Response Generalization

Similarly, the value of response generalization (or response induction), to you as a program designer and/or implementer may prove advantageous or not, depending on your aims. On the plus side, response generalization allows you to avoid having to teach minor behavioral variations completely from scratch. Instead, you can capitalize on response induction by using the variations to shape new behavior. The tennis coach may capitalize on her trainee's skill in badminton to promote an appropriate tennis swing. Rather than starting from the very beginning, all she has to do is teach a modified swing. The manager can heavily reinforce Willie's use of an especially fruitful problem-solving strategy or Mr. Busser's use of convincingly hearty praise. Because many of their critical features are well established within the person's behavioral repertoire, there is no need to teach those particular response topographies separately as new behaviors.

Trainers who deal with problem behavior in pets by teaching pet owners to use shaping and other reinforcement techniques occasionally report that some of their pet owner clients discover that the same techniques can be useful in dealing with the problematic behavior of their own children (see Pryor, 1999). This, too, might be regarded as an example of stimulus generalization (and probably response generalization as well, given the certain need to adjust the nature of the specific response components, as in shifting from training barking to promoting human speech).

Shaping depends on response variation because even minor behavioral shifts in the right direction permit us to reinforce those that more and more closely approximate the selected goal behavior. When Claude attempts to imitate a proper *eu* sound, his French teacher nods and smiles as his enunciation successively approximates the ideal French. Then later, response induction permits him to learn a different but related sound, *u* ("uh").

Mr. Valenzuela and the school principal, Helen, have agreed that she will wink, smile, nod, and signal "Okay" from the back of the room whenever she notices Mr. Valenzuela becoming increasingly enthusiastic. After several such visits, Mr. Valenzuela also starts becoming more proficient in giving behavior-specific feedback to students—a different but related behavior.

Unwanted response induction sometimes causes us grief, however. Behavioral variation in doling

"Generalization matters!"
- Who?
- Does what and what not?
- How?
- With and without whom & what?
- Where; where not?
- When; when not?
- For how long?
- Why?

out pills, landing an airplane, or performing brain surgery could lead to disaster. Fredrika, who has in the past been fairly successful in measuring ingredients for a pie shell "by eye," now attempts to use the same approach when baking a soufflé. Alas, on removing the dessert from the oven, it collapses into a sticky mess. Dr. Willie may succeed (or not) when using a shortcut like "guesstimating" the proper length of a sheet of wallpaper while re-decorating his bathroom at home; but were he to depend on an "educated guess" when programming a patient's defibrillator, that could prove lethal. As ethical ABA practitioners, we must do all we can to avoid causing harm by skipping essential steps in the behavior change process, or by applying procedures improperly. Examples might include bypassing the steps of identifying and delivering individually functional consequences, imposing overly-long timeout intervals, or failing to program for generalization.

## Assessing for Stimulus Generalization

In most advanced societies, agents of behavior-change depend heavily on such tools as lectures, demonstrations, admonitions, sermons, spoken advice, or even stand-alone "how-to" textbooks (even as in the present instance) to achieve their purposes. Many are convinced that presenting their message clearly and compellingly should be sufficient to produce general and lasting change. Unfortunately, evidence to the contrary often serves to chasten them. Nor is people's ability to recite or write acceptable performance rules any guarantee that they will practice those rules. Such "train and hope" techniques (Stokes & Baer, 1977) are chancy at best. To illustrate an oft-repeated experience, even when they were supplied with a written task analysis (Alavosius & Sulzer-Azaroff, 1990) and despite having learned to follow instructions for avoiding muscular-skeletal injuries by lifting and transferring their patients safely, three of four caregivers did not spontaneously transfer the skills to other job practices until they began to receive feedback on the job.

Other examples abound: Himle, Miltenberger, Gartheridge, and Flessner (2004) used a behavioral-skills training program to teach gun-play prevention skills to four- to five-year-olds. Within small group formats, they asked the children to role-play what they were supposed to do if they found a gun at home. Although they demonstrated the safety skills during assessment in the group setting, most failed to apply the skills during a home-based assessment. As a consequence, the same investigators (Himle, Miltenberger, Flessner, & Gartheridge, 2004) then incorporated *fluency training* within the protocol and found that about half of the four- to seven-year-olds participants successfully generalized the skill. The remaining youngsters were trained directly in their homes, which produced successful generalization. Follow-up assessments in the home from two weeks to five months after training revealed that the gun-safety skills persisted.

You can see the dangers of taking generalization for granted. We had better not teach a youngster to refrain from gun-play at home and then just hope that when he sees a gun at Uncle Joe's house he won't pick it up and play with it. Results of applied behavior analytic research conducted for over half a century has taught us we dare not assume that generalization can be expected to happen spontaneously. Rather, we must carefully design and incorporate generalization strategies within the change program from the very start. Transfer of the given behavior to all desired conditions (where, when, with whom, and what, plus other environmental features) depends on that.

## FORMALLY INTEGRATING GENERALIZATION TRAINING FROM THE VERY START

Beware of falling into the "*First let's just fix it and worry about generalization later!*" trap. Ignoring generalization is tempting. After all, we humans love instant gratification as much as any other species. Unfortunately, as mentioned, just hoping for generalization does NOT mean it will happen. When assessing whether infants would imitate their mother's sounds or playful actions, Paulson et al. (2002) found that maternal praise was the essential ingredient: No praise for a given response—no subsequent imitation of the response!

Yes, as is the case with discrimination, attaining generalization can be difficult. Consider the following illustration: a client with autism, whom we will call Refugio, was taught in a therapy room to touch his nose, head, mouth, etc. upon request. This illustration also was used in Chapter 16 to illustrate the sequencing method to help identifying hard to discover discriminative stimuli. The male school psychologist reported this improvement to the female teacher. However, when that teacher asked Refugio to touch his head, etc., he failed to comply. She reported this to the school psychologist who suggested maybe he needed to be present. Unfortunately, Refugio seemed to ignore his teacher's request despite the psychologist's presence. The male psychologist then tried making the requests of Refugio. Again—no compliance. Obviously, the requests were not functioning as $S^{D+}$s as they did in the therapy room. After the psychologist continued to test a variety of different conditions or materials, he, finally found out that if the table and chair from the therapy room were present, the child would touch his head, nose, etc., upon request. This phenomenon in which the behavior is controlled by one or more non-relevant stimuli is called stimulus over-selectivity. (Recall that earlier you have encountered other examples of over-selectivity and its remediation [e.g., by changing the background color, size of the print or pictures and their location.] Similarly, when teaching word recognition, you vary words with the same starting or ending letters and their size.)

The frequent failure of the "train and hope approach" (described by Stokes & Baer, 1977) is one of the reasons why focusing on generalization and discrimination aspects (helping the client respond correctly to $S^{Dr}$s) is such an important teaching/management skill; one that should be addressed from the very beginning of any behavior change program. Let's look at how we can do that.

You can begin by designing and demonstrating the validity of your own method or by choosing one or more established generalization-promotion strategies summarized below and described in detail by Baer and Stokes (1977), Chandler et al. (1992), Stokes and Baer (1977), and Stokes and Osnes (1989). To elaborate, Chandler et al. (1992) found prompting, positive reinforcement, and feedback to be the most effective promoters of generalization. As might be anticipated, combinations of antecedents and consequential strategies proved more successful than combinations of antecedent strategies alone (e.g., modeling plus rehearsal). As for the particular social skills that were found to be most successful at promoting peer interactions, those included initiations to peers, conversation or reciprocal interactions, and responding to and sharing with peers.

Try introducing minimally intrusive prompts, such as a gesture, a familiar facial expression or even directly requesting the behavior Should those fail to evoke the behavior after a reasonable trial period, you might progress on to stronger prompts like modeling the behavior yourself, asking the person's peer to demonstrate or gently physically guiding it yourself.

Frequently you will want the behaviors you plan to teach to occur in the presence of a various *people*, under numerous *circumstances*, and/or at different *times*. If so, you must incorporate strategies for promoting **stimulus generalization**. You can accomplish this by *expanding*, (rather than limiting, as with discrimination training) *the pool of $S^{Dr}$'s that set the occasion for* the emission of those particular behaviors across those circumstances. So, *plan for generalization from the beginning* by considering and enumerating the full range of circumstances under which the behavior is to occur. Be certain to specify in your clients' objectives the full set of conditions, such as the times and in the presence of whom, with what etc. you want them to emit the behaviors you are planning to teach. (Refer back to Chapter 4 to review how to develop goals and objectives)

Next you need to plan your strategies for promoting generalization training. Fortunately, behavior analysts (e.g., Stokes & Baer, 1977) have developed a number of options. Here we describe several:

## Request Generalization

When considering how to promote generalization, do not overlook the obvious. First try the simplest and most direct approach: *Ask for generalization*. Suggest your clientele use the skill(s) they already have mastered under other conditions (times, places, people, materials, and so on). "Why don't you try _____ (the skill you learned during the in-service) out here on the job?" Perhaps the respondent would agree, "Right! Good idea. I never thought of that!"

Here are a few other examples:

- "Remember how politely you asked to be excused from your chores so you could see the basketball finals at Grandma's house? Do you think you could use that tone of voice here instead of groaning and complaining? After that we can discuss the issue further."

- "Recall how enthusiastically you greeted customers when the general manager stopped by? Do you think you might try that every time?"

- If you were involved in teaching computer operators to adhere to safe posture practices on the job (e.g., McCann & Sulzer-Azaroff, 1996), a wise strategy would be to ask them to continue to practice those new skills and self-record progress while working on the computer at home.

- Strain, Kerr, and Ragland (1979) merely suggested that participants use their new helping skills in the new settings (e.g., "Say 'May I help?'"). "All participants learned to engage in appropriate helping behavior in the presence of nonverbal, verbal, and affective discriminative stimuli during both reinforced training trials and non-reinforced probe trials following an intervention consisting of multiple exemplar training, differential reinforcement, video modeling, and *prompting*" (italics added; p. 130).

Surely situations like these are familiar to you—so yes, *simply requesting generalization often works*. Asking people to practice any skill they have recently demonstrated under other conditions probably is one of the most direct ways to encourage generalization. However, if asking doesn't work, you need to be prepared to use a more systematic technique to assure that the altered behavior occurs under all relevant conditions. You can do this by becoming familiar with and skillful at using the following additional strategies for promoting generalization:

**Reinforce approximations.** Three male students in a special class included a nine-year-old third grader, a ten-year-old fourth grader (both diagnosed with serious emotional disturbance), and a five-year-old who was "diagnosed as developmentally delayed due to social and emotional concerns" (Mesmer, Duhon, & Dodson, 2007, p. 554). The special education classroom intervention consisted of three components: (1) A gradually more challenging goal statement indicating the required number of correct responses for the day, printed at the top of each student's worksheet. (2) A computer-generated thumbs-up icon placed at the top of the five- and nine-year-olds' papers, and a small digital timer for the ten-year-old. (3) Following each session, the teachers collected and scored the worksheets. Participants who exceeded their goals were immediately allowed to choose an item from the class prize box.

## Prompt Several People in Various Environments to Deliver Reinforcers

Generally speaking, *those mediating reinforcement for a particular behavior often become $S^{Dr}$s* for the recipients to engage in that behavior. Should you be alone in reinforcing your clients' demonstration of good sportsmanship (e.g., complimenting them for such target behaviors as sharing, improving in, or completing good plays, winning), they might limit those target behaviors to your presence. You have become a unique good-sportsmanship $S^{Dr}$. To avoid such narrowness, encourage others to prompt and reinforce the occurrence of the target behavior (e.g., sharing, etc.), and reinforce their attempts to comply. Eventually their presence will more apt to serve as $S^{Dr}$s, thereby increasing the range of $S^{Dr}$s that will evoke the behavior. Failure to take such measures across the clients' key environments runs the risk of the newly strengthened behavior undergoing extinction in your absence.

Five students with severe disabilities had been engaging in problematic behaviors as a vehicle for requesting particular objects and activities at school (Durand, 1999). After learning to use assistive communication devices instead to make those requests, their problematic behaviors decreased substantially, even out in the community. As Durand pointed out, the study "demonstrates the value of teaching skills to recruit natural communities of reinforcements in order to generalize intervention effects in meaningful nontraining environments" (p. 247).

In a related study, (Harding, Wacker, Berg, Rick, & Lee, 2004), investigators provided differential reinforcement in the form of supportive feedback to teach martial-arts students various punching and kicking techniques. The students' skill in using these new techniques spread to the sparring conditions, where they gained the reinforcers intrinsic to those circumstances.

Miltenberger (2008) also has cited several studies to support the contention that combining behavioral skills training with *in situ* training were "the most effective strategies for promoting generalization of safety skills" (p. 33). Having experienced equivalent success with similar methods, the developers of the Picture Exchange Communication System© (PECS) (Bondy & Frost, 2002) suggest that parents and service providers teach and support the program in all feasible settings not only across the school day, but also at home and in the community.

*Be cautious* about what you ask the parents, teachers and other agents to do. Those you conclude lack the skills essential to delivering reinforcement effectively probably will have a difficult time following your request. So before sending folks off on their own, model and ask them to practice those skills in your presence, as others (Crockett. Fleming, Doepke, & Stevens, 2005; Gillett & LeBlanc, 2007) did when training parents successfully to apply either discrete trial teaching, or a natural training paradigm, respectively, with their own children.

**Specify exact circumstances.** We have also found it helpful to specify the exact circumstances under which these agents are to provide reinforcers (e.g., when he first gets up, during breakfast, etc.), and, as they become more comfortable in delivering reinforcement, gradually to increase the variety of those situations. And, of course, we must be certain to recognize indications of their progressive competence as behavior managers.

**Provide recognition to others for delivering reinforcement.** Make every effort to involve and recognize spouses, siblings, care-givers and others who collaborate in implementing the program and make an extra point of commenting on how, specifically, their efforts apparently are positively influencing the client's behavior. Research (see Chapter 24) has shown that, perhaps because it tends to be so gradual, progressive child behavior in and of itself is often insufficient to reinforce the parents' or teachers' consistent implementation of the program, you even might profit by monitoring your own rates of delivering reinforcement to your client as well as to all participating caregivers and/or contingency managers. Thus, get in the habit of not only delivering reinforcement to your client's improvements, but also to the caregiver's and/or contingency manager's improvements.

**Become aware of contingencies in the natural environment that you use to help promote generalization.** One of the most prudent things you can do is to explore thoroughly in advance the environment(s) in which you want see the behavior(s) of concern occur. Observe those behaviors and record the consequences immediately following them to try to identify what social, material and environmental reinforcers and punishers naturally affect them. Among organizational staff, consequences might well include overt or subtle peer approval or disapproval, wages, recognition, opportunities for promotion, or particular assignments. In the home, powerful reinforcers might consist of attention, allowances, material goods, preferred chores, food, family activities. Punishers might include: unwanted tasks, unpleasant comments, vocal tones or facial expressions and so on. Clinical and school environments contain much to attract and repel, such as assignments, comments, grades, and the body language of teachers, counselors, peers and others. The time you invest in acquainting yourself with the setting in which you are or plan to be promoting generalization should pay off abundantly. Why? Because you will be better positioned to capitalize on those readily available, especially potent stimuli.

## Teach the Behavior in Various Environments Sequentially

Another way to promote generalization is to teach the behavior sequentially, first in one environment, then the next, then next, etc. This strategy was used with four- to six-year-old boys with autism to initiate conversations with peers in the presence of toys (Garcia-Albea, Reeve, Reeve, & Brothers, 2014). Conversations did not occur when novel toys were introduced until training was provided with multiple categories of toys. This illustration reminds us that not only must we be aware of the social cues in the environment, but also the physical cues (situations). When you do teach the skill in one situation after another, you are pairing the various antecedent stimuli with the behavior and its reinforcers. Many of these antecedents may begin to acquire discriminative properties ($S^{Dr}$s) for your client, again further promoting stimulus generalization by increasing the range of $S^{Dr}$s capable of evoking the behavior. When some of these $S^{Dr}$s are present in other environments, generalization to those settings becomes more predictable. Consequently, be certain to arrange a variety of settings across which clientele are to practice those skills designated for generalization.

As a case in point, three young children with language delays communicated their requests mainly by reaching, grabbing or leading someone to the desired item (Drasgow, Halle, & Ostrosky 1998). When taught an acceptable replacement behavior in one setting, it failed to generalize across settings. Generalization was achieved only after the investigators arranged sequentially to extinguish the old requests and reinforce those replacements across each of the settings.

In another example, two children with cognitive delays learned to describe a series of pictures orally within five-word complex sentences. (Garcia, Bullet, & Rust, 1977). The skill did not transfer to the classroom and home, however, until some of the instances actually were trained in those settings. Therefore, when generalization fails to occur spontaneously, that purpose can be achieved by a "systematic sequential modification in every non-generalized condition, i.e., across responses, subjects, settings, or experimenters" (Stokes & Baer, 1977 p. 352). This strategy permits you to develop additional discriminative stimuli ($S^{Dr}s$) within those varied environments, thereby increasing chances that some may promote additional stimulus generalization. This is the tactic that Miltenberger et al. (2005) applied in teaching gun safety to four and five-year-olds. Following schooling them in safety with guns, trainers followed with *in situ* training. The safety skills then generalized, not only across location—to the home—but over time, and persisted over a three month follow-up.

The moral of the story: If you wish to be absolutely certain that a particular skill has generalized across physical and social settings, materials, and coaches (supervisors etc.), check it out in each new setting. If need be, re-teach it; or at least train and intermittently reinforce it either simultaneously, or sequentially, under each and every one of those circumstances under which it is to be emitted, until it reaches a consistently high, steady performance level across all cases (See Chapters 22 & 23 on schedules of reinforcement.) Depending on your long-range objectives, this might mean shifting settings or teaching, training, coaching, or managing assignments across clients, students, or personnel—no simple task—but one that surely will pay off in the long run.

## Consider Using a Generalization Map

To assuring yourself that you have covered all key generalization bases in your objectives, consider constructing a "generalization map" similar to one devised by Drabman, Hammer, and Rosenbaum (1979). Essentially, the map reminds program developers and implementers of the various parameters across which they must plan to apply and demonstrate singly and in combination the effects of their generalization strategies: participants, coaches, behaviors/tasks, materials, settings, and times.

When you are planning and conducting an intervention, consider all the relevant features of generalization. Among many others, Stevenson and Fantuzzo (1984) included a generalization map when planning to teach their students a self-control procedure. In reporting their results, they examined the following key features of the generalization map: Behavior, Setting, Behavior-setting, Time, Setting-time, Behavior-Time, Behavior-Setting, Time, Subject, Subject-behavior, Subject-setting, Subject-behavior-setting, Subject-time, Subject-setting-time, Subject-behavior-time, Subject-behavior-setting. (See Figure 21.3.) Analyzing the results across each of the various elements of the generalization map should permit you determine the conditions under which generalization took place and those circumstances under which further teaching would be necessary. One of your clients (subject) may use the toilet (behavior) in school (setting), but not at home (not across behavior-setting). Referring to the map to analyze the circumstances controlling and not controlling behavior allows you to be more

Percentage of Generalized Treatment Effect from the Treated Student's Math Performance to Untreated Variables

| Generalization | Experimental phases | | |
|---|---|---|---|
| | B1 (%) | B2 (%) | A' (%) |
| Behavior | 161.7 | 96.5 | |
| Setting | 78.7 | 70.1 | |
| Behavior-setting | 93.6 | 108.7 | |
| Time | | | 134.0 |
| Setting-time | | | 127.6 |
| Behavior-time | | | −2.1 |
| Behavior-setting-time | | | −61.7 |
| Subject | 138.3 | 45.6 | |
| Subject-behavior | 44.7 | 54.4 | |
| Subject-setting | 138.3 | 43.9 | |
| Subject-behavior-setting | 95.7 | 94.7 | |
| Subject-time | | | 155.3 |
| Subject-setting-time | | | 161.7 |
| Subject-behavior-time | | | −12.7 |
| subject-behavior-setting-time | | | 59.6 |

**Figure 21.3.** Generalization map results from Stevenson & Fantuzzo's (1984) study on self-control procedures (p. 209).

thorough in your planning and conducting an intervention and in analyzing the efficacy of outcome.

You also can refer to the features of the generalization map if you are planning to use a multiple-baseline experimental design to demonstrate the functional relation between a given response (or response set) and a particular intervention. Let us say you have designed a new managerial strategy for promoting the quality of customer service. Monitoring performance along the way, you introduce the intervention following baseline with one participant. If performance improves and you are wondering about instituting that training throughout the company, you feel it would be prudent to demonstrate a functional relation between the intervention and performance improvement. So, as you learned in Chapter 9, you have a number of choices (incorporating the essential varied baseline lengths) try out the same technique with other participants or with the same participant in a different department; or with a different behavior, such as sales productivity; or the same technique at different times of the day.

Remember, counting on or hoping for spontaneous generalization often is futile. Rather, planning, assessing for, and reinforcing generalization from the very start (at least intermittently, as mothers did in a study of infant imitation by Poulson, Kymissis, Reeve, & Andreatos, 1991) is crucial.

## Incorporate Common Stimuli Across Instructional Environments

Just as numerous basic laboratory studies have shown, the more likely features of the environment resemble each other in particular ways (such as sharing common $S^{D}$s), the greater the likelihood that responding will generalize across environments (e.g., school, home, community, workplace, social setting etc.). Conversely, the greater the differences between the two stimulus conditions, the lower the probability of stimulus generalization (Skinner, 1938). In the world of human affairs, generalization is more predictable when discriminative stimuli are common to *both* the training and natural environments. In fact, the more discriminative stimuli various locations share in common, the more likely the response is to generalize across those settings. Consequently, during the early phases of skill training, strive to incorporate familiar materials, schedules of reinforcement, types of reinforcers used, etc. within the program. Crone and Mehta (2016) took advantage of this guideline by arranging to use stimuli common to the home (e.g., same place mats, plates and silverware, chairs, table, utensils, food items, and tangible reinforcers) when teaching their clientele appropriate mealtime behavior within a clinic setting.

*If you are unable to teach in the natural setting, do so in an environment that shares as closely as possible the conditions under which skills will be used in the future.* Lattimore et al. (2008) successfully taught new work tasks to adults with autism and profound intellectual disabilities by capitalizing on this rule. During simulation training, they employed a job coach and used work materials similar to those to be applied in the actual job setting. The *Picture Exchange Communication System*© (PECS) accomplishes this purpose by teaching students to carry their PECS books wherever they go—from class to class, from school to home, and once there, from room to room, and out in the community. Because the picture icons are practically universally understandable, reinforcers are just about guaranteed (see Schwartz, Garfinkle, & Bauer, 1998; Sulzer-Azaroff et al., 2009; Webb, 2000).

If no live role models are available to demonstrate a particular action, consider using video-modeling. After adults taught various social responses to children with autism attending a day care center (e.g., "Give it back please," "My turn," and "What do you want?"), the investigators (Jones, Lermon, & Lechago, 2014) noted that the children transferred the skills to other adults, but not to peers. Once shown a video of a peer engaging in the targeted social behavior and another peer providing reinforcement for the social responses, they began to apply the skills across peers. (This feature of incorporating common stimuli within video modeling interventions is analogous to selecting similar models, as described in Chapter 18.)

Don't be surprised that even if behavior does generalize, it fails to maintain in the new environment. Perhaps the reinforcement schedule is leaner there than in the original setting (Koegel & Rincover,

1977), or maybe additional contingencies take precedence. Suppose counselors use a rich intermittent schedule of reinforcement in the clinic to teach a young man a socially acceptable way to express his anger. Yet when the youth returns to his home, he receives only sparse reinforcement for applying that new skill, resulting in its rapid extinction. One way to avoid this kind of trap is to aim for closer correspondence between one set of circumstances and the next, by arranging for reinforcement features to extend across the various settings. In such cases you may need to become more creative. Should you, for example, recognize the need to increase the quantity of reinforcers delivered in the newer environment, you might coach your clients (e.g., via demonstration, guided practice and appropriate differential reinforcement) effective ways to solicit those. (Chapters 22 & 23 deal with the issue of persistence of an acquired behavior across time,)

When the risks are high, prudent designers of training programs tend especially to be sensitive to the *maintaining common stimuli across settings* guideline. Astronauts, airplane pilots and atomic-energy plant operators practice their routines using life-sized replicas of boards containing all the com-ponents present in actual control panels. Simulators of that nature also are used to train occupational skills of army tank operators, and other trainees whose performance accuracy can be a matter of life and death. Chemistry labs, woodworking shops, cooking classrooms, and other educational laboratories also are designed with the same concept of similarity in mind.

*As behavior analysts, we share a strong responsibility training our change-agent clients of the necessity for them to program for transfer (generalization) from preparatory, intensive, special, or remedial over to regular ongoing programs.* Indeed, Chandler et al. (1992) reported that only 29 percent of programs judged successful by their implementers explicitly programmed for transfer to stimuli common across settings. Absent this aspect of generalization training, behavior learned in such programs risks failing to transfer to natural settings (Walker & Buckley, 1972; Walker, Hops, & Johnson, 1975). To illustrate, many school districts set up special classrooms for students with various handicapping conditions. Frequently, each class has small numbers of students and at least one teacher plus one or more trained aides. Materials often are different from those in regular classrooms. While the students often succeed in such special environments, when mainstreamed back into regular classrooms, the gains they had made in the special classroom often fail to carry over. A major reason is that conditions have not been arranged to facilitate generalization: the reinforcement schedules, materials, level of support, or individual educational plan (IEP) objectives, and physical settings lack common features (Hunt et al., 1986; Meadows, Neel, Scott, & Parker, 1994; Schneider & Leroux, 1994). If generalization is to succeed, similar discriminative stimuli—rules, instructional materials, and schedules of activities—must be provided, with changes in reinforcement schedules gradual rather than abrupt. Some school districts use "halfway" classes to help bridge the gap between the two very different types of classrooms. Others gradually introduce students into regular classroom settings or train regular host teachers in the procedures used by special-education teachers (e.g., Walker et al., 1975).

Here are a few other school-related examples of programs explicitly designed to foster generalization among children with special needs:

- Using Mesmer's et al (2007) study that was describe earlier to illustrate the section on reinforcing approximations, three male students in a special class included a nine-year-old third grader, a ten-year-old fourth grader (both diagnosed with serious emotional disturbance), and a five-year-old who was "diagnosed as developmentally delayed due to social and emotional concerns" (Mesmer, Duhon, & Dodson, 2007, p. 554). The special education classroom intervention consisted of three components: (1) A gradually more challenging goal statement indicating the required number of correct responses for the day, printed at the top of each student's worksheet. (2) A computer-generated thumbs-up icon placed at the top of the five- and nine-year-olds' papers, and a small digital timer for the ten-year-old. (3) Following each session, the teachers collected and scored the worksheets. Participants who exceeded their goals were immediately allowed to choose an item from the class prize box.

Although only the first two components were incorporated in the general education settings, once this intervention was underway, the target responses increased to and maintained at high levels in both places. Results supported the value of incorporating common discriminative stimuli across settings.

- Jones, Feeley, and Takacs (2007) taught two three-year-old preschool boys with autism to respond spontaneously to particular events (what to say when someone sneezes; when they ask if you're okay). Both children used spoken language to communicate and had imitative vocal skills. "Spontaneous responses were defined as specific verbal utterances (e.g., the child says 'bless you') following non-spoken discriminative stimuli (e.g., adult sneeze)" (p. 565). They also were taught to say "What?" when someone whispered and "Are you okay?" when someone said "ouch!" Instruction consisted of immediate prompts, natural consequences, plus a reinforcing edible item and praise. After the child began to regularly anticipate the correct response, were he to respond incorrectly or fail to respond at all, he was told "no" or "uh uh" and prompted in a least-to-most fashion. Natural consequences (e.g., saying "thank you" when the child said "bless you" or talking more loudly when the child said "what?") followed all unprompted and prompted responses. For purposes of generalization, a teacher from a different classroom participated and the training was also introduced in novel settings (e.g., gym, playground). Both children's behaviors generalized across other people and settings.

(Note that the investigators not only used common stimuli—the same $S^D$s to evoke the appropriate verbal behavior—but also ensured a supportive environment for the generalized responses.)

- Petursdottir et al. (2007) introduced common play-related stimuli (parts of toys used in free play, such as a marble run) during peer-tutoring of a kindergarten child with autism. The child and his three peer tutors increased their social interactions during free play. (Note here that the common stimuli were not only the toys, but also the peers.)

- Preschool supervisors trained classroom and resource teachers to adapt class plans to support increased peer interactions among mainstreamed children and those with disabilities (Hundert & Hopkins, 1992). Both the students' and teachers' behavior generalized from the classroom to the playground.

- Similarly, Hundert (2007) asked four preschool supervisors to train classroom and resource teachers of children with disabilities to develop their own methods for promoting peer interactions among all the students, including the two in each classroom with disabilities. Supervisors provided the teachers with tactics (e.g., peer groupings, selection of materials, correspondence training, prompting, and group contingencies). As a result, children with and without disabilities increased their peer interactions. The teachers also generalized the use of their skills to successfully promote on-task behavior by students with and without disabilities during circle time—resulting in heightened rates of remaining on-task. If those in control of contingencies in the natural environment, such as a supervisor, conduct the training, common stimuli are assured (Green, Rollyson, Passante, & Reid, 2002).

- You, yourself, are using sound instructional methods when you incorporate within your own training arrangements as many physical and social elements as possible in common with those in the setting in which skills are to be practiced. An appreciation for the payoff derived from this sort of verisimilitude across conditions accounts for the increase in supervised practice required prior to allowing new practitioners to perform independently in many fields, including applied behavior analysis.[1]

Practice tends to promote skill fluency, which in turn may promote stimulus generalization.

## Promote Fluency

Behavior emitted rapidly, smoothly, and with apparent ease, that is, *"fluently,"* can be maintained and will tend to generalize more readily than behavior that is erratic. Simply put, "People are more likely to engage in a given behavior the less effort it requires" (Song & Schwarz, 2008, p. 986). When they fluently express new abilities, such as displaying appropriate social skills (Ducharme & Holborn, 1997), reading word passages (Martens, et al., 2007; Valleley & Shriver, 2003), and uttering smooth speech patterns (Onslow, Menzies & Packman, 2001) they are more apt to transfer those skills to new situations. (Watch tennis stars like the Williams sisters transfer their expertise across courts and continents!) Remember, by definition, any skill, basic or complex can be considered truly mastered only when emitted fluently and independent of prompts. Our clientele are less likely to emit behaviors they tend to perform awkwardly. So, determine whether the behavior is emitted with a reasonable level of fluency. If not, provide many opportunities for reinforced practice until it does achieve that level by eliciting and reinforcing the response so often that it appears to become "second nature."

Nonetheless, if the generalization you are seeking remains limited, then you should conduct a more formal assessment to investigate the contingencies at work. For example, as mentioned above, Himle et al. (2004) promoted fluency by praising and providing feedback to children as they rehearsed their gun-safety skills and also when, upon finding a gun in various situations, they exhibited the skills (don't touch, leave the area, tell an adult) correctly five times in a row. (For those eight out of 14 children who still failed to generalize the skills, the investigators persisted in implementing in situ training.)

Becoming fluent in performing an academic task can be especially supportive of generalization. Kubina, Young, and Kilwein (2004) taught students with learning disabilities to practice two component-spelling skills (oral word segmentation and letter sounds), until they applied those practices effortlessly. Even though the youngsters had not been directly taught how to spell the specific words, they applied these fluent skills to spelling at a 100 percent level of accuracy. Similarly, Bonfiglio, Daly, Martens, Lin, and Corsaut, (2004) suggested that generalization across reading passages "may occur partially as a function of a fluency threshold" (p. 114).

## Apply Strategies Designed to Facilitate Carry-Over into the Natural Setting

If you carefully assess the relation between the behavior of concern and the environment in which it is to be emitted, you should be able to identify conditions standing ready to support it. Lacking any, you may need to arrange new contingencies to reinforce and/or prompt (perhaps later fading those prompts) the behavior within the transfer setting. Training local personnel, peers, or parents are prime examples. Other methods might include activity schedules, pocket calendars, cellphone vibrator or other electronic signals, checklists, teaching the client tactfully to solicit reinforcers, and so on. (See Chapter 6 for ways to identify effective reinforcers and Chapters 15 through 19, 24, and 27 for other illustrative prompting strategies.)

**Correspondence training**, *delivering reinforcers contingent on the correspondence or agreement between verbal reports (saying) and actions (doing)*, is one technique for bringing overt behavior under the governance of rules. Teach people to match

---

[1] For an example of a formally programmed ABA field practice tool in the autism education field, see Sulzer-Azaroff & Associates (2007), *Applying Behavior Analysis across the Autism Spectrum: A Field Guide for Practitioners.* Cornwall-on-Hudson, NY: Sloan Publishing.

reports of their performance with what they actually are doing or have done (e.g., Israel & O'Leary, 1973), so that they will eventually depend on their verbal stated intentions to promote generalization. Diane, a typical four-year-old girl, hardly ever played with crayons, beads, or books, or in the kitchen area (Baer, Williams, Osnes, & Stokes, 1985). Thus, a program was designed to promote such play activities. If the child said "yes" when asked if she planned to play with the crayons, beads, or books, she was praised and given a token. Her rate of using those materials increased, but just temporarily. Subsequently, a doing-saying *correspondence training* (we might call it "truth telling") program was implemented. That is, Diane received reinforcers only if she actually played with the crayons after she had previously said she would. Crayon-play increased. Interestingly, after that, just reinforcing verbal statements of *intent* to play with the other play materials resulted in her actually following through, although correspondence was not reinforced for those other activities. Apparently, correspondence between saying and doing generalized from crayon play to the three other behaviors. Perhaps reinforcing correspondence at some times and only stated intentions at other times created an ambiguous situation. Diane may not have been able to discriminate which contingencies would be in effect at any given time, so she responded as if correspondence were being reinforced. In children of typical development, it is not unusual for correspondences between saying and doing to generalize across a range of settings. Once a child learns to tell the truth in response to questions like "What were you doing?" we would in fact want that to generalize across all settings.

*Specific problem-solving strategies* also may promote generalization across situations. After De Castro et al. (2003) taught aggressive boys to monitor and regulate their own emotions when provoked by peers, their aggressive acts decreased. Be certain, though, that the particular problem-solving method is an effective one. Not all are. In the same study, *considering the peer's emotions and intentions* and also *interposing a delay* actually *increased* the group's aggressiveness.

There is one particular technique that stands out as being ready to support your clients' tendency to emit a response more broadly once they have learned to emit it fluently: *Teach them to indicate where, when and with whom they will engage in the behavior*. For example, they might specify a goal such as, "When I eat some popcorn, I will share with my sister." Or, "When I play the board game with my sister, I will wait for my turn." Goals like those can function as MOs to encourage the client to emit the behavior more generally.

*Peer-mediation interventions* also appear promising for promoting generalization. MacFarland and Fisher (2020) found that video-based group instruction on social skills failed to encourage high school students to generalize those skills until a peer-mediated intervention was implemented (see Chapter 12 for peer-mediated interventions). Perhaps peer mediated interventions allow for providing on-going S$^D$s and feedback throughout various environments in the school (or other settings) that can help promote not only generalization but also maintenance.

## Pre-assess and Reduce Support for Functional Interfering, Maladaptive Behavior

Suppose you are quite convinced your client is capable of emitting a particular behavior, yet fails to transfer it across settings, materials, people, activities, and so on. Perhaps something is blocking its expression under those circumstances. To find out, conduct a functional assessment (review Chapter 10) of interfering behavior *under all generalization situations*. Then, for optimal results, reinforce alternative adaptive behaviors *incompatible with the unwanted behavior*, but that nonetheless yield the individual equivalent or more powerful reinforcers under each and every generalization circumstance.

## Provide Sufficient Exemplars

Despite an absence of specific instruction in practicing the new variants, the more **exemplars** (*examples containing the critical stimulus or response features*) your clients experience, the more fluent and general their response patterns will tend to become.

Suppose you are training your managerial staff to provide positive, constructive feedback. Instead of criticizing them, show personnel what *to* do, rather than pointing out what *not* to do by displaying video or role-played demonstrations of the skills, requesting they themselves role-play the skills, and setting an example by providing your own constructive feedback.

A number of professionals (e.g., Holth, 2017; Horner, Sprague, & Wilcox, 1982; Neef, Lensbower, Hockersmith, DePalma, & Gray, 1990; Repp & Karsh, 1991) have suggested that we can increase the likelihood of desired generalization by including multiple relevant examples of the stimuli that *are supposed to* occasion the related behavior (S+s). Or, as pointed out by Holth (2017), successful multiple exemplar training involves reinforcing an acceptable range of response topographies (greetings such as saying, "hi," "hello," a head nod and smile, etc.) under *varying* critical stimulus condition. For example, critical stimulus conditions for greetings might include relatives, friends, and teachers; for traffic lights at intersections they can be on the left side, the right side, or overhead. Given traffic lights in any of these locations, we not only want drivers to go, but also to stop, given corresponding locations of the red light. Imagine what chaos would erupt were we to teach braking, given a red light, but ignored going, given a green light. As new exemplars are added, the learner should become increasingly capable of generalizing to other stimuli possessing the same critical features. Look for several illustrations of this general rule in the literature on the prevention of child abduction (e.g., Poche et al., 1981; Johnson et al., 2005).

The multiple-exemplar rule is applicable to a variety of discrimination tasks, as illustrated in a study involving nine- to 19-year-olds with moderate intellectual disability (Repp, Karsh, Johnson, & VanLaarhoven, 1996.) All their examples consisted of words printed on cards, containing approximately the same number of letters, beginning with the same letter, often ending with the same letter, and sharing at least three letters in common. "noncritical dimensions (script and size of letters, positions of words on a card, color and size of card) were the same for all the words and did not change across trials" (p. 216). Presenting a *single example* of the correct word along with sequential examples of several incorrect words "was more efficient and was just as effective in generalization as the condition which presented multiple examples of *both* correct and incorrect words (p. 213)." However, when multiple examples of both the stated and unstated words were presented, the non-critical dimensions did change, thereby heightening each youngster's awareness of the range of stimuli. Changing these non-critical conditions, as in this strategy, may add to the complexity of the discrimination, and consequently to the sophistication of the learned concept or skill. When the discrimination is even more complex, (as in "If condition 1, then response 1 [e.g., given green, stepping on the gas] is correct but response 2 [stopping] is incorrect" and "If condition 2 [given red], then response 2 [stopping] is correct, but response 1 [stepping on the gas] is incorrect,") you want to provide many, many examples, including the critical and non-critical features of each set of conditions.

Despite offering no vocal prompting, Garcia-Albea et al. (2014) used an audio script and audio script fading procedure to teach four boys (four-to-six years old) to initiate conversations with peers in the presence of toys. Only after the investigators provided *multiple categories and exemplars* of toys, did the vocal interactions generalize across novel toys.

You may find it useful to use video media in which models teach sufficient exemplars, as Haring et al. (1987) did successfully. Those investigators taught three youths with autism to purchase items in one particular setting, but found that the youths failed to generalize their new skills to other settings. The investigators then played videotapes of same-aged, non-handicapped peers demonstrating each of the skills sequentially in various settings. During the presentation, the instructor asked the youths questions, stopping to model the relevant response following incorrect answers. Follow-up generalization probes showed that the *simulation* procedure was sufficient to induce and sustain near-perfect performance in the novel settings. Similarly, investigators (Day-Watkins, Murray, & Connell, 2014) combined displaying multi-exemplars, video modeling, verbal and physical prompting plus reinforcement successfully to teach adolescents with autism to help others wanting help and to promote generalization of that set of skills.

Eikeseth and Nesset (2003) investigated whether response-exemplar training of vocal imitation would improve the articulation of two boys, five and six, both with phonological disorder (i.e., a speech disorder characterized by inappropriate sound production and use). The articulation training consisted of requesting each participant to imitate specific target words (e.g., "Say 'cup'").

> Only one target word was trained at a time, but the target word was mixed with other mastered words and sounds to facilitate discrimination between the target word and other sounds and words, and to maintain high rates of correct responding. After the child had acquired correct imitation of the target word (i.e., the child responded correctly on at least nine of 10 consecutive presentations), that target word was presented in various two-and three-word sentences. (pp. 329–330)

Then, once the child responded correctly to nine of ten consecutive presentations within a three-word sentence, training was terminated for that target word. Were a child unable to imitate the individual parts of target words, prompting, chaining, and shaping procedures were added. Both participants began correctly to articulate the training words, as well as the names of other untrained objects within their conversational speech, even when monitored six months later.

Similarly, Carr (2003) used exemplar training with six children with autism to help them demonstrate *discrimination by exclusion*.

> The simplest form of exclusion trial follows a matching-to-sample or conditional discrimination format, in which a novel word is spoken as the sample and an unknown picture (i.e., one that has no established relation with a corresponding word for the participant) is presented along with one or more previously known pictures as comparisons. Demonstration of an exclusion-based conditional discrimination requires that the unknown picture is selected. (p. 508)

She found that presenting multiple examples of reinforced exclusion facilitated non-reinforced exclusion performances and reduced errors in new word-item discriminations. In each of these illustrations, generalization to untrained stimulus conditions or to untrained responses was taught by "training of sufficient exemplars (rather than all) of these stimulus conditions or responses" (Stokes & Baer, 1977, p. 355).

*To select appropriate exemplars, identify the critical defining features of the stimulus—those qualities that must be, and those that must **not** be present for the example to qualify for membership in the general stimulus class.* Critical features of a bus are that it: transports large numbers of people on the ground, usually along a fixed route; has wheels and an engine. Exemplars might be school buses, public buses, and airport buses. Assure yourself that incorrect examples are not included by generating a separate list of "non-examples" that contain most but not all the critical features—taxis, pedal bikes, boats, planes, moving vans, tractors, and so on. (See Figure 21.4.)

Pause for a moment to consider how this book is organized. Refer to the goals at the beginning of each chapter. Can you guess the kinds of skills we are hoping you acquire in dealing with the many concepts contained herein? Notice how we illustrate most key concepts several times and in various ways (words, charts, graphs, tables, images…). Why do you think we avoided limiting our presentation only to an abstract definition plus a single elaboration? Do you find yourself analyzing or interpreting the things you see people do in behavior-analytic terms? Have you begun to practice some of the skills about which you have read? If so, you are generalizing beyond your formal instructional experience. Good for you! And good for us, because apparently we provided you with sufficient exemplars.

**Figure 21.4** Identifying buses

## Train Loosely

Another generalization-promotion strategy is to apply the opposite to discrimination training. Instead of using a precisely repeated set of stimuli or formats, Stokes and Baer (1977) suggested you encourage transfer by conducting teaching "with relatively little control over the stimuli presented and the correct responses allowed, so as to maximize sampling of relevant dimensions for transfer to other situations and other forms of the behavior" (p. 357). This way, you associate a greater variety of stimuli with reinforcers; or said another way, a number of different stimuli now function as discriminative stimuli for you.

When you train loosely, you broaden the variety of stimuli serving a discriminative function for the learner. This helps limit overselectivity[2] (choosing or using a stimulus based on fewer than its full set of essential features, as in pointing to the two single-level buses, but not the double-decker bus); and it keeps irrelevant or narrow stimulus properties from inhibiting or suppressing generalization. To prevent her students on the autism spectrum from identifying her solely by some irrelevant feature such as the color of her shirt or shoes, the teacher would train loosely, taking pains to wear different clothing on different teaching days; sometimes stand; sometimes sit; assume different positions during teaching; vary her vocal tones; now and again use one form of requesting the response and sometimes another (e.g., "What's this?" "Tell me about this," "Tell me," "What's the answer?" "Next!") and vary reinforcement schedules, instructional settings she arranged, and so on. Such maneuvers may well serve to prevent the correct response from accidentally becoming associated with any stimulus fortuitously, but not meaningfully paired with the target stimulus, such as the teacher's face, voice, position, clothing, or the room.

If cheerful service is the restaurant manager's goal, she will target and reinforce her wait-staff's friendly greetings and smiling at their full array of customers, regardless of gender, race or dress; at different times of day and days of the week; whether the restaurant is packed or empty. To promote workers' maintaining safe surroundings, the foreman, managers, and peers would be trained periodically to compliment neatness at random times and in its various forms (table stacks of materials, clean floor area, safe body positions, use of protective equipment, and so on).

Suppose you are trying to promote your preschool students' use of descriptive adjectives. Among the many available instructional options, you might choose to:

- Set up formal lessons: select a set of pictures and ask for a description of each one, reinforcing those responses that contain descriptive adjectives.

- Make lots of enticing toys available and watch the children at play, instructing as opportunities present themselves. "I see you're playing with the big, green cement truck. Which one do you want to drive now? The little yellow one or the big brown one?" Next, after prompting, if necessary, you could reinforce by praising responses containing combinations of adjectives, while presenting the child's preference.

- Wait for the child to initiate an interaction, capturing that teachable moment: During free-play period, Sammy tugs at your jeans and asks, "Teacher, can I have that truck?" "Which truck do you want? Do you want the big, green cement truck or the little red fire truck?" "The big, green cement truck." "OK. Here you are." Receiving the truck is the natural reinforcer.

The last episode illustrates incidental teaching (Hart & Risley, 1975), about which you read in Chapter 18. You teach toward a specific, predetermined objective by capitalizing on natural unplanned opportunities or by displaying enticing objects just beyond the child's reach. There is a reasonable chance that when you implement various incidental teaching arrangements, such as teaching the use of prepositions, you might find, as McGee, Krantz, and McClannahan (1985) did, that your students generalize that class of skills more so than with more formalized drills. Perhaps one reason

---

[2]Overselectivity is the opposite of overgeneralization, which involves inappropriately including non-relevant exemplars with a given stimulus class.

incidental teaching promotes generalization so successfully is that it incorporates the element of loose training. That is, it permits students many opportunities to sample relevant dimensions of various stimulus situations. For instance, to teach the color green, materials might include green cars, green trucks, green apples, and green books. Note also, the various kinds of buses and non-buses we used to illustrate the concept of "bus" in Figure 21.3 above, along with the many different examples of behavior-analytic concepts we supply throughout this text.

The *natural language paradigm* (NLP) (Koegel, O'Dell, & Koegel, 1987) illustrates "loose teaching" very nicely. When applying the NLP, teachers or parents engage in play sessions during which they provide massed opportunities for children to initiate speaking. Laski, Charlop, and Schreibman (1988) described an investigation in which they used this method to promote speech among children on the autism spectrum. The adult presents a range of toys and takes turns with the student, playing with the toys while modeling a variety of words and phrases and using varied tasks and multiple exemplars. This encourages the child to speak, following which, regardless of quality, those speech efforts are reinforced by allowing the child access to the toys. "Thus, the NLP is a child-initiated protocol designed to increase motivation by varying tasks (Dunlap, 1984), increase responding by providing direct reinforcers (Koegel & Williams, 1980), and enhance generalization through loose structure and multiple exemplars (Stokes & Baer, 1977)" (Laski et al., p. 392).

Were you to learn all your behavior-analytic concepts only by identifying sets of examples that we present, you might have a difficult time transferring those concepts to new situations. That is our reason for embedding questions related to those concepts within this text and supplemental material, for asking you to generate original examples and to apply what you learn beyond your own study space. We count on your instructor, fellow students, and you yourself to seize upon natural opportunities to help you transfer concepts to novel cases. Survey news reports to conceptually analyze the behavioral contingencies operating within interesting current events: elections, court cases, ethnic strife, wars, murders, suicides, or, on the rare occasion when reported in the news, acts of heroism or altruism. Such events have stimulated animated discussions in our classes, while yielding us opportunities to "loosely train" important ABA concepts.

## Use Indiscriminable Contingencies

Although specific instructions abet precise task completion, after performance is well-established, yet you are seeking further generalization, begin to loosen the clarity of conditions under which the behavior is to be reinforced: Suppose you are driving along the highway on a sunny day, eight miles over the speed limit. Several cars coming toward you are blinking their headlights. "Why?" you wonder. "Is it foggy ahead? Is there an accident? Is a police car poised beyond the next bend?" You slow down. Or, in an analogous situation, you also might tend to reduce your speed where you've seen a police car previously parked and someone receiving a ticket. The response of driving within the speed limit transfers across all those situations, even though you yourself may have only received one speeding ticket and that was years ago. Why?

Because you are unable to discriminate the contingencies in effect at any particular moment in time, and are responding to only loosely related cues. In other words, *clear, situation-specific stimuli promote discrimination* (Bouxsein et al., 2008), and *indiscriminable contingencies tend to foster generalization*. So, when you are hoping for generalization, loosen the clarity of conditions under which the behavior will be reinforced.

A study by Guevremont, Osnes, and Stokes (1986) illustrates the latter point: The aim was to promote correspondence between what two four-year-olds *said* they did and what they actually *did* do. (We might call that "truth-telling.") First, they asked the children what they *would* (intended to) do; then observed; then asked the children to report what they *had* done; then provided rewards when reporting corresponded with what the youngsters actually had done, but not otherwise. After that intervention produced *say-do correspondence*, the experimenters switched over to one of the following contingency arrangements on a daily basis:

a. positive consequences delivered immediately following prompted verbalizations but not following correspondence;

b. positive consequences delivered after the observation for correspondence but not following the prompted verbalizations;

c. days on which no verbalizations were prompted and no consequences were delivered;

d. delayed positive consequences for prompted verbalizations but no consequences for correspondence; and

e. days on which no consequences were delivered for either prompted verbalizations or correspondence.

Delayed consequences for verbalizations (see Solnick & Baer, 1984) included only minimal consequences (e.g., "O.K.") immediately following the verbalization (p. 217).

Following that history of indiscriminable contingencies, the children's levels of say-do correspondence remained much higher and steadier during returns to baseline than they had during the original baseline, as well as just as high as during the correspondence-training phases. In other words, the children had learned to be much more truthful in reporting their behavior.

If your work involves teaching or managing personnel, try this tactic to encourage effective participation among all group members: First, take the time to establish correspondence between individuals' stating their intent to carry out a particular responsibility and actually executing the action. Then be certain to reinforce when their actions match the stated intention. Later, you can vary your reinforcement of either actual accomplishments or of statements of intention to accomplish something in particular, across different people and at random times. You will also be able intermittently to reinforce reports of previous accomplishments or of correspondence between verbal statements and actual performance. Because it will be difficult for group members to discriminate the contingencies in effect at any one time, correspondence is more apt to generalize. You will have taught the group members to keep the promises they make.

Remember, that delaying your delivery of reinforcers, or doing so intermittently, can be beneficial or detrimental: beneficial when your foremost concern is *maintaining a* behavior; detrimental, if you are hoping to diminish or eliminate it. Insofar as generalization is concerned, though, once a behavior is reasonably well established, if you hope to keep it going within, as well as beyond the training site, gradually switch over to delayed, intermittent reinforcement. When participants no longer gain reinforcers every time they emit a behavior, they may, at least for a while, begin to test it out at different times and places and with different people or materials. Assuming you are a sufficiently vigilant observer, you should be able to seize upon such episodes to reinforce behavior supportive of generalization. (For a vivid illustration of this point, examine the way Freeland and Noell [1999] capitalized on these principles to sustain the mathematics performances of several elementary school children.)

## Continue Training

You will want to refer back regularly to your statement of the behavioral objective: under what conditions, to how many correct trials in a row, over whatever sessions, days, weeks, or months you stipulated as the mastery criterion. Demonstrating the ability to perform a given behavior once or twice is no guarantee that it is firmly in place. Hence it is important to continue training in all relevant settings until the data inform you that the objective has been achieved, because such well-established behaviors are more apt to generalize.

Severe cases of refusal of nutritious food illustrate this situation. When their clients actively rejected nourishing foods, Peterson, Lerman and Nissen (2016) used a combined shaping and desensitization program consisting of a series of steps starting with (a) presenting the spoon with a bite in a bowl within arm's reach of the child, (b) removing the spoon and the bowl after the bite entered the child's mouth (c) presenting the next bite 30 seconds after the previous bite entered the child's mouth (with a few specific exceptions) or removing the spoon and bowl after 30 seconds if the child did not accept the bite. Personnel continued to implement that set plus several other specific steps over 100 or more sessions during which time the child eventually learned to accept nutritious foods.

## Teach Participants and Contingency Managers How to Promote and Support Generalization

Maintaining and supporting contingency managers' generalization strategies is just as challenging and demanding of correct programming as are those for maintaining and supporting the client-centered target behaviors they are intended to mediate. That is also the case when teaching self-management. Here are a few hints you might consider applying, especially in situations when conflicting demands on personnel are high.

So, to support our continued implementation of generalization (and other) strategies, we contingency managers can capitalize on practices like instructing ourselves aloud or covertly, arranging physical cues, or using other self-management techniques. Recognize that programming the generalization and maintenance of these mediating skills can really pay off far more broadly than simply teaching target behaviors one by one. A few examples of the kinds of readily available mediating responses follow.

Faloon and Rehfeldt (2008) used modeling, self-rules, and self-delivery of reinforcers successfully to teach three adults with mild developmental disabilities to iron their own pants. First, they used modeling, requesting that each participant watch the experimenter iron and listen to what he said. The experimenter then stated what he needed to do, demonstrated, and acknowledged his accomplishment ("good job") after completing each step. Withholding any praise, he then asked each participant to iron a pair of pants, while reciting both the instructions and the self-acknowledgement statements, first overtly; then, later, covertly for each step. If the participant made a discernible error, the experimenter corrected it, using least-to-most prompting. The training ended once the participant performed all steps with 100 percent accuracy for three consecutive sessions and recited the correct rules and self-acknowledgment statements without any prompts. Not only did each participant acquire the skill of ironing his pants independent of any extrinsic reinforcers, but each also transferred the skill to other settings. Apparently, teaching self-management this way can be an effective strategy for promoting generalization. Generally, colleagues tend to prefer to consult (Mayer & Wallace, 2020) with one another on a face-to-face basis. However, should that not be feasible, as we have learned, especially during the Covid epidemic, alternative communicative media are available, including, mail, the telephone, text, email, Zoom, teleconferencing, and other methods of communication. Also consider employing those media to set the occasion(s) for targeting behaviors, to supply feedback and merited social reinforcement, and to encourage your clients' maintenance and generalization of their newly acquired skills (Rivi & Roman, 2019).

**Self-record.** Participants and staff can mediate generalization by gaining proficiency in and regularly practicing self-recording. Sandy checks her "praise record," noting, as the consultant suggested, that she is praising much more than criticizing on the job. Be advised, though, that as with self-instruction, people will more faithfully and accurately self-record if, along with the reinforcement derived from graphic feedback or other evidence of progress, other folks intermittently continue to reinforce that self-recording. Absent some sort of reinforcing feedback like that derived from consistent and accurate self-recording, we risk seeing those gains diminish or disappear.

*Supported (reinforced)* self-recording has been found to be a powerful method for promoting generalization across various populations, including, among a multitude of others, encouraging:

- individual children with attention-deficit disorder to pay attention to their task during reading instruction (Edwards, 1995);
- 13- to 16-year-olds with learning disabilities to complete their homework (Trammel et al., 1994);

- students to conduct themselves acceptably in the absence of supervision (Ninness et al., 1991), and with entire classes (Mitchem & Young, 2001);
- children to reduce their inappropriate vocalizations (Mancina, Tankersley, Kamps, Kravits, & Parrett, 2000);
- lifeguards to improve their cleaning responsibilities, including vacuuming, lobby tidying, and pool-deck maintenance (Rose & Ludwig, 2009); and
- patients to manage their blood-pressure effectively (Feldman, Bacher, Campbell, Drover, & Chockalingam, 1998).

In the latter case, not surprisingly, the best results were achieved with a combination of "simplified medication regimens and a combination of behaviour strategies, including the tailoring of pill-taking to patients' daily habits and rituals, the advocacy of self-monitoring of pills and blood pressure, and the institution of a reward system… (p. 18)."[3]

**Consider Incorporating Cognitive Behavioral Strategies.** Given that any behavioral intervention is only as valuable as the specifically sought-after generality of the change it produces, we behavioral practitioners continuously hunt for strategies supportive of generalization. Using such challenges as social anxiety disorder (SAD) as a case in point, Swan, Carper, and Kendall (2016) have elaborated upon the list of previously identified generalization strategies for reinforcing the "positive opposite" (a desired alternative to the problem behavior—"Alt-R"). Among those are cognitive-behavioral techniques designed to foster coping and skill in anxiety-provoking situations, like providing clients increased opportunities to practice those skills while exposed to their particular bugaboos (i.e., conditioned aversive stimuli).

Further, they offer an extensive set of other approaches including, but not limited to:

- Reducing the extent to which family members accommodate to the client's anxiety symptoms (which affords the client the opportunity to practice and generalize his newly acquired coping skills within everyday situations).
- Training and coaching parents and/or caregivers to substitute attending to and reinforcing positive behaviors and set consistent limits instead of inadvertently reinforcing, by giving in, to problem behaviors. Some of these include:
  ○ Reinforcing and Rewarding Generalization by using such techniques as Kendall and Hedtke's (2006) "Coping Cat FEAR protocol" (Recognizing the physical sensations that indicate they Feel frightened; Expecting that bad things will happen; Attitudes and actions for coping by using such strategies as forming particular attitudes and executing certain actions; and Rewarding oneself for effort and approach).
  ○ Involving peers or parents in reinforcing desired behaviors across settings (DuPaul & Stoner, 2014), perhaps aided by means of token systems or daily report cards.
  ○ Capitalizing on technology, such as virtual reality exposure to anxiety-provoking stimuli (Powers & Emmelkamp, 2008) or using mobile technology to prompt use of the skills learned during treatment (Pramana, Patmanto, Kendall & Silk, 2014).
  ○ Promoting the practice of using cell-phone signals to prompt parental coaching or use coping thoughts such as "I can do it!" in place of the negative self-talk often accompanying depression (Peterman et al., 2015).

**Combine self-management methods.** Koegel and Koegel (1990) reported an especially compelling illustration of how children with autism were taught to manage their own stereotypic behavior. When a chronograph wrist-watch alarm sounded, the youngsters were to observe and record whether they were emitting the stereotypic behavior and to refrain from accepting reinforcers until they had met a criterion for diminished stereotypy. In under an hour, the

---
[3] See the literature on behavior therapy and on organizational-behavior management for numerous other examples involving adult participants.

youngsters mastered the self-management treatment package. Stereotypy diminished at the teaching site and later, elsewhere, after the self-management program had been maintained for a number of weeks.

As far as you, yourself, are concerned, whenever you learn about a new behavior-analytic principle or practice, apply it to your own activities at home, work, school, or out in the community, and find opportunities to teach it to others. This is no simple task. So be certain to supply varied and sufficient exemplars to hasten your mastery of and ability to apply each new element. You will learn the principle more efficiently and be better able to use it in novel situations. This is intuitively captured by the old precept that the best way to learn something is to teach it.

**Solicit reinforcers**. After they have mastered a skill, you can help participants gain support for its generalization by teaching them how to recruit reinforcers from the natural social environment (Craft, Alber, & Heward, 1998; Graubard, Rosenberg, & Miller, 1971). Craft et al. used modeling, error correction, role playing, and praise to teach fourth-graders with developmental disabilities to recruit their regular-education classroom teacher's attention by asking "How am I doing?" or "Look, I'm all finished" when completing their spelling assignments. Not only did the students' accuracy and number of spelling assignments completed in the regular classroom increase, but so did the amount of teacher praise. That is a recipe for converting a non-supportive to a supportive environment. (If your own work environment seems inadequately supportive, teach yourself various ways to solicit reinforcers from your peers, subordinates, and supervisors. See Chapter 24 for suggestions.)

**Provide positive performance feedback to peers, supervisors, and subordinates for generalization efforts.** If you hope to intervene successfully in an organization, invest some time initially identifying which stimulus events seem most powerfully to affect personnel performance. Positive verbal feedback from a supervisor, peer, or even a subordinate probably will appear high up on the list.

We ourselves have had the opportunity to put that suggestion to the test on various occasions. In one particular case (Sulzer-Azaroff & Harshbarger, 1995; described elsewhere in this text) we assisted a large manufacturing organization to save hundreds of thousands of dollars by systematically teaching quality inspectors and senior, junior, and middle managers how effectively to use performance feedback with their workers. It is truly amazing to observe how a subtle nod of approval can actually have such a powerful impact. (See numerous examples in Chapters 5, 6, 11, 12, and 24, and in the *Journal of Organizational Behavior Management*.)

## Record and Graph

As always, deciding whether to augment generalization depends on the data. Graphing and analyzing response measures allow us to determine whether and to what degree behavior has successfully generalized. If you are investigating generalization of easily-measured response classes such as written solutions to arithmetic problems solved on worksheets in class, and want to see how readily they transfer to solutions of homework problems, you can just collect, record, and plot both sets of data on a graph. Should very intensive measurement of generalization prove impractical, consider the pros and cons of assessing performance samples intermittently. For example, to assess the transfer of social skills taught outside of class to the natural social setting, you might count the number of times your adolescent participants socially initiate approaches toward classmates during a randomly selected period each week. The point is that you must obtain objective documentation that new behavioral skills have spontaneously generalized. If those data show that the desired behavior has been established not only locally, but has transferred and persists over time, you have reached your goal. Otherwise, as is often the case, you must implement additional generalization training.

## SUMMARY AND CONCLUSION

The ability to generalize is natural among higher-level organisms. Birds do it, bees do it, even three-toed sloths and chimps do it. We humans do it, too, and what a good thing that is! If you give the matter much thought, you will realize that your mastery of ways to teach and hasten adaptive forms of generalization is absolutely crucial. If we had to learn or teach every single skill separately, time would run out quickly. Nonetheless, natural generalization cannot be guaranteed, and its failure to occur when needed can pose various problems. For this reason, we agree with Haring (1988), who has suggested that *behavior analysts must include generalization criteria in the standards for judging achievement of objectives.*

Because success in a particular case depends upon newly acquired behavioral patterns extending to the natural environment, we should periodically probe for the intended spread of effect to determine whether further generalization training is necessary. Often our clients' need for learning and sustaining adaptive and/or constructive skills across situations is intense, while time is limited. So, the more proficient you become in promoting generalization, the more effective you will be in your role as an applied behavior analyst.

As you review this material, notice a general pattern in the placement of each strategy. That is intentional. We began by introducing you to those best included from the very beginning: setting goals and objectives likely to encourage generalization; identifying and incorporating naturally supportive conditions within the change program; asking for generalization, including requesting the behavior in the new setting, behaviors, responses and across time; programming common stimuli across conditions; using mediation strategies like correspondence training and applying problem solving techniques, as you continuing training. Then while the change program is ongoing, if any interfering behavior were noted to persist, you would assess its function and use that information to support acceptable functionally equivalent behavior. Meanwhile, you might decide to continue promoting fluency, providing sufficient exemplars, training loosely by using indiscriminable contingencies, and if appropriate, teaching behavior in different situations sequentially. After the desired behavior is reasonably well established, you then could begin delaying reinforcers and delivering them intermittently.

Assuming contingency managers and participants learn how to promote and maintain generalization, your family or colleagues can play an especially supportive part in promoting it. They can augment their positive influence by using self-instruction techniques like self-recording, self-management, and techniques for soliciting reinforcers not only with their clientele, but also by applying those to their own behavior. You can heighten positive outcomes even further by delivering positive feedback for such generalization efforts to peers, supervisors, subordinates, and even to yourself.

# Chapter 22

# Maintaining Behavior: Ratio and Related Schedules of Reinforcement

## Goals

1. Define, recognize, and give original illustrations for each of the following terms:
    a. ratio schedule
    b. fixed-ratio (FR) schedule
    c. variable-ratio (VR) schedule
    d. breaking point
    e. ratio strain
    f. progressive or adjusting schedule
    g. matching law
    h. differential reinforcement of rate schedule
    i. differential reinforcement of high rates (DRH)
    j. pacing schedules and differential reinforcement of paced responding (DRP)
    k. differential reinforcement of lower rates (DRL)
    l. differential reinforcement of diminishing rates (DRD)
    m. lag schedule
2. Develop a variable-ratio 5 schedule.
3. Describe why schedules of reinforcement used in the laboratory often do not produce the same results when applied in the "real world."
4. List and describe the typical characteristics of fixed- and variable-ratio schedule performance, explaining why each characteristic is specific to either fixed- or variable-ratio schedules.
5. Discuss the advantages of ratio schedules.

6. Describe how to use ratio scheduling effectively.
7. Describe several convenient techniques for delivering ratio reinforcement.
8. Discuss the disadvantages of ratio schedules and what might be done to minimize such disadvantages.
9. Describe and illustrate how to promote high rates of responding with ratio schedules.
10. Describe and illustrate how to maintain a selected target behavior at a high, steady rate.
11. Distinguish between *Differential Reinforcement of Paced Responding, Differential Rein-forcement of Low Rates, Differential Reinforcement of Diminishing Rates*, and *Lag Schedules*. Give an example of each and defend your choice of that particular schedule.

******

Every once in a while, Henrietta wins a blue ribbon for her painting.

Harry is up at bat. On the third pitch he connects with the ball for a base hit.

Whenever Helga has written the alphabet to her teacher's satisfaction three times, she receives a gold star.

Hugo's boss gives him a bonus about every fifth time Hugo negotiates a contract with a new customer.

Harley won a fistful of poker chips at roulette twice out of 73 attempts.

Try to recall your (reinforcing) delight when you finally completed enough strokes to propel yourself across the pool, or earned a point toward winning or actually did win a game.

Notice in all these examples that the individual performed an action (response) repeatedly, but reinforcement followed only a portion of those responses. Such *intermittent reinforcement* has the potential for maintaining the behavior over long time periods. That being the case, intermittent reinforcement can be a godsend or a curse, depending on the value of the response to those involved. Parents, teachers, and behavior managers of all stripes stand to profit by learning about how to use and avoid particular schedules of reinforcement. Just to whet your appetite, did you know that at some point you will promote greater durability of behavior change by reinforcing *less* frequently, but according to some specific pattern? On the other hand, you actually may inadvertently cause an unwanted behavior to persist by applying certain reinforcement schedules.

What is the best way to promote skill-mastery? As you learned in Chapter 20, one part of the equation for success— on the antecedent side—is to fade prompts or other forms of assistance. On the consequence side, we may gradually *thin the density* of reinforcers per response; that is, we may present reinforcers contingent on larger and larger numbers of responses, or *ratios* of responses to reinforcers. Or we may thin out the availability of reinforcers over time—presenting reinforcers contingent on a response only after longer and longer *intervals* of time since the last response was reinforced. For time-based delivery of reinforcement, the time between the delivery can be extended. Whether we thin with larger ratios or longer intervals, this kind of scheduling allows us to maintain behavior with fewer reinforcers. Furthermore, and probably more important, it creates behavior that is resistant to change because it builds a history in which many unreinforced responses have preceded one that is reinforced. In this chapter we will concentrate on *ratio schedules* and some of their relatives; in the next chapter we will concentrate on interval schedules and some of their relations.

In the material to follow, we cover schedules of reinforcement in some detail, describing how you can use these to generate particular performance patterns, such as the rate and consistency with which a behavior is emitted over time.[1] We also discuss the extent to which different schedules provide opportunities for competing behaviors to occur, both while the schedule is in effect and after reinforcers have been discontinued.

Along with those you encounter in your own daily life, many examples in this text involve attempts to increase the pace and/or pattern of specific performances. Educators hope to augment accurate academic or socially effective behavior. Other change agents aim to promote service excellence, production quality, compliance with medical regimens, specific job routines (e.g., adhering to organizational policies and regulations), self-management practices, alternatives to unwanted behaviors, and so forth. Sometimes we look mainly at the probability or likelihood of the behavior in tasks that are accomplished in well-defined trials or units. But often we are concerned with actual rates of responding in situations where the behavior can readily be repeated. Such conditions arise in many work tasks, such as sorting and quality control in industry. Fortunately, the results of considerable laboratory and applied research have informed us about methods for promoting and supporting high response rates. Ratio schedules are prime examples. We will examine the advantages and disadvantages of these schedules.

But there is another crucial reason to become familiar with the influences of schedules of reinforcement. Sometimes they are the culprit when you are concerned about addressing high frequencies of unwanted behavior, such as self-injurious or aggressive responding (see, for example, Hanley, Iwata, & Thompson, 2001.) When the reinforcers that maintain such behavior occur only occasionally, it can be easy to miss them. For example, Sis may assume she has efficiently ignored her brother's taunts. But if he gets through to her and her reaction reinforces the taunting, only once in every twenty or thirty tries on average, that may be sufficient to maintain his unpleasant taunting. Sometimes very few taunts produce her reaction; at other times she may be able to keep cool throughout very many instances. We would say that the brother's taunting was being reinforced on a *variable-ratio* or VR schedule.

## RATIO SCHEDULES DEFINED AND ILLUSTRATED

You remember Fern, the young woman with moderate developmental delay, who is employed in a sheltered workshop. The workshop contracts with various organizations to wrap gift items and place them in "goodie-bags." Sometimes orders differ in type and number of objects to be wrapped and packed. Fern has learned to locate the items she needs to wrap and include in each bag for that particular day by referring to a poster displaying the particular contents for the current contract. Fern earns her income according to a ratio schedule. What does the term "ratio schedule" mean?

We use the term **ratio schedule** to describe *an arrangement that delivers reinforcers contingent upon some number of responses*. Sometimes, as in a **fixed-ratio (FR) schedule**, *the response requirement remains constant*. Piecework in industry is a classic illustration of the FR schedule. Now, suppose Fern is packing goodie-bag orders containing six items. If reinforcers in the form of points toward her paycheck were delivered after Fern correctly packed each goodie-bag, she would be working on a fixed ratio six (FR 6) schedule. At school, awarding points toward a student's grade as soon as she completes three pages of a workbook illustrates a fixed-ratio of three, abbreviated *FR 3*.

The **variable-ratio (VR)** schedule is commonly used in applied settings. Under the VR schedule, *reinforcers are also contingent on a number of responses, but the particular number on any specific occasion varies. Usually VR schedules are identified by the average, i.e., a VR 20 schedule will on the average reinforce one out of every 20 responses*. In the pigeon laboratory, under a VR schedule, reinforcers (usually mixed grain) are arranged for the last of some number of pecks on a disk on the chamber wall (called a pigeon key). To create a VR 20 in contemporary laboratories, a

---
[1] For a thorough coverage of schedules of reinforcement, see Ferster & Skinner's full 1957 book on the subject and Catania's (2013) more recent coverage, as well as the extensive research literature on schedules of reinforcement that appears in the *Journal of the Experimental Analysis of Behavior* and other behavior analytic journals.

computer routine would randomly produce a reinforcer schedule that averages to 20 (e.g., 1, 39, 10, 30, 15, 25, 5, 35) and the reinforcer would be delivered according to the schedule. For example, after 1 response, then 39 responses, then 10 responses and so on (this kind of VR is sometimes called a *random ratio*, or RR). In the earlier days of this kind of research, such schedules were often arranged with predetermined sequences. For example, the sequence *4, 8, 12, 16, 20, 24, 28, 32, 36* averages to twenty. By making a list with these numbers in a mixed order (32, 4, 12, etc.), you could use these numbers to decide which of the pigeon's key pecks to reinforce. Pigeons usually peck rapidly given schedules like these, and the faster they peck the more quickly they produce the next reinforcer. Suppose you are working in the South Pacific to collect pearls from oysters. Sometimes you may open several oysters before you find an adequate pearl, but then you may find a pearl in two oysters in a row. If you find pearls in 10 percent of the oysters you open, on average, you would be working on a VR 10. Just about any task that involves searching for things where you will not be successful every time involves variable-ratio (VR) contingencies. It also has been shown that people appear to prefer the variable schedule over the fixed schedule, despite even larger ratio requirements (Mullane, Martens, Baxter, & Ver Steeg, 2017).

A variation of the ratio schedule has become a very useful research tool. In a **progressive** (or, as it is sometimes called, an *adjusting*) **ratio (PR) schedule** *the size of the response requirement increases in some systematic way, as in augmenting the requisite number of responses (on average) for reinforcers to be delivered*. At first the ratio requirement is 10, but after five reinforcers it increases to 20, and after another five to 30, and so on. Ratio requirements increase in value in a series of steps from one ratio to the next "…until the ratio becomes so high that the subject stops responding (the so-called breaking point)" (Schlinger, Derenne, & Baron, 2008, p. 44). An example might be the increasing number of push-ups an aerobics instructor requires of her students from one session to the next. Eventually, individual students will reach a point at which they can do no more. The breaking point has been reached and any further encouragement to perform more push-ups at that time will come to naught. Progressive ratio schedules have really impacted the way in which reinforcer assessments are now conducted. Davis et al. (2017) successfully used a progressive ratio schedule to help determine the reinforcing value of social interactions.

It should be noted that all ratio schedules have a breaking point. This ratio **breaking point** is defined as *when the individual stops responding*. When using a progressive ratio schedule, the therapist usually is trying to figure out where this point might be. A team of investigators (Russell, Ingvarsson, Haggar, & Jessel, 2017) implemented progressive ratio schedules to evaluate the relative strength of tokens as generalized conditioned reinforcers, versus specific reinforcers such as leisure items and edibles. Their results found that under the token condition, breaking points were higher than among the other conditions, which "suggest that the tokens functioned as generalized conditioned reinforcers" (p. 40). However, with planned FR and VR schedules, this point is talked about as **ratio strain** *(meaning the ratio has gotten too large and the individuals will no longer respond).*

# CHARACTERISTICS OF RATIO-SCHEDULE PERFORMANCE

Despite their species, under well-controlled laboratory conditions, given ratio contingencies, organisms tend[2] to produce fairly common response patterns (Ferster & Skinner, 1957). (Yes, humans often do volunteer to serve as subjects in studies conducted in laboratories,[3] where conditions

---

[2] In their studies of schedule arrangements consisting of sequences of variable ratio, then fixed interval reinforcement schedules, Baron and Leinenweber (1995) did find some distinct performance-pattern differences between humans and other species. According to Mace (1996) though, "The functional relationship between reinforcement and resistance to change has held across various reinforcement parameters including different types of multiple schedules of reinforcement…" (p. 560) including fixed- and variable-ratio schedules.

[3] In the United States and in a number of other nations, regardless of where they are set, investigators conducting experiments involving human subjects are required by law to inform participants in advance of the risks and benefits of the study, and to obtain their written consent, as well as to obtain

can be arranged more precisely than in natural settings.) The findings: Among very young children or in environments where verbal behavior is of lesser importance, human performances under both simple (Hutchinson & Azrin, 1961) and complex ratio reinforcement schedules tend to vary in fairly predictable ways (Bijou & Orlando, 1961; Bucklin & Dickinson, 2001; Davidson & Osborne, 1974; De Luca & Holborn, 1992; Field, Tonneau, Ahearn, & Hineline, 1996; Long, 1962, 1963; Mace, 1996; Schlinger, et al., 2008). Schedule performances characteristic of infants and nonhuman animals who cannot report what the current contingencies are, or when their verbal capacities are limited, do resemble those of other organisms. But as soon as humans begin to talk about their tasks, the talk can interact with their responding so that it deviates from the sorts of patterns we expect from nonhuman (and nonverbal) organisms such as rats, pigeons, and dogs. If someone merely gets to the point of saying something like "Pressing this button makes things happen, but it doesn't seem to work every time," that may be enough to change response patterns. It is important to understand the effects of schedule contingencies not only so we can identify their effects but also so we will be able to detect cases where those schedules do not produce the anticipated effect. Soon, we examine these schedule arrangements and their associated response configurations in more detail to guide planning of your own reinforcer delivery schedules.

In addition to the caution about the verbal repertoires of participants, also be aware that ratio response patterns are not as precisely predictable in natural settings. One reason is that in ordinary environments many reinforcement schedules may be operating simultaneously on many of the different classes of behavior in an individual's repertoire. The response classes maintained by these **concurrent schedules** *(meaning two or more schedules that are simultaneously available at a given time)* may interact with one another, causing responding to change in various ways (Bernstein & Sturmey, 2008).

Think about trying to conduct two or more tasks simultaneously, like studying while snacking and also texting. It should be intuitively obvious that study time will be reduced by the snacking and the texting, but those too will be reduced by the studying.[4]

## Ratio Schedules Usually Produce Fast Responding

Although exceptions have been noted (Yukl & Latham, 1975; Yukl, Latham, & Pursell, 1976), *ratio schedules generally produce high rates*. This makes intuitive sense because, as with piecework, the more rapidly participants respond, the sooner they gain their reinforcers within a given time period. Note that with the fixed-ratio schedule, a pause sometimes follows the completion of a ratio (a pause after reinforcement), after which rapid responding begins again. This pattern of FR responding is called *break and run*. The break should not be surprising with FR, because the first responses after the reinforcer will never be reinforced (unless it is on an FR1 schedule); only the last response at the end of the ratio will produce the reinforcer. This is not the case with VR, where another response can be reinforced very few responses after the last reinforcer. For this reason, pauses after reinforcement during VR are typically very brief if they occur at all.

Here are some additional examples from reports of ratio-schedule research involving human participants:

- With the amount of reinforcers held constant, part-time examination graders worked faster under VR 2 than CRF (continuous reinforcement) schedules (Yukl, Wexley, & Seymour, 1972).
- Despite earning equivalent amounts, experienced trappers working for a lumber company worked more rapidly when they earned on a VR 4 schedule than on a CRF schedule (Latham & Dossett, 1978).

---

the approval of a peer review committee. Animal laboratories in many modern nations also operate under policies ensuring humane treatment of their subjects.

[4]Multi-tasking like this probably also is distracting, thereby interfering with the precision with which each of the tasks is carried out. That may help explain why not only texting, but also even talking over a non-hand-held phone while driving tremendously increases one's odds of becoming involved in an accident.

- Workshop participants increased their rates of participating in job tasks under a FR (fixed-ratio) schedule with various food items (Saunders, McEntee, & Saunders, 2005; Saunders, Saunders, & Marquis, 1998; Saunders & Saunders, 2000).

Several factors affect rates of responding during ratio reinforcement and after those schedules are no longer in effect (i.e., extinction). Among those are the *size of the ratio requirement* (e.g., Everett, Studer, & Douglas, 1978), *reinforcer history*, including the age of the participant and how recently other schedules have been in effect (Chappell & Leibowitz, 1982; Lamal, 1978; Mace, Neef, Shade, & Mauro, 1994; Lattal & Neef, 1996; Weiner, 1981a, 1981b), *self-generated rules* (Horne & Lowe, 1993), and the *gradualness with which the reinforcement schedule is phased out*. In addition, as pointed out in Chapter 4, the criterion level that you set in your objective can influence fluency and maintenance of the behavior. To illustrate, investigators (Fuller & Fienup, 2018) compared the mastery levels of 50 percent vs. 80 percent vs. 90 percent, and found that setting the higher matter levels tended to promote not only more enduring responding but also greater fluency (known to facilitate maintenance).

How *fluently* the response pattern is being emitted is important too (Johnson & Layng, 1992; Lindsley, 1991; Twyman et al., 2005; Young et al., 1986). (The high, steady pace of the kinds displayed in Figure 22.1 can be described as *fluent* because responding remains regular or uninterrupted for long time periods. Eventually, of course, should the response never again be reinforced, as in extinction, responding eventually will become more and more irregular until generally it levels off at a very low rate, or no longer occurs.)

A number of investigators have studied the effects of the *size of the ratio requirement* upon patterns of responding (of course these vary as a function of whether a fixed or variable schedule of reinforcement is in effect). Hutchinson and Azrin (1961) and Weiner (1980) demonstrated that human responding is comparable to that of other species operating under ratio schedules (Boren, 1956; Skinner, 1938) in that the larger the response requirement, the more rapid the response rate (Everett et al., 1978). When ratio requirements become too large, however, response rates decrease. (How do you know it's too large? When responding falls off.) This increase in rate of responding within that limited range of increasing ratio size has been displayed in applied behavior analytic findings, such as those of Stephens, Pear, Wray, and Jackson (1975), who

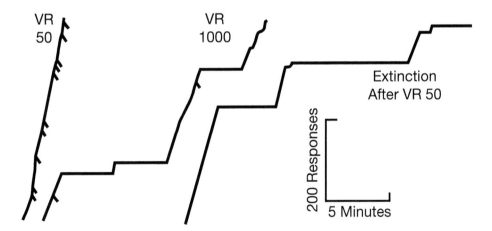

**Figure 22.1** Pigeon's responding during variable-ratio reinforcement

When, on average, one in fifty responses are reinforced, the pigeon's rate of pecking is extremely rapid. That high rate continues but is interspersed with long periods of pauses when only one reinforcer is obtained on average, per 1000 pecks. Notice that under extinction, after the pigeon no longer receives any grain at all, the very high rates continue but pauses between them become longer and longer. Eventually key-pecking will essentially come to a halt. From Catania (2007), p. 169 (with permission of the author).

compared various schedules of contingent candy delivery to determine the effects of ratio size on the rate at which developmentally-delayed children learned picture names. Both continuous and very low probability candy delivery (FR 25, or 4 percent) generated low response rates, while the children responded much faster when intermediate schedules were in effect. Probably in the former situation they rapidly became sated with the candy, while the response requirement under the very low probability condition produced *ratio strain*.

Fern will earn the same number of tokens for each goodie bag she packs: one token for each two (pair of) bags she packs. The rate with which she actually receives those tokens can vary: For instance, she might be given one token right after filling every other bag. That would be a simple FR2 schedule. Alternatively, she might be given five tokens after filling ten bags. Based on laboratory findings *she can be expected to pack more bags in proportionally less time under the latter condition than under the simple FR2 delivery schedule.* (This stands to reason, because with the FR2 schedule she may take time repeatedly to handle or exchange her tokens.)

At some point, *as the ratio requirement grows, the individual starts pausing, so that responding fluctuates between that at the usual high rate and periods of inactivity.* As mentioned, this effect of high ratios is called **ratio strain**. If ratio size continues to increase, or even simply remains at this high level, responding may drop out completely. Once reinforcers are produced infrequently, responding may reach the point where too few occur to complete the next ratio and produce the next reinforcer. Once responses are no longer producing reinforcers, this situation is functionally equivalent to extinction. Predicting exactly when this breakdown will occur usually is not possible. So, despite the benefits of high ratio requirements, we need to collect and analyze data on ongoing ratio performance for signs of ratio strain, especially because task requirements and individual learning histories vary. The avoidance and aggression we know to frequently accompany extinction often are associated with abrupt escalations in ratio requirements (Hutchinson, Azrin, & Hunt, 1968). Ultimately, responding can disappear altogether if we do not intervene with appropriate changes in contingencies.

## Consistency of Performance

As mentioned, especially under large FR requirements, usually nonhuman animals and sometimes humans pause immediately following reinforcer delivery. Perhaps because verbal behavior often mediates human schedule performances, human participants are somewhat less apt to pause under fixed-ratio schedules. An individual assigned to write a fixed number of pages before receiving bonus points may or may not stop working for a while after receiving the points. Pausing is more likely following reinforcers that follow completing a very large requirement than those that follow a shorter requirement. Pausing may also be affected by the magnitude of the reinforcer, the effort entailed in the responding, or the demand of the response requirement (Schlinger et al., 2008). During the pause, the individual may engage in sometimes unwanted other behavior, such as doodling, making cell-phone calls, texting, reading email messages, leaving the room, daydreaming, distracting others from their work, and so on. (Recall or observe your own study patterns as they relate to your quiz/examination schedules. Perhaps that will even more clearly illustrate this point.)

Although performance under variable-ratio (VR) schedules also may show ratio strain as the ratios grow large, they rarely are characterized by post-reinforcement pauses. Consider an illustrative VR reinforcement schedule: Fern is receiving reinforcers on a VR 5 schedule, which means she receives a voucher exchangeable for a portion of her pay on an *average* of every five bags packed. She has no way of anticipating when the next reinforcer will be delivered, whether after two or after eight bags are packed. After each reinforcer, as displayed in Figure 22.2 (vertical marks), she quickly resumes work with hardly a break. Such higher, steadier response rates under VR, as opposed to the post-reinforcement pauses we see sometimes with FR, are what Miltenberger and Fuqua (1983) found with work on a folder-assembly task by a male with delayed development.

The situation is analogous to one in which a teacher collects written assignments at random, as in spot checking on average every fifth page each stu-

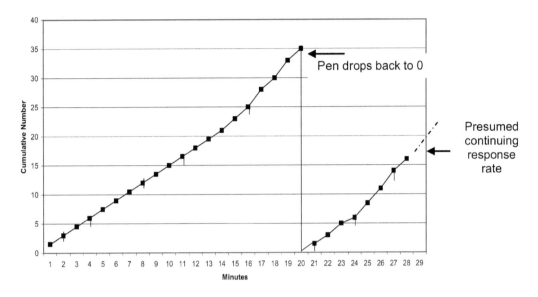

**Figure 22.2** Cumulative record of goodie bags packed

dent has completed. Some students could conceivably complete ten pages before the teacher checked and praised their performances. Others might have two pages checked in a row. So to avoid post-reinforcement pausing characteristic of FR schedules, give preference to VR schedules as Van Houten and Nau did in 1980. Those investigators provided evidence favoring variable- over fixed-ratio schedules: In an adjustment class for children with impaired hearing, they programmed a buzzer to sound every five minutes. If the five students were attentive and not disrupting when the teacher heard the buzzer,[5] the students earned checks exchangeable for an opportunity to win a prize. Checks were displayed on a chart. During the FR condition, whenever students earned eight checks, they could reach into a grab-bag for a possible reward. In the VR condition, each time the buzzer sounded, if they earned a check, they could draw a block from a bag containing seven brown blocks and one blue block (a VR 8 schedule) (this is also an example of a compound schedule because there is the time schedule and then the VR 8). Were they lucky enough to draw the blue block,

they would win a prize. Although solving problems correctly was not reinforced *per se*, attentiveness increased and disruptiveness decreased during both reinforcement conditions, with the very best performance level taking place under the VR condition.

## Continued Responding During Extinction

Ratio schedule histories, like those we will later discuss for interval schedules, produce sustained responding in extinction conditions (e.g., Beaman, Stoffer, Woods, & Stoffer, 1983). During extinction, after a ratio schedule has ended, responding often is characterized by bursts of responding at the same high rates emitted while the schedule was in effect followed by long pauses (Reynolds, 1968). This resembles the *break and run* pattern we described for FR responding, but no reinforcers are delivered during extinction, so the alternation between breaks and runs is typically highly variable, with the breaks or periods of non-responding becoming longer and the bursts or runs of high-rate responding becoming shorter. The following example illustrates this point:

---

[5]Today a preferable choice might be a pocket timer with a vibrating signal to avoid distracting others.

Cindy's mother usually refused her daughter's initial requests for money, assuming that if Cindy *really* needed it she would ask again. Over time, Cindy learned that it took three requests for her mom to give in and hand over the money (an FR 3 schedule). On Cindy's thirteenth birthday, her mother decided her daughter should earn her own spending money. The next time Cindy came with a request for funds, her mother told her to find a baby-sitting job. Cindy continued to plead; but to no avail. She went away for a while and then returned. (It had always worked before.) The pleading resumed. But her mother was steadfast, and the requests for money eventually stopped. (Had her mother relented, Cindy's requests for money probably would have returned to their former level almost immediately.)

The length of a person's earlier history of continuous reinforcement may make a difference. Some evidence suggests that the *longer* a person has been exposed to continuous reinforcement prior to partial reinforcement, the less resistant his responding is to extinction (Nation & Boyajian, 1980). Again, assuming your purpose is to see behavior continue, as suggested in Chapter 11, *shift from continuous to intermittent reinforcement before gradually reducing reinforcer delivery entirely.* Here we illustrate with a few fanciful examples:

- Professor Fogg sporadically gave a few pop quizzes during the first half of the semester; then stopped giving them altogether. Nonetheless, his students faithfully completed their assignments, "just in case."
- Of approximately 20 entries, Uncle Herman won a trip to Florida in one contest, a $5 gift certificate in another, and a case of dog food in a third. Although Uncle Herman has not won a thing for years after his streak of luck, he still spends all his spare time entering contests.
- After Jocelyn had taken her medication regularly for several weeks, her lab results began to improve and her doctor occasionally complimented her. Despite no longer receiving compliments later in the year, Jocelyn continued to take her medication regularly.

And here is a published example: Despite thorough medical examinations and a variety of physical treatments, Ten-year-old Josh continued either to retain his feces or soil himself (Bornstein et al., 1983). A simple daily point card, backed up by money for non-soiling and proper elimination, rapidly "cured" the problem. Beginning in the eleventh week, the schedule was thinned out gradually so that by the seventeenth week the point card was no longer used. Praise from the therapist continued, but also was thinned gradually until the twenty-eighth week, when contact with the therapist was terminated altogether. A year later the problem had not reappeared.

When extinction conditions are rigorously maintained following a reinforcement intervention, generally behavior eventually will return to its pre-intervention level, no matter the schedule history. In other words, when previously arranged reinforcers are discontinued and natural reinforcers fail to take over, behavior will extinguish, regardless of the schedule that had been operating. Some ratio-schedule histories (e.g., VR) simply delay the return to baseline performance. *Thus, if your goal is lasting behavior change, be sure the natural environment will take over and support the behavior before you terminate your reinforcement of that behavior.* This point is emphasized in Chapter 24 with examples of what you might do to help assure a supportive environment.

## ADVANTAGES OF RATIO SCHEDULES

Beyond its practical features, the main advantage of intermittent reinforcement is its ability to support maintained responding. Given that they are based on frequency of responses, ratio schedules offer a few specific advantages. The first and most obvious is that they tend to *generate high response rates*—a point that probably needs no repeating at this time. Second, given an initial phase of ratio reinforcement, the *high rates generated initially may continue even when the schedule is shifted to one that is interval-based* (see Chapter 23).

A third advantage of ratio schedules is that they are *particularly easy to use when the target response produces a permanent product.* On completion, products can simply be counted and reinforcers presented as scheduled: after so many goodie-bags packed, problems solved, answers to questions written, buttons buttoned, tables cleaned, beds made, pages typed, complimentary notes sent, and so on. (Recall that determining the reliability of measurement also is simplified through the use of permanent-product data.)

Fourth, ratio schedules may be *used to facilitate the transition from artificial to natural reinforcing contingencies*. This is accomplished through scheduling two sets of consequences for the target response: The weaker, but more natural, consequences are gradually provided more often; the more powerful artificial consequences, less often. As long as a stronger artificial reinforcer is continually correlated with the more natural weaker one, the latter should begin to acquire its own reinforcing properties.

Lucretia's mom sees her daughter meet her playmate's request to share a toy. Mom smiles, nods "Um-hum," and gives her daughter a hug, a powerful reinforcer for Lucretia. As the rate of sharing increases, her mother continues to smile and hug, but the ratio of hugs begins to diminish to about every other sharing response, then to about every third one, and so on. The contingent smiling and nodding seem to maintain the response successfully, and hugs have been reduced to a ratio that Lucretia's mother can easily manage. (Much later, when the rate of sharing is sufficiently high and stable, even smiling and nodding occasionally may be sufficient to continue to support Lucretia's sharing.)

Responding exclusively to just one among a complex set of stimuli, regardless of variations in stimuli and contingencies in effect, is called *stimulus overselectivity* (as was described in Chapter 17). Overselectivity, which characterizes many of those on the autistic spectrum, impedes discrimination learning. To illustrate, when the teacher presents Joey with an array of five flash cards and asks him to choose the one that says "Joey," he always picks the card containing a word beginning with J (e.g., John, Jack, Jenny, etc.). This tendency toward responding overselectively has been found to be more effectively modified when training has included a variable-ratio reinforcement phase rather than with continuous reinforcement throughout (Schreibman, Koegel, & Craig, 1977).

# USING RATIO SCHEDULES EFFECTIVELY

## Select Schedules to Sustain Desired Rates

In our earlier discussion of ratio schedules, we attempted to identify several response characteristics that directly bear upon programming for maintained responding. You have seen how ratio schedules promote high response rates (e.g. Bucklin & Dickinson, 2001). If consistency of responding is an issue, however, the ratio schedule should have a variable base. Individuals may display variations in their rates of responding under ratio schedules though, perhaps as a function of instructions (Catania, Matthews, & Shimoff, 1982), models, and history (Chappell & Leibowitz, 1982; Weiner, 1981a, 1981b, 1982).

**Individualizing schedules.** If you plan to use ratio reinforcement schedules to promote high success rates, you probably will need to adjust the specific schedule, or the density of the reinforcers, to the person's current response patterns. Depending on the task at hand, some people require dense external or extrinsic reinforcement; others, hardly any at all. This point was illustrated in a study by Platt, Harris, and Clements (1980), who, to determine the ideal level of reinforcers for each of their behaviorally-disordered students, developed a method of gradually thinning the reinforcement ratio while monitoring performance accuracy of math assignments completed. When a student's score began to fall below 90 percent, the experimenters judged the density of reinforcers had fallen just below its optimal level and adjusted the schedule accordingly. They used those results to provide students with sufficient but not excessive quantities of reinforcers; just the right amount to sustain their high-quality performance. (See also De Luca & Holborn, 1992, who chose specific schedule requirements for boys' bicycle pedaling on the basis of their earlier performance rates.)

Some evidence (Mace, McCurdy & Quigley, 1990) predicts that the *matching law* can apply to patterns of responding under ratio schedules. According to the **matching law**, *organisms distribute their* *behavior between two or more concurrent schedules of reinforcement* (Herrnstein, 1961). That is, if a shouting out an answer is reinforced with attention in the form of reprimands about 60 percent of the time and hand raising is reinforced (by being called on) about 40 percent of the time, the student would probably shout out answers more often (about 60 percent of the time) than raising his hand. Similarly, while playing basketball, should you make a 2-point more often than a 3-point basket, probably you will opt to shoot more 2-point than 3-point shots. That did seem to be the case in the Mace, et al. (1990) study. Two students receiving special education were provided with academic response alternatives. They could uniformly elect the response with the densest payoff or they could "match" by distributing their responses across the two according to each one's payoff rate. Rather than maximizing the payoff by uniformly choosing the denser schedule of reinforcement, one of the participants did at times change over to the response with the lower yield. The authors cite these results as reaffirming Balsam and Bondy's (1983) conclusion that rewards sometimes can have negative side effects.

## Thin Gradually

With a ratio schedule, thin the reinforcer density gradually.[6] You might select a given criterion for each thinning step, such as a minimum of 80 percent over 20 trials, before moving to the next less dense schedule. See Deckner, Deckner, and Blanton (1982) for an example of this approach used with young psychotic children. You can try the checklists they used, in which a starred blank designated that a reinforcer was to be delivered. You would just diminish the number of starred blanks each week. Similarly, you could modify the number of items signaling a reinforcer in a container or adjust the proportion of large to small dots on slips of paper, with one size dot indicating the reinforcer was earned according to the schedule you want to use. To shift from a 1:5 ratio (VR 5) to a 1:8 (VR 8), add three more items identical to the original set of four and one distinctive item that indicates a reinforcer is to be dispensed.

Adjusting the ratio requirement gradually is best because the same sort of disruption in responding (ratio strain) that tends to accompany extinction also occurs when a schedule increases too abruptly to a much higher ratio requirement. Along the way, supplement the schedule with other, perhaps less powerful reinforcers, such as praise or other social events. Then continue increasing the ratio requirement until it reaches its limit and the rate no longer increases (technically, its *break point*). Determining whether a "true" limit has been reached may be difficult, however, for ratio strain may be operating. A temporary reduction in the ratio requirement, perhaps followed by an even more gradual increase in the requirement, may inform you as to whether the absolute limit has been reached.

To increase (or decrease) response rates, you also can use an **adjusting or progressive schedule**—described previously as *one that increases or decreases gradually as a function of the client's performance*. Kirby and Shields (1972) did this by immediately praising a student and providing him with feedback on correctness following a gradually increasing number of assigned arithmetic problems. Haug and Sorensen (2006) have suggested using a progressive ratio (PR) schedule to reduce HIV risk behaviors, as evidenced by drug-free urine specimens, and to improve clients' adherence to their medication regimen. You also can use progressive schedules as a way to thwart clients' satiating on a given reinforcer or as a strategy for encouraging them to shift over to working for less-preferred reinforcers—especially when the schedule dictates that most-preferred reinforcers are also the most difficult to obtain (i.e., require the highest number of responses; Francisco, Borrero, & Sy, 2008).

Suppose Dexter has made very satisfactory progress with his studying by using a point system to manage his own contingencies. He has designed a reinforcer menu for himself, with a number of preferred activities costing specific numbers of points. He can go to the science museum for 50 points, read a chapter in his science-fiction book for 25 points, go online for ten minutes for 10 points, and visit a pal in another community for 500 points. During the first week the system is in operation he assigns him-

---

[6]To avoid confusion, we prefer the term *thin* rather than *fade*, as *fade* is the word conventionally used to describe the method for diminishing prompts to promote stimulus control.

self one point for each paragraph that he reads and is able to summarize to himself in a sentence. The next week he increases the requirement to two paragraphs per point; the next, to a page. Eventually he requires two pages, then five, then a chapter for a single point.

Over time, though, Dexter notes that his studying has begun to fall off sharply. He is finding all sorts of excuses for not working. One day he has a headache. He accidentally leaves his books at school a couple of times. His friends keep calling or emailing him, and he just cannot seem to end the conversations. Is it possible that the ratio requirement has something to do with the disruption? What he should try to do is to drop back a few steps, perhaps to the requirement of two pages per point, and to re-establish his previous high rate. Then he might proceed more cautiously—from two pages to three, four, six, and so on. If the more gradual progression does not induce a breakdown in rate, fine. But, if disruption occurs again, perhaps he should just drop back a little bit and stay there.

One way to avoid ratio strain is to increase the ratio requirement very gradually. Kirby and Shields (1972) programmed an *adjusting FR schedule* for a student who seldom completed his math assignments. (In an adjusting schedule, the response time or ratio requirement is altered gradually.) Starting with praising and marks of "correct" for each two problems accurately completed, the investigators gradually increased the FR schedule to four, then to eight, and so on until 20 problems had to be completed correctly before the student received praise.

Achievement remained high throughout. Eventually, however, a point may be reached at which the high, steady rate begins to disintegrate, as in a picture-naming study by Stephens et al. (1975). When this occurs, you can reduce the ratio requirement to the level at which rapid responding resumes, and then increase even more gradually.

In a related situation, the goal of a study (McLaughlin, 1981) was to improve the handwriting legibility of a group of special-education students. An adjusting fixed-ratio schedule was used as follows: To receive points exchangeable for privileges in an ongoing token economy, the students needed to write one additional legible letter (the adjusting aspect of the schedule requirement) on each successive trial. Students in the FR adjusting-schedule group improved significantly—from 35 at the pretest to 63.8 at the posttest. A no-token control group only improved from 31.1 at pretest to 41.1 at post-testing.

Let us suppose that the training staff at one of our favorite fictitious organizations, Purple Triangle, is concerned about increasing its employees' assignment-completion rates. The supervisor begins complimenting and writing notes to staff members each time they finish an assignment. This functions to increase their completion rates. Gradually the supervisor writes the notes less often, but continues to compliment as staff members finish each new assignment. As time goes by, reinforcers diminish, but the response rate keeps rising. Eventually, weeks go by without staff receiving any contingent reinforcers. At this point, the rate of completing assignments begins sporadically to decline. So the supervisor occasionally reinstates the reinforcers. The high rate of assignment completion recovers and remains at a reasonably successful level.[7]

We can use ratio schedules to sustain students' compliance with requests, as Neef, Shafer, Egel, Cataldo, and Parrish (1983) did. After first instituting the program successfully themselves, they then also successfully taught teachers how to use those compliance teaching techniques with target students. An especially positive outcome of the study was that the teachers began to use the methods with non-targeted students as well.

Investigators (Hagopian, Kuhn, Long, & Rush, 2005) used a related strategy to thin reinforcers during functional communication training (FCT). (Recall that functional communication training is widely used as treatment for individuals with developmental disabilities who exhibit severe behavior problems.) The investigators compared simple extinction to FCT with extinction plus access to competing stimuli. After conducting a functional analysis, they performed an assessment to identify competing stimuli that would produce reinforcers

---

[7]Organizational goal-setting practices are directly analogous. In coordination with their supervisors, the group jointly specifies a level of performance—often the number of accomplishments—to be achieved by the next meeting. Naturally, reinforcement is delivered whenever the goals are met. (See *Performance Management* media, e.g., Daniels, 1989, for numerous examples.)

that presumably would compete with the reinforcers currently maintaining the problem behavior. They hypothesized that combining FCT with those competing stimuli would result in more stable reductions in problem behavior during schedule thinning, along with a more rapid achievement of the treatment goal. In other words, problem behavior would diminish to a greater extent during the terminal reinforcement schedule for communication than FCT lacking competing stimuli. Results confirmed this hypothesis.

Prior to treating a client's functional communicative response, investigators (Wilson & Gratz, 2016) used a progressive ratio schedule of reinforcement to identify the breaking point. They then used that breaking point as the initial level at which to begin differentially reinforcing the functional communicative response.

## Consider Ongoing Reinforcement Schedules Prior to Implementing Extinction to Reduce Problematic Behavior

If at all possible, examine currently ongoing reinforcement schedules when attempting to reduce an unwanted behavior. For instance, you will want to *avoid* attempting extinction following behavior currently supported by a variable ratio schedule history, because such a history produces more resistance to extinction than a recent history of CRF. Unfortunately, under normal circumstances, variable schedules are more the rule than the exception, as contingency managers sometimes fail to restrain themselves from providing opportunities for escape, attention, or even tangible stimuli contingent on problematic behavior. So, as strange as it might seem, one option you might consider under such circumstances is first to shift over to continuously reinforcing (CRF) the unwanted behavior in advance of or along with the desired alternative, as Lerman, Iwata, Shore, and Kahng (1996) and Worsdell et al., (2000) did. In the latter case, "Results showed that one participant's problem behavior decreased and his alternative behavior increased during FCT when both behaviors were reinforced on FR 1 schedules" (p. 167).

Lalli and Casey (1996) found that when they reinforced compliance on a fixed-ratio (FR) 1 schedule and destructive behavior on a variable-ratio (VR) 5 schedule, the rate of their student's compliance increased and destructive behavior decreased. As they thinned the schedule of reinforcement for compliance, the student's destructive behavior increased while compliance decreased. Yet, when they combined the schedules by permitting escape on a VR 5 schedule and supplying adult attention for compliance on a VR 10 schedule, the youngster's low rates of destructive behavior and high levels of compliance persisted.

In general, though, if the goal of a particular program is to produce a high rate for a desired response, use an adjusting schedule to increase the ratio requirement gradually until the behavior reaches its peak—that is, until the increase stops and the rate levels off and remains steady (i.e., reaches its *asymptote*). If the rate of responding begins to disintegrate, temporarily reduce and then gradually resume adjusting the ratio requirement to solve the problem.

# DISADVANTAGES OF RATIO SCHEDULES

## Ratio Strain and Diminishing Performance Quality

We have already discussed the ratio-strain problem that may be encountered during too abrupt an increase in the ratio requirement, and offered some possible solutions. Additionally, though, at very high rates the topography (or quality) of the response may begin to disintegrate. (Think about what happens when you try to repeat "Peter Piper picked a peck of pickled peppers" really rapidly). Davidson and Osborne (1974) found that children produced a high proportion of errors immediately after reinforcers were delivered in an FR matching-to-sample task. Using a ratio schedule to maintain adequate amounts of practicing scales on the piano, Bruno von Burn awards himself a point for every ten scales that he practices. The points then can be exchanged for minutes during which he allows himself to play current hit tunes. His rate of practicing scales increases, but his technique begins to deteriorate. This sort of problem appeared when McLaughlin and Malaby (1975b) examined the effects of awarding points to fifth- and sixth-grade students for completion, rather than for accuracy, of math assignments. Rates of solving problems increased, but accuracy deteriorated.

If Bruno wanted to be sure that his technique would not disintegrate, he would have to define the response more carefully. Just completing scales would be inadequate. Only scales meeting a predetermined standard of acceptability would count toward the ratio. Consequently, to avoid the deterioration in response topography that might accompany the high rates promoted by ratio schedules, it is a good idea to set standards for acceptable quality beforehand. Then reinforcers would be delivered only contingent on the topographically correct number of responses required to complete the ratio. If errors persist, the ratio requirement can be reduced until the appropriate quality occurs reliably or else an additional rule can be appended to the contingency arrangement: All responses in the series must be topographically correct; or no more than X percent error will be allowed.

The mastery requirement in the *Personalized Systems of Instruction* (PSI) illustrates one way that inaccuracy of responding can be minimized. Students must complete a predetermined number of units to earn a grade; they must pass quizzes at a 90 percent level of correctness or better if the student is to be allowed to proceed. This prevents students from committing too many errors while rushing through the course material.

Ratio schedules require that response frequencies be counted, which sometimes can be inconvenient or impractical. This requirement can present a problem if clients cannot reliably keep track of their own rates of responding or if neither support staff nor instruments are available to accomplish this task. In such circumstances you may consider various alternatives: involving peers or volunteers, using inexpensive instruments like shopping counters, and others (see Chapter 8).

## Interval Schedules Often are Easier to Use

Maintained responding is very improbable in the total absence of reinforcers. So we must be prepared to build intermittent reinforcement into our programs, through either natural or other means. Program managers probably find it easier to implement interval (discussed in the next chapter) than ratio schedules. Clients may prefer interval schedules as well. When rates of payoff are kept essentially equal, humans and other species tend to choose time-dependent (interval) to response-dependent (ratio) schedules (Schaeffer, 1979). College students who could earn about the same number of points under either schedule generally chose the interval schedule. Only when payoff was substantially higher for the ratio schedules did they shift to the latter. (One might conclude that this preference for interval schedules is based on the fact that interval schedules require comparatively less responding than ratio schedules, thereby minimizing effort. Nevertheless, in the latter case, relative response rates were not significantly lower during the time-dependent schedule.)

Nevertheless, as previously mentioned, low response rates are a risk posed by interval schedules. Starting out with a ratio schedule is most practical when high rates are desired and keeping count of a response is not difficult. Once responding is well established, one can switch readily to an interval schedule. Other ways to provide high-rate histories are described next.

# PROMOTING HIGH RATES

## Provide Clear Instructions and Prompt Imitation of High Rates

If response rates under fixed ratio schedules are not as high as you would prefer, there are several things you can do. One is to *provide clear instructions*, such as "The machine is set so that you will earn a penny as soon as you press the button 40 times. The faster you press, the more pennies you will earn" (Weiner, 1981a, pp. 452–453). Another strategy is *to ask the client to imitate the rate of responding of someone else shown earning a reinforcer*. Bruno is having difficult time playing a *presto* movement rapidly enough. The maestro demonstrates the correct tempo, asks Bruno to do the same, and praises when the student's rate matches his own. Or, "Look, Paula.

Notice how rapidly Sal fills out her claims reports. If you work at that pace, soon you will earn your raise." And, you can promote higher rates by differentially reinforcing higher rates (DRH) as described below.

## DIFFERENTIALLY REINFORCING RATES

You can produce different rates of responding by reinforcing those rates directly, especially once you realize that each reinforcer has its effect not only on the most recent response, but also on those preceding it. One reason why reinforcing the last of five responses in FR 5 produces more behavior than reinforcing just a single response in continuous reinforcement (CRF) is that the effect of the reinforcer in FR 5 depends on its relation to all five responses, and not just on its relation to a single response, as in CRF. True, the earlier responses are followed by the reinforcer only after some delay, while the remaining responses are being emitted. Yet, a delayed reinforcer works even when a response occurs all by itself, so why shouldn't it work when the response is one of a sequence, as in FR 5? Said another way, we can think of FR as a way of using a single reinforcer to reinforce a sequence of five responses.

Those circumstances, by the way, account for ratio schedules producing higher rates than interval schedules. Because, in ratio schedules, delays between responses that come before the reinforced response are shorter than they are in interval schedules, those shorter delays strengthen responding more powerfully than longer ones. (Further details are beyond the scope of our story here, but for more information see Catania, 2005b).

When we conceive of an FR 5 as reinforcing a package of five responses, we recognize the importance of attending not only to the fifth response, but also the ones that came before it. For example, if a child makes an error in reading and then immediately corrects it, the teacher's praise may reinforce not just the correct reading but also the error that preceded it. Although the correct reading probably will be strengthened to a greater degree than the error, even so, the error has been somewhat reinforced and we should not be surprised if we see it recur in the future. As an alternative, if the student reads correctly often enough, the teacher should aim to reinforce the last several correct in a row rather than a correct reading immediately following an error.

In any case, if a reinforcer works on the last several responses in a sequence, then we can *differentially reinforce such sequences depending on whether the responses are occurring at a given rate: more slowly, at an intermediate or paced rate, or faster*. Such schedules are called **differential reinforcement of rate schedules**, and they come in various flavors. Each one described below is designed to do what its name says.

### Promoting More Rapid Responding

**Differential reinforcement of high rates (DRH)** is a schedule designed to promote consistently rapid responding. To establish a DRH schedule, we very closely observe sequences of responses and *deliver reinforcers only when several responses occur in rapid succession at or above a pre-established rate.* When pauses occur, we postpone reinforcer delivery. So, DRH involves differentially reinforcing rapid sequences of responses, and lower rates of responding are not reinforced. For example, DRH has been used to improve work productivity (McDuff et al., 2019) and increase the pace of self-feeding (Girolami, Kahng, Hilker, & Grolami, 2008).

Here are some other examples: "The crowd roars when the mile runner completes his run in less than four minutes. Its cheers are less enthusiastic for those finishing considerably later. When Chuck correctly comes to the end of all the problems in his workbook within a week, he receives an "A." If he takes longer, the grade is a "B." Grungy George rarely combs his hair or cleans his nails. When his friend visits, George combs his hair and cleans his nails every day for four days in a row. His parents privately compliment his improved appearance, and also reinforce his good grooming by increasing his allowance and offering him some extra money to entertain his friend. They decide to maintain contingencies that will reinforce a rate of at least one good-grooming session per day, and track whether George looks neat and clean at least once each day for at least four days in a row. With this DRH schedule, George's grooming is likely to remain high and steady.

But George's parents must be careful. If, for some reason, such as a falling out with his friend, his grooming falls off, it might be a long time before he again reaches the high-rate criterion for four days in a row. They might then have to resort to shaping, starting with a single day of proper grooming and gradually moving back up to four days in a row. In general, a disadvantage of DRH is that once an individual starts failing to meet the contingencies, reinforcement can fall off to the point where it is necessary to use shaping or other procedures to get performance back up to where it had been maintained by the DRH contingency. The more stringent the DRH contingency, the more likely that such a problem will arise.

## Promoting Paced Responding with Differential Reinforcement of Paced Responding (DRP)

Life conditions sometimes call for response sequences that are neither too fast nor too slow. When aiming for the basket, Herbie wants to shoot the ball rapidly, but not so fast that he misses because he fails to aim accurately. Our good buddy, Bruno, certainly wants to adhere to the pace set by Beethoven when he plays the sonata's *andante* movement—not as slowly as the *largo* (which might put him and his audience to sleep), nor as fast as *allegro*, which might cause him to hit the wrong keys, and naturally, would have offended Beethoven had he been able to hear it. **Pacing schedules** are defined as *those setting upper and lower limits on reinforceable response rates* (Catania, 2013). *Differential reinforcement of paced responding (DRP)* is characterized by reinforcement arranged to occur contingent only on response rates within those limits. They are suitable in any instances in which a particular tempo is important—as in performing certain intricate assembly tasks, driving, preparing foods, performing delicate surgery, and others you should be able to identify.

As with other reinforcement schedules, behavior analysts have investigated methods for promoting and supporting local temporal patterning. One example is a study conducted by Wearden and Shimp (1985). Student volunteers were instructed to operate a device by pushing a button, receiving no further instructions. Words flashed on the screen before them: either "good" or "poor." Various pacing contingencies were presented with the experimental goal of determining how well participants were able to match their pace with that programmed during particular phases of the study. While not all the participants were able to optimize their performance by matching the contingencies, those who did succeed reported having verbalized those contingency arrangements to themselves. Afterward, their matching improved even further. ("Oh I get it. This one wants me to respond once a second—no more; no less.")

Pacing schedules may be especially appropriate for students who tend to behave "impulsively," as many diagnosed with learning disabilities or attention-deficit hyperactivity disorder appear to do. Sometimes these students can benefit from slowing down and pausing, possibly reciting and giving themselves instructions before they act: "Oh. That's an addition, not a multiplication sign. I must add, not multiply these numbers!" The bottom line regarding pacing is that knowing and differentially reinforcing the optimal rate at which a particular individual should perform a given task would be most beneficial.

## Promoting Lower Rate Responding with Differential Reinforcement of Low Rates (DRL) and Diminishing Rates (DRD)

As used in laboratory studies, **differential reinforcement of lower rates (DRL)** is a procedure in which the delivery of reinforcers is contingent on responses emitted at low rates—that is, responses that are spaced relatively far apart. When DRL is in effect, a response is reinforced *only if it occurs following a specific period of time during which that response* *did not occur, or since the last time it occurred* (Ferster & Skinner, 1957). A monkey receives a banana pellet for pulling a chain only if he has not pulled that chain for at least 20 seconds. If the monkey pulls the chain too soon, a new 20-second period begins. In other words, chain-pulls cannot be reinforced unless they occur at least 20 seconds apart.[8]

Let us translate this contingency arrangement to the world of ordinary people. To reduce Ralph's excessive participation and thereby allow others an opportunity to have their say during English class, Ralph and Mrs. Olsen agree that if Ralph waits three minutes after participating until his next bid for recognition (raising his hand), she will call on him at the next opportunity. If not, she will ignore that bid and require him to wait at least three more minutes before she recognizes his next bid. In another example, a basketball coach praises her point guard if two minutes expire between her three-point shot attempts. As we will see in Chapter 28, where we will discuss further examples, DRL schedules are especially suitable to managing dangerously rapid responding, such as eating so rapidly as to risk choking.

Notice the DRL schedule is designed to reduce or maintain the rate of a behavior by reinforcing that very same behavior (*not* an alternative), but only when a specific time interval has passed in the absence of its having been emitted. We suggest you *limit your application of this schedule only to acceptable behavior that occurs too frequently or rapidly*, as illustrated above. Eventually, the rate of responding should drop to that set by the DRL contingency. Also, research with children with autism, three to seven years of age (Gaucher & Forget, 2020) indicates that those with higher IQs and receptive language scores adjusted more rapidly to DRLs of 5-seconds and 20-seconds for pressing on a touch screen. As the investigators pointed out, this indicates how some children's capacities appear to have provided them with a greater sensitivity to reinforcement contingencies than others

Similar to paced responding, when interval schedules are introduced after a history of DRL responding, low rates tend to persist. Baron and Galizio (1983) attributed the way instructions influence patterns of responding under reinforcement schedules to reinforcement history. Plaud, Gaither, and Lawrence (1997) used the descriptive term *behavioral momentum* (a term coined by Nevin and colleagues: Nevin et al., 1983; Nevin, 1988; 1992) to describe their own experiences with human subjects whose prior response patterns tended to persist despite changes in reinforcer contingencies.

Unlike DRL, **differential reinforcement of diminishing rates (DRD,** also called **full-session DRL**) can be used to reduce inappropriate behavior. When you use this schedule you *provide reinforcement when the occurrences of a behavior per a unit of time are less than how often the behavior typically occur*. For example, DRD was used successfully to reduce adults' excessive questioning in adult-day training centers by delivering "a reinforcer at the end of the day if the number of questions asked was less than a specified number during the entire session. Ques-tions, up to a specified number, were also reinforced within-session" (p. 545). Thus, it is a tolerant schedule recognizing that behavior change often occurs gradually, not all at once. DRD, like DRL, also is elaborated upon in Chapter 28.

## Promoting Variability of Responding with Lag Schedules

Not only can we influence rates of responding by schedules of reinforcement, but we also can influence variability of responding. When using a **lag schedule** (Lee, Sturmey & Fields, 2007), "*a response is reinforced only if it differs from a specified number of previous responses*" (Contreras & Betz, 2016, p. 4). For example, if you were using a lag of 2 schedule when teaching your client to identify similarities between two objects, you would only reinforce the third response if it was different from the previous two. If using a lag of 3, you would provide reinforcement only for the 4th response if it were different from the previous 3. Lag schedules

---

[8]The DRL schedule is used widely as a way of testing the influence of various physiological and medical conditions as well as within the pharmacological and biological research areas (e.g., McClure & McMillan, 1997, Stewart et al., 2006).

of reinforcement, then, are most useful in teaching similarities, differences, listing animals found in the zoo, having a client describe what is happing in a picture, increasing a response class, or any time you are promoting response variability, which is often considered an aspect of creativity (Goetz & Baer, 1973). Lee and Sturmey (2014) used a Lag-1 to help increase appropriate and varied responding by three children with autism. Wiskow and Donaldson (2016) used a lag-1 schedule with two typically developing girls (ages three and four) and a six-year-old boy with ADHD and high-functioning autism. The children not only increased the naming of different items in a category (e.g., animals) but were also more likely to repeat peer responses and increased their varied responses during individual testing. Lag schedules also have been used to reduce repetitive behavior (e.g., Napolitano, Smith, Zarcone, Goodkin, & McAdam, 2010), to increase varied mand responding during functional communication training (Adami, Falcomata, Muething, & Hoffman, 2017), and to improve social skills (Radley, Dart, Helbig, Schrieber, & Ware, 2019). In the Radley et al. study, they were better able to replace repetitive social communication responding with more novel responding by incorporating lag schedules within their social skills training of individuals with autism.

In a more recent study (Dracobly, Dozier, Briggs, & Juanico, 2017) with preschool-age children, lag schedules were found to produce substantially higher levels of variability and novelty than extinction. Also, leaner lag schedules (lag 4) produced "somewhat greater variability than denser lag schedules" (p. 618). In addition, lag schedules also appear to facilitate generalization by reinforcing multiple response exemplars (Silbaugh, et al., 2017).

Educators often combine lag schedules with progressive or adjusting schedules of reinforcement, as when investigators (Silbaugh & Falcomata, 2019) used a lag schedule to help a non-verbal child with autism learn to emit several signs to make requests (*mand*—see Chapter 19). Then, to help the alternative responses occur without prompting, they employed time delayed prompting to phase out the modeling.

## SUMMARY AND CONCLUSIONS

The nature of the schedule(s) of reinforcement previously and currently in effect heavily influences the configurations and rates of performance patterns. In this chapter we have discussed ratio schedules: what they are, how they operate, and their direct and indirect impact on performance. Depending on the size of the ratio requirement and the difficulty of the response, ratio schedules tend to support high rates of responding. Unlike variable ratios, post-reinforcement pauses more often accompany responding under fixed-ratio schedules. The exact appearance of an individual response pattern at any point in time, though, also is affected by numerous factors, including: the person's learning history, current state, contextual factors, rule-governance, the size of the ratio requirement, the difficulty of the response, other schedules simultaneously operating on the behavior of concern, and/or other classes of his or her behavior.

Responding is apt to continue longer under extinction when the individual has experienced a variable-ratio, as opposed to a fixed-ratio schedule. It also is likely to persist longer if the schedule should shift from a ratio to an interval format. Ratio schedules are especially convenient to use when the behavior produces a permanent product, because those products may be counted and used to prompt the delivery of reinforcers. The size of the ratio requirement also may easily be adjusted, depending on the person's observable response patterns. Recall, though, that in some instances, temporarily switching over from intermittent to continuous reinforcement prior to placing unwanted behaviors on extinction has proven beneficial.

In using ratio schedules, we must watch for instances of *ratio strain* induced by too challenging a schedule, and, if necessary, be prepared to reduce the response requirements temporarily. The impact of the schedule can be heightened, though, by providing clear instructions, imitative prompts, and differential reinforcement of high rates (DRH), and/or fluency training. Nevertheless, the multitude of schedules of reinforcement affecting any individual's given behavior at a point in time may affect the particular pattern of the behavior of concern. For example, differential reinforcement of rate schedules can increase or lower rates of responding, or result in paced or greater variability of responding. Also, it tends to be helpful to inform your clients about which differential contingencies they will be, or are, experiencing. Such information can prompt them to respond accordingly.

*Chapter 23*

# Maintaining Behavior by Arranging Time Based Schedules of Reinforcement

## Goals

1. Define, recognize, and provide original illustrations for each of the following terms:
    a. interval schedule
    b. fixed-interval (FI) schedule
    c. variable-interval (VI) schedule
    d. interreinforcement interval
    e. noncontingent reinforcement
    f. limited-hold schedule
    g. social facilitation
    h. behavioral contrast or contrast phenomenon (positive and negative)
    i. interspersal strategy
2. List and describe the characteristics characterizing performance under interval schedules of reinforcement.
3. Distinguish between *fixed-interval* and *fixed-time* schedules
4. Compare patterns of responding under FI and VI.
5. Describe under what conditions a fixed- versus a variable-interval schedule should be selected.
6. Describe how the (a) size of the interval, (b) quality of the reinforcer, (c) delay, (d) effort, and (e) magnitude of the reinforcer influence rate.
7. Provide possible explanations for the differences between the cumulative-response scalloping patterns produced by animals and humans while responding under FI schedules.

8. Describe why scalloping response patterns are unlikely to occur under a VI schedule of reinforcement.
9. Describe how impulsivity might be controlled under interval reinforcement.
10. Discuss the effects of schedule history on the effects of extinction.
11. Discuss the advantages and disadvantages of using interval schedules.
12. Discuss how (a) interval length, (b) history of ratio and differential reinforcement of rate schedules, (c) limited-hold restrictions, (d) presence of instructions and rules, (e) competitive contingencies, (f) behavioral contrast, and (g) interspersing easy tasks can influence rates of performance under interval schedules.
13. Give several examples of ways that different schedules can interact to influence performance.
14. Explain how to thin reinforcers when interval schedules are in effect.
15. Explain how to implement interval schedules to maintain a behavior at a high, steady rate.
16. Describe how reinforcing one response might influence another response

*************

Okay! Suppose you have successfully achieved your behavioral objective and are using a ratio-based intermittent reinforcement method to support its steady continuation. The chief upside of using such schedules is that while providing fewer reinforcers, such schedules maintain, or sometimes even support, an *increase* in the rate of a response. Their foremost down side, though, is that those schedules demand constant monitoring, because response ratios must be closely monitored. Permanent products, electro-mechanical recording devices, and so on may simplify that process, but you cannot avoid the simple fact that ratio schedules depend on response counts. A more practical approach is to substitute or eventually shift over to an interval rather than a ratio-dependent schedule.

In this chapter, we describe and illustrate how various interval-based schedules of reinforcement function, the types of performance patterns they generate, their advantages and disadvantages, and how you can optimize their effectiveness and utility. By introducing you to the characteristics of behavior under those schedules, we hope to help you to understand why certain classes of responding are or may become resistant to extinction. In addition, we offer several suggestions for implementing interval-based schedules effectively. Assuming you also will find it helpful to know the extent to which these various schedules provide opportunities for competing behavior, we discuss response patterns while the schedule is in effect and also after reinforcers have been discontinued.[1]

## INTERVAL SCHEDULES

### Defined and Illustrated

Under an **interval schedule**, *reinforcers are presented contingent on the first response emitted after some interval of time has ended*. Remembering that the reinforcer requires a response is crucial. Other responses can occur during the interval, but they have no effect on the delivery of the consequence. Only that first target response *after* the end of the

---
[1] Much more is known about the behavior of organisms under complex schedule arrangements, but a full treatment of such combinations transcends the scope of this book. Instead, we limit our presentation to relatively simple arrangements, because we feel those are most pertinent to practical application. Readers wishing more complete discussions of specific simple and complex reinforcement schedules should see, among others, the *Journal of the Experimental Analysis of Behavior*; Ferster and Skinner (1957), *Schedules of Reinforcement*, Appleton-Century-Crofts; Catania (2013), *Learning*, 5th Edition, Sloan Publishing; and Pierce & Cheney (2013), *Behavior Analysis and Learning*, 5th Edition, Taylor & Francis.

interval can produce the reinforcer, and the reinforcer will not occur without it. As with the ratio schedules, there are two fundamental types of interval schedules: *fixed-interval* and *variable-interval schedules*. We discuss both below.

## Fixed-Interval (FI) Schedules

Unlike ratio schedules, interval schedules depend on an interval of time plus one response. The number of responses during the interval has no effect, except for the particular response emitted following the end of the interval. In a **fixed-interval (FI) schedule**, *reinforcement is scheduled to be produced by the first response following a constant or fixed interval*. For example, Chuck and his teacher have agreed he should volunteer to speak in class more regularly during social studies discussion. His teacher defines volunteering as "raising his hand; then when recognized, responding with a novel comment directly relevant to the topic." The teacher then activates a timer that will vibrate following the passage of 15 minutes. The first time Chuck volunteers *after the teacher detects the vibration of her timer*, she tells him that he has received a checkmark in her record book and restarts the timer for the next 15-minute interval. At the end of the week, she tallies the checkmarks and allows Chuck to exchange them for activities of his choice from his "reinforcer menu." Fixed-interval schedules are abbreviated FI, and the schedule in this illustration would be called an "FI 15 min." or a "fixed-interval 15-minute" schedule. (Notice that the teacher used a clock stimulus that Chuck could not detect rather than a clicker or buzzer. Otherwise, he would simply have responded to those sounds as discriminative stimuli, and the timing of the interval would have been irrelevant.)

Some investigators (e.g., Floress, Cages, Poirot, & Estrada, 2020) now recommend delivering reinforcers on an FI interval as an antecedent for increasing the level of reinforcement in the school or home. As they point out, "Using praise as an antecedent-based strategy has the potential to establish and maintain high-quality student-teacher relationships, which positively impacts student behavior" (p. 84).

Such a strategy can enrich the climate of not only the classroom environment, but also the home, work, or almost any environment. (See Chapter 27 for additional antecedent strategies to increase appropriate behavior while preventing problem behaviors, by heightening the reinforcing quality of just about any environment.)

Here is another example from a work setting: Every two hours, Angela, the manager of patient-care personnel, checks her staff on video monitors. She then sends messages to those who are *on-task*, or working on their assigned responsibilities. She tries to compliment something they were doing well at the moment. ("Nice job of bathing Mr. J.M. I'm sure he's feeling more comfortable now.") Angela's schedule of reinforcement is an FI 2 hr.

With FI schedules, the reinforced response tends to occur at low rates early in the interval, and to increase gradually as the end of the interval approaches (this pattern is called a scallop, based on the appearance of FI performance in cumulative records). For this reason, it may not be a desirable schedule choice when the target is to maintain relatively consistent rates of responding over time.

## Distinguishing between Fixed-Interval and Fixed-Time Schedules

Take care not to assume that an FI schedule is in operation simply because reinforcers are being dispensed regularly. For a schedule to qualify as FI, reinforcers must be *contingent on* a given response that follows the end of the fixed interval. An FI reinforcer must be delivered contingently; a procedure that delivers reinforcers non-contingently is not an FI schedule. Rather, such procedures are *fixed-time* schedules (if the schedule of reinforcer delivery is the same amount of time between deliveries). In the example just presented, Angela defined on-task as "being engaged in a task meeting the person's job description" and made her compliments contingent on *being on-task*. Suppose, instead, that she complimented each person every two hours regardless of whether personnel were doing their assigned tasks, text messaging, or playing a computer game at that moment. Because reinforcer delivery was not contingent on specific behavior, such a procedure would be called a **fixed-*time* (FT) schedule**; that is, *reinforcers were delivered regularly after a fixed or constant time period, regardless of the ongoing behavior*. Actually, many white-collar workers are compensated according to fixed-time schedules, as in receiving their pay every two weeks despite what they actually do at any given time at work. Presumably, though, their retention on the job is based on their meeting certain standards of performance. Similarly, social security and retirement checks are delivered on FT schedule. Using a FT schedule can be a risky because *while the schedule is in effect, the only condition stipulated for the delivery of reinforcers is the passage of time*. As a result, the recipient may develop superstitious behavior (Ono, 1987), such as repeating acts previously contiguous with reinforcers (e.g., wearing certain items, parking in a certain location); but the reinforced acts may not necessarily be relevant to *appropriate* performance. (Time-based schedules are discussed in more detail in association with noncontingent reinforcement—see Chapter 27.) Like interval schedules, time schedules can either be fixed or varied. In a **variable-time schedule** *the reinforcers would be delivered noncontingently based upon an average amount of time*. For example, telling a parent to give Payton praise on a VT 15 minute schedule would mean that the parent should give Payton praise on average every 15 minutes.

### Variable-Interval (VI) Schedules

**Variable-interval schedules** *operate like fixed-interval schedules, except that the required time interval varies before a response can produce a reinforcer.* Chuck's teacher could have varied the interval from 0 to 10 minutes when she prepared the clock to prompt her with vibrations at the end of each interval, so that she would know whether to give him a checkmark the next time he volunteered. Eventually these intervals would average to about five minutes. Such a schedule would be called a "variable-interval 5-minute" or, abbreviated, a "VI 5 min." schedule.

Suppose, for their own well-being, the office and manufacturing personnel of the Brown's Med Tech Group are eager to improve their posture at the computer. Every hour, on average, a member of the safety staff observes the packaging operation and office and records each employee's posture score. They then compliment and provide specific feedback to every deserving worker for improvements in performance (a VI 1 hr.). (For actual examples of the effects of reinforcing feedback on worker performance, see Alavosius & Sulzer-Azaroff, 1990; Alvero, Bucklin, & Austin, 2001; Culig, Dickinson, Lindstrom-Hazel, & Austin, 2008; Gravina, Lindstrom-Hazel, & Austin, 2007; McCann & Sulzer-Azaroff, 1996.) Because the observations are on a VI schedule, some postures are reinforced by feedback events delivered very close together; and other by events far apart. This range of different intervals in VI schedules tends to create much more constant rates of responding within intervals, rather than the gradually increasing rates within intervals (scalloping) that occur with FI schedules.

## CHARACTERISTICS OF INTERVAL-SCHEDULE PERFORMANCE

Much of our earlier knowledge of the characteristics of performance under different schedules of reinforcement was derived from laboratory work with nonhumans. Today, given the growing wealth of data collected with humans in natural settings, we need to be more cautious about extrapolating the laboratory findings to humans acting within their daily surroundings. To illustrate, one reliable characteristic of fixed-interval response patterns observed in animals in laboratory settings was scalloping, typified by a gradually increasing rate of responding until a reinforced response at the end of each interval. With humans, outside of the laboratory and in real life, the picture is a bit more complicated. While human infants under six months of age do tend to pause following delivery of reinforcers (Darcheville, Riviere, & Wearden, 1993), more mature humans show different response patterns under *fixed*-interval (FI) schedules (Buskist & Miller, 1986), sometimes even responding at high rates with few pauses.

Variations in response patterns between laboratory animals and humans operating under fixed-

>
> **An Exercise**
>
> Many young people's group events are scheduled regularly: recreation and lunch periods, tests or other evaluations, progress reports, classes in specific subjects, and so on. At home, too, various activities take place at relatively fixed times: meals, chores, music practice, television shows, and so on. Some of these generally would be considered target responses; others reinforcing events. Can you differentiate those two classes? For the latter, what additional information would you need to help you decide whether you think they are operating on an FI or an FT schedule?

interval schedules probably are due to people's more complex verbal behavior (Bicard & Neef, 2002; Catania, Lowe, & Horne, 1990; Catania et al., 1982). Some have also cited individual learning histories or a tendency to be either "impulsive" or "self-controlled" (Darcheville et al., 1993). Barnes and Keenan (1993) demonstrated that verbal self-regulation can make a difference. When those investigators either did or did not provide access to alternative reinforcers in the form of reading material or television, the condition affected whether participants verbally regulated their response patterns. In the absence of the other activities, they did pause following reinforcer delivery. When the supplementary activities were available, they did not. As suggested by varied findings, many issues involving the interactions between verbal behavior and human performance maintained by interval schedules have yet to be resolved, but it is safe to say that when we use schedules with verbally-skilled humans, it is reasonable to assume that the schedule contingencies will combine with their verbal behavior to produce a broader range of outcomes than have been observed with nonhumans.

## Rate of Responding under Interval Schedules

In planning ABA interventions, specifying in advance the rate of responding desired during maintenance is important. If a relatively low rate is tolerable, an interval schedule may be the best solution, because its demands are simple: Reinforcer delivery depends only on the occurrence of a specific response just once following the end of the interval. A pigeon will ordinarily peck throughout the interval, but if it pecks just once after the required interval ends, despite strutting, cooing, and preening in between, it will still earn its grain. Technically, Chuck, who works on a fixed-interval five-minute schedule (FI 5 min.), can receive his token provided he contributes something to the discussion one time after the five-minute interval has elapsed. (Note how this differs from the FR schedule, which requires a particular number of responses as a condition for reinforcer delivery.) Single responses per interval are rare under FI schedules, though. As we have seen, laboratory studies have found that (non-human) animals tend to pause following reinforcer delivery, after which their response rates accelerate.

Under interval schedules, if responders pause *during* an interval, the moment of potential reinforcer delivery is unaffected; the next response after the end of the interval is still reinforced. The rate of responding during an interval could double, but this would not change the time at which the interval ends. This contrasts with ratio schedules, where slower rates of responding result in fewer reinforcers. In ratio schedules, the numbers of responses per reinforcer are determined but the time between reinforcers depends on rate of responding. In interval schedules, on the other hand, minimum times between reinforcers are determined but the numbers of responses per reinforcer depend on the subject/participant's idiosyncratic rate of responding. If Chuck were working on a VI 2 min. schedule, he would have to contribute at least once each two minutes on average to earn the maximum number of tokens. In an FI 9 min. schedule, as little as a single contribution at the end of each nine-minute interval would suffice for maximum payoff. The residents of the group home would tidy their rooms more regularly if they were inspected hourly, rather than on alternate days. Such assumptions have been borne out in results of research with human participants.

Response rates under interval schedules can be manipulated by shortening or extending the duration of the interval (Lowe, Harzem, & Bagshaw, 1978), just as the particular interval-schedule can influence students' specific performance patterns (Mace et al., 1990; Martens, Lochner, & Kelly, 1992). In general, though, the shorter the interval, the higher the maintained rate of responding, in both FI and VI schedules. This is illustrated for VI schedules in Figure 23.1. For FI and VI schedules of the same duration (e.g., FI 2-min and VI 2-min), the FI tends to produce somewhat lower response rates, perhaps depending on the low rates early during the FI scallop.

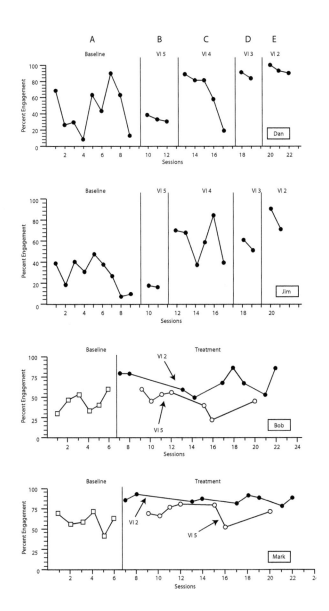

**Figure 23.1  Variable-interval schedule behavior**
Top two figures in A-B-C-D-E sequence: The shorter the interval to reinforcer delivery, the higher the engagement rate. The lower two display a similar effect within multi-element designs for two students under VI 2 and VI 5. From Martens et al. (1992). © 1992 by the Society for the Experimental Analysis of Behavior, Inc.

The *quality* of the reinforcer is another factor that may influence rate of responding under interval reinforcement. People often work more rapidly for more valuable consequences under interval scheduling, as Neef, Mace, and Shade (1993) have shown. Participants could earn money either in the form of "program money" (tokens) or cash. They found that one of their participants worked at a higher rate for the cash reinforcer than for tokens of fairly equivalent value. But when they manipulated the true value of the "money" (that is, actual versus "program money" of *lesser* value), the experimenters demonstrated that student responding shifted in tandem with the change in reinforcer value.

Reinforcer *delay* also can enter into the interval-schedule picture. Neef et al. (1993) found that one of their participants chose to work for immediate rather than for delayed reinforcers, even when the immediate reinforcers were of lower value than the delayed.

The *effort* required by a given interval schedule also may influence rate of responding, especially when choices are available. All other factors considered, people operating under interval schedules tend to choose the response format that demands less effort of them. (See Neef, Shade, & Miller, 1994.)

The *magnitude* (force or intensity) of the reinforcer has been thought to be a factor affecting the rate of responding under different schedules of reinforcement. Children who engaged in problem behavior participated in a study in which they responded to social attention according to different schedules of reinforcement (Trosclair-Lasserre, Lerman, Call, Addison, & Kodak, 2008). "Results indicated that preference for different magnitudes of social reinforcement may predict reinforcer efficacy and that magnitude effects may be mediated by the schedule requirement" (p. 203).

Individuals operating under interval reinforcement-schedule choice situations have been found to choose particular interval sizes, reinforcer quality, and delay periods. Other antecedent conditions also affect the potency of social attention as well. So, for individuals known to behave impulsively, use a data-based approach, such as a comparison design (Neef et al., 1993) if you are seeking to identify an optimal rate of social reinforcement under given circumstances. One size does not fit all.

## Maintaining Rates Originally Established under Ratio Schedules

The previous chapter elaborated upon the utility of ratio schedules as a means of supporting high response rates. Out in the field, though, it is much more convenient to implement interval schedules, because they do not require the constant vigilance demanded by ratio schedules. Suppose John, a student we have encountered before, now is working at an acceptably high rate under a ratio schedule. Economic and convenience factors cause the staff to decide to shift to a VI schedule. The supervisor tells John that he would like to see how many tasks the young man can complete while he himself is away helping other people. The supervisor selects a VI schedule of five minutes, the average time it takes John to complete five tasks under the VR 5 schedule. John will hardly notice the change. So, after approximately five minutes, the supervisor checks back, and if John is working on his task, the supervisor gives him a reinforcer.

The VI 5 schedule of social approval then is adjusted gradually to VI 8, VI 15, and VI 30. John's learning history with regard to ratio schedules encourages the boy to work quickly over extended periods, thereby heightening his eligibility for actual competitive employment. In addition, John now is earning more tokens because he completes more job-related tasks.

Permit us to inject a note of caution: Watch out before you switch from a ratio to an interval schedule when teaching functional communication. Hanley et al. (2001) compared the results of moving from continuous reinforcement of requests for help to various interval schedules (FI 1 s, 2 s, 4 s, 16 s, 25 s, 35 s, 46 s, and 58 s). The participants' communication responses skyrocketed (almost tripled in rate). Take home point: consider, in advance, the chosen range for the level of responding you are seeking, so you don't inadvertently create chaos in the form of too high, out-of-control, response rates after implementing excessively powerful intermittent reinforcement schedules.

## Consistency of Performance

As we have noted, among laboratory animals, fixed-interval responding usually is characterized by a fixed-interval *scallop:* after receiving reinforcement the responding drops. As the end of the interval approaches, the responding increases — sort of like the letter 'u' (see Figure 23.2). By its nature, the fixed-interval schedule does not demand that the organism emit the target response throughout the interval. Instead of immediately resuming pecking the disk, pigeons occasionally have been seen to pause, strut, coo, preen, or flap their wings early in the new interval, especially following long-interval FI reinforcement. After all, they have never received grain immediately following a reinforced peck. Similarly, under laboratory conditions, human adults (Lowe et al., 1978) and infants (Lowe, Beastay, & Bentall, 1983) have generated similar patterns of FI performance patterns as those of (other) animals (e.g., Ferster & Skinner, 1957). Human child and adult FI response patterns, though, tend to differ somewhat. Sometimes people continue consistently to perform at high rates throughout the interval instead of stopping or slowing down following reinforcer delivery (Weiner, 1964). At other times, they may stop responding altogether for a while, and then abruptly shift to a high rate pattern (Buskist & Morgan, 1987; Lowe et al., 1978). Such factors as the following may account for the differences:

- alternative sources of reinforcers (Hagopian, Crockett, van Stone, DeLeon, & Bowman, 2000)
- instructions and rules (Crozier & Tincani, 2005; Lippman & Meyer, 1967; Matthews, Catania, & Shimoff, 1985; Vaughan, 1985)
- other schedules currently in effect (Barnes & Keenan, 1993; Buskist & Morgan, 1987; McSweeney, 1983; Plaud, Gillund, & Ferraro, 2000; Skinner, 2002)
- schedule history (Dougan, McSweeney, & Farmer, 1985; Lattal & Neef, 1996; Weiner, 1964)
- reinforcer magnitude (Trosclair-Lasserre et al., 2008)

Yet, occasionally we can identify instances of post-reinforcement pauses in the natural situations. Figure 23.3 illustrates the acceleration in rate at which U.S. congressional representatives passed bills as adjournment approached. Notice the pattern produced: the typical FI scallop about which we spoke earlier.

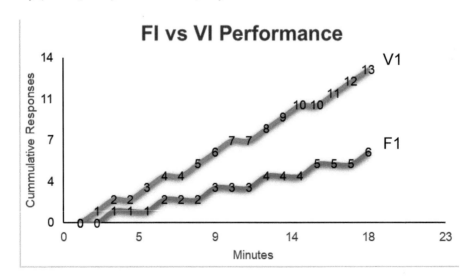

**Figure 23.2** Hypothetical demonstration of FI and VI schedule performance

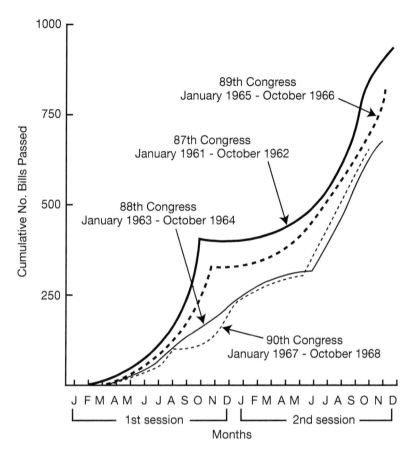

**Figure 23.3** Cumulative numbers of bills passed during the legislative sessions of Congress from January 1961 to October 1968. From Weisberg & Waldup (1972). © 1972 by the Society for the Experimental Analysis of Behavior, Inc.

In another analogous situation, students who are quizzed or graded at regular intervals often delay studying until just before the scheduled event. As the interval progresses, rates of studying accelerate. While study behavior is low, rates of other response categories are higher: playing, working on other assignments, and so on. Mawhinney, Bostow, Laws, Blumenfeld, and Hopkins (1971) measured minutes of college students' studying per day under daily and three-week quiz conditions. (Quizzes probably set up both positive and negative reinforcement contingencies.) Figure 23.4 indicates that studying was relatively consistent under the daily schedule, but during the three-week schedule it was slow at first and then increased. (Note that these are not cumulative records, so the increasing rates do not appear as a scallop. Can you figure out how to change these data into a cumulative record?)

During social studies class, Chuck conceivably could look out the window, disrupt, get a drink, doodle, and so on early within each five-minute interval. Yet, as long as he contributed a task-related response to the discussion at least once following each five-minute period, he still would remain eligible for and receive the maximum number of token reinforcers. How do you think the group-home residents' rooms might look on the day between fixed alternate-day inspections?

Performance of the kind just described does not usually occur under variable-interval schedules because participants cannot predict the time between reinforcement opportunities. So the individual tends

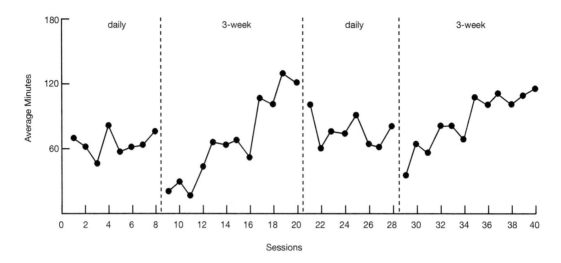

**Figure 23.4** Average minutes studied per session by all subjects during alternating daily and three-week testing conditions. From Mawhinney et al. (1971). © 1971 by the Society for the Experimental Analysis of Behavior, Inc.

to maintain a steady pace of responding. Suppose the pigeon pecks twice in succession and is presented with grain both times. It pecks again, despite having recently received the grain. Students whose instructors give irregular "pop" quizzes also tend to keep up better with their assignments. Their study may pay off at any time, and not just at some fixed dates after prior quizzes.

Whether the function is to avoid failure (negative reinforcement) or to repeat success (positive reinforcement), studying is maintained, and students are less likely to engage in competing activities. Following an unpredictable spot inspection by the safety manager, construction workers probably would continue to adhere to their safety practices fairly consistently, just in case there might be another inspection. Because performance under variable-intervals tends to remain consistent, whereas that under fixed-interval schedules may not, *if steady performance is your goal, a VI rather than an FI schedule would be your better choice.*

### Error Patterns

Different patterns of error production may emerge under some interval schedules. Not only do pigeons tend to produce the most errors in the second quarter under fixed-interval schedules (Ferster, 1960), but so do children. For example, in a study of matching-to-sample performance under fixed-interval schedules, children produced the most errors in the second quarter of each interval (Davidson & Osborne, 1974). Those operating under variable-interval schedules distributed errors more evenly within each interval.

### Managing Impulsivity

Although our clients' failure to respond or their low performance rates under interval reinforcement schedules sometimes can be troublesome, at other times our concern is different. Perhaps because interval schedules (FIs in particular) generally involve a delay between people's actions and their attaining the reinforcer, they may either act impulsively or quickly shift to behaviors designed to produce more immediate, though perhaps less valuable, reinforcers. In a laboratory study (Ainslie, 1974), pigeons had a choice between immediately earning a small quantity of food by pecking a key of one color, or waiting and later earning a large quantity by pecking a key of a different color. Only three of the ten pigeons learned to delay, i.e., to wait for the more valuable reinforcers. Schweitzer and Sulzer-Azaroff (1988) observed similar choices among several children with developmental delays.

Initially, they chose the more immediate, small (1), rather than the delayed, large (3), reinforcers. By starting with a very short delay to the more valuable reinforcer and slowly and systematically increasing it, the experimenters were able to teach the children better to manage that impulsivity by learning to wait for the reinforcer with the higher payoff. In another situation (Schweitzer & Sulzer-Azaroff, 1995), boys learned to control their "impulsive choices" of immediate smaller over delayed larger reinforcers by engaging in alternative reinforceable activities.[2] Dixon and Tibbetts (2009) conducted a related study with three adolescents with traumatic brain injury. Again, during baseline, the boys initially had chosen the smaller immediate reinforcer, but they changed their preference to the larger delayed reinforcer following self-control training program. (See also a closely related study by Dixon, Marley, & Jacobs, 2003.)[3]

## Responding During Extinction

As previously discussed, *a history of intermittent reinforcement tends to promote persistence under extinction* or non-reinforcement conditions (Ferster & Skinner, 1957). Remember, behavior may be intermittently reinforced occasionally, whether intended or not, as in the case of someone inadvertently reacting to complaining or disrupting. For better or worse, a little reinforcement can go a long way. As with ratio schedules, interval schedules teach people that although not all responses are followed by reinforcers, some are. As a result, responding previously reinforced under interval schedules, both fixed and variable, tend to persist during extinction much longer than after a history in which every response has been reinforced (continuous reinforcement). You may recall that extinction after ratio reinforcement usually consists of runs of responding, interrupted by longer and longer breaks.

After interval reinforcement, however, there may be some high-rate responding for a while; but then during extinction, response rates tend gradually to slow down, sometimes over very extensive periods of time. Extinction after FI is similar to extinction after VI because there is no basis for a scalloped pattern of responding (there cannot be post-reinforcement pauses once reinforcers are no longer delivered).

Lucretia's teacher praises her occasionally when the girl is playing nicely with the other children. Your boss drops by sporadically and praises the fine quality of your work. Neither Lucretia nor you have any way to anticipate when praise will be provided. So were the teacher or boss to discontinue the delivery of reinforcers altogether, discriminating the altered condition would take quite a while, especially if the interval between one reinforcer and the next were lengthy. Naturally, sooner or later, if no reinforcer ever were to materialize, the response probably would return to its baseline level. Even here, contingency managers don't get something for nothing.

How about unwanted behavior? Suppose such behavior produces irregular reinforcer delivery? Alas, the durability of the effect on the behavior is comparable. After learning of the nasty side-effects of punishment, the basketball coach is determined that he will shape progressively improving player performance. As his shaping skills improve, so do those of most of the team members. But at some point during practice, Boris, generally a consistently good player, but whom the coach has inadvertently ignored (deprived of attention), makes a poor shot. The coach stops to coach him individually, thereby unintentionally reinforcing the poor performance with his attention. No wonder Boris is "off his game" for several weeks.

Another familiar example is that of a non-speaking youngster on the autism spectrum whose functional assessment has revealed that he tends to hit himself when he does not gain the help or attention he seeks. His family has instituted a program in which they ignore self-hitting but try immediately to attend to the youngster when he presents a sign or pictorial cue to request what he wants. One day his mom, busily occupied with the laundry, fails to attend to fast enough when the picture is offered. As a result, he reverts to hitting himself. Now Mom turns to the boy, guesses what he wants, and gives it

---

[2] A fairly extensive literature on similar forms of impulsivity in gambling and drug use has been evolving, but is beyond the scope of this text.

[3] The topic of *delay discounting* also is relevant to the examination of impulsivity—in gambling, drug abuse, and other maladaptive forms of addiction (see, for example, Reynolds, 2006).

to him. What do you think will happen to the youngster's rate of hitting himself? Alas, self-hitting can be expected to return until differential reinforcement is reinstituted and practiced consistently over an extended period of time.

Yes, in contrast with continuous reinforcement, interval schedules tend to generate responding that continues longer during extinction. Additionally, the more powerful the reinforcers during training (i.e., higher frequency or larger amount), the greater will be the resistance to extinction (Shull & Grimes, 2006). Additionally, in general, if the interval that maintained a response was large, the response probably will continue longer than if the interval had been fairly short (Reynolds, 1968). These tendencies again underscore the value of using a program that progressively extends the interval prior to reinforcer delivery. Even if Chuck finally has achieved the terminal goal—contributing regularly to the social studies discussion under a VI 5 min. schedule, terminating the reinforcement program completely would be premature. His responding might not continue very long if reinforcers were suddenly withdrawn. A preferable tactic would be gradually to "thin" the schedule by slowly lengthening the interval until token delivery became contingent on Chuck's regular contributions over days or perhaps even weeks. By that time, Chuck might hardly notice that token-delivery had been discontinued altogether, and perhaps other natural reinforcement contingencies might have taken over.

Now, can you consider the reinforcement schedules you might include if you were to design a habit-change plan for a willing participant, or even for yourself?

## ADVANTAGES AND DISADVANTAGES OF INTERVAL SCHEDULES

Beyond their utility as a means of promoting maintained responding—not only during reinforcement but under extinction as well—a major advantage of using interval schedules is their ease of implementation. Because they are duration, rather than frequency-based, one simply has to periodically check a clock or calendar, or respond to a visual, auditory, or tactile timer-signal to be reminded to present the reinforcer (but the stimulus that prompts you to make the contingent reinforcer available cannot be discriminable to your client). The interval schedule is particularly appealing when other demands compete with contingency managers' time and attention.

Still one more advantage, as with other intermittent schedules of reinforcement, is that, compared to reinforcing every response, they delay satiation. This probably is responsible to some degree for maintained responding during reinforcement. Too much of a good thing—whether candy bars, mocha lattes, or  pats on the back—is too much. When flooded with those, your efforts to attain them cease. Satiation is forestalled when valued reinforcers are delivered just once in a while, as happens under interval schedules.

*Although FI schedules tend to produce changing response rates (scallops), variable-interval schedules promote more consistent responding.* So, if consistency is what you are after during reinforcement and afterward, substitute variable for fixed-interval schedules. You also have seen that interval schedules tend to generate lower response rates than ratio schedules. If that poses a problem for you, you can overcome that in other ways, to be discussed shortly.

Given that interval-schedule performance tends to be quite predictable, it can be used as a method for testing the impact of additional variables. In fact, numerous investigations use VI schedules to generate steady performance as a baseline for studying the effects of drugs. An example is an investigation of the effects of methylphenidate (MPH) on the sensitivity to reinforcers of children with attention-deficit hyperactivity disorder (Murray & Kollins, 2002). When medicated with MPH, two children solved more arithmetic problems.

Assuming no other schedules of reinforcement are operating simultaneously on the behavior of interest, another difficulty that might arise with FIs is that the individual may excessively display unrelated behaviors, such as snacking, drinking, moving about, self-stimulating, and so on, to fill the time between reinforcer delivery (Granger, Porter, & Christoph, 1984; Schweitzer & Sulzer-Azaroff, 1995). Or, as other investigators (Drifke, Tiger, & Lillie, 2020) have cautioned, "The introduction of delays may result in the resurgence [resurgence is discussed in more detail in Chapter 26] and maintenance of problem behavior and the weakening of the newly trained communicative response" (p. 1579). Such behaviors are more likely when other reinforceable activities are unavailable during the **inter-reinforcement interval** (*the time between reinforcer deliveries*). Discretion dictates, and some evidence suggests, that you avoid fixed-intervals with children who are hyperactive or who frequently engage in destructive or abusive behaviors, unless the delay period is structured to permit constructive alternative reinforceable activities. Schweitzer and Sulzer-Azaroff (1995) found that unless boys, particularly those diagnosed with attention-deficit hyperactivity disorder (ADHD), had access to other activities during their delay period, they left their seats, upset furniture, vocalized loudly, or became destructive in other ways. Hagopian et al. (2000) provided evidence supporting the value of providing alternative sources of reinforcement by using noncontingent reinforcement (NCR) while interval schedules are in effect. (**Noncontingent reinforcement (NCR)** *delivery is based on the passage of time, fixed or variable, regardless of the person's actions at the time*—e.g., noncontingent availability of toys, games, music, food, smiles, etc.—See Chapter 27 for more examples.) They concluded that making alternative sources of reinforcers available via NCR was responsible for reductions in problem behavior. Similarly, Drifke, et al. (2020) report that by **differentially reinforcing alternative responding** (i.e., using **DRA**, see Chapter 28) during delays they were able to obtain optimal treatment results.

## PROMOTING PREFERRED RATES OF RESPONDING UNDER INTERVAL SCHEDULES

As noted earlier, relying on the clock, calendar, or timer to prompt you to deliver a reinforcer is easier to manage than continuously counting a particular number of response repetitions. But the relatively

low response rates supported by interval schedules sometimes become problematic. Fortunately, after clarifying your purpose, several supplemental strategies are available to affect response rates under these schedules. These include:

- reducing or increasing the size of the interval for a while
- building a ratio history of reinforcing high (or low) rates of the response
- reinforcing high rates of responding (DRH)
- adding a limited-hold component
- using instructions or rules
- arranging competitive contingencies
- taking advantage of contrast effects
- interspersing easy tasks

We elaborate on some of these tactics below.

### Plan Your Reinforcement Schedule with Care

You may be able to use to your advantage the fact that the shorter the interval, the more rapid the response rate. Suppose you want to speed up the rate of production in your classroom or production plant. Circulate and frequently compliment students or employees for working rapidly and well. (A popular 1985 book by Tom Peters and Jane Austin called *A Passion for Excellence*, popularized this as "management by walking around.")

You also may want to consider *patterns of performance*. Is consistency of responding critical, or can you tolerate abrupt bursts and long pauses?

Once you are clear about the rates and patterns you are looking for, both during reinforcer delivery and afterward, you are in a better position to select the appropriate schedule. By judiciously combining it with other elements, such as instructions or supplementary discriminative stimuli such as a clock or calendar, you can plan how best to apply the schedule. So, let us now turn to the environmental factors known to influence interval-schedule performance and consider the nature of their influence.

## Provide a History Appropriate to Your Objective(s)

A particular response's schedule history can influence its subsequent rate under a different schedule (Okouchi, 2003). "The more a subject's history resembles current conditions in terms of temporal proximity and other common elements, the more likely it is to persist to affect current responding" (Weiner, 1983, p. 522). Although history effects occur with both humans and nonhumans, such effects are more typical and more dramatic with humans. Weiner (1964) found that if a different schedule, such as a differential reinforcement of high rates (DRH) or a variable-ratio schedule generated high rates, over time those patterns would be likely to persist, despite a shift to an interval schedule. Consequently, *when you seek high rates, we suggest that you provide a history of ratio and/or DRH reinforcement.*

If we arrange either ratio or interval schedules, we can often expect those contingencies to take hold without much additional intervention, but that is not the case with DRH schedules (described in Ch. 22). Sometimes before instituting a DRH schedule we need to interpose a phase designed to first produce a rate of responding that will satisfy the high-rate contingency. Suppose John is employed in a vocational workshop. The supervisor knows John can correctly sort items to be packed in a goodie-bag, because when he sits down with John on a one-to-one basis, the young man completes the task correctly. In a group setting, however, things are different. John hardly ever finishes his work, instead wandering around the room and annoying others.

After giving the matter careful thought, the job coach realizes that he has been giving attention to John for each task-completion. Given that the average assignment involves about 25 sorting tasks, the coach would ultimately like to be in the position of attending to John only about once an hour. Right now, though, that would be equivalent to extinguishing the boy's performance. So instead, he provides a small amount of attention each time John completes his task, offering a paper bag just big enough to contain the items for one sorting task.

He asks John to raise his hand after he finishes the task. When John raises his hand, the coach recognizes and reinforces the young man's efforts. After a while, though, he requires two completions by supplying John with a sheet of paper containing an outline of two completed sorting tasks and shows and asks the boy to raise his hand after finishing two tasks. He then prompts John to complete small but variable numbers of sorting tasks (2, 4, 3, etc.) before raising his hand. Essentially, he has gradually changed the contingency to VR 5; we could say that the VR performance was shaped. At this point, the supervisor notes the time John takes to complete each set of tasks.

With this information, the supervisor applies a DRH schedule that requires a rate of task completion equivalent to the highest that John had reached under VR 5. Henceforth, when the specified number of tasks is completed correctly within less time than average, John earns a bonus reinforcer (for example, an extra coffee break). But the VR shaping procedure was needed to get John up to the DRH criterion. Eventually, though, the coach probably would want to shift to a VI schedule, not only because that would lessen his need to remain constantly vigilant, but also because responding under VI contingencies is typically less fragile than responding under DRH contingencies.

## Place a Limited Hold on Responding

We all have experienced limited holds. For example, if a benefit holds a lottery to support some good cause and in announcing the winner says that the prize must be claimed within 24 hours, then claiming the prize is subject to a 24-hour limited hold.

A **limited hold** (sometimes abbreviated LH) *is imposed when a response is eligible to be reinforced only within some restricted period of time.* If a store will close in 15 minutes and you want to purchase something there, then you'll want to get there before the 15-minute limited hold ends or going there will not be reinforced by your opportunity to purchase what you needed. An LH can be applied to any schedule.

George's mom is tired of nagging him about his appearance during his last-minute rush to the school bus. Mom informs George that if he looks neat and clean when it is time for him to leave, he will receive his allowance. If not, there will be no allowance, and he will have to wait until the next day. The limited-hold contingency increases George's neatness. The client must respond more quickly to earn reinforcers when the LH contingency is added to interval schedules. When just the interval schedule is used, the client can delay responding and still receive reinforcement. Thus, interval schedules are often combined with LH to promote more rapid, consistent responding.

The teacher assigned a project in a seventh-grade social studies class. Each student was to bring in ten newspaper clippings. The students would present their current-events items to the class and receive credit toward their grades. The teacher did not specify a time by which the clippings were due. Some students went for several weeks without doing the assignment, and then, toward the end of the marking period, began bringing in reams of clippings. The last week before report cards were to be distributed, the class was overloaded with current-events presentations. The teacher was forced to postpone the next social studies unit, and some of the students never did complete that assignment. To avoid such a situation in the next marking period, the teacher added a (limited-hold) restriction: Credit would only be given for three news clippings once a week, on Friday. They would be given no credit for news clippings over three for any given week and they would not be given credit if they were not brought in by Friday. The opportunity to receive reinforcers was available only on Friday for the week's news clipping and only up to three news clippings. One way, then, to increase responding is to impose an additional restriction on performance. That restriction, the limited hold, *requires that if reinforcers are to be available, to be eligible for reinforcement, the response must occur within a specific span of time.* This contingency is one that many of us have probably learned to use without awareness. You receive approval or avoid criticism if you submit your monthly reports by the appropriate date, not afterward (when the *limited hold* has expired). Teachers give grades only when an assignment is completed within a certain time limit. Similarly, Annie, a 16-year-old with moderate intellectual disability, would receive a token and specific praise only if she were on-task within one second following each 30 second interval (Cihak, Alberto, & Fredrick, 2007). If not, the next 30-second interval was started.

Here is a homework example: A mom is adhering to a VI of 10 minutes to encourage her son to increase the amount time he attends to his homework. At the end of about 10 minutes she looks to see if he is on-task. Rather than waiting until on-task behavior occurs to deliver the reinforcer (as with a traditional VI schedule), an LH of one second is added. In other words, if her son is not working on his homework when she looks, he loses out on earning his token exchangeable towards a high preference reinforcer. The next VI begins. He can only earn his tokens if he is on-task at the immediate end of the VI schedule. (We used the term *on-task* to indicate that the LH can be combined with interval schedules on almost any on-task behavior and under a variety of settings (e.g., working on a production line, paying attention, exercising).

Notice that the limited hold is described in terms of a given duration, but it can be imposed on any type of schedule. For example, if an oyster shucker in a restaurant has an arrangement where he gets a share of the waiter's tip only if he shucks a dozen oysters within five minutes of receiving the order, the schedule is an FR 12, but it also includes a limited hold. It is an FR 12 with LH 5 min, in that his shucking will be reinforced by a share of the tip only if he completes it quickly enough.

Laboratory studies have demonstrated that the imposition of a short limited-hold schedule increases response rates (Reynolds, 1968). In the fictitious classroom situation described above, the new policy had a similar effect. To avoid losing the opportunity to earn credits, the students brought in the clippings more regularly and increasingly more often. In an actual study, Wesp (1986) found that by imposing a regular deadline (a *limited hold*), he encouraged students in his PSI course to consistently complete more units by requiring them to meet a given schedule than when allowed to set their own patterns. By incorporating limited holds on turning in assignments, the authors found that their students began to hand in fewer late papers. Beyond relying on ratio schedules, about which you read in the previous chapter, notice how you can speed up responding maintained by schedules by restricting to a brief period the time during which responses can be eligible to be reinforced.

Earlier, in Chapter 13, you read about how behavior-analytic methods were applied to resistant horses to allow themselves to be loaded into a trailer (Ferguson & Rosales-Ruiz, 2001). "Fancy," one of the horses, was particularly reluctant to enter the trailer where she could earn a reinforcer by touching a target. Instituting a limited hold, plus arranging for a companion horse to serve as a model, eventually resulted in Fancy's loading onto the trailer more quickly.

## Promote Higher Responding with Differential Reinforcement of High Rates (DRH)

*Differential reinforcement of high rates (DRH)*, as described in Chapter 22, is a schedule designed to promote consistently rapid responding. To establish a DRH schedule, we very closely observe sequences of responses and *deliver reinforcers only when several responses occur in rapid succession at or above a pre-established rate.* When pauses occur, we postpone reinforcer delivery. So, DRH involves differentially reinforcing rapid sequences of responses and lower rates of responding are not reinforced. The crowd roars when the mile runner completes his run in less than four minutes. Its cheers are less enthusiastic for those finishing considerably later. When Chuck correctly comes to the end of all the problems in his workbook within a week, he receives an "A." If he takes longer, the grade is a "B." As mentioned previously, Grungy George rarely combs his hair or cleans his nails. When his friend visits, George combs his hair and cleans his nails every day for four days in a row. His parents privately compliment his improved appearance, and also reinforce his good grooming by increasing his allowance and offering him some extra money to entertain his friend. They decide to maintain contingencies that will reinforce a rate of at least one good-grooming session per day, and track whether George looks neat and clean at least once each day for at least four days in a row. With this DRH schedule, George's grooming is likely to remain high and steady.

## Use Discriminative Stimuli

Various classes of verbal stimuli exert powerful influences over behavior while interval-reinforcement schedules are in effect. Examples of such classes include generating verbal discriminative stimuli for oneself, receiving instructions, describing the contingencies, and self-instructions. For instance, early on, Lowe et al. (1978) found that subjects reported counting to themselves as a method of estimating when to respond under a fixed-interval schedule. Later, in a series of studies among human adults, researchers (e.g., Horne & Lowe, 1993) examined the accuracy of the verbalizations of the contingencies (rules) that people generate for themselves and how that affects their performance under variable-interval schedules. When conditions such as cues and other features varied from one situation to the next, instead of adjusting to and eventually matching their response patterns to the altered contingencies, as would be expected, most did not match their responding to the reinforcement schedules in ways that were predicted by the matching law (which we discuss in Chapter 22 and later in this chapter). A post-experimental questionnaire suggested that rules interact with contingencies of reinforcement to influence response patterns. Knowing the rules in effect sometimes produces behavior that more closely follows the rules. Depending on your purposes as a behavior manager, you may decide either to clearly specify the rules in effect, to avoid your clients' generating and acting upon erroneous rules, or to maintain vague conditions to see if preferable behavioral patterns result.

Many investigators have studied how and why *instructions* sometimes override contingency effects (see Baron & Galizio, 1983, for a review). But first we need to recognize that rules are not the same as *instructions*. Saying that presses on the left button will produce coins (a rule), is different from saying one should press the left button (an instruction). The first describes what the button does; the second says what you should do. Although they seem equivalent, they may very well produce different patterns of button-pressing. Skinner (1969) has pointed out that behavior produced by interacting with contingencies is typically more sensitive to changed contingencies than behavior produced by the following of instructions, which tends to be more stereotyped and inflexible.

Under certain reinforcement schedules, people respond rapidly when instructed to do so, demonstrating that their response rates often are more powerfully affected by instructions than by consequences. College students were exposed for considerable time to an FI 30 second schedule in which the reinforcers were pennies (Buskist & Miller, 1986). When left to their own devices, without instructions, they began to wait about 30 seconds after each reinforcer before responding again, a pattern that allowed them to minimize effort and maximize payoff. The same happened with members of another group informed at the outset that obtaining the pennies was possible every 30 seconds. However, the response patterns of the latter group matched the contingency right from the start, in that they paced their responses to approximately one every 30 seconds. Another group was *misinformed*. They were told they could obtain pennies every 15 seconds. Within a few sessions, however, they learned to conform to the actual contingencies. They spaced their responding to 30, not 15, seconds. For the last group, though, when informed that the schedule was an FI 60 second, pauses were much longer than the optimal 30 seconds. In that case, instructions actually overrode the contingencies, producing longer pauses following reinforcer delivery than the schedules would produce. (Whether or not the behavior of these college-student subjects would have come under better contingency control had the reinforcers been more powerful is another question.)

Even young children's response rates of performing under FI schedules can be modified by instructions (Bentall & Lowe, 1987). Despite intervals of identical size, either experimenter- or self-generated instructions influenced the pace of the children's responding. Again, research suggests that if you teach people descriptions of the current contingencies, their responding may conform to those descriptions whether they are accurate or not (e.g., Catania et al., 1982; Rain, Shillingford, Miller, & Baier, 2000; and numerous others). Instructions may reduce rates that might otherwise be high, or raise rates that might otherwise be low. The moral of the story is that when you see unusual patterns of responding that seem inconsistent with actual contingencies in effect, you should consider the possibility that instructions or verbal behavior in other forms is complicating the picture.

 Assuming you adhere to *ethical rules* (obtaining informed consent, debriefing, and so on), try this: first, ask the responder to describe the schedule, and then reinforce statements ("You're getting close," etc.) that successively approximate the description of a contingency that would support a particular rate or pattern you have pre-selected. Finally, see whether the responder begins to behave in a way consistent with the description. You might also try the same exercise, but make the target description one that specifies what the responder should do. Does one of these have bigger or more consistent effects on behavior than the other?

We would not encourage you to misinform anyone other than as a didactic example, but you can begin to see how people might *misinform themselves* under ambiguous circumstances. They could generate hypotheses about contingencies and then begin to act as if those actually were operating. Convinced that the things one says to oneself can have an especially powerful impact on patterns of responding under various reinforcement schedules, many researchers posit that such self-statements may account for the differences in response patterns between humans and animals. Although Weiner (1983) argued that this is an oversimplification, it is clear that instructions about contingencies may influence performance, especially under relatively weak reinforcing contingencies. The main point is that people may behave differently from one another under ambiguous situations due to the instructions they give themselves. So, if you want to establish a pattern that is consistent with the contingencies in effect, you should first see if you can prevent verbalization altogether. But that can be exceedingly difficult, so the next best thing is to provide very clear and accurate descriptions of the reinforcement schedule in effect. (For example, "If you turn in your report at the end of every pay period, I will read and give you feedback on it within the following week.") If, instead, you would like to shift to a new schedule from one that has been supporting a high (or low) rate while hoping for the ongoing rate to persist, saying nothing may be best. The change may go unnoticed as folks continue their established patterns.

As we have seen, people are not always taken in by misleading rules. Note what happened when instructions regarding schedules were *deliberately* misleading, as in an investigation by Okouchi (1999). Three subjects were told to respond slowly but received reinforcers for responding rapidly (actually a DRH schedule), or were instructed to respond rapidly but gained reinforcers for adhering to a DRL schedule. Participants learned to do the *opposite* of what the instructions told them to do. Interestingly, they persisted with those contrary rates afterward, despite a shift to a fixed-interval schedule for which those particular rate contingencies were now irrelevant.

You already know that instructions can influence performance under interval schedules. Demonstrations may also be effective as instructions, as when the experimenter presses a button rapidly or slowly to show how an apparatus works. "Watch Willie," his teacher directs, as Willie dribbles the basketball. The others pick up Willie's tempo.

Other events can influence response rates or tempos, too. We are told, and for all we know it could be true, that some restaurants play music with a rapid beat to encourage their patrons to eat quickly so they can turn over the seating to new customers. Try applauding in a random pattern while others in the audience clap in unison. That's hard to do. When everyone else is enunciating slowly, speaking rapidly may be difficult. *The influence of the performance patterns of others on rates of responding* is called **social facilitation** (Hake & Laws, 1967).[4] While much needs to be learned about the fine details of control exerted by social stimuli (Hake et al., 1983), social facilitation may exert a powerful effect when you want to alter rates of responding within groups, as the research on modeling has indicated (see Chapter 18).

We guess that social facilitation will most probably influence response rates when many members of the group, especially prestigious leaders, support the pace. An interesting example is an episode that occurred in a noisy manufacturing plant in Israel (Zohar, Cohen, & Azar, 1980). The objective was to increase workers' rates of using earplugs to protect their hearing. Regular feedback was supplied, indicating the amount of temporary hearing loss employees suffered each day when failing to use ear plugs. Eventually, most of the workforce used the protection. This effect then carried over to new employees, who never received the feedback but who did see most of their co-workers using the protectors. (Some might say the *corporate culture* had been modified.)

You see something similar happening when you feel yourself compelled to conform because the audience hushes in preparation for the opening of the curtain, or shouts and cheers as the quarterback crosses over into the end zone. Generate a few examples of your own. The moral: Find a way to encourage many group members to meet a standard of performance, such as a rate or accuracy standard, and the others may fall in line (as in modeling). Then seize opportunities to reinforce the behavior of the group as a whole. ("Everyone is hard at work. That will give us time for an extra break today.") Ergo, if you find using interval schedules to be more practical, first interpose a phase during which you promote rates and sustain them for a while at the level more closely corresponding to your standard for success.

---

[4] A similar phenomenon may be at work with "group conformity," a concept studied extensively by social psychologists (See Feldman, 1985, pp. 334–346.)

## Arrange Competition

*Competition* describes a situation in which reinforcers are unequally accessible to members of a group or to individuals. Only one team can be victorious; just one student wins the spelling bee; a few out of many ticket purchasers succeed in winning small lottery prizes, only one the grand prize. But how do competitive contingencies affect response rates supported by fixed-interval reinforcer delivery? Buskist, Morgan, and Rossi (1984) conducted an experiment in which two individuals either worked alone, or competed for points during an FI 30 second schedule. Regardless of whether or not subjects were informed of the competitive contingency in effect, their rates of responding increased substantially under the competitive arrangement. When told about the competition in effect, subjects increased their rates rapidly; those left to discover the contingencies for themselves took a while to increase their responses.

In a somewhat different situation (Schmitt, 1987), however, college students worked under a low-paying individual contingency versus either concurrent individual or cooperative or competitive contingencies. While individual and cooperative contingencies produced higher response rates, during competitive contingencies those rates were quite a bit lower, and participants tended to avoid competing most of the time. Yet when those participants *did* opt to compete, they responded at very high rates. The picture became even more complicated as contests lengthened, as overall rates of competitive responding occurred, and as contests and lower paying alternative contingencies were unavailable. Schmidt concluded that the effect of group contingency arrangements depends on a number of variables including response alternatives, choice conditions, group size, task type, and others.

When one person's or team's win (reinforcement) means another's loss (extinction), conflict or (extinction-induced) aggression may result. Yet, as a contingency manager, you need not deny the loser(s) reinforcers entirely, but only partially or even not at all. Multiple winners may be feasible. Points for each exercise in a gymnastics competition or for each hand in a bridge game, offers of particular jobs when plenty are available, and being the winning team(s) in the Good Behavior Game (Barrish, Saunders, & Wolf, 1969) are examples, because if each team achieves a given criterion, each can win. (See Chapter 28 for a description of the Good Behavior Game.) You also saw earlier how a collective team effort may inspire mutual collaboration and support (Frankowsky & Sulzer-Azaroff, 1978). Ludwig, Biggs, Wagner, and Geller (2001) observed 82 pizza deliverers' use of turn-signals and safety-belts, and stopping completely at intersections. Each week the deliverer with the highest average performance was rewarded with a free vehicle-maintenance coupon. Turn-signal use increased 22 percent and stayed there during the withdrawal phase. Complete intersection stopping increased by 17 percent from baseline to the intervention phase and also was maintained. Winners, of course, displayed the most improvement, but non-winners also became safer drivers.

So, should you find yourself in a situation in which it would be impractical for you to *maintain* the kinds of schedules that promote high rates of responding, such as variable-ratio and differential reinforcement of high rates, *consider adding a bit of competition from time to time*. Make a game of it. You may find the rates increasing over those that ordinarily would be generated under interval-reinforcement schedules alone.

## Capitalize on Behavioral Contrast

Another way you might be temporarily able to alter the rate of responding under interval schedules, especially when direct-acting strategies are impractical, is to take advantage of the **behavioral contrast** phenomenon (Hantula & Crowell, 1994; McSweeney, 1982; see also Williams, 1997[5]). This is the phenomenon you observe when two (or more) different schedules alternate and reinforcement is discontinued for one of them. Typically, while the rate of responding during this component decreases, the rate of responding during the other component increases. *Sometimes the increase in one response*

---

[5]Actually, considerable laboratory research has been conducted on the behavioral contrast phenomenon. Williams' 1997 paper reviews a text covering that literature (Flaherty, *Incentive Relativity*, 1996).

*(in the unchanged environment) that accompanies a decrease in responding in the intervention environment* is called **positive behavioral contrast**, whereas *a decrease of responding (in the non-intervention environment) that accompanies an increase in the other* has been called **negative behavioral contrast**.

Whatever the interpretation of how it works, behavioral contrast is a phenomenon that you can observe. Watch your own behavior. You may see instances of a schedule change affecting one of your own unrelated performances, such as when your rates of study drop during the days preceding your going home for the holidays versus during your normal routine. An instance of *negative behavioral contrast* among developmentally-delayed clients is that as they began to receive extra reinforcers for progress, in other areas their rates of practicing self-help skills may fall off, despite an unchanging reinforcement schedule associated with progress in the latter area.

For further clarification, let us consider some additional examples: A teacher increases the reinforcers she delivers when her students perform well in spelling (but not when they improve in other areas). It would not be unusual in this situation to see their spelling improve but time spent on studying math *decrease*, even though no change was made in the reinforcement schedule of studying math. This phenomenon illustrates *negative behavioral contrast*. Now let us consider an example of positive behavioral contrast: You withhold reinforcers when students push one another at school. While pushing decreases at school, pushing siblings increases at home despite no change in the reinforcement schedule implemented in the home. Now, to assure yourself that you understand the concept, we suggest you generate a few examples of positive and negative behavioral contrast on your own and check them out with others in the know to make sure you understand the concept.

Of course, behavioral contrast is not always predictable. But, as Redmon and Farris (1987) advise:

> if a change in the schedule of reinforcement in one situation or setting is likely to have effects on behavior in other settings, then coordinated intervention is a necessity. Thus, in the case where children move from one environment to another or from activity to activity, program changes in one component should be coordinated with conditions in other components. (p. 331)

Depending on behavioral contrast effects, though, is not necessarily the most reliable approach, because the histories and current contingencies in each person's life differ from one to the next. So, you may not want to become overly dependent on generating contrast effects as a method for altering rates. Nevertheless, particularly when you recognize that circumstances will interfere with your own control over the contingencies for a while, and when other alternatives are unavailable, consider giving it a try. Behavioral contrast also is known to occur under extinction and/or DRO conditions. (See Chapter 26 for examples of behavioral contrast with extinction and Chapter 28 for DRO examples of behavioral contrast.)

**Differentiating behavioral contrast from the matching law.** Behavioral contrast occasionally is confused with the matching law (described in Chapter 22). Recall that the matching law involves *different behaviors*. Or as Catania (2013) emphasizes, the matching law maintains that "the relative rates of different responses tend to equal the relative reinforcement rates they produce" (p. 449). Behavioral contrast involves separate schedules of reinforcement across at least two separate environments for *the same* behavior.

## Heighten Response Rates under Interval Schedules by Interspersing Easy Tasks

Cates et al. (1999) posited that distributing easy tasks among more difficult ones may transform an activity into one that becomes more intrinsically reinforcing. By scattering additional brief easy tasks within more difficult assignments, they discovered that students' performance under interval schedules of reinforcement increased. Billington, Skinner, Hutchins, and Malone (2004) obtained similar results among college students when they distributed easy problems among more difficult sets. You might be able to capitalize on this phenomenon by occasionally interlacing easier tasks within the more difficult ones when attempting to teach your personnel or students new, challenging skills. Also, as pointed out in Chapter 27, this interspersal strategy has the advantage of supporting the development of greater fluency and retention because it provides additional practice opportunities.

## HOW MIGHT REINFORCING ONE RESPONSE AFFECT OTHER RESPONSES?

You already have seen the way one schedule of reinforcement can influence behavior under a different schedule. Interestingly, though, organisms, especially humans, do not necessarily limit their response choices to the one with the highest payoff. Rather, they tend to distribute their schedule choices across the various options available to them. In fact, when all other confounding factors presumably are controlled (a rare situation with humans living in open societies), human and other animals as pointed out in Chapter 22, often *match or distribute their responses in choice situations according to the proportion of payoff.* If pecking one key yields a pigeon grain 40 percent of the time and pecking the other yields the grain 60 percent of the time, the pigeon will tend to peck the first one about 40 percent of the time and the second about 60 percent. Or simply stated, we tend to engage in more or the behavior that produces the highest levels of reinforcement, and less in behavior that produces lower reinforcement. This phenomenon, labeled the **matching law** (Herrnstein, 1961; 1970), has been found to apply to behavior under certain circumstances. One example, reported by Borrero and Vollmer (2002), involved clients with severe behavior problems. Their participants tended to match their rates of maladaptive behavior to their historical payoff rates.

Be cautious when invoking the matching law, though, because such findings hold only under certain circumstances. Matching is usually studied with concurrent schedules, wherein each of two or more responses (e.g., a pigeon's pecks on a left key or on a right key) is maintained by a different schedule.

Furthermore, matching is most evident with clearly independent concurrent VI schedules. Matching also occurs with concurrent VR schedules, but only in a very limited sense. Responding usually drifts to one key or the other, typically the one with the lower ratio of responses to reinforcers (fewer responses per payoff), so that eventually all responses occur on that one key and all reinforcers are produced by pecks on that key. Eventually 100 percent of the responses are allotted to one key; 0 percent to the other, and 100 percent of the reinforcers are produced on that key and 0 percent on the other. This too is a form of readily analyzed matching.

Conceptual discussions aside, practitioners will want to know whether singling out one behavior to reinforce more frequently will affect other behaviors. Of course this can happen. As argued by Balsam and Bondy (1983), positive reinforcement, like punishment (as you will learn) tends to have collateral effects. Mace et al. (1990) pointed out: "Matching theory predicts that as the relative richness of reinforcement favors one behavior, responding on concurrent alternatives will decrease, regardless of whether the alternative behaviors are aberrant or adaptive" (p. 198). Dishion, Spracklen, Andrews, and Patterson (1996) analyzed data from 181 dyads and found that relative rates of discussing rule breaking by adolescents were proportional to the relative rates of reinforcers (laughing) provided by peers. Similarly, Borrero et al. (2007) found "positive correlations between relative response allocation and relative reinforcer rates" (p. 598) for college students discussing juvenile delinquency. (The reinforcer was a confederate making statements of agreement, e.g., "I agree with that point.") Remember, though, that beyond relative rates of payoff, other factors, including satiation, adaptation, and habituation also influence the way individuals distribute their responses.

Despite whether it is a general or global property of behavior or, more likely, a product of more basic processes as they interact within specific arrangements of reinforcement contingencies, you can still use the matching law to your advantage. Suppose an individual is spending too much time on one activity and not enough on another. Increasing the rate of reinforcer delivery for the lower-frequency activity might help balance the way the person allocates his/her time. To illustrate, one of us consulted with a teacher who had a student who frequently read even during times he was to do his math. The suggestion was that the teacher double her reinforcers, the attention she gave him, when the student worked on and completed math assignments. (She also decreased her attention to reading.) The boy's math work increased while the reading no longer occurred during math. A similar program could be designed for a worker who spends too much time on one activity and not enough on another. The supervisor could significantly increase the attention given to the second activity. But of course we do not need to know the quantitative details of matching to develop such applications.

*Recognize also that the interactions summarized in the matching law also can operate to your disadvantage.* Mace et al. (1990) worked with two boys, Glenn, a 16-year-old with a record of delinquency, and Phil, a 12-year-old functioning in the profound range of intellectual disability. When given equal rates of reinforcers for multiplication and division problems, Glenn distributed his responses almost equally to both. When the reinforcers were doubled for one type of problem and held constant for the other, his responding almost doubled for the academic task for which the reinforcers were doubled, but it diminished for the other academic task even though the reinforcement rate for that task was held constant. Phil responded similarly, gradually responding less to the academic task for which the rate of reinforcers was held constant. As Mace et al. noted, increasing the rate of reinforcer delivery for one response may "have undesirable effects on other behaviors that may be adaptive" (p. 203). This kind of negative behavioral contrast effect is most likely when each response has the same function, i.e., produces the same reinforcers.

As in our discussion above about concurrent ratio schedules, humans and other organisms (e.g., Paronis, Gasior, & Bergman, 2002) may maximize or restrict responding mainly, and perhaps exclusively, to alternatives that previously yielded the highest payoffs. For a dramatic example, watch a gambler who has experienced a "winning streak." She may forget about eating, sleeping, loving, or partaking in any alternative available reinforcers whatsoever.[6] Many years of follow-up research, however, have shown that additional factors may influence the way organisms distribute their responding under different schedules. These include whether the schedule is variable or fixed (Herrnstein, 1964, showed that pigeons prefer variable schedules to fixed schedules. Similarly, as mentioned in the previous chapter, Mullane, et al., 2017, found that humans also appear to prefer variable over fixed schedules). Also, regarding antecedent stimuli, people prefer informative stimuli to uninformative stimuli (Catania, 1975), and prefer free choice to forced choice (Catania & Sagvolden, 1980). (See also Fisher & Mazer, 1997, for coverage of basic versus applied research on choice behavior and Catania's 2013 text for a more extensive discussion of this topic.)

People's sensitivity to particular schedules may vary from one individual to the next. Some respond as though unaware of the schedule in effect, even though it might seem fairly obvious to others. This seems to be the case particularly with youngsters on the autism spectrum, who often fail to maximize (i.e., select the choice with the richest payoff) and are often less responsive to extinction conditions than their typical peers (Mullins & Rincover, 1985). Similarly, Murray and Kollins (2000) reported that Ritalin, or methylphenidate, makes the relative rates of responding of children with ADHD more consistent with that predicted by the matching law. But sub-optimal responding is by no means restricted to those with developmental challenges. Behavioral economists (e.g., Hursh, 1984; Myerson & Green, 1995; and others) have studied the influence of various parameters of reinforcement upon (often suboptimal) choice, as in deciding what and when to buy or sell in the stock market or making other significant economic decisions.

Making wise choices to maximize one's reinforcers is important in many situations in life: selecting the best job, mate, most supportive social group, and so on. You can see the kinds of problems that might arise when people are insensitive to

---

[6]This often is the case in addictions to drugs, alcohol, typical or atypical sexual acts, exercise, and others.

schedule variations. Conversely, though, not being affected by differences in schedules sometimes can be advantageous, as when people undergo transitions from managed reinforcer deliveries for adaptive behavior within school or work environments to the sporadic reinforcement contingencies of less-structured settings.

## SCHEDULE INTERACTIONS

Probably it has occurred to you that all of us behave under a multiplicity of antecedent stimuli and schedules of positive and aversive contingencies. Some affect what we do on the job; others, our interactions with people at home and in the community; still others relate to our own self-care, our inner thoughts and feelings, leisure and recreational activities, and so on. These complex contingencies vie for ascendance at any point in time. Do the events setting the occasion for meal preparation activities take precedence over looming deadlines at work, demanding that we remain at the computer? The same complexity affects those with whom we interact on a daily basis—our family members, friends, service providers, colleagues, clientele, and so on.

Familiarizing yourself with the behavioral characteristics associated with particular schedules of reinforcement should help you both to understand and manage current performance and anticipate future behavioral patterns. You would expect, for example, that rates will accelerate toward the end of the interval when a response has been reinforced on a *fixed-interval* schedule, and that those patterns will persist for a while during the early phases of extinction.

Nevertheless, many factors complicate our ability to predict, interpret, and manage specific response patterns on the basis of just one particular schedule. The picture is far more complex. We already have learned about individual variations in terms of schedule effectiveness and the influence of history and social variables (e.g., models). Another is that reinforcement schedules may influence one another in different ways.

People rarely spend their entire day repeating the same thing. One reason is that *the value of any given reinforcer alters from one time to another.*  Food is more reinforcing after we have not eaten for a while than following a big meal. Engaging in social interactions, performing job responsibilities, and/or enjoying recreational activities are similarly affected by prior and concurrent reinforcement schedules. Additionally, different concurrent or sequential schedules of reinforcement are often operating at any given point in time. One of the authors, for example, could work on this book, cook chicken soup, read the newspaper, and/or listen to music. Which one I actually do depends on many variables.

These complex schedule arrangements interact with one another, thereby influencing response distributions and patterns. When two fixed-ratio schedules, one short and one long, are in effect at the same time, people tend to emit the response required by the shorter ratio rather than the longer. So, if you want responding to continue under a fixed-ratio schedule, do not allow some other response to produce the reinforcer according to a shorter fixed-ratio reinforcement schedule. If you hope your staff will keep working at one task until break time, resist the temptation to give them a different, shorter task until after the first one is complete.

When two different schedules with different proportions of payoff operate simultaneously, you may see people distributing their responding across the two schedules. Bruno plays his favorite melodies and his playing is intrinsically reinforced by the music. His mother praises his performance of her favorite selections, some of which have passages that Bruno loves to hear while others contain parts he doesn't like at all. Bruno distributes his practicing rather than sticking with one category.

Perhaps the complexity of schedules of reinforcement discourages you. Are you holding your head and saying, "Why bother? The tangle of interacting schedules is so complicated, I might as well forget it." Please don't give up! Instead, use this information to help yourself to:

- try to understand mysterious changes in your own and others' behavioral patterns.
- alter rates indirectly by capitalizing on contrast effects (pour on the reinforcers for making acceptable choices or withhold them from all but the one you want to see increase).
- find ways to override the influence exerted by schedules over which you have little or no control. Despite those kinds of ongoing competing schedules, you may well achieve your objective by heavily reinforcing the target behavior.

Notice! You have finished reading a good portion of this book. Consider the schedules that have sustained your own diligence!

That answer brings us full circle: Recall how we need to *responsibly* revisit and re-prioritize the goals and objectives with and/or for our clients; choose, revise or design methods to measure the behavior of concern over time; identify powerful reinforcers or develop new, more promising ones—*contingencies that will take precedence over any others, especially those operating inefficiently or counterproductively*; select analytic designs; assess baseline performance, then apply, monitor, and, informed by the data, adjust the intervention as necessary and experimentally analyze the short- and long-term impact of the intervention. Then we must remember to maintain and expand the scope of the new, more preferred performance patterns.

## SUMMARY AND CONCLUSIONS

Identifying, selecting, and applying contingencies powerful enough to override those currently operating at a less efficient, effective, or even counterproductive level is no simple task. Nor should we overlook the moral responsibility we assume in so doing—to serve and benefit our clientele without causing harm to them or to others; not just now but in the foreseeable future.

Shifting to intermittent reinforcement is crucial to the long-term success of just about any behavioral intervention. In Chapters 22 and 23 we have covered several forms of intermittent reinforcement. (See Table 23.1 for a review and summary of an array of different schedules, the contingencies they arrange, and the general nature of their impact.) Interval schedules are among the most convenient to use in applied settings because they do not require constant vigilance. Instead, they permit reinforcers to be delivered contingent on the target behavior, following the passage of fixed or variable intervals. When applying interval schedules, be certain the response you are supporting has occurred before you apply any reinforcers. Otherwise, you may inadvertently reinforce and thereby strengthen the wrong responses or fail to strengthen the targeted response at all.

Responding is apt to continue longer under extinction when the individual has experienced a variable-ratio or variable-interval, as opposed to fixed schedules. It also is likely to persist longer if the schedule should shift from a ratio to an interval format. Differential reinforcement of either high or low rates of responding also may be used to shift the response patterns in the desired direction, as may paced-responding schedules. Also recall that in some instances, temporarily switching from intermittent to continuous reinforcement prior to placing *unwanted* behaviors on extinction has proven beneficial.

The impact of interval schedules can be heightened by providing clear instructions or rules; interspersing competitive contingencies; and combining with limited hold, imitative prompts, and DRH. Nevertheless, the multitude of schedules of reinforcement affecting any given individual at a given point in time may heighten or lessen the particular pattern of the behavior of concern.

**TABLE 23.1  Basic Schedules**

| Name and Abbreviation | | Contingency | Comment |
|---|---|---|---|
| Variable interval (Random interval) | VI (RI) | $t$ s, then 1 response | $t$ varies; with random intervals, response rate is roughly constant |
| Fixed interval | FI | $t$ s, then 1 response | $t$ constant; generates FI scallops |
| Variable ratio (Random ratio) | VR (RR) | $n$ responses | $n$ varies; high constant rates, but large $n$ may produce ratio strain |
| Fixed ratio | FR | $n$ responses | $n$ constant; generates postreinforcement pauses and high-rate runs |
| Lag schedule | LAG | Reinforcer provided only if response different from x previous responses | Promotes response variability |
| Variable time | VT | $t$ s | $t$ varies; reinforcers are response independent |
| Fixed time | FT | $t$ s | $t$ constant; reinforcers are response independent |
| Continuous reinforcement | (FR 1) | 1 response | All responses reinforced; also abbreviated CRF |
| Extinction | EXT | | As procedure, often used even if response has never been reinforced |
| Limited hold | LH | Reinforcer cancelled if no reinforced response within $t$ s | $t$ constant if not otherwise specified; LH, added to other schedules, cannot stand alone |
| Differential reinforcement of low rate (or long IRT) | DRL | $t$ s without response, then 1 response | Maintains responding easily; decreased responding increases reinforcement and thus prevents extinction |
| Differential reinforcement of high rate | DRH | 1 response within $t$ s or less of last response | Alternatively, at least $n$ responses within $t$ s; sometimes difficult to maintain, because decreased responding reduces reinforcement |
| Differential reinforcement of paced responding | DRP | 1 response between $t$ and $t'$ s of last response | Sets both upper and lower limits on reinforceable response rates |
| Differential reinforcement of other behavior | DRO | $t$ s without response | A negative-punishment or omission procedure; ordinarily decreases rate of designated response |

\* $t$ s = time in seconds; $n$ = number of responses

*Chapter 24*

# Organizational Performance Management Systems: Supervising and Supporting Contingency Managers

## Goals

1. Describe and explain the importance of behavioral-analytic programming in an organization's function.
2. Define and illustrate a *behavioral package* or program.
3. List and discuss the importance of each of the following stimulus control and reinforcement strategies for promoting program implementation:
    a. being present when program is initiated
    b. prompting, as needed
    c. feedback
    d. removing aversive stimuli
    e. combining feedback with prompts and reinforcers
    f. providing frequent feedback and reinforcement

4. Define *feedback* and describe how to provide and maximize the effect of feedback through:
    a. constructive, precise communication
    b. source
    c. form
    d. timing
    e. goal-setting
    f. prompting
    g. reinforcing

5. Offer examples of positive and negative reinforcers that have been used successfully on the program implementers' behavior.

6. List and discuss the importance of each of the following strategies for sustaining program implementation:
   a. using prompts as needed, and gradually decreasing them
   b. identifying and using a variety of reinforcing sources in the natural environment
   c. gradually decreasing the behavior analyst's support (while those from the natural environment remain intact)
   d. promoting generalization

*************

## FUNCTION MATTERS MOST

Organizations are designed to accomplish specific purposes: In business, ultimately to profit owners or shareholders; in service or educational establishments, to improve the lives and circumstances of clientele now and in the future; with families, to enable their members to move toward self-sufficiency and satisfaction, and so on. Only those whose members contribute toward those ends will survive and flourish.

If we accept the assumption that all members of an organization contribute toward the organization's mission, their performance, needs to be analyzed and emphasized immediately as well as over the long term. The actions of each and every person, staff member, and leader must clearly contribute to the mission of the organization. Managers, staff specialists, direct-line personnel, and others must consistently promote the production and delivery of top-quality goods and/or ethically acceptable and effective services at the lowest feasible cost.

Consider, then, your own responsibilities in your capacity as an applied behavior analyst. Is it to retain or expand the customer base of a business? To support assurance of quality products or services? To help promote and retain skilled personnel? To assist in cost containment? To advance client progress rates? These kinds of prospective and ongoing considerations can make a major difference because they will guide your choice of activities and allocation of time, effort, and human and material resources. Then observe and record the way you expend those, asking yourself in the meantime how good the fit is. There is a reasonable chance that you will make some changes as a result. If you do, then as you have learned repeatedly, be sure to find a doable way to monitor and analyze the impact of those changes.

During that process, remind yourself that just as your growing garden requires ongoing care if your plants and flowers are to flourish, your behavior-analytic programs need careful nurturing if their positive effects are to thrive. In Chapter 3, we presented ways to provide a supportive environment for selecting and developing programs, including supervisory methods for promoting *treatment integrity*, (i.e., ensuring that intervention programs are implemented as planned). Here we expand upon that topic. Earlier, we also shared methods for maximizing the effectiveness of particular behavior-change procedures, generally at the small-group level.[1] This chapter broadens the focus to include more complex **behavioral packages** (i.e., *the combination of two or more selected behavioral procedures*) designed to increase and maintain the high quality performance at an organization-wide level.

## PROGRAM IMPLEMENTATION

When faced with a behavioral challenge, our first response tends to be to try to fix it hurriedly by applying a familiar change program. But in our haste, we may pay insufficient attention to main-

---
[1] Also see Chapter 3 for methods of increasing rates of program implementation.

taining the program over time. As Sugai and Horner (1999) have pointed out, "the real challenge is not identifying and developing new strategies, but in delivering and maintaining these strategies..." (p. 12). In 2006, these same authors offered a model for expanding and sustaining positive behavioral support on a school-wide basis (See Figure 24.1). As emphasized in Chapter 3, if we fail to arrange properly in advance and to regularly support our programs, we risk their lapsing back to baseline.

To avoid this tendency, after a program has been jointly chosen and affirmed by those involved, and the date and time has been set for its implementation, we must plan ways to assure it continues intact. Fortunately, our field has devoted considerable effort toward designing and analyzing methods for promoting and supporting such efforts.[2] In this chapter we offer suggestions that may keep you from abandoning your efforts prematurely.

## Be Present and Supportive

Our presence is crucial to help solve problems that may develop or to demonstrate appropriate procedures, especially in the early stages of a new intervention. Suppose we had suggested that a teacher might use modeling[3] to instruct Johnny to raise his hand for attention. The teacher remembered to reinforce the model's appropriate hand-raising, but not Johnny's act of imitating the model's behavior. If we are on site, we can observe that omission, signal the teacher to add the missing piece (reinforcing the imitation) and convey approval when the teacher complies. (As we emphasize, instead of harping on examples of poor performance, behavior analysts need to provide heavy doses of positive recognition for meritorious personnel performance [Reid & Parsons, 2006]. Otherwise, they run the risk that their presence will become aversive and that they will be avoided by the behavior change agent.)

---

[2]*The Journal of Organizational Behavior Management* devotes itself to exactly these kinds of issues.

[3]See the section on effective use of modeling in Chapter 18 and Chapters 27 and 28.

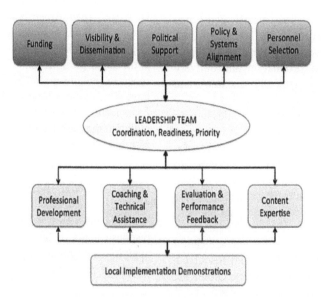

**Figure 24.1** Sugai & Horner (2006)

Our presence also has another advantage, in that it can prompt contingency managers[4] to implement the program as designed, particularly if we previously have been sure to reinforce proper program implementation. Safety directors who make it a point to detour through different areas of the plant each day and to compliment peers for supporting their fellow employees' adherence to safe practices, simply by their presence, will prompt peers to continue that practice.

## Use Prompts Temporarily and Only as Necessary

Change agents can become so wrapped up in their ongoing activities that they overlook using their newly learned behavioral skills. Under such circumstances, you might provide them with additional prompts (modeling, cues, reminders, instructions, directions, data displays). To illustrate, Hall, Lund, and Jackson (1968) found that holding up a colored piece of paper reminded staff to apply reinforcement.[5] However, be careful not to over-prompt, as too much prompting can lead to overdependence and/or resentment. Too many reminders (think "nagging") to a foreman to praise his deserving crew or to a parent to apply a token economy according to design certainly can cause resentment. Be particularly sensitive to any signs that you might be over-prompting.

As a tool for training four care-providers to apply reinforcement practices, Taber, Lambright, and Luiselli (2017) displayed a video model of staff interacting with a student in a program for students with ASD and related disabilities. The video showed a novel care provider offering labeled praise in a form that encouraged a reciprocal response (e.g., "You are doing a good job staying in your seat, *aren't you*?" p. 190). The model care-provider also demonstrated conversational exchanges further to promote reciprocal attention (e.g., the caregiver says, "What do you want to say to mommy and daddy?" The client responds, "I want to say hi to mommy and daddy.") The video also demonstrated using specific praise for other behaviors; including those not involving the promotion of reciprocal exchanges. After viewing the video just once, all four care providers increased their use of reciprocal and differential attention with an 18-year old female with ASD, whose aggressive behavior (e.g., slapping, biting, pushing, and hair pulling) in turn decreased substantially. So again, we see the importance of training personnel to maintain a richly reinforcing environment.

In addition to using modeling or imitative prompts, you might ask the contingency managers to collect observational data on one another's targeted behaviors, because those who observe others performing the new skill may find themselves prompted to implement the program. For example, Sasson and Austin (2004) requested computer-terminal operators to observe and collect observational data on other computer operators' safety-related behaviors. They reported that participants who conducted safety observations of other participants performed more safely than participants who did not participate in the observation process. In addition, these changes remained during a four-month follow-up evaluation. Thus, consider requesting that program implementers not only periodically observe, but also take data on the performance of other change agents. Also, be sure to fade your own prompts over time to enable the implementer to gain increasing independence while maintaining good behavioral practices (e.g., have them record data on themselves).

You also might want to consider using a "bug-in-ear" to help prompt those learning to apply ABA procedures. Investigators (Artman-Meeker, Rosenberg, Badgett, Yang, & Penney, 2017) found that by using the "bug-in-ear" they were able to improve fidelity of implementation, and create more verbal learning opportunities for pre-school children with autism.

---

[4]We use the terms "program implementer," "contingency manager" or "change agent" interchangeably to denote the manager of the programmatic contingencies. This individual may or may not be a qualified and/or a Registered Behavior Technician® (RBT).

[5]The effect was similar to that achieved when Zeilberger, Sampen, & Sloan (1968) nodded—a consequence—when personnel did follow through.

## Provide Feedback on Program Implementation

### What is Feedback?

*Miriam-Webster (*on line) defines *feedback* as "the transmission of evaluative or corrective information to the original or controlling source about an action, event, or process." Within the organizational behavior management field, **feedback** generally is viewed as *the return of information in a form that can influence behavior.* Delivering feedback is one of the most useful and powerful management tools you can use within a commercial, educational, or service organization, or within a family, and it appears to be a primary factor for improving treatment integrity (Codding, Livanis, Pace, & Vaca, 2008). Feedback can be natural, unintentional, or carefully managed. Its form can vary too, from a subtle facial expression or gesture, to a set of general spoken comments (e.g., "Nice job!" "Good going!" "Ah hah!" "That was awful!" "Aargh!"), to precise quantitative measures (e.g., "Your praise has increased from a baseline of about three times an hour to six times an hour. That's really great!" "That was the tenth time in a row you returned from your break on time!") In other words, as Mangiapanello and Hemmes (2015) have pointed out, productive feedback, simply consists of the application of good operant conditioning procedures.

Each of these actions shows that you observed and are acknowledging what the other(s) said or did. Notice, though, that feedback is not necessarily a reinforcer, though of course it can function as one. What, then, *is* the function of feedback? In simple terms, *feedback supplies information on performance.* Feedback can operate as a discriminative stimulus, signaling that reinforcers, or punishers, or something ambiguous, or nothing special is likely to follow that particular event. By recognizing the various possible functions of feedback, we then can apply it more wisely, primarily by making our own feedback into a stimulus that signals reinforcement (an $S^{Dr}$). Then, when repeated over time, ultimately the feedback will evolve into a conditioned reinforcer rather than becoming aversive.

### *Maximizing the Effects of Feedback for Improving Performance*

**Provide constructive, precise communication.** When your objective is to improve performance, making the feedback *specific* and *constructive* rather than vague or aversive is preferable; that is, you will want to communicate as precisely as possible what about the performance was done correctly. Generally, you can ignore non-exemplary performance, other than when correcting it right away is imperative. Your audience probably will catch on to the aspects you are not mentioning pretty fast, especially if those features are listed for all to see. *Clear* performance feedback provides precise instructions to guide correct future performance. Therefore, to be effective, *feedback must be specific and comprehensible.* To illustrate, Rice, Austin, and Gravina (2009) found that they could increase employee's correct greetings, from 11.5 percent to 66 percent, and closing behaviors from eight percent to 70 percent, by combining task clarification and manager-delivered social praise. Similarly, when we attempted to heighten worker safety, instead of providing general feedback about the way workers arranged their environments or used their equipment ("Good job!" or "You're being safe!"), we supplied them with checklists specifying exactly what they did well and, by implication, what they might do in the future to improve their performance.

Your skills in setting and defining behavioral objectives, and in counting, measuring, recording and graphing, will come in handy because you will know precisely how to phrase your comments: "Nice going! You bent your knees and not your back. That will help keep your back safe." "Great! You waited a full six seconds before providing a prompt. That takes patience."

**Consider the source of feedback.** Feedback can derive from many sources: natural ones, like watching a nail enter a board as you hammer it; actions of others, like the boss's congratulatory handshake or pats on the back; mechanisms like performance reports; inventory printouts; speeding tickets; audience ratings. Familiar examples of feedback sources in service settings include, among others:

- periodic performance appraisals
- tallies of products (lesson plans written, presentation slides prepared, quarterly reports submitted, etc.)
- spoken feedback
- video recordings
- checklists completed during or right after an activity

To illustrate, assume the program's behavior analyst is working on improving her own presentation skills. She and the senior manager have agreed on clear definitions of performance criteria: "Is responsive to audience" was defined as "Scans audience regularly"; "Invites questions and comments"; "Responds with simple clear, direct explanations." The behavior analyst asks her clinical supervisor to provide her with feedback after the presentation. Soon after the session, each takes a copy of the checklist and completes it independently, rating each item as occurring rarely, sometimes, often, very often, or as too often. The two then match their ratings and discuss instances of especially well-executed performances and suggestions for the future. Then they target a new level for the next time.

**Select forms of feedback.** You can use a variety of formats to provide reinforcing feedback: email, phone calls, texts, graphs paired with recognition and praise, thank-you notes, tokens of appreciation, complimentary notes copied to the individual's supervisor and others related to the change agent's success. (See Mayer & Wallace, 2020, for numerous other examples.) Formal systems of feedback are useful not only with parents and educators, but also in promoting all types of employee performances in a range of settings such as hockey teams (Anderson, Crowell, Domen, & Howard, 1988), electrical utilities industries (Petty, Singleton, & Connell, 1992), bank tellers (Crowell, Anderson, Abel, & Sergio, 1988), textile factories (Welsh, Luthans, & Sommer, 1993), hotel banquet staff (LaFleur & Hyten, 1995), and nursing-home staff (Hawkins, Burgio, Lanford, & Engel, 1992). However, recall that because of contextual variables, such as motivational operations, the reinforcing value of any given stimulus can vary from person to person and time to time.

As emphasized in Chapter 11, to support behavior change, select reinforcers integral to the natural environment and likely to function effectively with the recipient under the circumstances.

Programs lacking ongoing feedback risk failure. To illustrate, MacDonald, Gallimore, and MacDonald (1970) noted that parents and relatives needed support (feedback and reinforcement) in the form of face-to-face meetings or phone conversations *at least twice a week* for them to maintain behavioral contracts made with their adolescents for increasing school attendance. In a related study, Hunt and Sulzer-Azaroff (1974) contacted one group of parents regularly twice a week beginning the day after a behavior-management program was developed for their child. A second group was not contacted for several weeks. All the parents in the regularly-contacted group but only 25 percent of those in the second (non-contacted) group continued to implement the program. In other words, 75 percent of the non-contacted parents failed to help their child. Comparable studies with teachers (Holden & Sulzer-Azaroff, 1972) and staff in a residential care facility (Mozingo et al., 2006) reported similar results. Delivering feedback regularly is necessary until the altered behaviors are well-established. As you will note below, afterward you may gradually reduce your reinforcing feedback, *assuming the environment begins naturally to support the program*. (Notice how similar this approach is to how you manage reinforcers to change a client's behavior.) Later, we also discuss the value of involving people within the natural environment as additional important sources of feedback.

**Provide immediate feedback.** Feedback is a *behavioral consequence*, because it *follows* behavior. And, as you have learned, when it comes to consequences, *sooner is better*! To illustrate: noting that rather than immediately providing teachers with feedback on an on-going basis, feedback is often provided to teachers on the next day (Sweigart, Landrum, & Pennington, 2015). The investigators intervened by showing a middle school teacher in a mathematics resource classroom how much positive feedback she was providing to her students each session. (They transferred this information from an Excel laptop workbook to the iPad that the teacher kept within view during each session in order to provide immediate feedback). Not only did the teacher increase her use of positive feedback, but there were positive student collateral effects, including improved engagement and a decrease in student classroom disruptions.

Another example aimed to reduce selector errors in a southeastern United States food-service distributor warehouse by using a voice-assisted selecting tool that provided immediate feedback when errors occurred (Berger & Ludwig, 2007). The intervention reduced selector errors from 2.44 per 1,000 cases to 0.94, most strongly affecting on those employees who had generated the most errors during baseline. So, regardless of whether any particular feedback episode is or is not, by definition, a reinforcer or a punisher, if you deliver that consequence clearly and as soon as you possibly can, the message can begin to acquire instructional control.

**Provide feedback related to selected goal(s).** Goal-setting is a management method designed to encourage personnel to try harder—to *stretch* toward a new level, or to maintain a high level of performance. One form capitalizes on recent performance records, that serve as a basis for determining how high or far the individual or group can reasonably be expected to reach, either in the immediate and/or distant future. In *collaborative goal-setting*, as described in Chapters 3, 4, and 27, participants set the goals jointly. In other situations, the manager or supervisor may select the next and/or final level to be achieved. In either case, the proposed goal generally represents an important step forward. Box 24.1 uses a hypothetical example to illustrate the process.

**Transform feedback into a secondary reinforcer.** Assuming that at this point you have mastered the basics of behavior analysis, let us remind you of the key advantages *positive reinforcement* has over punishment and extinction: that it increases desirable behavior and promotes a beneficial spread of effect and good cheer that may encourage recipients to choose to remain in and return to the situation. So, as you might imagine, we encourage you to emphasize making your feedback as positively reinforcing as possible. Check out the contrasting scenarios in Box 24.2 to see how teachers' experi-

ence with prior consultants' style might affect their reactions to the visiting behavior analyst.

Feedback is known to be most effective when it signals reinforcement (Baron, Kaufman & Stauber, 1969). In the first example within Box 24.2, we might infer that on previous visits the behavior analyst (or other consultants) probably had emphasized criticisms and corrections, while in the second, comments were positive and supportive. (This works for individual clients, too. In Chapter 27 we point out that when Todd et al. [2002] increased specific feedback to a 4:1 ratio of positive to corrective feedback, client problem behavior decreased substantially while staff satisfaction increased.)

As a consultant or manager, certainly you want to be welcomed as helpful, rather than avoided as a threat. So, as we have said many times, try to *accentuate the positive* whenever possible, in this case by *providing more supportive than corrective feedback.*

Assuming your positive feedback *is* reinforcing, you will recognize this as differential reinforcement of incompatible behavior (DRI—see Chapter 28). Instead of waiting for the opposite of what you typically see, pausing until you *do* notice what you are looking for, does require considerable patience. But in the long run, it pays off; and this works with adults and associates just as well as with youngsters.

**Feedback alone often is insufficient.** *To be on the safe side, we suggest you augment feedback by providing a rationale, goal-setting, prompting (as necessary), problem solving, and, as always, by reinforcing progress.* Dengerink and Mayer (2018)

### Box 24.1: An Example of Goal-Setting

Especially when employee injuries are minor, the incidence reports required by law and by Port Pembroke's Paper Products' insurance carriers are often submitted much later than required by company and governmental policy. To address this deficiency, the Director of Operations assembles the supervisors and elaborates upon all the reasons why rapid reporting is important (legal, ethical, monetary, and so on). She then displays a graph of the percentage of reports turned in on time. The gap between the present level and perfection is far too wide to reasonably expect perfection to be achieved overnight. So the group decides to set a goal of 55 percent, for the next week. This is indicated with an arrow on the graph. During the following two weeks, the group meets the goal and the manager congratulates everyone. Next they discuss whether to raise the goal still higher, to 75 percent. All agree. She draws a line at the 75 percent level. They reach it twice. Heartened by their success they decide to go for 100 percent. But the team only reaches that goal once during the next four weeks. After discussing the matter and realizing that emergencies such as absent supervisors and various unanticipated crises might occur, they consent to lowering the final level to 90 percent. By the end of the nineteenth week, they have succeeded twice. "That's probably as high as any program like ours should be expected to sustain," the manager announces. "As you can see, the effort you've all made has really paid off. So, in appreciation, during the lunch break this Friday, there'll be a pizza party —on us!"

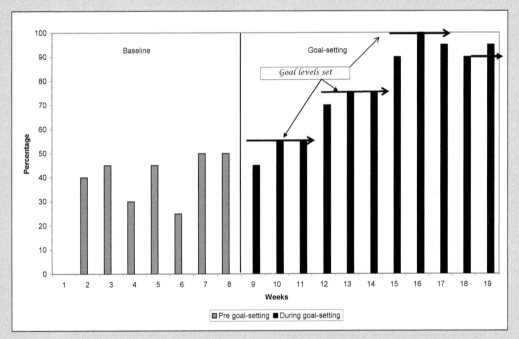

**Figure 24.2** Percentage of incident reports turned in on time prior to and during goal-setting (fictitious data).

combined these antecedent strategies in a study (described earlier in Chapter 3) involving training parents to interact more effectively with their non-compliant children. The two workshops alone produced little to no change in parent-child interactions. When, subsequently, in-home coaching, in the form of *offering rationales, prompting, modeling, feedback*, and selecting goals jointly, was added to the mix, parental approving statements increased and disapproving statements and actions decreased.

> **Box 24.2: Experience with the Consultant**
>
> There is a knock at the classroom door and it swings open. "May I come in?" the consulting behavior analyst inquires.
>
> 1. "Sure," (thinking to yourself: "Uh- oh. What am I doing wrong? Are all the kids and staff on task?
>    "Darn it. I didn't get around to organizing the new centers we talked about last week. And there's Carlos, wandering about the room instead of working on his language program.")
>    You feel your stomach tying into knots, dreading what will happen next.
>
> 2. "Great," (thinking to yourself: "Good timing! This gives me a chance to show her how I've reorganized the students' progress records.
>    "She'll see Carlos wandering the room, and probably be able to suggest how to encourage him to keep working. And, oh, right, I wanted to ask if she can help me find some new materials for the dress-up and crafts centers.")

This, in turn, resulted in significantly improved child compliance. Again, we note the value of providing follow-up support if behavior change is to be achieved. Unfortunately, training workshops limited solely to verbal instruction rarely produce meaningful, lasting behavior change in personnel performance. Rather, if parental and change-agents' efforts are to succeed and endure, prompting and positive recognition usually need to be incorporated temporarily into the program. (Periodic follow-up data collection will inform you as to when it might be appropriate to gradually begin to diminish the intensity of the program. Your best bet would be to lessen the prompting; then reduce the density of the feedback to a comfortable ongoing level.).

These feedback strategies have been found to be effective in a range of settings, beyond the classroom and the home. For example, one of the most classic employee complaints is a sense of feeling under-valued. "Our boss ignores us when we work hard or accomplish something new because, he says, this is our job and we're *supposed* to be doing it. But it sure would be nice to be recognized or rewarded for our efforts, at least once in a while." (See Mayer & Wallace, 2020, for potential reinforcers for program implementers.)

Be cautious, though, about limiting your support to feedback alone (DiGennaro et al., 2007). Rather, supplementing it by explaining why the act is important, setting goals, temporarily prompting, and especially supplying dense reinforcement initially, tapering it off a bit later on, should encourage progress (Alvero et al., 2001; Balcazar et al., 1985-86; Cossairt et al., 1973; Rose & Church, 1998). As a case in point, Huberman and O'Brien (1999) trained therapists serving adult chronic mental patients residing in group homes to set measurable goals, and to deliver verbal and graphic feedback and praise to their patients as a function of their progress toward those goals. The experimenters then provided the therapists with written and spoken feedback, praise, and monetary reinforcers contingent on their own implementation of those skills. The number of weekly staff goals and indicators of patient goal progress and activity levels increased substantially. Similarly, Jessup and Stahelski (1999) used goal-setting, performance feedback, and tangible rewards in an aluminum production plant to reduce product defects. They achieved, "a dramatic performance improvement (lowered rate of rejects)" (p. 6). Apparently, when both staff and participants are involved in the goal-setting process, both become winners. (See also Fellner & Sulzer-Azaroff, 1984 and Fellner & Sulzer-Azaroff, 1985).

Combining reinforcement with feedback also produces change more successfully. Early on, Cossairt et al. (1973) found that pairing social praise with feedback, in the form of sharing the number of intervals during which students attended to their teacher's instructions with those of teacher praise for student attending, produced more teacher praise and student attending than feedback without praise. Also, teachers found feedback without praise unpleasant or aversive to them. In a related study, feedback to teachers about how closely they were following program recommendations were combined with specific positive comments about the program implementation. That combination also improved implementation fidelity and reduced student problem behavior (Rodriguez, Loman, & Horner, 2009). Similarly, others (Rantz, Dickinson, Sinclair, & Van Houten, 2009) found pilots' compliance with items on a checklist ranged from 53 to 91 percent when they were given technical feedback alone. However, when graphic feedback and praise for improvements was added to the mix, each participant demonstrated near perfect levels of checklist performance, during seven subsequent simulated flights. Similarly, Clark, Wilder, Kelly, and Ryan (2020) found that while teaching three different parents a structured meal procedure to decrease food over-selectivity among their children with autism, just one was successful with instructions plus video modeling alone. The other two parents also required in vivo prompts and feedback to be successful.

Although it may be tempting to attack an unwanted problem directly, we remind you to try to promote the desired alternative goal behavior instead. You can accomplish that by providing personnel with a rationale for engaging in the goal performance and by supporting its acquisition through modeling and feedback (Boyce & Geller, 2001). To illustrate, four supervisors working in group homes for individuals with cognitive delays were trained to provide paraprofessional staff with rationales, verbal instructions, modeling, prompts to practice, goal-setting, praise, and feedback (Fleming, Oliver, & Bolton, 1996). "Changes in supervisor performances (in the use of the trained skills) were in turn associated with increases in or maintenance of correct teaching by paraprofessional staff" (pp. 3–4).

Following a one-hour initial training session, Printer, East, and Thrush (2015) used a combination of video feedback, self-recording, and goal setting to train middle school and high school teachers on the benefits and use of praise. More specifically, the training included how to use four different types of praise: specific individual and group praise and general individual and group praise. Teachers watched video recordings of themselves about three times per a week, for about 15 minutes each. They were requested to first record every time they used each of the four types of praise and each time they directed negative comments to an individual or to a group of students. Second, after reflecting on their number of praise and negative statements, they then selected goals for the next day. All increased their use of praise and decreased their negative statements.

Minor, DuBard, and Luiselli (2014) also found that neither correction and praise, nor feedback alone, successfully promoted teachers' rates of implementing behavior intervention programs. However, once they added problem-solving consultation, in the form of discussing potential barriers to implementation and how to overcome those, and jointly addressed procedural modifications to correct procedural misapplications, uniform improvement resulted.

Investigators (Madzharova, Sturmey, & Jones, 2012) compared two training programs for teaching staff to teach their clients how to mand (request). They compared the package of instructions, modeling, rehearsal, and feedback to modeling and feedback only. They concluded that feedback combined with modeling alone might be sufficient to train staff to acquire teaching peer-to-peer manding. It was unclear, however, if social praise was part of the feedback in this study.

Yet, "Despite a rich body of empirical evidence that supports the use of teacher praise to improve student outcomes, it continues to be underused in practice. (A recent book by Mayer (2020) describes various ways to enhance the application of reinforcement in the classroom.) Performance feedback is a promising practice to increase teacher's use of praise" (Sweigart, Collins, Evanovich, & Cook, 2016, p. 419). So, you should remember to add some form of specific recognition to your package of feedback to *change agents* (e.g., "The way you smiled and praised Mary for completing her work really seemed to please her, don't you think?" "Your pat on the back was just what John needed to give him that extra encouragement to get his report in on time." "Mike's mother called and said she was so delighted to read the progress note you sent home with her son; said it made her day." "Your clients seem to be doing so much better since you started implementing….").

Sometimes feedback relating to overall group performance produces a more powerful impact than when presented to a specific individual (Alvero et al., 2001; Boyce & Geller, 2001).[6] In such cases, peers often are observed to encourage one another to excel (Sulzer-Azaroff & Harshbarger, 1995). Nor do reinforcers necessarily need to be costly, as in the latter instance, when edible treats were occasionally offered during group celebrations for quality improvement. As Boyce and Geller (2001) also noted, simple rewards often are sufficient when attempting to promote and maintain staff performance).[7]

As a supervisor or mentor, also be sure to *provide feedback on both staff program implementation as well as with client progress.* The findings of DiGennaro et al. (2007) and others (Alvero et al., 2001; Balcazar et al., 1985–1986; Cossairt et al., 1973; Rose & Church, 1998) have demonstrated that limiting feedback to client progress alone (which can be slow and variable) may be insufficient to maintain program implementation.

Certainly, it is true that the numerous demands of the workplace can thwart our intentions to pause to assess personnel performance on the job. If that is your situation, we suggest that you, as a manager or supervisor, *schedule* a time into your daily activities to reinforce ongoing personnel efforts (and record your actual visits—perhaps by making a simple checkmark on your calendar and tallying and perhaps graphing the weekly results). Encourage your fellow managers, administrators, or supervisors to do likewise. If you are unable to undertake this particular responsibility yourself, identify others whose perspective matters to recipients so they can take the responsibility of serving as agents of feedback and reinforcement.

Accentuating positive feedback and reinforcement isn't always easy, though. This is especially true when delivering feedback under unpleasant circumstances. It seems that annoyances demand our immediate attention, which makes finding something nice to say especially difficult. When caught in that kind of bind consider the following to augment your use of positive feedback:

Prepare in advance by reminding yourself of a few praiseworthy performances that you can count on in the particular situation: Maybe the person tends to be especially neat, to maintain a well-organized setting, to help out her peers, or to have a friendly smile. You should be able to identify *something*. This personal list should supply you with a sufficient source of positive comments.

Many personnel find surprise visits punishing. Until you become sufficiently well acquainted with each person's tendencies in this regard, give them advance notice about your planned visit—the reason and the approximate time you expect to be there. Then be sure to follow through accordingly.

When you note something needs correcting, use that as a cue for shaping the alternative action (progressing via small steps—see Chapter 13). If the group is out of control, wait until the staff does something constructive to calm them down. Seize that as an opportunity to comment positively or to signal approval. If a teacher prompts too often, look for an episode when she waits for the student to initiate independently; then compliment her patient waiting.

Combining frequent performance feedback with reinforcement is essential. As mentioned in Chapter 3, we counsel you to *postpone initiating a program until you are certain that its implementers will receive ongoing feedback, along with merited reinforcers* (e.g., weekly, or more often if possible), *especially during its early phases.* To avoid programmatic failure, and any subsequent unwillingness of personnel to implement the approach in the future, continue to provide ongoing feedback and reinforcement until their new habit patterns are solidly established (DiGennaro et al., 2007), and you have assisted natural contingency managers (e.g., parents, teachers, supervisors) to assume contingency control.

---

[6] Could this relate to whether the organizational milieu is competitive or cooperative?

[7] The effectiveness and applicability of these potential reinforcers will vary with the program implementer and setting. Therefore observing their effects and using those that work for the implementer being assisted is important. To obtain other ideas, solicit suggestions from supervisors, program implementers, clients, and other staff or employees.

Be sensitive at the same time, though, to the frequency of feedback. Just as you want to avoid *overprompting,* recognize that excessively frequent or detailed feedback could begin to become aversive. Think of how you might feel if your boss congratulated you every single day for a month for arriving at work on time: "Yes! On time again, for the seventeenth day in a row this month." The rule, then, is to provide feedback that is sufficient enough to convey to personnel your awareness of exactly what they are doing well (or not so well), but not so much that they find it irritating.

## Contingently Remove Aversive Stimuli (Negative Reinforcement)

Sometimes change agents may ask for help in ridding themselves of aversive conditions, as in the case of parents appealing for advice in dealing with their child's tantrums. If you enable them to quickly lessen the tantrums, you are providing negative reinforcement (i.e., the skill you have taught them reduces tantrums, permitting them, thereby, to avoid or terminate the aversive stimulus).

When an organization finds particular personnel behaviors intolerable, such as an over-punitive supervisor's abuse of staff, it must be made clear that should the practice continue, appropriate disciplinary actions will be taken. That might prompt the supervisor to seek out the behavior analyst's help in changing those patterns.[8] By effectively assisting such supervisors, the behavior analyst may enable them to retain their staff positions. That's negative reinforcement!

DiGennaro et al. (2007) used a unique form of negative reinforcement to increase treatment integrity. They provided daily written feedback about client progress, along with the contingency managers' intervention-implementation fidelity scores. Staff members failing to achieve 100 percent fidelity were required to attend a meeting with the consultant to practice missed steps. Once they achieved 100 percent fidelity, their attendance was no longer required.

Personnel in challenging fields often need to unwind after a particularly trying day (a form of negative reinforcement). You, as an interested listener, can provide that function. However, be careful not to fall into the trap of reinforcing complaining or serving as a "crying towel" rather than assisting. "Attention should be given to bolstering adequate performance, not inefficiency" (Brown, 1974, p. 196). Before terminating such sessions, try to shift over to the positive, perhaps by posing questions such as "So, what was the *best* thing that happened at work today?" The answer may supply opportunities to reinforce some more positive and/or constructive thoughts or actions.

## Addressing Program Implementation Problems

Inadequate program implementation can be the result of a number of factors. The Performance Diagnostic Checklist-Human Services (PPC-HS), developed by Carr et al. (2013), is an assessment tool used to identify variables contributing to poor employee performance (e.g., contingency manager or RBT) in human services settings, such as schools, clinics, hospitals (Hays & Romani, 2021), and residential facilities. As indicated by Wilder, Cymbal and Villacorta (2020), several studies have demonstrated that interventions based on the PDC-HS have been shown to be more effective than interventions like checklists not based on an assessment of the variables that might be contributing to the poor performance. The PDC-HS includes interviewing, observation and scoring, and evaluates three major domains: *Training, Task Clarification, and Prompting; Resources, Materials, and Processes;* and, *Performance Consequences, Effort, and Competition.* This tool can help identify variables influencing program implementation, other than the behavior's function, such as the availability of materials, insufficient verbal feedback, insufficient training, and necessary task clarification and prompting.

---
[8]Except in the most dangerous or life threatening of situations and operating under strict legal and ethical guidelines, behavior analysts should not allow themselves to be placed in the position of supporting or condoning staff use of corporal punishment. Among their primary responsibilities is to identify and encourage the application of positive behavioral supports.

## PROGRAM MAINTENANCE

Regardless of whether an intervention is directed at clients, students, or organizational personnel, program maintenance is always an issue to be confronted: "… behavior will only be durable if there are contingencies maintaining it" (Malott, 2001, p. 100). It should come as no surprise, then, that Mathew et al (2014) found that availability of additional support was a characteristic of sustained program implementation. And although self-incentives often are suggested as an aid to program implementation and maintenance, a meta-analysis (Brown, Smith, Epton & Armitage 2017) hints that relying *solely* on that that strategy might be questionable. In your own practice, then, suppose an organization or family has temporarily employed an external behavioral consultant to design a promising new program. Successfully transferring control back to local contingency managers would be wise, rather than assuming the program will persist under its own power.

## Gradually Decrease Prompts

*As personnel begin to master their new skills, consultants should phase out their own verbal reminders, signals, or other intrusive cues.* Inviting the individual you are coaching to collaborate in designing your prompting strategies is a good idea, too. If the intervention is complex (as with a token economy), fade out prompts and gradually reduce reinforcers for each separate key component (e.g., delivering tokens contingently, pairing with descriptive praise etc.) once the person has mastered it. Then, if necessary, prompt combinations, such as praise paired with tokens and/or backup reinforcers, or whatever other skill needs to be addressed next. "Natural teachers" seem to do this "intuitively."

In general, our intent should be to prompt just barely enough to bring about whatever response you are working on. As we discuss, over-prompting can lead to dependence or resentment; to being seen as an effort to control or to diminish the person's autonomy. Therefore, as the learner begins to demonstrate proficiency in the skill, you need to gradually fade the prompts. An increase in error rates will inform you that you have been fading prompts *too* abruptly. In that case, drop back to a denser schedule, followed by a more gradual reduction in prompts.

## Set Goals Jointly

*Participative goal-setting* is a related strategy, as mentioned previously. Agreeing on sub- and final goals jointly, rather than unilaterally, is one way to promote and guide and progress incrementally toward and then maintaining the ultimate objective. This approach has been functionally analyzed in various organizations, such as factories (Fellner & Sulzer-Azaroff, 1984), hospital operating rooms (Cunningham & Austin, 2007), and schools (Gillat & Sulzer-Azaroff, 1994). Suppose your goal is to encourage schoolchildren to learn their multiplication tables or to increase the amount they read. Using a tactic similar to Gillat's, you might ask the principal to visit the classroom briefly (a few moments or less) to view a wall chart on which individual students had set weekly goals (e.g., the percentage correct they would try to achieve on their arithmetic assignments) and to praise evidence of progress they actually were making toward those goals. If you refer to the paper you'll learn that the children made quite rapid progress under those circumstances. Similar improvement was achieved by Fellner and Sulzer-Azaroff (1984) when they applied goal-setting to improve the safe performance of industrial workers.

Suppose you were working on a skill such as your own frequency of delivering reinforcers. In general, after constructing a baseline composed of repeated performance measures, you, as the behavior analyst and implementer, might jointly set a challenging yet achievable level to be attained during the next few days or weeks (e.g., "I will complement the commendable behavior of at least four employees during the next three consecutive days"). Demonstrating achievement of that level creates an occasion for feedback and reinforcement. Once the previous goal, complimenting four employees on each of three consecutive days, has been established, you set a new goal. Meanwhile, you gradually remove the reinforcers and prompts from the old goal and soon make them contingent only on the new one. You continue this until the ultimate objective is accomplished. Nicol and Hantula (2001) have provided some compelling evidence supporting the effectiveness of that tactic. When those investigators used a similar combination of feedback and setting successive goal levels, delivery drivers' punctuality in providing meals to elderly clients increased. (See Cunningham & Austin, 2007 and Reber & Wallin, 1984, for comparable demonstrations.)

Goals need not be restricted to progress levels nor to group efforts. They also can consist of discrete tasks to be completed by individuals or teams. Undoubtedly, you are familiar with "to-do lists," day timers, activity charts, assignment sheets, and other comparable ways of indicating tasks to be completed, by when and, maybe, to what level of precision. Fellow staff and supervisors certainly can support their own achievements by working in partnership with others or by sharing evidence of their progress with their supervisors. This was the case in a successful effort to promote professionals' completion of their tasks at a treatment program serving clients with developmental disabilities (Sulzer-Azaroff et al., 1998).

Box 24.3 describes a case in which goal-setting and shaping were combined to transform a classroom into a pleasant teaching and learning environment. (Note that the procedure implemented initially was similar to current teacher practices. Further, the behavior analyst *did not begin by suggesting novel techniques until success was achieved with the initial strategy*; one that the teacher felt comfortable using.)

---

### Box 24.3

"Mrs. Jones" asked for help with her junior high school class of highly disruptive students. Observation revealed that she was quite skillful in identifying and administering aversive consequences to individual students when they misbehaved, but her baseline of providing reinforcers for good behaviors was zero. She indicated that given 34 students in her class, reinforcing appropriate behavior would be impossible. (Actually, though, Mrs. Jones was delivering individual punitive consequences quite frequently.)

The consultants and Mrs. Jones agreed to set and pursue sub-goal levels of prompting and shaping. Because the teacher was skillful in identifying misbehaviors and applying aversive consequences, the initial step was to involve her in using a modified response cost program: Each student began each day with a total of ten points listed on a point card on his or her desk. Whenever Mrs. Jones observed an instance of misbehavior, she crossed out one of the points. Near the end of the period, students could exchange the points for time in a reinforcing Activity Center the behavior analyst helped Mrs. Jones organize in the rear of her classroom. The behavior analyst visited the classroom frequently to assist Mrs. Jones, to answer any questions and reinforce her efforts in implementing the program. The students reported they liked the program because "Mrs. Jones isn't yelling at us as much."

Next, the behavior analyst suggested that when the class had spent ten to fifteen minutes without misbehaving, which they had started to do, she might compliment the whole class's performance and award them an extra point (e.g., "I'm so pleased with the way all of you are working. Each of you may put a *plus one* on your card.") Again, as he continued to do throughout, the behavior analyst carefully monitored progress and complimented the teacher whenever he could.

After measures of the teacher's use of positive reinforcers and of student behavior showed improvement, the third step was implemented. The investigators prompted her to compliment Hector, a student who responded positively to Mrs. Jones' helping him with an assignment. So when she saw Hector at work, she complimented him. Once she became skillful in reinforcing Hector's behavior, another student who resembled Hector was added as a subject. Then other students were included; then small groups. Before long, the program was altered from students starting out with ten points, which they risked losing, to beginning with none and earning their points for constructive classroom behavior. Within about three months, the classroom environment was transformed into an agreeable setting in which learning, studying, and teaching became more pleasurable. (Based on Mayer & McGookin, 1977.)

Do not become discouraged if your clients resist your advice initially. As Patterson and Chamberlain (1994) pointed out, initial success in the form of improvements in the child's behavior leads to parents' greater willingness to teach their children. Similarly, Cautilli, Riley-Tillman, Axelrod, and Hineline (2005), have noted that contingency managers become less opposed to implementing recommended strategies once they have experienced success by following a method suggested by the behavior analyst: "Parents become resistant to using the techniques offered by the behavior therapist until they begin to experience the benefit of those techniques in the child's behavior. At the point of the technique's success, the parents begin to become more compliant" (p. 154).

In summary, here are some guidelines for effectively shaping the performance of program implementers:

- Initially, begin by choosing methods resembling current practices (see Chapter 3).
- Select prompts, directions, models, cues, or any other antecedent arrangements already known to promote each desired step or approximation to the alternative goal behavior.
- Assure that each successful step is reinforced. (Without frequent reinforcement, the implementer of the program is likely to revert to using prior practices, such as aversive control methods.)
- Once the newly acquired behavior has been established, gradually and progressively reduce the number of prompts and reinforcers.

## Identify and Use Various Reinforcing Sources

*Altered behavior will only maintain if ongoing, current contingencies support their continuation.* Identifying and using a variety of reinforcing sources to support and maintain program implementation efforts become especially critical as you gradually

> Should you feel under-appreciated in the organization in which you are operating, you might consider planning and implementing a similar set of strategies. Expressing your appreciation to your boss, spouse, roommate, offspring, co-worker or dorm counselor when they make a move in a direction promises to encourage a repetition of that act in the future!

begin to withdraw your support. Draw upon other willing professionals, supervisors, peers, clients, consumers, parents, other family members, colleagues, or friends. *Do not depend exclusively on your own prompts and reinforcers to sustain parent or staff improvement or maintain program implementation.* If working in an institution or work environment, seek the collaboration of behavioral team members in supporting change. Among the advantages of involving other key people are: (1) the natural social environment begins to serve as a source for prompting and reinforcing the desired behaviors in your absence, and (2) it makes it possible for you to gradually reduce your own prompts and reinforcers as control shifts back to the natural contingencies. In addition, the targeted behaviors are more likely to sustain when supported by those normally present, rather than being limited to when researchers or consultants are the sole providers of reinforcers (Boyce & Geller, 2001). Also noteworthy is that personnel who experience support from their networks of peers and colleagues are less likely to report burnout (Corrigan et al., 1998). For additional reinforcing sources, see Mayer and Wallace (2020).

### Parents

If a parent is implementing the program, solicit the help of the spouse, domestic partner, friends, relatives, neighbors, and others to regularly recognize his and/or her efforts. If the change-agent is the child's care provider, teacher, counselor, speech and language professional, or psychologist, parental cooperation and expressions of appreciation often can serve as powerful reinforcers. Therefore, keep parents regularly informed about what is happening and how this is helping their child. Encourage parents to let service providers know how much they appreciate what they are doing to help their child.

*Clients*

The clients, themselves, also can serve as sources of reinforcement for program implementation. The reinforcers derive, as mentioned, not only from evidence of their progress but also positive comments, smiles, compliments, and so on, directed toward the program manager. Depending on circumstances, such as under what conditions, who is giving and who is receiving them, congratulatory comments made in the presence of the recipient's peers may often serve a powerful reinforcing function. Therefore, teach others, including the clients themselves, to reinforce behaviors that facilitate ongoing progress. In a classic study, Graubard et al. (1971) taught twelve 15-year-old students to increase their teachers' rates of praise and to decrease negative comments and punishment by using the following techniques: (1) contingent verbal compliments (e.g., "Gee, it makes me feel good and I work better when you praise me"; "I like the way you teach this lesson"); (2) asking for extra assignments; and (3) contingent nonverbal behaviors (e.g., making eye contact, sitting up straight, and nodding in agreement as their teacher spoke). They also learned to look down and remain quiet while receiving any negative comments or punishers from their teacher. Within a short time, these strategies were effective in that the teacher dramatically increased her use of praise and diminished her disapproving comments. Also, the students reported how much nicer their teachers had become; the teachers how much more mature their students seemed to be. Craft, Alber, and Heward (1998) used a similar strategy when teaching fourth graders with developmental disabilities to recruit teacher attention while they worked on spelling assignments in their regular education classroom. Not only did their use of teacher attention statements increase in the regular classroom, but so did teacher praise received by these students, their percentage of worksheet items completed, and their accuracy on spelling assignments. (Review Chapter 14 for teaching clients social skills of that nature.)

*Peers*

Peers can improve behavior by serving both as models who demonstrate preferred skills and as reinforcing agents for one another's behavior by providing recognition, compliments, materials, and suggestions. Both clients' and contingency managers' peers can become a source of support for lasting change, as in the following example: After attempting to teach four typically developing preschool students to attend to their teachers when their individual names were called, or when the class was asked to pay attention, their levels of compliance decreased during maintenance. However, once classroom peers were taught to remind and praise one another for attending, attending maintained at high levels (Beaulien et al., 2013).

Well designed and supported organizational teams can promote peer cooperation, positive programming, and staff retention while alleviating stress and reducing burnout in the process (Corrigan, et al., 1998; Gersten, Keating, Yovanoff, & Harniss, 2001; Whitaker, 2000). Accordingly, try to:

- encourage program implementers to meet in groups to discuss new procedures and techniques they have found helpful in serving their clients.
- encourage change agents to observe, and when feasible, simultaneously collect data on the behavioral procedures that specific (model) program implementers are using.
- let fellow contingency managers know when their colleagues need help.
- assist and reinforce peers' offering of mutual assistance to one another by complimenting and communicating appreciation to one another.

*Supervisors, Managers, Administrators*

Because supervisors, managers and administrators are chiefly responsible for seeing to it that their subordinates do a good job, programmatic success depends on how effectively they support and assist their subordinates. By their very nature, those positions typically entitle them to initiate particular reinforcing and perhaps disciplinary actions. Depending on the character of the organization, these could affect decisions related to job assignments, hiring and firing, setting wages, awarding salary increases, expressing approval, dispensing privileges, scheduling breaks and vacations, recommending promotions, and assigning and maintaining quality assurance over tasks or products.

The extent to which staff involved in a behavior-change program cooperate or compete, and/or experience stress depends in good part on the nature of the supervisory support they receive. Such factors can even influence personnel to decide whether or not to remain on the job (Brunsting, Sreckovic, & Lane, 2014; Cancio, Albrecht & Johns, 2013; Gersten et al., 2001). When special education teachers reported experiencing appreciation, opportunities for growth, and trust from their supervisors, they were more likely to express an intent to remain in the field (Cancio et al., 2013). Clear administrative direction and support also serve to counteract teacher burnout (Brunsting et al., 2014).

According to Gallessich (1973), the principal is usually the most influential person in the school. Their "educational orientation, administrative style, decision-making patterns and relations with central administration, faculty, and community affect all aspects of the school" (p. 60). Support for this conclusion derives from an intervention designed to reduce school vandalism. Vandalism rates decreased in schools in which the administrators were seen by personnel to be highly involved and supportive, but increased in schools with less involved administrators (Mayer, Butterworth, Komoto, & Benoit, 1983). Similarly, McIntosh et al. (2014) found that along with team functioning, teachers rated administrative support as the most important feature for both schoolwide program implementation and sustainability.

In the Gillat and Sulzer-Azaroff (1994) study, following baselines on student performance, the senior investigator taught school principals specific skills in time management, goal-setting, praising, and non-vocal approval. Principals then scheduled a few minutes a week to visit the classrooms, review wall charts displaying student performance, and compliment both students and teachers on the students' progress. Grade-school students memorized their multiplication tables much more quickly and middle-school students independently read substantially more pages as a function of those increases in positive attention. As Sulzer-Azaroff (2000) pointed out, "the trickle-down effect again was demonstrated" (p. 156). Remember too, in the study by Cossairt et al. (1973), how student progress alone was insufficient to increase teachers' use of praise, but when the principals intermittently complimented them when they did praise, those rates maintained and even increased further.

Another example was set in a residential care facility (Mozingo et al., 2006). The experimenters evaluated the impact of a staff training and management package designed to increase frequency of accurate recording of problem behavior. Following in-service training, only two of eight participants increased their accuracy, but when the supervisor was present and provided support and feedback, all eight improved. On achieving parallel results, Cooper (2006) concluded that "management's demonstrable support was significantly associated with behavioral safety performance" (p. 1).

Examples of ways you as a supervisor or manager can display "active or demonstrable support" are:

- positively recognizing personnel who implement programs as planned.
- being present at behavior support team meetings.
- providing resources.
- releasing personnel from their assigned work to train, assist, and observe other program implementers.
- aiding in establishing needed policy and community contacts.
- compensating staff involvement in committee work by subtracting other duties or responsibilities.
- recognizing client improvements.

### Others

Also, don't overlook peer influence. Teachers tend to be more accepting of an intervention plan developed by a school team. (See comments on the influence of teams in Chapter 3 and Chapter 18 for a rationale and justification for peer rather than expert modeling (Crone, Hawken, & Bergstrom, 2007). Additionally, anyone else who observes or also works with the clientele in the organization can be called on to provide reinforcers. Inspire those others to join in and support the change process by emphasizing the program implementer's aims and accomplishments.

## PROGRAM GENERALIZATION

Promote generalization by voicing the expectation that it will be addressed, by drawing attention to similarities between situations, and in other ways (see Chapter 21). Recall our earlier example of how the behavior consultant noted commonalities among some of Mrs. Jones' students for the purpose of prompting Mrs. Jones to use her newly-acquired positive management skills across students and situations. In Chapter 21, you learned many other ways to promote generalization across clients, situations, time, and behaviors. Stop and think about those you can apply toward heightening the broad-based and lasting implementation of behavior-analytic methods within your own present or future organization.

### Consider the Big Picture within the Organization

Before we bring this chapter to a close, allow us to remind you of how essential it is to pause to consider the big picture. Stop! Look! Listen! And take note as you identify the important general and specific contingencies of reinforcement operating within your organization. Although the key purpose of your involvement may be to assist with one or a few local challenges (e.g., personnel performance, students' social, academic, or communication problems, family members' support of effective programming, health aspects, managerial or similar issues), other reinforcing and punishing stimuli of all kinds continue to function behind the scenes: Compensation and other personnel policies; job assignments; internal and external sources of social approval or disapproval; everyone's individual learning histories, current challenges, satisfactions, and future aspirations; even weather conditions, plus countless others remain to influence the outcome.

Seek the cooperation of natural leaders, who can abet progress. Watch out, too, for notorious or concealed "control freaks," who unless you garner their cooperation from the start, may fight to retain or expand their power by doing what they can to undermine your efforts. Acquaint yourself with key organizational evaluation measures, such as profit and loss figures; production, test, quality, and injury scores; sales records; personnel satisfaction; performance appraisal and retention figures; and so on, and factor that information into your planning. In the long run, if you can convince others that the methods you propose for abetting the pursuit of their objectives are likely to succeed at a reasonable cost, you should be "good to go." Otherwise, reconsider either the behavioral objective or your anticipated methods.

Also, always look for and implement ways to make the environment more nurturing. As Biglan (2015) points out, it is important to help people move from using escalating punitive measures to using positive reinforcement to nurture prosocial and productive behaviors.

### Contemplate the Even Broader Picture

Meaningful behavior change sometimes requires modifying contingencies external to the organization. For example, in 2008, Bill Gates, founder and former CEO of Microsoft®, wrote a stimulating article on creative capitalism. He suggested incentives (i.e., reinforcers) beyond the direct profit motive to encourage organizational leaders, such as heads of pharmaceutical companies, to invest more resources toward assisting (e.g., providing medicine to) underserved people:

- Incentives can be as straight-forward as giving public praise to the companies that are doing work that serves the poor. This summer, a Dutch nonprofit called the Access to Medicine Foundation started publishing a report card that shows which pharmaceutical companies are doing the most to make sure that medicines are made for—and reach—people in developing countries. When I talk to executives from pharmaceutical companies, they tell me that they want to do more for neglected diseases—but they at least need to get credit for it. ...
- Publicity is very valuable, but sometimes it's still not enough to persuade companies to get involved. Even the best P.R. may not pay the bill for 10 years of research into a new drug. That's why it's so important for governments to create more financial incentives. Under a U.S. law enacted last year, for example, any drug company that develops a new treatment for a neglected disease like malaria can get a priority review from the [FDA] for another product it has made. If you develop a new drug for malaria, your profitable cholesterol drug could go on the market as much as a year earlier. Such a priority review could be worth hundreds of millions of dollars. It's a fantastic way for governments to go beyond the aid they already give and channel market forces so they improve even more lives (p. 44).
- In other words, creative capitalism is already under way. But we can do much more. Governments can create more incentives like the FDA voucher. We can... make sure the rankings get publicity so companies get credit for doing good work. Consumers can reward companies that do their part by buying their products. Employees can ask how their employers are contributing (p. 45).

It should be apparent by now that reinforcers not only can abet the constructive progress of clients, students, personnel, customers, organizations, or institutions, but also can influence behavior on national and international levels. As Gates pointed out, the longer we wait to apply such contingencies, "the more people suffer needlessly" (p. 45).

## SUMMARY AND CONCLUSIONS

Designing a successful and sustainable behavioral program requires a supportive environment. Toward this end, we remind you of the value of taking the following steps toward achieving this aim drawn from this chapter and elsewhere in this text.

- Prepare personnel.
- Develop a system within the natural environment to prompt, if necessary, and to support and provide ongoing reinforcement for continued program implementation.
- Analyze the current context to permit you to capitalize on available assets and to avoid impediments to productive change.
- Select effective procedures.
- Ensure treatment integrity.
- Assure contextual fit.
- Select goals and interventions jointly.
- Use specific and comprehensible language.
- Incorporate intervention prompts within the natural environment, as necessary.
- Collaboratively design, use, and share the results of performance inventories with appropriate parties.
- Provide ongoing support while your change programs are in place by:
  ◦ Being present when a program is initiated.
  ◦ Removing aversive stimuli.
  ◦ Identifying and using a variety of sources of reinforcement to augment natural stimulus controls.
  ◦ Providing frequent feedback for program implementation.
  ◦ Prompting, as necessary; then fading prompts.

- Supplementing feedback with suggestions and reinforcement.
- As always, maintain ongoing data collection and evaluation systems (see Chapters 7 through 9 and 25)

• Take the "big picture" into account

The bottom line: *Programs with the best chances of thriving and surviving, particularly in your absence, are those supported by the natural environment.* Otherwise they risk deteriorating or failing altogether. Much of your work, then, will have been for naught. The attached checklist (Figure 24.4) is designed to help you to heighten your chances of success.

Remember, that should your purpose be to encourage a behavior change agent to practice an important behavior skill (e.g., implementing the plan) while they are engaging in inappropriate behavior (e.g., reinforcing problem behavior, overusing punishment) then use the same approach that you would take with a client. That is, search to determine if an important behavior is not occurring due to either a skill deficit, not being adequately evoked, or not being reinforced. Whereas if an inappropriate behavior is occurring, discover if it is being reinforced and whether the function needs to be addressed either by way of antecedent manipulations, extinction, differential reinforcement, or some combination of the three.

See the *Summary Table (page 567) for Transferring, Expanding, and Maintaining Responding.*

| **Support Strategies** | Yes/No |
|---|---|
| 1. Are the objectives of the program specific, clear, related to the mission of the organization, ethically justifiable, and reasonably achievable? | _____ |
| 2. Have you arranged your schedule to permit your regular presence on site? | _____ |
| 3. Have you chosen *prompting* strategies to use, if necessary? | _____ |
| 4. Have you planned the steps you will take to deliver *feedback*? | _____ |
| 5. Will your feedback system be specific enough? | _____ |
| 6. Will your feedback system be sufficiently clear? | _____ |
| 7. Upon what *sources* will you base your feedback? | _____ |
| 8. Identify the *recipients* of your feedback. | _____ |
| 9. Will you provide feedback to individuals or to a group? | _____ |
| 10. What is the basis for this plan? | _____ |
| 11. Will you provide *immediate feedback*? If *No*, list the changes you can make to accomplish that aim. | _____ |
| 12. Are you planning on using *goal-setting*? If *Yes*, describe. If *No*, say why not. | _____ |
| 13. What steps will you take to transform your feedback into a *secondary reinforcer*? | _____ |
| 14. Have you planned a *rationale* to offer to program implementers? If *Yes,* state it here. If *No*, say why not. | _____ |
| 15. In what form will you supply *feedback* (e.g. spoken, written, graphed, tokens, etc.)? Why? | _____ |
| 16. What reinforcers will you combine with your feedback? Why? | _____ |
| 17. Have you provided an appropriate level of feedback? (i.e., Not too much nor an insufficient amount.) Comment please. | _____ |
| 18. Do you plan to use negative reinforcement? If so, describe. | _____ |
| 19. Have you made specific plans to fade prompts? Describe briefly. | _____ |
| 20. Did you plan for involving sources of reinforcement beyond yourself? List them and describe what the others will do to enable this purpose to be achieved. | _____ |
| 21. Have you planned ways to foster generalization? Describe briefly. | _____ |

**Figure 24.4** Checklist: How well have you arranged to support the implementation and continuation of behavior change programs? (Where the yes/no column has been shaded, if you need more space, write out your response on the back of the form.)

# Summary Table
# Transferring, Expanding, and Maintaining Responding

## Transferring and Expanding Stimulus Control

| Operation/ Procedure | Maximizing Effectiveness | Temporal Properties | Durability of Effect | Other Features |
|---|---|---|---|---|
| **Delayed prompting:** Interposing a gradually increasing period of time between the natural discriminative stimulus and prompts | 1. Interpose delay between S⁺ and prompt<br>2. Gradually Increase delay<br>3. Differentially reinforce response in presence of S⁺<br>4. Assess for acquisition using pre-planned random sequence trials<br>5. Sustain reinforcement until target response emitted at high and steady rate over several sessions in a row | As delay increases, time to evoke response also increases until *moment of transfer* | Depends on length of time required to reach *moment of transfer* | Increases opportunity for independence; may permit errorless learning; *moment of transfer* immediately apparent |
| **Graduated prompting:** Applying prompts of increasing intrusiveness until target response occurs | 1. Give less intrusive prompts a fair try<br>2. Assess by locating functional S^D and begin at that point<br>3. Differentially reinforce response in presence of least intrusive prompt<br>4. Sustain reinforcement until target response emitted at high and steady rate over several sessions in a row | Depending on initial instructional level may be time consuming, | Depends on how firmly stimulus control established | Maximizes success; unless highly intrusive prompts lead to overdependence on those prompts |
| **Fading:** Gradually withdrawing artificial prompts as stimulus (S+) acquires appropriate discriminative control | 1. Remove prompts gradually<br>2. Block or remove S⁻s for unwanted responses<br>3. Prevent overdependence on prompts<br>4. Try *graduated guidance* to fade physical prompts,<br>5. Fade modeling and instructional prompts<br>6. To minimize errors: Initially select S⁺s very different from S⁻s; then introduce S⁻s briefly and at weak intensity<br>7. Highlight critical elements of target stimuli<br>8. Remove irrelevant stimuli | Gradual | Depends on how firmly established S^D control has become | Essential for independence from artificial supports; when done with care, can establish powerful stimulus control; prevents over-dependence on artificial prompts |

# Transferring and Expanding Stimulus Control (cont.)

| Operation/ Procedure | Maximizing Effectiveness | Temporal Properties | Durability of Effect | Other Features |
|---|---|---|---|---|
| | 1. Consider using response delay<br>2. Reinforce S⁺—R combination heavily until firmly established; then thin schedule of reinforcement gradually contingent on the S^D—R combination | | | |
| **Stimulus Generalization Training:** In the presence of a new stimulus sharing key characteristics with previously taught discriminative stimulus, promoting similar antecedent stimulus-response relation | 1. Program for generalization from the very start<br>2. Set objectives supportive of generalization<br>3. Train to fluency<br>4. Identify and make use of naturally supportive conditions<br>5. Reinforce the behavior when it occurs in other related contexts<br>6. Request generalization<br>7. Program common stimuli across conditions<br>8. Use mediation strategies<br>9. Train behavior in all relevant settings, perhaps sequentially<br>10. Pre-assess and reduce support for interfering maladaptive behavior<br>11. Provide sufficient exemplars<br>12. Train loosely<br>13. Use indiscriminable contingencies<br>14. Teach contingency mangers to promote and support appropriate generalization<br>15. Manage continued promotion and support of appropriate generalization<br>16. Record and graph generalization data | Gradual, although may occur spontaneously | Long-lasting as long as intermittently reinforced in context | Generalization training enables people use their skills in various environments |

## Maintaining Behavior

| Operation/ Procedure | Maximizing Effectiveness | Temporal Properties | Durability of Effect | Other Features |
|---|---|---|---|---|
| **Fixed ratio (FR) schedule:** Reinforcing every nth emission of the behavior | 1. Begin at baseline rates, increase ratio gradually and progressively<br>2. Individualize to person's response patterns<br>3. Promote fluency<br>4. If responding begins to disintegrate, temporarily reduce and gradually reinstate ratio requirement<br>5. Reduce value of reinforcers<br>6. Change over to a variable schedule<br>7. Identify and capitalize on natural reinforcement contingencies and contextual supports | Gradual | Continues as long as reinforcement quantify and/or quality reduced gradually yet continues intermittently | Produces high response rates; requires counting; post-reinforcement pause not likely but possible following high rates |
| **Variable ratio (VR) schedule:** Reinforcing the response following an average of n responses | 1. Match ratio requirement to individual's initial response patterns<br>2. Increase ratio requirement gradually and progressively<br>3. Promote response fluency<br>4. If responding begins to disintegrate, temporarily reduce ratio requirement<br>5. Reduce value of reinforcers<br>6. Identify and capitalize on natural reinforcement contingencies and contextual supports | Gradual | Continues as long as density of reinforcement reduced gradually yet continues periodically | Produces high, consistent response rates; requires counting; approximates contingencies in natural environment |

## Maintaining Behavior (cont.)

| Operation/ Procedure | Maximizing Effectiveness | Temporal Properties | Durability of Effect | Other Features |
|---|---|---|---|---|
| **Fixed-interval (FI) schedule:** Reinforcing the first response following a constant or fixed interval (or fixed time period) | 1. Begin with short intervals; increase gradually and progressively<br>2. Temporarily shorten interval requirement if responding begins to disintegrate<br>3. To diminish response rate, expand interval length<br>4. For a more rapid rate: schedule shorter intervals and or DRH; Promote response fluency; combine with limited-hold<br>5. To promote a particular moderate rate, differentially reinforce paced responding (DRP), that is, reinforce when rate falls within a high and low zone<br>6. To promote low rates, combine with differential reinforcement of low rates (DRL)<br>7. Use discriminative stimuli to prompt or abate the behavior<br>8. Consider incorporating periodic competition<br>9. Capitalize on behavioral contrast (e.g., thin schedule in one environment to increase rate in unchanged environment)<br>10. Intersperse easy tasks<br>11. Identify and capitalize on natural reinforcement contingencies and contextual supports<br>12. Progressively lengthen delay, reduce value of reinforcers, and thin reinforcers | Gradual | Moderate | Easy to use; avoids need to count responses; produces less consistent responding than VI |

## Maintaining Behavior (cont.)

| Operation/ Procedure | Maximizing Effectiveness | Temporal Properties | Durability of Effect | Other Features |
|---|---|---|---|---|
| **Variable-interval (VI) schedules:** Reinforcing the first response following a pre-determined variable interval | Same as FI above | Gradual | Long-lasting; effect more durable than FI | Easy to use; avoids counting behavior; approximates contingencies of natural environment; promotes more consistent responding than FI |
| **Limited hold (LH):** Reinforcing the response only if it occurs within a specific time span following the interval | 1. Select time unit on basis of observational records<br>2. Consider practical demands of the situation, and if necessary, gradually adjust to situational demands | Rapid | Depending on size of limited-hold interval may promote higher rates than interval schedules | May be combined with most any schedule |
| **Differential reinforcement of high rates (DRH):** Reinforcing only after several responses occur at or above a pre-established rate | 1. Determine current response rate<br>2. Select rate slightly above current rate to reinforce<br>3. Increase rate criterion gradually until desired rate is achieved<br>4. Lower rate requirement temporarily if rate begins to disintegrate | Moderate | Long lasting | Can combine with ratio of interval schedules |

## Maintaining Behavior (cont.)

| Operation/ Procedure | Maximizing Effectiveness | Temporal Properties | Durability of Effect | Other Features |
|---|---|---|---|---|
| **Differential reinforcement of paced responding (DRP):** Reinforcing responses that fall within a range of high and low limits | 1. To obtain optimal tempo, select upper and lower rate limits<br>2. Reinforce only when the response occurs within the set limits | Gradual | Long lasting | Useful to manage behavior that tends to be impulsive or that needs to be emitted at neither a too rapid nor slow pace |
| **Differential reinforcement of low rates (DRL):** Reinforcing only if behavior occurs following, not during interval | 1. Apply to excessively rapid current rates of behavior<br>2. Differentially reinforce the emission of the behavior following a given time period of non-responding<br>3. Extend interval gradually until response desired rate stabilizes | Gradual | Long lasting | Best when used with desired behavior that is occurring excessively difficult to use in applied settings on undesired behavior |
| **Lag schedule:** Reinforce only if response is different from X previous responses | 1. Determine current response rate<br>2. Select rate slightly above current rate to reinforce<br>3. Increase variability criterion gradually until desired variability is achieved<br>4. Lower rate requirement temporarily if rate begins to disintegrate | Moderate | Long lasting | Good for teaching associations, similarities, differences, & response classes |

# Maintaining Behavior (cont.)

## General Suggestions for Supervisory Support of Peak Personnel Performance

1. Set goals jointly
2. Remove, minimize or otherwise compensate for aversive aspects of conducting the response cost program
3. Be present when program is initiated
4. Prompt as necessary
5. Provide frequent feedback and reinforcers for improvements and for optimal program implementation
6. Apply implementation guidelines to promote and sustain generalization of ABA skills
7. Gradually decrease prompts
8. Gradually decrease supervisory presence and reinforcers until steady-state performance achieved.
9. Identify and capitalize upon various discriminative stimuli and reinforcing features of the natural environment.
10. Assure natural contingencies provided by others in the natural environment are maintained at a reasonable level.
11. Assess the effectiveness of the natural contingencies. If they are inadequate, enhance them by involving additional support and additional social, tangible, or other currently functional consequences

*Chapter 25*

# Identifying Effective Interventions with Complex Research Designs

## Goals

1. List and discuss three questions that can be legitimately raised before a behavioral program is adopted on a broad scale.
2. Define, recognize, and give original illustrations for each of the following terms:
    a. internal validity
    b. external validity
    c. changing-criterion design
    d. multiple-probe design
    e. sequence effects
    f. multiple-treatment interference
    g. alternating-treatment (multi-element) design
    h. parametric analysis
    i. experimental significance
    j. clinical (social, personal) significance
    k. educational significance and social validity
    l. direct replication
    m. systematic replication
3. Identify and describe the advantages and possible limitations of the changing-criterion design.
4. Describe how to enhance the changing-criterion design's validity.
5. Describe the purpose and advantage of intermittently using multiple probes, and differentiate between using multiple probes and intermittent sampling.
6. Describe how withdrawal methods can be used to compare treatments and to assess for maintenance.

7. List, describe, and illustrate with a new example the advantages and possible limitations of the alternating-treatment design, and discuss how to minimize those disadvantages.
8. Discuss how best to determine which component, or combination of components, is responsible for the effectiveness of an intervention package.
9. For each of the designs compared in Table 25.1, describe a novel situation for which that specific design would be the most appropriate. Be sure to clearly justify your selection.
10. List and discuss the criteria for determining the significance of a demonstrated functional relation.
11. Explain how to determine cost effectiveness and discuss its importance.
12. Discuss the importance that replication plays in developing behavioral laws and in establishing generality of findings.
13. Discuss the value of conducting preplanned probes of generality and maintenance.
14. Be prepared to conduct single-subject experimental designs.

\*\*\*\*\*\*\*\*\*\*\*\*\*

## PRELIMINARY CONSIDERATIONS PRIOR TO ADOPTING PROGRAMS

A large banking firm is planning on instituting a Personnel Performance Improvement Program (PPIP). It will consist of specifying the key facets of each job: what individuals should be doing and accomplishing; measuring those job performances; planning a schedule for observing and recording how well personnel are performing their tasks; and systems for conveying that information back to them and for rewarding progress toward group goals. Senior management's big concerns are how well the plan will work, and if so, whether it will net more than it costs. They decide that before deploying the program on a system-wide basis it would be wise to analytically validate the intervention at one of their branches.

"What evidence can you supply that your procedures are effective?" is increasingly asked in many areas of human endeavor, including human services, education, health care, business, and elsewhere. Certainly, we cannot, nor should we expect, skeptics unfamiliar with the accomplishments of behavior analysis to embrace its methods in the absence of confirmation of its effectiveness. Nor should we expect such funding sources to fund ineffective intervention programs lacking validation. Such caution is reasonable when one considers adopting any behavior-change program or procedure. Decision-makers should legitimately raise questions about the internal and external validity of the program and its impact on the bottom line.

### How Internally Valid is the Program?

Questions of **internal validity** are concerned with *"whether there is a causal relationship from one variable to another in the form in which the variables were manipulated or measured"* (Cook & Campbell, 1979, p. 38).[1] For behavioral programs, the question becomes one of how convincingly the behavioral changes can be shown to relate functionally to the procedures. (Were the changes in behavior functionally related to the intervention? Or, how

---

[1]See also Shadish, Cook, & Campbell (2002), *Experimental and quasi-experimental designs for generalized causal inference*.

> ### A Summary of Experimental Analytic Terms
>
> **What is a variable?** To review, in behavior analysis a variable is some feature of behavior or of the environment that is capable of changing in value.
> *Examples*: Number, size, shape, intensity.
>
> **What are control variables?** These are the conditions that you hold constant (that don't change) in an experiment.
> *Examples*: Unless they are the subject of investigation, these often are materials, setting, managers, personnel, tools, and so on.
>
> **What are dependent variables?** These are the measures that validly depict the behavior(s) of interest or concern.
> *Examples*: Among others,
> *Frequency*, as in number of days skipping school or the number of suggestions the doctor makes
> *Rate* (number per standard unit of time), such as number of products completed per hour or miles covered per hour
> *Latency*, or the amount of time it takes before the individual responds to a signal, as in the number of seconds between the starter's whistle and beginning to run or for the class to quiet down after the teacher flicks the lights
> *Duration*, the time the behavior is ongoing—from onset to offset: the length of time spent texting, studying, daydreaming
> *Topography*, the shape or form of the response: i.e., the judge's rating of the quality of the skater's performance; the precision with which engraver reproduces a design
>
> **What are experimental variables?** These are the conditions, or independent variables, that you systematically vary to determine the effect of those variations on the dependent variables—the measures that change accordingly.
> *Examples*: Reinforcement of particular behaviors; shaping of behavior to be acquired; application of particular training packages.

well does the study control for confounding variables or potential sources of error?) As we already have learned in Chapter 9, single-subject designs are eminently well-suited to this concern because they eliminate competing explanations for the findings. Remember internal validity is not just important in formal ABA research, but is at the very core of applied behavior analysis. We must demonstrate that the procedures we implement are functionally related to the change in behavior.

## How Externally Valid is the Program?

Cook and Campbell have used the term **external validity** to refer to the *"approximate validity with which conclusions are drawn about generalizability of a causal relationship to and across populations of persons, settings, and times"* (p. 39). In behavior analysis we want to know whether the procedures have generality beyond the original set of cases—to other people, behaviors, or settings. Before investing in an expensive curriculum designed to train managerial skills, for example, we may wish to feel fairly confident that the program would be exportable to other units of the organization and that the effects will endure after the behavior analyst departs.

The designs previously described in Chapter 9 are well suited to demonstrating external validity. As you saw in that chapter, one way to test such generality is by conducting multiple-baselines across settings, behaviors, or people. Moreover, replication (i.e., duplication) of specific effects using single-subject design also speaks to the external validity of the intervention (that is, if it has been shown to work successfully for several, then there is a good chance that it will do the same for others under similar situations). Collecting measures repeatedly prior to, during, and following intervention also informs us about the *durability* of effect.

## Will Changes in Performance Impact the Bottom Line?

If Mel learns a set of dating skills, will he succeed in getting more dates and will the women he dates be willing to see him again? If personnel increase their safe practices, will accidents rates decrease? When students remain on-task, do they actually learn more? If managers use more praise and recognition, will their subordinates become more productive? Behavior analysts need to compare the net benefit of their interventions to those achieved by ongoing methods in terms of how *rapidly* and *durably* goals or standards are achieved, the cost of the investment, and other *short-* and *long-term benefits*. They can satisfactorily address these concerns by collecting baseline, intervention, and maintenance data, before, during, and after formally intervening.

The most stringent program evaluation methods incorporate scientific methods to address such validation questions. In behavior analysis, that means conducting careful within-subject (or single-subject) functional analyses. These permit us to reject competing explanations for how results were achieved, as well as to examine the intervention's impact on the context in which the change takes place. Both the withdrawal and multiple-baseline designs, about which you read in Chapter 9, permit you to demonstrate *internal validity* (generalizability within the individual—your praise works on timeliness of the individual's completion of tasks, also on quality of job performed and so on.). Additionally, multiple-baselines lend themselves to evaluating aspects of *external validity* (generalizability to other individuals, responses, or settings). In this chapter we offer some additional methods for functionally analyzing the relation between treatments and behavior, especially when we wish to examine more complex behaviors or to compare one method against another. Included are methods for analyzing individuals' progress in acquiring and/or maintaining new skills, for comparing the effects of different strategies of change, and for assessing the significance of the changes achieved.

## FUNCTIONALLY ANALYZING INCREASES AND DECREASES IN BEHAVIOR

Fern's job coach has decided to test the functional effectiveness of the methods she is using to shape Fern's acquisition of a new task: box-packing skills. Mr. Ernie, the psychologist, hopes to help Helen, his client, acquire a set of social coping skills, while Paula's boss, Angela, plans to teach Paula a new system of accounting via a backward chaining approach. How might they evaluate the relation between those treatment methods and the performances of concern?

As discussed in Chapter 9, withdrawal designs are unsuitable for functionally analyzing nonreversible patterns of behavior, such as mastering new skills. Despite response levels increasing during the treatment phase, one would not expect measures of those skills to return to baseline levels during a withdrawal phase. We would not fail to recall how to ride a bicycle or to read, despite a lack of external support. Nor would we expect Fern, Helen, and Paula to forget the skills they had mastered following termination of reinforcement.

By contrast, recall, too, from Chapter 9 that multiple-baselines are capable of revealing reliable changes in levels of responding as a function of treatment without requiring the reversal of performance patterns. The power of the demonstration lies in demonstrating that reliable change occurs *when and only when* the intervention is put into effect for each particular baseline. But what can we do when no other behaviors, settings, or people are available for purposes of replication? Or, suppose we hope to demonstrate that our treatment is responsible while we are shaping a behavior by reinforcing approximations? One alternative is to use the *changing-criterion design*.

# CHANGING-CRITERION DESIGN

Early on, Hall (1971a) described the operation of the **changing-criterion design** as follows:

> In using the changing criterion design, the experimenter successively changes the criterion for consequation, usually in graduated steps, from baseline levels to a desired terminal level. If the behavior changes successively at or close to the set criterion levels, experimental control can be demonstrated (p. 24).

The changing-criterion design, then, involves a step-wise introduction of different criterion values above or below baseline. The steps consist of progressive increases or decreases in the response requirement. The power of the demonstration, then, rests on a close match between the intervention and the response patterns generated. Don't forget your POVs (prediction, obtained results & verification — see Ch. 9). In the changing-criterion design, POVs are achieved by responding correlating with the new criterion after each criterion change. Moreover, each achieved criterion becomes a projected level against which to compare the behavior obtained in the next criterion (see Chapter 9 for a review of projected levels and obtained level with respect to analyzing single-subject data).

## Changing-Criterion Designs Illustrated

Hall's demonstration (1971b) focused on stopping a 23-year-old male graduate student's smoking, after having smoked 20 to 30 cigarettes a day for several years. He and the behavior analyst agreed that if he smoked more than 15 cigarettes in a day, he would tear a dollar bill into tiny pieces and throw it away. This criterion of 15 cigarettes remained in effect for five days. Then it was lowered to no more than 13 cigarettes each day for the next five days, and so on. Hall noted that "the systematic stair step ceiling was never exceeded and in most cases was closely approximated.... Each five-day phase acted as a baseline for the next five-day phase and demonstrated that the self-imposition of the consequence of having to tear up a dollar bill was effective in keeping smoking below the criterion level" (p. 55).

In a more recent demonstration, Grey, Healy, Leader, and Hayes (2009) used a changing-criterion design across settings to evaluate the effects of a predictive stimulus (a "Time Timer") plus delayed reinforcement (from one second to ten minutes) on a child's appropriate waiting, as well as on problematic behavior currently maintained by access to tangibles. It was possible to successfully increase the duration of the participant's appropriate waiting behavior while extending the reinforcement delay from one second to ten minutes (see Figure 25.1). Notice that the behavior closely matches the step-wise increase in criteria across phases. Especially noteworthy is the correspondence between the criterion and the obtained behavior after the criterion was reduced and subsequently increased (i.e., a mini-reversal).

Skinner, Skinner, and Armstrong (2000) also used the changing-criterion design to heighten the persistence with which an adult with schizophrenia increased the time spent in leisure reading. Reinforcers were dependent on his achieving the criterion set for the number of pages to be read each day.

In another case, Gorski and Westbrook (2002) used differential reinforcement within a changing-criterion design to increase the adherence to his physical therapy regimen of an 18-year-old male with leukocyte adhesion deficiency (a rare primary immunodeficiency). By gradually advancing the criterion for reinforcement, the experimenters ultimately were able to increase to 80 percent the average time he used his crutches.

## Advantages of Changing-Criterion Design

As with the multiple-baseline design (Chapter 9), the changing-criterion design does not *require* a reversal phase to demonstrate experimental control. This is especially advantageous when dealing with irreversible changes in behavior like learning to ride a bicycle, reading, speaking, or when even a very brief reversal is ethically questionable. Experimental control does not depend on reversals. Changing-criterion designs can demonstrate experimental control with a single individual, behavior, or within

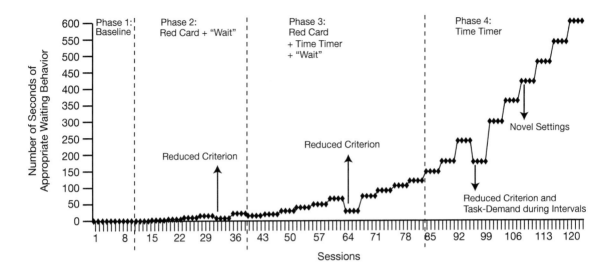

**Figure 25.1** Example of changing-criterion design. Reprinted from *Research in Developmental Disabilities, 30*. Grey et al., Using a Time Timer™ to increase appropriate waiting behavior in a child with developmental disabilities, pp. 359–366, 2009, with permission from Elsevier.

one setting. Also, they are ideally suited to programs in which criteria are changed gradually and progressively, as in differential reinforcement of high (DRH), diminishing (DRD), or low (DRL) rates and shaping programs.

## Disadvantages of Changing-Criterion Design

Hartmann and Hall (1976) suggested that performance stability at each criterion level is "crucial to producing a convincing demonstration of control" (p. 531). This can be cumbersome, though, because each phase basically serves as the baseline for the next. Moreover, phases can become unduly long if the behavior is slow to change or stabilize. Another concern with the changing-criterion design is that it requires control over both *direction* and *level* of change. Therefore, program designers must concern themselves not only with it increasing or decreasing behavior, but also predicting what change magnitudes are apt to be achievable from one step to the next. To affect progress, criterion changes must be sufficiently challenging, yet remain sufficiently achievable to permit behavior to match these changes. Another "risk" (offset by the silver lining of achieving the goal more rapidly) is losing experimental control due to the behavior's progressing more rapidly than anticipated to the desired end level. Consequently, you need to set levels of criterion change with care, which can be somewhat daunting.

## Using and Demonstrating Control via the Changing-Criterion Design

One attraction of the changing-criterion design is the wealth of possible ways to adjust its different components, including varying the length of the phases, the magnitude of change demanded by the criterion levels, and the number of phases. These variations may impact the experimental control achieved, as each phase serves as a baseline for the next. Although phase lengths may be varied, experimental control depends on behavioral stability within each phase prior to changing the criterion. Moreover, *varying the lengths of each phase increases the design's validity.* Should you wish to make a *really* powerful case for the functional relation between the changing criteria and progress, you might also consider temporarily reversing the direction of the criterion level requisite for reinforcement, as was demonstrated in Figure 25.1. Also see Figure 25.2. To ensure experimental control via a changing-

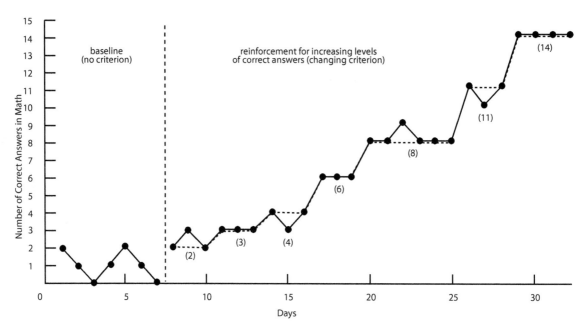

**Figure 25.2** Demonstrating control over number of correct answers in math via a changing-criterion design. From Hall (1971a). Permission to reprint granted by R. Vance Hall, Ph.D., H & H Enterprises, Inc.

criterion design, remember you must demonstrate three POVs. In a changing-criterion design a POV is secured when the obtained response pattern in the first criterion phase not only does not overlap with the prediction from baseline, but also when it closely matches the criterion. Thus, you must have at least three changes in the criterion to demonstrate experimental control. In addition to demonstrating three POVs, consider several additional suggestions or rules when using changing-criterion designs to demonstrate functional relationships: not only should each sub-phase vary in length (as mentioned to help rule out time as a controlling variable) but to be convincing, one of the sub-phases should last longer than baseline. Moreover, avoid forced or guided responding. Rather, responding should consistently be unrestricted (Klein, et al., 2017). Adherence to these rules is essential to avoid a loss of experimental control. A recent review of the current literature using the changing-criterion design found that only 25 percent met the full requirements for demonstrating experimental control (see Klein, et al., 2017).

**Choosing and varying phase lengths.** Among Hall's early studies was one (1971a) in which he used the changing-criterion design to demonstrate control by reinforcement over the number of a student's correct answers in math (Figure 25.2). Note the number of days doubled for criterion level 8. Assuming a match between the criterion level and response patterns, this *variation in the number of sessions* can provide especially strong evidence that the intervention was exerting functional control.

Suppose you hope to encourage a youngster, Dean, to practice the piano without protest for 30 minutes, six days a week. At first you set a goal[2] of four minutes; then, after five days, advance it to five minutes; then to eight, and so on. When Dean meets the goal, you praise him enthusiastically. One time he even exceeds the goal; but another time he fails to reach it. You are fairly certain that your praise is powerful and you bestow it consistently, but you want to find out whether setting the goal matters. So, (as depicted in Figure 25.3) you lower the level for three days. Lo and behold, Dean practices for only 15 minutes on days 25 to 27. When you reinstate the previous goal level of 20 minutes, the rate

---

[2] Goals and goal-setting are discussed further in Chapters 4, 17, and 26.

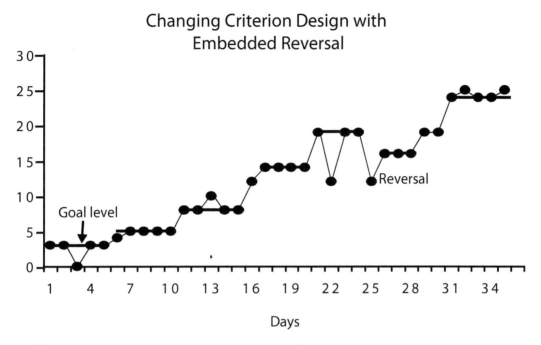

**Figure 25.3** A changing-criterion design with a reversal embedded in the sequence (hypothetical data)
Notice that in most, though not all instances, measures of behavior tend to approach the goal line for the week, represented by the solid horizontal line. The close correspondence between the goal set and performance suggests functional control.

recovers. By now you are quite confident that goal-setting adds to the effectiveness of the contingency arrangement.

**Setting criterion levels.** Change agents must set criterion levels cautiously, because the changing-criterion design depends on the match between the value of the dependent variable and the pre-established criterion level. If set at too easy a level, the behavior may "run away with itself," thereby failing to correspond to the set criterion levels. If that happens, control over extraneous variables is lost. To reestablish control, the level will need to be made more stringent. The same issue can occur if the individual fails to reach a criterion performance. Again, control over extraneous variables is lost. In an effort to try and reestablish control, the requirement will have to be lowered.

Usually the changing criteria are set at a specific point or level. However, researchers (McDougall, 2005; McDougall, Hawkins, Brady, & Jenkins, 2006) have proposed a variation in which the criteria are set in the form of an upper- and lower-level *range* of acceptability, rather than at one specific level. For example, instead of setting a criterion for decreasing calories consumed from 3000 to 2800, then to 2600, the first criterion might be 2700–2900; next, from 2400–2650. McDougall (2005) termed the design a *"range-bound changing-criterion design."* That investigator nicely illustrated the design by describing a case of an obese adult's efforts to increase his amount of running. In that case, following baseline, the runner obtained reinforcers as a function of achieving any point within a preset range of 10 percentile points. Over time, as performance improved, those criterion ranges were raised. The source of control in this design depends on the behavior falling within the step-like criterion bands (i.e., lower and upper criterion levels).

Although, from an experimental control standpoint, larger changes are more impressive, if the criterion is unachievable, experimental control is lost. Ergo: choose criterion changes large enough to be detected, yet small enough to be achievable.

## Overall Number of Criterion Changes

Another way the changing-criterion design can vary is in the number of criterion changes. Again, although the number of phases to include is up to the discretion of the program designer (however, a minimum of three POVs are required to demonstrate experimental control), the more often measures of the behavior change conform closely to a new criterion, the more convincing the demonstration of experimental control. If you replicate your changing-criterion design across (individuals or groups of) participants and also vary the number of days spent at each criterion level, your results can be even more convincing. (For an example, see Sulzer-Azaroff et al., 1990).

# MULTIPLE-PROBE DESIGN

Within the changing-criterion design, unless we collect data on sub-components of the behavior or on related behaviors, we risk losing the opportunity to see whether the latter were improving simultaneously, or if we could have achieved change more rapidly by some other means. In an unlikely scenario, suppose we had set a criterion level of 90 percent safe worker performance at the onset of our interventions rather than raising the standard gradually. Safety performance might have improved to that level immediately, thereby averting any need to shape gradual improvement. Another possible alternative was suggested in Chapter 9: using multiple-baselines to determine whether responding has generalized from one baseline to another. A different technique would be to *probe* related performances during the main intervention, by intermittently measuring those associated behavior(s) while they remained under baseline conditions. During the **multiple-probe design**, *data are collected only intermittently on other baselines*. Depending on whether or not those data co-vary with the more intensive data set, we can decide whether or not to intervene on the others.

To assess progress in shaping or chaining, you can break the skill you are teaching down into its separate elements; then collect baseline measures of them and apply the intervention sequentially to each element's baseline. You then would examine whether change appears to depend upon their receiving the intervention directly or if some of the elements co-vary with the others. Maybe acquiring one chain immediately produces mastery of a different though related one, as in the case of any reasonably proficient organist's being able to perform simple pieces on the piano.

You can apply the same logic to assessing whether intervention with one element of a task analysis or performance level influences that of another by intervening to promote one skill or rate while watching what happens to the others not yet treated, in multiple-baseline fashion. An example would be a student learning to do long division. His mastery of multiplication, one of the steps in the chain, would influence his success with other untutored steps (based on Horner & Baer, 1978). A multiple probe design also can be useful when working with feeding issues. For example, you could probe if the intervention with the child eating broccoli affects eating other vegetables not targeted during the intervention (e.g., carrots).

As you consider this tactic for a moment, though, perhaps you realize that taking continuous baselines for unlearned behavioral segments might be impractical or punishing for the evaluator and/or the learner. Just as a nurse does not take a person's temperature continuously but occasionally probes instead, here *"probing" the untreated baselines intermittently* would be preferable (Horner & Baer, 1978). Intermittently, you would apply multiple-probes by providing learners with an opportunity to perform the untrained responses, to ascertain whether the skills were being acquired or just changing by happenstance. Horner and Baer suggested that such opportunities or probes be conducted:

- initially on each of the training steps.
- again "on every step in the training sequence after criterion is reached on any training step" (p. 190).
- then in a series, just prior to teaching a particular segment.

To illustrate, consider the steps in teaching an abbreviated word-processing operation:

> **Minerva Loses Experimental Control along with Weight**
>
>  To encourage herself to lose weight, Aunt Minerva decides to use a point system exchangeable for a bikini and a trip to the south of France. She wants to find out whether the points actually are closely influencing her eating habits. For the next week, she sets the criterion for awarding herself points at an intake level 20 calories below that of the previous week. The following week, she sets the criterion 20 calories lower, and so on. Yet the data show that her intake is reduced far more substantially than the preset average of 20 calories per week. She loses weight, but also experimental control. Because her caloric-intake level does not match the pre-established criteria, whether or not the point system has served a controlling function is obscured. Maybe other unidentified factors could have influenced the outcome, and she doesn't know whether the point system had any influence at all. Had Aunt Minerva set the criteria at a more challenging level, she might have been able to demonstrate experimental control.

1. Turn on the computer.
2. Access the word-processing program.
3. Open a file.
4. Type a paragraph.
5. Save the file.
6. Print the file.

Instead of asking the student to perform each step repeatedly, you might ask her to perform each just once. Next, you would take a few baseline measures on Step 1; then train that step by telling, showing, and reinforcing. Once Step 1 has been learned, you would again assess Steps 2 through 6; then you would probe Step 2 in a series, followed by training in a similar manner. Again, you would probe the remaining steps and take a sequence of measures for Step 3, and so on. Perhaps you would see performance beginning to improve at the more advanced levels, even in the absence of intensive instruction. Further teaching would then need to be kept to a minimum.

## The Multiple-Probe Design Illustrated

Figure 25.4 displays probe data for one of three developmentally-delayed young men learning laundry skills (Thompson, Braam, & Fuqua, 1982). The probes measured each response in the entire chain right before baseline and training of each component. No reinforcers were delivered during probes. The baseline data only measured components previously trained, plus, as the data indicate, the component to be trained next. Note that Chester did know how to do some of the untrained steps prior to the intervention, but fully mastered those following the intervention at that level. In a more recent application of a multiple-probe design, Nava, et al. (2019) evaluated the effects of using peer-generated examples to augment examples contained in textbook and lectures on undergraduate performance on knowledge assessments. Although the peer-generated examples did not enhance their knowledge assessment performance, the students did rate them as more highly preferred, culturally responsive, and diverse than those in the textbook (hence, we have tried to be more sensitive to these perspective in this current edition).

Eighteen third-grade students participated in an investigation of the effects of an audiotaped teaching intervention on their multiplication fluency (McCallum, Skinner, Turner, & Saecker, 2006). To experimentally analyze the program's impact, the investigators used a multiple-probes-across-tasks design consisting of three sets of problems. During the intervention, students were given lists of problems and instructed to attempt to complete each one before an audiotape player provided the correct answer. Initially, the delay between problems and answers was brief. Subsequently, delays were varied. Results showed that after the intervention was implemented across all three sets of problems, multiplication-fact fluency immediately increased.

If you want to be able to assess learning trends, avoid confusing the multiple-probe method with

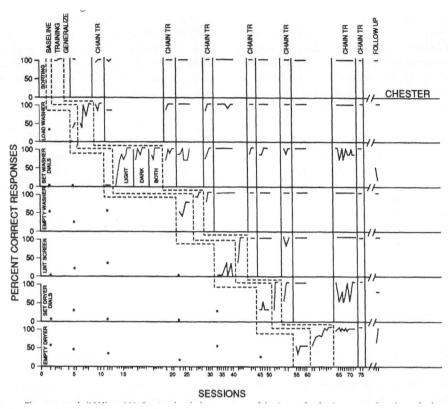

**Figure 25.4** Example of multiple-probe design. From Thompson et al. (1982), Figure 1. © 1982 by the Society for the Experimental Analysis of Behavior, Inc.

intermittent sampling of skill acquisition. Multiple-probes include closely repeated measures of performance at the step being taught. That is not the same as quizzing weekly, monthly, or twice a semester—an all-too-familiar practice. As Munger, Snell, and Loyd (1989) have mentioned, among the several disadvantages of infrequent assessments are that, in the absence of graphic data showing systematic improvement in performance, the instructor's judgment about the influence of the procedures on changes in level, trends, or variability may be distorted. Unwise program recommendations could result.

The design strategies presented so far permit behavior analysts to assess the functional relation between a given intervention and performance by revealing patterns of responding prior to and during the intervention. Suppose your concern is broader, though, in that you are seeking to discover those interventions promising to work more rapidly, durably, or economically, or to be more or less practical or acceptable to consumers. For instance, you may want to know which is preferable among a number of alternative strategies. Perhaps you are wondering whether oral instructions are sufficient to teach word-processing or if modeling might hasten learning. Suppose you want to analyze the effects of three different consequences on schoolchildren's completion of tasks: no extra recess (treatment A), extra recess time with planned activities (treatment B), and extra recess time with free play (treatment C). Here, you might compare the three by using a design strategy based on repeatedly measuring their various impacts within individual subjects.

Actually, determining whether a particular behavioral intervention is effective or not is fairly straightforward. But how do we choose the most promising alternative when more than one treatment option is available? Comparing the effectiveness of one intervention against that of another (a **comparative analysis**) is somewhat more complicated. Suppose, along with the specific focus of the intervention, say, to reduce Marty's classroom disruptions, a teacher is wondering whether to implement either noncontingent reinforcement (NCR—you remember, distributing reinforcers regardless of the participant's behavior at the time) or differential reinforcement of alternative behaviors (DRA). How would you decide which is most promising with respect to ease of implementation and associated side effects? Given the success of behavioral interventions in general, and the multitude of suitable change programs currently available, facing this kind of dilemma is not unusual.

You possibly could compare the effectiveness of different interventions by using a reversal design (e.g., A-B-A-B-A-C-A-C, A-B-C-A-B-C, etc.). But such comparisons are fraught with limitations. If, for example, treatment B regularly is presented in advance of treatment C, *B treatment conditions may influence subsequent performance* in C (**sequence effects**) Or we may say that the **carry-over** from whatever sequential pattern has become established **under B** may influence or confound the subsequent results in C. To illustrate, were we to use a reversal design to compare the effects of non-contingent reinforcement (NCR) versus those of differential reinforcement of alternative behaviors (DRA) by exposing the student to NCR prior to DRA, we would be unable to determine whether or not DRA produced its effects simply because it followed NCR. You cannot conclude that the outcome was the effect of DRA alone, because the student was exposed to NCR first. To rule out this potential confound, we could reverse the order of treatments on replication (e.g., A-C-A-B), preferably within or across subjects and/or by counterbalancing the order across subjects.

Beyond sequence effects, another concern is the possibility of **multiple-treatment interference**, derived from the participant's current and past history, in your setting and elsewhere. Suppose you were comparing the effects of timeout and response cost, but the participant had and continues to experience long timeouts in his home environment. That history also would confound your results. So, when designing a study, you need to be aware of the possibility of multiple-treatment interference, in the sense that *the participant's learning history may impact his or her performance under subsequent treatment.* (We elaborate upon these concepts later.)

Another disadvantage of using the reversal design as the basis for comparing interventions is the extended time required to complete the evaluation. (Note the eight phases in the above example.) Yet, behavior-change agents generally are called upon to alter behavior as quickly as possible, which is not compatible with extended reversal designs. Nevertheless, identifying the most promising intervention in a particular situation remains a frequent concern. The answer may lie in the alternating-treatment designs, our next topic.

## ALTERNATING-TREATMENT (MULTI-ELEMENT) DESIGNS

Experimental designs consisting of *treatment conditions rapidly alternated within or across sessions or days, and that permit us to examine any emerging differences in the rates as a function of each intervention*, are identified by a number of different names, including **multi-element**[3] (Bittle & Hake, 1977, Ulman & Sulzer-Azaroff, 1975), **alternating-treatment** (Barlow & Hersen, 1984), *simultaneous treatment* (Kazdin & Hartmann, 1978), *multiple schedule* (Leitenberg, 1973), or *concurrent schedules* (Hersen & Barlow, 1976). "The multi-element design… involves the repeated measurement of a behavior under alternating conditions of the independent variable" (Ulman & Sulzer-Azaroff, 1975, p. 379). According to Barlow and Hersen (1984), in the alternating-treatment design, *the same person is the recipient of two or more rapidly alternating conditions.* Were we to use an alternating-treatment design to compare the effects of NCR versus

---

[3]Technically, the multi-element design differs slightly from the alternating-treatment design in that in the former, "distinctive (potentially discriminative) stimulus is correlated with each condition…" (Ulman & Sulzer-Azaroff, 1975, p. 379).

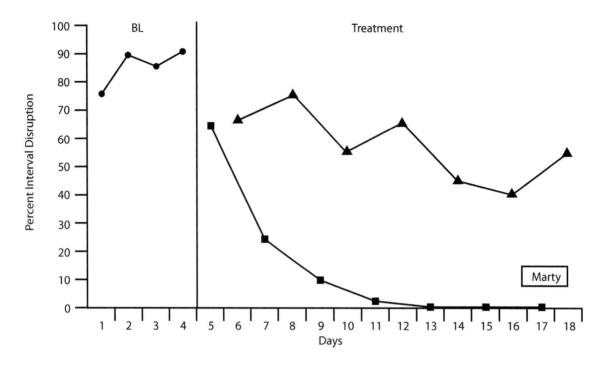

**Figure 25.5** Hypothetical example of the use of an alternating-treatment design. Note how each condition is functionally related to distinct levels of disruption (triangle = treatment A and square = treatment B).

DRA on Marty's behavior, we would rapidly alternate the two treatments (e.g., every other day) and examine problem behavior during each condition (see Figure 25.5).

Using a distinctive stimulus or set of stimuli with each contingency should ease the participant's ability to discriminate between the different conditions within the multi-element baseline (alternating-treatment) design (Ulman & Sulzer-Azaroff, 1975). Like multiple schedule and mix schedule, the use of the term multi- is used to describe the use of a discriminative stimulus with each condition (schedule). When response patterns are unique to each condition—that is, if "the subject's behavior is fractionated by stimulus control over each separate element" (Sidman, 1960; responses are distributed distinctively according to the stimuli associated with each element)—then experimental control has been demonstrated. The clearly discriminative conditions are intended to signal the particular ongoing intervention to the participant while observers assess for any distinctive responding under each. Obviously, the participant must be able to discriminate the stimuli associated with each condition; otherwise, differential response rates are unlikely to evolve. Consequently, behavior analysts usually try to intensify the distinctiveness of those discriminative stimuli (e.g., a different room, desk, or therapist; a sign; a different-colored worksheet; etc.). To illustrate, Conners et al. (2000) used diversely colored rooms and different therapists to support differential responding while using an alternating-treatment design to conduct a functional assessment. Moreover, in the absence of such discriminative stimuli, participants frequently failed to respond differentially across conditions.

As with other functional analytic approaches, the purpose of the alternating-treatment design is to be able to predict and replicate particular behavioral patterns. What is unique about it is that each data point serves as the basis for predicting the next and subsequent data points for each condition. Moreover, it permits treatments to be compared to an original baseline or to a baseline held constant throughout the treatment.

## The Alternating-Treatment Design Illustrated

The alternating-treatment design often is used as a tool for functionally analyzing the conditions associated with self-injurious and destructive behavior. Note that in Figure 25.6, data revealed that both interventions were effective in reducing self-injurious behavior (SIB), but noncontingent reinforcement (NCR) was associated with either more rapid or greater overall response suppression. This alternating-treatment analysis revealed the most effective intervention for each of these three participants.

Of course, various other interventions, including educational methods, rehabilitation practices, and so on can be compared using the alternating-treatment design. Neef, McCord, and Ferreri (2006) used the design to analyze college students' quiz performance as a function of guided notes (students needed to actively respond by completing notes themselves) versus notes pre-completed by the instructor (a more passive method). As shown in Figure 25.7, although both methods produced

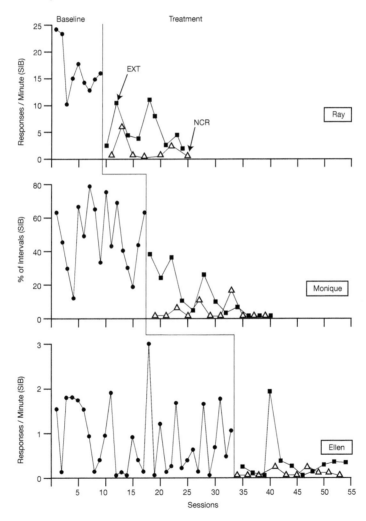

**Figure 25.6** Use of an alternating-treatment design to evaluate the effects of noncontingent reinforcement (NCR) and sensory extinction on the self-injurious behavior of three individuals with developmental disabilities. From Roscoe, Iwata, & Goh (1998), Figure 2. © 1998 by the Society for the Experimental Analysis of Behavior, Inc.

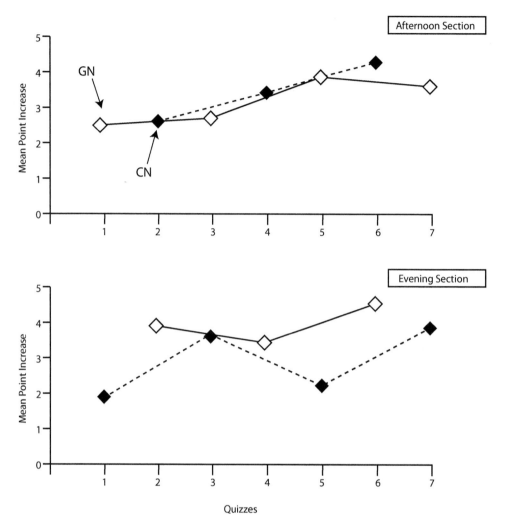

**Figure 25.7** An alternating treatment comparison between guided (GN) and pre-completed (CN) notes on student quiz performance. From Neef et al. (2006), Figure 1. © 2006 by the Society for the Experimental Analysis of Behavior, Inc.

roughly equivalent performances by those in the afternoon session, the guided notes produced superior results among the evening session students.

Weems (1998) used an alternating-treatment design to compare feedback methods intended to enable a patient to manage his own heart-rate. The patient learned best when supplied with visual heart-rate feedback. In another medically-related investigation, Coyle and Robertson (1998) also used a multi-element design to determine which of two passive mobilizing techniques increased the range of patients' wrist extension following particular types of wrist fractures.

## Using the Alternating-Treatment Design

**Emphasize distinctiveness of relevant discriminative stimuli.** If we want unique performances to evolve under different stimulus conditions, we must be certain the participant is able to discriminate between the stimuli *associated with* each condition. Otherwise, differential response rates are unlikely to evolve. Therefore, we advise you to *make each associated $S^D$ reasonably salient by using a different room, desk, therapist, sign, different-colored worksheet, and so on*, for *each*. When conducting an alternating-treatment design for functional analytic purposes, Conners, et al. (2000) used different-colored rooms and therapists to facilitate differential responding. Moreover, they demonstrated that when discriminative stimuli were not used, the clients responded differentially to diverse functional analysis conditions, more slowly or not at all.

**Consider using design variations.** You can vary the ways you use alternating-treatment designs to compare the functions of two or more independent variables. For example: to evaluate performance under a single-treatment versus baseline conditions (B versus A, within a single phase), especially if some kind of intervention is occurring during baseline; to compare two treatments absent a no-treatment control (B versus C within a single-phase); to compare two treatments within two phases (baseline is measured during phase one and the two treatments are compared during phase two—A then B versus C); and/or to extend the previous comparison by adding a third and final phase, wherein the most effective intervention is continued (either B or C). Another variation can strengthen findings revealed by an alternating-treatment design by applying the most successful intervention to the behaviors that were not acquired through the less-successful method(s). Ollendick, Matson, Esveldt-Dawson, and Shapiro (1980) used this tactic to demonstrate the value of using positive practice with their students (see Figure 25.8).

During the alternating-treatment design phase, words from Set A were assigned to the *positive practice plus positive reinforcement* condition; words from Set B were assigned to the *traditional* (study the words you got wrong) *plus positive reinforcement* condition; words from Set C

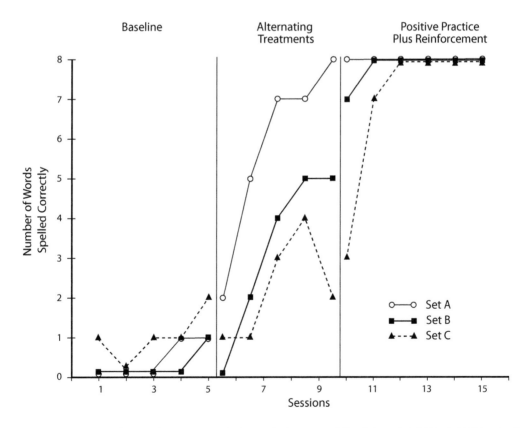

**Figure 25.8** Illustration of alternating-treatment design variation. From Ollendick et al. (1980). © 1980 by the Society for the Experimental Analysis of Behavior, Inc.

were assigned to the *traditional alone* condition. During the last phase, all three words sets were assigned to the *positive practice plus reinforcement* condition.

By presenting and withdrawing particular contingencies during the assessment phase, Day, Horner and O'Neill (1994) demonstrated that SIBs were functionally related to both escape from difficult task demands and to access to preferred items. They then instituted phases during which they taught the participant to use an appropriate form of communication first to obtain preferred objects and next to escape from difficult tasks (see Figure 25.9).

What about the POVs? In a multi-element design you assess POVs from the data point in one condition to the data point in the next condition by predicting what would happen if the intervention was not switched and ensuring the obtained level of behavior is different than that prediction. This can be very tricky. For example, if the two interventions work similarly, it will be difficult to obtain POVs with just the multi-element design unless you have a baseline condition and a combined design. Thus, if you are not sure how the two interventions will compare, it is best to ensure that POVs can be obtained by including a baseline as well as a combined design (e.g., multiple baseline across participants with a multielement design comparing two interventions).

## Advantages of Alternating-Treatment Designs

Alternating-treatment designs are especially useful for analyzing complex behavior, in that they

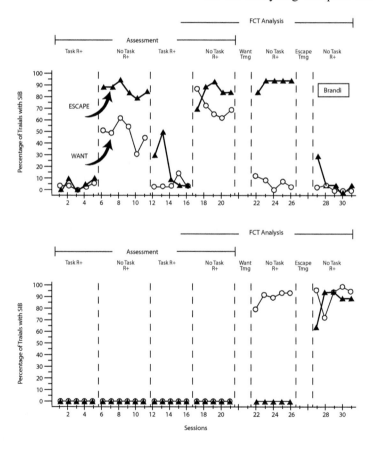

**Figure 25.9** Demonstration of the utility of the alternating treatment design when attempting to analyze the function of self-injurious behavior (SIB) and identify an acceptable solution. From Day et al. (1994). © 1994 by the Society for the Experimental Analysis of Behavior, Inc.

permit the effects of one or more independent variables to be compared. Although separate baseline phases ordinarily are a preferred way to show "naturally" ongoing behavioral patterns, baselines are not essential for demonstrating experimental control within alternating-treatment designs. This can be a key benefit, especially when the participant's ongoing behavior is harmful in some way, as with aggression or self-injury. Additionally, long baselines are unnecessary when alternating-treatment designs rapidly reveal distinct differences as a function of each diverse treatment. Rather, following a brief or even nonexistent original baseline period, baseline conditions can subsequently be interspersed among alternating-treatment conditions throughout the program. Although this design does not completely eliminate multiple-treatment interference, it does minimize it because exposure to each of the different interventions is brief, not extended, as in withdrawal or multiple-baseline designs. Sequence effects also are held to a minimum given the participant's limited exposure to one condition in advance of the next.

Another advantage of the alternating-treatment design is that it permits the variables to be compared within the context of a more slowly-changing background, such as seasonal changes, variations in available materials, and so on. Suppose you wanted to know whether hourly or daily supervisory feedback affected product quality differently. Were you to use an A-B-A-C design, with each phase lasting several weeks, seasonal variations in orders for goods (for example, the pre- versus post-holiday season) might also shift in tandem with the phase changes. Then you wouldn't be able to determine whether any distinctive effects were a function of the two different schedules or of the numbers or kinds of orders to be filled. Because the alternating-treatment design enables you to shift conditions far more rapidly, any differences within closely related time periods would be revealed when patterns of orders remain relatively stable from one day to the next.

The alternating-treatment design possesses other distinct advantages (Ulman & Sulzer-Azaroff, 1975), including:

- Its appropriateness for studying "irreversible" dependent variables (i.e., when behavior changes are less likely to reverse following protracted presentations of the independent variable).
- Its allowance for the rapid emergence of distinctive effects, thereby allowing the evaluation to be concluded quickly.
- Its utility in circumstances of baseline variability that do not require baseline stability.
- For the above reasons, its readier acceptance by families and personnel.

In addition, the alternating-treatment design is well suited to conducting *parametric analyses*; that is, *examining response patterns under different quantitative values of the independent variable*. For example, you can use the design to determine the minimal essential quantity or quality of a reinforcer, as in how often you need to monitor and compliment workers' good safety practices on the job or parents on their use of praise, or how many points toward a prize are sufficient to encourage apartment dwellers to recycle their trash or elder-care givers to conduct exercise routines with their clients.

In general, the alternating-treatment design opens avenues to more sophisticated analyses of complex behavior in applied settings and is especially well suited to *parametric*, *component*, and *comparative* analyses.

## Disadvantages of Alternating Treatment Designs

A major concern in any form of behavioral research is with sequencing effects, a form of the more general multiple-treatment interference. *Sequence, carryover, or alternation effects all refer to situations in which one experimental treatment influences behavior within other treatment phases* (Barlow, Nock, & Hersen, 2008). While the alternating-treatment design minimizes this type of threat to validity, one must carefully schedule and monitor the different conditions to see to it that each is implemented exactly as planned and that no single intervention is continued too long or inadvertently implemented along with other environmental changes. Withdrawal or multiple-baseline schedules are preferable methods of analyzing simple operant behaviors, such as performance rates, as a function of simple reinforcement schedules.

We also need to concern ourselves with two kinds of sequence-effect confounds within the alternating-treatment design. One relates to the *order* of treatments. Suppose A is the baseline condition; B uses tangibles plus praise as a combined treatment; and C uses praise alone. B always precedes C. As Theobald and Paul (1976) noted, behavioral patterns during a later A phase actually could be a function of whether its history included C alone or B then C. Probably the history of praise plus tangible reinforcers affected the subsequent patient responses to praise alone. Would treatment C have supported a different effect if not preceded by B? To minimize (though not eliminate entirely) this sequence effect, the order of presentation of treatments could, instead, be counterbalanced and delivered for only brief periods of time. The sequence might be A (baseline), A, C, A, C, B, B, A, C, B, A, B, C, and so on. Also, different sequences may be used within the same subjects for different behaviors.

Another sequence effect relates to the influence of the treatments on one another (i.e. multiple-treatment interference), irrespective of which one came first. For example, if you compared reinforcing effects of $5 versus $10 for participants with roughly equivalent learning histories performing the same task, the $5 might well weaken as a reinforcer. ("Why should I do it for $5 when I've gotten $10 earlier for doing it?") By contrast, were the $5 the *only* monetary reward presented, it may well maintain its reinforcing strength.[4] You cannot be certain in any given instance, though, that this sort of multiple-treatment interference affected outcomes. In one case (Maydak, Stromer, Mackay, & Stoddard, 1995), sequencing skills emerged among developmentally-disabled students who had been trained in matching-to-sample. Yet, unlike college students, their matching-to-sample skills were not facilitated by receipt of training in sequencing skills.

This disadvantage may be turned into an advantage, however, as Hains and Baer (1989) indicated.

Sometimes the alternating-treatment design is applied with sets of variables that naturally must interact with one another. (For example, consider how contextual variations, such as the deprivation and non-deprivation inherent in daily meal scheduling, might influence the effect of contingent and noncontingent delivery of food.) Here, the design may reveal how these different variables interact with one another. As Hanes and Baer (1989) contended, that feature permits the use of single-subject designs to examine interactive effects more efficiently and, by so doing, to begin to determine the degree to which currently understood behavioral phenomena are general or restricted to a single person, time, and/or place.

Another potential disadvantage of alternating-treatment designs is that participants may fail to discriminate between conditions that are rapidly alternating. This problem can be easily overcome by tying distinctive stimuli to each condition: colored lights, placemats, room wall-colors, tee-shirts worn by the change agents, location within the room (e.g., front vs. back of the classroom), and so on.

# CONDUCTING COMPONENT AND PARAMETRIC ANALYSES

## Component Analysis

Behavior-change interventions often consist of combinations or "packages" of treatments. In such cases, we may not know if and how much each component contributes to any observed change. Consider this situation: written and verbal instructions, modeling, and feedback commonly are combined within parent training programs (e.g., Kuhn, Lerman, & Vorndran, 2003; Mueller, et al., 2003; Neef, 1995). In such cases, conducting **component analyses**, (*identifying which and to what extent individual or combinations of elements influenced behavior measured change*), may be difficult. To solve this dilemma, the contribution of each component would have to be analyzed separately and in combination with the others: written instructions in the absence of the other procedures; verbal instruction alone; and so on, until each of the components

---
[4] A substantial amount of work in the area of "behavioral economics" concerns itself with these sorts of learning history effects. See, for instance, Johnson and Bickel (2006).

was separately investigated. Or, we might begin with one, then add the next, and so on. For example, Howard et al. (2020) used an add-in analysis and reversal design to demonstrate the effects of four self-management components (goal setting, self-monitoring, self-evaluation, and self-reinforcement). Specifically, they systematically evaluated the components with respect to effectiveness and efficiency with two high school students with emotional disturbance by beginning with goal setting, adding in self-monitoring, next self-evaluation, and finally self-reinforcement. Results demonstrated that the effects of the self-management were only maximized after they implemented the full intervention. It also is possible to evaluate a package by removing one component and then another to demonstrate the active component of a treatment package. For example, Donaldson et al. (2021) evaluated different components of the *Good Behavior Game* (see Chapter 28) at reducing disruptive classroom behaviors. Initially, they implemented all components to reduce particular classroom behavior across two pre-school classes. Subsequently, they removed various features of the intervention, ultimately concluding that vocal teacher feedback was essential to preventing disruptive behavior. You can use a number of single-case research designs can to evaluate components of interventions (e.g., reversal, withdrawal, multiple baseline, multielement), just remember you must obtain three POVs with all investigated components. Thus, although different designs can permit a component analysis, multielement designs are generally preferred due to its efficiency in complex analyses. The alternating-treatment design, then, is preferable when we hope to discover the active variable(s) within an intervention, and/or the relative contribution of different aspects of the intervention, or to pinpoint its essential elements. Cooper, Wacker, McComas, and Brown (1995) used both an alternating-treatment as well as a reversal design to investigate the active component(s) of treatment packages geared toward increasing food acceptance among children with feeding disorders. They found that escape-extinction promoted food acceptance. Similarly, Freeman (2006) conducted a component analysis to determine which component(s) were critical to success in treating bedtime resistance. Combining both a "bedtime pass" and extinction produced the best outcome.

## Parametric Analysis

Sometimes we want to find out how best to fine-tune our particular intervention, as in choosing the most effective reinforcer magnitude. *Parametric analyses* are well suited to such investigations and are commonly used to evaluate the differential effects of a range of values of an independent variable. In **parametric analyses**, *one parameter is held constant while other variables, within a family of functions, change to help determine their relative effects* (Catania, 2013). In a habit-reversal intervention, Twohig and Wood (2001) used a parametric analysis to search for the most effective competing response (CR) practice duration for nail biters. They compared increases in nail length as a function of five seconds, one minute, and three minute CR durations. Results showed that only the one minute and three minute durations produced lasting effects. Similarly, Carr, Bailey, Ecott, Lucker, and Weil (1998) conducted a parametric analysis of the suppressive effects of different magnitudes of noncontingent reinforcement on maladaptive responding. When compared to the other two magnitudes (medium and low), high-magnitude schedules produced the most significant and consistent response rate reductions. In addition to determining the most effective magnitude of an intervention, parametric analyses also have been used to assess what happens if an intervention is not implemented with fidelity. Why would that be important? Well sometimes after professionals have successfully implemented an intervention in a clinical setting but when the intervention is applied in the home setting, or by parents, they don't necessarily implement with 100 percent fidelity. Thus, it becomes imperative to understand what will happen to treatments when implemented at various fidelity levels in applied situations to predict any issues or loss in treatment effects that may arise. Are some interventions more durable when not implemented with 100 percent fidelity in these applied settings? In a recent example, Colón and Ahearn (2019) undertook a parametric analysis to assess the effectiveness of response interruption and redirection when inconsistently implemented. Results demonstrated that with 50 percent or above fidelity, the intervention was effective. Findings of this nature help to inform those who train and manage caregiver performance by allowing them to identify and specify the levels of treatment integrity required of various interventions to support effective treatment gains. Like component analyses, various single-subject research designs are available for such analyses (e.g., reversal, multielement, multiple baseline). The pros and cons of each design must be analyzed when deciding on which particular design to utilize to answer the specific questions at hand.

## SELECTING APPROPRIATE SINGLE-SUBJECT DESIGNS

Our discussion of research designs capable of demonstrating a functional relation between an *independent variable(s)* (or *treatments*) and a dependent variable (target behavior) has been by no means exhaustive. In addition to the designs discussed and illustrated in this text, various other combinations have been used in complex research (see Johnston & Pennypacker, 2008). As one of many such examples, Figure 25.10 illustrates a combined multiple-baseline-and-reversal (A-B-A-C) design (Mace, Page, Ivancic, & O'Brien, 1986).

Examine the figure closely to discover the experimenters' reasons for using such a combination of the various interventions. Yes, we can use experimental designs to answer experimental questions, instead of altering experimental questions to "fit" existing designs. *The question always comes first!* Bearing that in mind, review Table 25.1, which compares different experimental designs, conditions for selecting and avoiding them, and other advantages. The table may help you select designs best suited to answering your experimental or clinical questions. Moreover, when conducting applied research, it is always best to stay on the safe side by combining designs to ensure that experimental control is achieved one way or another.

Suppose at the onset you believed that the behavioral pattern would reverse, but after the initial baseline you noticed that indeed the behavior actually was irreversible, you preserved your experimental control by planning at the outset to use both a reversal and multiple-baseline-across-participants design. Your safest bet is to base the design of your experiment so as to control for all the possibilities you can imagine, not on a whim.

A few other issues are worth considering relative to single-subject designs. First, no hard-and-fast rules exist as to the number of withdrawals, multiple baselines, criteria, alternating conditions, or participants necessary to demonstrate convincingly the effects of the independent variable. This is not unlike the sorts of judgments we must make when selecting suitable inferential statistics for group design analyses. In either single-subject or group designs, "the judgments required are highly qualitative, and rules cannot always be stated profitably" (Baer et al., 1968, p. 95). The question remains open.

## OTHER CONSIDERATIONS WITH SINGLE-SUBJECT DESIGNS

### Irreversibility and Sequence Effects

Sometimes well-established behavior like reading, riding a bicycle, baking a chocolate cake, or using a safer and more comfortable position while at work, seems to become insensitive to extinction (i.e., they do not readily reverse in an A-B-A-B design). Perhaps reinforcers available in natural environments have taken over, or perhaps the habit has become "reinforcing in its own right," that is, *intrinsically reinforcing* (very often these are two ways of saying the same thing). Other times the position of a particular response within a sequence—the *eating* part of a chain of steps involved in baking a chocolate fudge cake—may powerfully influence subsequent performance.

Jones, Ollendick, and Shinske (1989) found it more expedient to compare different methods of teaching clients the skills involved in evacuating a building during a fire by statistically analyzing the results of a group design. Of course, the most prom-

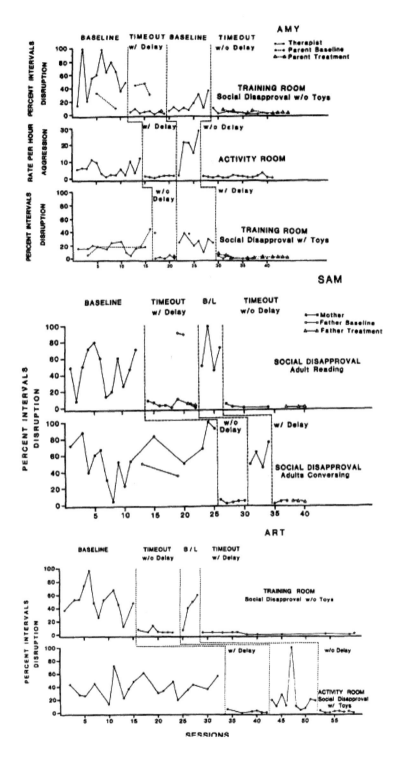

**Figure 25.10** Illustration of design combination. From Mace et al. (1986), Figure 1. © 1986 by the Society for the Experimental Analysis of Behavior, Inc.

**TABLE 25.1  Single-Subject Designs**

| Design | Operation | Select When | Avoid When | Other Advantages |
|---|---|---|---|---|
| Withdrawal (ABAB) | Measure baseline (A); apply procedure (B); return to baseline conditions (A); repeat procedure (B) | Extended baseline conditions can be tolerated before and during intervention | behaviors not reversible; rapid results required; reversal of specific targete behavior ethically irresponsible | Alternating A and B conditions may facilitate client's discrimination of relevant stimuli in the situation and transfer from CRF to intermittent schedules |
| Withdrawal (with reinforcement not contingent on target behavior during A condition) | Same as ABAB, except reinforcers not contingent on the targeted behavior during A and contingent on the targeted behavior during B | Comparing effects of noncontingent reinforcement; when overall level of reinforcement needs to be maintained | Same as ABAB; independent variable expected to produce only slight effect | Same as ABAB; reinforcers available throughout |
| Reversal | Following intervention (B), apply contingencies to ommision of target or to alternatives to target behavior during reversal phase (A) | Target behavior resistant to reversal; rapid demonstration of control desirable | Same as ABAB; "other" behaviors may be dangerous or otherwise undesirable | Same as ABAB; reinforcers available throughout |
| Multiple-baseline (General) | Measure baselines of several behaviors; apply procedure to one behavior, continuing baseline measures of other behaviors; apply procedure to second behavior; continue measuring treated and untreated behaviors; and so on | Target behavior is nonreversible or reversal is undesirable | All behaviors require rapid change | Intervention not interrupted once instituted, consequently more acceptable to clients and staff than reversals or withdrawals |
| Multiple-baseline across behaviors | Apply procedure to different behaviors one at a time with the same individual | Same as multiple-baseline; several behaviors of one individual targeted for change and independent of one another, demonstrating control of procedure across behaviors | Same as multiple-baseline design; effects of procedure may spread to baselines of other behaviors | Same as multiple-baseline design |

**TABLE 25.1 Single-Subject Designs (cont.)**

| Design | Operation | Select When | Avoid When | Other Advantages |
|---|---|---|---|---|
| Multiple-baseline across situations | Apply procedure to behaviors of one or more subjects across situations and at different times | Same as multiple-baseline design; same behaviors of one or more individuals are targeted for change in more than one setting; demonstrating control of procedures across situations | Same as multiple-baseline design; behavior change in one situation may spread to baselines in other situations | Same as multiple-baseline design |
| Multiple-baseline across individuals | Apply procedure to same behavior of different individuals at different times | Same as multiple-baseline design; same behavior targeted for change among several individuals; demonstrating control of procedure across individuals | Same as multiple-baseline design; changes in one individual's behavior may affect other individuals' baselines | Same as multiple-baseline design |
| Changing criterion | Apply intervention when behavior meets criterion level; change value of criterion at irregular intervals | Teaching new behaviors; intervention consists of graduated steps (as with DRL, and *progressive* or adjusting schedule changes) | Responding is likely to exceed the criterion | May ideally serve programming needs when criteria are changed gradually and progressively |
| Multiple probes | Probe performance intermittently prior to intervention (and more regularly during intervention) | To assess acquisition of skills; more frequent assessments would interfere with learning or are difficult practically | More frequent data required | May use to assess for steps acquired without formal training |
| Alternating treatment | Successively apply different interventions under distinctive stimulus conditions in rapid alternation with equivalent behaviors | Evaluating one or more different procedures; targeting behaviors unlikely to be reversed; stable baseline difficult to achieve; sequence and contrast effects minor or the subject of analysis | Unwilling or unable to continue alternating conditions until clear differences are manifest | More acceptable than reversals in applied settings; can show rapid effects over a limited time |

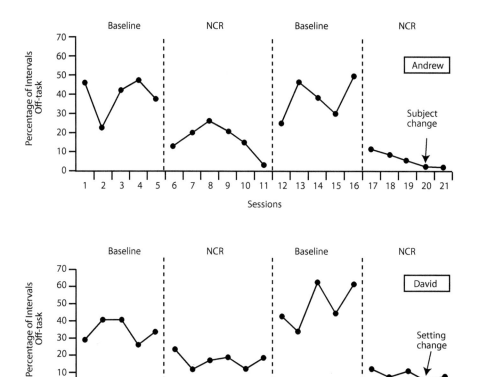

**Figure 25.11** Percentage of intervals in which off-task behaviors were observed across baseline and noncontingent reinforcement conditions for Andrew (top) and David (bottom). From Austin & Soeda (2008), Figure 1. © 2008 by the Society for the Experimental Analysis of Behavior, Inc.

ising method could be applied afterward to other individuals in multiple-baseline fashion. Baer et al. (1987) eloquently summarizes the issue of selecting experimental designs: "a good design is one that answers the question convincingly... and needs to be constructed in reaction to the question and then tested through argument in that context rather than imitated from a textbook" (p. 319).

## Determining the Significance of a Demonstrated Functional Relation

Yes, applied behavior analysts generally use single-subject designs to meet concerns of internal validity by demonstrating reliable, and sometimes replicable (as in A-B-A-B) differences in levels, trends, and/or variability of behaviors, under baseline and one or more intervention conditions. Now we address *external* validity. A key question is "Of what *significance* is any demonstrated functional relation?"

A traditional way to answer that question has been to turn to probability theory, by asking, "What is the likelihood that these results could have been obtained by chance alone?" If the numbers convince us that any differences between treated and untreated groups were very unlikely to have been produced solely by chance, we tend to accept the findings as "statistically significant." "Sometimes measurement and control is so good that a very small difference turns out to be *statistically* significant, but if it is small it might turn out to have *no practical* significance whatsoever" (personal communication from A. Charles Catania, 9/20/10). In applied behavior analysis, however, the emphasis is more on the impact of the intervention on each individual's personal, academic, vocational, social, and/or other behavior classes.

## Determining Experimental Significance

We may determine **experimental significance** by asking *how the behavior looks now, under treatment, versus how we would have expected it to look had the experimental intervention not occurred* (Risley, 1970). Kazdin (2010) has described several ways to determine which single-subject results clearly meet the criterion for experimental significance.

**Overlap in plotted performance.** The first method is to look at *overlap in plotted performance* by examining how often the data recorded during the intervention overlap with those during baseline, especially for treatments over time within or across subjects, settings, or behaviors. Figure 25.11, illustrates this point by displaying the results of a teacher's use of a noncontingent reinforcement procedure to decrease the off-task behavior of two third-grade students. Note that for both participants the percent of intervals off-task during both baseline and intervention rarely overlaps.

**Trend analysis.** Another way to infer that the treatment has been effective is to examine systematic changes in the *trend* occurring as a function of treatment conditions. Notice how David's data in Figure 25.11 showed an increasing trend in off-task behavior during the second baseline, while during the second NCR phase, after noncontingent reinforcement was reinstated, that trend reversed, shifting to a downward direction.

**Time-series statistical analysis.** A third way to meet the criterion is by demonstrating statistical significance on the basis of time-series analyses of the patterns of repeated measures of individuals' performance under each experimental condition. This method is especially useful when visual displays are insufficiently convincing or when measures are not independent of one another (i.e., are serially dependent on one another, Hartmann et al., 1980). If the data are so variable that the actual magnitude of an effect becomes obscure, important results might inadvertently be discarded as insignificant. Various statistical methods have been devised to assess the significance of change in single cases (see Barlow et al., 1984; Kazdin, 2010; Satake, Jagaroo, & Maxwell, 2008; Tryon, 1982; the series of articles in the *Journal of Applied Behavior Analysis, 7*, 1974, 627–653; and others). Moreover, additional research has focused on the comparison of effect sizes (Campbell, 2004) and on statistical process control (SPC) methods and illustrations (e.g., Pfadt, Cohen, Sudhalter, Romanczyk, and Wheller, 1992) as they relate to single-subject design. In a more recent review, Craig and Fisher (2019) provide a rationale and guide to using "randomization tests statistical analyses" as an alternative to visual inspection for analyzing behavior analytic data. Moreover, they provide a lens for looking at practical barriers to using certain standard statistical methods with behavior analytic results, to help behavior analyst understand and use statistical analyses. You may be asking yourself why this is important, given that most other science professions utilize statistical analyses and that some funding agencies require their use, understanding how they can be applied to behavior analytic data can be important. Craig and Fisher argue that the use of randomization tests (which is a specific type statistical analyses) are better suited because they do not require any distributional assumptions or randomization, and because the method more closely aligns with the purpose of behavior analytic questions (i.e., individual differences vs. population statistics).

For those of us whose primary concern is enhancing important personal, educational, vocational, and social behavior, however, another approach is available. Instead of mining the data for evidence of statistical significance, all might be better served by modifying the intervention methods. Suppose, for instance, our aim is to increase a behavior—say the amount of time a person spends exercising each day. Yet our data seems to be quite variable, with many "high" days during baseline and "low" days during treatment. We are better advised to modify the program, rather than to try to tease out the subtle effects within the data. In general, we concur with Jack Michael's recommendation:

> When a dependent variable is not under good control—when there is considerable unexplained variability even though the independent variable being studied is at a constant value—it is not usually necessary to go ahead with other planned manipulations. Further efforts can be made to obtain a more stable dependent variable or to discover and eliminate some of the sources of uncontrolled variation. (1974, p. 651)

## Other Forms of Significance

**Personal and social significance.** In addition to the significance of the functional relation between the behavior and treatment(s), the applied behavior analyst also asks about the importance of the outcome for particular individuals, their family members, associates, and/or their local or broader societies (Baer et al., 1968; Risley, 1970). Identifying ways to measure such responses in advance of an intervention should enable consumers to determine whether the client and others have benefited from the intervention or not.

**Clinical significance.** Some program evaluation models are based on the discrepancy between expected outcomes and those actually achieved. This same approach can be used to assess the value of change achieved by applying behavioral procedures. Chapter 4 discussed specification of behavioral objectives. Recall that beyond the description of the response and the conditions under which it is to occur, a behavioral objective includes a standard or criterion for determining its attainment. In applied behavior analysis, we judge a behavior change to be **clinically significant** if we accomplish *the pre-stated objective*. According to a series of papers on the topic of clinical significance (social and personal) in the journal *Behavioral Assessment* (Number 2, 1988), the criteria for describing clinical significance may derive from normative studies, meta-analyses, clarification of goals, statistical significance, social evaluation, termination of the complaints of the clinician and client, and other sources. Should the behavior improve to the pre-established criterion level as stated in the objective and be shown to be functionally related to the intervention, we certainly can conclude that the outcome is significant in the clinical sense.

Alternatively or in addition, we can agree upon the social, personal, or clinical significance of an outcome by assessing changes in the individual's ecological context. Has *the behavior change proven beneficial or detrimental to the participants, and/or their physical surroundings and social milieu*? Enabling a worker to be more productive may result in an increase of wages as a benefit. Yet at the same time that may endanger her or her coworkers if her work rate becomes too rapid to maintain adequate safety. Or, promoting one employee's innovations may result in bonuses or promotions as a benefit, while simultaneously causing difficulties for others in the organization by making their jobs obsolete.

**Educational significance and social validity.** How do you determine whether your efforts have been educationally or socially valid? **Educational significance**, according to Voeltz and Evans (1983), depends not only on whether change has occurred as a function of the program, but also on *whether the intervention was implemented as specified and beneficial to the client and those in his own environment*. Regarding **social validity**, Wolf (1978) advised that three factors be considered:

- the social significance of the goals
- the social appropriateness of the procedures
- the social importance of the effects

The first two issues were discussed in Chapters 4 and 12 on goal and procedural selection. In terms of social importance, Wolf suggested that we find out *whether consumers are satisfied with the results, both planned and unplanned*. No matter how experimentally effective an intervention may be shown to be, what is the use if consumers are dissatisfied with the outcome? Should they find the behaviors too costly, bothersome, intrusive, or unpalatable in some other way, they would be unlikely to continue to use the treatment.

To examine social validity, we can ask people about results. As other behavior analysts are increasingly doing, we might consider employing well-designed questionnaires or structured interview formats. In one case, Marmolejo, Wilder, and Bradley (2004) evaluated the effects of response cards on students' quiz scores and their participation in an upper-division course. Both performance plus social validity questionnaire results showed not only increases in quiz scores and continued student participation, but also that students approved of the use of these response cards. Similarly, Codding et al. (2005) used performance feedback as a means for increasing treatment integrity among teachers implementing school-based interventions. According to a social validity rating measure, the teachers rated the intervention favorably. In another case (Alavosius & Sulzer-Azaroff, 1990), nurses were asked a set of consumer satisfaction questions about the value of the training they had received in safely lifting and transferring clients. All agreed that the methods were helpful and acceptable. Maybe that explains why some participants reported that they had initiated teaching the techniques to their fellow workers. The findings also have encouraged further work along these lines. (e.g., Jostad, Miltenberger, Kelso, & Knudson, 2008; Nikopoulos & Nikopoulou-Smyrni, 2008).

A different approach is to ask uninformed judges to make global assessments of change, as Schreibman, Koegel, Mills, and Burke (1981) did to socially validate change among their autistic clients. Judges were able to distinguish those children whose behavior had been experimentally shown to have improved from children whose behavior had not.

Subjectivity is always an issue of concern when using human opinion measures. Often respondents are concerned about supplying the answer they think the inquirer wants to hear. When feasible, an alternative is to provide opportunities for consumers to choose. After the program has been completed, you can offer to repeat it or to conduct other viable alternatives, such as repeating the previous methods with other behavior, people, or in other settings. See which, if any, they elect.

# MAKING DECISIONS APPLICABLE TO LARGE GROUPS

As previously discussed, the single-subject design is not necessarily the most practical way to arrive at normative group decisions. Sometimes such purposes are better served by group experimental-research designs or meta-analyses of single-subject research. Suppose the special-education departmental staff of a jurisdiction wanted to decide whether they should train and support teachers' use of the *Picture Exchange Communication System*©. In an actual case in the United Kingdom (Howlin et al., 2007) decision-makers determined that the most expedient way to decide would be to test the statistical significance of differences in average student gains from pre-test to post-test between population samples drawn from the group trained in PECS and a control group not so trained. Results revealed that while the program was in effect, the experimental group did engage in functional communication significantly more often than the control group.

In addressing the broader question of identifying the best strategy for treating children on the autism spectrum, a study (McEachin, Smith, & Lovaas, 1993) was designed to assess the long-term outcomes of providing such children with early *intensive behavioral intervention* (an approach based on applied behavior analysis). The early-intervention program demonstrated that in 47 percent of the cases the children "recovered from autism," while there was a major reduction in the severity of 42 percent of the remaining cases. As might be anticipated, that report was criticized (as almost any study of this level of intensity, size, and complexity is bound to be) on various methodological grounds (e.g., Gresham & MacMillan, 1998). Nonetheless, findings were sufficiently compelling to encourage further simple (controlled to be as similar as feasible) and systematic (containing variations on the basic theme) replications of the program. Since then, findings from several group comparison studies have supported those results (e.g., Remington et al., 2007).

Using a meta-analysis, Kane, Connell, and Pellecchia (2010) looked at the effects of language interventions in a naturalistic interventions versus contrived interventions on children with autism. They evaluated percentage of non-overlapping data and concluded that naturalistic interventions are more effective than contrived interventions for teaching and maintaining skills, but that contrived interventions resulted in greater generalization than naturalistic interventions.

Remember, though, that if a behavior analyst, manager, supervisor, clinician, nurse, counselor, psychologist, teacher, or parent, among others, wants to know whether a promising set of materials actually will aid a particular individual client, their best choice is to use a single-subject design.

## COST EFFECTIVENESS

Beneficial or detrimental outcomes to people and their environments are primary considerations when you evaluate the value of an intervention program. So is consumer satisfaction. Yet no matter how pleased any constituencies may be with the outcome, their enthusiasm will be tempered by the expenses involved. Practitioners, as well, should be aware of the costs they incur if they are to charge reasonably for their services.

Yates (1985) offered a useful strategy that scientist/practitioners may use to determine cost effectiveness. Basic steps involve:

1. Decide which program or technique to analyze.
2. Use experimental analyses.
3. Decide how to assess costs and benefits in advance.
4. Use multiple measures and comparison procedures.

You may assess *cost/benefit* by identifying the necessary resources for a program (personnel, materials, facilities, equipment, and so on) and then determining the value of each. The total then may be contrasted with the costs of applying those resources to the best alternative method. Calculate also clients', families', staff and volunteer time and psychological cost (if you can gain a handle on that), inflationary adjustments, other expenses suggested by interested parties plus any other relevant cost features. Besides effectiveness and satisfaction, the value of interventions may be assessed in terms of actual fiscal savings, present and future income by the agency and clients, and others. Refer to Yates (1985) for additional details, including methods for assessing the relationship between costs and effectiveness.

Regardless of which formulae you select, be sure to contrast the various immediate and long-term outcomes of your particular program with results that have been or might be achieved by others, such as previous interventions. Perhaps you will conclude that on balance, the intervention you have evaluated is preferable despite the added costs.

## EVALUATING THE SIGNIFICANCE OF FINDINGS

Once you can successfully defend your conclusions as to the experimental and social significance of your findings, you may wish to ask how general they are. Where direct replication helps establish "the generality of phenomena among the members of a species ... systematic replication can accomplish this and at the same time extend its generality over a wide range of situations" (Sidman, 1960, p. 111). Recall how earlier in the discussion of single-subject designs we mentioned that such designs generate principles of behavior for particular individuals. When experimenters **directly replicate** procedures and obtain *common outcomes across similar behaviors, individuals, or settings,* they begin to acknowledge the generality of the outcomes. Examples are presented repeatedly throughout this book. We become even more convinced of the power and generality of a principle when *results are reproduced despite variations in the basic procedural parameters, such as the task, setting, change agent, or others,* as in the **systematic replication** tactic. A couple of illustrations follow.

The CLASS (Contingencies for Learning Academic and Social Skills) program was developed by Walker and his colleagues (e.g., Walker & Hops, 1979) to correct the opposition and acting out of pupils in the primary grades. The clearly delineated package of components, including teacher praise, individual and group contingencies, school and home rewards, contracting, and response cost had been applied successfully in numerous students, classrooms, and schools. Then Walker, Retana, and Gersten (1988) decided to try the program in Costa Rica, where many environmental variables, such as class size, level of parental involvement, financial support, and other aspects differ from those in the United States. Results achieved by this systematic replication were similar to those achieved previously (although not quite as dramatic), lending credence to the hardiness and generality of the CLASS package.

The fundamental elements of an injury-prevention program designed by Sulzer-Azaroff and her colleagues include pinpointing behavioral targets related to previous injuries or "near misses" in particular settings, devising valid measures of those performances, assessing participant's baseline performance, then regularly feeding back the results of those and subsequent assessments to the workers and/or their supervisors. A series of systematic replications by numerous investigators have demonstrated the general effectiveness of the package across varied conditions: different safety targets, job settings, augmented rewards and social events, schedules of feedback, group size, and others. (See Sulzer-Azaroff & Austin, 2000, for a review of the effect of these procedures on reducing accident rates.)

Similarly, the early intensive behavioral intervention strategies reported by McEachin et al. (1993) and others, mentioned earlier, constitute another cogent example of the systematic replication approach to treating youngsters on the autism spectrum. Still one more example is the broad-based application of functional-analysis methodology for the purpose of identifying the circumstances responsible for the self-abusive and aggressive behaviors of clients on the autism spectrum. This method has solidly demonstrated its ability to serve as a broadly general assessment strategy. In fact, it has been used to determine the function of numerous problematic behaviors across various populations (Hanley, Iwata, & McCord, 2003) in a wide range of settings.

# PROBING FOR GENERALITY AND PERSISTENCE OF CHANGE

As we reliably reproduce the results of given ABA methods under the same, as well as under altered circumstances, our confidence in the dependability and generality of the intervention grows. Measures of the social importance and cost effectiveness of the method allow us to feel ever more confident about its value. Evaluation is not complete, however, until we conduct periodic preplanned probes of generality and persistence while the intervention is in effect, and afterward. This quantification will inform us about whether the natural community of contingencies has assumed sufficient control over the change or whether environmental arrangements must be restructured to support the generalization and maintenance of the behavior change (Chapters 21–24).

# PRACTICING ANALYTICALLY

Remember one of the key dimensions of applied behavior analysis is its analytical feature. Consequently, to properly practice as a behavior analyst requires that you demonstrate functional relationships between the conditions in effect and the related behavior. It is not sufficient simply to collect data, operationally define behavior (i.e., be behavioral), precisely describe the interventions implemented (i.e., technological), and/or discuss behavior change principles incorporated with the procedure in a conceptually systematic way. One must also demonstrate that the results are a function of (i.e., are functionally related to) the specific interventions that have been implemented. (In the language of the layman, one might conclude that the intervention(s) fostered the results.) We demonstrate this lawful relationship between the behavior of concern and the intervention by employing single-case designs. Recall that single-case designs are not reserved only for researchers (remember those myths we discussed in Ch. 9), but are essential to your own performance as a competent behavior analyst. This is not to assert that you won't encounter hurdles to overcome to truly demonstrate a functional relationship between the intervention you implement and related behavior change. But, given solid planning, you can overcome these barriers to ensure that your ongoing practice remains analytical. It is insufficient for us to contend that our intervention was effective. Rather, we must offer evidence that what happened resulted directly from what we did. (Now would be a good time review Chapter 9 and decide how you will put single-case designs into practice in the analyses of behaviors of concern to you).

## SUMMARY AND CONCLUSIONS

Any program of behavior change needs to be evaluated for its validity and significance. Single-subject designs lend themselves especially well to the requirements of rigorous research methodology, permitting the assessment of internal validity, an essential of program evaluation.

Chapter 9 began with simpler designs, such as the withdrawal and multiple-baseline, which permit us to analyze how a given set of conditions is functionally related to behavior change. In this chapter we have described, illustrated, and discussed the more complex changing-criterion and alternating-treatment designs. Table 25.1 displays the full set covered in this text, including displays of the operation, conditions for and against its selection, and other advantages of each design. In general, assuming extended phases can be tolerated, we suggest you use withdrawal and multiple-baseline designs to demonstrate functional control. Select the withdrawal design if the target behavior is capable of readily changing direction. Use changing-criterion and multiple-probe designs to demonstrate experimental control over skill acquisition or other irreversible varieties of learning. Choose the alternating-treatment method to compare different treatments and/or to probe for any interactions between treatments and contexts. In general, though, adjust your experimental strategies to the particular question being posed; not the other way around.

This chapter also has considered questions of significance, generality, cost/benefit, and especially, the social importance of results. Finally, we have emphasized the need to follow up to evaluate and/or to support the durability and generality of the intervention.

*Chapter 26*

# Reducing Behavior: Extinction

## Goals

1. List and discuss several important factors to consider prior to targeting a behavior for reduction.
2. Discuss contextually inappropriate behavior, including a justification for its consideration.
3. Discuss the relevance of peer-reviewed research in the development of interventions aimed at reducing problem behavior.
4. Discuss the circumstances under which a nonrestrictive procedure could be considered highly restrictive and how those considerations might affect one's perspectives on clients' rights to effective treatment.
5. Define and illustrate *extinction*.
6. Discuss each property of extinction and how to minimize potential side-effects that may interfere with progress.
7. Define and differentiate between an *extinction burst* and *extinction-induced aggression*.
8. Define and illustrate *escape extinction*.
9. Define, differentiate and illustrate:
    a. *spontaneous recovery*
    b. *resurgence* and *regression*
10. Distinguish *positive behavioral contrast* from *behavioral contrast* in general.
11. Describe how to use extinction effectively.
12. Illustrate several methods for achieving extinction within group settings.
13. Define *learned helplessness* and describe what may contribute to its occurrence.
14. What is meant by the *Dead Man's Test*?
15. Discuss when it might and might not be appropriate to use extinction.

## DECIDING TO PREVENT OR REDUCE BEHAVIOR

For better or worse, the members of every family, organization, or every other social group, are affected by the behaviors of members of their cohort. They notice who directs what actions to themselves or others, and the immediate, and sometimes longer, term effect of those actions. Mom praises Sally for cleaning her plate, so Sally's sister begins to clean her plate. An office worker can't help overhearing the boss reprimanding his coworker for spending too much time chatting on the phone or playing games on his computer, so as soon as he notices the boss entering the area, he, himself rushes to open the file he is supposed to be addressing. Despite his doctor's warnings and his own dissatisfaction with his girth, Roger regularly loads his plate with and consumes highly caloric foods that already have resulted in his unhealthy weight gain. These sorts of maladaptive actions are universal and by now, probable you can understand why: they have been powerfully reinforced.

In this text, so far, you have been learning about the way reinforcement functions to promote and teach personally and socially valued behaviors. In most cases, if you begin and continue to employ those strategies meticulously, the frequency of those preferred behaviors begin to accelerate, while many un- or less-preferred acts begin to fall by the wayside.

Nonetheless, sometimes the individuals for whose deportment we are responsible continue to act in non-constructive or even destructive ways. So, in advance of even starting the search for strategies to diminish or eliminate those kinds of unwanted behaviors, you have a responsibility to thoroughly observe the contingencies currently operating within the person's environment. Is there sufficient ongoing reinforcement to sustain people's adaptive performance? Are you, yourself, so enmeshed in trying to put out fires that you fail to attend to *what's right* in your social milieu?

When you find yourself pressed to handle unpleasant, disruptive, dangerous, or even moderately or seriously irritating behavior, your first reaction might be to use an intervention to reduce its occurrence. Before applying any procedure designed to reduce behavior, we urge that, first, you assess, and then, if necessary, give a fair trial (many weeks, perhaps even months) to enriching the level of ongoing reinforcement within the environment in which the person(s) of concern misbehave. If addressing that fails, you may need to tailor an individual program for that person, including addressing ongoing environmental supports and impediments to that change.

## TARGETING A BEHAVIOR FOR REDUCTION

Once a decision has been made to reduce a behavior, next comes determining what behaviors should be targeted for prevention and/or reduction. Should just any behavior be targeted for prevention or reduction? Ask yourself first, *"To whom does the problem belong?"*—to the person who is disturbing you, or to you? Who will benefit now and in the future from a resolution of the problem? You, your organization, or those you are serving?

In and of itself, just about any specific behavior is neither good nor bad. Just to cite a few examples, hitting in a boxing ring, shouting or throwing at a sports event, saying nasty things in a dramatic rendition, running around in a game of tag, or pushing someone out of the path of danger are acceptable behaviors. Screaming is not acceptable while the teacher is talking to the class, but it is encouraged during the big game of the season. So when you say "unwanted behavior," think **contextually inappropriate behavior,** or **CIB**, *behavior unsuitable in the particular context.* CIB is a term used by Bondy and Sulzer-Azaroff (2002) to describe classes of behavior that might reasonably be targeted for prevention or reduction given specific circumstances.

Then we need to consider whether to concentrate simply on eliminating a behavior *per se*, or to choose and promote alternative, appropriate behaviors. From an *ethical* perspective, aiding in the construction of acceptable alternative behavior is more advantageous than simply eliminating behavior from people's repertoires. From a *practical* viewpoint, if they engage in the CIB to gain reinforcement and they do not have an appropriate means for gaining said reinforcement, it would be better to give them an acceptable replacement behavior rather than waiting to see what behavior in which they begin to engage while their problem behavior diminishes. For example, if someone engages in aggression to get attention, it would be better to teach them to use an "attention card," rather than chancing their selecting an even more undesirable attention-getting behavior. Moreover, focusing on the development of behaviors incompatible with the unwanted ones encourages individuals to remain and continue working and progressing in the situation, and to see themselves in a more positive light. (Refer back to Chapter 4 to remind yourselves of the guidelines for selecting sound behavioral objectives and the value of the constructional approach.)

Nevertheless, despite everyone's combined best efforts, sometimes circumstances require us to shift our focus to methods designed to prevent or reduce particularly serious behaviors, preferably through supportive, or, in the *most extreme cases*, temporarily punitive methods. That might be done on the grounds that clients or their advocates and/or those representing the perspectives of their families, teachers, care-providers, or society at large deem the treatment to be to *everyone's mutual benefit*. Consider a few examples: Lucretia's severe eye-poking threatens to cause her irreversible eye damage. Fernando's habit of flinging sharp and heavy tools in the workshop places others at risk. Paula's chronic procrastination slows down her team's completion of its assigned projects, and also prevents Paula and others from receiving promotions and salary increases. Mr. Kelley's sarcasm is so punishing that his students' performance rates and satisfaction with school are seriously impaired; as a result, many of them drop out of school. Howard's careless handling of hazardous materials and equipment places him and his co-workers in jeopardy.

Angela's habit of twirling her hair every now and then is a different story, however. It is neither harmful nor disruptive, nor does it interfere with her learning. She completes all work assignments competently. Unless Angela is really eager to address the issue, directly applying any reductive procedure is not justifiable.

Once you have made an ethically responsible decision to target an action for reduction, before going any further, you need to *attempt to discover why it is happening* or *what is supporting it*. This analysis not only makes sense but adheres to the Behavioral Analysts Certification Board's Professional and Ethical Compliance Code for Behavior Analysts which states, "When behavior analysts are developing a behavior-reduction program, they must first conduct a functional assessment" (Code 3.01-a). (Functional assessments are described in Chapter 10.) You might find that the behavior serves a calming effect or possibly enables the person to progress toward a more pleasurable activity sooner. For some behavior problems, looking at how the environment triggers the issue, might be altered instead of or prior to addressing the CIB. For example, is the behavior a natural and predictable reaction to punishment or extinction conditions (i.e., is the person aggressive to escape or avoid an aversive situation)? In such cases, alter your focus from changing the person's behavior to reducing the aversiveness of the situation, or substituting current circumstances with ones that contain a higher density of reinforcement. Examples are:

- Shifting particularly vulnerable students from Mr. Kelley's class to one taught by a teacher who dispenses reinforcement liberally, but rarely invokes punishment, or by teaching Mr. Kelley to change his methods (the later would probably be more advantageous).
- Adjusting disruptive students' tasks to those that are both productive and fun: instead of teaching arithmetic facts with flashcards, embed them in the context of dramatic play such as a store, a sports contest, or a fantasy drama.
- Making Howard's job easier by providing wastebaskets and storage niches within reach of his work surface.
- Helping Paula to subdivide her tasks carefully into smaller units and providing her with a chart to check.
- Instructing Paula, and perhaps her coworkers, to deliver small reinforcers to her as she completes each subtask.
- Changing Fernando's workshop assignment to one that involves handling or arranging

colorful objects, materials he is known to be capable of and to enjoy manipulating.

If practical environmental changes such as *extinction* (Thompson, Iwata, Hanley, Dozier, & Samaha, 2003) or, antecedent methods of the type described in the next chapter are not feasible and the behavior of concern remains so problematic that it cannot be ignored, try other positive constructive methods listed in Chapter 28. If those simpler methods are unsuccessful, carefully examine the results of the functional behavioral assessment. Does the troublesome behavior allow the individual to avoid or escape a difficult or demanding task, or produce attention or access to some reinforcing objects or activities (Carr & Durand, 1985b)? The answer may guide you toward a solution in which you can use antecedent and positive methods based on your FBA.

When intervention methods give close consideration to the function of problem behavior(s), resorting to punitive methods rarely becomes necessary. Should the functional behavioral assessment strongly suggest the root of the problem, you might be able to use positive behavioral interventions by altering the antecedents that set the occasion for its occurrence and/or by teaching new, socially desirable responses that yield equivalent or possibly even more potent reinforcers.

Fortunately, positive behavioral interventions of the kind described in the next two chapters can be as effective as punitive ones and generate far fewer aggressive and escape reactions (see Carr & Durand, 1985a, 1985b; Durand & Carr, 1987; Durand & Kishi, 1987; Horner & Budd, 1985; Iwata et al., 1994). A case in point is an individual's inability to achieve fulfillment of his or her wants and needs. Several researchers have reported that when people who were previously unable to communicate effectively learned a functional substitute, such as using pictures or signs, their aggression subsided (Bondy & Frost, 1998; Charlop-Christy et al., 2002; Frea, Arnold, & Vittimberga, 2001; Webb, 2000).

Next, examine the peer-reviewed research literature to *ensure that the procedures you are considering have been empirically demonstrated to be effective among the types of populations your client represents and for the behaviors of concern.* From that array, select the most promising, benign, natural, contextually appropriate, and least intrusive procedures available (or design a tightly-constructed experimental analysis yourself).

After that, you will want to *check federal, state, and local laws and organizational policies* to ensure the procedure is not on a *Do Not Conduct* list. With developmentally-disabled children, for example, you will need to abide by contemporary legislative guidelines. Also, in that the federal legislation of *Every Student Succeeds Act* (Dec., 2015) gives states more power over education policy, be sure to check the policies and laws within your state, and stay abreast of judicial decisions rendered in your own jurisdiction (Etscheidt, 2006). In general, if your client is a student, you will be required to provide free appropriate education under the least restrictive conditions feasible. The latter has been defined in detail by various state and local agencies. In Massachusetts, for example, state policy (Commissioner of Mental Retardation, 104, CMR 20.15) regulates three different levels of intrusiveness. The first requires only supervisory approval; the second, fairly elaborate human rights and professional and advocate reviews and approvals; and the third, court approval. State educational policies regulate disciplinary teacher methods, and labor departments and/or union agreements often govern disciplinary practices in work settings.

*Choose the most contextually appropriate, constructive, least restrictive and least intrusive procedures feasible.* This means you begin by considering positive approaches first, such as teaching functional communication or other skills (e.g., Hanley, Piazza, Fisher, & Maglieri, 2005; Schwartz et al., 1998), as described in Chapters 27 and 29. Consider temporarily augmenting or supplementing positive methods with reductive methods such as *negative punishment* (e.g., removing reinforcers—*response cost*, or removing the opportunity to earn reinforcers—*time-out*), or *positive punishment* methods (e.g., requiring the problem behavior to be corrected—*overcorrection*, or in rare cases, by presenting aversive stimuli contingent on the behavior—*punishment)*, only if the non-punitive interventions are deemed either inappropriate or work dangerously slowly or have failed after having been applied appropriately (e.g., Ganz, Cook, Corbin-Newsome, Bourgeois, & Flores, 2005). But even then, *it is critical that any and all punitive procedures be combined with reinforcement procedures for alternative behavior in the behavior change program.* In fact, based on research findings, we strongly recommend that *any procedure used for reducing inappropriate behavior be combined with both differential reinforcement and non-contingent reinforcement* (see Chapters 27 & 28).

## NONRESTRICTIVE PROCEDURES AND THE CLIENT'S RIGHT TO EFFECTIVE TREATMENT

What is "least restrictive" can be a matter of judgment. As Van Houten et al. (1988, p. 383) pointed out:

Consistent with the philosophy of *least restrictive yet effective treatment*, exposure of an individual to restrictive procedures is unacceptable unless it can be shown that such procedures are necessary to produce safe and clinically significant behavior change. It is equally unacceptable to expose an individual to a nonrestrictive intervention (or a series of such interventions) if assessment results or available research indicate that other procedures would be more effective. Indeed, a slow-acting but "nonrestrictive" procedure should be considered highly restrictive if prolonged treatment increases risk, significantly inhibits or prevents participation in needed training programs, delays entry into a more favorable social or living environment, or leads to adaptation to the aversive stimuli and the eventual need to apply an even more restrictive procedure. Thus, in some cases, a client's right to effective treatment may dictate the immediate use of faster-acting, but temporarily more restrictive, procedures.[1]

Note the emphasis is on the *temporary* use of restrictive procedures. When caregivers rely solely on delivering intense punitive consequences, they are harshly restricting the types of environments in which their clients can live or work. In the rare case in which no other approach seems to control a clearly dangerous behavior and you elect to use a punitive procedure, be sure to:

- conduct a functional assessment
- adhere to ethical guidelines. (See Chapter 31).
- select the least restrictive procedure that's contextually appropriate and likely to be effective
- use a very dense schedule of positive consequences contingent upon approximations to preferred alternative behaviors.
- carefully monitor effects.
- *phase out the punishment as soon as feasible* (see Chapters 29 & 30).

## EXTINCTION

Unless the behavior of concern is really threatening and must be immediately terminated, extinction generally is the first procedure we consider when challenged to reduce or prevent an unwanted behavior. In extinction the reinforcement that has been maintaining or supporting it is terminated. Along with the other positive attributes described elsewhere in this text, extinction helps prevent novel unwanted or contextual inappropriate behavior from becoming established because it does not produce reinforcement. It also is a very useful procedure, as it is combined with, or part of, many of the procedures throughout this book.

### Extinction Defined and Illustrated

Earlier we defined the reinforcement process as the increase or maintenance in the rate of a behavior as a function of particular contingent consequences, while **extinction** was defined as a *decrease in behavior due to its no longer producing reinforcers contingent on that behavior.* As with reinforcement, extinction is a normal condition of daily life. We win some; we lose some. When we intentionally design a given **extinction procedure**, though, *we*

---

[1]Minor editorial changes included.

*deliberately withhold or block the particular reinforcing stimuli currently supporting the unwanted behavior of concern.* Any time the purpose is to reduce a behavior, by whatever means, we generally will want also to program for extinction by placing the inappropriate behavior on extinction so it is not reinforced.

Of course, using extinction is nothing new for any of us. All of us employ extinction in our daily interactions with others. Participants in informal social discussions show interest (the reinforcer) in certain aspects of the conversation, while they ignore other aspects. Which topics does the group continue to discuss? Yes, those for which the speakers receive reinforcement; the rest fall by the wayside. Similarly, if Bonnie is no longer given any candy before lunch, she will eventually learn to stop asking for it. As previously indicated, *those behaviors that serve a function for the individual (i.e., produce reinforcement) are more apt to persist*; those that don't, gradually fade away. Behavior-change agents may take advantage of this natural reductive effect of extinction by applying it as a strategy for lowering the rates of unwanted behavior.

In applied behavior analysis, extinction often is employed for another purpose: as a control procedure in single-subject experimental analyses. As we have seen, this generally is done by comparing patterns of behavior under the extinction phase against those during the phase(s) within the change procedures being investigated. Thompson et al. (2003, p. 221) demonstrated the utility of using this approach by comparing three control procedures: (1) extinction, (2) reinforcement of the absence of the behavior (omission training: DRO—see the next chapter), and (3) noncontingent reinforcement (NCR—see previous chapter). They found that extinction produced "the most consistent and rapid reversal effects, along with few negative side effects." Because extinction is used so widely, conscientious contingency managers must inform themselves about its properties and master the methods for its effective application.

## Properties of Extinction

When, contingent on a given behavior all reinforcement permanently ends, the rate of that behavior tends gradually to return to its pre-reinforcement level, which could be as low as zero. (Note, though, that although no longer reinforced, the learned behavior probably is not erased from the organism's repertoire, e.g., Baeyens et al., 2005; Bouton, 2004; Epstein, 1985; Shull & Grimes, 2006; Wilson & Hayes, 1996.) *During* the extinction process, however, the behavior often is characterized by predictable patterns. These include a diminishing response rate; particular temporal features; initial increases in aggression, response rates, intensities, and variability; plus *regression or resurgence* (a tendency to engage in former behaviors, which also contributes to response variability).

**Gradual behavioral reduction.** Once they are no longer reinforced, established patterns of behavior continue for some indeterminate amount of time before stopping (Skinner, 1953). The whining child and the nagging spouse keep whining and nagging for a while, even when those behaviors yield them no further satisfaction (i.e., reinforcement). Eventually that rate declines. This pattern, however, generally tends to be irregular, not monotonic or linear.

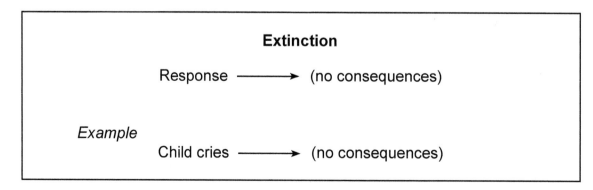

"Instead, individuals exposed to extinction tend to respond sporadically, ...gradually pausing for longer periods of time" (Lerman & Iwata, 1996, p. 348).

Several factors are known to influence the behavior's rate and pattern of diminishing under extinction conditions.[2] Among others, these include:

- The number *of trials previously reinforced* (depending on the reinforcement schedule). Generally, the greater the number of trials reinforced, the greater the resistance to extinction.
- *The density of rates or amounts of reinforcers.* The higher the behavior's rate, or the larger the reinforcer's value, the greater the resistance to extinction.
- The *schedules* on which the response previously has been reinforced. As opposed to a denser and more fixed schedule of reinforcement, a historically thinner and more variable schedule generates greater resistance to extinction.
- *Cues associated with acquisition and extinction* conditions, such as the setting. Resistance to extinction is greater when stimuli are correlated with features present when the response was originally acquired or reinforced.
- The individual's *level of deprivation* with respect to the specific reinforcer. The greater the deprivation, the greater the resistance to extinction.
- Other *motivational operations* (e.g., recent seizures, drug state) may promote or retard the rate of extinction.
- The availability of *reinforcers for competing behaviors.* If more reinforcers are available for the latter, extinction tends to be more rapid.
- The *effort* required to engage in the response. The greater the effort required to engage in the response, the more rapid the rate of extinction.
- *Other contingencies* currently operating that can affect the rate of extinction.

When we contemplate using extinction as a method of reducing unwanted behavior patterns, we need to consider the known characteristics of the extinction process. For instance, related to the point about the greater longevity of behavior under variable as opposed to fixed schedules, Lerman et al. (1996) have suggested that prior to implementing extinction, change agents might initially place the unwanted behavior that was on an intermittent schedule of reinforcement on a continuous schedule of reinforcement:

> If, before extinguishing them, Mrs. Hendricks intentionally laughed or groaned at her husband's tactless jokes every single time she heard them, the bad jokes would disappear faster when ultimately placed on extinction than if she were to laugh at his jokes inconsistently.

> In the past, Fran, the pharmacist, has sometimes agreed to stay late and finish filling the prescriptions assigned to her work partner, Chet. Now, she has planned that before placing his request for her help on total extinction, she will devote several days to completing his assigned tasks. After that she will inform him, "No Chet. From now on, you'll have to do them yourself. I meet all my assigned tasks, so henceforth I plan to leave on time," and she will stick to her resolve. (Mrs. Hendricks and Fran had better prepare themselves for the side-effects of extinction, though, if they hope to succeed in their efforts.)

Note that our above list of historical factors includes such variables as "motivating operations" including *deprivation and satiation.* The more deprived of a given reinforcer a person has been, the longer the behavior that previously functioned to secure that reinforcer will persist under extinc-

---

[2]See, among others, Catania (2007); Donahoe & Palmer (1994); Epstein (1985); and Skinner (1938, 1957) for general analyses of extinction as an aspect of the learning process, and Arkhipov (2002); Leslie et al. (2005); Prados, Manteiga, & Sansa (2003); Shull & Grimes (2006); and Vansteenwegen et al. (2006) for more specific cases.

tion conditions. This factor is especially important when the behavior has been maintained by primary reinforcers (Holland & Skinner, 1961). Although whining may have produced no cookies for weeks, a child may whine for a cookie longer and at a higher rate when hungry than after having eaten a large meal. Similar effects also may be seen with generalized reinforcers like attention (O'Reilly et al., 2007). In the latter investigation, children who were provided with considerable attention just prior to a session during which attention was withheld, sought less of it than those who received little of it in advance.

A response that requires considerable *effort* will extinguish more rapidly than an easy one. Marco, whose main task was to repair electrical wires atop high poles, used to ride out to repair sites together with his supervisor. During the ride, Marco often seized the opportunity to complain about having to secure his safety belt while working at a certain height above ground. Although his supervisor tried to ignore the complaints, they persisted. Now the supervisor no longer has Marco join him on the ride to the work site, but plans his arrival to coincide with Marco's being well into his task, often atop a utility pole. Marco rarely complains now, because to do so would require that he climb down and back up a utility pole to air his grievances.

When extinction is combined with *reinforcement* of an *alternative incompatible and/or functionally equivalent behavior*, the unwanted response will diminish more rapidly (Worsdell et al., 2000), and extinction bursts are less likely (Lerman & Iwata, 1996; Freeman, 2006). Reese, Howard, and Rosenberger (1974) found that males with cognitive delays produced far fewer errors when an alternative, acceptable response was available for caregivers to reinforce than when errors were placed on extinction. (The same is true of applying extinction in combination with other reductive procedures, such as response cost, timeout, punishment, and contingent effort, about which you will learn shortly.) Were Mrs. Hendricks not only to stop laughing at her husband's jokes but also raise an eyebrow (aversive to him) to imply their tastelessness, he might stop telling those kinds of jokes sooner than if the only thing she did was to ignore them.

**Extinction bursts**, *transitory increases in response rate, intensity, aggression, and variability*, have been observed in both animals and humans (Kelly, 1969; Skinner, 1953) immediately after the cessation of reinforcement, especially when a large proportion of the previous responses have been reinforced. Woods and Borrero (2019) have reported that extinction bursts occur in 24 to 39 percent of the cases they reviewed for which extinction was implemented, and in 30 percent of the pediatric food refusal studies (Woods & Borrero, 2019). However, there are ways to decrease its likelihood of occurrence, as you will see as you continue to read this chapter.

What do you do when a vending machine fails to deliver? Probably you pull the plunger or push the button more and more frequently with greater vigor and/or hit or kick the machine before you give up and go away. The youngster whose crying  is totally ignored for the first time may continue to scream with increasing intensity before the crying eventually subsides. (The term **extinction-induced aggression** serves as a technical descriptor when there is a *temporary increase in the aggressive aspect alone*.)

These corollaries to extinction have been extensively studied in the past. For instance, discontinuing positive reinforcement has been shown to produce aggression in pigeons (Azrin, Hutchinson, & Hake, 1966) and in squirrel monkeys (Hutchinson et al., 1968). Kelly (1969) demonstrated a similar response in human males who received money for pulling a knob. When money delivery was suspended, several forcibly hit the apparatus. Lovaas, Freitag, Gold, and Kassorla (1965) observed increases in self-injurious behavior (SIB) during extinction of clapping and singing, while Goh and Iwata (1994) noted increases in aggression during extinction of self-injury. About 40 percent of the clients in a study by Reed et al. (2004) displayed extinction bursts when extinction was the sole intervention used for food refusal. Similarly, Lerman,

Iwata, and Wallace (1999) found that nearly one-half of 41 clients whose SIB had been extinguished exhibited increases in aggression or full-blown extinction bursts.

Numerous examples of such reactions are seen in natural settings: the top student who cries in exasperation when he does not receive a high enough grade; the employee who picks a fight with one of his coworkers when someone else is awarded the promotion he anticipated for himself; the students who don't succeed in school and turn to violence and vandalism; roommates who trash the belongings of the one who fails to perform her cleanup assignment. All probably are exhibiting extinction-induced aggression.

Extinction bursts or extinction-induced aggression also can occur as a result of using escape extinction. **Escape extinction** involves *blocking escape attempts so that escape responses no longer provide reinforcement*. Extinction bursts have been reported by Lerman, Iwata, and Wallace (1999), and physical aggression by Lerman and Iwata (1995), especially when physical guidance is necessary (Piazza et al., 1996). (Escape extinction is discussed more thoroughly in Chapter 29.)

Beyond aggression directed toward others or oneself, early researchers noted temporary increases in variability of a response in terms of its *duration, location, interresponse time, latency, and amplitude* (Antonitis, 1951; Millenson & Hurwitz, 1961; Morris, 1968; Stebbins & Lanson, 1962; Trotter, 1957). Increases in the variability and number of novel behaviors have also been reported (Schwartz, 1982). Actually, these novel behaviors sometimes can provide unexpected teaching opportunities. As Lerman and Iwata (1996) have suggested, "extinction bursts might be desirable in certain situations" (p. 347). How could that be? Because behavior tends to become more variable during extinction bursts, "clinicians should be prepared to detect and reinforce these appropriate behaviors as soon as they occur" (p. 348). Similarly, extinction conditions may induce an approximation that can then be treated by shaping. Suppose a client speaks too quietly (low amplitude), extinction "could induce instances of higher amplitude behavior, which then could be maintained through reinforcement" (p. 348).

Nevertheless, extinction bursts apparently are not universal. In fact, in a comparison of the side effects of DRA versus extinction, Petscher and Bailey (2008) noted that "desirable collateral effects of academic engagement tended to be higher during EXT than DRA" (p. 468). Of the five participants, they did note one instance of extinction-induced aggression, though.

**Contributors to extinction bursts.** Research has shed additional light on factors contributing to extinction bursts (aggression, increases in rate, withdrawal). In general, as mentioned earlier, behaviors treated with optimal or continuous reinforcement are more likely to produce an extinction burst than one operating under an intermittent schedule of reinforcement. Extinction bursts also are more apt to occur during the initial phases of extinction, when clients recently have been deprived of the reinforcer that has been supporting the problem behavior. Those reactions *do* gradually decrease (O'Reilly et al., 2006; Todd, Morris, & Fenza, 1989). If, for instance, attention has maintained a particular problem behavior and the client has not been receiving attention for other behaviors, imposing extinction conditions would more likely result in an extinction burst. This is what O'Reilly et al. (2006) found when working with two individuals with autism. Sam, 14, engaged in SIB (self-injurious behavior in the form of head hitting, head banging, and hand biting) and aggression (biting, punching, and kicking), which were maintained by access to food. Twenty-year-old John's issues included body hitting, skin picking, inappropriate self-touching, hair eating, and eloping that were found to have been maintained by attention. When these reinforcers were provided continuously ten to fifteen minutes prior to the start of the extinction period (Sam was provided with unlimited access to snacks, John with continuous social interactions), hardly any extinction bursts occurred. However, if those reinforcers were withheld for a period of time prior to the start of the extinction interval, the problem behaviors increased dramatically while extinction was in effect. This research further indicates that problem behaviors are less likely to occur in an environment that includes NCR prior to the use of extinction.

**Spontaneous recovery and resurgence.** As noted, another phenomenon often observed in connection with extinction is *the reappearance of the "extinguished" (target) response at the beginning of a new session, despite no resumption of reinforcement.* In other words, following a period of reinforcement (intervention), if the "extinguished" behavior reappears when you start a new session, it is called *spontaneous recovery*. This **spontaneous recovery** (Skinner, 1953) often appears with extinction (Lerman & Iwata, 1996; Lerman, Kelley, Van Camp, & Roane, 1999).

**Resurgence**[3] *refers to the recurrence of previously reinforced behavior when a target, or dominant, behavior is no longer reinforced.* Several investigators (Lieving, Hagopian, Long, & O'Connor, 2004; Volkert, Lerman, Call, & Trosclair-Lasserre, 2009) point out that a previously reinforced behavior tends to reoccur when another behavior is no longer reinforced. Or, as Greer and Shahan (2019) point out with slightly different wording, *"Resurgence is an increase in a previously suppressed behavior resulting from a worsening in reinforcement conditions for current behavior"* (p. 816), This might include a reduction in the density or termination of reinforcement that was previously obtained as a consequence of an alternative replacement behavior. Some (e.g., Lerman, Kelley, Van Camp, & Roane, 1999) prefer to use the term *spontaneous recovery*, when a behavior that has been placed on extinction over a period of time, emerges once again. The (generally unwanted) behavior re-emerges because the preferred alternative no longer produces any or sufficient reinforcers as a consequence of the target and/or alternative behavior, the phenomenon is called *resurgence*.

Volkert et al. found that the behavioral problems of four of five children diagnosed with autism or developmental disabilities, who had received functional communication treatment, re-emerged when the communicative response was no longer reinforced or when very thin schedules of reinforcement were used. Although this sort of resurgence tends to be transitory, recognizing its existence can save contingency managers from committing the tactical error of giving up on extinction prematurely.

When reinforcement is being thinned too rapidly for the functional alternative behavior, the client might react as if total extinction conditions were in effect. To illustrate, investigators (Briggs, Fisher, Gree, & Kimball, 2018) were working with 25 individuals aged 2 to 19 years old with an average age of 7.5 being treated for destructive behavior. They found that when they thinned reinforcement for three alternative behaviors, the destructive behaviors resurged among 19 of 25 (76%) of the clients. Also, the magnitude of the destructive behavior exceeded that of baseline levels in some cases. A more recent study (e.g., Sullivan, et al., 2020) has reported that in addition to an increased probability of resurgence, other non-targeted forms of problem behaviors often emerge after a previously reinforced behavior is placed on extinction. Consequently, to minimize the likelihood of resurgence, plan, whenever possible, to combine extinction with other reductive procedures that generate reinforcement described in Chapters 27 and 28 (e.g., noncontingent reinforcement, modeling, & DRA).

As suggested, beyond the nuisance of the unwanted behavior cropping up after it presumably has disappeared, the big danger is that practitioners may be tempted to give up and move impulsively on to more severely aversive procedures, such as timeout, response cost, or punishment. The more you understand this phenomenon, the less likely you are to be caught in the trap of prematurely increasing the coerciveness of the procedures you select. Appreciate, then, that the probability of spontaneous recovery or resurgence is greater when extinction conditions (schedule, setting, competing reinforcers, and other elements) are similar to those under which the behavior was initially reinforced (Epstein & Skinner, 1980; Wilson & Hayes, 1996). The latter investigators found that when they reinforced participants' responding to conditional discriminations within a matching-to-sample format first on one schedule, and then switched to a different matching-to-sample schedule, the participants did acquire the new rules. Yet when reinforcement stopped altogether (extinction conditions), participants tended to return to the earlier response levels, the ones they had generated during the initial reinforcement schedule. In other words, if the more recently successful strategy didn't work, they regressed to and

---

[3]Clinicians call a similar occurrences *symptom substitution* or *regression*.

tended to persist with the initial (now also unsuccessful) strategy.

Reed and Morgan (2006) conducted an analogous study with rats. They observed resurgence during extinction, again following an orderly pattern of returning to the initially successful schedule (*resurgence*): After initially emitting the immediately previously-trained response, the subjects then started to display the response sequence they first were trained to perform. Apparently resurgence during extinction is general across human and other animal species.

Perhaps *the tendency to return to previously successful though currently ineffective behavioral rates (resurgence)*, explains how presumably mature, responsible adults sometimes act childishly while experiencing extinction conditions—whining or crying, say, as a result of a poor grade at school, loss of a job or of a sale, or withdrawal of attention or affection from a loved one.

Resurgence is less likely to occur for responses that require effort. In other words, response effort diminishes the likelihood of resurgence occurring (Wilson, Glassford, & Koekenmeier, 2016). So, a response that took considerable effort before it was put on extinction is less likely to occur again in the future than one that took little effort. Also, resurgence appears less likely to occur with NCR when NCR is combined with EXT rather than used alone (Saini, Fisher, & Pisman, 2017).

**Behavioral contrast.** Behavioral contrast was defined and discussed in Chapter 23. Here we review that phenomenon as it relates to extinction.

Many studies with humans and nonhumans have documented *behavioral contrast* (see Lerman & Iwata, 1996, for a review). According to Reynolds, (1961, p. 57), a "change in behavior is called a contrast when the change in the rate of responding during the presentation of one stimulus is in a direction away from the rate of responding generated during the presentation of the other stimulus." The term *positive behavioral contrast applies to the phenomenon of a behavior declining during the extinction condition, while increasing during another condition or setting in which reinforcers are not withheld.*

Suzie enjoys sharing her drawings with her parents. One day her mother has stopped attending to her "masterpieces," while her father continues to express his interest. The father begins to note that Suzie is now sharing her drawings with him much more often than before. During dismissal time, watch children who have just been released from a school that maintains very rigid disciplinary policies, or observe college freshmen from highly restrictive families suddenly living independently for the first time. Some seem to go completely wild for a time before settling down. Although the contingencies in place vary at the different locations, the contrast between the two may in and of themselves contribute to the striking differences in levels of acceptable and unacceptable behavior. In a controlled demonstration of this phenomenon, Wahler, Vigilante, and Strand (2004) reported the occurrence of behavioral contrast with a nine-year-old boy who demonstrated oppositional behavior. The mother was taught to use extinction on the behavior, but the teacher was not. The child's oppositional behavior decreased in the home, but *increased* in the classroom. More to the current point, the investigators noted that the child's increases  in oppositional behavior did "not correspond to measures of his teacher's inappropriate attention because she maintained her reactions at a steady level across observations" (p. 49). Take-home point: if you are going to implement extinction in one setting (home), it would be wise to ensure that extinction is implemented across settings (school) to avoid contrast effects.

## Using Extinction Effectively

Given the rich body of research on extinction, we are in the fortunate position of being able to offer a set of promising guidelines for practitioners to apply when using extinction. These follow.

**Identify and withhold all sources of reinforcement contingent on the behavior of concern.** This is easier said than done because while sometimes, reinforcing consequences are fairly obvious, at other times they are not. In the latter case, you can use an A-B-C analysis; or in more difficult situations, a functional behavioral analysis, to discover the reinforcers maintaining the problem behavior (refer to Chapters 6 and 10). Identifying *all* reinforcers operating on the behavior of concern is crucial if extinction is to function effectively, because each and every one must be consistently withheld contingent on the target response. However, when combining extinction combined with reinforcement for alternative behaviors (DRA–see Chapter 29), it appears that if you are able to minimize the reinforcement for the problem behavior while maximizing it for the alternative behavior, the intervention will usually still tend to be effective (Volmer, et al., 2020).

The manner in which extinction is implemented will depend on the reinforcement contingency identified as maintaining the unwanted behavior. In fact, Iwata et al. (1994) demonstrated that behavioral reductions in SIB were observed only when extinction was based on the maintaining function. To illustrate this point, here are some fanciful, though credible scenarios:

> Margaret, a middle-aged woman working as an administrative assistant, consistently gossips about her fellow employees. By watching her in the process, one suspects that Margaret might gossip so much because that is the only time the others pay attention to her. Hoping to dissuade her from gossiping, her coworkers agree to use extinction by withdrawing their attention when the gossiping begins; but they will make a concerted effort to chat with her during the break by asking about more neutral topics like her golf game and her dog, Bogie. Although a good effort, if Margaret's gossiping behavior function to escape  work tasks rather than attention, having the others ignore her gossiping but still engage with her would actually not decrease her gossiping.
>
> Whenever his wife asks him to take out the trash, Charles says he has a headache. So his wife Penny takes out the trash for him. For Penny to implement extinction, she would need to make sure that she never takes out the trash if he complains of a headache following her request.

Extinction is somewhat trickier for behavior maintained by automatic reinforcement (i.e., sensory stimulation). In these situations, it is not only important to identify the precise function of the behavior targeted for reduction, but also to identify the exact source of reinforcement and find a way to block it when the behavior occurs. (See Rincover, Cook, Peoples, & Packard, 1979 for illustrations.)

Let us look at some other examples where the maintaining function may not be so obvious. Take, for instance, the simple behavior of students frequently leaving their seats without permission. What might the reinforcers be? Some may do this to obtain teacher attention. So, consistently withholding teacher attention when those youngsters are out of their seats, and providing it when they are seated and working, probably would effectively reduce their rates of leaving their seats. Others, however, might stand up because the assignment is too difficult for them, and the behavior allows them to escape having to work on the aversive assignment. Still others may go to talk with peers or find moving around reinforcing, and so on. Obviously, if the teacher were to ignore these other students' behavior (the ones who do it because they want to get out of doing the assignment or because of the attention they get from their peers), extinction would not be in effect, because teacher attention is not the reinforcer maintaining that behavior. Research has demonstrated that unless the appropriate reinforcers are withheld from the response (i.e., based on the function of the behavior), the behavior will not diminish and actually may increase in rate (Iwata et al., 1994).

Suppose one of the players on the soccer team frequently makes weird noises. The coach sometimes laughs along with the others. At other times, the coach or the other players tell him to cut it out. Here, the reinforcers derive from both the leader and the other group members. To achieve extinction conditions in this situation, everyone, peers and leader, has to ignore the noises. (Recall the earlier discussion in Chapter 12, in which we illustrated how dependent and interdependent group contingencies could achieve extinction conditions when peers are the source of reinforcement.)

In one last example, Ross and Horner (2009) implemented an extinction procedure to reduce two students' bullying at each of three elementary schools. Operating on the assumption that the major function of the bullying was, as it often is, peer attention, they taught the participants to adhere to the following guidelines:

1. Distinguish between respectful and non-respectful (e.g., bullying) behavior (e.g., hitting, kicking, spitting, biting, choking, stealing, throwing objects, restricting movement, teasing, taunting, threatening, negative body language or gestures).
2. Do not laugh, cheer, complain, fight back or whine if you are being bullied or if you see another being bullied. Here the students were being taught to withhold reinforcement for non-respectful (i.e., bullying) behavior.
3. Say "stop," and use the stop gesture (hand held up) if someone is not respectful to you.
4. Walk away if, after saying "stop," the disrespectful behavior continues.
5. If you see someone being treated disrespectfully, say "stop" and take the victim away.
6. If after you walk away, disrespectful behavior continues, tell an adult.
7. If someone says "stop" to you, stop what you are doing, take a breath, and go about your day.

Instructional, administrative, and supervisory staffs also were instructed to teach those guidelines to *all* students in each school. Also, in addition to the normal standards for protection and safety, playground supervisors were taught the following steps:

1. If a student reports a problem behavior, ask, "Did you say 'stop'?" or "Did you walk away?"
2. If the reporting student did not indicate having practiced saying "stop" and walking away, encourage him/her to apply the responses the next time and go no further.
3. If the reporting student did say "stop" or did walk away, interact with the student identified as engaging in the problem behavior.
4. Ask the offending student if he or she was asked by others to stop.
5. Then ask if he or she did in fact stop.
6. Have the youngster practice the steps to follow when asked to stop.

All six participants reduced their rates of bullying.

**Consider context when applying extinction.** Just as reinforcement history may be context-dependent, the same is true of extinction. Indeed, both basic and applied studies have demonstrated its effects are more successful when extinction takes place under original learning conditions. This seems to be true across species. (See, for instance, Parker, Limebeer, & Slomke, 2006, who suggested that extinction should be used in the context in which the behavior was originally established.)

A related effect was found in a basic study with human volunteers (Milad, Orr, Pitman, & Rauch, 2005). First, subjects experienced correlations of stimuli with mild but unpleasant shock; then underwent fear-extinction trials. Following those trials, participants engaged in less fearful types of responding in the setting in which the fear first had been acquired and then extinguished, than elsewhere. But they also re-acquired the "extinguished response" more readily under the original learning conditions.

Here is a fanciful example of the same point: Ingmar, employed by a biotechnology organization, is working to improve his public-speaking skills because he is often called upon to use them in his sales work. He has been told that his habit of using filler words such as "like," "you know," "umm," and "you know what I'm saying?" convey a lack of confidence, thereby probably negatively impacting his sales. He enlists the help of the partner with whom he splits commissions. During practice sessions, the partner agrees to look away (a form of social extinction), rather than to nod whenever one of those fillers pops up. He will look up again when Ingmar speaks more fluently. By this means, Ingmar's use of filler words declines. His delivery in his partner's presence becomes so fluent that soon Ingmar has generalized his now well-established fluency to his work in the field. Now his audience sees Ingmar as appearing to convey greater confidence in the product. Lo and behold, sales increase!

Our advice to practitioners, then, is to *teach under all the conditions under which the new behavior is to be emitted.* Also, when the goal is to reduce or eliminate a response by means of extinction, minimize resurgence by seeing to it that all *reinforcers are withheld from the response under every circumstance in which you hope to see it diminish.*[4]

**Clearly specify the conditions for extinction.** Mom told Abner that while she is working at her desk, she will not respond to his pestering. Mom has stuck to her resolve and Abner has quickly learned that Mom-at-the-desk means that pestering will not work; he had best seek out his dad. Had no information been exchanged about the conditions under which extinction would occur, eventually Abner would learn not to interrupt his mother while she worked at the desk, but it might have taken much longer. This combination of instructions and extinction worked to reduce Abner's pestering.

"Remember: First a drink, then a trip to the potty, then a story. That's all," Dad reminds Baby Bonnie as he puts her to bed. Dad holds to the contingencies by not responding to Bonnie's overtures for additional attention. Bonnie learns to settle down and go to sleep after the story.[5]

Recall how in our earlier discussion of stimulus control we elaborated on the importance of specifying the conditions under which extinction and reinforcement occur within an instructional sequence. The same holds with extinction. Again, the important point is *simply and clearly to communicate in advance the rules of the game—the conditions in effect during the event of concern* and consistently to follow through with the consequences as pre-stated. Be sure to avoid long explanations following the event, for such attention may serve a reinforcing function.

Naturally, however, at the appropriate time you would reinforce the absence of the undesirable behavior (i.e., you might use a DRO procedure, described in the next chapter). When Mom leaves her desk, she tells Abner how much she has appreciated his not interrupting, offers him a snack, and plays his favorite game with him.

**Combine extinction with other procedures to manage intolerable behaviors.** Certain behaviors require immediate reduction. They cannot be tolerated for even a moment. Although ignoring a youngster's rudeness for a while may be feasible, paying no attention to a preschooler's running out into a street full of traffic would be absurd and dangerous. Because extinction, especially when used as the sole procedure, can take time to produce its effect, it is not a good choice under such circumstances. Rather, dangerous acts demand that extinction be combined with interventions producing more immediate effects, such as those involving aversive consequences (see Chapters 29 & 30).

**Avoid using extinction as the sole intervention with aggressive behaviors, especially in group settings.** Intolerable actions like aggressive and destructive behaviors may be imitated by peers, especially when ignored by adult supervisors[6] (Bandura & Walters, 1963; Bandura, 1965b). Managers who intend to remove reinforcing attention by ignoring that kind of misconduct need to be aware of this potential trap and may want to opt for an alternative. Additionally, they need to realize that total extinction would be very difficult to accomplish in a group setting, because victims and peers are almost certain to react.

**Maintain extinction conditions for a sufficient time.** Extinction bursts can be very distressing. The first time the teacher ignored Reggie's colorful language, he responded by bursting forth with a hair-raising stream of profanities. The teacher

---

[4]See Wilson & Hayes (1996) for a basic experimental analysis of resurgence with humans in matching-to-sample; also Milad et al. (2005) and Parker et al. (2006) for other human and nonhuman examples of basic research on resurgence.

[5]See Brown & Piazza (1999) for a commentary on ABA sources for relief from children's bedtime problems.

[6]Perhaps because the functional reinforcer is not adult but peer attention.

might well have branded his technique of ignoring swearing a failure. But was it? The only way the teacher could find out would be to ride the crest of the wave for a while (and hope the other students were no more sophisticated than the teacher himself had been at their age) and to see if the foul language would begin to subside. Assuming that the teacher's frowning and scolding were the key reinforcing events, the behavior would ultimately diminish.

At such challenging times, data collection can be a tremendous asset. The number of class periods during which Reggie did *not* swear could be tallied, perhaps with the help of an electronic counter. If the frequency of non-swearing days slowly but steadily increased, then there would be room for optimism. Sometimes improvement is so gradual that it remains undetected in the absence of graphed data. The point is that you need to *prepare yourself for extinction bursts, and plan to persist long enough*—at least a few weeks—to give the procedure a fair try.

**Complement extinction with other procedures.** Although extinction can be effective as the sole intervention, we *strongly* recommend you combine it with other procedures, especially reinforcing acceptable alternatives (DRA—see the next chapter) or noncontingent reinforcement (NCR). *Such alternatives are more positive than extinction.* Note that this is what was done in the Ross and Horner (2009) bullying illustration described above. Students were taught specific alternative responses (e.g., saying "stop," holding hands up, walking away, telling a teacher) when reacting to bullying.

*Combining the reinforcement of alternative behaviors (DRA) with extinction has "consistently demonstrated that DRA eliminates the response burst and reduces resistance to extinction"* (Lerman & Iwata, 1996, p. 367). Freeman (2006) combined extinction with DRA and/or differential reinforcement of diminishing rates (DRD—see the next chapter) to eliminate extinction bursts. He eliminated the bedtime problems (e.g., frequently getting up after being put to bed) of four typically-developing, unrelated three-year-old children by combining extinction with a bedtime pass, the pass exchangeable for one trip out of the bedroom for less than three minutes for a specific activity (e.g., use of restroom, one more hug). After the pass was used once, the child surrendered it to the parents for the night. Calling out was ignored, and if the child got up again, he was returned to his room without comment. Using either extinction alone or the bedtime pass alone accomplished little, but the combination of extinction and reinforcement successfully reduced extinction bursts. (Refer to Box 28.1 for a scenario of how extinction and reinforcement might play out within an ordinary family.)

Similarly, Lerman et al. (1999) found that spontaneous recovery could be reduced by liberally applying reinforcers in a differential reinforcement procedure. Also, dense, ongoing noncontingent reinforcement (NCR) can decrease extinction bursts and resistance to extinction (Lerman & Iwata, 1996; Reed et al., 2004; Vollmer et al., 1998). So, *be sure to provide lots of noncontingent reinforcement along with contingent reinforcement of appropriate behaviors to help prevent problems from emerging while extinction is in effect.*

The bottom line is that: "Behavior will go to where there is reinforcement" (Daniels & Lattal, 2017). Thus, by withholding reinforcement from the inappropriate behavior, and providing it to behavior that is more functional and appropriate, constructive behavior change is likely.

**Implement and sustain extinction within all contexts in which the behavioral reduction is to take place.** Responses of a given type tend to stay suppressed longer in those locations in which extinction has been carried out, than elsewhere (e.g., Parker et al., 2006). Three-year-old Kelly used to throw quite a tantrum whenever her request for candy was ignored. Her preschool teacher has decided to use extinction along with differential reinforcement of other behaviors, by ignoring Kelly's requests for candy and any subsequent tantrums. She did receive more nutritious snacks when she sat quietly at the table and asked for them during regularly scheduled snack times. Eventually, Kelly's tantrums for candy were practically eliminated at school. Kelly's parents, however, were incredulous at hearing that their daughter hardly ever had a tantrum any longer at school, because things at home seemed to be worse than ever on that score. (That was not surprising because as Epstein, 1985, and others have found, school was the context under which the extinction was instituted. Also, as mentioned earlier, because reinforcement continued in the home setting, behavioral contrast was in effect.) They asked for help. After the home-school coordinator started making regular visits to Kelly's home to teach both parents how to extinguish the tantrums and prepared them for possible resurgence, along with suggesting more frequent healthy snacks, the tantrums eventually became a thing of the past.

**Use extinction to promote response variability as a basis for choosing acceptable alternative behaviors to reinforce.** What can you do in a situation in which you hope to use differential reinforcement and/or shaping, yet the individual fails to emit any remotely acceptable response within the category you plan to build upon? One possibility, as mentioned earlier (Lerman and Iwata, 1996), is to use extinction as a way of generating an array of novel behaviors. Grow, Kelley, Roane, and Shillingsburg (2008) did that by exposing problem behavior (whining and aggression) to extinction to induce response variability. They first choose one of the response variations as an appropriate alternative (saying "no" or "don't" or reaching for an object) to promote during functional communication training. Contingent on the newly selected alternative behavior, they then delivered the reinforcer previously identified in the functional analysis as having maintained problem behavior. The targeted problem behaviors (whining and aggressions) diminished in all cases.

**Enrich the environment with an adequate supply of reinforcers for acceptable behaviors.** Because extinction involves the discontinuation, or withholding of reinforcers contingent on a particular response, determining whether individuals have sufficient reinforcement available from other sources is critical. Recognize that by its nature (i.e., extinction involves withholding reinforcers), extinction can produce deprivation—an establishing operation with evocative effects. If Harry's temperamental responses no longer yield him attention, his manager would be well advised to make sure that Harry does not lose out on receiving his attention altogether. Otherwise, if Harry can find no constructive way to make the boss notice him, he probably will continue trying different, perhaps even more irritating behaviors, until one succeeds. Consequently, if you intend to apply extinction, plan to provide the individual with a dense schedule of reinforcement for desirable behaviors. For instance, Harry's boss could comment on the apparent care with which Harry performs his job assignments, smile at any friendly overtures, and so on.

In residential facilities serving people with severe developmental delays, it is not unusual to see the inhabitants repeating puzzling rituals—stereotypic responses like head weaving, hand or finger movements, rocking, or pacing a given area nonstop. What explains the development and maintenance of such seemingly functionless acts? Perhaps extinction is the answer. When people lack sufficient repertoires of adaptive or constructive communicative behaviors that allow them readily to acquire natural reinforcers (such as attention, affection, material goods, and so on), many will continue to express maladaptive behaviors for the meager reinforcers those yield: sensory stimulation by means of changing visual, tactile, or auditory patterns, or social attention from peers or staff members, who inadvertently reinforce through attention. Alternatively, having no way of controlling their world, they may give up altogether and curl up in bed or in a corner. Such a response to the environment has been labeled "**learned helplessness**" (Seligman, 1975) or *abulia* (*a state in which an individual seems to have lost will or motivation, Encyclopedia of Neurological Disorders*, 2008).

Such adverse reactions are far less prevalent in enriched environments; those with stimulating activities, toys, equipment, refreshments, and challenging yet achievable task assignments matched to the repertoires and preferences of the participants. Increasingly, due in good part to national or federal legislation in many farsighted nations, educational and service programs serving individuals with special needs promote such environments. In the case of developmentally-challenged preschoolers, for example, children often busily engage in arts and crafts, dramatic play, singing, dancing, enjoying snacks, pretend play, or enjoying indoor or outdoor exercise equipment, and they receive lots of special attention for progressing toward the objectives as designated in their individual educational plans and nested within the program. In places like these, the stereotypic and self-abusive behavior thought to be so characteristic of many people with autism rarely is seen. Additionally, the dense reinforcement makes the children, like everyone else, feel good and more positive about themselves (Ludwig & Maehr, 1967; Wisocki, 1973).

Beyond the inexcusable omission of all sources of programmed reinforcement, the main problem with using extinction alone is that no alternative constructive behaviors are designated to replace those to be eliminated (i.e., it doesn't pass the **Dead Man's Test**: "*If a dead man can do it, it isn't behavior*"). For these reasons, always select and reinforce other *preferred* performances in concert with extinction.

As you already know, that combination requires differential reinforcement. Supplementing extinction with differential reinforcement has the added advantage of attenuating the negative side effects, such as the extinction bursts that often accompany the procedure. Now, the individual has a reliable source of reinforcement for engaging in alternative behaviors. In the next chapter we elaborate further upon ways to apply *differential reinforcement of alternative behaviors* effectively.

## SUMMARY AND CONCLUSIONS

Behavior analysts who have elected to apply reductive procedures need to choose those with the greatest promise for success in that particular situation. Various methods are available, including preventive methods (Chapter 27), extinction, several differential reinforcement techniques (Chapter 28), and various negative and positive punishment procedures (Chapters 29 & 30). Each has advantages and limitations. In this chapter, we discuss extinction. In subsequent chapters we cover the other possibilities.

Noncontingent reinforcement (see Chapter 27) is natural to environments enriched with lots of stimulating and achievable tasks, materials, and social events. Often such arrangements are sufficient to prevent or minimize problematic performance. If NCR or other preventive methods fail to reduce unwanted behavior sufficiently, adding extinction is a reasonable choice.

Used alone or combined with other procedures, carefully designed and implemented extinction methods can effectively reduce an array of undesirable behaviors. To help you to decide whether extinction is an appropriate choice in a particular situation, we suggest you address the following questions.

- Can the behavior of concern be tolerated temporarily?
- Can a transitory worsening of that behavior be tolerated?
- Is the behavior not likely to be imitated?
- Can all the reinforcers currently supporting the behavior be identified?
- Is it feasible to withhold all those reinforcers?
- Can acceptable alternative behaviors be identified and reinforced?

If each question can be answered "yes," then implementing extinction is a feasible option. But be prepared for possible extinction bursts and resurgence, though. If you answer one or more of those questions with a "no," consider alternative procedures or complement extinction with more constructive and/or more rapidly-acting alternative methods.

Extinction is a reasonable choice in situations in which the behavior to be reduced is not serious, temporary setbacks can be tolerated, and all the reinforcers for the unwanted behavior can be withheld over an extended period of time. As with all reductive procedures, e*xtinction's effectiveness will be advanced when combined with various preventive methods, including noncontingent reinforcement* (Chapter 27) *and various differential reinforcement procedures* (see Chapter 28), *including differential reinforcement of alternative behaviors.*

*Chapter 27*

# Preventing Challenging Behavior by Enriching the Environment

## Goals

1. Specify the disadvantages of punitive approaches.
2. Define positive behavior interventions (PBIs) and explain why emphasizing them is important.
3. Discuss the implication of IDEA and IDEIA with respect to developing behavior plans in educational settings.
4. Define and illustrate *antecedent control strategies*.
5. Discuss and illustrate how to use stimulus change to prevent and reduce problem behavior.
6. Describe how to promote rule and instruction following.
7. Illustrate the strategy of removing barriers to goals.
8. Provide examples of several means of presenting prompts,
9. List, briefly describe, and provide novel examples of a set of empirically tested antecedent strategies designed to prevent or reduce troublesome behaviors including:
   a. *prompting*
   b. *interrupting* and *redirecting responding*
   c. *preparing activity schedules*
   d. *greeting clients*
   e. *incorporating behavioral momentum* or *high-probability requests*
   f. *providing (permitting) choice*
   g. *setting goals* and *behavioral contracts collaboratively*
   h. *reducing response effort*
   i. *applying the interspersal strategy*
   j. *responding chorally*
   k. *using response cards*
10. Define the term mnemonics and provide at least two examples of its use as learning aids

11. Justify the importance of a highly reinforcing environment
12. Define and illustrate *noncontingent reinforcement (NCR)*
13. List the advantage and disadvantages of incorporating NCRs within programs of behavior change
14. Describe how to use NCR effectively
15. Define and illustrate the NCR plus extinction *(NCR/EXT) combination*
16. Discuss and illustrate how to use modeling to reduce and prevent problem behavior
17. Define and illustrate social stories.

*************

This chapter focuses on the use of antecedent methods, such as adding and removing discriminative stimuli, abolishing or establishing motivating operations (MOs), and adjusting response effort to help prevent problematic behaviors. Chapter 28 presents consequential interventions designed to help prevent and reduce problem behavior. But first, we argue for the value of selecting alternatives to punishment and defend a preference for selecting positive behavioral interventions.

## WHY CHOOSE ALTERNATIVES TO PUNISHMENT?

As Carr, Taylor, Carlson, and Robinson (1991) and Cataldo (1991) have noted, at one time, punishment and related aversive approaches were considered the most effective means of reducing severe behavior problems. As research has revealed, though, such punitive approaches, however, foster aggression (e.g., violence, assaults, and vandalism), escape (e.g., tardiness, truancies, and dropouts), negative self-statements, and negative attitudes toward oneself and school (Azrin, Hake, Holz, & Hutchinson, 1965; Berkowitz, 1983; Mayer & Sulzer-Azaroff, 1991). Critics also see them as dehumanizing. Moreover, *given the identification of the behavior's function, punishment-based approaches are often no more effective than antecedent and reinforcement-based approaches* (Pelios et al., 1999).

Remember antecedent manipulations tend to fall into one of the following categories: manipulation of the discriminative stimuli and either establishing or abolishing MOs, and altering the response effort involved with the response targeted for reduction. Given these parameters of antecedent manipulations, we provide specific examples and consider the categories to which they belong.

## POSITIVE BEHAVIOR INTERVENTIONS

**Positive behavioral interventions (PBIs)** are *designed to reduce inappropriate behavior by prompting and reinforcing substitute alternative constructional behaviors* (Carr & Sidener, 2002). PBIs often involve arranging appropriate MOs in addition to addressing consequences for the CIB. Fortunately, as mentioned previously, in comparison to punitive procedures, when based on a behavior's *function* and applied appropriately, positive (non-punitive) antecedent and consequential behavior interventions:

- usually prevent and/or reduce problematic behavior as effectively as punitive procedures, while being less restrictive and intrusive.
- are *less* likely to provoke violence, escape, and aggression or to lower the recipients' views of themselves, of those delivering the contingencies, and of associated tasks.[1]

---

[1] For a compelling exposition of the many downsides of using coercive approaches, see Sidman's *Coercion and its fallout* (Revised Edition), Cambridge Center for Behavioral Studies: Authors Cooperative Publications (2001).

- are *more* likely to emphasize teaching how *to* behave than how *not to* behave.
- are *more* likely to elevate the person's general level of reinforcement, resulting in more prosocial behavior (Todd et al., 2002; Zanolli & Daggett, 1998).

Additionally, when discipline programs/interventions take a positive approach and address related contextual factors, a number of valuable outcomes have been achieved (Mathews, McIntosh, Frank, & May, 2014; Mayer & colleagues, 1979, 1981, 1983a, 1987, 1991, 1993, 2001, 2002; Metzler, Biglan, Rusby, & Sprague, 2001; Sprague et al., 2001). These include *decreases* in antisocial behaviors, including vandalism costs, discipline referrals, dropout and suspension rates; *increases* in prosocial behaviors, including attendance, time spent on assigned tasks, perceptions of school safety, and cooperation and positive feelings among students and staff. These results appear particularly relevant now in that states are required by Federal Legislation (*Every Student Succeeds Act*—ESSA, 2015) to develop a plan to reduce suspensions and expulsions.

In the U.S., results like those above have led to *Individuals with Disabilities Education Act* (IDEA, IDEIA) policies that state when students exhibit behavior that interferes with their learning or that of others, school individual education plan (IEP) teams must consider "positive behavioral interventions, strategies, and supports to address that behavior" and incorporate them into the student's IEP. Dwyer and Osher (2000) also point out that positive behavioral strategies not only help youngsters in special education, but are also useful for addressing behavior that interferes with social and emotional development and learning among those in regular education.

## ANTECEDENT CONTROL STRATEGIES

Below we present a variety of activities that have been shown to help prevent problematic behavior. They are all antecedent control strategies, including reinforcement when it is used as a motivational operation (MO). **Antecedent control strategies** involve *manipulating some aspect of the physical or social environment to "evoke" (or set the stage for) a desired response, or to reduce the likelihood of unwanted behaviors being emitted.* In this chapter we illustrate some constructive antecedent manipulations commonly used to promote agreeable instead of disagreeable behavior. Antecedent manipulations that *increase the likelihood* of a desired response include:

- *Presenting* discriminative stimuli that signal reinforcement ($S^{Dr}$), or presenting supplemental antecedent stimuli that maintain control over the desired behavior.
- *Removing* discriminative stimuli that signal punishment ($S^{Dp}$) and that block the desired behavior.
- *Decreasing* the necessary response effort (i.e., the work or effort involved with engaging in the response) for the desirable behavior and/or increasing the effort required to engage in the problem behavior (if feasible).
- *Presenting or arranging* a motivational operation (MO) that heightens the reinforcing value of the consequences of the desirable behavior (see Table 27.1 for examples).

Other antecedent manipulations that reduce the likelihood that problematic responses will be emitted include:

- *Adding* a discriminative stimulus that signals punishment ($S^{Dp}$);
- *Removing* the discriminative stimuli that cue ($S^{Dr}$s) the problem behavior;
- *Reducing or eliminating* motivational operations (MOs) that contribute to occurrence of the problem behavior; and
- *Combining or using* packages of antecedent-control strategies, such as establishing rules, modeling, and social stories.

# CHAPTER 27  PREVENTING CHALLENGING BEHAVIOR BY ENRICHING THE ENVIRONMENT • 625

**TABLE 27.1  Promoting Goal Attainment by Managing Antecedent Conditions**

| Antecedent Strategy | ➡ Increase Desirable Behavior | Decrease Undesirable Behavior |
|---|---|---|
| **Stimulus Change** | *Add $S^D$ or Remove $S^{Dp}$* | *Add $S^{Dp}$, $S^\Delta$ or Remove $S^{Dr}$* |
| Goal: Increase on-task behavior and decrease "goofing off" in class. | Add a timer to indicate whether the student has remained on-task for 5 minutes and reinforcement will be forthcoming. <br><br> Separate from the group a peer who calls student a "teacher's pet" because he does his school work. | Move a youngster's seat next to the teacher's desk, which not only adds a stimulus that indicates that "goofing off" will not be reinforced, but also removes the stimulus (the other children) whose presence signals he will gain reinforcement in the form of attention. |
| Goal: Increase on-time arrival at work. | Instead of reprimanding staff lateness, install a time-clock and allow staff arriving on time every day of the week to leave early on the day of their choice the following week. | Assign late staff to bus-arrival check-in duty the following week. Remove an opportunity to sleep a few minutes later. |
| **MO** | ➡ *Arrange* | *Eliminate* |
| Goal: Increase on-task behavior and decrease aggression maintained by escape. | Enrich break area with preferred activities, to which the child can have access only by being on-task for a specified amount of time. (Combining both MO and differential reinforcement to increase working by making this break more preferable as well as by supplying contingent reinforcement.) | Eliminate the need for contingent breaks by scheduling *noncontingent* breaks in an enriched break area every 15 minutes. |
| **Response Effort** (An MO) | ➡ *Decrease Response Effort* | *Increase Response Effort* |
| Goal: Increase eating healthy food and decrease consuming junk food. | Always have favored pre-cut veggies and fruits available in the refrigerator, thereby diminishing the likelihood of the person's choosing less healthy food. | Keep all junk food out of the house, signaling response effort required to drive to the store to get it. |
| **Modeling** | ➡ *Present Imitative Prompt* | *Develop $S^\Delta$* |
| Goal: Increase concise, carefully conceived contributions during staff meetings. | Comment positively on the constructiveness, clarity, and conciseness of the model's contributions. | Shift attention away from or interrupt a person continuing to digress or complain. |
| Goal: Increase hand-raising and decrease shouting out maintained by attention. | Reinforce models' hand-raising in the presence of the client and, of course, reinforce the client's act of imitation. (Contingency manager will likely become an $S^{Dr}$ for hand-raising.) | Ignore (withhold reinforcement) all students who are shouting out. (Contingency manager will likely become an $S^\Delta$ for shouting out.) |

## USING STIMULUS-CHANGE PROCEDURES TO PREVENT PROBLEMATIC BEHAVIOR

As discussed in Chapter 17, *stimulus change* consists of *presenting or withdrawing motivating operations and/or $S^{Dr}s$, $S^{Dp}s$, or $S^{De}s/S^{\Delta}s$ (antecedent stimuli that occasion or reduce [abate or diminish] behavior)*.

### Removing Impediments to Goal Behaviors

Removing impediments to positive behavior change is one stimulus-change procedure among many for preventing and reducing behaviors like off-task or non-goal behavior and generally is *easier than adding or removing consequence*. Changing the seating of students who distract others by talking can improve performance by decreasing that source of disruption. Removing sweets from the house supports sticking to your diet, eventually leading to weight loss. Turning off the television can reduce distractions, thereby enabling students to complete homework and be more productive. Simply by revising an adolescent's school curriculum, Dunlap, Kern-Dunlap, Clarke, and Robbins (1991) reduced a student's troublesome behavior.

Table 27.1 presents a brief summary of antecedent strategies aimed at supporting goal-attainment.

After we have identified well-established motivational operations and/or manageable $S^{Dr}s$ and $S^{De}s$, we can present or withdraw those for the purpose of changing the rate of a behavior. Given that the focus of this chapter is on positive behavior interventions, we emphasize presenting or removing stimuli that signal reinforcement ($S^{Dr}s$), rather than those that signal punishment ($S^{Dp}s$).

## PROMPTING STRATEGIES FOR PREVENTING/REDUCING PROBLEM BEHAVIOR

### Presenting Rules or Instructions

Clearly stating and explicitly reinforcing adherence to rules or standards frequently facilitates acceptable deportment. The problem is that parents, educators, supervisors, and other managers often erroneously assume that their children, students, and personnel already understand behavior standards; that they know or *should* know how to behave and that they *should* follow rules. In such cases, behavioral expectations tend to be communicated ambiguously, if at all (i.e., clear $S^D$s have not been developed). Participants then must learn the rules through trial and error; that is, by coming in contact with the contingencies. Unfortunately, if contingency managers do not articulate rules clearly, rule violations tend to be more frequent, hence punished more often. In such circumstances the fault actually lies with the failure of the environment to support or set the occasion for appropriate behavior, not with the transgressor.

Recognizing that inappropriate behavior differs from non-compliant behavior is important. "Noncompliance occurs when the learner does not do something that is directly commanded. Inappropriate behaviors are those that the learner may produce while complying" (Englemann & Colvin, 1983, p. 1).

The main point is that before barging in to prevent or reduce repeatedly occurring problematic behaviors in a given situation, STOP! First, clearly establish and communicate the rules or instructions for the individual, group, family, or organization. For example, before working on a student's behavior of noncompliance, were the deadline and expectations stated clearly? As one set of examples, Mayer and colleagues (1999, 2002, 2003, 2005) developed guidelines for clearly communicating rules in educational settings.[2] We briefly review those below. Recognize, though, that many of these guidelines can be applied in various other situations.

---

[2] For an elaboration of using rules, or classroom expectations, for school personnel, see the book: *The positive classroom: Improving student learning and behavior* by Mayer (2020).

**Involve participants in the development of the rules or expectations.** Participants can be involved in establishing the rules as an aspect of setting goals for participants' performance. Involvement in rule-setting heightens everyone's awareness and understanding of those rules and increases the likelihood of their adopting and adhering to them (Cotton et al., 1988; Fellner & Sulzer-Azaroff, 1985; Gillat & Sulzer-Azaroff, 1994).

**State the rules or expectations positively.** Once rules have been listed, review and state them positively. "Don't be late" fails to communicate expectations clearly. Are people not late as long as they place at least one foot in the establishment by the deadline? Or, must they be at their work stations? The rules "Be at your work station by starting time" or "Be in your seat with materials out before the tardy bell ring," are clearly stated instructions. They precisely communicate the desired or expected behavior. Note that the focus has moved from teaching "what *not* to do" to "what *to* do," and the rules are stated in a positive and supportive manner rather than coming across as negative and suppressive. The focus here is to develop an $S^{Dr}$, not an $S^{Dp}$.

**Keep the rules simple and short.** People are less likely to remember long lists of rules. Thus, after stating the list in a positive format, help participants condense them into a total of about three to eight of the most essential ones. Then, to reinforce recalling the rules by removing the rules from view, ask group members to re-generate the list in writing or orally, depending upon which is more effective with your particular group. That will provide you and group members the opportunity to practice saying and thereby to better recall the rules in the future.

**Keep rules developmentally appropriate.** Rules need to match the developmental level of the individuals. For example, most preschool children "do not benefit from conceptually complex rules or general guidelines (e.g., 'Be respectful') that are not grounded within concrete activities" (Fox & Little, 2001, p. 252). According to Fox and Little (2001), the statement "touch your friends gently" may be an appropriately stated rule for two-year-olds, while "solve your problems by talking, not hitting" may

---

**Generating Participant Rules**

Julie Smith, a Performance-Management trainer, asks participants in a strategic planning meeting to generate a list of "participant agreements" before addressing the main tasks. These often include such items as: "Adhere to the schedule when arriving, taking breaks, or leaving," "Turn off cell phones," "Participate actively in the discussion by contributing ideas and expressing concerns"....
Because the rules are derived from the group, and are discussed and agreed to by all, participants remain on-task and feel more satisfied with the process.

---

be more suitable for four-year-olds. If a preschooler is frustrated with a difficult task, the teacher might instruct: "Say, 'Teacher, I need help.'" When the child imitates the modeled request, the teacher follows up by helping. Or, when students are coming in from the play-yard, a statement such as "bikes stay on the playground" might be appropriate. *Rules of this nature can be designed to apply to specific activities or to informal social interactions.*

**Consider developing a common set of rules.** Some organizations opt to generate a set of rules applicable to most everyone involved. A common set of rules helps avoid confusion for students with multiple teachers or employees with more than one supervisor.

**Teach the rules.** We have found that presenting rules both visually and orally helps promote communication and reduce misunderstanding. Display the rules prominently on a poster or whiteboard, or as printed handouts and/or copied by the participants. An especially helpful method for explaining the rules to preschoolers and primary students and those with cognitive handicaps is to have them role-play each rule. Skits and role-playing situations involving peers teaching one another can also be helpful strategies. In sum, help participants to actively learn the code of conduct, rather than just providing them with a paper or booklet and leaving them to their own devices. Remember, *we want the rules to serve as $S^{Dr}s$. Thus it is important* to ensure that the rules are followed in the presence of the rule, so that positive consequences can occur to foster stimulus control (i.e., establish the neutral rule into an $S^{Dr}$ by reinforcing the rule following behavior in the presence of the rule).

**Select positive consequences for following rules.** *Rules alone do not produce appropriate behavior.* To operate effectively and to teach the *expectations, rule or instruction following must be reinforced*. People learn to behave differently in different contexts by having experienced distinctive consequences for acts performed in those contexts. Healthcare workers at the geriatric ward of City Hospital rarely wash their hands as they move from patient to patient. Why? Because hardly anyone notices or does anything about it whether they do or not. But if they see the floor supervisor, Eva, watching, they make quite a show of scrubbing up. Students learn to raise their hands in Ms. Smith's classroom because she only recognizes students who have their hands up, while they learn to speak out freely in Ms. Foster's classroom because she sometimes acknowledges students who speak out. Such differential reinforcement teaches people to discriminate which rules to adhere to under what circumstances. However, if instruction-following is not reinforced, it may eventually diminish, or it may occur only under circumstances where it is likely to be monitored. If Ms. Foster fails to call on those who raise their hands, hand-raising in her classroom probably will fade away. Therefore, according to Horner and Sugai (2000), a key feature of successful school-wide discipline programs is to provide an ongoing recognition system for student performance that matches behavioral expectations.

From a more general perspective, the management plan in any organization must frequently reinforce appropriate behavior. *People are bound to follow rules or instructions more consistently when compliance and noncompliance produce differential consequences.* Differential reinforcement works as much here as we would expect it to anywhere else. When we consistently reinforce rule-following but not infractions, the following of rules becomes a class of behavior that has been created by differential reinforcement (recall that such classes are called *operant classes*). Once instruction-following has become such a class, individuals may begin to adhere to new instructions, and so we may be able to produce desired behavior and inhibit problematic behavior even without exposing every instance of rule following or breaking to the relevant contingencies. If the child has learned to follow instructions such as "don't touch the hot stove," then maybe the child will obey when told "don't play with that sharp knife," even though the child is hearing that instruction for the first time.

In the early stages of instruction-following, adherence to rules needs to be reinforced very frequently. A teacher might, for instance, plan to terminate instruction five minutes early whenever students have complied with the code, offering them a special event instead—a song, a dance, free time, or something similar. Later on, once rule-adherence reaches a high and steady rate for several weeks, she can deliver those consequences less frequently, but never eliminate them entirely. In sum, *combining clearly communicated rules and periodically reinforcing adherence to those expectations is an effective way to establish instruction-following (sometimes also called* rule-governed behavior*), and instructions then can be used to prevent or minimize problem behavior*. In a study conducted by Johnson, Perrin, Salo, Deschaine, and Johnson (2016), they were able to reduce procrastination, missed deadlines, and produce better writing quality when rules were used within a university course.

## Presenting Prompts

Sometimes removing all the impediments to a goal is not feasible. An alternative is to use a conspicuous prompt to occasion the goal behavior. (*Prompts*, as pointed out in Chapters 17 and 18, are stimuli that *temporarily set the occasion for desired behavior and/or for reducing the rate of an unwanted behavior*.) Parents, teachers, therapists, and employers use directions, prompts, cues, and demonstrations to occasion desired behavior as substitutes for problem behavior. Sometimes, the process can be as easy as adding an image or sign to remind someone of the reinforcer to be gained by engaging in a desired behavior. For example, April places a picture of a new outfit she is eager to purchase on the refrigerator to "remind" her of the reinforcer she will permit herself to buy when she eats healthy food and loses weight. On the graph displaying the team's progress toward meeting their safety goal, Harry writes a comment (the prompt) "nearly there," at which time, he will treat them to a pizza party. Simpson (2006) discouraged adults from using their cell phones and persuaded them to buckle up while driving by placing two signs ($S^D$s) near the exit of a university parking lot. The signs simply said: "Please Hang Up, I Care" and "Please Buckle Up, I Care." After discovering that in-service training failed to teach adult instructional assistants to effectively manage disruptions, Petscher and Bailey (2006) found that a combination of a vibrating pager (a tactile prompt), self-monitoring, and bonus points for accurate program implementation substantially improved their performances.

Vibrating pagers also have been used successfully to prompt youngsters with autistic spectrum disorders (ASD) to increase their verbal initiations during play activities (Shabani et al., 2002; Taylor & Levin, 1998), and to increase their use of communication cards to request help when lost (Taylor, Hughes, Richard, Hoch, & Coello, 2004). They can be useful in reminding their teachers to scan for and present reinforcers as merited. In a far simpler demonstration, Hall et al. (1968) had classroom observers hold up a small square piece of colored paper, in a manner not likely to be noticed by the pupil, whenever the pupil engaged in particular goal behaviors. This served to signal ($S^D$) the teacher to reinforce student behavior, instead of ignoring the student's appropriate behavior. Similarly, Zeilberger et al. (1968) successfully cued parents to apply selected tactics for reducing their children's aggressive behavior. Often a simple nod of the head can serve such a function.

To help reduce behavior issues during transitions, Guardino and Fullerton (2014) used prompts to clarify what kindergarten and first grade students were to do. These prompts, or classroom modifications, included providing lines on the rug to indicate seating rows, easy access to needed materials, visual aids to indicate choices, and chimes to begin and end transitions. These prompts helped to reduce transition time an average of 1 minute, 36 seconds across four classrooms.

How the prompt is presented also can influence compliance. For example, evidence and experience (Ducharme & Worling, 1994; Hagopian & Adelinis, 2001; Mayer, 2000; Walker et al., 2004) suggests that *noncompliance is more probable following "a terminating than an initiating request"* or prompt (Mayer, p. 79). For example, rather than telling children to "stop playing," they would be more likely to comply if they were told, "Come now, we are going to eat."

Woods and Poulson (2006) used scripts to teach three children, two six-year-olds with autism and one five-year-old diagnosed with "other health impairment," to initiate social interactions with typically-developing peers. All participants increased those initiations, while some also generalized their unscripted initiations to a different activity. Additionally, after the students with disabilities began using the scripts, the typically-developing cohort of peers became more accepting of them. Script fading has been found to support independent peer interactions among youngsters on the autism spectrum (Krantz & McClannahan, 1998).

Social stories (addressed later in this chapter) are short, individualized vignettes prepared in storybook format describing the client or student acting in a particular socially-acceptable way. While social stories typically are combined with other procedures, Scattone, Tingstrom, and Wilczynski (2006) found that two of three youngsters in their study were able to use social stories alone to increase their social initiations and responses.

Those with whom we have consulted have used assembly diagrams and models to guide production workers to refine the quality of their products (Sulzer-Azaroff & Harshbarger, 1995); and signs and demonstrations to assist workers to work more safely on the job (McCann & Sulzer-Azaroff, 1996). (Of course, in both cases, adding socially reinforcing consequences further heightened those improvements.)

Sometimes one reinforcer can serve as a prompt for providing others. Mandelker et al. (1970) reported that teachers' use of tokens led them to increase their use of social reinforcers like praise. (As many researchers in this field have found, reinforcing environments help to prevent problematic student behavior—e.g., Doughty & Anderson, 2006; Favell, et al., 1982; Lalli, Casey, & Kates, 1997; O'Callaghan, et al., 2006; Roberts-Gwinn, Luiten,

Derby, Johnson, & Weber, 2001; Todd, et al., 2002.). Also, always be aware that *prompts combined with reinforcing feedback is more effective than prompts or feedback alone* (Massar, 2018).

## Response Interruption and Redirection

**Redirecting** involves *taking action to interrupt people's inappropriate behavior and prompting their engagement in more acceptable alternative behavior*. Redirection can also be viewed as a stimulus-change procedure, in that it functions as a prompt for acceptable alternative behavior. To illustrate, Hagopian and Adelinis (2001) found that a 26-year-old man with moderate retardation and bipolar disorder became aggressive when staff blocked his high rates of pica (e.g., eating pieces of paper and other inedible objects). However, once the investigators started to redirect him to preferred alternative foods, the pica was peacefully reduced. Similarly, Ahearn, Clark, MacDonald, and Chung (2007) used redirection with four children, ages seven to 11, diagnosed with autism to successfully reduce their vocal stereotypy (i.e., repetitive vocal responses). The redirection consisted of the child's teacher issuing a series of vocal demands the child typically complied with during the day immediately after any stereotypy until the child complied with three consecutively issued demands without any stereotypy. Not only did stereotypy diminish for all four children, but three of the children also increased their appropriate communication. More recent research (Toper-Korkmaz, Lerman & Tsami, 2018) though, indicates that a single redirection demand, rather than a series of repeated demands, not only saved time, but effectively reduced vocal stereotypy of children with autism following response interruption.

Response interruption and redirection (RIRD) also were found to be effective in reducing vocal stereotypy for a five-year-old child (Dickman, Bright, Montgomery, & Miguel, 2012). When differential reinforcement of appropriate vocalizations, the stereotypy decreased further and the appropriate vocalization also increased. Though some have found verbal reprimands effective in reducing stereotypy (Cook, Rapp, Gomes, Frazer, & Lindblad, 2014), response interruption and redirection (RIRD) are used commonly as an effective intervention for stereotypy (Martinez & Betz, 2013) and minimize the negative side effects of using such punishment.

Redirection also can be used to help promote compliance. As mentioned previously, we now know that *noncompliance is more probable following a terminating than an initiating request* (Hagopian & Adelinis, 2001; Walker et al., 2004). Thus, rather than saying, don't, stop, etc., redirect with comments such as "OK, now we get to do ____", "What's our next activity?" "What time is it? Oh, now it is time to ____."

We must be cautious in using redirection, especially *when the function of the problem behavior is attention*. The act of redirecting necessarily provides attention, thereby possibly reinforcing the behavior of concern and inadvertently strengthening it. Also, *avoid redirecting the individual to a different activity when the function of the problem behavior is escape from an aversive one*, because in so doing, redirection will negatively reinforce the problem behavior. However, redirection can work well when the function of the inappropriate behavior is gaining access to some reinforcing activity or item, or when it provides automatic reinforcement. The method often works well in these situations because by being redirected, the individual no longer is treated to the contingencies that had been reinforcing the disruptive behavior.

DeRosa, Novak, Morley, and Roane, (2019) reported on their comparison of RIRD with blocking the response in their effort to promote the reduction of motor stereotypy among three male youngsters with ASD, ages 6, 9, and 19. While they found both successfully reduced the motor stereotypy, response blocking worked faster and lasted longer. Whether such results hold true for verbal stereotypy remains to be seen. Also, in our opinion, blocking is more punishing and less educative than RIRD.

Response cost (see Chapter 29), a negative punishment procedure, also was found to be somewhat less effective on vocal stereotypy than RIRD (McNamara & Civicini-Motta, 2019). RIRD has been shown to be effective in treating pica as reported in a study by Taylor (2020). Their four-year-old male participant with autism engaged in pica, food selectivity, and food stealing. The assessment revealed that the pica was maintained by automatic reinforcement, and occurred at its highest levels, and across various contexts, in the absence of competing stimuli; but levels were lower when differentially reinforced by access to highly preferred tangibles, and at its lowest when highly preferred edibles were available across various contexts. "The participant learned to independently throw away, put away, and use appropriately some materials and to refrain from touching other items he previously consumed inappropriately. Pica decreased by 97 percent, independent discards increased by 100 percent, and 100 percent of admission goals were met" (p. 40).

After reviewing 71 studies on reducing motor stereotypy, researchers (Akers, Davis, Gerow, & Avery, 2020) concluded that access to competing stimuli and differential reinforcement of alternative behavior (DRA—see Chapter 28) are evidence-based interventions for motor stereotypy.

Implementing RIRD accurately can be challenging for more junior therapists. Their most common errors appear to be maintaining the integrity of the procedure while initiating and terminating the procedure (Giles, Swan, Quinn, & Weifenbach, 2017). The importance of this fact is that results have indicated that levels of stereotypy diminish faster under 100 percent integrity levels than at 33 percent levels of integrity (Gaughier, Ahern, and Colon, 2020), as one would expect.

Some evidence suggests that augmenting RIRD with noncontingent music successfully suppresses vocal stereotypy and improves on-task behavior. This combination also is reported to work faster than RIRD alone (Gibbs, Tullis, Thomas, & Elkins, 2018).

Investigators (Cividni-Motta, Moore, Fish, Priehs, & Ahern, 2020) compared response interruption and redirection (RIRD) with response interruption (RI) for treating the duration of public masturbation among individuals with ASD. They found both procedures to be effective, but "RI required fewer resources and less time" (p. 394).

## Using Activity Schedules: A Behavior Management Problem-Prevention Package Comprised of Several Antecedent Procedures

Activity schedules combine a set of methods for decreasing disruptive behaviors, especially during transition times, into a package. Just as the entries in your own appointment book do, **activity schedules** *specify in words, or display in pictures, the daily sequence of activities the student or client is to complete by the time a cue is provided* (e.g., lights on and off, spoken instructions, a timer buzzes) *to signal time to change to the next activity.*[3] These $S^D$s prompt participants to move from one activity to the next. These schedules are displayed to permit them to be referred to periodically throughout the day. Generally, the time sequence for word or picture cards is displayed in vertical format to enable the student to move each one from the "to be completed" to the "completed" column.

In one illustrative application, Dooley, Wilczenski, and Torem (2001) reported using an activity schedule with a three-year-old child with autism who had engaged in hitting, kicking, biting, crying, and screaming during transitions from one activity to another. The activity schedule

> board consisted of line drawings representing various settings and daily activities. Pictures were secured with Velcro strips. Upon his arrival at school, Chris and the teacher or assistants reviewed the schedule board together. Chris then removed the first picture and was led to the first activity. He matched his picture with one on a container and engaged in the activity. Upon completion of the task, the picture was deposited in the container.... Transitions in this preschool class were signaled by turning the lights off and by a verbal cue. Those signals prompted Chris to return to the schedule board for his next pictured assignment (pp. 58–59).

As a result of implementing the activity schedule, Chris's disruptions fell from about 12 to 14 to between zero and one per day. Compliance, which had been at zero, occurred in nine of ten to ten of ten times per day, allowing more time for learning.[4]

---

[3]Braille or textured images or vibrating signals may be substituted as needed for the visually or hearing impaired.

[4]For a more complete description of the use of activity schedules with clients on the autism spectrum, see Krantz and McClannahan (1993).

Activity schedules frequently are used in classrooms, as in the case of assisting students with attention-deficit/hyperactive disorder (ADHD) to increase their time on-task (Cirelli, Sidener, Reeve, & Reeve, 2016). All teachers and students reported finding the use and results of using the activity schedule highly acceptable. Similarly, using activity schedules with middle school students with various disabilities, increased the participants time on-task and work completion in math and language arts (Mattson & Pinkelman, 2020). In addition, students and teachers reported enjoying the activity schedules.

The physical format of most activity schedules consists of schedule books containing printed pictures attached to physical pages. Sometimes a list is posted as to what order various activities will occur. Also, Reinert, Higbee and Nix (2020) point out, technology-based activity schedules are beginning to be used increasingly. The authors "provide a task analysis for creating both simple and complex digital activity schedules using Google Slides, a freely available, web-based technology that operates on a variety of digital platforms" (p. 577). They also provide "suggestions for how behavior analysts can train parents to use this technology with their children using telehealth procedures" (p. 577). (Telehealth procedures are described in Ch. 10.)

In terms of modality, some prefer to use a tablet, such as the iPod™ Touch. Its effectiveness appears to be on par with the book-based picture activity schedule (Giles & Markham, 2017). Others have successfully used the wearable Octopus watch® to prompt typical developing children to adhere and independently complete the activities on their schedules, and to prompt those with autism to engage in play activities in a clinical setting (Jimenez-Gomez, Haggerty, & Topcuoglu, 2021). Similarly, interactive computerized training, "a self-paced program that incorporates instructions videos, and interactive questions" (Gerencser, Higbee, Akers, & Contreras, 2017, p. 567) has been used to teach parents to implement photographic activity schedules.

Investigators (Brodhead, Courtney, & Thaxton, 2018) evaluated the effects of embedding an activity schedule within an iPad on increasing the variety of play activities in which participants engaged. They used a graduated guidance procedure (Chapter 20) to teach three children with autism ages four, six, and nine to follow their activity schedules. All three increased the variety of play activities to four a session, and used the activity schedule independently and correctly. Furthermore, they continued to respond correctly even when asked to engage in novel applications.

An activity schedule one of the authors actually used with her seven- and 11-year-old grandchildren when they came to visit (see Figure 27.1). The separate pictures could be re-ordered by joint agreement. After the particular activity was completed, the picture was moved over to the empty (completed) column. The children generally were delighted to discover what new, exciting things were in store for them and we never heard, "I don't know what to do. I'm bored!"

It is important to note, however, when utilizing such schedules for disruptive behavior maintained by escape, that schedules alone will not be effective. In fact, Waters, Lerman, and Hovanetz (2009) demonstrated that without the addition of extinction (e.g., making the individual move on to the next scheduled activity) the schedule did not improve problem behavior associated with task avoidance.

## PREVENTING OR REDUCING PROBLEMATIC BEHAVIOR BY BUILDING A MORE REINFORCING ENVIRONMENT

Surely at this point we recognize how features of the environment may heighten or lessen the probability of individuals' misbehaving (e.g., Dishion, 1992; Loeber & Dishion, 1983; Mayer, 1995; Mayer, Nafpaktitis, Butterworth, & Hollingsworth, 1987; Mayer & Ybarra, 2003, 2006; Patterson et al., 1989; Tolan & Guerra, 1992).

Antecedent events, or motivational operations, that appear to contribute to problem behavior in the *school* include:

- *Students* having experienced academic failure and/or lack of appropriate social skills.
- *Staff* maintaining an ongoing punitive environment, abandoning efforts toward help-

| | | |
|---|---|---|
| Eat breakfast |  | |
| Go to beach | 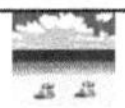 | |
| Swim or dig in the sand |  | |
| Find at least 5 different shells |  | |
| Eat lunch |  | |
| Clean shells |  | |
| Take pictures of shells |  | |
| Have a snack |  | |
| 15 minute break: read, nap, or watch Disney Channel |  | |
| Identify shells with Grandma | 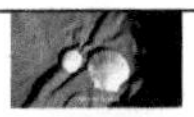 | |
| Make pages for your own shell book | 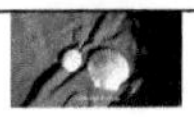 | |
| Help cook dinner or rest |  | |
| Dinner |  | |
| Read, TV, or games |  | |
| Bedtime |  | |

**Figure 27.1** Activity schedule

ing students or accepting a subculture that devalues individual differences.

- Inconsistencies by *staff* in setting and enforcing rules.
- *Educators* failing to train, or training ineffectually, staff in constructive intervention strategies and ways of organizing the classroom or school; providing unclear rules of student deportment.
- *Staff* and *parents* failing to support constructive programs.

In the *home*, the partial list includes:

- Parents or caregivers failing to monitor the child's behavior.
- The child having experienced frequent coercive behavior-management procedures.
- The child having experienced inconsistencies in rule-setting and enforcement.
- The child having experienced low levels of affection, attention, and parent involvement.
- The child having experienced sexual or physical abuse.

Those in the *community* include, among others:

- A number of antisocial networks (e.g., family, peers) in the community.
- Neighborhood and community disorganization.
- Lack of jobs.
- High availability of drugs.
- Insufficient constructive and enjoyable after-school and summer activities for youngsters.
- Displays of aggressive acts in the media.

Recognizing the influence of those sorts of detrimental environmental factors has spurred behavior analysts to design ways to heighten the reinforcing properties in the milieus in which clientele live, learn, work, and relax. The happy result: problematic behaviors have often diminished. This section briefly describes a number of those "reinforcement packages." While possibly none of these may be directly applicable in your situation, you might consider using some as templates for designing similar packages more closely suited to your needs. To illustrate, when antecedent conditions, such as those listed above, have been reduced and replaced by positive and constructive alternative conditions, antisocial behavior has diminished (Dishion, 1992; Mayer & colleagues, 1979, 1983, 1993; Metzler et al., 2001; Sprague et al., 2001). Below we offer several examples of programs incorporating the conditions supportive of prosocial behavior.

## Greeting

Allday and Pakurar (2007) found that by having teachers greet middle-school students at the door by name, along with positive statements such as "I'm glad to see you" or "I like your new shirt," resulted in on-task improvement from a mean of 45 percent to a mean of 72 percent. The investigators concluded that, "Teacher greetings represent an antecedent manipulation that can easily be implemented in classrooms to improve students' on-task behavior" (p. 317). Similarly, another study based in a middle school compared the effects of the teacher's offering positive greetings at the door to the lack of such greetings (Cook, Fiat, & Larson, 2018). Data indicated that the positive greetings were associated with "significant improvements in academic engaged time and reductions in disruptive behavior" (p. 149). Furthermore, the teachers found the intervention to be reasonable, feasible, and acceptable. Similarly, investigators (Browring & Toogood, 2019) found that being greeted at the door by personnel in a vocational training center for adults with intellectual disabilities, increased on-task behavior of clientele and appeared to prompt staff to interact more frequently with participants. Further, investigators (Allday, Bush, Ticknor, & Walker, 2011) report that when teachers greeted their students, the students initiated work on their assigned tasks more rapidly. As Cook, et al. suggest, it appears that *positive greetings at the door appear to be a low-cost, high-yield proactive classroom management strategy.* So consider frequently greeting your students, clients, and/or personnel and you may find it functions as a motivating operation to initiate their assigned tasks sooner and keep going longer.

Similarly, Edwards and Johnston (1977) taught bus drivers to greet the first student, plus any other student who greeted the driver at each bus stop. As a result, a survey found that students who rode these experimental buses rated their drivers as more friendly and the ride as more favorable than did students who rode control buses on which greetings never occurred. Also, Brown and Sulzer-Azaroff (1994) found that greetings paired with smiles by bank tellers were positively correlated with customer satisfaction. In addition, when housekeeping staff provided handwritten greeting cards and name-introduction cards, the tips they received increased (Shih, Jai, Chen, & Blum, 2019). Perhaps the initial tone that is set, or the personal attention or recognition that is provided, helps to establish a positively reinforcing environment that promotes favorable behaviors.

## Distracting with Preferred Events

A common means of reducing anxiety and frustration is to apply distractions. For example, researchers have emphasized how watching TV during dental procedures, and during sexual and reproductive healthcare procedures can lower the patient's anxiety and subsequently reported pain associated with the procedure (Akintomide, Doshi, Power, & Wilkinson, 2016). Similarly, teachers have used preferred events to help children transition to less preferred activities. When faced with situations likely to evoke problem behavior, such as transitions to less-preferred activities or to less-structured surroundings, personnel can distract the individual by providing reinforcing events in advance of, or during, the transition (a form of noncontingent reinforcement or NCR). Such distractions function as motivational operations setting the stage for more adaptive behaviors. In one case, Davis, et al. (2000) presented a preferred item (e.g., paired with a favorite peer, stopwatch, blue race car, action figures) immediately prior to the teacher delivering a request to transition to a less-preferred activity. The investigators have pointed out that a distracter (and high-probability requests—see next topic) "can be used to increase a student's responsiveness to requests during undesired events and activities that he typically tries to escape or avoid" (p. 439). It also can help moderate the person's negative reaction to the non-preferred event or activity because it adds reinforcers to the mix.

In a related case report, Vaughn et al. (2002) identified their distracters based on functional and reinforcer assessments for a seven-year-old boy with autism, severe intellectual disabilities, and a long history of difficult behaviors. The behaviors they focused on were climbing on tables and chairs in a fast-food restaurant, running away, and refusing to leave the restaurant's playground. It was determined that attention was a major function for his behaviors during mealtime at the restaurant. After reinforcers, such as a tape recorder, musical book, animated car-racing screen, and bubbles, were identified, they were provided to him during the meal as distracters. Additionally, his mother poured on the attention by talking with him about the toys and took turns playing with them. During the departure phase of the routine, the mother called the boy and began to blow bubbles through a plastic wand until the child arrived at her side. They then alternated blowing bubbles as they left. As a result, problem behaviors decreased substantially.

A similar strategy of providing preferred stimuli, such as toys or activities, throughout the meal also has been used to help reduce food refusal. To illustrate, Wilder, Normand, and Atwell (2005) helped to reduce their clients' self-injury and to improve their food acceptance by providing continuous access to a video during meals. Stark et al. (1989) attempted unsuccessfully to use distraction with four children who expressed high levels of anxious and disruptive behavior when visiting the dentist. Apparently, the negative reinforcement derived from escaping the situation was more powerful than that of the distracting activity. Consequently, if you use this method be sure that the distracting activities you choose are more reinforcing than those inherent in the unwanted behavior. Also, be careful not to present the preferred stimuli contingent on the unwanted behavior because that could inadvertently reinforce it.

In the following example of the use of distracting with preferred events, an elderly man with dementia residing in a nursing home was frequently physically and verbally aggressive. Rather than choosing to use anti-psychotic medication and/or restraints, the investigators (Fisher & Buchanan, 2018) provided him with a preferred stimulus that was available continuously during caregiving sessions. Both verbal and physical aggression diminished significantly. Again, *the results of these studies underscore the importance of incorporating reinforcers within' environments in which people learn, work, play, and live.*

## Behavioral Momentum or High-Probability Request (or Instructional) Sequence

An especially promising operation for gaining compliance and productive participation is to establish **behavioral momentum** by *making requests known to promote high rates of compliance in advance of the activity less likely to be performed.* Behavioral momentum sometimes is described as being similar to Newton's laws of motion: an object in motion is likely to continue in motion unless presented with an equal and opposite force or disruptor (Trump, Herrod, Ayres, Ringdahl, & Best, 2020). A meta-analysis of interventions to improve compliance of students with disabilities found using high-probability requests in a school setting as "potentially evidence based" (Losinski, Sanders, Katsiyannis, Wiseman, 2017). Tania delivers several easy requests she is quite certain Bert will respond to rapidly—wash the board, carry out the waste-basket, feed the fish, draw a picture, and write the alphabet (i.e., *high-probability request sequence*) and complete his arithmetic problems, (i.e., a low-probability request; something he is capable of doing, but rarely does on request). Sula presents several cards for Irma to read aloud. The first six or seven contain words that Irma can read easily, while the next few are harder for her. Her initial string of reinforced successes encourages her to persist with the more difficult ones. This strategy has been shown to decrease defiance, noncompliance, transition problems, and other escape-motivated behaviors (Austin & Agar, 2005; Banda & Kubina, 2006; Davis, Brady, Williams, & Hamilton, 1992; Davis, et al., 2000; Ray, Skinner, & Watson, 1999; Mace & Belfiore, 1990) as well to increase a number of socially-appropriate behaviors (see Killu, 1999 for a review) including social interactions (Davis, Brady, Hamilton, McEvoy, & Williams, 1994). Behavioral momentum also has been used successfully to help a three-year-old boy with autism, who readily engaged in motor imitation, but he seldom imitated vocal responses (Hansen, DeSouza, Stuart, & Shilliingsburg, 2019). Following his imitating several motor responses (a high probability behavior), the child was asked to imitate a vocal response (a low probability behavior). We believe that using high-probability requests promotes momentum, thereby setting up a condition for compliance as a general response class (Lee, Belfiore, Scheeler, Hua, & Smith, 2004). If the low-probability request has aversive properties, then frequently augmenting reinforcers may reduce its aversiveness and increase compliance (Lee, 2005; Lee et al., 2004).

Lipschultz and Wilder (2017) provide several recommendations when using behavioral momentum:

- Make sure the high-p requests or instructions have been empirically identified before using them. That is, be sure to have observed the client following the request before you use them as high-p requests.
- Be sure to reinforce compliance with the high probability requests. If compliance is not obtained, check and eliminate any stimuli associated with low-p request, and/or use different high probability requests.
- Reinforce compliance with the low-probability request.

Once again, research indicates that stressing the positive pays. Be aware, though, of one important point: As Mace, Mauro, Boyajian, and Eckert (1997) demonstrated, *when using this type of high-probability request intervention, differential reinforcement is essential to success.* The unwanted responses must be placed on extinction, while compliance with desired, low-probability responses must be contingently rewarded by delivering powerful reinforcers (Zarcone, Iwata, Hughes, & Vollmer, 1993; Zarcone, Iwata, Mazaleski, & Smith, 1994). Moreover, investigators (Wilder, Majdalany, Sturkie, & Smeltz, 2015) demonstrated the importance of differential reinforcement for compliance with the high-p request to get compliance with the low-p request. They demonstrated that increases in low-p compliance only occurred when the high-p request was differentially reinforced with edibles. In addition, they demonstrated that the value of the reinforcer delivered for compliance with the high-p request affected the compliance with the low-p request in the procedure. In other words, the most common form of reinforcement for compliance (e.g., praise) was not effective in increasing compliance with the low-p request if that was the reinforcer delivered for compliance with the high-p request. However, when they provided a more powerful reinforcer, edibles for compliance with the high-p request, the participants complied with the low-p request. Thus, to increase the likelihood that behavioral momentum will be effective, we suggest that you use high preference reinforcers of sufficient magnitude when reinforcing compliance to both high and low probability requests. Behavioral momentum now is considered an evidence-based practice for individuals with autism spectrum disorder (Brosh, Fisher, Wood, & Test, 2018).

## Providing Choice

In Chapter 11, we discussed providing opportunities for choice as a means of increasing the effectiveness of reinforcement. We also pointed out how allowing choice can help prevent problem behaviors. Carter (2001) used play opportunities to compare the effects of choice to non-choice in a naturalistic language intervention procedure among children with autism. The youngsters could choose among various toys and games during the play. When they were permitted to choose during language intervention within a play context, the children's disruptive behaviors diminished considerably, while their levels of appropriate social play/pragmatic skills increased, and the targeted language generalized to the home.

Similarly, choice was used to eliminate two children's behaviors of disrobing at school and urinating on their clothing (Carlson, Luiselli, Slyman, & Markowski, 2008). Both students, a 13-year-old girl diagnosed with autism and a five-year-old boy with pervasive developmental disorder, not otherwise specified, seemed to engage in these behaviors to gain access to new and more preferred clothing. The more effective intervention for both children was simply to give "the children a choice to change into high-preference clothes at scheduled opportunities during the day" (p. 86).

Stenhoff et al. (2008) assisted a 15-year-old ninth-grade student with a learning disability, who usually refused to complete his biology class assignments. The intervention consisted of allowing the student to choose between two academic assignments. One was the regular class assignment; the alternative had questions on one side and answers on the other side. The student chose the regular class assignment every session, and his completion rate went from a mean of two percent to a mean of 99 percent. His rate of accuracy averaged 81 percent during the final intervention phase. (No baseline data were collected; however, during the withdrawal phase of the design his accuracy went down to zero percent.) Also, his grade for the class improved from 52 percent (failing) to 76 percent (passing). Similarly, Ramsey, Jolivette, Patterson, and Kennedy (2010) found that by allowing five adolescents with emotional/behavioral disorders who lived in a residential facility to choose the sequence of their tasks, the youngsters improved both their on-task and task-completion rates, although not their accuracy. Also, Tasky, Rudrud, Schulze, and Rapp (2008) found that

choice among tasks increased the on-task behavior of three adults with traumatic brain injury.

Choice also plays an important role in educational game development. Researchers (Lomas, et al., 2017) found that with over 10,000 subjects, moderately difficult levels were most motivating when self-selected. In another study, individuals were allowed to choose the *sequence* in which they were to complete their tasks (Kern, Mantegna, Vorndran, Bailin, & Hilt, 2001). This intervention resulted in improved behavior for each participant, and the investigators concluded that simply being able to choose *may, in and of itself, be reinforcing.* Schmidt, Hanley, and Layer's (2009) findings tend to support the value of permitting choice. When identical consequences were available for both choice and no-choice conditions, they found that the children demonstrated a preference for choice, regardless of whether the consequences were more or less preferred. Others (Toussaint, Kodak, & Viadescu, 2016) also report that clients prefer choice-making opportunities and that they often result in increased treatment efficacy.

Similar findings have been reported for a range of human and nonhuman subject populations in varied settings (See Catania & Sagvolden, 1980; Moore & Fantino, 1975; Romaniuk & Miltenberger, 2001.) Therefore, *offer choices as a motivating operation whenever possible, especially when the function of the problem behavior appears to be escape- or access-motivated* (Berotti, 1996; Dyer et al., 1990; Sigafoos, 1998).

Moreover, providing antecedent choice of reinforcers within demand contexts also demonstrated improved performance and actually preference for choice as an antecedent method (Peterson, Lerman, & Nissen, 2016).

## Using Participative Goal-Setting: Promoting Success and Preventing Problem Behaviors

Goal setting may serve a valuable supportive function within the behavior-change process, as mentioned in Chapter 17, in that goals may function as motivating operations (MOs). Suppose you notice that the garage needs to be cleaned (an SD). If you set a goal, like "On Wednesday I'm going to clean the garage." you would be much more apt to clean it than if not. We find that inviting people to participate in setting goals in advance of choosing an activity also can improve rule compliance, job performance (e. g., increased safety, production), and physical activity over simply assigning goals (Cotton, et al., 1988; Fellner & Sulzer-Azaroff, 1985; Kuhl, Rudrud, Witts, & Schulze, 2015; Sulzer-Azaroff et al., 1990). For example, in evaluating effective management styles, investigators (Posadzinska, Shupska, & Karaszewski, 2020) conclude that a participative leadership style results in "a more open approach in interactions with employees," and "stimulates the development of innovative solutions and fosters creativity in employees" (p. 488). Similarly, Chan (2019) noted that the participative leadership style tends to result in an increase in employees' work engagement and job satisfaction. Kuhl et al (2015) sought to increase children's physical activity. They reported that individual goal setting, along with individual feedback, rather than classroom goal setting and feedback, helped to increase the average number of steps taken per day. Similarly, Hayes and Van Camp (2015) increased children's steps by tailored goals, self-monitoring, reinforcement and feedback. Mellalieu, Hanton, and O'Brien (2006) found that when members of a collegiate rugby team were invited to participate in goal-setting, their execution of task-specific field skills (number of tackles, successful kicks, and number of ball carries) improved. Similarly, collegiate football players (Ward & Carnes, 2002) improved their performance during practice and games when they collaborated in setting goals. Similarly, when Thai athletic shoe production teams participated in setting their goals and reviewing weekly quality scores (and of course, received peer and supervisor approbation and other tangible reinforcers), product quality increased by over 9 percent and defects dropped from over 7 percent to about 4.4 percent. This translated into a yearly savings of over $10 million (Sulzer-Azaroff & Harshbarger, 1995; see Figure 17.2 in Chapter 17 for the graphic representation).

Participative goal-setting is often used as an aspect of behavioral contracting and has been effective in reducing problem and establishing preferred replacement behaviors. (For guidelines on setting goals and developing behavioral contracts, see Chapter 4.) Therefore, *involve participants in setting goals and/or establishing behavioral contracts whenever feasible.* Also, as always, follow progress toward goals and attainment with reinforcement.

## Reducing Response Demand

**Response effort** relates to *the amount of force, exertion, or time requisite to engaging in a response.* Other factors being equal, *we can avoid problematic reactions by temporarily reducing the level of the demand*; that is, by reducing or temporarily removing the aversive properties inherent in the response requirement (Friman & Poling, 1995). Reducing demand often works because less challenging behaviors are more likely to be emitted than those requiring more effort. Horner and Day (1991) applied this premise to reduce problematic behavior maintained by escape from tasks. Paul, a 12-year-old boy, was aggressive during academic work periods as a way to avoid doing his assignments. Paul was taught two different replacement behaviors requiring less effort than becoming aggressive. These included a simple sign language gesture to request a break and more effortful signing sequence (*"I want to go, please"*). When Paul was permitted to sign *"break"* to escape having to work for a while, he was more likely to choose the former over aggressing. However, when Paul could earn a break only by signing the more difficult *"I want to go, please,"* he engaged in aggression instead.

In a similar case, Brothers, Krantz, and McClannahan (1994) manipulated the response effort required to save recyclable paper. Rather than requiring people to dispose of paper in the trash can, they placed a small container on each employee's desk. (Of course, the method actually combined a prompt, the presence of the container, paired with the greater effort required to get up and throw the paper in the trash.) As a result of this simple manipulation, far less recyclable paper was wasted.

Failure to comply may be due to response effort. For example, investigators (Wilder, Fishetti, Myers, Leon-Enriquez, & Majdalany, 2013) reported that compliance is effected by the amount of effort required. Young children are more likely to comply when there is less effort involved. So, if non-compliance is an issue, you might try initially reducing the effort involved. Once compliance is established and reinforced, then you can try to increase the effort involved gradually. Similarly, Felde, Hagagerty, Sleiman, and Gravina (2020) noted that therapists were better prepared to conduct social skills training groups when less response effort was required by making materials more easily accessible, and by issuing email prompts.

Failing to fulfill requested tasks sometimes can set the stage for problematic behavior. In fact, Lee et al. (1999, p. 200) contend that there are "strong functional relationships between a student's capacity to succeed on difficult academic tasks and the occurrence of a variety of problem behaviors." Further, according to Gold and Mann (1982, p. 313), "poor scholastic experiences are significant causes of delinquent and disruptive behavior."

As in other instances of extinction-induced aggression (see Chapter 26), students generally find repeated academic failure to be especially punishing, which predictably results in escalating behavioral problems (see Chapter 30). Yet, as Ysseldyke et al. (1997) pointed out, mismatches between students' assignments and their actual levels of academic functioning are not at all unusual. For example, those investigators found that high-school students capable of reading only at the third-grade level often were assigned reading material at the eleventh-grade level, which, in turn, required extreme effort. The aversiveness of their readily-predictable rates of failure elevated their levels of misbehavior *both in and outside of the classroom*. Perhaps educators are not adequately informed about or fail to act upon the fact that *mismatching assignments to students' ability levels is a recipe for academic failure*. That, in turn, may partially explain why "approximately four of every five disruptive students can be traced to some dysfunction in the way schools are organized, staff members are trained, or schools are run" (U.S. Department of Education, 2000, p. 10).

## Promoting Academic/task Success While Preventing Problem Behavior

As we have seen, overly challenging assignments tend to promote a variety of problem behaviors. Interestingly, too, we have learned that people are more likely to complete tasks, engage in fewer problem behaviors, and choose to do more work, not only when the work is at their functional or skill level, but also when the **interspersal strategy** is used: *intersperse easier items or activities within their assignments* (e.g., Cates et al., 1999; Guilhardi, Smith, Rivera, & Ross, 2017; Johns et al., 2000; Logan & Skinner, 1998; Sanford & Horner, 2013). This holds true even when the length of the task is increased. Not only do individuals usually *prefer* tasks composed of both difficult and easy tasks, but they tend to *accomplish more and remain on task longer*, probably due to heightened rates of gaining immediate reinforcement for completing problems. Also, because the *interspersal technique* provides practice opportunities, students achieve higher retention and fluency levels.

Al-hinai, Shourbagi, and Emara (2019) found that using an interspersal strategy to teach fourth grade students with learning disabilities to solve mathematics problems resulted in the students performing better than the control group that was not exposed to the interpersonal strategy. Also, in their meta-analytic review of the interspersal strategy, Bottini, Vetter, McArdell, Wiseman, and Gillis (2018) found that "no procedural variation presents a significant benefit over any other, suggesting that task interspersal may be an instructional procedure easily adapted to a client's needs or preferences. Further, task interspersal was effective across a range of target skills" (p. 119).

Other antecedent techniques for heightening students' success rates (including increased task engagement, work productivity, and accuracy), and for reducing levels of problem behaviors include: breaking assignments or tasks down into their component parts; adding visual cues, such as enlarging

---

To maximize reinforcement and minimize the frequency of troublesome behaviors:

1) adjust tasks to match participants' functional levels; and

2) intersperse easier ones among the more challenging tasks.

print size, underlining, or highlighting words; adding illustrations; and incorporating choice (Dunlap, White, Vera, Wilson, & Panacek, 1996; Lee et al., 1999).

Beware, though, to avoid assigning overly easy tasks, because that situation also has been associated with increases in problem behaviors. Umbreit et al. (2004) addressed ten-year-old Jason's excessive talking and wandering around the classroom by assigning him more challenging material. When Jason was permitted to work ahead on his assignments and workbooks until he reached one in which he was unable to answer all questions correctly within ten minutes of continuous work, that assignment was deemed to be more challenging. At that point his behavior improved, and both the student and his teacher gave the intervention a very positive acceptability rating. Again, this study points out the importance of *adjusting task assignments to the functional levels (neither too high nor too low) of each participating individual.* See Boxes 27.1 and 27.2 for additional interventions for improving academic performance.

Twyman and Heward (2018) suggest that choral responding and response cards are easy-to-use teaching tactics "that consistently yield measurably superior learning outcomes… across curriculum content and students' age and skill levels" (p. 78). Why are teaching strategies like **choral responding** and **response cards** (see Boxes 27.1 & 27.2) more effective than the standard practice of asking students to raise their hands? Probably because by both doing and saying, students are more engaged in learning skills. We learn what we do, so teachers who concentrate on getting their students to behave more often and more appropriately to the material they are learning are probably more effective than those teachers who concentrate mainly on their lecture style or other features of their own classroom behavior. Also, as pointed out by Munro and Stephenson (2009), when teachers use response cards, they tend to provide more feedback than when they request only hand-raising; and, as you have learned, the more frequent and immediate the reinforcement, the more rapid the learning. In addition, when Clarke, Haydon, Bauer, and Epperly (2016) introduced response cards to a science and social studies general education class, they found that

> **Box 27.1**
> **Choral Responding**
>
>
> In **choral responding**, *participants answer questions or imitate modeled statements in unison*. Within the process, the group leader identifies those who fail to respond appropriately and assists them afterward. Because everyone is engaged, individual students have less opportunity to misbehave. Choral responding has been shown to improve learning rates more successfully than more traditional recitation methods. In one case, Sterling, Barbetta, Heward, and Heron (1997) examined the added impact of choral responding to the teacher's modeling of correct answers to health questions. The teacher displayed a card containing a health fact question to five fourth-grade students (four challenged with developmental delays and one with a learning disability). She then modeled the correct response, and instructed the students immediately to repeat the correct response three times. On end-of-the-day and two-week post-assessments, all five responded correctly more often than they had in the absence of the choral-responding feature.

mainstreamed students with intellectual disabilities increased their active responding and the duration of their remaining on-task. This prompted the authors to conclude that response cards can help make the classroom more inclusive.

Response cards also have been used as instructional tools at the college level. Bulla, Wertalik and Crafton, (2020) wondered what questioning format with the cards might be most suitable. So, they compared asking college students for definitions with asking them to discriminate between examples and non-examples of concepts. The discrimination questions produced better performance than the definitions questions, as measured by class quizzes.

Choral responding appears to be even more effective when it is combined with mnemonic strategies (Hayden, Musti-Rao, & Alter, 2017; Scruggs & Mastropieri, 2000). A **mnemonic** is *a strategy*

## Box 27.2
### Response Cards

Response cards consist of a piece of paper, an index card, a small erasable board, a white laminated tile board, or any object large enough to permit the student to write on it multiple times. (Randolph, 2007, suggests that the specific nature of the response card appears to be irrelevant.) Students are instructed to write their answers to questions large enough to allow them to be seen from the front of the room, and to display their answers only when instructed to do so. For example, the teacher might ask students in a high-school chemistry class, "What is the atomic symbol for hydrogen?" The students write their answers on their cards, and when the teacher says "Show me," they hold up their cards. The teacher then scans the cards and affirms the correct answer (e.g., "Yes, the symbol is H.") in a constructive, not a negative or demeaning way. Students are not regarded as cheating when they look at other students' cards because they learn from their peer models. Also, the teacher can identify those who appear to be experiencing difficulty and provide them with extra instruction later on. When compared to the traditional method of hand-raising, in which only one student is called upon to provide an answer, use of response cards has been found to prevent problematic and increase on-task behavior (Armendariz & Umbreit, 1999; Gardner, Heward, & Grossi, 1994). The method also has functioned to raise quiz scores more effectively than the traditional hand-raising system in elementary, secondary-school, and college classrooms (Bulla, et al., 2020; Cavanaugh, Heward, & Donelson, 1996; Narayan, Heward, Gardner, Courson, & Omness, 1990). Randolph's (2007) review of 18 studies on the use of response cards concluded that they significantly and consistently enhance test and quiz achievement, plus class participation, and reduce disruptive behavior.

*designed to improve memory or recall by tying new information more closely to the learner's existing knowledge base.* For example, when Hayden, Musti-Rao and Alter (2017) taught students with mild to moderate disabilities who were in grades seven through nine to identify states on a map, they compared combining choral responding with mnemonics to choral responding by itself. For example, students were asked to identify key words that were similar to each state's name (e.g., a picture of a hamster was associated with the state of New Hampshire, crayons for the state of Colorado). Choral responding was then used for each state, sometimes with the mnemonic and other times without it. They found that the combined intervention was more effective than choral responding by itself for increasing on-task behavior and accuracy on daily quizzes.

## THE IMPORTANCE OF A REINFORCING ENVIRONMENT

The importance of maintaining high levels of reinforcement in the local environment was mentioned earlier in Chapters 3, 5, 6, and 11 on reinforcement and bears repeating here. Group managers seeking to develop a supportive environment conducive to learning and cooperative, safe, healthy, and productive performance as replacements for problem behaviors must maintain a highly reinforcing ambiance. People prefer to remain in densely reinforcing environments. Other factors being equal, they will be more productive and less destructive and disruptive. Vandalism, aggression, and attendance problems are likely to diminish as a function of having lots of events that those involved find reinforcing—typically praise, recognition, special rewards, and activities, provided both directly contingent on performance improvement as well as noncontingently. The latter might include enjoyable educational events, audiovisual presentations, entertaining art, music, dramatic or dance performances, arts and crafts activities, sports events, and trips, distributed freely as well as contingent on progress and behavioral improvements.

You may have noticed that many of the strategies described in this and the previous chapter serve to heighten the reinforcing properties of the environment. For example, Favell et al. (1982) found that simply making toys available non-contingently resulted in less self-injury than sterile surroundings. As part of a school-wide strategy, Todd et al. (2002) increased rates of specific feedback to students to a ratio of four positive comments to each corrective comment. Problem behavior decreased substantially while staff satisfaction increased. Similarly, Cook et. al. (2016) increased rates of specific praise, approval, and positive gestures by general education elementary and middle school teachers who had a higher ratio of negative-to-positive interactions with their students to a ratio of five positive to one negative, resulting in fewer disruptions and more student engaged time. Also, Zanolli and Daggett (1998) found that two socially withdrawn preschoolers, one with autism, made more spontaneous initiations after high rates of reinforcement than after low rates. Actually, results of numerous studies suggest that environmental enrichment automatically serves to reduce a variety of problematic behaviors that previously had been maintained by automatic reinforcement (Gover, Fahmie, & McKeown, 2019). Gover et al. illustrate that such enrichment can be even more effective when combined with prompts, differential reinforcement, and blocking. Some evidence suggests that environmental enrichment also "can reduce alcohol seeking behavior following a period of abstinence (Campbell, Jin, & Lawrence, 2019). (See our Web page and Mayer et al., 1983b, for a variety of practical reinforcing programs that were used as part of an overall strategy to reduce vandalism, aggression, and attendance problems, and to increase students' on-task and paying-attention behaviors.) As Nevin (1988) has demonstrated, dense or constant reinforcement helps promote and maintain prosocial behavior.

Antecedent operations also appear to play a major role in students' academic and social performance. This conclusion has been supported by findings by Mayer et al. (1987) and later by West, Taylor, Wheatley, and West (2007), who discovered that clear standards or expectations, positive relationships with teachers, positive social skills, in relating to peers, doing well on assignments and tests, receiving praise and recognition for effort, and doing good work in school were better predictors of achievement and safety than such traditional measures as economic status, home language, family bonding, neighborhood stability, and peer associations. Clearly, more reinforcing school environments support lower rates of problem behavior than punitive ones. Mayer (2020) offers further strategies for promoting a positive classroom environment in his book on the positive classroom.

## USING NONCONTINGENT REINFORCEMENT (NCR) TO PREVENT INAPPROPRIATE BEHAVIOR[5]

We have mentioned that providing noncontingent reinforcement (NCR) serves to heighten the general level of reinforcement in the current environment. Settings rich in reinforcement tend to support adaptive and constructive behaviors, while staving off the misconduct that ordinarily might occur were those reinforcers absent. As we shall illustrate below, contingency managers have used NCR effectively as an MO to diminish or eliminate various problematic behaviors.

### NCR Defined and Illustrated

Under **noncontingent reinforcement (NCR)**, *reinforcers are added to environments independent of participants' behavior. Regardless of participants' actions at the time, these conditions are maintained on an ongoing basis, or presented according to a fixed-time (FT) or variable-time (VT) schedule of reinforcement.* Under FT schedules, *reinforcers are programmed for regular noncontingent delivery*, while under VT schedules, *they are delivered according to a specific mean length of time* (e.g., on average of, say, every five minutes), regardless of the person's ongoing behavior. Fortunately, this kind of environmental enrichment is becoming standard practice among those who arrange programs for people housed in institutions or group homes. In general, such conditions may include noncontingently arranging pleasant social events, providing

---

[5]Some researchers prefer the language of free reinforcement to that of NCR

---

**Noncontingent Reinforcement (NCR)**

Following the passage of each "t" time period ⟶ reinforcers delivered, regardless of the nature of the intervening behaviors.

Example:
After T time (e.g., 10 minutes) ⟶ the teacher compliments the class or a group of students for working hard or for paying attention, regardless of what they are actually doing.

---

clients with access to items such as toys or games, music, preferred food, smiles, affection, and so on. VT reinforcement strategies also have become a more commonplace practice by zoo workers, resulting in an improvement in the animals' health, apparent contentment, and well-being (Carmignani, 2010). A number of researchers (e.g., Davis et al. 2016; Horner & Day, 1991) also have pointed out that for maximal benefit, the reinforcers provided through the NCR should be functionally equivalent to the consequences maintaining the challenging behavior. So, be sure a do a functional behavior assessment to help you determine what those reinforcers are.

When contemplating using procedures that might involve extinction, we must concern ourselves with the fact that eliminating the response-reinforcer relation may create problems because it may increase the individual's motivation for that reinforcer. NCR allows us to break the contingent relation between the response and the reinforcer without depriving the individual of important reinforcers. When deprived of reinforcers, people's actions (tantruming, destructiveness, aggression) remind us how important those reinforcers can be. For that reason, when people with seriously challenging behaviors are involved, those actions need to be functionally assessed to inform us as to the choice of particular reinforcers. (Recall, from Chapter 10, these functions often include attention, obtaining tangible objects, or escape from difficult or unpleasant tasks.) However, less formal functional behavior assessments also may prove useful in designing solutions to more everyday challenges.

For example, suppose Howie has decided to try to discover the function of his wife Jen's nagging. After observing their interactions over a couple of weeks, he concludes that Jen nags him to gain his attention and affection. He decides to increase the quantity of those reinforcers on a time-based schedule, delivering them every 30 minutes (FT 30). While generally ignoring her nagging, he uses his pocket timer with a vibrating signal to prompt himself to tell her he loves her, give her kisses, or to make a pleasant comment. Needless to say, besides reducing the nagging, his approach might also lead to a happier relationship. (If this sounds creepy to you, try it. But be truthful—stick to actually merited comments. You even can ask the recipient's permission in advance by stating that you recognize that you have been neglecting her/him and are using this method to remind yourself to let them know what you really value about what they do.) NCR, then, is designed to provide clients the reinforcers they value, thereby lessening the likelihood of their seeking those reinforcers in less acceptable ways. In other words, a heavy schedule of NCR can reduce the motivational operations and have an abative, or abolishing, effect for various misbehaviors (Wallace, Iwata, Hanley, Thompson, & Roscoe, 2012). That is, *an individual is no longer is motivated to misbehave to gain attention or access to various items or activities* when such reinforcers readily are available non-contingently. This is what O'Reilly et al. (2006) found when working with a 20-year-old male with an intellectual disability who engaged in inappropriate self-touching primarily to gain attention. Their client engaged in less inappropriate self-touching following pre-sessions in which he had access to attention as compared to sessions that followed no access to attention. Similarly, Hagopian et al. (2002) used NCR, combined with differential reinforcement of alternative behavior (DRA, see Chapter 28) and exclusionary timeout (see Chapter 29), to reduce inappropriate sexual behaviors (ISBs) by a 14-year-old boy diagnosed with an intellectual disability, attention deficit hyperactivity disorder, depression, and oppositional defiant disorder. The ISBs consisted of public masturbation, displaying his genitals, and inappropriately touching of others. An experimental functional analysis indicated that these ISBs were maintained by attention. The NCR consisted of delivering attention every five minutes (FI 5). Attention also was provided contingent on appropriated requests for attention (DRA). And, because the child also engaged in aggression, disruption, and elopement (leaving the area without permission) for attention, timeout was contingent on dangerous levels of behavior. As a result of this intervention package, ISBs and his other inappropriate behaviors were almost entirely eliminated.

Investigators (Phillips, Innaccone, Rooker, & Hagopian, 2017) sought to determine how NCR affected 21 different subjects with intellectual or developmental disabilities, who ranged in age from five to 33 years, and displayed various severe problem behaviors. They found "NCR effectively treated problem behavior maintained by social reinforcement in 14 of 15 applications, using either the functional reinforcer or alternative reinforcers" (p. 357). However, when they provided non-contingent reinforcement for the problem behavior being maintained by automatic reinforcement, they often found it necessary to provide additional treatment components like differential reinforcement of alternative behavior (DRA) and/or punishment to produce clinically significant effects.

NCR also can minimize the need to engage in escape-related responses to aversive environments. For example, Allen and Wallace (2013) investigated the use of non-contingent escape, or negative reinforcement, in a pediatric dental clinic with 151 children ages two to nine years old. Their "results demonstrated that the routine delivery of scheduled breaks from treatment significantly reduced the vocal and physical disruptive behavior and the need for restraint in a nonclinical sample of children undergoing restorative dental treatment. In addition, the treatment did not add significantly to the typical time spent on behavior management by dentists" (p. 723). As the authors concluded, "brief breaks from ongoing dental treatment has good efficacy, acceptability, and generality" (p. 723). Similarly, frequent, brief breaks from difficult academic or job-related work may produce similar results.

Noncontingent reinforcement is an effective treatment for a wide range of targeted behaviors maintained by social and automatic reinforcement (e.g., Carr et al., 2000; Doughty & Anderson, 2006; Lindberg, Iwata, Roscoe, Worsdell, and Hanley, 2003; Horner, 1980; Roberts-Gwinn et al., 2001; Vollmer, Marcus, & LeBlanc, 1994). Below, to illustrate how NCR might be implemented, we summarize several published studies.

Freddie was an 11-year-old boy with autism spectrum disorder (ASD) who engaged in aggressive and disruptive behavior. The investigators (Roberts-Gwinn et al., 2001) found that noncontingent exposure to kinesthetic stimuli (e.g., textured toys, a vibrator, or water) reduced Freddie's hitting, kicking, removal of clothes, and eloping to near zero levels. Apparently, the noncontingent kinesthetic stimuli produced greater reinforcing stimulation than his aberrant behavior. Once given access to the kinesthetic stimuli contingent on manding (requesting), Freddie's appropriate alternative responses also increased and were maintained during six-month and nine-month follow-up probes. Similarly, NCR of attention every one minute (FT 1) was used successfully with two students with autism who engaged in problem behaviors in an after-school program (Noell & Getch, 2016), and investigators (Lanovaz, Sladeczek, & Rapp, 2012) also have reported that non-contingent music immediately reduced vocal stereotypy for three of four children, ages nine to 11 with autism. NCR also was used successfully with a seven-year-old boy with ASD who frequently engaged in perseverative speech maintained by attention (Noel & Rubow, 2018).

As an intervention with two boys with developmental delays and histories of problem behavior, Doughty and Anderson (2006) combined NCR with functional communication training. Lyle, a 13-year-old with mild to moderate intellectual disability, injured himself, was aggressive, and destroyed property. Two-year-old Nicholas, functioning in the severe to profound range of intellectual disability, injured himself and was aggressive and disruptive. Noncontingently providing both participants with alternative preferred stimuli, such as attention and treats, on a fixed-time schedule (NCR) and also reinforcing mands (or requests) with contingent attention, increased mands and reduced problem behaviors.

Using a teacher-selected modified NCR schedule of delivering praise every four minutes (FT 4 min), Austin and Soeda (2008) reported how a teacher reduced the off-task behavior of two third-graders. One was identified as having a specific learning disability; the other was not receiving any special education services. Every four minutes, the teacher praised each of the two youngsters in alternating order for remaining on-task and redirected them when their behavior was inappropriate. No attention was scheduled for appropriate or inappropriate behaviors that occurred in the interim. Off-task behavior immediately diminished for both children.

Standing up in the bathtub can endanger toddlers. So when a typically-developing 16-month-old girl refused to sit down in the tub, Ward and Higbee (2008) randomly provided noncontingent reinforcement in the form of highly-preferred bath toys (e.g., foam alphabet letters and numbers, plastic cups, bath-time book with pictures of various sea animals) for 30 seconds on a fixed-time schedule (FT 30 sec). The child stopped standing in the tub.

Slocum, Grauerholz-Fisher, Peters, and Vollmer (2018) also found that to treat aggression successfully, they initially made functional reinforcers continuously available (NCR). Next, they gradually decreased the availability of the NCRs, yet aggression remained absent, or nearly absent. However, the environment remained reinforcing (as it should) in that alternative reinforcers were available throughout the sessions for various activities.

Hodges, Shuler, Wilder and Errel (2021) point out that research suggests that response-independent delivery of preferred stimuli can increase subsequent compliance to low-probability instructions. However, their research shows that the effectiveness of such an antecedent intervention approach appears to be dependent on at least two factors:

(1) How much of the reinforcer is delivered (i.e., the *stimulus magnitude*). They found that a five edible pretrial was much more effective than giving the client just one edible.

(2) How much *time is allowed to interact with the preferred items* prior to the request to comply. A three minute pretrial duration of access to preferred (leisure) items produced considerably more compliance than shorter durations (e.g., 30 seconds) of access to the items.

Thus, when NCR is used with sufficient magnitude and/or time, it *can help prevent non-compliance*. Also, it would be wise to consider how the magnitude and/or time allowed to experience any preventive intervention might influence its effectiveness.

## Advantages and Disadvantages of NCR

**Advantages.** NCR possesses the advantages of being easy to implement (Kahng et al., 2000), of raising the general level of reinforcement by enriching or adding preferred reinforcing and stimulating materials/activities to the environment, of minimizing or eliminating the negative side effects of extinction (e.g., extinction bursts, increases in aggression) (Catania, 2005a; Van Camp et al., 2000), and can result in inadvertently strengthening desirable behaviors through chance pairings of appropriate behavior with the delivery of the reinforcer (Roscoe et al., 1998; Dozier et al., 2001). Also, according to Vollmer, Ringdahl, Roane, and Marcus (1997), NCR has several advantages over differential reinforcement of alternative behavior (DRA; see Chapter 28) in that it is easier to implement while promoting high rates of reinforcement delivery and lower rates of problem behaviors (e.g., Hagopian, Fisher, & Legacy, 1994; Lalli et al., 1997; O'Callaghan et al., 2006), reductions that have been shown to persist for up to a year (Lindberg et al., 2003).

As we often have pointed out, children with various handicapping conditions, or those who frequently act out, tend to receive low rates of positive attention. This is what investigators (Rubow, Noel, & Wehby, 2019) found for children with emotional and behavioral disorders (EBD). After implementing a program of ongoing noncontingent attention, not only did those youngsters' disruptive behavior decrease and their on-task behavior increase, but teacher reprimands also decreased in tandem.

Given their potential advantages, time-based schedules can serve a valuable function, provided (1) the behaviors occurring at the time are those you hope to nurture; and (2) that they have achieved a *reasonable momentum—are occurring at a high, steady rate* (Nevin et al., 1983). Group managers can periodically circulate about, delivering reinforcers without actually checking to see if personnel, children, students, or patients are doing what they have been asked to do.

The main advantage of using VT over FT schedules of NCR is their expedience: behavior managers can deliver reinforcers more or less at their own convenience, as long as they meet the essential time requirement. And, as already mentioned, managers need not present those reinforcers contingent on any specific behavior, which relieves them of the need to observe exactly *what* behaviors the client is emitting at the moment.

**Disadvantages.** In that it does not teach specific functional replacement or alternative behaviors, NCR shares the same disadvantages as differential reinforcement procedures that do not involve reinforcing preferred alternative behavior (e.g., differential reinforcement of diminishing or zero rates—Chapter 28). For a more constructive approach, you may want to augment NCR with other interventions such as modeling, differential reinforcement of alternative behaviors (DRA), or functional communication training (FCT). Take special care when trying to combine NCR with other procedures that teach alternative behavior, though, because the dense schedules of NCR may cause the client to become satiated with the reinforcing stimuli (i.e., Goh, Iwata, & DeLeon, 2000). Goh and colleagues evaluated the effects of NCR plus DRA. During the NCR plus DRA condition, they delivered attention or access to a preferred item according to a dense NCR schedule *and* contingent on each emission of the alternative response. Subsequently, the authors thinned the NCR schedule while keeping the DRA procedure intact. During the dense NCR schedule, plus DRA, problem behavior was eliminated; but the alternative response failed to emerge. Rather, the alternative response happened only after they thinned the NCR schedule.

NCR also can promote accidental learning: Sixteen-year-old Kato has been struck by the radiance of his classmate Leanna's smile. While glancing over at her one day, Leanna happens to bestow that smile in Kato's direction. Now, even during a fascinating illustrated lecture on the role of debauchery during the fall of the Roman Empire, Kato spends more time looking in Leanna's direction than at the teacher. Afterwards, although Leanna rarely smiles in Kato's direction, the young man regularly loses track of the class, teacher, and topic under discussion. The only thing that matters is Leanna's rare and wonderful smile.

Whatever behavior is ongoing may become quite resistant to extinction under time-based schedules, such as Leanna's smiling irregularly and not contingent on Kato's behavior. (Kato watches Leanna almost without pause, whether she smiles back or not.) If your goal is to reduce or eliminate a behavior, you are taking a big risk with NCR, especially if the behavior of concern already has gained momentum (Nevin et al., 1983). Ahearn, Clark, Gardenier, Chung, and Dube (2003) studied variable-time schedules with clients who engaged in very high rates of stereotypic behavior. When the clients were given periodic access to preferred reinforcers, "their rates of stereotypy were more resistant to disruption following periods of access to preferred stimuli delivered on a variable-time schedule than following periods without access to preferred stimuli" (p. 439). So, as a behavior manager, be very careful about how, where, and when you distribute reinforcers noncontingently. They may inadvertently strengthen the very behavior you are hoping to reduce.

When NCR seems ineffective as a means of reducing unwanted behaviors, the problem may be traced to certain conditions: (1) given a long history under intermittent reinforcement schedules, NCR has not been continued for a long enough period of time; (2) other weak reinforcers were maintaining the problem behavior that went undetected during assessment, yet they continued to operate during

NCR; (3) the reinforcers that were provided via the NCR procedure were not actually functional; (4) the behavior was supported by circumstances other than reinforcing contingencies—e.g., such as tics produced by neurological disorders.

Vollmer et al. (1997) reported that reinforcement might accidentally result in maintenance rather than elimination of the disruptive behavior, especially when the NCR schedule accidentally provides reinforcement in close proximity to the behavior problem. One way this potential has been overcome is to *combine NCR with extinction* **(NCR/EXT)** *by delaying delivery of the scheduled reinforcer should an unwanted behavior just have been emitted or still be ongoing*. Suppose the schedule called for your providing attention every five minutes, yet the person began to engage in the problem behavior at four minutes 59 seconds. You then would withhold delivery of the attention for five seconds after the misbehavior ended before delivering the NCR. Horr and Michael (2021) used NCR/EXT to reduce the perseverative speech by an 11-year-old boy with autism. They provided attention on a fixed time schedule and placed perseverative speech on extinction (that was being maintained by attention) resulting in a 98.5 percent decrease in the perseverative speech that maintained over a 28-month period.

The logistics involved in implementing NCR may raise an additional issue. Specifically, the requisite density of the initial NCR schedule can often be cumbersome. Most reports of the effective implementation of NCR to reduce behavior problems among clients with severe challenges have involved very dense reinforcement schedules (e.g., from continuously to FT 5 min schedules—Hagopian et al., 1994; Kahng et al., 2000). Given that demand on the time of caregivers during the early stages of NCR, it is often difficult for them to do anything else until the schedule is thinned to become more manageable. If you find yourself in this situation, Kahng et al. (2000) have kindly designed a set of automated thinning programs you might make use of during the maintenance phase of your behavioral-reduction program (e.g., constant time increases, proportional time increases, session-to-session time increases). Moreover, researchers have demonstrated that lean NCR schedules can be effective (Wallace et al. 2012). However, it has been suggested that the mechanism responsible for effectiveness during lean schedules is not just a motivational intervention but also extinction. Thus, if a dense schedule cannot be used, a lean schedule is available—however, when implementing, behavior-change agents should consider possible negative side effects of extinction and be prepared that they may occur.

Unfortunately, thinning the NCR schedule may disrupt progress. To illustrate, Goh, Iwata, and Kahng (1999) addressed the problem of four individuals who ate cigarettes (pica). Although the investigators were able to successfully reduce two of the participants' cigarette pica by using highly-preferred edible reinforcers within a dense schedule of NCR, after the experimenters thinned the NCR schedule the effects failed to maintain. Subsequently, though, after adding DRA (exchanging the cigarette for edible reinforcers), three of the four participants' rates of pica were successfully reduced.

More recently, Saini et al. (2016) compared the relative effectiveness of NCR with response blocking. The subjects consisted of a five-year-old boy and a six-year-old girl with autism who engaged in pica, and a four-year old boy with autism who engaged in self-injurious behavior. The investigators found that neither NCR nor blocking was sufficient to reduce the problem behaviors, but the combination of the two was very effective in reducing these automatically reinforced behaviors.

## Using NCR Effectively

If you choose NCR to reduce a behavior and are unable to manage the reinforcers currently maintaining the behavior (e.g., as in certain forms of self-stimulation), select stimuli that match or exceed their current reinforcing qualities (Goh et al., 1995; Piazza et al., 1998): Noncontingently deliver the reinforcer(s) maintaining the behavior targeted for change (Richman, Barnard-Brak, Grubb, Bosch, & Abby, 2015), or use **competing reinforcers**—*powerful reinforcers, such as musical toys, art materials, etc. that interfere with the reinforcing function of the problem behavior* (Fisher, DeLeon, Rodriguez-Catter, & Keeney, 2004; Fisher, O'Connor, Kurtz, DeLeone, & Gogjen, 2000). Be sure the reinforcers you use are more powerful than those produced by the unwanted response (Roscoe, Iwata, & Rand, 2003). As Fisher et al. (2004) point out, when high-magnitude reinforcers are used, "noncontingent delivery of competing stimuli can effectively reduce rates of destructive behavior maintained by social-positive reinforcement, even when the contingency for destructive behavior remains intact" (p. 171). Also, unless the nature and delivery schedule of the noncontingent reinforcers are especially powerful, be certain to *combine NCR with extinction for the unwanted response* (e.g., Reed et al., 2004). To hedge your bets, though, as investigators (Lindberg et al., 2003) pointed out: "Most applications of NCR include an extinction component. That is, "the reinforcer responsible for behavioral maintenance is delivered according to some response-independent schedule, but is not delivered following occurrences of the target behavior" (p. 1). Recognize that when you use such a combination, the procedure is no longer a simple NCR procedure. Wallace et al. (2012) suggest that the combination of NCR and extinction be called NCR/EXT (as we started using earlier in this chapter). Be careful to *avoid using only NCR if you notice or even suspect that your clients often engage in unwanted behavior.* You do not want inadvertently to nurture those. Also, though NCR has a number of advantages, it is not as effective as contingent reinforcement when trying to increase a specific behavior, such as moderate-to-vigorous physical activity (e.g., Zerger, Normand, Goga, & Patel, 2016).

NCR, however, does appear to work for some clients without using extinction. In working with five children, ages three to nine, all with autism and one also with obsessive-compulsive disorder (OCD), investigators (Fritz, et al., 2017) used NCR without extinction on property destruction, screaming, kicking people and other surfaces, and SIB (all clients exhibited a different behavior, except two were treated for screaming). The function for each one's inappropriate behavior was to re-gain access to a preferred item that was removed. The reinforcer they used with each client during the NCR was access to the preferred item, starting with continuous access. Access periods of 20 seconds were gradually thinned to once every five minutes. The NCR was effective by itself for three of the clients. For the other two, the investigators also implemented a DRA in which the two clients were taught to present a card with the picture of the item they wanted to obtain access to it. This combined intervention strategy worked effectively to stop the problem behavior (OCD and screaming) for both of them.

While NCR has rarely been formally investigated within business, industrial, health, community, or other organizational settings, the message is clearly relevant for all: Benefits will accrue to your organization if you maintain an ongoing density of reinforcers.

## OTHER PRIMARY PREVENTION METHODS

The list of antecedent events designed effectively to reduce the probability of unwanted behavior is long. In addition to the ones we have covered above, below we discuss two more important primary prevention packages: *modeling* and *social stories*.

### Modeling

Modeling was introduced in Chapter 18. Here we focus on how to use modeling effectively to reduce unwanted behavior. The *modeling procedure* consists of *demonstrating the appropriate or replacement behavior* (e.g., working on-task), *or positively recognizing others* (e.g., peers, colleagues) *for engaging in the replacement behavior* (e.g., being on-task). The desired behavior serves as an imitative prompt or $S^{Dr}$ for others to imitate. For example, Johnson and Brown (1969) found modeling to be more effective than direct instructions or group discussions in producing rapid parent behavior change.

A good behavior-management rule to follow is: *When you notice a person engaged in some minor violation* (e.g., being away from his work, calling out, talking to neighbors), *rather than punishing the behavior, use the behavior as a reminder to look for others who are doing what they should, and audibly praise their appropriate behavior.* For example, Hilda is out of her seat. You might say to Socorro, Hilda's friend, "I'm so pleased to see that you are in your seat doing your work. You too, Tyrone. In fact, this whole row is working very well!" When

Hilda gets back in her seat and starts doing her work, be sure to compliment her behavior, too. *(Always remember to reinforce the imitation or this strategy will not work effectively.)* In another example, Phil, a store manager, notices Jamie and Sarah off in a corner gossiping instead of working. Instead of reprimanding them, he looks around and praises Jim, loudly enough for Jamie and Sarah to hear, for straightening up the shelves, and then allows Jim to take a five-minute break. After Jamie and Sarah get back to work, Phil makes sure he praises them for working hard for a while, and then allows them a five-minute break.

**Using modeling effectively.** Several factors influence the effectiveness of using modeling as a method for reducing unwanted behavior. One is model selection. Remember from Chapters 15 through 18 on stimulus control, there are several basic factors to consider when selecting models:

- observer's previous experience with the model(s)
- multiple models who are:
  - similar to the observer
  - competent (although may have had similar problems in the past—Warner & Swisher, 1976)
  - have a good measure of prestige in the group (i.e., receives more than the average amount of reinforcement from peers and supervisors)

Model selection appears to be particularly important in work with youth who engage in high rates of antisocial behavior such as aggression, vandalism, rule infractions, and defiance. A number of studies (e.g., Boivin & Vitaro, 1995; Cairns & Cairns, 1992; Dishion, French, & Patterson, 1995) have reported that association with antisocial or delinquent peers increases levels of current and future antisocial behavior. This peer influence is particularly potent with moderately disruptive boys. When they associate with aggressive friends, their own delinquency increases correspondingly (Vitaro, Tremblay, Kerr, Pagani, & Bukowski, 1997). Consequently, it should come as no surprise that treating youths in groups composed exclusively of antisocial peers appears to be less effective than treating them in mixed groups (Feldman, 1992).

In addition, the contingency manager can heighten the effectiveness of the procedure by arranging a number of antecedent operations. These include:

- highlighting the similarity between observers and models.
- encouraging behavioral rehearsal.
- providing instructions, rules, and rationales.
- keeping the modeled behavior simple.
- reinforcing the modeled behavior.
- reinforcing acts of imitation of the modeled behavior.

If your use of modeling is to be maximally effective, you need to consider and address each of the above factors.[6]

**Advantages of modeling.** Understandably, teachers and other contingency managers often give a disproportionate amount of their attention to students who are misbehaving than to those behaving appropriately. For example, the child who sits quietly and works rarely receives attention when another child is running around the classroom throwing papers on the floor. The modeling procedure turns the situation around so that those who deserve the recognition and attention are more likely to get it. (But be careful to avoid responding to those who shout out "I did that too" in an attempt to be recognized. You do *not* want to reinforce that type of disruptive behavior and encourage others to imitate it.)

Another advantage of modeling is that it teaches appropriate replacement behaviors. Because the focus is not on punishment but on teaching, modeling produces an environment that is more positive and conducive to learning. Thus, we recommend that you use this strategy frequently throughout the day as a regular management tool.

**Disadvantages of modeling.** The major disadvantage of modeling is that it does not produce

---

[6]See Chapter 18 for an elaboration of these factors.

immediate change. Rather, its effects can take a while. For this reason we suggest that to manage serious, intolerable problem behavior that must stop immediately, you combine it with some more rapidly-acting strategy. Select modeling to reduce minor infractions and to help prevent problem behavior from occurring. Another downside to using modeling to manage unwanted behavior is that it seems more natural to many people to notice and provide attention (reinforcement) when people do the *wrong thing* rather than when they behave appropriately. (You will discover in Chapter 31 that punishment provides more immediate reinforcement to the person administering it than do efforts to promote prosocial behavior.) So, contingency managers may overlook opportunities to recognize prosocial imitative acts. Under such conditions, people soon stop imitating the positive models because doing so no longer is reinforced. Instead, they revert to or escalate the misbehavior that worked in the past. Therefore, be sure you reinforce imitation of positive models, even if you need to create your own prompts to remind yourself to reinforce (e.g., timers, beepers or buzzers that provide auditory cues, clocks or light flashes that provide visual cues, or vibrating timers that provide tactile signals).

Also, don't simply assume that praise will function as a reinforcer for the behavior of everyone at any given time. Positive recognition by the teacher or manager works best when functional analyses, and/or preference assessments, have demonstrated attention is a powerful reinforcer for the individual (see Chapters 5 and 6).

## Using Social Stories

Gray and Garand (1993) first introduced **social stories** to help children with autism become more aware of how to act acceptably in social situations. Though not designed as a specific behavior analytic tool, from a behavior analytic perspective, *social stories are a specific antecedent strategy designed to enable children to better follow a particular social protocol*. Social stories contain short episodes, usually consisting of one concept per page, written in the first person, and designed to provide the children with answers to questions of the *who, what, when, where,* and *why* of a given social situation (Gray & Garand, 1993). They include the likely reactions of others in a situation (e.g., what others may be saying to themselves or experiencing) and provide information about the appropriate social response tailored to the individual (Delano & Snell, 2006). They also provide a sentence to help the client recall the story or deal with the situation. To heighten their effectiveness, they often are combined with pictures, such as Mayer-Johnson's (1981) picture communication symbols (Lorimer et al., 2002), or videotaped models (Hagiwara & Myles, 1999; Swaggart, Gagnon, Bock, and Earles, 1995). Visual modeling (Volkmar, Lord,, Bailey, Schultz, and Klin, 2004) provides opportunities for the children to view their own and others' social interactions. Social stories also are individualized to specific situations and to the individual's ability and environment. They appear to be effective with individuals with a minimum verbal mental age of approximately three years (Hutchins & Prelock, 2013). (See Gray, 1996, 2000; Gray & Garand, 1993, for guidelines in writing social stories.) However, other forms of behavioral support (see below) must be added for social stories to yield their maximal value.

Tsai's (2006) review of 29 empirical investigations of social stories concluded that even though social stories are designed to prompt children's social interactions and positive behavior, most studies concentrated solely on inappropriate behavior and did not measure the prosocial target behavior contained in the participant's storybooks. Also, many studies incorporated the social story into a package rather than using it in isolation. Therefore, it is difficult to know which specific aspects brought about the behavior change. To investigate this issue further, Tsai used a withdrawal design nested within a multiple-baseline across-subjects design with three elementary students with autism. None of the participants' behavior improved as a function of the social story alone. Similarly, investigators (Daneshvar, Charlop, & Maimberg, 2018) compared social stories to a photo activity schedule as tools for teaching social skills to children with autism and found that the photo activity intervention was highly effective, while the social stories were ineffective in teaching the targeted social behaviors. However, as in studies investigating other antecedent practices, when social stories were combined with reinforcement, peer/

adult prompting, and opportunities to practice the new skills, not only did disruptive behavior decrease, but all participants' conversation skills, play skills, and on-task behavior improved dramatically.

Other studies also have shown that social stories in isolation produce limited or questionable success (e.g., Sansosti & Powell-Smith, 2006; Sansosti & Powell-Smith, 2008; Scattone, 2002; Shahrestani, Symon, & Campbell, 2009; Tsai, 2006). Yet, after combining them with behavior analytic methods, such as reinforcement and role playing, they can effectively increase positive behavior (e.g., Hagiwara & Myles, 1999; Moore, 2004; Sansosti & Powell-Smith, 2008; Shahrestani et al., 2009; Staley, 2002; Swaggart et al., 1995; Thiemann & Goldstein, 2001; Tsai, 2006). Consequently, in the interest of producing more promising outcomes, we encourage investigators and change agents to incorporate the features derived from behavior analytic studies of reinforcement and model selection into their social story procedures, follow-up role-playing, and real-life practice across various situations.

## SUMMARY AND CONCLUSIONS

One of the most important points about alternatives to punishment is that they can be used not only to prevent and reduce problem behaviors but also to design effective learning environments. Not simply approaches for reducing problem behaviors, they are effective strategies for building new, desirable behavior, and preventing some problem behaviors from ever emerging. We need to determine what it is that we want our students or clients to do as we design environments, rather than waiting until they fail and then designing remediation programs. The intervention strategies contained in this and in Chapter 28 can support the achievement of such outcomes.

Stimulus change and several prompting strategies for preventing and/or reducing problem behavior have been introduced. They are empirically based, minimally intrusive antecedent methods that can serve to promote positive behavior and prevent inappropriate behavior.

Recognize that the need to reduce behavior often involves ethical and sometimes organizational and legal issues. Consequently, before selecting and applying a reductive procedure, make sure the decision is ethically responsible by using the most reinforcing and least restrictive, aversive, or intrusive procedure that has been scientifically demonstrated to be effective. Be certain to emphasize ethical, positive, and constructive behavior interventions whenever possible.

Behavior often can be improved temporarily simply by altering antecedent conditions. In the present chapter we have presented a variety of empirically based, minimally restrictive or intrusive antecedent-control methods to promote acceptable behavior. Note, too, that each intervention discussed in this chapter has been responsible for successfully preventing and reducing behavior without resorting to punishment, and can be manipulated in isolation or in combination with other constructive behavior-change methods. These strategies allow us to avoid the disadvantages inherent in using punitive approaches. They also promote a more enriched reinforcing environment for clients. And, as you now recognize, *environments enriched with reinforcement serve to prevent problem behavior and are more apt to promote constructive learning or behavior change.*

Noncontingent reinforcement (NCR) used as an MO has been shown to be an effective strategy for dealing with a wide range of troublesome behaviors maintained especially by social, tangible, and automatic reinforcement. Results of applied behavior-analytic studies have shown that if these reinforcers are readily available on a noncontingent basis, people do not have to misbehave to obtain them. Generally, when levels of reinforcement are elevated, problem behaviors decrease, and the environment becomes more supportive of desirable behaviors. Therefore, it is important to distribute generous portions of NCR, especially within settings designed to prevent problem behavior and support productive performance. Consider combining extinction with preventive and reductive programs, as necessary, to avoid inadvertently reinforcing even more serious behavior problems.

We remind you, however, that various methods of antecedent control need to be developed and maintained if the antecedent control is to remain effective. Always:

(1) assess for and select effective (high preference) reinforcers.

(2) determine the appropriate magnitude of the selected reinforcers.

(3) determine the amount of time allowed for any antecedent reinforcing activity.

In addition, assuming that new acceptable replacement behaviors are sufficiently reinforced, they are more likely to continue to increase and gain precedence over former inappropriate behavior. Ongoing positive behavioral support, in the form of differential reinforcement of behavioral improvements is essential if, as Bird and Luiselli (2000) and many others have shown, antecedent controls are to remain effective.[7] Differential reinforcement will be the focus of our next chapter.

Don't forget, as well, to see to it that reinforcement plays a major role in your interactions with your friends, relatives, peers, associates, staff, and even your own administrators and supervisors. Assume responsibility for guaranteeing that all receive lots of social and other reinforcers to improve and maintain high levels of satisfaction and cohesiveness within the group. In other words, be certain to emphasize ethical, positive, and constructive behavior interventions whenever possible.

---

[7] An excellent source for further information on positive behavioral support is the *Journal of Positive Behavior Interventions* by Sage Publications.

*Chapter 28*

# Preventing and Reducing Behavior through Differential Reinforcement

## Goals

1. Define and illustrate:
   - *differential reinforcement (DR)*
   - *differential reinforcement of alternative behaviors (DRA)*
   - *differential reinforcement of incompatible behaviors (DRI)*
   - *escape extinction*
   - *differential reinforcement of other behavior (DRO)*
   - *progressive differential reinforcement of other behavior (DROP)*
   - *differential reinforcement of low rates of behavior (DRL) or spaced-responding DRL*
   - *differential reinforcement of diminishing rates (DRD) or complete or full-session DRL*
2. Describe and discuss how (a) the *Catch 'em Being Good game* and (b) the *Activity Table* capitalize on well-documented behavioral principles.
3. Review the definition of *differential reinforcement* and explain its function as a procedure for reducing particular unwanted behaviors.
4. Specify and discuss the (a) advantages and (b) disadvantages and c) the effective application of DRO and of DRA.
5. Explain how to minimize or avoid the occurrence of resurgence when using DRA.
6. Define, illustrate, compare and contrast at least three commonly used *correction procedures*.
7. Define and illustrate *whole-interval*, *momentary*, and *progressive DRO* (DROP), and say how they differ from one another and from DRA.
8. List and discuss the advantages and disadvantages of using *differential reinforcement of other behaviors (DRO)*, including definitions and illustrations of *behavioral contrast*.

9. Describe how to use DRO effectively.
10. Define, illustrate and distinguish between and discuss the advantages and disadvantages of using *differential reinforcement of low rates (DRL)* and *differential reinforcement of diminishing rates (DRD) of behavior.*
11. Illustrate and describe the essential features of the *Good Behavior Game.*
12. Defend the value of providing a reinforcing environment.

\*\*\*\*\*\*\*\*\*\*\*\*\*

*Each day, Carmine's teacher leaves school with her stomach tied in knots. Despite her threats and scolding, Carmine simply refuses to work, instead bothering the other students attempting to learn. He hums his favorite songs, wanders around the room, "accidentally" bumps into other students, taps his pencil on the desk, often crunching his paper into a ball, throwing it in the direction of the wastepaper basket, but never quite reaching it. One day, he even tried to climb out the window.*

*How on earth, his teacher wonders, will her students ever score well on their achievement tests when Carmine refuses to let them concentrate? She wants to avoid punishing the boy's misbehavior, but doesn't know what else to do.*

In previous chapters, we discussed several non-punitive procedures incorporating extinction and antecedent manipulations that can be used to prevent or reduce behaviors of concern without having to resort to punishment. A third class of non-punitive reductive procedures relies on differential reinforcement. In fact, Carr, Taylor, Carlson and Robinson (1991) and Cataldo (1991) have noted, at one time, punishment and related aversive approaches were considered the most effective means of reducing severe behavior concerns. As research has revealed, though, such punitive approaches foster aggression (e.g., violence assaults and vandalism) escape (e.g., tardiness, truancies, or skipping work, and dropouts), negative self-statements, and negative attitudes toward oneself, school, or work (Azrin, Hake, Holz, & Hutchinson, 1965, Berkowitz, 1983; Mayer & Sulzer-Azaroff, 1991). Critics also see them as dehumanizing. Moreover, given the identification of the behavior's function, punishment-based approaches are often no more effective than antecedent and reinforcement-based approaches (Pelios et al.,1999), or positive behavior interventions.

**Positive behavior interventions** (PBI) *are designed to reduce inappropriate behavior by prompting and reinforcing substitute alternative constructional behaviors* (Carr & Sidener, 2002). PBIs often involve arranging appropriate MOs in addition to addressing consequences for the target behavior. Fortunately, as mentioned previously, in compari-son to punitive procedures, when based on a behavior's function and applied appropriately, positive (non-punitive) antecedent and consequential behavior interventions:

- usually prevent and/or reduce behaviors of concern as effectively as punitive procedures, while being less restrictive and intrusive.
- are less likely to provoke violence, escape, and aggression or to lower the recipients' vies of themselves, of those delivering the contingencies, and of associated tasks.
- are more likely to emphasize teaching how to behave than how not to behave.
- are more likely to elevate the person's general level of reinforcement, resulting in more prosocial behavior (Todd et al., 2002; Zanolli & Daggett, 1998).

Additionally, when discipline programs/interventions take a non-punitive approach and have addressed related contextual factors, a number valuable outcomes have been achieved. These include decreases in antisocial behaviors, including vandalism costs, discipline referrals, dropout and suspensions rates; increase in prosocial behaviors, including attendance, time spent on assigned tasks, perceptions of school safety, and co-operation and positive feelings among students and staff (Mathews McIntosh, Frank, & May, 2014; Mayer & Colleagues, 1979, 1981, 1983a, 1987, 1991, 1993, 2001, 2002; Metzler, Biglan, Rusby, & Sprague, 2001; Sprague et al., 2001). Among the most effective non-punitive approaches are differential reinforcement procedures.

# DIFFERENTIAL REINFORCEMENT

As you learned earlier, *differential reinforcement* involves reinforcing particular members of a given behavioral class (or form, or topography) and not another; that is, we reinforce a response when it occurs under specific stimulus conditions but not under other stimulus conditions. In this chapter, we describe several differential reinforcement procedures you can use to reduce unwanted behaviors. We begin with *differential reinforcement of specific alternative behaviors*, one of the most commonly used procedures for reducing misconduct, by teaching the client to discriminate *how to* from *how not to* behave, or to engage in more contextually appropriate behavior. As we do, you may agree with the conclusion presented by Karsten and Carr (2009) that "differential reinforcement of unprompted responses may be the most appropriate default approach to reaching children with autism" (p. 327).

# DIFFERENTIAL REINFORCEMENT OF ALTERNATIVE (DRA) AND INCOMPATIBLE (DRI) BEHAVIOR

## DRA and DRI Defined, Illustrated, and Distinguished from One Another

**Differential reinforcement of alternative behavior (DRA)** *involves reinforcing a specified alternative(s) to the unwanted behavior, while treating or withholding reinforcement from the unwanted behavior.* Rather than making disapproving comments or reacting automatically to problem behavior, the contingency manager (1) first tries to determine what stimuli currently have reinforcing value for the client; (2) then identifies what acceptable alternative behavior should yield a similar consequence; and (3) next, while simultaneously withholding reinforcement from the unwanted behavior(s), reinforces the alternative behavior when it occurs.

Actually, placing behaviors of concern on total extinction is not always feasible. However, Vollmer, et al. (2020) report that should you be able to minimize the reinforcing consequences of the problem behavior while maxmizing those for the selected alternative behavior, the DRA strategy will likely remains effective. (The reinforcement for the alternative behavior must "outweigh" the reinforcement for the problem behavior.) Of course, whenever possible, total extinction conditions for the problem behavior should remain the component of choice.

Sometimes we are challenged by an individual engaging in a severely dangerous or destructive behavior that needs to be terminated immediately. In such instances, we can combine DRA with negative or positive punishment (see Chapters 29 and 30), or you can hasten the cessation of the behavior by combining DRA with other differential reinforcement procedures and introducing some of the preventive procedures describe in Chapter 27.

To illustrate, suppose a functional behavioral assessment has revealed that Stanley refuses to comply with demands because Barney inadvertently reinforces the refusal by telling Stanley how important his job is and that when he stops working it interferes with others' ability to work. Were Barney to use DRA instead, he would ignore Stanley's refusals, but pay close attention to Stanley when he actually complies with Barney's requests or when he requests a short break (e.g., "Can I take a five-minute break"). Similarly, if a student shouts out for attention, the teacher needs to ignore the shouting and reinforce only hand-raising. This functional approach is basically what investigators (Wilder, Masuda, O'Connor, & Baham, 2001) took with a 43-year-old man diagnosed with schizophrenia after discovering that his bizarre vocalizations were maintained by attention. Instead, they differentially reinforced or provided attention to his *appropriate* vocalizations, while ignoring his bizarre vocalizations. This DRA strategy reduced bizarre vocalizations while increasing appropriate communication.

**Determine that the individual is capable of performing the desired behavior.** Of course if the individual has not yet learned the desired alternative behavior, the first step is to teach it. As a case in point (Greenwald, Wiliams, & Seniuk, 2014), an eight-year-old girl with autism who would frequently tantrum (e.g., scream, cry, kick, hit, drop to the floor and/or/ run) while in the grocery store, initially lacked the critical skills of gathering particular items to purchase. The experimenters then decided to teach her a set of appropriate grocery-gathering skills consisting of the following:

- reading aloud the word on an index card
- walking to the identified item
- picking it up
- placing it in the cart

The child's mother was taught how to use this procedure, while the number of items the child was to gather was systematically increased from one to over 15. The child learned to match word cards to the correct items and then collect each item and place it in a shopping cart. The tantrums rapidly subsided after the girl began to gain attention for gathering groceries appropriately but not following any tantrums.

Note, though, that not all concerning behaviors are maintained by attention. Attending differentially to three two- to three-year-olds with developmental delays who engaged in food refusal did not effectively increase food acceptance or a clean mouth (as a result of swallowing) (Patel et al., 2002). However, "acceptance and mouth clean increased for all 3 participants once *escape extinction* was added to the differential reinforcement procedures" (p. 363). (**Escape extinction** involves *blocking escape attempts so that escape responses no longer provide reinforcement*.) To block escape, the therapist held the spoon or cup to the child's mouth until he or she took a bite or drink. If the child expelled it, it was scooped back up and re-presented until swallowed. Once this escape extinction was implemented, DRA worked successfully to increase the children's rates of eating presented foods. Notice that for DRA to work effectively, you need to identify and be sure to withhold all sources of reinforcement, positive and/or negative, from the problem behavior. (Dowdy, Tincani, Nipe, and Weiss (2018) have found that if a highly preferred item is provided for compliance, escape extinction may be unnecessary. So, you would be wise to conduct a reinforcer preference assessment prior to introducing a compliance program.)

In a similar case, DRA was combined with negative reinforcement and demand fading to treat food selectivity or refusal (Najdowski, Wallace, Doney, & Ghezzi, 2003). Jack, a five-year-old diagnosed with autism, ate mainly candy, chips, chicken nuggets, and French fries. A functional assessment determined that his refusal behavior was most likely maintained by escape. Jack's mother then instructed him to take one bite of food that she held within one inch of his mouth until he either took the bite or 30 minutes had elapsed. If he accepted the bite, his mother praised him and removed the non-preferred food (NPF), replacing it with preferred foods. "During the first four dinners of this phase, if a bite was initially accepted but then expelled or vomited, Jack was still provided access to the high-preferred foods. However, beginning with the fifth dinner and thereafter, bites expelled or vomited resulted in a new bite of the same NPF being presented until Jack swallowed it" (Najdowski et al., p. 384). This intervention increased Jack's acceptance of more nutritious food at home and in a restaurant.

**Differential reinforcement of incompatible behaviors (DRI)** *is a sub-class of DRA, with a further restriction: the alternative behavior cannot be emitted simultaneously with the unwanted behavior.* In our earlier example, Stanley's working at the work station was incompatible with leaving the work station (both behaviors could not occur at the same time). So, technically, the procedure might more accurately be labeled "DRI." By comparison, a student *might* be able to blurt-out with his hand up, so we would label the differential reinforcement procedure as a "DRA." In Stanley's case, were his supervisor to withhold attention for non-compliance and only reinforce Stanely's performing his job instead of refusing, that would be a DRA.

A client with autism known to the authors engaged in the stereotypic behavior of waving her hands before her face. Her therapist targeted this and several other behaviors that interfered with her attending to relevant environmental stimuli. DRI was selected and a large group of hand-involved instructional and play behaviors were reinforced: using the sand table, assembling puzzles, piling blocks, painting, and so on. With sufficient reinforcement, the girl began to engage in those constructive play activities more often. Stereotypic hand movements were never attended to, neither positively, nor punitively. Yet, because they could not coexist with the more constructive behaviors and were not as functional, they gradually diminished. When her teacher used a similar approach, parallel results were achieved in school.

Slifer, Koontz, and Cataldo (2002) used DRI to teach four children to hold their heads still and follow instructions during functional magnetic resonance imaging (used to study brain function during behavioral tasks). Each child chose a prize to earn for improved performance. After their participation, the children were given immediate feedback along with praise and the previously selected prize if they had met the improvement criteria for holding a still head and engaging in the required tasks.

Given the near chaos reigning in an elementary-school lunch room, Wheatley et al. (2009), taught students to discard their trash appropriately, sit in their seats, and walk, not run, in the lunch room. School staff members learned to look for, specifically commend, and write and sign a note recognizing and praising by name those students they observed behaving accordingly. Later, recipients of the notes took them to the school's office, where at the end of the day the principal drew five notes at random and announced the names of the winning students over the school's intercom. Winners then went to the office, where they chose a small reward such as an eraser, sticker, pencil, folder, and so forth. The praise notes also were posted on a board in the main hallway. After the notes completely covered the board, students received a group reward: as extra recess or an ice-cream party (i.e., an interdependent group contingency). To heighten staff participation, "teachers whose names were on the five selected Praise Notes were also entered into a weekly drawing for a gift certificate or service voucher donated by businesses in the community" (p. 560). The results: "Litter left in the lunchroom decreased by 96 percent, the average number of instances of sitting inappropriately decreased by 64 percent, and the average number of instances of running in the lunch room decreased by 75 percent" (p. 551). Managers used DRI to reduce the aggressive acts of two children with ASD during public outings (Romani et al., 2019). Apparently, each child's behavior functioned to gain them access to a tangible item. To handle the problem, before entering either a gift shop or cafeteria, each child was told and shown pictorially that if they followed directions (incompatible with aggressive acts) they would earn a prize, such as a preferred candy or access to a preferred activity. This strategy resulted in a decrease in aggressive behaviors and an increase in compliance.

## DRA and DRI: Group Management Programs

DRA serves as the foundation of many effective group management programs. Here we describe two. [Chapters 14 & 24 contain several others including social skills training (SST) and functional communication training (FCT)].

The **"Catch'em Being Good Game"** *combines DRA with modeling and can be used to teach appropriate behavior in varied situations.* Participants find this game enjoyable and exciting. You can conduct it by following these steps:

1. Obtain a roll of tickets at a stationary supplier.
2. Identify one or more behaviors you want your students or clients to regularly practice (e.g., completing class- or homework, getting to class on time, raising hands, working quietly, helping classmates with their work).
3. With the group's input, list an array of appropriate reinforcing activities and items.
4. Explain to the group that you will be:

a. Searching for members who are performing the identified behaviors (i.e., completing class-work, raising hands to make requests, or other behaviors of your choosing.)

b. Distributing tickets to and complimenting those you "catch" engaging in those behaviors.

5. Ask recipients to write their names on the back of the ticket as soon as they receive it.

6. At an appropriate time, have participants place their tickets in a container. The more tickets the participant receives, the greater chance he or she will have of being chosen to play.

7. Place four or five paper cups upside-down on a flat surface. Under each, place a piece of paper on which you have written one of the reinforcing items or activities.

8. Have each student whose name was called select a cup and read aloud what reward he or she is to receive. (Notice how this program also incorporates modeling.)

9. Every so often, initially about three times a session, draw one to five tickets from the container and call out the holder's name. Congratulate and provide the designated rewards to the participants who won them.

10. After a few days, gradually reduce the game's frequency. Eventually, after the desired effects have been achieved, just play periodically, as a special treat for the group. However, be sure to continue your compliments and praise.

Adaptations of the "Catch'em Being Good Game" include:

- Selecting participants based on their behavior at the moment you decide to play the game.
- At the primary-school level, you can read the notes aloud to the students, or use pictures to represent the rewards.

Yi (2000) tested the game's efficacy with a regular fifth-grade classroom containing 29 students, nine of whom were receiving special education services for various learning disabilities. Improvements were noted in percentage of homework assignments handed in, hand-raising, and lining up appropriately. In fact, the latter improved from zero percent to 100 percent in one day and stabilized at about 90 percent.

Similar to the previous game, you can use an **activity table** to teach specific behaviors or to achieve control in disruptive classrooms or other group settings. You conduct it like this:

- On a table, display an assortment of reinforcing activities appropriate to the developmental level and interests of the youngsters—interesting reading materials, checkers and chess sets, cards, a computer, television or CD player with headphones, and so on (see Chapter 6 for further ideas).

- Identify one or more target behaviors appropriate to the situation. (e.g., for a classroom, these might include: arriving in class on time, completing class work, raising hands to obtain teacher attention, working quietly and helping classmates with their work).

- Award points, tickets, or checkmarks to individuals for performing the behavior(s).

- Allow youngsters immediate access to the activity table for five minutes once they have obtained their tickets, points, or checks; or allow them to bank their checks for up to a total of 20 minutes.

Notice how the **activity table** program *combines DRA and modeling in a novel, exciting and enjoyable way to teach youngsters appropriate behavior.*

## Advantages of DRA

**Constructive.** Identifying one or more beneficial alternative behaviors usually is possible. In the illustrations cited, increased social interactions, task completion, and participation in group play undoubtedly contributed to the individuals' progress personally, educationally, and socially. They learned what *to* do instead of what *not* to do. This advantage contrasts with other reductive procedures, such as extinction, punishment, response cost, and timeout that focus primarily on eliminating behavior.

Because it is constructive, it is one of the interventions that is most commonly used to teach behavior. To provide another example, Hood, Luczynski, and Mitteer (2017) worked with three students, a 16-year-old boy with Asperger's Syndrome, a 15-year-old girl with ASD and an eight-year-old boy with ASD. All three were doing well academically in regular classrooms without special education supports, and had no history of recent behaviors of concern. However, their interpersonal skills of greeting and having conversations with others were very weak, and each participant expressed a desire to improve in both of these areas. Using a combination of *NCR*, consisting of a non contingent five-minute break, *modeling*, by providing multiple examples, and *DRA*, earning an additional 30 seconds of additional time for each correct response, the investigators were able to "produce robust acquisition, generalization, maintenance, and treatment extension for 15 of the 16 targeted skills across participants" (p. 459).

**Benign.** Extinction, response cost, timeout, and positive punishment all possess negative qualities, requiring either that reinforcers be withheld or withdrawn or aversive consequences presented. With DRA, reinforcers continue, so a carefully planned program will yield regular reinforcement and all the good things that go along with it. Any generalized responding to stimuli in the setting is likely to be positive. People also are more likely to remain in situations in which reinforcers are delivered. In our clinical illustration, the child who learned to use her hands in useful ways always attended sessions willingly and never attempted to leave. Had we scolded or withheld attention whenever the stereotypic hand movements occurred, she may have found the situation aversive and tried to leave or at least refused to cooperate in the program.

**Acceptable.** Practitioners who see their jobs as helping individuals to develop to their fullest possible potential often are unwilling to use aversive contingencies and tend to rate them as less acceptable (Meunier, Kissell, & Higgins, 1983). Jones, Eyberg, Adams, and Boggs (1998) asked 20 mothers of children referred for treatment of disruptive behavior to rate the acceptability of positive reinforcement procedures, response cost, timeout, overcorrection, and spanking. Procedures that emphasized positive reinforcement were rated as most acceptable. Similarly, the parents of the three children in the above mentioned study by Hood et al. (2017) reported high levels of satisfaction with both the intervention and outcomes. Many prefer not to spend their time scolding, punishing, threatening, or intentionally ignoring clients' behaviors, choosing instead more appropriate methods to help them acquire beneficial skills. Reinforcing a productive, desirable alternative to an unwanted behavior is well suited to those ideals. Also, as mentioned in the previous chapter, DRA helps to eliminate extinction bursts and enhances effectiveness (Lerman & Iwata, 1996; Freeman, 2006). Additionally, children as well as parents report a preference for DRA as opposed to other procedures (Kazdin, 1981).

**Helps to prevent problem behavior.** Not only does DRA/DRI reduce problem behaviors, but its use also helps the environment to become more reinforcing and less punitive, resulting in less problem behavior. For example, Taber et al (2017) used video modeling to teach four care-givers in a non-public school to use differential reinforcement with specific praise, and to ask the client's opinion of the reinforced behavior to encourage reciprocity. They found that not only did the care-givers increase their use of their reinforcing statements, but that the non-targeted client's aggressive behavior (e.g., hair pulling, slapping, biting, pushing) decreased substantially. As pointed out in previous chapters, *reinforcing environments can help prevent problem behavior.* Busch, Saini, Zorzos, and Duyile (2018), combined DRA with noncontingent access to edible items, response effort manipulations, and response blocking to reduce life-threatening pica with a 19-year-old man diagnosed with autism, epilepsy and severe intellectual disability. Pica was reduced to near zero levels and remained there during a five-year follow-up. The authors point out that "live-threatening behaviors such as pica can be effectively reduced with nonrestrictive interventions, and treatment results can be maintained in the absence of restrictive behavior management practices [the authors point out that restraint and punishment are frequently used] in typical settings" (p. 335). Pica also was reduced for a four-year old male with autism by combining response interruption and redirection with differential reinforcement to teach him to throw away, put away and appropriately use some materials and to refrain from touching other items that he previously consumed inappropriately (Taylor, 2020).

**Helps promote improved tolerance to delayed reinforcement.** As mentioned in Chapter 11, investigators (Drifke, et al., 2020), reported that when thinned fixed time schedules of reinforcement are in effect, you can heighten clients' tolerance to delayed reinforcement by *reinforcing the occurrence of alternative behaviors as they occur during the time delay.* This strategy was found to be more effective than using just a fixed time schedule of reinforcement alone, or by reinforcing the absence of the problem behavior during the passage of time (DRO—see below). The DRA schedule has further advantages of teaching, strengthening and establishing other appropriate behaviors.

**Lasting change.** Once the alternative behavior occurs at a high and steady enough rate to block the unwanted behavior, the latter is suspended. As long as the alternative behavior is *maintained* at a reasonable pace, the original one is not apt to return. Foxx, McMorrow, Fenlon, and Bittle (1986) found this to be the case when they reinforced an alternative behavior to replace public masturbation by a 16-year-old male with severe developmental delays. Following the rules for maintaining high rates of behavior (review Chapters 22 & 23), then, enables us to achieve maintenance of the desired behavior while blocking the undesirable behavior.

## Disadvantages of DRA

**Effect may be delayed.** Reinforcement procedures can take time to produce results, particularly if the alternative response is not firmly established in the client's repertoire. Unless the replacement behavior occurs at a fairly high and steady rate, time remains to permit the undesirable behavior to be expressed. Until Violet interacts with others frequently, she still has lots of opportunity to remain alone. While Desmond's rate of remaining on-task increases, he can continue to disrupt. Fortunately, you may be able to speed up the process by combining DRA with other procedures, such as modeling, DRO and DRD (differential reinforcement of diminishing rates, discussed below). Also, using response cost or stimulus change to reduce the undesirable behavior more rapidly while reinforcing its replacement may help reduce the time lag. But again, once an aversive consequence like response cost is introduced, some of the major advantages of DRA (i.e., that it is a positive and constructive approach) are lost.

**Other adaptive behaviors may decrease.** In Chapters 23 and 26 we described what happens in other settings when a behavior increases as a result of reinforcement in one particular setting. Those other behaviors, adaptive as well as problematic, that serve a similar function, tend to decrease in the other settings (negative behavioral contrast). To minimize that potential adverse impact, be sure regularly to reinforce *all* (or as many as possible) alternative desired or adaptive behaviors across all appropriate settings.

## Using DRA Effectively

**Select appropriate replacement behavior(s).** In previous chapters, we discussed at length the selection of alternative behaviors or goals. To review, the targets you select to replace the unwanted behavior should be constructive, likely to be supported in the natural environment, readily achievable, acceptable to all concerned, and functional[1] in the sense that they enable the person to earn the same (or better) reinforcers than those previously obtained by means of the unwanted behavior. (Review Chapters 4 & 10 for illustrations of functionally equivalent replacement behaviors.)

To select the most promising replacement behaviors, try identifying the situations or conditions under which the behavior of concern *tends to* or *tends not to* be emitted. For example, in a manner similar to that used by Lanomaz, Rapp, and Fergu-

---

[1]Fortunately, as Pelios et al. (1999) have found, "once maintaining variables for problem behavior are identified, experimenters tend to choose reinforcement-based rather than punishment-based procedures as treatment for both SIB and aggressive behavior" (p. 185).

son (2013) described in Chapter 16, investigators determined that sitting was associated with lower levels of stereotypy than while watching TV. After they reinforced the combination of sitting while watching TV, they then were able to progress toward reducing vocal stereotypy while the TV was on.

**Strive for behavioral incompatibility.** When you select responses to reinforce, emphasize alternatives that are not apt to occur simultaneously with the unwanted behavior (although as Young & Wincze, 1974, have shown, success is not guaranteed even then). If both are capable of being emitted at the same time, the unwanted behavior may be strengthened inadvertently. Suppose Vernon not only gets into trouble while he is truant during school hours, but also manages to steal and destroy property while in school. Simply reinforcing school attendance will not reduce his misbehavior, and may even accidentally strengthen it within the school setting. So you have to be very specific about the alternative reinforceable behaviors you select and the conditions under which they are to be emitted. Depending on the situation, doing schoolwork at his desk, participating in group activities, or engaging in woodworking and art projects may be incompatible with stealing and destruction. Strengthening different activities like allowing Vernon to go on errands, remain alone without supervision, or have access to free and unstructured time must be avoided, because these are not incompatible with theft and vandalism. Vernon could conceivably write on walls while on an errand, rifle through students' desks while alone in the room, and so on. Whenever feasible, then, select a replacement behavior fully incompatible with the undesired behavior, in which case you would be using DRI.

In an applied example, one of the authors was successful in reducing aggression maintained by peer attention during class passing periods of a middle school student, by allowing for peer-talk time contingent on keeping his hands in his pockets during the transition. *He could not hit others if his hands were in his pockets during transitions.*

**Avoid Resurgence.** DRA and FCT (functional communication training) are not always long lasting due to resurgence of the previous concerning behavior. Resurgence of the behavioe targeted for reduction *tends to happen when extinction conditions occur for the alternative behavior too soon or lasts too long* (i.e., the contingency manager does not continue to provide sufficient reinforcement). However, over time with continual treatment implementation, resurgence becomes less likely (Mace et al., 2010; Mace & Nevin, 2017; Wacker et al., 2011, 2017). Besides gradually thinning out your reinforcement, there is some evidence (Mace & Nevin, 2017) that generalization training (teaching the alternative behavior in more than one setting) also appears to reduce the likelihood of resurgence. It may be that resurgence is more likely to occur when the targeted behavior continues to receive reinforcement in other situations. Thus, it is important to implement generalization training and/or weaken the contingencies maintaining the problem behavior in those situations in which the problem behavior occurs (Ringdahl & St. Peter, 2017). Also, try to avoid lapses in treatment integrity or allowing your client to see another receiving reinforcement for engaging in the targeted problem behavior. Any of these situations might promote resurgence.

**Supplement with other procedures.** In addition to the factors to consider when you select replacement behaviors and use reinforcement and extinction, recognize that supplementing DRA with other behavioral procedures can further increase its effectiveness. You can combine *DRA with most other procedures* (e.g., prevention strategies, extinction, punishment, and other differential reinforcement procedures) *for preventing and reducing behavior*. Such procedural combinations usually produce more *rapid* results than either alone. However, one exception is combining noncontingent reinforcement (NCR) with DRA. A dense NCR schedule has been shown to possibly suppress the acquisition of appropriate behavior. "Thus, the strengthening of socially appropriate behaviors as replacements for problem behavior during NCR interventions might best be achieved if the NCR schedule is first thinned" (Hoh, Iwata, & DeLeon, 2000, p. 33).

If a promising alternative behavior is absent from the person's repertoire, try *differential reinforcement, shaping, or chaining* to promote its development. But, should the individual reveal s/he *is* capable of performing the behavior, your challenge becomes one of bringing it under reasonable *stimulus control,* perhaps by emphasizing the stimulus conditions in effect and/or modeling the behavior.

Other methods for teaching replacement behaviors involve giving verbal directions and presenting other S$^D$s to occasion and subsequently strengthen the response with reinforcement. If, for instance, a youngster who seems to have a difficult time attending to one activity for very long responds correctly to the direction, "Please, do your work," giving that instruction while reinforcing increasingly longer periods of staying on-task would make sense.

As a last resort you might turn to using a slightly more aversive or punitive correction procedure, such as telling the child "No, that is not ____," then removing the stimulus; or have him/her repeat the correct response five to ten times following an incorrect or non-response. (See positive practice in Chapter 30).

As always, change agents must be very sensitive to the effects of instructions like these. Do they just occasion the desired behavior, or do they also reinforce unwanted behavior by providing contingent attention? To find out, you can implement instructions for a few days and observe changes in the frequency or duration of the unwanted behavior. If, for example, the extra attention you provide functions as a reinforcer, that behavior will increase. Waiting for the sought-after behavior to occur by itself, or prompting and reinforcing a nearby peer's performance to occasion it, might be preferable to the directive. Then, delivering reinforcers following that wanted behavior should boost its rate. It is important that if you are going to use prompting to evoke the alternative behavior, that you do NOT prompt contingent on the problem behavior. Doing so is likely to create an inappropriate behavior chain (e.g., problem behavior → therapist prompting → alternative behavior → reinforcement). Again, it doesn't matter how benign it seems (e.g., "use your words"), sometimes, inserting a prompt to engage in the alternative behavior contingent on problem behavior can function as a form of reinforcing attention, creating and strengthening the unwanted behavior chain.

The following case (Fowler et al., 1986) illustrates several of the aforementioned points: Three seven-year-old boys, Chuck, Bob, and Adam, who frequently misbehaved during recess, were trained, then appointed as peer monitors. Their job was to award or subtract points depending on their assigned buddies' conduct on the playground. The monitors recorded the points by moving beads on a string and also received feedback on the quality of their monitoring and their own deportment during play. Monitors and the rest of the class shared in the backup activities earned by the buddies they supervised. The three monitors' own negative interactions diminished substantially during the recess periods during which the program was in effect, but not within other recess periods. Notice how the behavior, being a monitor, tended to be incompatible with misbehaving and how the reinforcers correlated with that role supported the children's job performance.

*Modeling* can be an especially helpful adjunct to DRI, as well as to other procedures. Although some members of a group might misbehave, you can highlight the exemplary deportment of others as imitative prompts. "Ebenezer, I sure am pleased to see you working quietly"; "Wow, Clyde is really working now, too." Comments like these may set the occasion for peers to imitate the behavior, and in turn their behaviors receive reinforcers as well.

Another key advantage of combining modeling with DRI is that it prompts positive scanning, modulating the contingency manager's natural inclination to respond disproportionately to negative behavior: "Roberto, sit down!" "Eric, be quiet!" "Stop that!" "Don't you know any better?" "Get back to work." Modeling helps to turn the tables so the deserving individuals obtain their share of recognition. (Please refer to Chapters 18 and 27 for using modeling effectively.)

In case you are unable to identify the most effective **corrective procedure** to apply with a given individual, consider modeling (see Chapter 18) the desired response yourself; then encouraging the client to imitate it (Barbetta, Heron, & Heward, 1993). Modeling is minimally intrusive and has been found to be an especially effective way to correct the unwanted behaviors of many children on the autism spectrum (McGhan & Lerman, 2013).

# DIFFERENTIAL REINFORCEMENT OF OTHER BEHAVIOR (DRO)

## DRO Defined and Differentiated from DRA

**Differential reinforcement of other behaviors (DRO),** (sometimes referred to as **differential reinforcement of zero occurrences** or as **omission training**) refers to *the differential reinforcement of any **other** behavior(s) the individual is emitting at a specified **time** and/or to reinforcing the absence, omission, or non-occurrence of the (particular unwanted) behavior of concern during a period of time*. Because the "other" behaviors are not necessarily specified, no particular behaviors will reliably yield reinforcers, instead the absence of the problem behavior will be associated with the delivery of reinforcers. Therefore, no particular acts are likely to *increase* very much, if at all. What *does* happen is that the unwanted behavior begins to *decrease* because reinforcement is limited to moments when it is absent. To illustrate, Carmine's teacher might compliment him or congratulate the class as a whole during the rare moments when neither Carmine nor anyone else is being disruptive.

Remember, DRO differs from DRA in that with DRA, reinforcers are contingent on specific acceptable, alternative behavior(s), not just the absence of the target behavior. (See the distinction in Figure 28.1.) Practitioners generally find DRO an especially appealing method for reducing behavior, because, unlike DRA, the schedule does not require the same degree of vigilance as reinforcing *specific* alternative behaviors, or the use of prompts to get the individual to emit a particular behavior. Rather than giving her daughter a reinforcer whenever Julie engages in a particular alternative response, such as asking appropriately for something instead of whining, Julie's mom gives her daughter a reinforcer if the child has *not* whined for the entire afternoon. Note that with DRO, reinforcers are provided contingent on zero occurrences of the unwanted behavior either within a period of time, or else at given moments. Unlike DRA, DRO is not response-dependent, because no particular alternative response is required. Let us examine this procedure more closely to help you see what we mean.

## Whole-Interval and Momentary DRO Defined and Illustrated

*Conceptually,* the notion of differentially reinforcing the absence of a response can be confusing. Reinforcement is said to have occurred when a response-contingent consequence leads to an increase in the rate of the target response. Techni-

---

**Differential Reinforcement of Alternative Responses (DRA)**

Response(s) serving as a specific alternative to the unwanted behavior
Specific alternative $R \longrightarrow S^r$

E.g., When Carmine raises his hand rather than yelling out $\longrightarrow$ the teacher provides $S^r$

---

**Differential Reinforcement of Zero Rates of the Response (DRO)**

The absense of the unwanted behavior (over a given time period) $\longrightarrow$ S

E.g., When Carmine has not been calling out, humming, staring out the vindow, tapping his pencil, or crumpling up paper and throwing it across the room for 15 minutes $\longrightarrow$ the teacher provides $S^r$

---

**Figure 28.1** Differentiating between DRA and DRO

cally, a non-response can't be reinforced. Yet *procedurally,* within DRO you can deliver reinforcers contingent upon the passage of a period of time, or at the moment during which a given response is absent. (Presumably, whatever behavior—good, bad, or indifferent—*is* ongoing at the time would be reinforced, posing a risk of that response increasing slightly in rate.) The rule stipulates *only* that *the unwanted behavior must be absent* for reinforcers to be delivered.

Two variations of DRO methods include *whole-interval DRO* and *momentary DRO*. In addition to these two variations, the DRO interval can either be *fixed* (the same interval size each time; e.g., "DRO 5 min" requires that each and every interval would be five minutes in length), or it can be *variable* (the interval may vary around an average or *mean, say, of five minutes*). With a DRO variable interval of five minutes, the intervals could be one minute, five minutes, two minutes, seven minutes, etc. as long as they average out to five.

**Whole-interval DRO.** As Figure 28.2 illustrates, **whole-interval DRO** requires monitoring throughout the interval because in whole-interval DRO**,** *a reinforcer is delivered following a period of time during which the individual has omitted engaging in a given behavior.* Implementing this method requires continuous observation to ensure that the unwanted target behavior has not occurred during the interval. No reinforcers would be delivered if the target behavior occurred at any time during that interval. Because emitting the unwanted behavior no longer yields reinforcers, but completing time periods marked by its absence *does*, the rate of that unwanted behavior begins to diminish. Read on, and you will discover examples of how useful a tool DRO can be in dealing with highly interfering, dangerous, disturbing, or socially repugnant behaviors.

Several of the children in a third-grade class frequently disrupted during math and language-arts instruction by running around the room, making noise, or annoying other children or their property in various ways (Allen, Gottselig, & Boylan, 1982). The teacher used a clever DRO procedure to eliminate the problem almost completely: After explaining and posting rules, she set a timer for five minutes. When the timer signaled the end of the interval, if the children had not disrupted, the

---

**Whole-interval DRO**

Behavior of concern *absent completely* between
time 1 and time 2 ⟶ reinforcement.

For example, under a whole-interval 5 min DRO, reinforcement would be provided at the end of the five minute interval provided the individual did not engage in the behavior throughout the interval.

versus

**Momentary DRO**

Behavior of concern *absent at the moment* when
the interval terminates ⟶ reinforcement.

For example, were you adhering to a momentary 5 min DRO, you would provide enforcement at the 5 min mark, provided the individual is not engaging in the behavior of concern at that particular moment.

---

**Figure 28.2** Differentiating between whole-interval DRO and momentary DRO.

teacher flipped over a card displaying the numeral 1, indicating that the class had earned a minute of free play. Subsequently, for each five-minute period during which no one in the class disrupted, the teacher displayed the next numeral in the sequence. This continued until the period ended and the class was able to cash in its earned minutes for the free time. (Note that in this example the DRO procedure resembles a token economy, in that the numerals were later exchanged for the reinforcer, in this case free play.) The teacher reported that despite the instructional time lost due to dispensing the free-time reward, not only did the children disrupt less, but they actually increased the number of assignments they completed. Presumably the diminishing disruptions permitted the students to attend and comply better with the task assignment.

In a verbal instruction/DRO comparison study among four nine- to 11-year-old children with Tourette's syndrome, participants were told "Do whatever you need to do to keep your tics from happening during the next five minutes (Woods & Himle, 2004). Within the *verbal condition*, they provided the children with a list of targeted tics and asked to prevent their occurrence. The *DRO condition* combined the verbal instructions with a token system, whereby a token was delivered every ten seconds during which a tic did not occur. These tokens were exchangeable for "a few cents for each token." Results indicated that while the verbal instructions alone resulted in a 10.3 percent reduction, they were much less effective than the verbal-instructions-plus-DRO method, which led to a 76.3 percent reduction from baseline across all children. DRO has been used successfully to increase the period of time during which three young children with autism omitted targeted forms of stereotypy (Rapp, Cook McHugh, & Mann, 2017). "In addition, results showed that the participants' non-targeted stereotypy either decreased or was unchanged when DRO was provided for the targeted stereotypy" (p. 42).

Severe self-injurious nail biting was the behavior of concern for a child with autism (Heffernan & Lyons, 2016). After an FBA determined that the nail biting was reinforced by automatic reinforcement, the investigators implemented the DRO procedure that provided reinforcing stimuli similar to nail biting (i.e., dried rice, pasta, cereal, and lentils) the "nail biting was successfully reduced and maintained at near zero levels (p. 251).

Flood and Wilder (2004) used DRO to treat an 11-year-old boy's *separation anxiety disorder*. While separated from his mother, they allowed the boy access to preferred items or activities contingent upon an absence of emotional behavior across gradually increasing periods of time. First, the mother progressively increased her physical distance from the boy right in the therapy room. By session 23, she started leaving the room. During baseline, the boy engaged in emotional behavior as soon as the mother attempted to leave. Eventually, he was able to be away from her for 90 minutes with no signs of a meltdown, and the mother reported that when used in the home, the same procedure increased the time he could tolerate being away from both her and his father.

The blood-glucose levels of an 18-year-old patient diagnosed with autism, severe learning disabilities, and Type 2 diabetes needed to be regularly monitored; but he fought the process all the way. Shabani and Fisher (2006) came to the rescue by combining DRO with stimulus fading to help diminish the young man's interfering reactions by negotiating the following deal: If during the ten seconds when the lancet was placed gradually closer and closer to his hand, the patient did not move his hand and arm outside an outline on a poster-board, he immediately received access to highly-preferred food items. Eventually the method worked, allowing daily blood samples to be drawn. Similarly, Dufour and Lanovaz (2020) used a whole interval DRO to teach a five-year-old and a nine-year-old boy with autism to stop removing a heart rate monitor. The intervention resulted in 100 percent compliance in wearing the medical device.

Whole-interval DRO was used with a 19-year-old man with Asperger syndrome whose chronic skin picking resulting in scarring and open wounds to his forehead, nose, mouth, and hands (Tiger, Fisher, & Bouxsein, 2009). The initial DRO interval was five minutes: For each interval of non-skin picking, he was given ten cents. The DRO interval was changed later on to ten minutes. After that, implementation of the DRO procedure was turned over to the client. Next, the interval was increased to 15 minutes. While observational recordings taken every ten seconds (partial-interval time sampling) during baseline showed that the client engaged in skin picking in about 56 percent of the intervals, the rate dropped to almost zero once the DRO treatment was implemented, and remained there after the client managed the treatment delivery himself.

Besides those illustrated above, examples of other behaviors successfully reduced by means of DRO have included aggression by developmentally-delayed (Luiselli & Slocumb, 1983) and brain-injured clients (Hegel & Ferguson, 2000; Teichner, Golden & Giannaris, 1999), noncompliance (Kodak et al., 2003), public masturbation (Foxx, Bittle, Bechtel, & Livesay, 1986), "repetitive vocalizations in the form of meaningless sounds, shrieks, and incoherent statements" (Luiselli & Reisman, 1980, p. 279), screaming by a child with autism in the presence of music (Buckley & Newchok, 2006), rumination (O'Neil, White, King, & Carek, 1979); self-stimulation (Harris & Wolchik, 1979), vomiting and spitting (Garcia & DeHaven, 1974), wandering by people with dementia (Heard & Watson, 1999), and many others.

**Momentary DRO.** The observation procedure *momentary time sampling* provides the foundation for momentary DRO (see Figure 28.2). With **momentary DRO**, *reinforcers are delivered at preset moments, provided the response is* not *occurring at those moments* (Repp & Deitz, 1974). To use momentary DRO, you observe the participant at a particular point in time, and if the behavior of concern is not occurring at that instant, you deliver a reinforcer. For example, Michele gains a reinforcer if she is at her work station at the very second when the preset interval is reached. Momentary DRO does not require the change agent to observe the individual throughout the interval, only at its end. Polvinale and Lutzker (1980) used momentary DRO by delivering attention on a variable interval schedule contingent on the nonoccurrence of public masturbation, and enticing or coercing other children in school into sexual interactions, by a 13-year-old boy with Down syndrome. After 19 days, the inappropriate sexual behavior (ISB) was eliminated. Follow-ups one month, six months, and one year later found no further occurrence of ISB.

To help you distinguish between whole interval DRO and momentary DRO, recall the case of Julie's whining. In whole-interval DRO, her mom would deliver a reinforcer at the very end of the hour if Julie had not been whining at any time during the previous hour. With momentary DRO, it would not matter if Julie had been whining five or forty minutes earlier, as long as she was not whining at the termination of the interval (i.e., on the hour).

**Whole-interval versus momentary DRO.** Lindberg, Iwata, Kahng, and DeLeon (1999) used a DRO strategy with three individuals with severe learning disabilities who engaged in self-injurious behavior (SIB), previously identified as being maintained by social reinforcement. Personnel monitored the clients according to a predetermined schedule: either a whole interval (reinforcement was contingent on an absence of the SIB throughout the interval) or on a variable interval DRO schedule. Both schedules successfully diminished the SIB rates. They then switched to a *variable-momentary differential-reinforcement-of-other-behavior (VM DRO) schedule: that is,* assuming the SIB was absent at the moment of observation, they delivered a reinforcer. The investigators found that the variable-momentary schedule successfully maintained the absence of the self-injurious behaviors. The authors concluded that "These findings suggest that VM DRO schedules may represent attractive alternatives to traditional FI schedules, because momentary schedules do not require continuous monitoring and may result in higher rates of reinforcement." (p. 123).

The advantage of using a momentary DRO should be obvious. It is useful for busy people like most of us, in that it does not require the continuous monitoring of whole-interval DRO. When signaled to observe, we can stop for a moment to note the presence or absence of the unwanted behavior and provide reinforcers if merited; then continue our regular activities.

Suppose you were trying to eliminate a nervous habit, like tugging your sideburns, twirling your hair, or sucking your fingers while studying. You could set your wrist timer to sound every X seconds. At the sound, you would determine whether you were displaying your habit and give yourself a reward if merited. Then you could return to your studies. That is much easier than trying to concentrate on both at once.

According to Lindberg et al. (1999), momentary DRO actually may result in higher rates of reinforcement than whole-interval DROs. You probably can guess why. With momentary DRO, the unwanted behavior still can be emitted at other times during the interval, because reinforcers are contingent only on the absence of the response at the very moment when the interval terminates. Were Herbie to use a momentary DRO to control his nail biting, he could still bite his nails, as long as he wasn't doing it at the precise moment when his wrist alarm sounded. By contrast, the whole-interval DRO schedule would not permit the behavior of concern to receive reinforcement were to occur at *any* time within the interval.

This phenomenon may have explained Repp, Barton, and Brulles' (1983) and Barton, Brulle, and Repps' (1986) findings when they compared the effectiveness of whole-interval versus momentary DRO. As you probably anticipated, the whole-interval DRO was more effective. Yet, interestingly, when the momentary DRO had been *preceded* by a phase of whole-interval DRO, during which the rate of the unwanted response had diminished substantially, the momentary approach functioned quite well. The effectiveness of momentary DRO, then, may be influenced by the history provided during the initial phase in a study. In the 1986 case, the rate of the behavior was initially diminished through whole-interval DRO. Then, during the subsequent momentary DRO phase, the new lower rate pattern was correlated with reinforcers.

Recall, though, that Lindberg et al. (1999) found variable-momentary (VM DRO) was just as effective as whole-interval DRO for decreasing one participant's SIB, previously supported by social reinforcement. They suggested that the reason for the discrepancies between their results and those of earlier studies might be that the previous research did not identify nor withhold the reinforcers that played the most powerful role in maintaining the target behavior. Also, Lindberg et al. set their initial DRO interval lengths according to each participant's rate of SIB during baseline, a very rich DRO schedule indeed.

To summarize, you may find momentary DRO to be as effective as whole-interval DRO if you adhere to the following steps:

- First, identify and withhold the reinforcers maintaining the unwanted behaviors.
- Then, while maintaining these extinction conditions, use related stimuli to differentially reinforce the omission of the behavior by initially applying a dense momentary DRO schedule.
- Then, as the response continues to diminish, you begin to lengthen the size of that interval until it is large enough to manage conveniently.

Varying the interval length also may help prevent your client from discriminating the end of the DRO interval. Suppose you decided to use momentary DRO to reduce a student's rate of wandering around the classroom. You deliver reinforcers every 30 minutes to those children in class who are seated. But suppose some begin to catch on to the fact that they only need to be on their good behavior when the clock approaches the hour and half-hour, not necessarily at other times. In between, they could roam about freely. To avoid problems associated with predictable interval sizes like those, you would be better off using a variable-momentary DRO schedule. In the current instance, you might monitor the children every 30 minutes on average: in 30, then 15, then 20, then 45 minutes and so on (~30 min). (Later, we suggest practical techniques contingency managers can use to remind themselves to pause to deliver reinforcers. Also for other techniques designed to sustain lasting change, review the sections on maintaining behavior)

**Progressive DRO (DROP).** Another DRO variation is called differential reinforcement of other behavior on a progressive schedule (Carr, Linehan, O'Reilly (2016), which some wittily choose to label "DROP." Here, you increase the quantity of reinforcers you deliver to some preset maximum, in tandem with expanding the length of time during which the unwanted behavior is absent. But should the unwanted behavior occur, you return to the original reinforcer quantity. In other words, the

## Bonus Tokens

| 2 five-minutes-in-a-row with no problem behavior | 3 five-minutes-in-a-row with no problem behavior | 5 five-minutes-in-a-row with no problem behavior | 8 five-minutes-in-a-row with no problem behavior | 12 five-minutes-in-a-row with no problem behavior |
|---|---|---|---|---|
| 1 extra | 2 extra | 3 extra | 4 extra | 5 extra |

**Figure 28.3** Bonus tokens

longer the participant goes without engaging in the problem behaviors, the larger the reinforcer she or he receives.

Carmine and his teacher make a deal. For every five-minute period during which the boy does not disrupt, he will receive a token. He will be able to save his tokens until he earns twenty-five, the price of being able to play computer games for ten minutes. But there is a bonus provision as well—notice their arrangement as displayed in Figure 28.3.

Carmine's tokens accumulate rapidly. But one day another boy in the class accidentally bumps into him, causing Carmine to shout a string of obscenities. Although, Carmine fails to earn any tokens for that time block, he still will be able to during the next, but he must wait for ten minutes before he can earn any *extra* tokens.

As you can see, the *progressive DRO* method is designed to extend the length of time during which the unwanted behavior remains absent. Even in the case of a mishap like the one above, Carmine does not become bankrupt, though he does pay a certain penalty for "losing it." Additionally, the system has generated a learning history of good behavior that may influence his future performance, in the sense that he had begun to experience bonanza periods of reinforcement. Histories of this kind have been found to influence subsequent performance rates (e.g., Ono & Iwabuchi, 1997; see Lattal and Neef, 1996, to review other variations of DRO schedules studied both in the laboratory and in applied settings).

## Advantages of DRO

**Widely applicable.** You already have been alerted to the fact that DRO is benign and relatively easy to use, at least when compared to the dense reinforcement required of DRA. Given appropriate training, both sophisticated and neophyte change agents have been able to use the method successfully to address a wide breadth of behaviors (Homer & Peterson, 1980), and as seen by the many illustrations in this chapter.

**Relatively rapid.** Although its effects can be more delayed than with punishment procedures, DRO may function more rapidly than extinction alone, sometimes producing substantial behavioral decrements within a few or even a single session (Homer & Peterson, 1980; Shabani & Fisher, 2006). Be cautious when interpreting the results of such comparisons, though, because as mentioned previously, outcomes differ depending on the variables applied within each procedure. "Unless we know how to make each treatment optimally effective, it will be pointless in many cases to compare techniques" (Van Houten, 1987, p. 109). If the most optimal arrangements are unknown, the one identified as the best currently available should be used as

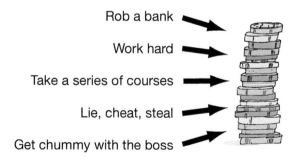

**Figure 28.4** Behaviors reinforced by money

a basis for making any comparisons between different procedural techniques.

**Often durable and general.** Especially when *behavioral function* has been a primary consideration in prescribing DRO, the method often has produced lasting response suppression. (See Vollmer & Iwata, 1992, for a review.)

**May enable contingency managers to avoid or replace aversive techniques.** We have just provided you with a number of examples of the benign application of DRO procedures with humans. DRO can be used equally well as non-abusive substitutes for widely used abusive animal management techniques, as in a case in which Fox, Bailey, Hall and St. Peter (2012) used the method to teach horses to refrain from biting, chewing, or pawing.

**Effectiveness independent of functionality of reinforcer.** The effectiveness of DRO procedure does not necessarily depend upon the relationship between the functional reinforcer and the problem behavior. In fact, if the reinforcer used in the DRO is more powerful than those reinforcing the unwanted behavior, it may be possible to override the reinforcement value of the functional reinforcer (see Chapters 6 and 11 for how to increase the value of a reinforcer). As such, DRO procedures can successfully supplement other interventions aimed at reducing the problematic behavior.

## Disadvantages of DRO

DRO is not without its disadvantages. These include a resurgence of the problematic behavior, its failure to meet the "Dead-Man's Test," its focus on the negative, its risk of reinforcing other unwanted behaviors, and behavioral contrast.

**Participant may return to previous problem behavior ("resurgence").** If the *other* behavior produces reinforcers of lesser value, or requires more time or effort to attain some of equivalent value, returning to the previously (maladaptive) behavior is more likely. So, it should come as no surprise that DRA has been found less likely to result in resurgence than DRO (Romano & St. Peter, 2017).

The fact that you are reading this book suggests that your own reinforcement history has taught you that the most productive way to achieve your goals is to study and learn. Others may have gotten what they wanted in risky ways, like copying classmates' answers on a quiz, because studying is not always easy and its reinforcers tend to be delayed.

**Fails the "Dead Man's Test."** As Axelrod (1987) has rightly contended, DRO may fail the "Dead Man's Test." (As mentioned in the previous chapter, a dead person will *not* engage in just about any behavior you could name.) That is, the procedure is not necessarily constructive unless one or more beneficial replacement behaviors are incorporated within the program. To illustrate, should we specify that *reinforcers are to be provided for not blurting out*, anyone, living or dead would qualify for receiving those reinforcers. To avoid this pitfall, then, be certain to avoid specifying a *non*-behavior as your goal. Instead change or add a constructive substitute procedure to it, such as modeling, DRA or DRI.

The latter point was dramatically supported in a study by Leitenberg, Burchard, Burchard, Fuller, and Lysaght (1977). The investigators compared the effectiveness of DRA versus DRO as a method of reducing sibling conflict (physical and verbal attacks—hitting, pushing, throwing objects, taking another's belongings, making threats, name calling, and so on) among six families with 16 children aged two to ten. During the DRO phase, children were praised and given a penny following each one-minute interval in which they were ignored. During DRA, praise and pennies were distributed following episodes of such appropriate interactions as playing, helping, or sharing. Both procedures were equally effective in reducing sibling conflict, but only during DRA did the children increase their *appropriate* interactions. The point is, as mentioned previously, if you elect to use a DRO procedure, other more-preferred behaviors are not likely to improve unless they are specifically targeted for consistent reinforcement.

**Accentuates attending to the "negative."** Using DRO requires keeping the unwanted behavior under surveillance, thereby riveting the manager's attention on the behavior of concern. As a result of their constant attention on the unwanted behavior, and because gaining attention of any kind at all sometimes can be more reinforcing than being ignored, the problem behavior might inadvertently begin to receive reinforcement. Moreover, if a caregiver or behavior change agent is focused on monitoring and reinforcing the absence of the targeted behavior, they may inadvertently fail to notice, and consequently fail to reinforce appropriate behavior. This point can extend to self-management as well. For instance, McFall (1970) found that smokers who counted the number of cigarettes they smoked *increased* their smoking rates, whereas those who recorded the number of *urges not followed by smoking* decreased their rates. Therefore, when using DRO, monitor for signs of reactivity by noting any worsening of the target behavior that could possibly be traceable to the increased attention it is receiving. If that should be the case, either adjust the observational recording method to an instrument or person outside of the client's normal social network or switch over to DRA.

**Risks reinforcing other unwanted behavior.** Beyond the one to be eliminated, under DRO conditions *all* behaviors are equally eligible for reinforcement. This arrangement could conceivably mean that you find yourself in the position of reinforcing a behavior that was just as bad as, or perhaps even worse than, the one to be eliminated. Pearl is given a small piece of fruit or a raisin every five minutes, provided that she has not been flicking her fingers. If she is rocking when the fruit is delivered, her rocking may increase. This sort of problem is more apt to happen to people with a large number of unsuitable behaviors in their repertoires. When working with these clients, turn to one or more of these alternatives: (1) either apply DRO to several of the most serious unwanted behaviors, provided that a sufficient number of reinforceable intervals will be available to give the program a chance to work; (2) withhold reinforcers until desired or neutral behavior occurs (provided this does not extend the DRO interval too long); or (3) select another reductive procedure. Research findings, such as those by Hangen, Romero, Neidert, and Borreto (2020), suggest that extinction-induced variability may account for any observed increase in rate of other non-targeted behaviors during DROs. Consequently, we encourage you to select alternative (2) above.

**Behavioral contrast.** When using DRO or any other procedure designed to reduce a given behavior, ensure that the behavior does not receive reinforcement at other times or places. Otherwise, the behavior may *increase* at those other times or in those other places. Support for this assertion derives from a classic study performed by Reynolds (1961). Pigeons' key pecking continued to be reinforced under one discriminative stimulus ($S^D$), whereas non-key pecking was reinforced under a different $S^D$. Although the rate of key pecking under the DRO-correlated stimulus was practically eliminated, responding under the non-DRO stimulus conditions increased to a level higher than previously. Reynolds (1961) labeled this phenomenon **behavioral contrast**, (defined in Chapter 23 as *occurring when behavior in the non-treatment condition changes in the direction opposite from that in the treatment condition*.) Although we have not encountered human data on this phenomenon with DRO per se, they have been reported for extinction, a key component of DRO (see Chapter 26). For this reason, watching for the possible contrast effect during the use of DRO seems advisable. For instance, Pearl's hand stereotypy should be measured in those environments in which the DRO is operating *and* in those in which it may not. An increase in stereotypy in those latter settings would suggest the emergence of a contrast effect.

| Sec | 15 | 30 | 45 | 60 | 75 | 90 | 105 | 120 | 135 | 150 | 165 | 180 | 195 | 210 | 225 | 240 | 255 | 270 | 285 | 300 |
|---|---|---|---|---|---|---|---|---|---|---|---|---|---|---|---|---|---|---|---|---|
| Obs.1 | y | y | y | y | y | n | n | n | n | n | n | n | N | n | n | n | n | y | y | y |
| Obs.2 | y | y | n | n | n | n | n | y | y | n | n | n | N | n | n | n | n | n | n | n |

**Figure 28.5** Summary data sheet

## Using DRO Effectively

**Determine the function of the behavior.** DRO appears to be most effective when the challenging behavior is maintained by positive reinforcement in the form of attention or access to tangibles (Hanley & Tiger, 2011). You may not want to restrict your use to these functions of behavior, but you probably should consider DRO when the function of your target behavior is seeking attention or gaining access to tangibles. Remember the other possible reinforcing functions of challenging behavior (e.g., social negative reinforcement in the form of escape from demands or automatic reinforcement), or when using the non-functional reinforcers within the DRO schedule, because it will be important to tip the scales. That is, *the value of the reinforcers delivered in the DRO should be greater than that derived from the behavior of concern.*

**Maximize opportunities for reinforcement.** Because DRO is a differential reinforcement procedure, all the methods for effectively using differential reinforcement apply here as well. To maximize the person's opportunity for reinforcement under whole-interval DRO, look closely at the baseline performance. Determine the average period of time the individual successfully omits the unwanted behavior and set the DRO interval just below that. Recall that for a differential reinforcement procedure to work, the individual must receive the reinforcer. If the DRO interval you set is too long, and the person fails to earn the reinforcer, then DRO procedure will be ineffective.

Pearl's caregivers are convinced that hardly a moment goes by without her flicking her fingers. Yet when they closely study the data, they find that Pearl actually spends an average of 2.7 minutes between bursts of that form of stereotypy. So, they reason, beginning with a DRO interval of 2.5 minutes should permit Pearl to receive reinforcers frequently. Figure 28.5 displays a portion of the summary data sheet. The shaded cells represent 10 cells (150 seconds or 2.5 minutes); intervals during which Pearl did not flick her fingers. Depending on who was designated the primary observer, one of the black arrows indicates the moment at which she would be eligible to receive a reinforcer.

Another way to increase reinforcement is to reset the time period immediately following the behavior of concern, rather than waiting for the entire interval to expire. This is the method we recommend as it provides more opportunity for the individual to earn reinforcers. However, it should be pointed out that simply resetting the time might be less effective. For example, if Pearl engages in the stereotypy on average every 2.7 minutes and the DRO interval were set at five minutes, even the resetting feature would not permit her to earn reinforcers. Therefore, *first carefully consider the size of the initial interval prior to combining it with a resetting feature.* The initial interval should insure that the client is highly likely to earn reinforcers.

**Articulate both the DRO rules in effect and the consequences as you present those.** In civilized societies, most tend to adhere to rules, especially those tied to predictable consequences (e.g., "If I don't stop at the red light, that patrol officer in the car right behind me probably will give me a ticket"). So clearly articulate the rules in effect for those with adequate listener repertoires (Watts et al., 2013). E. g., "If you don't ___ (target behavior) for ___ (time) you get ___ (reinforcer)." Hence, to promote a more rapid behavior change, unless your audience thrives on (gains reinforcers for) being oppositional, clearly communicate the rules in effect when using DRO.

In addition to stating the DRO rule, consider articulating at the end of the DRO the consequence the person earned or failed to earn. Iannaccone, Hagopian, Javed, Borrero, and Zarcone, (2020), in working with 9- to 16-year olds with severe behaviors, found that combining the specification of exactly what reinforcer the youngster lost, such as a preferred edible or access to a preferred toy, (e.g., "You hurt yourself so you don't get a jellybean.") reduced problem behavior much more effectively for all participants than simply specifying the rule (We assume that these youngsters paid little attention to rules because their behaviors had been contingency shaped, not rule-governed). Specifying the consequence while they were experiencing them might help them more quickly to identify the actual consequences in operation under this new contingency arrangement, and help them to learn some new rules to govern their behavior (i.e., help the youngsters' behaviors to become more rule governed).

**Adjust schedule gradually.** After the objectionable behavior has begun to diminish in rate, you can gradually extend the length of the intervals of time during which the offending behavior must be omitted for reinforcement to follow. For example, Herbie bites his nails, a habit that has caused him distress for many years. Familiar with self-management methods, he decides to use a DRO procedure to rid himself of the behavior. He sets his wrist alarm to sound every ten minutes while he is reading, studying, and watching television (peak nail-biting times). When the timer sounds, he records whether his fingers touched his teeth in the interim. If not, he praises and awards himself a token. Later, he exchanges the requisite tokens for the opportunity to read emails from his girlfriend, to call her, or to engage in his hobby, computer photography. When the frequency of his nail biting has diminished by, say, 50 percent for a few days in a row, he lengthens the interval to 20 minutes. Herbie maintains this pattern until his nails remain unbitten for three months. The same "adjusting DRO" tactic could be used with Pearl or anyone else for whom the goal is to diminish or eliminate an unwanted behavior.

Rosen and Rosen (1983) used this sort of schedule during omission training to produce a gradual reduction in, and ultimately eliminate a child's stealing. They proceeded by adjusting the frequency with which they checked items stored in the child's desk to determine whether any were marked to indicate they did not belong to him. Initially they checked every 15 minutes; then gradually extended the time interval until ultimately it reached every two hours.

**Combine with other procedures.** As you have already learned, to make the most of DRO, combine it with other procedures, especially reinforcing acceptable incompatible (DRI), or at least alternative behaviors (DRA). An early laboratory study with children (Long, 1962) underscored this fundamental guideline: In that case, the investigator found that providing a clock assisted children to distinguish when any particular schedules of reinforcement were in effect (i.e., how long they needed to refrain from unacceptable behavior to receive their reinforcers). Such combinations produce speedier and more effective outcomes. Hedquist and Roscoe, (2020) used a combined DRI and DRO by reinforcing the completion of a product (DRI) in the absence of any motor stereotypy (DRO) while they were engaged in their task. This combination was much more effective than DRO alone, and it effectively reduced the clients' stereotypy while also increasing their task engagement and completion without having to resort to response blocking or interruption. Apparently, resurgence tends to be minimized under this combination of interventions. So, *while the DRO is in effect, reinforce desired alternative behaviors as they occur.* Also whenever possible, reinforce, especially, the behaviors that clearly are incompatible with those targeted for reduction. You can do this by complimenting a person for omitting a response, not only at the end of the interval but also whenever any desired, incompatible response is occurring. To illustrate, Shumate and Wills (2010) helped a second-grade teacher use a combination of DRO and DRA with three students of typical intelligence who were disruptive and at risk for reading failure. Following brief periods of not being disruptive or off-task (i.e., DRO), they gave the students considerable attention, previously determined to be the function of their behavior. In addition, they implemented DRA and DRI by reinforcing students' appropriate strategies for recruiting teacher attention. All three students' disruptive behavior decreased to near zero levels. In fact, one of the authors routinely uses a DRO procedure combined with other procedures as a *bonus contingency.* For example, teaching the client to use an alternative response to obtain reinforcement, while specifying that if the client goes a whole week without engaging in problem behavior, she will receive a *bonus reinforcer* (e.g., getting to go to a favorite hot spot).

When you design an DRO intervention, try to make the "other behavior" more intrinsically appealing by choosing things the person already enjoys doing or that are bound to generate praise or other positive reactions from those near and dear. For instance, you might consider shaping, differential reinforcement, chaining, and/or other methods to teach the individual to dance, play an instrument, or engage in track and field sports in place of rocking or jumping about.

*When using DRO,* be certain, as always, to *program for generalization rather than leaving it up to chance.* To illustrate, in cases of thumb sucking (Lowitz & Suib, 1978) and of separation anxiety (Flood & Wilder, 2004), generalization was carefully programmed. In the thumb-sucking instance, results were so successful and long-lasting that a follow-up call a year later revealed that the child's dentist no longer planned to prescribe braces to straighten the previously threatening malocclusion of the child's teeth.

Should your combinations of DRO with DRA fail, as you would with any program, analyze each of the variables you are applying. See whether the procedure can be made more powerful by reassessing client choices, setting events, quality, amount, and/or intensity of reinforcers; try reducing the size of the DRO interval and/or examine $S^D$s, motivating operations, and schedules of reinforcement. Give the most optimal arrangements you can identify a reasonable chance. If those methods don't work, then, assuming the target behavior isn't intolerable, consider "shaping" the reduction in response rate by interposing a *differential reinforcement of diminishing rates* (DRD) procedure, described next.

# DIFFERENTIALLY REINFORCING LOWER AND DIMINISHING RATES OF BEHAVIOR

Sometimes our intention is to reduce a behavior's rate rather than eliminate it. Consuming small quantities of alcohol may not be harmful, whereas, as we all are aware, too much can be detrimental. Ludwig writes too quickly and ends up handing in a sloppy paper. When Lotte races, the precision of her butterfly stroke deteriorates. During team meetings, Ralph tends to dominate group discussions, Desmond constantly asks harebrained questions, and Ida complains excessively. Those examples illustrate behaviors that need not necessarily be eliminated, just lessened. Ralph and Desmond should continue to participate in the workshop by asking questions and providing examples—but just not as often. Two behavioral procedures are especially well-suited to *reducing* (not eliminating) rates of behavior: *differential reinforcement of* (1) *lower* or of (2) *diminishing rates.*

## DRL Defined and Illustrated

**Differential reinforcement of low rates (DRL)** (also called **Differential reinforcement of spaced responding**) was defined and illustrated in Chapter 23. To review, DRL consists of *delivering reinforcers contingent on a sequence of responses emitted at low rates*—that is, responses that are spaced relatively far apart. When **DRL** is in effect, *a behavior is reinforced only if it occurs following a specific period of time during which it **did not occur**, or since the last time it occurred* (Ferster & Skinner, 1957). As pointed out in Chapter 23, to reduce Ralph's excessive participation, so as to allow others an opportunity to have their say during English class, Ralph and Mrs. Olsen agree that if Ralph waits three minutes after participating until his next bid for recognition, she will call on him at the next opportunity. If not, she will ignore what he says and require him to wait three more minutes to be called on. In another example, a basketball coach praises her point guard if two minutes have expired between her three-point shot attempts.

DRL schedules are especially suitable to managing dangerously rapid responding like eating so fast as to risk choking. Lennox, Miltenberger, and Donnelly (1987) only permitted rapid eaters to take a bite following a 15-second pause. Similarly, Wright and Vollmer (2002) used a DRL schedule with Millie, a 17-year-old girl diagnosed with profound mental retardation and cerebral palsy. Millie ate her finely chopped and pureed foods too quickly, and as a result would often choke in the process. An *adjusting* DRL was used to slow her down. During some of the training sessions, she also was prompted to "eat slowly" following each bite. The DRL intervals ranged from averages of eight to 15 seconds, and were marked by a beep at the end of the interval. Following the beep, she was permitted a bite of food, provided she had not attempted to eat during the scheduled intervals. If she did try to take a bite prior to the DRL interval, the attempt was blocked, and Millie was physically guided to place the eating utensil on the table and to place her hand in her lap, and the timer was reset. This treatment package was delivered twice a day, five days a week, for 10 to 20 minutes each session, over 45 sessions. It successfully reduced her rate of eating; bites decreased from a mean average of 8.6 seconds apart to 15 seconds apart. Also, the unpleasant side effects of screaming, crying, and self-injury gradually diminished and remained low (now ranging from zero to five percent of the time) throughout the latter half of the treatment, regardless of whether the experimenter or the mother provided the food. Similarly, positive results have been achieved by using DRL to assist people with neurological problems (Knight, Rutterford, Alderman, & Swan, 2002).

Remember, the DRL schedule is designed to reduce or maintain the rate of a behavior by reinforcing that very same behavior (*not* an alternative), but only when a specific time interval has passed during which it was absent. This can pose ethical issues with aggressive, self-injurious, and other problem behaviors. For these reasons, *we recommend you limit your application of this schedule only to otherwise acceptable behaviors currently occurring too frequently or rapidly* (e.g., dominating discussions in class or taking excessive breaks at work) as illustrated above. Eventually, the rate of responding should begin to approach that set by the DRL contingency. Evidence also indicates that some children are more sensitive and/or responsive to DRL schedules than others (Gaucher & Forget, 2020). So, be sure to clearly specify to your clients the schedule in effect, especially the behavior upon which the reinforcement is contingent. This is what several investigators (Becraft, Borrero, Davis, Mendres-Smith, & Castillo, 2018) did and found that signals "facilitated and maintained responding in both types of DRL schedules (spaced-responding DRL and full-session DRL).

## Differential Reinforcement of Diminishing Rates (DRD) Defined and Illustrated

DRD is closely related to DRL, but in this case *reinforcement is delivered explicitly "when the number of responses in a specified period of time is less than, or equal to, a prescribed limit,"* (Deitz

### DRL and DRD Differentiated

**Differential Reinforcement of Low Rates (DRL)**

If at least "t" time has passed since the last response of concern was emitted, that behavior, then ⟶ reinforcement

DRL is similar to reinforcing longer and longer Interresponse Times (IRTs) and that is what results in the behavior's reduction.

**Differential Reinforcement of Diminishing Rates (DRD)**

If no more than "x" occurrences of that behavior occur in "t" time ⟶ reinforcement

DRD involves reinforcing lower and lower rates, and that is what results in the behavior's reduction.

**Figure 28.6** Differentiating between DRL and DRD

& Repp, 1973, p. 457). Sometimes it is called **full-session DRL** *(f-DRL) rather than DRD* (Becraft, et al., 2018). As in whole-interval DRO, you observe behavior during the interval. With DRO, reinforcers are provided if the behavior was absent. Here, though, at the end of the interval you would reinforce contingent on a reduced number of occurrences during the preceding time interval. In the laboratory analogue of this variation, a monkey automatically received a banana pellet at the end of a preset interval (whether he pulled the chain or not), as long as he had pulled the chain *fewer than* "x" times during the interval. Using this schedule may be easier than other differential reinforcement procedures especially with groups, because all that is required is counting responses up to "x" number within an interval. If the number is exceeded before the end of the interval, reinforcers are withheld when the interval comes to an end. Otherwise, reinforcers are scheduled for delivery, presumably, even if the target behavior is occurring at that moment. (Should such a case arise, we suggest you impose a brief delay following that occurrence.)

DRD was used to reduce the number of questions by two adults with intellectual disabilities (Otalvaro, Krebs, Brewer, Leon, & Steifman, 2020). The investigators delivered a reinforcer at the end of the day if the participants asked fewer than a specified number of questions. Also, only a specified maximum number of questions were reinforced within the sessions. As a result, both participants asked fewer questions.

Another variation of DRD is analogous to shaping and to progressive differential reinforcement. Here the rule states that *the size of the interval between responses is to lengthen, or the preset maximum number of targeted responses within the interval is to decrease gradually.*

Two more examples, one of each procedure, should help to clarify the distinction between DRL and DRD (see Figure 28.6): Ralph's excessive talking during group counseling has become a real nuisance. The counselor decides it is only fair to allow the other youths also to have a chance to participate. So, for the DRL case, she makes an agreement with Ralph. She explains she will use her stopwatch to measure the amount of time since he has last spoken. If that time is longer than the previous interval, she will call on Ralph. Otherwise, she will not.

In the DRD situation, reinforcement would be provided after intervals of fewer contributions; that is, if Ralph participated only twice in ten minutes, he would be called upon. This is a relatively painless way of gradually weaning Ralph from dominating the counseling session. Another instance might be the rule Jim sets for himself: "If I only smoke four cigarettes, rather than the usual seven in the morning, I will be able to watch the DVD I rented this evening. Otherwise, I'll have to wait."

## Advantages of DRL and DRD

**Benign.** Numerous options exist for lowering response rates: reprimanding people for going too fast or doing too much, ignoring them altogether, continually reminding them to slow down, feeding them tranquilizing drugs, and so on. But both DRL and DRD permit reinforcement to continue; thereby, sharing many of the advantages with other positive procedures: Good things still continue to happen! But here is a situation in which reinforcement continues, as people go merrily on their way. So, when you are seeking a non-aversive method for reducing the rate of a behavior, consider DRD or DRL.

**Tolerant.** DRL and DRD reflect a built-in tolerance for the target behavior, communicating the message, "What you're doing is okay, as long as it is not done to excess." *So, consider using the procedures to foster moderation.* Although too much clowning is a nuisance, an occasional antic can relieve the monotony. Dominating the conversation is inappropriate, but contributing to it from time to time is socially acceptable. Everyone complains once in a while. That is okay. Mrs. Kvetch just should not complain all the time. So consider DRD and DRL procedures when the goal is to moderate, but not necessarily eliminate habits like eating junk food, consuming alcohol, talking on the phone, watching television, playing video games, or procrastinating. Fortunately, the techniques are particularly amenable to self-management.

**Convenient and effective.** DRD has been shown to be effective among an assortment of populations. Early on, Deitz and Repp (1973) described their experience with a group of ten noisy children who were severely developmental delayed, and with an office-procedure class of 15 typical high-school senior girls who frequently wasted time discussing social topics in class. With the children with developmental delays, the baseline averaged 32.7 "talk outs" per 50-minute session. The contingency was then set so that if they produced five or fewer talkouts in 50 minutes, each member would be allowed to select two pieces of candy. The rate of talking out immediately declined to an average of 3.13 instances per session. The senior girls had averaged 6.6 social discussions per 50-minute session. For them, the DRD procedure was instituted in a series of phases: Initially, when fewer than six social discussions occurred during the period for each of the first four days of the week, the Friday class would be a "free" period. For the next week, fewer than three discussions were allowed. Eventually the criterion was reduced to zero (technically evolving into a DRO schedule). In addition to finding the DRD procedure very easy to use, the high-school teacher reported that the "free time" worked well as a reinforcer. "She found it more useful to have four days in which the students are not disruptive and are working than to have five relatively disruptive days" (Deitz & Repp, 1973, p. 462).

The DRD procedure also successfully served to reduce an 11-year-old fifth-grade boy's rate of talking out and a sixth-grader's rate of leaving her seat (Deitz & Repp, 1974). In each instance, the unwanted behavior diminished when two or fewer responses per period earned them gold stars. Differential reinforcement with either gold stars or access to a sand table (Deitz et al., 1978) also was applied successfully in a learning disabilities class to reduce a number of a seven-year-old's inappropriate behaviors and a group of five-year-old handicapped children's non-permissible talk-outs. Similarly, the DRD approach also was successful in promoting weight loss among obese children by progressively reinforcing their rates of engaging in exercise (Epstein, et al 1995).

The advantages of these procedures seem to appeal especially to developers and implementers of educational programs designed to serve students faced by particular challenges. Included are students facing socio-economic hardships (Mayer, 1999), those with various disabilities (Cavalier, Ferretti, & Hodges, 1997) and those needing to "catch up" academically for a range of reasons (Johnson & Layng, 1994).

DRD has been successfully combined with DRO. For example, investigators (Sloman, Reyes, & Vollmer, 2014) described an independent group contingency with 18- to 63-year-olds with disabilities who resided in a secure residential treatment facility with 20 residents. Each resident had commented at least one felony. The intervention's group contingency consisted of a bi-weekly special activity that included a catered luncheon, music and socializing. During each week before the special activity, residents who had no more than one instance of a minor inappropriate behavior (DRD) and no instances of severe inappropriate behavior (DRO) were allowed to attend the special activity. Lower levels of inappropriate behavior occurred during weeks in which the contingency was in effect (each week before the contingency) than during the weeks when the special activity was not in effect (each week following the contingency).

**Helpful in social skills training.** As Gadaire, Marshall, and Brissett (2019) have pointed out, "Social skills are unique in that excessive rates of responding may be just as socially undesirable as deficient responding" (p. 20). They found that applying DRD effectively maintained participants' responding at appropriate levels without eliminating the social skill.

## Disadvantages of DRL and DRD

**Time.** Compared to the more rapidly-acting reductive methods to be discussed in Chapters 29 and 30 (e.g., punishment, response cost), DRD and DRL procedures may take a while to produce the outcomes sought. However, they may be combined with other positive reductive procedures (e.g., modeling, DRO, DRA), to hasten their rates of success.

**May not be suitable for dangerous or objectionable behaviors.** We caution you against choosing DRL or DRD as your sole intervention with aggressive and self-abusive behaviors, though, because that may mislead your client into concluding that the behavior is acceptable in moderation. When the unwanted behavior is sufficiently dangerous or otherwise seriously objectionable, augment DRL or DRD with or substitute a different reductive method.

**Focus on undesirable behavior**. As with DRO, DRL and DRD procedures require the contingency manager and program recipient to monitor the behavior of concern. This poses a risk that preferred behaviors may be overlooked or unwanted ones unduly attended to, and thereby be inadvertently reinforced by the extra attention. Adding DRA and modeling procedures and/or stipulating that managers provide a minimum of three positive comments per hour for desirable behaviors might serve to counteract this potential hazard.

## Effective Use of DRL and DRD

We apply DRL and DRD in much the same way as DRO; that is by using optimal reinforcing contingencies and basing the sizes of intervals on the participant's previous performance patterns. Additionally, we want to increase the size of the interval gradually because delaying reinforcement too long will produce the same sort of disruption as selecting too large a step in shaping. Instead, increase the interval size slowly and patiently. The individual's behavior will tell you how close to the mark you have been with your programming. Any major signs of relapse should mandate a rapid retreat to a shorter interval. Also, as mentioned previously, limit using DRL with otherwise acceptable behaviors, but just those occurring at excessive rates.

DRD can be used for a wide range of behaviors, but should you chose to apply it with serious problems such as aggression or self-abuse, be sure to combine it with other procedures, including modeling as an antecedent cue and/or DRA, DRI, DRO, extinction and/or even, in the worst case scenario, punishment, as a consequential event. Meanwhile, to avoid inadvertently reinforcing serious behaviors, postpone your delivery of reinforcers until the client has been behaving acceptably for a while.

## The Good Behavior Game: An Illustrative DRD Behavior-Management Package

The **Good Behavior Game** is an example of an interdependent group contingency package in which modeling, rules, and DRD are combined to produce rapid improvement in the deportment of the members of a group (see Brockman & Leibowitz, 1982; Barrish, et al., 1969; Dolan, et al., 1993; Embry, 2002; Harris & Sherman, 1973; Swiezy, Matson, & Box, 1992). The game has been shown effectively to reduce disruptive behavior across many settings and populations (Flower, McKenna, Bunuan, Juething, & Vega, 2014), including from pre-school (e.g., Foley, Dozier, & Lessor, 2019; Wiskow, Matter & Donaldson, 2019) through the high school level (e.g., Groves & Austin, 2019; Embry, 2002). Wiskow et al. also reported that combining the game with verbal prompts, such as, "Remember to raise your hand," was more effective at the pre-school level. The object of the game is for *groups to compete against one another by holding their penalty points below a given limit*. The team or teams scoring below a gradually decreasing specific number, or who have the fewest infractions, win various reinforcers.

The Good Behavior Game has been implemented not only by adults, but also children as young as kindergarten age have been taught to lead the GBG (Donaldson, Matter, & Wiskow, 2018). As the authors emphasize, though, some teachers prefer to implement the game, while others prefer to have a child manage it in the classroom. So, be sure to consider teacher preference when designing the class-wide intervention procedure.

A very successful variation of the Good Behavior Game involved replacing the DRD with a DRA, within an interdependent group contingency, to reduce fourth-graders' disruptive behavior in the library (Fishbein & Wasik, 1981). The children had been noisy, failed to use the library as intended for reading or reference, pushed one another, and playfully shocked each other after rubbing their shoes on the carpeted floor. Together, the librarian and the class developed a set of rules for appropriate conduct in the library:

a. If you talk, talk quietly.
b. Choose a library book or look at library materials during the library period.
c. When walking, be very careful not to shock one another.
d. Treat one another with respect at all times, being careful not to push or fight (p. 91).

The class was divided randomly into two teams. The librarian looked up several times during the period and awarded a team a point only if all its members were following the rules; that is, performing the specified desired alternative behaviors (DRA). To win the game, a team needed to obtain three out of four possible points. The winning team(s) could choose between working on an art project or listening to a story read by the regular classroom teacher during the last ten minutes of the afternoon. Any losing team would continue with its regular classroom work. Both teams usually won the game and presumably all students played the game. Perhaps the more positive thrust of this variation of the Good Behavior Game, plus the greater involvement of the students in establishing the rules, accounted for the "increased student motivation to behave appropriately" (Fishbein & Wasik, 1981, p. 93).

There is some strong evidence to support the fact that the Good Behavior Game actually may have desirable long-term effects (Kellam & Anthony, 1998; Reid, Eddy, Fetrow, & Stoolmiller, 1999). Surprisingly, in 1998, six years after having participated in it, Kellam & Anthony, 1998 found that males who had been exposed to the Good Behavior Game were less likely to initiate smoking, were less aggressive, and were rated by their teachers as better behaved than those in a control group who never were exposed to the game). Similarly, Reid et al. (1999) reported reductions in playground aggression and when the youngsters were post-tested 30 months later they were found significantly less likely to have been arrested.

The Good Behavior Game (GBG) appears to be very robust across different populations. According to Joslyn and Vollmer (2020), when used with students attending alternative schools and diagnosed with EBD who engaged in severe problem behaviors, the GBG resulted in substantial reductions in the problem behaviors despite low treatment integrity.

Galbraith and Normand (2017) evaluated a modified version of the Good Behavior Game (i.e., they used an interdependent group contingency) on the number of steps taken by general education third grade students during recess. They divided a class into two teams, and awarded the team with the highest step counts during recess raffle tickets for a school-wide lottery. Recess periods during which the game was in effect produced more steps than those in which the game was not in effect. Investigators (Rubow, Vollmer, & Josllyn, 2018) also have demonstrated that the Good Behavior Game was effective with fourth- through eighth-grade students in an alternative school with emotional and behavioral disorders. Not only did it reduce their disruptions, but it also appeared to increase their teacher's use of praise relative to reprimands.

As Embry (2002) has pointed out, there have been a number of replications of the Good Behavior Game "across different grade levels, different types of students, different settings, and some with long-term follow-up show strong, consistent impact on impulsive, disruptive behaviors of children and teens as well as reductions in substance use or serious antisocial behaviors" (p. 273). Because of such findings, Embry (2002) has suggested that use of the Good Behavior Game might be considered a "behavioral vaccine." However, the Good Behavior Game is strictly a group-management strategy. Based on the studies cited in this text, we are convinced that *any* program that helps minimize the use of punitive consequences, increases the level of reinforcement, recognizes and harnesses peer support for pro-social behavior, and/or includes positive behavioral interventions as alternatives to punishment, will help prevent or minimize misbehavior.

One precaution to consider relates to some evidence that the positive effects of the Good Behavior Game sometimes may be limited to those circumstances during which it is in effect, for as Donaldson, Wiskow, and Soto, (2015) found, it did not appear to affect rates of disruption during preceding or following activity periods. We encourage those who use the game to interweave it across the day and perhaps to augment it with other procedures directed toward task accomplishment.

Some teachers have expressed concerns about the Good Behavior Games's potential for evoking negative peer interactions toward students who break the rules. However, research studies in both primary and secondary classrooms (Groves & Austin, 2019) have indicated that the good behavior game resulted in an increase in positive, not negative, peer interactions, in addition to reducing disruptive behaviors. But remember, unless combined with DRA, methods that produce a reduction in disruption do not necessarily guarantee that more task-relevant or adaptive behaviors will emerge.

## SUMMARY AND CONCLUSIONS

In this chapter, we have focused on constructive ways to manage behavior. Differential reinforcement of alternative behaviors (DRA) is designed to teach clientele specifically how *to* behave. When constructive alternatives are carefully selected and reinforced, not only does the undesirable behavior rapidly diminish in rate, but the individual also learns a more appropriate set of behaviors.

The DRA procedure reduces unwanted behavior indirectly because it promotes increases in the selected alternative constructive behavior, thereby interfering with the unwanted behavior as it undergoes extinction. If the preferred alternatives are properly strengthened and maintained, the DRA procedure can produce long-lasting results. Because the approach is benign, practitioners can use it with comfort. Applying appropriate reinforcement techniques toward strengthening behaviors totally incompatible with and/or functionally equivalent to the unwanted target, while withholding those reinforcers found to be maintaining the problem behavior (placing the undesirable behavior on extinction) are most promising. Although slower acting than some reductive procedures, DRA has many advantages that make it a worthy choice as a management procedure. Additionally, you can expedite the DRA process by using modeling to prompt the preferred alternative. And perhaps its most compelling advantage is that by paying attention and combining modeling and DRA, you distribute attention and recognition for positive and constructive, not problematic, performances.

Differential reinforcement of the nonoccurrence (zero-occurrence or omission) of a behavior (DRO) has been shown rapidly and effectively to reduce behaviors of concern, provided that you withhold reinforcers every time the undesirable behavior is emitted and, at least initially, you program reinforcement frequently, contingent on the completion of a time interval absent the target behavior.

Although it demands close monitoring, the whole-interval DRO is a particularly powerful reductive procedure. To avoid inadvertently reinforcing other classes of unwanted behaviors, though, we advise you to avoid using DRO to treat individuals apt to display a multitude of challenging behaviors.

Using DRL and DRD to reinforce low and diminishing rates of a behavior is an excellent method for decelerating excessively high-rate behaviors. These methods are easily adapted for group application and can be combined with other procedures rapidly to reduce unwanted behavior.

As with the DRA and modeling procedures, positive reinforcement is integral to each of the reductive methods described in this chapter. However, DRA and modeling also are constructive in that they teach individuals what they *should* be doing, whereas DRD and the various forms of DRO teach how *not* to behave. For this reason, whenever possible, we advise that you combine DRDs and DROs with DRA and modeling. In addition, if you have chosen your methods primarily for the purpose of reducing seriously challenging behaviors, you should add extinction of the maladaptive behavior to the mix, so you do not inadvertently reinforce it.

Due to the adverse side-effects associated with punitive procedures, the positive reductive behavioral interventions presented in this and the previous chapters generally are preferred. Reserve punishment for imminently dangerous or extremely objectionable performance. But even then, for greater effectiveness, try to add positive reductive methods such as appropriate antecedent and differential reinforcement procedures. Also, you can combine most of the positive preventive/reductive methods. In fact, such combinations tend to yield more rapid results, which, in turn, may counteract the need for using any punishment at all. (See Table 28.1 for a comparison of the features of the various differential reinforcement methods discussed in this chapter.)

In these last three chapters we have presented several strategies, all of which stress the value of providing a reinforcing environment. Let us review some of these points:

- Punitive procedures generate adverse reactions.
- Positive antecedents and consequences help prevent and reduce troublesome behaviors because they those are less likely to occur in reinforcing environments, as elaborated here:
  ○ Aggression tends to increase when an individual is deprived of reinforcers (e.g., attention/recognition/rewards) for other behaviors. So remember, a densely enriched environment generally hastens the rate at which a selected behavior diminishes under extinction.
  ○ Research has consistently demonstrated that when extinction is combined with reinforcement of alternative (DRA) or of diminishing behavior (DRD), extinction-induced response bursts, or acts of aggression, are less likely.
  ○ When children with autism are provided with reinforcing environments, the stereotypic and self-abusive behaviors so characteristic of many of these children diminish.
  ○ When the general level of reinforcement is enriched by adding preferred materials and /or activities noncontingently, a wide range of challenging behaviors decrease, particularly those maintained by social and automatic reinforcement.
  ○ When specific feedback is made more reinforcing (e.g., by implementing a high ratio of positive to corrective comments, as described in Chapter 24), children's behaviors of concern decrease substantially, while staff satisfaction increases.
  ○ Preschoolers have been found to increase their rates of spontaneously initiating prosocial behaviors during high rates as opposed to low rates of noncontingent reinforcement.
  ○ Dense or high rates of reinforcement (contingent and noncontingent) help to maintain prosocial and prevent challenging behavior.
  ○ High rates of reinforcement decrease people's need to engage in inappropriate behaviors to:
    · Attain attention because they now receive attention for many appropriate behaviors.
    · Escape or avoid aversive stimuli because those are removed or replaced with reinforcers.
    · Gain access to activities or objects because many are readily available.

For all these reasons, selecting positive strategies in preference to punishment permits your behavior-management methods to be more constructive and usable in a broad array of situations. Your clientele will be the greatest beneficiaries, while you will feel better about yourself and your work.

TABLE 28.1  A Comparison of Reinforcement-Based Reductive Procedures

| Procedure | Illustrative Targeted Behavior | | |
|---|---|---|---|
| | **Criticizing**<br>*Positive reinforcers are dispensed:* | **Leaving the Work Station**<br>*Positive reinforcers are dispensed:* | **Eating Junk Food**<br>*Positive reinforcers are dispensed:* |
| DRA | for complimenting someone | for remaining at work station | for eating healthy foods |
| DRL (spaced-responding DRL) | following criticism after an interval containing no criticisms | following departing from the work station after an interval of not leaving | for eating junk food after an interval of not eating junk food |
| DRD (full-session DRL) | when intervals contain fewer critical statements than previously | following intervals containing lower rates of leaving the work station than previously | at the end of interval containing less than previous amount of junk food eaten |
| Whole-interval DRO | following intervals without criticizing | following intervals of not leaving the work station | following intervals of not eating junk food |
| Momentary DRO | for not criticizing at the moment the person is observed | for not being away from the work station at the moment the person is observed | for not eating junk food at the moment the person is observed |
| NCR | every 5 minutes whether criticizing or not | every 5 minutes regardless of whether at work station or not | every 5 minutes regardless of whatever food has been consumed |

*Chapter 29*

# Reducing Behavior with Negative Punishment: Response Cost and Timeout

## Goals

1. Discuss why studying punishment is important and when one might consider using it.
2. Define and differentiate between each of the following:
   a. *punishment procedures* and *reinforcement procedures*
   b. *reinforcers* and *punishers*
   c. *negative reinforcement* and *negative punishment*
3. Define, recognize, and give original illustrations of each of the following terms:
   a. *response cost* and *bonus response cost*
   b. *timeout*, differentiating from *response cost* and *extinction*
   c. *inclusion timeout* (provide examples of each of the four applications)
   d. *exclusion timeout*, including *facial screening*
   e. *seclusion timeout*, including *required relaxation*, and discuss the reasons why the use of seclusion timeout is controversial
   f. *restrained timeout*
4. Define, differentiate between, and illustrate *planned ignoring* and *extinction*.
5. List and discuss the advantages of *response cost* and *timeout*.
6. List and discuss the disadvantages of *response cost* and *timeout*.
7. List the three ethical guidelines endorsed by the Behavior Analyst Certification Board® (BACB) regarding the use of aversives and discuss how each applies to response cost and timeout.
8. List safeguards for minimizing adverse reactions to seclusion timeout.
9. Tell how to use response cost and timeout effectively.

10. Discuss the importance of learning history and how it can influence the effectiveness of a selected response cost or timeout program. Also, discuss the adverse effects of using heavy fines and long timeout periods.
11. Define, illustrate, and explain the purpose of including a provision for *contingent delay* in a timeout program and why it should be used with caution.
12. Describe specific situations in which (a) response cost and (b) timeout would and would not be the behavioral procedure of choice; justify your position

Unplanned non-socially mediated punishment happens frequently to virtually all human beings as we merely make our way through the day. Turning the wrong knob in the shower, touching a hot stove, taking an incorrect golf club swing are all examples of behavior that is punished.... Punishment is a fact of nature; it just happens. (Vollmer, 2002, p. 470)

Punishment is a natural and ongoing part of life, and we need to better understand the role of punishment if we are to be successful in our efforts to engineer environments in which children and adults with deviant behavior are successful. (Horner, 2002, p. 465)

Although the use of punishment often raises ethical issues, such procedures may be needed when the reinforcers that maintain behavior cannot be identified or controlled, or when competing reinforcers cannot be found. (Lerman, Iwata, Shore, & DeLeon, 1997, p. 187)

Understanding of punishment processes is needed to develop a systematic, effective technology of behavior change. (Lerman & Vorndran, 2002, p. 456)

Understanding punishment can help us figure out why a person might act aggressively or behave unacceptably in some other way. Also, in those rare cases in which a punitive procedure is deemed necessary, we need to make the best procedural choice and use it appropriately and effectively.

In Chapters 26 through 28 we pointed out that when behavioral procedures promote acceptable alternatives to problematic behaviors, resorting to punitive methods often becomes unnecessary. Certainly, from having read the earlier chapters, you are familiar with an array of alternative, non-punitive interventions consonant with Lovaas' and Favell's (1987) position:

> if a program cannot conduct alternative interventions in a high quality fashion, then it should not employ aversive procedures. It is perhaps less obvious, that if a program cannot insure the necessary degree of quality in the use of the alternative treatments, then the facility or agency should not purport or attempt to treat severe problem behavior at all. (p. 320)

We concur with this perspective and urge you to avoid using punitive procedures except when you can neither identify nor control the reinforcers maintaining *serious problem behavior*, nor find competing reinforcers. However, in those rare cases in which you have unsuccessfully given alternative positive reinforcement-based interventions a fair try or have found them inappropriate, you might consider using one of the *negative* (as in "take away or subtract reinforcers") *punishment* procedures. In this chapter, we define *punishment* in general, and *negative punishment* in particular. Then we discuss two negative punishment procedures: *response cost* and *timeout*.

## NEGATIVE PUNISHMENT DEFINED

Recall that reinforcement procedures consist of applying reinforcers contingently to increase or maintain behavior. **Punishment procedures** produce the reverse outcome: *stimuli are applied or withdrawn contingently to decrease behavior*. Also recall that negative reinforcement involves removing an aversive stimulus (negative reinforcer) as a consequence of a response, to strengthen that response. Similarly, **negative punishment** entails *removing or reducing positive reinforcers as a consequence of a response, to reduce the rate of that response*. (We remind you that the descriptor "negative" merely means the removal or subtraction of a stimulus and is not intended to imply that the procedure is harmful or destructive.) Review Table 29.1 for a simple operational description of procedural terms and their effects.

*Response cost* and *timeout* are two major, yet distinctly different, classes of negative punishment. To choose and use each effectively and responsibly, behavior analysts and program implementers need to be informed of the procedures' particular features. As we review and discuss punitive methods, realize that basic (laboratory) research on punishment of all types has been declining rapidly, probably due to ethical concerns. This, in turn, has resulted in a paucity of *new* knowledge on the topic (see Catania, 2008; Lerman & Vorndran, 2002).

## RESPONSE COST

Response cost is commonly applied in homes, schools, institutions, sports, and sometimes even in business and commercial organizations (see Figure

29.1). Because response cost is not constructive and tends to set the occasion for many of the negative side effects of other aversive procedures, like positive punishment and timeout, its application raises ethical and legal concerns. Consequently, before using response cost, program planners need to review governmental policies and laws, conduct institutional reviews, and negotiate contracts with the concerned parties or their surrogates. Applying the method to reduce acts harmful to individuals or society at large should not be too difficult to justify.

### Response Cost Defined

First used by Weiner (1962), the term **response cost ($S^{rc}$)** refers to *the removal or withdrawal of some quantities of reinforcers contingent on a response*. Technically, to merit the label *response cost*, the procedure must function to reduce the rate of the response on which it is contingent. Behavior change-agents are applying response cost when they implement a program calling for withdrawing a specific number of reinforcers (tokens, points or stickers, possibly even money) as a consequence of unwanted behavior. It is important to note that failing to earn a reinforcer is not equivalent to the removal of a reinforcer contingent on a response, as in response cost.

Response cost differs from positive punishment (see Chapter 31) in that *positive punishment* involves *presenting* an aversive stimulus contingent

**TABLE 29.1   Reductive Procedures**

| Term | Contingent Operation (as a consequence of a given response) | Indended Outcome |
|---|---|---|
| *Positive* reinforcement | *Add* (+) favorable stimulus | *Increase* (+) behavior |
| *Negative* reinforcement | *Remove* (-) aversive stimulus | *Increase* (+) behavior |
| Extinction | *Withhold* favorable stimulus | *Decrease* (-) behavior |
| *Positive* punishment | *Add* (+) aversive stimulus | *Decrease* (-) behavior |
| *Negative* punishment: Response cost | *Remove* (-) given amount of favored stimulus | *Decrease* (-) behavior |
| *Negative* punishment: Timeout | *Remove* (-) access to favorable consequences for a given time period | *Decrease* (-) behavior |

> Speeding $\rightarrow$ $250 fine
> Clipping $\rightarrow$ 20-yard penalty
> "Copying from your neighbor? $\rightarrow$ Three points off your grade!"
> "Being rude? $\rightarrow$ You lose a dollar from your canteen fund."
> Breakage $\rightarrow$ "We're deducting 10 dollars from your paycheck."

**Figure 29.1** Everyday applications of response cost ($S^{rc}$)

on a response (e.g., a reprimand), thereby reducing the rate of the response. Response cost involves *withdrawing* some quantity of reinforcing stimuli, resulting in reduced rates of the response. Fining a youth ten points from his point-saving system for fighting reduces the rate of fighting.

Response cost may involve tangible as well as symbolic reinforcers. A parent may deduct a dollar from the child's allowance contingent on some misbehavior such as visiting a friend without permission instead of coming right home after school. The section manager may reduce the amount size of or cancel the yearly bonus of an employee who ignores rules for safety or civility. When used systematically in educational and service settings—applied settings—response cost usually is limited to the withdrawal of symbolic or other learned reinforcers such as grades, points, or tokens.

To remove specified amounts of a reinforcer, the individual must have "some level of positive reinforcement...available in order to provide the opportunity for...withdrawing that reinforcement" (Azrin & Holz, 1966, p. 392). Little would be accomplished by imposing a fine on someone without any money.

## Illustrations of Response Cost Programs

In an early classroom token economy program (Sulzer et al., 1971), point penalties were imposed for certain severe disruptive behaviors such as throwing objects.[1] Similarly, Rapport et al. (1982) indicated that response cost in the form of loss of free time for not working on assignments did a better job of increasing two boys' rates of remaining on-task and improving their academic performance than did Ritalin®.

Switzer, Deal, and Bailey (1977) imposed a response cost contingency to reduce stealing in three second-grade classrooms. They compared the effects of an anti-stealing lecture alone with those of an interdependent group[2] response cost program that combined (1) loss of free time for the entire class if items were not returned, (2) access to regular free time if stolen items were returned, and (3) extra free time for no thefts. The lecture was ineffective, while the group response cost contingency effectively reduced stealing.

Kahng, Tarbox, and Wilke (2001) used response cost to assist a five-year-old boy who had been diagnosed with mild to moderate intellectual disability to diminish his refusal of food at home. If the child did not accept a bite or engaged in problematic behavior (e.g., spitting the food out, gagging, vomiting, batting the spoon away, kicking, or hitting), they blocked access to customarily available highly-preferred tangible items such as books and audiotapes. "Treatment resulted in an increase in food acceptance to 100 percent of bite offers and near-zero rates of problem behavior" (p. 93).

An 11-year-old boy with Down syndrome and autism displayed vocal stereotypy, which occurred

---

[1] Now a grandmother, the same author used a token/point system when her granddaughters visited to attend summer day camp. The girls earned tokens by adhering to a mutually-determined daily schedule: arising on time, making the bed, eating breakfast, washing up, brushing teeth, and so on. Points could be traded in for books, prizes, trips, and treats. Tantrums resulted in a loss of points. (Tantrums were so costly that even when tempted, the children elected not to waste their points on such a frivolity.)

[2] Refer back to Chapter 12 for a review of group contingencies.

as "loud, repetitive, non-contextual verbalizations (e.g., saying "banana" when this was not contextually appropriate) and repetitive, loud, unintelligible vocalizations (e.g., "ahhh")" (Athens, Vollmer, & Sloman, 2008, p. 291). Response cost paired with contingent demands were used to reduce that troublesome behavior. If the stereotypy occurred following a demand, a second demand was delivered (e.g., "What color is this?"). If it occurred after the second demand was delivered, response cost was implemented, which consisted of the boy losing access to the toy he was playing with for ten seconds (other toys were available in the room and were not removed). After the ten seconds, the toy was returned to him. The stereotypy reduced significantly. Shillingsburg, Lomas, and Bradley (2012) also addressed vocal stereotypy that was maintained by automatic reinforcement by a 12-year-old boy with autism. The youth could earn a token based on a varying DRO schedule. The tokens were exchangeable for time on the computer. However, if he engaged in vocal stereotypy during the DRO, he lost a token. If he engaged in vocal stereotypy while on the computer, the response cost was loss of the computer. Vocal stereotypy was reduced to near zero levels in the classroom.

To reduce public smoking among youth, Jason et al. (2005) also used a response cost contingency. The youth in town "A" were given a warning in which they were told that if they were observed possessing tobacco again they would be fined and their tobacco confiscated. In town "B," the youth were penalized with a ticket "that could be paid for by sending a fee to the city clerk (in addition a note was sent home to their parents about the tobacco being confiscated and the ticket being issued) (p. 303). In both towns, "the rates of visible youth tobacco use decreased in the locations of the observations" (p. 303).

Falcomata, Roane, Hovanetz, and Kettering (2004) compared the reductive effects of applying noncontingent reinforcement (NCR) with and without response cost as a consequence of inappropriate vocalizations by an 18-year-old man with autism. The vocalizations previously had been maintained by automatic reinforcement. They found that the combination of NCR and response cost was much more effective than the NCR alone.

## A Variation of Response Cost: Bonus Response Cost

A **bonus response cost** system may enable contingency managers to avoid the aggressive reactions often found to accompany being subjected to a fine. *Rather than the contingency manager taking away points or tokens that clients have earned, clients are given a pool of bonus reinforcers from which a specific amount is subtracted, contingent on each occurrence of a serious problem behavior.* For example, Ms. Charming awards tokens to her workshop clients who perform their job tasks correctly. Also, she holds ten bonus tokens in reserve for them at the start of each day. When a client misbehaves, she subtracts bonus tokens from the reserve. If she does not need to impose any penalties, she awards the client all ten bonus tokens at the end of the day.

Reynolds and Kelley (1997) used a bonus response cost package, in this case for managing the aggressive behavior of five preschoolers. Each child was given five smiley faces at the beginning of a 40-minute observation period. A smiley face was removed immediately following a child's aggressive act (e.g., hitting, kicking, taking a toy from another child, destroying class materials, throwing toys, calling another child a name or excluding him/her from an activity). If the child retained one or more smiley faces at the end of the observation period, he was allowed to choose from a list of rewards generated by the teacher and child (e.g., access to a favorite toy, crayon, or sticker, becoming "teacher's helper," playing in a preferred center, special snack). "The response cost treatment package substantially decreased aggressive behavior and was a highly acceptable classroom treatment to teachers and parents" (p. 216). The teachers also reported an increase in the children's positive social interactions while the treatment was in effect. For instance, Jacob's teacher reported that because he was less aggressive, his classmates liked him more and were more eager to play with him.

Bonus response cost systems are worth trying when you worry that applying a typical response cost procedure might produce a violent reaction. Nevertheless, avoid depending on bonus response cost alone. As with any reductive procedure, augment it with a procedure designed to increase the rate of an acceptable replacement behavior, such as DRA, because the delay of reinforcement imposed by even this modified system is much too long for many clients to tolerate.

## TIMEOUT FROM REINFORCEMENT

Seymour, Jacqueline, Esmerelda, and Jose form the "Hard-Core Four." Despite their new teacher, Mr. F. R. Vincent's extensive collection of fine lesson plans and instructional materials, he is rapidly becoming discouraged. Although the other students staunchly attempt to complete their assignments, the Hard-Core Four continually interfere. Egged on by one another, they steal the other students' pencils, hide their work, tell inappropriate jokes, clown around, and gang up on peers who have "ratted" to the teacher during recess. In general, these four are ruining the learning atmosphere. Well aware of the long histories of punishment shared by these four students, Mr. Vincent is reluctant to repeat that practice. Yet, he finally realizes that if the other students are to learn, he will have to use some reductive procedures. Besides response cost, he is considering using *timeout from reinforcement*. Like response cost and positive punishment procedures, timeout can effectively reduce unwanted behavior and may be an appropriate choice for such a group.

### Timeout Defined and Differentiated from Extinction and Response Cost

*Timeout* was first discussed in the applied literature a half a century ago (Baer, 1961). Since then, it has been incorporated into countless behavior-management plans to address a wide range of maladaptive behaviors. **Timeout** is *a procedure in which access to varied reinforcers is barred for a specific time, contingent upon a response.*[3] As with response cost, timeout involves subtracting or taking away reinforcement opportunities, so we refer to it as a *negative punishment procedure*. Also, similar to response cost, both procedures involve the contingent withdrawal of reinforcement. The two differ in that timeout does not stipulate that specific amounts of reinforcers be removed; instead, access to an array of usually accessible reinforcers is withdrawn for a specified period of time contingent on a particular unwanted response. Timeout incorporates extinction as one of its components. However, with extinction alone, only the stimuli identified as reinforcers for the behavior of concern are withheld, while reinforcement continues in typical fashion as a consequence of *all but* that behavior. When Clarissa stops coming to the phone when her suitor calls, she is using extinction to reduce his calling. (The suitor's telephoning Clarissa leads to neither reinforcement nor to any change in the environment for calling.) If when Tracy whines for a cookie she no longer receives it, extinction is being used. Crying and demanding produce no reinforcement or change in the environment—no cookies are delivered. (See Figure 29.2.)

With *timeout*, however, access to the full range of ordinarily available reinforcers is denied for a time period. Therefore, timeout is more aversive than extinction, in that with extinction the individual's other responses remain eligible for reinforcement. During timeout, however, social reinforcement is eliminated for an interval of time. The opportunity to gain socially mediated or material reinforcement is minimized[4]: *Either the individual is removed from the reinforcing environment* (as in isolation, or the placement in a nonreinforcing location) *or the reinforcers or reinforcing environment is removed from the individual for some stipulated duration.* Timeout from token-earning is one example (Winkler, 1971).

Removing Tracy from the kitchen for a specific time contingent on crying for and demanding cookies illustrates timeout. The opportunity to receive cookies or almost any other reinforcer is unavailable for five minutes. (Alternatively, Tracy's mother might have contingently removed herself and the

---

[3]This definition is a variation of one offered by Reese (1966) combined with Ferster and Skinner's (1957) laboratory-derived definition.

[4]We say "minimized" and not "eliminated" because not every single source of reinforcement is necessarily removed during timeout periods.

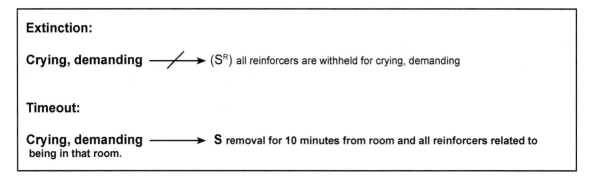

**Figure 29.2** Examples characterizing the distinction between extinction and timeout

box of cookies from the kitchen for a few minutes, leaving the child in the now non-reinforcing environment.) We would diagram timeout to indicate that crying or demanding results in the contingent removal of access to the reinforcing environment for ten minutes. (See Figure 29.2.)

## Variations of Timeout

Timeout can be engineered in various ways. Ryan, Peterson, and Rozalski (2007) have categorized the method into four categories: (1) inclusion, (2) exclusion, (3) seclusion, and (4) restrained timeout, all of which have ethical implications.

### *Inclusion Timeout*

**Inclusion timeout** is the least intrusive/aversive and the most commonly used form of timeout (Ryan et al., 2007). *The individual may be moved to an area where he or she can hear and see what is happening (or may even stay put), but for a brief period of time (e.g., three to five minutes) gains no response from others nor is allowed to participate.* Examples of this procedure include: (a) withdrawal of materials, (b) planned ignoring, (c) contingent observation, and (d) the timeout ribbon.

**Withdrawal of materials.** This variation of timeout *involves removing reinforcing materials, such as toys, from an individual contingent upon the infraction.* Though not extensively researched, the method has been used successfully to reduce noncompliance by students with cognitive delays (Burchard & Barerra, 1972; Gresham, 1979). It also was used by Ward et al. (2017) to reduce noncompliance, related behavioral excesses, as well as low effort, all maintained at least in part by attention. By removing the materials and not allowing four- to six-year-old students to return to work until readiness was demonstrated (e.g., calmed and oriented toward teacher, and when asked, informed teacher that s/he was ready to work again), compliance with non-preferred activities increased. They also maintained that this procedure was less likely to produce extinction bursts and aggression than escape extinction. Of course, if the function of the student's behavior was primarily escape, not attention, this strategy would result in negative reinforcement and you would not use it.

**Planned ignoring.** This variation of inclusion-timeout *involves withholding any attention, physical contact, and/or verbal interactions with the individual for a brief fixed duration[5] contingent upon the occurrence of the unwanted behavior.* The therapist or contingency manager working individually with the client might turn away from and not interact with the client for three minutes. Or the therapist might combine planned ignoring with withdrawing materials by removing the materials from the desk and turning his or her back on the client for a set number

---

[5]In that the time is brief, planned ignoring is unlike the prolonged pretense that the person does not exist, as practiced in some highly-aversive school and military training programs.

of minutes. This procedure can be applied quickly and conveniently, but its broad-ranging effectiveness remains to be conclusively demonstrated (Nelson & Rutherford, 1983; Ryan et al., 2007). Further, *planned ignoring is not extinction in that during planned ignoring, reinforcement is not provided to other behaviors, as with extinction.*

A related practice is *timeout from speaking.* Onslow, Packman, Stocker, Doorn, and Siegel (1997) were able successfully to reduce stuttering in school-age children by implementing a timeout from speaking. Whenever the youngster stuttered, s/he was required to stop talking for five seconds. Two of three children showed clear reductions in stuttering as a result of this timeout procedure.

**Contingent observation.** Contingent observation (Porterfield, Herbert-Jackson & Risley, 1976) is another relatively benign form of timeout. Just as it is used in competitive sports like ice hockey, upon a rule violation, *the client is relocated to an area in which s/he can observe what is going on but not participate in the activities.* For example, a child who misbehaves while working in a group is relocated a few feet away from the table. She can see what is happening but not participate in the (presumably) reinforcing activities. Another instance would be Kevin's dad ordering the boy to sit on a bench for ten minutes instead of swimming, after his son pushed his younger sister, Debbie, into the pool.

Murphy, Hutchinson, and Bailey (1983) used contingent observation as a general management procedure to control aggression on the playground. In that study, offenders committing aggressive acts during organized games were treated with a two-minute timeout on the bench. This version of timeout also has been found to be as effective as the more restrictive exclusion timeout in reducing undesirable behaviors  by children with emotional and behavioral disturbances (Gallagher, Mittelstadt, & Slater, 1988; Mace & Heller, 1990). When, occasionally, clients have failed to remain in their penalty area or timeout chair, the offender has been required to remain in another room for a minute or two, as a consequence. Roberts (1988) found this method to be just as effective as a parental spank with defiant preschool children.

**Timeout ribbon.** Another relatively benign form of timeout involves separating the clients from the reinforcing environment. Foxx and Shapiro (1978) accomplished this form of timeout by providing a ribbon to be worn like a necktie (sometimes referred to as the "timeout ribbon") to each of their students with severe educational handicaps. If a child engaged in one of any specifically designated set of misbehaviors, the tie (or ribbon) was removed for three minutes, or longer if necessary, until that misbehavior stopped. Students wearing ties received treats and praise every few minutes. (Note the ribbon, which becomes a secondary reinforcer, was *removed*, not added, contingent on the misbehavior. If the child had been required to wear the ribbon contingent on the misbehavior and decrease in the misbehavior resulted, the procedure would have been labeled a *positive* punishment procedure.) The timeout ribbon also was used successfully with a noncompliant four-year-old (Yeager & McLaughlin, 1995). Compliance increased even further when very precise requests were made. Further, in both community and school settings, use of the procedure resulted in two middle-school students with moderate cognitive delays (Alberto, Heflin, & Andrews, 2002), resulting in reducing and maintaining their disruptions at zero during a two-week follow-up. Other examples of the successful use of the timeout ribbon procedure in elementary general education (Fee, Matson & Manikam, 1990) and special education (Salend & Gordon, 1987; Salend & Maragulla, 1983) classrooms include reducing talking out of turn and students' leaving their seats without permission.

## *Exclusionary Timeout*

 **Exclusionary timeout** *involves relocating the individual from a reinforcing to a non-reinforcing environment or separating the reinforcing environment from the individual.* Due to ethical considerations, under the exclusionary timeout practice, the person is not to be physically prevented from leaving the timeout area. Nor is the door to be locked, nor is the individual blocked from leaving. (National Alliance for the Mentally Ill, 2001; Ryan, Sanders, Katsiyannis, & Yell, 2007.) This variant of timeout is more restrictive than inclusionary timeout in that *it denies the individual the opportunity to observe and/or hear what is occurring in the original setting.* Suppose Esmerelda throws a book at another student; Mr. Vincent directs her to stand behind a room divider for two minutes. An analogous teacher practice is requiring the student to sit outside in the hallway, the school office, or in another classroom. Ramon screams for a cookie, so his mother takes the cookie jar and leaves Ramon alone in the dining room. Maria is rude to her mother, so she is sent to sit in the bathroom for five minutes.

By combining reinforcement of alternative behaviors with exclusionary timeout, Kee, Hill, and Weist (1999) systematically analyzed a similar situation. Whenever a ten-year-old girl with profound intellectual disability, Anne, hit or spit, she was removed to a nearby school bathroom for three minutes. Then, before being allowed to return to the classroom she needed to remain quiet for 30 seconds. Anne's aggressive behaviors remained near zero throughout the remainder of the school year. Similarly, Fabiano et al. (2004) found using five-minute timeouts to be an effective means of reducing aggression, property destruction, and chronic noncompliance in recreational and classroom settings, regardless of the child's age or parental reports of oppositional or conduct problems at home. Further, when compared to no-timeout conditions, the procedure appeared to have no negative effects on staff-child interactions. You probably can provide further illustrations of both informal and planned timeout from your own experience, because teachers and parents commonly use exclusionary timeout as a disciplinary technique.

**Facial screening.** Facial screening is a variant of exclusionary timeout. It has been successfully used with fairly severely delayed clients (Foxx & Garito, 2007), for whom watching what was going on around them served as a reinforcing experience. **Facial screening** *involves the contingent application of a face cover* (e.g., a terry-cloth bib, Horton, 1987), a blindfold (Murphy, Ruprecht, & Nunes, 1979), or the contingency manager's hands (McGonigle, Duncan, Cordisco, & Barrett, 1982). To be effective, *the visual input must be contingently blocked for about five to 15 seconds* (Demetral & Lutzker, 1980; Gross, Farrar, & Liner, 1982; Horton, 1987) *following each occurrence of the unwanted behavior.* As with all other reductive procedures, to optimize effectiveness, facial screening should also be combined with a differential reinforcement strategy, such as DRA and/or DRO (Gross et al., 1982; Rapp et al., 2000). Client attempts to remove the facial screen have been handled successfully with a stern "No," then physically guiding the client's hands down to his or her side (Gross et al., 1982).

Facial screening has proven to be very successful with a variety of self-injurious behaviors, including, among others: slapping, hitting, or scratching the head or face (Demetral & Lutzker, 1980; Winston, Singh, & Dawson, 1984; Zegiob, Alford, & House, 1978), chronic hand- or thumb-biting (Demetral & Lutzker, 1980; Singh, 1980), and trichotillomania (chronic hair-pulling that results in spotty baldness; Gross et al., 1982; Rapp et al., 2000); stereotypy, such as hand-clapping (Zegiob, Jenkins, Becker, & Bristow, 1976), tongue-clicking, repetitive fabric-pulling, visual fixation on finger movements (McGonigle et al., 1982), pica (Bogart, Piersel, & Gross, 1995), and excessive screaming (Singh, Winton, & Dawson, 1982). Facial screening also was found to be more effective than water-mist spray and forced arm exercise with two 17-year-old girls with profound intellectual disabilities for self-injurious finger-licking and excessive ear-rubbing (Singh, Watson, & Winton, 1986).

Facial screening also has been used with rumination (DeRosa, Roane, Bishop, & Silkowski, 2016). (Rumination is relatively common among individuals with intellectual disabilities. It involves repeated regurgitation of previously ingested food, which then can be re-chewed, re-swallowed, or spit out. Health risks include weight loss, malnutrition, tooth decay, esophageal damage and death.) DeRosa et al. reported that neither NCR nor facial screening substantially reduced rumination for an 18-year-old man with autism, but the combination of the two procedures eliminated the behavior.

Seeing the screening procedure in operation may upset unprepared visitors, though, and colleagues tell us that it is not universally effective.

Also, in some jurisdictions, even though it is only mildly aversive, its use may be illegal. For example, in the California public schools (Title 5, EC Section 3052[l]) applying any procedure that deprives a student of one or more of his senses is illegal. So be certain to check the legal regulations in your locality before using facial screening.

## Seclusion Timeout

Though similar to exclusionary timeout, **seclusion timeout** *involves removing the individual from the environment and, for a brief period of time, placing him or her alone in a room or other environment designated for this purpose; also, if necessary, preventing him or her from leaving (i.e., locking or blocking the door) until the end of the timeout period* (Busch & Shore, 2000; Ryan et al., 2007). This is obviously one of the most restrictive forms of timeout. It removes the individual from the reinforcing environment, including peers, and others. It is mainly used to contain violent behavior and/or to protect either the individual or others (Busch & Shore, 2000). Seclusion timeout should not be used for minor misbehaviors.

The use of seclusion timeout has been steeped in controversy: "Advocates cite the necessity and efficacy of these procedures as interventions for dangerous behaviors, while opponents question their effectiveness and focus on their potential for misuse" (French & Wojcicki, 2018, p. 35). There seems to be a consensus, however, toward minimizing its use. As pointed out by the Association for Behavior Analysis' International (ABAI) task force (March, 2010) and by the United States Department of Education (2012), seclusion should be avoided whenever possible and should not be used except in situations where a person's behavior poses imminent danger or serious physical harm to self or others. However, Marx and Baker (2017) observed that states vary in how closely their practices adhere to such guiding principles. Also, when using seclusion or restraint to address such dangerous behavior, the interventions should address the behavior's function and its effects carefully monitored. Further, the task force pointed out that its use should be continued only if it has been demonstrated to be safe and effective, and should be reduced and eliminated as soon as feasible. In addition, be aware that, like facial screening, some states prohibit its use in particular settings. In fact, as pointed out by Ryan et al. (2007), "it has been the use of seclusionary timeout procedures which has been most often the focus of controversy" (p. 219). Numerous lawsuits have been brought against school districts claiming that the way seclusionary timeout was implemented violated student rights. "In addition, advocacy organizations have lobbied for the elimination of seclusionary timeout in all child caring agencies including schools" (Ryan et al., 2007, p. 215).

Several factors underlie the controversy. A key one is that little research exists on the effectiveness of seclusion timeout and the few studies that do exist were conducted over a quarter century ago. Those studies also present us with contradictory findings concerning timeout's effectiveness (Ryan et al., 2007). Additionally, the passage of the *No Child Left Behind Act* (NCLB) of 2001 also has stimulated concerns regarding its use, since NCLB implies that only evidence-based interventions should be used.

A second basis for concern is that seclusion timeout has often been applied inappropriately. As pointed out by Ryan et al. (2007, p. 219):

> Some students were left in timeout for extended periods of time either because they were "forgotten" or because of conscious decisions by staff. Over the years there have also been numerous instances of students committing suicide, or suffering severe injuries or death while in "unsafe" exclusionary or seclusionary timeout settings. (AACAP, 2002; Maden, 1999)

Another reason for the controversy is that seclusion timeout sometimes has been confused with traditional seclusion or solitary confinement. As Budd and Baer (1976) pointed out some time ago:

> By contrast, traditional seclusion or solitary confinement procedures are usually employed on an unsystematic basis and, when used contingently, they are probably used for only

extreme examples of the behavior. They are typically lengthy procedures, lasting hours or even several days, and with little or no monitoring of their effectiveness in modifying the undesirable behavior. Because of these important differences between the correct use of timeout and use of other seclusion practices, timeout would seem to be a humane and acceptable treatment procedure. (p. 215)

Similarly, Connolly Moore, and Adamy (2019) report that seclusion, resulting in due process hearings, is often avoidable but used due to ineffective special education practices, loose legal boundaries, and sometimes "expert" recommendations.

If you are considering using timeout, especially of the seclusionary type, we recommend that you familiarize yourself with and adhere to legal restrictions and professional ethical codes. A number of states have policies, varying in comprehensiveness, regarding the use of seclusion timeout procedures (Ryan et al., 2007). For example, one may not use locked seclusion in California, unless it is in a facility otherwise licensed or permitted by the state law to use a locked room (Title 5, EC Section 3052[l]). Other states, such as Oklahoma, have considered abolishing its use. For example, the Oklahoma Disability Law Center, Inc., *a system of protection & advocacy* (2016) has taken the position that schools and the Oklahoma State Department of Education must establish as a top priority the reduction and eventual elimination of restraint and seclusion. Also, be prepared to address the concerns that various people may have and implement safeguards, such as those described later, before implementing timeout. In addition, make every effort to structure environments so that using exclusion timeout is unnecessary.

Just as the other forms of timeout have their variations, so does seclusionary timeout:

**Required relaxation** is a version of seclusion timeout that *requires the individual lie down*, usually on a bed. It has been successfully used to reduce adult men's rates of severe violence and/or destructiveness (Webster & Azrin, 1973). The purpose is to help the person terminate the problem by relaxing and regaining control. For those with histories of extreme violence, rooms without furniture or breakable windows have been used. Such isolation areas are best reserved for those who are dangerously out of control (see "Legal Sanctions," discussed below in this chapter). As mentioned, evidence of the effectiveness of seclusion timeout is mixed (Webster, 1976; Smith, 1981), with possible reasons for such results discussed below.

**Restrained timeout**, a variation of seclusion timeout, often is referred to as either (a) *movement suppression* or (b) *therapeutic holding/restraining* (Ryan & Peterson, 2004). (Here the distinction between negative and positive punishment becomes less clear in that the act of holding and/or restraining to achieve non-reinforcing or timeout conditions may function as positive punishment.) Physically restraining or therapeutic holding is the more severe of the two variations, and are often combined to reduce seriously dangerous behaviors, such as ingesting non-edible objects like rocks, poking one's eyes, or hitting one's head against the wall. These behaviors were rapidly suppressed by having the person remain totally immobile in a corner for a few minutes (Rolider & Van Houten, 1985). If the individual did not remain motionless for the brief timeout period (e.g., three minutes) he or she was told: "Don't move," or "Don't talk" in a very firm voice and physically guided and held into position as necessary. Restrained timeout also has been used to reduce aggressive behaviors among youngsters with cognitive delays (Luiselli, Suskin, & Slocumb, 1984), and aggressive and self-injurious behaviors among youngsters with emotional and/or behavioral disorders (Noll & Simpson, 1979; Rolider & Van Houten, 1985a).

A mother was taught to use movement-suppression timeout with her seven-year-old son by requiring him to sit on his hands when he violently waved and flapped them, and to use DRO for non-flapping (Hanley, Perelman, & Homan, 1979). (This movement-suppression method resembles the "freeze" technique that Allison & Ayllon [1980] used successfully to coach football, tennis, and gymnastics skills. In commenting on this freeze technique, which required instant immobility to permit their errors to be analyzed, trainees said, "It was uncomfortable in the 'frozen' position, but it helped me learn a lot" [p. 313].)

Be very cautious, though, if a decision has been made to use physical restraint. Besides using it only in situations that pose imminent danger of serious physical harm to self or others, the U. S. Department of Education (2012) points out that "Schools should never use mechanical restraints to restrict a child's freedom of movement" (p 2). In addition, federal law (ESSA —*Every Student Succeeds Act*, Dec., 2015) stipulates that each state in the U.S. must develop a plan as to how they are going to reduce restraint and seclusion in their schools.

## ADVANTAGES AND DISADVANTAGES OF RESPONSE COST AND TIMEOUT

When beset by serious behavioral challenges, we hope to terminate them as quickly as possible. Response cost and timeout may fulfill that purpose. The methods have other advantages as well.

### Strong and Rapid Behavioral Reduction

Both response cost and timeout generally reduce behavior effectively when applied appropriately; that is, according to guidelines for ethically sound and effective application. According to Campbell (2003), behavior analytic methods have been found to reduce problematic behaviors among the developmentally disabled, in general, particularly when based on functional analyses. This finding re-emphasizes the general success of these methods when they are applied according to the guidelines suggested by behavior analytic research. From a historical perspective, after Weiner (1964b, 1969) discovered that *response cost* tended to reduce the response rates of many of their subjects' fairly rapidly, response cost has been found subsequently to suppress problematic behaviors quickly in applied settings: violence by psychiatric patients (Winkler, 1970), aggression and disruptions in the classroom (Forman, 1980; Reynolds & Kelley, 1997; Sulzer et al., 1971), aggressive statements and tardiness among pre-delinquent boys (Phillips, 1968; Phillips, Phillips, Fixsen, & Wolf, 1971), plus stealing (Switzer, Deal, & Bailey, 1971), off-task and rule violation in classrooms (Iwata & Bailey, 1974; Rapport et al., 1982), food refusal (Kahng et al., 2001), youth's smoking in public (Jason et al., 2005), inappropriate vocalizations (Falcomata et al., 2004), excessive local directory-assistance phone calls (McSweeny, 1978), fingernail-biting (Long, Miltenberger, Ellingson, & Orr, 1999), time off-task (even more effectively than Ritalin® for youngsters with ADHD, Rapport et al., 1982), and mine accidents (Fox et al., 1987).

Timeout has been used effectively to reduce: complaints of pain (Miller & Kratochwill, 1979), aggression (Fabiano et al., 2004; Olson & Roberts, 1987; Kee et al., 1999; Zeilberger et al., 1968), noncompliance (e.g., Fabiano et al., 2004; McClellan, Cohen, & Moffett, 2009; Yeager & McLaughlin, 1995; Zeilberger et al., 1968), verbal tics (obscene vocalizations accompanied by facial twitches; Lahey, McNees, & McNees, 1973), stuttering (Franklin, Hennesy, & Beilby, 2008; McClellan, Lindsey, Cohen, & Moffett, 2009, Onslow et al., 1997), home accidents (Mathews et al., 1987), aggression on the playground (Murphy et al., 1983), and many other unwanted behaviors.[6]

A number of schools in Jigawa, Nigeria, reported that student's lateness continued to be a recurring problem (Sara, 2017). Their previous use of "conventional punitive punishment procedures of whipping and hard labor" had failed to ameliorate the problem. In seeking to identify an alternative management strategy, they decided to substitute response cost (RC) in 12 high schools and timeout (TO) in another 12 schools, then compared the results. Interestingly, once they implemented RC and TO, lateness diminished significantly regardless of which of the two new interventions they applied.

---

[6] See Johnston and Pennypacker's (1980) survey of timeout for an extensive review of the early evolution of research on this procedure, and Ryan's et al. (2007) review on the use of seclusion timeout in the schools.

## Promotes Discrimination Learning

Assuming the appropriate alternative behaviors receive reinforcers as well, timeout or response cost can promote rapid discrimination learning. In a basic experiment, Trent (1983) found that the combination of response cost and reinforcement taught adults to discriminate a single light switch problem (i.e., which "of six opaque buttons was connected to each of six red lights" [p. 209]) faster than feedback, reinforcement, or response cost alone. Similarly, combining use of the timeout ribbon for misbehavior, and treats and praise for appropriate behavior, helped students with severe intellectual disability to discriminate to behave appropriately in the presence of the experimenter (Foxx & Shapiro, 1978).

## Potential for Long-Lasting Effects

Several studies have found that negative punishment has produced *persistent* suppression of unwanted behaviors, such as speech disfluencies (Kazdin, 1973; Siegel, Lenske, & Broen, 1969), noncompliance (Gresham, 1979; Handen, Parrish, McClung, Kerwin, & Evans, 1992), and weight gain (Harmatz & Lapuc, 1968). Others, however, have noted the recovery of such responses when negative punishment was removed (Birnbrauer, Wolf, Kidder, & Tague, 1965; Falcomata et al., 2004; Iwata & Bailey, 1974). Although the explanations for the differences remain to be determined, we surmise that the individuals' histories of reinforcement in reference to those procedures uniquely affect the persistence of the behavioral suppression. Particularly relevant would be the presence or absence of internal or covert reinforcement, motivational operations, and discriminative stimuli for desirable alternative behaviors; magnitude of the fine or duration of the timeout period; length of the time contingencies remaining in effect; the schedule for removing contingencies; and the stimulus conditions associated with the punishment. Or, perhaps in some situations in which DRA and modeling were used, the acquired skills may have produced their own reinforcers, as reading eventually shifts from artificial consequences like teacher praise to the natural consequences of "becoming involved in the plot" or pleased by learning new information.

## Convenient and Socially Acceptable

Response cost is relatively convenient, especially when used in conjunction with point and token systems. Upon the emission of the unwanted behavior, a token or point can be removed, usually quietly and effortlessly. Similarly, depending on its form, timeout can be applied conveniently as well. Watch out, though, because using these procedures is comparatively easy and it may be tempting to apply them more often or punitively than necessary. George insults Jennifer, and the contingency manager says: "Okay, George. You're teasing. That will cost you ten points!" Or, he sends George to timeout for ten minutes. (Posting a response cost or timeout chart should remove the potential for that kind of arbitrariness.)

Nor is it uncommon to encounter token economies designed to penalize *all* infractions, major and minor. Such a heavy penalty system creates an aversive environment, as all participants, contingency manager included, continually scan for unwanted behaviors. (The obvious solution is to *add* to a program, emphasizing behaviors meriting positive reinforcement, rather than using such a self-defeating, heavy penalty system.)

When used with discretion, response cost can help eliminate behaviors very efficiently, without necessarily disrupting ongoing activities. Subtracting a few of George's points as a consequence of a major disruption is much easier than removing him from the room (timeout), scolding him (punishment), or changing his seat (stimulus change). Perhaps this is why Frentz and Kelley (1986) found that 82 mothers from a variety of settings rated response cost (i.e., taking away privileges) significantly more acceptable as a method of treating behavior problems than differential attention, timeout, spanking, or timeout combined with spanking. Similarly, parents and teachers rated response cost and positive reinforcement (praise and privileges) significantly more acceptable than timeout (ten minutes of isolation), spanking, or medication (Elliott, Witt,

Peterson, & Galvin, 1983; Heffer & Kelley, 1987; Reynolds & Kelley, 1997).

Timeout, though, appears to be more acceptable than scolding or spanking (Gross & Gavery, 1997). Interestingly, 85 percent of over 200 surveyed parents believe timeout is appropriate for serious behavior problems for children as young as two years of age, but its rated appropriateness decreases as the child gets older (Socolar & Stein, 1996). Additionally, non-exclusionary has been rated more acceptable than exclusionary timeout (Kazdin, 1980a). Parental or personnel preferences aside, U.S. Department of Education and other public laws require that we *select the least restrictive procedure likely to alleviate a behavior problem effectively*. Also, as Jason et al. (2005) have pointed out, such negative punishment programs are more likely to achieve their goals when affected members (family, staff, and others in regular contact with the client) are involved, and the program is responsive to the needs and resources in the environment.

Take local values into consideration when choosing a particular intervention, though, because in one survey (Borrego, Ibanez, Spendlove, & Pemberton, 2007), the authors found that Mexican-American parents saw response-cost as a more acceptable management strategy than "positive reinforcement-based techniques," like differential attention. Learning more about your consumers may enable you better to choose which route to pursue—in this case, whether to try to re-educate parents or to rely more heavily on response-cost.

Most of the disadvantages of these two negative punishment procedures are similar; however, others are unique to each procedure. First, we discuss the common disadvantages, then additional disadvantages specific to timeout.

## Not Universally Effective: Misuse Decreases Effectiveness

We cannot assume that on balance, using negative punishment will prove successful over time. Doleys, Wells, Hobbs, Roberts, and Cartelli (1976) found their students with developmental disabilities who were noncompliant improved only slightly or actually became even more noncompliant when as a consequence they were required to sit in the corner for 40 seconds. As you will see, the effectiveness of the intended punitive method depends on the availability of a heavily reinforcing environment, the client's learning history, the managers' ability to control reinforcers, and many other factors. In particular, "timeout" is unlikely to be effective if the problem behavior is maintained by negative reinforcement in the form of providing the individual the opportunity to escape from an aversive situation.

## Punitive, Non-Constructive Contingency

Because the negative punishment procedure involves the removal of reinforcers or separating the person from a reinforcing environment, it is essentially non-constructive. Stimuli correlated with punishment, such as the person administering it, may acquire aversive properties. People usually will work to avoid or escape from such stimuli, and even may become aggressive in their presence. Similarly, response cost also may provoke escape and aggression. Boren and Colman (1970) found that when they imposed fines for not attending meetings on a group of delinquent soldiers, the men rebelled and stayed away from meetings. Similarly, Hogan and Johnson (1985) eliminated the response-cost facet of a token economy for emotionally disturbed adolescents because the cost element promoted rather than lessened aggression. Eliminating response cost reduced reports of misbehavior and violence. Doty, McInnis, and Paul (1974) reported emotional reactions of a similar kind when extremely aggressive residents refused to pay their fines. It would appear that individuals with a history of becoming violent are more likely to turn to violence in reaction to response cost. However, most managers, educators, and clinicians prefer that clients achieve positive goals, such as social effectiveness, knowledge, skills, and other productive accomplishments, rather than avoiding aversive circumstances like non-reinforcing or punitive environments.

Timeout fails to add anything useful to an individual's repertoire, and as a punitive strategy, it often engenders such counter-productive responses as avoidance, escape, and aggression. So, wisdom suggests that we identify potential alternative constructive strategies before instituting timeout. As an option, consider using a high-probability instructional sequence (behavioral momentum) that Rortvedt and Miltenberger (1994) tested with some success: Identify constructive instructions to which your client is especially apt to comply. These could be as simple as "Touch your nose," or "Give me a high five." Record what happens after you consistently praise following compliance and ignore following non-compliance. After achieving an acceptable level of compliance with those high-probability requests, over a period of time, perhaps, days, (i.e., establishing momentum), you can begin to slowly introduce the sorts of instruction to which the individual usually fails to comply. Should this pan out, great! If not, you still can temporarily add pairing non-compliance with timeout (but remember attempts at using timeout can be reinforcing if it allows your clients to escape the demand. In such a situation, you would be using negative reinforcement, not timeout. Eventually there is a good chance that praise alone will work to sustain reasonable rates of compliance. (Also, review the strategies presented in Chapters 26–28 for other possible alternatives.)

The reactions just noted are by no means totally predictable (Bucher & Hawkins, 1971; Falcomata et al., 2004; Kahng et al., 2001; Long et al., 1999; Reynolds & Kelley, 1997; Schnake, 1986). If you follow the guidelines for maximal effectiveness (discussed later), you have a better chance of avoiding problems of the nature just described.

## Potential for Abuse

Both response cost and timeout, as with other punishment procedures, can be especially susceptible to abuse. Particularly when frustrated, contingency managers may be tempted to apply those methods to even minor infractions, or more restrictively than necessary (Regalado, Sareen, Inkelas, Wissow, & Halfon, 2004). Why? Timeout not only rapidly reduces unwanted behavior, but also, when offenders are removed from the environment, their aversive behavior leaves along with them. That, in turn, immediately provides relief (negative reinforcement) for the person administering timeout. Similarly, the temptation to use response cost too often or to impose overly harsh and unjustified penalties has also been reported. This is not difficult to understand. Its ease of application keeps the "cost" (i.e., effort) low for the managers, and its rapid effect provides them with immediate relief (an important feature of successfully reinforcing the manager's behavior of using the procedure via negative reinforcement).

An unfortunate outcome of excessive cost is that program participants then need to exert inordinate effort to recoup their losses, which, in turn may lead to their giving up. Once they realize that whatever they earn is likely to be taken away from them, they may decide to opt out of the program. (This is particularly true for people who emit numerous problematic behaviors. Using response cost to treat the total array of unacceptable behaviors is apt to cause them to wind up in "debtor's prison."). Moreover, you cannot get "blood from a stone," so if clients no longer have anything to take away because everything has already been taken away, they have nothing to lose.

Assuming you wish to avoid making yourself and your staff overly dependent on negative punishment, we suggest you see to it that its application is limited to only seriously intolerable behaviors. Restrict using it to acts that more constructive, benign, and optimally applied procedures have failed to suppress. For less resistant violations, the non-aversive procedures described in previous chapters are best. Remember, too, that although behavior managers may find the doctrine of least restrictiveness difficult to adhere to, as a law-abiding applied behavior analyst you must see to it that the policy is followed. Also, be certain to combine any aversive procedures with the kinds of constructive, non-aversive methods previously described, such as supporting preferred alternative acts. As a manager, you will need to devise and adhere to a plan for closely supervising contingency managers, to prevent their yielding to this tempting form of abuse. Thus, although it is recommended to ensure treatment integrity with all behavior analytic interventions, the cogency with doing so when implementing punishment-based procedures cannot be overstated.

## Suppression of Other Behaviors

In addition to the risk of abuse, timeout or response cost may simultaneously suppress acceptable responses as well. If Clyde is charged ten points every time he swears, he soon will be bankrupt with no chance of being able to earn access to the activity of his choice. He may then stop trying altogether (i.e., stop participating in class and not talk at all).

Related adaptive behaviors are more apt to be suppressed along with the target responses, especially when cues permitting clients to discriminate between acceptable (reinforceable) and unacceptable (punishable) behaviors are absent. In a study by Pendergrass (1972), two children with severe developmental delays were isolated for persistent misbehavior. According to the records, while the timeout program was in effect, the misbehavior diminished; but so did social interactions.

## ADDITIONAL DISADVANTAGES OF TIMEOUT

Additional disadvantages of timeout include loss of learning time, ethical and legal concerns, as well as negative public reactions.

## Loss of Learning Time

Depending on the form of timeout used, the procedure may interfere to a greater or lesser extent with learning opportunities. Students or trainees removed from classrooms obviously miss ongoing instruction. Those remaining in a modified timeout situation may be denied active participation in instruction or access to reinforcement as they progress. By its nature, contingent observation limits learning opportunities to those of a "vicarious" nature.

## Legal and Ethical Considerations

From a legal perspective, case law related to *seclusion* applies to placing a client in an isolated room. Below, we briefly summarize a set of illustrative historic legal decisions on the topic of timeout. We suggest that practitioners contemplating using timeout familiarize themselves in advance with the relevant contemporary law in their own jurisdictions:

- Adults, including those in seclusion, are entitled to adequate food, heat, light, ventilation, bedding, hygiene supplies, and clothing (Ennis & Friedman, 1973).
- The landmark *Wyatt* decision (1972) established legal protections connected with seclusion of institutionalized residents with mental handicaps. That decision prohibits seclusion, but "legitimate," professionally supervised timeout may be used in "behavior-shaping programs" (a term not defined in the decision). Emergency isolation of patients who harm themselves or others is limited to no longer than one hour. A qualified mental-health professional must give the appropriate order in writing, and it must be put into effect within 24 hours or not at all. During seclusion, the patient's physical and psychiatric condition is charted, and bathroom privileges must be allowed. Another decision, *New York State Association for Retarded Children v. Rockefeller* (1973), also prohibited seclusion of residents with intellectual disability.
- *Wëlsch v. Likins* (1974) required establishing a baseline before timeout or seclusion could be used, and the frequency of the objectionable behavior had to have shown a decrease after the intervention. Otherwise, timeout had to be stopped.

In 1975, a special task force for the state of Florida (May et al., 1976) prepared a report containing a set of procedural guidelines, including those related to timeout. This included the policy of the *least restrictive environment* (Ennis & Friedman, 1973) that mandates confinement be in the most minimally restrictive form that will permit treatment purposes to be met. To enable policy-makers and practitioners to judge the "level of restrictiveness" of any given timeout strategy, the procedure has been classified into various categories (Brantner & Doherty, 1983) with inclusion or non-exclusionary methods considered the least restrictive, exclusionary timeout (moving the individual to another part of the room or area) the next least intrusive, and *seclusion* or *isolation* (placing the person in a separate room or behind a physical barrier) the most restrictive.

After reviewing a large number of court decisions, Singer and Irvin (1987) concluded that: "For intrusive or restrictive procedures to be used, they must be aimed at educational objectives and must clearly be the least restrictive alternatives" (p. 51).

The ethics of using timeout have been questioned for some time. For example, in 2003, McDowell reviewed a case from New York State:

> a jury in New York awarded $75,000 in damages and attorney fees to a family in the Peters v. Rome City School District (2002) decision for false imprisonment and violating a student's fourth amendment rights by inappropriately using a timeout room. Staff members had placed a second-grade student in a timeout room for excessive periods (i.e., over an hour) and physically held the door shut to lock the student in.

Similar court cases have cropped up across the country including Arizona (Rasmus v. State of Arizona, 1996), Colorado (Padilla v. Denver School district, 1999), Michigan (Sabin v. Greenville Public Schools, 1999), Tennessee (Covington v. Knox County School System, 2000), and Washington (Washougal School District, 1999). Each of these cases was filed by parents concerned that school districts had violated the rights of their children through the use of timeout procedures. As a result, educational law organizations have cautioned schools about the possibility of litigation related to seclusion, and have called on them to establish policies (LRP Publications, 2006) (p. 222).

In a split (2:1) decision, the 9th circuit court in Pennsylvania (June, 2010) blocked considering a case brought by parents objecting to the use of timeout with their son. Possibly similar cases will be brought to the attention of the courts and be permitted to proceed.

As a result of litigation and professional ethical concerns about the use of any aversive procedure,[7] not just timeout, the Behavior Analyst Certification Board (see Shook, 2005, and the Professional and Ethical Compliance Code for Behavior Analysts, 2016) has developed a set of evolving ethical guidelines regarding the use of such procedures. Of present relevance are the following key points, extracted from Section 2: Responsibility in Practice and Section 3: Responsibility to Clients and Stakeholders of the ethics code for behavior analysts (2020):

- Behavior analysts "prioritize positive reinforcement procedures" and "consider relevant factors" such as risks and side effects when developing and implementing behavior change plans (see 2.14 Selecting, Designing, and Implementing Behavior-Change Interventions).

- Behavior analysts "recommend and implement restrictive or punishment-based procedures only after demonstrating that desired results have not been obtained using less intrusive means, or when it is determined by an existing intervention team that the risk of harm to the client outweighs the risk associated with the behavior-change intervention" (see 2.15 Minimizing Risk of Behavior-Change Interventions).

- Behavior analysts monitor, evaluate, and potentially discontinue non-effective interventions in a timely manner (see 2.15

---

[7]Important issues related to the ethics and acceptability of using various punitive procedures have been reviewed in a variety of sources (e.g., Donnellan & LaVigna, 1990; Emerson, 1992; Jacob-Timm, 1996; Sidman, 2001).

Minimizing Risk of Behavior-Change Interventions).

- Behavior analysts "comply with any required review processes" (see 2.15 Minimizing Risk of Behavior-Change Interventions).
- Behavior analysts "act in the best interest of the *clients*" and "do no harm" (see 3.01 Responsibility to Clients).
- Behavior analysts must advocate and educate others regarding the best evidence-based behavior-change procedures for their clients (see 3.12 Advocating for Appropriate Services).

## Public Concern with Timeout

Depending on its form, timeout has been known to excite public controversy. Early on, Kazdin (1980a) found that respondents rated non-exclusionary timeout as more acceptable than exclusionary timeout, and general timeout as less aversive and more acceptable than drug or shock therapy (Kazdin, 1980b).

When isolation is involved, the story can be somewhat different: Suppose a visitor, who has not been adequately briefed, passes a cubicle labeled "timeout booth." Concluding that some poor child is being kept in solitary confinement, the guest raises a ruckus, thereby threatening the viability of the program, along with improvement in the client's behavior.

Maybe we, too, might respond similarly to witnessing the application of seclusionary timeout if we didn't know that it was being used to manage severely dangerous, destructive, highly disruptive, or unhealthy acts. To minimize adverse public reactions, Rozalski, Yell, and Boreson (2006) have proposed a number of safeguards (see Box 29.1). If you are employed by a school system, be aware that most states have established policies related to the use of seclusion timeout in their facilities. So, be certain to check with your district's *current* policies with regard to the use of timeout.

Now that you are familiar with negative punishment procedures, how they operate, their advantages and disadvantages and reasonable precautions to take before implementing them, next we offer you set of guidelines for using these methods effectively.

## USING RESPONSE COST AND TIMEOUT EFFECTIVELY

Some aspects of the effective application of response cost and timeout are common to both, while others are distinctively different. First, we discuss the former; then those unique to each. Note that many of the rules mirror those for reinforcement: Every time you detect the unwanted behavior: Immediately apply strong enough (but not too costly) and meaningful penalties immediately following the violation. Be cautious, though, because just as inflated prices alienate potential customers, an overly priced response cost also can inadvertently suppress desirable behavior. Under such circumstances, you can reverse the situation by identifying and removing that particular cost contingency. In one relevant instance, after noting that "lost" ads greatly outnumbered "found" ads in classified sections of newspapers, a group of investigators (Goldstein, Minkin, Minkin, & Baer, 1978) arranged to remove the fee for the "found" ads in three newspapers. As a result, they discovered that the "found" ads increased in each newspaper and more personal property was returned.

### Apply Immediately

As mentioned, it is important to apply consequences immediately. Immediate application facilitates discrimination and subsequent behavior change. However, it is not always possible to apply a punitive consequence immediately. For example, when out in the community shopping, you may find it difficult to apply a consequence. To increase the effects of delayed negative punishers, Coppage and Meindl (2017) video-recorded the problem behavior and showed the video to the child at home immediately before delivering a 15-minute delayed timeout. This delayed intervention was found to be effective in reducing problem behavior. Slocum, Vollmer, and Donaldson (2019) reported that delayed timeouts (two minutes or less) were effective with four preschool students who displayed some combination of

> **Box 29.1**
> **Safeguards for the Use of Seclusion or Restraint Timeout in Educational Settings**
>
> If seclusion or restraint timeout is used with a participant who qualifies for special education or other public services (in a school, sheltered workshop, or other program serving dependant populations):
>
> • Describe it in the person's Individual Educational (504) or Service Plan.
>
> • Obtain the clients' or their advocates', parents', or guardians' informed consent, as well as permission from supervisors, before using seclusion or restraint timeout with any client. (Refer back to Chapter 11 where we discuss informed consent and check the current version of the BACB's *Ethics Code for Behavior Analysts*.)
>
> • Only use seclusion or restraint timeout on behaviors that present a risk of injury to others.
>
> • Ensure adequate lighting and carpeting. Placing a client in a dark room devoid of furniture with nothing but a cold floor on which to sit is unnecessarily harsh.
>
> • Remove all potentially dangerous objects, such as items that can be torn from walls, objects with sharp corners, and anything that can be thrown or swallowed.
>
> • To prevent injury, be sure clients can be observed/supervised at all times. Also, set a timer to remind yourself when the timeout period has expired.
>
> • Check current policies and laws regulating the use of timeout and seclusion procedures.
>
> • Use a neutral descriptor for the timeout area, such as "quiet area" or "relaxation room" rather than "timeout booth," a rather mechanical sounding term. Timeout areas do serve the purpose of quieting and relaxing people whose behavior is out of control.
>
> • Brief visitors before they enter the setting. Mention all the safeguards that have been instituted, and show and interpret the baseline and intervention data that document the effectiveness of the procedure.
>
> • Consider forming a Human Rights Committee. Some schools have expanded their IEP (Individual Education Planning) procedures to including review of the treatment program (Brakman, 1985; Irvin & Singer, 1984). The function of the committee is to: (a) provide due process and safeguards for clients, (b) ensure appropriate educational treatment, and (c) protect staff (Singer & Irvin, 1987). Minimally, as Brantner and Doherty (1983) recommend, determine the acceptability of your timeout procedure to the concerned public prior to implementing exclusionary timeout. This can help avoid adverse reactions, thereby impeding the program's survival.
>
> • Above all, continually monitor, prepare and make available graphic and written summaries of the effects of the program.

aggression, rule breaking and property destruction. So, *short* delays in applying timeout might still be effective.

However, it should be noted that generally delayed punishment has not been successful, thus utilizing such procedures needs to be done with caution until further replications of success of delayed punishment has been shown to be effective.

## Combine with Other Procedures

Undoubtedly, by now you realize that behavioral procedures need not be applied in their "pure form," but can, and often should, be combined for greater success. Dougherty, Fowler, and Paine (1985) combined response cost with timeout and differential reinforcement of alternative behavior within a dependent group contingency to reduce aggressive behaviors (e.g., hitting, pushing, threats, offensive gestures, property destruction) and playground rule infractions committed by two nine- and ten-year-old boys. After starting recess with four to six bonus points, the boys lost points for instances of aggression or rule infractions, but could earn points for prosocial behavior (e.g., cooperative play, refusal to fight). Boys who lost all points were placed in timeout for the remainder of the recess. Those still retaining points by the end of the recess could exchange them for a five-minute game with two or three chosen peers. In addition, points were accumulated toward a special class reward (e.g., popcorn, field trip, film) selected weekly by the class—an excellent way to garner social support.

Three special-education students could both lose (response cost) and gain (bonus) points as a function of how well they performed on a spelling test Truchlicka, McLaughlin, and Swain (1998). When compared to baseline performance, the implementation of the cost and bonus contingencies led to greater accuracy.

Similarly, combining reinforcement of correct responding with timeout heightened the imitation learning of a four-year-old child with developmental delays beyond that accomplished by differential reinforcement alone (Parsons & Davey, 1978). Timeout was only minimally effective when subjects had access to just a single alternative response, whereas the addition of a second alternative almost immediately eliminated the unwanted behavior. These findings underscore the importance of the Behavior Analysts Certification Board (2020) *ethics code for behavior analysts*, section 2.14, which states: "Behavior analysts select, design, and implement behavior-change interventions that.... (4) prioritize positive reinforcement procedures" (p. 12). Additionally, as you are aware, when applying any reductive method, including response cost or timeout, be sure that extinction conditions for the unwanted behavior are in effect. And, it is good to know that combining response cost with DRA and extinction, appears to have no adverse effect on subsequent resurgence (Kestner, Romano, Peter & Mesches, 2018).

## Create a Reinforcing Natural Environment

Recall that timeout *only* accomplishes its purpose if the stimuli in the individual's "time-in" environment are reinforcing, not aversive. Solnick, Rincover, and Peterson (1977) found timeout initially ineffective in reducing the spitting and self-injurious behavior of a 16-year-old boy with intellectual disability. Only after the regular environment was enriched with new toys, verbal prompts, and praise did the timeout procedure succeed. Consequently, if timeout is to be effective, the normal time-in environment must provide sufficient ongoing reinforcement. Mathews et al. (1987) demonstrated that when time-in was reinforcing (they taught the parents how to play and reinforce safe behaviors), using a brief timeout during free play without the parents, the dangerous behavior of one-year old infants was immediately decreased, and response suppression at the seven-month follow-up was achieved.

Similarly, participants need a reserve of points, tokens, or other generalized reinforcers if response cost is to function effectively. Because reinforcement systems usually are instituted to strengthen weak behaviors, certainly you will want to distribute such reinforcers very frequently at first, only thinning the schedule as the behavior increases in rate and/or stabilizes at an acceptable level. Of course, you would *avoid using response cost until participants have accumulated a reserve. Penalizing someone who is bankrupt is futile.*

## Remove as Many Reinforcers as Feasible During Timeout

For timeout to be effective, the natural ("time-in") environment in which the infraction tends to occur must contain reinforcing properties; the timeout environment must not. Sometimes we fail to recognize the availability of various reinforcers in the timeout environment. For example, one of the authors had an experience while teaching in an inner-city school. Children who misbehaved while preparing for dismissal were told to return to their classroom to remain after school. Although this approach proved effective with some, others actually appeared to solicit the "timeout." On analyzing the situation further, she realized that remaining in class while the teacher decorated the room and performed other duties actually may have been a reinforcing experience for those children. A switch in procedure supported that conjecture. The teacher used staying after school and helping the teacher as a reinforcer for meritorious performance. The approach proved to be a powerful incentive for several students. Likewise, a parent who sends her child to the bedroom for timeout may discover that access to the computer in the bedroom is highly reinforcing.

Identifying, then removing all reinforcers in a setting may be impossible; but contingently removing access to those items and events most responsible for sustaining the unwanted behavior may be sufficient. McReynolds (1969) used ice cream as a reinforcer to support a child's speech development. When the child lapsed into meaningless jargon (presumably reinforced in the past by attention), a timeout (i.e., planned ignoring) was instituted. It consisted of the experimenter's taking the ice cream and turning her chair away from the child. This timeout signaled non-reinforcement and reduced the jargon.

## Determine Magnitude Empirically

The more powerful the intensity of a punitive consequence, the greater the response suppression tends to be (Azrin & Holz, 1966). With response cost, intensity is reflected by the amount of the penalty; with timeout, by duration. Indeed, Burchard and Barrera (1972) found that more severe costs, a 30- as opposed to a five-token fine, suppressed maladaptive behaviors much more effectively.

History appears to play an important part in determining whether a fine of a given size, or the duration of the timeout period, will be sufficient to diminish the rate of a behavior. *If the individual has recently experienced heavy fines, or long timeouts, a small cost or timeout duration will not be effective.* In Burchard and Barrera's study (1972), the clients had historically experienced contingencies that combined a five-token penalty with five minutes of isolation (timeout) for serious infractions. Yet, when results of either five minutes of timeout or a five-token response cost were compared to those of either 30 minutes of timeout or a 30-token response cost, the separate and smaller contingencies showed weaker effects. Given the boys' earlier experience with the stronger combined contingency, the five-token fine probably seemed insignificant by comparison.

White, Nielsen, and Johnson (1972) determined whether the rates of suppression of severely disruptive behaviors by 20 institutionalized people with intellectual disabilities was differentially affected by durations of three different timeout lengths: one minute, 15 minutes, and 30 minutes. On the average, both the 15- and 30-minute timeout periods produced greater suppression than the one-minute duration. While the one-minute duration did suppress behaviors effectively among five of six subjects for whom it was the first duration encountered, it had hardly any effect among the other subjects who had already experienced longer durations.

Pace and Forman (1982) also compared varied reinforcement and fine levels to determine if these might have a differential effect on the disruptive behavior of four second-graders. In this particular case, the authors reported that "the degree of aversiveness of the procedure did not appear to be strongly related to effectiveness" (p. 365). The authors suspected it was just the fact that they were losing *something* that had the greatest influence. Again, history surely plays a strong role in the power of any behavioral procedure.

The way to select the proper cost or duration to levy is to approach the problem empirically. The unwanted behavior must be monitored and various cost magnitudes attempted until the desired response reduction is reliably achieved. One word of caution, though: *Do not increase the cost in small increments*, because people adapt more to gradually increasing intensities of punishment (as we discuss in the next chapter). Instead, return to baseline conditions for an extended period of time and then implement the selected response cost magnitude, or implement a much stronger cost abruptly, maintaining it for several days while monitoring the effects.

Here is an example: Clyde loves shocking and distracting the counselor and the other members of the discussion group by shouting obscenities. A system is in place consisting of awarding points for constructive contributions. The points are redeemable for optional activities. Everyone agrees that too much of the group's time has already been wasted, so they reject applying extinction along with the positive procedures. Rather, they decide to try a response cost of one point for each obscenity uttered. But that accomplishes little. The expletives continue. Would a harsher fine, say, ten points, work better? That notion is rejected as excessively punitive. So the cost contingency is dropped altogether for a while, and then a three-point fine is instituted, this time successfully. Here, adaptation to aversive consequences is avoided by making the contrast sharper. Rather than following one point directly by three points, the sequence is one point, no points, then three points—thereby making the difference more apparent.

Also, besides permitting people to adapt to gradually increased stimulus intensities, prior experience with any punishing event can influence its effectiveness (Lerman & Vorndran, 2002). In other words, *if you use a particular intensity level of response cost or timeout too frequently*, the recipients may begin to adapt to that level and *the procedure is likely to lose its effectiveness.* (This is another reason why the use of punitive procedures must be kept to a minimum.) Therefore, instead of yielding to the temptation to intensify the aversive conditions, program managers might discontinue the punishment for a period of time (Rachlin, 1966), and/or choose an alternative reductive procedure (Charlop, Burgio, Iwata, & Ivancic, 1988).

## Use the Smallest Magnitude of Aversive Conditions Found to be Effective

While findings such as those above seem to promise greater success when cost magnitudes or timeout durations are extreme, this logic is flawed.[8] Numerous studies of response cost have reported just as much success under conditions of minimal fines or timeout periods as under harsh conditions. To encourage an 11-year-old electively mute girl to talk, Sanok and Striefel (1979) successfully combined awarding a penny and praise for understandable verbal responses, combined with a one-cent fine for either nonvocal responses (e.g., gestures) or no speaking. Similarly, early studies also have demonstrated the effectiveness of short duration timeouts (Corralejo, Jensen, & Greathouse, 2018; Zimmerman & Baydan, 1963; Zimmerman & Ferster, 1963). For example, Corralejo, et al. reported the success of timeouts as brief as one minute for low-level sibling aggressions among three- to seven-year-old girls. Also, often the imposition of longer timeouts has been found to provide no further reductive effect, and sometimes even seems to disrupt behavior in other ways: long timeouts may teach clients new, less constructive ways to obtain reinforcers for themselves, via self-stimulation, fantasizing, destruction of the surroundings, and so forth. Long timeouts certainly interfere with clients' productivity more than shorter ones.

Another argument for minimizing the magnitude of negative punishment is that large timeout or response cost magnitudes can result in the suppression of not only the behavior of concern but also others simultaneously present. While Jeanne is in the process of composing some brilliant prose, the teacher may send her to the back of the room for popping her forbidden chewing gum. Guess how that might affect her future flashes of brilliance? Then, of course, there are ethical concerns about excessive harshness, along with the increased likelihood of extinction- or punishment-induced aggression (Hogan & Johnson, 1985).

Given the above, as a behavior analyst, you must see to it that timeout intervals are kept brief and response costs minimal, avoiding permitting those to inflate due to anger or forgetfulness.[9] Otherwise, the new history of longer durations or heavier fines may cause the lesser ones to lose their effectiveness. To circumvent this pitfall, busy personnel often find it helpful to use a signaling system, such as a vibrating timer or an alarm clock, to remind them that the timeout interval has expired. Alternatively, you may ask a staff person, friend, or volunteer to monitor the timeout from a vantage point invisible to the client. The monitor also can ensure that dependent clients are not in any danger.

## Clearly Communicate Response Cost or Timeout Conditions

As with all behavior-analytic procedures, informing individuals of the specific contingencies in operation is a way of involving them more actively as participants in the system. Sometimes members can

---

[8]International conventions *against* use of extended isolation make sense not only on humane but, as we can see, scientific grounds!

[9]This is one justification for providing periodic respite to caregivers working in challenging situations. It is best to prevent frustration from escalating in the first place than to wait until it is too late.

share in setting the consequences or even apply contingencies to their own behavior to achieve the goals they seek. Shirley was very eager to attend the college of her choice, so to help her achieve the necessary grade-point average she imposed response-cost contingencies when she procrastinated in her studies. For every hour she watched television beyond the first two, she donated a dollar to an organization she despised.

Watch how you label your procedure, though, because depending on the participant's learning history such labels may generate quite distinctive results (Northup, Kodak, Lee, & Coyne, 2004). Despite holding conditions constant, a five-year-old girl responded quite differently as a function of how the procedure was labeled. When the contingency was called "taking a break," the rate of her misbehavior was high, but was low when it was called "timeout."

When Giselle and Griselda become embroiled in a fist fight, each is sent to a quiet place to calm down. When Dad hears the twins just beginning to become upset with each other, he warns them, "Remember, if you can't play nicely with one another, you'll each have to go to your timeout area for a while." Assuming this contingency has been regularly paired with "fighting → timeout" in the past, that warning ($S^{Dp}$) should inhibit the fighting. Kendall, Nay, and Jeffers (1975) used warnings of that nature in their successful timeout program.

Role-playing or guided practice sessions can help people better understand "the rules of the game." Also, consistently correlating rules with given consequences for adherence or violation begins to transform the rules into motivational operations. People generally learn to discriminate more rapidly when the rules are available to them (e.g., "If I play nicely with my sister, then I get to play the video game. If I hit my sister, then I lose television time for the day.") Publicly posting rules related to costs and earnings for all participants to review is a good idea. With response cost, for instance, these postings serve as reminders that certain behaviors will lead to specific quantities of gains or losses (see Figure 29.3). Used in this manner, rules may begin to inhibit (occasion low rates of) undesirable behaviors.

Data seem to suggest that while the system is *being implemented*, explanations do little to augment the value of timeout (Alevizos & Alevizos, 1975; Gast & Nelson, 1977). In fact, caregivers who yield to the temptation to lecture clients en route to timeout may inadvertently be reinforcing those acts with attention. To avoid such a situation, rules of conduct should be reviewed regularly at other times, especially when participants are calm and attentive, such as during opening exercises or weekly meetings.

## Use Consistently

Most experienced practitioners know the importance of consistency. You will recall that we have already discussed the need for consistently maintaining reinforcement and extinction conditions. The same holds for response cost and timeout (Zimmerman & Baydan, 1963). To reduce a behavior, these methods should initially be applied as regularly as possible. However, once the performance reduction has reached the predetermined criterion, (for instance "no more than N responses per T time period,") shifting to an intermittent schedule may be possible. In other words, "intermittent schedules should be considered only if the continuous schedule remains effective in suppressing problem behavior to low levels over a considerable amount of time" (Ler-

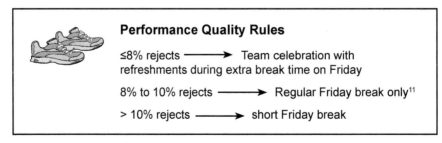

**Figure 29.3** Explaining the Rules of the Reinforcement and the Response-Cost Game

man & Vorndran, 2002, p. 447). Such a shift was accomplished effectively in a 1973 study by Clark, Rowbury, Baer, and Baer. An eight-year-old child with intellectual disability displayed behaviors that were considered disruptive and dangerous to other children, such as choking, attacking people, and destroying materials. Timeout was instituted consistently, in sequential order, for each category of behavior. Following substantial reductions in each of the behaviors, various timeout schedules were attempted. Low levels of the behaviors were maintained when the child was placed in timeout after an average of each third response, but not when the rate averaged only one in eight responses. However, before any firm conclusions can be drawn as to the effective use of intermittent punishment, further research is needed to clarify what intermittent schedules, operating under what parameters of reinforcement and punishment, are effective.[10]

## Consider Delivering Response-Cost Points to a Peer

The disposition of the reinforcers might influence the effectiveness of a given response-cost procedure. Center and Wascom (1984) showed that instead of simply removing points, transferring lost points to another student who was behaving appropriately (i.e., modeling appropriate ways to earn reinforcement) at the time, suppressed the inappropriate behavior more effectively. Try and see if this works in your setting, though we caution you to watch for hints that the penalized student might focus his *punishment-induced aggression* on the new recipient.

## Avoid Opportunities for Self-Injury, Self-Stimulation, and Escape during Timeout

Using a mild form of timeout, like withholding all attention for a period of time, as Harris and Wolchik (1979) did, may be insufficient—especially with people who do not find attention reinforcing in the first place. Nor is it wise to seclude a client in timeout who frequently engages in self-injury or self-stimulation. This point is especially crucial when the performance targeted for reduction is being maintained by negative reinforcement (escape-avoidance), as mentioned earlier, or reinforced by sensory stimulation (e.g., rocking, eye-poking, head-banging, throwing oneself on the floor, masturbating, or daydreaming) (Lovaas & Favell, 1987). In such cases, the requisite non-reinforcing environment required for timeout conditions cannot be readily achieved with clients who use the occasion to engage in such self-reinforcing activities. Such powerful conditions of reinforcement pose the risk of promoting rather than diminishing the rate of the unwanted behavior. For example, timeout was attempted to reduce tantrums by a six-year-old girl with autism, but the child frequently engaged in self-stimulation (Solnick et al., 1977). Instead of retreating, the tantrums increased. Apparently, timeout conditions were not achieved, because the isolation provided her with an opportunity to engage in self-stimulation.

If you suspect that self-injury is being sustained by tactile stimulation, try using protective equipment, such as a padded helmet for head-hitting or padded gloves for hand-biting, while the timeout is in effect (Dorsey, Iwata, Reid, & Davis, 1982). Another alternative is to remove access to a reinforcer, such as a hand-held vibrator, contingent on self-injury (Nunes, Murphy, & Ruprecht, 1977).

However, timeout *can* work to reduce self-injury maintained by positive social reinforcement. Therefore, before implementing a timeout program for self-injury or self-stimulation, you need to try to functionally assess what events are supporting and maintaining the behavior. Is it reinforcement in the form of escape from or avoidance of an aversive situation, such as excessive demands (Carr, Newsom, & Binkoff, 1976)? Is engaging in the act itself reinforced through sensory stimulation? Or, is it reinforced by attention or other social stimuli? Obviously, different treatment strategies would be indicated, depending on the function of the self-injury (Lovaas & Favell, 1987; Repp, Felce, & Barton, 1988). Thus, it should come as no surprise that Taylor and Miller (1997) found that *timeout's effectiveness was related not only to*

---

[10]See Sulzer-Azaroff & Harshbarger (1995) for a similar application, though their actual program used only positive consequences.

*treatment integrity but also to the function of the problem behavior.*

## Monitor Implementation and Progress

As always, record data under baseline, intervention, any reversal and follow-up conditions; otherwise you may find yourself actually reinforcing rather than penalizing a behavior. The latter actually happened in a study by McGee and Ellis (2001) when they applied a "basket-hold-timeout" (students' arms were physically restrained against their bodies) contingent on students' inappropriate classroom behavior.

Further, any time a reductive procedure is implemented, *you must not only monitor its effects on the client's behavior but also the fidelity of its implementation.* Ongoing data collection is not only a recommended BACB ethical guideline, but when it comes to punitive procedures, failing to monitor the program application and effects on client behavior is ethically irresponsible. If the program is not producing the expected outcome, it should be discontinued and/or revised based on a more detailed functional assessment.

## Design the Program to Minimize Emotional Outbursts

You can take steps to minimize aggression, escape, and other emotional reactions when using either response cost or timeout. However, because the actual methods vary for each procedure, we address each separately below.

**Response cost.** Sometimes collecting fines can be problematic, as Doty et al. (1974) found. Aggression, escape, and other emotional reactions to fines or removal of reinforcers can be minimized by clearly communicating the cost rules, retaining the smallest magnitude found to be effective, imposing the fines without fanfare, and ignoring emotional outbursts. A particularly successful strategy in elementary-school classes has been to display the cost of violations on the token price chart, as if they too were backup rewards. For instance, participants had the opportunity to purchase time to play a game for 20 points and to throw things about the room for 100 points. When an object was thrown, we simply remarked: "Oh, I see you just purchased the opportunity to throw something. I'll collect the 100 points." The dazed student surrendered the points, but was less eager to repeat such an expensive purchase in the future.

Another method that often works well is to return part of the fine if the client reacts "responsibly," for example, paying the fine immediately and returning to work right away. This procedure has the added advantage of reinforcing responses incompatible with escape or aggression.

**Timeout.** Timeout is not a logical choice when clients are highly resistant (i.e., it is almost impossible to move the client to or keep the client in timeout; e.g., Azrin & Wesolowski, 1975). Although most individuals will obey an authority figure and go to and remain in timeout for the required duration, many do resist (Foxx, Foxx, Jones, & Kiely, 1980) and/or once in timeout engage in emotional outbursts or other inappropriate behavior. In the former case, if two attendants had not been available to escort the enraged client to social isolation, the program could not have been accomplished. You must consider such factors before selecting the procedure, especially with large children or handicapped adults. It usually is best to avoid becoming embroiled in a physical exchange with a wrongdoer (Benoit & Mayer, 1975). Primarily, you want to avoid harm to anyone. Secondly, struggling with an authority figure in the presence of one's peers actually may contribute to the person's social status. If the resistance can be overcome readily, without causing undue commotion, however, timeout still may prove effective.

One method that holds promise to promote compliance for going to timeout is to reduce the timeout interval contingent on compliance with the timeout instruction. Investigators (Donaldson, Vollmer, Rakich, & Van Camp, 2013) found, for preschool-aged boys, when timeout was reduced from four minutes to one minute contingent on the child immediately going to timeout, compliance with the verbal timeout instruction increased for four out of six participants, and the procedure effectively reduced the problem behavior of all six participants.

In other words, negative reinforcement was used to motivate and help teach compliance with the timeout instruction while keeping the effectiveness of the timeout. (This strategy resembles the response cost practice of returning a portion of the fine for responsible behavior.)

Remember, given that the timeout environment is an aversive situation, escape from that situation can be very reinforcing. Therefore, be certain that release from timeout is not contingent upon a maladaptive response; otherwise, you might inadvertently reinforce it (Harris & Ersner-Hershfield, 1978). Given all these caveats, *if you are unable to implement and maintain timeout responsibly, optimally, safely, or without major disruption*, it is not a feasible choice. Additionally, to avoid negatively reinforcing maladaptive behavior, we suggest you only *release the client from timeout contingent on acceptable deportment*.

**Contingent delay** might help you avoid the latter pitfall. This technique involves *extending the timeout interval contingent on any inappropriate behavior that occurs during timeout* (Bostow & Bailey, 1969). *An individual would not be permitted to leave timeout until his or her behavior was acceptable for at least 15 to 30 seconds*. Adding contingent delay does reduce inappropriate behavior during timeout; but findings are mixed regarding whether it enhances timeout's effectiveness in reducing the unwanted behavior (Hobbs & Forehand, 1975; Mace et al., 1986). In addition to its inconclusive effectiveness, as pointed out by Mace et al. (1986), several potential liabilities are associated with the use of contingent delay:

- Clients are likely to be retained in timeout for lengthy durations for minor offenses that would not normally result in timeout, such as crying or getting out of their seats.
- To ensure correct application, more demands such as time, training, and supervision are required of contingency managers.
- The situation could "result in a control-control struggle between the client and caretaker" (p. 83).

Also, individuals highly resistant to the placement may be kept in timeout for periods beyond that necessary for effectiveness (Hobbs, Forehand, & Murray, 1978; Mace et al., 1986). We recommend that contingent delay only be applied when its necessity and utility can be justified on the basis of objective evidence with the particular client.

Resistance during timeout has been overcome by holding or locking the door (the latter is currently disallowed by law in certain jurisdictions),[11] while maintaining proper supervision, placing the individual in a more restrictive timeout (Roberts, 1988), and using physical restraint (Foxx et al., 1980) or some form of punishment (Roberts, 1988). A sharp verbal "No!" may work for some individuals. (See Chapter 31 for considerations in using positive punishment.) However, as previously mentioned, be sure to check legal and ethical guidelines and obtain appropriate permission before implementing such consequences. Or, consider reducing the time spent in timeout if the client goes there willingly and remains in timeout quietly.

## SUMMARY AND CONCLUSIONS

We discussed two negative punishment procedures in this chapter: *response cost* and *timeout*. You might consider using these for serious behavioral problems when: (1) more positive interventions alone are ineffective, (2) reinforcers maintaining the problem behavior cannot be identified or controlled, or (3) when competing reinforcers cannot be found.

Various factors must be considered before you select and effectively implement a negative punitive procedure. When these are attended to, each procedure has often been found to reduce unwanted behaviors quickly and conveniently. However, response cost generally is a more publicly acceptable procedure than timeout. It does not induce the controversy that some timeout procedures do, and is simpler and more straightforward than timeout. Despite this, provided with appropriate safeguards

---

[11]Danielle (1987). The Pennsylvania district's use of a locked timeout box violated the IDEA. Case #320. (Cited by Lohrmann-O'Rourke & Zirkel, 1998).

and protections for the client, contingent timeout can be very effective and acceptable. Remember, though, that neither procedure should be used unless those implementing it are properly trained and supervised, both the fidelity of the intervention and client progress are carefully monitored, and alternative behaviors are reinforced. Because negative punishment is an aversive approach, these procedures can promote aggression, avoidance, and escape. For these reasons, we advise you to use negative punishment procedures sparingly, only as a temporary expedient to treat serious behavior problems, and as always, according to the ethical guidelines of your profession.

## Chapter 30

# Reducing Behavior with Positive Punishment while Minimizing Coercion

## Goals

1. Define, illustrate, and differentiate *positive punishment* from *negative punishment*, *positive reinforcement*, and *negative reinforcement*.
2. Define and illustrate:
    a. aversive stimulus (intrinsic and extrinsic)
    b. unconditioned or primary aversive stimulus
    c. conditioned or secondary aversive stimulus
3. Describe and illustrate *intrinsic aversive stimuli*.
4. Describe how one might develop *masochism*.
5. Describe how to transform an aversive stimulus into a neutral or reinforcing stimulus.
6. Define, illustrate, and differentiate:
    a. contingent effort
    b. simple correction
    c. overcorrection, including restitution and positive practice
    d. negative practice
7. List the advantages and disadvantages of positive punishment.
8. List and describe how to maximize the effectiveness of positive punishment procedures.
9. Describe the *self-injurious behavior inhibiting system (SIBIS)*.
10. Describe how to choose and effectively use contingent effort.
11. Describe when it is appropriate and not appropriate to include reinforcement as part of the positive practice component of overcorrection.

*************

## ILLUSTRATIVE CASE

The following report based on one of the authors' cases describes how a punishment-based procedure successfully eliminated a client's seriously harmful behavior: Liam, now 38, has lived in a group home for people with developmental disabilities all his life. Diagnosed at the time with profound intellectual disability, Liam had no functional speech. He could follow two-step directions and was generally compliant. However, whenever out in public, he would pick up and consume cigarette butts ("cigarette pica"). Health concerns made this behavior problematic, as did the fact that he was unable to gather socially with others when smokers were present (or the remnants of smoking are around). Given that the functional behavioral assessment indicated that no reinforcers were clearly apparent, by exclusion, it was concluded that Liam's cigarette pica was being maintained by automatic reinforcement (possibly in the form of nicotine). The behavior analyst and Liam's staff tried a number of reinforcement-based procedures, such as noncontingent reinforcement and differential reinforcement of other or zero occurrences (DRO), but none successfully eliminated his pica. After meeting with Liam's team and attaining its approval, the behavior analyst and his staff proposed and discussed the merits of designing and implementing a punishment-based overcorrection procedure. The procedure consisted of the following: If Liam picked up a cigarette butt and started to place it in his mouth, staff were immediately to block the action and physically guide him to place the butt in the garbage, or, if no trash bin was available, to hand it to a staff member. Then they guided him to pick up five additional objects off the floor and place them in the garbage or staff's hands as well.

Before implementing the program, to build treatment fidelity, all relevant staff were trained through role-playing until they were able to demonstrate their ability to implement the program at an accuracy level of 90 percent or above. Additionally, if Liam picked up a cigarette butt and gave it to a staff member or independently put it in the garbage, the staff were to use DRA in the form of praising him and giving him a piece of his favorite snack (DRA).

Data were collected on Liam's attempts to eat butts, the number of times the overcorrection procedure was used, the number of times Liam handed a butt to a staff member or placed it in the garbage, and the frequency with which Liam was praised and given reinforcers. On the first day, the overcorrection procedure was applied 15 times. Within a couple of days, however, Liam no longer picked up cigarette butts and placed them in his mouth.

In Chapter 29, we discussed why studying punishment is so important and elaborated on those particular punishment procedures that are based on *subtracting* reinforcers (response cost) or denying access to them (timeout). Now we discuss *adding* aversive stimuli (positive punishment procedures); what they are, their advantages, disadvantages, and when and how to use them effectively.

## POSITIVE PUNISHMENT DEFINED

To the lay audience, the term *punishment* tends to share various connotations:

- Inflicting physical pain, as when a mother slaps her son's hand hard enough for it to hurt, to convince him not to pull the tablecloth off the china-laden table.
- Causing a symbolic or "psychological" wound, for instance, when the teacher ridicules a student before the class.
- Saying or doing something that society generally views as punishment, such as a grounding or scolding, regardless of the effect on the offender (as in several of the situations described earlier).

Before we discuss the topic meaningfully, allow us to clarify the ambiguities related to our use of the term *punishment*. Recall that **positive reinforcement** is a term describing *the "strengthening" (increase in rate) of a response as a function of an individual receiving a reinforcing stimulus following that response*. **Positive punishment** produces the reverse outcome. Consequently, we define positive punishment analogously as the "weakening" (decrease in rate) of a response as a function of the individual receiving an *aversive stimulus following* *that response*. As with positive reinforcement, when justified on ethical grounds, applied behavior analysts apply positive punishment to reduce or eliminate particularly dangerous, harmful, or obnoxious behavior. Consequently, a positive punishment **procedure** entails *reducing the rate of a response by presenting an aversive stimulus contingent on the (unwanted) response* (Azrin & Holz, 1966). Punishment can be said to have occurred only if the individual's rate of emitting the treated behavior has been demonstrably reduced. Like reinforcement, a punishment procedure is defined solely by its effect on behavior. As long as the event involves presenting a stimulus contingent on a behavior that reduces its subsequent rate, any given procedure may be labeled punishing. Moreover, just as with reinforcement, wherein the reinforcing potency of a given stimulus varies from one individual and circumstance to the next, the same is true for the strength of aversive stimuli within punishment. Notice that the definition of *punishment* refers to its effect on a specific behavior. So stimuli punishing for the behavior of one person may not be equivalent for others; or, the same stimulus may actually reinforce rather than punish the behavior of others (think of highly-spiced food, cold weather, personal partners, and so on).

If a father reprimands his child for interrupting, and the interruptions then cease, the reprimand has punished the interruptions. If interrupting continues unabated, however, the reprimand was not punishing. Suppose that the rate of interrupting actually *increases*. Then, the reprimand has *reinforced the interruptions* rather than punishing them.[1] Similarly, if the boss praises a worker in the presence of his coworkers for increasing his productivity and the worker *decreases* that rate in the future, then the boss's praise probably was (probably unintentionally) punishing, not reinforcing. (See Table 31.1 for a comparison of reinforcement and punishment procedures.)

Just as there were two main types of negative punishment procedures, *response cost* and *timeout*, there are two major positive punishment procedures: those involving the *presentation of aversive stimuli* and those requiring effort to the point of aversiveness (i.e., *contingent effort*). We present, discuss, and compare each separately because the operations differ from one another. But first, to help you understand these procedures, we discuss *aversive stimuli*.

## AVERSIVE STIMULI DEFINED AND ILLUSTRATED

Stimuli that function as punishers are called *aversive stimuli*. Along with other organisms, people tend vigorously to avoid aversive stimuli. Although this rule has occasional unusual variations (as in masochism, mentioned below; also in laboratory investigations: Church, 1963; Solomon, 1964). As briefly mentioned in Chapter 5, we use the term

[1] According to Van Houten & Doleys (1983), reprimands, or verbal or nonverbal expressions of disapproval, are the most common form of punishment used by parents, teachers, employers, and peers.

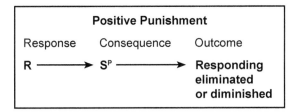

TABLE 30.1  A Comparison of Positive and Negative Reinforcement and Punishment

|  | *Positive Reinforcement* | *Positive Punishment* | *Negative Reinforcement* | *Negative Punishment* |
|---|---|---|---|---|
| Nature of Stimulus | $S^r$ consequence | Aversive consequence | Aversive consequence | $S^r$ consequence |
| Action | Added | Added | Subtracted | Subtracted |
| Outcome | Behavior increases or maintains | Behavior decreases | Behavior increases or maintains | Behavior decreases |

**aversive stimulus** to apply to all stimuli labeled *reductive, punishing, abative, or those whose termination is negatively reinforcing at that point in time.* Recognize, though, that any particular stimulus condition may be reinforcing, aversive, or neutral to varying degrees depending on its context (Catania, 2008). In freezing weather, putting on a heavy sweater is reinforcing; but punishing in hot, humid weather.

## Unconditioned or Primary Aversive Stimuli

Some types of stimuli are just about universally punishing, even in the absence of learning. Forceful blows, intense electric shocks, noxious odors, sudden exposure to overly brilliant lights and to deafening sounds are examples. Should those stimuli consistently occur contingent on a specific behavior, the rate of the behavior usually diminishes (unless individuals learn to habituate to those intense stimuli, as in learning to enjoy listening to earsplitting music). Generally, a small child who has experienced little in the way of corporal punishment and is spanked for dashing out into the street will be less likely to repeat the act in the future. Like many of us, you may have learned the hard way not to get shocked by handling a frayed electric cord or have been burned by touching a hot stove. In general, *a stimulus that is aversive in the absence of any prior learning history is called a* **primary or unconditioned aversive or punishing stimulus**, abbreviated here as **S<sup>P</sup>**.

## Conditioned or Secondary Aversive Stimuli

**Secondary or conditioned aversive stimuli** are *those that have gained their punitive properties by having previously been contiguously associated with powerful aversive stimuli,* much in the same way that a formerly neutral stimulus acquires reinforcing properties (see Chapter 6). A universal example of a conditioned aversive (punishing) stimulus ($S^p$) is the word "No!" spoken in a loud, sharp tone. Most people have experienced this "No!" in tandem with other strongly aversive stimuli. Baby Bonnie's mother shouts "No!" as the child touches the hot stove. Both the loudness of the sound and the pain of the burn contribute to the child's learning the meaning of "No!" (i.e., "No!" has become a conditioned aversive stimulus for Baby Bonnie).

Henceforth, any behavior followed by a loud, sharp "No!" probably will diminish, at least temporarily, as long as it occasionally predicts the delivery of powerful aversive stimuli. Other examples of conditioned aversive stimuli include frowns; gestures, like an authority shaking a finger; or motions, like clenching a fist or swinging a hand as if preparing to deliver a spanking or a blow. Stimuli like warnings and threats presented repeatedly just before timeout, response cost (the coach requiring a team member to do pushups for taunting a fellow player), or other aversive events also may become conditioned aversive stimuli ($S^{Dp}s$). However, as with other conditioned responses, if warnings and threats are not at least intermittently followed by the aversive consequence, eventually they will lose their power. For example, suppose Monica warns her son that if he spits he will have to go to wash his mouth out with soap. He then spits, but Mom doesn't invoke the washing his mouth out. The "warning or threat" will eventually fail to control the boy's behavior. (Recall how neutral stimuli acquire and lose their discriminative stimulus properties.)[2]

**Attention!**

Programming the application of unconditioned aversive stimuli with dependent clients, in places like schools, hospitals, clinics, or institutions, raises numerous legal, ethical, and practical issues. Although we discuss ethics further in the next chapter, a thorough coverage of the topic is well beyond the scope of this text. We advise you to avoid applying aversive stimuli in other than the most serious circumstances and to familiarize yourself with and strictly adhere to the ethical and legal guidelines of the professional practice of applied behavior analysis and of your own profession.

---

[2]O'Donnell et al. (2000) have concluded that conditioned and

## Intrinsic and Extrinsic Aversive Stimuli

In the natural course of events, the probabilities of certain behaviors being reduced when followed by such nasty experiences as painful shocks or burns from an electrical cord or a hot stove are high. These experiences are **intrinsic aversive stimuli**, in that *the aversive properties are integral or natural to the particular acts*. In purposeful behavior management, though, applied behavior analysts generally are concerned with specifically arranging aversive stimuli to reduce or eliminate unwanted behavior, in general or under particular circumstances. *Aversive stimuli delivered by an external agent* are **extrinsic aversive stimuli**. Intentionally designed punishment programs often involve managing stimuli of the extrinsic variety: reprimanding an employee for malfeasance, ticketing drivers observed failing to yield the right of way to pedestrians in a designated crosswalk or for other vehicular violations, or shouting a warning to a student or client showing signs of losing control.

Just as *reinforcing* stimuli may be intrinsic to an act, so may *aversive* stimuli. Performing difficult or highly repetitive motions, especially when no reinforcer follows, can turn the repetitive motion into aversive stimuli. So do instances in which the performer is obliged to increase the rate of a behavior far beyond its typical baseline range. Try doing a hundred pushups, and unless you are in superb physical condition, you will understand the concept of intrinsic aversiveness. Soon we shall describe

several illustrations of the management of these types of aversive activities: *contingent effort, positive* and *negative practice, restitution*, and *response-suppression procedures*. First, however, let us define and illustrate basic punishment features; then positive punishment procedures.

## Stimuli that Signal Non-reinforcement

Stimuli that signal non-reinforcing conditions can acquire punitive or aversive qualities. In the Good Behavior Game, for instance, marks on a board may signal loss of recreational time. Ultimately the marks (previously neutral stimuli) begin to acquire conditioned aversive properties, as a result of being correlated with periods of non-reinforcement. (Similarly, recall how antecedent or contextual stimuli regularly correlated with extinction begin to acquire aversive properties—$S^{De}$s, Azrin & Holz, 1966.)

Clyde's mom asks him to go to his room to do his homework, where attention from friends and family, and his access to his electronic gadgets, television, or other highly-preferred reinforcers are absent. The instruction "Go to your room!" becomes aversive. Debbie's parents call her Deborah only when they are upset, angry, or about to punish her. Debbie eventually begins to dislike being called Deborah. Ms. Charming repeatedly has requested that her supervisor, Ann Thrope, provide funds for tokens, backup reinforcers, and recording equipment for her workshop program. Ms. Thrope never delivers. After a while, Ms. Charming begins to dislike Ms. Thrope and avoids joining her for lunch. Ms. Thrope's presence has become aversive.

## Conditioning that Transforms Typically Aversive Stimuli into Reinforcers

How can events almost universally considered punitive become reinforcers? Think about some people who receive insufficient reinforcers for their efforts and accomplishments *except* following some punishing event. For example, overwhelmed by other concerns, Tim's mother generally ignores the boy. One sure way of gaining Mom's attention is to suffer

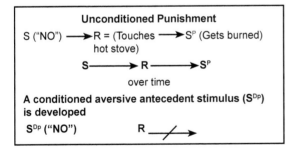

---

unconditioned punishers may not be functionally identical. They drew that conclusion after the therapist reprimanded eye-poking only while the client wore a wristband. The result was that eye-poking diminished in the absence of the therapist only when the client wore the wristband, but not quite to the same extent as when the therapist directly reprimanded the behavior.

an injury, because under those circumstances Tim's mom cuddles and reassures him. Just as moderately strong shocks can begin to serve a reinforcing function under laboratory conditions (Holz & Azrin, 1961), Tim soon learns that getting hurt is one sure way to obtain affection from his mother. (Some might label this **masochism**—*seeking out or inflicting punishment upon one's self.*)

Similarly, as we saw in earlier discussions of functional assessment, dependent people often learn to engage in maladaptive behaviors, like hurting themselves or others, as a way of requesting particular reinforcers. This is especially likely when their parents, teachers, peers, or caregivers are preoccupied, overworked and/or are unskilled in behavior analysis. Despite the additional punishment the clients receive by hurting themselves or others, those maladaptive behaviors may be their primary or even *only* functionally effective way of obtaining reinforcers. Under such circumstances, consider how difficult it might be to try to remove every single source of reinforcement for punished behavior. When faced with such a problem, our best recourse is to enable the client to establish new, constructive functional response repertoires instead.

Fear-provoking stimuli also can become neutral or reinforcing. To illustrate with just one of an enormous array of such studies, ponder the sorts of prompts you might use to teach people to manage their own behavior under situations they find extremely fear provoking. As Rothbaum et al. (2000) have shown, one way to approach the challenge is to place the individual in a situation known to be safe but closely resembling the fear-inducing circumstances, as in simulating being a passenger during an airplane flight. The authors integrated computer graphics, various displays, and input technologies to design a virtual-reality exposure "to give the user a sense of *presence* or *immersion* in the virtual environment" (pp. 1020–1021). They provided a head-mounted display consisting of "separate display screens for each eye, along with some type of display optics, stereo earphones, and a head-tracking device," and presented the user with a computer-generated view of a virtual world that seemed to change in a natural way, along with head and body motion. That arrangement permitted the subjects to become "desensitized" (the stimuli no longer set the occasion for fear-related responses) to the stimuli that previously prompted the inappropriate fear responses, especially during simulated take-offs and landings in an airplane during both calm and stormy weather.

Of course, in the latter, as one aspect of a *desensitization treatment*,[3] the aim was to simulate typical fear-evoking responses while clients know themselves to be safely on the ground. Participants are aware of how completely unreasonable their fears are. When combined with therapeutic input, the new conditions prompt the individual to become calmer in the face of the previously fear-inducing stimuli. Ultimately, the subject remains calm while the fear-provoking classes gradually become more actual, until eventually they participate in real flight without becoming terrified.

## ILLUSTRATIVE PUNISHMENT-BASED BEHAVIORAL PACKAGES

Just as procedures may be productively combined into packages or programs to increase rates of current, or to teach new behavior, the same is true of reductive methods. Here we describe four such packages that you might consider using after you have attempted the full array of constructional procedures: *contingent effort, positive practice, overcorrection,* and *negative practice.* Then, assuming you are employed by an organization, the procedure must be approved by the appropriate ethical review board and be closely monitored for treatment fidelity; and, of course, control of contingencies must be in the hands of those implementing the procedure. Now let us look at some examples.

### Contingent Effort

**Contingent effort** (also called **contingent exercise** or **contingent exertion**) is *a form of punishment that*

---

[3]*(Cognitive) behavior therapists* have used and reported on numerous desensitization methods analogous to these to support patients' learning to cope with a broad array of "irrational" fears and phobias.

*requires the individual to perform effortful exercises as a consequence of committing the problematic behavior* (e.g., Luce, Delquadri, & Hall, 1980). The procedure relies on the intrinsically aversive nature of particular stimuli and the effort may take various forms. Examples include arm and hand exercises to reduce inappropriate foot movements and vocalizations (Epstein, Doke, Sajwaj, Sorrell, & Rimmer, 1974); ten minutes of window washing to decrease swearing (Fischer & Nehs, 1978); standing up and sitting down ten times to eliminate aggressive acts and comments, such as "I'm going to step on your face" or "I'm going to kill you" (Luce et al., 1980). Perhaps you have used this method as a coach to discipline team members, by requiring them to run laps or do pushups or sit-ups following transgressions. Military sergeants are notorious for ordering disciplinary routines such as trench digging, forced hikes, potato peeling, and pushup repetitions to turn their rookies into compliant soldiers. Probably everyone is familiar with teachers who require students to write "I will not ____" several hundred times. Parents may supplement their disapproval of a particular misdeed by insisting that their youngsters clean their rooms or do dishes or yard work as punishment. All illustrate forms of contingent effort or exertion.

Interestingly, sleep deprivation can affect a person's perception of the difficulty of, or preference for, a particular task (Massar, Lim, Sasmita, & Chee, 2019). Illnesses can have a similar effect (Draper, et al., 2018). Current circumstances of that sort may explain why client choices may vary from session to session. So, always be prepared to adjust the form of the interventions you select depending on your client's recent history and/or conditions currently in effect (including a change in MOs).

Sometimes, **simple correction**, *requiring the learner just to restore the environment to its previous state*, is sufficient to treat unintentional, infrequent, undesirable behaviors (Azrin & Besalel, 1999): righting a desk that was knocked over or requiring the person who cuts into line to move to the last position. When the misdeed is of a more serious or dangerous nature, and contingent effort, after being given a reasonably fair trial, does not remedy the situation, we may need to go beyond the mere correction to *overcorrection*. **Overcorrection** is *a relevant and educational form of contingent effort that involves both* (1) *restitution* (being required to repair environmental disruption or extensive destruction) *and* (2) *positive practice: i.e., to intensively practice optimal forms of a constructive, alternative behavior* (Foxx & Azrin, 1973). For example, for the **restitution** component, a boy who has overturned his desk would first be told "No," (a learned aversive stimulus), "you overturned your desk" (a specification of the behavior), immediately after which he would be required not only to return the desk to its correct upright position but also to dust and clean it.

As well as being aversive, **positive practice** is designed to be educative by *requiring the individual repeatedly to practice a positive alternative behavior*. For the positive practice element of overcorrection, the youth who overturned his desk might be required to dust and clean additional desks in the room. Beyond erasing his own "artistry," the youth who marks up a wall could be instructed to clean the entire wall, and perhaps to practice writing on appropriate materials, such as copying patterns or words onto a piece of paper. A worker caught attempting to repair a machine without first deactivating it might be required to spend extra hours practicing the appropriate lock-out procedure and carrying out preventive maintenance procedures with several machines. Notice that in these examples, the offenders are taught positive or correct ways of treating desks; where and how to use pencils, crayons, or markers; and how to follow the appropriate safety practices.

Variations of overcorrection have been used as a technique for enhancing academic productivity among a wide range of students, from those with major developmental delays to those whose skills fall within the normal range (Lenz, Singh, & Hewett, 1991). Those authors concluded that the procedure promoted the children's achievement levels. They also proposed substituting the term "directed rehearsal" when used alone or in combination with positive reinforcement of constructive alternatives to enhance academic performance.

In general, although not universally effective, overcorrection often has been demonstrated to be effective in the management of a range of undesirable behaviors. (See Carey & Bucher, 1986; Cole, Montgomery, Wilson, & Milan, 2000). For example, sometimes one or just a few trials (e.g., suppressing drooling: see Van der Berg, Didden, Jongerius, & Rotteveel, 2007) may be as effective as multiple positive practice requirements. Among others, successful examples of the use of the standard or modified method include:

- Bruxism (i.e., the clinching, grinding and/or gnashing of one's teeth) reduced in normal adults (Watson, 1993).
- Spelling skills increased by typically-developing youngsters, those with cognitive delays, and children and adolescents with severe learning disabilities (Foxx & Jones, 1978; Ollendick et al., 1980; Stewart & Singh, 1986).
- Vocational and self-care skills acquired by adult clients with developmental delays (Carey & Bucher, 1981, 1983, 1986).
- Oral reading proficiency increased among children with developmental delays (Singh, 1987; Singh & Singh, 1986).
- Appropriate toy play increased among children with autism (Wells, Forehand, Hickey, & Green, 1977).
- Sharing of materials more frequent among kindergarten children with hearing impairment, those with multiple handicaps, and normal preschool children (Barton & Osborn, 1978).
- Drooling (Trott & Maechtlen, 1986; Van der Berg et al., 2007)
- Pica (McAdam, Sherman, Sheldon, & Napolitano, 2004) reduced among disabled clients.
- Urinary incontinence reduced among children with autism (LeBlanc, Carr, Crossett, Bennett, & Detweiler, 2005; Perez, Bacotti, Peters, & Vollmer, 2020).

When it functions as planned, one reason why *overcorrection* appears to produce such rapid results is that it substitutes new and functionally effective responses apt to be supported by the natural environment for the previously maladaptive behaviors. However, Foxx and Livesay (1984) have posited that, in contrast to results with most groups, the reductive effects of overcorrection tend not to be as durable for individuals operating at very low-functioning levels. They offer several possible explanations: First, given their severely limited behavioral repertoires, low-functioning individuals tend to express fewer competing reinforceable behaviors. Second, should the person's maladaptive behavior return after a period of time, staff may fail to re-implement the complex and time-consuming overcorrection procedure, reverting instead to less demanding (and less effective) methods used previously, such as timeout or physical restraint (Foxx & Livesay, 1984). Third, to be educative, the restitution aspect must be relevant to the misbehavior. Sometimes figuring out just what that activity should be is difficult. (What would be an appropriate restitution procedure for the behavior of peeking under female visitors' skirts?) When immediate action is called for, identifying an appropriately relevant aversive activity on the spot can pose a problem. Perhaps further research and experience with overcorrection will help to resolve such difficulties.

In terms of consumer satisfaction, perhaps because overcorrection is explicitly designed to have an educative component, school personnel, administrators, parents, the public, and participants tend to prefer it to other aversive activities (Blampied & Kahan, 1992; Foxx & Bechtel, 1982; Horner et al., 2002; Ollendick et al., 1980; Polvinale & Lutzker, 1980). Interestingly, as Horner et al. (2002) reported, parents preferred it to reinforcement for treating children with stereotypy. However, parents of children with cancer rated both timeout and overcorrection as unacceptable methods to apply with their children (Miller, Manne, & Palevsky, 1998).

*Negative practice* also involves contingent effort. However, with **negative practice**, *after the individual has emitted an unwanted behavior s/he is required to repeatedly practice that same unwanted behavior for a predetermined time.* Secan and Egel (1986) implemented negative practice contingent on the self-stimulatory hand-clapping of three students with developmental delays. As soon as a youngster's hands made contact, a staff member would say, "If you want to clap, you will clap" (p. 33), and the youngster was instructed to clap until he had clapped

60 times. If he did not comply, clapping was physically guided until 60 claps were completed. Teachers reported the advantages "that the procedure was implemented throughout the day with success, took very little time to implement (approximately 45–60 seconds), and, with these students, did not result in side-effects such as aggression or resistance" (p. 36). In addition, the lower rate of self-stimulatory hand-clapping permitted the youngsters' greater access to reinforcing activities such as catching, rolling, and throwing a ball. (As mentioned elsewhere in this text, providing a reinforcing milieu is essential for maintenance of behavioral change.)

Naturally, negative practice would not be used for dangerous behaviors; only for those whose infrequent repetition can be tolerated. One of the author's mothers applied the procedure for swearing and door slamming. It must have worked reasonably well because to this day it takes a lot of provocation for us to swear or slam the door. Negative practice probably works for three reasons: effort, extinction, and satiation. The response occurs repeatedly without extrinsic reinforcement, and the person begins to satiate on whatever conditioned intrinsic reinforcement it contains. Hearing yourself say "Damn!" or slamming the door a hundred times does begin to get old.

## ADVANTAGES OF POSITIVE PUNISHMENT

### Effectively Stopping Behavior

Numerous cases have been reported in the literature to demonstrate that the presentation of aversive stimuli can effectively stop behavior, which is no surprise, because the punishment procedure is *defined* by its successful reduction in rates of the treated behavior. (See Azrin & Holz, 1966; Gershoff, 2002; Lerman & Vorndran, 2002; Matson & Taras, 1989; for reviews.) As reported in the applied-research literature, punishment generally has been used to diminish behaviors that seriously interfere with learning and performance or are especially dangerous or destructive. These have included stereotypy, self-injury (Hanley, Piazza, Fisher, & Kristen, 2005; Vorndran & Lerman, 2006), aggression (Dixon, Helsel, Rojahn, & Cipollone, 1989; Hanley et al., 2005), disruption, safety, and traffic violations (Van Houten & Malenfant, 2004), combinations of these (Fisher, Piazza, Cataldo, Harrell, Jefferson, & Conner, 1993; Hagopian, Fisher, Sullivan, Acquisto, & LeBlanc, 1998), failure to use ear protection (Sadler & Montgomery, 1982), and behaviors of a similar nature. The procedure also has been used to condition minimally aversive methods as substitutes for powerful aversive stimuli, as in the case of Dixon et al. (1989), who taught a child with violently destructive behaviors to respond to a mild aversive stimulus (facial screening) instead of a stronger one (aromatic ammonia). It also has served as a supplement to promoting the development of adaptive behaviors such as discrimination, attention, and word recognition (Guess, Helmstetter, Turnbull, & Knowlton, 1987).[4]

In working with four youngsters with autism (ages 6, 8, 11, and 14), Verriden and Roscoe (2019) compared the additive effectiveness of various punitive procedures to DRA and NCR to successfully decrease troublesome, automatically reinforced behavior. The individualized client analysis consisted of alternating four to five punishment procedures (response cost, hands down, positive practice overcorrection, contingent demands, response blocking, and reprimands) in a random order in conjunction with the ineffective DRA and NCR. They found that the use of DRA and NCR became effective in reducing automatically reinforced problem behavior when combined with powerful punishment procedures; however, the effective punisher differed among clients. These results emphasize the importance of assessing punitive procedures to determine which actually functions as punishment, or that actually works, for each specific client.

### Halting the Behavior Rapidly; Perhaps Lastingly

Occasionally, you need to change dangerous behavior rapidly (e.g., to stop a child from running into

---

[4]Knowing that punishment reduces the rate of a behavior may enable you to analyze puzzling situations, such as a person's failure to emit a response you are certain he is capable of performing.

a busy street or from attempting to push another child over a guard rail). Beyond restraining the individual, using an intense punishing stimulus, like a loud, sharp verbal reprimand or a swat, may be appropriate, because optimal application of punishment offers the advantage of halting the behavior quickly; sometimes over a reasonably long-time span (Azrin, 1960; Scotti, Evans, Meyer, & Walker, 1991). In their 20-year review of the literature on punishment and other methods for reducing the problem behaviors of developmentally-delayed persons, Matson and Taras (1989) concluded that aversive procedures can rapidly and significantly maintain treatment effects over the span of a month or longer. Similarly, Kazdin (2001) and Lerman and Vorndran (2002) have pointed out that a wide variety of punishers (e.g., verbal reprimands, shock, water mist, lemon juice, removal of reinforcers) produce immediate, substantial suppression of problem behaviors. More recently, investigators (Dominguez, Wilder, Cheung, & Rey, 2014) used a verbal reprimand to decrease rumination by an 11-year-old boy with autism who did not communicate vocally (he used pointing and leading to communicate). Rumination was reduced to near-zero levels and the effects were shown to maintain at 6, 12, and 18-month follow-ups. Also, used in conjunction with procedures based on functional assessments, punishment may enable a major reduction in severe behavior, as it did for every circumstance in which Hagopian et al. (1998) applied it. However, the long-term suppressive effects remain in question, probably dependent on factors such as whether extinction conditions accompany the punishment (Lerman & Vordran, 2002) and if functionally-equivalent replacement behaviors are promoted and reinforced.

One can readily be misled into concluding prematurely or inaccurately that particular applications of punishment have been effective, thereby reinforcing the agent's use of the procedure. Michael (2004) has illustrated this point as follows:

> when a small child's misbehavior is followed by a severe reprimand, the misbehavior will cease immediately, but primarily because the reprimand controls behavior incompatible with the misbehavior—attending to the adult who is doing the reprimanding, denying responsibility for the misbehavior, emotional behavior such as crying, etc. This sudden and total cessation of the misbehavior does not imply, however, that the future frequency of its occurrence has been reduced, which would be the true effect of punishment. (p. 37)

Therefore, prior to concluding that your punishment approach has "worked," keep recording the subsequent frequency of the punished behavior. Also, watch to be sure you haven't been beguiled into overusing punishment by being able to terminate the noxious behavior(s) rapidly (negative reinforcement). As a supervisor, for instance, you may have experienced the pleasure of being able to move a meeting agenda along by making sarcastic remarks to those who seem to be dominating the conversation. Don't be surprised when they and a few others of your subordinates stop contributing to the discussion during team meetings!

## Facilitating Adaptive Behavior

Given that punishment is designed to reduce the rates of particular behaviors, can it also be applied to support constructive outcomes, either directly or collaterally? Yes. When objectionable behavior has been punished and preferred alternatives reinforced, the individual can learn to discriminate acceptable from unacceptable conduct. For example, Pfiffner and O'Leary (1987) found that *following a period of enhanced positive consequences*, students who received firm, brief, specific reprimands, contingent on off-task behavior, began rapidly to increase their time on-task and improve the accuracy of their academic performance. Once these gains were established, a *gradual* shift over to a primarily positive approach permitted the improvement to maintain successfully.

Sometimes anecdotal or experimental evidence indicates that recipients of punishment have collaterally improved adaptive skills, such as appropriate play and improved attending to environmental events. Newsom, Favell, and Rincover (1983) described a number of instances in which the toy play by children with developmental delays increased in conjunction with a reduction in their rates of self-stimulation. Similarly, Newsom et al. and Rolider, Cummings, and Van Houten (1991) reported that eye contact, attention to task, and attention to peers and surroundings in general have improved as a side effect of punishment. Facilitation of social interactions and cooperation is, according to Newsom et al. (1983), "the most frequently noted side effect of punishment" (p. 302; i.e., among developmentally-delayed children with high rates of self-stimulatory, aggressive, and self-injurious behavior). Cases cited included those clients whose reduced aggression, destructiveness, self-injury, and rumination were followed by enhanced social responsiveness or cooperation. Of the 25 studies with aversive components involving participants with developmental delays that Matson and Taras (1989) reviewed, the authors indicated that 96 percent resulted in positive side effects, such as weight gain, improved self-help, social interactions, and responsiveness to the environment, plus reduced crying and disrupting.

**Decreasing collateral inappropriate behavior.** Some evidence hints that aggression, emotional reactions, stereotypic, and other maladaptive behavior may decrease along with the main target of the program (Duker & Seys, 1996; Thompson, Iwata, Conners, & Roscoe, 1999). "The prevalence of these side effects is unknown, however, because relatively few studies have directly examined the effects of punishment on unpunished behavior" (Lerman & Vorndran, 2002, p. 454).

**Increasing responsiveness to reinforcement.** After reviewing the literature on punishment, Lerman and Vorndran (2002) concluded that "punishment may enhance the efficacy of reinforcement for establishing appropriate behavior that competes with or replaces inappropriate behavior, an outcome that in turn may increase the likelihood that punishment can be withdrawn" (p. 450). For example, investigators (e.g., Koegel, Firestone, Kramme, & Dunlap, 1974; Rolider et al., 1991) found that punishment of problem behavior was associated with increases in compliance and toy play.

**Instructive to peers.** A behavior is more likely to be imitated in a situation in which it is followed by either no consequences or by reinforcement, rather than by punishment (Bandura, 1965a, 1965b). When a particular misbehavior is punished, others are less likely to copy the unwanted act in that context. As a case in point, when some students were reprimanded for being disruptive, others disrupted less (Van Houten, Nau, MacKenzie-Keating, Sameoto, & Colavecchia, 1982).

**May facilitate acquisition of a range of skills.** As one of many such examples, in Chapter 16 on stimulus control, you discovered that learners often acquire concepts not through point-by-point instruction for each and every relationship among its members, but through the formation of equivalence classes. As Perkins, Dougher, and Greenway (2007) have demonstrated, punishment may facilitate learners' discovery of which stimuli do and which do not belong to a given equivalence class. If little Edgar is learning about *neighborhood helpers*, the teacher may reinforce Edgar's inclusion of *firemen, police officers, and refuse collectors*, but may punish (say "No") to his insertion of investment brokers within the set.

# DISADVANTAGES OF POSITIVE PUNISHMENT

If punishment works rapidly to reduce the rate of a behavior, why not use it as the first line of defense against unwanted behavior? Actually, many do with children in the home and school, not to speak of their use of fines, penalties, and demotions in the world of adults. Although generally outlawed elsewhere, 19 states in the U.S. permit use of corporal punishment in the schools (Gehoff, Sattler & Holden, 2020). Researchers (Heekes, Krugher, Lester & Ward, 2020) indicate that despite a global shift toward preventing corporal punishment in schools, the practice remains widespread, including in locations where in the practice is banned. Boys, black students (in the U.S.) and those exposed to violence at home appear especially to be at risk of corporal punishment. However, students with disabilities are even more likely to receive corporal punishment (MacSuga-Gage, Gage, Katslyannis, Hirsch, & Kisner, 2020) in school. Also of interest, is the fact that those who experienced corporal punishment in school were more likely to spank their own children and to experience depression as adults (Gehoff et al., 2020). Moreover, Gershoff, Goodman, Miller-Perrin, Holden, Jackson, Kazdin, and Alan (2018) have pointed out that "physical punishment is linked with the same harms to children as is physical abuse and summarize the extensive research that finds links between physical punishment and detrimental outcomes for children that are consistent across cultural, family, and neighborhood contexts" (p. 626). They recommend that "parents should avoid physical punishment, psychologists should advise and advocate against it, and policymakers should develop means of educating the public about the harms of and alternatives to physical punishment" (p. 626). As you read about punishment's disadvantages,[5] though, you will begin to understand the information that has been causing those numbers to diminish slowly and steadily since the early 1980s.

## Provoking Withdrawal

Generally, people or animals react to punishment by attempting to withdraw (Azrin et al., 1965; Hutchinson, 1977). You probably have seen exaggerated instances of this phenomenon illustrated in cartoons and situation comedies: the victim of a nagging spouse stomping out of the house; the severely rebuked child heading around the corner carrying his hobo pack; the employee who quits after being chewed out by the boss. Examples from everyday life are just as common: the staff member whose efforts are regularly criticized is often absent or late and may eventually resign; the student who is repeatedly reprimanded develops feigned or actual illnesses, tunes out, cuts class, or drops out of school altogether. Children avoid adults who rely on punitive methods of control (Morris & Redd, 1975; Redd, Morris, & Martin, 1975), and teachers avoid teaching children with problem behaviors, probably because they find it difficult or punishing to work with them (Carr, Taylor, & Robinson, 1991). Escape also may be symbolic or indirect, rather than literal. For example, the student may doodle or hum; the spouse, turn away and sulk in response to criticism. In all cases, the social process is disrupted and communication breaks down.

## Suppressing Responses

When punishment is used excessively, too intensively, and/or without reinforcement for alternative behaviors, other responses are likely to be suppressed as well. A woman whose close relative is gravely ill stiffens when the phone rings. After disappointing news, she puts the phone down, and instead of returning to her normal daily routine, she falls into her easy chair and stares out the window. The aversive circumstances immobilize her, resulting in her accomplishing nothing else for the rest of the day. A child stops talking in front of the teacher who curtly corrects the youngster's misuse of grammar. Yes, ongoing aversive circumstances can suppress responding. In fact, recently one of the authors was working with a client with a severe history of being punished, and the client just sat and did nothing. One could hypothesize that the client has been so severely punished for various responses that he had just stopped responding all together.

Blocking a response also may be associated with decreases in adaptive responding (e.g., leisure-item interactions) and increases in other stereotypic responses (Bradshaw, Szabadi, & Bevan, 1977; Lerman, Kelley, Vorndran, & Van Camp, 2003). For example, in one case, blocking stereotypic behavior (head- and tooth-tapping) was associated with increased hand-wringing. In addition, results suggested that the reductions in rates of interactions were due to accidental or *adventitious* punishment. Prompts to access an alternative source of reinforcement attenuated the side effects somewhat, but the undesirable effects of response-blocking were found to be fairly durable. So when you see an inert student, employee, patient, or client, try to detect whether aversive stimuli are operating. The threat

---
[5] As Crosbie, Williams, Lattal, Anderson, & Brown (1997) have found, the side effects of punishment vary among individuals. Probably this is a function of their long-term learning histories.

of punishment also can have a negative influence on information processing. For example, Ballard, Sewell, Cosgrove, and Neal, (2019) have reported that: "The threat of punishment lowered the average quality and quantity of information processed, compared with the prospect of reward or no performance incentive at all." Apparently even *the threat of punishment appears to lead to poorer decision making and accomplishment; another major reason to promote reinforcing environments.*

## Promoting Aggression

We are already aware that extinction can be a precursor to aggression. Punishment is similar. Although some applied studies report no evidence of aggression (e.g., Linscheid & Reichenbach, 2002), others do. For instance, Hutchinson (1977) discussed how both people and animals tend to become aggressive in response to aversive stimulation, especially when escape is blocked. Our ability to identify factors that promote aggression is critical to our understanding of the world, to maintaining our control over our own lives, and to fulfilling our responsibilities and protecting society. For instance, ponder the fact that young children who are aggressive have an increased likelihood of "criminal behavior, number of moving traffic violations, convictions for driving while intoxicated, aggressiveness toward spouses" (Eron, 1987, p. 439), and turning to punishment to manage the behavior of their own children.

Eron (1987) has noted that in the natural home environment, low levels of reinforcement and high levels of punishment have been related to excessive aggression in school by eight-year-olds. Similarly, investigators (Taylor, Manganello, Lee, & Rice, 2010) found that mothers who reported using *spankings* two or more times the previous month with three-year-olds, were more likely to experience higher aggression levels by their child when he or she was five years of age, even when levels of aggression at age three were accounted for. Mayer and his colleagues (Mayer, 1995; Mayer & Butterworth, 1979; 1981; Mayer, et al., 1983a; Mayer et al., 1987; Mayer & Sulzer-Azaroff, 1991, 2002)

discovered that vandalism rates in schools correlated positively with a heavy reliance on punitive disciplinary techniques and unsuitable academic assignments. Presumably, the latter are punishing because they are either insufficiently or overly challenging. Similarly, Carr et al. (1980) established that people often use counter-aggression to terminate the aversive stimuli inflicted by others, and Berkowitz and his colleagues (Berkowitz, 1983; Berkowitz, Cochran, & Embree, 1981) have found that aversive stimulation induces the victim to harm others. Numerous instances of "punishment-induced aggression" also emerge in our normal daily lives. One example, is reciprocal domestic violence (i.e., one partner hits the other partner to punish him or her for going out with friends, and the partner that was hit responds by hitting back).

## Promoting Inappropriate Generalization

Stimulus generalization is a risk associated with punishment. As you saw in Chapters 15–18 on stimulus control, people respond to stimuli that resemble or share properties of those present while the behavior was being conditioned. Stimuli similar to those present during punishment may, at least temporarily, evoke the same sorts of reactions as those stimuli actually present during the punishment. In one classic study (Watson & Rayner, 1920), an 11-month-old child's conditioned fear of a white rat generalized to all furry objects. If the objective is to accomplish generalized suppression, as with self-injury or acts of violence, such a spread of effect can be advantageous. As Newsom et al. (1983) have noted, however, the effects tend to dissipate "as the subject has additional opportunities to discriminate the actual contingencies of punishment in force" (p. 299).

Generalization to stimuli related to punishment can be problematic. Unintended reactions, such as the inclination to escape or retaliate, or worse yet, to become immobile, can spread from the particular unwanted behavior to the punishing agents themselves, such as to the manager who rebukes his employees, or the teacher or parents who discipline the child. Or they may transfer to the context—

the job or school setting. A student, scolded for speaking out of turn, may respond with aggression toward or withdrawal from the teacher, the principal, the subject he is studying, the school, and so forth. One story we heard was of an art teacher who scolded misbehaving students and required them to stand in a corner or repeatedly to write rules if they talked too much or misbehaved in other minor ways. To retaliate, one day the students hid her glasses; on another occasion, they broke them. The art teacher "had no clue as to why the students disliked her." Other familiar stories have included students attempting to escape or to stop responding altogether in school, not speaking, writing, reading, or working, at least for a while, as a function of a school authority, parent, or peer having punished their behavior. Sometimes students escape by dropping out of school. Mayer et al. (1993) showed that when school personnel learned to substitute positive behavior-management procedures for punishment, high-risk students' rates of dropping out of high-school diminished.

Another danger is *learned helplessness* (Maier, Seligman, & Solomon, 1969) or *abulia*. Rats who received inescapable shock in one situation failed to take advantage of the available opportunity to escape in other situations. When you are perplexed by a person who has real options and yet does nothing to rid himself of aversive circumstances such as an abusive partner or a punishing job, recognize that this sort of overgeneralization may be at work.

Ultimately, as in a number of cases cited by Newsom et al. (1983), recipients do tend to learn to discriminate that the punishment is delivered for a specific behavior and/or under particular conditions. Sometimes this can be detrimental, as when you would prefer to see a behavior disappear across all contexts. Otherwise, when unwanted only under particular circumstances (remaining quiet at a religious observance, funeral, or in the library), learning to discriminate these from other settings can be beneficial. You can't count on the latter happening spontaneously, though. So, to ensure it is acquired, you need to clearly inform clients about the specific acts for which punishment was delivered. Clear antecedents for the desired alternative behavior, followed by lavish reinforcement for compliance, should help them make the necessary distinctions.

## Setting Conditions for Recovery or Resurgence Afterwards

Unless punishment has been combined with optimal reinforcement of functionally-equivalent alternative behaviors or is so powerful that it totally suppresses the behavior (a rare phenomenon because behaviors that are targeted for reduction usually have an extended history of having been reinforced), the unwanted behavior(s) are likely to gradually recover their rates (a phenomenon called *resurgence*, see Chapter 28). Think about how initially after receiving a speeding ticket you follow the speed limits, but after some time passes you go back to your old ways of being a speed demon. Sometimes that rate even exceeds the level prior to treatment. This predictable phenomenon adds another risk factor to choosing punishment as a management mechanism. In other words, applying, then discontinuing punishment can produce a pattern worse than before punishment was implemented. (Perhaps this explains the recidivism of criminals who commit increasingly appalling crimes or the escalation of various forms of abuse.)

## Promoting Behavioral Contrast

Earlier, we discussed behavioral contrast in association with various procedures, such as extinction and differential reinforcement of other behavior (DRO). To review, *behavioral contrast describes a behavioral rate change that occurs in a direction opposite from that happening within the treatment setting*, despite constant conditions in a second setting. Behavioral contrast also has been observed in applied settings when punishment has been included in the disciplinary mix. For example, Risley (1968) noted that while a punishment program designed for a child with autism to suppress his climbing on a bookcase was in effect, his rate of climbing on a chair increased. Foxx and Azrin (1973) used overcorrection (see below for details) to reduce one of their participant's mouthing of objects in a daycare center. While the behavior decreased in the center, the problem increased at home. Similarly, while punishment appeared to reduce a client's self-injury rates at school, the rates increased slightly at home (Merbaum, 1973).

Because behavioral contrast appears more probable when the individual is obtaining insufficient reinforcement for constructive alternative behaviors, as an adjunct to all reductive programs, *you need to be certain to differentially reinforce acceptable alternative behavior (DRA)*. Additionally, any time you use a procedure involving aversive stimuli, you need to *assess rate changes in other classes of problematic behavior and under other circumstances as well as taking any steps necessary to remedy the situation*.

## Modeling Punishment

In our discussion of the advantages of punishment, we mentioned that clients are less likely to imitate a punished behavior. There is a real risk, though, that they may duplicate the *act of delivering punishment* (Bandura & Walters, 1963; Bandura, 1965c). In her frustration, Miranda's mom spanks her for throwing her food on the floor (a consequence we would not recommend for food throwing). Miranda goes outside and swats her baby sister for playing with her toys. (Her sister stops playing with Miranda's toys.) Peer aggression, in particular, tends to be imitated (Kniveton, 1986a; Ling & Thomas, 1986), especially by youngsters with three or more siblings (Kniveton, 1986b). For example, youngsters who viewed videotapes of aggressive and nonaggressive play behavior by children similar to themselves became more aggressive only after viewing the aggressive models.[6]

A number of other studies have now linked increased young adult, adolescent and childhood aggression with watching aggressive acts in the media (e.g., Huesmann, Moise-Titus, Podolski, & Eron, 2003; Mestel, 2002), interacting with violent video games (Hasan, Begue, Scharkow, & Bushman, 2013), or date violence with experiencing harsh corporal punishment at home (Simons, Burt, & Simons, 2008). Several other investigations have shown that individuals often imitate the kind of punishment or other reductive methods they have experienced (Gelfand et al., 1974; Mischel & Grusec, 1966), such as being spanked, being required to stand in the corner, or being deprived of a meal. Be cautious, then, when using or exposing young people to viewing punishment, in that it may serve as an act to be imitated. (We would guess that the tendency for abusive families and societies to reproduce themselves from one generation to the next can be explained by this phenomenon.)

In Chapter 18 we discussed how the behaviors of prestigious persons tend to be imitated, especially when observed receiving reinforcers as a result of those behaviors. Probably unintended teaching of that kind can take place in any sort of organizational, work, educational, or community setting where use of punishment is reinforced by the immediate cessation of aversive events—that is, by negative reinforcement. Sometimes new managers learn to be punitive toward their employees by watching their own supervisors gain (often negative, sometimes positive) reinforcement in that way.

By now, you can begin to understand why violence is so widespread in many societies.[7] In addition to extinction and punishment-induced aggression, here is another to add to the list: People with prestige and power (those in control of contingencies) may actually be teaching aggression by modeling it! If you want to avoid becoming an unwitting trainer of violence, then, be sure you avoid punishing whenever possible, especially in the presence of those who respect you.

## Diminishing "Self-Esteem"

Being the frequent recipient of punishment may negatively impact the way people describe not only their surroundings but also themselves (as measured by responses on paper-and-pencil tests of "self-

---

[6]Extrapolating further, Eron (1987) found that youngsters who were exposed to aggressive models at age eight tended to be more aggressive ten and 22 years later. In addition, he found that: "One of the best predictors of how aggressive a young man would be at age 19 was the violence of the television programs he preferred when he was 8 years old." (p. 438). Apparently there is good reason to monitor and manage young children's television to avoid repeatedly exposing them unduly to aggression (delivering punishment to others).

[7]Read Sidman's "Coercion and Its Fallout," (2001) for a thorough and very readable analysis of punishment's unfortunate impact on society and its members along with his suggestions for making the world a more benign and better place.

esteem") in a more negative light, particularly if the aversive stimuli were directed at *them*, rather than their *behavior* ("You're a bad boy"; "Jim is immature. Sometimes he acts like a two-year-old"; "Clarence is irresponsible"). The significance of this point should not be taken too lightly because studies (e.g., Wattenberg and Clifford, 1964) have indicated that what people, especially the young, say about themselves can influence their performance and achievement. Other studies (Flanders, 1965; Ludwig & Maehr, 1967) also have indicated that when teachers directed their comments to individual students, rather than to their behavior, the content of the students' self-reports (i.e., self-esteem) shifted in a negative direction. *If disapproving comments must be used, they should never be directed at the individual ("You're a bad boy") but at the behavior ("No, hitting is wrong!").* That sort of specificity enables people to recognize that the particular behavior is unacceptable; not that they, themselves are generally unworthy. Therefore, *just as we are well advised to use specific or labeled praise* (Bernhardt & Forehand, 1975), *we should do the same with punishment* (Van Houten & Doleys, 1983).

Again, to help clients discriminate among the circumstances in which explicit behaviors will and will not be tolerated, reinforce acceptable alternative behaviors. Furthermore, we suggest you apply reinforcement in the form of praise, because it is likely not only to occasion and strengthen desired behaviors, but also to heighten people's evaluative statements about themselves and their surroundings (Bandura, Grusec, & Menlove, 1967; Flanders, 1965).

## Overusing Punishment

Why is punishment used so frequently? By now you probably understand that reinforcement is responsible, because just as with any other behavior, if it persists, then it is being reinforced. The threat and use of punishment rapidly gets people what they want, and rids them of what they don't want; or maybe they have observed others using and/or receiving reinforcement for applying punishment. (Think: the bully on the block, tyrannical rulers of nations.) Furthermore, if their own behavior was punished recently, they will find reinforcing for a time the opportunity to hurt someone else (Azrin, Hutchinson, & Hake, 1963).

A study by Martin (1974) illustrates the reinforcing effect of punishment on its users' behavior. When requested to play with objects like beads or blocks, a group of young children was praised sometimes for staying on-task, and at other times reprimanded when off-task. When reprimanded, their rates of staying on-task were higher than during the praise for the on-task condition. The latter circumstances would undoubtedly reinforce the contingency manager's use of reprimands over the use of reinforcement. However, don't allow yourself to be trapped by these contingencies!

One problem is that the negative side effects that might discourage the use of punishment may be delayed or obscure. In the Martin (1974) study, a follow-up phase demonstrated that despite their working faster when reprimanded, the children later avoided the activities in which they had been involved while the reprimands were delivered. The punishing agent may fail to observe the avoidance pattern right away—if ever. That may explain why people naive about the principles of behavior may continue to dispense punishers and why many parents and teachers rely so heavily on reprimands or disapproving comments (Hart & Risley, 1995; Van Acker et al., 1996; White, 1975). The unfortunate result can be that reprimands or disapproving comments appear to worsen, not improve, noncompliance or other objectionable behavior (Van Acker et al., 1996). *To prevent misuse of punishment, we need to encourage program implementers to rely more heavily on preventative antecedents and differential reinforcement than on punitive methods.*

## Promoting Habituation to Aversive Stimuli

"Prior experience with the punishing stimulus either contingently or noncontingently can decrease a behavior's sensitivity to punishment" (German & Vorndran, 2002, p. 435). People begin to adapt or *habituate* to stimuli they repeatedly experience. Just as the reinforcing value of a stimulus will diminish with overuse, so will the suppressive influences of excessively repeated aversive stimuli. Most eventually learn to tune out constant nagging or overly frequent spankings or reprimands unless the stimuli are extremely harsh. This is the sort of phenomenon that leads to physical or psychological abuse—one more reason why punishment is best reserved for only the most severe transgressions. Accordingly, we need to *avoid using punishment for extended periods*.

## Generating Public Antipathy

Many oppose the formal application of punishment in some or all of its facets. The reasons include, among others:

- sensational media coverage of misapplications of punishment
- attributing to others personal perspectives on the subject
- personal experiences
- legal, professional, or ethical considerations
- objective evidence

Professionals and governmental agencies that have spearheaded anti-aversive movements and many members of the public represent that viewpoint. According to Elliott (1988), "people generally rate positive treatment procedures as more acceptable than negative procedures for changing children's behavior" (p. 72). Nevertheless, this opposition is by no means universal, and often respondents will sanction using more intrusive or restrictive methods to treat truly severe and resistant problems (e.g., Elliott, 1988; Kazdin, 1980a), *especially when provided with information about treatment fidelity and reliable evidence of effectiveness* (Von Brock & Elliott, 1987). Beyond informing themselves of and adhering to professional guidelines, applied behavior analysts should check with representatives of the community and related professional and paraprofessional employees and clients to find out where they stand locally in this regard. Informing those concerned about problem severity, treatment effectiveness, and the need to adhere to ethical standards also should help.

## Increasing Costs in the Short Term

To be effective, aversive procedures must be instituted immediately and for a sufficient duration, requiring the undivided attention of staff. Otherwise, if the procedure is discontinued prematurely, the targeted behavior may recover or even exceed its previous rate. If, for instance, the restitution aspect of an overcorrection protocol requires that a student right all the desks he has overturned, and then some, a staff member would need to be available to enforce that requirement and to use physical guidance if necessary. Foxx and Livesay (1984) have suggested that after initial preparation with less-challenging clients, personnel be trained in the specialized procedure and given extra pay for implementing overcorrection correctly. So, before electing to employ intricate methods like these, consider the following costs: time to assess client strengths and weaknesses, tangible reinforcers, extra compensation for specially-trained personnel to implement the program, funds to support the collection of reliable and valid data on client performance and treatment fidelity, and powerful staff performance-management systems. (Review Chapter 24 for further suggestions.) Of course, assuming your intervention is successful, the net long-term savings in terms of lower medical bills, personnel and supervisory costs, and quality-of-life factors may justify the investment.

## Review of Negative Side Effects

In their review of 382 applied studies with the developmentally disabled, Matson and Taras (1989) concluded that side effects have not generally been found universally to accompany aversive methods. However, a number of such instances *have* been documented across many species, including volunteer human subjects, especially when their escape from the aversive stimulus is blocked. These have included stimulus generalization, behavioral contrast, accelerated rates of scanning the environment, "freezing," manipulating objects, moving about, and becoming aggressive (Hutchinson, 1977). Behavior analysts also worry about imitation, peer reactions, negative "self-esteem," and risk of abusive overuse by staff, along with ethical, safety, and legal issues.

Further bases for caution derive from the results of a large meta-analysis of 88 reports specifically on *parental use of corporal punishment* (Gershoff, 2002). Among the outcomes listed were: increased child aggression, child delinquent and antisocial behavior, risk of becoming a victim of physical abuse, adult aggression, risk of abusing one's own child or spouse, adult criminal and antisocial behavior, decreased quality of the relationship between parent and child, a decrease in the child's mental health, and a subsequent decrease in adult mental health. "Corporal punishment was associated with only one desirable behavior, namely, increased immediate compliance" (p. 541). Since unwanted behavior is terminated immediately following the presentation of a punishing stimulus, the immediate compliance of a child reinforces the parent's use of punishment, thereby increasing the probability of the parent's using this procedure in the future on other problem behaviors. Certainly similar outcomes could be reflected in out-of-the-home settings.

*Many behavior managers wisely suggest that to balance out the negative impact of each punisher they deliver, they apply at least three to four reinforcers contingent on those clients' desirable behavior.* In work in which Rasmussen and Newland (2008) compared monetary gain versus loss, they found that punishment (monetary loss) "subtracted more value [about three times] than a single reinforcer added, indicating an asymmetry on the law in effect" (p. 157). More recently, *research indicates that for youngsters with emotional and behavioral disorders (EBD), a nine to one ratio appears needed to improve behavior* (Caldarella, Larsen, Williams, Wills, & Wehby, 2019). Similarly, Robinson and Peter (2019) found that 10-year-olds with ADHD, and who engaged in chronic, severe problem behavior, reduced those troublesome behaviors and increased the time spent on academic responding once they began to accumulate reinforcers throughout the session. Perhaps it may be the case that those with more severe disorders, or who are at risk, require more reinforcement to counter the effects of punishment and/or insufficient reinforcement. Similarly, it seems like whenever punishers or periods of non-reinforcement are used, especially with youngsters, it is important to teach a variety of appropriate or replacement behaviors to ensure contact with reinforcers. Whether such ratios persist against the test of time, especially when verbal mediation is held constant, is to be seen, but nevertheless, *it does appear that the value of the two procedures is neither necessarily opposite nor equal and that some youngsters will need more reinforcement than others to help compensate for, or counteract, the damage that punishment has wrought.* These studies remind us of the importance of remaining cautious when electing to use punishment as our initial intervention, if at all.

## Effects of Torture

A report of research findings appeared in the *New York Times* (2016) on "How U. S. Torture Left a Legacy of Damaged Minds" after September 11th. According to the report, acts of torture, or "interrogation methods," occurred in secret C.I.A. prisons and at Guantanamo, and the results revealed the following persistent mental health problems: permanent headaches, anxiety, disturbed sleep, severe nightmares, post-traumatic stress disorder, paranoia, depression, and psychosis. The acts of torture, or severe punishment, that were used included: beatings, sleep deprivation, waterboarding, dousing with ice water, locking in a coffin-like box, sensory deprivation, menacing with dogs, isolation, head forced into toilet water, death threats, sexual taunts (including threatening rape), forced nudity, aggressive body cavity searches, kept in diapers, spit in face, slammed against wall, shackled in painful contortions, and others. In short, severe punishment often results in severe mental health problems.

Such research findings compel us to consider seriously whether, beyond its apparent benefits, systematically choosing and using punishment to deal with unwanted behavior is truly warranted. By now, the reasons why punishment has become the most controversial of all behavior-modification procedures should be clearly apparent to you. So, we urge you to proceed cautiously on the path to using this method, and *try to avoid the use of severe punish-*

ment acts completely, including corporal punishment or beatings.

## USING POSITIVE PUNISHMENT EFFECTIVELY

If we are to promote rapid and enduring suppression of unwanted behavior, we should heed the results of the multitude of studies conducted on positive punishment. Many of the resultant strategies mirror those for applying positive reinforcement, though generally the circumstances are more complicated.

### Take Preliminary Steps Prior to Instituting a Positive Punishment Procedure

**Conduct a functional behavioral assessment.** Given all the potential negative side effects of punishment, you probably would be relieved to be able to avoid using it altogether. So, at this point, take the time to investigate what conditions probably are maintaining the unwanted behavior. Once those are identified, alternative approaches may be open to you. For instance, in the case of self-injurious and aggressive behavior, as Pelios et al. (1999) have found, it pays to stop, look, listen, and analyze why the person is behaving unacceptably in the first place. The answer may lead you back to choosing several of the many more constructive methods contained in this book or, at least, combining the latter with punishment for a package that produces an even more rapid effect and is possibly preferred by clientele (Hanley et al., 2005).

**Obtain informed consent.** The practice of obtaining informed consent (See Chapter 11 and/or the Behavior Analyst Certification Board (2020) *Ethics code for behavior analysts*) is based on the recognition that the clients (or their advocates) and/or parents and caregivers have the right to be informed about proposed experimental or programmatic procedures and their anticipated outcomes. The practice also permits consumers to learn about the advantages and disadvantages of possible alternative interventions and provides them with the opportunity to be invited to participate in the selection of specific goals and procedures. If consent or refusal is to be considered "informed," this information must be communicated at a level comprehensible to the client or advocate. As you know, the change-process may be abetted by involving the client in the process and clearly delineating the rules of the game. Thus, if the client is judged sufficiently capable of understanding and providing it, obtain his or her *informed consent*. Otherwise, seek the permission of parents, guardians, or advocates. If you negotiate a reasonable contract that includes powerful reinforcers for alternative acceptable behaviors, you are even more likely to achieve success.

### Reinforce Acceptable Alternative Behaviors

According to the Behavior Analyst Certification Board's (2020) *ethics code for behavior analysts*:

They recommend and implement restrictive or punishment-based procedures only after demonstrating that desired results have not been obtained using less intrusive means, or when it is determined by an existing intervention team that the risk of harm to the client outweighs the risk associated with the behavior-change intervention. When recommending and implementing restrictive or punishment-based procedures, behavior analysts comply with any required review processes (e.g., a human rights review committee). Behavior analysts must continually evaluate and document the effectiveness of restrictive punishment-based procedures and modify or discontinue the behavior-change intervention in a timely manner if it is ineffective. (Code 2.15, p. 12)

As with any responsible behavior-analytic practice, we certainly support the notion that you *pair differential reinforcement of alternative behaviors (DRA) with the application of any punitive proce-*

*dures*. Also, consider including modeling, DRO, NCR, DRD, and preventive interventions (Chapters 27 & 28). When concerned with behaviors that provide their own intrinsic reinforcement, the solution may depend upon providing the individual with the opportunity to attain reinforcers of equivalent or stronger value from more acceptable sources. As an example, when addressing aggression among 15-year-old and four-year-old boys with mild intellectual disabilities, Borrero, Vollmer, and Wright (2002) found that when "the probability of reinforcement for aggression was equal to the probability of reinforcement for the nonoccurrence of aggression, rates of aggression were suppressed to low levels" (p. 337). Similarly, to cope with stealing, providing alternative socially desirable behaviors by, for example, training in a skill that is both intrinsically reinforcing and regularly and reasonably remunerative may solve the problem.[8] As long as successful thieves have no socially acceptable way to earn the goods and services they covet, they probably will continue to steal. But if they receive heavy reinforcement for acceptable alternative behaviors while stealing is punished, there would be even more room for optimism.[9]

*Mild* punishment also may augment the effect of a pharmacological intervention (Durand, 1982). Apparently, by combining the interventions, dramatic reductions in the subject's self-injurious behavior were achieved. Durand posited that the drug may have served as a "setting event" for using the punishment successfully.[10]

The good news, as we can see, is that weaker punishment may have a more powerful effect if combined with other procedures, such as drug therapy or DRA. Although intense punishment generally is more successful in reducing well-established maladaptive behaviors (Azrin & Holz, 1966), milder, less restrictive punishment[11]—"No," a frown, or a head shake—promises to function just as well *provided the person is allowed access to an alternative reinforceable behavior* (Thompson et al., 1999). This effect is illustrated nicely in the graphed results of the research conducted by Thompson et al. with four adults with developmental disabilities who engaged in self-injurious behavior.

Figure 30.1 illustrates the effects of no punishment versus punishment for unwanted behavior, along with augmented reinforcement or not for acceptable behavior. An alternating-treatment design format was used in one instance (Shelly). Note that the greatest success in reducing Shelly's spitting was achieved when mild punishment (e.g., wiping saliva from spitting with a soft cloth, or holding her arms immobile for several seconds) was combined with access to reinforcing activities (while she was not engaged in SIB). Also, when punishment and reinforcement were paired, less punishment was required to maintain adaptive behavior. Bottom line: *punishment works better in reinforcing environments*. Also, of course, combining punishment with preventive methods, DRA and other positive reductive procedures whenever possible, works best of all.

## Select Functionally-Effective Aversive Consequences

In your reading so far, you have seen numerous examples of aversive stimuli. Yet, just as reinforcers are distinctively different from one individual to another, depending on stimulus conditions, so are aversive stimuli. Roane et al.'s (2003) comment highlights this point in the following way: "the reward contingency functioned as punishment

---

[8]This discussion is predicated on the assumption that the function of stealing generally is obtaining material rewards. Sometimes, though, the reinforcer is different, as in receiving pleasure from obtaining objects without having to pay for them or the thrill of escaping detection.

[9]Publications in various behavior therapy journals (see, for example, *Behavior Therapy, Behaviour Research and Therapy, Behavior Therapy and Experimental Psychiatry, Child and Family Behavior Therapy, Cognitive Therapy and Research, Behavior Therapy and Experimental Psychiatry*, and others included in our reference list) have reported how similar procedural combinations have effectively changed behaviors associated with a range of antisocial behaviors.

[10]Investigations with nonhuman animals suggest that certain drugs also may potentiate the effectiveness of reinforcing stimuli (e.g., Donny et al., 2004).

[11]See the Behavior Analysis Certification Board's® (BACB®) Professional and Ethical Compliance Code for Behavior Analysts for using positive punishment procedures: www.bacb.com.

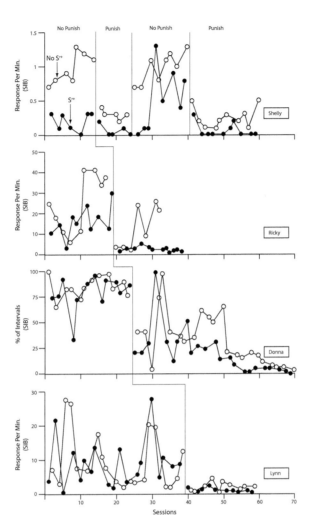

**Figure 30.1** Reducing maladaptive responding with mild punishment. SIB during alternative S^r+ and no S^r+ conditions across no-punishment and punishment phases. Note that different y-axis scales are used for each participant. From Thompson et al. (1999). © 1999 by the Society for the Experimental Analysis of Behavior, Inc.

(because the participant preferred the task to the rewards)" (p. 35). Additionally, whether a given aversive stimulus will be effective at any particular time often depends on the context in which it is delivered. Probably you have anticipated at least one of the reasons why different stimuli influence people distinctively: their learning histories. Learning affects whether any particular formerly neutral (or sometimes, even a primary aversive event, like hitting one's head or being restrained) begins to acquire reinforcing properties. The same is true of conditioned aversive stimuli. In some households, arguing is considered quite obnoxious; in others, it is recreational. Some children melt in response to reprimands, whereas others appear oblivious to scolding, no matter how harsh. The peculiarly individual nature of aversive stimuli poses a problem for policymakers attempting to restrict their use. One temptation is to categorize such stimuli according to their apparent degrees of intrusiveness or restrictiveness. But those classifications may well vary as a function of local values. Also, such arbitrary designations may be inappropriate for any specific individual. For instance, Favell, McGimsey, and Jones

(1978) noted that physically restraining clients for self-injurious behavior functioned not as a punisher but as a positive reinforcer. *Consequently, we can only designate a given stimulus as a punisher on the basis of the function it serves for a given individual under particular circumstances.*

## Vary Effective Aversive Stimuli

Similar to avoiding satiating with given reinforcers, you can *minimize your client's adapting to punishing stimuli by varying the aversive stimuli.* For example, Charlop et al. (1988) found that when they altered the punishers (overcorrection, timeout, or the word "No") instead of limiting themselves to using a single punisher, children with developmental delays misbehaved less frequently. The authors postulated several reasons for this effect:

- Individuals might adapt to the repeated presentation of a single punisher.
- Perhaps the variety of multiple punishers increased the salience of the consequences.
- The literature on avoidance behavior (e.g., Dunlap & Johnson, 1985; Sidman, 1953) indicates that "unpredictable contingencies promote a more steady rate of avoidance behavior" (p. 94).
- "The varied-punisher condition may be viewed as a combination of a continuous schedule of punishment with the unpredictability of specific punishers, thus maximizing the effect" (p. 95).

## Prevent Escape

Escape is a natural reaction to aversive stimulation. When escape is blocked, the effect of punishment is even more acute (Azrin et al., 1965; Dinsmoor & Campbell, 1956). If Pearl runs out of the room instead of participating in an overcorrection routine for self-injurious acts, the procedure can have no effect. Were escape prevented, the procedure would have a better chance of working.

Some escape behaviors merit encouragement, however, because they are acceptable alternatives to the unwanted target behavior. Permitting Lucretia to escape from contingent observation by becoming compliant and indicating her readiness to play nicely is one example. An appropriate way for Pearl to escape overcorrection would be by cooperating in the positive-practice routine and returning to active participation in instructional tasks, rather than to self-stimulation. Such situations actually are episodes of negative reinforcement (the removal of aversive stimuli contingent on the behavior). Naturally, when *appropriate* escape behaviors are emitted for a time, they should be positively reinforced. (Guard against making acceptable escape behaviors the only occasion for reinforcement, though. Soon you will see why.)

## Apply Immediately and Consistently

As with reinforcement, punishment tends to operate more effectively when the aversive stimuli (or stimulus) are applied every time the offense occurs (Acker & O'Leary, 1988; Lerman et al., 1997) and as soon as possible afterward (Azrin, 1956; Michael, 2004). In their study of traffic violations, Wagenaar and Maldonado-Molino (2007) concluded that the effectiveness of the deterrence policy they devised for speeders seemed to be more strongly affected by how rapidly the punishment was delivered than by the severity of the penalty. Therefore, by immediately and consistently applying punishment whenever an employee acts recklessly, you should note a rapid drop in his rate of risk-taking and an increase in his ability to distinguish unsafe from safe acts.

Suppose a toddler has run into the street:

> To teach him the danger associated with being in the street, the child's parent might give the child one sharp spank as he picks the child up out of the street. This spanking would teach the child to associate the middle of the street with danger, but a spanking after he is safely back in the curb is poor timing. The child should associate the street with danger; the curb, with safety. (Krumboltz & Krumboltz, 1972, p. 206)

However, rather than a "sharp spank" we would recommend a sharp reprimand of the behavior.

Circumstances may prevent you from administering punishment immediately and consistently. When confronted with such a situation, consider *recreating the episode*, so at a later time the early links in the chain of unacceptable behaviors are eventually followed by the punisher, as in two successful studies with clients with developmental delays (Rolider & Van Houten, 1985a; Van Houten & Rolider, 1988). One of these clients in the 1985 study, a multiply-handicapped 17-year-old girl, stole and hoarded objects belonging to others. When confronted with the (planted) items she was known regularly to steal and required immediately to remain immobile in a padded corner for one minute, her rates of stealing rapidly diminished. The authors concluded that the *recreating the episode* procedure "provides an opportunity for trained personnel to apply restrictive procedures to low frequency behavior that occurs in their absence rather than relying on less qualified staff to implement the procedure immediately after the behavior occurs" (p. 190).

The same authors used a similar procedure successfully to diminish children's tantrums in public places (Van Houten & Rolider, 1988). The tantrum was recorded, an illustrative segment of about one minute extracted, and several hours later their parents replayed the recording at home. They then implemented a timeout procedure following each of four repetitions. The experimenters concluded that this type of punishment procedure has several advantages: rapid behavioral reduction, enabling punishment of behaviors that are not easily detected or dealt with when they occur, and permitting the behavior analyst or someone trained in the procedure to apply it reliably and safely. Moreover, videotaping the behavior may have additional compensations. For example, if the behavior is dangerous, it might be more ethical to punish "video-trials" rather than waiting for the dangerous behavior to occur to permit a "teaching" moment.

Be alert to the dangers of using punishment inconsistently, because each time the violation succeeds, both positive and negative reinforcement are the likely consequences—and that will encourage a repetition of the misbehavior. Support for this contention can be seen in a study by Tarbox, Wallace, and Tarbox (2002), who demonstrated that a previously identified effective punishment procedure (response blocking for hand-mouthing) proved unsuccessful when employed intermittently. However, Lerman et al. (1997) did find that the self-injurious behavior of some (three out of five) clients with profound intellectual disabilities remained low *if the schedule of delivered punishment was gradually thinned out following a phase during which every response was punished.* However, for the other two subjects, such "intermittent punishment was ineffective, despite repeated attempts to thin the schedule" (p. 187). Only schedules of continuous punishment delivery were effective. It is best then, *to be prepared to deliver a very dense, preferably continuous, schedule of punishment if the data support that necessity.*

Delayed punishment has its special pitfalls as well. When the aversive stimuli are delivered at a time other than right away, the behavior immediately prior to the application of the punishers may be impacted rather than offensive behavior. For example, Timmy hits his sister while his mother is on the phone. Twenty minutes letter, when she gets off the phone, Timmy is doing his homework. At that point she scolds him for hitting his sister. Consequently, the punishment doesn't follow hitting, but instead, doing homework. Guess how that might affect Timmy's rate of doing his homework? Or instead, when Timmy's dad returns from work, the boy's mother regales her husband with tales of the child's misdeeds, insisting that dad discipline the child. The main effect of Dad's disciplining is to prompt Timmy to avoid his dad. Of course, rules can aid in bridging the gap, "Wait till your father gets home and he hears what you've done. He'll let you have it!" But, as we have seen, rules in governing behavior are not always as effective as current contingencies. (For example, when you delay the delivery of the reinforcer, you actually may reinforce the behavior it follows rather than the target behavior.) So the moral of the story is, if you are unable to use it regularly and immediately following the unwanted behavior (or cannot find a powerful way to bridge the time gap), don't use punishment. Otherwise you might make matters worse.

## Select Appropriate Intensity

One property of aversive stimulation makes it all the more dangerous—that all other factors being equal, the more intense the aversive stimulus, the more powerful its effect. A sharp retort is more influential than a mild one; so is a more intense blow or a longer regimen of effortful exercises. Low-intensity aversive stimuli may or may not be effective, depending on the learning history of the individual. Those who have rarely experienced that particular form of punishment in that particular context may be influenced by the mildest of aversive stimuli. One of the authors (Wallace), who was never shouted at as a child, finds any loud comments very aversive. Others with long histories of exposure to punishing stimuli in a particular setting may habituate to those that most find especially aversive. Many of our readers may have habituated to shouting as a general form of communication in their families, or to high decibel levels of music that the rest of us find downright painful! In general, though, all else being equal, the effect of mild punishment is less durable than that of the more severe variety (Azrin & Holtz, 1966; Boe & Church, 1967).

Nonetheless, milder forms of punishment can prove successful with weakly-established behaviors. As mentioned earlier, the frequency and schedule with which the behavior has been reinforced influences its strength. Feeble behaviors obviously are easier to eliminate, so mild punishment should be sufficient to eliminate those. When little Bonnie reached for her dog's tail for the first time, his growl and/or Mom's "No" or head shake probably would successfully prevent the recurrence of the behavior. Conversely, reducing well-established performances may require more intense punishment to override their reinforcing effects. If Bonnie habitually torments her dog, mild punishment probably would be insufficient to override the effects of the reinforcement she gains from hanging onto his tail. Lerman and Vordran's (2002) recommendation makes sense:

> While the punishing stimulus needs to be intensive enough for an effective application, it should not be more intense than necessary. Until further applied research on magnitude is conducted, practitioners should select magnitudes that have been shown to be safe and effective in clinical studies, as long as the magnitude is considered acceptable and practical by those who will be implementing treatment. (p. 443)

Yet, we would add that the level of intensity necessary at one time and place with any individual client, given his or her recent and extended histories, may not be the same as with the next client or situation. Also, there are alternative ways to avoid needing to resort to the use of intense punishment. One is to support milder aversive applications by combining those with other procedures—our next topic.

## Combine Positive Punishment with Extinction

Punishment works more rapidly when combined with extinction for the targeted behavior than when applied in isolation (Azrin & Holz, 1961, 1966). Achieving rapid results requires that, as feasible, reinforcers maintaining the unwanted behavior be removed or withheld and made contingent only on desirable alternative behaviors. Recall that a stimulus acquires conditioned aversive properties when it signals that no reinforcement is forthcoming. Such conditioning would be delayed or prevented if the behavior received reinforcement simultaneously from some other source, such as peer attention or hastening the completion of the task.

Similarly, the effectiveness of a punishing event can be diluted if the unwanted behavior is followed by aversive paired with reinforcing stimuli. Investigators have found that misconduct like blurting out (Acker & O'Leary, 1988) or aggression (Sawin & Parke, 1979) tend to persist rather than decline, and become more resistant to extinction when they produce both punishment and reinforcement. However, basic research (e.g., Epstein, 1984; Rodriguez & Logan, 1980) indicates that the timing and placement of punishment and reinforcement can influence the outcome. It does appear that when punishment precedes reinforcement, the punishment is less effective than when the reinforcement takes place first (Lerman & Vorndran, 2002).[12]

---

[12]This might help explain or enable the development of masochism.

When consequences are under your control, the best option is to block any reinforcement for the violation altogether. But how to accomplish this may not always be apparent. Some clientele may find the extra attention they garner from lengthy verbal reprimands reinforcing. Perhaps this is why Abramowitz, O'Leary, and Futtersak (1988) found that for seven hyperactive second- and third-graders, "short reprimands resulted in significantly lower rates of off-task behavior than did long reprimands" (p. 243).

The person whose disruptive behavior provokes not only an aversive scolding but also the approval of peers will be more likely to disrupt in the future than if peers did not display their approval. Sometimes, however, removing reinforcement for engaging in a specific behavior is extremely difficult, especially when the act itself provides immediate reinforcement. (Think pleasures of the flesh.) In such cases, externally delivered punishment will contribute little other than to teach the person to be more discreet. Circumstances like these probably are at the root of many of our most serious social problems, such as theft, rape, child molestation, unsafe sex, substance abuse, and some forms of self-injury. The powerful reinforcement yielded by those behaviors is immediate, whereas any punishment that others administer is usually delayed and intermittent—and, as a result, not too effective. This explains in part why criminal recidivism rates are so high.

Regardless of whether it is or is not possible to punish consistently, be sure to continue to withhold reinforcement whenever each violation does occur. A group of investigators (Sherrill, O'Leary, Albertson-Kelly, & Kendziora, 1996) found that teacher reprimands remained highly effective when delivered continuously, provided students' inappropriate attempts at soliciting their teacher's attention were ignored. Otherwise, if attended to (by providing feedback, asking the child to elaborate, answering the question, etc.) the inappropriate solicitations did not effectively diminish in the absence of the reprimand. The investigators concluded, "If you can reprimand only a small proportion of the child's solicitations for attention, ignore rather than attend to the rest" (p. 234). (However, in such a situation, DRA and modeling probably may have just as effectively reduced the behavior without the need for any punishment.)

## Consider and If Possible, Manage Contextual Factors

Establishing or motivational operations can strongly influence the extent to which punishment works. Probably the person's physical state, such as sleep or food deprivation, matters, especially when reinforcers for the unwanted response are influenced by those circumstances. Watch a normally compliant child throw a tantrum when tired!

Antecedent *stimuli*, such as the time, setting, agent, rules, and so on, can influence the outcome too, in terms of how successfully punishment works. Close physical proximity appears to increase the effectiveness of reprimands (Van Houten et al., 1982), as do a fixed stare and a firm grasp of the child's upper arm (Van Houten et al., 1982). Just as specifying the desired behavior while praising (Bernhardt & Forehand, 1975; Goetz & Salmonson, 1972) and/or smiling and a pat on the back increase the effectiveness of praise (Kazdin, Silverman, & Sittler, 1975), using specific reprimands can increase the effectiveness of punishment (Van Houten & Doleys, 1983).

As with other procedures, when the conditions under which punishment will be delivered are clear, its effect should be more powerful: "Do not smoke. Violators will be prosecuted" functions as a discriminative stimulus for punishment ($S^{Dp}$), informing people that smoking in that situation has a probability of being punished. Phrases like "Falling rock zone," "High voltage lines—danger"; and the sound so familiar to dwellers in tornado county—the tornado warning siren—have a similar function. As we described in Chapter 15, the $S^{Dp}$ develops by being consistently present when a given response is regularly punished in the presence of a stimulus.

The impact of a given episode of punishment also may depend on the agent delivering it. In the opera *Boris Godounov*, Tsar Boris threatens: "But should you lie to me, I promise you a death so terrible, so frightful, that Tsar Ivan himself will shudder in his grave in horror!" Prince Schuisky replies, "I fear no death—but fear [only] *your* displeasure" (Moussosrgky, 1874). Each of us has people in our lives whose approbation or disapproval is terribly important; others whose opinions hardly matter at all. Just a hint of dissatisfaction from the former can be more punishing than a severe reaction from the latter. In all likelihood, those whose reactions count are people in control of many important reinforcing contingencies in our lives: our parents, children, close relatives and friends, lovers and bosses. Although experimental evidence regarding this parameter of punishment remains to be studied, the results of the few studies known to us on source of feedback (e.g., Fox & Sulzer-Azaroff, 1989) hint that the specific agent of punishment may matter a lot.

## Program for Generalization and Maintenance

Generalization of the effects of punishment is by no means a foregone conclusion; nor is maintenance. In fact, sparse research is available on this topic, and most conclusions seem to be based on case reports. As far as we know at this point, rather than risking that the response only be suppressed under narrow stimulus conditions, we suggest you conduct the program *in all settings* in which the response reduction is desired and also design a technique to prevent relapse. (Chapters 21–23 detailed such methods.) At a minimum, train and check the fidelity of the treatment as conducted by all managers, staff, parents, peers, clients, and others who control contingencies.

## Monitor Regularly

Recall that the Behavior Analyst Certification Board *ethics code for behavior analysts,* (2020) code 2.15, states: *Behavior analysts must continually evaluate and document the effectiveness of restrictive or punishment-based procedures and modify or discontinue the behavior-change intervention in a timely manner if it is ineffective* (p. 12, italics added). As always, you need to keep records to document the integrity with which the procedure is implemented. This is one procedure where you should really record when and how often it is being implemented, not just whether it is being implemented correctly. Beside serving as a monitoring system, it allows you to analyze the true nature of the procedure (e.g., it should not take 25 applications to see a reduction in the problem behavior). Also, consistently and reliably record and graph the rate of the target behavior under baseline and treatment conditions. Data patterns will permit you to regularly assess change and to decide whether to stay the course, revise, or discontinue the procedure. Because punishment may generate various side effects, other problematic and adaptive behaviors need to be measured as well. Evidence of behavioral contrast, suppression of other behaviors, attempts to withdraw from the situation, aggressive responses, detrimental peer reactions, and negative self-statements ("self-esteem") all should be noted. Data hinting at marked increases or decreases in such side effects will be useful in assessing the general success of the program.

## Teach Optimal Choice Selection Up Front

Consider the case of choosing between small amounts of reinforcers now versus larger amounts of reinforcers later on. A basic research literature, *behavioral economics*, revolves about this issue, because often, the rapid (*impulsive*) choice is disadvantageous to the individual and to society in the long run. (Think: party versus study now, leading to marginal versus better job later; spend versus save money now, leading to no versus some earned interest later; cheat versus learning the assignment now, leading to being unskilled or skilled on the job later.)

## An Illustration of Optimal Application of Punishment for Extremely Dangerous Self-Abusive Behavior: SIBIS

Once in a while, extremely self-abusive clients are brought to the attention of behavior analysts, because everything else of a more constructive and benign nature has failed to terminate the injuries they heap upon themselves. In some cases, for instance, continued self-abuse has threatened imminent loss of vision or other sensory or brain function. The **self-injurious behavior inhibiting system (SIBIS)**, *an apparatus designed to reduce severe self-injury by delivering electric shock as punishment*, was invented to incorporate all the key features of an effective punishment strategy for the purpose of discouraging this class of behavior (Linscheid, Iwata, Ricketts, Williams, & Griffin, 1990). Specifically, the apparatus responds to severe self-blows to the head by delivering a response-contingent electric shock to the client's arm or leg, while automatically recording the stimulus delivery.

Linscheid et al., presented five cases where individuals with severe, longstanding, and previously unmanageable self-injury were successfully treated (i.e., self-injury was immediately and almost completely eliminated) using the SIBIS unit to deliver contingent electrical stimulation. In fact, results not only demonstrated the effective use of the SIBIS unit, but also that a mild, brief electric stimulation eliminated previously untreatable self-injury (i.e., other reinforcement based methods had been unsuccessful). Although follow-up data indicate maintenance in the original evaluation, published long-term follow-up reports have yielded conflicting evidence regarding long-term effectiveness. In one case, after years during which SIBIS functioned effectively, the self-injury returned (e.g., Rickett, Goza, & Matese, 1993). Perhaps the client had adapted to the repeated exposure to the stimulus, or maybe self-injury was being used as his attempted and perhaps sole medium of communication. (Hitting head = "I feel bad.") The latter possibility is partly supported by results from another case (Linscheid & Reichenbach, 2002), for when the researchers were sensitive to and rapidly addressed medical problems such as ear infection, fevers, and medication status, the self-injury rates remained low over a period of five years. These long-term follow-up reports remind us that *it is important to think of the durability of the effects of the interventions we implement and to remember that punishment alone should never be the sole intervention.*

## APPLYING CONTINGENT EFFORT

In addition to assessing the function of the unwanted behavior and applying the above guidelines for optimizing the effect of "generic punishment," you might consider the following suggestions for choosing and using *contingent effort* activities.

## Select Activities Relevant to the Misbehavior

When you use aversive activities like overcorrection, try to choose those that are relevant to the misbehavior. Foxx and Bechtel (1982) have argued that using irrelevant responses does not constitute overcorrection, even when the methods share characteristics in common with over-correction. Foxx and Azrin (1972) also noted, "This characteristic of relevance should also motivate the educator to apply the restitution procedure since the educator would otherwise be forced to correct the general disturbance himself" (p. 16).

The misbehaving client should directly experience the effort normally required by others to undo the damage created by the client's misbehavior. For example, the person who overturns the desk is instructed to set it upright and to dust and clean it. Clients who frequently had their hands in their mouths (Foxx & Azrin, 1973) or bit their hands, which resulted in formation of irritated, reddened, and torn, open calluses, were required to engage in an oral-hygiene procedure by brushing their gums and teeth with a toothbrush that had been partially immersed in a container of oral antiseptic (mouthwash) and to wipe their outer lips with a washcloth dampened with the antiseptic. According to Foxx and Azrin, this restitution activity was initially selected because "mouthing of objects or parts of one's body results in exposure to potentially harmful microorganisms through unhygienic oral contact. The Restitutional Overcorrection rationale suggests that this possibility of self-infection be eliminated" (1973, p. 4).

In another case (Barnard et al., 1974), guided by a kitchen timer, clients were required to engage in two minutes of washing the affected areas, using a cotton swab and mild soap; one minute of hand drying; and two minutes of rubbing hand-cream into the affected area. As a result, mouthing or biting hands was substantially reduced among all children in both studies. More recently, Ricciardi, Luiselli, Terrill, and Reardon (2003) required a seven-year-old boy with autism to repeatedly practice discarding objects contingent on attempted or actual pica, rather than eating the objects. His pica was successfully reduced to near zero levels.

## Maintain Consistency of Performance of Aversive Activities

As already implied, aversive activities need to be performed without pause. Furthermore, additional work and effort are included, for as Foxx and Azrin have indicated in relation to overcorrection, "an increased work or effort requirement is known to be annoying and serves as an inhibitory event" (1972, p. 16). However, ethics demand that, to avoid injury, *excessive force be avoided*. Wait patiently until major resistance subsides; being emotionally distraught competes with learning.

## Extend Duration of Aversive Activities

Foxx and Azrin (1972) suggested that the restitution duration extend two to ten minutes beyond the time needed to restore the disrupted environment; not excessive but longer than that needed simply to correct a wrong (for example, setting a chair upright) and to restore the environment.

## Consider Reinforcing Positive Practice

Originally, Foxx and Azrin (1972) and Foxx and Bechtel (1982) cautioned against using reinforcement during positive practice out of concern that the targeted behavior might increase under other circumstances as a result. In using positive practice with adults with developmental delays, though, Carey and Bucher (1981) did reinforce the correct behavior. Yet, their clients' stereotypy diminished and the correct motor tasks they were instructed to implement accelerated. The authors concluded that in situations in which the outside environment would be expected to positively reinforce correct practices, "the use of reinforcement for positive practice would appear to be the treatment to be tried in preference to the traditional version" (p. 90). Your own choice should depend on what the data tell you. You could try withholding versus applying reinforcement for the positive practice efforts under controlled conditions (e.g., in a multi-element design) to determine which produces the more productive outcome. Along with various antecedents and differential reinforcement methods, you might find that combining positive practice with reinforcement provides a constructive alternative to simple punishment. The procedure may even act more rapidly than DRO alone, in that the client's behavior would yield a denser reinforcement schedule.

Other examples of reinforced positive practice might include reinforcing Tricia's moving her head as instructed, or Wayne's repeated practice of correctly-written previously misspelled words.

# RIGHT TO EFFECTIVE TREATMENT

It would be amiss for us to provide you with all this information regarding the definition of punishment, descriptions and effectiveness of punishment based procedures, the do's and don'ts, the side effects, and not discuss the notion of the *right to effective treatment*. The Behavior Analyst Certification Board (2020) *Ethics code for behavior analysts* stipulates in code 2.01 on "Providing Effective Treatment" the following:

> Behavior analysts prioritize clients' rights and needs in service delivery. They provide services that are conceptually consistent with behavioral principles, based on scientific evidence, and designed to maximize desired outcomes for and protect all clients, stakeholders, supervises, trainees, and research participants from harm. Behavior analysts implement non-behavioral services with clients only if they have the required education, formal training, and professional credentials to deliver such services. (p. 10)

The idea of ensuring the right to effective treatment within applied behavior analysis has a long-standing history. In fact, Van Houten et al. (1988) provide a very detailed discussion on this very topic. The argument is made that effective services (reinforcement or punishment-based) should not be withheld, especially when withholding said treatment poses risks to the client (e.g., think of someone who engages in severe head banging). This includes effectively treating behaviors that are barriers to independence and social acceptability. Moreover, the judgement of restrictiveness needs to be cogently evaluated in that it might be that a slower acting procedure based upon reinforcement may actually be more restrictive than a faster acting procedure based upon punishment, especially with severe behavior problems. Vollmer (2002) stated: "to ignore punishment as an application is akin to ignoring the benefits and limitations of medical technology" (p. 469). Thus, although we firmly recommend the use of reinforcement based procedures, there are circumstances in which the client has the right to have punishment utilized within a treatment package.

## SUMMARY AND CONCLUSIONS

Punishment is an integral aspect of daily life. Although its use as a management tool sometimes can be justified, as in the opening case in this chapter, it tends to be relied upon much too heavily and is often applied inappropriately. One antidote is to teach personnel serving dependent populations, such as jailers, custodians, parents, and teachers, about its effects on behavior and how to apply it successfully when required. Here we have reviewed various types of aversive stimuli, defined and discussed variations of aversive stimuli and punishment's advantages, disadvantages, and its effective use. Punishment in its simplest form was described as a procedure involving the presentation of an aversive stimulus, resulting in a reduction of the rate of the behavior. Additionally, we discussed various kinds of contingent effort. These included (1) *contingent effort* (or *contingent exertion or exercise*): requiring the performance of effortful movements as a consequence of committing misdeeds, (2) *overcorrection*: requiring the use of a relevant, educative form of contingent effort, along with *positive practice*, and when environmental disruption occurs, providing restitution, and (3) *negative practice*: being required to expend effort practicing the unwanted behavior repeatedly, with the goal of achieving satiation or transforming the response sequence into an aversive situation.

Traditionally, discipline has been practiced by punishing misbehaviors and reinforcing desired or goal behavior (a two-pronged approach). Today, however, thanks to the research efforts of several generations of behavior analysts, a number of non-punitive alternatives are available, including: antecedent methods that have demonstrated effectiveness for preventing inappropriate behavior, a variety of effective differential reinforcement procedures, and social-skills and other training. All of these alternatives can be used to prevent the escalation of behaviors of concern in the first place and to reduce the behavior should it become necessary. No longer are we primarily dependent on punitive procedures for reducing severe behaviors. This is a promising development in that punitive procedures have, as described in this and previous chapters, a number of serious disadvantages. Given the current state-of-the-art practice of behavior management, punitive procedures (whether negative or positive) should only be considered after all others (the methods contained in Chapters 26–28) fail, when the reinforcers that maintain *serious behavior* cannot be identified and/or controlled, or when competing reinforcers cannot be found or used. Even then, under most all circumstances, *avoid the use of severe forms of positive or negative punishment*, including corporal punishment, restraint, and seclusion, due to their potential for causing long-term mental health problems. When punishment is deemed the only option, it should be combined with a variety of non-punitive constructive alternatives, particularly DRA, along with various antecedent methods appropriate to the situation. In addition, when punishment is the only available recourse for treating dangerous and serious behaviors, we need to apply our procedures faithfully (including assessing and reporting treatment fidelity) and carefully and reliably monitor, record, and report ongoing direct and indirect effects on the client's behavior.

Also, we strongly recommend that you review Table 10.6 on selecting interventions based on function. We believe that you will find this table a helpful guide in addressing various behaviors of concern.

See the *Summary Table for Preventing and Reducing Behavior* starting on the next page.

# SUMMARY TABLE: PREVENTING AND REDUCING BEHAVIOR

## Antecedent Methods and Procedural Packages for Preventing/Reducing Behavior

| Procedure/ Operation | Maximizing Effectiveness | Temporal Properties | Durability of Effect | Other Features and Comments |
|---|---|---|---|---|
| **Redirecting:** Interrupt inappropriate and prompt more acceptable alternative behavior | 1. Prompt and reinforce engaging in acceptable alternative behavior<br>2. Avoid redirecting to alternative activity if escape is function of unwanted behavior<br>3. Avoid redirecting if function of behavior is attention seeking | Rapid | Often temporary; sometimes long lasting, particularly when activity to which redirected is heavily reinforced | |
| **Distracting with preferred event:** Distract the individual by providing reinforcing events in advance of, or during, the transition. | 1. Use in advance of situations likely to provoke problem behavior, such as transitioning to a less preferred activity<br>2. Provide high-preference item during transition<br>3. Provide reinforcers for transitioning appropriately | Rapid when works | Varies with reinforcing value of distraction | Such distractions function as motivational operations setting the stage for more adaptive behaviors. May reduce tantrums during transitions |
| **Establishing behavioral momentum:** Program behavior known to produce high rates (e.g., of compliance) in advance of low rate (less preferred) activity | 1. Program several high rate (i.e., high preference) activities prior to requesting lower rate (i.e., preference) activity<br>2. Combine with differential reinforcement (i.e., unwanted responses on extinction;, compliance with desired, low probability responses contingently rewarded with powerful reinforcers) | Rapid | Long lasting provided differentially reinforced | (Functions as an MO). May promote greater compliance |

| Procedure/Operation | Maximizing Effectiveness | Temporal Properties | Durability of Effect | Other Features and Comments |
|---|---|---|---|---|
| **Reducing response effort:** Temporarily reduce the level of demand or effort | 1. Reduce amount or difficulty level of requested activity<br>2. Adjust tasks to match participants' functional levels<br>3. Differentially reinforce compliance<br>4. Gradually increase amount of work or difficulty level as reinforcement continues for compliance<br>5. Intersperse easier tasks to provide success, review and fluency development | Rate of problem behavior rapidly reduced; desired behavior, gradually achieved | Long lasting as long as participation in activity reinforced | Help avoid problematic reactions during situations that call for compliance. Situation made less aversive. Participants tend to accomplish more and remain on task longer when easy tasks interspersed with more difficult tasks |
| **Applying noncontingent reinforcement (NCR):** Presenting reinforcers on a fixed-time (FT) or variable-time (VT) schedule, regardless of the client's actions at the moment (unless clearly misbehaving) | 1. Select effective reinforcers<br>2. Deliver reinforcers on a fixed or variable time schedule<br>3. If seeking to reduce problem behaviors, frequently use reinforcer(s) currently maintaining the problem behavior, or powerful reinforcers that interfere with the reinforcing function of the problem behavior<br>4. Avoid using NCR if you notice or even suspect that your clients often engage in unwanted behavior, or combine with extinction of the problem behavior | Gradual | Long lasting as long as NCR is continued | Enriches reinforcing. value of environment Easy to use. Often used as an antecedent intervention for preventing and reducing unwanted behavior. Minimizes or eliminates the negative side effects of extinction (e.g., extinction bursts). |

739

| Procedure/Operation | Maximizing Effectiveness | Temporal Properties | Durability of Effect | Other Features and Comments |
|---|---|---|---|---|
| **Applying noncontingent reinforcement (NCR) (cont.)** | 5. Combine with DRA and perhaps modeling to teach replacement behavior | | | Does not teach specific functional replacement or alternative behaviors. If not combined with extinction of unwanted behavior, can promote accidental learning or reinforcement of problem behavior |
| **Modeling:** Demonstrate the appropriate or replacement behavior, and positively recognize others — e.g., popular peers, colleagues — for engaging in the replacement behavior | 1. Reinforce group members demonstrating appropriate behavior (i.e., use their behavior as imitative prompts) <br> 2. When noting person engaged in violation, use that to cue yourself to look for others who are complying and publicly recognize their appropriate behavior <br> 3. Highlight similarity between observers and models <br> 4. Encourage behavioral rehearsal <br> 5. Provide instructions, rules, and rationales | Moderate | Long lasting provided differential reinforcement consistent | Helps prevent and reduce problem behavior AND teaches how to behave. Behaviors deserving of recognition and attention more likely to receive those |

| Procedure/Operation | Maximizing Effectiveness | Temporal Properties | Durability of Effect | Other Features and Comments |
|---|---|---|---|---|
| **Modeling (cont.)** | 6. Keep the modeled behavior simple<br>7. Reinforce acts of imitation of the modeled behavior<br>8. Select multiple models who are: (a) similar to the observer, (b) demonstrate the desired behavior competently (even though they may have had similar problems in the past), (c) have a good measure of prestige in the group (i.e., receives more than the average amount of reinforcement from peers and supervisors), and have (d) had previous positive experience with the observer | | | |
| **Using activity schedule:** Specify in words, or display in pictures, the daily sequence of activities the student or client is to complete by the time a cue is provided (e.g., lights on and off, spoken instructions) to signal time to change to the next activity. | 1. Display schedule to permit periodic client review throughout the day<br>2. Words or pictures displayed vertically to enable client to move each symbol from the *to-be-completed* to the *completed* column<br>3. Gradually fade out activity schedule as spoken instructions acquire discriminative control<br>4. Reinforce smooth transitioning<br>5. Gradually thin reinforcement as client learns to transition appropriately | Rapid, after masters use of activity schedule | Long lasting as long as activity schedule present | Often used to facilitate transitions. |

741

| Procedure/ Operation | Maximizing Effectiveness | Temporal Properties | Durability of Effect | Other Features and Comments |
|---|---|---|---|---|
| **Social stories:** stories containing brief episodes, consisting of one concept per page, written in first person, and designed to provide the children with answers to questions of the *who, what, when, where,* and *why* of a given social situation. They include the likely reactions of others the situation and provide information about the appropriate social response tailored to the individual | 1. Tailor social story to individual's specific situations, ability and environment<br>2. Combine written and/or verbal story with visuals such a s pictures or video of models<br>3. Combine with peer/adult prompting<br>4. Incorporate into your social story procedures the various features derived from behavior analytic studies including:<br>  a. select behavioral goals that are likely to be supported by the natural environment<br>  b. select appropriate models<br>  c. provide follow-up role-playing<br>  d. provide real-life practice across various situations<br>  e. differentially reinforce the particular social skill in all relevant situations | Gradual | May be long lasting assuming necessary skills in client's repertoire and all relevant environments continue to support newly learned social skill | Focus is on teaching how to behave. A form of social skills training |

| Procedure/Operation | Maximizing Effectiveness | Temporal Properties | Durability of Effect | Other Features and Comments |
|---|---|---|---|---|
| **Social skills training:** Teach socially acceptable behaviors that will be naturally recognized and accepted (reinforced) by high status, productive peers and significant others | 1. Identify social skill deficit through observation or use of social skill inventory<br>2. Do a task analysis of social skill to be taught<br>3. Use chaining, modeling, other prompts such as instructions, role-playing, and provide real-life practice across various situations once social skill has reached a degree of fluency<br>4. Use differential reinforcement throughout training | | | Focus is on teaching how *to* behave. By learning to pay attention, take turns, wait patiently, and so on, youngsters are less likely to become inattentive, impulsive, impatient, or engage in other inappropriate behavior |

## Consequential Methods for Preventing/Reducing Behavior

| Procedure/ Operation | Maximizing Effectiveness | Temporal Properties | Durability of Effect | Other Features and Comments |
|---|---|---|---|---|
| **Reductive Procedures in General** | 1. Obtain informed consent if indicated by organizational policy<br>2. Conduct a functional behavioral assessment for serious problems<br>3. Monitor behavior and treatment fidelity throughout<br>4. Implement procedures for maintenance and generalization of acceptable replacement behaviors<br>5. Prepare and maintain densely reinforcing environment<br>6. Combine with antecedent methods for reducing behavior | | | |
| **Extinction:** Withhold contingent reinforcers as a consequence of a behavior | 1. Identify all reinforcers for a particular behavior and withhold completely<br>2. Avoid using extinction as the sole intervention especially with aggressive behaviors, in group settings and with intolerable behaviors<br>3. Supplement with other reductive methods, especially differential reinforcement of alternative behaviors (DRA)<br>4. Provide NCR<br>5. Specify conditions under which extinction conditions are in effect and follow through consistently<br>6. Maintain procedure long enough to begin to show effect<br>7. Implement and sustain extinction within all contexts in which the behavioral reduction is to take place, including, if possible, the context in which the behavior was originally established | Gradual | Long lasting provided extinction conditions maintained and alternative behaviors reinforced | Possible behavioral contrast, extinction burst, spontaneous recovery and/or resurgence. May be difficult to withhold all reinforcers. Does not depend on application of aversive stimuli. |

| Procedure/ Operation | Maximizing Effectiveness | Temporal Properties | Durability of Effect | Other Features and Comments |
|---|---|---|---|---|
| **Extinction (cont.)** | 8. Consider using extinction to promote response variability as a basis for choosing acceptable alternative behaviors to reinforce | | | |
| **Differential reinforcement of alternative behavior (DRA):** Reinforce alternative(s) to unwanted behavior while withholding reinforcement from unwanted behavior | 1. Identify selected alternative to/replacement for the problem behavior<br>2. Reinforce replacement behavior and other alternatives to the problem behavior<br>3. When possible, select and reinforce alternative behavior that cannot coexist with the unwanted behavior (DRI)<br>4. Withhold reinforcers from the problem behavior<br>5. Combine with other differential reinforcement procedures (DRD & DRO), modeling and other prompts<br>6. Adhere to guidelines for effective reinforcement and extinction procedures<br>7. Plan for and apply methods to promote generalization and maintenance of desired response | Moderate | Long lasting | Constructive, positive, benign and acceptable. Need to monitor for and reinforce alternative behavior throughout |
| **Differential reinforcement of other behavior (DRO) or Omission Training:** Differentially reinforce absence, omission or non-occurrence of a (particular) behavior | 1. All methods for effectively using differential reinforcement listed above apply<br>2. Maximize person's opportunity for reinforcement under whole interval DRO by examining baseline performance. Determine average period of time individual successfully omits the unwanted behavior; set DRO interval just below that.<br>3. Reset requisite time period immediately following the behavior of concern, rather than waiting for entire interval to expire<br>4. To minimize behavioral contrast, ensure targeted not reinforced at other times/elsewhere | Gradual, but more rapid if combined with DRA | Can be long lasting provided omission of target behavior or occurrence of alternative behavior | DRO may strengthen other ongoing behavior(s) Procedure widely applicable. Unless combined with DRA, may result in behavioral contrast, |

| Procedure/ Operation | Maximizing Effectiveness | Temporal Properties | Durability of Effect | Other Features and Comments |
|---|---|---|---|---|
| **Differential reinforcement of other behavior (DRO) or Omission Training (cont.)** | 5. Withhold reinforcement delivery if other unwanted behaviors occurring at the time. Wait for desired or neutral behavior.<br>6. After objectionable behavior has begun to diminish in rate, gradually extend the intervals<br>7. Combine with other procedures such as DRA | | intermittently reinforced | increased attending to negative behaviors and fails "dead man's test" |
| **Differential reinforcement of low rates (DRL):** Reinforce behavior if occurs following specific period of time during which absent | 1. Extend interval gradually until desired rate reached<br>2. Base size of interval on previous performance patterns<br>3. Limit application to acceptable behaviors occurring too frequently or rapidly (e.g., eating too fast; talking excessively or participating in group discussion)<br>4. Combine with other procedures such as stimulus control (e.g., modeling, rules, goal setting), DRA, and DRO<br>5. If undesired behavior occurring, postpone delivery of reinforcers, behavior acceptable | Gradual | May be long-lasting | Benign, tolerant, convenient; focus on unwanted behavior |
| **Differential reinforcement of diminishing rates (DRD):** Deliver reinforcers when number of responses per time period less than, or equal to, prescribed limit | 1. Same as above, except for #3<br>2. Extend interval, or reduce the number of targeted response within the interval, gradually<br>3. Retreat to shorter intervals if regression occurs | Gradual | May be long-lasting | Same as above. May not be suitable for dangerous or objectionable behaviors |

| Procedure/ Operation | Maximizing Effectiveness | Temporal Properties | Durability of Effect | Other Features and Comments |
|---|---|---|---|---|
| **Response cost:** Remove or withdraw quantities of reinforcers contingent on unwanted response | 1. Allow for buildup of reinforcement reserve<br>2. Empirically determine effective magnitude of response cost<br>3. Communicate conditions of application<br>4. Apply every time<br>5. Combine with other procedures such as DRA and modeling<br>6. Consider using bonus response cost<br>7. Consider delivering response cost points to a peer<br>8. Design program to minimize emotional outbursts | Rapid | Long-lasting, when combined with DRA | Promotes discrimination; socially acceptable; convenient; effect depends on reinforcement history; may occasion aggression and escape; associated stimuli may become aversive; potential for abuse; other behaviors may be suppressed; does not teach how to behave |
| **Timeout:** Deny access to varied reinforcers for specific time contingent upon a unwanted response | 1. Make time-in as reinforcing as possible<br>2. Avoid use if time-in is aversive<br>3. Empirically determine effective magnitude of timeout<br>4. Use least intrusive, but effective form of timeout<br>5. Communicate conditions for use of timeout<br>6. Remove reinforcers during timeout<br>7. Apply every time<br>8. Combine with other procedures such as DRA and modeling<br>9. Avoid opportunities for self-injury or escape during timeout<br>10. Design program to minimize emotional outbursts — consider using contingent delay<br>11. Consider using contingent delay<br>12. Implement safeguards if seclusion or restraint timeout used | Rapid | Long-lasting when combined with DRA | All the above plus: loss of learning time; may be legally restricted; public concern (non-exclusionary timeout is more acceptable than exclusionary timeout) |

| Procedure/ Operation | Maximizing Effectiveness | Temporal Properties | Durability of Effect | Other Features and Comments |
|---|---|---|---|---|
| **Overcorrection:** Require individual to repair environmental disruption or destruction (restitution) and to intensively practice optimal forms of a constructive, alternative behavior (positive practice) | 1. Obtain informed consent<br>2. Make restitution relevant to misbehavior<br>3. Combine restitution activity with extinction and timeout like conditions<br>4. Extend duration of restitution several minutes beyond time needed to restore disrupted environment<br>5. Consider reinforcing positive practice responding<br>6. Apply consistently<br>7. Apply immediately<br>8. Arrange environment to block escape<br>9. Keep performance consistent during procedure<br>10. Combine with reinforcement of alternative behavior at times other than during overcorrection<br>11. Avoid using excessive force | Rapid | Long-lasting | Minimizes disadvantages of punishment but still aversive; educative; instructive to peers; may facilitate acquisition of various skills; provokes withdrawal, escape, and aggression |
| **Negative practice:** Require individual repeatedly to practice unwanted behavior for predetermined time | 1. Use in reinforcing environment<br>2. Use on behavior for which repetition can be tolerated<br>3. Do not use with dangerous behavior | Moderate | Can be long-lasting | Probably works due to required effort, extinction, and satiation |
| **Punishment:** Present aversive stimulus contingent on a response | 1. Obtain informed consent<br>2. Select and use minimal, yet effective, aversive consequences<br>3. Vary the aversive stimuli that you use<br>4. Combine with extinction<br>5. Combine with reinforcement of alternative behavior<br>6. Arrange environment to block escape<br>7. Apply consistently<br>8. Apply immediately | Rapid | May be long-lasting in context in which used | Provokes escape, withdrawal, and aggression; can decrease or increase collateral problem behavior; instructive to peers; increases responsiveness to reinforcement; can promote inappropriate generalization; act of |

| Procedure/ Operation | Maximizing Effectiveness | Temporal Properties | Durability of Effect | Other Features and Comments |
|---|---|---|---|---|
| **Punishment (cont.)** | 9. Consider, and if possible, manage contextual factors<br>10. Avoid excessive force<br>11. Implement maintenance and generalization of replacement behavior | Rapid | | punishment may be imitated; negative impact on "self-esteem"; tendency to be overused; habituation to punisher possible; can generate public antipathy |

*Chapter 31*

# Achieving Lasting Change Ethically

## Goals

1. Specify where and with whom behavioral procedures can be responsibly applied.
2. Once you have mastered the material in this book, describe what you need to do next within your professional development.
3. Describe steps for minimizing malpractice.
4. Describe the mission and purpose of the Behavior Analysis Certification Board®.
5. Describe the foundation upon which ethical perspectives are based.
6. List and describe elements of the code for professional and ethical conduct, endorsed by the Behavior Analysis Certification Board®.
7. Point out the advantages of using ethical guidelines.
8. Draw a conclusion about the ways knowledge of ABA concepts, principles, and practices can benefit your clientele, you yourself, your families, and your local and broader societies.

*************

At last, we have just about completed our survey of many ways to analyze and change behavior and keep it changed. To recall where we began and how far we have progressed, turn back to Figure 1.1. Yes, we have considered what applied behavior analysis is, its historical and philosophical underpinnings, and the way it functions. Then we noted that ABA generally operates according to a customary plan: In response to a practical or conceptual challenge, behavior analysts take a series of preliminary steps, pursuing a particular path toward the goals and objectives chosen to meet that challenge. Prior to actually initiating any change strategies, we make ethically responsible plans for measuring and analyzing ways to demonstrate the functionality of the relationship between the particular procedures and behavioral changes. Then, during and/or after assessing baseline performance, we identify current functional contingencies, choose new ones to test, and plan ways to analyze and evaluate patterns of change. Given proper permissions and that foundation in place, we implement the jointly selected program and monitor progress toward our goals.

The thousands of references to reports of successful outcomes noted in this text and elsewhere corroborate the power and utility of applied behavior-analytic principles and procedures. In a way, this science-based technology works so well because:

- Functional assessments reveal what contingencies currently support the behavior(s) of interest (why the person is doing what s/he does) and guide our selection of the most promising change methods.
- Preference assessments help to identify highly effective reinforcers for the purpose of motivating clients.
- Measurement during baseline and treatment reveals ongoing behavior patterns prior to and during our implementation of any change strategies.
- Experimental analysis of the impact of those strategies permits us to determine the extent to which our plans are succeeding, and/or whether we need to alter our change procedures or perhaps even revisit our objectives.

Of course, there are and will be more tribulations. Unsolved behavioral challenges continue to confront us at every level, from the minor and personal to the major and social. What is it that causes and how do we prevent an army psychiatrist from turning a gun on his colleagues and murdering 13 of them? What prompts societies to drop bombs on or blow up their adversaries or even themselves? How can we help prevent such horrors? Why do hordes of people die needlessly of preventable diseases or injuries and what can be done to reverse this situation? Are there systematic methods for modifying the wasteful behavior that imperils the future of life on earth? And even when successes are documented, reproducing those outcomes more efficiently and lastingly remains an ongoing challenge. The need for the services of skillful applied behavior analysts will persist well beyond our collective lifetimes.

## WHERE AND WITH WHOM MAY WE APPLY BEHAVIORAL PROCEDURES?

If you are convinced of the validity, generality, and applicability of ABA's research findings, the short answer to "where and with whom does ABA work?" is: everywhere, with everyone, including ourselves, *provided our activities conform to ethical standards.* Why? Because applying principles of behavior, based as they are on scientific evidence, is simply a case of using good teaching, training, counseling, coaching, or management practices. Ignoring your newfound expertise or selecting change strategies of lesser effectiveness would be foolish. So, ethically applying behavioral principles to achieve your own goals or those of your family members, significant others, colleagues, managers, friends, pets, and everyone else over whose contingencies you maintain sufficient control, makes sense. With that said, it is important to make sure that we are practicing within our scope of competency. For example, although I know that ABA interventions work with children with feeding disorders, if I do not have competency-based training in this area I should not "wing it" and work with such children. But the authors of this book are well known for utilizing ABA procedures and principles within their everyday lives.

# HUMAN VALUES IN APPLIED BEHAVIOR ANALYSIS

"I will keep them from harm and injustice."
—Hippocrates

Until this point in the text, we have emphasized the scientific and methodological aspects of applied behavior analysis. Surely during this journey, you have been impressed by ABA's potential power as a means of altering behavior. By mastering information about this increasingly powerful technology, you have attained a certain amount of potential power—power capable of being applied for the benefit or to the detriment of others. As ABA becomes more professionalized, such ethical considerations rise in their level of importance. *You, above all, are responsible for seeing to it that you do no harm.*

## Professional and Ethical Considerations

Behavior analysis is not applied in a vacuum, but within society. As soon as we begin to consider influencing the behavior of our fellow humans or of other organisms (e.g., pets, farm animals, animals in zoos or circuses, and so on), we must pause to examine our own, our participant's, our consumer agency's, and our society's philosophical and ethical values. *Responsible* applied behavior analysts routinely ask themselves and other collaborators in the process (clients and/or their advocates, teachers, managers, parents, colleagues, etc.) whether the goals and methods they contemplate pursuing and applying are constructive and ethically defensible. Will they protect others from harm and injustice?

Additionally, especially if the change agent's job description includes practicing applied behavior analysis, they, their employers, and clientele probably will want them to become and remain certified by a well-recognized board or agency, such as the Behavior Analysis Certification Board.®

## ABA Practice within Other Areas of Specialization

As mentioned, ABA practice increasingly is recognized for its value in various specialty areas, including, among many others: education; training; psychology; counseling; various forms of behavioral, physical, and other therapeutics; consulting; management; coaching; healthcare; and safety. Recall Table 1.2, which included a *partial* listing of those classes of behavior addressed by ABA, to which we have referred in this text alone. Ask yourself what sphere of expertise the coordinators of each particular behavioral intervention represent.

Perhaps you may already have earned a license, credential or certification to practice within your own particular field. Organizations specializing in education, medicine, counseling, psychology, sociology, recreational sports, speech and language, safety, commerce, industry, and numerous others increasingly seek well-qualified ABA professionals. Inevitably, when demand outstrips supply, the job market expands and draws many candidates to the field. Among those are some whose training and/or performance may be marginal. So, although many of us might be pleased to see the number of self-identified Applied Behavior Analysts expanding, potential employers need to be especially careful to avoid hiring lesser-skilled or unscrupulous practitioners.

Yes, malpractice can happen. Sometimes it is reflected in the practitioner's failure to remain current with the state of this technology. We ourselves have seen instances of under-prepared and/or inadequately supervised personnel or administrators who, in the name of applied behavior analysis, fail to analyze the function of particular behaviors in advance of substituting others that would serve the same purpose more productively and wholesomely. They have used overly punitive procedures; or overlooked the teaching of adaptive behaviors to replace those selected for eradication; or overused non-functional or unhealthy consequences; or selected inappropriate, especially narrow or non-relevant instructional or behavioral objectives; or failed to assess for and secure appropriate environmental supports for constructive behavioral objectives or to analyze the impact of their interventions before applying them ineffectually or counterproductively... and the list goes on.

Of course, comparable acts of omission or commission are by no means limited to ABA. Whether through naiveté or malevolence, similar examples of accidental or deliberate misconduct can be found in just about any field of human endeavor. To keep these to a minimum, professional organizations often develop and institute competency standards and codes of ethics. If you already specialize in a particular area (e.g., psychology, education, nursing, medicine, business, health and safety, speech and language, occupational therapy, and so on) your practice probably is already guided by ethical standards. Now, assuming you wish to identify yourself as a *professional behavior analyst,* solely or additionally, the same applies to your practice within this field.

## PROFESSIONALIZING PRACTICE: THE BEHAVIOR ANALYSIS CERTIFICATION BOARD®

As successful applied behavior analytic intervention services began to proliferate, a group of concerned ABA specialists decided to form the **Behavior Analysis Certification Board® (BACB®)**. The BACB was established in 1998 to meet professional needs. The Board's stated **mission** is *to "protect consumers of behavior-analytic services by systematically establishing, promoting, and disseminating professional standards of practice." The BACB oversee and operates certification programs that include establishing practice standards, administering examinations, developing and monitoring ethical standards, along with any disciplinary systems deemed necessary."*

Today, several states in the United States and a growing number of nations give hiring preference to, and/or require that personnel identifying themselves as applied behavior analysts to be officially certified by the BACB® as **Board Certified Behavior Analysts (BCBA®s)** or **Board Certified Associate Behavior Analysts (BCaBA®s)** (the latter a position requiring lesser levels of training). (BCBA®s, who have earned doctoral degrees, have become eligible for a special designation: BCBA-D®.) The BACB also registers behavior technicians (RBTs) who collect and graph data, implement ABA programs under the direction and supervision of a BCBA or BCaBA. (For a book describing RBTs and designed to help train them, see Wallace & Mayer, 2020). Increasingly, states in the United States require that the responsible providers of ABA services be BACB®-certified and/or to be licensed.

To become certified, one must meet eligibility requirements (coursework and experiential standards), formally apply to take, and pass an examination. Moreover, there are requirements to maintain certification, such as one must continue to adhere to ethics requirements. Because its standards and task lists change periodically, if you wish to become certified or to familiarize yourself with current guidelines, we suggest you visit http://www.bacb.com. As appropriate in an evolving field such as this one, the Behavior Analysis Certification Board® reviews and revises its standards and guidelines periodically. A copy of the January 1, 2022 task list can be found in Appendix 1. It is your responsibility, during your training and afterward, to keep current. (You will find the requirements current at the time of the completion of this text in an addendum located just prior to the glossary.

## YOUR LEGAL AND ETHICAL RESPONSIBILITIES AS AN APPLIED BEHAVIOR ANALYST

In addition to knowing and practicing in accordance with the *Ethics Code for Behavior Analysts*, certainly you will want to (1) become familiar with the laws of the jurisdiction (nation, state or province, town or city) in which you intend to practice; and (2) be aware of and adhere to accepted standards for national certification programs.

## Guidelines and the *Code* for Responsible Conduct for Behavior Analysts

Unlike the science-based technology of applied behavior analysis, *ethical* perspectives rest on a philosophical foundation. They reflect contemporary values of local and broader societies about right and wrong, good and bad, acceptable or unacceptable. Given that a key function of the BACB is to protect ABA consumers, the organization has established the: *Ethics Code for Behavior Analysts* (*Code*). Four principles underlie the *Code* that behavior analysts commit to following, including to: "benefit others, treat others with compassion, dignity, and respect, behave with integrity, and ensure their own competence" (BACB, 2020, p. 4).

The BACB's ethical *Code* for behavior analysts (2020) became effective, January 1, 2022. In addition to the section on ethical standards, the BACB's ethical code contains several other sections: a Table of Contents, an Introduction, including the Scope of the Code, Core Principles, Application of the Code, Enforcement of the Code and a Glossary. It is best to go on line to the BACB and review the entire code. To assure your knowledge of and adherence to the current code, you must regularly review and integrate its features throughout your day-to-day practice of behavior analysis.

The code expands on other aspects of the standards we already have covered, and addresses ABA ethical responsibilities as a teacher/supervisor, ethical practices in the workplace, responsibilities to colleagues and society, as well as ethical research activities. Please understand, though, that as in the other helping professions (e.g., the American Psychological Association's *Ethical Principles of Psychologists and Code of Conduct*), these perspectives on ethical applications of behavior analysis probably will expand and change over time. As our science progresses and social values alter, we anticipate that these standards will be modified periodically. Your responsibility as an ABA practitioner is to remain currently familiar with and adhere to the Board's current official guidelines for accurately representing intervention efficacy and demonstrating professional competence. Accordingly, beyond further coursework on the topic, we suggest you visit *BACB.com* now, and regularly thereafter, to review the complete set of current standards. To provide you with a flavor of the kinds of items the BACB subsumes under "Ethics Standards," we include several boxes containing illustrative (*not* the complete set) tasks relevant to the topic under discussion.

## Use Scientifically-Validated Assessments and Interventions

> **Box 31.1**
> **Code Elements 2.01, 2.13 & 2.14**
> **Reliance on Scientific Knowledge**
>
> *Behavior analysts select, design, and implement assessments and behavior-change interventions that are "based on scientific evidence" (p. 12). Moreover, "they provide services that are conceptually consistent with behavioral principles, based on scientific evidence, and designed to maximize desired outcomes for and protect all clients, stakeholders, supervisees, trainees, and research participants from harm" (p. 11).*

We are familiar with several forward-looking organizations serving young people with developmental challenges, in which staff are required to restrict their interventions to those reported in the peer-reviewed research literature as being safe and effectual with comparable populations. Similarly, many public and private school districts are demanding that their teaching staff base their practices on valid evidence of effectiveness. The training literature is beginning to reflect that perspective. (See, for example, the National Autism Center's *Evidence-Based Practice and Autism in the Schools*.)

Nor is ABA alone. In the medical field, for example, Sackett, Rosenberg, Gray, Haynes, and Richardson (1996) have described in detail the levels of scientific support, (including findings from "n of one" or single-subject design protocols), necessary before medical personnel may ethically elect to apply particular treatment protocols. Other specialty application areas are beginning to demand similar degrees of scientific support before they include given treatment and intervention methods within their daily practices.

Those who use applied behavior analysis, as defined by its original designers (see Baer, Wolf, & Risley, 1968), meet this stricture, because experimental analysis is a defining feature of ABA. Each time we apply behavior analysis to assess and intervene, we are using within- and/or across-participant replication. Results ultimately lead to our staying the course, adjusting the intervention protocol, or rejecting it altogether. Because they undergo rigorous peer evaluation, reports of particular behavioral analyses published in peer-reviewed scholarly journals merit our strongest respect. Assuming our populations resemble those in the published studies, we should feel especially confident about replicating the procedures in our home territories.

After thoroughly searching, should you find that the particular challenge facing you seems not to have been addressed adequately by the ABA community, you might plan, with permission and support from your organization and agreement from your participant(s) (or their agents), to try a novel approach (just be sure it is conceptually systematic). If that succeeds, replicate the method as a within- or across-subject experimental design, write up your procedure and results, and submit the report to a journal for publication. (See the most recent edition of the *Publication Manual of the American Psychological Association* for guidance in preparing your report.) You will have performed a real service!

Even if you do not take the publication route, given appropriate permissions, you still can replicate and report the results of your novel method in-house. At least your organization's clientele and your fellow service providers will be able to profit from your successes.

Whatever you do, though, remember that unlike scientific discovery, which is based on solid data derived from research, ethical guidelines are fluid, value-based, and changing from one time, place, and society to another. They are shaped by cultural contingencies. Your responsibility as an investigator and/or practitioner is to stay abreast of your field's current local, regional, and national ethical guidelines. Especially if the cultural values veer from the tried and true, then arranging to have your intended practices reviewed by participants, advocates, administrators, and/or peers is the most sensible way to proceed.

## Practice within Professional Competence

> **Box 31.2**
> **Code Element 1.05 and 1.06**
> **Boundaries of Competence**
>
> *Behavior analysts practice only within their identified scope of competence. They engage in professional activities in new areas (e.g., populations, procedures) only after accessing and documenting appropriate study, training, supervised experience, consultation, and/or co-treatment from professionals competent in the new area. Otherwise, they refer or transition services to an appropriate professional (p. 9). Moreover, behavior analysts engage in professional development to build and maintain their scope of practice.*

Suppose, an individual with a solid ABA background is competing for a tempting job, but one that requires *expertise* in (not simple familiarity with) using a particular method such as the *Picture Exchange Communication System* (PECS©). Having attended a PECS© workshop, the candidate asserts that she has the requisite competence, though she knows full well she has not successfully demonstrated and received certification as a PECS© implementer. She then would be in violation of Standard 1.05.

Another instance might be a candidate's exaggerating his familiarity with business management, when shifting to that field from the learning disabilities area. Actually his acquaintance with the latter is limited to what he has read in the newspaper. A preferable posture would be to acknowledge his lack of business expertise and to suggest that, at a minimum, the management of the organization choose the behavioral goals and contribute to the identification of appropriate objectives and powerful reinforcing contingencies.

Remind yourself that applied behavior analysis is a methodology, not a particular content area. You are responsible for having mastered the special knowledge, skills, and values of the field in which you intend to implement ABA. Otherwise, collaborate with others so qualified, and/or first undertake mastering those essential skills yourself.

Obviously, ABA is a rapidly expanding field. New areas of application, instruments, methods, technological refinements, experimental analytic techniques, and other information and methods emerge almost daily. Values and perspectives about their application change too. Years ago, professionals in our field did not realize they would need to know *how to analyze the function of* severe aggressive or self-abusive behavior. Today, functional assessments are conducted under those circumstances. We who were trained in the olden days have had to stay abreast of new developments by reading journal reports and/or attending courses, workshops, practicing under supervision, and so on. Just as you would expect your own physician, attorney, or tax advisor to remain up-to-date with progress in their fields, applied behavior analysts also must fulfill that responsibility on an ongoing basis. In fact, the Behavior Analysis Certification Board® requires that behavior analysts continue their education to maintain their status as certified behavior analysts. A number of organizations provide continuing education units (see Authorized Continuing Education Provider Directory on the BACB website).

## Being Truthful and Documenting Professional Work

> **Box 31.3**
> **Code Element 1.01**
> **Being Truthful**
>
> *Behavior analysts are truthful and arrange the professional environment to promote truthful behavior in others. They do not create professional situations that result in others engaging in behavior that is fraudulent or illegal or that violates the Code. They also provide truthful and accurate information to all required entities (e.g., BACB, licensure boards, funders) and individuals (e.g., clients, stakeholders, supervisees, trainees), and they correct instances of untruthful or inaccurate submissions as soon as they become aware of them. (p. 9)*

The interesting aspect of this particular code is that behavior analysts must arrange professional environments that promote and support integrity. How does one promote such an environment? Here the contents of this book extend beyond simply assessing and intervening with clients. Long-range success requires that we assess and (re)organize the environment to generate ongoing support for maintaining programmatic integrity. In your role as behavior analyst you will have numerous opportunities to model performance integrity. Consider, for example, a situation in which a funding provider approves 20 hours per month for a particular client, but the supervisor is unable to schedule all those hours in a particular month. This would provide an opportunity to model for the BCaBA or the RBT how to handle a failure to meet billing requirements honestly, with the intention of promoting the BCaBA's future billing integrity.

> **Box 31.4**
> **Code Elements 3.11 & 6.08**
> **Documenting Professional and Scientific Work**
>
> *Throughout the service relationship, behavior analysts create and maintain detailed and high-quality documentation of their professional activities to facilitate provision of services by them or by other professionals, to ensure accountability, and to meet applicable requirements (e.g., laws, regulations, funder and organization polices). Documentation must be created and maintained in a manner than allows for timely communication and transition of services, should the need arise. (p. 14)*
>
> *Behavior analysts give appropriate credit (e.g., authorship, author-note acknowledgement)...(p. 18).*

Fully documenting all assessment and intervention procedures as well as behavioral data is a basic requirement for each and every client to whom one provides services. Remember, as well, that one of the key dimensions of ABA is to be technological. Consequently, you should detail these records in a manner that enables another person completely to understand what services have been provided and what additional and current services are currently being provided. Moreover, it should be apparent where a particular client started behaviorally and where they are now, and what interventions produced those changes. But it isn't sufficient to just be technological:, remember that being conceptually systematic is one of the key dimensions of ABA. Given that it combines science and practice, teamwork in applied behavior analysis is much more the rule than the exception. When you prepare case and research reports, be sure to credit accurately who did what within the program. Usually, the name of the leader(s) with major responsibility for the project or research program and/or those coordinating the team's activities head the list of authors of in-house reports as well as publication submissions. (In the latter case, refer to the current edition of the *Publication Manual of the American Psychological Association [APA]*, which serves as the standard for many professional and scientific publications.) Indicate other names in the order of the importance of their contribution to the program. Within the body of reports to be submitted for publication, include a section on personnel, describing their job titles, background, qualifications, and specific responsibilities. When you wish to reference the work of others, the *APA Publication Manual* also specifies guidelines and restrictions you should follow related to authorship of published reports, including published research or descriptive reports, forms, tables, charts, figures, inventories, and other tools.

## Identify and Reconcile Conflicts of Interest

> **Box 31.5**
> **Code Element 1.11, 1.13, & 1.14**
> **Multiple and Exploitive Relationships**
>
> *Because multiple relationships may result in a conflict of interest that might harm one or more parties, behavior analysts avoid entering into or creating multiple relationships, including professional, personal, and familial relationships with clients and colleagues. Behavior analysts communicate the risks of multiple relationships to relevant individuals and continually monitor for the development of multiple relationships. If multiple relationships arise, behavior analysts take appropriate steps to resolve them. When immediately resolving a multiple relationship is not possible, behavior analysts develop appropriate safeguards to identify and avoid conflicts of interest in compliance with the Code and develop a plan to eventually resolve the multiple relationship. Behavior analysts document all actions taken in this circumstance and eventual outcomes. (p. 10)*
>
> *Behavior analysts do not abuse their power or authority by coercing or exploiting persons over whom they have authority (e.g., evaluative, supervisory). (p. 10)*
>
> This includes romantic and sexual relationships with clients, stakeholders, trainees, and supervisors.

When approached by those with whom you already have a relationship—your friends, relatives, employers, employees, co-workers, students, or neighbors, your best option is to refer them elsewhere for formal behavior analytic services related to serious personal issues. Sometimes, though, multiple relationships develop even with the most cautious behavior analysts. For example, you find your son on the same baseball team as your client. Or your client's mom enrolls in the same doctoral program as yours. The important thing is to be aware of the nature of the relationship. So, if a multiple relationship develops, take steps to resolve the issue. In such cases it would be reasonable and responsible for you to ask to be replaced by another BCBA for the particular case.

Be certain to avoid exploiting others such as employees, students, supervisees, research participants, and clients over whose reinforcing contingencies you have control. Resist the inducement to request payment, or demand extra work, or sexual or other favors. Were you to scan the ethical review records across a range of educational, human service, and other professions, you should not be surprised to note numerous instances in which therapists, teachers, and supervisors have destroyed their careers and done damage to their clientele by yielding to such attractions. Our advice: with the first twinge of temptation, gently but immediately refer the individual elsewhere.

## Protect Clients' Dignity, Health, and Safety

> **Box 31.6**
> **Code Element 2.15, 2.18, 3.01, & 3.12**
> **Protecting Clients and the Profession**
>
> *Behavior analysts select, design, and implement behavior-change interventions (including the selection and use of consequences with a focus on minimizing risk of harm to the client and stakeholders. They recommend and implement restrictive or punishment-based procedures only after demonstrating that desired results have not been obtained using less intrusive means, or when it is determined by an existing intervention team that the risk of harm to the client outweighs the risk associated with the behavior-change intervention. When recommending and implementing restrictive or punishment-based procedures, behavior analysts comply with any required review processes (e.g., a human rights review committee). Behavior analysts must continually evaluate and document the effectiveness of restrictive or punishment-based procedures and modify or discontinue the behavior-change intervention in a timely manner if it is ineffective. (p. 12)*
>
> *When a behavior analyst is concerned that services concurrently delivered by another professional are negatively impacting the behavior-change intervention, the behavior analyst takes appropriate steps to review and address this issue with the other professional. (p. 12)*
>
> *Behavior analysts act in the best interest of the clients, taking appropriate steps to support clients' rights, maximize benefits, and do no harm. They also are knowledgeable about and comply with applicable laws and regulations related to mandated reporting requirements. (p. 13)*
>
> *Behavior analysts advocate for and educate clients and stakeholders about evidence-based assessment and behavior-change intervention procedures.*

Many of us in the United States know firsthand how dreadful many custodial institutions housing those with delayed development and psychiatric issues were, prior to the legislation emanating from such cases as *Wyatt v. Stickney* (1972). To describe conditions as unhygienic and lacking any reasonable (no less evidence-based) programs of effective client treatment would be a major understatement. Were you to enter such places, your senses would be assaulted by moans, screeches, thumps, groans, and a combination of unpleasant odors and sights. Seeing young children or fully-grown adults endlessly rocking; hitting or assaulting themselves or others; ritualistically manipulating items like strings, articles of clothing, and (rarely) toys or parts of their own bodies, would not be unusual. The few staff present would be scrambling to treat injuries, restrain clients from committing further damage to themselves and others, clean up messes, serve meals, change clothing, or when the rare opportunity presented itself, attempting a bit of teaching or coordinating recreational activities.

Then, those judicial decisions and laws began to come into play. Many more federal and state resources were disbursed for educational and rehabilitation services to people with disabilities and behavioral disorders. Clients were relocated into foster, small group, and other more humane living arrangements and their lot improved incrementally.

Now, having reached this point in the text, you know that today far more fruitful and humane methods exist for educating and supporting the development of people facing a breadth of challenges, and you can specify the services that you will be offering. Functional assessments enable the analysis and much more humane treatment of problematic behaviors; functional and augmentative communicative systems such as picture exchange (e.g., PECS©), computerized, and gestural systems supplant aggression as communicative mechanisms to permit people to attain more of what they want and need and less of what they don't. And, of course, as you have seen, behavior-analytic based instructional technology has enabled vast numbers of people to constructively expand their skill repertoires.

This is not to say that unsafe, unhealthy, or inhumane living, working, or learning conditions do not still exist to greater or lesser degrees in the United States and throughout the world. Should that be the case in your community or place of employment, you have a professional and moral responsibility to take steps toward remedying the situation. Certainly, if you have another professional affiliation, say as a psychologist affiliated with the American

Psychological Association or with an educational organization, you are already guided by its ethical standards. As a certified behavior analyst, you also have a duty to report serious health and safety issues to your supervisors or managers and to adhere to the Board's current ethical guidelines. And, of course, you will make the promotion of humane, constructive client behavior a top priority.

We also remind you of the foolishness of attempting to kill a fly with an elephant gun. Certainly, you could not readily justify a full ABA program if simply asking the person to alter his behavior or shaping progressive changes in a given direction worked quickly. Nor would you continue a costly program, like requiring continuous round-the-clock monitoring and managing an annoying but not profoundly dangerous behavior like thumb-sucking, nail biting, or scowling. On the other hand, suppose the behavior of concern *is* seriously detrimental, as in disrupting other people's ability to conduct their important daily activities or causing injury to oneself or others; *and* suppose you have conducted a full functional assessment to identify the responsible reinforcers; *and* you have given all positive approaches a fair trial. Then you might seek permission to use aversive consequences temporarily.

## Protect Confidentiality

> **Box 31.7**
> **Code Element 2.03, 2.04, 5.10 & 5.11**
> **Maintaining Confidentiality**
>
> *Behavior analysts take appropriate steps to protect the confidentiality of clients, stakeholders, supervisees, trainees, and research participants; prevent the accidental or inadvertent sharing of confidential information; and comply with applicable confidentiality requirements (e.g., laws, regulations, organization polices). The scope of confidentiality include service delivery (e.g., live, teleservices, recorded sessions); documentation and data; and verbal, written, or electronic communication. (pp. 10–11)*
>
> *Behavior analysts only share confidential information about clients, stakeholders, supervisees, trainees, or research participants: (1) when informed consent is obtained; (2) when attempting to protect the client or others from harm; (3) when attempting to resolve contractual issues; (4) when attempting to prevent a crime that is reasonably likely to cause physical, mental, or financial harm to another; (5) when compelled to do so by law or court order. When behavior analysts are authorized to discuss confidential information with a third party, they only share information critical to the purpose of the communication. (p. 11)*
>
> *Behavior analysts... do not publish information and/or digital content of clients on their **personal** social media accounts and websites. When publishing... on **professional** social media accounts or websites, behavior analysts ensure that for each publication they: (1) obtain informed consent before publishing; (2) include a disclaimer than informed consent was obtained and that the information should not be captured and reused without express permission; (3) publish on social media channels in a manner that reduces the potential for sharing; and (4) make appropriate efforts to prevent and correct mis-use... (p. 17)*
>
> *Before publicly sharing information about clients using digital content, behavior analysts ensure confidentiality, obtain informed consent before sharing, and only use content for the intended purpose and audience. (p. 17)*

Perhaps among the various reasons you have been drawn to the field of applied behavior analysis is your fascination with behavior in general; your curiosity about why humans and other organisms behave the way they do and what can be done to change that. Naturally you witness or hear about cases you would be tempted to share with others inside and maybe even outside of the field. Resist that temptation. If others inquire about specific experiences with your clientele, explain that as an ABA professional you are constrained from divulging such information. Given today's digital age, it is extremely important to maintain client confidentiality, especially in publicly accessible domains, such as social media.

As mentioned earlier, if you are teaching, training, or supervising others, you may want to illustrate a particular point by referring to an experience with a client. In that circumstance, first obtain written informed consent from the people involved and/or their responsible representatives. Also, you are well advised to disguise the identity of those individuals by changing distinguishing characteristics, historical background, and so on, so that no one could possibly recognize them.

If your client is transferring elsewhere, you may feel or actually be obligated to pass his or her records along to your successor. Again, ask your clients (or their parents or guardians) to provide their written consent to transfer those materials.

Today, teachers, trainers, and consultants often use live or recorded video displays to demonstrate a particular point or for training purposes. An example would be demonstrating safe body position while working at a computer; another, showing how to interpose gradually extended delays between "Oh, you want..." (delay) "...that puzzle piece," when attempting to encourage a child learning to communicate with PECS©. Before proceeding, be absolutely certain that the person and/or parents or guardians agree in writing to have the material shared with the audience. Again, unless performers or those in other capacities specifically ask or agree to be publicly recognized, do everything feasible to respect their anonymity.

## EVALUATING AND MONITORING APPROPRIATE SERVICES

> **Box 31.8**
> **Code Element 2.18, 3.12, & 5.06**
> **Appropriate Services**
>
> *Behavior analysts engage in continual monitoring and evaluation of behavior-change interventions. If data indicate that desired outcomes are not being realized, they actively assess the situation and take appropriate corrective action. When a behavior analyst is concerned that services concurrently delivered by another professional are negatively impacting the behavior-change intervention, the behavior analyst takes appropriate steps to review and address the issue with the other professional. (p. 12)*
>
> *Behavior analysts advocate for and educate clients and stakeholders about evidence-based assessment and behavior-change intervention procedures. They also advocate for the appropriate amount and level of behavioral service provision and oversight required to meet defined client goals. (p. 13)*
>
> *Behavior analysts do not advertise nonbehavioral services as behavioral services. If behavior analysts provide nonbehavioral services, those services must be clearly distinguished from their behavioral services and BACB certification with the following disclaimer: "These interventions are not behavioral in nature and are not covered by my BACB certification." This disclaimer is placed alongside the names and descriptions of all nonbehavioral interventions. (p. 15)*

As with all other professional practitioners, the conduct of behavior analysts is subject to the influence of powerful contingencies of reinforcement. Consider, for example, a situation in which the prospective client's parents are convinced that using *facilitated communication* (Bicklin, 1990) would enable them at last to break the communicative barrier between them and their "non-verbal" son. Although aware that this technique has been discredited and lacks evidence of efficacy (Jacobson, Mulick, & Schwartz, 1995), the candidate omits mentioning that fact and agrees to train the youngster to use FC. She then is violating the Behavior Analyst Certification Board® ethical guidelines stated in Box 31.8.

Understandably, family members, associates, educators, and managers of various stripes seek to accomplish the most in behavioral improvement for the least cost and effort. You may find yourself approached by prospective clients requesting a particular "quick fix," about which they have heard from the media, colleagues, friends, or family members, for rapidly repairing a problematic behavioral situation: "cures" for autism by arranging for the client to swim with dolphins, ride horses, or consume special diets; reversing poor job performance or inappropriate social skills based on unsubstantiated claims for fast-acting training packages, and so forth. While such interventions may be enjoyable for participants and relatively economical for those handling the purse strings, they can also be harmful to the extent that they might delay or be offered as a substitute for the application of effective, scientifically validated change strategies.

One highly successful autism educational treatment program with which we are familiar restricts the use of educational/behavior-change procedures to those that have been reported in at least three peer-reviewed scientific journal papers as effective with like challenges, individuals, and/or groups. Another, similar but much broader and intensive thrust, has been the creation of the National Autism Center, which selected as its first major initiative, "an unprecedented effort to produce a set of standards for effective, research-validated education and behavioral intervention for children with Autism Spectrum Disorders (ASD)." According to its website, (http://www.nationalautismcenter.org), an "expert panel" composed of renowned scientists, practitioners, researchers, and clinicians well-known for their influential work in the field of Autism Spectrum Disorders" collaborated to identify and fulfill the Center's aims to:

- provide the strength of evidence supporting educational and behavioral treatments that target the core characteristics of these neurological disorders.
- describe the age, diagnosis, and skills/behaviors targeted for improvement associated with treatment options.
- identify the limitations of the current body of research on autism treatment and offer recommendations for engaging in evidence-based practice for ASD.

Today the Center has gathered and displayed lists of demonstrably effective practices, many of which are the fruit of scientifically sound applied behavior-analytic investigations.

There is no reason why specialists in other areas of behavior-analytic application cannot collaborate similarly in identifying effective behavioral interventions of special relevance to their concerns. In the educational arena, examples might include scientifically demonstrated, successful school-wide student learning and behavior-management systems; in the safety area, methods demonstrating per capita reductions in accidental injuries, and so on.

## Obtain Written Service Agreement

> **Box 31.9**
> **Code Element 2.11 & 3.04**
> **Informed Consent**
>
> *Behavior analysts are responsible for knowing about and complying with all conditions under which they are required to obtain informed consent from clients, stakeholders, and research participants (e.g., before initial implementation or assessments or behavior-change interventions, when making substantial changes to interventions, when exchanging or releasing confidential information or records). They are responsible for explaining, obtaining, re-obtaining, and documenting required informed consent. They are responsible for obtaining assent from clients when applicable. (p. 11)*
>
> *Before implementing services, behavior analysts ensure that there is a signed service agreement with the client and/or relevant stakeholders outlining the responsibilities of all parties, the scope of behavioral services to be provided, the behavior analyst's obligations under the Code, and procedures for submitting complaints about a behavior analyst's professional practices to relevant entities (e.g., BACB, service organizations, licensure boards, funders). Undated service agreements must be reviewed with and signed by the client and/or relevant stakeholders. (p. 13)*

When determining services for clients, including which assessments and interventions will be implemented, it is important to obtain a written service agreement and informed consent. In addition, if significant modifications are to be implemented, it is important to re-obtain written consent. Remember consent can only be given by someone who has reached legal age (i.e., 18 years in the U.S.). When initiating services with individuals who cannot give consent, consent must be obtained by their legal guardian AND you must obtain assent from the client. Just as important as it is for services, obtaining consent becomes relevant when disclosing client information regarding clients as well.

The behavior analyst should avoid disclosing confidential information to anyone else without fully informing consumers about the purpose of the disclosure—that is, when dealing with mature, competent organizational or individual adult participants. If the main consumers are children or otherwise not competent clients, then their parents or guardians must be so informed. So, as a behavior analyst, even after you obtain parental informed consent to video-record a child with developmental challenges while he progresses toward a learning objective, you would also obtain the parent's consent before showing the recording to others outside of the child's school.

Or suppose you were consulting with the management of a chain of restaurants about ways to heighten service quality. To assess the wait-staff's quality of service, you have video-recorded and scored a set of positive and negative examples. Then, at a later date, while training new personnel, you use those materials to analyze and illustrate good and poor service. You only would do so after obtaining the consent of the managers and of the personnel whose data and images you plan to display.

If the individual, organizational client, or other "legally authorized person on behalf of the client" permits it, behavior analysts may disclose confidential information to others, unless the law prohibits it. There are situations, however, that call for disclosure of confidential information without the consent of the individual involved. According to the BACB® guidelines, those cases are mandated or permitted by law for such valid purposes as providing "needed professional services by the individual or organizational client"; to "obtain appropriate professional consultations," "protect the client or others from harm," or to obtain payment for services, "in which instance disclosure is limited to the minimum necessary" to obtain that payment.

In an episode one of us witnessed years ago, a caregiver remarked "watch this!" as he laughingly discarded a cigarette butt on the floor, where clients with known histories of pica snatched and consumed the butt. After those actions were disclosed to and investigated by the organizational administrators, the person's employment was terminated.

In another situation, we disclosed several safety hazards to the local managers and off-site owners of an overseas manufacturing plant: a barricaded fire-exit door and an open elevator shaft into which workers could fall. Happily, those conditions were quickly repaired.

## Continuity, Discontinuing, and Transitioning of Services

> **Box 31.10**
> **Code Element 3.14, 3.15, & 3.16**
> **Continuity of Services**
>
> *Behavior analysts act in the best interest of the client to avoid interruption or disruption of services. They may appropriate and timely efforts to facilitate the continuation of behavioral services in the event of planned interruptions (e.g., relocation, temporary leave of absence) and unplanned interruptions (e.g., illness, funding disruption, parent request, emergencies). They ensure that service agreements or conflicts include a general plan for action of service interruptions. When service interruptions occur, they communicate to all relevant parties the steps being taken to facilitate continuity of services. Behavior analysts document all actions taken in this circumstance and the eventual outcomes. (p. 14)*
>
> *Behavior analysts include the circumstances for discontinuing services in their service agreement. They consider discontinuing services when: (1) the client has met all behavior-change goals; (2) the client is not benefiting from the services; (3) the behavior analyst and/or their supervisees or trainees are exposed to potentially harmful conditions that cannot be reasonably resolved; (4) the client and/or relevant stakeholder requests discontinuation; (5) the relevant stakeholders are not complying with the behavior-change despite appropriate efforts to address barrier; or (6) services are no longer funded. Behavior analysts provide the client and/or relevant stakeholders with a written plan for discontinuing services, document acknowledgment of the plan, review the plan throughout the discharge process, and document all steps taken. (p. 14)*
>
> *Behavior analysts include in their service agreement the circumstances for transitioning the client to another behavior analyst within or outside of their organization. They make appropriate*

> *efforts to effectively manage transitions; provide a written plan that includes target dates, transition activities, and responsible parties, and review the plan throughout the transition. When relevant, they take appropriate steps to minimize disruptions to services during the transition by collaborating with relevant service providers. (p. 14)*

From the outset, the concerned parties need clearly to specify and mutually agree how those services will be obtained and delivered, as well as the conditions under which they will be terminated. Assuming behavior analysts deliver their behavior change services effectively, eventually those services should no longer be required.

In your own case, how will you know that it is time to terminate your services? What level of behavior change will clearly indicate those services no longer are needed? Suppose things don't progress as planned, then what? Suppose the unforeseen happens, such as a pandemic (e.g., COVID-19). How will you as a behavior analyst plan for such emergency situations? What steps will you take to facilitate the continuity or transitioning of services? Remember Murphy's Law, "If anything can go wrong it will." It is better to plan for such situations than to be left with holding the bag. Colombo, Wallace, and Taylor (2020) recently provided a service decision model for practitioners during crises. The point is that any interruption in services, even those of a temporary nature, can significantly affect our clients' progress.

Sometimes despite your best efforts, you may encounter impediments to the effectiveness of your services. Just as we don't blame clients for their behavioral challenges, neither should we blame the source of the barrier. Rather we should be wise to try to address the situation before terminating our services. Yet, despite all, should we determine that service discontinuation or transfer is necessary, we should attempt to undertake the process by developing a mutually agreeable written plan of action if one is not specified in the original contract.

## Cultural Humility in Practice

> **Box 31.11**
> **Code Element 1.07, 1.08, 1.10, 2.09**
> **Building Relationships with Clients & Stakeholders**
>
> *Behavior analysts actively engage in professional development activities to acquire knowledge and skills related to cultural responsiveness and diversity. They evaluate their own biases and ability to address the needs of individuals with diverse needs/backgrounds (e.g., age, disability, ethnicity, gender expression/identity, immigration status, marital/relationship status, national origin, race, religion, sexual orientation, socioeconomic status). Behavior analysts also evaluate biases of their supervisees and trainees, as well as their supervisees' and trainees' ability to address the needs of individuals with diverse needs/backgrounds. (p. 9)*
>
> *Behavior analysts do not discriminate against others. They behave toward others in an equitable and inclusive manner regardless of age, disability, ethnicity, gender expression/identity, immigration status, marital/relationship status, national origin, race, religion, sexual orientation, socioeconomic status, or any other basis proscribed by law. (p.9)*
>
> *Behavior analysts maintain awareness that their personal biases or challenges (e.g., mental or physical health conditions; legal, financial, marital/relationship challenges) may interfere with the effectiveness of their professional work. Behavior analysts take appropriate steps to resolve interference, ensure that their professional work is not compromised, and document all actions taken in this circumstance and the eventual outcome. (p.9)*
>
> *Behavior analysts make appropriate efforts to involve clients and relevant stakeholders throughout the service relationship, including selecting goals, selecting and designing assessments and behavior-change interventions, and conducting continual progress monitoring. (p. 11)*

Behavior analysis does not happen in a vacuum. Rather, the world in which we live and practice, is a melting pot. Understanding how historical and contemporary cultural variables affect behavior as well as how current cultural variables influence contingencies of reinforcement is essential to the design of any behavior analytic endeavor. Skinner (1981) discussed how those factors intersect as well as their combined effects on behavior.

Beyond understanding how cultural variables effect our clients, we must also account for the way these variables influence the behavior of caregivers and stakeholders. In fact, you might find yourself in a situation where in a caregiver's religious beliefs influence the selection of target behaviors (e.g., masturbation). It will be important to not only understand the intersection of the caregiver's beliefs, but also to assess your own biases and the potential influence of these biases on your practice. In fact, one of the authors' students had to become familiar with the belief system of a far-right group to which the parents of a client subscribed to prior to being able to build rapport and develop treatment goals with them. It would have been amiss for the behavior analyst to dismiss the family's belief system because it did not match their own. It also could have potentially led to ineffective services, especially while selecting targets, assessing contingencies, and developing interventions.

Essential to taking cultural variables into account is taking stock of one's own level of cultural humility, awareness, and biases (Fong, et al., 2016). In keeping with that perspective, we encourage you to obtain professional development in diversity, equity, and inclusion (DEI). In fact, many behavior analytic professional organizations have developed DEI boards and special interest groups to foster and develop equitable and inclusive environments within the science and practice of behavior analysis. Moreover, one might take advantage of any of a number of DEI trainings and certificate programs offered. Applying the core principles, consulting the ethics code (benefit others; treat others with compassion, dignity, and respect; behave with integrity, and ensure competence), enables practitioners to provide services from a cultural humble perspective.

## Practicing Ethically Beyond the Client and Stakeholder

> **Box 31.12**
> **Code Element 1.15 & 1.16,**
> **Practice Information**
>
> *Behavior analysts make appropriate efforts to respond to requests for information from and comply with deadlines of relevant individuals (e.g., clients, stakeholders, supervisees, trainees) and entities (e.g., BACB, licensure boards, funders). They also comply with practice requirements (e.g., attestations, criminal background checks) imposed by the BACB, employers, or governmental entities. (p. 10)*
>
> *Behavior analysts remain knowledgeable about and comply with all self-reporting requirements of relevant entities (e.g., BACB, licensure boards, funders). (p. 10)*

The concept of practicing ethically extends well beyond populations of clients and stakeholders to include, among others, case and trainee supervisors. In recent texts, Le-Blanc, Sellers, and Ala'i (2020) have provided a detailed task analysis for building and sustaining effective supervisor-supervisee relationships and provide practical exercises for developing and maintaining these relationships; and, Mayer and Wallace (2020) describe the consulting relationship, and how it can determine to what degree intervention programs achieves fidelity. We encourage our readers to not only familiarize themselves with the ethic code as it pertains to one's own particular responsibility to supervisees and trainees (Section 4), but to continue to build one's knowledge and skills with respect to engaging in this class of behavior. First and foremost, it is important to understand and adhere to supervision requirements established by funding providers as well as professional credentialing entities. For example, the BACB has very specific requirements regarding supervision for RBTs that are different for future BCaBAs and BCBAs. Knowing these specifics is mandatory in providing ethical supervision.

Understanding one's own supervision competency and volume ability is also very important when providing both case and trainee supervision. For example, if one does not have the competency to provide feeding interventions, one should not be providing supervision on a feeding case or a trainee learning how to run a feeding intervention. Moreover, given the intense nature of supervision, it is wise to periodically access one's time availability for providing quality and ethical supervision (volume or number of supervisees and cases). It is unrealistic to provide case supervision for 50 cases or 100 supervisees!

It is also important to know what knowledge a trainee has before assigning or delegating tasks. For example, it would not be okay to assign a functional analysis to a trainee if they have never had specific instruction and training on functional analyses. This is also why it is important to keep records of what specific concepts and procedures have been taught to trainees (i.e., performance monitoring). Just as accountability with respect to what has been taught and how well trainees perform specific tasks, supervisors are also accountable for their performance. As such, it is important to include continual evaluation of one's own supervisory practices (and not just trainee outcomes).

Finally, continuity of supervision is important. Thus, it is necessary for supervisors to minimize interruption or disruption of supervision and develop a plan in the event of unplanned or planned interruptions. Moreover, if it is necessary to terminate supervision, behavior analysts develop a plan for termination that minimizes the impact to the trainee, supervisee, or case.

Additionally, it is important to understand that as a behavior analyst one has a responsibility to the certification board itself, both with respect to communication and practice requirements.

Responding to inquiries from the BACB, licensure boards, and funders is important, but one must maintain a currently updated BACB portal including any name changes, as well as, designation of supervisor status for registered behavior technicians (RBTs). For example, suppose you are the designated supervisor for a particular RBT, who subsequently leaves the agency, or you, yourself leave the agency, it is your responsibility to delete your name as the supervisor from the BACB portal.

# EVALUATE THE ETHICAL PRACTICES IN ORGANIZATIONS PRIOR TO YOUR EMPLOYMENT

As Brodhead, Quigley and Cox (2018) suggest, it is helpful to verify that an organization practices ethically before you apply to affiliate with it. Seek this information from your ABA advisors and/or instructors, and/or from that organization's previous employees, consumer advocacy organizations, and by carefully inspecting that organization's online review platforms (e.g., Yelp® & Google®). Pre-screening potential employers will enable you avoid affiliating with organizations that engage in questionable practices.

Brodhead et al. (2018) provided a table of sample interview topics and questions for use during the interview. Answers to questions, such as those displayed in Table 31.1, many of which are based on Brodhead's et al. questions, can guide your choice in finding a proffered position.

# PROMOTE AND SUPPORT FREEDOM AND DIGNITY

Some have taken exception to the scientific analysis of human behavior and its application to the betterment of society and its individual members because they say it imposes control on individuals who would otherwise have been free. But as B. F. Skinner masterfully treats this particular concern in his book *Beyond Freedom and Dignity* (1971), freedom is an illusion if one's behavior is determined by contingencies one does not even recognize. It is not as if we introduce contingencies where there once were none; instead, every instance of behavior-analytic application substitutes new, clearly identified contingencies for those often inadequate or destructive ones that are already in place. We have done our job once we have replaced the old contingencies that created problems with new ones that solve those problems.

To those who object that contingencies of reinforcement can be used to the detriment of others, we stress how important it is to recognize that contin-

**Table 31.1**

1. How does this organization support the behavior analyst's access to the behavior analytic literature, as well as access to and support for formal professional development, such as funding to support in-service training and attendance at professional conferences, and so forth?
2. What system does it have in place that supports their employees' on-going engagement in ethical behavior?
3. What degree or type of supervision does it provide for its employees?
4. How does the organization address internal problems between supervisors and supervisees?
5. Does the organization anticipate any changes in the populations it serves? If so, what training will it provide to employees to qualify them to serve the new population?
6. How do they manage electronic records?
7. How does the organization collaborate with others who provide services to their clients?
8. How does the organization accommodate to clients' varying cultural backgrounds?
9. What steps does it take to promote continuity of supervision?

gencies that are undetected and/or unacknowledged, such as being naively seduced into trying dangerous drugs or risky social or sexual practices, are far more likely to place people in danger than those that have been subjected to the detailed scrutiny of the scientifically- and ethically-sensitive applied behavior analyst. When we can identify the contingencies that operate on our own and others' behavior, all of us are much less likely to be victimized by the (mis) application of principles of behavior. As Sir Francis Bacon reminded us back in the sixteenth century, "Knowledge is power."

## SUMMARY AND CONCLUSIONS

Before completing our survey of applied behavior analysis, we need to remind ourselves of the essential features of ABA's scientific and technological underpinnings and methods of application. If you are wondering whether to apply the concepts, principles, and change strategies described in this text within your daily lives, (if you haven't already started to do that), our answer is "Why not?"—that is, assuming you have sufficient control over powerful contingencies of reinforcement and can do so honestly, fairly, and responsibly. After all, throughout history, effective parents, teachers, managers, counselors, spiritual leaders, sovereigns, and others have successfully applied many of the methods we have surveyed. But if you hope to apply behavior analysis at a professional level, you must learn your chosen field's common language and master its store of information, resources, tools, skills, and standard practices. And, of course, you need to responsibly apply the full ABA model, including functionally analyzing reliable and valid measures of behavior prior to, during, and after intervening.

While this text has mainly emphasized a science-based technology of behavior change, if clientele are to be protected from harm and injustice, certainly ethics and morality must also play a role in the application of behavior analysis. So, in addition to ABA practitioners becoming and remaining informed and skilled with their particular fields of practice, they also share a responsibility for adhering to a set of ethical guidelines of the kind that the Behavior Analysis Certification Board® endorses. Reflecting the current values of our local and broader societies, we are responsible for:

- treating our clients honestly and kindly;
- accurately representing the likelihood of success of our proposed intervention(s);
- practicing only within our limits of competency;

- maintaining competence through professional development activities;
- obtaining legal and ethically-sound informed consent;
- setting lifestyle or system-change goals and targets of behavior-change in conformance with applicable laws, and ethical and professional ABA standards;
- considering cost/benefit when initiating, continuing, modifying, or discontinuing ABA services;
- identifying and reconciling contingencies compromising the practitioner-client covenant;
- using the most effective and least intrusive assessment and behavior-change methods;
- protecting confidentiality;
- representing one's own and others' contributions to the ABA field truthfully;
- protecting clients' dignity, health, and safety

We thank you for staying the course. Our fondest hope is that the power you have gained through your expanding knowledge of applied behavior-analytic concepts and methods will enrich the lives of the clients you serve, as well as your own and those of your nearest and dearest. "Applied correctly, these well-grounded and optimistic principles about the human condition can help us all make wiser and more respectful choices that make the world a better place in which to live" (Daniels & Lattal, 2017, p. 161). An understanding of how behavioral contingencies work and the ability to manage them responsibly are among the most supreme forms of empowerment available to humanity.

> **The Puzzle about Ethics**
>
> *Answer:*
>
> Ethical guidelines reflect the values of the local society. Beyond consumer acceptability, when practices are consonant with local ethical values, community members are more likely to support and maybe even to supplement procedural contingencies. In so doing, they are more apt to contribute in a more general way to the application of behavior analysis for productive and lasting change.
>
>

# APPENDIX

## Behavior Analyst Certification Board® Fifth Edition Task List[1]
with page references to the text

### Introduction

The BCBA/BCaBA task list covers tasks that a practicing behavior analyst will perform with some, but probably not all, clients. These tasks include "the knowledge and skills that serve as the foundation for the BCBA and BCaBA examinations" (BACB: BCBA/BCaBA Task List, 5th ed., p. 1). This list is provided mainly as a resource for instructors and a study tool for candidates. Candidates for the BCBA and BCaBA credentials should have a thorough understanding of these topics.

The BCBA/BCaBA Task List is organized in two major sections, Foundations, which includes basic skills and underlying principles and knowledge, and Applications, which includes more practice-oriented skills (BACB:BCBA/BCaBA Task List, 5th ed., p. 1).

The BCBA Fifth Edition Task List is presented for those who wish to review and are seeking a quick reference. Chapter(s) and/or the primary pages in which each specific task is addressed are presented. Some tasks are more general than others so an entire chapter or chapters may be cited. Others are comprehensive in nature, resulting in the entire book being cited.

Be sure to review the glossary for terms. (Caution: reading just a section on a term is not likely to provide an integrative understanding of the term. A comprehensive understanding is needed to understand many of the terms. Thus, we highly recommend that the entire book be studied if your background in ABA is weak.) You can also download your own copy of the Task List from BACB.com.

---

© 2020 by the Behavior Analyst Certification Board,® Inc. ("BACB®") all rights reserved. Reprinted here with the permission of the BACB. Unauthorized reproduction, dissemination or distribution in any medium is strictly prohibited. Requests to reprint, copy, or distribute this document and questions about this document must be submitted in writing directly to the BACB. To confirm this is the most recent version of the Task List, go to www.bacb.com.

| Section I: Foundations ||||
|---|---|---|
| Task # | A. Philosophical Underpinnings | Page reference |
| A-1 | Identify the goals of behavior analysis as a science (i.e., description, prediction, control). | 7–8; 730–731 |
| A-2 | Explain the philosophical assumptions underlying the science of behavior analysis (e.g., selectionism, determinism, empiricism, parsimony, pragmatism). | 5–6 |
| A-3 | Describe and explain behavior from the perspective of radical behaviorism. | 15–17 |
| A-4 | Distinguish among behaviorism, the experimental analysis of behavior, applied behavior analysis, and professional practice guided by the science of behavior analysis. | 3–5; 8–11 |
| A-5 | Describe and define the dimensions of applied behavior analysis (Baer, Wolf, & Risley, 1968). | 7–10 |
| Task # | B. Concepts and Principles | Page reference |
| B-1 | Define and provide examples of behavior, response, and response class. | 7; 24–25 |
| B-2 | Define and provide examples of stimulus and stimulus class | 25–27; 351 |
| B-3 | Define and provide examples of respondent and operant conditioning. | 27–29; 99–101; 206 |
| B-4 | Define and provide examples of positive and negative reinforcement contingencies. | 29–30; 81–92; 684 |
| B-5 | Define and provide examples of schedules of reinforcement. | Chapters 22–23; 503 |
| B-6 | Define and provide examples of positive and negative punishment contingencies. | Chapters 30–31; 87; 685–688; 695–696; 670–671; 701–703 |
| B-7 | Define and provide examples of automatic and socially mediated contingencies. | 103–104; 200–202; 265, 321 |
| B-8 | Define and provide examples of unconditioned, conditioned and generalized reinforcers and punishers. | 99–103; 686–687 |

© 2020 by the Behavior Analyst Certification Board,® Inc. ("BACB®") all rights reserved. Reprinted here with the permission of the BACB. Unauthorized reproduction, dissemination or distribution in any medium is strictly prohibited. Requests to reprint, copy, or distribute this document and questions about this document must be submitted in writing directly to the BACB. To confirm this is the most recent version of the Task List, go to www.bacb.com.

| | | |
|---|---|---|
| B-9 | Define and provide examples of operant extinction | Chapter 28; 30–31; 49t; 618; 705–706 |
| B-10 | Define and provide examples of stimulus control. | Chapters 15–16, 345 |
| B-11 | Define and provide examples of discrimination, generalization and maintenance. | Chapters 21–23; 345–349; 455; 459, 462–463; 543–544; 550t |
| B-12 | Define and provide examples of motivating operations. | 32;112–113; 202; 337–339; 340–341; 597–598 |
| B-13 | Define and provide examples of rule-governed and contingency-shaped behavior. | 385–386 |
| B-14 | Define and provide examples of the verbal operants | 411–413 & Chapter 19 |
| B-15 | Define and provide examples of derived stimulus relations. | 354–357; 428–430; 430–432 |

| Task # | C. Measurement, Data Display, and Interpretation | Page reference |
|---|---|---|
| C-1 | Establish operational definitions of behavior. | 67;149 box |
| C-2 | Distinguish among direct, indirect, and product measures of behavior. | 129–132; 203–211;145t |
| C-3 | Measure occurrence (e.g. count, frequency rate percentage). | 130–132; 145t |
| C-4 | Measure temporal dimensions of behavior (e.g., duration, latency, interresponse time). | 130–133; 145t |
| C-5 | Measure form and strength of behavior (e.g., topography, magnitude). | Chapter 7 |
| C-6 | Measure trials to criterion. | 134; 145t |
| C-7 | Design and implement sampling procedures (i.e., interval recording, time sampling). | 133–138 |
| C-8 | Evaluate the validity and reliability of measurement procedures. | 37,125–127; 141–143 |
| C-9 | Select a measurement system to obtain representative data given the dimensions of behavior and the logistics of observing recording. | Chapter 7 |

© 2020 by the Behavior Analyst Certification Board,® Inc. ("BACB®") all rights reserved. Reprinted here with the permission of the BACB. Unauthorized reproduction, dissemination or distribution in any medium is strictly prohibited. Requests to reprint, copy, or distribute this document and questions about this document must be submitted in writing directly to the BACB. To confirm this is the most recent version of the Task List, go to www.bacb.com.

| Task # | | Page reference |
|---|---|---|
| C-10 | Graph data to communicate relevant quantitative relations (e.g., equal-interval graphs, bar graphs, cumulative records). | Chapter 8 |
| C-11 | Interpret graphed data. | 165–169 |

| Task # | D. Experimental Design | Page reference |
|---|---|---|
| D-1 | Distinguish between dependent and independent variables. | 174 |
| D-2 | Distinguish between internal and external validity. | 557–558; 579–582 |
| D-3 | Identify the defining features of single-subject experimental designs (e.g., individuals serve as their own controls, repeated measures, prediction, verification, replication). | 177 & Chapters 9 & 25 |
| D-4 | Describe the advantages of single-subject experimental designs compared to group designs. | 173–176 |
| D-5 | Use single-subject experimental designs (e.g., reversal, multiple baseline, multielement, changing criterion). | Chapters 9 & 25 |
| D-6 | Describe rationales for conducting comparative, component, and parametric analyses. | 519–530 |

## Section Two: Applications

| Task # | E. Ethics | Page reference |
|---|---|---|
| E-1 | Responsible conduct of behavior analysts. | Chapter 32 & the BACB's ethical code (all tasks in this section) |
| E-2 | Behavior analysts' responsibility to clients. | |
| E-3 | Assessing behavior. | |
| E-4 | Behavior analysts and the behavior-change program. | |
| E-5 | Behavior analysts as supervisors. | |
| E-6 | Behavior analysts' ethical responsibility to the profession of behavior analysis. | |
| E-7 | Behavior analysts' ethical responsibility to colleagues. | |
| E-8 | Public statements. | |
| E-9 | Behavior analysts and research. | |
| E-10 | Behavior analysts' ethical responsibility to the BACB. | |

© 2020 by the Behavior Analyst Certification Board,® Inc. ("BACB®") all rights reserved. Reprinted here with the permission of the BACB. Unauthorized reproduction, dissemination or distribution in any medium is strictly prohibited. Requests to reprint, copy, or distribute this document and questions about this document must be submitted in writing directly to the BACB. To confirm this is the most recent version of the Task List, go to www.bacb.com.

# APPENDIX 1: BEHAVIOR ANALYSIS CERTIFICATION BOARD FIFTH EDITION TASK LIST

| Task # | F. Behavior Assessment | Page reference |
|---|---|---|
| F-1 | Review records and available data (e.g., educational, medical, historical) at the outset of the case. | 67–68; 202–211 |
| F-2 | Determine the need for behavior-analytic services. | Chapters 4, 10 & 26 |
| F-3 | Identify and prioritize socially significant behavior-change goals. | 67–73 |
| F-4 | Conduct assessments of relevant skill strengths and deficits. | 132; 203–210; 426 |
| F-5 | Conduct preference assessments. | 106–112 |
| F-6 | Describe the common functions of problem behavior. | 200–202 |
| F-7 | Conduct a descriptive assessment of problem behavior. | 206–211 |
| F-8 | Conduct a functional analysis of problem behavior. | 211–214 |
| F-9 | Interpret functional assessment data. | 214–218 |

| Task # | G. Behavior Change Procedures | Page reference |
|---|---|---|
| G-1 | Use positive and negative reinforcement procedures to strengthen behavior. | Chapters 5, 6, & 11 |
| G-2 | Use interventions based on motivating operations and discriminative stimuli. | Chapters 15–19 |
| G-3 | Establish and use conditioned reinforcers. | 100–102 |
| G-4 | Use stimulus and response prompts and fading (e.g., errorless, most-to-least, least-to-most, prompt delay, stimulus fading). | Chapter 20 |
| G-5 | Use modeling and imitation training. | 390–403; 470; 475; 530; 544 |
| G-6 | Use instructions and rules. | 385-389; 593-596; 625–626; 639; 678–679 |
| G-7 | Use shaping. | Chapter 13 |
| G-8 | Use chaining. | Chapter 14 |
| G-9 | Use discrete-trial, free-operant and naturalistic teaching arrangements. | 390–392; 415–418; 427 |
| G-10 | Teach simple and conditional discriminations. | 349–354 |
| G-11 | Use Skinner's analysis to teach verbal behavior. | Chapter 19 |

© 2020 by the Behavior Analyst Certification Board,® Inc. ("BACB®") all rights reserved. Reprinted here with the permission of the BACB. Unauthorized reproduction, dissemination or distribution in any medium is strictly prohibited. Requests to reprint, copy, or distribute this document and questions about this document must be submitted in writing directly to the BACB. To confirm this is the most recent version of the Task List, go to www.bacb.com.

| | | |
|---|---|---|
| G-12 | Use equivalence-based instruction. | 354–359 |
| G-13 | Use the high-probability instructional sequence. | 601–602 |
| G-14 | Use reinforcement procedures to weaken behavior (e.g., DRA, FCT, DRO, DRL, NCR). | Chapter 29; 417–418 |
| G-15 | Use extinction. | Chapter 28 |
| G-16 | Use positive and negative punishment (e.g., time-out, response cost, overcorrection). | Chapters 30 & 31 |
| G-17 | Use token economies. | 258–267 |
| G-18 | Use group contingencies. | 30; 248–255; 618–630 |
| G-19 | Use contingency contracting. | 74; 232–235 |
| G-20 | Use self-management strategies. | 239–245 |
| G-21 | Use procedures to promote stimulus and response generalization. | Chapter 21 |
| G-22 | Use procedures to promote maintenance. | Chapters 22 & 23 |
| Task # | **H. Selecting and Implementing Interventions** | **Page reference** |
| H-1 | State intervention goals in observable and measurable terms. | 58–60 |
| H-2 | Identify potential interventions based on assessment results and the best available scientific evidence. | 103–118; 223–224; 231 |
| H-3 | Recommend intervention goals and strategies based on such factors as client preferences, supporting environments, risks, constraints, and social validity. | Chapters 3, 4 & 24; 81–82; 103–112 |
| H-4 | When a target behavior is to be decreased, select an acceptable alternative behavior to be established or increased. | 630–636 |
| H-5 | Plan for possible unwanted effects when using reinforcement, extinction, and punishment procedures. | Chapter 11; 93–97; 615–620; 665–679; 691–698 |
| H-6 | Monitor client progress and treatment integrity. | Chapter 7; 42–43; 127–129; 283 |
| H-7 | Make data-based decisions about the effectiveness of the intervention and the need for treatment revision. | Chapter 8 |

© 2020 by the Behavior Analyst Certification Board,® Inc. ("BACB®") all rights reserved. Reprinted here with the permission of the BACB. Unauthorized reproduction, dissemination or distribution in any medium is strictly prohibited. Requests to reprint, copy, or distribute this document and questions about this document must be submitted in writing directly to the BACB. To confirm this is the most recent version of the Task List, go to www.bacb.com.

| | | |
|---|---|---|
| H-8 | Make data-based decisions about the need for ongoing services. | Chapter 8 |
| H-9 | Collaborate with others who support and/or provide services to clients. | Chapters 4 & 24 |

| Task # | I. Personnel Supervision and Management | |
|---|---|---|
| I-1 | State the reasons for using behavior-analytic supervision and the potential risks of ineffective supervision (e.g., poor client outcomes, poor supervisee performance). | Chapter 24 |
| I-2 | Establish clear performance expectations for the supervisor and supervisee. | Chapters 4 & 24 |
| I-3 | Select supervision goals based on an assessment of the supervisee's skills. | Chapters 4 & 24 |
| I-4 | Train personnel to competently perform assessment and intervention procedures. | Chapter 24 |
| I-5 | Use performance monitoring, feedback, and reinforcement systems. | Chapters 3 & 24 |
| I-6 | Use a functional assessment approach (e.g., performance diagnostics) to identify variables affecting personnel performance. | Chapter 10 |
| I-7 | Use function-based strategies to improve personnel perfor-mance | Chapters 10 & 24 |
| I-8 | Evaluate the effect of supervision (e.g., on client outcomes, on supervisee repertoires). | Chapters 4 & 24 |

# Glossary

Note: Numerals at the end of each definition indicate the chapter(s) in which the term was defined and/or further illustrated. Also, several other common terms are listed without a chapter number in that they are used in context, but not separately defined in a particular chapter. They are listed here should you wish to re-familiarize yourself with the term's meaning.

**Abate.** To decrease the likelihood of the emission of a response. Used as an action verb in relation to operant behavior, wherein the response bears a probabilistic relationship (not inferring a one-to-one relationship, as with inhibit or block). The $S^{\Delta}$s and $S^{D p}$s abate behavior. 15

**A-B-C Analysis.** A method for analyzing relationships among the behavior (B) and its consequences, (C) and its antecedents (A). 2, 10

**Abolishing operation (AO).** A motivation operation (MO) that reduces reinforcer effec-tiveness relative to baseline.

**Abscissa.** The x value, on the x-axis or horizontal line of a graph, usually expressed in observational sessions or standard units of time, such as hours, days, weeks or months. 8

**Accountability.** Objective demonstration and communication of the effectiveness of a given program: functional relations, behavioral outcomes, cost-benefit, consumer satisfaction, and so on. 9, 25

**Accuracy.** The extent to which the response meets standards or is correct. 4

**Across-behavior multiple-baseline design.** A single-subject or intensive experimental design that involves: (1) Obtaining a validly representative set of pretreatment measures (baseline) of several *different behaviors*; (2) applying the intervention or experimental procedure to one of the behaviors until its measurement pattern changes substantially, while continuing to record the baseline measures of the other behaviors; (3) applying the identical intervention to a second behavior; then to a third and so on. The procedure continues until it becomes apparent that each behavioral measurement changes concurrent with the intervention. 9

**Across-individuals multiple-baseline design.** A single-subject or intensive experimental design that involves: (1) collecting baseline measures on the same behavior of several *different individuals*; (2) applying the intervention first with one individual while the baseline conditions are continued with the other individuals; then (3) applying the intervention to the second individual's behavior as in item (2). This procedure is continued until it becomes apparent that each individual's behavior systematically changes only when the intervention is applied. 9

**Across-situations multiple-baseline design.** A single-subject or intensive experimental design that involves: (1) Collecting baselines on a behavior of one or more individuals across *different situations;* (2) testing the effects of the intervention *(independent variable)* first in one situation, while the baseline conditions are continued through the other situations; and (3) applying the intervention in the second situation as in item 2. This procedure is continued until it becomes apparent that behavior systematically changes only in those situations in which the intervention is applied. 9

**Activity reinforcer.** Contingent access to activities (watching TV, skating, playing, and so on) that support the increase or maintenance of the target behavior. 6

**Activity schedules.** Written or pictorial displays of the daily sequence of activities in which the client is assigned to engage or to complete by the time a cue ($S^D$) is activated (e.g., lights on and off, verbal instructions, a timer) to signal time-to-change to the next activity. Generally the schedules are displayed in vertical format to permit participants to review and move the depiction of each activity from the *to-be-completed* to the *completed* column, as the day progresses. 27

**Activity table.** A surface on which materials for a variety of reinforcing activities are displayed. Individuals may earn access to time at the table for accomplishments, such as completing their work or following various classroom rules. 27

**Adaptation.** Refers to the gradual reduction in the rates of responding evoked by a stimulus over repeated or prolonged presentations (as when the client no longer reacts to the presence of an observer). A period of time during which reactivity subsides. When the rate of the behavior has stabilized, adaptation is assumed to have been accomplished. The term adaptation tends to be used in operant conditioning. Also see Habituation. 7, 11

**Adjusting schedule.** See Ratio schedules of reinforcement. 22

**Advocate.** A person or group serving to protect a client's interests; not one who is employed by the organization or institution delivering services. Advocates, who may be community representatives such as clergymen, law students, or a panel of interested citizens, consider a program's goals and procedures in terms of what they believe is best for the *individual* client and argue on the client's behalf. 4, 11

**Alternating-treatment design.** (Also often called multi-element, simultaneous treatment, multiple schedule, and concurrent schedules design.) A within-subject or intensive experimental design consisting of alternating presentations of two or more independent variable arrangements. The term multi-element has sometimes been reserved for situations in which each arrangement is correlated with a distinctive discriminative stimulus. The distinctive response patterns generated under each condition then are revealed by comparing performance under each of the variables. 25

**Alternation effects.** *See* Sequence effects. 25

**Alt-R.** *See* Differential reinforcement of alternative behaviors; when alternatives are not compatible with the original behavior of interest, the term *reinforcement of incompatible behaviors* is applicable. 28

**Alternative goals.** While these behavioral goals are not necessarily designed to serve the same function for the client as his misbehavior did, they are designed to teach alternative ways to behave. These might include either other appropriate ways of behaving, and/or ceasing inappropriate behavior. Such goals may be added to the mix, assuming the constructive behaviors are emphasized. Also see Goals and Functional goals. 28

**Anecdotal assessment.** See Indirect assessment. 10

**Antecedent control strategies.** These involve the manipulation of some aspect of the physical or social environment to "evoke" (set the stage for) a desired response or to reduce the likelihood of occurrence of a competing response. Generally speaking, antecedent control procedures can be categorized into three approaches: manipulating discriminative stimuli, motivational operations, and/or various complex combinations of antecedent control strategies. 15–20 & 27

**Antecedent stimulus.** A stimulus that precedes or accompanies a behavior and may exert discriminative control over that behavior. 2

**Applied behavior analysis (ABA).** ABA connotes a scientific method, a technology, and a professional approach. It is a system designed to analyze and change behavior in a precisely measurable and accountable manner. ABA is an evidence-base method of examining and changing what people (and other living creatures) say and do. 1

**Applied behavior analysis program.** A systematic approach to analyzing and changing behavior. The program essentially incorporates the full behavior analysis model (see Figure 1.1): Establishment of behavioral objectives; selection and application of valid and reliable measures; regular recording; consistent application of selected procedures based upon principles of behavior; plus an experimental evaluation of results. An applied behavior analysis program sometimes is referred to as a *behavior analysis program, behavioral program,* or a *behavior modification* or *therapy program.* 1

**Applied behavior analyst.** An individual who has demonstrated mastery of the professional competencies involved in assessing behavior and designing, implementing, functionally analyzing, and communicating the results of an applied behavior analysis program. 1, 31

**Applied research.** Research directed toward an analysis of the variables that can be effective in improving the behavior under study (Baer et al., 1958). In applied behavior analysis, research involves examining socially important behaviors. Applied research usually is conducted in natural settings rather than in the laboratory. 1, 9, 25

**Artificial discriminative stimulus.** A prompt or discriminative stimulus that is not naturally present in the environment. Because an artificial stimulus is intrusive, before the learner has been judged to have achieved of the goal, it should be faded or gradually eliminated. (E.g., Verbal instructions may be used as artificial stimuli while a student learns a new motor skill. Those verbal prompts are faded as the skill is refined.) 17, 18, 20

**Artificial reinforcer.** A reinforcer not usually present in the natural setting or not a natural consequence of the behavior. For example, trinkets are artificial reinforcers, used to reward good performance in many school programs. 10

**Asymptote.** The point at which the behavior reaches its peak – that is, when the increase stops and the rate levels off and remains steady, possibly before declining. 22

**Augmentative verbal communication.** Methods of supporting communication beyond the typical means of speaking, writing, gesturing etc. Augmentative methods may include, among others, using signs, touching images or vocal key pads, activating computer generated and other mechanical devices, and exchanging images. See also PECS. 19

**Automatic reinforcer.** The reinforcement is inherent in the response itself (i.e., thumb sucking, twirling hair, masturbation, or rocking back and forth may produce a reinforcing sensation for the client). 6, 10

**Aversive stimulus.** A stimulus, also called a *punisher,* with the function of decreasing the strength (e.g., rate) of a behavior when presented as a consequence of (is contingent on) that behavior. A stimulus, also called a *negative reinforcer,* the contingent *removal* of which results in an *increase* in the rate of the behavior. Organisms will work to avoid aversive stimuli. A stimulus that abates (halts) a behavior from occurring ($S^{Dp}$). The term aversive stimulus is used to apply to all stimuli labeled reductive, punishing, abating, or those whose termination is negatively reinforcing at that point in time. Non-technically: A noxious object or event. (Note: There is no *d* in the word aversive.) See also Negative reinforcer; Punisher, $S^{Dp}$, Primary aversive stimulus, Secondary aversive stimulus, intrinsic and extrinsic aversive stimuli. 5, 29, 30

**Avoidance behavior.** A class of behavior that postpones or circumvents an aversive stimulus. The act of avoidance cannot remove an aversive stimulus because it has not yet occurred, but rather it prevents it occurrence or postpones it. Avoidance behaviors protect or prevent the individual from being subjected to an aversive stimulus for the time being. Related *to negative reinforcement* in that the avoidance behavior increases in rate when it completely postpones or avoids an aversive stimulus. Nontechnically: An action the individual does to keep from getting punished. 5, 29, 30

**Awareness of being assessed**. See Observer awareness of being assessed. 7

**BACB**. See Behavior Analysis Certification Board. 31

**Back-up reinforcer.** An object or event that already has demonstrated its reinforcing function for the behavior of an individual. It is distributed in exchange for a specific number of tokens, points, or other exchangeable reinforcers. For example, points might be exchanged for the back-up reinforcer of free time. 12

**Backward chaining procedure.** Effecting the development of a behavioral chain of responses by reinforcing the last response, element, or link in the chain first; the last two next; and so on, until the entire chain is emitted as a single complex behavior. 14

**Bar graphs.** Graphic depictions in bar form; generally used to compare discrete sets of data that relate to one another; or to summarize performance within a condition or group of individuals. 8

**BARS**. See behaviorally anchored rating scale. 7

**Baseline.** Repeated measures of the strength or level (e.g., frequency, intensity, rate, duration, or latency) of behavior prior to the introduction of an experimental variable (treatment, intervention, or procedure). Baseline measurements are continued until performance has stabilized and can be used as a basis for assessing the effects of the intervention or experimental variable. 8, 9

**Basic research.** Research typically conducted in a laboratory setting where it is possible to arrange tight experimental control. 9

**BCBA**. See Board Certified Behavior Analyst. 31

**Behavior.** Any living organism's, including people's directly measurable actions or physical functions, including both saying and doing. In this text we use the term *behavior* synonymously with *response* and *performance,* and the term *behavior* as an abbreviated way of saying "classes of behavior." Two functional classes of behavior (i.e., behaviors that lead to reinforcers) include those acting directly on the environment (e.g., the male gathering fruit for himself) and the other is that mediated by the behavior of others—verbal behavior. 1, 2, 19

**Behavior Analysis.** Experimental investigation of variables that influence the behavior of any living organism. 1

**Behavior Analysis Certification Board (BACB).** An organization concerned with developing, promoting and implementing performance standards in the form of an international certification program for those alleging to provide behavior-analytic services. Its purpose is to protect clientele, and to promote ethically sound "best practice." 31

**Behavior analytic procedure.** See Behavioral procedure. 2

**Behavioral assessment.** Behavioral assessment is used to investigate first, an individual's typical patterns of behavior; then depending on findings, to identify and describe specific challenges, and to plan, execute, and evaluate treatment as objectively, validly and clearly, as possible. Depending on the behavior and its context, specific valid and reliable measures are selected, and applied in order validly to depict the characteristics of the behavior of interest prior to any intervention (the pre-intervention baseline). Should an intervention subsequently be undertaken, the measures are collected repeatedly and results analyzed during, and after any systematic intervention or treatment. Though direct observation forms the core of behavioral assessment, indirect methods sometimes also are added to guide our selection of the most appropriate treatment strategy. Also see Sensitive measure, Objective measure, Reliable measure, and Valid measures. 7

**Behavior chain.** See chain, behavioral. 14

**Behavioral contract.** The negotiated goals and procedures of a behavior analysis program, mutually agreed upon by the client or advocate and other involved persons, and modifiable by joint consent. A behavioral contract often communicates *who* is to do *what with or to whom,* by *when,* and *anticipated outcomes.* Also called a *contingency contract.* 4, 11

**Behavioral contrast.** When a procedure that decreases behavior (e.g., DRO, extinction, or punishment) is introduced into one context, the behavior maintained in other contexts may increase, despite no other change in contingencies directly affecting the latter. This increase is called *positive behavioral contrast*. Behavioral contrast also has been observed when the schedule of reinforcement has been increased in one situation while remaining constant in the other. In this case performance may *decrease* in the constant situation producing a *negative behavioral contrast.* 23, 26, 28

**Behavioral cusp.** A behavior (or behavioral class) that affords clients greater access to reinforcers, by expanding their repertoires and enabling more rapid learning. Similar to *pivotal behavior*. Listening, following instructions etc. are examples. 4

**Behavioral dimensions.** Measurable parameters or descriptive characteristics that describe particular aspects of the performance, such as frequency, rate, intensity, duration, topography, and accuracy. Behavioral dimensions are included in *behavioral objectives (see below).* 4

**Behavioral goal.** Behavioral goals state the direction (increased, decreased, maintained, developed, expanded, or restricted) and level to which the target behavior is to be changed: A behavioral goal should be translated into a set of behavioral objectives prior to designing a program. *Also see* goal. 4

**Behavioral laws.** Principles of behavior that have been demonstrated to possess very broad generality. The predictable functions of immediacy and schedules of reinforcement are examples. 2

**Behaviorally anchored rating scale (BARS).** A method of assessing performance by assigning a numerical value to one's judgments. Each number on the scale represents a specific set of observable behaviors, such as steps, tasks, severity of a behavior, or skills involved in a complex task. These numbers and their corresponding behaviors are located on a rating scale. 7

**Behavioral momentum.** Strength of force or motion. In behavior analysis, when a behavior is repeated at a high, steady rates. Promoting behavioral momentum is a strategy used to increase the likelihood that a low probability behavior will occur by presenting stimuli known to promote a high probability of responding (e.g., compliance) ahead of an activity less likely to be performed. For example, Sula presents several cards for Irma to read aloud. The first six or seven contain words that Irma is known to label (tact) automatically, while the next few are more difficult for her. The initial string of successes encourages her to persist with the more difficult ones. 27

**Behavioral objective.** Precise specification of a goal behavior, including three essential elements: (1) The behavior; (2) the givens – situations, context, or conditions under which the behavior is to occur; and (3) the standard of acceptability or *criterion* level of performance. When the objective is related to formal instruction, it is called an *instructional objective*. 4

**Behavioral package.** A combination of two or more selected behavioral procedures. 24

**Behavioral principles.** Lawful relations between behavior and the variables that control it, discovered through experimental analyses of behavior. Behavioral principles may help to explain previous and present performance and to predict future behavior, because the relations have been found to apply across responses, people, and contexts. 2

**Behavioral procedure or strategy.** Interventions or treatments used to induce behavioral change (e.g., the application of behavioral principles). Behavioral procedures, or strategies, are used to occasion, teach, maintain, increase, extend, restrict, inhibit, or reduce behaviors and constitute the core of most applied behavior analysis programs. 2

**Behavioral product recording.** See Permanent product recording. 7

**Behavioral rehearsal.** Reinforced practice of a complex skill under simulated conditions. Role playing is one form of behavioral rehearsal. 16

**Behavioral repertoire.** The total complement of behaviors that an individual previously has demonstrated. It has been shaped, or, if it has been extinguished, it may be rapidly reconditioned. 5

**Behavioral skills training (BST).** A behavioral intervention package consisting of instructions, modeling, rehearsal, and feedback (including differential reinforcement). 18

**Behavioral technicians.** Auxiliary workers, such as observers and data recorders, whose services may be required to conduct some of the technical aspects of a behavior analysis program: e.g., designing and implementing observational recording systems; designing and executing graphing schemes and so on. 8

**Behavior modification.** Interventions based on the science of behavior and designed to change behavior in a precisely measurable manner. Term often used interchangeably with *applied behavior analysis* and *behavior therapy*. "Applied behavior analysis," though, is further restricted to those interventions that include an experimental analytic design to assess treatment effects. The term *behavior therapy* often is used when respondent (i.e., "Pavlovian") procedures are emphasized. Treatment involving modification of self-communication ("thoughts" and "images" "phobic reactions") usually is labeled "Cognitive Behavior Therapy." 1

**Board Certified Behavior Analyst (BCBA).** An individual who has completed a BACB approved academic program, participated in a BACB specified field experience under supervision of a BCBA, passed the BCBA examination, and has completed at least a master's degree. (Those with a doctorate are designated BCBA-D.) A Board Certified Assistant Behavior Analyst (BCaBA) meets similar requirements, but has less training and must work under the supervision of a BCBA. 31

**Bonus response cost.** See Response cost. 29

**Breaking Point.** The abrupt cessation of responding, usually due to thinning reinforcers too rapidly or to a level that is too thin. 22

**Carry-over effects.** See Sequence effects. 25

*Catch 'em being good game.* Sometimes called the *Slot machine game*. A game of chance in which participants receive reinforcers as prizes. Several cups are placed upside down, concealing paper slips on which the names of reinforcing items or events are written. Each participating client or staff member (selected on the basis of having engaged in the desired target behavior) chooses one cup, thereby gaining the indicated reinforcer. This game incorporates modeling and DRA. 28

**Celeration chart.** See Standard celeration chart. 8, 17

**Chain, behavioral.** A complex behavior consisting of two or more response segments that occur in a definite order. "... a sequence of responses that are functionally linked to the same terminal reinforcer" (Kuhn, Lerman, Vorndran, & Addison, 2006, p. 263). A chain can be homogeneous or heterogeneous. Homogeneous chains consist of responses that are similar to one another, as in lifting or throwing. Heterogeneous chains consist of responses that differ from one another, as in playing football or assembling a barbecue. 14

**Chaining procedure.** A procedure in which intact responses are reinforced in sequence to form more complex behaviors ultimately emitted as a single cohesive performance. See also Backward chaining procedure and Forward chaining. 14

**Change in level.** Depicts the amount (often assessed as the average frequency, rate, accuracy or other response measure emitted within a given time-span) by which the behavior has changed; that is, whether the average (mean, median or mode) performance rate is higher, lower or remaining the same as compared to previous average performance 8

**Changing criterion design.** An applied behavior analytic design involving successive changes in the criterion for delivering consequences, usually in graduated steps from baseline levels to a desired terminal goal. Experimental control is demonstrated if the behavior changes to meet or closely approximate each successively set criterion level. 25

**Choral responding.** Answering questions or imitating modeled statements as a group in unison. Within the process, the group leader identifies those who fail to respond appropriately and assists them afterward. Because everyone is engaged, individual students have less opportunity to misbehave. 27

**CIB.** See Contextually inappropriate behavior. 27

**Classical conditioning.** See respondent conditioning. 2

**Client.** The person who receives the services of a behavior analyst, and/or of an agency or organization; the individual whose behavior is targeted for change. Often labeled the "participant" in an applied behavior analysis program. The terms *subjects, students, learners,* and *patients* also are used interchangeably with *client*s. 3

**Clinical significance.** The change is considered clinically significant if the pre-stated objective is obtained, and/or when the behavior change has spurred correlated (ecological) changes for the participants, and their physical and social environments. 25

**Coefficient of agreement.** See Reliability. 7

**Coercion.** Coercion occurs in two forms: 1) oppressive or aversive force and 2) disproportionately powerful incentives; often involves threats, severely punitive contingencies, or disproportionately powerful incentives for the purpose of inducing a behavioral change toward an objective unwanted by the client (or their surrogates). Coercion is said to be increasing as the value of incentives and threats increase beyond socially or personally acceptable norms and the client becomes progressively less involved in goal selection. 4

**Collateral behaviors.** Behaviors not treated directly, yet whose rates may change as another behavior is directly treated. Also, behaviors, other than those intentionally treated, that might be influenced by the treatment. (Sometimes labeled *adjunctive behaviors.*)

**Collateral measures.** Measures of variables that relate indirectly to changes in the target behavior. Included would be assessing the impact on the "bottom line" as well as the un-programmed spread of effect to other people, places or behaviors.

**Communicative stimuli.** See Verbal stimuli. 19

**Competing reinforcers.** Powerful reinforcers, such as social attention, musical toys, art materials, etc. that interfere with the reinforcing function of the problem behavior. 27

**Complete stimulus control.** *See* Stimulus control, strong. 16

**Component analysis.** Analysis conducted for the purpose of identifying the separate contributions of each of a combination of elements to the overall behavioral change. 25

**Computer assisted or aided instruction (CAI).** Instruction aided by computer technology, including presenting curriculum, directing student responses and providing feedback and reinforcement. It may permit responses to be analyzed immediately, and allow instructional material to branch into remedial or advanced levels depending on the learner's performance. 18

**Concept.** One or a set of abstract critical properties shared, perhaps only in part, among a number of critical antecedent stimuli. Among the features common to dogs (with unusual minor exceptions) are that they are canines, have hair, tails, and four legs; they bark; and they are readily domesticated. That omits many creatures including rodents, raccoons, and cats, who don't bark, and seals, who don't have four legs, turtles, who don't have hair and wolves, not easily domesticated. 16

**Conceptual analysis of behavior.** Verbally addresses historical, philosophical, theoretical, and methodological issues and relations among different behavioral properties. 1

**Conceptual task analysis.** See task analysis. 4, 14

**Concurrent schedules.** Two or more schedules that operate simultaneously and independently, each for a different response. 22

**Concurrent schedules design**. See alternating treatment design. 25

**Concurrent task method of chaining.** (Also known as total or whole task method of chaining.) A simultaneous teaching method, in which all or several elements are taught concurrently, as opposed to joining or adding one link at a time, as in the serial methods of forward and backward chaining. 14

**Conditional discriminations.** See Discrimination, conditional. 16, 17

**Conditioned aversive stimulus.** See Secondary aversive stimulus 2, 4, 30

**Conditioned motivating operation (CMO)**: See Motivating operations, conditioned. 15

**Conditioned respondent stimulus.** See respondent conditioning. 2

**Conditioned reinforcer ($S^r$).** See Secondary reinforcer. 2, 6

**Conditioned respondent.** Respondents can be *conditioned*, as in Pavlov's famous experiments with the conditioning of dogs' salivation response to a bell. Also see respondent behavior. 2

**Confounding variables.** Uncontrolled variables that influence the outcome of an experiment to an unknown extent, making impossible the precise evaluation of the effects of the independent on the dependent variable(s). 9, 25

**Constructional approach.** An approach to changing behavior that emphasizes building behaviors rather than reducing or eliminating them. It involves

(1) observing or interviewing to determine the goal; (2) identifying the current repertoires on which to build; (3) selecting change procedures to permit building on current repertoires in achievable steps; and, (4) selecting and using natural reinforcers that will maintain the goal behavior. 4, 28

**Contact desensitization.** See Desensitization, contact. 13

**Context.** The surrounding conditions and limitations, under which the response occurs, including the setting, furnishings, materials, personnel, and so on. 4

**Contextual factors.** See Context. 3, 11, 27

**Contextual fit.** Contextual fit is the condition achieved when an appropriate intervention is selected that suits the skills, resources, schedules, and values of the contingency managers i.e., program implementers). 3

**Contextually inappropriate behavior** (CIB). Behavior unacceptable in a particular situation. 27

**Contiguity.** Occurring simultaneously or nearly simultaneously.

**Contingencies.** The specified dependencies or relations between behavior and its antecedents and consequences. Contingencies can occur naturally or be managed intentionally by presenting, withdrawing, or withholding stimuli to affect either other people's or one's own behavior. 2

**Contingency analysis.** A description of an individual's goal and/or problem behavior and the events that are noted to precede and follow those behaviors. Used to begin to identify contingencies that may be functionally related to goal and problem behaviors. 10

Contingency contract. See Behavioral contract. 4, 11

**Contingency control.** The capability effectively to manage the functional antecedents and consequences of given responses. 10

**Contingency managers.** Individuals—parents, nurses, teachers, counselors, therapists, and/or the clients themselves—who conduct the day-to-day operation of a behavioral program by systematically applying behavioral strategies or procedures; program implementers. 3

**Contingency-shaped behavior.** Behavior learned by experiencing consequences directly. Behavior shown to be more susceptible to generally prevailing contingencies than to verbal stimuli such as instructions or rules. 18

**Contingent delay.** An extension of the timeout interval by a period of time contingent on inappropriate behavior during timeout. For example, until behavior is acceptable for at least a minute beyond the occurrence of the inappropriate behavior, the individual would not be permitted to leave the timeout setting. See Timeout (TO). 29

**Contingent effort.** See Contingent exertion. 30

**Contingent exertion** (also called *contingent effort* and *contingent exercise*). Physical exertion or effort required as a consequence of misbehavior. E.g., an individual is required to perform an exercise routine such as standing up and sitting down rapidly ten times following each occurrence of the unwanted response. An aspect of overcorrection. 30

**Contingent exercise.** See contingent exertion. 30

**Contingent observation.** See Inclusion timeout. 29

**Contingent relation.** The relation between a behavior and its antecedents and/or consequences. 10

**Continuous behavior.** A response lacking a clearly discriminable beginning or end. Pouting, smiling, eye contact, and other behaviors often are treated as continuous responses because determining when the behavior begins and terminates is difficult. 7

**Continuous reinforcement (CRF).** A schedule of reinforcement in which each occurrence of a response is followed by a reinforcer. 11

**Contrast phenomenon.** See Behavioral contrast. 23

**Control condition.** Condition under which extraneous or potential confounding variables are held constant; used in applied behavior analysis for the purpose of eliminating alternative explanations for the results of an experimental analysis. 9, 10

**Control variables.** Variables held constant (that don't change) in an experiment (e.g., unless they are the subject of investigation, these are often materials, tools, setting, mangers, teachers, and so on). 25

**Cooperative learning.** *Interdependent* and/or *dependent* group contingencies arranged to promote productive peer influence. Reinforcers are shared among group members 12

**Coping model.** See Model, coping. 18

**Correction procedures.** These usually involve prompts, DRA, DRI, modeling, or sometimes punishment in form of a "no" along with positive practice. The purpose is to teach the client to discriminate and engage in the appropriate behavior. For example, a teacher might say, "Please do your work," or provide reinforcement for another student's engagement in the target behavior, and then reinforce the client's act of imitation. 30

**Correspondence training.** Delivering reinforcers contingent on correspondence or agreement between verbal reports (saying) and actions (doing). e.g., teacher praises Diane only after she actually has played with the crayons after previously saying she would. Because mother saw that he did actually help Jan with her math after he said he did, Mother loaned Bob the car. 21

**Criteria.** Constitute the part of the behavioral objective that states the standards used to determine its accomplishment; the specification of acceptable levels of performance to be achieved. Criteria used to evaluate the success of a given behavior analysis program are expressed as measurable behavioral dimensions (parameters like frequency, rate, acceleration, quantity and so on) that characterize particular aspects of the performance. 4

**Criterion analysis.** See Task analysis 4, 14

**Criterion level.** The level of performance to be achieved. 4

**Critical features of stimuli.** The distinctive properties of stimuli, such as size, shape, position, and color, that enable one stimulus class to be discriminated from another. Stimuli sharing a number of critical features often can be grouped to characterize a particular concept. Example: Mammals: creatures sharing these *critical features*: having fur, a backbone, and a spinal chord, and who suckle their young. Yet other critical features shared only among subsets of the stimuli, such as particular shapes, habits, genetic qualities, and so on, distinguish one subclass of stimuli from another, as with different species of mammals. 15

**Cumulative records.** A display of the rates of a behavior in the form of changes in the slope or curve of the response patterns (number of responses /a specific time period) generated as a function of conditions in effect. The steeper the line, the more rapid the response rate. The cumulative record also permits one to view at a glance the total number of responses accumulated during recording periods, as each new measure is added onto the previous total. 8

**Cusp.** See Behavioral cusp. 4

**Daily report card.** A arrangement among educational personnel, students, and their families; designed to coordinate the contingencies across settings. In one setting (e.g., the school), each day, the teacher reports the presence or absence of the target behavior and sends it to the other setting (usually the home), where a delayed consequence is presented. 11

**Data.** The numerical results of measuring some quantifiable aspect of behavior from which conclusions are often drawn. 7, 8, 9

**Datum.** The singular form of data.7, 8, 9

**Dead man's test**. Used in goal selection. If a "dead man" can do it, the goal is not acceptable and needs to be changed into something constructive. 26, 28

**Delayed matching-to-sample.** See Matching to sample, delayed. 16

**Delayed prompting.** A procedure, sometimes referred to as *time-delayed prompting or delayed cuing*, designed to teach a behavior by interposing a time delay between the presentation of the natural and an artificial prompt. When the natural antecedent stimulus ($S^+$) fails to evoke a given response, an artificial $S^D$ (prompt), usually a portion of or even the full correct answer, is inserted to occasion the behavior and thereby permitting it to be reinforced. Initially, the natural discriminative stimulus is presented concurrently with an effective artificial $S^D$, or prompt, to evoke and reinforce the appropriate response. Teaching using *progressive or graduated delayed prompting* (also called *progressive time delay*) usually progresses by gradually extending the time between the $S^+$ (e.g., a math problem) and the prompt (the answer), until the client emits the correct response reliably in advance of the prompt. *See also* Transfer of stimulus control. 20

**Delay of gratification.** Time between the response and its contingent reinforcer(s). 11

**Dependent group contingency.** A contingency arrangement in which the performance of an individual or several members of a group forms the basis for the group's access to reinforcement. For example, when the average of the lowest three student scores improve, everyone in the class receives reinforcers.12

**Dependent variable.** A variable that changes systematically, as a direct function of a change in another variable (the *independent variable)*. When systematic changes in the independent variable are reliably accompanied by changes in the dependent variable, we say the two are *functionally relate—* that the level or value of the dependent variable is in fact *dependent* on the level or value of the independent variable. In applied behavior analysis, the dependent variable usually is some behavioral measure; the independent variable, some condition or treatment that may affect a parameter (e.g., level, trend, variability) of that behavior. 9

**Deprivation.** The absence or reduction of a reinforcer for a period of time. Deprivation is a motivating operation that increases the effectiveness of the reinforcer and the rate of behavior. 6

**Derived stimulus relations.** A relation between two or more stimuli that is not directly trained and not based on physical properties of the stimuli. Often used to describe an aspect of stimulus equivalence. 16

**Descriptive assessments.** Involves observing the setting events, direct antecedents and the consequences that appear to correlate with the behavior of concern to predict its function. Descriptive assessments are often the initial step toward true functional (i.e., a cause and effect) relations between the behavior of concern and the events controlling its emission; The more closely given antecedents, behaviors, and consequences relate, the higher the probability that a functional relationship exists. 4, 10

**Desensitization, contact.** Based on shaping, an intervention, that involves differentially reinforcing closer and closer approximations toward approaching an object the client fears or avoids, while the participant continues to relax.13, 18, 29

**Determinism**. Doctrine that acts of will, occurrences in nature, or social or psychological phenomena are causally determined by preceding events or natural laws. 1

**Differential observing responses (DOR)**. The DOR method is designed to gain the client's attention and to teach him or her to discriminate the defining characteristics, or critical features, of each sample stimulus, prior to the matching-to-sample task. For example, the client could be required to distinguish the distinctive letters (e.g., n, t, r) of the word ("e**n**te**r**" as opposed to "o**t**he**r**"), immediately prior to having him match the whole words.17

**Differential reinforcement (DR).** Consists of reinforcing particular behavior(s) of a given class (or form, pattern or topography) while placing those same behaviors on extinction and/or punishing them when they fail to match performance standards or when they occur under inappropriate stimulus conditions, Also,. 15, 16, 27, 28

**Differential reinforcement of alternative behavior (DRA).** A reinforcement procedure usually designed to reduce a given behavior by reinforcing alternative behavior while withholding reinforcement (e.g., using extinction and/or punishment) for the unwanted response. A procedure used for developing stimulus control. 28

**Differential reinforcement of diminishing rates (DRD**, also called **Full session DRL)**. A schedule according to which *reinforcement is delivered "when the number of responses in a specified period of time is less than, or* *equal to, a prescribed limit*" (Deitz & Repp, 1973, p. 457). Also see Progressive DRD. 22 & 28

**Differential reinforcement of high rates (DRH).** A schedule specifying that reinforcers are delivered only after several responses occur in rapid succession at or above a pre-established rate. Increasingly higher rates of the behavior are differentially reinforced until they reach a specific criterion level. 22

**Differential reinforcement of incompatible behaviors (DRI).** A sub-class of DRA, with a further restriction: the alternative behavior cannot be emitted simultaneously with the unwanted behavior. (E.g., reinforcing completion of work reduces those forms of disruption that are incompatible with working.) 28

**Differential reinforcement of low rates (DRL,** also called **spaced DRL).** A behavior is reinforced only if it occurs following a specific period of time during which it did not occur, or since the last time it occurred. *Example:* A teacher only compliments and calls on a student who waits for at least 3 minutes before participating again. For full session DRL, see Differential reinforcement of diminishing rates." 22, 28

**Differential reinforcement of other behaviors (DRO).** The differential reinforcement of the absence, omission or non-occurrence of a (particular) behavior. The reinforcement operation may strengthen whatever other behavior(s) the individual is emitting at the time; and, this explains why it is called differential reinforcement of other behavior. Sometimes called *omission training,* or *differential reinforcement of zero occurrences. See also* Momentary, Whole interval and Progressive DROs. [When a particular "other behavior" is identified as the one to be reinforced, the preferred term is DRA (differential reinforcement of an alternative behavior).] 28

**Differential reinforcement of paced responding (DRP)** is characterized by reinforcement arranged to occur contingent only on response rates emitted within set upper and lower limits. 22

**Differential reinforcement of rate schedules.** Under these schedules, various response sequences are differentially reinforced, depending on their rates: slowly, at an intermediate or paced rate, or faster. These include DRD, DRH, DRL and DRP (described above). 22

**Direct instruction.** A teaching method that involves using a prepared curriculum (i.e., DISTAR™) consisting of: (1) following a very carefully organized and detailed sequence of instruction; (2) teaching skillfully in small groups when appropriate; (3) evoking unison responses; (4) using signals to encourage all students to participate; (5) pacing presentations quickly; (6) applying specific techniques for correcting and preventing errors; and (7) using praise. 18

**Direct observational recording.** A method, sometimes called *observational recording,* in which human observers objectively record ongoing (or video-recordings of ongoing) behavior. Event and time sampling are both direct observational recording methods. 7, 8

**Direct replication.** *See* Replicate. 25

**Discrete behavior.** A behavior, such as a lever press, sneeze, hit, or a correct answer to an addition problem, that has a clearly discriminable beginning and end. The frequencies of discrete behaviors can be easily counted by using frequency recording or event recording. 7

**Discrete trial.** See Discrete trial training. 18

**Discrete trial training.** Here, tasks are broken down into short, simple trials. A *discrete trial* is a single cycle of behaviorally-based instructional routine consisting of four or five parts: (1) Presenting, if necessary, the $S^D$ or $S^+$ -- a short, clear instruction or cue to which the client is to respond. (2) Providing a *temporary* prompt, if necessary, such as *showing* (or *telling* or *guiding*) the client's correct responding. (3) Waiting for the skill or instructional target behavior to occur. (4) Providing the reinforcer, such as positive feedback, praise or a high preference item, designed to motivate the client to continue responding correctly contingent on the behavior. (5) Ending with an inter-trial interval consisting of a brief pause between consecutive trials. The trial is called *discrete* because it has a definite beginning and end. 18

**Discriminated operant.** A response operating under stimulus control. The response occurs only when the particular $S^D$ is present. Discrete Trail Training (DTT) is an example of a method based on the use of discriminated operants. 15

**Discrimination, conditional.** A form of complex stimulus control in which the role of one discriminative stimulus is conditional on the presence of other discriminative stimuli (sometimes a *motivating operation*). Conditional discriminations involve a four term rather than a three-term contingency: conditional stimuli, antecedent stimuli, responses (behaviors), and consequences. In contrast with simple discriminations, each antecedent stimulus is discriminative for reinforcement, or not, conditional on the presence of another particular antecedent (e.g., a figure to match, as in matching to sample). Also, different contexts can change the effects of discriminative stimuli on behavior. For example, if bad weather causes a school closing, then the student may ignore the due date for a term-paper and immerse himself in his favorite video-game. Also see stimulus control, complex, and matching-to-sample. 16, 17

**Discrimination, simple.** An antecedent evokes or abates (inhibits) the behavior. Three elements, or a three term contingency, are involved: A discriminative stimulus, behavior (response), and consequence. Also see stimulus control, simple. 16

**Discrimination, stimulus.** A form of tight stimulus control in which responding is restricted to certain stimulus situations: those in which the response has been reinforced, and not to those in which it has not been reinforced. The ability to identify under which conditions, a behavior will lead to reinforcement, or not. Stimulus discriminations may be established by *differentially reinforcing* responding in one stimulus situation and extinguishing or punishing that response in other situations, and/or by reinforcing other behavior in the other situations. 2, 16, 21

**Discriminative control.** When an individual responds consistently in the presence of a particular antecedent stimulus or stimuli, the response is said to be under the *control* of that stimulus or those stimuli. 15

**Discrimination learning.** Discrimination learning is demonstrated when, under specific conditions, the individual reliably (consistently) emits a particular behavior often leading to reinforcement and does not emit that behavior under other conditions -- those under which the response does not lead to reinforcement. 15

**Discriminative stimuli ($S^Ds$).** Stimuli are said to be discriminative when they control behavior differentially, after having been present reliably when a response either has been reinforced, placed on extinction, or punished. Their presence or absence systematically alters the probability of the rate of response. Discriminative stimuli are antecedents that influence given subsequent behavior. They either evoke (trigger or set the occasion for) or abate (inhibit) the occurrence of the behavior. There are several types of discriminative stimuli. These include: 2, 15

$S^{Dr}s$—An antecedent stimulus in the presence of which a given response is likely to be reinforced. It is discriminative for reinforcement due to its having preceded, or accompanied, the behavior-reinforcer combination. An $S^{Dr}$ tends to occasion or evoke a particular response because reinforcement has tended to follow it in the past. 2, 15

$S^Δs$ (S-deltas)—An antecedent stimulus in the presence of which a given response is not likely to be reinforced. An $S^Δ$ abates (inhibits or suppresses) the response, in that the response is not likely to be reinforced in its presence (i.e., extinction is the likely consequence). 2, 15

$S^{Dp}s$— An antecedent stimulus that has been repeatedly paired with punishment. An antecedent stimulus in the presence of which a given response is likely to produce aversive consequences, such as punishment, timeout, or response cost. 2, 15

**Discriminative stimulus, natural.** See Natural discriminative stimulus. 15

**DISTAR™.** See Direct Instruction. 18

**DOR method.** See Differential observing responses. 17

**DR.** *See* Differential reinforcement. 16, 26, 28

**DRA.** *See* Differential reinforcement of alternative behaviors. 28

**DRD.** *See* Differential reinforcement of diminishing rates. 22, 28

**DRH.** *See* Differential reinforcement of high rates. 22

**DRI.** *See* Differential reinforcement of incompatible behaviors. 28

**DRL.** *See* Differential reinforcement of low rates. 22

**DRO.** *See* Differential reinforcement of other behaviors. 28

**DROP.** *See* Progressive DRO. 28

**DRP.** *See* Differential reinforcement of paced responding. 22

**DTT.** *See* discrete trial training. 18

**Duplic.** "When the controlling variable is a verbal stimulus and the response has point-to-point correspondence (the beginning, middle, and end of the stimulus matches the beginning, middle and end of the response) with formal similarity (when the controlling antecedent stimulus and the response share the same mode and physically resemble each other) we may label the response duplic behavior" (Michael 1982, p. 3). The duplicated stimulus can be a spoken word, a sign, a gesture, a matching image, or a written stimulus. Also, see echoics and imitation -- types of duplic behavior. 19

**Duration.** The length of time that passes from onset to offset of a behavior or a stimulus. 4, 7

**Duration recording.** Recording the time that elapses from the onset to the offset of a response (e.g., the length of time a person spends talking on the phone). 7

**Echoics.** A type of duplic behavior in which another person's verbal behavior is repeated, as in parroting what another has said. 19

**Ecobehavioral assessment.** Examining behavior in relation to its context—ongoing and previous contingencies. Ecobehavioral assessment considers how a behavior change may affect *and* be affected by contextual conditions including changes in the social and physical environment. 10

**Edible reinforcer.** Consumable items - like milk and snacks that serve a reinforcing function. 6

**Educational significance.** The extent to which the change has contributed toward the educational progress of the student. 25

**Elicit.** In respondent or classical conditioning of reflexes, a verb used to denote the effect of an antecedent conditioned or unconditioned stimulus on a conditioned or unconditioned response. In describing the salivary reflex of a dog, we would say that the unconditioned stimulus, meat, *elicits* salivation. Following conditioning, another stimulus, such as a tone, also might elicit salivation. *See also* Respondent behavior. 2, 15

**Emit.** A verb that describes the occurrence of an operant behavior. In this text, familiar verbs, such as express, perform, respond, and behave are used as equivalents. See also Operant behavior. 5

**Empirical.** Derived from or guided by experience or experiment. 1

**Empirical task analysis.** See Task analysis. 14

**Empiricism:** Derived from or guided by experience, observation or experiment. 1

**Environment.** The context in which the behavior occurs. 2

**Episodic severity (ES).** A measure of the intensity or gravity of a response. 7

**Equal interval graphs.** Line graphs, bar graphs, and cumulative graphs generally are labeled equal interval graphs because the units on the y- and x-axis are spaced equally, as opposed to those in standard celeration charting, which uses logarithmic units. 8

**Equivalence class.** Complex behavior that consists of three defining relations of reflexivity, symmetry, and transitivity. Reflexivity refers to identity matching (e.g., Daddy is a specific man, 9 is always nine regardless of size, color, etc.); *symmetry* refers to functional reversibility (e.g., given a picture of a dog, select the word dog, and given the word dog, the picture of the dog is selected); and, *transitivity,* which refers an action with a direct object that can be recombined into classes having the same function. If A =B and B = C, then A = C (or visa versa). 16

**Error correction procedure.** A procedure used as part of *discrete trial training, and in many other interventions,* following each error. Correction procedures, including modeling, are designed to reduce client errors and help teach appropriate responding. See the section on *discrete trail training* in Chapter 18 for illustrations of its effective use. 18

**Errorless learning.** Instructional methods specifically designed to prevent or substantially minimize any learner errors are used to teach particular discriminations. Most-to-least prompting and fading methods are especially suitable for teaching new skills errorlessly. For example, sequences of artificial discriminative stimuli are arranged carefully and faded slowly and systematically so that control eventually shifts to the natural stimuli identified ultimately to evoke the response. Also, using *within stimulus prompts, stimulus equalization* and *response delay can facilitate errorless learning.* 20

**Escape behavior.** Behavior that reduces or removes aversive stimulation, thereby producing negative reinforcement. See *also* Negative reinforcement. 5, 28, 29

**Escape extinction.** Escape responses no longer provide reinforcement as a result of escape attempts being blocked. 26

**Establishing operation.** *A motivational operation (MO) that increases reinforcer effectiveness relative to baseline.* 2, 15

**Establishing stimulus ($S^E$).** A stimulus that, having been paired with an establishing operation, and having evoked a given response, now becomes a conditioned stimulus for that operation. It cues or prompts the occurrence of the establishing operation. In this text, this term is replaced by the term *motivating stimulus ($S^M$).* 15

**Ethics.** Operating according to ethical precepts: providing for voluntariness and/or informed consent by clients or advocates; arranging the least intrusive or restrictive and most benign yet effective procedures; being accountable; obtaining, maintaining, and con-tinuing development of competence, and others. 31

**Event measure.** The number of times the response occurs. Also called frequency. 7

**Event recording.** An observational recording procedure in which the number of occurrences of a given discrete behavior – number of times correct answers are given, blows delivered, and so on—are counted over a specified period of time – within an interval, session, class period, day, week, month, or observation period. 7

**Evidence-based practices.** Practices, programs, or procedures scientifically demonstrated to be effective with like populations. 9

**Evoke.** To increase the likelihood of the emission of a response by arranging prior stimulus conditions. Also used as an action verb in reference to operant behavior, wherein the response bears a probabilistic relationship (not a one-to-one relationship, as with *elicit)* to the occurrence of the $S^D$. The terms *set the occasion for, occasion, promote, cue,* and *signal* often are used as synonyms. 2, 15

**Exchangeable reinforcers.** See Token Reinforcers. 12

**Exclusionary timeout.** This version of timeout involves relocating the individual from a reinforcing to a non-reinforcing environment or separating the reinforcing environment from the individual. With exclusion timeout, the person is not physically prevented from leaving the timeout area. It is not locked, nor is the individual blocked form leaving. However, it does deny the individual the opportunity to observe and/or hear what is occurring in the original setting. *Facial screening* is a variant of exclusionary timeout. It involves the contingent application of a face cover (e.g., a terry-cloth bib, a blindfold or the contingency manager's hands). The visual input is contingently blocked for about 5 to 15 seconds following each occurrence of the unwanted behavior. The use of facial screening, though mild, is not legal in some settings, such as in the California schools. 29

**Exemplars.** Examples containing the critical stimulus or response features. For example, the critical features of a bus are that it transports more than six people on the ground, has wheels and an engine. Exemplars would include public busses, school busses and airport busses. Non-exemplars would be pedal boats, airplanes and horse drawn single-seated wagons.

**Experimental analysis of behavior.** A scientific method designed to discover the functional relation between behavior and the variables that control it. Also called functional analysis assessment. 2, 7, 9, 10, 25

**Experimental design.** An aspect of an experiment directed toward unambiguously establishing experimental control; in behavior analysis, to demonstrate a functional relation between response patterns and interventions. Experimental designs control for extraneous influences such as placebo and Hawthorne effects, passage of time, and other subject, task and environmental potentially confounding variables. See *also* Withdrawal design, Multiple baseline design, Alternating-treatment design, and other specific design strategies. 9, 25

**Experimental relation.** See Functional relation. 9, 10

**Experimental significance.** Experimental significance is determined by asking what the behavioral pattern of concern would be if the experimental intervention had not occurred and comparing it with that achieved via the behavioral intervention. Simply stated, "Did the treatment result in a meaningful change in the behavior?" 25

**Experimental variable.** See Independent variable. 25

**External validity.** The correctness or validity of conclusions about the generalizability of a functional or causal relationship, to and across other people, settings, or times. 25

**Extinction.** The phenomenon of extinction (or "extinction *process*") is the diminished rate (or eventual total absence) of a behavior, resulting from the discontinuation of reinforcement contingent on a particular target behavior. An extinction *procedure* is one in which the reinforcement of a previously reinforced behavior is discontinued, usually by withholding all sources of reinforcement contingent on the occurrence of the behavior. 2, 26

**Extinction burst.** A predictable, temporary increase in the rate, variability, and intensity of an array of (presumably previously reinforced) responses. These often consist of the behavior targeted for reduction, along with aggression, and crying) and occur immediately after the cessation of reinforcement or the introduction of extinction. Also see Extinction-induced aggression. 26

**Extinction-induced aggression.** Describes the temporary increase in aggression that often accompanies extinction in its early phases, in the absence of any other identifiable precipitating events. Also see Extinction burst. 26

**Extraneous variables.** *See* Confounding variables. 9

**Extra-stimulus prompts.** These prompts are not naturally inherent in the stimulus, as are *within-stimulus prompts*. They are provided as external supplements to the stimulus. Examples include *imitative prompts*, gestures, *response delay*, and *graduated guidance*. 20

**Extrinsic aversive stimuli.** Aversive stimuli external to the behavior that may be delivered by an outside agent. 30

**Facial screening.** *See* Inclusion timeout. 29

**Fading.** A procedure used for transferring control of responding from one stimulus or set of stimuli to another by gradually and systematically removing one while the other is gradually introduced. For example, in teaching the word red, you might fade out the color red while you fade in the intensity of the lines for the letters r, e, & d. It is frequently used to gradually fade out physical guidance, modeling, instructions, and other prompts as S⁺s in the natural environment become $S^D$s. 20

**Feedback.** Information transmitted back to the responder following a particular performance in a form that may influence behavior: seeing or hearing about specific features of the results. Feedback may function as a reinforcer or punisher; and/or may serve a discriminative function. Feedback can be natural, unintentional, or carefully managed. Its form can vary too, from a subtle facial expression or gesture, to a set of general spoken comments (e.g., "Nice job!" "Good going!" "Ah hah!" "That was awful or awesome!"), to precise quantitative measures (e.g., "Your praise has increased from a baseline of about 3-times an hour to 6-times an hour. That's really great!" "That was the tenth time in a row you came back late from your break!") 24

**FERG.** See Functional goals. 4

**Fidelity of implementation**. Also known as **treatment integrity, treatment fidelity,** or **procedural fidelity**. Implementation fidelity refers to the accuracy with which the intervention or treatment is implemented. Fidelity of implementation affects intervention outcomes: Generally, given a well-designed plan of intervention, the higher the treatment integrity, the more effective the intervention. Some researchers use the label "process research," to describe the integrity with which the procedure is implemented, as opposed to "outcome research," which seeks to determine client behavior change. 3, 7

**Fixed interval (FI)**. *See* Interval schedules of reinforcement. 23

**Fixed ratio (FR)**. *See* Ratio schedules of reinforcement. 22

**Fixed time (FT) schedule.** See Time schedules of reinforcement. 23, 27

**Fluency.** See Response fluency. 17, 21

**Forward chaining.** Effecting the development of a chain of responses by training the first response or link in the chain initially, then joining the second link, and so on until the entire chain is emitted as a single complex behavior. 14

**Four-term contingency.** A four-term contingency includes the following elements: 1) motivating or establishing operations, 2) antecedent stimuli (discriminative stimuli), 3) responses (behaviors), and 4) consequences. The phrase communicates the interrelationship among those four elements. 16

**Frame.** A finely graded instructional step. Part of a teaching segment in programmed instruction. Confirmation for responding correctly to each step is assumed to furnish reinforcement. *See also* Programmed instruction. 13

**Free operant.** A free operant *is a* response that is emitted without any constraints or prompts, thereby leaving the individual in a position "freely" to emit the next identical or similar response (Catania, 2007). Within an instructional or training situation, the participant's free-operant behavior is not dependent on an instruction, prompt, or any supportive discriminative stimulus provided by another individual. Whatever discriminative control is present is natural to the environment. Examples include, running aimlessly and pushing a lever in the absence of any instructions or cues. 18

**Frequency.** The number of times a behavior occurs. Often expressed as rate—that is, in relation to a given period of time. Also called event. 4, 7

**Frequency recording.** Counting the occurrences of a behavior, such as the number of interruptions or balls thrown, without regard to time. 7

**Freeze technique.** Instructing individuals to become immobile while maintaining their current behavioral topography. Used to teach people to discriminate positive and negative examples of particular motor forms. (Think, a ballet or gymnastic position).

**Full session DRL.** See Differential reinforcement of diminishing rates (DRD). 28

**Function.** The term functional, or function, implies the lawful manner in which the rate, form or other pattern with which the behavior is repeated relates to the way its consequences have influenced it in the past. When we say that behavior occurs because it is functional, we are saying it occurs because it has a history of producing particular reinforcing events.

**Functional analysis or functional analysis assessment.** *See* Experimental analysis of behavior. 9, 10, 25

**Functional assessment.** See Functional behavioral assessment. 4, 10

**Functional behavior.** Behavior that results in functional consequences that gains the individual what s/he is seeking. Also see replacement behavior and functional goals. 10

**Functional behavioral assessment.** Also called functional assessment. A method of inquiring about why a person repeats particular behaviors, such as simple behaviors like raising one's hand to especially puzzling, dangerous or disruptive behaviors. A method of determining the function of a particular behavior. 4, 10

**Functional Communication Training (FCT).** FCT is based on DRA (differential reinforcement of alternative behavior). Once the function of a problem behavior is determined, that function, or reinforcer, is provided for more socially appropriate behavior. 19

**Functional consequences.** Consequences that are effective positive reinforcers or that rid the client of aversive stimuli (i.e., what is not wanted at that moment). 10

**Functional equivalence.** "When changes in the contingencies controlled by one pair of stimuli are sufficient to change the subject's behavior with respect to other pairs" (Sidman et al, 1989, p. 272). "Physically dissimilar stimuli come to be treated as equivalent to, or substitutable for, one another in certain contexts" (Green, 2001, p. 79). For example, a picture of a dog, the written and/or spoken word dog, and an actual dog are functionally equivalent. Without functional equivalence, we could not read. Also see Equivalence class. 16

**Functional goals.** Functional goals are behaviors that produce functional reinforcers. Based on the findings of a functional assessment, they focus on teaching clients how to obtain their reinforcers in socially acceptable ways. For example, if a client yells out for attention, he might be taught to raise his hand or to speak in a quiet voice to obtain attention. Also called Functionally equivalent replacement goals (FERGs). 4

**Functionally equivalent replacement goals (FERGs).** See Functional goals. 4

**Functional relation.** A lawful relation between values of two variables. In behavior analysis, a *dependent variable* (treated behavior) and a given *independent variable* (intervention or treatment procedure) are *functionally related* if the behavior changes systematically with changes in the value of the independent variable or treatment. For example, the more intense an aversive stimulus, the stronger the response suppression. Experimental research designs also prevent people from attributing the behavior change to non-related or extraneous causes. 9, 10, 22

**Functional skill.** See replacement behavior. A substitute skill that enables the individual to obtain reinforcement. Usually it is age, or at least developmentally appropriate, socially significant, and likely to be reinforced or supported by the natural environment in both the short *and* long run. 4

**Functional utility** refers to the person obtaining what s/he wants (particular reinforcers). A behavior is functional when it permits individuals to get what they seek. 19

**Generalization.** See Generalization, response and Generalization, stimulus. 21

**Generalization, response.** (Also called *response induction)* The spread of effects to other classes of behavior, when one class of behavior is modified by reinforcement, extinction, and so on. The shift in the form or topography of a behavior. For instance, the way a particular letter is shaped or formed may vary in ways that are similar but not identical to the formation of the letter as it was originally reinforced. 21

**Generalization, stimulus.** The occurrences of the response in the presence of antecedent stimuli sharing certain characteristics with those previously correlated with reinforcement; a broadening of the range of stimuli or $S^D$s (objects, sounds, times, places, other people, and so on) that "set the occasion for" or evoke particular behaviors. Generalization occurs when stimulus control is absent, incomplete, or when responding occurs in the presence of stimuli sharing certain characteristics with those previously associated with reinforcement. The child who calls all quadrupeds "doggie" is generalizing (we often refer to this type of behavior as "over-generalizing"), as you are when you say "What's up?" to both your friend April as well as to Julie whenever you see them. Stimulus generalization, then, is the repetition of the same response at other times, in other places, or in the presence of other people. 2, 21

**Generalization training.** A method designed to occasion a behavior emitted in one stimulus situation in another (usually novel) stimulus situation; programming for stimulus generalization. For instance, students who have learned a set of skills in one setting (i.e., the resource room) may be taught to apply those skills in other settings (i.e., the classroom). 21

**Generalized imitation.** As a response class, using the imitation skill not only in response to familiar examples, but with novel examples as well. Duplicating modeled behavior in novel instances, beyond those explicitly taught. 18

**Generalized reinforcer.** A conditioned reinforcer effective for a wide range of behaviors as a result of having been paired with a variety of previously established reinforcers (primary and conditioned). Due to this history, the effectiveness of a generalized reinforcer tends not to depend on any one state of deprivation, and is only minimally affected by satiation. Money is a prime example of a generalized reinforcer. It has been associated with and can be exchanged for a variety of other reinforcers. 6, 11

**Generative learning.** The class of learning of new material resulting from previous learning. Training to fluency helps to promote generative learning as does teaching behavioral cusps. 13

**Goal.** The intended broad or abstract purpose of an intervention. Also see behavioral goals, functional goals, and alternative goals. 4

**Goal levels**. A goal level refers to a preset value of performance to be reached at a given time. *See also* Goal-setting. 24

**Goal, outcome.** A specification of the end product or behavior sought as a result of the treatment program. Examples include decreases in vandalism cost or reductions in the number of absences. 4

**Goal, process (or treatment).** A target, the accomplishment of which enables the achievement of an outcome goal. For example, increasing a teacher's rates of giving approval might be a *process goal* enabling the *outcome goal* of improving students' scholastic achievement. 4, 9

**Goal-setting.** Specifying a performance quality and/or level to be attained, often by a particular time. A goal might be set to attain a certain number of accomplishments, level of quality, percentage of correct answers, and so forth. A term often used in organizational management. 17

**Good behavior game.** A group management package in which the group is divided into two or more teams and rules are specified. In its original form, a team was penalized by being assigned a check-mark against it if a member violated one of the rules. Reinforcers were provided to each team with fewer than the criterion number of marks or for the team with the fewest marks at the end of a preset period. More currently it frequently involves reinforcing consequences as well as punishment, such as periodically providing points exchangeable for reinforcers for a team when its members act according to the rules. 28

**Graduated guidance.** The combined use of physical guidance and fading, resulting in a systematic gradual reduction of the intensity of physical guidance. To use this procedure, begin while the client is being cooperative, using the minimal amount of physical guidance necessary to evoke the correct response; then gradually fade out the physical guidance. 20

**Graduated delayed prompting.** See Delayed prompting. 20

**Graduated prompting.** A stimulus control method, also called *minimum to maximum prompting* or increasing assistance, that begins with the natural $S^+$ and progresses from the least-to-most artificial or restrictive prompts until the desired behavior occurs. An example would be shifting from gestural to spoken, to imitative, to physically guided prompts. 20

**Graph.** A diagram displaying data in the form of one or more points, lines, line segments, curves, or areas, representing the variation of a variable in comparison with that of one or more other variables. (See Line graphs and Bar graphs.) 8

**Group contingencies.** Arrangements in which consequences are delivered to some or all members of a group as a function of the performance of one, several, or all of its members. *See also* Interdependent, dependent, and independent group contingencies. 12

**Guiding.** See Physical guidance. 20

**Habit reversal.** An intervention package for reducing annoying habits, consisting of awareness training, DRI, imagery training, social support and contingency awareness.

**Habituation.** Refers to reductions in the responding <u>elicited</u> by a stimulus over repeated presentations (as when the startle response to a loud noise diminishes with repeated presentations). The term habituation is primarily used in respondent or classical conditioning. 11, 16

**High probability requests.** See Behavioral momentum. 27

**Imitation.** Matching the behavior of a model, or engaging in a behavior similar to that observed. A type of duplic behavior in which the point to point correspondence of the physical action of another, such as producing a communicative sign, is duplicated. 18, 19

**Imitative prompt.** A discriminative stimulus consisting of a behavior that is modeled in order to occasion an imitative response. 18

**Incidental teaching.** Teaching toward specific, predetermined objectives, by capitalizing on natural unplanned opportunities, as in temporarily blocking a child's access to an item until particular adjectives are used to request the object. 19, 21

**Inclusion timeout.** The least intrusive/aversive and the most commonly used form of timeout. The individual may be moved to an area where he or she can hear and see what is happening (or may even stay put), but for a brief period of time (e.g., 3-5 minutes) is not responded to nor allowed to participate. Examples include: a) *withdrawal of materials* (removing reinforcing materials from and ignoring an individual contingent him or her for a brief period of time upon committing the infraction, , b) *planned ignoring* (withholding any attention, physical contact, and/or verbal interactions with the individual for a short duration contingent upon the occurrence of the unwanted behavior—(NOT equivalent to an extinction procedure because it is intentionally temporary and reinforcement is withheld from a number of behaviors, not just the target behavior), c) *contingent observation* (contingent on the occurrence of a rule violation, the client is relocated to an area in which s/he can observe what is going on but not participate in the activities). May also include removing a *ribbon* for X, usually 3, minutes or longer if necessary, contingent on each occurrence of an infraction,. (Only students wearing the ribbon-ties receive periodic treats and praise). 29

**Incompatible behavior.** A specific alternative response class (DRA) incapable of being emitted simultaneously with another behavior; behavior that interferes with another specific behavior. 28

**Incomplete stimulus control.** *See* Stimulus control, weak. 16

**Increasing assistance.** *See* Graduated prompting. 20

**Independent group contingency** Applying the same consequences to the same or to a different behavior of each member of a group. The reinforcement of one member's behavior does not depend upon the performance of others. For example, "Each assembly line worker who meets the production quota will earn a bonus;" "Each student must have 9 out of 10 math problems correct to earn their two tokens." 12

**Independent variable.** The experimental variable that is managed or manipulated. In behavior analysis, the independent variable often is a behavioral procedure, package, or other intervention or treatment program. 9, 25

**Indirect assessment.** Indirect assessments are used initially to gather background information about the behaviors of interest. Tools include client self-reports, recalled anecdotes supplied by those significant in the person's life (e.g., parents, teachers, spouses, co-workers). Generally, information is obtained about the circumstances under which the behavior is said to or not to occur, with an emphasis on ecological variables. Often interviews, along with instruments such as checklists, rating scales and client records (e.g., previous incident reports, Individual Education Plans – IEPs, psychological evaluations, medical reports and so on) are used to help provide a more detailed picture of the client's behavioral patterns and the stimuli that appear to relate to those. 4, 10

**Induction.** See Generalization, response. 21

**Informed consent.** Clients (or their advocates) and/or parents and caretakers have the right to be informed about problem behaviors, previously attempted interventions, proposed experimental or programmatic outcomes and methods, as well as alternative interventions, including the procedures' advantages and disadvantages, methods of data collection, Assuming consent or rejection is to be considered "informed," they also are to be invited to participate in the selection or rejection of specific goals and procedures. This information must be communicated at a level that will be understood by the clients and/or their advocates. For a more complete definition, see the Behavior Analysts Certification Board's (BACB's) definition in its ethics code for behavior analysts. 11, 30

**Instructional demand.** In an experiment, an unintended alteration in behavior occurring as a function of variations in the way instructions are delivered. 7, 18

**Instructional objective.** See Behavioral objective. 4

**Intensity.** The strength or force with which a stimulus is delivered or a behavior expressed. Sounds, lights, and physical blows can vary in intensity. Similar to *magnitude*. 4, 7

**Intensive designs.** See Single-subject experimental designs. 9, 25

**Interdependent group contingencies.** Contingency arrangement in which members of the group are treated as if they were a single behaving individual. The group's performance determines the reinforcer each member receives. For example, "If the group averages 90% on the test, everyone will have free time." 12

**Intermittent reinforcement.** A schedule of reinforcement in which some, but not all, of the occurrences of a response are reinforced. 11, 22, 23

**Internal validity.** A feature that describes how correct or valid conclusions are about the functionality of the relationship between two variables, such as an intervention procedure and changes in behavior. Internal validity, then, addresses the validity of the answer to the question, " Did the treatment, and not some other factor, bring about the behavior change?" 25

**Interobserver agreement assessment (IOA)**. Also, called assessment of interobserver reliability. A method for estimating the reliability of a behavioral observation system. A coefficient of agreement is calculated by comparing scores obtained by two or more independent observers and determining the number of times they agreed and/or disagreed in proportion to the number of observations scored. Depending on the observational method used, there are several methods of calculating IOA. To calculate IOA for: 1) **permanent product recording**, use the formula: the number of agreements divided by the number of agreements plus disagreements, then multiply the fraction by one hundred. 2) **event or frequency recording**: the smaller total number of agreements is divided by the larger total of agreements plus disagreements. A more accurate method is the *block by block method*: the observation session is broken further into intervals, and events or frequencies are recorded per interval. Scores are compared on an interval by interval basis to obtain an IOA score. Intervals in which both observers agree exactly receive a score of 1; those for which they they do not agree are assigned a zero and a coefficient of agreement is calculated by dividing the smaller total by the larger. Next, those separate coefficients are summed and divided by the total number of intervals. 3) For **duration and IRT recording**, the formula: shorter duration/ longer duration X 100 is used. 4) For **time sampling observational recordings**, formula: # of intervals agreed/ # of intervals agreed + # of interval disagreed X 100 is used. If the behavior occurs at low rates, the more conservative calculation is based on scored intervals while for behavior that occurs at high rates, unscored intervals are more conservative. *See also* Reliability. 7

**Interreinforcement interval.** The time scheduled between reinforcements. 23

**Interresponse time (IRT).** IRT is measured by recording the duration of elapsed time from the offset of one response to the onset of the next response. 7

**Interval spoilage.** See Partial interval time sampling. 7

**Interval schedules of reinforcement.** A schedule according to which reinforcers are presented contingent on the first response emitted after the termination of a given interval of time: (a) *Fixed interval (FI)* schedule—following a constant time period; (b) *Variable interval (VI)* schedule—similar, but reinforcement is delivered following the completion of intervals averaging that time period. 23

**Interval time-sampling.** See Time sampling. 7

**Intervention.** See Treatment. 9

**Intraverbals.** Verbal stimuli controlled by verbal stimuli without point-to-point correspondence or formal similarity and are reinforced by nonspecific reinforcers (Skinner, 1957). Intraverbal behavior can assume many forms, such as social interchanges (e.g., "You're welcome," when someone says "Thank you"), word associations (e.g., "black" when someone says "white"), and translations from one language to another. 19

**Intrinsic aversive stimuli.** Aversive properties integral or natural to particular acts, such as fatigue or muscle strain inherent to excessive exercise, or to remaining totally inactive, or repeating the same movement excessively. 30

**Intrinsic motivation.** An inferred state based on observing an individual expressing a particular behavior at high rates in the absence of any identifiable external reinforcing consequences. Emitting the behavior itself is assumed, in and of itself, to be reinforcing; behavior that actually may be under the control of a very thin schedule of subtle reinforcers. 11

**IOA.** See Interobserver agreement assessment. 7

**Ipsative data.** Data based on the behavior of an individual; used as the basis for demonstrating functional relations. Because ipsative data are derived from the behavior of a particular individual rather than from group norms, they can be used to investigate what conditions lawfully affect the behavior of the individual, rather than that of a group in general. 9

**IRT.** See Interresponse time. 7

**Isolation.** *See* Timeout. 29

**Job analysis.** *See* Task analysis. 14

**Labeled praise.** *See* Specific praise. 11

**Lag Schedule.** A response is reinforced only if it differs from a specified number of previous responses. They are used to produce response variability, or what some call an aspect of creative responding. 22

**Latency.** The elapsed time from the presentation of an antecedent stimulus (cue, prompt, signal) and the response. 4, 7

**Learned helplessness.** A state in which the individual seems to have lost motivation. Does not respond to reinforcers. 26

**Learned reinforcer.** See Conditioned reinforcer. 6

**Learning.** Any enduring change in behavior produced as a function of the interaction between the behavior and the environment. Or, learning = change in behavior. Often used to describe motor or cognitive skills, but term also may refer to social, affective, personal, and other classes of operant behavior. 2

**Learning history.** The sum of an individual's behaviors that have been conditioned or modified as a function of his or her interaction with environmental events. See Behavioral repertoire. 5

**Level.** See Change in level. 8, 9

**Limited hold.** A restriction placed on an interval schedule requiring that to be eligible for reinforcement, the *primed response* (the first response following termination of the required interval) must occur within a specific span of time following that interval. 23

**Line graphs.** A graphic display of data scaled along some dimension, such as time or the order of responses in a sequence. Lines connect data points within a phase. In ABA, line graphs generally are used to display relations among sets of variables across units of time. See Chapter 8 for illustrations. 8

**Link.** An intact response, or performance, that combined with others form a behavioral chain; small teachable units that may configure a series of sequentially ordered links within more complex behavioral chains. 14

**Magnitude.** Greatness of size, volume, or extent (i.e., of a response or a stimulus). 7

**Maintenance procedures.** Strategies used to promote the persistence of behaviors under natural environmental conditions, such as alterations in reinforcing contingencies, fading prompts, and teaching self-management. 20, 22, 23, 24

**Mands.** A verbal response consisting of a "request" for some object or action (i.e., a specific reinforcer). The "requesting" (or demanding) is controlled by a specific relation between the motivating antecedent and the reinforcer. People use mands to request a reinforcing object or event. Being able to mand heightens individuals' likelihood of getting what they want when they want it. 19

**Masochism.** The appearance of seeking out or inflicting "punishment" upon one's self. 30

**Matching law.** A description of a phenomenon according to which organisms match or distribute their responses according to the proportion of payoff during choice situations (i.e., if a behavior is reinforced about 60% of the time in one situation and 40% in another, that behavior tends to occur about 60% of the time in the first situation, and 40% in the second). Sometimes called matching theory. 23

**Matching theory.** See Matching law. 23

**Matching-to-sample.** A form of *conditional discrimination*. Matching-to-sample entails an individual selecting from two or more alternatives (e.g., *objects, figures, letters, or sounds*) the stimulus that matches or corresponds to a standard or sample. Matching-to-sample can occur simultaneously or following a delay. Also see "Matching-to-sample, simultaneous" and "Matching-to-sample, delayed." 16

**Matching-to-sample, delayed.** A type of matching-to-sample in which the sample picture or item is removed prior to the presentation of choices. 16

**Matching-to-sample, simultaneous.** A type of matching-to-sample in which the sample item, often an image or printed word though sometimes a three dimensional object, may be presented while the choices remain exposed. Both the sample and choices are present at the same time. 16

**Maximum-to-minimum prompting.** Begins with a prompt known reliably to evoke the behavior and gradually shifts to less intrusive, more natural prompts. (Most to least.) A prompting method that is used to promote *errorless learning.* 17

**Measurement complexity.** Refers to the complexity or the number of behaviors observed. Observers are more likely accurately to assess three or four behaviors than eight or nine. 7

**Minimum-to-maximum prompting.** Also called *graduated prompting.* or increasing assistance. Prompting begins with minimal cues, that gradually increase in level of assistance, only as necessary, until the behavior occurs (e.g., prompts may include requests, modeling, physical guidance, gestures and so on). (Least to most prompting.) 17

**Mission.** An organization's fundamental purpose for existing. 4

**Mnemonic.** A strategy designed to improve memory or recall by tying new information more closely to the learner's existing knowledge base. For example, the state of New Hampshire could be paired with a hamster. 27

**MO.** See Motivating operation. 2, 10, 15, 27

**Model.** A person whose behavior is (or is to be) imitated. 18

**Model, coping.** A model known previously to have experienced difficulty with the behavior to be imitated, but who now is capable of demonstrating that skill.

**Modeling procedure.** A stimulus control procedure that uses demonstrations to prompt an imitative response; colloquially, a *show or demonstration procedure.* 18, 27

**Modeling, video.** Video demonstrations of a behavior, generally used for the purpose of cueing an imitative response. 18

**Momentary DRO.** A variation of the DRO procedure. Reinforcers are delivered at particular preset moments, contingent of the absence of (a) particular behavior(s) at the time. 28

**Momentary time-sampling.** A time-sampling procedure in which a response is recorded only if it is occurring at the specific point in time when the interval terminates. E.g., a timer goes off at the end of a 10-minute interval, and the observer checks to see whether the youngster has his thumb in his mouth *at that moment.* 7

**Moment of transfer.** In *delayed prompting* the point at which the person begins to "anticipate," or respond in advance of the presentation of the prompt. 20

**Motivating event.** See Motivating operations. 2, 15

**Motivating operations (MOs). MOs** (sometimes called establishing operations – EOs, or setting events – SEs) MOs are antecedent events that (a) change the value of the consequence, or, (b) along with the immediate discriminative stimulus ($S^D$), may alter the behavior. The value altering effect consists of either (a) an increase in the reinforcing or punitive effectiveness of some stimulus, or (b) a decrease in reinforcing or punitive effectiveness. With respect to the behavior altering effect, it either (a) increases the current frequency of the behavior that has been reinforced by some stimulus-- an evocative effect (this MO is referred to as an establishing operation) or (b) decreases the current frequency of behavior, an abative effect (this MO is referred to as an abolishing operation). Or, said more parsimoniously, an event that alters the reinforcing or punishing value of a stimulus, and increases or decreases the rates of behaviors that produce that consequence. **MOs** occasion (evoke) and abate responding by changing the discriminative strength of the antecedent and the reinforcing value of the consequence. MOs usually are present prior to and/or concurrent with the presentation of the $S^D$. Examples: Having just eaten a large meal will diminish the effectiveness of edible reinforcers, while food deprivation will increase the effectiveness of edible reinforcers. A history of recent punishment when attempting a task is more likely to evoke aggression the next time the task is presented. 2, 10, 15

**Motivating operation, conditioned (CMO):** A learned relation between the nature and value of an antecedent stimulus and the nature of a response. 15

**Motivating operation, conditioned-transitive:** "An environmental variable that establishes (or abolishes) the reinforcing effectiveness of another stimulus and evokes (or abates) the behavior that has been reinforced by that other stimulus" (Michael, 2007, p. 391). E.g., food deprivation establishes food and the stimuli associated with food, such as eating utensils, as reinforcers. Also see Motivating stimulus. 15

**Motivating operation, reflexive:** A conditioned reflexive MO that acquires its MO effectiveness by preceding particular improving or worsening situations (Michael, 2007). E.g., repeated failure has been shown to lead to an escape reaction (e.g., aggression, self-injury, leaving the situation, etc.) A history of failure, then, becomes a reflexive MO. Alternatively, gradually approaching one's goal may function as an MO to encourage continued performance. 15

**Motivating operation, surrogate: A** surrogate MO "is a stimulus that acquires its MO effectiveness by being paired with another MO, and has the same value-altering and behavior-altering effects as the MO with which it was paired" (Michael, 2007, p. 390). 15

**Motivating operation, unconditioned (UMO):** The antecedent value–altering effect of a unconditioned motivating operation that does not depend on one's learning history. 15

**Motivating stimulus ($S^M$).** Also called conditioned-transitive motivating operation. A stimulus that must be present to allow the individual to engage in the behavior. A stimulus (e.g., car keys) that the individual has learned (conditioned) must be present to allow him or her to engage in the behavior (driving the car). Its absence evokes seeking it out. A stimulus upon which reinforcement of an $S^D$-R relation depends. Also see Establishing stimulus. 15

**Movement suppression timeout.** Preventing movement during timeout by means of physical restraint and/or verbal instructions. Often used in combination with other reductive procedures to manage violent and/or self-destructive behavior. 29

**Multielement design.** See Alternating treatment design. In the multi-element design distinctive discriminative stimuli are paired with each treatment condition. 25

**Multiple-baseline designs.** A single-subject or intensive experimental design that attempts to replicate the effects of a procedure (treatment or intervention) across (1) different subjects, (2) different settings, or (3) different classes of behavior. Intervention introduced independently to each subject (or setting or class of behavior) in succession across baselines of differing lengths to control for such time-dependent extraneous variables as history, maturation, reaction to being measured for longer or shorter periods, seasonal influences, and so on. See *also* Across-behaviors multiple-baseline; Across-subjects multiple-baseline; Across-situations multiple-baseline; Within-subject experimental design. 9

**Multiple probes.** Measuring untreated responses intermittently to assess any variations in those responses due to generalization or unidentified conditions; also used to enable learners (or others) to ascertain whether the untreated skills actually were being acquired or just varying randomly. See also Probe. 9, 25

**Multiple-schedule design.** See Alternating treatment design. 25

**Multiple-treatment interference.** A condition in which the participant's treatment *history* (inside or outside the experiment) influences performance under a subsequent treatment. Observed changes in the dependent variable (the behavior receiving treatment) then would be confounded by the prior treatment, rather than being a function of the designated independent variable. 25

**Narrative recording.** A written description of behavior in progress. The recorded events then can be ordered into a *sequence analysis* that specifies a behavior, its antecedents, and its consequences. 10

**Natural discriminative stimulus.** A discriminative stimulus indigenous to the natural environment; not one artificially introduced. The printed word is a natural $S^D$ for reading the word; a hint is not. The hour that marks the beginning of the work day is a natural $S^D$ for starting to work. 15

**Natural reinforcer.** A reinforcer indigenous to the natural environment. A good mark is usually a natural reinforcer in a school setting as is pay for a worker. 5, 6

**Needs assessment.** A systematic method for identifying goals to target for programmatic change. Needs assessment may include observations, tests, interviews, questionnaires, and other sources of input.

**Negative behavioral contrast.** See Behavioral contrast. 23, 26

**Negative discriminative stimuli.** See Discriminative stimuli, $S^{D\text{p}}$. 2

**Negative practice.** A punishment procedure that requires the client repeatedly to practice the target behavior for a predetermined time period, contingent on the occurrence of the unwanted behavior. Negative practice often transforms the response (conditioned) into an aversive stimulus to be avoided. 30

**Negative punishment.** The removal or reduction of positive reinforcers as a consequence of a response, resulting in the reduction in the rate of that response. (The descriptor "negative" merely means the removal or subtraction of a stimulus and is not intended to imply that the procedure is harmful or destructive.) Two major types of negative punishment include Timeout and Response cost. 2, 29

**Negative reinforcement.** A behavior has been negatively reinforced if it increases or is maintained as a function of the contingent removal or reduction of a stimulus. In the negative reinforcement *procedure*, the change agent intentionally removes, reduces, subtracts, or postpones an aversive stimulus (negative reinforcer) as a consequence of a response, for the purpose of strengthening that response. Sometimes referred to as escape conditioning. 2, 5

**Negative reinforcer.** An aversive stimulus; a stimulus that, when removed, reduced, or postponed as a consequence of a response, results in an *increase* in or *maintenance* of that response. See also Aversive stimulus. 5

**Neutral stimulus.** An object or event that is neutral with respect to some property that it later may acquire. A neutral stimulus does not affect behavior reliably in a particular context until it has been paired sufficiently often with some event that does have controlling properties (i.e., it has not yet evolved into an $S^D$, reinforcer, and so on). 2

**Noncontingent reinforcement (NCR).** In NCR the reinforcer is presented on a fixed-time (FT) or variable-time (VT) schedule of reinforcement, regardless of the client's actions at the time. NCR enriches environments by making reinforcing stimuli freely available.. Often used as an antecedent to prevent unwanted behavior. 27

**Normative data.** Data based on group behavior, such as group averages. One may compare the data recorded on an individual's behavior to those from a norm group, to a sample group, or the data based on one group's average performance to another's. See how this differs from *Ipsative data*.

**Objective measurement.** Publicly verifiable measures free of feelings, interpretations, or inferences. The operationalized behavior is clearly observable and measurable. 7

**Observational recording.** See Direct observational recording. 7

**Observer awareness of being assessed.** When observers are aware that their own scoring is being monitored. This often results in more accurate observers data. 7

**Observer bias.** A situation in which the data recordings may have been influenced by the observer(s)' expectation of change in a particular direction. 7

**Observer drift.** A phenomenon in which observational data move away from the true (valid) measures. In many cases indexes of agreement between observers begin to diverge from or coalesce toward one another over time, irrespective of the "true" value of the measure. 7

**Occasion** (verb). To increase the likelihood of the emission of a response by arranging prior stimulus conditions; used as an action verb in relation to operant behavior, wherein the response bears a probabilistic relationship (not a one-to-one relationship, as with *elicit*) to the occurrence of the $S^D$. The terms *set the occasion for, evoke, promote, cue,* and *signal* may serve as synonyms. 2, 15

**Omission training.** See Differential reinforcement of other behaviors (DRO). 28

**Ontogeny.** The origin and development of an individual organism from embryo to adult. 1

**Operant behavior.** That class of behavior primarily controlled by its consequences, and often, following a given learning history by particular antecedent stimuli. 2

**Operant class.** See Response class. 2

**Operant learning.** The basic process by which "voluntary" learning occurs. Operant learning can be encouraged through the use of various teaching strategies, including reinforcement, differential reinforcement, stimulus change, or shaping or discouraged via extinction, differential reinforcement and various other reductive methods. (Sometimes called operant conditioning.) 2

**Operant level.** The strength (e.g., rate or duration) of behavior prior to any known or designed conditioning. *(Baseline,* which subsumes operant level, refers to the strength of behavior prior to the introduction of an experimental variable but does not preclude earlier conditioning.) 8

**Operation.** An act or behavior that affects the environment. 4

**Operationally defined.** Terms (often colloquial psychological) that are broken down into observable and measurable components. 4

**Operational definition or statement.** The product of breaking down a broad concept, such as "aggressiveness," into its *observable* and reliably *measurable* component behaviors (frequency of hitting or biting others, duration of scream, and so on). Sometimes referred to as a *pinpointed* or *targeted behavior.* 4, 8

**Ordinate.** The y value, on the y-axis of a graph, usually expressed in numerals such as frequency, number or percentage. 8

**Outcome goal.** See Goal, outcome. 4

**Outcome recording.** See Permanent product recording. 7

**Outcome variables.** Those "bottom line" measurable factors that characterize the outcome goal, such as annual profit, and improved academic and social performance. 25

**Overcorrection.** A reductive procedure composed of a relevant and educative form of contingent exertion. Overcorrection consists of one or both of two basic components: (1) *Restitutional training* (or restitutional overcorrection), which requires the individual to restore the environment to a state substantially improved from that which existed prior to the act; and (2) *positive-practice* (or positive-practice overcorrection), which requires the individual repeatedly to practice a positive alternative behavior. When no environmental disruption occurs, only the positive-practice procedure is used. *Simple correction*, just requiring the learner to restore the environment to its previous state, is often sufficient to treat unintentional, infrequent, mildly undesirable behaviors. 30

**Overdependence.** Sometimes called *prompt dependence,* describes a condition in which a response becomes dependent on artificial or irrelevant prompts. Overdependence can be minimized by avoiding unnecessary prompts (over-prompting), as in using least-to-most prompting. Also see Stimulus overselectivity. 17

**Overgeneralization.** Emitting a response appropriate to some contexts in an inappropriate context. For example, calling all men "dada." An inappropriate generalization. 21

**Overjustification effect.** Belief that reward contingencies have a pervasive negative effect on intrinsic motivation. (Child comes to expect a reward, and tends not to engage in behavior unless rewarded for doing so.) 5

**Overselectivity.** Stimulus overselectivity refers to behavior under the control of a single feature of complex stimulus, as in only calling apples "red" if they are red. Or calling tomatoes "apples" because they are red. 17

**Pacing schedules.** These schedules are defined as those in which the upper and lower limits on reinforceable response rates are set. 23

**Package.** See Behavioral package. 24

**Parameter.** Any of a set of physical properties whose values determine the characteristics of a behavior, such as schedule and quantity or quality of reinforcers. Differences in parametric values may influence how rapidly, effectively, safely, constructively, durably, and so on, a given behavior changes. 5

**Parametric analyses**. When one parameter is held constant while other variables, within a family of functions change to help determine their relative effects. 25

**Parsimony.** The simplest theory that fits the facts of a problem is the one that should be selected. 1

**Partial-interval time-sampling.** A time-sampling procedure whereby a response is recorded if it occurs at any time(s)—even momentarily—during the interval, and not necessarily throughout the interval, as in *whole-interval* time-sampling; sometimes called *interval spoilage,* because any instance of the behavior (especially an unwanted behavior) "spoils" the interval. 7

**PBST.** See positive behavior support team. 3

**PECS.** See Picture exchange communication system. 19

**Peer influence strategies.** Arrangements of group contingencies that promote peer influence (e.g., peer tutoring and peer reinforcement). Illustrative are cooperative learning structures that rely on *dependent* and *interdependent* group contingencies in which group members share reinforcers. 12

**Peer-mediated strategy.** Involving trained, supervised, and monitored peers as direct service providers (e.g., contingency managers, co-therapists, or tutors). 12

**Peer review.** A panel of unbiased professional colleagues who review issues and methods related to programs under review, and recommend any changes to enhance the quality of care and treatment of clients. 31

**Percentage of opportunities.** Frequency/opportunities x 100. 7

**Performance feedback.** *See* Feedback. 24

**Permanent products.** A tangible outcome produced by the behavior that exists for a period of time so observers need not be present at the exact moment the behavior occurs. 7

**Permanent product recording.** A behavioral recording method in which durable products of a behavior—such as the number of windows broken, widgets produced, homework problems handed in, rejects, percentage of test questions correct, and so on—are assessed. Sometimes called outcome recording or behavioral product recording. Not suited to measuring *transitory behaviors.* 7

**Personalized system of instruction (PSI)**. *PSI* resembles programmed instruction, in that goals are clearly defined, step sizes relatively small, study questions prompt correct responses, and feedback and reinforcement delivered consistently and with minimal delay. PSI is characterized by self-pacing, use of proctors, unit mastery, emphasis on the written word, and occasional motivational lectures and demonstrations; also known as the "Keller Plan," after Fred Keller, its originator. 15

**Phase change lines.** Vertical lines on a graph indicating a change in the "treatment" or independent variable. E.g., the vertical line between the last baseline session and the first treatment session. 8

**Phase label.** The phase label describes, or names, the condition(s) in place (e.g., baseline, treatment, follow-up, etc.). 8

**Phylogeny.** Those historical patterns of relationships among their genetic endowments, past experiences, and the internal and external environmental contingencies of reinforcement currently affecting them. 1

**Physical guidance.** A form of response priming, or prompting, in which the coach or trainer physically guides the participant to perform the proper motion. E.g., a swimming coach guiding the movement of a youth's arm to demonstrate the proper stroke. 18

**Picture Exchange Communication System (PECS).** An augmentative verbal communication system that uses images rather than spoken or written words as the communicative medium. 3, 19

**Pivotal behavior.** Behaviors, that as learned, produce change in other adaptive untrained behavior. Similar to Behavioral cusp. 4

**PLA-Check (Planned activity check).** An observational recording system in which, according to a preset schedule, the observer counts the number of individuals engaged in the assigned task at that moment and compares that to the total number present. (The total engaged is divided by the total number of individuals assigned to the activity.) See also Momentary time sampling. 7

**Planned ignoring.** See Inclusion timeout. 29

**Positive behavior support team (PBST).** The PBST includes representative stakeholders and focuses most heavily on primary prevention programs; responsible for examining contextual factors, or motivational operations (e.g., histories of student failure, an over-reliance on punitive methods of control and an under-reliance of positive reinforcement by personnel) and designing programs with the aim of preventing problem behaviors in the first place. 3

**Positive behavioral interventions.** Designed to reduce aberrant behavior by reinforcing alternative, rather than punishing unwanted behaviors. (Carr & Sidener, 2002). 27, 28

**Positive behavioral contrast.** See Behavioral contrast. 23

**Positive practice (overcorrection).** See Overcorrection. 30

**Positive punishment.** An event in which a stimulus (typically unpleasant) occurs contingent on a response, resulting in a decrease in the future probability of that response. 2, 30

**Positive punishment procedure.** Intentionally *reducing* the rate of a response by presenting an aversive stimulus contingent on the (unwanted) response. Punishment can be said to have occurred only if the individual's rate of emitting the treated behavior has been demonstrably reduced. Like reinforcement, a punishment procedure is defined solely by its effect on behavior. 30

**Positive reinforcement process:** Inferred when the rate of a response maintains or increases as a function of contingent consequences (positive reinforcers). 2, 5

**Positive reinforcement procedure.** The planned application of a positively reinforcing stimulus for the purpose of increasing or maintaining the rate of a response. A carefully planned reinforcement program designed with maximal effectiveness, whereby the rate of a response maintains or increases as a function of the contingent presentation of a stimulus (a positive reinforcer) following the response. 5

**Positive reinforcer.** A stimulus, such as an object or event, that follows or is presented as a consequence of a response and results in the rate of that response increasing or maintaining. Food, praise, attention, recognition of achievement and effort, special events, and activities often serve as positive reinforcers. Nontechnical terms for positive reinforcers include *incentives, rewards,* and *strokes.* 5

**Positive scanning.** Focusing one's attention on desirable rather than unwanted behavior, often abetted by recording it. Positive scanners tend to "notice" and hence reinforce positive behaviors more and negative behaviors less often. 28

**Positive discriminaitive stimuli.** See Discriminative stimuli, $S^{Dr}$.

**POV.** To confirm that the behavior change is due to the intervention, or to demonstrate experimental control, we can do this via Prediction (P) which is what would happen if nothing changed; Obtain data (0) or results, which is what happens to the target behavior when we implement the intervention; and we verify (V) when the P and O don't overlap (the O increases or decreases compared to baseline. 9

**Pragmatism.** A practical approach to problems in which truth is found in the process of verification. 9

**Praise.** See Positive reinforcer; Specific praise. 5

**Precision Teaching.** A formal, individualized instructional method that emphasizes rate building (fluency), charting of performance (celeration charting), designing and implementing teaching, and that reinforces the emission of each specific behavior under all the conditions in which it is expected to occur. 8, 17

**Precursors.** Precursors reliably occur prior to the target behavior and are functional related to it. 14

**Premack principle.** Statement that contingent access to higher-probability behavior ("preferred activities") reinforces lower-probability behavior. See *also* Response deprivation hypothesis. 6

**Primacy effect.** The tendency to return to previously highly successful though perhaps currently ineffective behavioral patterns. 27

**Primed response.** The first response following termination of the required interval (in interval schedules of reinforcement). Also see Limited hold. 28

**Principles of behavior.** See Behavioral principles. 2

**Primary aversive stimulus ($S^P$).** A stimulus (object, or event) that functions aversively in the absence of any prior learning history (a painful electric shock, a bee sting, or a sudden loud noise) resulting in a decrease in the rate of the behavior it follows. Its cessation (e.g., of physical discomfort, hunger pangs, and unpleasant noises) is reinforcing, regardless of prior learning or conditioning (i.e., negative reinforcement). (Sometimes called unconditioned aversive stimulus.) 6, 30

**Primary prevention.** Addressing factors contributing to problem behavior among all clients in the setting, (e.g., punitive environments), to prevent the occurrence of problem behaviors. 3

**Primary positive reinforcer ($S^R$).** A stimulus, such as food, water, or sexual activity, that usually is reinforcing in the absence of any prior learning history; often used interchangeably with primary reinforcer. Primary reinforcers function as reinforcers the very first time they occur under given circumstances (e.g., deprivation, discomfort), leading to an increase or maintenance of the rate of the response. (Sometimes called unconditioned reinforcer.) 6

**Probe.** A brief *withdrawal* phase in a behavior analytic investigation, designed to examine the behavioral effect of a given intervention. 9

**Procedural fidelity.** See "fidelity of implementation." 3

**Procedural package.** See Treatment. 9

**Procedure.** See "behavioral procedures." 2

**Process goal.** See Goal, process. 4, 9

**Program integrity.** See Fidelity of implementation. 3, 7

**Programmed instruction.** An educational application based on shaping, characterized by contingencies managed in such a way that the student progresses successfully in steps from one level of difficulty to the next. Confirmation of correct responses is assumed to provide a reinforcing function. 13

**Progressive delay prompting.** Gradually extending the length of time between the presentation of a discriminative stimulus and the intended response; designed to serve as a device for promoting eventual prompt independence. See Delayed prompting. 20

**Progressive DRO (DROP).** Presenting reinforcers, perhaps in increasing quantity, to some pre-set maximum, in tandem with expanding the length of time during which the unwanted behavior is absent. 28

**Progressive ratio (PR) schedule.** "A schedule in which requirements change progressively with each reinforcer" (Catania, 2007). 22

**Prompt.** A functional but irrelevant discriminative stimulus, such as a "hint" or "reminder," designed to set the occasion for a desired response. Prompts usually are faded before the terminal goal is judged to have been achieved. (For example, the "f" sound serves as a prompt in "2 + 2 are f____" The "f" sound must be faded completely to conclude that the student has achieved the goal of knowing how to add 2 + 2.) Also see Response prompts and Stimulus prompts. 17

**Prompting.** Prompting denotes applying a functional but irrelevant or contrived discriminative stimulus that sets the occasion for the desired response. 17, 27

**Prompt dependence.** See Overdependence. 17

**Prompting, delayed.** See Delayed prompting. 20

**Proprioceptive cues.** The stimuli or sensations that arise from within one's own body. 18

**PSI.** *See* Personalized system of instruction (PSI). 15

**Punisher.** A stimulus that, when presented immediately following a response, effects a *reduction* in the rate of the response. This text uses the term *aversive stimulus* interchangeably with *punisher* or *punishing stimulus*. 5, 29, 30

**Punishment.** An event occurring contingent on a response that decreases the future probability of the response. Like reinforcement, punishment can be broken into two separate categories: *See* positive punishment and negative punishment. 2, 29, 30

**Qualitative praise.** See Specific praise. 11

**Rate.** The average frequency of behavior emitted during a standard unit of time. Formula: Number of responses divided by the number of time units. For example, if 20 responses occur in 5 minutes, the rate is 4 responses per minute. 4, 7

**Rate of criterion level.** Before shifting over to a maintenance mode by thinning out reinforcer delivery, we must ask ourselves "How consistently, often and/or over what period of time the criterion level should be sustained before we will conclude that the behavior is sufficiently established in the person's repertoire?" In other words this measure of rate can provide a guide as to when to begin maintenance. 4

**Rational task analysis.** See Task analysis. 14

**Ratio schedules of reinforcement.** A schedule in which reinforcement is delivered contingent on the last of a *number* of responses: (a) *Fixed ratio (FR) schedule—A* reinforcement schedule in which a constant number of responses must occur prior to the reinforced response. (b) *Variable ratio (VR) schedule—* A schedule in which a variable number of responses must occur prior to the reinforced response. The number of responses usually varies around a specified average. (c) *Progressive ratio (PR) or adjusting schedule–* a schedule in which the response requirement gradually increases within a session as a function of performance and time until responding no longer occurs for some time period (the "break point"). A schedule that increases or decreases gradually according to the client's performance. 22

**Ratio strain.** A disruption in performance when ratio requirements are very high or are raised abruptly. An individual is said to be suffering from "ratio strain" when previously high rates of responding disintegrate. 22

**Reactivity.** An artificial effect produced by the process of conducting the assessment or as a result of experimental activities other than the selected independent (treatment) variable. It is the influence of the assessment procedures themselves (not any treatment or intervention) on the client's behavior pattern, compromising, thereby, the validity of the data. 7.

**Recalibrate.** Retraining observers to achieve interobserver agreement scores at acceptable levels of accuracy. 7

**Recording products of behavior.** See Permanent product recording. 7

**Recovery.** The reemergence of the baseline rate of a recently punished or extinguished response.

**Redirection.** Interrupting a person's inappropriate behavior and reinforcing a more acceptable alternative behavior. 27

**Reductive procedure.** A procedure, such as *DRA, DRL, punishment, response cost,* and *timeout,* used to reduce the rate of a behavior. 26–30

**Reflexive motivating operation**: See Motivating operation, reflexive. 15

**Reinforced positive practice.** A positive practice procedure in which the positive practice activity is reinforced. See *also* Overcorrection. 30

**Reinforcement.** A process in which a behavior is strengthened (i.e., the behavior's frequency, rate, duration, intensity, or other dimensions increase or persist) as a function of an event that occurs as a consequence of, or contingent on, the response; a natural process or managed procedure that increases the rate or supports the maintenance of a given response. Both *positive reinforcement* and *negative reinforcement* increase or maintain behavior. Also see Reinforcement procedure. 2, 5

**Reinforcement density.** Frequency or rate at which responses are reinforced or the quantity of reinforcers delivered per presentation. The lower the ratio or shorter the interval required by a given reinforcement schedule, the *denser* the reinforcement. 22, 23

**Reinforcement procedure.** The carefully planned presentation of positive reinforcers, or removal of negative reinforcers or aversive stimuli, as a function of a given response for the explicit purpose of increasing the future rate of that response under similar circumstances. Systematically planned, goal-directed applications of principles of effective reinforcement. 5

**Reinforcement reserve.** The unconsumed quantity of reinforcers in the possession of an individual or group. Often used to refer to a number of tokens or other exchangeable reinforcers. 12

**Reinforcement schedule.** *See* Schedule of reinforcement. 11, 22, 23

**Reinforcer.** A specific behavioral consequence, the addition of which functions, to increase or maintain the rate of a behavior. A reinforcer is defined solely by its function – that is, by demonstrating an increase or by maintaining the strength (rate, duration, and so on) of the behavior on which it is contingent. *See also* Positive; Negative; Conditioned; Edible; Tangible; Unconditioned; and other classes of reinforcers. 5

**Reinforcer menu.** An array of possible reinforcers from which respondents may select as a consequence of given (or set of) behavior(s). 6

**Reinforcer, natural.** *See* Natural reinforcer. 6, 7, 11

**Reinforcer preference assessments** (RPAs) Repeatedly presenting to an individual several items at a time, in counterbalanced order to determine which items s/he repeatedly (1) approaches, (2) selects, and/or (3) with which s/he spends the most time. There are several variations of preference assessments, including duration based, single-stimulus, paired-stimulus, and multiple stimulus assessments (with and without replacement). Results inform reinforcer-selection for a particular intervention program. 6

**Reinforcer sampling.** Enabling an individual to come in contact with a potential reinforcer to experience the positive characteristics of the stimulus. Used to develop new reinforcing consequences for particular individuals. 6

**Reinforcer survey.** A set of questions designed to help identify an array of reinforcers effective for a particular individual. 6

**Reliable measurement.** Measurement that remains consistent regardless of who conducts it and what conditions prevail. *See also* Reliability. 7

**Reliability of Measurement.** Consistency of measurement across time, observers and conditions. Also see Interobserver agreement assessment. 7

**Repeated measures experimental designs.** See Single subject experimental designs. 9, 25

**Repertoire, behavioral.** *See* Behavioral repertoire. 5

**Replacement behavior.** Behavior chosen to yield reinforcers equivalent to or greater than those previously yielded by the problem behaviors. 10

**Replicate.** To repeat or duplicate an experimental procedure, usually to demonstrate its reliability by reproducing the results. *See also* Systematic replication. 25

**Required relaxation.** *See also* Seclusion timeout. 29

**Respondent behavior.** A response that is lawfully elicited by antecedent stimuli. Also, *reflexive behavior*. *Unconditioned respondent behavior* is an autonomic response that requires no previous learning, like a startle response or knee jerk. Other respondent behavior may be *conditioned*, as in Pavlov's famous experiments with the conditioning of dogs' salivation. *See also Elicit,* and *Conditioned* and *Unconditioned respondent behavior.* 2

**Respondent conditioning** (also referred to as **classical conditioning**) is said to take place when a neutral stimulus (NS), (one that does not automatically elicit an unconditioned response – an UR), is paired with an unconditioned stimulus (US), producing, thereby, an UR. As those pairings continue, the formerly neutral stimulus gradually gains the eliciting properties of the US, eventually evolving into a conditioned stimulus (CS) capable of eliciting a response almost identical to the UR, the conditioned response (CR). 2

**Response.** A directly measurable behavior. Used interchangeably in this book with *behavior* and *performance*. 1, 2

**Response cards.** Cards that students write their answers on to questions. 27

**Response class.** The composite set of behaviors controlled by a particular reinforcing or punishing event, (e.g., yelling, crying, or throwing things, are each specific behaviors; yet if they equally gain a child access to a desired toy, yelling, crying and throwing are said to be members of the same response class. 2

**Response cost.** A reductive procedure in which a specified quantity of available reinforcers are contingently withdrawn following the response, resulting in a decrease in the rate of the response. Usually these reinforcers are withdrawn from the client's reserve, as with loss of points, yardage, or fines. In *bonus response cost,* reinforcers are subtracted from a reserved pool of potential bonus reinforcers. 29

**Response delay.** A procedure designed to prevent the client from responding too quickly ("impulsively") by requiring a preset time delay between the $S^+$ or $S^D$ and the response. 20

**Response deprivation hypothesis (RDH).** A hypothesis stating that when access to an activity is restricted to below baseline levels, the person will engage in the targeted activity at a level exceeding baseline rates. Restricting access to below baseline levels, then, serves as a motivating operation. 6

**Response effort.** The amount of force, exertion, or time required to engage in a response. Other factors being equal, problematic reactions may be prevented or minimized by temporarily reducing the level of the demand or effort in the task. By contrast, increasing the requisite response effort may serve a punishing function. 27

**Response fluency.** A state achieved when a participant's targeted behavior occurs smoothly, rapidly, and with little apparent effort; a condition that facilitates generalization and maintenance and helps prevent relapse. 17, 21

**Response generalization.** See Generalization, response. 21

**Response induction.** See Generalization, response. 21

**Response prompts.** Prompts that directly act on the response and include behavior from a therapist (e.g, verbal instructions, modeling, and physical guidance). 17

**Restitutional training.** See Overcorrection. 30

**Restrained timeout.** See Seclusion timeout. 29

**Resurgence.** *An increase in a previously suppressed behavior resulting from a worsening in reinforcement conditions in general.* Resurgence contributes to variability of responding during extinction. 26, 28

**Return to baseline experimental design.** This design incorporates the withdrawal and its several variations, including the reversal design. 9

**Reversal phase.** A return to baseline phase in which reinforcers are delivered contingent on the occurrence of the undesired, instead of the desired behavior. The $A_2$ experimental phase. Also see withdrawal phase. **9**

**Reversal design.** An experimental design in which the effects of the *independent variable* are tested by introducing a phase (e.g., a DRA or DRO treatment phase) during which the direction of the change reverses (i.e., reinforcement of being out-of-seat instead of in-seat). A reversal design, then, requires an intervention crafted for the purpose of turning behavior around in the opposite direction, as in intervening to *promote* the unwanted behavior. **9**

**Reward.** A reward is an arbitrarily selected item or event assumed to motivate an individual to repeat a given behavior. A reward is not a reinforcer unless it has demonstrated its effectiveness as a contingent stimulus that increases or sustains a person's behavior under given (setting, establishing) conditions. 5

**Role-playing.** Performance of a sequence of responses to simulate the action of another individual or the same individual under other circumstances. A method of *behavioral rehearsal.* 18

**Rule-governed behavior.** See Verbally controlled behavior. 18

**S.** See Stimulus. 15

**S⁺.** A neutral stimulus designated to become discriminative for reinforcement (i.e., to become an $S^{Dr}$.) 15

**S⁻.** A neutral stimulus designated to become discriminative for punishment: (i.e., to become an $S^{Dp}$.) 15

**S⁰.** A neutral stimulus designated to become discriminative for non-reinforcement: (i.e., to become an S-delta or $S^\Delta$.)

**$S^D$.** See *Discriminative stimuli.* 2, 15

**$S^\Delta$ (S-delta).** See *Discriminative stimuli.* 2, 15

**$S^{Dr}$.** See *Discriminative stimuli.* 2, 15

**$S^{Dp}$.** See *Discriminative stimuli.* 2, 15

**$S^E$.** See *Establishing stimulus.* 15

**$S^M$.** See *Motivating stimulus.* 15

**Satiation.** The reduction in performance or reinforcer effectiveness that occurs after the participant has received a large amount of a particular reinforcer usually within a short time period following the behavior. 11

**Scatter plot.** A grapic depiction of recorded instances of the behavior of concern. Those instances are plotted according to when (and by implication where) they are emitted. *Time of day* is plotted on the ordinate (y-axis); *days* on the abscissa (x-axis). Used to reveal elusive environmental stimuli that may be influencing the behavior. 16

**Schedule of reinforcement.** The rule followed by the environment that determines which among the many occurrences of a response will be reinforced. See *also* Interval schedules, Fixed and Variable time, Ratio schedules of reinforcement, Limited hold, Differential reinforcement of high rates (DRH), and Adjusting schedules. 11, 22, 23

**Scientific method.** A method of research in which a problem is identified, relevant data are gathered, a hypothesis or question is formulated from the gathered data, and the hypothesis or experimental question is empirically tested. 1

**Seclusion timeout.** The most restrictive form of timeout: For a set time-period, removing the individual from the environment and, for a brief period of time, placing him or her alone in a room or other environment designated for this purpose; also, if necessary, preventing him or her from leaving (i.e., locking or blocking the door) until the end of the timeout period. This restrictive form of timeout is used mainly to contain violent behavior and/or to protect either individuals themselves or others. And, like facial screening, some states in the U.S. restrict its use. Variations of seclusion timeout include: a) *required relaxation*, which requires that the individual lie down, usually on a bed; b) *restrained timeout*, often referred to as either 1) *movement suppression* or 2) *therapeutic holding/ restraining.* Physically restraining or therapeutic holding is the more severe of the two variations, but these often are combined to reduce seriously dangerous behaviors, such as ingesting non-edible objects like rocks, poking one's eyes, or hitting one's head against the wall. 29

**Secondary aversive stimulus ($S^p$).** A stimulus that initially has no aversive properties but acquires them as a result of its having repeatedly been accompanied by or of occurring just prior to (1) the withdrawal or absence of reinforcers, or (2) the delivery of primary or other learned aversive stimuli. Also called conditioned aversive stimulus. 6, 30

**Secondary prevention.** Using strategies like small-group social skills training and tutoring, with clients who are at-risk for failure and/or behavioral problems. 3

**Secondary reinforcer ($S^r$).** A stimulus that initially lacked reinforcing properties, but has acquired those by being paired with primary or strong secondary reinforcers. Also called *conditioned or learned reinforcer*. 6

**Selectionism.** Behaviors evolve and persist through natural selection (based on the contingencies — antecedents, or precursors, and consequences related to the behavior's occurrence — in the environment interacting with biology). 1

**Self-control.** Choosing more valuable but delayed, over a smaller more immediate reinforcers. (e.g., completing a work assignment instead of watching TV, visiting friends on the weekend rather than during the work-week, to complete assignments and thereby avoid the pressure of a last-minute rush.) Sometimes referred to as *self-management*. 11

**Self-injurious behavior inhibiting system (SIBIS)**. An apparatus designed to reduce severe self-injury by delivering electric shock as punishment. It is activated by severe self-blows to the head, delivering response-contingent electric shock to the client's arm or leg, while automatically recording the stimulus delivery. 30

**Self-instruction.** Guiding one's own learning, usually by reciting a sequence of verbal prompts or using other prompting, fading, and reinforcement strategies. 11

**Self-management.** A procedure in which individuals change some aspect of their own behavior. One or more of five major components are generally involved: (1) Self-selection of goals; (2) monitoring one's own behavior; (3) self-selection of procedures; (4) implementation of procedures, including reinforcing one's own behavior; and, (5) self-evaluating, including monitoring and determining the effectiveness of the procedures. 11

**Self-modeling, video.** A form of video modeling in which trainees are shown videotaped segments of the best samples of their own behavior, while external prompts and flawed examples are edited out. Self-modeling is designed to prompt imitation of one's own exemplary performance. 18

**Self-monitoring.** Observing and recording one's own behavior. 11

**Sensitive measure of behavior.** A measure that reflects subtle changes in the the response of interest. E.g., using using a watch that displays tenths of a second, not just minutes to measure how fast someone runs the 50 yard dash. 7

**Sequence analysis.** A description of an individual's behaviors and the events observed to precede and follow those behaviors. Used to provide clues about the possible functional properties of various antecedent and consequential stimuli. 10

**Sequence effects**. (Also called carryover or alternation effects.) A situation in which one experimental treatment phase *within the experiment* influences subsequent performance during another treatment phase. 25

**Sequencing method.** A method for identifying antecedent stimuli controlling a response -- by trying first one, then combining two, three, (and so on) potential $S^D$s to determine which one or combination evokes or abates the behavior. 16

**Sequential withdrawal design.** An experimental design in which first one element of the treatment is withdrawn, then a second, and so on, until all elements have been withdrawn; particularly well suited to assessing behavior for maintenance.

**Setting events.** See "motivating operations." 2, 15

**Shaping.** Teaching new behaviors by differentially reinforcing *successive approximations* toward the behavioral objective. Sometimes PSI or individualized instruction is referred to as *shaping*. 13

**"Show" procedure.** See Modeling procedure. 18

**SIBIS.** *See* Self-injurious behavior inhibiting system. 30

**Significant others.** Individuals with substantial knowledge of, contact with, and/or control over many of the client's contingencies, such as family members, teachers, and close friends. 6

**Simple correction** A single corrective action as opposed to *Overcorrection*. 30

**Simple discrimination contingency.** This contingency consists of an antecedent stimulus, **A** (or $S^D$), a behavior, **B** (or response, **R**), and the consequence **C** (or reinforcer, $S^r$). 16

**Simple stimulus control.** See Stimulus control, simple. 16

**Simultaneous matching to sample**. See Matching to sample, simultaneous. 16

**Simultaneous treatment design.** Two or more baseline and/or treatment options are simultaneously in place and the participant's performance under each condition is assessed separately. *See* Alternating treatment design. 25

**Single-subject experimental designs.** Used to evaluate unambiguously the effects of the independent variable on the behavior. Demonstrates the relation between the experimental manipulation of a specific independent variable, or treatment, on the change in behavior (the dependent variable). Behavioral research designs based on repeated measurement of a behavior under the same and under different conditions of the independent variable (phases). During each phase, sufficient data are collected to depict a convincingly valid representation of the behavior under that condition. Sometimes referred to as intensive designs, single case designs, *repeated measures, time-series experimental designs* or within-subject designs. *See also* Experimental design; Alternating treatment design; Multiple baseline design; Reversal design; Withdrawal design. 9, 25

**Single-case designs.** See Single-subject experimental designs. 9, 25

**Skill card.** A *task analysis* of a social skill often printed on a 3x5 card. Skill cards can serve as $S^D$s to prompt the client's actions. 14

**Skills analysis.** See Task analysis. 14

**Social facilitation.** Said to occur when rates of responding are influenced by the performance patterns of others. 23

**Socially mediated reinforcers.** Reinforcers delivered by another person. 6

**Social reinforcer.** An interpersonal act that serves a reinforcing function. Reinforcers mediated by other people, such as recognition, compliments ("What a good boy!"), or peer approval. 6

**Social stories.** A specific individualized stimulus control strategy designed to suit a child's specific situation, ability, and environment; designed to prompt children to follow a particular social protocol that addresses the *who, what, when, where,* and *why* of a given social situation, along with the likely reactions of others. 27

**Social validity.** A feature of measured results that includes (1) the social significance or importance of the goals, (2) the social appropriateness of the procedures, and (3) the social importance of the effects. 25

**Specific praise.** Involves specifying the particular target behavior, providing the reason or rationale for its delivery, providing eye contact, and speaking in a sincere, enthusiastic tone of voice. Designed to reinforce a given behavior *and* assist the learner to discriminate the conditions under which the response is to be emitted. Often called *labeled* or *qualitative praise.* 11

**Spontaneous recovery.** The reappearance of a presumably "extinguished" response *at the beginning of a new session or under new conditions,* despite no resumption of reinforcement. 26

$S^r$. See Conditioned reinforcer; Positive reinforcer; Reinforcement. 5, 6, 15

$S^R$. See Unconditioned reinforcer ($S^R$). 5, 6, 15

**Standard celeration chart.** A variation of a semi-logarithmic chart, which shows proportional or relative changes in behavior. Because the units on the y-axis in standard celeration charting are not equally distanced from each other, but rather represent a proportional increase, it is not considered an equal interval graph. Precision Teaching relies on using standard celeration charts. 8, 17

**Strategic planning.** "Strategic planning determines where an organization is going over the next year or more, how it's going to get there and how it'll know if it got there or not" (McNamara, 2008). 4

**Step size.** The number of new responses in a subset, or the extensiveness of the change in topography that constitutes a *successive approximation* in a specific shaping procedure 14

**Stereotypy.** The persistent and inappropriate repetition of phrases, gestures, or acts. 5

**Stimulus (S).** A specific or combination of physical objects or events, (stimuli), which affect the behavior of an individual. Stimuli may be internal (e.g., pressure, pain, covert statements) or external to the person. Stimuli frequently arranged in behavior analysis programs include reinforcing, aversive, and discriminative stimuli. 2, 15

**Stimulus change.** The presentation or removal of motivational operations or discriminative stimuli that evoke or abate [inhibit] behavior. 16, 27

**Stimulus class:** A group of antecedent stimuli that have a common effect on an operant class. Group members tend to evoke or abate the same behavior or response class, yet may vary across physical dimensions. 2, 16

**Stimulus control.** The process (when it takes place naturally) or procedure (when intentionally programmed) that enables an antecedent stimulus to gain control over one or more particular behaviors as a function of the individual's experience of response-consequence correlation in the presence of that antecedent. The relation between a discriminative stimulus and a response that is correlated with a consequence. A term used to describe responding governed by stimuli that precede a given behavior. Depending on circumstances, these antecedent stimuli may be labeled *discriminative stimuli ($S^Ds$).* See also Discriminative stimuli. 2, 15

**Stimulus control, simple.** A reliable relation between an antecedent stimulus and a response, in the sense that a given discriminative stimulus ($S^D$) dependably evokes or abates a particular behavior. Also see Discrimination, simple and Simple discrimination contingency. 16

**Stimulus control, strong.** Sometimes called tight, complete, or powerful stimulus control, particularly when a given response occurs at a much higher or a much lower frequency depending on the presence or absence of the identified discriminative stimluli. 16

**Stimulus control, weak.** Sometimes called incomplete stimulus control. Inferred when a particular behavior occurs irregularly or diminishes in the presence of a given discriminative stimulus; that the antecedent stimulus does not consistently regulate the behavior; that the behavior does not reliably occur or fail to occur, respectively, in response to the presence or absence of the stimulus). 16

**Stimulus delay procedure.** *See* Delayed prompting and Time delay procedure. 20

**Stimulus discrimination**. See Discrimination, stimulus 2, 21

**Stimulus equalization.** An error reduction procedure in which the complexity of a set of stimulus dimensions is abruptly, but temporarily reduced by eliminating irrelevant dimensions. 20

**Stimulus equivalence.** See Functional equivalence. 16

**Stimulus fading.** *See* fading. 20

**Stimulus generalization.** *See* Generalization, stimulus. 2, 21

**Stimulus property.** An attribute or parameter of the stimulus such as topography, texture, volume, size, color, position, and intensity. *See also* Parameter.

**Stimulus prompts.** Prompts that directly act on the stimuli that cue the response and are either within stimulus prompts (e.g., changing the color or size of the cue) or are extra stimulus prompts (e.g., adding a picture to the original cue). 17

**Stimulus overselectivity.** A form of prompt overdependence in which responding is controlled by one or more non-relevant stimuli are among the full array of stimuli. For example, child with autism will respond to request to touch his nose only when table and chair are present from therapy room. 17

**Strategic planning.** A organizational method that includes determining goals, how their attainment will be evaluated and what are to be scheduled to accomplish the goals. 4

**Strong stimulus control.** See Stimulus control, strong. 17

**Student success team (SST).** A group organized within a school for the purpose of identifying, addressing and preventing problems exhibited by the 10 - 20% specific individual students who have not responded satisfactorily to the programs implemented by the

**positive behavior support team (PBST)** and/or who remain *at-risk* for severe academic or behavioral problems. 3

**Sub-goals.** Short-term goals, usually expressed in numerical quantities designating particular accomplishments to be attained toward the purpose of achieving the end goal. 17

**Subjective measures.** Non-publically verifiable measures; measures that cannot be repeated by others. 7

**Subset of behavior.** The group of simpler response components that may combine to form a more complex behavior. 14

**Successive approximations.** The gradual changes in the form or shape or other features of a behavior as it increasingly approaches its intended topography. 13

**Supplementary reinforcers.** Reinforcers used to augment the natural reinforcers to help bridge the time gap before the natural reinforcer is delivered. They are designed to signal that a stronger reinforcer is apt to be forthcoming. 11

**Surrogate motivating operation.** See Motivating operation, surrogate. 15

**Systematic replication.** A method designed to repeat or duplicate experimental findings by applying the core features of an experimental investigation, despite variations in a number of conditions, such as task, setting or other parameters of the basic procedures. 25

**Tacts.** Verbal operants under the functional control of nonverbal discriminative stimuli, whose emission is reinforced by generalized conditioned reinforcement. Tacting includes saying a word in the *presence* of an object, an event, or a feature of an abstract stimulus class. (Notice that we cannot tact things that are not present. Naming things not present is simply called naming.) 19

**Tangible reinforcers.** Tangible items (magazines, jewelry, toys, cars, and so on) the contingent delivery of which increases or maintains a behavior. 6

**Target behavior.** The behavior to be changed. In this book, we often use the term interchangeably with *pinpoint, dependent variable,* or *wanted* or *unwanted behavior.* 4

**Task analysis.** Breaking down a complex skill, job or behavioral chain into its component behaviors, sub-skills, or subtasks. Components are is stated in its order of occurrence and are designed to set the occasion for the occurrence of the next behavior. Task analyses are particularly useful in planning specific stimulus control and chaining procedures. 14

**Task analysis, empirical,** Task analysis based on systematically observing performers in action. Also see Chain. 14

**Task analysis, rational.** Components of a task analysis derived from studying the subject matter and specifying the process or procedure that is presumed to be involved in performing the task. 14

**Teaching.** Promoting learning, by any or a combination of various means: showing, telling, guiding, and differentially reinforcing accuracy and rate and/or otherwise arranging matters so that reinforcement follows a reasonable proportion of those efforts directed towards meeting behavioral objectives. 2

**Telehealth.** A service delivery model that delivers services via information and communication technologies. 10

**Tell procedure.** An instructional or stimulus-control procedure that uses oral, written, signed, or other instructions or rules to prompt the emission of a correct response under appropriate conditions, thereby enabling it to become eligible for reinforcement. 18

**Terminal behavior.** The behavior ultimately to be achieved as the outcome of a behavior analysis program; described according to all its relevant behavioral dimensions or parameters. Usually it is assigned a criterion or standard level of performance by which its acceptability is to be judged. Often used interchangeably with *behavioral* or *instructional objective, goal behavior,* and *target behavior;* occasionally denoted by the noun *pinpoint.* 4

**Tertiary prevention.** Individualized strategies (e.g., functional behavior assessments and individualized behavior plans, including positive behavior interventions) designed to assist clients who regularly exhibit severe social and/or academic problem behaviors. 3

**Therapeutic holding/restraining.** See Seclusion timeout. 29

**Three-term contingency.** A phrase used to describe the interdependency among antecedents, behavior and consequences: A-B-C's. Example: When a given behavior (B) occurs under specific stimulus conditions (the antecedents—A), it is to be reinforced (the consequences—C). 2, 15

**Tiered** or **level token economies.** Economies in which participants are able (or required) to move up (or down) a hierarchy of levels, contingent upon their improved (or worsening) behavior by meeting set criteria. The higher the level attained, the greater their access to various back-up reinforcers. 12

**Time delay prompting.** See Delayed prompting. 20

**Timeout.** A procedure in which access to varied sources of reinforcement is removed or reduced for a particular time period contingent on an unwanted response, for the purpose or reducing the rate of the response. Access to reinforcement is contingently removed for a specified time either by contingently removing the behaving individual from the reinforcing environment, or the reinforcing environment is contingently removed for some stipulated duration. There are several levels of timeout. *See Inclusion timeout, Exclusionary timeout, and Seclusion timeout.* 29

**Timeout ribbon.** See Inclusion timeout. 29

**Timeout room.** A physical space arranged to minimize the reinforcement that an individual is apt to receive during a given time period, sometimes referred to as *timeout booth* or *quiet place*. Procedures for using such facilities must conform to ethical and legal standards. 29

**Time-sampling.** A direct observational procedure in which the presence or absence of specific behaviors is recorded within short uniform time intervals. (E.g., an observer observes for 10 seconds and records the occurrence or nonoccurrence of a behavior during the following 5 seconds.) This procedure may continue for a specific time period each day. Time-sampling variations include: (1) Whole-interval time-sampling, (2) partial-interval time-sampling, and (3) momentary time-sampling. 7

**Time schedules of reinforcement.** Reinforcement is contingent on the passage of time, regardless of ongoing behavior (a) *Fixed time schedule (FT)* – a schedule of reinforcement in which reinforcers are delivered following the passage of a specific amount of time and not dependent on a particular response. (b) *Variable time schedule (VT)* – A schedule in which reinforcement is delivered contingent on the passage of a variable time interval, not upon the occurrence of a particular response. 27, 23

**Time series experimental designs.** See Single subject experimental designs. 9, 25

**Token.** A conditioned reinforcer in the form of a ticket, voucher, checkmark, or other symbolic item, which is exchangeable at a later time for a coveted reinforcing item or event (the *back-up reinforcer*). The extent to which tokens serve as reinforcers depends on the individual's experience with them and the available back-up items. 6, 12

**Token economy.** A contingency package. Tokens (exchangeable reinforcers) are given as soon as possible following the emission of a target response. The recipient later exchanges the tokens for a reinforcing object or event. Also called token system. 12

**Token system.** See Token economy. 12

**Topography of response.** The configuration, form, appearance, or shape of a response. The correct topography of a behavior can be determined by photographing an expert performing the behavior. 4, 7

**Total task method of chaining.** *See* Concurrent task method of teaching. 14

**Transfer of stimulus control.** A process by which a new antecedent stimulus begins to evoke a response in place of a previous antecedent stimulus. In applied behavior analysis this is often deliberately arranged by using *fading* or *delayed prompting*. 20

**Transitive motivating operation.** See Motivating operation, transitive. 15

**Transitory behavior.** A behavior that does not leave an enduring product or outcome (e.g., smiling, paying attention, or teasing). Such a behavior needs to be observed and recorded as it occurs or preserved by means of audio/video recording. See the various recording methods: Event, Duration, Latency, IRT, and various Interval time sampling methods. 7

**Treasure box.** A motivational tool used in schools and homes. Toys, games, and arts and crafts materials are contained in colorful boxes and used as reinforcers for young people. Items within a box will vary from time to time or, if used in a school, boxes can be exchanged periodically among classrooms to increase novelty. 11

**Treatment.** The behavioral procedures, intervention program, or independent variable(s) being applied. May be referred to as a *treatment-* or *contingency-package* when specific behavioral procedures are combined into a cohesive treatment. 9

**Treatment drift.** A term used to describe the application of the intervention veering off course from its originally intended path, thereby violating the fidelity of the implementation or treatment. 7

**Treatment fidelity.** See Fidelity of implementation. 3, 7

**Treatment integrity.** See Fidelity of implementation. 3, 7

**Treatment phase.** The period of time during which the intervention is in effect. 9

**Treatment utility of assessment.** The degree to which assessment is demonstrated to contribute to desired or beneficial treatment outcomes. 7

**Trend.** The general direction and rate of increase or decrease in which data move over time. 8, 9

**Trendline.** A standard of reference line derived by examining measures of central tendency of a series of data setst over time; used to determine the rate and direction of change (trend); that is, whether the rate of the behavior is accelerating or decelerating. 8, 9

**Trials to criterion.** The number of responses for the participant has emitted in order to meet the criterion or standard set for success. 7

**Unchaining.** Sometimes called "disrupting" or "unlinking" a chain; a method designed to lessen behavior by unlinking one element of the chain from the next so that one link no longer serves as a discriminative stimulus for the next link, nor as the reinforcer for the prior link. This sometimes may be accomplished by reinforcing the last response in a chain, despite its occurring in the absence of the other responses in the chain. 14

**Unconditioned aversive stimulus ($S^p$).** See primary aversive stimulus. 15, 30

**Unconditioned motivating operation.** See Motivating operation, unconditioned. 15

**Unconditioned reinforcer ($S^R$).** See primary reinforcer. 2, 6

**Unconditioned respondent behavior.** Behaviors reliably elicited by stimuli that precede those behaviors (i.e., unconditioned antecedent stimuli), despite any prior learning. Unconditioned respondent behaviors are also known as reflexes and generally are thought of as behaviors with which the individual was endowed at birth. 2

**Unconditioned stimuli (USs).** Particular preceding stimuli that directly produce ("elicit") respondent behaviors. A familiar US is, a bright light shined into the eyes causing the pupils to contract (UR). 2

**Vaganotic measurement system.** The measurement scale or units are not equal. 10

**Valid measures.** The extent to which measures actually measure what they are purported to measure. 7

**Variability.** The degree to which the rate of the behavior varies (sometimes from the measure of central tendency) from one assessment to another. 8

**Variable(s).** Any behavior or condition in the individual's internal or external environment that may assume any one of a set of values (e.g., number, size, shape, intensity). *See also* Control variable, Dependent variable; Experimental variable, Independent variable. 9, 25

**Variable interval (VI) schedule.** *See* Interval schedules of reinforcement. 23

**Variable ratio (VR) schedule of reinforcement.** *See* Ratio schedules of reinforcement. 22

**Variable time schedule.** See Time schedules. 23, 27

**Verbal behavior.** Behavior reinforced through the mediation of other persons. Included are spoken or non-spoken forms of communication that help people get what they want and avoid what they don't want, faster and more efficiently. Included under the rubric of verbal behavior are speaking, gestures, writing, typing, touching, and so on. There is no specific one form, mode or medium. Verbal behavior, then, refers to a particular class of behavior that serves as a vehicle or mediator for allowing organisms to obtain reinforcers. 19

**Verbally-controlled behavior.** Behavior under the control of as rules and instructions, rather than behavior shaped by reinforcing or aversive consequences. Because it covers a broader array of verbal stimuli, the term "rule-governed behavior" generally has been replaced by the term "verbally-controlled behavior." 18

**Verbal relating.** Responding to one event in terms of another that is controlled by contextual cues beyond the nonarbitrary stimulus properties. For example, a traveler can be taught that a Canadian quarter is less than an American quarter and can automatically derive that an American quarter is worth more than a Canadian quarter. With respect to early language learners, the goal is to teach them how to discriminate between the relevant and irrelevant features of a task (i.e., get them to respond relationally to the contextual cues rather than the physical stimulus properties or nonarbitrary stimulus properties — the size of the coins). 19

**Verbal stimuli.** Words, gestures, and other symbolic stimuli that serve to mediate reinforcement. 19

**Vertical phase change lines.** See Phase change lines. 8

**Video modeling.** See modeling, video. Also see Self-modeling. 18

**Video self-modeling.** See self-modeling, video. 18

**Voluntary.** The client's voicing agreement with the terms of the behavior-change program under non-coercive circumstances. Behavior is assumed to be voluntary when the individual chooses and/or initiates action toward a goal, in the absence of threats or highly intrusive, unusually powerful, incentives. 4

**Weak stimulus control.** See Stimulus control, weak. 16

**Whole-interval DRO.** A reinforcer is delivered following a period of time during which the individual has not engaged in a given behavior. 28

**Whole-interval time-sampling.** A time-sampling procedure, often referred to simply as interval recording, that requires the response to be emitted throughout the entire interval for its presence to be scored. *See also* Time-sampling. 7

**Whole task.** *See* Concurrent task method of teaching. 14

**Withdrawal design.** An experimental (design that involves the removal of the intervention in order to test its effect. For example, one frequently used withdrawal design involves: (1) Obtaining a base rate measure of the target behavior; (2) repeatedly applying the intervention or procedure; (3) withdrawing the intervention for a time, under the same conditions as those that were in effect during the baseline period; and (4) reapplying the intervention. This design is used to determine whether the effect of the intervention can be reproduced. (Often abbreviated as ABAB design.) Also see Reversal design. 9

**Withdrawal of treatment phase.** The phase in the return-to-baseline design in which the intervention is temporarily removed to demonstrate experimental control. The $A_2$ phase. 9

**Within-stimulus prompts.** Increases errorless learning by altering "the physical characteristics of the stimuli to be discriminated to increase the likelihood that correct responses will occur early in training" (Green, 2001, p. 78). 20

**Within-subjects experimental designs.** See Single subject experimental designs. 9

**X-axis.** The horizontal line on the graph. The x axis displays the label for the observational sessions. These may be composed of specific observational sessions (usually described in more detail in the accompanying narrative) or standard units of time, such as hours, days, weeks or months. 8

**Y-axis.** The vertical line on a graph.. The *y axis,* usually is used to depict a measure of the dependent variable (the behavior), often is assigned a label such as *"Frequency," "Number," "Percentage"* etc.), and contains the *axis scales or numerals*. 8

**Zone system.** An observational system similar to partial-interval time-sampling in which not time but space—such as the school yard—is divided into specific pre-designated areas. Each area, or zone, is relatively small and provides equivalent opportunities for the target behavior to occur in it. The observer watches and counts the presence or absence of the behavior, or the frequency or results of a given behavior within a particular area. Sometimes the design is planned to function on an interval spoilage basis—that one or more scored instances of the targeted behavior recorded within that zone during the observational interval (e.g., 10 seconds, a day) indicate the occurrence of the behavior or result. Alternatively, the observer may score behavior within 1 zone over several time intervals, before moving on to the next. 7

# References

AACAP (2002). See American Academy of Child and Adolescent Psychiatry (2002).

Abramowitz, A. J., O'Leary, S. B., & Futtersak, M. W. (1988). The relative impact of long and short reprimands on children's off-task behavior in the classroom. *Behavior Therapy, 19,* 243–247.

Acker, M. M., & O'Leary, S. G. (1988). Effects of consistent and inconsistent feedback on inappropriate child behavior. *Behavior Therapy, 19,* 619–624.

Adami, S., Falcomata, T.S., Muething, C. S., & Hoffman, K. (2017). An evaluation of lag schedules of reinforcement during functional communication training: Effects on varied and responding and challenging behavior. *Behavior Analysis in Practice, 10,* 209–213. doi 10.1007/s40617-017-0179-7.

Adamo, E. K., Wu, J., Wolery, M., Hernmeter, J. L., Ledford, J. R., & Barton, E. E. (2015). Using video modeling, prompting and behavior-specific praise to increase moderate-to-vigorous physical activity for young children with down syndrome. *Journal of Early Intervention, 37,* 270–285.

Adams, G. L., & Engelmann, S. (1996). *Research on Direct Instruction: 25 years beyond DISTAR.* Seattle, WA: Educational Achievement Systems.

Adams, G. L., Tallon, R. J., & Rimell, P. (1980). A comparison of lecturer versus role-playing in the use of positive reinforcement. *Journal of Organizational Behavior Management, 2,* 205–212.

Agran, M., Sinclair, T., Alper, S., Cavin, M., Wehmeyer, M., & Hughes, C. (2005). Using self-monitoring to increase following-direction skills of students with moderate to severe disabilities in general education. *Education and Training in Developmental Disabilities, 40*(1), 3–13.

Ahearn, W. H., Clark, K. M., Gardenier, N. C., Chung, B. I., & Dube, W. V. (2003). Persistence of stereotypic behavior: Examining the effects of external reinforcers. *Journal of Applied Behavior Analysis, 36,* 439–448.

Ahearn, W. H., Clark, K. M., MacDonald, R. P. F., & Chung, B. I. (2007). Assessing and treating vocal stereotypy in children with autism. *Journal of Applied Behavior Analysis, 40,* 263–275.

Ainslie, G. (1974). Impulse control in pigeons. *Journal of the Experimental Analysis of Behavior, 21,* 485–489.

Ainsman, L, & Mayer, G. R. (2018). Utilizing a self-monitoring behavior package in an early intervention classroom: An implementation of a group self & match system. Manuscript submitted for publication.

Akers, J. S., Davis, T. N., Gerow, S., & Avery, S. (2020). Decreasing motor stereotypy in individuals with autism spectrum disorder: A systematic review. *Research in Autism Spectrum Disorders, 77,* 101611. doi: 10.1016/j.rasd.2020.101611

Akintomide, H., Doshi, J., Power, J., & Wilkinson, C. (1016). Television: a way of distracting patients during sexual and reproductive healthcare procedures. *Journal of Family Planning and Reproductive Health Care, 42,* 220–221. doi:10.1136/fprhc-22015-101289.

Alabiso, F. (1975). Operant control of attention behavior. A treatment for hyperactivity. *Behavior therapy, 6,* 39–42.

Alavosius, M. P., & Sulzer-Azaroff, B. (1985). An on-the-job method to evaluate patient lifting technique. *Applied Ergonomics, 16,* 307–311.

Alavosius, M. P., & Sulzer-Azaroff, B. (1986). The effects of performance feedback on the safety of client lifting and transfer. *Journal of Applied Behavior Analysis, 19,* 261–267.

Alavosius, M. P., & Sulzer-Azaroff, B. (1990). Acquisition and maintenance of health-care routines as a function of feedback density. *Journal of Applied Behavior Analysis, 23,* 151–162.

Alberto, P., Heflin, L. J., & Andrews, D. (2002). Use of the timeout ribbon procedure during community-based instruction. *Behavior Modification, 26,* 297–311.

Albin, R. W., Lucyshyn, J. M., Horner, R. H., & Flannery, K. B. (1996). Contextual fit for behavioral support plans: A model for "goodness of fit." In L. K. Koegel, R. L. Koegel, & G. Dunlap (Eds), *Positive behavior support plans: Including people with difficult behavior in the community* (pp. 81–98). Baltimore: Brookes.

Alevizos, K. J., & Alevizos, P. N. (1975). The effects of verbalizing contingencies in time-out procedures. *Journal of Behavior Therapy and Experimental Psychiatry, 6,* 253–255.

Alford, B. A., & Lantka, A. L. (2000). Processes of clinical change and resistance: A theoretical synthesis. *Behavior Modification, 24,* 566–579.

AL-hinai, M. A., Shourbagi, S.E., & Emara, E. (2019). The effectiveness of interspersal strategy in the improving accuracy level to solve mathematics problems and task engagement among grade 4 students with learning disabilities at the sultanate of Oman. *Journal of Educational and Psychological studies, 13* (3), 475–495. doi.org/10.24200/jeps

Allday, R. A., Bush, M. N., Ticknor, N., & Walker, L. (2011). Using teacher greetings to increase speed to task engagement. *Journal of Applied Behavior Analysis 44*(2), 393–396.

Allday, R. A., & Pakurar, K. (2007). Effects of teacher greeting on student on-task behavior. *Journal of Applied Behavior Analysis, 40,* 317–320.

Allday, R. G., & Pakurar, K. (2008). Effects of teacher greetings on student on-task behavior. *Teaching Exceptional Children Plus, 4,* 1–14.

Allen, J. S., Tarnowski, K. J., Simonian, S. J., Elliott, D., & Drabman, R. S. (1991). The generalization map revisited: Assessment of generalized treatment effects in child and adolescent behavior therapy. *Behavior Therapy, 22,* 393–405.

Allen, K. D. (1998). The use of an enhanced simplified habit-reversal procedure to reduce disruptive outbursts during athletic performance. *Journal of Applied Behavior Analysis, 31,* 489–492.

Allen, K. D., Barone, V. J., & Kuhn, B. R. (1993). A behavioral prescription for promoting applied behavior analysis within pediatrics. *Journal of Applied Behavior Analysis, 26,* 493–502.

Allen, K. D., & Stokes, T. F. (1987). Use of escape and reward in the management of young children during dental treatment. *Journal of Applied Behavior Analysis, 20,* 381–390.

Allen, K. D., & Wallace, D. P. (2013). Effectiveness of using noncontingent escape for general behavior management in a pediatric dental clinic. *Journal of Applied Behavior Analysis, 46,* 723–737.

Allen, L. C., Gottselig, M., & Boylan, S. (1982). A practical mechanism for using free time as a reinforcer in classrooms. *Education and Treatment of Children, 5,* 347–353.

Allen, M. B., Baker, J. C., Nuernberger, J. E., & Vargo, K. K. (2013). Precursor manic behavior in the assessment and treatment of episodic problem behavior for a woman with a dual diagnosis. *Journal of Applied Behavior Analysis, 46*(3), 685–688. https://doi-org.mimas.calstatela.edu/10.1002/jaba.57

Allison, A. G., & Ayllon, T. (1980). Behavioral coaching in the development of skills in football, gymnastics, and tennis. *Journal of Applied Behavior Analysis, 13,* 297–314.

Allsopp, D. H. (1997). Using classwide peer tutoring to teach beginning algebra problem-solving skills in heterogeneous classrooms. *Remedial & Special Education, 18,* 367–380.

Alnemary, F., Wallace, M., Alnemary, F., Gharapetian, L., & Yassine, J. (2017). Application of a pyramidal training model on the implementation of trial-based functional analysis: A partial replication. *Behavior Analysis in Practice, 3,* 301–306.

Alter, P. J., Conroy, M. A., Mancil, G. R., & Haydon, T. (2008). A comparison of functional behavior assessment methodologies with young children: Descriptive methods and functional nalysis. *Journal of Behavioral Education 17*(2), 200–219.

Alvero, A. M., Bucklin, B. R., & Austin, J. (2001). An objective review of the effectiveness and essential characteristics of performance feedback in organizational settings (1985–1998). *Journal of Organizational Behavior Management, 21*(1), 3–29.

Alvero, A.M., Struss, K. & Rappaport, E. (2007). Measuring safety performance: A comparison of whole, partial, and momentary time-sampling recording methods. *Journal of Organizational Behavior Management, 28*(1), 1–28.

American Academy of Child and Adolescent Psychiatry. (2002). Practice parameter for the prevention and management of aggressive behavior in child and adolescent psychiatric institutions, with special reference to seclusion and restraint. *Journal of the American Academy of Child and Adolescent Psychiatry, 41*(2), 4s-25s.

American Psychological Association. (2004). Ethical principles of psychologists and code of conduct. *American Psychologist, 57,* 1060–1073.

American Psychological Association. (2010). *Publication manual of the American psychological association, 5th Edition.* Washington, DC.

Anderson, C. A., & Anderson, D. C. (1984). Ambient temperature and violent crime: Tests of the linear and curvilinear hypotheses. *Journal of Personality and Social Psychology, 46,* 91–97.

Anderson, C.A., & Bushman, B.J. (2002, March). Psychology: The effects of media violence on society. *Science, 295,* 2377–2379.

Anderson, D. C., Crowell, C. R., Domen, M., & Howard, G. S. (1988). Performance posting, goal setting and activity-contingent praise as applied to a university hockey team. *Journal of Applied Psychology, 73,* 87–95.

Anderson, D. C., Crowell, C. R., Hantula, D. A., & Siroky, L. M. (1988). Task clarification and individual performance posting for improving cleaning in a student-managed university bar. *Journal of Organizational Behavior Management, 9*(2), 73–90.

Anderson, D. C., Crowell, C. R., Sponsel, S. S., Clarke, M., & Brence, J. (1983). Behavior management in the public accommodations industry: A three-project demonstration. *Journal of Organizational Behavior Management, 4* (1/2), 33–66.

Anderson, M. A. (1985). Cooperative group tasks and their relationship to peer acceptance and cooperation. *Journal of Learning Disabilities, 18,* 83–86.

Anderson, R. C. (1967). Educational psychology. *Annual Review of Psychology, 18,* 129–164.

Antonitis, J. J. (1951). Response variability in the white rat during conditioning, extinction, and reconditioning. *Journal of Experimental Psychology, 42,* 273–281.

Apolloni, T., Cooke, S. A., & Cooke, T. P. (1976). Establishing a normal peer as a behavioral model for developmentally delayed toddlers. *Perceptual and Motor Skills, 43,* 1155–1165.

Apuzzo, M., Fink, S., & Risen, J. (Oct., 9, 2016). How the U. S. torture left a legacy of damaged minds. *New York Times.*

Ardoin, S. P., Martens, B. K., & Wolfe, L. A. (1999). Using high-probability instruction sequences with fading to increase student compliance during transitions. *Journal of Applied Behavior Analysis, 32,* 339–351.

Argott, P. J., Townsend, D B., & Poulson, C. L. (2017). Acquisition and generalization of complex empathetic responses among children with autism. *Behavior Analysis in Practice, 10,* 107–117. doi: 10.1007/s40617-016-0171-7.

Arkhipov, V. (2002). Delayed impairment of response extinction after single seizures induced by picrotoxin. *Behavioural Brain Research, 12*(8), 109–111.

Arkoosh, M. K., Derby, K. M., Wacker, D. P. Berg, W., McLaughlin, T. F., & Barretto, A. (2007). A descriptive evaluation of long-term treatment integrity. *Behavior Modification, 31,* 880–895.

Armendariz, F., & Umbreit, J. (1999). Using active responding to reduce disruptive behavior in a general education classroom. *Journal of Positive Behavior Interventions, 1,* 152–158.

Arrington, R. E. (1943). Time-sampling in studies of social behavior: A critical review of techniques and results with research suggestions. *Psychological Bulletin, 40,* 81–124.

Artman-Meeker, K., Rosenberg, N., Badgett, N., Yang, N., & Penney, A. (2017). The effects of bug-in-ear coaching on pre-service behavior analysts' use of functional communication training. *Behavior Analysis in Practice, 10,* 228-241. doi: 10.1007/s40617-016-0166-4.

Athens, E. S., Vollmer, T. R., & Pipkin, C. C. P. (2007). Shaping academic task engagement with percentile schedules. *Journal of Applied Behavior Analysis, 40,* 475–488.

Athens, E. S., Vollmer, T. R., Sloman, K. N., & Pipkin, C. C. P. (2008). An analysis of vocal stereotypy and therapist fading. *Journal of Applied Behavior Analysis, 41,* 291–297.

Athens, E. S., Vollmer, T. R., & Sloman, K. N. (2008). An analysis of vocal stereotypy an therapist fading. *Journal of Applied Behavior Analysis, 41,* 291–297.

Atkinson, R. K., Renkl, A., & Merrill, M. M. (2003). Transitioning from studying examples to solving problems: Effects of self-explanation prompts and fading worked-out steps. *Journal of Educational Psychology, 95,* 744–783.

Attila, A., Priplata, A., Niemi, J.B., Harry, J.D., Lipsitz, L.A, & Collins J. (2003). Vibrating insoles and balance control in elderly people, *Lancet , 362,* 1123–24

Austin, J. L., & Agar, G. (2005). Helping young children follow their teachers' directions: The utility of high-probability command sequences in pre-K and kindergarten classrooms. *Education and Treatment of Children, 28,* 222–236.

Austin, J., Weatherly, N. L., & Gravina, N. E. (2005). Using task clarification, graphic feedback, and verbal feedback to increase closing-task completion in a privately owned restaurant. *Journal of Applied Behavior Analysis, 38,* 117–120.

Austin, J. L., & Soeda, J. M. (2008). Fixed-time teacher attention to decrease off-task behaviors of typically developing third graders. *Journal of Applied Behavior Analysis, 41,* 279–283.

Austin, J. E., & Tiger, J. H. (2015). Providing alternative reinforcers to facilitate tolerance to delayed reinforcement following functional communication training. *Journal of Applied Behavior Analysis, 48,* 663–668. doi: 10.1002/jaba.215.

Austin, J., & Wilson, K. G. (2001). Response-response relationships in organizational behavior management. *Journal of Organizational Behavior Management, 21*(4), 39–53.

Axelrod, S. (1973). Comparison of individual and group contingencies in two special classes. *Behavior Therapy, 4,* 83–90.

Axelrod, S. (1987). Book review: Doing it without arrows: A review of LaVigna and Donnellan's Alternative to punishment: Solving behavior problems with non-aversive strategies. *The Behavior Analyst, 10,* 243–251.

Axelrod, S., & Greer, R. D. (1994). Cooperative learning revisited. *Journal of Behavioral Education, 4,* 41–48.

Ayllon, T., & Azrin, N. H. (1965). The measurement and reinforcement of behavior of psychotics. *Journal of the Experimental Analysis of Behavior, 8,* 357–383.

Ayllon, T., & Azrin, N. (1968). *The token economy: A motivational system for therapy and rehabilitation.* New York: Appleton.

Ayllon, T., & Azrin, N. H. (1964). Reinforcement and instructions with mental patients. *Journal of the Experimental Analysis of Behavior, 7,* 327–331.

Ayllon, T., & Kelly, K. (1972). Effects of reinforcement on standardized test performance. *Journal of Applied Behavior Analysis, 5,* 477–484.

Azrin, N. H. (1956). Effects of two intermittent schedules of immediate and non-immediate punishment. *Journal of Psychology, 42,* 3–21.

Azrin, N. H. (1960). Effects of punishment intensity during variable-interval reinforcement. *Journal of the Experimental Analysis of Behavior, 3,* 128–142.

Azrin, N. H., & Armstrong, P. M. (1973). The "mini-meal": A method for teaching eating skills to the profoundly retarded. *Mental Retardation, 2,* 9–13.

Azrin, N. H., & Besalel, V. A. (1999). *How to use positive practice, self-correction, and overcorrection* (2nd ed.). Austin, TX: Pro-Ed.

Azrin, N. H., Hake, D. G., Holz, W. C., & Hutchinson, R. R. (1965). Motivational aspects of escape from punishment. *Journal of Experimental Analysis of Behavior, 8,* 31–44.

Azrin, N. H., & Holz, W. C. (1961). Punishment during fixed-interval reinforcement. *Journal of the Experimental Analysis of Behavior, 4,* 343–347.

Azrin, N.H., & Holz, W. C. (1966). Punishment. In W. A. Honig (Ed.). *Operant behavior: Areas of research and application* (pp. 380–447). New York: Appleton.

Azrin, N. H., Hutchinson, R. R., & Hake, D. J. (1966). Extinction-induced aggression. *Journal of the Experimental Analysis of Behavior, 9,* 191–204.

Azrin, N. H., Hutchinson, R. R., & Hake, D. J. (1963). Pain-induced fighting in the squirrel monkey. *Journal of the Experimental Analysis of Behavior, 6,* 620.

Azrin, N., Jones, R. J., & Flye, B. (1968). A synchronization effect and its application to stuttering by a portable apparatus. *Journal of Applied Behavior Analysis, 1,* 283–295.

Azrin, N. H., & Nunn, R. G. (1973). Habit reversal: A method for eliminating nervous habits and tics. *Behaviour Research and Therapy, 11,* 619–628.

Azrin, N. H., & Nunn, R. G. (1977). *Habit control in a day.* Simon & Schuster.

Azrin, N. H., Shaeffer, R. M., & Wesolowski, M. D. (1976). A rapid method of teaching profoundly retarded persons to address by a reinforcement-guidance method. *Mental Retardation, 14,* 29–33.

Azrin, N. H., & Wesolowski, M. D. (1975). Eliminating habitual vomiting in a retarded adult by positive practice and self-correction. *Journal of Behavior Therapy and Experimental Psychiatry, 6,* 145–148.

Babcock, R, A., Sulzer-Azaroff, B., Sanderson, M., & Scibak, J. (1992). Increasing nurses' use of feedback to promote infection-control practices in a head injury treatment center. *Journal of Applied Behavior Analysis, 25,* 621–627.

Bacon, D. L., Fulton, B. J., & Malott, R. W. (1982). Improving staff performance through the use of task checklists. *Journal of Organizational Behavior Management, 4* (1), 17–25.

Baer, D. M. (1961). The effect of withdrawal of positive reinforcement on an extinguishing response in young children. *Child Development, 32,* 67–74.

Baer, D. M., Peterson, R. F., & Sherman, J. A. (1967). The development of imitation by reinforcing behavior of similarity to a model. *Journal of the Experimental Analysis of Behavior, 10,* 405–416.

Baer, D. M., & Stokes, T. F. (1977). Discriminating a generalization technology. In P. Mittler (Ed.) *Research to practice in mental retardation. Vol. II. Education and training.* University Park Press, Baltimore. Pp. 331–336.

Baer, D. M., Wolf, M. M., & Risley, T. R. (1968). Some current dimensions of applied behavior analysis. *Journal of Applied Behavior Analysis, 1,* 91–97.

Baer, D. M., Wolf, M. M., & Risley, T. R. (1987). Some still-current dimensions of applied behavior analysis. *Journal of Applied Behavior Analysis, 20,* 313–327.

Baer, R A., Williams, J. A., Osnes, P. G., & Stokes, T. F. (1985). Generalized verbal control and correspondence training. *Behavior Modification, 9,* 477–489.

Baeyens, F., Vansteenwegen, D., Beckers, T., Hermans, D., Kerkhop, I., & De Ceulaer, A. (2005). Extinction and renewal of Pavlovian modulation in human sequential feature positive discrimination learning. *Learning and Memory, 12,* 178–192.

Bailey, J. S. (1991). Marketing behavior analysis requires different talk. *Journal of Applied Behavior Analysis, 24,* 445–448.

Bailey, J. S., & Burch, M. R. (2002). *Research methods in applied behavior analysis.* Sage Publications.

Bailey, J.S. & Burch, M. (2005). *Ethics for behavior analysts: A practical guide to the Behavior Analysis Certification Board Guidelines.* Mahwah, N.J.: Lawrence Earlbaum Associates, Inc.

Bailey, J. S., & Pyles, D. A. M. (1989). Behavioral Diagnostics. In E. Cipani (Ed.), *The treatment of severe behavior disorders: Behavior analysis approach.* (pp. 85–107).

Bailey, J., McComas, J. J., Benavidas, C., & Lovascz, C. (2002). Functional assessment in a residential setting: Identifying an effective communicative replacement response for aggressive behavior. *Journal of Developmental and Physical Disabilities, 14,* 353–369.

Bailey, J. S., Timbers, G. D., Phillips, E. L., & Wolf, M. M. (1971). Modification of articulation errors of pre-delinquents by their peers. *Journal of Applied Behavior Analysis, 4,* 265–281.

Baillargeon, L., Demers, M., & Ladouceur, R. (1998). Stimulus-control: Nonpharmacologic treatment for insomnia. *Canadian Family Physician, 44,* 73–79.

Bakeman, R., & Gottman, J. M. (1986). *Observing interaction: An introduction to sequential analysis.* New York: Cambridge University Press.

Baker, S. D., Lang, R., & O'Reilly, M. (2009). Review of video modeling with students with emotional and behavioral disorders. *Education and Treatment of Children, 32,* 403–420.

Balcazar, F., Hopkins, B. L., & Suarez, Y. (1985–86). A critical, objective review of performance feedback. *Journal of Organizational Behavior Management, 7,* 65–89.

Ballard, K. D., & Glynn, T. (1975). Behavioral self-management in story writing with elementary school children. *Journal of Applied Behavior Analysis, 8,* 387–398.

Ballard, T., Sewell, D. K., Cosgrove, D., & Neal, A. (2019). Information processing under reward versus under punishment. *Psychological Science, 30,* 757–764. https://doi.org/10.1171/0956797619835462

Balsam, P. D., & Bondy, A. S. (1983). The negative side-effects of reward. *Journal of Applied Behavior Analysis, 16,* 283–296.

Bamford, C., Lamont, S., Eccles, M., Robinson, L., May, C., & Bond, J. (2004). Disclosing a diagnosis of dementia: A systematic review .*International Journal of Geriatric Psychiatry, 19,* 151–169 .

Bancroft, S. L., & Bourret, J. C. (2008). Generating variable and random schedules of reinforcement using Microsoft Excel macros. *Journal of Applied Behavior Analysis, 41,* 227–235.

Banda, D. R., & Kubina, R. M. (2006). The effects of a high-probability request sequencing technique in enhancing transition behaviors. *Education and Treatment of Children, 29,* 507–516.

Banda, D. R., McAfee, J. K., & Hart, S. L. (2012). Decreasing self-injurious behavior and fading self-restraint in a student with autism and Tourette syndrome. *Behavioral Interventions, 27,* 164–174. doi: 10.1002/bin.1344

Bandura, A. (1965a). Various processes: A case of no-trail learning. In L. Berkowitz (Ed.), *Advances in experimental social psychology.* Vol. 2. New York: Academic Press, pp. 1–55.

Bandura, A. (1965b). Influence of models' reinforcement contingencies of the acquisition of imitative responses. *Journal of Personality and Social Psychology, 1,* 589–595.

Bandura, A. (1965c). Behavioral modification through modeling procedures. In L. Krasner & L. P. Ullman (Eds.), *Research in behavior modification* (pp. 310–340). New York: Holt, Rinehart & Winston.

Bandura, A. (1968). Social-learning theory of identification processes. IN D. A. Goslin & D. C. Glass (Eds.), *Handbook of socialization theory and research.* Chicago: Rand McNally.

Bandura, A. (1969). *Principles of behavior modification.* New York: Holt, Rinehart & Winston.

Bandura, A. (1977). *Social learning theory.* Englewood Cliffs, NJ: Prentice-Hall.

Bandura, A. (1986). *Social foundations of thought and action: A social cognitive theory.* Englewood Cliffs, NJ: Prentice-Hall.

Bandura, A. (1989) Social cognitive theory. In R. Vasta, Ed., *Annals of child development. Six theories of child development,* 1–60, Greenwich, CT: JAI Press.

Bandura, A., Grusec, J., & Menlove, F. (1967). Some social determinants of self-monitoring reinforcement systems. *Journal of Personality and Social Psychology, 5,* 449–455.

Bandura, A., & Kupers, C. J. (1964). Transmission of patterns of self-reinforcement through modeling. *Journal of Abnormal and Social Psychology, 69,* 1–19.

Bandura, A., Ross, D., & Ross, S. (1963a). Vicarious reinforcement and imitative learning. *Journal of Abnormal and Social Psychology, 67,* 601–607.

Bandura, A., Ross, D., & Ross, S. A. (1963b). Imitation of film-mediated aggressive models. *Journal of Abnormal and Social Psychology, 66,* 3–11.

Bandura, A., & Walters, R. H. (1963). *Social learning and personality development.* New York: Holt, Rinehart & Winston.

Barbera, M. L., & Kubina, R. M. Jr. (2005). Using transfer procedures to teach tacts to a child with autism. *The Analysis of Verbal Behavior, 21,* 155–161.

Barbetta, P. M., Heron, T. E., & Heward, W. L. (1993). Effects on active student response during error correction on the acquisition, maintenance, and developmental disabilities. *Journal of Applied Behavior Analysis, 26,* 111–119. doi: 10.1901/jaba.1993.26=11

Barker, M. R., Bailey, J. S., & Lee, N. (2004). The impact of verbal prompts on child safety-belt use in shopping carts. *Journal of Applied Behavior Analysis, 37,* 527–530.

Barlow, D., Agras, W. S., Leitenberg, H., & Wincze, J. P. (1970). Experimental analysis of the effectiveness of "shaping" in reducing maladaptive avoidance behavior: An analogue study. *Behavior Research and Therapy, 8,* 165–173.

Barlow, D. H., Hayes, S. C., & Nelson, R. O. (1984). *The scientist practitioner: Research and accountability in clinical and educational settings.* New York: Pergamon Press.

Barlow, D., & Hersen, M. (1984). *Single case experimental designs: Strategies for studying behavior change in the individual.* (2nd ed.). Esmsford, NY: Pergamon Press.

Barlow, D. H., Nock, M. K., & Hersen, M. (2008). Single case experimental designs: Strategies for studying behavior change (3rd ed.). New Jersey: Prentice Hall.

Barish, H. H. Saunders, M., & Wolf, M. M. (1969). Good Behavior Game: Effects of individual contingencies for group consequences on disruptive behavior in a classroom. *Journal of Applied Behavior Analysis, 2,* 119–124.

Barnard, J. K., Christophersen, E.R., Altman, K., & Wolf, M. (1974). Parent mediated treatment of self-injurious behavior using overcorrection. Paper presented at the meeting of the American Psychological Association, New Orleans.

Barnes, C. S., Mellor, J. R., & Rehfieldt, R. A. (2014). Implementing the Verbal Behavior Mile-stones Assessment and Placement Program (VB-MAPP): Teaching assessment techniques. *The Analysis of Verbal Behavior, 30,* 36047.

Barnes, D., & Keenan, M. (1993). Concurrent activities and instructed human fixed-interval performance. *Journal of Experimental Analysis of Behavior, 59,* 501–520.

Barnes, D., & Keenan, M. (1994). Response-reinforcer contiguity and human performance on simple time-based reinforcement schedules. *The Psychological Record, 44,* 63–90.

Barnes-Holmes, D., Barnes-Holmes, Y., & Cullinan, V. (2000a). Relational frame theory and Skinner's *Verbal Behavior*: A possible synthesis. *The Behavior Analyst, 23,* 69–84.

Barnes-Homes, C., Barnes-Homes, Y., & Cullinan, V. (2000b). Education. In S.C. Hayes, D. Barnes-Holmes, & B. Roche (Eds). *Rational frame theory: A post-Skinnerian account of human language and cognition* (pp. 181–196). N. Y.: Plenum

Barnes-Holmes, Y., Barnes-Holmes, D., McHugh, L., & Hayes, S C. (2004). Relational frame theory: Some implications for understanding and treating human psychopathology. *International Journal of Psychology and Psychological Therapy, 4,* 355–376.

Barnes-Holmes, D., Staunton, C., Whelan, R., Barnes-Holmes, Y., Commins, S., Walsh, D., et al. (2005). Derived stimulus relations, semantic priming, and event-related potentials. Testing a behavior theory of semantic networks. *Journal of Experimental Analysis of Behavior, 84,* 417–433.

Baron, A., & Galizio, M. (1983). Instructional control of human operant behavior. *The Psychological Record, 33,* 495–520.

Baron, A., & Galizio, M. (2005). Positive and negative reinforcement: Should the distinction be preserved? *The Behavior Analyst, 28,* 85–98.

Baron, A., & Galizio, M. (2006). The distinction between positive and negative reinforcement: Use with care. *The Behavior Analyst, 29,* 141–151.

Baron, A., Kaufman, A., & Stauber, K. A. (1969). Effects of instructions and reinforcement feedback on human operant behavior maintained by fixed interval reinforcement. *Journal of the Experimental Analysis of Behavior, 12,* 701–712.

Baron, A., & Leinenweber, A. (1995). Effects of a variable-ratio conditioning history on sensitivity to fixed-interval contingencies in rats. *Journal of the Experimental Analysis of Behavior, 63,* 97–110.

Barrera, R. D., Lobato-Barrera, D., & Sulzer-Azaroff, B. (1980). A simultaneous treatment comparison of three expressive language training programs with a mute autistic child. *Journal of Autism and Developmental Disorders, 10,* 21–37.

Barrera, R. D., & Sulzer-Azaroff, B. (1983). An alternating treatment comparison of oral and total communication training programs with echolalic autistic children. *Journal of Applied Behavior Analysis, 16,* 379–394.

Barreras, R. B. (2009). *Identifying adolescents at-risk of developing emotional or behavioral disorders (EBD): An Effectiveness study.* Paper presented at the meeting of the California Association for Behavior Analysis for Behavior Analysis, San Francisco, CA.

Barretto, A., Wacker, D. P., Harding, J., Lee., J., & Berg, W. K. (2006). Using telemedicine to conduct behavioral assessments. *Journal of Applied Behavior Analysis, 39,* 333–340.

Barrish, H. H., Saunders, M., & Wolf, M. M. (1969). Good Behavior Game:

Effects of individual contingencies for group consequences on disruptive behavior in a classroom. *Journal of Applied Behavior Analysis, 2,* 199–124.

Barry, L. M., & Burlew, S. B. (2004). Using social stories to teach choice and play skills to children with autism. *Focus on Autism and Other Developmental Disabilities, 19*(1), 45–51.

Barry, L., Holloway, J., & Gunning, C. (2018). An investigation of the effects of a parent delivered stimulus-stimulus pairing intervention on vocalizations of two children with Autism Spectrum Disorder. *The Analysis of Verbal Behavior, 35*(1), 57–73. https://doi.org/10.1007/s40616-018-0094-1

Barry, N. J., & Overman, P. B. (1977). Comparison of the effectiveness of adult and peer models with EMR children. *American Journal of Mental Deficiency, 82,* 33–36.

Barton, E. J. (1981). Developing sharing: an analysis of modeling and other behavioral techniques. *Journal of Abnormal and Social Psychology, 66,* 3–11.

Barton, E. J., & Bevirt, J. (1981). Generalization of sharing across groups: Assessment of group composition with preschool children. *Behavior Modification, 5,* 503–522.

Barton, R., & Reichow, B. (2012). Guidelines for graphing data with Microsoft® office 2007TM, office 2010TM, and Office for MaTM 2008 and 2011. *Journal of Early Intervention, 34,* 129–150.

Barton, E. J., & Osborn, J. G. (1978). The development of sharing by a teacher using positive practice. *Behavior Modification, 2,* 231–250.

Barton, L. E., Brulle, A. R., & Repp, A. C. (1986). Maintenance of therapeutic change by momentary DRO. *Journal of Applied Behavior Analysis, 19,* 277–282.

Baruni, R. R., Rapp, J. T., Lipe, S. L., Novotny, M. A. (2014). Using lag schedules to increase toy play variability for children with intellectual disabilities. *Behavioral Interventions, 29,* 21–35. doi: 10.1002/bin.1377.

Bass, J. D., & Mulick, J. A. (2007). Social play skills enhancement of children with autism using peers and siblings as therapists. *Psychology in the Schools, 44,* 727–735.

Bates, D.M., Renzaglia, A., & Wehman, P. (1981). Characteristics of an appropriate education for severely and profoundly handicapped students. *Education and Training of the Mentally Retarded, 16,* 142–149.

Beaman, A. L., Stoffer, G. R., Woods, A., & Stoffer, J. E. (1983). The importance of reinforcement schedules in the development and maintenance of altruistic behaviors. *Academic Psychology Bulletin, 5,* 309–317.

Beaulieu, L., Hanley, G. P., & Roberson, A. A. (2013). Effects of peer mediation on preschoolers' compliance and compliance precursors. *Journal of Applied Behavior Analysis, 46,* 555–567 doi: 10.1002/jaba.66.

Becirevic, A., Critchfield, T. S., & Reed, D. D. (2016). On the social acceptability of behavior-analytic Terms: Crowdsourced comparisons of lay and technical language. *The Behavior Analyst, 39,* 3050317. doi: 10.1007/s40614-016-0067-4.

Becker, W. C., & Carnine, D. W. (1981). Direct instruction: A behavior theory model for comprehensive educational intervention with the disadvantaged. In S. W. Bijou & R. Ruiz (Eds.), *Behavior modification: Contributions to education.* Hillsdale, NJ: Lawrence Erlbaum Associates.

Becker, W. C., Engelmann, S., Carnine, D. W., & Maggs, A. (1982). Direct instruction technology–making learning happen. In P. Karoly & J. J. Steffen (Eds.), *Advances in child behavior analysis and therapy: Vol. 1* (pp. 151–206). New Your: Garner Press.

Becker, W. C., Engelmann, S., & Thomas, D. R. (1975). *Teaching 2: Cognitive learning and instruction.* Chicago: SRA.

Becker, W. C., & Gersten, R. (1982). A follow-up of Follow Through: The later effects of the Direct Instruction model on children in fifth and sixth grades. *American Educational Research Journal, 19,* 75–92.

Becraft, J. L., Borrero, J. C., Davis, B., Medres-Smith, A. E., & Castillo, M. I. (2018). The role of signals in two variations of differential reinforcement-of-low-rate procedures. *Journal of Applied Behavior Analysis, 51,* 3–24. doi: 10.1002/jaba.431.

Becraft, J. L., & Rolider, N. U. (2015). Reinforcer variation in a token economy. *Behavioral Interventions, 30,* 157–165. doi: 10.1002/bin.1401.

*Behavior analyst certification board guidelines for responsible conduct for behavior analysts.* (July, 2010).http://www.bacb.com/pages/conduct.html

*Behavior analyst certification board's professional and ethical compliance code for behavior analysts.* (March, 2016). bacb.com.

Belisle, J., Paliliunas, D., Lauer, T., Giamanco, A., Lee, B., & Sickman, E. (2020). Derived relational responding and transformations of function in children: A review of applied behavior-analytic journals. *The Analysis of Verbal Behavior, 36*(1), 115–145. https://doi.org/10.1007/s40616-019-00123-z

Belisle, J., Stanley, C. R., Schmick, A., Dixon, M. R., Alholail, A., Galliford, M. E., & Ellenberger, L. (2020). Establishing arbitrary comparative relations and referential transformations of stimulus function in individuals with autism. *Journal of Applied Behavior Analysis, 53*(2), 938–955. https://doi-org.mimas.calstatela.edu/10.1002/jaba.655

Bellini, S., & Hopf, A. (2007). The development of the autism social skills profile: A preliminary analysis of psychometric properties. *Exceptional Children, 73,* 246–287. doi: org/10.1177/00144029707300301

BenitaezSantiago, A., & Miltenberger, R. G. (2016). Using video feedback to improve martial arts performance. *Behavioral Interventions, 31,* 12–27. doi: 10.1002/bin.1424.

Bennett, M. K., Manal, H., & Van Houten, R. (2014). A comparison of gateway in-street sign configuration to other driver prompts to increase yielding to pedestrians at crosswalks. *Journal of Applied Behavior Analysis, 47,* 3–15.

Benoit, B. (1972). An example of chaining in math. *The Learning Analyst Newsletter, 1,* 6–7.

Benoit, R. B., & Mayer, G. R. (1975). Timeout: Guidelines for its selection and use. *The Personnel and Guidance Journal, 53,* 501–506.

Bentall, R. P., & Lowe, C. F. (1987). The role of verbal behavior in human learning: III. Instructional effects in children. *Journal of Experimental Analysis of Behavior, 47,* 177–190.

Berens, N. M., & Hayes, S. C. (2007). Arbitrarily applicable comparative relations: Experimental evidence for a relational operant. *Journal of Applied Behavior Analysis, 40,* 45–71.

Berg, W. K., Peck, S., Wacker, D. P., Harding, J., McComas, J., Richman, D., & Brown, K. (2000). The effects of presession exposure to attention on the results of assessments of attention as a reinforcer. *Journal of Applied Behavior Analysis, 33,* 463–477.

Berg, W. K., & Wacker, D. P. (1989). Evaluation of tactile prompts with a student who is deaf, blind, and mentally retarded. *Journal of Applied Behavior analysis, 22,* 93–99.

Berg, W. K., Wacker, D. P., Ringdahl, J. E., Stricker, J., Vinquist, K., Salil Kumar Dutt, A., Dolezal, D., Luke, J., Kemmerer, L., & Mews, J. (2016). An integrated model for guiding the selection of treatment components for problem behavior maintained by automatic reinforcement. *Journal of Applied Behavior Analysis, 49*(3), 617–638. https://doi.org/10.1002/jaba.303

Bergarmann, S. C.,Kodak, T. M., LeBlanc, B. A. (2017). Effects of programmed errors of omission and commission during auditory-visual conditional discrimination training with typical developing children. *The Psychological Record, 67,* 109–119.

Berger, S. M., & Ludwig, T. D. (2007). Reducing warehouse employee errors using voice-assisted technology that provided immediate feedback. *Journal of Organizational Behavior Management, 27*(1), 1–31.

Bergstrom, R., Najdowski, A. C., Alvarado, M., & Tarbox, J. (2016). Teaching children with autism to tell socially appropriate lies. *Journal of Applied Behavior Analysis, 49,* 405–410. doi: 10.1002/jaba.295.

Bergstrom, R., Najdowski, A. C., & Tarbox, J. (2014). A systematic replication of teaching children with autism to respond appropriately to lures from strangers. *Journal of Applied Behavior Analysis, 47,* 861–865. DOI: 10.1002/jaba.175.

Berkowitz, L. (1983). Aversively stimulated aggression: Some parallels and difference in research with animals and humans. *American Psychologist, 38,* 1135–1144.

Berkowitz, L., Cochran, S. T., & Embree, M. C. (1981). Physical pain and the goal of aversively stimulated aggression. *Journal of Personality & Social Psychology, 40,* 687–700.

Bernal, M. E., Gibson, D. M., Williams, D. E., & Pesses, D. I. (1971). A device for automatic audio tape recording. *Journal of Applied Behavior Analysis, 4,* 151–156.

Bernhardt, A. J., & Forehand, R. (1975). The effects of labeled and unlabeled praise upon lower and middle class children. *Journal of Experimental Child Psychology, 19,* 536–543.

Bernstein, H., & Sturmey, P. (2008). Effects of fixed-ratio schedule values on concurrent mands in children with autism. *Research in Autism Spectrum Disorders, 2,* 362–370.

Berotti, D. (1996). *Effects of preference and choice on problem behavior.* Unpublished doctoral dissertation, State University of New York, Albany.

Berzins, L. G., Trestman, R. L. (2004). The development and implementation of dialectical behavior therapy in forensic settings. *International Journal of Forensic Mental Health, 3,* 93–101.

Bicard, D. E., & Neef, J. A. (2002). Effects of strategic versus tactical instructions on adaptation to changing contingencies in children with ADHD. *Journal of Applied Behavior Analysis, 35,* 375–389.

Bicklin, D. (1990). *Communication unbound: Autism and Praxis.* Harvard Educational Review.

Biglan, A. (2015). *The nurture effect: How the science of human behavior can improve our lives and our world.* Oakland, CA: New Harbinger Publications, Inc.

Biglan, A. (2015). *The future effect: How the science of human behavior can improve our lives & our world.* Oakland, CA: New Harbinger Publications, Inc.

Bijou, S. W., Birnbrauer, J. S., Kidder, J. D., & Tague, C. (1967). Programmed instruction as an approach to teaching of reading, writing, and arithmetic to retarded children. In S. W. Bijou & D. M. Baer (Eds.), *Child development: Readings in experimental analysis.* New York: Appleton.

Bijou, S. W., & Orlando, R. (1961). Rapid development of multiple-schedule performances with retarded children. *Journal of the Experimental Analysis of Behavior, 4,* 7–16.

Bijou, S. W., Peterson, R. F., & Ault, M. H. (1968). A method to integrate descriptive and experimental field studies at the level of data and empirical concepts. *Journal of Applied Behavior Analysis, 1,* 175–191.

Billington, E., Skinner, C., Hutchins, H., & Malone, J. (2004). Varying problem effort and choice: Using the interspersal technique to influence choice towards more effortful assignments. *Journal of Behavioral Education, 13,* 193–207.

Binder, C. (1994). Measurably superior instructional methods: Do we need sales and marketing? In R. Gardner, III, D. M. Sainato, J. O. Cooper, T.E. Heron, W. L. Heward, J. Eshleman, & T. A. Grossi (Eds.). *Behavior Analysis in education: Focus on measurably superior instruction* (pp. 21–31). Belmont, CA: Brooks/Cole.

Binder, C. (1996). Behavioral fluency: Evolution of a new paradigm. *The Behavior Analyst, 19,* 163–197.

Binder, C., & Watkins, C.L. (2010). Precision teaching and direct instruction: Measurably superior instructional technology in schools. *Performance Improvement Quarterly, 3* 74–96.

Binder, L. M., Dixon, M. R., & Ghezzi, P. M. (2000). A procedure to teach self-control to children with attention deficit hyperactivity disorder. *Journal of Applied Behavior Analysis, 33,* 233–237.

Binnendyk, L., & Lucyshyn, J. M. (2009). A family-centered positive behavior support approach to the amelioration of food refusal behavior: An empirical case study. *Journal of Positive Behavior Intervention, 11,* 47–62.

Bird, F. L., & Luiselli, J. K. (2000). Positive behavioral support of adults with developmental disabilities: Assessment of long-term adjustment and habilitation following restrictive treatment histories. *Journal o Behavioral Therapy and Experimental Psychiatry, 31,* 5–19.

Birnbrauer, J. S., Wolf, M. M., Kidder, J. D., & Tague, C. (1965). Classroom behavior of retarded pupils with token reinforcement. *Journal of Experimental Child Psychology, 2,* 219–235.

Bisen-Hersh, E. B., Swope, B. W., Lorah, E. R., Barnard, J. C., Campbell, A., McElrath, K., & Wade, J. A. (2010, May). Alternative behavioral interventions revisited: Which approach for which children? In P. N. Hineline (Chair), *Alternative behavioral interventions revisited: Which approach, for which children, with what resources?* Symposium conducted at the annual meeting of the Association for Applied Behavior Analysis International, San Antonio, TX.

Bittle, R., & Hake, D. F. (1977). A multi-element design model for component analysis and cross-setting assessment of a treatment package. *Behavior Therapy, 8,* 906–914.

Black, L. I., Vahratian, A., Hoffman, H. J. (2015). Communication disorders and use of intervention services among children aged 3–17 years, *USA NCHS data brief, no. 205,* Hyattsville, MD, National Center for Health Statistics.

Blair, B. J., Tarbox, J., Albright, L., Mac-Donald, J. M., Shawler, L. A., Russo, S. R., & Dorsey, M. F. (2019). Using equivalence-based instruction to teach the visual analysis of graphs. *Behavioral Interventions, 34*(3), 405–418. https://doi-org.mimas.calstatela.edu/10.1002/bin.1669

Blakely, E., & Schlinger, H. (1987). Rules: Function-altering contingency-specifying stimuli. *The Behavior Analyst, 10,* 183–187.

Blampied, N. M., & France, K. G. (1993). A behavioral model of infant sleep disturbance. *Journal of Applied Behavior Analysis, 26,* 477–492.

Blampied, N.M., Kahan, E. (1992). Acceptability of alternative punishments. *Behavior Modification, 16,* 400–413.

Blew, P. A., Schwartz, I. S., & Luce, S. C. (1985). Teaching functional community skills to autistic children using nonhandicapped peer tutors. *Journal of Applied Behavior Analysis, 18,* 337–342.

Blick, D.W. & Test, D.W. (1987). Effects of self-recording on high-school students' on-task behavior. *Learning Disability Quarterly,* 10, 203–213.

Blom, D. E., & Zimmerman, B. J. (1981). Enhancing the social skills of an unpopular girl: A social learning intervention. *Journal of School Psychology, 19,* 295–303.

Bloom, B. S. (1980). The new direction in educational research: Alterable variables. *Phi Delta Kappan, 61,* 382–385.

Bloom, B. S. (1984). The 2 sigma problem: The search for methods of group instruction as effective as one-to-one tutoring. *Educational Researcher, June/July,* 4–16.

Bloom, S. E., Iwata, B. A., Fritz, J. N., Roscoe, E. M., & Carreau, A. B. (2011). Classroom application of a trial-based functional analysis. *Journal of Applied Behavior Analysis, 44,* 19–31. doi: 10:1901/jaba.2011. 44-19.

Bloomfield, H. H. (1973). Assertive training in an outpatient group of chronic schizophrenics: A Preliminary report. *Behavior Therapy, 4,* 277–281.

Blume, Arthur W. 2001. Negative reinforcement and substance abuse: Using a behavioral conceptualization to enhance treatment. *The Behavior Analyst Today 2*(2): 86–90. doi:10.1037/h0099916.

Bogart, L. C., Piersel, W. C., & Gross, E. J. (1995). The long-term treatment of life-threatening pica: A case study of a woman with profound mental retardation living in an applied setting. *Journal of Developmental and Physical Disabilities, 7*(1), 39–50.

Boe, E. E., & Church, R. M. (1967). Permanent effects of punishment during extinction. *Journal of Comparative and Physiological Psychology, 63,* 486–492.

Boivin, M., & Vitaro, F. (1995). The impact of peer relationships on aggression in childhood: Inhibition through coercion or promotion through peer support. In J. Mc Cord (Ed.), *Coercion and punishment in long-term perspectives* (pp. 183–197). New York: Cambridge University Press.

Bondy, A., & Frost, L. (1994). The picture exchange communication system. *Focus on Autism and Other Developmental Disabilities,* 9, 1–19.

Bondy, A., & Frost, L. (1998). The picture exchange communicatino system. *Seminars in Speech and Language, 19,* 373–389.

Bondy, A., & Frost, L. (2001a). *A picture's worth: PECS and other visual communication strategies in autism.* Bethesda, MD: Woodbine House.

Bondy, A., & Frost, L. (2001b). The picture exchange communication system. *Behavior Modification, 25,* 725–744.

Bondy, A., & Frost, L. (2002). *A picture's worth.* Bethesday, MD, Woodbine House.

Bondy, A., & Sulzer-Azaroff, B. (2002). *The pyramid approach to education in autism.* Newark, DE, Pyramid Educational Products, Inc.

Bonfiglio, C. M., Daly, E. J., Martens, B. K., Lin, L. R., & Corsaut, S. (2004). An experimental analysis of reading interventions: generalization across instructional strategies, time, and passages. *Journal of Applied Behavior Analysis, 37,* 111–114.

Bonfonte, S. A., Boudrret, J. C., & Lloveras, L. A. (2020). Comparing the reinforcing efficacy of tokens and primary reinforcers. *Journal of Applied Behavior Analysis, 53,* 1593–1605. doi: 10.1002/jaba.675

Boren, J. (1956). Response rate and resistance to extinction as functions of the fixed ratio. *Dissertation Abstracts, 14,* 1261.

Boren, J. J., & Colman, A. D. (1970). Some experiments on reinforcement principles within a psychiatric ward for delinquent soldiers. *Journal of Applied Behavior Analysis, 3,* 29–37.

Borlase, M. A., Vladescu, J. C., Kisamore, A. N., Reeve, S. A, & Fetzer, J. L. (2017). Analysis of precursors to multiply controlled problem behavior: A replication. *Journal of Applied Behavior Analysis, 50,* 668–674. doi: 10.1002/jaba.398

Bornstein, P. H., Balleweg, B. J., McLellarn, R. W., Wilson, G. L., Sturm, C. A., Andre, J. C., et al. (1983). The "Bathroom Game": A systematic program for the elimination of encopretic behavior. *Journal of Behavior Therapy and Experimental Psychiatry, 14,* 67–71.

Borrego, J. Jr., Ibanez, E. S., Spendlove, S.J., & Pemberton, J.R. (2007). Treatment acceptability among Mexican American parents. *Behavior Therapy, 38*(3), 218–227.

Borrero, J. C., Crisolo, S. S., Tu, Q., Rieland, W. A., Ross, N. A., Francisco, M. T., et al. (2007). An application of the matching law to social dynamics. *Journal of Applied Behavior Analysis, 40,* 589–601.

Borrerro, J. C., & Vollmer, T. R. (2002). An application of the matching law to severe problem behavior. *Journal of Applied Behavior Analysis, 35,* 13–27.

Borrero, J. C., Vollmer, T. R., & Wright, C. S. (2002). An evaluation of contingency strength and response suppression. *Journal of Applied Behavior Analysis, 35,* 337–347.

Bosch, S., & Fuqua, W. R. (2001). Behavioral cusps: A model for selecting target behaviors. *Journal of Applied Behavior Analysis, 43,* 123–125.

Bostow, D. E., & Bailey, J. B. (1969). Modification of severe disruptive and aggressive behavior using brief timeout and reinforcement procedures.

*Journal of Applied Behavior Analysis, 2,* 31–37.

Boudreau, J., & Harvey, M T. (2013).. Increasing recreational initiations for children who have ASD using video self-modeling. *Education and Treatment of Children,* 36, 49–60.

Bourret, J., Vollmer, T. R., & Rapp, J. T. (2004). Evaluation of a vocal mand assessment and vocal mand training procedures. *Journal of Applied Behavior Analysis, 37,* 129–144.

Bouton, M.E. (2004). Context, ambiguity, and unlearning: sources of relapse after behavioral extinction. *Biological Psychiatry,* 52(10), 976 – 986.

Bouxsein, K. J., Tiger, J. H., & Fisher, W. W. (2008). A comparison of general and specific instructions to promote task engagement and completion by a young man with Asperger syndrome. *Journal of Applied Behavior Analysis, 41,* 113–116.

Bovi, G. M. D., Vladescu, J. C., DeBar, R. M., Carroll, R. A., & Sarokoff, R. A. (2017). Using video modeling with voice-over instruction to train public school staff to implement a preference assessment. *Behavior Analysis in Practice, 10,* 72–76.

Bowman, L. G., Fisher, W. W., Thompson, R. H., & Piazza, C. C. (1997). On the relation of mands and the function of destructive behavior. *Journal of Applied Behavior Analysis, 30,* 251–265.

Bowman-Perrot, L., deMarin, S., Mahadevan, L., & Etchells, M. (2016). Assessing the academic, social, and language production outcomes of English language learners en-gaged in peer tutoring: A systematic review. *Education and Treatment of children, 39,* 359–388.

Bowman-Perrott, L. J., Greenwood, C. R., & Tapia, Y. (2007). The efficacy of CWPT used in secondary alternative school classrooms with small teacher/pupil rations and students with emotional and behavioral disorders. *Education and Treatment of Children, 30,* 65–87.

Bowring, D. L., & Toogood, S. (2019). The use of positive greetings at the door to increase on-task behaviour in a vocational training centre. *International Journal of Positive Behavioural Support,* 9, 38–46.

Boyce, T. E., & Geller, E. S. (2001). Applied behavior analysis and occupational safety: The challenge of response maintenance. *Journal of Organizational Behavior Management, 21,* 31–60.

Boyer, E., Miltenberger, R. G., Batsche, C., & Fogel, V. (2009). Video modeling by experts with video feedback to enhance gymnastics skills. *Journal of Applied Behavior Analysis, 42,* 855–860.

Boyle, J. R., & Hughes, C. A. (1994). Effects of self-monitoring and subsequent fading of external prompts on the on-task behavior and task productivity of elementary students with moderate mental retardation. *Journal of Behavioral Education,* 4, 439–457.

Braam, S. J., & Poling, A. (1983). Development of intraverbal behavior in mentally retarded individuals through transfer of stimulus control procedures: Classification of verbal responses. *Applied Research in Mental Retardation,* 4, 279–302.

Bradley-Johnson, S., Graham, D. P., & Johnson, C. M. (1986). Token reinforcement on WISC-R performance for white, low-socio-economic, upper and lower elementary-school age students. *Journal of School Psychology, 24,* 73–79.

Bradley-Johnson, S., Sunderman, P., & Johnson, C. M. (1983). Comparison of delayed prompting and fading for teaching preschoolers easily confused letters and numbers. *Journal of School Psychology, 21,* 327–335.

Bradshaw, C. M., Szabadi, E., & Bevan, P. (1977). Effect of punishment on human variable-interval performance. *Journal of the Experimental Analysis of Behavior, 27,* 275–279.

Bradshaw, M. F., Watt, S. J., Elliott, K. M., & Riddell, P. M. (2004). The effects of a pre-movement delay on the kinematics of prehension in middle childhood. *Human Movement science, 23,* 771–784.

Brakman, C. (1985). A human rights committee in a public school for severely and profoundly retarded students. *Education and Training of the Mentally Retarded, 20,* 139–147.

Brantner, J. P., & Doherty, M. A. (1983). A review of timeout: A conceptual and methodological analysis. In S Axelrod & J. Apsche (Eds.), *The effects of punishment on human behavior* (pp. 87–132). New York: Academic Press.

Braukmann, C. J., Maloney, D., M., Fixsen, D. L., Phillips, E. L., & Wolf, M. M. (1974). An analysis of a selection interview training package for predelinquents at achievement place. *Criminal Justice and Behavior, 1,* 30–42.

Brechner, K. C., Linder, D. E., Meyerson, L., & Hays, V. L. (1974). A brief report on a device for unobtrusive visual recording. *Journal of Applied Behavior Analysis, 7,* 499–500.

Breevaart, K., Bakker, A. B., & Demerouti, E. (2014). Daily self-management and em-ployee work engagement. *Journal of Vocational Behavior, 84,* 31–38.

Breyer, N. L., & Allen, C. (1975). Effects of implementing a token economy on teacher attending behavior. *Journal of Applied Behavior Analysis, 8,* 373–380.

Briere, D. E., Simonsen, B., Sugai, G., & Myers, D. (2015). Increasing new teachers' specific praise using within-school consultation intervention. *Journal of Positive Behavior Interventions, 17,* 50–60. DOI: 10.1177/1098300713497098 jpbi.sagepub.com

Briesch, A. M., & Briesch, J. M. (2016). Meta-analysis of behavioral self-management interventions in single-case research. *School Psychology Review,* 45(1), 3–18.

Briggs, A. M., Fisher, W. W., Geer, B. D., & Kimball, R. T. (2018). Prevalence of resurgence of destructive behavior when thinning reinforcement schedules during functional communication training. *Journal of Applied Behavior Analysis, 51,* 620–633. doi: 10.1002/jaba.472

Brodhead, M. T., Courtney, W. T., & Thaxton, J. R. (2018). Using activity schedules to promote varied application use in children with autism. *Journal of Applied Behavior Analysis, 51,* 80–86. doi: 10.1002/jaba.435

Brodhead, M. T., Higbee, T. S., Gerencser, K. R., & Akers, J. S. (2016). The use of a discrimination training procedure to teach and variability to children with autism. *Journal of Applied Behavior Analysis 49,* 34–48. doi: 10.1002/jaba.280

Brodhead, M.T., Quigley, S. P., & Cox, D. J. (2018). How to identify ethical practices in organizations prior to employment. *Behavior Analysis in Practice, 11,* 165-173.

Brockman, M. P., & Leibowitz, J. M. (1982). Effectiveness of various omission training procedures as a function of reinforcement history. *Psychological Reports, 50*, 511–530.

Brobst, B., & Ward, P. (2002). Effects of public posting, goal setting, and oral feedback on the skills of female soccer players. *Journal of Applied Behavior Analysis, 35*, 247–257.

Broden M., Hall, R. V., & Mitts, B. (1971). The effect of self-recording on the classroom behavior of two eighth-grade students. *Journal of Applied Behavior Analysis, 4*, 191–198.

Brody, G. H., & Brody, J. A. (1976). Vicarious language instruction with bilingual children through self-modeling. *Contemporary Educational Psychology, 1*, 138–145.

Brody, G. H., Lahey, B. B., & Combs, J. L. (1978). Effects of intermittent modeling on observational learning. *Journal of Applied Behavior Analysis, 11*, 87–90.

Brooks, B. D. (1974). Contingency management as a means of reducing school truancy. *Education, 95*, 206–211.

Brosh, C. R., Fisher, L. B., Wood, C. L., & Test, D. W. (2018). High-probability request sequence: An evidence-based practice for individuals with autism spectrum disorder. *Education and Training in Autism and Developmental Disabilities, 53*, 276–286.

Brothers, K. J., Krantz, P. J., & McClannahan, L. E. (1994). Office paper recycling: A function of container proximity. *Journal of Applied Behavior Analysis, 27*, 153–160.

Broussard, C., & Northup, J. (1997). The use of functional analysis to develop peer interventions for disruptive classroom behavior. *School Psychology Quarterly, 12*, 65–76.

Browder, D. M., Morris, W. W., & Snell, M. E. (1981). The use of time delay to teach manual signs to a severely retarded student. *Education and Training of the Mentally Retarded, 16*, 252–258.

Brown, E. M., Smith, D. M., Epton, T., Armitagee, C. J. (in press, 2017). Do sel-incentives change behavior? A systematic review and meta-analysis. *Behavior Therapy.* doi.org/10.1016/j.beth.2017.09.004

Brown, C. S., & Sulzer-Azaroff, B. (1991). Immediate customer feedback: High return with low cost. *Performance Management Magazine*, 18–19.

Brown, C. S., & Sulzer-Azaroff, B. (1994). An assessment of the relationship between customer satisfaction and service friendliness. *Journal of Organizational Behavior Management, 14*, 55–75.

Brown, D., & Frank, A. R. (1990). Let me do it! Self-monitoring in solving arithmetic problems. *Education and Treatment of Children, 13*, 239–348.

Brown, K.A., & Piazza, C.C. (1999). Commentary: Enhancing the effectiveness of sleep treatments: Developing a functional approach. *Pediatric Psychology, 24*, (6) 487–489.

Brown, K. E., & Miranda, P. (2006). Contingency mapping: Use of a novel visual support strategy as an adjunct to functional equivalence training. *Journal of Positive Behavior Interventions, 8*(3), 155–164.

Brown, L., Branston, M.B., Hamre-Nietupski, S., Pumpian, I., Cerro, N., & Gruenewald, L. (1979). A strategy for chronological-age-appropriate and functional curricular content for severely handicapped adolescents and young adults. *Journal of Special Education, 13*, 624–630.

Brown, M. A. (1974). Nonreinforcement for teachers: Penalties for success. In R. Ulrich, T. Stachnik, & J. Mabsy (Eds.). *Control of human behavior. Behavior modification in education, Vol. 3.* Glenview, Ill.: Scott, Foreman & Co.

Brown, N., & Redmon, W. K. (1989). The effects of a group reinforcement contingency on staff use of unscheduled sick leave. *Journal of Organizational Behavior Management, 10* (2), 3–17.

Browning-Wright, D., Mayer, G. R., Cook, C. R., Crews, S. D., Kraemer, V. R., & Gale, B. (2007). A preliminary study on the effects of training using Behavior Support Plan Quality Evaluation Guide (BSP-QE) to improve positive behavioral support plans. *Education and Treatment of Children, 30*(3), 89–106.

Bruzek, J. L., & Thompson, R. H. (2007). Antecedent effects of observing peer play. *Journal of Applied Behavior Analysis, 40*, 327–331.

Bryan, L., & Gast, D.L. (2000). Teaching on-task and on-schedule behaviors to high-functioning children with autism via picture activity schedules. *Journal of Autism and Developmental Disorders, 30*, 553–567.

Bucher, B., & Reaume, J. (1979). Generalization of reinforcement effects in a token program in the home. *Behavior Modification, 3*, 63–72.

Bucher, B., & Hawkins, J. (1971, September). *Comparison of response cost and token reinforcement systems in a class for academic underachievers.* Paper presented at the meeting of the association of the Advancement of Behavior Therapy, Washington, D. C.

Buckley, J., Luselli, J. K., Harper, J. M., & Shlesinger, A. (2020). Teaching students with autism spectrum disorder to tolerate haircutting. *Journal of Applied Behavior Analysis, 53*, 2081–2089. doi: 10.1002/jaba.713

Buckley, S. D., & Newchok, D. K. (2005). Differential impact of response effort within a response chain on use of mands in a student with autism. *Research in Developmental Disabilities, 5*, 203–216.

Buckley, S.D., & Newchok, D.K. (2006). Analysis and treatment of problem behavior evoked by music. *Journal of Applied Behavior Analysis, 39*, 141–144.

Bucklin, B.R. & Dickinson, A. M. (2001). Monetary incentives: A review of different types of arrangements between performance and pay. *Journal of Organizational Behavior Management, 23*, 45 – 137.

Budd, K., & Baer, D. M. (1976, Summer). Behavior modification and the law: Implications of recent judicial decisions. *The Journal of Psychiatry & Law; a special reprint*, 171–274.

Buggey, R. (2007). A picture is worth.... Video self-modeling applications at school and home. *Journal of Positive Behavior Interventions, 9*, 151–158.

Buggey, R., Toombs, K., Gardner, P., & Cerveti, M. (1999). Self-modeling as a technique to train response behaviors in children with autism. *Journal of Positive Behavior Interventions, 1*, 205–214.

Bukala, M., Hu, M. Y., Lee, R., Ward-Horner, J. C., & Fienup, D. M. (2015). The effects of work schedules on performance and preference in participants with autism. *Journal of Applied Behavior Analysis, 48*, 215–220. doi: 10.1002/jaba.188

Bulla, A. J., Wertalik, J. L., & Crafton, D. (2020). A preliminary investigation of question type used during response card activities on establishing concept formation in an introductory college class. *European Journal of Behavior Analysis*, DOI:10.1080/15021149.2020.1737406

Burch, M.R., Clegg, J.C., & Bailey, J.S. (1987). Automated contingent reinforcement of correct posture. *Research in Developmental Disabilities, 8,* 15–20.

Burchard, J. D., & Barrera, F. (1972). An analysis of timeout and response cost in a programmed environment. *Journal of Applied Behavior Analysis, 5*(3), 271–282.

Burg, M. M., Reid, D. H., & Lattimore, J. (1979). Use of a self-recording and supervision program to change institutional staff behavior. *Journal of Applied Behavior Analysis, 12,* 363–375.

Burns, M. K., Aguilar, L. N., Young, H., Preast, J. L., Taylor, C. N., & Walsh, A. D. (2019). Comparing the effects of incremental rehearsal and traditional drill on retention of mathematics facts and predicting the effects of memory. *School Psychology, 34,* 521–530. doi.org/10.1037/apq0000312

Busch, A. B., & Shore, M. F. (2000). Seclusion and restraint: A review of recent literature. *Harvard Review of Psychiatry, 8,* 261–270.

Busch, L. P. A., Saini, V., Zorzos, C., & Duyile, L. (2018). Treatment of life-threatening pica with a 5-year follow-up. *Advances in Neurodevelopmental Disorders, 2,* 335–343. https://doi.org/10.1007/s41252-018-0053-9

Buskist, W., Cush, D., & DeGrandpre, R. J. (1991). The life and times of PSI. *Journal of Behavioral Education, 1,* 215–234.

Buskist, W. F., & Miller, H. L. (1986). Interaction between rules and contingencies in the control of human fixed-interval performance. *The Psychological Record, 36,* 109–116.

Buskist, W. F., Morgan, A. B., & Rossi, M. (1984). Competitive fixed interval performance in humans: Role of "orienting" instructions. *The Psychological Record, 34,* 241–257.

Buskist, W. F., & Morgan, D. (1987). Competitive fixed-interval performance in humans. *Journal of Experimental Analysis of Behavior, 47,* 145–158.

Butler, C., & Graff, R. B. (2021). Stability of preference and reinforcing efficacy of edible, leisure, and social attention stimuli. *Journal of Applied Behavior Analysis, 54,* 684–699. doi: 10.1002/jaba.807

Byra, K., L., White, S., Temple, M., & Cameron, J. J. (2018). An approach to cleanliness training to support bathroom hygiene among children with autism spectrum disorder. *Behavior Analysis in Practice, 11,* 139–143.

Byrne, B. (1969). Attitudes and attraction. In L. Berkowitz (Ed.), *Advances in experimental social psychology*. Vol. 4, New York: Academic Press.

Byrne, B., & Griffitt, W. (1969). Similarity and awareness of similarity of personality characteristics as determinants of attraction. *Experimental Research in Personality, 3,* 179–186.

Cagliani, R. R., Ayres, K. M., Whiteside, E. et al. *J Dev Phys Disabil.* (2017). https://doi.org/10.1007/s10882-017-9564-y

Cairns, R. B., & Cairns, B. D. (1992). The sociogenesis of aggressive and antisocial behaviors. In J. McCord (Ed.), *Facts, frameworks, and forecasts* (pp. 157–191). New Brunswick, NJ: Transaction Publishers.

Caldarella, P., Larsen, R. A. A., Williams, L., Wills, H. P., Wehby, J. H. (2019). Teacher praise-to-reprimand ratios: Behavioral response of students at risk for EBD compared with typically developing peers. *Education and Treatment of Children, 42,* 447–468.

Caldarella, P., Williams, L., & Jolstead, K. A. (2017). Managing student behavior in an elementary school music classroom: A study of class-wide function related intervention teams. *Journal of Applied Research in Intellectual Disabilities, 30,* 423–432.

Caldwell, N. K., Wolery, M., Werts, M. G., & Caldwell, &. (1996). Embedding instructive feedback into teacher-student interactions during independent seating work. *Journal of Behavioral Education, 6,* 459–480.

Cameron, J. (2001). Negative effects of reward on intrinsic motivation – A limited phenomenon: Comment on Deci, Koestner, and Ryan. *Review of Educational Research, 71,* 29–42.

Cameron, J., Banko, K. M., & Pierce, W. D. (2001). Pervasive negative effects of rewards on intrinsic motivation: The myth continues. *The behavior analyst, 24,* 1–44.

Cameron, J., & Pierce, W. D. (1994). Reinforcement, reward, an intrinsic motivation: A meta-analysis. *Review of Educational Research, 64,* 363–423.

Cameron, M. J., & Cappello, M. J. (1993). We'll cross that hurdle when we get to it: Teaching athletic performance within adaptive physical education. *Behavior Modification, 17,* 136–147.

Campbell, E., Jin, S., & Lawrence, A. J. (2019). Environmental enrichment reduces the propensity to relapse following punishment-imposed abstinence of alcohol seeking. *Physiology & Behavior, 210.* https://doi.org/10.1016/j.physbeh.2019.112638

Campbell, J. M. (2003). Efficacy of behavioral interventions for reducing problem behavior in persons with autism: a quantitative synthesis of single-subject research. *Research in Developmental Disabilities, 24*(2), 120–138.

Campbell, J. M. (2004). Statistical comparison of four effect sizes for single-subject design. *Behavior Modification, 22,* 234–246.

Campbell, S., & Skinner, C. H. (2004). Combining explicit timing with an interdependent group contingency program to decrease transition times: An investigation of the timely transitions game. *Journal of Applied School Psychology, 20*(2), 11–27.

Caprara, G. V., Barbaranelli, C., Pastorelli, C., Bandura, A., & Zimbardo, P. G. (2000). Prosocial foundations of children's academic achievement. *Psychological Science, 11,* 302–306.

Cardon, T., Wangasgard, N., & Dobson, N. (2019). Video modeling using classroom peers as models to increase social communication skills in children with ASD in an integrated preschool. *Education and Treatment of Children, 42,* 515–536.

Carey, R. G., & Bucher, B. D. (1981). Identifying the educative and suppressive effects of positive practice and restitutional overcorrection. *Journal of Applied Behavior Analysis, 14,* 71–80.

Carey, R. G., & Bucher, B. D. (1983). Positive practice overcorrection: The effects of duration of positive practice on acquisition and response reduction. *Journal of Applied Behavior Analysis, 16,* 101–109.

Carey, R. G., & Bucher, B. D. (1986). Positive practice overcorrection: Effects of reinforcing correct performance. *Behavior Modification, 10,* 73–92.

Cariveau, T., Hunt, Katelyn, H., & McCord, M. (2021). Recommendations for using PowerPoint 2016/2020 to create individualized matching to sample sessions on the iPad. *Behavior Analysis in Practice, 14,* 161–165. http://doi.org/10.1007/s40617-020-00484-1

Cariveau, T., & Kodak, T. (2017). Programming a randomized dependent group contingency and common stimuli to promote durable behavior change. *Journal of Applied Behavior Analysis, 50,* 121–133. doi: 10.1002/jaba.352

Cariveau, T., Kodak, T., & Campbel, V. (2016). The effects of inter trail interval and instructional format on skill acquisition and maintenance for children with autism spectrum disorders. *Journal of Applied Behavior Analysis, 49,* 809–825. doi: 10.1002/jaba.322

Carlile, K. A., DeBar, R. M., Reeve, S. A., & Reeve, K. F. (2018). Teaching help-seeking when lost to individuals with autism spectrum disorder. *Journal of Applied Behavior Analysis, 51,* 191–206. doi: 10.1002/jaba.447

Carlson, J. D., & Mayer, G. R. (1971). Fading: A behavioral procedure to increase independent behavior. *The School Counselor, 18,* 193–197.

Carlson, J. I., Luiselli, J. K., Slyman, A., & Markowski, A. (2008). Choice making as intervention for public disrobing in children with developmental disabilities. *Journal of Positive Behavior Interventions, 10,* 86–90.

Carmignani, K. (2010). Training tigers: The cat's meow. *San Diego Zoonooz. February, 29–31.*

Carnegie, D. (1936). *How to win friends and influence people.* New York: Simon and Schuster.

Carnine, D. W. (1976). Effects of two teacher-presentation rates on off-task behavior, answering correctly, and participation. *Journal of Applied Behavior Analysis, 9,* 199–206.

Carr, A., Linehan, C., & O'Reilly, G. (2016). *Clinical psychology practice.* https://books.google.com/books? isbn: 1317576021.

Carr, D. (2003). Effects of exemplar training in exclusion responding on auditory-visual discrimination tasks with children with autism. *Journal of Applied Behavior Analysis, 36,* 507–524.

Carr, E. G. (1996). The transfiguration of behavior analysis: Strategies for survival. *Journal of Behavioral Education, 6,* 263–270.

Carr, E.G, Dunlap, G., Horner, R.H., Koegel, R.L., Turnbull, A.P., Sailor, W., Anderson, J.L., Albin, R.W., Koegel, L.K., & Fox , L. (2002) Positive Behavior Support: Evolution of an applied science. *Journal of Positive Behavior Interventions, 4,* 4–16.

Carr, E. G., & Durand, V. M. (1985a). Reducing behavior problems through functional communication training. *Journal of Applied Behavior Analysis, 18,* 111–126.

Carr, E. G., & Durand, V. M. (1985b). The social-communicative basis of severe behavior problems in children. In S. Reiss & R. Bootzin (Eds.), *Theoretical issues in behavior therapy.* (pp. 219–254). New York: Academic Press.

Carr, E.G., Horner, R.H., Turnbull, A.P., Marquis, J.G., McLaughlin, D., Magito, D., McAtee, M.L., Smith, C.E., Ryan, K.A., Ruef, M.B., Doolabh, A., & Braddock, D.E. (1999). *Positive behavior support for people with dDevelopmental disabilities: A rResearch synthesis.* Washington, D.C.: American Association on Mental Retardation.

Carr, E. G., & Newsom, C. D. (1985). Demand-related tantrums: Conceptualization and treatment. *Behavior Modification, 9,* 403–426.

Carr, E. G., Newsom, C. D., & Binkoff, J. A. (1976). Stimulus control of self-destructive behavior in a psychotic child. *Journal of Abnormal Child Psychology, 4,* 139–153.

Carr, E. G., Newsom, C. D., & Binkoff, J. A. (1980). Escape as a factor in the aggressive behavior of two retarded children. *Journal of Applied Behavior Analysis, 13,* 101–117.

Carr, E. G., Taylor, J. C., Carlson, J. I., & Robinson, S. (1991). Reinforcement and stimulus-based treatments for severe behavior disorders in developmental disabilities. In U.S. Department and Health and Human Services. *Treatment of destructive behaviors in persons with developmental disabilities* (pp. 173–229) (NIH Publication No. 91–2410). Bethesda, MD: National Institutes of Health.

Carr, E.G., Taylor, J.C., & Robinson, S. (1991). The effects of severe behavior problems in children on the teaching behavior of adults. *Journal of Applied Behavior Analysis, 24,* 523–35.

Carr, E. G., Yarbrough, S. C., & Langdon, N. A. (1997). Effects of idiosyncratic stimulus variables on functional analysis outcomes. *Journal of Applied Behavior Analysis, 30,* 673–686.

Carr, J. E. (1996). On the use of the term "noncontingent reinforcement." *Journal of Behavior Analysis and Therapy, 1,* 33–37.

Carr, J. E., Bailey, J. S., Ecott, C. L., Lucker, K. D., & Weil, T. M. (1998). On the effects of noncontingent delivery of differing magnitudes of reinforcement. *Journal of Applied Behavior Analysis, 31,* 313–321.

Carr, J. E., & Burkholder, E. O. (1998). Creating single-subject design graphs with Microsoft excel™. *Journal of Applied Behavior Analysis, 31,* 245–251.

Carr, J. E., Coriatry, S., Wilder, D. A., Gaunt, B. T., Dozier, C. L. Britton, L. N., et al. (2000). A review of "noncontingent" reinforcement as treatment for the aberrant behavior of individuals with developmental disabilities. *Research in Developmental Disabilities, 21,* 377–391.

Carr, J. E., Nosik, M. R., & Luke, M. M. (2018). On the use of the term 'frequency' in applied behavior analysis. *Journal of Applied Behavior Analysis, 51,* 436-439. doi: 10.1002/jaba.449

Carr, J. E., & Sidener, T. M. (2002). On the relation between applied behavior analysis and positive behavioral support. *The Behavior Analyst, 25,* 245–253.

Carr, J. E., & Severtson, J. M. (2005). On the appropriateness of the term "noncontingent reinforcement." *European Journal of Behavior Analysis, 6,* 21–24.

Carr, J. E., Wilder, D. A., Majdalany, L., Mathisen, D., & Strain, L. A. (2013). An assessment-based solution to a human-service employee performance problem. *Behavior Analysis in Practice, 6,* 16–32. doi.org/10.1007/bf03391789.

Carroll, R. A., & Klatt, K. P. (2008). Using stimulus-stimulus pairing and direct reinforcement to teach vocal verbal behavior to young children with autism. *Analysis of Verbal Behavior, 24,* 135–146.

Carrol, R. A., & Kodak, T. (2015). Using instructive feedback to increase response varia-bility during intraverbal training for children with autism spectrum disorder. *Analysis of Verbal Behavior, 31* 183–199. doi: 10.1007/s40616-015-0039-x.

Carroll, R. A., Kodak, T., & Fisher, W. W. (2013). An evaluation of programmed treatment-integrity errors during discrete trial instruction. *Journal of Applied Behavior Analysis, 46,* 379–394.

Carroll, R. J., & Hesse, B. E. (1987). The effects of alternating mand and tact training on the acquisition of tacts. *The Analysis of Verbal Behavior, 5,* 55–65.

Carroll, R. A., Owsiany, J., & Cheatham, J. M. (2018). Using an abbreviated assessment to identify effective error-correction procedures for individual learners during discrete-trial instruction. *Journal of Applied Behavior Analysis, 51,* 482–501. doi: 10.1002/jaba.460

Carter, C. M. (2001). Using choice with game play to increase language skills and interactive behaviors in children with autism. *Journal of Positive Behavior Interventions, 3,* 131–151.

Carter, M., & Grunsell, J. (2002). The behavior chain interruption strategy: A review of research and discussion of future directions. *Journal of the Association for Persons with Severe Handicaps, 26*(1), 37–49.

Carton, J. S., & Schweitzer, J. B. (1996). Use of a token economy to increase compliance during hemodialysis. *Journal of Applied Behavior Analysis, 29,* 111–113.

Catagnus, R. M., Hineline, P. N., & Brown, T. W. (2020). Transferring cues for cooperation: Helping students follow group instructions. *Behavioral Interventions, 35*(3), 414–431. https://doi-org.mimas.calstatela.edu/10.1002/bin.1715

Cataldo, M. F. (1991). The effects of punishment and other behavior reducing procedures on the destructive behaviors of persons with developmental disabilities. In U. S. Department of Health and Human Services. *Treatment of destructive behaviors in persons with developmental disabilities* (pp. 231–341) (NIH Publication No. 91–02410). Bethesda, MD: National Institutes of Health.

Catania, A. C. (1968). *Contemporary research in operant behavior.* Glenview, IL: Scott, Foresman.

Catania, A. C. (1969). Concurrent performances: Inhibition of one response by reinforcement of another. *Journal of the Experimental Analysis of Behavior, 12,* 731–744.

Catania, A. C. (1975). Freedom and knowledge: An experimental analysis of preference in pigeons. *Journal of the Experimental Analysis of Behavior, 24,* 89–106.

Catania, A. C. (2017). *The ABCs of behavior analysis: An introduction to behavior and learning.* Cornwall-on-Hudson, NY: Sloan Publishing.

Catania, A. C., & Sagvolden, T. (1980). Preference for free choice over forced choice in pigeons. *Journal of the Experimental Analysis of Behavior, 34,* 77–86.

Catania, A. C. (2005a). The nonmaintenance of behavior by noncontingent reinforcement. *European Journal of Behavior Analysis, 6,* 898–914.

Catania, A. C. (2005b). The operant reserve: A computer simulation in (accelerated) real time. *Behaviorural Processes, 69,* 257–278.

Catania, A. C. (2005c). Attention-deficit/hyperactivity disorder (ADHD): One process or many? *Behavioral and Brain Sciences, 28,* 446–450.

Catania, A. C. (2013). *Learning,* 5th Ed. Cornwall on Hudson, NY: Sloan Publishing.

Catania, A.C. (2008, March). Basic operant contingencies: Main effects and side effects. In W. Fisher, *Handbook of applied behavior analysis.* Center for Effective Discipline Website

Catania, A. C., Lowe, C. R., & Horne, P. (1990). Nonverbal behavior correlated with the shaped verbal behavior of children. *Analysis of Verbal Behavior, 8,* 43–55.

Catania, A. C., Matthews, B. A., & Shimoff, E. (1982). Instructed versus shaped human verbal behavior: Interactions with nonverbal responding. *Journal of the Experimental Analysis of Behavior, 38,* 233–248.

Catania, A. C., Sagvolden, T. (1980). Preference for free choice over forced choice in pigeons. *Journal of the Experimental Analysis of behavior, 34,* 77–86.

Catania, A.C., Sagvolden, R., & Keller, K. J. (1988). Reinforcement schedules: Retroactive and proactive effects of reinforcers inserted into fixed-interval performances. *Journal of the Experimental Analysis of Behavior, 49,* 49–73.

Cautela, J. R., & Groden, J. (1978). *Relaxation: A comprehensive manual for adult, children, and children with special need.* Champaign, IL: Research Press.

Cautilli, J., Riley-Tillman, C., Axelrod, S., & Hineline, P. (2005). Current behavioral models of client and consultee resistance: A critical review. *International Journal of Behavioral Consultation and Therapy, 2*(1), 147–164.

Cates, G. L., Skinner, C. H., Watkins, C. E., Rhymer, K. N., McNeill, S. L., & McCurdy, M. (1999). Effects of interspersing additional brief math problems on student performance and perception of math assignments: Getting students to prefer to do more work. *Journal of Behavioral Education, 9,* 177–192.

Cavalier, A.R., Ferretti, R.P., & Hodges, A.E. (1997). Self-management within a classroom token economy for students with learning disabilities. *Research in Developmental Disabilities, 18*(3) 167–178.

Cavanaugh, R. A., Heward, W. L., & Donelson, F. (1996). Effects of response cards during lesson closure on the academic performance of secondary students in an earth science course. *Journal of Applied Behavior Analysis, 29,* 403–406.

Cengher, M., Budd, A., Farrell, N., & Fienup, D. M. (2018). A review of prompt-fading procedures: Implications for Effective and Efficient skill acquisition. *Journal of Developmental and Physical Disabilities, 30,* 155–173.

Cengher, M., & Fienup, D. M. (2020). Presession attention affects the acquisition of tacts and intraverbals. *Journal of Applied Behavior Analysis, 53,* 1742–1767. doi: 10.1002/jaba.657

Cengher, M., Shaman, I. Moss, P., Roll, D., Feliciano, G., & Flenup, D. M. (2016). A comparison of the effects of two prompt-fading strategies on skill acquisition in children with autism spectrum disorders. *Behavior Analysis in Practice, 9,* 115–125.

Center, D. B., & Wascom, A. M. (1984). Transfer of reinforcers: A procedure to enhance response cost. *Educational and Psychological Research, 4,* 19–27.

Chafouleas, S. M., Riley-Tillman, T. C., & Sassu, K. A. (2006). Acceptability and reported use of daily behavior report cards among teachers. *Journal of Positive Behavior Interventions, 8*(3), 174–182.

Chafouleas, S. M., Riley-Tillman, R. C., Sassu, K. A., LaFrance, J. J., & Patwa, S. S. (2007). Daily behavior report cards: An investigation of the consistency of on-task data across raters and methods. *Journal of Positive Behavior Interventions, 9,* 30–37.

Chan, P. E., Crosland, K. A., & Fogel, V. A. (2016). Reducing phobic behavior near wa-ter and increasing water approach skills. *Behavioral Interventions, 31,* 163–179. doi: 10.1002/bin.1443

Chan, S. C. H. (2019). Participative leadership and job satisfaction: mediating role of work engagement and the moderating role of fun experienced at work. Leadership & Or-ganization Development Journal, 40(3), 319-333. https://doi.org/10.1108/LODJ-06-2018-0215

Chandler, L.K., Lubeck, R.C. & Fowler, S.A. (1992). Generalization and maintenance of preschool children's social skills: a critical review and analysis. *Journal of Applied Behavior Analysis, 25,* 415–428.

Chappell, L. R., & Leibowitz, J. M. (1982). Effectiveness of differential reinforcement as a function of past reinforcement and present schedule. *Psychological Reports, 51,* 647–659.

Charlop-Christy, M.H., Carpenter, M., Le, L., LeBlanc, L.A., & Kellet, K. (2002). Using the picture exchange communication system (PECS) with children with autism: Assessment of PECS acquisition, speech, social-communicative behavior, and problem behavior. *Journal of Applied Behavior Analysis, 35,* 213–231.

Charlop-Christy, M. H., & Daneshvar, S. (2003). Using video modeling to teach perspective taking to children with autism. *Journal of Positive Behavior Interventions, 5,* 12–21.

Charlop-Christy, M. H., & Milstein, J. P. (1989). Teaching autistic children conversational speech using video modeling. *Journal of Applied Behavior Analysis, 22,* 275–285.

Charlop, M., Malmberg, D.B., & Berquist, K.L. (2008). An application of the picture exchange communication system (PECS) with children with autism and a visually impaired therapist. *Developmental Physical Disabilities, 20,* 509–525.

Charlop, M. H., Burgio, L. D., Iwata, B. A., & Ivancic, M.T. (1988). Stimulus variation as a means of enhancing punishment effects. *Journal of Applied Behavior Analysis, 21,* 89–95.

Charlop, M. H., & Walsh, M. E. (1986). Increasing autistic children's spontaneous verbalizations of affection: An assessment of time delay and peer modeling procedures. *Journal of Applied Behavior Analysis, 19,* 307–314.

Chase, P. N. (2006). In response: Teaching the distinction between positive and negative reinforcement. *The Behavior Analyst, 29,* 113–115.

Chase, P. N., & Danforth, J. S. (1991). The role of rules in concept learning. In L. J. Hayes & P. N. Chase (Eds.), *Dialogues on verbal behavior* (pp. 205–225). Reno, NV: Context Press.

Cheung, S. (2017). Effects of administration conspicuous rounding on acute care staff pain rounding. Master Thesis, CSULA.

Cheung, C. C., & Winter, S. (1999). Class-wide peer tutoring with or without reinforcement: Effects on academic responding, content coverage, achievement, intrinsic interest and reported project experiences. *Educational Psychology, 19,* 191–214.

Chomsky, N. (1959). A review of B.F. Skinner's Verbal Behavior. *Language, 35,* 26–58.

Christensen, A., Wallace, M. D., Romick, K., Houchins, N., Landaburu, H., Tarbox, J., & Tarbox, R. (2002, February). *The systematic development of an indirect assessment: Indirect Functional behavioral assessment.* Presented at the annual meeting of the California Association for Behavior Analysis, San Francisco, CA.

Christensen, L., Young, K. R., & Marchant, M. (2004). The effects of peer-mediated positive behavior support program on socially appropriate classroom behavior. *Education and Treatment of Children, 27,* 199–234.

Christy, P. R. (1975). Does use of tangible rewards with individual children affect peer observers? *Journal of Applied Behavior Analysis, 8,* 187–196.

Chung, K., Reavis, S., Mosconi, M., Drewry, J., Matthews, T., & Tasse, M. J. (2006). Peer-mediated social skills training program for young children with high-functioning autism. *Research in Developmental Disabilities, 28* (4), 423–436.

Church, R. M. (1963). The varied effects of punishment on behavior. *Psychological Review, 70,* 369–402.

Cicero, F.R., & Pfadt, A. (2002). Investigation of a reinforcement-based toilet training procedure for children with autism. *Research in Developmental Disabilities, 23,* 5, 319–331.

Cihak, D., Alberto, Pl A., & Fredrick, L. D. (2007). Use of brief functional analysis and intervention evaluation in public settings. *Journal of Positive Behavior Interventions, 9,* 80–93.

Cihak, D., Fahrenkrog, C., Ayres, K. M., & Smith C. (2010). The use of video modeling via a video iPod and a system of least prompts to improve transitional behaviors for students with autism spectrum disorders in the general education classroom. *Journal of Positive Behavior Interventions, 12,* 103–115.

Cihelkova, D., Hursh, D., Durica, K., Stausbaugh, E., Yurich, K., Tucci, V., & Schlosnagle, L. (2012). *The impact of the competent learner model on the GARS, Viineland, and PLS outcomes for children with autism spectrum disorder.* AUCD Conference Poster.

Cihon, J. H., Ferguson, J. L., Milne, C. M., Leaf, J. B., McEachin, J., & Leaf, R. (2019). A preliminary evaluation of a token system with a flexible earning requirement. *Behavior Analysis in Practice, 12,* 548–565. doi: org/10.1007/s40617-018-00316-3

Cirelli, C. A., Sidener, T. M., Reeve, K. F., & Reeve, S. A. (2016). Using activity schedules to increase on-task behavior in children at risk for attention-deficit/hyperactivity disorder. (2016). *Education and Treatment of Children, 39,* 283–300.

Cividini-Motta, C., Moore, K., Fish, L. M., Priehs, J. C., & Ahearn, W. H. (2020). Reducing public masturbation in individuals with ASD: An assessment of response interruption procedures. *Behavior Modification, 44,* 394–428. https://doi.org/10.1177/0145445518824277

Claerhout, S., & Lutzker, J. R. (1981). Increasing children's self-initiated compliance to dental regimens. *Behavior Therapy, 12,* 165–176.

Clare, L., Wilson, B.A., Carter, G., Breen, K., Gosses, A., & Hodges, J.R. (2000). Intervening with everyday memory problems in dementia of Alzheimer type: An errorless learning approach. *Journal of Clinical and Experimental Neuropsychologia, 22*(1), 132–146.

Clark, H. B., Brandon, F. G., Macrae, J. W., McNees, M. R., Davis, F. L., & Risley, T. R. (1977). A parent advice package for family shopping trips: development and evaluation. *Journal of Applied Behavior Analysis, 10,* 605–624.

Clark, H. B., Rowbury, T., Baer, A. M., & Baer, D. M. (1973). Timeout as a punishing stimulus in continous and intermittent schedules. *Journal of Applied Behavior Analysis, 6,* 443–455.

Clark, K. M., & Green, G. (2004). Comparison of two procedures for teaching dictated-word/symbol relations to learners with autism. *Journal of Applied Behavior Analysis, 37,* 503–507.

Clark, R. J., Wilder, D. A., Kelley, M. E., & Ryan, V. (2020). Evaluation of instructions and video modeling to train parents to implement a structured meal procedure for food selectivity among children with autism. *Behavior Analysis in Practice, 13,* 674–678. doi.org/10. 1007/s40617-120-00419-w

Clarke, L. S., Haydon, R., Bauer, A., & Epperly, A. C. (2016). Inclusion of students with an intellectual disability in the general education classroom with the use of response cards. *Preventing School Failure: Alternative Education for Children and Youth, 60* (1), 35–42. https://doi.org/10.1080/1045988X.2014.966801

Clarke, S., Remington, B., & Light, P. (1986). An evaluation of the relationship between receptive speech skills and expressive signing. *Journal of Applied Behavior Analysis, 19,* 231–239.

Clauser, B., & Gould, K. (2006). Visual screening as a reductive procedure: An examination of generalization and duration. *Behavioral Interventions, 3*(1), 51–61.

Clayton, M., Helms, B., & Simpson, C. (2006). Active prompting to decrease cell phone use and increase seat belt use while driving. *Journal of Applied Behavior Analysis, 39,* 341–349.

Clement, P. W. (1999). *Outcomes and incomes: How to evaluate and improve your psychotherapy practice by measuring outcomes.* New York: Guilford.

Codding, R. S., Feinberg, A. B., Dunn, E. K., & Pace, G. M. (2005). Effects of immediate performance feedback on implementation of behavior support plans. *Journal of Applied Behavior Analysis, 38,* 205–219.

Codding, R. S., Livanis, A., Pace, G. M., & Vaca, L. (2008). Using performance feedback to improve treatment integrity of classwide behavior plans: An investigation of observer reactivity. *Journal of Applied Behavior Analysis, 41,* 417–422.

Cohen, P. A., Kulik, J. A., & Kulik, C. C. (1982). Educational outcomes of teaching. *American Educational Research Journal, 19,* 237–297.

Cohen, S., Richardson, J., Klebez, J., Febbo, S., & Tucker, D. (2001). EMG feedback: The effects of CRF. FR, VR, FI, & VI schedules of reinforcement on the acquisition and extinction of increases in forearm muscle tension. *Applied Psychophysiology and Biofeedback, 26, 3,* 227–248.

Cohrs, C. M., Shriver, M. D., Burke, R. V., & Allen K. D. (2016). Evaluation of increas-ing intecededent specificity in goal statements on adherence to positive behavior-management strategies. *Journal of Applied Behavior Analysis, 49,* 768–779. doi: 10.1002/jaba.321.

Cole, G. A., Montgomery, R.W., Wilson, K.M., & Milan, M.A. (2000). Parametric analysis of overcorrection duration effects. Is longer really better than shorter? *Behavior Modification, 24,* 359–378.

Collier-Meek, M. A.,Sanetti, L. M., Fallon, L. M. (2017). Incorporating applied behavior analysis to assess and support educators' treatment integrity. *Psychology in the Schools, 54,* 446–460. doi:10:1002/pits.22001

Collins, M., Carnine, D., & Gersten, R. (1987). Elaborated corrective feedback and the acquisition of reasoning skills: A study of computer-assisted instruction. *Exceptional Children, 54,* 254–262.

Collins, S., Higbee, T. S., & Salzberg, C. L. (2009). The effects of video modeling on staff implementation of a problem-solving intervention with adults with developmental disabilities. *Journal of Applied Behavior Analysis, 42,* 489–854.

Collins, T. R., Gresham, F. M., & Dart, E. H. (2016). The effects of peer mediated check-in/check-out on the social skills of socially neglected students. *Behavior Modification, 40,* 568–588.

Colombo, R. A., Wallace, M., Taylor, R. (2020). An essential service decision model for ABA providers during crises. *Behavior Analysis in Practice, 13,* 306–311.

Colón, C.L. and Ahearn, W.H. (2019), An analysis of treatment integrity of response interruption and redirection. *Journal of Applied Behavior Analysis, 52,* 337–354. https://doi-org.mimas.calstatela.edu/10.1002/jaba.537

Common, E.A., Bross, L. A., Oakes, W. P., Cantwell, E. D., Lane, K. L., & Germer, K. A. (2019). Systematic review of high probability requests in K-12 settings: Examining the evidence base. *Behavioral Disorders, 45,* 3–21. doi.org.10.1177/0198742916800029

Conine, D. E., Vollmer, T. R., & Bolivar, H. A. (2020). Response to name in children with autism: Treatment, generalization and maintenance. *Journal of Applied Behavior Analysis, 53,* 744–766. doi: 10.1002/jaba.635

Conn, V.S., Hafdahl, H.R., Brown, S. A., & Brown, L. M. (2008). Meta-analysis of patient education interventions to increase physical activity among chronically ill adults. *Patient Education and Counseling, 70,* 157–172.

Connell, J. E., & Witt, J. C. (2004). Applications of computer-based instruction: using specialized software to aid letter-name and letter-sound recognition. *Journal of Applied Behavior Analysis, 37,* 67–71.

Conners, J., Iwata, B. A., Kahng, S. W., Hanley, G. P., Worsdell, A. S., & Thompson, R. H. (2000). Differential responding in the presence and absence of discriminative stimuli during multielement functional analyses. *Journal of Applied Behavior Analysis, 33,* 299–308.

Connolly, J. F., Moore, A., & Adamy, P. H. (2019). Seven underlying conditions that led to the use of seclusion and resulted in due process hearings. *Journal of Special Education Leadership, 32*(2), 86–102.

Conroy, M.A., Fox, J.J., Bucklin, A., & Good, W. (1996). An analysis of the reliability and stability of the motivation assessment scale in assessing the challenging behaviors of persons with developmental disabilities. *Education and Training in Mental Retardation and Developmental Disabilities, 31,* 243–250.

Constantine, B., & Sidman, M. (1975). The role of naming in delayed matching to sample. *American Journal of Mental Deficiency, 79,* 680–689.

Contreras, B. P., & Betz, A. M. (2016). Using lag schedules to strengthen the intraverbal repertoires of children with autism. *Journal of Applied Behavior Analysis, 49,* 3–16. doi:10.1002/jaba.271.

Conyers, C., Miltenberger, R. G., Peterson, B., Gubin, A., Jurgens, M., Selders, A., et al. (2004). An evaluation of in vivo desensitization and video modeling to increase compliance with dental procedures in persons with mental retardation. *Journal of Applied Behavior Analysis, 37,* 233–238.

Cook, C.R., Crews. S.D., Browning Wright, D., Mayer, G.R., Gale, B., Kraemer, B., & Gresham, F.M. (2007). Establishing and evaluating the substantive adequacy of positive behavioral support plans. *Journal of Behavioral Education,* 16, 191–206.

Cook, C. R., Fiat, A., Larson, M., Daikos, C., Slemrod, T., Holland, E. A., Thayer, A. J. & Renshaw, T. (2018). Positive greetings at the door: Evaluation of a low-cost, high-yield Proactive classroom management strategy. *Journal of Positive Behavior Interventions, 20,* 149–159. doi.org/10.1177/1098300717753831

Cook, C. R., Mayer, G. R., Browning-Wright, D., Kraemer, B., Wallace, M., Dart, E., & Collins, T. (2010). Exploring the link between evidence-based behavior intervention plans and student outcomes: An initial effectiveness study. *The Journal of Special Education, 41,* (Published online before print, May, 2010. http://sed.sagepub.com/content/early/2010.)

Cook, C. R., Grady, E. A., Long, A. C., Renshaw, R., Codding, R. S., Fiat, A., & Larson, M. (2016). Evaluating the impact of increasing general education teachers ratio of positive-to-negative interactions on students' classroom behavior. *Journal of Positive Behavior Interventions, 18,* 1–11. doi: 10:1177/1098300716679137

Cook, J. L., Rapp, J. T., Goes, L. A., Frazer, T. J., & Lindblad, T. L. (2014). Effects of verbal reprimands on targeted and untargeted stereotypy. *Behavioral Interventions, 29,* 106–124. doi: 10.1002/bin.1378

Cook, T. D., & Campbell, D. T. (1979). *Quasi-experimentation: Design & analysis issues for field settings.* Chicago: Rand McNally College Publishing Company.

Cooke, T. P., & Apolloni, T. (1976). Developing positive social-emotive behaviors: A study of training and generalization effects. *Journal of Applied Behavior Analysis, 9,* 65–78.

Cooper, J. O., Heron, T. E., & Heward, W. L. (1987). *Applied behavior analysis.* Columbus, OH: Merill Publishing Co.

Cooper, L. J., Wacker, D. P., Brown, K., McComas, J. J., Peck, S.M., Drew, J., et al. (1999). Use of a concurrent operants paradigm to evaluate positive reinforcers during treatment of food refusal. *Behavior Modification, 23,* 3–40.

Cooper, L. J., Wacker, D. P., McComas, J. J., Brown, K., et al. (1995). Use of a component analysis to identify active variables in treatment packages for children with feeding disorders. *Journal of Applied Behavior Analysis, 28,* 139–153.

Coppage, S., & Meindl, J. N. (2017). Using video to bridge the gap between problem behavior and a delayed time-out procedure. *Behavior Analysis in Practice, 10,* 285–289. doi: 10.1007/s40617-017-0197-5

Corralejo, S. M., Jensen, S. A., Greathouse, A. D. (2018). Time-out for subling aggression: An analysis of effective durations in a natural setting. *Child & Family Behavior Therapy, 40,* 187–203. http://doi.org/10.1080/07317107.2018.1487701

Correa, V. I., Poulson, C. L., & Salzberg, C. L. (1984). Training and generalization of reach-grasp behavior in blind, retarded young children. *Journal of Applied Behavior Analysis, 17,* 57–69.

Corrigan, P. W., William, O. B., McCracken, S. G., Kommana, S., Edwards, M., & Brunner, J. (1998). Staff attitudes that impede the implementation of behavioral treatment programs. *Behavior Modification, 22,* 548–562.

Cosden, M., Gannon, D., & Haring, T.G. (1995). Teacher-control versus student-control over choice of task and reinforcement for students with severe behavior problems. *Journal of Behavioral Education, 5,* 11–27.

Cossairt, A., Hall, R. V., & Hopkins, B. L. (1973). The effects of experimenter's instructions, feedback, and praise on teacher praise and student attending behavior. *Journal of Applied Behavior Analysis, 6,* 89–100.

Costello, K. M., & Smyth, S. (2017). Group contingencies increase school and project attendance in at-risk adolescents: A pilot study. *Education and Treatment of Children, 40,* 379–400.

Cote, C. A., Thompson, R. H., Hanley, G. P., & McKerchar, P. (2007). Teacher report and direct assessment of preferences for identifying reinforcers for young children. *Journal of Applied Behavior Analysis, 40,* 157–166.

Cotton, J. L., Vollrath, D. A., Froggatt, A. L., Lengnick-Hall, M. L., & Jennings, K. R. (1988). Employee participation: Diverse forms and different outcomes. *Academy of Management Review, 13,* 8–22.

Coyle, J.A., & Robertson, J. (1998). Comparison of two passive mobilizing techniques following Colles' fracture: A multi-element design. *Manual Therapy, 3*(1), 34–41.

Craft, M. A., Alber, S. R., & Heward, W. L. (1998). Teaching elementary students with developmental disabilities to recruit teacher attention in a general education classroom: Effects on teacher praise and academic productivity. *Journal of Applied Behavior Analysis, 31,* 399–415.

Craig, A. R., & Fisher, W. W. (2019). Randomization tests as alternative analysis methods for behavior analytic data. *Journal of the Experimental Analysis of Behavior, 111,* 309–328.

Craighead, W. E., Mercatoris, M., & Bellack, B. (1974). A brief report on mentally retarded residents as behavioral observers. *Journal of Applied Behavior Analysis, 7,* 333–340.

Creer, T. L., Kotses, H., Wigal, J. K. (1992) A second-generation model of asthma self-management. *Pediatric Asthma, Allergy & Immunology, 6*(3) 143-165.

Critchfield, T. S. (1999). An unexpected effect of recording frequency in reactive self-monitoring. *Journal of Applied Behavior Analysis, 32,* 389–391.

Critchfield, T. S. (2017). Visuwords®: A handy online tool for estimating what non-experts may think when hearing behavior analysis jargon. *Behavior Analysis in Practice, 10*, 318-322. doi: 10.1007/s40617-017-0173-0

Critchfield, T. S., Doepke, K. J., Epting, L. K., Becirevic, A., Reed, D. D., Fienup, D. M., Kremsreiter, J. L., & Ecott, C. L. (2017). Normative emotional responses to behavior analysis jargon or how not to use words to win friends and influence people. *Behavior Analysis in Practice, 10*, 97–106. doi: 10.1007/s40617-016-0161-9

Critchfield, T. S., & Kollins, S. H. (2001). Temporal discounting: Basic research and the analysis of socially important behavior. *Journal of Applied Behavior Analysis, 34*, 101–122.

Cronbach, L.J., & Meehl, P.E. (1955). Construct validity in psychological tests. *Psychological Bulletin, 52*(4), 281–302.

Crone, D. A., Hawken, L. S., & Bergstrom, M. K. (2007). A demonstration of training, implementing and using functional assessment in 10 elementary and middle school settings. *Journal of Positive Behavior Intervention, 9*, 15–29.

Crone, R. M., & Mehta, S. S. (2016). Parent training on generalized use of behavior analytic strategies for decreasing the problem behavior of children with autism spectrum. *Education and Treatment of Children, 39*, 64–94.

Croner, M. D., & Willis, R. G. (1961). Perceived differences in task competency and asymmetry of dyadic influence. *Journal of Abnormal Psychology, 31*, 68–95.

Cronin, J. (1982). A comparison of two types of antecedent control over supervisory behavior. *Journal of Organizational Behavior Management, 4*, 37–47.

Cronin, K. A., & Cuvo, A.G. (1979). Teaching mending skills to mentally retarded adolescents. *Journal of Applied Behavior Analysis, 12*, 401–406.

Crosbie, J., Williams, A.M., Lattal, K.A., Anderson, M.M., & Brown, S.M. (1997). Schedule interactions involving punishment with pigeons and humans. *Journal of the Experimental Analysis of Behavior, 68*, 161–175.

Crowell, C. R., Anderson, D. C., Abel, D. M., & Sergio, J. P. (1988). Task clarification, performance feedback and social praise: Procedures for improving the customer service of bank teller. *Journal of Applied Behavior Analysis, 21*, 65–71.

Crozier, S., & Tincani, M. J. (2005). Using a modified social story to decrease disruptive behavior of a child with autism. *Focus on Autism an Other Developmental Disabilities, 20*(2), 150–157.

Culig, K., M., Dickinson, A. M., Lindstrom-Hazel, D., & Austin, J. (2008). Combining workstation design and performance management to increase ergonomically correct computer typing postures. *Journal of Organizational Behavior Management, 28*(3), 148–175.

Cummings, C., & Saunders, K. J. (2019). Using PowerPoint 2016 to create individualized matching to sample sessions. *Behavior Analysis in Practice, 12*, 483–490. https://doi.org/ao.1007/s40617-018-0223-2

Cunningham, C. E., Bremner, R., & Boyle, M. (1995). Large group community-based parenting programs for families of preschoolers at risk for disruptive behavior disorders: Utilization, cost effectiveness, and outcome. *Journal of Child Psychology and Psychiatry, 36*, 1141–1159.

Cunningham, T. R., & Austin, J. (2007). Using goal setting, task clarification and feedback to increase the use of hands-free technique by hospital operating room staff. *Journal of Applied Behavior Analysis, 40*, 673–677.

Cuvo, A. J. (1978). Validating task analyses of community living skills. *Vocational Evaluation and Work Adjustment Bulletin, 11*, 13–21.

Cuvo A. J, Lerch, L. J., Leurquin, D.A, Gaffaney, T.J., & Poppen, R. L. (1998). Response allocation to concurrent fixed-ratio reinforcement schedules with work requirements by adults with mental retardation and typical preschool children. *Journal of Applied Behavior Analysis, 31*, 43–63.

Dalton, T., Martella, R. C., & Marchand-Martella, N. E. (1999). The effects of a self-management program in reducing off-task behavior. *Journal of Behavioral Education, 9*, 157–176.

Dalrymple, A.J., & Feldman, M.A. (1992). Effects of reinforced directed rehearsal on expressive sign language learning by persons with mental retardation. *Journal of Behavioral Education, 2*, 1–16.

Danaher, B. G., Boles, S., Akers, B., Gordon, J. S., & Severson, J. H. (2006). Defining participant exposure measures in web-based health behavior change programs. *Journal of Medical Internet Research, 8*, 3, e (15).

Daneshvar, S. D., Charlop, M. H., & Malmberg, D. B. (2019). A treatment comparison study of a photo activity schedule and social stories for teaching social skills to children with autism spectrum disorder; brief report. *Developmental Neurorehabilitation, 22*, 209-214. doi.org/10.1080/17518423.2018.1461947

Danielle, S., Pennsylvania Case No. 320, EHLR 509:142 (Pa. SEA 1987)

Daniels, A. C. (1989). *Performance management.* Tucker, GA: Performance Management Publications.

Daniels, A.C. (1994). *Bringing out the best in people.* New York: McGraw Hill.

Daniels, A. C. (2001). *Other people's habits: How to use positive reinforcement to bring out the best in people around you.* New York: McGraw-Hill.

Daniels, A. C., & Daniels, J. E. (2004). *Performance management: changing behaviors that drive organizational effectiveness.* Atlanta, GA: Performance Management Publications.

Daniels, A. C., & Lattal, A. D. (2017). *Life's a PIC/NIC® ... when you understand behavior.* Cornwall on Hudson, NY. Sloan Publishing.

Darcheville, J. C., Riviere, V., & Wearden, J. H. (1993). Fixed-interval performance and self-control in infants. *Journal of Experimental Analysis of Behavior, 60*, 239–254.

Darwin, C. (1872/1958). *The origin of species* (6th ed.). New York: Mentor. (Original work published in 1872.)

Davidson, N. A., & Osborne, J. G. (1974). Fixed ratio and fixed interval schedule control of matching-to-sample errors by children. *Journal of the Experimental Analysis of Behavior, 21*, 27–36.

Davis, D. R., Bostow, D. E., & Heimisson, F. T. (2007). Strengthening scientific verbal behavior: An experimental comparison of progressively prompted and unprompted programmed instructions and prose tutorials. *Journal of Applied Behavior Analysis, 40*, 179–184.

Davis, C. A., Brady, M. P., Hamilton, R., McEvoy, M. A., & Williams, R. E. (1994). Effects of high-probability requests on the social interactions of young children with severe disabilities. *Journal of Applied Behavior Analysis, 27,* 619–637.

Davis, C. A., Brady, M., Williams, R., & Hamilton, R. (1992). Effects of high-probability requests on the acquisition and generalization of responding to requests in young children with behavior disorders. *Journal of Applied Behavior Analysis, 25,* 905–916.

Davis, C. A., Reichle, J. E., & Southard, K. L. (2000). High-probability requests and a preferred item as a distractor: Increasing successful transitions in children with behavior problems. *Education and Treatment of Children, 23,* 423–440.

Davis, T. N., Hodges, A., Weston, R., Hogan, E., & Padilla-Mainor, K. (2017). Correspondence between preference assessment outcomes and stimulus reinforcer value for social interactions. *Journal of Behavioral Education, 26,* 238–249. doi:10.1007/s10864-017-9271-x.

Davis, T. N., Machalicek, W., Scalzo, R., Kobylecky, A., Campbell, V., Pinkelman, S., Chan, J. M., & Sigafoos, J. (2016). A review and treatment selection model for individuals with developmental disabilities who engage in inappropriate sexual behavior. *Behavior Analysis in Practice, 9,* 389–402. doi: 10.1007/s40617-015-0062-3

Dawson, G., & Adams, A. (1984). Imitation and social responsiveness in autistic children. *Journal of Abnormal Child Psychology, 12,* 209–226.

Day, H. M., Horner, R. H., & O'Niell, R. E. (1994). Multiple functions of problem behaviors: Assessment and intervention. *Journal of Applied Behavior Analysis, 27,* 279–289.

Day-Watkins, J., Murray, R., & Connell, J. E. (2014). Teaching helping to adolescents with autism. *Journal of Applied Behavior Analysis, 47,* 850-855. DOI: 10.1002/jaba.156

DeBaryshe, B. D., Patterson, G. R., & Capaldi, D. M. (1993). A performance model for academic achievement in early adolescent boys. *Developmental Psychology, 29,* 795–804.

DeCasper, A. J., & Fifer, W. P. (1980). Of human bonding: Newborns prefer their mother's voices. *Science, 208,* 1174–1176.

De Castro, B. O., Bosch, J. D., Veerman, J. W., & Koops, W. (2003). The effects of emotion regulation, attribution, and delay prompts on aggressive boys' social problem solving. *Cognitive Therapy and Research, 27,* 153–166.

Deckner, C. S., Deckner, P. O., & Blanton, R. L. (1982). Sustained responding under intermittent reinforcement in psychotic children. *Journal of Abnormal Child Psychology, 10,* 203–213.

Deitz, S. M., & Malone, L. W. (1985). Stimulus control terminology. *The Behavior Analyst, 8,* 259–264.

Deitz, S. M., & Repp, A. C. (1973). Decreasing classroom misbehavior through the use of DRL schedules of reinforcement. *Journal of Applied Behavior Analysis, 6,* 457–463.

Deitz, S. M., & Repp, A. C. (1974). Differentially reinforcing low rates of misbehavior with normal elementary school children. *Journal of Applied Behavior Analysis, 7,* 622.

Deitz, S. M., Slack, D. J., Schwarzmueller, E. B., Wilander, A. P., Weatherly, T. J., & Hilliard, G. (1978). Reducing inappropriate behavior in special classrooms by reinforcing average interresponse times: Interval DRL. *Behavior Therapy, 9,* 37–46.

Delano, M. E. (2007). Improving written language performance of adolescents with Asperger syndrome. *Journal of Applied Behavior Analysis, 40,* 345–351.

Delano, M., & Snell, M. E. (2006). The effects of social stories on the social engagement of children with autism. *Journal of Positive Behavior Interventions, 8,* 29–42.

DeLeon, I. G., Chase, J. A., Frank-Crawford, M. A., Carreau-Webster, A. B., Triggs, M. M., Bullock, C. E., & Jennett, h. K. (2014). Distributed and accumulated reinforcement arrangements: evaluations of efficacy and preference. *Journal of Applied Behavior Analysis, 47,* 293–313. doi:10.1002/jaba.116

DeLeon, I. G., Iwata, B. A., Conners, J., & Wallace, M. D. (1999). Examination of ambiguous stimulus preferences with duration-based measures. *Journal of Applied Behavior Analysis, 32,* 111–114.

DeLeon, I. G., Neidert, P. L., Anders, B. M., & Rodriguez-Catter, V. (2001). Choices between positive and negative reinforcement during treatment for escape-maintained behavior. *Journal of Applied Behavior Analysis, 34,* 521–525.

Deliperi, P., Viadescu, J. C., Reeve, K. F., Reeve, S. A., & DeBar, R. M. (2015). Training staff to implement a paired-stimulus preference assessment using video modeling with voiceover instruction. *Behavioral Interventions, 30,* 241–332. doi: 10.1002/bin.1421

Delprato, D. J. (2001). Comparisons of discrete-trial and normalized behavioral language intervention for young children with autism. *Journal of Autism and Developmental Disorders, 31,* 315–325.

Delquadri, J., Greenwood, C. R., Whorton, D., Carta, J. J., & Hall, R. V. (1986). Classwide peer tutoring. *Exceptional Children, 52,* 535–542.

De Luca, R. V., & Holborn, S. W. (1985). Effects of a fixed-interval schedule of token reinforcement on exercise with obese and non-obese boys. *The Psychological Record, 35,* 525–533.

De Luca, R. V., & Holborn, S. W. (1992). Effects of a variable-ratio reinforcement schedule with changing criteria on exercise in obese and nonobese boys. *Journal of Applied Behavior Analysis, 25,* 671–679.

Demchak, M. (1990). Response prompting and fading methods: A review. *American Journal of Retardation, 94,* 603–615.

Demetral, F. D., & Lutzker, J. R. (1980). The parameters of facial screening in treating self-injurious behavior. *Behavior Research of Severe Developmental Disabilities, 1,* 261–277.

Dengerink, K., & Mayer, G. R. (2018). Parent training: The effects of in-home coaching following workshops in Huaycan, Peru. Manuscript submitted for publication.

Deochand, N. (2017). Automating phase change lines and their labels using Microsoft Excel®. *Behavior Analysis in Practice, 10,* 279–284. doi: 10.1007/s40617-016-0169-1.

Deochand, N., Costello, M. S., & Fuqua, R W. (2015). Phase-change lines, scale breaks, and trend lines using Excell 2013. *Journal of Applied Behavior Analysis, 48,* 476–493.

DePaolo, J., Gravina, N. E., & Harvey, C. (2019). Using a behavioral intervention to improve performance of a women's college lacrosse team. *Behavior Analysis in Practice, 12,*

407–411. doi:.org/10.1007/s40617-018-0272-6.

DeRosa, N. M., Novak, M. D., Morley, A. J., & Roane, H. S. (2019). Comparing re-sponse blocking and response interruption/redirection on levels of motor stereotypy: Effects of data analysis procedures. *Journal of Applied Behavior Analysis, 52,* 1021–1033. doi: 10.1002/jaba.644.

DeQuinzio, J. A., & Taylor, B. A. (2015). Teaching children with autism to discriminate the reinforced and nonreinforced responses of others: Implications for observational learning. *Journal of Applied Behavior Analysis, 48,* 38–51. doi: 10.1002/jaba.192

DeQuinzio, J. A., Townsend, D. B., Sturmey, P., & Poulson, C. L. (2007). Generalized imitation of facial models by children with autism. *Journal of Applied Behavior Analysis, 40,* 755–759.

DeRicco, D. A., & Niemann, J. E. (1980). In vivo effects of peer modeling on drinking rate. *Journal of Applied Behavior Analysis, 13,* 149–152.

DeRosa, N. M., Roane, H. S., Bishop, J. R., & Silkowski, E. L. (2016). The combined effects of non contingent reinforcement and punishment on the reduction of rumination. *Journal of Applied Behavior Analysis, 49,* 680–685. doi: 10.1002/jaba.304

DeSouza, A. A., Akers, J. S., & Fisher, W. W. (2017). Empirical application of Skinner's verbal behavior to interventions for children with autism: A review. *Analysis of Verbal Behavior, 33,* 229–259. doi: 10.1007/s40616-017-0093-7

Devany, J. M., Hayes, S. C., & Nelson, R. (1986). Equivalence class formation in language-able and language-disabled children. *Journal of the Experimental Analysis of Behavior, 46,* 243–257.

Dibley, S., & Lim, L. (1999). Providing choice making opportunities within and between daily school routines. *Journal of Behavioral Education, 9,* 117–132.

Dickinson, A. M. (1989). The detrimental effects of extrinsic reinforcement on "intrinsic motivation," *The Behavior Analyst, 12,* 1–15.

Dickes, N. R., & Kodak, T. (2015). Evaluating at the emergence of reverse intraverbals following introverts training in young children with autism spectrum disorder. *Behavioral Interventions, 30,* 169–190. doi: 10.1002/bin.1412

Dickman, S. E., Bright, C. N., Montgomery, D. H., & Miguel, C. F. (2012). *Behavioral Interventions, 27,* 185–192. doi: 10.1002/bin.1348

DiGennaro, F. D., Martens, B. K., & Kleinmann, A. E. (2007). A comparison of performance feedback procedures on teachers' treatment implementation integrity and students' inappropriate behavior in special education classrooms. *Journal of Applied Behavior Analysis, 40,* 447–461.

Dineen J. P., Clark, H. B., & Risley, T. R. (1977). Peer tutoring among elementary students: Educational benefits to the tutor. *Journal of Applied Behavior Analysis, 10,* 231–238.

Dingman, L. A. (1978). How well-managed organizations develop their executive. *Organizational Dynamics,* Autumn, 63–77.

Dinsmoor, J. A., & Campbell, S. L. (1956). Escape-from-shock-training following exposure to inescapable shock. *Psychological Reports, 2,* 43–49.

Dishion, T. J. (1992, October). *An applied model of antisocial behavior.* Paper presented at a workshop for potential applicants for NIMH research grants to prevent youth violence, Bethesda, MD.

Dishion, T. J., French, D. C., & Patterson, G. R. (1995). The development and ecology of antisocial behavior. In D. Cicchetti & D. J. Cohen (Eds.), *Developmental psychopathology* (pp. 421–471). New York: John Wiley & Sons.

Dishion, T. J., Spracklen, K. M., Andrews, D. W., & Patterson, G. R. (1996). Deviancy training in male adolescent friendships. *Behavior Therapy, 27,* 373–390.

Dittlinger, L. H., & Lerman, D. C. (2011) Further analysis of picture interference when teaching word recognition to children with autism. *Journal of Applied Behavior Analysis 44*(2), 341–349.

Dixon, J.A., Helsel, W.J., Rojahn, J., & Cipollone, R. (1989). Aversive conditioning of visual screening with aromatic ammonia for treating aggressive and disruptive behavior in a developmentally disabled child. *Behavior Modification, 13,* 91–107.

Dixon, L.S. (1981). A functional analysis of photo-object matching skills of severely retarded adolescents. *Journal of Applied Behavior Analysis, 14,* 465–478.

Dixon, M. (1976). Teaching conceptual classes with receptive labale training. *Acta Symbolica, 7,* 17–35.

Dixon, M. R., Belisle, J., Stanley, C., Rowsey, K., Daar, J. H., & Szekely, S. (2015). Toward a behavior analysis of complex language for children with autism: Evaluating the relationship between PEAK and the VB-MAPP. *Journal of Developmental and Physical Disabilities, 27,* 223–233.

Dixon, M., Belisle, J., Stanley, C. R., Speelman, R. C., Rowsey, K. E., Kime, D., & Daar, J. H. (2017). Establishing derived categorical responding in children with disabilities using the PEAK-E curriculum. *Journal of Applied Behavior Analysis, 50,* 134–145. doi: 10.1002/jaba.355

Dixon, M. R., & Cummings, A. (2001). Self-control in children with autism: Response allocation during delays to reinforcement. *Journal of Applied Behavior Analysis, 34,* 491–495.

Dixon, M. R., Hayes, L. J., Binder, L. M., Manthey, S., Sigman, C., & Zdanowski, D. M. (1998). Using a self-control training procedure to increase appropriate behavior. *Journal of Applied Behavior Analysis, 31,* 203–210.

Dixon, M. R., Hayes, S. C., Stanley, C., Law, S., & al-Nasser, T. (2020). Is acceptance and commitment training or therapy (ACT) a method that applied behavior analysts can and should use? *Psychological Record, 70*(4), 559–579. https://doi-org.mimas.calstatela.edu/10.1007/s40732-020-00436-9

Dixon, M. R., Jackson, J. W., Small, S. L., Horner-King, M. J., Lik, N. M. K., Garcia, Y., & Rosales, R. (2009). Creating single-subject design graphs in Microsoft Excel™ 2007. *Journal of Applied Behavior Analysis, 42,* 277–293.

Dixon, M. R., Marley, J., & Jacobs, E. A. (2003). Delay discounting by pathological gamblers. *Journal of Applied Behavior Analysis, 36,* 449–458.

Dixon, M. R., & Tibbetts, P. A. (2009). The effects of choice on self-control. *Journal of Applied Behavior Analysis, 42,* 243–252.

Dodge, K. A., Schlundt, D.C., Schocken, I., & Delugach, J. D. (1983). Social competence and children's sociometric status: The rule of peer group entry strategies. *Merrill-Palmer Quarterly, 29,* 309–336.

Dogan, R. K., King, M. L., Fischetti, A. T., Lake, C. M., Mathews, T. L., & Warzak, W. J. (2017). *Journal of Applied Behavior Analysis, 50,* 805–818. doi: 10.1002/jaba.411

Doke, L. A., & Risley, T. R. (1972). The organization of day-care environments: Required versus optional activities. *Journal of Applied Behavior Analysis, 5,* 405–420.

Dolan, L.J., Kellam, S.G., Brown, C.H., Werthamer-Larsson, L., Rebok, G.W., Mayer, L.S., Laudoff, J., Turkkan, J.S., Ford, C., & Wheeler, L. (1993, July-September). The short-term impact of two classroom-based preventive interventions on aAggressive and shy behaviors and poor achievement. *Journal of Applied Developmental Psychology, 14*(3), 317–345.

Doleys, D. M., Wells, K. C., Hobbs, S. A., Roberts, M. W., & Cartelli, L. M. (1976). The effects of social punishment on noncompliance: A comparison with timeout and positive practice. *Journal of Applied Behavior Analysis, 9,* 471–482.

Dominguez, A., Wilder, D. A., Cheung, K., & Rey, C. (2014). The use of a verbal reprimand to decrease rumination in a child with autism. *Behavioral Interventions, 29,* 339–345. doi: 10.2002/bin.1390

Donahoe, J. W., & Palmer, D. C. (1994). *Learning and complex behavior,* Needham, MA.: Allyn & Bacon.

Donaldson, J. M., Lozy, E. D., & Galjour, M. (2021). Effects of Systematically Removing Components of the Good Behavior Game in Preschool Classrooms. *Journal of Behavioral Education, 30*(1), 22–36. https://doi-org.mimas.calstatela.edu/10.1007/s10864-019-09351-8

Donaldson, J. M., Matter, A. L., & Wiskow, K. M. (2018). Feasibility of and teacher preference for student-led implementation of the good behavior game in early elementary classrooms. *Journal of Applied Behavior Analysis, 51,* 118–129. doi: 10.1002/jaba.432

Donaldson, J. M., Vollmer, R. R., Yakich, T. M., & Van Camp, C. (2013). Effects of reduced timeout intervals on compliance with the timeout instructions. *Journal of Applied Behavior Analysis, 46,* 369–378.

Donaldson, J. M., Wiskow, K. M., & Soto, P. L. (2015). Immediate and distal effects of the good behavior game. *Journal of Applied Behavior Analysis, 48,* 685–689. doi: 10.1003/jaba.229

Donnellan, A. M., & LaVigna, G. W. (1990). Myths about punishment. In A. C. Repp & N. N. Singh (Eds.), *Perpectives on the use of nonaversive and aversive interventions for persons with developmental disabilities (*pp. 33–57). Sycamore, II.: Sycamore.

Donnelly, M. G., & Karsten, A. M. (2017). Effects of program teaching errors on acquisition and durability of self-care skills. *Journal of Applied Behavior Analysis, 50,* 511–528. doi: 10.1002/jaba390

Donny, E.C., Lanza, S.T., Balster, R.L., Collins, L.M., Caggiula, A., & Rowell, P. P. (2004). Using growth models to relate acquisition of nicotine self-administration to break point and nicotinic receptor binding. *Drug and Alcohol Dependence, 75*(1), 23–35.

Donnerstein, E., & Wilson, D. W. (1976). Effects of noise and perceived control on ongoing and subsequent aggressive behavior. *Journal of Personality and Social Psychology, 34,* 774–781.

Dooley, P., Wilczenski, F. L., & Torem, C. (2001). Using an activity schedule to smooth school transitions. *Journal of Positive Behavior Interventions, 3,* 57–61.

Dorsel, T. N. (1977). Implementation of variable schedules of self-reinforcement procedures. *Behavior Therapy, 8,* 489–491.

Dorsel, T. N., Anderson, M. L., & Moore, E. M. (1980). A further simplification of variable schedule self-reinforcement procedures. *Journal of Behavior Therapy and Experimental Psychiatry, 11,* 35–36.

Dorsey, B. L., Nelson, R. O., & Hayes, S. C. (1986). The effects of code complexity and of behavioral frequency on observer accuracy and interobserver agreement. *Behavioral Assessment, 8,* 349–363.

Dorsey, M. F., Iwata, B. A., Reid, D. H., & Davis, P. A. (1982). Protective equipment: Continuous and contingent application in the treatment of self-injurious behavior. *Journal of Applied Behavior Analysis, 15,* 217–230.

Doty, D. W., McInnis, T., & Paul, G. L. (1974). Remediation of negative side effects of an on-going response-cost system with chronic mental patients. *Journal of Applied Behavior Analysis, 7,* 191–198.

Dougan, J. D., McSweeney, F. K., & Farmer, V. A. (1985). Some parameters of behavioral contrast and allocation of interim behavior in rats. *Journal of the Experimental Analysis of Behavior, 44,* 325–335.

Dougherty, B. S., Fowler, S. A., & Paine, S. C. (1985). The use of peer monitors to reduce negative interactions during recess. *Journal of Applied Behavior Analysis, 18,* 141–153.

Doughty, A. H., & Lattal, K. A. (2001). Resistance to change of operant variation and repetition. *Journal of the Experimental Analysis of Behavior, 76,* 195–215.

Doughty, S. S., & Anderson, C. M. (2006). Effects of noncontingent reinforcement and functional communication training on problem behavior and mands. *Education and Treatment of Children, 29,* 23–50.

Doughty, S.S., Anderson, C.M., Doughty, A.H., Williams, D.C. & Saunders, K.J. (2007). Discriminative control of punished stereotyped behavior in humans. *Journal of the Experimental Analysis of Behavior 87, 3,* 325–336.

Dowdy, A., & Jacobs, K. W. (2019). An empirical evaluation of the disequilibrium model to increase independent seatwork for an individual diagnosed with autism. *Behavior Analysis in Practice, 12*(3), 617–621. https://doi.org.mimas.calstatela.edu/10.1007/s40617-018-00307-4

Dowdy, A., Tincani, M., Nipe, T., & Weiss, J. J. (2018). Effects of reinforcement without extinction on increasing compliance with nail cutting: A systematic replication. *Journal of Applied Behavior Analysis, 51,* 924–930.

Downs, A. F. K., Rosenthal, T. L., & Lichstein, K. L. (1988). Modeling therapies reduce avoidance of bathtime by the institutionalized elderly. *Behavior Therapy, 19,* 359–368.

Dowrick, P. W., & Dove, D. (1980). The use of self-modeling to improve the swimming performance of spina bifida children. *Journal of Applied Behavior Analysis, 13,* 51–56.

Dozier, C. L., Carr, J. E., Enloe, K., Landaruru, H., Eastridge, D., & Kellum K. K. (2001). Using fixed-time schedules to maintain behavior: A preliminary investigation. *Journal of Applied Behavior Analysis, 34,* 337–340.

Drabman, R. S., Hammer, D., & Rosenbaum, M. S. (1979). Assessing generalization in behavior modification with children: The generalization map. *Behavioral Assessment, 1,* 203–219.

Dracobly, J. D., Dozier, C. L., Briggs, A. M., & Juanico, J. F. (2017). An analysis of procedures that affect response variability. *Journal of Applied Behavior Analysis, 50,* 600–621. doi: 10.1002/jaba.392

Draper, A., Koch, R. M., van der Meer, J. et al. (2018). Effort but not reward sensitivity is altered by acute sickness induced by experimental edotoxemia in humans. *Neuropsychopharmacology 43,* 1107–118. https://doi.org/10.1038/npp.2017.231

Drasgow, E., Halle, J. W., & Ostrosky, M. M. (1998). Effects of differential reinforcement on the generalization of a replacement mand in three children with severe language delays. *Journal of Applied Behavior Analysis, 31,* 357–374.

Drasgow, E., & Yell, M. L. (2001). School-wide behavior support: Legal implications and requirements. *Child & Family Behavior Therapy, 24,* 129–145.

Drifke, M. A., Tiger, J. H., & Lillie, M. A. (2020). DRA contingencies promote improved tolerance to delayed reinforcement during VCT compared to DRO and fixed-time schedules. *Journal of Applied Behavior Analysis, 53,* 1579–1592.

Dube, W.V., Iennaco F. M., Rocco, F. I., Kledaras, J.B., & McIlvane, W. J. (1992). *Journal of Behavioral Education, 2,* 29–51.

Dube, W. V., & McIlvane, W. J. (1997). Reinforcer frequency and restricted stimulus control. *Journal of Experimental Analysis of Behavior, 68,* 303–316.

Dube, W., & McIlvane, W.J. (1999). Reduction of stimulus overselectivity with nonverbal differential observing responses, *Journal of Applied Behavior Analysis, 32,* 25–33.

Dube, W. V., McIlvane, W. J., Mackay, H. A., & Stoddard, L. T. (1987). Stimulus class membership established via stimulus-reinforcer relations. *Journal of the Experimental Analysis of Behavior, 47,* 159–175.

Ducharme, D.E., & Holborn, S.W. (1997). Programming generalization of social skills in preschool children with hearing impairments. *Journal of Applied Behavior Analysis, 30,* 639–651.

Ducharme, J. M., & Worling, D. E. (1994). Behavioral momentum and stimulus fading in the acquisition and maintenance of child compliance in the home. *Journal of Applied Behavior Analysis, 27,* 639–647.

Duenas, A. D., Plavnick, J. B., & Bak, M. Y. S. (2018). Effects of joint video modeling on unscripted play behavior of children with autism spectrum disorder. *Journal of Autism and Developmental Disorders,* Published online. doi.org/10.1007/s10803-018-3719-2

Dufrene, B. A., Doggett, R. A., Henington, C., & Watson, T. S. (2007). Functional behavioral assessment and intervention for disruptive classroom behaviors in preschool and head start classrooms. *Journal of Behavioral Education, 16,* 368–388.

Dufour, M.-M., & Lanovaz, M. J. (2020). Increasing compliance with wearing a medical device in children with autism. *Journal of Applied Behavior Analysis, 53,* 1089–1096. doi: 10.1002/jaba.628

Duker, P. C., & Seys, D. M. (1996). Long-term use of electrical aversion treatment with self-injurious behavior. *Research in Developmental Disabilities, 17,* 293–301.

Dukes, C., Brady, M. P., Scott, J., & Wilson, C. L. (2016). Using modeling and rehearsal to teach fire safety to children with autism. *Journal of Applied Behavior Analysis, 49,* 699–704.

Dunkel-Jackson, S. M., Dixon, M. R., & Szekely, S. (2016). Self-control as generalized operant behavior by adults with autism spectrum disorder. *Journal of Applied Behavior Analysis, 49,* 705–710. doi: 10.1002/jaba.315.

Dunlap, G. (1984). The influence of task variation and maintenance tasks on the learning and affect of autistic children. *Journal of Experimental Child Psychology, 37,* 41–64.

Dunlap, G., dePerczel, M., Clarke, S., Wilson, D., Wright, S., White, R., et al. (1994). Choice making to promote adaptive behaviors for students with emotional and behavioral challenges. *Journal of Applied Behavior Analysis, 27,* 505–518.

Dunlap, G., & Johnson, J. (1985). Increasing the independent responding of autistic children with unpredictable supervision. *Journal of Applied Behavior Analysis, 18,* 227–256.

Dunlap, G., Kern-Dunlap, L., Clarke, S., & Robbins, F. R. (1991). Functional assessment, curricular revision, and severe behavior problems. *Journal of Applied Behavior Analysis, 24,* 387–397.

Dunlap, G., White, R., Vera, A., Wilson, D., & Panacek, L. (1996). The effects of multi-component, assessment-based curricular modifications on the classroom behavior of children with emotional and behavioral disorders. *Journal of Behavioral Education, 6,* 481–500.

Dunn, J., & Clare, L. (2007). Learning race-name associations in early-stage dementia: Comparing the effects of errorless learning and effortful processing. *Neuropsychological Rehabilitation, 17,* 735–754.

Dunn, M. E., Shelnut, J., Ryan, J. B., & Katsiyannis, A. (2017). A systematic review of peer-mediated interventions on the academic achievement of students with emotional/behavioral disorders. *Education and Treatment of Children, 40,* 497–524.

Durand, V.M. (1982). Analysis and intervention of self-injurious behavior. *Journal of the Association for the Severely Handicapped, 7,* 44–53.

Durand, V. M. (1985). Employee absenteeism: A selective review of antecedents and consequences. *Journal of Organizational Behavior management, 7,* 135–167.

Durand, V. M. (1999). Functional communication training using assistive devices: Recruiting natural communities of reinforcement. *Journal of Applied Behavior Analysis, 32,* 247–267.

Durand, V. M., & Carr, E. G. (1987). Social influences on "self-stimulatory" behavior: Analysis and treatment application. *Journal of Applied Behavior Analysis, 20,* 119–132.

Durand, V. M., & Carr, E. G. (1992). An analysis of maintenance following functional communication training. *Journal of Applied Behavior Analysis, 25,* 777–794.

Durand, V. M., & Crimmins, D. B. (1988). Identifying the variables maintaining self-injurious behavior. *Journal of Autism and Developmental Disorders, 18*, 99–117.

Durand, V. M., & Kishi, G. (1987). Reducing severe behavior problems among persons with dual sensory impairments: An evaluation of a technical assistance model. *Journal of the Association for Persons with Severe Handicaps, 12*, 2–10.

Dustin, R. (1974). Training for institutional change. *The Personnel and Guidance Journal, 52*, 422–427.

Dwyer, K., & Osher, D. (2000). *Safeguarding our children: An action guide*. Washington, D. C.: U. S. Departments of Education and Justice, American Institutes for Research.

Dyer, K. (1987). The competition of autistic stereotyped behavior with usual and specially assessed reinforcers. *Research in Developmental Disabilities, 8*(4), 607–626.

Dyer, K., Christian, W. P., & Luce, S. C. (1982). The role of response delay in improving the discrimination performance of autistic children. *Journal of Applied Behavior Analysis, 15*, 231–240.

Dyer, K., Dunlap, G., & Winterling, V. (1990). The effects of choice making on the problem behaviors of students with severe handicaps. *Journal of Applied Behavior Analysis, 23*, 515–524.

Dyer, K., & Osher, D. (2000). *Safeguarding our children: An action guide*. Washington, D. C., U.S. Departments of Education and Justice, American Institutes for Research.

Dyer, K., Santarcangelo, S., & Luce, S.C. (1987). Developmental influences in teaching language forms to individuals with developmental disabilities. *Journal of Speech and Hearing Disorders, 52*, 335–347.

Edgar, R., & Clement, P. (1980). Teacher-controlled and self-controlled reinforcement with underachieving black children. *Child Behavior Therapy, 2*, 33–56.

Edmunds, S. R., Rozga, A., Li, Y., Karn, E. A., Lbanez, L. V., Rehg, J. M., & Stone, W. L. (2017). Brief report: Using a point-of-view camera to measure eye gaze in young children with autism spectrum disorder during naturalistic social interactions: A pilot study. *Journal of Autism and Developmental Disorders, 47*, 898–904.

Edwards, L. (1995). Effectiveness of self-management on attentional behavior and reading comprehension for children with attention deficit disorder. *Child and Family Behavior Therapy, 17*, 1–17.

Edwards, K. A., & Johnston, R. (1977). Increasing greeting and farewell responses in high school students by a bus driver. *Education and Treatment of Children, 1*, 9–18.

Edwards, L. J. (2000). Modern statistical techniques for the analysis of longitudinal data in biomedical research. *Pediatric Pulmonology, 30*(4), 330–344.

Edwards, L., Salant, V., Howard, V. F., Brougher, J., & McLaughlin, T. F. (1995). Effectiveness of self-management on attentional behavior and reading comprehension for children with attention-deficit disorder. *Child and Family behavior Therapy, 17*(2), 1–17.

Edwards, T. L., Lotfizadeh, A. D., & Poling, A. (2019). Rethinking motivation operations: A reply to commentaries on Edwards, Lotfizadeh, and Poling, (2019). *Journal of the Experimental Analysis of Behavior, 112*, 47–59

Egel, A. L. (1981). Reinforcer variation: Implications for motivating developmentally disabled children. *Journal of Applied Behavior Analysis, 14*, 345–350.

Egel, A. L., Richman, G. S., & Koegel, R. L. (1981). Normal peer models and autistic children's learning. *Journal of Applied Behavior Analysis, 14*, 3–12.

Egervari, G. (2016). AMPA Receptor Plasticity in the Nucleus Accumbers Mediates Withdrawal-Related Negative-Affective States. *Journal of Neuroscience, 36*, 10505–10507.

Eid, A. M., Aljaser, S. M., AlSaud, A. N., Asfahani, S. M., Alhaqbani, O. A., Mohtasib, R. S., Aldhalaan, H. M., Fryling, M. (2017). Training parents in Saudi Arabia to implement discrete trial teaching with their children with autism spectrum disorder. *Behavior Analysis in Practice 10*(4) 402–406.

Eikeseth, S. (2009). Outcome of comprehensive psycho-educational interventions for young children with autism. *Research in Developmental Disabilities, 30*, 158–178.

Eikeseth, S., & Nesset, R. (2003). Behavioral treatment of children with phonological disorder: The efficacy of vocal imitation and sufficient-response-exemplar training. *Journal of Applied Behavior Analysis, 36*, 325–337.

Eisner Hirsch, S., Healy, S., Judge, J. P., & Lloyd, J. W. (2016). Effects of an interdependent group contingency on engagement in physical education. *Journal of Applied Behavior Analysis, 49*, 975–979. doi: 10.1002/jaba.328

Elliott, D. S. (1992, October). *Correlates of youth violence, and designing evaluations of interventions*. Paper presented at a workshop for potential applicants for NIMH research grants to prevent youth violence, Bethesda, MD.

Elliott, S. N. (1988). Acceptability of behavioral treatments: Review of variables that influence treatment selection. *Professional Psychology: Research and Practice, 19*, 68–80.

Elliott, S. N., Witt, J. C., Peterson, R., & Galvin, G. A. (1983). *Acceptability of behavioral interventions: Factors that influence teachers' decisions*. Unpublished manuscript.

Embry, D. D. (2002). The Good Behavior Game: A best practice candidate as a universal behavioral vaccine. *Clinical Child and Family Psychology Review, 5*, 273–297.

Emerson, E. (1992). Self-injurious behavior: An overview of recent trends in epidemiological and behavioural research. *Mental Handicap Research, 5*, 49–81.

Engelmann, S., & Colvin, G. (1983). *Generalized compliance training: A direct-instruction program for managing severe behavior problems*. Baltimore: MD. Paul H. Brookes.

Ennis, B. J., & Friedman, P. R. (Eds.). (1973). *Legal rights of the mentally handicapped*. Vols. 1–2. Practicing Law Institute. The Mental Health Law Project, Washington, D. C.

Ennis, C. R., Blair, K. C., & George, H. P. (2016). An evaluation of group contingency interventions: the role of teacher preference. *Journal of Positive Behavior Interventions, 18*, 17–28.

Ennis, R. P., Royer, D. J., Lane, K. L., & Dunlap, K. D. (2020). Behavior-specific praise in pre-K-12 settings. Mapping the 50-year knowledge base. *Behavioral Disorders, 45*, 131–147.

Epstein, L. H., Doke, L. A., Sajwaj, T. E., Sorrell, S., & Rimmer, B. (1974). Generality and side effects of overcorrection. *Journal of Applied Behavior Analysis, 7,* 385–390.

Epstein, L. H., Paluch, R. A., Kilanowski, C. K., Raynor, H. A. (1995). The effect of reinforcement or stimulus control to reduce sedentary behavior in the treatment of pediatric obesity. *Health Psychology 23*(4), 371–s380.

Epstein, L. H., Parker, L., McCoy, J. F., & McGee, G. (1976). Descriptive analysis of eating regulation in obese and nonobese children. *Journal of Applied Behavior Analysis, 9,* 407–415.

Epstein, R. (1984). Self-injurious behaviour: An overview of recent trends in epidemiological and behavioural research. *Mental Handicap Research, 5,* 49–81.

Epstein, R. (1985). Extinction-induced resurgence: Preliminary investigations and possible applications. *Psychological Record, 35,* 143–153

Epstein, R., & Gross, C. M. (1978). A self-control procedure for the maintenance of nondisruptive behavior in an elementary school child. *Behavior Therapy, 9,* 109–117.

Epstein, R., Lanza, R. P., & Skinner, B. F. (1980). Symbolic communication between two pigeons. *Science, 207,* 543–545.

Epstein, R., & Skinner, B. F. (1980). Resurgence of responding after the cessation of response-independent reinforcement. *Proceedings of the National Academy of Sciences, U.S.A., 77,* 6251–6253.

Erken, N., & Henderson, H. (1976). *Practice skills mastery program.* Logan, UT: Mastery Programs, Ltd.

Eron, L. D. (1987). The development of aggressive behavior from the perspective of a developing behaviorism. *American Psychologist, 42,* 435–442.

Esch, B. E., Carr, J. E., & Michael, J. (2005). Evaluating stimulus-stimulus pairing and direct reinforcement in the establishment of an echoic repertoire of children diagnosed with autism. *Analysis of Verbal Behavior, 21,* 43–58.

Esch, J. W., Esch, B. E., McCart, J D., & Petursdottir, A. I. (2010). An assessment of self-echoic behavior in young children. *The Analysis of Verbal Behavior, 26,* 3–13.

Etscheidt, S. (2006). Behavior intervention plans: Pedagogical and legal analysis of issues. *Behavior Disorders, 31,* 89–109.

Evans, G. W. (1979). Behavioral and physiological consequences of crowding in humans. *Journal of Applied Social Psychology, 9,* 27–46.

Everett, G. E., Olmi, D. J., Edwards, R. P., & Tingstrom, D. H. (2005). The contributions of eye contact and contingent praise to effective instruction delivery in compliance training. *Education and Treatment of Children, 28,* 48–62.

Everett, P. B., Studer, R. G., & Douglas, T. J. (1978). Gaming simulation to pretest operant-based community interventions: An urban transportation example. *American Journal of Community Psychology, 6,* 327–338.

Fabiano, G. A., Pelham, W. E., Manos, M. J., Gnagy, E. M., Chronis, A. M., Onyango, A. N., et al. (2004). An evaluation of three time-out procedures for children with attention-deficit/hyperactivity disorder. *Behavior Therapy, 35,* 449–469.

Fairbank, J. A., & Prue, D. M. (1982). Developing performance feedback systems. In L. W. Frederiksen (Ed). *Handbook of organizational behavior management.* New York: Wiley.

Fahmie, T. A., & Hanley, G. P. (2008). Progressing toward data intimacy: A review of within-session data analysis. *Journal of Applied Behavior Analysis, 41,* 319–331.

Falcomata, R. S., Roane, H. S., Hovanetz, A. N., & Kettering, T. L. (2004). An evaluation of response cost in the treatment of inappropriate vocalizations maintained by automatic reinforcement. *Journal of Applied Behavior Analysis, 37,* 83–87.

Faloon, B. J., & Rehfeldt, R. A. (2008). The role of overt and covert self-rules in establishing a daily living skill in adults with mild developmental disabilities. *Journal of Applied Behavior Analysis, 41,* 393–404.

Farber, H., & Mayer, G. R. (1972). Behavior consultation in a barrio high school. *The Personnel and Guidance Journal, 51,* 273–279.

Fahmie, T. A., Iwata, B. A., Harper, J., & Querim, A. C. (2013). Evaluation of the divided attention condition during functional analyses. *Journal of Applied Behavior Analysis, 46,* 71–78.

Farone, S.V., Spencer, T., Aleardi, M., Pagano, C., & Biederman, J. (2004). Meta-analysis of the efficacy of methylphenidate for treating adult attention-deficit/hyperactivity disorder. *Journal of Clinical Psychopharmacology, 24*(1), 24–29.

Farrimond, S. J., & Leland Jr., L. S. (2006). Increasing donations to supermarket food-bank bins using proximal prompts. *Journal of Applied Behavior Analysis, 39,* 249–251.

Fauke, J. Burnett, J., Powers, M. A., & Sulzer, B. (1973). Improvement of handwriting and letter recognition skills. A behavior modification procedure. *Journal of Learning Disabilities, 6,* 296–300.

Favell, J. E., Azrin, N. H., Baumeister, A. A., Carr, E. G., Dorsey, M. F., Forehand, R., et al. (1982). The treatment of self-injurious behavior. *Behavior Therapy, 13,* 529–554.

Favell, J. E., McGimsey, J. F., & Jones, M. L. (1978). The use of physical restraint in the treatment of self-injury and as positive reinforcement. *Journal of Applied Behavior Analysis, 11,* 225–241.

Fee, V. E., Matson, J. L., & Manikam, R. (1990). A control group outcome study of a nonexclusionary time-out package to improve social skills with preschoolers. *Exceptionality, 1,* 107–121.

Felde, A., Haggerty, K., Sleiman, A. A. et al. (2020). Reducing response effort to improve employee preparedness in a human service organization. *Behavior Analysis in Practice, 13.* https://doi.org/10.1007/s40617-020-00512-0

Feldman, E. K., & Matos, R. (2012). Training paraprofessionals to facilitate social interactions between children with autism and their typically developing peers. *Journal of Positive Behavior Interventions, 15,* 169–179.

Feldman, R. (1985). *Social psychology.* New York: McGraw-Hill.

Feldman, R. A. (1992). The St. Louis experiment: Effective treatment of antisocial youths in prosocial peer groups. In J. McCord & R. E. Tremblay (Eds.), *Preventing antisocial behavior: Interventions from birth through adolescence* (pp. 233–252). New York: Guilford Press.

Feldman, R., Bacher, M., Campbell, N., Drover, A., & Chockalingam, A. (1998). Adherence to pharmacologic management of hypertension. *Canadian Review of Public Health, 89,* 1–16.

Fellner, D. J., & Sulzer-Azaroff, B. (1984). A behavioral analysis of goal setting. *Journal of Organizational Behavior Management, 6,* 33–51.

Fellner, D. J., & Sulzer-Azaroff, B. (1985). Occupational safety: Assessing the impact of adding assigned or participative goal setting. *Journal of Organizational Behavior Management, 7,* 3–24.

Ferguson, D. L., & Rosales-Ruiz, J. (2001). Loading the problem loader: The effects of target training and shaping on trailer-loading behavior of horses. *Journal of Applied Behavior Analysis, 34,* 409–424.

Ferguson, J., & Brink, B. (2004). Caught in a bind: Student teaching in a climate of state reform. *Teacher Education Quarterly,* 55–64.

Fernald, P. S., & Jordan, E. A. (1991). Programmed instruction versus standard text in introductory psychology. *Teaching of Psychology, 18,* 205–211.

Ferritor, D. E., Buckhold, D., Hamblin, R. L., & Smith, L. (1972). The noneffects of contingent reinforcement for attending behavior on work accomplished. *Journal of Applied Behavior Analysis, 5,* 7–17.

Ferster, C. B. (1960). Intermittent reinforcement of matching to sample in the pigeon. *Journal of the Experimental Analysis of Behavior, 3,* 259–272.

Ferster, C. B., & Skinner, B. F. (1957). *Schedules of reinforcement.* New York: Appleton.

Ferster, C. B., & Skinner, B. F. (1957). *Schedules of reinforcement.* New York: Appleton-Century-Crofts.

Fettig, A., & Barton, E. E. (2013). Parent implementation of function-based intervention to reduce children's challenging behavior. *Journal of Early Intervention, 35,* 194–219.

Fettig, A., Schultz, T. R., Sreckovic, M. A. (2015). Effects of coaching on the implementation of functional assessment-based parent intervention in reducing challenging behaviors. *Journal of Positive Behavior Interventions, 17,* 170–180. DOI:10.1177/1098300714564164 jpbi.sagepub.com

Field, D. P., Tonneau, F., Ahearn, W. H., & Hineline, P. N. (1996). Preference between variable-ratio and fixed-ratio schedules: Local and extended relations. *Journal of the Experimental Analysis of Behavior, 66,* 283–295.

Fienup D. M. (2019). The future of verbal behavior: Integration. *The Analysis of Verbal Behavior, 34*(1–2), 18–23. https://doi.org/10.1007/s40616-018-0108-z

Fienup, D. M., Ahlers, A. A., & Pace, G. (2011). Preference for fluent versus disfluent work schedules. *Journal of Applied Behaviors Analysis, 44,* 847–858. doi:1-.1901/jaba.2011.44-847.

Finkel, A. S., & Williams, R. L. (2001). A comparison of textual and echoic prompts on the acquisition of intra-verbal behavior in a six-year-old boy with autism. *The Analysis of Verbal Behavior, 18,* 61–70.

Fishbein, J. E., & Wasik, B. H. (1981). Effect of the good behavior game on disruptive library behavior. *Journal of Applied Behavior Analysis, 14,* 89–93.

Fischer, C. (1999–2000). An effective (and affordable) intervention model for at-risk high-school readers. *Journal of Adolescent & Adult Literacy, 43,* 326–335.

Fisher, J., & Nehs, R. (1978). Use of commonly available chores to reduce a boy's rate of swearing. *Journal of Behavior Therapy and Experimental Psychiatry, 9,* 89–93.

Fisher, J. E., & Buchanan, J. A. (2018). Presentation of preferred stimuli as an intervention for aggression in a person with dementia. *Behavior Analysis: Research and Practice, 18*(1), 33–40. http://dx.doi.org/10.1037/bar0000086

Fisher, M. H., Burke, M. M., & Griffin, M. M. (2013). Teaching young adults with disabilities to respond appropriately to lures from strangers. *Journal of Applied Behavior Analysis, 16,* 528–533.

Fisher, P. A., & Laschinger, H. S. (2001). A relaxation training program to increase self-efficacy for anxiety control in Alzheimer family caregivers. *Holistic Nursing Practice, 15*(2), 47–58.

Fisher, W.W., DeLeon, I.G., Rodriguez-Catter, V., & Keeney, K.M. (2004). Enhancing the effects of extinction on attention-maintained behavior through noncontingent delivery of attention or stimuli identified via a competing stimulus assessment. *Journal of Applied Behavior Analysis, 37,* 171–184.

Fisher, W. W., Kodak, T., & Moore, J. W. (2007). Embedding an identity-matching task within a prompting hierarchy to facilitate acquisition of conditional discriminations in children with autism. *Journal of Applied Behavior Analysis, 40,* 489–499.

Fisher, W. W., Kuhn, D. E., & Thompson, R. H. (1998). Establishing discriminative control of responding using functional and alternative reinforcers during functional communication training. *Journal of Applied Behavior Analysis, 31,* 543–560.

Fisher, W. W., & Mazur, J. E. (1997). Basic and applied research on choice responding. *Journal of Applied Behavior Analysis, 30,* 387–410.

Fisher, W.W., O'Connor, J.T., Kurtz, P.F., DeLeon, I.G., & Gotjen, D.L. (2000). The effects of noncontingent delivery of high- and low-preference stimuli on attention-maintained destructive behavior. *Journal of Applied Behavior Analysis, 33,* 79–83.

Fisher, W. W., Pawich, T. L., Dickes, N., Paden, A. R., & Toussaint, K. (2014). Increasing the saliency of behavior-consequence relations for children with autism who exhibit persistent errors. *Journal of Applied Behavior Analysis, 47,* 738–747. doi:10.1002/jaba.172

Fisher, W. W., Piazza, C. C., Bowman, L. G., & Amari, A. (1996). Integrating caregiver report with a systematic choice assessment. *American Journal of Mental Retardation, 101,* 15–25.

Fisher, W. W., Piazza, C. C., Bowman, L. G., Hagopian, L. P., Owens, J. C., & Slevin, I. (1992). A comparison of two approaches for identifying reinforcers for persons with severe and profound disabilities. *Journal of Applied Behavior Analysis, 25,* 491–498. doi: 10.1901/jaba.1992.25-491

Fisher, W., Piazza C., Cataldo, M., Harrell, R., Jefferson, G., & Conner, R. (1993). Functional communication training with and without extinction and punishment. *Journal of Applied Behavior Analysis, 26,* 23–36.

Fisk, K. E. (2008). Treatment integrity of school-based behavior analytic interventions: A review of the research. *Behavior Analysis in Practice, 1*(2), 19–25.

Fiske, K. E. (2008), Treatment integrity of school-based behavior analytic interventions: A review of the research. *Behavior Analytic Practice, 1*(2), pp. 19–25.

Fitterling, J. M., & Ayllon, T. (1983). Behavioral coaching in classical ballet. *Behavior Modification, 7,* 345–368.

Fixsen, D. L., Phillips, E. L., & Wolf, M. M. (1972). Achievement Place: The reliability of self-reporting and peer-reporting and their effects on behavior. *Journal of Applied Behavior Analysis, 5*, 19–30.

Fixsen, D. L., Phillips, E. L., & Wolf, M. M. (1973). Achievement Place: Experiments in self-government with pre-delinquents. *Journal of Applied Behavior Analysis, 6*, 31–47.

Flaherty, C. F. (1996). *Incentive reality*. New York, NY: Cambridge University Press.

Flanders, N. A. (1965). *Teacher influence, pupk. Attitudes, and achievement*. Cooperative Research Monograph, No. 12.

Flanagan, S., Adams, H. E., & Forehand, R. (1979). A comparison of four instructional techniques for teaching parents to use timeout. *Behavior Therapy, 10*, 94–102.

Fleming, R. K., Oliver, J. R., & Bolton, D. M. (1996). Training supervisors to train staff: A case study in a human service organization. *Journal of Organizational Behavior Management, 16*(1), 3–25.

Fleming, R. K., & Sulzer-Azaroff, B. (1988). Enhancing quality of teaching by direct-care staff through performance feedback on the job. *Behavioral Residential Treatment, 4*, 377–395.

Fleming, R. K., & Sulzer-Azaroff, B. (1989). Enhancing quality of teaching by direct care staff through performance feedback. *Behavioral Residential Treatment, 4*, 377–395.

Fleming, R., & Sulzer-Azaroff, B. (1992). Reciprocal peer management. Improving staff instruction in a vocational training program. *Journal of Applied Behavior Analysis, 25*, 611–620.

Fleming, R.K., & Sulzer-Azaroff, B. (2002) eABA: Designing a PSI-type curriculum in Autism education. 28th Annual Convention of the Association for Behavior Analysis International, Toronto, Ontario, May.

Flood, W. A., Wilder, D. A., Flood, A. L., & Masuda, A. (2002). Peer-mediated reinforcement plus prompting as treatment for off-task behavior in children with attention deficit hyperactivity disorder. *Journal of Applied Behavior Analysis, 35*, 199–204.

Flood, W. A., & Wilder, D. A. (2004). The use of differential reinforcement and fading to increase time away from a caregiver in a child with separation anxiety disorder. *Education and Treatment of Children, 27*, 1–8.

Flores, M. T., Gates, G. L., Poirot, K. E., & Estrada, N. J. (2020). Conceptualizing fixed-interval praise delivery. *Intervention in School and Clinic, 56*(2), 84–91. https//doi.org/10.1177/1053451220914889

Flower, A., McKenna, J. W., Bunuan, R. L., Muething, C.S., & Vega, Jr. R. (2014). Effects of the Good Behavior Game on challenging behaviors in school settings. *Review of Educational Research, 84*, 546–571. doi: 10.3102/0034654314536781

Foley, E. A., Dozier, C., & Lessor, A. L. (2019). Comparison of components of the good behavior game in a preschool classroom. *Journal of Applied Behavior Analysis, 52*, 84–104. doi: 10.1002/jaba.506

Fong. E. H,., Catagnus, R., Brohead, M., Quigley, S., & Field, S. (2016). Developing the cultural awareness skills of behavior analysts. *Behavior Analysis in Practice, 9*, 84–94.

Fonger, A. M., & Malott, R. W., (2019). Using shaping to teach eye contact to children with autism spectrum disorder. *Behavior Analysis in Practice, 12*, 216–221. doi: org/10.1007/s40617-018-0245-9

Forman, S. G. (1980). A comparison of cognitive training and response cost procedures in modifying aggressive behavior of elementary school children. *Behavior Therapy, 11*, 594–600.

Fowler, S. A., Baer, D. M., & Stolz, S. B. (Eds.). (1984). *Analysis and intervention in developmental disabilities: Special Issue: self-management tactics for the developmentally disabled, 4*. New York: Pergamon.

Fowler, S. A., Dougherty, B. S., Kirby, K. C., & Kohler, F. W. (1986). Role reversals: An analysis of therapeutic effects achieved with disruptive boys during their appointments as peer monitors. *Journal of Applied Behavior Analysis, 19*, 437–444.

Fowler, S. A., Rowbury, T. G., Nordyke, N. S., & Baer, D. M. (1976). Color-matching technique to train children in the correct use of stairs. *Physical Therapy, 56*, 903–910.

Fox, A. E., Bailey, S. R., Hall, E. G., & St. peter, C. C. (2012). Reduction of biting and chewing of horses using differential reinforcement of other behavior. *Behavioral Processes, 91*, 125–128. doi: 10.1016/j.beproc.2012.05.001

Fox, A. E. & Belding, D. L. (2015). Reducing pawing inheres using positive reinforcement. *Journal of Applied Behavior Analysis, 48*, 936–940. doi: 10.1002/jaba.241

Fox, C. J., & Sulzer-Azaroff, B. (1983). Effectiveness of performance feedback from a supervisor vs. a non-supervisor in promoting paraprofessionals' implementation of basic fire-evacuation training. Paper presented at the association for Behavior Analysis, Ninth Annual Convention, Milwaukee, WI.

Fox, C. J., & Sulzer-Azaroff, B. (1989). The effectiveness of two different sources of feedback on staff teaching of fire evacuation skills. *Journal of Organizational Behavior Management, 10(2)*, 19–35.

Fox, C. J., & Sulzer-Azaroff, B. (1989). The effectiveness of two different sources of feedback on staff teaching of fire evacuation skills. *Journal of Organizational Behavior Management, 10*, 19–35.

Fox, D. K., Hopkins, B. L., & Anger, W. K. (1987). The long-term effects of a token economy on safety performance in open-pit mining. *Journal of Applied Behavior Analysis, 20*, 215–224.

Fox, E. (n.d.). *How is RFT different from stimulus equivalence?* Retrieved from https://contextualscience.org/how_iw_rft_defferent_froom_stimulut_equivalence.

Fox, E.J., & Ghezzi, P.M. (2003). Effects of computer-based fluency training on concept formation. *Journal of Behavioral Education, 12*(1), 1–21.

Fox, L., & Little, N. (2001). Starting early: Developing school-wide behavior support in a community preschool. *Journal of Positive Behavior Interventions, 3*, 251–254.

Foxx, C. L., Foxx, R. M., Jones, J. R., & Kiely, D. (1980). Twenty-four hour social isolation: A program for reducing the aggressive behavior of a psychotic-like retarded adult. *Behavior Modification, 4*, 130–144.

Foxx, R. M. (1996). Translating the covenant: The behavior analyst as ambassador and translator. *The Behavior Analyst, 19*, 147–161.

Foxx, R. M., & Azrin, N. H. (1972). Restitution: A method of eliminating aggressive-disruptive behavior of retarded and brain damaged patients. *Behavior Research and Therapy, 10,* 15–27.

Foxx, R. M., & Azrin, N. H. (1973). The elimination of autistic self-stimulatory behavior by overcorrection. *Journal of Applied Behavior Analysis, 6,* 1–14.

Foxx, R. M., & Bechtel, D. R. (1982). Overcorrection. *Progress in Behavior Modification, 13,* 227–228.

Foxx, R. M., Bittle, R. G., Bechtel, D. R., & Livesay, J. R. (1986). Behavioral treatment of the sexually deviant behavior of mentally retarded individuals. *International Review of Research in Mental Retardation, 14,* 291–317.

Foxx, R. M., & Garito, J. (2007). The long term successful treatment of the very severe behaviors of a preadolescent with autism. *Behavioral Interventions, 22*(1), 69–82.

Foxx, R. M., & Jones, J. R. (1978). A remediation program for increasing the spelling achievement of elementary and junior high school students. *Behavior Modification, 2,* 211–230.

Foxx, R. M., & Livesay, J. (1984). Maintenance of response suppression following overcorrection: a 10-year retrospective of eight cases. *Analysis and Intervention in Developmental Disabilities, 4,* 65–79.

Foxx, R. M., McMorrow, M. J., Fenlons, S., & Bittle, R. G. (1986). The reductive effects of reinforcement procedures on the genital stimulation and stereotypy of a mentally retarded adolescent male. *Analysis and Intervention in Developmental Disabilities, 6,* 239–248.

Foxx, R. M., & Shapiro, S. T. (1978). The timeout ribbon: A nonexclusionary timeout procedure. *Journal of Applied Behavior Analysis, 12,* 125–136.

Frampton, S. E., Shillingsburg, M. A., & Simeone, P. J. (2020). Feasibility and preliminary efficacy of Direct Instruction for Individuals with autism utilizing speech-generating devices. *Behavior Analysis in Practice, 13,* 648–658. doi.org/10.1007/s40617-020-412-3.

Francisco, M. T., Borrero, J. C., & Sy, J. R. (2008). Evaluation of absolute and relative reinforcer value using progressive-ratio schedules. *Journal of Applied Behavior Analysis, 41,* 189–202.

Franklin, D. E., Hennesy, C. L., & Beilby, J. M. (2008). Investigating factors related to the effects of time-out on stuttering in adults. *International Journal of Language and Communication Disorders 43*(3), 283–299.

Franklin, D. E., Taylor, C. L., Hennessey, N.W., & Beilby, J. M. (2008). Investigating factors related to the effects of timeout on stuttering in adults. *International Journal of Language & Communication Disorders, 43*(3), 283–299.

Frankowsky, R. J., & Sulzer-Azaroff, B. (1975, December). *Individual and group contingencies and collateral social behaviors.* Paper presented at the meeting of the Association for the Advancement of Behavior therapy, San Francisco.

Frankowsky, R. J., & Sulzer-Azaroff, B. (1978). Individual and group contingencies and collateral social behaviors. *Behavior Therapy, 9,* 313–327.

Frea, W., Arnold, C., & Vittimberga, G. (2001). A demonstration of the effects of augmentative communication on the extreme aggressive behavior of a child with autism within an integrated preschool setting. *Journal of Positive Behavior Intervention, 3,* 194–198.

Frea, W.D., & Hughes, C.H. (1997). Functional analysis and treatment of social-communicative behavior of adolescents with developmental disabilities. *Journal of Applied Behavior Analysis, 30,* 701–704.

Freeland, J.T., & Noell, G.H. (1999). Maintaining accurate math responses in elementary school students: The effects of delayed intermittent reinforcement and programming ommon stimuli. *Journal of Applied Behavior Analysis, 32,* 211–215.

Freeman, K. A. (2006). Treating bedtime resistance with the bedtime pass: A systematic replication and component analysis with 3–year-olds. *Journal of Applied Behavior Analysis, 39,* 423–428.

Freeman, K. A., Anderson, C. M., & Scotti, J. R. (2000). A structured descriptive methodology: Increasing agreement between descriptive and experimental analyses. *Education and Training in Mental Retardation and Developmental Disabilities, 35,* 406–414.

Freeman, K. A., & Dexter-Mazza, E. T. (2004). Using self-monitoring with an adolescent with disruptive classroom behavior —preliminary analysis of the role of adult feedback. *Behavior Modification, 28,* 402–419.

Freeman, K. A., & Piazza, C. C. (1998). Combining stimulus fading, reinforcement, and extinction to treat food refusal. *Journal of Applied Behavior Analysis, 31,* 691–694.

French, D. D., & Wojcicki, C. A. (2018), Restraint and seclusion: Frequency, duration, and rate of injury for students with emotional and behavioral disorders. *School Mental Health, 10,* 35–47. https://doi.org/10.1007/s12310-017-9240-5

Frentz, C., & Kelley, M. L. (1986). Parents' acceptance of reductive treatment methods: The influence of problem severity and perception of child behavior. *Behavior Therapy, 17,* 75–81.

Fryling, M. J., Wallace, M. D., & Yassine, J. N. (2012), Impact of treatment integrity on intervention effectiveness. *Journal of Applied Behavior Analysis, 45*(2) pp. 449–453.

Fricchione, G. (2004). Generalized anxiety disorder. *Clinical Practice, 351,* 675–682.

Friman, P., & Poling, A. (1995). Making life easier with effort: Basic findings and applied research on response effort. *Journal of Applied Behavior Analysis, 28,* 583–590.

Frisch, M. B., & Higgins, R. L. (1986). Instructional demand effects and the correspondence among role-play, self-report, and naturalistic measures of social skills. *Behavioral Assessment, 8,* 221–236.

Fritz, J. N., Jackson, L. M., Stiefler, N. A., Wimberly, B. S., & Richardson, A. R. (2017). Noncontingenet reinforcement without extinction plus differential reinforcement of alternative behavior during treatment of problem behavior. *Journal of Applied Behavior Analysis, 50,* 590–599. doi: 10.1002/jaba.395

Frost, L., & Bondy, A. (2002). *The picture exchange communication system.* Newark, DE Pyramid Educational Products.

Frost, L., & Bondy, A. (2006). A common language: Using B.F. Skinner's verbal behavior for assessment and treatment of communication disabilities on SLP-ABA. *SLP-ABA, 1*(2) 103–119.

Frying, M. J., Wallace, M. D., & Yassine, J. N. (2012). Impact of treatment integrity on intervention effectiveness. *Journal of Applied Behavior*

*Analysis, 45,* 449–453. doi: 10.1901/jaba.2012.45-449.

Fuchs, L. S., & Fuchs, D. (2001). Principles for sustaining research-based practice in the schools: A case study. *Focus on Exceptional Children, 33*(6), 1–14.

Fuchs, L. S., Fuchs, D., & Kazdan, S. (1999). Effects of peer-assisted learning strategies on high school students with serious reading problems. *Remedial & Special Education, 20,* 309–318.

Fujita, Y., & Hasegawa, Y. (2003). Weight control: Selection of low-calorie food. *Japanese Journal of Behavior Analysis, 18,* 3–9.

Fulcher, R., & Cellucci, T. (1997). Case formulation and behavioral treatment of chronic cough. *Journal of Behavior Therapy and Experimental Psychiatry, 28,* 291–296.

Fuller, J. L., & Fienup, D. M. (2018). A preliminary analysis of mastery criterion level: Effects on response maintenance. *Behavior Analysis in Practice, 11,* 1–8. doi.org/10.1007/s40617-017-0201-0

Funk, M., Kosch, T., & Schmidt, A., (2016). Interactive worker assistance: comparing the effects of in-situ projection, head-mounted displays, tablet, and paper instructions. ACM International Joint Conference on Pervasive and Ubiquitous Computing, 934-939. doi.org/10.1145/2971648.2971706

Gable, R. A., Park, K. L., & Scott, T. M. (2014). Functional behavioral assessment and students at risk for or with emotional disabilities: Current issues and considerations. *Education and Treatment of Children, 37,* 111–135.

Gadaire, D. M., Marshall, G., & Brissett, E. (2019). Differential reinforcement of low rate responding in social skills training. *Learning and Motivation, 65,* 20–32. https://doi.org/10.1016/j.lmot.2017.08.005

Gardner, S. J., & Wolfe, P. S. (2019). Results of a video prompting intervention package impacting dishwashing skill acquisition for adolescents with autism. Journal of Special Education Technology, 34, 147-161. doi.org/10.1177/01626434188002666

Gaff, R. B., Gibson, L., & Galiatsatos, G. T. (2006). The impact of high- and low-preference stimuli on vocational and academic performances of youths with severe disabilities. *Journal of Applied Behavior Analysis, 39,* 131–136.

Gajar, A. H., Schloss, P. J., Schloss, C. N., & Thompson, C. K. (1984). Effects of feedback and self-monitoring on head trauma youths' conversation skills. *Journal of Applied Behavior Analysis, 17,* 353–358. Galbraith, L. A., & Normand, M. P. (2017). Step it up? Using the good behavior game to increase physical activity with elementary school students at recess. *Journal of Applied Behavior Analysis, 50,* 856–860. doi: 10.1002/jaba.403

Gallagher, M. M., Mittelstadt, P. A., & Slater, B. R. (1988). Establishing time-out procedures in a day treatment facility for young children. *Residential Treatment for Children & Youth, 5,* 59–68.

Ganz, J. B., Bourgeois, B. C., Flores, M. M., & Campos, B. A. (2008). Implementing visually cured imitation training with children with autism spectrum disorders and developmental delays. *Journal of Positive Behavior Interventions, 10,* 56–66.

Ganz, J. B., Cook, K. E., Corbin-Newsome, J. Bourgeois, B., & Flores, M. (2005). Variations on the use of a pictorial alternative communication system with a child with autism and developmental delays. *Teaching Exceptional Children Plus, 1*(6), 2005.

Garcia, E. E., Bullet, J., & Rust, F. P. (1977). An experimental analysis of language training generalization across classroom and home. *Behavior Modification, 1,* 531–550.

Garcia, E. E., & DeHaven, F. (1974). Use of operant techniques in the establishment and generalization of language: a review and analysis. *American Journal of Mental Deficiency, 79,* 169–178.

Garcia-Albea, E., Reeve, S. A., Reeve, K. F., & Brothers, K. J. (2014). Using audio script fading and multiple-exemplar training to increase vocal interactions in children with autism. *Journal of Applied Behavior Analysis, 47,* 325–343.

Gardner, R. III, Heward, W. L., & Grossi, T. A. (1994). Effects of response cards on student participation and academic achievement: A systematic replication with inner-city students during whole-class science instruction. *Journal of Applied Behavior Analysis, 27,* 63–72.

Garfinkle, A. N., & Schwartz, I. S. (2002). Peer imitation: Increasing social interactions in children with autism and other developmental disabilities in inclusive classrooms. *Topics in Early Childhood Special Education, 22,* 26–38.

Gast, D. L., & Nelson, C. M. (1977). Legal and ethical considerations for the use of timeout in special education settings. *The Journal of Special Education, 11,* 457–467.

Gast, D. L., Van Biervliet, A., & Spradlin, J. E. (1979). Teaching number-word equivalences: A study of transfer. *American Journal of Mental Deficiency, 83,* 524–527.

Gates, B. (2008, August, 11). How to fix Capitalism. *Time, 172*(6), 20–45.

Gaucher, M., & Gorget, J. (2010). Temporal regulation of children with autism spectrum disorder exposed to a differential-reinforcement-of-low-rates schedule. *Experimental Analysis of Behavior, 113,* 515–529. https://doi.org/10.1002/jeab.592

Gaul, K., Nietupski, J., & Cerro, N. (1985). Teaching super-market shopping skills using an adaptive shopping list. *Education and Training of the Mentally Retarded, 20,* 53–59.

Gauthier, K. A., Ahearn, W. H., & Colon, C. L. (2020). Further evaluation of treatment integrity for response interruption and redirection. *Behavior Intervention, 35,* 571-580. doi.org/10.1002/bin.1738

Geer, B. D., & Shahan, T. A. (2019). Resurgence as choice: Implications for promoting durable behavior change. *Journal of Applied Behavior Analysis, 52,* 816–846. doi: 10.1002/jaba.573

Gelfand. D. L. (1962). The influence of self-esteem on rate of verbal conditioning and social matching behavior. *Journal of Abnormal and Social Psychology, 65,* 259–265.

Gelfand, D. M., Hartmann, D. P. Lamb, A. D., Smith, C. L., Mahan, M. A., & Paul, S. C. (1974). The effects of adult models and described alternatives on children's choice of behavior management techniques. *Child Development, 45,* 585–593.

Geller, E. S. (2001). From ecological behaviorism to response generalization: Where should we make discriminations? *Journal of Organizational Behavior Management, 21*(4), 55–73.

Geren, M. A., Stromer, R., & Mackay, H. A. (1997). Picture naming, matching to sample, and head injury: A stimulus control analysis. *Journal of Applied Behavior Analysis, 30,* 339–342.

Gerencser, K. R., Higbee, T. S., Akers, J. S., & Contreras, B. P. (2017). Evaluation of interactive computerized training to teach parents to implement photographic activity schedules with children with autism spectrum disorder. *Journal of Applied Behavior Analysis, 50,* 567–581. doi: 10.1002/jaba.386

Gershoff, E. T. (2002). Corporal punishment by parents and associated child behaviors and experiences: A meta-analytic and theoretical review. *Psychological Bulletin, 128,* 539–579.

Gershoff, E. T., Foodman, G. S., Millelr-Perrin, C. L., Holden, G. W., Jackson, Y., Kazdin, A. E. (2018). The strength of the causal evidence against physical punishment of children and its implications for parents, psychologists, and policymakers. *American Psychologist, 73,* 626–638.

Gettinger, M. (1986). Issues and trends in academic engaged time of students. *Special Services in Schools, 2,* 1–17.

Ghaemmaghami, M., Hanley, G. P., & Jessel, J. (2021). Functional communication training: From efficacy to effectiveness. *Journal of Applied Behavior Analysis, 54,* 122–143. doi: 10.1002/jaba.762.

Ghezzi, P. M. (2007). Discrete trials teaching. *Psychology in the Schools, 44,* 667–679.

Gibbs, A. R., Tullis, C. A., Thomas, R., & Elkins, B. (2018). The effects of noncontingnet music and response interruption and redirection on vocal stereotypy. *Journal of Applied Behavior Analysis, 51,* 899914. doi.org/10.1002/jaba.485

Giles, A., & Markham, V. (2017). Comparing book- and tablet-based activity schedules: Acquisition and preference. *Behavior Modification, 41*(5), 647–664. doi.org/10.1177/45445517700817

Giles, A., Swain, S., Quinn, L., & Welfenbach, B. (2018). Teacher-implemented re-sponse interruption and redirection: Training, evaluation, and descriptive analysis of treatment integrity. *Behavior Modification, 42,* 148–169. doi.org10.1177/0145445517731061

Gillat, A., & Sulzer-Azaroff, B. (1994). Promoting principals managerial involvement in institutional improvement. *Journal of Applied Behavior Analysis, 27,* 115–129.

Girolami, K. M., Kahng, S., Hilker, K. A., & Girolami, P. A. (2008). Differential reinforcement of high rate behavior to increase the pace of self-feeding. *Behavioral Interventions, 24,* 17–22. https://dor.org/10.100s/bin.273

Glenn, I. M., & Dallery, J. (2007). Effects of internet-based voucher reinforcement and a transdermal nicotine patch on cigarette smoking. *Journal of Applied Behavior Analysis, 40,* 1–13.

Glover, J., & Gary, A. L. (1976). Procedures to increase some aspects of creativity. *Journal of Applied Behavior Analysis, 9,* 79–84.

Goetz, E. M., Ayala, J. M., Hatfield, V. L., Marshall, A. M., & Etzel, B. C. (1983). Training independence in preschoolers with an auditory stimulus management technique. *Education & Treatment of Children, 6,* 251–261.

Goetz, E. M., & Baer, D. M. (1973). Social control of form diversity and the emergence of new forms in children's blockbuilding. *Journal of Applied Behavior Analysis, 6,* 209–217. doi: 10.1901/jaba.1973.6-209

Goetz, E. M., & Salmonson, M. M. (1972). The effect of general and descriptive reinforcement on "creativity" in easel painting. In G. Semb (Ed.), *Behavior analysis and education.* Lawrence: University of Kansas.

Goh, A. E., & Bambara, L. M. (2012). Individualized positive behavior support in school settings: A Meta-Analysis. *Remedial and Special Education, 33,* 271–286.

Goh, H. L., & Iwata, B. A. (1994). Behavioral persistence and variability during extinction of self-injury maintained by escape. *Journal of Applied Behavior Analysis, 27,* 173–174.

Goh, H. L., Iwata, B. A., & DeLeon, I. G. (2000). Competition between noncontingent and contingent reinforcement schedules during response acquisition. *Journal of Applied Behavior Analysis, 33,* 195–205.

Goh, H. L., Iwata, B. A., & Kahng, S. (1999). Multicomponent assessment and treatment of cigarette pica. *Journal of Applied Behavior Analysis, 32,* 297–315.

Goh, H. L., Iwata, B. A., Shore, B. A., DeLeon, I. G., Lerman, D. C., Ulrich, S. M., & Smith, R. G. (1995). An analysis of the reinforcing properties of hand mouthing. *Journal of Applied Behavior Analysis, 28,* 269–283.

Goings, K., Carr, L., Maguire, H., Harper, J. M., & Luiselli, J. K. (2019). Improving classroom appearance and organization through a supervisory performance improvement intervention. *Behavior Analysis in Practice, 12,* 430–434. doi: org/10.1007/s40617-018-00304-7.

Gold, M., & Mann, D. W. (1982). Alternative schools for troublesome secondary students. *Urban Review, 14,* 305–316.

Goldstein, H., & Brown, W. H. (1989). Observational learning of receptive and expressive language by handicapped preschool children. *Education and Treatment of Children, 12,* 5–37.

Goldstein, R. S., Minkin, B. L., Minkin, N., & Baer, D. M. (1978). Finders, keepers: An analysis and validation of a free-found-ad policy. *Journal of Applied Behavior analysis, 11,* 465–473.

Goldstein, A. P., Sprafkin, R. P., Gershaw, N. J., & Klein, P. (1980). *Skillstreaming the adolescent.* Champaign, IL.: Research Press.

Goldiamond, I. (1968). *Stuttering and fluency as manipulatable operant response classes.* New York: Houghton Mifflin.

Goldiamond, I. (1974). Toward a constructional approach to social problems: Ethical and constitutional issues raised by applied behavior analysis. *Behaviorism, 2,* 1–85; also reprinted as a Classic Article in 2002: *Behavior and Social Issues, 11,* 108–197.

Goldiamond, I. (2002). Toward a constructional approach to social problems: Ethical and constitutional issues raised by applied behavior analysis. *Behavior and Social Issues, 11,* 108–197.

Goldsmith, T. R., LeBlanc, L. A., & Sauter, R. A. (2007). Teaching intraverbal behavior to children with autism. *Research in Autism Spectrum Disorders, 1,* 1–13.

Goldstein, G., & Wickstrom, S. (1986). Peer intervention effects on communicative interaction among handicapped and nonhandicapped preschoolers. *Journal of Applied Behavior Analysis, 19,* 209–214.

Gorski, J. A. B., & Westbrook, A. C. (2002). Use of differential reinforcement to treat medical non-compliance in a pediatric patient with leukocyte adhesion deficiency. *Pediatric Rehabilitation, 5,* 29–38.

Gorthmaker, V. J., Dally III, E. J., McCurdy, M., Persampieri, M. J., & Hergenrada, M. (2007). Improving reading outcomes for children with learning disabilities: Using brief experimental analysis to develop parent-tutoring interventions. *Journal of Applied Behavior Analysis, 40,* 203–221.

Gouboth, D., Wilder, D. A., & Bocher, J. (2007). The effects of signaling stimulus presentation during noncontingent reinforcement. *Journal of Applied Behavior Analysis, 40,* 725–730.

Goucher, M., & Forget, J. (2020). Temporal regulation of children with autism spectrum disorder exposed to a differential-reinforcement-of-low-rates schedule. *Journal of Experimental Analysis of Behavior, 113,* 515–528. doi.org/10.1002/jeab.592

Gover, H. C., Fahmie, T. A., & McKeown, C. A. (2019). A review of environmental enrichment as treatment for problem behavior maintained by automatic reinforcement. *Journal of Applied Behavior Analysis, 52,* 299-314. doi: 10.1002/jaba.508

Grabe, M. (1988). Technological enhancement of study behavior: on-line activities to produce more effective learning. *Collegiate Microcomputer, 6,* 253–259.

Grace, R. C., & Nevin, J. A. (1997). The relation between preferences and resistance to change. *Journal of the Experimental Analysis of Behavior, 67,* 43–65.

Graff, R. B., Gibson, L., & Galiatsatos, G. T. (2006). The impact of high- and low-preference stimuli on vocational and academic performances of youths with severe disabilities. *Journal of Applied Behavior Analysis, 39,* 131–135.

Graham, S., & Harris, K. R. (2003). Students with learning disabilities and the process of writing: A meta-analysis of SRSD studies. In H. L. Swanson, K. R. Harris, & S. Graham (Eds.), *Handbook of learning disabilities* (pp. 323–3344). New York: Guilford.

Gramling, S. E., Neblett, J., Grayson, R., & Townsend, D. (1996). Temporomandibular disorder. Efficacy of an oral habit reversal treatment program. *Journal of Behavior Therapy and Experimental Psychiatry, 27,* 245–256.

Granger, R. G., Porter, J. H., & Christoph, N. L. (1984). Schedule induced behavior in children as a function of inter-reinforcement interval length. *Physiology and Behavior, 33,* 153–157.

Graubard, P. S., Rosenberg, H., & Miller, M. B. (1971). Student applications of behavior modification to teachers and environments or ecological approaches to social deviancy. In E. A. Ramp & B. L. Hopkins (Eds.). *A new direction for education: Behavior Analysis, 1971.* (pp. 80–101). Lawrence, Kansas: University of Kansas.

Grauvogel-MacAaleese, A. N., & Wallace, M. D. (2010). Use of peer-mediated intervention in children with attention deficit hyperactivity disabilities. *Journal of Applied Behavior Analysis, 43,* 547–551.

Gravina, N., Lindstrom-Hazel, D., & Austin, J. (2007). The effects of workstation changes and behavioral interventions on safe typing postures in an office. *Work, 29*(3), 245–253.

Gray, C. A. (1996). *Social stories and comic strip conversations: Unique methods to improve social understanding* [Videotape]. Arlington, TX: Future Horizons.

Gray, C. A. (2000). *The new social story book.* Arlington, TX: Future Horizon.

Gray, C., & Garand, J. (1993). Social stories: Improving responses of students with autism with accurate social information. *Focus on Autistic Behavior, 8,* 1–10.

Green, C. W., Rollyson, J. H., Passante, S. C., & Reid, D. H. (2002). Maintaining proficient supervisor performance with direct support personnel: An analysis of two management approaches. *Journal of Applied Behavior Analysis, 35,* 205–208.

Green, D. R., Ferguson, J. L., Cihoon, J. H., Torres, N., Leaf, R., McEachin, J., Rudrud, E., Schulze, K., & Leaf, J. B. (2020). The teaching interaction procedure as a staff training tool. *Behavior Analysis in Practice, 13,* 421–433. doi.org/10.1007/s40617-019-00357-2

Green, G. (1992). Stimulus control technology for teaching number/quantity equivalences. *Proceedings of the Conference of the National Association for Autism (Australia),* pp. 51–63. Melbourne, Australia: Victorian Autistic Children's & Adults' Association.

Green, G. (2001). Behavior analytic instruction for learners with autism: Advances in stimulus control technology. *Focus on Autism and Other Developmental Disabilities, 16*(2), 72–85.

Green, L., & Rachlin, H. (1996). Commitment using punishment. *Journal of the Experimental Analysis of Behavior, 65,* 593–601.

Green, R. B., Hardison, W. L., & Greene, B. F. (1984). Turning the table on advice programs for parents: Using placemats to enhance family interaction at restaurants. *Journal of Applied Behavior Analysis, 17,* 497–508.

Green, V. A., Prior, T., Smart, E., Boelema, T., Drysdale, H., Harcourt, S., Roche, L., & Waddington, H. (2017). The use of individualized video modeling to enhance positive peer interactions in three preschool children. *Education and Treatment of Children, 40,* 353–378.

Greene, B. F., Winnett, R. A., Van Houten, R., Geller, E. S., & Iwata, B. A. (1987). *Behavior analysis in the community, 1968–1986.* Reprint series, Volume 2, by the Society for the Experimental Analysis of Behavior, Inc. Lawrence, Kansas.

Greene, D., & Lepper, M. R. (1974). Intrinsic motivation: How to turn play into work. *Psychology Today, 8,* 49–54.

Greenwald, A. E., Williams, W. L., & Seniuk, H. A. (2014). Decreasing supermarket tantrums by increasing shopping tasks: Advantages of Pre-Teaching. *Journal of Positive Behavior Interventions 16,* 56–59.

Greenwood, C. R. (2001). Class wide peer tutoring learning management system. *Remedial & Special Education, 22,* 34–48.

Greenwood, C. R., Baskin, A., & Sloane, H. N. (1974). Training elementary aged peer behavior managers to control small group programmed mathematics. *Journal of Applied Behavior Analysis, 7,* 103–114.

Greenwood, C. R., Carta, J. J., & Hall, V. H. (1988). The use of peer tutoring strategies in classroom management and educational instruction. *School Psychology Review, 17,* 258–275.

Greenwood, C. R., & Delquadri, J. (1995). Classwide peer tutoring and the prevention of school failure. *Preventing School Failure, 39*(4), 21–25.

Greenwood, C. R., Delquadri, J. C., & Carta, J. J. (1997). *Together we can! Classwide peer tutoring to improve basic academic skills.* Longmont, CO: Sopris West.

Greenwood, C. R., Delquadri, J. C., & Hall, R. V. (1989). Longitudinal effects of classwide peer tutoring. *Journal of Educational Psychology, 81,* 371–383.

Greer, D. G. (1985). A pedagogy for survival. In A. Brownstein (Ed.), *Progress in the science of behavior.* Hillsdale, N.J.: Laurence Erlbaum.

Greer, R. D. (1980). *Design for music learning.* New York: Teachers College Press.

Greer, R. D. (1981). An operant approach to motivation and affect: Ten years of research in music learning. In *Documentary report of the Ann Arbor Symposium: Applications of psychology to the teaching and learning of music.* (pp. 102–121). Music Educators' National Conference, Reston, VA.

Greer, R. D., & Speckman, J. M. (2009) The integration of speaker and listener responses: A theory of verbal development. *The Psychological Record 59,* 449-488.

Gresham, F. M. (1979). Comparison of response cost and timeout in a special education setting. *The Journal of Special Education, 13,* 199–206.

Gresham, F. M. (2005). Response to intervention: An alternative means of identifying students as emotionally disturbed. *Education and Treatment of Children, 28,* 328–244.

Gresham, F. M., Cook, C. R., Crews, S. D., & Kern, L. (2004). Social skills training for children and youth with emotional and behavioral disorders: Validity considerations and future directions. *Behavioral Disorders, 30,* 32–46.

Gresham, F. M., & MacMillan, D. L. (1997). Autistic recovery? An analysis and critique of the empirical evidence on the early intervention project. *Behavioral Disorders, 22*(4), 185–201.

Gresham, F. M., & Nagle, R. J. (1980). Social skills training with children: Responsiveness to modeling and coaching as a function of peer orientation. *Journal of Consulting and Clinical Psychology, 48,* 718–729.

Gresham, F. M., Van, M. V., & Cook, C. R. (2006). Social skills training for teaching replacement behaviors: Remediating acquisition deficits in at-risk students. *Behavioral Disorders, 31,* 363–377.

Grey, I., Healy, O., Leader, G., & Hayes, D. (2009). Using a time timer to increase appropriate waiting behavior in a child with developmental disabilities. *Research in Developmental Disabilities, 30,* 359–366.

Grindle, A. C., Dickinson, A. M., & Boettcher, W. (2000). Behavioral safety research in manufacturing settings: A review of the literature. *Journal of Organizational Behavior Management, 20*(1), 29–68.

Groman, S. M., James, A. S., Seu, E., Tran, S., Clark, T. A.,... Jentsch, J. D. (2014). In the blink of an eye: relating positive-feedback sensitivity to stratal dopamine D2-like receptors through blink rate. *Journal of Neuroscience, 34,* 14443–14454. doi: 10.1523/jneurosci.3037-14.2014.

Groskreutz, N. C., Groskreutz. M. P., Bloom, S E., & Slocum, T. A. (2014). Generalization of negatively reinforced hands in children with autism. *Journal of Applied Behavior Analysis, 47,* 560–579. doi: 10.1002/jaba.151.

Gross, A. M., Farrar, M. J., & Liner, D. (1982). Reduction of trichotillomania in a retarded cerebral palsied child using overcorrection, facial screening, and differential reinforcement of other behavior. *Education and Treatment of Children, 5,* 133–140.

Gross, A. M., Heimann, L., Shapiro, R., & Schultz, R. M. (1983). Children with diabetes: Social skills training and hemoglobin A1c levels. *Behavior Modification, 7,* 151–164.

Gross, D., & Gravey, C. (1997). Scolding, spanking and timeout revisited. *The American Journal of Maternal/Child Nursing, 22*(4), 209–213.

Grossman, L.S., Martis,B., & Fichtner, C. G. (1999). Are sex offenders treatable? A research overview (1999). *Psychiatric Services, 50,* 349–361.

Groves, E. A., & Austin, J. (2017). An evaluation of interdependent and independent group contingencies during the good behavior game. *Journal of Applied Behavior Analysis, 50,* 552–566. doi: 10.1002/jaba393.

Groves, E. A., & Austin J. L. (2019). Does the Good Behavior Game evoke negative peer pressure? Analyses in primary and secondary classrooms. *Journal of Applied Behavior Analysis, 52,* 3–16. doi: 10.1002/jaba.513

Grow, L. L., Carr, J. E., Kodak, T., Jostad, C. M., & Kisamore, A. N. (2011). A comparison of methods for teaching receptive labeling to children with autism spectrum disorders. *Journal of Applied Behavior Analysis, 44,* 475–498. doi: 10.1901/jaba.2011,44-475.

Grow, L. L., Kelley, M. E., Roane, H. S., & Shillingsburg. M. A. (2008). Utility of extinction-induced response variability for the selection of mands. *Journal of Applied Behavior Analysis, 41,* 15–24.

Grow, L. L., Kodak, T., & Carr, J. E. (2014). A comparison of methods for teaching receptive labeling to children with autism spectrum disorders: A systematic replication. *Journal of Applied Behavior Analysis, 47,* 600–605. doi: 10.1002/jaba.141

Gruber, B., Reeser, R., & Reid, D. H. (1979). Providing a less restrictive environment for profoundly retarded persons by teaching independent walking skills. *Journal of Applied Behavior Analysis, 12,* 285–297.

Gruber, D., & Poulson, C. L. (2016). Graduated guidance delivered by parents to teach yoga to children with developmental delays. *Journal of Applied Behavior Analysis, 49,* 193–198. dos: 10.1002/jaba.260.

Guardino, C., & Fullerton, E.K, (2014). Taking the time out of transitions. *Education and Treatment of Children, 37,* 211–228.

Guess, D. (1969). A functional analysis of receptive language and productive speech: Acquisition of the plural morpheme. *Journal of Applied Behavior Analysis, 2,* 55–64.

Guess, D., Helmstetter, E., Turnbull, H. R., & Knowlton, S. (1987). Use of aversive procedures with persons who are disabled: An historical review and critical analysis. *Monograph of the Association for Persons with Severe Handicaps.*

Guevremont, D.C., Osnes, P.G., & Stokes, T. (1986). Programming maintenance after correspondence training interventions with children. *Journal of Applied Behavior Analysis, 19,* 215–219.

Guevremont, D. & Woonsocket, D., & Spiegler,M.D., 2002, *Contemporary behavior therapy.* Cengage Publishing.

Guilhardi, P., Smith, J., Rivera, C., Ross, R. K. (2017). Learner preference between massed- and alternating-trial sequencing when teaching stimulus relations to children with autism.

*Behavior Analysis in Practice, 10*, 77–82.

Gulotta, C. S., Piazza, C. C., Patel, M. R., & Layer, S. A. (2005). Using food redistribution to reduce packing in children with severe food refusal. *Journal of Applied Behavior Analysis, 38,* 39–50.

Gustafson, C., Hotte, E., & Carsky, M. (1976). *Everyday living skills.* Unpublished manuscript, Mansfield Training School, Mansfield Depot, CT.

Haas, A., Vannest, K., & Smith, S. D. (2019). Utilizing peers to support academic learning for children with Autism Spectrum Disorder. *Behavior Analysis in Practice, 12,* 734–740.

Hackenberg, T. D. (2018). Token reinforcement: Translational research and application. *Journal of Applied Behavior Analysis, 51,* 393–435. doi: 10.1002/jaba.439

Hagopian, L. P., & Adelinis, J. D. (2001). Response blocking with and without redirection for the treatment of pica. *Journal of Applied Behavior Analysis, 34,* 527–530.

Hagopian, L. P., Crockett, J. L. van Stone, M., DeLeon, I. G., & Bowman, L. G. (2000). Effects of noncontingent reinforcement on problem behavior and stimulus engagement: The role of satiation, extinction, and alternative reinforcement. *Journal of Applied Behavior Analysis, 33,* 433–449.

Hagopian, L. P., Farrell, D. A., & Amari, D. (1996). Treating total liquid refusal with backward chaining and fading. *Journal of Applied Behavior Analysis, 29,* 573–575.

Hagopian, L. P., Fisher W. W., & Legacy, S. M. (1994). Schedule effects of noncontingent reinforcement on attention-maintained destructive behavior in identical quadruplets. *Journal of Applied Behavior Analysis, 27,* 317–325.

Hagopian, L.P., Fisher, W.W., Sullivan, M.T., Acquisto, J., & LeBlanc, L.A (1998). Effectiveness of functional communication training with and without extinction and punishment: A summary of 21 inpatient cases. *Journal of Applied Behavior Analysis, 31,* 211–235.

Hagopian, L. P., Kuhn, A. C., Long, E. S., & Rush, K S. (2005). Schedule thinning following communication training: Using competing stimuli to enhance tolerance to decrements in reinforcer density. *Journal of Applied Behavior Analysis, 38,* 177–193.

Hagopian, L. P., Paclawskyj, T. R., & Kuhn, S. C. (2005). The use of conditional probability analysis to identify a response chain leading to the occurrence of eye poking. *Research in Developmental Disabilities, 26,* 393–397.

Hagopian, L.P., Rush, K.S., Lewin, A.B., & Long, E.S. (2001). Evaluating the predictive validity of a single stimulus engagement preference assessment. *Journal of Applied Behavior Analysis, 34,* 475–485.

Hagopian, L. P., Rush, K. S., Richman, D. M., Kudrtz, P. F., Contrucci, S. A., & Crosland, K. (2002). The development and application of individualized levels systems for the treatment of problem behavior. *Behavior Therapy, 33,* 65–s86. doi: 10.1016/S0005-7894(02)80006-5

Hains, A., & Baer, D. M. (1989). Interaction effects in multielement designs: Inevitable, desirable, and ignorable. *Journal of Applied Behavior Analysis, 22,* 57–69.

Hake, D. F., Donaldson, T., & Hyten, C. (1983). Analysis of discriminative control by social behavioral stimuli. *Journal of the Experimental Analysis of Behavior, 39,* 7–23.

Hake, D. F., & Laws, D. R. (1967). Social facilitation of responses during a stimulus paired with electric shock. *Journal of the Experimental Analysis of Behavior, 10,* 387–392.

Hall, R. V. (1971a). *Managing behavior: Behavior modification: The measurement of behavior.* No. 1. Lawrence, KS: H & H Enterprises.

Hall, R. V. (1971b). *Managing behavior: Behavior modification: Applications in school and home.* No. 3. Lawrence, KS: H & H Enterprises.

Hall, R. V., Delquadri, J., Greenwood, C. R., & Thurston, L. (1982). The importance of opportunity to respond in children's academic success (pp. 107–149). In E. D. Edgar, N. Haring, J. R. Jenkins & C. Pious (Eds.). *Serving young handicapped children: Issues and research.* Austin, TX: Pro-Ed.

Hall, R. V., Lund, D., & Jackson, D. (1968). Effects of teacher attention on study behavior. *Journal of Applied Behavior Analysis, 1,* 1–12.

Halle, J. W., Baer, D. M., & Spradlin, J. E. (1981). Teachers' generalized use of delay as a stimulus control procedure to increase language use in handicapped children. *Journal of Applied Behavior Analysis, 14,* 389–409.

Halle, J. W., & Holt, B. (1991). Assessing stimulus control in natural settings: An analysis of stimuli that acquire control during training. *Journal of Applied Behavior Analysis, 24,* 579–589.

Halle, J. W., Marshall, G. M., & Spradlin, J. E. (1979). Time delay: A technique to increase language usage and facilitate generalization in retarded children. *Journal of Applied Behavior Analysis, 12,* 431–439.

Hamblin, R. L., Hathaway, C., & Wodarski, J. (1974). Group contingencies, peer tutoring, and accelerating academic achievement: Experiment 1. In E. Ramp & B. L. Hopkins (Eds.) *A new direction for education: Behavior Analysis* (pp. 41–53). Lawrence: University of Kansas.

Handen, B. L., & Zane, T. (1987). Delayed prompting: A review of procedural variations and results. *Research in Developmental Disabilities, 8,* 307–330.

Handen, B. L., Parish, J. M., McClung, T. S., Kerwin, M. E., & Evans, L. D. (1992). Using guided compliance versus timeout to promote compliance. *Research in Developmental Disabilities, 13,* 157–170.

Hangen, M. M., Romero, Neidert, & Borrero (2020). "Other" behavior and the DRO: The roles of extinction and reinforcement. *Journal of Applied Behavior Analysis, 53,* 2385–2404. doi: 10.1002/jaba.736

Hanley, E. M., Perelman, P. G., & Homan, C. I. (1979). Parental management of a child's self-stimulation behavior through the use of timeout and DRO. *Education and Treatment of Children, 2,* 305–310.

Hanley, G. P. (2012). Functional assessment of problem behavior. Dispelling myths, overcoming implementation obstacles, and developing new lore. *Behavior Analysis in Practice, 5,* 54–72. https://doi.org/10.1007/BF03391818.

Hanley, G. P., Cammilleri, A. P., Tiger, J. H., & Ingvarrson, E. T. (2007). A method for describing preschoolers' activity preferences. *Journal of Applied Behavior Analysis, 40,* 603–618.

Hanley, G. P., Heal, N. A., Tiger, J. H., & Ingvarsson, E. T. (2007). Evaluation of a classwide teaching program for developing preschool life skills. *Journal of Applied Behavior Analysis, 40*, 277–300.

Hanley, G. P., Iwata, B. A., & McCord, B. E. (2003). Functional analysis of problem behavior: A review. *Journal of Applied Behavior Analysis, 36*, 147–185.

Hanley, G. P., Iwata, B. A., & Roscoe, E. M. (2006). Some determinants of changes in preference over time. *Journal of Applied Behavior Analysis, 39*, 189–202.

Hanley, G. P., Iwata, B. A., Roscoe, E. M., Thompson, R. H., & Lindberg, J. S. (2003). Response-restriction analysis II: Alteration of activity preference. *Journal of Applied Behavior Analysis, 36*, 59–76.

Hanley, G.P., Iwata, B.A. & Thompson, R.H., (2001). Reinforcement schedule thinning following treatment with functional communication training. *Journal of Applied Behavior Analysis, 34*, 17–38.

Hanley, G. P. Iwata, B. A., Thompson, R. H., & Lindberg, J. S. (2000). A component analysis of stereotypy as reinforcement for alternative behavior. *Journal of Applied Behavior Analysis, 33*, 285–297.

Hanley, G. P., Jin, C. S., Vanselow, N. r., & Hanratty, L. A. (2014). Producing meaningful improvements in problem behavior of children with autism via synthesized analyses and treatments. *Journal of Applied Behavior Analysis, 47*, 15–36. doi: 10.1002/jaba.106

Hanley, G. P., Piazza, C. C., Fisher, W. W., & Maglieri, K. A. (2005). On the effectiveness of and preference for punishment and extinction components of function-based interventions. *Journal of Applied Behavior Analysis, 38*, 51–65.

Hanley, G. P., & Tiger, J. H. (2011). Differential reinforcement procedures. In W. W. Fisher, C. C. Piazza, & H. S. Roane (Eds.), *Handbook of applied behavior analysis* (pp. 229–249). New York, NY: Guilford Press.

Hanna, E. S., De Souza, D. V., De Rose, J. C., & Fonseca, M. (2004). Effects of delayed constructed-response identity matching on spelling of dictated words. *Journal of Applied Behavior Analysis, 37*, 223–227.

Hannum, J. S., Thoresen, C. E., & Hubbard, D. R. (1974). A behavioral study of self-esteem with elementary teachers. In M. J. Mahoney & C. E. Thoresen (Eds.), *Self-control: Power to the person*. Monterey, CA: Brooks/Cole.

Hansen, B., DeSouza, A. A., Stuart, A. L., & Shillingsburg, M. A. (2019). *Behavior Analysis in Practice, 12*, 199–203. https://doi.org/10.1007/s40617-018-00280-y

Hansen, B. D., & Wills, H. P. (2014). The effects of goal setting, contingent reward, and instructions on writing skills. *Journal of Applied Behavior Analysis, 47*. 171–175.

Hansen, B. D., Wills, H. P., & Kamps, D. M. (2014). The effects of function-based self-management interventions on student behavior. *Journal of Emotional and Behavioral Disorders, 22*, 149–159.

Hansen, D. J., Tisdelle, D. A., & O'Dell, S. L. (1985). Audio recorded and directly observed parent-child interactions: A comparison of observation methods. *Behavioral Assessment, 7*, 389–399.

Hansen, G. D. (1979). Enuresis control through fading, escape, and avoidance training. *Journal of Applied Behavior Analysis, 12*, 303–307.

Hantula, D.A., & Crowell, C.R. (1994). Behavioral contrast in a tow-option analogue task of financial decision making. *Journal of Applied Behavior Analysis, 27*, 607–617.

Hardiman, S. A., Goetz, E. M., Reuter, K. E., & LeBlanc, J. M. (1975). Primes, contingent attention and training: Effects on a child's motor behavior. *Journal of Applied Behavior Analysis, 8*, 399–209.

Harding, J. W., Wacker, D. P., Berg, W. K., Rick, G., & Lee, J. F. (2004). Promoting response variability and stimulus generalization in martial arts training. *Journal of Applied Behavior Analysis, 37*, 185–195.

Harding, J.W., Wacker, D.P., Berg, W.K., Winborn-Kemmerer. L., Lee, J.F., & Ibrahimovic, M. (2009). Analysis of multiple manding topographies during functional communication raining. *Education and Treatment of Children, 32*, 21–36.

Haring, T. G. (1988). *Generalization for students with severe handicaps*. Seattle: Washington University Press.

Haring, T. G., Kennedy, C. H., Adams, M. J., & Pitts-Conway, V. (1987). Teaching generalization of purchasing skills across community settings to autistic youth using videotape modeling. *Journal of Applied Behavior Analysis, 20*, 89–96.

Haring, T. G., Roger, B., Lee, M., Breen, C., & Gaylord-Ross, R. (1986). Teaching social language to moderately handicapped students. *Journal of Applied Behavior Analysis, 19*, 159–171.

Harmatz, M. G., & Lapuc, P. (1968). Behavior modification of overeating in a psychiatric population. *Journal of Consulting and Clinical Psychology, 32*, 583–587.

Harmon, T. M., Nelson, R. O., & Hayes, S. C. (1980). The differential effects of self-monitoring mood versus activity in depressed patients. *Journal of Consulting and Clinical Psychology, 48*, 30–38.

Harris, F. R., Wolf, M. M., & Baer, D. M (1967). In S. W. Bijou & S. M. Baer (Eds.), *Child development: Readings in experimental analysis*. New York: Appleton.

Harris, M., Casey, L. B., Meindl, J. N., Powell, D., Hunter, W. C., & Delgado, D. (2020). Using behavioral skills training with video feedback to prevent risk of injury in youth female soccer athletes. *Behavior Analysis in Practice, 13*, 811–819. https://doi.org/10.1007/s40617-020-00473-4

Harris, R. E., Marchand-Martella, N., & Martella, R. C. (2000). Effects if a peer-delivered corrective reading program. *Journal of Behavioral Education, 10*, 21–36.

Harris, S. L., & Ersner-Hershfield, R. (1978). Behavioral suppression of seriously disruptive behavior in psychotic and retarded patients: A review of punishment and its alternatives. *Psychological Bulletin, 85*, 1352–1375.

Harris, S. L., & Wolchik, S. A. (1979). Suppression of self-stimulation: Three alternative strategies. *Journal of Applied Behavior Analysis, 12*, 185–198.

Harris, V. W., & Sherman, J. A. (1973). A use and analysis of the "good behavior game" to reduce disruptive classroom behavior. *Journal of Applied Behavior Analysis, 6*, 405–417.

Harrison, A. M., & Piles, D A. (2013). The effects of verbal instructions and shaping to improve tackling by high school football players. *Journal of Applied Behavior Analysis, 46,* 518–522.

Hart, B., & Risley, T. R. (1975). Incidental teaching of language in the preschool. *Journal of Applied Behavior Analysis, 8,* 411–420.

Hart, B., & Risley, T. R. (1980). In vivo language intervention: Unanticipated general effects. *Journal of Applied Behavior Analysis, 13,* 407–432.

Hart, B., & Risley, T. (1995). *Meaningful differences in the everyday experience of young American children.* Baltimore: Brookes Publishing Co.

Hart, S.L., & Banda, D.R. (2009). Picture exchange communication system with individuals with developmental disabilities: A meta-analysis of single subject studies. *Remedial and Special Education,* OnlineFirst, published on August 26, 2009.

Hartman, D. P., & Hall, R. V. (1976). The changing criterion design. *Journal of Applied Behavior Analysis, 9,* 527–532.

Hartmann, D. P., Gottman, J. M., Jones, R. R., Gardner, W., Kazdin, A. E., & Vaught, R. (1980). Interrupted time-series analysis and its application to behavioral data. *Journal of Applied Behavior Analysis, 13,* 543–559.

Hausman, N. L., Ingvarsson, E. T., and Kahng, S. W. (2014). A comparison of reinforcement schedules to increase independent responding in individuals with intellectual disabilities. *Journal of Applied Behavior Analysis, 47,* 155–159.

Hasiam, C., Gilroy, D., Black, S., & Beesley, T. (2006). How successful is errorless learning in supporting memory for high and low-level knowledge in dementia? *Neuropsychological Rehabilitation, 16,* 505–536.

Haskett, G. J., & Lenfestey, W. (1974). Reading-related behavior in an open classroom: Effects of novelty and modeling on preschoolers. *Journal of Applied Behavior Analysis, 7,* 233–241.

Hatch, J. P. (1980). The effects of operant reinforcement schedules on the modification of human heart rate. *Psychophysiology, 17,* 559–567.

Haug, N. A., & Sorensen, J. L. (2006). Contingency management interventions for HIV-related behaviors. *Current HIV/AIDS Reports, 3,* 144–149.

Haupt, E. J., Van Kirk, M. J., & Terraciano, T. (1975). An inexpensive fading procedure to decrease error and increase retention of number facts. In E. Ramp & G. Semb (Eds.), *Behavior analysis: Areas of research and application* (pp. 225–232). Englewood Cliffs, NJ: Prentice-Hall.

Hawkins, A. M., Burgio, L. D., Lanford, A., & Engel, B. T. (1992). The effects of verbal and written supervisory feedback on staff compliance with assigned prompted voiding in a nursing home. *Journal of Organizational Behavior Management, 13,* 137–150.

Hawkins, R. P. (1985). Comment: On Woolfolk and Richardson. *American Psychologist, 40,* 1138–1139.

Hawkins, R. P. (1986). Selection of target behaviors. In R. O. Nelson & S. C. Hayes (Eds.). *Conceptual foundations of behavioral assessment* (pp. 331–385). New York: Guilford.

Hawkins, R. P., & Dotson, V. A. (1975). Reliability scores that delude: An Alice in Wonderland trip through the misleading characteristics of interobserver agreement scores in interval recording. In E. Ramp & G. Semp (Eds.), *Behavior Analysis: Areas of research and application* (pp. 359–376). Englewood Cliffs, NJ: Prentice-Hall.

Hawkins, R. O., Haydon, T., Denune, H., Larkin, W., Fite, N. (2015). Improving the transition behavior of high school students with emotional behavioral disorders using a randomized interdependent group contingency. *School Psychology Review, 44,* 208–223.

Hayden, M., Wheeler, M., & Carnine, D. (1989). The effects of an innovative classroom networking system and an electronic gradebook on time spent scoring and summarizing student performance. *Education and Treatment of Children, 12,* 353–264.

Hayden, T., Musti-Ran, S., & Later, P. (2017). Comparing choral responding and choral responding plus mnemonic device during geography lessons for students with mild to moderate disabilities. *Education and Treatment of Children, 40,* 77–96.

Haydon, T., Masti-Rao, S., & Alter, P. (2017). Comparing choral responding and choral responding plus mnemonic device during geography lessons for students with mild to moderate disabilities. *Education and Treatment of Children, 40,* 77–96.

Hayes, L. J., Aguiar, M. J. & Hayes, S. C. (1991). Communicative behavior. In B. Sulzer-Azaroff & G. R. Mayer (Eds.), *Behavior analysis for lasting change* (pp. 351–369). New York: Holt-Rinehart-Winston.

Hayes, L. J., Tilley, K., & Hayes, S. C. (1988). Extending equivalence class membership to gustatory stimuli. *The Psychological Record, 38,* 473–482.

Hayes, S. C. (1994). Relational frame theory: A functional approach to verbal events. In S. C. Hayes, M. Sato, & K. Ono, (Eds.), *Behavior analysis of language and cognition* (pp. 11–30). Reno, NV: Context Press.

Hayes, L. B., & Van Camp, C. M. (2015). Increasing physical activity of children during school recess. *Journal of Applied Behavior Analysis, 48,* 690–695. doi: 10.1002/jaba.222.

Hayes, S. C., & Barnes, D. (1997). Analyzing derived stimulus relations requires more than the concept of stimulus class. *Journal of Experimental Analysis of Behavior, 68,* 235–270.

Hayes, S. C., Barnes-Holmes, D., & Roche, B. (2001). *Relational frame theory: A post-Skinnerian account of human language and cognition.* New York: Kluwer Academic/Plenum Publishers.

Hayes, S. C., & Hayes, L. J., (1989). The verbal actions of the listener as a basis for rule-governance. In S. C. Hayes (Ed.), *Rule-governed behavior: Cognition, contingencies and instructional control* (pp. 153–190). New York: Plenum Press.

Hayes, S. C., & Hayes, L. J. (1992). Verbal relations and the evolution of behavior analysis. *American Psychologist, 47,* 1383–1395.

Hayes, S. C., Munt, E. D., Korn, Z., Wulfert, E., Rosenfarb, I., & Zettle, R. D. (1988). The effect of feedback and self-reinforcement instructions on studying performance. *The Psychological Record, 36,* 27–37.

Hayes, S. C., Nelson, R. O., & Jarrett, R. B. (1987). The treatment utility of assessment. A functional approach to evaluating assessment quality. *American Psychologist, 42,* 963–974.

Hayes, S. C., Strosahl, K., & Wilson, K. G. (2012). *Acceptance and commitment therapy: The process and practice of mindful change* (2nd edition). New York; NY: Guilford Press.

Haynes, S. N. (1978). *Principles of behavioral assessment.* New York: Gardner Press.

Haynes, S. N., & Horn, W. F. (1982). Reactivity in behavioral observation: A review. *Behavioral Assessment, 4,* 369–385.

Haynes, S. N., & Wilson, C. C. (1979). *Behavioral assessment: Recent advances in concepts, methods, and outcomes.* San Francisco: Jossey-Bass.

Hays, T., & Romani, P. W. (2021). Use of the performance diagnostic checklist-human services to assess hand hygiene compliance in a hospital. *Behavior Analysis in Practice, 14,* 51–57. https://doi.org/10.1007/s40617-020-00461-s

Health Resources and Services Administration, HRSA, (2005). Glossary of HIV/AIDS-Related Terms 5th Edition. October, US Department of Health and Human Services.

Heal, N. A., & Hanley, G. P. (2007). Evaluating preschool children's preferences for motivational systems during instruction. *Journal of Applied Behavior Analysis, 40,* 249–261.

Heard, K., & Watson, T. S. (1999). Reducing wandering by persons with dementia using differential reinforcement. *Journal of Applied Behavior Analysis, 32,* 381–384.

Heatherton, T. F., & Sargent, J. D. (2009). Does watching smoking in movies promote teenage smoking? *Current Directions in Psychological Science, 18,* 63–67.

Heckaman, K. A., Alber, S., Hooper, S., & Heward, W. L. (1998). A comparison of least-to-most prompts and progressive time delay on the disruptive behavior of students with autism. *Journal of Behavioral Education, 8,* 171–201.

Hedquist, O.. B., & Roscoe E. M. (2020). A comparison of differential reinforcement procedures for treating automatically reinforced behavior. *Journal of Applied Behavior Analysis, 53,* 284–295. doi:10.1002/jaba.561

Heekes, S., Kruger, C. B., Lester, S. N., & Ward, C L. (2020). Systematic review of corporal punishment in schools: Global prevalence and correlates. *Trauma, Violence & Abuse.* (on-line) https://doe.org/a0.1177/1524838020925787

Heering, P. W., & Wilder, D. A. (2006). The use of dependent group contingencies to increase on-task behavior in two general education classrooms. *Education and Treatment of Children, 29,* 459–468.

Heffer, R. W., & Kelley, M. L. (1987). Mothers' acceptance of behavioral interventions for children: The influence of parent race and income. *Behavior Therapy, 18,* 153–163.

Heffernan, T., & Richards, C. S. (1981). Self-control of study behavior: Identification and evaluation of natural methods. *Journal of Counseling Psychology, 28,* 361–364.

Heffernan, L., & Lyons, D. (2016). Differential reinforcement of other behaviour for the reduction of severe nail biting. *Behavior Analysis in Practice 9*(3), 253–256.

Hegel, M.T., & Ferguson, R.J. (2000). Differential reinforcement of other behavior (DRO) to reduce aggressive behavior following traumatic brain injury. *Behavior Modification, 24,* 94–101

Heiby, E. M. (1983). Toward the prediction of mood change. *Behavior Therapy, 14,* 110–115.

Heinicke, M. R.., Carr, J. E., & Copsey, C. J. (2019). Assessing preferences of individuals with developmental disabilities using alternative stimulus modalities: A systematic review. *Journal of Applied Behavior Analysis, 52*(3), 847–869. https://doi-org.mimas.calstatela.edu/10.1002/jaba.565

Heldt, J., & Schlinger, H D. (2012). Increased variability in teaching under a lag 3 schedule of reinforcement. *Analysis of Verbal Behavior, 28,* 131–136.

Henderson, H. S., Jenson, W. R., & Erken, N. F. (1986). Using variable interval schedules to improve on-task behavior in the classroom. *Education and Treatment of Children, 9,* 250–263.

Hernandez, E., Hanley, G.P., Ingvarsson, E.T., & Tiger, J.H. (2007). A preliminary evaluation of the emergence of novel mand forms. *Journal of Applied Behavior Analysis, 40,* 137–156.

Herrnstein, R. J. (1961). Relative and absolute strength of response as a function of frequency of reinforcement. *Journal of the Experimental Analysis of Behavior, 4,* 266–267.

Herrnstein, R. J. (1964). Aperiodicity as a factor in choice. *Journal of the Experimental Analysis of Behavior, 7,* 179–182.

Herrnstein, R. J. (1970). On the law of effect. *Journal of the Experimental Analysis of Behavior, 13,* 243–266.

Herrnstein, R. J. (1989). IQ and falling birth rates. *The Atlantic Monthly, 263,* 73–79.

Herrnstein, R.J. (1997). *The matching law.* In H. Rachlin & D. I. Laibson (Eds.), *Papers in psychology and economics.* Harvard University Press.

Herrnstein, R. J., & Loveland, D. H. (1975). Maximizing and matching on concurrent ration schedules. *Journal of the Experimental Analysis of Behavior, 24,* 107–116.

Hersen, M. H., & Barlow, P. H. (1976). *Single case experimental designs.* New York: Pergamon.

Hesse, K. D., Robinson, J. W., & Rankin, R. (1983). Retention and transfer from morphemically based direct instruction spelling program in junior high. *The Journal of Educational Research, 76,* 276–279.

Heward, W. L., & Eachus, H. T. (1979). Acquisition of adjectives and adverbs in sentences written by hearing impaired and aphasic children. *Journal of Applied Behavior Analysis, 12,* 391–400.

Heyman, G. M. (1992). Effects of methylphenidate on response rate and measures of motor performance and reinforcement efficacy. *Psychopharmacology, 109,* 145–152.

Hicks, K. G. (1965). Imitation and retention of film-mediated aggressive peer and adult models. *Journal of Personality and Social Psychology, 2,* 97–100.

Hieneman, M., & Dunlap, G. (2001). Factors affecting the outcomes of community-based behavioral support. *Journal of Positive Behavior Interventions, 2,* 67–74.

Hienz, R. D., Brady, J. V., Hursh, S. R., Ragusa, L. C., Rouse, C. O., & Gasior, E. D. (2005). Distributed communication and psychosocial performance in simulated space dwelling groups. *Acta Astronautica, 56*(9–12), 937–948.

Higbee, T. S., Aporta, A. P., Resende, A., Nogueira, M., Goyos, C., & Pollard, J. S. (2016). Interactive computer training to teach discrete trial instruction to undergraduates and special educators in Brazil. *Journal of Applied Behavior Analysis, 49,* 780–793. doi: 10.1002/jaba.329

Higgins, S.T., & Budley, A.J. (1993). *Treatment of drug dependence through the principles of behavior analysis and behavioral pharmacology.* NIH, NIDA Monographs, 97–126.

Higgins, J. W., Williams, R. L., & McLaughlin, T. F. (2001). The effects of a token economy employing instructional consequences for a third-grade student with learning disabilities: A data-based case study. *Education and Treatment of Children, 24,* 99–106.

Himle, M. B., Chang, S., Woods, D. W., Pearlman, A., Buzzella, B., Bunaciu, L., & Piacentini, J. C. (2006). Establishing the feasibility of direct observation in the assessments of tics in children with chronic tic disorder. *Journal of Applied Behavior Analysis, 39,* 429–440.

Higgins, W.J., Luczynski, K. C., Carroll, R. A., Fisher, W. W., & Mudford, O.C. (2017). Evaluation of a telehealth training package to remotely train staff to conduct a preference assessment. *Journal of Applied Behavior Analysis, 50,* 238–251. doi: 10.1002/jaba.370

Himle, M. B., Miltenberger, R. G., Flessner, C., & Gatheridge, B. (2004a). Teaching safety skills to children to prevent gun play. *Journal of Applied Behavior Analysis, 37,* 1–9.

Himle, M. B., Milternberger, R. G., Gatheridge, B., & Flessner, C. (2004b). An evaluation of two procedures for training skills to prevent gun play in children. *Pediatrics, 113*(1), 70–77.

Himle, M. B., Woods, D. W., Piacentini, J. C., & Walkup, J. T. (2006). Reversal training for Tourette Syndrome. *Journal of Child Neurology, 21,* 719–725.

Hineline, P. N. (1984). The several roles of stimuli in negative reinforcement. In P. Harzem and M. D. Zeiler (Eds.). *Predictability, correlation, and contiguity* (pp. 203–246). New York: Wiley.

Hinshaw, S. P. (1992). Externalizing behavior problems and academic underachievement in childhood and adolescence: Causal relationships and underlying mechanisms. *Psychological Bulletin, 111,* 127–155.

Hively, W. (1962). Programming stimuli in matching to sample. *Journal of the Experimental Analysis of Behavior, 5,* 279–298.

Hobbs, S. A., & Forehand, R. (1975). Effects of differential release form timeout on children's deviant behavior. *Journal of Behavior Therapy and Experimental Psychiatry, 6,* 256–257.

Hobbs, S. A., Forehand, R., & Murray, R. G. (1978). Effects of various durations of timeout on noncompliant behavior of children. *Behavior Therapy, 9,* 652–656.

Hobson, R. P., & Lee, A. (2003). Imitation and identification in autism. *Journal of Child Psychology and Psychiatry, 40,* 649–659.

Hodes, J. W., Meppelder, M., de Moor, M., Kef, S., & Schuengel. (2016). Alleviating parenting stress in parents with intellectual disabilities; A randomized controlled trial of a video-feedback intervention to promote positive parenting. *Journal of Applied Research in Intellectual Disabilities, 30,* 423–432. doi: 10.1111/jar.12302.

Hoffmann, A. N., Samaha, A. L., Bloom, S. E., & Boyle, M. A. (2017). Preference and reinforcer efficacy of high- and low-tech items. A comparison of time type and duration for access. *Journal of Applied Behavior Analysis, 50,* 222–237. doi: 10.1002/jaba.383

Hofmeister, A., Engelmann, S., & Carnine, D. (1989). Developing and validating science education videodiscs. *Journal of Research in Science Teaching, 26*(7), 655–677.

Hogan, S., & Prater, M. A. (1993). The effects of peer tutoring and self-management training on on-task, academic, and disruptive behaviors. *Behavior Disorders, 18,* 188–128.

Hogan, W. A., & Johnson, D. P. (1985). Elimination of response cost in a token economy program and improvement in behavior of emotionally disturbed youth. *Behavior Therapy, 16,* 87–98.

Hoko, J. A., & LeBlanc, J. M. (1988). Stimulus equalization: Temporary reduction of stimulus complexity to facilitate discrimination learning. *Research in Developmental Disabilities, 9,* 255–275.

Holden, B., & Sulzer-Azaroff, B. (1972). Schedules of follow-up and their effect upon the maintenance of a prescriptive teaching program. In G. Semb, I. R. Green, R. P. Hawkins, J. Michael, E.L. Phillips, J. A. Sherman, H. Sloane, & D. R. Thomas (Eds.) *Behavior analysis and education.* Kansas: University of Kansas.

Holland, J. G., & Skinner, B. F. (1961). *The analysis of behavior: A program of self-instruction.* New York: McGraw-Hill.

Holth, P. (2017). Multiple exemplar training: Some strengths and limitations. *The Behavior Analyst, 40,* 225–241. doe: 10.1007/s40614-017-0083-z

Holtz, W. C., & Azrin, N. H. (1961). Discriminative properties of punishment. *Journal of the Experimental Analysis of Behavior, 6,* 399–406.

Holtz, W. C., Azrin, N. H., & Allyon, T. (1963). Elimination of behavior of mental patients by response produced extinction. *Journal of the Experimental Analysis of Behavior, 6,* 407–412.

Homer, A. L., & Peterson, L. (1980). Differential reinforcement of other behavior: A preferred response elimination procedure. *Behavior Therapy, 11,* 449–471.

Honeywell, J. A., Dickinson, A. M., & Poling, A. (1997). Individual performance as a function of individual and group pay contingencies. *Psychological Record, 47,* 261–274.

Hood, S. A., Luczynski, K. C., & Mitteer, D. R. (2017). Toward meaningful outcomes in teaching conversation and greeting skills with individuals with autism spectrum disorder. *Journal of Applied Behavior Analysis, 50,* 459–486. doi: 10.1002/jaba.388

Hood, S. A., Olsen, A. E., Luczynski, K. C., & Randle, F. A. (2010). Improving accepting and giving compliments with individuals with developmental disabilities. *Journal of Applied Behavior Analysis, 53,* 1013–1028. doi: 10.1002/jaba.662

Hoogeveen, F. R., Smeets, P. M., & Lancioni, G. E. (1989). Teaching moderately mentally retarded children basic reading skills. *Research in Developmental Disabilities, 10,* 1–18.

Hopkins, B. L. (1987). Comments of the future of applied behavior analysis. *Journal of Applied Behavior Analysis, 20,* 339–346.

Horne, P. J., & Lowe, C. F. (1993). Determinants of human performance on concurrent schedules. *Journal of the Experimental Analysis of Behavior, 59,* 29–60.

Horne, P.J., & Lowe, C.F. (1996). On the origins of naming and other symbolic behavior. *Journal of the Experimental Analysis of Behavior, 65,* 185–241.

Horne, P.J., & Lowe, C.F. (1993). Determinants of human performance on concurrent schedules. *Journal of the*

*Experimental Analysis of Behavior, 59,* 29–60.

Horne, P.J., Lowe, C. F., & Harris, D.A. (2007). Naming and categorization in young children: V. Manual sign training. *Journal of the Experimental Analysis of Behavior, 87,* 367–381.

Horner, R. D. (1980). The effects of an environmental "enrichment" program on the behavior of institutionalized profoundly retarded children. *Journal of Applied Behavior Analysis, 13,* 473–492.

Horner, R. D., & Baer, D. M. (1978). Multiple-probe technique: A variation of the multiple baseline. *Journal of Applied Behavior Analysis, 11,* 189–196.

Horner, R. D., & Keilitz, I. (1975). Training mentally retarded adolescents to brush their teeth. *Journal of Applied Behavior Analysis, 8,* 301–309.

Horner, R. H. (1994). Functional assessment: Contributions and future directions. *Journal of Applied Behavior Analysis, 27,* 401–404.

Horner, R. H. (2002). On the status of knowledge for using punishment: A commentary. *Journal of Applied Behavior Analysis, 35,* 465–467.

Horner, R. H., & Budd, C. M. (1985). Acquisition of manual sign use: Collateral reduction of maladaptive behavior and factors limiting generalization. *Education and Training of the Mentally Retarded, 20,* 39–47.

Horner, R.H., Carr, E.G., Halle, J., McGee, G.., Odom, S. & Wolery, M. (2005). The use of single-subject research to identify evidence-based practice in special education, *Exceptional Children, 71,* 165–179.

Horner, R. H., Carr, E. G., Strain, P. S., Todd, A. W., & Reed, H. K. (2002). Problem behavior interventions for young children with autism: A research synthesis. *Journal of Autism and Developmental Disabilities, 32,* 423–446.

Horner, R. H., & Day, H. M. (1991). The effects of response efficiency on functionally equivalent competing behaviors. *Journal of Applied Behavior Analysis, 24,* 719–732.

Horner, R. H., Sprague, J., & Wilcox, B. (1982). General case programming for community activities. In B. Wilcox & G. T. Bellamy (Eds.), *Design of high school programs for severely handicapped students* (pp. 61–98). Baltimore: Brookes.

Horner, R. H., & Sugai, G. (2000). School-wide behavior support: An emerging initiative. *Journal of Positive Behavior Interventions, 2,* 231–232.

Horr, J. A. M., & Michael, A. V. (2021). Functional analysis of noncontingent reinforcement with extinction in the treatment of perseverative speech. *Behavior Analysis in Practice, 14,* 208-213. https://doi.org/10.1007/s40617-020-00523-x

Horton, S. B. (1987). Reduction of disruptive mealtime behavior by facial screening. A case study of a mentally retarded girl with long-term follow-up. *Behavior Modification, 11,* 53–64.

Hosford, R. E. (1980). Self-as-a-model: A cognitive social learning technique. *The Counseling Psychologist, 9,* 45–61.

Hosford, R. E., Moss, R. E., & Morrell, G. (1976). Developing law abiding behavior. The-self-as-a-model technique: Helping prison inmates change. In J. D. Krumboltz and C. E. Thoresen (Eds.). *Counseling methods.* (pp. 487–495). New York: Holt, Rinehart & Winston.

Houchins, N., & Boyce, T. E. (2001). Response generalization in behavioral safety: Fact or Fiction? *Journal of Organizational Behavior Management, 21*(4), 3–11.

Houten, R. V., Malenfant, J. E. L., Austin, J., & Lebbon, A. (2005). The effects of a seatbelt-gearshift delay prompt on the seatbelt use of motorists who do not regularly wear seatbelts. *Journal of Applied Behavior Analysis, 38,* 195–203.

Houvouras, A. J., & Harvey, M. T. (2014). Establishing fire safety skills using behavioral skills training. *Journal of Applied Behavior Analysis, 47,* 1–5. doi: 10.1002/jaba.113.

Howard, A. J., Morrison, J. Q., & Collins, T. (2020). Evaluating self-management interventions: Analysis of component combinations, *School Psychology Review, 49*:2, 130–143

Howie, P. M., & Woods, C. L. (1982). Token reinforcement during the instatement and shaping of fluency in the treatment of stuttering. *Journal of Applied Behavior Analysis, 15,* 55–64.

Howlin, P., Gordon, R. K., Pasco, G., Wade, A., & Charman, T. (2007). The effectiveness of picture exchange communication system (PECS) training for teachers of children with autism: A pragmatic, group randomized controlled trial. *Journal of Child Psychology & Psychiatry, 48,* 473–481.

Hranchuk, K., Greer, R. D., & Longano, J. (2019). Instructional demonstrations are more efficient than consequences alone for children with naming. *Analysis of Verbal Behavior, 35,* 1–20.

Huberman, W. L., & O'Brien, R. M. (1999). Improving therapist and patient performance in chronic psychiatric group homes through goal-setting, feedback, and positive reinforcement. *Journal of Organizational Behavior Management, 19*(1), 13–36.

Huesmann, L.R., Moise-Titus, J., Podolski, C., & Eron, L.D. (2003). Longitudinal relations between children's exposure to TV violence and their aggressive and violent behavior in young adulthood. *Developmental Psychology, 39,* 201–221.

Hughes, C. A., & Hendrickson, J. M. (1987). Self-monitoring with at-risk students in the regular class setting. *Education and Treatment of Children, 10,* 225–236.

Hughes, M.W., Schuster, J.W., & Nelson, C.M. (1993). The acquisition of independent dressing skills by students with multiple disabilities. *Journal of Developmental and Physical Disabilities, 5,* 233–252.

Hundert, J. P. (2007). Training classroom and resource preschool teachers to develop inclusive class interventions for children with disabilities. *Journal of Positive Behavior Interventions, 9,* 159–173.

Hundert, J., & Hopkins, B. (1992). Training supervisors in a collaborative team approach to promote peer interaction of children with disabilities in integrated preschools. *Journal of Applied Behavior Analysis, 25,* 385–400.

Hunkin, N. M., Squires, E. J., Parkin, A. J., & Tidy, J. A. (1998). Are the benefits of errorless learning dependent on implicit memory? *Neuropsychologia, 36,* 25–36.

Hunt, P., Goetz, L., & Anderson, J. (1986). The quality of IEP objectives associated with placement on integrated versus segregated school sites. *Journal of the Association for Persons with Severe Handicaps, 11,* 125–130.

Hunt, S., & Sulzer-Azaroff, B. (1974). *Motivating parent participation in home training sessions with pre-trainable retardants.* Paper presented at the American Psychological Association, New Orleans, Louisiana.

Hursh, S. R. (1984). Behavioral economics. *Journal of Experimental Analysis of Behavior, 42,* 435–452.

Husan, Y., Begue, L., Scharkow, M. G., & Bushman, B. J. (2013). The more you play the more aggressive you become: A long-term experimental study of cumulative violent video game effects on hostile expectations and aggressive behavior. *Journal of Experimental Social psychology, 49,* 224–227. doi: 10.1016/j.jesp2012.10.016

Hutchins, T. L., & Prelock, P. A. (2013). Parents perceptions of their children's social behavior: The social validity of social storiesTM and comic strip conversations. *Journal of Positive Behavior Interventions, 15,* 156–168.

Hutchinson, R. R. (1977). By-products of aversive control. In W. K. Honig & J. E. R. Staddon (Eds.), *Handbook of operant behavior.* Englewood Cliffs, NJ: Prentice Hall, 415–431.

Hutchinson, R. R., & Azrin, N. H. (1961). Conditioning of mental hospital patients to fixed-ratio schedules of reinforcement. *Journal of the Experimental Analysis of Behavior, 4,* 87–95.

Hutchinson, R. R., Azrin, N. H., & Hunt, G. M. (1968). Attack produced by intermittent reinforcement of a concurrent operant response. *Journal of the Experimental Analysis of Behavior, 11,* 489–495.

Hyten, C., Madden, G. J., & Field, D. P. (1994). Exchange delays and impulsive choice in adult humans. *Journal of Experimental Analysis of Behavior, 62,* 225–233.

Iannaccone, J. A., Hagopian, L. P., Javed, N., Borrero, J. C., & Zarcone, J. R. (2020). Rules and statements of reinforcers loss in differential reinforcement of other behavior. *Behavior Analysis in Practice, 13,* 81–89. doi.org/10.1007/s40617-019-00352-7

Individuals with Disabilities Education Act Amendments of 1997, 20 U.S.C. § 1400 *et seq.*

Individuals with Disabilities Education Act of 2004, P. L. 105–17, 20 U.S.C. para. 1400 *et seq.*

Ingvarsson, E. T., & Hanley, G. P. (2006). An evaluation of computer-based programmed instruction for promoting teachers' greetings of parents by name. *Journal of Applied Behavior Analysis, 39,* 203–214.

Ingvarsson, E T., Tiger, J. H., Hanley, G. P., & Stephenson, K. M. (2007). An evaluation of intraverbal training to generate socially appropriate responses to novel question. *Journal of Applied Behavior Analysis, 40,* 411–429.

Irvin, L. K., & Singer, G. S. (1984). *Human rights review manual.* Eugene, OR: Oregon Research Institute.

Irvin, L. K., & Singer, G. S. (1985). *Informed consent for intrusive behavioral treatments.* Eugene, OR. Oregon Research Institute.

Isquierdo, A., Brigman, J. L., Radke, A. K., Rudebeck, P. H., & Holmes, A. (2017). the neural basis of reversal learning: An updated perspective. *Neuroscience, 345,* 12–26.

Israel, A. C., & O'Leary, K. D. (1973). Developing correspondence between children's words and deeds. *Child Development, 44,* 575–581.

Iwata, B. A. (1987). Negative reinforcement in applied behavior analysis: An emerging technology. *Journal of Applied Behavior Analysis, 20,* 361–378.

Iwata, B. A. (1995). *Functional analysis screening tool.* Gainesville, FL: The Florida Center on Self-injury.

Iwata, B. A. (2006). On the distinction between positive and negative reinforcement. *The Behavior Analyst, 29,* 121–123.

Iwata, B. A., & Bailey, J. S. (1974). Reward versus cost token systems: An analysis of the effects on students and teachers. *Journal of Applied Behavior Analysis, 7,* 567–576.

Iwata, B. A., Dorsey, M. F., Slifer, K. J., Bauman, K. E., & Richman, G. S. (1982). Toward a functional analysis of self-injury. *Analysis and Intervention in Developmental Disabilities, 3,* 1–20.

Iwata, B. A., Dorsey, M. F., Slifer, K. J., Bauman, K. E., & Richman, G. S. (1994). Toward a functional analysis of self-injury. *Journal of Applied Behavior Analysis, 27,* 197–209. (Reprinted form *Analysis and Intervention in Developmental Disabilities, 2,* 3–20, 1982).

Iwata, B. A., Pace, G. M., Cowdery, G. E., & Miltenberger, R. G. (1994). What makes extinction work: An analysis of procedure form and function. *Journal of Applied Behavior Analysis, 27,* 131–144.

Iwata, B. A., Pace, G. M., Kalsher, M. J., Cowdery, G. E., & Cataldo, M. F. (1990). Experimental analysis and extinction of self-injurious escape behavior. *Journal of Applied Behavior Analysis, 23,* 11–27.

Jackson, J., & Dixon, M. (2007). A mobile computing solution for collecting functional analysis data on a pocket PC. *Journal of Applied Behavior Analysis, 40,* 359–384.

Jacobs, K. W., Morford, Z. H., King, J. E., & Hayes, L. J. (2017). Predicting the effects of interventions: A tutorial on the disequilibrium model. *Behavior Analysis in Practice, 10*(2), 195–208. https://doi-org.mimas.calstatela.edu/10.1007/s40617-017-0176-x

Jacobsen, N.K., (1982). Temporal and procedural influences on activity estimated by time-sampling, *Journal of Wildlife Management, 46*(2), 1982.

Jacobson, J.W., Mulick, J.A. & Schwartz, A.A. (1995). A history of facilitated communication: Science, pseudoscience and antiscience. *American Psychologist,* 750–765.

Jacob-Timm, S. (1996). Ethical and legal issues associated with the use of aversives in the public schools: The SIBIS controversy. *School Psychology, Review, 25,* 184–198.

James, S. D., & Egel, A. L. (1986). A direct prompting strategy for increasing reciprocal interactions between handicapped and nonhandicapped siblings. *Journal of Applied Behavior Analysis, 19,* 173–186.

Jason, L., Billows, W., Schnopp-Wyatt, D., & King, C. (1996). Reducing the illegal sales of cigarettes to minors: Analysis of alternative enforcement schedules. *Journal of Applied Behavior Analysis, 29,* 333–344.

Jason, L. A., Pokorny, S. B., Turner, P. L., Freeland, M., Corbin, S., & Driscoll, M. (2005). Decreasing public smoking among youth: A preliminary study. *Education and Treatment of Children, 28,* 299–307.

Jenson, W. R. (1980). The individual point card: Incorporating fixed and variable ratio schedules of reinforcement. *Child Behavior Therapy, 2,* 65–67.

Jenson, W. R., Neville, M., Sloane, H. N., & Morgan, D. (1982). Spinners and chart moves. *Child & Family Behavior Therapy, 4*, 81–85.

Jerome, J., Frantino, E. P., & Sturmey, P. (2007). The effects of errorless learning and backward chaining on the acquisition of internet skills in adults with developmental disabilities. *Journal of Applied Behavior Analysis, 40*, 185–189.

Jessup, P. A., & Stahelski, A. J. (1999). The effects of a combined goal setting, feedback and incentive intervention on job performance in a manufacturing environment. *Journal of Organizational Behavior Management, 19*(3), 5–26.

Jimenez-Gomez, C., Haggerty, K., & Topcuoglu, B. (2021). Wearable activity schedules to promote independence in your children. *Journal of Applied Behavior Analysis, 54*, 197–216. doi: 10.1002/jaba.756

Jones, S. H., St. Peter, C. C., & Ruckle, M. M. (2020). Reporting of demographic varia-bles in the Journal of Applied Behavior Analysis. Journal of Applied Behavior Analysis, 53, 1304-1315. doi: 10.1002/jaba.722Johns, G. A., Skinner, C. H., & Nail, G. L. (2000). Effects of interspersing briefer mathematics problems on assignment choice in students with learning disabilities. *Journal of Behavioral Education, 10*, 95–106.

Johnson, B. M., Miltenberger, R. G., Egemo-Helm, K., Jostad, C. M., Flessner, C., & Gatheridge, B. (2005). Evaluation of behavioral skills training for teaching abduction-prevention skills to young children. *Journal of Applied Behavior Analysis, 38*, 67–78.

Johnson, C., White, D., Green, G., Langer, S., & MacDonald, R. (2000, May). *A discrimination and stimulus equivalence curriculum for individual with severe learning difficulties.* Paper presented at the annual meeting of the Association for Behavior Analysis, Washington, DC.

Johnson, D. W., & Johnson, R. T. (1983). Effects of cooperative, competitive, and individualistic learning experience on social development. *Exceptional Children, 49*, 323–329.

Johnson, D. W., Johnson, R. T., Warring, D., & Maruyama, G. (1986). Different cooperative learning procedures and cross-handicap relationships. *Exceptional Children, 53*, 247–252.

Johnson, D. W., Maruyama, G., Johnson, R., Nelson, D., & Skon, L. (1981). Effects of cooperative, competitive, and individualistic goal structures on achievement: A meta-analysis. *Psychological Bulletin, 89*, 47–62.

Johnson, K. A., Vladescu, J. C., Kodak, T., & Sidener, T. M. (2017). An assessment of differential reinforcement procedures for learners with autism spectrum disorder. *Journal of Applied Behavior Analysis, 50*, 290–303. doi: 10.1002/jaba.372

Johnson, K. R., & Layng, T. V. J. (1992). Breaking the structuralist barrier: Literacy and unmeracy with fluency. *American Psychologist, 47*, 1475–1490.

Johnson, K. R., & Layng, T. V. J. (1994). The Morningside model of generative instruction. In Gardner, R, Sainato, D. M., Cooper, J. O., Heron, T. E., Eshleman, J. W., & T. A. Grossi (Eds.), *Behavior analysis in education: Focus on measurably superior instruction* (pp. 173–197). Belmont CA: Wadsworth, Inc.

Johnson, K. R., & Ruskin, R. S. (1977). *Behavior instruction: An instructive review.* Washington, D. C.: American Psychological Association.

Johnson, K. R., Street, E. M., Kieta, A. R., & Robbins, J. K. (2021). *The Morningside model of generative instruction: Building a bridge between skills and inquiry teaching.* Cornwall-on-Hudson, NY: Sloan Publishing, LLC.

Johnson, L., McComas, J., Thompson, A., & Symons, F. J. (2004). Obtained versus programmed reinforcement: Practical considerations in the treatment of escape-reinforced aggression. *Journal of Applied Behavior Analysis, 37*, 239–242.

Johnson, M.W., & Bickel, W.K. (2006). Replacing relative reinforcing efficacy with behavioral economic demand curves. *Journal of the Experimental Analysis of Behavior, 85*, 73–93.

Johnson, P. E., Perrin, C. J., Salo, A, Deschaine, E., & Johnson, C. (2016). Use of an explicit rule decreases procrastination in university students. *Journal of Applied Behavior Analysis, 49*, 346–358. doi: 10.1002/jaba.287

Johnson, S., & Brown, R. (1969). Producing behavior change in parents of disturbed children. *Journal of Child Psychology and Psychiatry, 10*, 107–121.

Johnston, J. M., & Pennypacker, H. S. (1980). *Strategies and tactics of human behavioral research.* Hillsdale, NJ: Lawrence Erlbaum Associates.

Johnston, J. M., & Pennypacker, H. S. (2020). *Strategies and tactics of behavioral research* (4rd ed.). New York: Routledge/Taylor & Francis Books.

Jolivette, K., Wehby, J. H., Canale, J., & Massey, G. (2001). Effects of choice-making opportunities on the behavior of students with emotional and behavioral disorders. *Behavioral Disorders, 26*, 131–145.

Jones, E. A., Feeley, K. M., & Takacs, J. (2007). Teaching spontaneous responses to young children with autism. *Journal of Applied Behavior Analysis, 40*, 565–570.

Jones, F. H., Fremouw, W., & Carples, S. (1977). Pyramid training of elementary school teachers to use a classroom management "skill package." *Journal of Applied Behavior Analysis, 10*, 239–253.

Jones, F. H., Simmons, J. Q., & Frankel, F. (1974). An extinction procedure for eliminating self-destructive behavior in a 9-year-old autistic girl. *Journal of Autism and Childhood Schizophrenia, 4*, 241–250.

Jones, G., Ostojic, D., Menard, J., Picard, E., & Miller, C. (2017). Primary prevention of reading failure: Effect of universal peer tutoring in the early grades. *Journal of Educational Research, 110*, 171–176.

Jones, J., Lerman,D. C., & Lechago, S. (2014). Assessing stimulus control and promoting generalization via video modeling when teaching social responses to children with autism. *Journal of Applied Behavior Analysis, 47*, 37–50.

Jones, K. M., Drew, H. A., & Weber, N. L. (2000). Noncontingent peer attention as treatment for disruptive classroom behavior. *Journal of Applied Behavior Analysis, 33*, 343–346.

Jones, M. L., Eyberg, S. m., Adams, C D., & Boggs, S R. (1998). Treatment acceptability of behavioral interventions for children – An assessment by mothers of children with disruptive behavior disorders. *Child & Family Behavior Therapy, 20*(4), 15–26

Jones, R. T., Nelson, R. E., & Kazdin, A. E. (1977). The role of external variables in self-reinforcement. A review. *Behavior Modification, 1,* 147–178.

Jones, R. T., Ollendick, T. H., & Shinske, F. K. (1989). The role of behavioral versus cognitive variables in skill acquisition. *Behavior Therapy, 20,* 293–302.

Jones, S. H., St. Peter, C. C., & Ruckle, M. M. (2020). Reporting of demographic variables in the *Journal of Applied Behavior Analysis. Journal of Applied Behavior Analysis, 53,* 1304–1315. doi: 10.1002/jaba.722

Joslyn, P. R. & Vollmer, T. R. (2020). Efficacy of teacher-implemented Good Behavior Game despite low treatment integrity. *Journal of Applied Behavior Analysis, 53,* 465–474. doi: 10.1002/jaba.614

Jostad, C.M., Miltenberger, R.G., Kelso, P., & Knudson, P. (2008). Peer tutoring to prevent firearm play: Acquisition, generalization, and long-term maintenance of safety skills. *Journal of Applied Behavior Analysis, 41,* 117–143.

Juanito, J. F., Dozier, C. L., Payne, S. W., Brandt, J. A. A., & Hirst, E. S. J. (2016). Ann evaluation of toy quality for increasing self-control in typically developing preschool children. *Journal of Applied Behavior Analysis, 49,* 460–471. doi: 10.1002/jaba.320

Jusczyk, A. M. (1993). Infant's sensitivity to the sound patterns of native language words. *Journal of Memory and Language, 32,* 402–420.

Kahana, S. Y., Frazier, T. W., & Drotar, D. (2008). Preliminary quantitative investigation of predictors of treatment non-adherence in pediatric transplantation: A brief report. *Pediatric Transplantation, 12,* 656–660.

Kagan N. (1972). *Influencing human interaction.* East Lansing: Michigan State University, Instructional Media Center.

Kagel, J., & Winkler, R. (1972). Behavioral economics: Areas of cooperative research between economies and applied behavior analysis. *Journal of Applied Behavior Analysis, 5,* 335–342.

Kagohara, D. M., van der Meer, L., Ramdoss, s., O'Reilly, M. F., Lancioni, G. E., Davis, T. N., ...Sutherland, D., (2013). Using iPods and iPads in teaching programs for individuals with developmental disabilities: A systematic review. *Research in Developmental Disabilities, 34,* 147–156.

Kahlow, T. A., Sidener, T. M., Kisamore, A. N., & Reeve, K. F. (2019). Teaching the mand "when?" to children with autism spectrum disorder. *The Analysis of Verbal Behavior, 35*(2), 221–234. https://doi.org/10.1007/s40616-019-00115-z

Kahng, S., & Iwata, B. A. (1998). Computerized systems for collecting real-time observational data. *Journal of Applied Behavior Analysis, 31,* 253–261.

Kahng, S., Iwata, B. A., DeLeon, I. G., & Wallace, M. D. (2000). A comparison of procedures for programming noncontingent reinforcement schedules. *Journal of Applied Behavior Analysis, 33,* 223–231.

Kahng, S., Iwata, B. A., Fischer, S. M., Page, T. J., Treadwell, K. R. H., Williams, D. E., & Smith, R. G. (1998). Temporal distributions of problem behavior based on scatter plot analysis. *Journal of Applied Behavior Analysis, 31,* 593–604.

Kahng, S. W., Tarbox, J., & Wilke, A. E. (2001). Use of a multicomponent treatment for food refusal. *Journal of Applied Behavior Analysis, 34,* 93–96.

Kahnt, T., & Tobler, P. N. (2016). ilife 2016;5:e12678 Doi: 10.7554/elife.12678

Karlson, T., & Chase, P. N. (1996). A comparison of three prompting methods for training software use. *Journal of Organizational Behavior Management, 16,* 27–44.

Karsten, A. M., & Carr, J. E. (2009). The effects of differential reinforcement of unprompted responding on the skill acquisition of children with autism. *Journal of Applied Behavior Analysis, 42,* 327–334.

Kameenui, E. J., Simmons, D. C., Chard, D., & Dickson, S. (1997). Direct Instruction reading. In S. A. Stahl & D. A. Hayes, Eds.), *Instructional models in reading* (pp. 59–84). Mahwah, NJ: Erlbaum.

Kamps, D. M., Barbetta, P. M., Leonard, B. R., & Delquadri, J. (1994). Classwide peer tutoring: An integration strategy to improve reading skills and promote peer interactions among students with autism and general education peers. *Journal of Applied Behavior Analysis, 27,* 49–61.

Kamps, D. M., Dugan, E., Potucek, J., & Collins, A. (1999). Effects of cross-age peer tutoring networks among students with autism and general education students. *Journal of Behavioral Education, 9,* 97–115.

Kamps, D., Royer, J., Dugan, E., Dravits, T., Gonzalez-Lopez, A., Garcia, J., et al. (2002). Peer training to facilitate social interaction for elementary students with autism and their peers. *Exceptional Children, 68,* 173–187.

Kanareff, V., & Lanzetta, J. T. (1960). Effects of success-failure experiences, and probability of reinforcement upon acquisition and extinction of an imitative response. *Psychological Reports, 7,* 151–166.

Kane, M., Connell, J. E., & Pellecchia, M. (2010) A quantitative analysis of language interventions for children with autism. *The Behavior Analyst Today, 11*(2), 128–144.

Karla, M. S., & Ozkan, S. Y. (2015). Effects of class-wide self-monitoring on on-task behaviors of preschoolers with developmental disabilities. *Education and Training in Autism and Developmental Disabilities, 50,* 418–432.

Karlsson, T., & Chase, P. N. (1996). A comparison of three prompting methods for training software use. *Journal of Organizational Behavior Management, 16,* 27–44.

Karsten, A. M., & Carr, J. E. (2009). The effects of differential reinforcement of unprompted responding on the skill acquisition of children with autism. *Journal of Applied Behavior Analysis, 42,* 327–334.

Kartal, M. S., Ozkan, S. Y. (2015). Effects of class-wide monitoring on on-task behaviors of preschoolers with developmental disabilities. *Education and Training in Autism and Developmental Disabilities, 50,* 418–432.

Kastak, D. & Schusterman, R.J., (1994). Transfer of visual identity matching-to-sample in two California sea lions (Zalophus californianus). *Animal Learning and Behavior, 22,* 427–435.

Kazdin, A. E. (1973). The effect of response cost and aversive stimulation in suppressing punished and nonpunished speech disfluencies. *Behavior Therapy, 4,* 73–82.

Kazdin, A. E. (1974a). Self-monitoring and behavior change. In M. J. Mahoney & C. E. Thoresen (Eds.), *Self-control: Power to the person* (pp. 218–246). Monterey: Brooks/Cole.

Kazdin, A. E. (1974b). Covert modeling, model similarity, and reduction of avoidance behavior. *Behavior Therapy, 5,* 325–340.

Kazdin, A. E. (1980a). Acceptability of alternative treatments for deviant child behavior. *Journal of Applied Behavior Analysis, 13,* 259–273.

Kazdin, A. E. (1980b). Acceptability of time-out from reinforcement procedures for disruptive child behavior. *Behavior Therapy, 11,* 329–344.

Kazdin, A. E. (1981). Acceptability of child treatment techniques: The influence of treatment efficacy and adverse side effects. *Behavior Therapy, 12,* 493–506.

Kazdin, A. E. (1982). *Single-case designs Methods for clinical and applied settings.* New York: Oxford Univ. Press.

Kazdin, A. E. (1993). *Single-case designs: Methods for clinical and applied settings.* New York: Oxford Univ. Press.

Kazdin, A. E. (2010). *Behavior modification in applied settings* (9th Edition). Belmont, CA: Wadsworth.

Kazdin, A. E., & Erickson, L. M. (1975). Developing responsiveness to instructions in severely and profoundly retarded residents. *Journal of Behavior Therapy and Experimental Psychiatry, 6,* 17–21.

Kazdin, A. E., Silverman, N. A., & Sittler, J. L. (1975). The use of prompts to enhance vicarious effects of nonverbal approval. *Journal of Applied Behavior Analysis, 8,* 279–286.

Kazdin, A. E., & Hartmann, D. P. (1978). The simultaneous treatment design. *Behavior Therapy, 9,* 912–922.

Kee, M., Hill, S. M., & Weist, M. D. (1999). School-based behavior management of cursing, hitting, and spitting in a girl with profound retardation. *Education & Treatment of Children, 22,* 171–178.

Keller, F. S. (1968). Goodbye, teacher. *Journal of Applied Behavior Analysis, 1,* 79–90.

Keller, F. (2009). *At my own pace.* Cornwall-on-the Hudson: Sloane Publishing.

Keller, F. S., & Schoenfeld, W. N. (1950). *Principles of psychology.* New York: Appleton.

Kellam, S. G., & Anthony, J. C. (1988). Targeting early antecedents to prevent tobacco smoking: Findings from an epidemiologically based randomized field trial. *American Journal of Public Health, 88,* 1490–1495.

Kellogg, W. N. (1941). Electric shock as a motivating stimulus in conditioning experiments. *Journal of General Psychology, 25,* 85–97.

Kelly, J. F. (1969). *Extinction induced aggression in humans.* Unpublished master's thesis, Southern Illinois University.

Kelly, H., & Miltenberger, R. G. (2016). Using video feedback to improve horseback-riding skills. *Journal of Applied Behavior Analysis, 49,* 138–147. dos: 10.1002/jaba.272

Kelly, S., Green, G., & Sidman, M. (1998). Visual identify matching and auditory-visual matching: A procedural note. *Journal of Applied Behavior Analysis, 31,* 2376–243.

Kelso, P. D., Miltenberger, R. G., Waters, M. A., Egemo-Helm, K., Bagne, A. G. (2007). Teaching skills to second and third grade children to prevent gun play: A comparison of procedures. *Education and Treatment of Children, 30*(3), 29–48.

Kendall, P. C., Nay, W. R., & Jeffers, J. (1975). Timeout duration and contrast effects: A systematic evaluation of a successive treatments design. *Behavior Therapy, 6,* 609–615.

Kennedy, C. H. (1992). Concurrent operants: A model for stimulus control transfer using delayed prompting. *The Psychological Record, 42,* 525–540.

Kennedy, C. H. (1994). Manipulating antecedent conditions to alter the stimulus control of problem behavior. *Journal of Applied Behavior Analysis, 27,* 161–170.

Kennedy, C. H. (2005). *Single-case designs for educational research.* Boston: Allyn and Bacon.

Kennedy, C. H., & Meyer, K. A. (1996). Sleep deprivation, allergy symptoms, and negatively reinforced problem behavior. *Journal of Applied Behavior Analysis, 29,* 133–135.

Kent, R. N., Kanowitz, J., O'Leary, K. D., & Cheiken, M. (1977). Observer reliability as a function of circumstances of assessment. *Journal of Applied Behavior Analysis 10*(2), 317–324.

Kercood, S., & Grskovic, J. A. (2009). The effects of highlighting on the math computation performance and off-task behavior of students with attention problems. *Education and Treatment of Children, 32,* 231–241.

Kern, L., Childs, K. E., Dunlap, G., Clarke, S., & Falk, G. D. (1994). Using assessment-based curricular interventions to improve the classroom behavior of a student with emotional and behavioral challenges. *Journal of Applied Behavior Analysis, 27,* 7–19.

Kern, L., Dunlap, G., Clarke, S., & Childs, K. E. (1994). Student-assisted functional assessment interview. *Diagnostique, 19,* 29–39.

Kern, L., Mantegna, M. E., Vorndran, C. M., Bailin, D., & Hilt, A. (2001). Choice of task sequence to reduce problem behaviors. *Journal of Positive Behavior Interventions, 3,* 3–10.

Kern, L., Ringdahl, J. E., Hilt, A., & Sterling-Turner, H. E. (2001). Linking self-management procedures to functional analysis results. *Behavioral Disorders, 26,* 214–226.

Kern, L., Vorndran, C. M., Hilt, A., Ringdahl, J. E., Adelman, B. E., & Dunlap, G. (1998). Choice as an intervention to improve behavior: A review of the literature. *Journal of Behavioral Education, 8,* 151–170.

Kern R.S., Green, M. F., Mintz, J., Liberman, R.P. (2003). Does "errorless learning" compensate for neurocognitive impairments in the work rehabilitation of schizophrenic patients? *Psychological Medicine, 33,* 433–442.

Kern, R. S., Wallace, C. J., Hellman, S. G., Womack, L. M., & Green, M. F. (1996). A training procedure for remediating WCST deficits in chronic psychotic patients: an adaptation of errorless learning principles. *Journal of Psychiatric Research, 30,* 283–294.

Kestner, K. M., Romano, L. M., St.Peter, C.C., & Mesches, G. A. (2018). Resurgence following response cost in a human-operant procedure. *The Psychological Record, 68,* 81–87. https://doi.org/10.1007/s40732-018-0270-7

Kheterpal, S., Gupta, R., Blum, J. M., Tremper, K. K., O'Reill, M., & Kazanjian, P. E. (2007). Electronic reminders improve procedure documentation compliance and professional fee reimbursement. *Anesthesia Analog, 104,* 592–597.

Killeen, P. R., & Jacobs, K. W.. (2016). Coal is not black, snow is not white, food is not a reinforcer: The roles of affordances and dispositions in the analysis of behavior. *The Behavior Analyst, 39,* 1–22.

Killu, K. (1999). High-probability request research: Moving beyond compliance.

*Education and Treatment of Children, 22,* 470–494.

Kincaid, M. S., & Weisberg, P. (1978). Alphabet letters as tokens: Training preschool children in letter recognition and labeling during a token exchange period. *Journal of Applied Behavior Analysis, 11,* 199.

Kinder, D., & Carnine, C. (1991). Direct Instruction: What it is and what it is becoming. *Journal of Behavioral Education, 1,* 193–213.

King, B., Radley, K. C., Jenson, W. R., Clark, E., & O'Neill, R. E. (2014). Utilization of video modeling combined with self-monitoring to increase rates of on-task behavior. *Behavioral Interventions, 29,* 125–144. doi: 10.1002/bin.1379

King, G. R., & Logue, A. W. (1987). Choice in a self-control paradigm with human subjects: Effects of changeover delay duration. *Learning and Motivation, 18,* 421–438.

Kirby, F., & Shields, F. (1972). Modification of arithmetic response rate and attending behavior in a seventh grade student. *Journal of Applied Behavior Analysis, 5,* 79–84.

Kirsch, I., Wolpin, M., & Knutson, L. N. (1975). A comparison of in vivo methods for rapid reduction of "stage fright" in the college classroom: A field experiment. *Behavior Therapy, 6,* 165–171.

Kisamore, A. N., Karsten, A. M. & Mann, C. C. (2016). Teaching multiply controlled intraverbals to children and adolescents with autism spectrum disorders. *Journal of Applied Behavior Analysis, 49,* 826–847. doi: 10.1002/jaba.344

Kistner, J., Hammer, D., Wolfe, D., Rothblum, E., & Drabman, R. S. (1982). Teacher popularity and contrast effects in a classroom token economy. *Journal of Applied Behavior Analysis, 15,* 85–96.

Klahr, D., Nigam, M. (2004). The equivalence of learning paths in early science instruction: effects of direct instruction and discovery learning. *Psychological Science, 15,* 661–667.

Klein, L., Houlihan, D., Vincent, J., & Panahon, C. (2017). Best practices in utilizing the changing criterion design. *Behavior Analysis in Practice, 10*(1), 52–61.

Knight, C., Rutterford, N. A., Alderman, N., & Swan, L. J. (2002). Is accurate self-monitoring necessary for people with acquired neurological problems to benefit from the use of differential reinforcement methods? *Brain Injury, 16* (1), 75–87.

Kniveton, B. H. (1986a). Peer models and classroom violence: An experimental study. *Educational Research, 28,* 111–116.

Kniveton, B. H. (1986b). Peer modeling of classroom violence and family structure: An experimental study. *Educational Studies, 12,* 87–94.

Kodak, T., Campbell, V., Bergmann, S., LeBlanc, B., Kurtz-Nelson, E., Cariveau, T., Haq, S., Semantik, P., & Mahon, J. (2016). Examination of efficacious, efficient, and socially valid error-correction procedures to teach sight words and prepositions to children with autism spectrum disorder. *Journal of Applied Behavior Analysis, 49,* 532–547. doi: 10.1002/jaba.310.

Kodak, T., Fisher, W. W., Kelley, M. E., & Kisamore, A. (2009). Comparing preference assessments: Selection- versus duration-based preference assessment procedures. *Research in Developmental Disabilities, 30,* 1068–1077.

Kodak, T., Miltenberger, R. G., & Romaniuk, C. (2003). The effects of differential negative reinforcement on other behavior and noncontingent escape on compliance. *Journal of Applied Behavior Analysis, 36,* 379–382.

Koegel, L. K., Carter, C. M., & Koegel, R. L. (2003). Teaching children with autism self-initiations as a pivotal response. *Topics in Language Disorders, 23* (2), 134–135.

Koegel, L. K., Koegel, R. L., Hurley, C., & Frea, W. D. (1992). Improving social skills and disruptive behavior in children with autism through self-management. *Journal of Applied Behavior Analysis, 25,* 341–353.

Koegel, L. K., Park, M. N., & Koegel, R. L. J. (2014). Using self-management to improve the reciprocal social conversation of children with autism spectrum disorder. *Journal of Autism and Developmental Disorders, 44,* 1055–1063. doe: 10.1007/s 10803-013-1956-y

Koegel, R. L., Camarata, S., Koegel, L. K., Ben-Tall, A., & Smith, T. (1998). Increasing speech intelligibility in children with autism. *Journal of Autism and Developmental Disabilities, 28,* 241–251.

Koegel, R. L., Dunlap, G.., & Dyer, K. (1980). Intertrial interval duration and learning in autistic children. *Journal of Applied Behavior Analysis, 13,* 91–99.

Koegel, R. L., Dyer, K., & Bell, L. K. (1987). The influence of child-preferred activities on autistic children's social behavior. *Journal of Applied Behavior Analysis, 20,* 243–252.

Koegel, R. L., Firestone, P. B., Kramme, K. W., & Dunlap, G. (1974). Increasing spontaneous play by suppressing self-stimulation in autistic children. *Journal of Applied Behavior Analysis, 7,* 521–528.

Koegel, R. L., & Koegel, L. K. (1988). Generalized responsivity and pivotal behaviors. In R. H. Horner, G. Dunlap, & R. L. Koegel (Eds.), *Generalization and maintenance: Life-style changes in applied settings* (pp. 41–66). Baltimore: Paul H. Brookes.

Koegel, R.L. & Koegel, L.K. (1990). Extended reductions in stereotypic behavior of students with autism through a self-management treatment package. *Journal of Applied Behavior Analysis, 23,* 119–127.

Koegel, R. L., & Koegel, L. K. (2006). *Pivotal response treatments for autism: communication, social, and academic development.* Baltimore: Brookes Publishing Co.

Koegel, R. L., O'Dell, M. C., & Koegel, L. K. (1987). A natural language teaching paradigm for non-verbal autistic children. *Journal of Autism and Developmental Disorders, 17,* 187–200.

Koegel, R. L., & Rincover, A. (1976). Some detrimental effects of using extra stimuli to guide learning in normal and autistic children. *Journal of Abnormal and Child Psychology, 4,* 59–71.

Koegel, R. L., & Rincover, A. (1977). Research on the difference between generalization and maintenance in extra-therapy responding. *Journal of Applied Behavior Analysis, 10,* 1–12.

Koegel, R. L., Schreibman, L., Britten, K., & Laitinen, R. (1979). The effects of schedule of reinforcement on stimulus overselectivity in autistic children. *Journal of Autism and Developmental Disorders, 9,* 383–397.

Koegel, R.L., & Williams, J. (1980). Direct versus indirect response-reinforcer relationships in teaching autistic children. *Journal of Abnormal Child Psychology, 4,* 536–547.

Kohler, F. W. (1986). *Classwide peer tutoring: Examining natural contingencies of peer reinforcement.* Doctoral Dissertation. Department of Human Development and family Life, University of Kansas.

Kohler, F. W., & Greenwood, C. R. (1986). Toward a technology of generalization: The identification of natural contingencies of reinforcement. *The Behavior Analyst, 9,* 19–26.

Kohler, F. W., Strain, P. S., Hoyson, M., Davis, L., Donina, W. M., & Rapp, N. (1995). Using a group-oriented contingency to increase social interactions between children with autism and their peers. *Behavior Modification, 19,* 10–32.

Kohn, A. (1993). *Punished by rewards: The trouble with gold stars, incentive plans, A's, praise, and other bribes.* New York: Houghton Mifflin.

Komaki, J., & Dore-Boyce, K. (1978). Self-recording: Its effects on individuals high and low in motivation. *Behavior Therapy, 9,* 65–72.

Konarski, E. A. Jr., Johnson, M. R., Crowell, C. R., & Whitman, T. L. (1980). Response deprivation and reinforcement in applied settings: A preliminary analysis. *Journal of Applied Behavior Analysis 13,* 595–609.

Konarski, E. A., Jr., Johnson, M. R., Crowell, C. R., & Whitman, T. L. (1981). An alternative approach to reinforcement for applied researchers: Response deprivation. *Behavior Therapy, 12,* 653–666.

Konarski, E. A. Jr., Crowell, C. R., & Duggan, L. M. (1985). The use of response deprivation to increase the academic performance of EMR students. *Applied Research in Mental Retardation, 6,* 15–31.

Kornhaber, R., & Schroeder, H. (1975). Importance of model similarity and extinction of avoidance behavior in children. *Journal of Clinical and Consulting Psychology, 43,* 601–607.

Kraemer, B. R., Cook, C. R., Browning-Wright, D., Mayer, G. R., & Wallace, M. D. (2008). Effects of training on the use of the behavior support plan quality evaluation guide with autism educators: A preliminary investigation examining positive behavior support plans. *Journal of Positive Behavior Interventions, 10,* 179–189.

Krantz, P. J., MacDuff, M. T., & McClannahan, L. E. (1993). Programming participation in family activities for children with autism: Parent' use of photographic activity schedules. *Journal of Applied Behavior Analysis, 26,* 137–138.

Krantz, P.J., & McClannahan, L.E. (1993). Teaching children with autism to initiate to peers: Effects of a script-fading procedure. *Journal of Applied Behavior Analysis, 26,* 121–132.

Krantz, P. J., & McClannahan, L. E. (1998). Social interaction skills for children with autism: A script-fading procedure for beginning readers. *Journal of Applied Behavior Analysis, 31,* 191–202.

Krentz, H., Miltenberger, R., & Valbuena, D. (2016). Using token reinforcement to increase walking for adults with intellectual disabilities. *Journal of Applied Behavior Analysis, 49,* 745–750. doi: 10.1002/jaba.326

Kritch, K. M., & Bostow, D. E. (1998). Degrees of constructed-response interaction in computer-based programmed instruction. *Journal of Applied Behavior Analysis, 31,* 387–398.

Krumboltz, J. D., & Krumboltz, H. G. (1972). *Changing children's behavior.* Englewood Cliffs, NJ: Prentice-Hall.

Krumboltz, J. D., & Thoresen, C. E. (1964). The effects of behavioral counseling in groups and individual settings on information seeking behavior. *Journal of Counseling Psychology, 11,* 324–333.

Krumhus, K. M., & Malott, R. W. (1980). The effects of modeling and immediate and delayed feedback in staff training. *Journal of Organizational Behavior Management, 2,* 279–293.

Kubany, E. S., & Sloggett, B. B. (1973). Coding procedure for teachers. *Journal of Applied Behavior Analysis, 6,* 339–344.

Kubina, R. M., Young, A. E., & Kilwein, M. (2004). Examining an effect of fluency: Application of oral word segmentation and letter sounds for spelling. *Learning Disabilities: A multidisciplinary Journal, 13,* 17–23.

Kubinyi, E., Topál, J., Mikási, A., & Csányi, V. (2003). Dogs (Canis familiaris) learn from their owners via observation in a manipulation task. *Journal of Comparative Psychology, 117,* 2, 156–165.

Kuhl, S., Rudrud, E. H., Witts, B. N., & Schulze, K. A. (2015). Classroom-based interdependent group contingencies increase children's physical activity. *Journal of Applied Behavior Analysis, 48,* 602–612. doi: 10.1002/jaba.219.

Kuhn, S. A. C., Lerman, D. C., & Vorndran, C. M. (2003). Pyramidal training for families of children with problem behavior. *Journal of Applied Behavior Analysis, 36,* 77–88.

Kuhn, S. A. C., Lerman, D. C., Vorndran, C. M., & Addison, L. (2006). Analysis of factors that affect responding in a two-response chain in children with developmental disabilities. *Journal of Applied Behavior Analysis, 39,* 263–280.

Kuttler, S., Smith-Myles, B., & Carlson, J. K. (1998). The use of social stories to reduce precursors to tantrum behavior in a student with autism. *Focus on Autism and Other Developmental Disabilities, 13,* 176–182.

Kyong-Mee, C., Reavis, S., Mosconi, M., Drewry, J., Matthews, T., & Tassé, M. J. (2007). Peer-mediated social skills training program for young children with high-functioning autism, *Research in Developmental Disabilities, 28*(4), 423–436.

Lafleur, N. K., & Johnson, R. G. (1972). Separate effects of social modeling and reinforcement in counseling adolescents. *Journal of Counseling Psychology, 19,* 291–295.

LaFleur, T., & Hyten, C. (1995). Improving the quality of hotel banquet staff performance. *Journal of Organizational Behavior Management, 15,* 69–93.

Lahey, B. B., McNees, M. P., & McNees, M. C. (1973). Control of an obscene "verbal tic" through timeout in an elementary school classroom. *Journal of Applied Behavior Analysis, 6,* 101–104.

Lalli, J. S., Casey, S. D., & Kates, K. (1997). Noncontingent reinforcement as treatment for severe problem behavior: Some procedural variations. *Journal of Applied Behavior Analysis, 30,* 127–137.

Lalli, J. S., & Mauro, B. C. (1995). The paradox of preference for unreliable reinforcement: The role of context and conditioned reinforcement. *Journal of Applied Behavior Analysis, 28,* 389–394.

Lalli, J. S., Casey, S. D. (1996). Treatment of multiply controlled problem behavior. *Journal of Applied Behavior Analysis, 29,* 391–395.

Lalli, J. S., Vollmer, T. R., Progar, P. R., Wright, C., Borrero, J., Daniel, D., Barthold, C. H., Tocco, K., & May, W. (1999). Competition between positive and negative reinforcement in the treatment of escape behavior. *Journal of Applied Behavior Analysis, 32,* 285–296.

Lamal, P. A. (1978). Reinforcement schedule and children's preference for working versus freeloading. *Psychological Reports, 42,* 143–149.

Lambert, J. M., Copeland, B. A., Karp, E. L. et al. (2016). Chaining functional basketball sequences (with embedded conditional discriminations) in an adolescent with autism. *Behavior Analysis in Practice, 9,* 199–210.

Lambert, N. K., Nihira, K., & Leland, H. (1993). *Adaptive Behavior Scale – School* (2nd ed.). Austin, TX: Pro-Ed.

Landa, R. K., Frampton, S. E. and Shillingsburg, M. A. (2020), Teaching children with autism to mand for social information. *Journal of Applied Behavior Analysis, 53*: 2271–2286. https://doi-org.mimas.calstatela.edu/10.1002/jaba.733

Landa, R. K., Hansen, B., & Shillingsburg, M. A. (2017). Teaching mands for information using "when" to children with autism. *Journal of Applied Behavior Analysis, 50,* 538–551. doi: 10.1002/jaba.387

Lane, J. D., Gast, D. L., Ledford, J. R., & Shepley, C. (2017). Increasing social behaviors in young children with social-communication delays in a group. *Education & Treatment of Children, 40,* 115–144.

Lane, S. D., & Critchfield, T. S. (1998). Classification of vowels and consonants by individuals with moderate mental retardation: Development of arbitrary relations via match-to-sample training with compound stimuli. *Journal of Applied Behavior Analysis, 31,* 21–41.

Lane, K. L., Gresham, F. M., MacMillan, D. L., & Bocian, K. (2001). Early detection of students with antisocial behavior and hyperactivity problems. *Education and Treatment of Children, 24,* 294–308.

Lancioni, G. E., Smeets, P. M., & Oliva, D. (1987). Introducing EMR children to arithmetical operations: A program involving pictorial problems and distinctive-feature prompts. *Research in Developmental Disabilities, 8,* 467–485.

Landry, L., & McGreevy, P. (1984). The paper clip counter (PCC): An inexpensive and reliable device for collecting behavior frequencies. *Journal of Precision Teaching, 5,* 11–13.

Lang, R., O'Reilly, M., Lancioni, G., Rispoli, M., Machalicek, W., & Chan, J. M. (2009). Discrepancy in functional analysis results across two settings: Implications for intervention design. *Journal of Applied Behavior Analysis, 42,* 393–397.

Lanovaz, M. J., Rapp, J. T., & Ferguson, S. (2013). Assessment and treatment of vocal stereotypy associated with television: A pilot study. *Journal of Applied Behavior Analysis, 46,* 544–548.

Lanovaz, M. J., Sladeczek, I. E., & Rapp, J. T. (2012). Effects of non contingent music on vocal stereotypy and toy manipulation in children with autism spectrum disorders. *Behavioral Interventions, 27,* 207–223. doi: 10.1002/bin.1345

Laraway, S., Snycerski, S., Michael, J. & Poling, A. (2001). Antecedent events that reduce operant responding. *Analysis of Verbal Behavior, 18,* 101–104.

Laraway, S., Snycerski, S., Michael, J., & Poling, A. (2003). Motivating operations and terms to describe them: Some further refinements. *Journal of Applied Behavior Analysis, 36,* 407–414.

Laski, K.E., Charlop, M.H. & Schreibman, L. (1988). Training parents to use the natural language paradigm to increase their autistic children's speech. *Journal of Applied Behavior Analysis, 21,* 391–400.

Lattal, K. A., & Neef, N. A. (1996). Recent reinforcement-schedule research and applied behavior analysis. *Journal of Applied Behavior Analysis, 29,* 213–230.

Latham, G. I. (1994). *The power of positive parenting: A wonderful way to raise children.* Logan, UT: P & T ink.

Latham, G. P., & Baldes, J. J. (1975). The 'practical significance' of Locke's theory of goal setting. *Journal of Applied Psychology, 60,* 122–124.

Latham, G. P., & Dossett, D. L. (1978). Designing incentive plans for unionized employees: A comparison of continuous and variable ratio reinforcement schedules. *Personnel Psychology, 3,* 47–61.

Lattal, K. A., & Neef, N. A. (1996). Recent reinforcement-schedule research and applied behavior analysis. *Journal of Applied Behavior Analysis, 29,* 213–230.

Lattimore, L. P., Parsons, M. B., & Reid, D. H. (2008). Simulation training of community job skills for adults with autism: A further analysis. *Behavior Analysis in Practice, 1*(1), 24–29.

Lauterback. W. (1990). Situation-response (S-R) questions for identifying the function of problem behavior: the example of thumb sucking. *British Journal of Clinical Psychology, 29,* 51–57.

LaVigna, G. W., & Willis, T. J. (2005). Episodic severity: An overlooked dependent variable in the application of behavior analysis to challenging behavior. *Journal of Positive Behavior Interventions, 7,* 47–54.

Layng, T. V. J., Twyman, J. S., & Strikeleather, G. (2003). Headsprout early reading™: Reliably teaching children to read. *Behavioral Technology Today, 3,* 7–20.

Layng, T. V. J., Twyman, J. S., & Strikeleather, G. (2004). Selected for success: How headsprout reading basics™ teaches beginning reading. In D. J. Moran & R. Malott (Eds.), *Evidence-based educational methods* (pp. 171–195). St. Louis, MO: Elsevier Science/Academic Press.

Leaf, J. B., Cihon, J. H., Ferguson, J. L., Milne, C. M., Leaf, R., & McEachin, J. (2020). Recommendations for behavior analysts regarding the implementation of Social Stories for individuals diagnosed with autism spectrum disorder. *Behavioral Interventions, 35*(4), 664–679. https://doi-org.mimas.calstatela.edu/10.1002/bin.1736

Leaf, J. B., Sheldon, J. B., & Sherman, J. A. (2010). Comparison of simultaneous prompting and no-no prompting in two-choice discrimination learning with children with autism. *Journal of Applied Behavior Analysis, 43,* 215–228.

LeBel, T. J., Chafouleas, S. M., Britner, P. A., & Simonsen, B. (2013). Use of daily report card in an intervention package involving home-school communication to reduce disruptive behavior in preschoolers. *Journal of Positive Behavior Interventions, 15,* 103–112.

LeBlanc, J. M., & Ruggles, T. R. (1982). Instructional strategies for individual and group teaching. *Analysis and Intervention in Developmental Disabilities, 2,* 129–137.

LeBlanc L. A., Carr J. E., Crossett, S. E., Bennett, C. M., & Detweiler D.D. (2005). Intensive outpatient behavioral treatment of primary urinary incontinence of children with autism. *Focus on Autism and Other Developmental Disabilities, 20*(2), 98–105

LeBlanc, L.A., Coatee, A.M., Deneshvar, S, Charlop-Christy, M.H., Morris, C., & Lancaster,B.M. (2003). Using video modeling and reinforcement to teach perspective-taking skills to children with autism. *Journal of Applied Behavior Analysis, 36,* 253–257.

LeBlanc, L. A., Hagopian, L. P., & Maglieri, K. A. (2000). Use of a token economy to eliminate excessive inappropriate social behavior in an adult with developmental disabilities. *Behavioral Interventions, 15,* 135–143.

LeBlanc, L. A., Piazza, C. C., & Krug, M. A. (1997). Comparing methods for maintaining the safety of a child with pica. *Research in Developmental Disabilities, 18,* 215–220.

LeBlanc, L. A., Raetz, P. B., Sellers, T. P., Carr, J. E. (2016). A proposed model for selecting measurement procedures for the assessment and treatment of problem behavior. *Behavior Analysis in Practice, 9,* 77–83.

LeBlanc, L. A., Selllers, T. P., Ala'i, S. (2020). *Building and sustaining meaningful and effective relationships as a supervisor and mentor.* Sloan Publishing: Cornwall on Hudson, NY.

Lecomte, T., Liberman, R. P., & Wallace, C. J. (2000). Identifying and using reinforcers to enhance the treatment of persons with serious mental illness. *Psychiatric Services, 51,* 1312–1314.

Ledbetter-Cho, K., Lang, R., Davenport, K., Moore, M., Lee, A., O'Reilly, M., Watkins, L., & Falcomata, T. (2016). Behavioral skills training to improve the eduction-prevention skills of children with autism. *Behavior Analysis in Practice, 9,* 26–-270. doi:10.107/s40617-016-0128-x

Lee, C., & Tindal, G. A. (1994). Self-recording and goal-setting: Effects o non-task and math productivity of low-achieving Korean elementary school students. *Journal of Behavioral Education, 4,* 459–479.

Lee, D. (2005). Increasing compliance: A quantitative synthesis of applied research on high-probability request sequences. *Exceptionality, 13,* 141–154.

Lee, D. L., Belfiore, P. J., Scheeler, M. C., Hua, Y., & Smith, R. (2004). Behavioral momentum in academics: Using embedded high-p sequences to increase academic productivity. *Psychology in the Schools, 41,* 789–801.

Lee, R., & Sturmey, P. (2014). The effects of script-fading and a lag-1 schedule on varied social responding in children with autism. *Research in Autism Spectrum Disorders, 8,* 440–448. doi: org/10.1016/j.rasd.2014.01.003.

Lee, R., Sturmey, P., & Fields, L. (2007). Schedule-induced and operant mechanisms that influence response variability: A review and implications for future investigations. *The Psychological Record, 57,* 429–455.

Lee, Y., Sugai, G., & Horner, R. H. (1999). Using an instructional intervention to reduce problem and off-task behaviors. *Journal of Positive Behavior Interventions, 1,* 195–204.

Leigland, S. (1997). Is a new definition of verbal behavior necessary in light of derived relational responding? *The Behavior Analyst, 20,* 3–9.

Leigland, S. (2007). Fifty years later: Comments on the further development of a science of verbal behavior. *The Behavior Analyst Today, 8,* 336–346.

Leitenberg, H. (1973). The use of single case methodology in psychotherapy research. *Journal of Abnormal Psychology, 82,* 87–101.

Leitenberg, H., Burchard, J. D., Burchard, S. N., Fuller, E. J., & Lysaght, T. V. (1977). Using positive reinforcement to suppress behaviors: Some experimental comparisons with sibling conflict. *Behavior Therapy, 8,* 168–182.

LeLaurin, K., & Risley, T.R. (1972). The organization of day-care environments: "zone" versus "man-to-man" staff assignments. *Journal of Applied Behavior Analysis, 5,* 225–232.

Lennox, D. B., Miltenberger, R. G., & Donnelly, D. R. (1987). Response interruption and DRL for the reduction of rapid eating. *Journal of Applied Behavior Analysis, 20,* 279–284.

Lenz, M., Singh, N.N., & Hewett, A.E. (1991). Overcorrection as an academic remediation procedure: A review and reappraisal, *Behavior Modification, 15,* 64–73 .

Lepper, M. R., Green, D., & Nesbitt, R. E. (1973). Undermining children's interest with extrinsic rewards: A test of the overjustification hypothesis. *Journal of Personality and Social Psychology, 28,* 129–137.

Lepper, T. L., & Petursdottir, A. I. (2017). Effects of respondse-contingent stimulus pairing on vocalizations of nonverbal children with autism. *Journal of Applied Behavior Analysis, 50,* 750–774. doi: 10.1002/jaba.415

Lequia, J., Machalicek, W., & Lyons, G (2013). Parent education intervention results in decreased challenging behavior and improved task engagement for students with disabilities during academic tasks. *Behavioral Interventions, 28,* 322–343. doi: 10.1002bin/1369

Lerman, D. C., & Iwata, B. A. (1993). Descriptive and experimental analyses of variables maintaining self-injurious behavior. *Journal of Applied Behavior Analysis, 26,* 293–319.

Lerman, D. C., & Iwata, B. A. (1995). Prevalence of the extinction burst and its attenuation during treatment. *Journal of Applied Behavior Analysis, 28,* 93–94.

Lerman, D. C., & Iwata, B. A. (1996). A methodology for distinguishing between extinction and punishment effects associated with response blocking. *Journal of Applied Behavior Analysis, 29,* 231–234.

Lerman, D. C., & Iwata, B. A. (1996). Developing a technology for the use of operant extinction in clinical settings: An examination of basic and applied research. *Journal of Applied Behavior Analysis, 29,* 345–382.

Lerman, D. C., Iwata, B. A., Shore, B. A., & DeLeon, I. G. (1977). Effects of intermittent punishment on self-injurious behavior: An evaluation of schedule thinning. *Journal of Applied Behavior Analysis, 30,* 187–201.

Lerman, D. C., Iwata, B. A., Shore, B. A., & Kahng, S. W. (1996). Responding maintained by intermittent reinforcement: Implications for the use of extinction with problem behavior in clinical settings. *Journal of Applied Behavior Analysis, 29,* 153–171.

Lerman, D. C., Iwata, B. A., Smith, R. G., Zarcone, J. R., & Vollmer, T. R. (1994). Transfer of behavioral function as a contributing factor in treatment relapse. *Journal of Applied Behavior Analysis, 27,* 357–370.

Lerman, D. C., Iwata, B. A., & Wallace, M. D. (1999). Side effects of extinction: Prevalence of bursting and aggression during the treatment of self-injurious behavior. *Journal of Applied Behavior analysis, 32,* 1–8.

Lerman, D. C., Kelley, M. E., Van Camp, C. M., & Roane, H. S. (1999). Effects of reinforcement magnitude on spontaneous recovery. *Journal of Applied Behavior Analysis, 32,* 197–200.

Lerman, D. C., Kelley, M. E., Vorndran, C. M., & Van Camp, C. M. (2003). Collateral effects of response blocking during the treatment of stereotypic behavior. *Journal of Applied Behavior Analysis, 36,* 119–123.

Lerman, D. C., & Vorndran, C. M. (2002). On the status of knowledge for using punishment: Implications for treating behavior disorders. *Journal of Applied Behavior Analysis, 35,* 431–464.

Lerman, D. C., Vorndran, C., Addison, l., & Kuhn, S. A. (2004). A rapid assessment of skills in young children with autism. *Journal of Applied Behavior Analysis, 37,* 11–26. doi: 10.1901/jaba.2004.37-11

Leslie, J. C., Shaw, D., Gregg, G., McCormick, N., Reynolds, D. S., & Dawson, G. R. (2005). Effects of reinforcement schedule on facilitation of operant extinction by chlordiazepoxide. *Journal of the Experimental Analysis of Behavior, 84,* 327–338.

Levin, H., Glass, G., & Meister, G. (1984). *Cost-effectiveness of four educational interventions.* (Report No. 84–A11). Institute for Research in Educational Finance and Governance (IFG), Stanford University, Stanford, CA.

Levy, A., DeLeon, I. G., Martinez, C.K., Fernandez, N., Gage, N. A., Sigurdsson, S. O., & Frank-Crawford, M. A. (2017). A quantitative review of over justification effects in persons with intellectual and developmental disabilities. *Journal of Applied Behavior Analysis, 50,* 206–221. doi: 10.1002/jaba.359

Levy, E. A., McClinton, B. S., Rabinowitz, F. M., & Wolkin, J. R. (1974). Effects of vicarious consequences on imitation and recall: Some developmental findings. *Journal of Experimental Child Psychology, 17,* 115–132.

Lewis, T. J., Scott, T. M., & Sugai, G. (1994). The problem behavior questionnaire: A teacher-based instrument to develop functional hypotheses of problem behavior in general education classrooms. *Diagnostique, 19,* 103–115.

Lewis, T. J., & Sugai, G. (1996). Descriptive and experimental analysis of teacher and peer attention and the use of assessment-based intervention to improve pro-social behavior. *Journal of Behavioral Education, 6,* 7–24.

Libby, M. E., Weiss, J. S., Bancroft, S., & Ahearn, W. H. (2008). A comparison of most-to-least and least-to-most prompting on the acquisition of solitary play skills. *Behavior Analysis in Practice, 1* (1), 37–43.

Liber, D. B., Frea, W. D., & Symon, J. B. G. (2007). Using time-delay to improve social play skills with peers for children with autism. *Journal of Autism and Developmental Disorders, 38,* 312–323.

Lieving, G. A., Hagopian, L. P., Long, E. S., & O'Connor, J. (2004). Response-class hierarchies and resurgence of severe problem behavior. *The Psychological Record, 54,* 621–634.

Lieving, G. A., & Lattal, K. A. (2003). Recency, repeatability, and reinforcer retrenchment: An experimental analysis of resurgence. Journal of the *Experimental Analysis of Behavior, 80,* 217–233. doe: 101901/jeab.2003.80-217.

Lifter, K., & Bloom, L. (1989). Object knowledge and the emergence of language. *Infant Behavior and Development, 12,* 395–413.

Lifter, K., Sulzer-Azaroff, B., Anderson, S. R., & Cowdery, G. E. (1993). Teaching play activities to preschool children with disabilities: The importance of developmental considerations. *Journal of Early Intervention, 17*(2), 139–159.

Lillie, M. A., & Tiger, J. H. (2019). Acquisition and generative responding following print-to-braille construction response training with sighted learners. *Journal of Applied Behavior Analysis, 52*(1), 286–298. https://doi-org.mimas.calstatela.edu/10.1002/jaba.516

Lindberg, J. S., Iwata, B. A., Kahng, S. W., & DeLeon, I. G. (1999). DRO contingencies: An analysis of variable-momentary schedules. *Journal of Applied Behavior Analysis, 32,* 123–136.

Lindberg, J. S., Iwata, B. A., Roscoe, E. M., Worsdell, A. S., & Hanley, G. P. (2003). Treatment efficacy of noncontingent reinforcement during brief and extended application. *Journal of Applied Behavior Analysis, 36,* 1–19.

Lindsley, O. R. (1968). A reliable wrist counter for recording behavior rates. *Journal of Applied Behavior Analysis, 1,* 77–78.

Lindsley, O. R. (1991). Precision teaching's unique legacy from B. F. Skinner. *Journal of Behavioral Education, 1,* 253–266.

Lindsley,, O. R. (1991). From technical jargon to plain English for application. *Journal of Applied Behavior Analysis, 21,* 449–458. doi: 10.1901/jaba.1991.13-83.

Ling, P. A., & Thomas, D. R. (1986). Imitation of television aggression among Maori and European boys and girls. *New Zealand Journal of Psychology, 15,* 47–53.

Linscheid, T. R., Iwata, B. A., Ricketts, R. W., Williams, D. E., & Griffin, J. C. (1990). Clinical evaluation of the Self-injurious Behavior Inhibiting System (SIBIS). *Journal of Applied Behavior Analysis, 23,* 53–78.

Linscheid, T. R., & Reichenbach, H. (2002). Multiple factors in the long-term effectiveness of contingent electric shock treatment for self-injurious behavior: A case example. *Research in Developmental Disabilities, 23,* 161–177.

Lionello-DeNolf, K. M., da Silva Barros, R., & McIlvane, W. J. (2007). A novel method for teaching the first instances of simple discrimination to nonverbal children with autism in a laboratory environment. *Psychological Record, 58,* 229–244.

Lipinski, P., & Nelson, R. (1974). Problems in the use of naturalistic observation as a means of behavioral assessment. *Behavior Therapy, 5,* 341–351.

Lippman, L. G., & Meyer, M. E. (1967). Fixed-interval performance as related to instructions and to subject's verbalizations of the contingency. *Psychonomic Science, 8,* 135–136.

Lipschultz, J., & Wilder, D. (2017). Recent research on the high-probability instructional sequence: A brief Review. *Journal of Applied Behavior Analysis, 50*, 424–428. doi: 10.1002/jaba.378

Litow, L., & Pumroy, D. K. (1975). A brief review of classroom group-oriented contingencies. *Journal of Applied Behavior Analysis, 8*, 341–347.

Lloyd, J. L., Riley, G. A., & Powell, T. E. (2009). Errorless learning of novel routines through a virtual town in people with acquired brain injury. *Neuropsychological Rehabilitation, 19*, 98–109.

Loeber, R., & Dishion, J. J. (1983). Early predictors of male delinquency: A review. *Psychological Bulletin, 94*, 68–99.

Logan, P., & Skinner, C. H. (1998). Improving students' perceptions of a mathematics assignment by increasing problem completion rates: Is problem completion a reinforcing event? *School Psychology Quarterly, 13*, 322–331.

Logue, A. W., Pena-Correal, T. E., Rodríguez, M. L., & Kabela E. (1986). Self-control in adult humans: Variation in positive reinforcer amount and delay. *Journal of the Experimental Analysis of Behavior, 46*, 159–173.

Lohaus, A., & Klein-Hessling, J. (2003). Relaxation training in children: Effects of extended and intensified training. *Psychology & Health, 18*, 237–249.

Lohrmann-O'Rourke, S., & Zirkel, P. A. (1998). The case law on aversive interventions for students with disabilities. *Exceptional Children, 65*, 101–123.

Lomas, I. D., Koedinger, K., Patel, N., Shodhan, S., Poonwala, N., & Forlizzi, J. L. (2017). Is difficulty overrated?: The effects of choice, novelty and suspense on intrinsic motivation in educational games. In *Proceedings of the 2017 CHI conference on human factors in computing systems*, Ch. 17, 1028-1039. https://doi.org1-.1145/3025453.3025638

Long, E.R., (1962). Additional techniques for producing multiple-schedule control in children. *Journal of the Experimental Analysis of Behavior, 5*, 443–455.

Long, E. R. (1963). Chained and tandem scheduling with Children. *Journal of the Experimental Analysis of Behavior, 6*, 459–472.

Long, E. S., Miltenberger, R. G., Ellingson, S. A., & Orr, S. M. (1999). Augmenting simplified habit reversal in the treatment of oral –digital habits exhibited by individuals with mental retardation. *Journal of Applied Behavior Analysis, 32*, 353–365.

Long, E. S., Miltenberger, R. G., & Rapp, J. T. (2000). Simplified habit reversal plus adjunct contingencies in the treatment of thumb-sucking and hair-pulling in a young child. *Child and Family Behavior Therapy, 21*, 45–58.

Lopez, C., & Dubois, D. L. (2005). Peer victimization and rejection: Investigation of an integrative model of effects on emotional, behavioral, and academic adjustment in early adolescence. *Journal of Clinical Child and Adolescent Psychology, 34*, 25–36.

Lopez, A. R., & Wiskow, K. M. (2020). Teaching children with autism to initiate social interactions using textual prompts delivered via apple watches®. *Behavior Analysis in Practice, 13*, 641–647. doi.org/10.1007/s40167-019-00385-y

Lorimer, P. A., Simpson, R. L., Myles, B. S., & Ganz, J. B. (2002). The use of social stories as a preventative behavioral intervention in a home setting with a child with autism. *Journal of Positive Behavior Interventions, 4*, 53–60.

Losinski, M., Sanders, Katsiyannis, & Wiseman, N. (2017). A meta-analysis of interventions to improve the compliance of students with disabilities. *Education and Treatment of Children, 40*, 435–464.

Lovaas, O. I. (1977). *The autistic child: Language development through behavior modification*. New York: Irvington.

Lovaas, O. I., Berberich, J. P., Perloff, B. F., & Schaeffer, B. (1966). Acquisition of imitative speech in schizophrenic children. *Science, 151*, 705–707.

Lovaas, O. I., Berberich, J. P., Perloff, B. F., & Schaeffer, B. (1991). Acquisition of imitative speech by schizophrenic children. *Focus on Autistic Behavior, 6*, 1–5.

Lovaas, O. I., & Favell, J. E. (1987). Protection for clients undergoing aversive/restrictive interventions. *Education and Treatment of Children, 10*, 311–325.

Lovaas, O. I., Freitag, G., Gold, M. J., & Kassorla, I. C. (1965). Experimental studies in childhood schizophrenia: Analysis of self-destructive behavior. *Journal of Experimental Child Psychology, 2*, 67–84.

Lovaas, O. I., Koegel, R., Simmons, J. Q., & Long, J. S. (1973). Some generalization and follow-up measures on autistic children in behavior therapy. *Journal of Applied Behavior Analysis, 6*, 131–166.

Lovaas, O. I., Schreibman, L., Koegel, R. L., & Rehm, R. (1971). Selective responding by autistic children to multiple sensory input. *Journal of Abnormal Psychology, 77*, 211–222.

Lowe, C. F., Beastay, A., & Bentall, R. P. (1983). The role of verbal behavior in human learning: Infant performance on fixed interval schedules. *Journal of the Experimental Analysis of Behavior, 39*, 157–164.

Lowe, C. F., Harzem, P., & Bagshaw, M. (1978). Species differences in temporal control of behavior II: Human performance. *Journal of the Experimental Analysis of Behavior, 29*, 351–161.

Lowery, C.T. & Mattaini, M.A. (1999). The science of sharing power: Native American thought and behavior analysis. *Behavior and Social Issues, 9*, 3–23.

Lowitz, G. H., & Suib, M. R. (1978). Generalized control of persistent thumbsucking by differential reinforcement of other behaviors. *Journal of Behavior Therapy & Experimental Psychiatry, 9*, 343–346.

LRP Publications. (November 10, 2006). Time-out rooms: Advice to avoid liability while disciplining students with disabilities. *The Special Educator, Bonus Report.*

Luce, S. C., Delquadri, J., & Hall, R. V. (1980). Contingent Exercise: A mild but powerful procedure for suppressing inappropriate verbal and aggressive behavior. *Journal of Applied Behavior Analysis, 13*, 583–594.

Luciano, M. C. (1986). Acquisition, maintenance, and generalization of productive intraverbal behavior through transfer of stimulus control procedures. *Applied Research in Mental Retardation, 7*, 1–20.

Luczynski, K. C., & Hanley, G. P. (2013). Prevention of problem behavior by teaching functional communication and self-control skills to preschoolers.

*Journal of Applied Behavior Analysis, 46,* 355–368.

Ludwig, D. J., & Maehr, M. L. (1967). Changes in self-concept and stated behavioral preferences. *Child Development, 38,* 453–467.

Ludwig, T. D., Biggs, J., Wagner, S., & Geller, E. S. (2001). Suing public feedback and competitive rewards to increase the safe driving of pizza deliverers. *Journal of Organizational Behavior Management, 21,* 75–104.

Ludwig, T. D., Gray, T. W., & Rowell, A. (1998). Increasing recycling in academic buildings: A systematic replication. *Journal of Applied Behavior Analysis, 31,* 683–686.

Luiselli, J. K., Putnam, R. F., & Sunderland, M. (2002). Longitudinal evaluation of behavior support interventions in a public middle school. *Journal of Positive Behavior Interventions, 4,* 182–188.

Luiselli, J. K., & Reisman, J. (1980). Some variations in the use of differential reinforcement procedures with mentally retarded children in specialized treatment settings. *Applied Research in Mental Retardation, 1,* 227–288.

Luiselli, J.K., & Slocumb, P.R. (1983). Management of multiple aggressive behaviors by differential reinforcement, *Journal of Behavior Therapy and Experimental Psychiatry, 14,* 343–347.

Luiselli, J.K., Suskin, L. L., & Slocumb, P.R. (1984). Application of immobilization time-out in management programs with developmentally disabled children. *Child and Family Behavior Therapy, 6,* 1–15.

Luyben, P. D., Funk, D. M., Morgan, J. K., Clark, K. A., & Delulio, D. W. (1986). Team sports for the severely retarded: Training a side-of-the-foot soccer pass using a maximum-to-minimum prompt reduction strategy. *Journal of Applied Behavior Analysis, 19,* 431–436.

Lynch, D. C., & Cuvo, A J. (1995). Stimulus equivalence instruction of ration-decimal relations. *Journal of Applied Behavior Analysis, 28,* 115–126. doi: 10.1901/java, 1995 28-115

MacCorquodale, K., & Meehl, P. (1948). On a distinction between hypothetical constructs and intervening variables. *Psychological Record, 55,* 95–10–7.

MacDonald, J., & Ahearn, W. H. (2015). Teaching observational learning to children with autism. *Journal of Applied Behavior Analysis, 48,* 800–816. doi: 10.1002/jaba.257.

MacDonald, R.P.F., Dickson, C.A., Martineau, M., & Ahearn, W.H. (2015). Prerequisite skills that support learning through video modeling. *Education and Treatment of Children, 38,* 33–47.

MacDonald, W. S., Gallimore, R., & MacDonald, G. (1970). Contingency counseling by school personnel: An economical model of intervention. *Journal of Applied Behavior Analysis, 3,* 175–182.

MacDuff, G.S., Krantz, P.J., & McClannahan, L.E. (1993). Teaching children with autism to use photographic activity schedules: Maintenance and generalization of complex response chains. *Journal of Applied Behavior Analysis, 26,* 89–97.

MacDuff, G. S., Krantz, P. J., & McClannahan, L. E. (2001). Prompts and prompt-fading strategies for people with autism. In C. Maurice, G. Green, & R. M. Foxx (Eds.), *Making a difference: Behavioral intervention for autism.* Austin, TX: PRO-ED.

Mace, F. C. (1996). In pursuit of general behavioral relations. *Journal of Applied Behavior Analysis, 29,* 557–563.

Mace, F., & Belfiore, P. (1990). Behavioral momentum in the treatment of escape-motivated stereotypy. *Journal of the Applied Behavior Analysis, 23,* 507–514.

Mace, F. C., & Heller, M. (1990). A comparison of exclusion time-out and contingent observation for reducing severe disruptive behavior in a 7–year-old boy. *Child & Family Behavior Therapy, 12*(1), 57–68.

Mace, F. C., & Kratochwill, T. R. (1985). Theories of reactivity in self-monitoring: A comparison of cognitive-behavioral and operant methods. *Behavior Modification, 9,* 323–343.

Mace, F. C., Mauro, B. C., Boyajian, A. E., & Eckert, T. L. (1997). Effects of reinforcer quality of behavioral momentum: Coordinated applied and basic research. *Journal of Applied Behavior Analysis, 30,* 1–20.

Mace, F. C., McComas, J., Mauro, B. C., Progar, P. R., Taylor, B., Ervin, R., & Zangrillo, a. N. (2010). Reinforcement of alternative behavior increases resistance to extinction: Clinical demonstration, animal modeling, and clinical test of one solution. *Journal of the Experimental Analysis of Behavior, 93,* 349–367.

Mace, F. C., McCurdy, B., & Quigley, E. A. (1990). A collateral effect of reward predicted by matching theory. *Journal of Applied Behavior Analysis, 23,* 197–205.

Mace, F. C., Neef, N. A., Shade, D., & Mauro, B. C. (1994). Limited matching on concurrent-schedule reinforcement of academic behavior. *Journal of Applied Behavior Analysis, 27,* 585–596.

Mace, F. C., & Nevin, J. A. (2017). Maintenance, generalization and treamtne relapse: A behavioral momentum analysis. *Education and Treatment of Children, 40,* 27–42.

Mace, F. C., Page, T. J., Ivancic, M. T., & O'Brien, S. (1986). Effectiveness of brief time-out with and without contingent delay: A comparative analysis. *Journal of Applied Behavior Analysis, 19,* 79–86.

MacFarland, M. C., & Fisher, M. H. (2020). Peer-mediated social skill generalization for adolescents with autism spectrum disorder and intellectual disability. *Exceptionality, 28.* doi.org/10.1080/09362835.2019.1579722

MacIver, M. A., & Kemper, E. (2002). Guest editors' introduction: Research on Direct Instruction reading. *Journal of Education for Students Placed At-Risk, 7,* 107–116.

Mackay, H. A., & Sidman, M. (1984). Teaching new behavior via equivalence relations. In P. H. Brooks, R. Sperber, and C. McCauley, (Eds.), *Learning and cognition in the mentally retarded* (pp. 292–313). Hillsdale, NJ: Lawrence Erlbaum Associates.

MacPherson, M. M., Merry, K. J., Locke, S. R., & Jung, M. E. (2019). Effects of mobile health prompts on self-monitoring and exercise behaviors following a diabetes prevention program: Secondary analysis from a randomized controlled trial. *JMIR MhealthUhealth, 7*(9), 12956. doi: 10.2196/12958

MacSuga-Gage, A. S.,, Gage, N. A., Katslyannis, A., Hirsch, S., & Eisner, H. (2020). *Journal of Disability Policy Studies.* (on-line) https://doi.org/10.1177/1044207320949960

Maden, T. (1999). Seclusion. *The Journal of Forensic Psychiatry, 10*(2), 242–244.

Madzharova, M., Sturmey, P., & Jones, E. (2012). Training staff to increase manding in students with autism: Two preliminary case studies. *Behavioral Interventions, 27*(4), 224–235.

Magee, S.K., & Ellis, J. (2001). The detrimental effects of physical restraint as a consequence for inappriate classroom behavior. *Journal of Applied Behavior Analysis, 34,* 501–504.

Mager, R. F. (1962). *Preparing instructional objectives.* Palo Alto: Fearon.

Mager, R. F. (1972). *Goal analysis.* Palo Alto: Fearon.

Mager, R. F. (1997a). Goal analysis: How to clarify your goals so you can actually achieve them, 3rd ed. Atlanta: The Center for Effective Performance, Inc.

Mager, R. F. (1997b) *Preparing instructional objectives: A critical tool in the development of effective instruction* (3rd ed.). Atlanta, GA: Center for Effective Performance.

Maheady, L., & Sainato, D. (1985). The effects of peer tutoring upon the social status and social interaction patterns of high and low status elementary students. *Education and Treatment of Children, 8,* 51–65.

Mahoney, G., & MacDonald, J. (2007). *Autism and developmental delays in young children: The responsive teaching curriculum for parents and professionals.* Austin TX: Pro-ed.

Maier, S. F., Seligman, M. E. P., & Solomon, R. L. (1969). Pavlovian fear conditioning and learned helplessness: Effects on escape and avoidance behavior of (a) the CS-US contingency and (b) the independence of the US and voluntary responding. In B. A. Campbell and R. M. Church (Eds.), *Punishment and aversive behavior.* New York: Appleton Century Crofts.

Majdalany, L. M., Wilder, D. A., Greif, A., Greif, A., Mathisen, D., & Saini, V. (2014). Comparing massed-trial instruction, distributed-trial instruction, and task interspersed to teach tacts to children with autism spectrum, disorders. *Journal of Applied Behavior Analysis, 47,* 657–662. doi: 10.1002/jaba.149

Malone, J. C. (2014). Edi John B. Watson really "found" behaviorism? *Behavior Analyst, 37,* 1–12.

Malott, R. W. (2001). Occupational safety and response maintenance: An alternate view. *Journal of Organizational Behavior Management, 21,* 85–102.

Malott, R. W., & Trojan, E. A. (2008). *Principles of behavior, 6th Ed.* New York: Prentice Hall.

Mancil, G. R. (2006). Functional communication training: A review of the literature related to children with autism. *Education and Training in Developmental Disabilities, 41,* 213–224.

Mancina, C., Tankersley, M., Kamps, D., Kravits, T., & Parrett, J. (2000). Brief report: Reduction of inappropriate vocalizations for a child with autism using a self-management treatment plan. *Journal of Autism and Developmental Disorders, 30,* 599–606.

Mandelker, A. B., Brigham, T. A., & Bushell, D. Jr. (1970). The effects of token procedures on a teacher's social contacts with her students. *Journal of Applied Behavior Analysis, 3,* 169–174.

Mangiapanello, K. A., & Hemmes, N. S. (2015). An analysis of feedback from a behavior analytic perspective. *Behavior Analyst, 38,* 51–75. DOI: 10.1007/s40614-014-0026-x

Mann, P. H. (Ed.) (1975). *Mainstream special education: Issues and perspective in urban centers.* (USOE Project No. CEG-0-72-3999[609].) Reston, Va: Council For Exceptional Children.

Manos, M. J. (1983). Effects of verbal elaborations and social reinforcement on children's discrimination learning. *Education and Treatment of Children, 6,* 263–275.

March, R., Horner, R. H., Lewis-Palmer, T., Brown, D., Crone, D., Todd, A. W. et al. (2000). *Functional Assessment Checklist for Teachers and Staff (FACTS).* Eugene, OR: University of Oregon, Department of Educational and Community Supports.

Marcus, A., & Wilder, D. A. (2009). A comparison of peer video modeling and self video modeling to teach textual responses in children with autism. *Journal of Applied Behavior Analysis, 42,* 335–341.

Marckel, J. M., Neef, N, a., & Ferreri, S J. (2006). A preliminary analysis of teaching improvisation with the picture exchange communication system to children with autism. *Journal of Applied Behavior Analysis, 39,* 109–115.

Markham, V. A., Giles, A. F., Roderique-Davis G., Adshead, V., Tamiaki, G., & May, R. J. (2020). Applications of within-stimulus errorless learning methods for teaching discrimination skills to individuals with intellectual and developmental disabilities: A systematic review. *Research in Developmental Disabilities, 97.* doi.org/10/1016/j.ridd.2019. 103521.

Marmolejo, E. K., Wilder, D. A., & Bradley, L. (2004). A preliminary analysis of the effects of response cards on student performance and participation in an upper division university course. *Journal of Applied Behavior Analysis, 37,* 405–410.

Marr, M. J. (2016). Complexity revisited. *Inside Behavior Analysis, 8*(2), 2–3.

Marsteller, T. M., & St. Peter, C. C. (2014). Effects of fixed-time reinforcement schedules on resurgence of problem behavior. *Journal of Applied Behavior Analysis, 47,* 455–469. doi: 10.1002/jaba.2014.134.

Martella, R. C., Leonard, I. J., Marchand-Martella, N. E., & Agran, M. (1993). Self-monitoring negative statements. *Journal of Behavioral Education, 3,* 77–86.

Martens, B. K., DiGennaro, F. D., Reed, D. D., Szczech, F. M., & Rosenthal, B. D. (2008). Contingency space analysis: An alternative method for identifying contingent relations from observational data. *Journal of Applied Behavior Analysis, 41,* 69–81.

Martens, B. K, Eckert, T. L., Begeny, J. C., Lweandowski, L. J., DiGennaro, F. D., Montarello, S. A. et al. (2007). Effects of a fluency-building program on the reading performance of low-achieving second and third-grade students. *Journal of Behavioral Education, 16,* 38–53.

Martens, B. K., Hilt, A. M., Needham, L. R., Sutterer, J. R., Panahon, C. J., & Lannie, A. L. (2003). Carryover effects of free reinforcement on children's work completion, *Behavior Modification, 27,* 560–577.

Martens, B. K., Lochner, D. G., & Kelly, S. Q. (1992). The effects of variable-interval reinforcement on academic engagement: A demonstration of matching theory. *Journal of Applied Behavior Analysis, 25,* 143–152.

Martin, J. A. (1974, August). *Children's task preferences: Effects of reinforcement and punishment.* Paper presented at the meeting of the American Psychological Association, New Orleans.

Martin, J. A. (1975). Generalizing the use of descriptive adjectives through modeling. *Journal of Applied Behavior Analysis, 8,* 203–209.

Martin, J. E., Rusch, F. R., James, L., Decker, P. J., & Trtol, K. A. (1982). The use of picture cues to establish self-control in the preparation of complex meals by mentally retarded adults. *Applied Research in Mental Retardation, 3,* 105–119.

Martin, T. L., Pear, J. J., & Martin, G. L. (2002a). Analysis of proctor marking accuracy in a computer-aided personalized system of instruction course. *Journal of Applied Behavior Analysis, 35,* 309–312.

Martin, T. L., Pear, J. J., & Martin, G. L. (2002b). Feedback and its effectiveness in a computer-aided personalized system of instruction course. *Journal of Applied Behavior Analysis, 35,* 427–430.

Martinez, C. K., & Betz, A. M. (2013). Response interruption and redirection: Current research trends and clinical application. *Journal of Applied Behavior Analysis, 46,* 549–554.

Martner, S. G., & Dallery, J. (2019). Technology-based contingency management and e-cigarettes during the initial weeks of a smoking quit attempt. *Journal of Applied Behavior Analysis, 52*(4), 928–943. https://doi-org.mimas.calstatela.edu/10.1002/jaba.641

Marx, T. A., & Baker, J. N. (2017). Analysis of restraint and seclusion legislation and policy across states: Adherence to recommended principles. *Journal of Disability Policy Studies, 28*(1), 23–31. https://doi.org/10.1177/1044207317702069

Masataka, W. (2002). Independent travel skills and social interactions in a natural environment: Teaching a student with autism. *Japanese Journal of Behavior Therapy, 28,* 83–95.

Mash, E. J., & McElwee, J. D. (1974). Situational effects on observer accuracy: Behavioral predictability, prior experience, and complexity of coding categories. *Child Development, 45,* 367–377.

Mason, S. A., McGee, G. G., Farmer-Dougan, V., & Risley, T. R. (1989). A practical strategy for ongoing reinforcer assessment. *Journal of Applied Behavior Analysis, 22,* 171–179.

Massar, M. (2018). Effects of coach-delivered prompting and performance feedback on teacher use of evidence-based classroom management practices and student behavior outcomes. Scholars' Bank, University of Oregon. URI: http//hdl.handle.net/1794/23123

Massar, S. S. A., Lim, J., Sasmita, K., & Chee, M. W. L. (2019). Sleep deprivation in-creases the costs of attentional effort: Performance, preference and pupil size. *Neuropsychologia, 123,* 169–177. https://doi.org/10.1016/jheropsychologia.2018.03.032

Masterlinck, M. (1901). *La vie des abeilles (The life of the bee).* London: Ruskin House. Translated into English by K. Sutro. (1928). New York, N.Y. Dodd, Mead & Co.

Mathews, B., Catania, A. C., & Shimoff, E. (1985). Effects of uninstructed verbal behavior on nonverbal responding: Contingency descriptions versus performance descriptions. *Journal of the Experimental Analysis of Behavior, 43,* 155–164.

Mathews, B. A., Friman, P. C., Barone, V. J., Ross, L. V., & Christophersen, E. R. (1987). Decreasing dangerous infant behaviors through parent instruction. *Journal of Applied Behavior Analysis, 20,* 165–169.

Mathews, K., & Hagopian, L. (2014). A comparison of two data analysis training methods for paraprofessionals in an educational setting. *Journal of Organizational Behavior Management, 34*(2), 165–178.

Mathews, S., McIntosh, K., Frank, J. L., & May, S. L. (2014). Critical features predicting sustained implementation of school-wide positive behavioral interventions and supports. *Journal of Positive Behavior Interventions, 16,* 168–178.

Matson, J. L., & Taras, M. E. (1989). A 20-year review of punishment and alternative methods to treat problem behaviors in developmentally delayed persons. *Research in Developmental Disabilities, 10,* 85–104.

Matson, J. L., & Vollmer, T. R. (1995). *User's guide: Questions about behavioral function (QABF).* Baton Rouge, LA: Scientific Publishers, Inc.

Mattson, S. L., & Pinkelman, S. E. (2020). Improving on-task behavior in middle school students with disabilities using activity schedules. *Behavior Analysis in Practice, 13,* 104–118. doi:org/10.1007/s40617-019-00373-2

Matthews, K., & Hagopian, L. (2014). A comparison of two data analysis training methods for paraprofessionals in an educational setting. *Journal of Organizational Behavior Management, 34*(2), 165–178.

Matthews, B. A., Catania, A. C., & Shimoff, E. (1985). The effects of uninstructed verbal behavior on nonverbal responding: Contingency descriptions versus performance descriptions. *Journal of the Experimental Analysis of Behavior, 43,* 155–164.

Matthews, B. A., Shimoff, E., & Cantania, A. C. (1987). Saying and doing: A contingency-space analysis. *Journal of Applied Behavior Analysis, 20,* 69–74.

Maurice, C. (1993). *Let me hear your voice. A family's triumph over autism.* Fawcett Columbine: New York.

Maurice, C., Green, G., & Luce S. C. (1996) *Behavioral Intervention for Young Children With Autism: A Manual for Parents and Professionals.* (Austin, TX: Pro-Ed)

Mausner, B. (1954). The effect of prior reinforcement in the interaction of observer pairs. *Journal of Abnormal and Social Psychology, 49,* 65–68.

Mausner, B., & Block, B. L. (1957). A study of the additivity of variables affecting social interaction. *Journal of Abnormal and Social Psychology, 54,* 250–256.

Mawhinney, V. T., Bostow, D. E., Laws, O. R., Blumenfeld, G. T., & Hopkins, B. L. (1971). A comparison of students' studying behavior produced by daily, weekly, and three-week testing schedules. *Journal of Applied Behavior Analysis, 4,* 257–264.

May, J. G., Risley, T. R., Twardosz, S., Friedman, P., Bijou, S., Wexler, D., et al. (1976). *Guidelines for the use of behavioral procedures on state programs for retarded persons.* NARC Monograph, MR Research, Arlington, TX.

Maydak, M., Stromer, R., Mackay, H.A., & Stoddard, L.T. (1995). Stimulus classes in matching to sample and sequence production: The emergence of numeric relations. *Research in Developmental Disabilities, 16, 3,* 179–204.

Mayer, G. R. (1995). Preventing antisocial behavior in the school. *The Journal* of *Applied Behavior Analysis, 28*(4), 467–478.

Mayer, G. R. (1999). Constructive discipline for school personnel. *Education and Treatment of Children, 22,* 36–54.

Mayer, G. R. (2000). *Classroom management: A California resource guide.* Los Angeles County Office of Education, Safe Schools. Downey, CA.

Mayer, G. R. (2001). Antisocial behavior: Its causes and prevention in our schools. *Education and Treatment of Children, 24*(4), 414–429

Mayer, G. R. (2002). Behavioral strategies to reduce school violence. *Child and Family Behavior Therapy, 24,* 83–100.

Mayer, G. R. (2003, February). *Maintaining schoolwide change.* Paper presented at the meeting of the California Association for Behavior Analysis's 23rd Annual Western Regional Conference, Newport Beach, CA.

Mayer, G. R. (2005). Schoolwide Discipline. In M. Hersen, G. Sugai, & R. Horner (Eds.), *Encyclopedia of behavior modification and cognitive behavior therapy: Educational applications, vol. 3.* (pp. 1496–1506). Thousand Oaks, CA: Sage Publications.

Mayer, G. R. (2009). Gang prevention strategies for schools. In H. Walker, M. Shinn, and G. Stoner (Eds.), *Interventions for achievement and behavior in a three-tier model including RTI (3rd Edition).* Bethesda, MD: National Association of School Psychologists Monograph.

Mayer, G. R. (2020). *The positive classroom: Improving student learning and behavior.* Cornwall-on-Hudson, NY: Sloan Publishing, LLC.

Mayer, G. R., & Butterworth, T. (1979). A preventive approach to school violence and vandalism: An experimental study. *The Personnel and Guidance Journal, 57,* 436–441.

Mayer, G. R. & Butterworth, T. W. (1981). Evaluating a preventive approach to reducing school vandalism. *Phi Delta Kappan, 62,* 498–499.

Mayer, G. R., & McGookin, R. B. (1977). *Behavioral consulting.* Los Angeles: Office of the Los Angeles County Superintendent of Schools.

Mayer, G. R., Butterworth, T., Nafpaktitis, M., & Sulzer-Azaroff, B. (1983a). Preventing school vandalism and improving discipline: A three-year study. *Journal of Applied Behavior Analysis, 16,* 355–369.

Mayer, G. R., Butterworth, T., Spaulding, H. L., Hollingsworth, P., Amorim, M., Caldwell-McElroy, C., Nafpaktitis, M., & Perez-Osorio, X. (1983b). *Constructive discipline: Building a climate for learning. A Resource manual of programs and strategies.* Downey, CA: Office of the Los Angeles County Superintendent of Schools.

Mayer, G. R., & McGookin, R. B. (1977). *Behavioral consulting.* Los Angeles: Office of the Los Angeles County Superintendent of Schools.

Mayer, G. R., Mitchell, L., Clementi, T., Clement-Robertson, E., Myatt, R., & Bullara, D. T. (1993). A dropout prevention program for at-risk high school students: Emphasizing consulting to promote positive classroom climates. *Education and Treatment of Children, 16,* 135–146.

Mayer, G. R., Nafpaktitis, M., Butterworth, T., & Hollingsworth, P. (1987). A search for the elusive setting events of school vandalism: A correlational study. *Education and Treatment of Children, 10,* 259–270.

Mayer, G. R., Rohen, T. H., & Whitley, A. D. (1969). Group counseling with children: A cognitive-behavioral approach. *Journal of Counseling Psychology, 16,* 142–149.

Mayer, G. R., & Sulzer-Azaroff, B. (1991). Interventions for vandalism. In G. Stoner, M. K. Shinn, & H. M. Walker, (Eds.), *Interventions for achievement and behavior problems.* Washington, DC: National Association of School Psychologists Monograph.

Mayer, G. R., & Sulzer-Azaroff, B. (2002). Preventing school violence and vandalism. In M. R. Shinn, H. M. Walker, & G. Stoner (Eds.), *Interventions for academic and behavior problems II: Preventive and remedial approaches.* (2nd Ed.). Bethesda, MD: National Association of School Psychologists Monograph.

Mayer, G. R., Sulzer-Azaroff, B., & Wallace, M. D. (2012). *Behavior analysis for lasting change* (2nd Ed.). Cornwall on Hudson NY: Sloan Publishing.

Mayer, G. R., & Wallace, M. D. (2020). *Behavioral consulting: Improving client and consultee learning and behavior.* Cornwall on Hudson, NY: Sloan Publishing, LLC.

Mayer, G. R., & Wallace, M. D., (2022). *Preventing problematic behavior at home, school, and at work.* Cornwall on Hudson, NY: Sloan Publishing.

Mayer, G. R., & Ybarra, W. J. (2003). *Teaching alternative behaviors schoolwide: A resource guide to prevent discipline problems.* Los Angeles: Los Angeles County Office of Education.

Mayer, G. R., & Ybarra, W. J. (2003). *Teaching alternative behaviors schoolwide (TABS). A resource guide to prevent discipline problems.* The Los Angeles County Office of Education, Safe Schools: Downey, CA.

Mayer, G. R., & Ybarra, W. (2006). *Gang violence: Prevention and intervention strategies for schools.* The Los Angeles County Office of Education, Safe Schools: Downey, CA.

Mayer-Johnson, R. (1981). *The picture communication symbols book.* Solana Beach, CA: Mayer-Johnson.

Mayfield, K. H., & Vollmer, T. R. (2007). Teaching math skills to at-risk students using home-based peer tutoring. *Journal of Applied Behavior Analysis, 40,* 223–237.

Mazur, J. E. (2002). *Learning and behavior.* Upper Saddle River, NJ: Prentice Hall.

McAdam, D. B., Klatt, K. P., Koffarnus, M., Dicesare, A., SLolberg, K., Welch, C., et al. (2005). The effects of establishing operations on preferences for tangible items. *Journal of Applied Behavior Analysis, 38,* 107–110.

McAdam, D.B., Sherman, J.A., Sheldon, J.B., & Napolitano, D.A. (2004). Behavioral interventions to reduce pica of persons with developmental disabilities. *Behavior Modification, 28,* 45–72.

McCallum, E., Skinner, C. H., Turner, H., & Saecker, L. (2006). The taped-problems intervention: Increasing multiplication fact fluency using a low-tech, classwide, time-delay intervention. *School Psychology Review, 35,* 419–434.

McCandless, B. R. (1967). *Children, behavior and development.* Hinsdale, IL: Dryden.

McCann, K.B., & Sulzer-Azaroff, B. (1996). Cumulative trauma disorders: Behavioral injury prevention at work. *Journal of Applied Behavioral Science, 32*(3), 277–291.

McClannahan, L. E., & Krantz, P. J. (1999). *Activity schedules for children with autism: Teaching independent behavior*. Bethesda, MD: Woodbine House.

McClellan, C. B., Cohen, L. L., & Moffett, K., (2009). Time out based discipline strategy for children's non-compliance with cystic fibrosis treatment. *Disability and Rehabilitation 31*(4), 327–336.

McClure, G. Y., & McMillan, D.E. (1997). Effects of drugs on response duration differentiation. VI: differential effects under differential reinforcement of low rates of responding schedules. *Journal of Pharmacology and Experimental Therapeutics, 28*(3), 1368–1380.

McComas, J. J., Lalli, J. S., & Benavides, C. (1999). Increasing accuracy and decreasing latency during clean intermittent self-catheterization procedures with young children. *Journal of Applied Behavior Analysis, 32,* 217–220.

McConnachie, G., & Carr, E. G. (1997). The effect of child behavior problems on the maintenance of intervention fidelity. *Behavior Modification, 21,* 121–158.

McConnell, S. R. (2002). Interventions to facilitate social interactions for young children with autism. Review of available research and recommendations for educational intervention and future research. *Journal of Autism and Developmental Disorders, 32,* 351–372.

McCord, B. E., Grosser, J. W., Iwata, B. A., & Powers, L. A. (2005). An analysis of response-blocking parameters in the prevention of pica. *Journal of Applied Behavior Analysis, 38,* 391–394.

McCord, B. E., Thomson, R. J., & Iwata B. A. (2001). Functional analysis and treatment of self-injury associated with transitions. *Journal of Applied Behavior Analysis, 34,* 195–210. doi: 10.1901/jaba.2001. 34-195

McCullagh, P. (1987). Model similarity effects on motor performance. *Journal of Sport Psychology, 9,* 249–260.

McCurdy, B. L., Mannella, M. C., & Eldridge, N. (2003). Positive behavior support in urban schools: Can we prevent the escalation of antisocial behavior? *Journal of Positive Behavior Interventions, 5,* 158–170.

McDonnell, J. J. (1987). The effects of time delay and increasing prompt hierarchy strategies on the acquisition of purchasing skills by students with severe handicaps. *The Journal of the Association for Persons with Severe Handicaps, 12,* 227–236.

McDonnell, J., & Ferguson, B. (1989). A comparison of time delay and decreasing prompt hierarchy strategies in teaching banking skills to students with moderate handicaps. *Journal of Applied Behavior Analysis, 22,* 85–91.

McDonnell, J., & McFarland, S. (1988). A comparison of forward and concurrent chaining strategies in teaching Laundromat skills to students with severe handicaps. *Research in Developmental Disabilities, 9,* 177–194.

McDonnell, J., Thorson, N., Allen, C., & Mathot-Buckner, C. (2000). The effects of partner learning during spelling for students with severe disabilities and their peers. *Journal of Behavioral Education, 10,* 107–121.

McDougall, D. (1998). Research on self-management techniques used by students with disabilities in general education settings. *Remedial and Special Education, 19,* 310–320.

McDougall, D. (2005). The range-bound changing criterion design. *Behavioral Interventions, 20,* 129–137.

McDougall, D., & Brady, M. P. (1998). Initiating and fading self-management interventions to increase math fluency in general education classes. *Exceptional Children, 64,* 151–166.

McDougall, D., Hawkins, J., Brady, M., & Jenkins, A (2006). Recent innovations in the changing criterion design: Implications for research and practice in special education. *Journal of Special Education, 40,* 2–15.

McDowell, K. C. (2003). Indiana Department of education, Unpublished Memorandum to Members of the National Council of State Education Attorneys (NCOSEA).

McDowell, L. S., Gutierrez, A., & Bennett, K. D. (2015). Analysis of live modeling plus prompting and video modeling for teaching imitation to children with autism. *Behavioral Interventions, 30,* 333–351. doi: 10.11002/bin.1419

McDuff, E., Lanovaz, M., Morin, D., Vona, J., Kheloufi, Y., & Giannakakos, A. R. (2019). Using differential reinforcement of high rates of behavior to improve work productivity: A replication and extension. *Journal of Applied Research in Intellectual Disabilities, 32,* 1288–1293. https://diu,irg/10.1111/jar.12614

McEachin, J. J., Smith, T., & Lovaas, O. I. (1993). Long-term outcome for children with autism who received early intensive behavioral interventions. *American Journal on Mental Retardation, 97,* 359–372.

McFall, R. M. (1970). Effects of self-monitoring on normal smoking behavior. *Journal of Consulting and Clinical Psychology, 35,* 135–142.

McGhan, A. C., & Lerman, D. C. (2013). An assessment of error-correction procedures for learners with autism. *Journal of Applied Behavior Analysis, 46,* 626–639. DOI: 10.1002/jaba.65

McGee, S. G., Almeida, C., Sulzer-Azaroff, B., & Feldman, R. S. (1992). Promoting reciprocal interactions via peer incidental teaching. *Journal of Applied Behavior Analysis, 25,* 117–126.

McGee, G.G., & Daly, T. (2007). Incidental teaching of age-appropriate social phrases to children with autism. *Research and Practice for Persons with Severe Disabilities, 32,* 112–123.

McGee, G. G., Krantz, P. J., & McClannahan, L. E. (1985). The facilitative effects of incidental teaching on preposition use by autistic children. *Journal of Applied Behavior Analysis, 18,* 17–31.

McGill, P. (1999). Establishing operations: Implications for assessment, treatment, and prevention of problem behavior. *Journal of Applied Behavior Analysis, 32,* 393–418.

McGinnis, J. C., Friman, P. C., & Carlyon, W. D. (1999). The effect of token rewards on "intrinsic" motivation for doing math. *Journal of Applied Behavior Analysis, 32,* 375–379.

McGinnis, E., & Goldstein, A. P. (1997). *Skillstreaming the elementary school child: A guide for teaching prosocial skills.* Champaign, Ill.: Research Press.

McGonigle, J. J., Duncan, D. V., Cordisco, L., & Barrett, R. P. (1982). Visual screening: An alternative method for reducing stereotypic behavior. *Journal of Applied Behavior Analysis, 15,* 461–467.

McKelvey, J. L., Sisson, L.A., Van Hasselt, V.B., & Hersen, M. (1992). An approach to teaching self-dressing to a child with dual sensory impairment. *Teaching Exceptional Children, 25,* 12–15.

McLaughlin, T. F. (1981). An analysis of token reinforcement: A control group comparison with special education youth employing measures of clinical significance. *Child Behavior Therapy, 3*, 43–50.

McLaughlin, T. F., & Malaby, J. E. (1975a). Elementary school children as behavioral engineers. In E. Ramp & G. Semp (Eds.), *Behavior analysis: Areas of research and application* (pp. 319–328). Englewood Cliffs, NJ: Prentice-Hall.

McLaughlin, R. F., & Malaby, J. E. (1975b). The effects of various token reinforcement contingencies on assignment completion and accuracy during variable and fixed token exchange schedules. *Canadian Journal of Behavioral Science, 7*, 411–419.

McLaughlin, T. W., Snyder, M. K., & Welsh, J. L. (2012). Behavior support interventions implemented by families of young children examination of contextual fit. *Journal of Positive Behavior Interventions, 14*(2) pp. 87–97.

McIlvane, W. J., Dube, W. V., Green, G., & Serna, R. W. (1993). Programming conceptual and communication skill development: A methodological stimulus class analysis. In A. P. Kaiser & D. B. Gray (Eds.), *Enhancing children's communication* (Vol. 2, pp. 242–285). Baltimore: Brookes.

McIntosh, C. K., Brown, J. A., & Borgmeier, C. J. (2008). Validity of functional behavior assessment within a response to intervention framework: Evidence, recommended practice, and future directions. *Assessment for Effective Intervention, 34*, 6–14.

McIntosh, K., Predy, L. K., Upreti, G., Hume, A. E., Turri, M. G., & Mathews, S. (2014). Perceptions of contextual features related to implementation and sustainability of school-wide positive behavior support. *Journal of Positive Behavior Interventions, 16*, 31–43.

McIntyre, L. L., Gresham, F. M., DiGennaro, F. D., & Reed, D.. D. (2007). Treatment integrity of school-based interventions with children in the journal of Applied Behavior Analysis 1991–2005. *Journal of Applied Behavior Analysis, 40*, 659–672. doi: 10.1901/jaba.2007.659-672.

Mclain, L. (2011, Winter). Is it normal for my dog to be so "amorous"? *Healthy Pet Magazine, 28*.

McLaughlin, T. W., Denny, M. K., & Snyder, P. A. (2012). Behavior support interventions implemented by families of young children. *Journal of Positive Behavior Interventions, 14*, 87–97. doi: 10.1177/1098300711411305

McNamara, C. (2008). *A field guide to nonprofit strategic planning*. Authenticity Publishing.: WWW.

McNeely, C. A., Nonnemaker, J. M., & Blum, R. W. (2002). Promoting school connectedness: Evidence from the national longitudinal study of adolescent health. *Journal of School Health, 72*(4), 138–146.

McNeil, M. (1994). Creating powerful partnerships through partner learning. In J. S. Thousand, R. A. Villa, & A. I. Nevin (Eds.), *Creativity and collaborative learning: A practical guide to empowering students and teachers* (pp. 243–261). Baltimore: Paul H. Brookes.

McNeill, K. L., Lizotte, D. J., Krajcik, J., & Marx, R. W. (2006). Supporting students' construction of scientific explanations by fading scaffolds in instructional materials. *Journal of Learning Sciences, 15*, 153–191.

McReynolds, L.V. (1969). Application of timeout from positive reinforcement for increasing the efficiency of speech training. *Journal of Applied Behavior Analysis, 2*, 199–205.

McReynolds, W. T., & Church, A. (1973). Self-control, study skills development and counseling approaches to the improvement of study behavior. *Behavior Research and Therapy, 11*, 233–235.

McSweeny, A. J. (1978). Effects of response cost on the behavior of a million persons: Charging for directory assistance in Cincinnati. *Journal of Applied Behavior Analysis, 1*, 47–51.

McSweeney, F. K. (1982). Positive and negative contrast as a function of component duration for key pecking and treadle pressing. *Journal of Experimental Analysis of Behavior, 37*, 281–293.

McSweeney;, F. K. (1983). Positive behavioral contrast when pigeons press treadles during multiple schedules. *Journal of Experimental Analysis of Behavior, 39*, 149–156.

McSweeney, F. K. (2004). Dynamic changes in reinforcer effectiveness: Satiation and habituation have different implications for theory and practice. *The Behavior Analyst, 27*, 171–188.

McSweeney, F. K., Kowal, B. P., Murphy, E. S., & Wiediger, R. S. (2005). Stimulus change dishabituates operant responding supported by water reinforcers. *Behavioural Processes, 20*, 235–246.

Meadows, N., Neel, R., Scott, C., & Parker, G. (1994). Academic performance, social competence, and mainstream accommodations: A look at mainstreamed and non-mainstreamed students with serious behavior disorders. *Behavioral Disorders, 19*, 170–180.

Melchiori, L. E., De Souza, D. G., & De Rose, J. C. (2000). Reading, equivalence, and recombination of units: A replication with students with different learning histories. *Journal of Applied Behavior Analysis, 33*, 97–100.

Melekoglu, M. A. (2019). Evidence-based fluency interventions for elementary students with learning disabilities. *European Journal of Education Studies, 6*, 411–423. doi: 109287/zenodo.3404991

Melin, L., & Gotestam, K. G. (1981). The effects of rearranging ward routines on communication and eating behaviors of psychogeriatric patients. *Journal of Applied Behavior Analysis, 4*, 47–51.

Mellalieu, S. D., Hanton, S., & O'Brien, M. (2006). The effects of goal setting on rugby performance. *Journal of Applied Behavior Analysis, 39*, 257–261.

Merbaum, M. (1973). The modification of self-destructive behavior by a mother-therapist using aversive stimulation. *Behavior Therapy, 4*, 442–447.

Mesmer, E. M., Duhon, G. J., & Dodson, K. G. (2007). The effects of programming common stimuli for enhancing stimulus generalization of academic behavior. *Journal of Applied Behavior Analysis, 40*, 553–557.

Mestel, R. (2002, March 29). Adolescents' TV watching is linked to violent behavior. *Los Angeles, Times*, A-18.

Metoyer, C. N., Fritz, J. N., Hunt, J. C., & Fletcher, V. I. (2020). Teaching caregivers to respond safely during agitated states before aggression using simulation training. *Journal of Applied Behavior Analysis, 53*, 2250–2259. doi: 10.1002/jaba.751

Metzler, C. W., Biglan, A., Rusby, J. D., & Sprague, J. R. (2001). Evaluation of a comprehensive behavior management program to improve school-wide positive behavior support. *Education and Treatment of Children, 24*, 448–479.

Meunier, G. F., Kissell, R., & Higgins, T. (1983). Scale of aversiveness of behavioral decelerators. *Perceptual Motor Skills, 56*(2), 611–614.

Michael, J. (1974). Statistical inference for individual organism research: Mixed blessing or curse? *Journal of Applied Behavior Analysis, 7,* 647–653.

Michael, J. (1975). Positive and negative reinforcement: A distinction that is no longer necessary: or a better way to talk about bad things. *Behaviorism, 3,* 33–44.

Michael, J. (1982). Distinguishing between discriminative and motivational functions of stimuli. *Journal of the Experimental Analysis of Behavior, 37,* 149–155.

Michael, J. (1982). Skinner's elementary verbal relations: Some new categories. *The Analysis of Verbal Behavior, 1,* 1–4.

Michael, J. (1993). Establishing operations. *The Behavior Analyst, 16,* 191–206.

Michael, J. (1985, March). *Stimulus change decrement.* Paper presented at the meeting of the Northern CA Association of Behavior analysis, San Mateo, CA.

Michael, J. (1988). Establishing operations and the mand. *The Analysis of Verbal Behavior, 6,* 3–9.

Michael, J. (2000). Implications and refinements of the establishing operation concept. *Journal of Applied Behavior Analysis, 33,* 401–410.

Michael, J. (2004). *Concepts and principles of behavior analysis* (rev. ed.) Kalamazoo, MI: Society for the Advancement of Behavior Analysis.

Michael, J. (2007). Motivating operations. In Cooper, J. O., Heron, T. E., & Heward, W. L. (2007). *Applied behavior analysis,* (2nd ed.). Columbus: Pearson/Merrill Prentice Hall.

Michelson, L., Dilorenzo, T. M., Calpin, J. P., & Williamson, D. A. (1981). Modifying excessive lunchroom noise: Omission training with audio feedback and group contingent reinforcement. *Behavior Modification, 5,* 553–564.

Miguel, C. F., Carr, J. E., & Michael, J. (2002). Effects of stimulus-stimulus pairing procedure on the vocal behavior of children diagnosed with autism. *The Analysis of Verbal Behavior, 18,* 3–13.

Miguel, C. F. & Kobari-Wright, V. V. (2013). The effects of tact training on the emergence of categorization and listener behavior in children with autism. *Journal of Applied Behavior Analysis, 46,* 669–673.

Miguel, C. F., Petursdottir, A. I., & Carr, J. E. (2005). The effects of multiple-tact and receptive-discrimination training on the acquisition of intraverbal behavior. *The Analysis of Verbal Behavior, 21,* 27–41.

Mihalic, S. F. (2003). Blueprints for violence prevention. *Youth violence and juvenile justice, 1* (4), 307–329.

Milad, M.R., Orr, S.P., Pitman, R.K., & Rauch, S.L. (2005). Context modulation of memory for fear extinction in humans. *Psychophysiology, 42(4),* 456–464.

Miles, N. I., & Wilder, D. A. (2009). The effects of behavioral skills training on caregiver implementation of guided compliance. *Journal of Applied Behavior Analysis, 42,* 405–410. doi: 10.1901/jaba.2009.42-405

Millar, D.C., Light, J.C., & Schlosser, R.W. (2006). The impact of augmentative and alternative communication intervention on the speech production of individuals with developmental disabilities: A research review. *Journal of Speech, Language, and Hearing Research, 49,* 248–264.

Millenson, J. R. (1967). *Principles of behavior analysis.* New York: Macmillan.

Millenson, J. R., & Hurwitz, H. M. B. (1961). Some temporal and sequential properties of behavior during conditioning and extinction. *Journal of the Experimental Analysis of Behavior, 4,* 97–106.

Miller, A. J., & Kratochwill, T. R. (1979). Reduction of frequent stomachache complaints by time-out. *Behavior Therapy, 10,* 211–218.

Miller, D.L., Manne, S., & Palevsky, S. (1998). Brief report: acceptance of behavioral interventions for children with cancer: perceptions of parents, nurses, and community controls. *Journal of Pediatric Psychology, 23,* 267–271.

Miller, M. L., & Malott, R. W. (1997). The importance of overt responding in programmed instruction even with added incentives for learning. *Journal of Behavioral Education, 7,* 497–503.

Miltenberger, R. G. (2001a). *Behavior modification: Principles and procedures.* Belmont, CA: Wadsworth/Thompson Learning.

Miltenberger, R. G. (2008). Teaching safety skills to children: Prevention of firearm injury as an exemplar of best practice in assessment, training, and generalization of safety skills. *Behavior Analysis in Practice, 1*(1), 30–36.

Miltenberger, R. G. (2008). *Behavior modification: Principles and procedures,* 4th Ed. Pacific grove, CA: Thomson/Wadsworth.

Miltenberger, R. G., & Fuqua, R. W. (1981). Overcorrection: A review and critical analysis. *The Behavior Analyst, 4,* 123–141.

Miltenberger, R. G., & Fuqua, R. W. (1983). Effects of token reinforcement schedules on work rate: A case study. *American Journal of Mental Deficiency, 88,* 229–232.

Miltenberger, R. G., Fuqua, R. W., & Woods, D. W. (1998). Applying behavior analysis to clinical problems: Review and analysis of habit reversal. *Journal of Applied Behavior Analysis, 31,* 447–469.

Miltenberger, R. G., Gatheridge, B. J., Satterlund, M., Egermo-Helm, K. R., Johnson, B. M., Jostad, C., et al. (2005). Teaching safety skills to prevent gun play: An evaluation of in situ training. *Journal of Applied Behavior Analysis, 38,* 395–398.

Minkin, N., Braukmann, C. J., Minkin, B. L., Timbers, G. D., Timbers, B. J. Fixsen, D. L., et al. (1976). The social validation and training of conversational skills. *Journal of Applied Behavior Analysis, 9,* 127–139.

Minor, L., DuBard, M., & Luiselli, J. K. (2014). Improving intervention integrity of direct service practitioners through performance feedback and problem solving consultation. *Behavioral Interventions, 29,* 145–156. doi: 10.1002/bin.1382

Mirenda, P.M., & Donnellan, A.L. (1986). Effects of adult interaction style on conversational behavior in students with severe communication problems. *Language, Speech, and Hearing Services in Schools, 17,* 126–141.

Mirenda, P. (2001). Autism, augmentative communication and assistive technology: What do we really know? *Focus on Autism and Other Developmental Disabilities, 16*(3), 141–151.

Miriam-Webster on-line Dictionary (2008). Retrieved June 16, 2008.

Mischel, W., & Grusec, J. E. (1966). Determinants of the rehearsal and transmission of neutral and aversive behaviors. *Journal of Personality and Social Psychology, 3,* 197–205.

Mitchem, K., & Young, K.R. (2001). Adapting self-management programs for classwide use: Acceptability, feasibility, and Effectiveness. *Remedial and Special Education, 22,* 75–88.

Moffitt, T. E., Caspi, A., Harrington, H., & Milne, B. J. (2002). Males of the life-course-persistent and adolescence-limited antisocial pathways: Follow-up at age 26 years. *Development and Psychopathology, 14,* 170–207.

Montegar, C. A., Reid, D. H., Madsen, C. H., & Ewell, M. D. 91977). Increasing institutional staff to resident interactions through inservice training and supervisor approval. *Behavior Therapy, 8,* 533–540.

Moore, D. W., Anderson, A., Glassanbury, M., Lang, R., & Didden, R. (2013). Increasing on-task behavior in students in a regular classroom. Effectiveness of a self-management procedure using a tactile prompt. *Journal of Behavioral Education, 22,* 302–311.

Moore, J., & Fanino, E. (1975). Choice and response contingencies. *Journal of the Experimental Analysis of Behavior, 23,* 339–347.

Moore, J. W., & Fisher, W. W. (2007). The effects of videotape modeling on staff acquisition of functional analysis methodology. *Journal of Applied Behavior Analysis, 40,* 197–202.

Moore, L., & Carnine, D. (1989). Evaluating curriculum design in the context of active teaching. *Remedial and Special Education, 10,* 28–37.

Moore, P. S. (2004). The use of social stories in a psychology service for children with learning disabilities: A case study of a sleep problem. *British Journal of Learning Disabilities, 32*(3), 133–138.

Morgan, C. A., & Wine, B. (2018). Evaluation of behavior skills training for teaching work skills to a student with autism spectrum disorder. *Education and Treatment of Children, 41,* 223–232.

Morgenthaler, T. I., Owens, J., Alessi, C., Boehlecke, B., Brown, T. M., Coleman, J., et al. (2006). Practice parameters for behavioral treatment of bedtime problems and night wakings in infants and young children. *Sleep, 29,* 1277–1281.

Morris, E. K., & Redd, W. H. (1975). Children's performance and social preference for positive, negative, and mixed adult-child interactions. *Child Development, 46,* 525–531.

Morris, E. K., & Rosen, H. S. (1982). The role of interobserver reliability in the evaluation of graphed data. *Behavioral Assessment,* 387–399.

Morris, J. P. (1968). Changes in response force during acquisition and extinction in retarded children. *American Journal of Mental Deficiency, 73,* 384–390.

Morrison, R.S., Sainato, D.M., Benchaaban, D., & Endo, S. (2002). Increasing play skills of children with autism using activity schedules and correspondence training. *Journal of Early Intervention, 25* (1), 58–72.

Mortenson, B. P., & Witt, J. C. (1998). The use of weekly performance feedback to increase teacher implementation of a prereferral academic intervention. *School Psychology Review, 27,* 613–627.

Moussorgsky. (1874). *Boris Bodonov. Angle Records.*

Mouzakitis, A., Codding, R. S., & Tryon, G. (2015). The effects of self-monitoring and performance feedback on the treatment integrity of behavior intervention plan implementation and generalization. *Journal of Positive Behavior Interventions, 17,* 223–234. DOI: 10.1177/1098300715573629 jpbi.sagepub.com

Mozingo, D. B., Smith, T., Riodan, M. R., Reiss, M. L., & Bailey, J. S. (2006). Enhancing frequency recording by developmental disabilities treatment staff. *Journal of Applied Behavior Analysis, 39,* 253–256.

Mueller, M. M., Piazza, C. C., Moore, J. W., Kelley, M. E., Bethke, S. A., Pruett et al. (2003). Training parents to implement pediatric feeding protocols. *Journal of       Applied Behavior Analysis, 36,* 545–562.

Mueller, M. M., Piazza, C. C., Patel, M. R., Kelley, M. E., & Pruett, A. (2004). Increasing variety of foods consumed by blending nonpreferred foods into preferred foods. *Journal of Applied Behavior Analysis, 37,* 159–170

Mueller, M. M., Palkovic, C. M., & Maynard, C. S. (2007). Errorless learning: Review and practical application for teaching children with pervasive developmental disorders. *Psychology in the Schools, 44,* 691–700.

Mueller, M. M., Wilczynski, S. M., Moore, J. W., Fusilier, I., & Trahant, D. (2001). Antecedent manipulations in a tangible condition: The effects of stimulus preference on aggression. *Journal of Applied Behavior Analysis, 34,* 237–240.

Mulick, J., Hoyt, R., Rojahn, J., & Schroeder, S. (1978). Reduction of a "nervous habit" in a profoundly retarded youth by increasing toy play: A case study. *Journal of Behavior Therapy and Experimental Psychiatry, 9,* 381–385.

Mulick, J. A., Leitenberg, H., & Rawson, R. A. **(1976)**. Alternative response training, differential reinforcement of other behavior, and extinction in squirrel monkeys (*Saimiri sciureus*). *Journal of the Experimental Analysis of Behavior, 7,* 311–320.

Mullane, M. P., Martens, B. K., Baxter, E. L., & Ver Steeg, D. (2017). Children's preference for mixed-versus fixed-ratio schedules of reinforcement: A translational study of risky choice. *Journal of the Experimental Analysis of Behavior, 107,* 161–175. doi.org/10.1002/jeab.234

Mullins, M., & Rincover, A. (1985). Comparing autistic and normal children along the dimensions of reinforcement maximization, stimulus sampling, and responsiveness to extinction. *Journal of Experimental Child Psychology, 40,* 350–374.

Munger, G. F., Snell, M. E., & Loyd, B. H. (1989). A study of the effects of frequency of probe data collection and graph characteristics on teachers' visual analysis. *Research in Developmental Disabilities, 10,* 109–127.

Munk, D. K., & Repp, A. C. (1994). Behavioral assessment of feeding problems of individuals with severe disabilities. *Journal of Applied Behavior Analysis, 27,* 241–250.

Monro, D. W., & Stephenson, J. (2009). The effects of response cards on student and teacher behavior during vocabulary instruction. *Journal of Applied Behavior Analysis, 42,* 795–800.

Murph, D., & McCormick, S. (1985). Evaluation of an instructional program designed to teach minimally literate juvenile delinquents to read road signs. *Education and Treatment of Children, 8,* 133–151.

Murphy, G., MacDonald, S., Hall, S., & Oliver, C. (2000). Aggression and the termination of "rituals": A new variant of the escape function for challenging behavior? *Research in Developmental Disabilities, 21*(1), 43–59.

Murphy, H. A., Hutchinson, J. M., & Bailey, J. S. (1983). Behavioral school psychology goes outdoors: The effect of organized games on playground aggression. *Journal of Applied Behavior Analysis, 16,* 29–36.

Murphy, R. J., Ruprecht, M., & Nunes, D. L. (1979). Elimination of self-injurious behavior in a profoundly retarded adolescent using intermittent time-out, restraint, and blindfold procedures. *AAESPH Review, 4,* 334–345.

Murray, L.K., & Kollins, S.H. (2000). Effects of methylphenidate on sensitivity to reinforcement in children diagnosed with attention deficit disorder: An application of the matching law. *Journal of Applied Behavior Analysis, 33,* 573–591.

Murzynski, N. T., & Bourret, J. C. (2007). Combining video modeling and least-to-most prompting for establishing response chains. *Behavioral Interventions, 22,* 147–152. doi: 10.1002/bin.224

Myerson, J., & Green, L. (1995). Discounting of delayed rewards: Models of individual choice. *Journal of Experimental Analysis of Behavior, 64,* 263–276.

Najdowski, A. C., Wallace, M. D., Doney, J. K., & Ghezzi, P. M. (2003). Parental assessment and treatment of food selectivity in natural settings. *Journal of Applied Behavior Analysis, 36,* 383–386.

Najdowski, A. C., Wallace, M. D., Ellsworth, C., MacAleese, A., & Cleveland, J. (2008). Treating problem behavior according to maintaining variables identified by a functional analysis of precursor behaviors. *Journal of Applied Behavior Analysis, 41,* 97–105.

Nagatomi, K., & Wemura, H. (2017). Positive effects of instruction and self-recording on the on-task behavior of a student with autism spectrum disorder in a home setting. *Japanese Journal of Behavior Analysis, 31,* 144–152.

Najdowski, A, C., Bergstrom, R., Tarbox, J., & Clair, M. S. (2017). Teaching children with autism to respond to disguised bands. *Journal of Applied Behavior Analysis, 50,* 723–743. doi: 10.1002/jaba.413

Najdowski, A. C., St. Clair, M., Fullen J. A., Child, A., Persicke, A., & Tarbox, J. (2018). Teaching children with autism to identify and respond appropriately to the preferences of others during play. *Journal of Applied Behavior Analysis, 51,* 890–898.

Najdowski, A. C., Wallace, M. D., Penrod, B., & Cleveland, J. (2005). Using stimulus variation to increase reinforcer efficacy of low preference stimuli. *Behavioral Interventions, 20,* 313–328.

Najdowski, A. C., Wallace, M. D., Penrod, B., Tarbox, J., Reagon, K., & Higbee, T. S. (2008). Caregiver-conducted experimental functional analyses of inappropriate mealtime behavior. *Journal of Applied Behavior Analysis, 41*(3), 459–465. https://doi-org.mimas.calstatela.edu/10.1901/jaba.2008.41-459

Napolitano, D. A., Smith, T., Zarcone, J. R., Goodkin, K., & McAdam, D. B. (2010). Increasing response diversity in children with autism. *Journal of Applied Behavior Analysis, 43,* 265–271. doi: 10.1901/jaba.2010.43-265

Narayan, J. S., Heward, W. L., Gardner III, R., Courson, F. H., & Omness, C. K. (1990). Using response cards to increase students' participation in an elementary classroom. *Journal of Applied Behavior Analysis, 23,* 483–490.

Nation, J. R., & Boyajian, L. G. (1980). Continuous before partial reinforcement: Effect on persistence training and resistance to extinction in humans. *American Journal of Psychology, 93,* 697–710.

National Alliance for the Mentally Ill. (2001). *Where we stand: Seclusion and restraint, MANI.* 1–6l. Retrieved October 30, 2002 from http://www.nami.org/update/unitedrestraint.html

National Autism Center (2009). *Evidence-Based Practice and Autism in the Schools. 41* Pacella Park Drive, Randolph, MA, 02368.

National Institute on Deafness and Other Communication Disorders (NIDCD) website (2009).

National Research Council (2001). *Educating children with Autism.* Washington, D.C. National Academy Press.

National Weather Service (2004). Mission statement. U.S. Department of Commerce.

Nava, C. E., Fahmie, T. A., Jin, S., & Kumar, P. (2019). Evaluating the Efficacy, Preference, and Cultural Responsiveness of Student-Generated Content in an Undergraduate Behavioral Course. *Behavior Analysis in Practice, 12*(4), 747–757.

Naylor, A. S., Kamps, D., & Wills, H. (2018). The effects of the CW-FIT group contingency on class-wide and individual behavior in an urban first grade classroom. *Education and Treatment of Children, 41*(1).

Neef, N. A. (1995). Pyramidal parent training by peers. *Journal of Applied Behavior Analysis, 28,* 333–337.

Neef, N. A., Bicard, D. F., & Endo, S. (2001). Assessment of impulsivity and the development of self-control by students with attention deficit hyperactivity disorder. *Journal of Applied Behavior Analysis, 34,* 397–408.

Neef, N. A., Lensbower, J., Hockersmith, I., DePalma, V., & Gray, K. (1990). In vivo versus simulation training: An interactional analysis of type and range of training exemplars. *Journal of Applied Behavior Analysis, 23,* 447–458.

Neef, N. A., Mace, F. C., Shade, D. (1993). Impulsivity in students with serious emotional disturbance: The interactive effects of reinforcer rate, delay, and quality. *Journal of Applied Behavior Analysis, 26,* 37–52.

Neef, N. A., Mace, F. C., Shea, M. C., & Shade, D. (1992). Effects of reinforcer rate and reinforcer quality on time allocation: Extensions of matching theory to educational settings. *Journal of Applied Behavior Analysis, 25,* 691–700.

Neef, N. A., Marckel, J., Ferreri, S. J., Bicard, D. F., Endo, S., Aman, M. G., et al. (2005). Behavioral assessment of impulsivity: A comparison of children with and without attention deficit hyperactivity disorder. *Journal of Applied Behavior Analysis, 38,* 23–37.

Neef, N. A., Marckel, J., Ferreri, S., Jung, S., Nist, L., & Armstrong, N. (2004). Effects of modeling versus instructions on sensitivity to reinforcement schedules. *Journal of Applied Behavior Analysis, 37,* 267–281.

Neef, N. A., McCord, B. E., & Ferreri, S. J. (2006). Effects of guided notes versus completed notes during lectures on college students' quiz performance. *Journal of Applied Behavior Analysis, 39,* 123–130.

Neef, N. A., Shade, D., & Miller, M. S. (1994). Assessing influential dimensions of reinforcers on choice in students with serious emotional disturbance. *Journal of Applied Behavior Analysis, 27,* 575–583.

Neef, N. A., Shafer, M. S., Egel, A. L., Cataldo, M. F., & Parrish, J. M. (1983). The class specific effect of compliance training with "do" and "don't" requests: Analogue analysis and classroom application. *Journal of Applied Behavior Analysis, 16,* 81–99.

Neely, L. C., Ganz, J. B., Davis, J. L., Boles, M. B., Hong, E. R., Ninci, J., & Gilliland, W. D. (2016). Generalization and maintenance of functional living skills for individuals with autism spectrum disorder: A review and meta-analysis. *Review Journal of Autism and Developmental Disorders, 3,* 37–47.

Neely L., MacNaul, H., Gregori, E., & Cantrell, K. (2021). Effects of telehealth-mediated behavioral assessments and interventions on client outcomes; A quality review. *Journal of Applied Behavior Analysis, 54,* 484–510. doi: 10.1002/jaba.818

Nelson, C. M., & Rutherford, R. B. (1983). Timeout revisited: Guidelines for its use in special education. *Exceptional Education Quarterly, 3,* 56–67.

Nelson, R. O. (1983). Behavioral assessment: Past, present, and future. *Behavioral Assessment, 5,* 195–206.

Nevin, J. A. (1988). Behavioral momentum and the partial reinforcement effect. *Psychological Bulletin, 103,* 44–56.

Nevin, J. A. (1992). An integrative model for the study of behavioral momentum. *Journal of the Experimental Analysis of Behavior, 57,* 301–316.

Nevin, J. A., Mandell, C., & Atak, J. R. (1983). The analysis of behavioral momentum. *Journal of Experimental Analysis of Behavior, 39,* 49–59.

Newell, F. M. (1996). Effects of a cross-age tutoring program on computer literacy learning of second-grade students. *Journal of Research on Computing in Education, 28,* 346–358.

Newman, D. L., Moffitt, T. E., Caspi, A., Magdol, L., Silva, P. A., & Stanton, W. R. (1996). Psychiatric disorder in a birth cohort of young adults: Prevalence, comorbidty, clinical significance, *and* new case incidence form ages 11 to 21. *Journal of Consulting and Clinical Psychology, 64,* 552–562.

Newsom, C., Favell, J., & Rincover, A. (1983). The side effects of punishment. In S. Axelrod & J. Apsche (Eds.). *The effects of punishment on human behavior* (pp. 285–316). New York: Academic Press.

New York State Association for the Retarded Children v. Rockefeller, 357 F. Supp. (E. D. N.Y., 1973).

Nicol, N., & Hantula, D. A. (2001). Decreasing delivery drivers' departure times. *Journal of Organizational Behavior Management, 21*(4), 105–116.

Niedelman, M. (1991). Problem solving and transfer. *Journal of Learning Disabilities, 24,* 322–329.

Nihira, K., Leland, H., & Lambert, N. K. (1993). *Adaptive Behavior Scale—Residential and Community* (2nd ed.). Austin, TX: Pro-Ed.

Nikopoulos, C.K., & Nikopoulou-Smyrni, P.G. (2008). Teaching complex social skills to children with autism; advances of video modeling. *Journal of Early and Intensive Behavior Intervention, 5*(2), 30–43.

Ninness, H. A. C., Fuerst, J., Rutherford, R., & Glenn, S. S. (1991). Effects of self-management training and reinforcement on the transfer of improved conduct in the absence of supervision. *Journal of Applied Behavior Analysis, 24,* 499–508.

Noel, C. R., & Getch, Y. Q. (2016). Non contingent reinforcement in after-school settings to decrease classroom disruptive behavior for students with autism spectrum disorder. *Behavior Analysis in Practice, 9,* 261–265.

Noel, C. R., & Rubow, C. C. (2018). Using noncontingent reinforcement to reduce perseverative speech and increase engagement during social skills instruction. *Education and Treatment of Children, 41,* 157–168.

Noell, G. H., Gresham, F. M., & Gansle, K. A. (2002). Does treatment integrity matter? A preliminary investigation of instructional implementation and mathematics performance. *Journal of Behavioral Education, 11,* 51–61.

Noell, G. H., Witt, J. C., LaFleur, L. H., Mortenson, B. P., Rainier, D. D., & LeVelle, J. (2000). Increasing intervention implementation in general education following consultation: A comparison of two follow-up strategies. *Journal of Applied Behavior Analysis, 33,* 271–284.

Noldus, L. P., Spink, A. J., & Tegelenbosch, R. A. J. (2001). EthoVision: A versatile video tracking system for automation of behavioral experiments. *Behavior Research Methods, Instruments, & Computers, 33*(3), 398–414.

Noll, M.B., & Simpson, R. L. (1979). The effects of physical time-out on the aggressive behaviors of a severely emotionally disturbed child in a public school setting. *AAESPH Review, 4,* 399–406.

Normand, M. P., & Knoll, M. C. (2006). The effects of stimulus-stimulus pairing procedures on the unprompted vocalization of a young child diagnosed with autism. *Analysis of Verbal Behavior, 22,* 81–85.

Northup, J. (2000). Further evaluation of the accuracy of reinforcer surveys: A systematic replication. *Journal of Applied Behavior Analysis, 33,* 335–338.

Northup, J., Broussard, C., Jones, K., George, T., Vollmer, T. R., & Herring, M. (1995). The differential effects of teacher and peer attention on the disruptive classroom behavior of three children with a diagnosis of attention deficit hyperactivity disorder. *Journal of Applied Behavior Analysis, 28,* 227–228.

Northup, J., Fusilier, I., Swanson, V., Roane, H., & Borrero, J. (1997). An evaluation of methylphenidate as a potential establishing operation for some common classroom reinforcers. *Journal of Applied Behavior Analysis, 30,* 615–625.

Northup, J., Kodak, T., Lee, J., & Coyne, A. (2004). Instructional influences on analogue functional analysis outcomes. *Journal of Applied Behavior Analysis, 37,* 509–512.

Northup, J., Vollmer, T. R., & Serrett, K. (1993). Publication trends in 25 years of the Journal of Applied Behavior Analysis. *Journal of Applied Behavior Analysis, 26,* 527–537.

Nosik, M. R., & William, W. L. (2011). Component evaluation of a computer based format for teaching discrete trial and backward chaining. *Research in Developmental Disabilities, 32,* 1694–1702. doi: 10.1016/j.ridd.2011.02.022.

Nosik, M. R., Williams, W. L., Garrido, N., & Lee, S. (013). Compariosn of computer based instruction to behavior skills training for teaching staff implementation of discrete-trial instruction with an adult with autism. *Research in Developmental Disabilities, 34*, 461–468. doi: 10.1016/j.ridd.2012.08.011

Nunes, D. L., Murphy, R. J., & Ruprecht, M. L. (1977). Reducing self-injurious behavior of severely retarded individuals through withdrawal of reinforcement procedures. *Behavior Modification, 1*, 499–516.

Nuzzolo-Gomez, R., Leonard, M. A., Ortiz, E., Rivera, C. M., & Creer, R. D. (2002). Teaching children with atuism to prefer books or toys over stereotypy or passivity. *Journal of Positive Behavior Interventions, 4*, 80–87.

O'Brien, F., Azrin, N. H., & Bugle, C. (1972). Training profoundly retarded children to stop crawling. *Journal of Applied Behavior Analysis, 2*, 131–137.

O'Callaghan, P. M., Allen, K. D., Powell, S., & Salama, F. (2006). The efficacy of noncontingent escape for decreasing children's disruptive behavior during restorative dental treatment. *Journal of Applied Behavior Analysis, 39*, 161–171.

O'Carroll, R.E., Russell, H.H., Lawrie, S.M., & Johnstone, E.C. (1999). Errorless learning and the cognitive rehabilitation of memory-impaired schizophrenic patients. *Psychological Medicine, 29*, 105–112.

O'Neill, S. J., McDowell, C., & Leslie, J. C. (2018). A comparison of prompt delays with trial-and-error instruction in conditional discrimination training. *Behavior Analysis in Practice, 11*, 370–380. doi.org/10.1007/s40617-018-0261-9

O'Neill, S. J., McDowell, C., & Leslie, J. C. (2020). A comparison of variations of prompt delay during instruction on an expressive labeling task. *Journal of Behavioral Education*. doi.org/10.1007s10864-020-09407-0

Odom, S. L., Brown, W. H., Frey, T., Karasu, N., Smith-Canter, L. L., & Strain, P. S. (2003). Evidence-based practices for young children with autism: Contributions for single-subject design research. *Focus on Autism and Other Developmental Disabilities, 18*, 166–175.

O'Donnell, J. O. (2001). The discriminative stimulus for punishment or $S^{Dp}$. *The Behavior Analyst, 24*, 261–262.

O'Donnell, J., Crosbie, J., Williams, D. C., & Saunders, K. J. (2000). Stimulus control and generalization of point-loss punishment with humans. *Journal of the Experimental Analysis of Behavior, 73*, 261–274.

O'Hora, D., & Maglieri, K.A. (2006). Goal statements and goal-directed behavior: A relational frame account of goal-setting in organizations. *Journal of Organizational Behavior Management, 26*, 131–170.

Okouchi, H. (1999). Instructions as discriminative stimuli. *Journal of the Experimental Analysis of Behavior, 72*, 205–214.

Okouchi, H. (2003) Effects of differences in interreinforcer intervals between past and current schedules on fixed interval responding. *Journal of the Experimental Analysis of Behavior, 79*, 49–64.

O'Leary, K. D., Kaufman, K. F., Kass, R. E., & Drabman, R. (1970). The effect of loud and soft reprimands on the behavior of disruptive students. *Exceptional Children, 37*, 145–155.

Oien, I., Fallang, B., & Ostensjo, S. (2009). Goal-setting in pediatric rehabilitation: Perceptions of parent and professional. *Child: Care, Health & Development, 36*, 558–565. doi:10.1111/j.1365-2214.s009.01038x

Oklahoma Disability Law Center, Inc. a system of protection & advocacy. (2016). *Statement of opposition to restraint and/or seclusion of students with disabilities in public schools*. www.peapods.us/wp-content/.../statement-of-opposition-to-restraint-and-seclusion.

Olive, M., de la Cruz, B., Davis, T., Chan, J., Lang, R., O'Reilly, M., & Dickson, S. (2007). The effects of enhanced milieu teaching and a voice output communication aid on the requesting of three children with autism. *Journal of Autism and Developmental Disorders, 37*, 1505–1513.

Ollendick, T. H., Dailey, D., & Shapiro, E. S. (1983). Vicarious reinforcement: Expected and unexpected effects. *Journal of Applied Behavior Analysis, 16*, 485–491.

Ollendick, T. H., Matson, J. L., Esveldt-Dawson, K., & Shapiro, E. S. (1980). Increasing spelling achievement: An analysis of treatment procedures utilizing an alternating treatments design.

*Journal of Applied Behavior Analysis, 13*, 645–654.

Olson, R. L., & Roberts, M. S. (1987). Alternative treatments for sibling aggression. *Behavior Therapy, 18*, 243–250.

Olsen, R., & Winchester, J. (2008). Behavioral self-monitoring of safety and productivity in the workplace: A methodological primer and quantitative literature review. *Journal of Organizational Behavior Management, 28*(1), 9–75.

O'Neil, P. M., White, J.L., King, C.R., & Carek, D.J. (1979). Controlling childhood rumination through differential reinforcement of other behavior. *Behavior Modification, 3*, 355–372.

O'Neill, R. E., Horner, R. H., Albin, R. W., Storey, K., & Sprague, J. R. (1990). *Functional analysis of problem behavior: A practical guide*. Sycamore, IL: Sycamore.

Ono, K. (1987). Superstitious behavior in humans. *Journal of the Experimental Analysis of Behavior, 47*, 261–271.

Ono, K., & Iwabucki, K. (1997). Effects of histories of differential reinforcement of response rate on variable-interval responding. *Journal of the Experimental Analysis of Behavior, 67*, 311–322.

Onslow, M., Menzies, R. G., & Packman, A. (2001). An operant intervention for early stuttering, *Behavior Modification, 25*, 116–139.

Onslow, M., Packman, A., Stocker, S., Doorn, J. V., & Siegel, G. M. (1997). Control of children's stuttering with response-contingent time-out. *Journal of Speech, Language, and Hearing Research, 40*, 121–133.

Oppenheimer, M., Saunders, R. R., & Spradlin, J. E. (1993). Investigating the generality of the delayed prompt effect. *Research in Developmental Disabilities, 14*, 425–444.

O'Reilly, M. F. (1995). Functional analysis and treatment of escape-maintained aggression correlated with sleep deprivation. *Journal of Applied Behavior Analysis, 28*, 225–226.

O'Reilly, M. F. (1997). Functional analysis of episodic self-injury correlated with recurrent otitis media. *Journal of Applied Behavior Analysis, 30*, 165–167.

O'Reilly, M., Edrisinha, C., Sigafoos, J., Lancioni, G., Machalicek, W., & Antonucci, M. (2007). The effects of precession attention on subsequent attention-extinction and alone conditions. *Journal of Applied Behavior Analysis, 40,* 731–735.

O'Reilly, M. F., & Lancioni, G. (2000). Response covariation of escape-maintained aberrant behavior correlated with sleep deprivation. *Research in Developmental Disabilities, 21,* 125–136.

O'Reilly, M. F., Sigafoos, J., Edrisinha, C., Lancioni, G., Cannella, H., Choi, H. Y., & Barretto, A. (2006). A preliminary examination of the evocative effects of the establishing operation. *Journal of Applied Behavior Analysis, 39,* 239–242.

O'Reilly, M., Tiernan, R., Lancioni, G., Lacey, C., Hillery, J., & Gardiner, M. (2002). Use of self-monitoring and delayed feedback to increase on-task behavior in a post-institutionalized child within regular classroom settings. *Education and Treatment of Children, 23,* 91–102.

Orlando, R., & Bijou, S.W. (1960). Single and multiple schedules of reinforcement in developmentally retarded children (1960). *Journal of the Experimental Analysis of Behavior, 3,* 339–348.

Otalvaro, K. A., Krebs, C. A., Brewer, A. T., Leon, Y., & Steifman, J. S. (2020). Reducing excessive questions in adults at adult-day training centers using differential-reinforcement-of-low rates. *Journal of Applied Behavior Analysis, 53,* 545–553. doi: 10.1002/jaba.edu

Ortega, R., & Fienup, D. M. (2015). Effects of a preferred stimulus and mother's attention on infant behavior during tummy time. *Behavior Analysis in Practice, 8,* 66–69. doi: 10.1007/s40617-014-0032-1

Pace, D. M., & Forman, S. G. (1982). Variables related to the effectiveness of response cost. *Psychology in the Schools, 19,* 365–370.

Pace, G. M., Ivancic, M. T., Edwards, G. L., Iwata, B. A., & Page, T. J. (1985). Assessment of stimulus preference and reinforcer value with profoundly retarded individuals. *Journal of Applied Behavior Analysis, 18,* 249–255.

Pace, G. M., Iwata, B. A., Edwards, G. I., & McCosh, K. C. (1986). Stimulus fading and transfer in the treatment of self-restraint and self-injurious behavior. *Journal of Applied Behavior Analysis, 19,* 381–389.

Paclawskyj, T. R., Matson, J. L., Rush, K. S., Smalls, Y., & Vollmer, T. R. (2001). Assessment of the convergent validity of the questions about behavioral function scale with analogue functional analysis and the motivation assessment scale. *Journal of Intellectual Disability Research, 45,* 484–494.

*Padilla v. Denver School District No. 1,* 35 F.Supp.2d 1260 (D. Colo., 1999).

Page, S., & Neuringer, A. (1985). Variability is an operant. *Journal of Experimental Psychology, 11,* 429–452. https://doi.org/10.1037/0097-7403.11.3.429.

Page, S.V., Griffith, K., & Penrod, B. (2017). Reduction of rapid eating in an adolescent female with autism. *Behavior Analysis in Practice 10,* 87–91. https://doi.org/10.1007/s40617-016-0143-y

Page, T. G., & Iwata, B. A. (1986). Interobserver agreement: History, theory, and current methods. In A. Poling & R. W. Fuqua (Eds.), *Research methods in applied behavior analysis: Issues and advances* (pp.99–126). New York: Plenum.

Page, M., Wilson, B. A., Shiel, A., Carter, G., & Norris, D. (2006). What is the locus of the errorless-learning advantage? *Neuropsychologia, 44,* 90–100.

Palmer, D.C. (2006). On Chomsky's appraisal of Skinner's Verbal Behavior: A half-century of misunderstanding. *Behavior Analysis, 29,* 253–267.

Palmer, D. C. (2016). On intraverbal control and the definition of the intraverbal. *The Analysis of Verbal Behavior, 32,* 96–106.

Parker, L.A., Limebeer, C.L., & Slomke, J. (2006). Renewal effect: Context-dependent extinction of a concise- and a morphine-induced conditioned floor preference in rats. *Psychopharmacology, 187,* 133–137.

Parnell, S. (2005, Oct.). Direct instruction narrows Wisconsin's achievement gap. *School Reform News.* Heartland Institute.

Paronis, C. A., Gasior, M., & Bergman, J. (2002). Effects of cocaine under concurrent fixed ratio scheduled of food and IV drug availability: A novel choice procedure in monkeys. *Psychopharmacology, 163,* 283–291.

Parrott, K. A., Schuster, J. W., Collins, B. C., & Gassaway, L. J. (2000). Simultaneous prompting and instructive feedback when teaching chained tasks. *Journal of Behavioral Education, 10,* 3–19.

Parsons, J., & Davey, G. C. L. (1978). Imitation training with a 4–year-old retarded person: The relative efficiency of timeout and extinction in conjunction with positive reinforcement. *Mental Retardation, 16,* 241–245.

Partington, J. W., & Bailey, J. S. (1993). Teaching intraverbal behavior to preschool children. *Analysis of Verbal Behavior, 11,* 9–18.

Patel, M. R., Piazza, C. C., Kelly, M. L., Ochsner, C. A., & Santana, C. M. (2001). Using a fading procedure to increase fluid consumption in a child with feeding problems. *Journal of Applied Behavior Analysis, 34,* 357–360.

Patel, M. R., Piazza, C. C., Martinez, C. J., Volkert, V. M., & Santana, C. M. (2002). An evaluation of two differential reinforcement procedures with escape extinction to treat food refusal. *Journal of Applied Behavior Analysis, 35,* 363–374.

Patel, R. R., Normand, M. P., & Kohn, C. S. (2019). Incentivizing physical activity using token reinforcement with preschool children. *Journal of Applied Behavior Analysis, 52,* 499–515. doi: 10.1002/jaba.536

Patterson, G. R. (1965). An application of conditioning techniques to the control of hyperactive child. In L. P. Ullman & Krasner, (Eds.), *Case studies in behavior modification* (pp. 370–375). New York: Holt, Rinehart & Winston.

Patterson, G. R. (1971). *Families: Applications of social learning to family life.* Champaign, IL.: Research Press Company.

Patterson, G. R., DeBaryshe, B. D., & Ramsey, E. (1989). A developmental perspective on antisocial behavior. *American Psychologist, 44,* 329–335.

Patterson, G. R., & Chamberlain, P. (1994). A functional analysis of resistance during parent training. *Clinical Psychology: Science and Practice, 1*(1), 53–70.

Patterson, G. R., Reid, J. B., & Dishion, T. J. (1992). *Antisocial boys.* Eugene, OR: Castalia.

Paul, G. L., Licht, M. H., Mariotto, M.J., Power, C.T., & Engel, K.L. (1988). The staff-resident interaction chronograph: Observational assessment instrumentation for service and research. Champaign, Il: Research Press.

Paulus, P. B., & Matthews, R. W. (1980). When density affects task performance. *Personality and Social Psychology Bulletin, 6,* 199–124.

Pawlicki, R. E., & Morey, T. M. (1976). A low cost instrument for "thinning" self-directed schedules of reinforcement. *Behavior Therapy, 7,* 120–122.

Payne, S. W., Dozier, C. L., Briggs, A. M.,et al. (2017). An analysis of group-oriented contingencies and associated side effects in preschool children. *Behavioral Interventions, 26,* 27–52. doi.org10.1007/s10864-016-9225-2

Pear, J. J., & Crone-Todd, D. E. (1999). Personalized system of instruction in cyberspace. *Journal of Applied Behavior Analysis, 32,* 205–209.

Pear, J. J., & Crone-Todd, D. E. (2002). A social constructivist approach to computer-mediated instruction. *Computers & Education, 38,* 221–231.

Pelios, L., Morren, J., Tesch, D., & Axelrod, S. (1999). The impact of functional analysis methodology on treatment choice for self-injurious and aggressive behavior. *Journal of Applied Behavior Analysis, 32,* 185–195.

Pellegerino, R., Sinding, C., de Wijk, R. A., & Hummel, T. (2017). Habituation and adaptation to orders in humans. *Physiology & Behavior, 177,* 13–19.

Pence, S., Roscoe, E. M., Bourret, J. C., & Ahearn, W. H. (2009). Relative contributions of three descriptive methods: Implications for behavioral assessment. *Journal of Applied Behavior Analysis, 42,* 425–446.

Pence, S. T., & St. Peter, C. C. Evaluation of treatment integrity errors on mand acquisition. *Journal of Applied Behavior Analysis, 48,* 575–589. doi: 10.1002/jaba.238

Pendergrass, V. E. (1972). Timeout from positive reinforcement following persistent, high-rate behavior in retardates. *Journal of Applied Behavior Analysis, 5,* 85–91.

Penrod, B., Wallace, M. D., & Dyer, R. (2008). Assessing potency of high- and low-preference reinforcers with respect to response rate and response patterns. *Journal of Applied Behavior Analysis, 41,* 177–188.

Perez, B. C., Bacotti, J. K., Peters, K. P., & Vollmer, T. R. (2020). An extension of commonly used toilet-training procedures to children with autism spectrum disorder. *Journal of Applied Behavior Analysis, 53,* 2360–2375. doi: 10.1002/jaba.727

Perkins, D.R., Dougher, M.J., & Greenway, D.E. (2007). Contextual control by function and form of transfer of functions. *Journal of the Experimental Analysis of Behavior, 88,* 87–102.

Perri, M. G., Richards, C. S., & Schultheis, K. R. (1977). Behavioral self-control and smoking reduction: A study of self-initiated attempts to reduce smoking. *Behavior Therapy, 8,* 360–365.

Peterson, C., Lerman, D.C., & Nissen, J. A. (2016). Reinforcer choice as an antecedent versus consequence. *Journal of Applied Behavior Analysis, 49,* 286–293. doi: 10.1002/jaba.284

*Peters v. Rome City School District,* 747, N. Y. S.2d 867 (N.Y.A.D. 4 Dept., 2002).

Peters, T. J., & Austin, N. (1985). *A passion for excellence.* New York: Random House.

Peterson, G. B. (2004). A day of great illumination: B.F. Skinner's discovery of shaping. *Journal of the Experimental Analysis of Behavior, 82,* 317–328.

Peterson, L. D., Young, K. R., Salzberg, C. L., West, R. P., & Hill, M. (2006). Using self-management procedures to improve classroom social skills in multiple general education settings. *Education and Treatment of Children, 29,* 1–21.

Petscher, E. S., & Bailey, J. S. (2006). Effect of training, prompting, and self-monitoring on staff behavior in a classroom for students with disabilities. *Journal of Applied Behavior Analysis, 39,* 215–226.

Petscher, E.S., & Bailey, J.S. (2008). Comparing main and collateral effects of extinction and differential reinforcement of alternative behavior. *Behavior Modification, 32,* 468–488.

Petty, M. M., Singleton, B., & Connell, D. W. (1992). An experimental evaluation of an organization incentive plan in the electric utility industry. *Journal of Applied Psychology, 77,* 427–436.

Petursdottir, A.I., Carr, J. E., & Michael, J. (2005). Emergence of mands and tacts of novel objects among preschool children, *The Analysis of Verbal Behavior, 21,* 59–74.

Petursdottir, A., McComas, J., McMaster, K., & Horner, K. (2007). The effects of scripted peer tutoring and programming common stimuli on social interactions of a student with autism spectrum disorder. *Journal of Applied Behavior Analysis, 40,* 353–357.

Pfadt, A., Cohen, I. L., Sudhalter, V., Romanczyk, R. G., & Wheller, D. J. (1992). Applying statistical process control to clinical data: An illustration. *Journal of Applied Behavior Analysis, 25,* 551–560.

Pfiffner, L. J., & O'Leary, S. G. (1987). The efficacy of all-positive management as a function of the prior use of negative consequences. *Journal of Applied Behavior Analysis, 20,* 265–271.

Phaneuf, L., & McIntyre, L. L. (2007). Effects of individualized video feedback combined with group parent training on inappropriate maternal behavior. *Journal of Applied Behavior Analysis, 40,* 737–741.

Phillips, C. L., Iannaccone, J. A., Rooker, G. W., & Hagopian, L. P. (2017). Noncontin-gent reinforcement of the treatment of severe problem behavior; An analysis of 27 consecutive applications. *Journal of Applied Behavior Analysis, 50,* 357–376. doi/org/10.1002/jaba.376

Phillips, E. L. (1968). Achievement Place: Token reinforcement procedures in a home-style rehabilitation setting for "pre-delinquent" boys. *Journal of Applied Behavior Analysis, 1,* 213–223.

Phillips, E. L., Phillips, E. A., Fixsen, D., & Wolf, M. M. (1971). Achievement place: Modification of behavior of predelinquent boys within a token economy. *Journal of Applied Behavior Analysis, 4,* 45–61.

Phillips, E. L., Phillips, E. A., Fixsen, D., & Wolf, M. M. (1972). *The teaching family handbook.* Lawrence: University of Kansas, Department of Human Development.

Phillips, E. L., Phillips, E. A., Wolf, M. M., & Fixsen, D. L. (1973). Achievement Place: Development of the elected manager system. *Journal of Applied Behavior Analysis, 6,* 541–561.

Piazza, C. C., & Fisher, W. (1991). A faded bedtime with response cost protocol for treatment of multiple sleep problems in children. *Journal of Applied Behavior Analysis, 24,* 129–140.

Piazza, C. C., Moes, & Fisher, W. W. (1996). Differential reinforcement of alternative behavior and demand fading in the treatment of escape-maintained destructive behavior. *Journal of Applied Behavior Analysis, 29,* 569–572.

Piazza, C. C., & Roane, H. S. (2009). Assessment of pediatric feeding disorder. In J. L. Matson, F. Andrasik, & M. Matson (Eds.). *Assessing childhood psychopathology and developmental disabilities.* Pp. 471–490. New York, NY: Springer Science & Business Media.

Pierce, W. D., & Cheney, C. D. (2008). *Behavior analysis and learning (4th Ed.).* New York: Routledge

Pinter, E. B., East, A., & Thrush, N. (2015). Effects of Video-Feedback Intervention on Teachers' Use of Praise. *Education and Treatment of Children, 38,* 451–472.

Plaud, J.J., Gaither, G.A., & Lawrence, J.B. (1997). Operant transformations and human behavioral momentum. *Journal of Behavior Therapy and Experimental Psychiatry, 28,* 169–179.

Plaud, J. J., Gillund, B., & Ferraro, F. R. (2000). Signal detection analysis of choice behavior and aging. *Journal of Clinical Geropsychology, 6,* 73–81.

Poche, C., Brouwer, R., & Swearingen, M. (1981). Teaching self-protection to young children. *Journal of Applied Behavior Analysis, 14,* 169–176.

Poling, A. (2010). Progressive-ratio schedules and applied behavior analysis. *Journal of Applied Behavior Analysis, 43,* 347–349.

Poling, A., Lotfizadeh, A. D., & Edwards, T. L. (2020). Motivating operations and discriminative stimuli: Distinguishable but interactive variables. *Behavior Analysis in Practice, 13,* 502–508. http://doi.org/10.1007/s40617-019-00400-

Poling, A., Methot, L. L., & LeSage, M. G. (1995). *Fundamentals of behavior analytic research.* New York: Plenum.

Polvinale, R. A., & Lutzker, J. R. (1980). Elimination of assaultive and inappropriate sexual behavior by reinforcement and social restitution. *Mental Retardation, 18,* 27–30.

Poterfield, J. K., Herbert-Jackson, E., & Risley, T. R. (1976). Contingent observation: An effective and acceptable procedure for reducing disruptive behavior of young children in a group setting. *Journal of Applied Behavior Analysis, 9,* 55–64.

Piazza, C. C., Contrucci, S. A., Hanley, G. P., & Fisher, W. W. (1997). Nondirective prompting and noncontingent reinforcement in the treatment of destructive behavior during hygiene routines. *Journal of Applied Behavior Analysis, 30,* 705–708.

Piazza, C. C., Fisher, W. W., Hanley, G. P., LeBlanc, L. A., Worsdell, A. S., Lindauer, S. E., et al. (1998). Treatment of pica through multiple analyses of its reinforcing functions. *Journal of Applied Behavior Analysis, 31,* 165–189.

Pierce, W. D., & Cheney, C. D. (2008). *Behavior analysis and learning, 3rd Ed.* Nahwah, N. J.: Lawrence Erlbaum Assoc's., Inc.

Pigott, H. E., Fantuzzo, J. W., & Clement, P. W. (1986). The effects of reciprocal peer tutoring and group contingencies on the academic performance of elementary school children. *Journal of Applied Behavior Analysis, 19,* 93–98.

Platt, J. S., Harris, J. W., & Clements, J. E. (1980). The effects of individually designed reinforcement schedules on attending and academic performance with behaviorally disordered adolescents. *Behavioral Disorders, 5,* 197–205.

Podsakoff, P. M. (1982). Effects of schedule changes on human performance: An empirical test of the contrasting predictions of the law of effect, the probability-differential model, and the response-deprivation approach. *Organizational Behavior and Human Performance, 29,* 322–351.

Poling, A., Methot, L. L., & LeSage, M. G. (Eds.). (1995). *Fundamentals of behavior analytic research.* New York: Plenum Press.

Poling, A., & Normand, M. (1999). Noncontingent reinforcement: An inappropriate description of time-based schedules that reduce behavior. *Journal of Applied Behavior Analysis, 32,* 237–238.

Polirstok, S. R., & Greer, R. D. (1986). A replication of collateral effects and a component analysis of a successful tutoring package for inner-city adolescents. *Education and Treatment of Children, 9,* 101–121.

Pollack, M.J., Fleming, R.K., & Sulzer-Azaroff, B. (1994). Enhancing professional performance through organizational change. *Behavioral Interventions, 9,* 27–42.

Pollard, J. S., Higbee, T. S., Akers, J. S., & Brodhead, M. T. (2014). An evaluation of interactive computer training to teach instructors to implement discrete trials with children with autism. *Journal of Applied Behavior Analysis, 47,* 765–776. doi: 10.1002/jaba.152.

Popkin, J. (2003). Enhancing academic performance in a classroom serving students with serious emotional disturbance: Interdependent group contingencies with randomly selected components. *School Psychology Review, 32,* 384–397.

Porter, B.E., Anderson, D.S., Kristie L., Martinez, K.L., & Anderson, K.B. (2005). *The Virginia Strategic Plan for Pedestrian Safety: Focusing on Behavior Change.* Project report: The Virginia Department of Motor Vehicles.

Posadzinska, I., Shupska, U., & Karaszewski, R. (2020). The attitudes and actions of the superior and the participative management style. *European Research Studies, 23,* 488–501.

Poulson, C. L., Kymissis, E., Reeve, K. F., Andreatos, M., & Reeve, L. (1991). Generalized vocal imitation in infants. *Journal of Experimental Child Psychology, 51,* 267–279.

Powell, J., Martindale, A., & Kulp, S. (1975). An evaluation of time-sampling measures of behavior. *Journal of Applied Behavior Analysis, 8,* 463–469.

Powell, S., & Nelson, B. (1997). Effects of choosing academic assignments on a student with attention deficit hyperactivity disorder. *Journal of Applied Behavior Analysis, 30,* 181–183.

Prados, J., Manteiga, R. D., & Sansa, J. (2003). Recovery effects after extinction in the Morris swimming pool navigation task. *Learning & Behavior, 31*(3), 299–304.

Prater, M. A., Hogan, S., & Miller, S. R. (1992). Using self-monitoring to improve on-task behavior and academic skills of an adolescent with mild disabilities across special and regular education settings. *Education and Treatment of Children, 15,* 43–55.

Premack, D. (1959). Toward empirical behavior laws: I. Positive reinforcement. *Psychological Review, 66,* 219–233.

Pronovost, P. J., Wu, A. W., & Sexton, J. B. (2004) Acute decompensation after removing a central line: Practical approaches to increasing safety in the intensive care unit. *Annals of Internal Medicine, 140,* 1025–1033.

Pryor, K. (1999). *Don't shoot the dog! The new art of teaching and training* (rev. ed.). New York: Bantam Books.

Pryor, K., & Norris, K.S. (1991). *Dolphin societies: Discoveries and puzzles.* Berkeley: University of California Press.

Quattrochi-Tubin, S., & Jason, L. A. (1980). Enhancing social interactions and activity among the elderly through stimulus control. *Journal of Applied Behavior Analysis, 13,* 159–163.

Querim, A. C., Iwata, B. A., Roscoe, E. M., Schichenmehyer, K. J., Ortega, J. V., & Hurl, K. E. (2013). Functional analysis screening for problem behavior maintained by automatic reinforcement. *Journal of Applied Behavior Analysis, 46,* 47–60.

Quinn, M., Miltenberger, R., Abreu, A., & Narozanick, T. (2017). An intervention featuring public posting and graphical feedback to enhance the performance of competitive dancers. *Behavior Analysis in Practice, 10,* 1–11.

Rachlin, H. (1966). Recovery of responses during mild punishment. *Journal of Experimental Analysis of Behavior, 9,* 251–263.

Radley, K. C., Dart, E. H., Helbig, K A., Schrieber, S. R., & Ware, M. E. (2018). An evaluation of the additive effects of lag schedules of reinforcement. *Developmental Neurorehabilitation, 22,* 180–191. doi.org/ao.1080/17518423.2018.1523242

Raia, C.P., Shillingford, S.W., Miller, H.L., & Baier, P.S. (2000). Effects of differences in interreinforcer intervals between past and current schedules on fixed-interval responding. *Journal of the Experimental Analysis of Behavior, 74,* 265–281.

Rajagopal, S., Nicholson, K., Putri, T.R., Addington, J. and Felde, A. (2021), Teaching children with autism to tact private events based on public accompaniments. *Journal of Applied Behavior Analysis, 54*: 270–286. https://doi-org.mimas.calstatela.edu/10.1002/jaba.785

Ramsey, M. L., Jolivette, K., Patterson, D. P., & Kennedy, C. (2010). Using choice to increase time on-task, task-completion, and accuracy for students with emotional/behavior disorders in a residential facility. *Education and Treatment of Children, 33*(1), 1–21.

Randolph, J. J. (2007). Meta-analysis of the research on response cards: Effects on test achievement, quiz achievement, participation, and off-task behavior. *Journal of Positive Behavior Interventions, 9,* 113–128.

Rantz, W. G., Dickinson, A. M., Sinclair, G. A., & Van Houten, R. (2009). The effect of feedback on the accuracy of checklist completion during instrument flight training. *Journal of Applied Behavior Analysis, 42,* 497–509.

Rapp, J. T., Cook, J. L., McHugh, C., Mann, K. R. (2017). Decreasing stereotypy using NCR and DRO with functionally matched stimulation: Effects on targeted and non-targeted stereotypy. *Behavior Modification, 41*(1), 45–83. doi.org/10.1177/0145545516652370

Rapp, J. T., Dozier, C. L., & Carr, J. E. (2001). Functional assessment and treatment of pica: A single-case experiment. *Behavioral Interventions, 16,* 111–125.

Rapp, J. T., Miltenberger, R. G., Galensky, T. L., Ellingson, S. A., Stricker, J., Garlinghouse, M., & Long, E. S. (2000). Treatment of hair pulling and hair manipulation maintained by digital-tactile stimulation. *Behavior Therapy, 31*(2), 381–393.

Rapp, J. T., Vollmer, R. R., & Hovanetz, A. N. (2005). Evaluation and treatment of swimming pool avoidance exhibited by an adolescent girl with autism. *Behavior Therapy, 36,* 101–105.

Rapport, M. D., Murphy, H. A., & Bailey, J. S. (1982). Ritalin vs. response cost in the control of hyperactive children: A within-subject comparison. *Journal of applied Behavior Analysis, 15,* 205–216.

Rasmus v. State of Arizona, 939, F.Supp. 709 (D. Ariz., 1996).

Rasmussen, E. B., & Newland, M. C. (2008). Asymmetry of reinforcement and punishment in human choice. *Journal of the Experimental Analysis of Behavior, 89,* 157–167.

Rauer, S. A., Cooke, T. P., & Apolloni, T. (1978). Developing nonretarded toddlers as verbal models for retarded classmates. *Child Study Journal, 8,* 1–8.

Ray, K. P., Skinner, C. H., & Watson, R. S. (1999). Transferring stimulus control via momentum to increase compliance in a student with autism: A demonstration of collaborative consultation. *School Psychology Review, 28,* 622–628.

Reber, R.A., & Wallin, J.A. (1984). The effects of training, goal-setting, & knowledge of results on safe behavior: A component analysis. *The Academy of Management Journal, 27,* 544–560.

Redd, W. H., Morris, E. K., & Martin, J. A. (1975). Effects of positive and negative adult-child interactions on children's social preference. *Journal of Experimental Child Psychology, 19,* 153–164.

Redford, P. M., & Ervin, R. A. (2002). Employing descriptive functional assessment methods to assess low-rate, high-intensity behaviors: A case example. *Journal of Positive Behavior Interventions, 4*(3), 146–155, 164.

Redmon, W. K., & Farris, H. E. (1987). Application of basic research to the treatment of children with autistic and severely handicapped repertoires. *Education and Treatment of Children, 10,* 326–337.

Reed, D. D., & Azulay, R. L. (2011). A microsoft Excel® 2010 based tool for calculating inter observer agreement. *Behavior Analysis in Practice, 42,* 45–52.

Reed, P., & Morgan, T.A. (2006). Resurgence of response sequences during extinction in rats shows a primacy effect. *Journal of the Experimental Analysis of Behavior, 86,* 307–315.

Reed, G. K., Piazza, C. C., Patel, M. R., Layer, S. A., Bachmeyer, M. H., Bethke, S. D., & Gutshall, K. A. (2004). On the relative contributions of noncontingent reinforcement and escape extinction in the treatment of food refusal. *Journal of Applied Behavior Analysis, 37,* 27–42.

Reese, E. P. (1966). *The analysis of human operant behavior.* Dubuque, IA: Wm. C. Brown.

Reese, E. P. (1971). *Skills training for the special child.* Behavior Films, 202 West St., Granby, MA, 01033.

Reese, H. W. Commentary on Malone: Who founded Behaviorism? *Behavior Analyst, 38,* 109–114. DOI: 10.1007/s40614-014-0020-3 Reese, E. P., Howard, J. S., & Reese, T. W. (1977). *Human behavior: An experimental analysis and its applications.* Dubuque, IA: Wm. C. Brown.

Reese, E. P., Howard, J., & Rosenberger, P. (August, 1974). *A comparison of* three reinforcement procedures in assessing visual capacities of profoundly retarded individuals. Paper presented at the meeting of the American Psychological Association, New Orleans.

Reeve, S., A., Reeve, K. F., Townsend, D. B., & Poulson, C. L. (2007). Establishing a generalized repertoire of helping behavior in children with autism. *Journal of Applied Behavior Analysis, 40,* 123–136.

Regalado, M., Sareen, H., Inkelas, M., Wissow, L. S., & Halfon, N. (2004). Parents' discipline of young children: Results from the national survey of early childhood health. *Pediatrics, 113*(6), 1952–1958.

Rehfeldt, R. A., & Barnes-Holmes, Y. (Eds.). (2009). *Derived relational responding applications for learners with autism and other developmental disabilities: A progressive guide to change.* Context Press: Oakland, CA.

Rehfeldt, R., & Root, S. (2005). Establishing derived requesting skills in adults with severe developmental disabilities. *Journal of Applied Behavior Analysis, 38,* 101–105.

Reid, D. H., & Parsons, M. B. (2006). *Motivating human service staff: Supervisory strategies for maximizing work effort and work enjoyment* (2nd ed.). Vol. 3. Morganton: Habilitative Management Consultants, Inc.

Reid, D. H., Parsons, M. B., & Jensen, J. M. (2017). Maintaining staff performance following a training intervention: Suggestions from a 30-year case example. *Behavior Analysis in Practice, 10,* 12–21.

Reid, D. H., Parsons, M. B., McCarn, J. E., Green, C. W., Phillips, J. F., & Schepis, M. M. (1985). Providing a more appropriate education for severely handicapped persons. Increasing and validating functional classroom tasks. *Journal of Applied Behavior Analysis, 18,* 289–301.

Reid, J. B., Eddy, J. M., Fetrow, R. A., & Stoolmiller, M. (1999). Description and immediate impacts of a preventative intervention for conduct problems. *American Journal of Community Psychology, 24,* 483–517.

Reid, R. (1996). Research in self-monitoring with students with learning disabilities: The present, the prospects, the pitfalls. *Journal of Learning Disabilities, 29,* 317–331.

Reid, R., Trout, A. L., & Schartz, M. (2005). Self-regulation interventions for children with attention deficit/hyperactivity disorder. *Exceptional Children, 71,* 361–377.

Reinert, K. S., Higbee, T. S., & Nix, L. D. (2020). Creating digital activity schedules to promote independence and engagement. *Behavior Analysis in Practice, 13,* 577–595. doi.org/10.1007/s40617-020-00437-8

Reitman, D., Hupp, S. D. A., O'Callaghan, P. M., Gulley, V., & Northup, J. (2001). The Influence of a token economy and methylphenidate on attentive and disruptive behavior during sports with ADHD-diagnosed children. *Behavior Modification, 25*(2), 305–323.

Remington, B. (1994). Augmentative and alternative communication and behavior analysis: A productive partnership? *Augmentative and Alternative Communication, 10,* 3–13.

Remington, B., Hastings, R. P., Kovshoff, H., degli Espinosa, F., Jahr, E., Brown, T., et al. (2007). Early intensive behavioral intervention: Outcomes for children with autism and their parents after two years. *American Journal on Mental Retardation, 112,* 418–438.

Renne, C. M., & Creer, T. L. (1976). Training children with asthma to use inhalation therapy equipment. *Journal of Applied Behavior Analysis, 9,* 1–11.

Repp, A. C., Barton, L. E., & Brulle, A. R. (1983). A comparison of two procedures for programming the differential reinforcement of other behaviors. *Journal of Applied Behavior Analysis, 16,* 435–445.

Repp, A. C., & Dietz, S. M. (1974). Reducing aggressive and self-injurious behavior of institutionalized retarded children through reinforcement of other behaviors. *Journal of Applied Behavior Analysis, 7,* 313–325.

Repp, A. C., Felce, D., & Barton, L. E. (1988). Basing the treatment of stereotypic and self-injurious behaviors on hypotheses of their causes. *Journal of Applied Behavior Analysis, 21,* 281–289.

Repp, A. C., & Karsh, K. G. (1991). The Task Demonstration Model for teaching persons with severe handicaps. In R. Remington (Ed.). *Severe mental handicap and applied behaviour analysis* (pp. 263–284). Chichester: John Wiley.

Repp, A. C., Karsh, K. G., Johnson, J. W., & VanLaarhoven, T. (1996). A comparison of multiple versus single examples of the correct stimulus on task acquisition and generalization by persons with developmental disabilities. *Journal of Behavioral Education, 6,* 213–230.

Repp, A. C., Roberts, D. M., Slack, D. J., Repp, C. F., & Berkler, M. S. (1976). A comparison of frequency, interval, and time-sampling methods of data collection. *Journal of Applied Behavior Analysis, 9,* 501–508.

Reppucci, N. D. (1977). Implementation issues for the behavior modifier as institutional change agent. *Behavior Therapy, 8,* 594–605.

Reppucci, N. D., & Saunders, J. T. (1974). Social psychology of behavior modification: Problems of implementation in natural settings. *American Psychologist, 29,* 649–660.

Resnick, L. B., & Ford, W. W. (1978). Analysis of tasks for instruction: An information processing approach. In A. C. Catania & T. A. Brigham (Eds.). *Handbook of applied behavior analysis: Social and instructional processes* (pp. 378–409). New York: Irvington Publishers.

Reynolds, B. (2006). A review of delay-discounting research with humans: relations to drug use and gambling. *Behavioural Pharmacology, 17,* 651–66.

Reynolds, G., & Reed, P. (2018). The effect of stimulus duration on overselectivity: Evidence for the role of within-compound associations. *Journal of Experimental Psychology: Animal Learning and Congntion, 44,* 293–308. doi.org/10.1037/xan0000175

Reynolds, G. S. (1961). Behavioral contrast. *Journal of the Experimental Analysis of Behavior, 4,* 57–71.

Reynolds, G. S. (1968). *A primer of operant conditioning.* Glenview, IL: Scott, Foresman.

Reynolds, G. S. (1968). *A primer of operant conditioning.* Glenview, IL: Scott, Foresman.

Reynolds, L. K., & Kelley, M. L. (1997). The efficacy of a response cost-based treatment package for managing aggressive behavior in preschoolers. *Behavior Modification, 21,* 216–230.

Ricciardi, J. N., Luiselli, J. K., & Camare, M. (2006). Shaping approach responses as intervention for specific phobia in a child with autism. *Journal of Applied Behavior Analysis, 39,* 445–448.

Ricciardi, J. N., Luiselli, J. K., Terrill, S., & Reardon, K. (2003). Alternative response training with contingent practice as interventions for pica in a school setting. *Behavioral Interventions, 18,* 219–226.

Rice, A., Austin, J., & Gravina, N. (2009). Increasing customer service behaviors using manager-delivered task clarification and social praise. *Journal of Applied Behavior Analysis, 42,* 665–669.

Richards, C. S. (1981). Improving college students' study behaviors through self-control techniques: A brief review. *Behavioral Counseling Quarterly, 1,* 159–175.

Richter, K. P., Harris, K. J., Paine-Andrews, A., Fawcett, S. D., Schmid, T. L., Lankenau, H. H., et al. (2000). Measuring the health environment for physical activity and nutrition among youth: A review of the literature and applications for community initiatives. *Preventive Medicine, 31*(2), s98–s111.

Rickard, H. C., Melvin, K. D., Creel, J., & Creel, L. (1973). The effects of bonus tokens upon productivity in a remedial classroom for behaviorally disturbed children. *Behavior Therapy, 4,* 378–385.

Richardson, A. R., Lerman, D. C., Nissen, M. A., Luck, K. M., Neal, A. E., Bao, S., & Tsami, L. (2017). Can pictures promote the acquisition of sight-word reading? An evaluation of two potential instructional strategies. *Journal of Applied Behavior Analysis, 50,* 67–86. doi: 10.1002/jaba.354

Richardson, W. K., & Warzak, W. J. (1981). Stimulus stringing by pigeons. *Journal of Experimental Analysis of Behavior, 36,* 267–276.

Richman, D. M., Barnard-Brak, L., Grubb, L., Bosch, A., & Abby, L. (2015). Meta-Analysis of noncontingent reinforcement effects on problem behavior. *Journal of Applied Behavior Analysis, 48,* 131–152. doi: 10.1002/jaba.189.

Rickert, V. I., Sottolano, D. C., Parrish, J. M., Riley, A. W., Hunt, F. M., & Pelco, L. E. (1988). Training parents to become better behavior managers. *Behavior Modification, 12,* 475–496.

Ricketts, R.W., Goza, A.B., & Matese, M. (1993). A 4-year follow-up of treatment of self-injury. *Journal of Behavior Therapy and Experimental Psychiatry, 24,* 57–62.

Rieth, S. R., Stahmer, A. C., Suhrheinrich, J., & Schreibman, L. (2015). Examination of the prevalence of stimulus overselectivity in children with ASD. *Journal of Applied Behavior Analysis, 48,* 71–84. doi: 10.1002/jaba.165

Rilling, M. (1977). Stimulus control and inhibitory processes. In W. K. Honig & J. E. R. Staddon (Eds.), *Handbook of operant behavior* (pp. 432–480). Englewood Cliffs, NJ: Prentice-Hall.

Rincover, A., Cook, R., Peoples, A., & Packard, D. (1979). Sensory extinction and sensory reinforcement principles for programming multiple adaptive behavior change. *Journal of Applied Behavior Analysis, 12,* 221–233.

Ringdahl, J. E., & St. Peter, C. (2017). Resurgence: The unintended maintenance of problem behavior. *Education and Treatment of Children, 40,* 7–26.

Risley, T. R. (1968). The effects and side effects of punishing the autistic behavior of a deviant child. *Journal of Applied Behavior Analysis, 1,* 21–35.

Risley, T. R. (1970). Behavior modification: An experimental-therapeutic endeavor. In L. A. Hamerlynck, P. O. Davidson & L E. Acker (Eds.), *Behavior modification and ideal mental health services,* (pp. 103–127). Calgary: University of Calgary Press.

Risley, T. R. (1997). Montrose M. Wolf: The origin of the dimensions of applied behavior analysis. *Journal of Applied Behavior Analysis, 30,* 377–381.

Risley, T. (2005). Montrose M. Wolf (1935–2004). *Journal of Applied Behavior Analysis, 38,* 279–287.

Risley, T. R., & Cataldo, M. F. (1973). *Planned activity check: Materials for training observers.* Lawrence, KS: Center for Applied Behavior Analysis.

Rivera, C. J., Hudson, M. E., Weiss, S. L., & Zambone, A. (2017). Using multicomponent multimedia shared story intervention with an iPad to teach content picture vocabulary to students with developmental disabilities. (2017). *Education and Treatment of Children, 40,* 327–352.

Rizvi, S. L., & Roman, K. M. (2019). Generalization modalities: Taking the treatment out of the consulting room—Using telephone, text, and email. In M. A. Swales (Ed.), *The Oxford handbook of dialectical behaviour therapy* (p. 201–215). Oxford University Press.

Roane, H.S., Fisher, W.W., & McDonough, E.M. (2003). Progressing from programmatic to discovery research: A case example with the overjustification effect. *Journal of Applied Behavior Analysis, 36,* 35–46.

Roane, H. S., Vollmer, T. R., Ringdahl, J. E., & Marcus, B. A. (1998). Evaluation of a brief stimulus preference assessment. *Journal of Applied Behavior Analysis, 31,* 605–620.

Roberts-Gwinn, M. M., Luiten, L., Derby, K. M., Johnson, T. A., & Weber, K. (2001). Identification of competing reinforcers for behavior maintained by automatic reinforcement. *Journal of Positive Behavior Interventions, 3,* 83–97.

Roberts, M. W. (1988). Enforcing chair timeouts with room timeouts. *Behavior Modification, 12,* 353–370.

Robertson, J., Green, K., Alper, S., Schloss, P. J., & Kohler, F. (2003). Using peer-mediated intervention to facilitate children's participation in inclusive childcare activities. *Education and Treatment of Children, 26,* 182–197.

Robinson, J. D., & Hesse, K. D. (1981). A morphemically based spelling program's effect on spelling skills and spelling performance of seventh grade students. *The Journal of Educational Research, 75,* 56–62.

Robinson, K. E., & Rapport, L. J. (2002). Strategies for behavioral change: Outcomes of a school-based mental health program for youth with serious emotional disorders. *Psychology in the Schools, 39,* 661–675.

Robinson, N., & St. Peter, C. C. (2019). Accumulated reinforcers increase academic responding and suppress problem behave for students with Attention-Deficit Hyperactivity Disorder. *Journal of Applied Behavior Analysis, 52,* 1076–1088. doi:10.1002/jaba.570.

Robinson, P. W., Newby, J. J., & Ganzell, S. L. (1981). A token system for a class of underachieving hyperactive children. *Journal of Applied Behavior Analysis, 14,* 307–315.

Robinson, P.W., & Storm, R.H. (1978). Effects of error and errorless discrimination acquisition on reversal learning. *Journal of the Experimental Analysis of Behavior, 29,* 517–525.

Rock, M. L. (2005). Use of strategic self-monitoring to enhance academic engagement, productivity, and accuracy of students with and without exceptionalities. *Journal of Positive Behavior Interventions, 7*(1), 3–17

Rodriguez, B. J., Loman, S. L., & Horner, R. H. (2009). A preliminary analysis of the effects of coaching feedback on teacher implementation fidelity of first step to success. *Behavior Analysis in Practice, 2*(2), 11–21.

Rodriguez, J. O., Montesinos, L., & Preciado, J. (2005). A 19th century predecessor of the token economy. *Journal of Applied Behavior Analysis, 38,* 427.

Rodriguez, W. A., & Logan, F.A. (1980). Preference for punishment of the instrumental or the consummatory response. *Animal Learning & Behavior, 8,* 116–119.

Roeyers, H., Van Oost, P., & Bothyune, S. (1998). Immediate imitation and joint attention in young children with autism. *Development and Psychopathology, 10,* 441–450.

Rogalski, J. P., Roscoe, E. M., Fredericks, D. W., & Mezhoudi, N. (2020). Negative reinforcer magnitude manipulations for treating escape maintained problem behavior. *Journal of Applied Behavior Analysis, 53,* 1514–1530. doi: 10.1002/jaba.683

Rogers, R. W., Rogers, J. S. Bailey, J. S., Runkle, W., & Moore, B. (1988). Promoting safety belt use among state employees: The effects of prompting and a stimulus-control intervention. *Journal of Applied Behavior Analysis, 21,* 263–269.

Rogers, S. J. (2000). Interventions that facilitate socialization in children with autism. *Journal of Autism and Developmental Disorders, 30,* 399–409.

Rogers, S. J., Hepburn, S. L., Stackhouse, T., & Wehner, E. (2003). Imitation performance in toddlers with autism and those with other developmental disorders. *Journal of Child Psychology and Psychiatry, and Allied Disciplines, 44,* 763–781.

Rogers-Warren, A. K. (1984). Ecobehavioral analysis. *Education and Treatment of Children, 7,* 283–303.

Rogers-Warren, A. K., Warren, S. F., & Baer, D. M. (1977). A component analysis: Modeling, self-reporting, and reinforcement of self-reporting in the development of sharing. *Behavior Modification, 1,* 307–322.

Rohan, K. J. (2005). Clinical Psychiatry News – High-Beam Research - Oct 1, 2005.

Rohena, E. I., Jitendra, A. K., & Browder, D. M. (2002). Comparison of the effects of Spanish and English constant time delay instruction on sight word reading by Hispanic learners with mental retardation. *The Journal of Special Education, 36,* 171–186.

Rolider, A., Cummings, A., & Van Houten, R. (1991). Side effects of therapeutic punishment on academic performance and eye contact. *Journal of Applied Behavior Analysis, 24,* 763–773.

Rolider, A., & Van Houten, R. (1993). The interpersonal treatment model. In R. Van Houten & S. Axelrod (Eds.), *Behavior analysis and treatment.* (pp. 127–168). New York: Plenum.

Rolider, A., & Van Houten, R. (1985a). Movement suppression time-out for undesirable behavior in psychotic and severely developmentally delayed children. *Journal of Applied Behavior Analysis, 18,* 275–288.

Rolider, A., & Van Houten R. (1985b). Suppressing tantrum behavior in public places through the use of delayed punishment mediated by audio recording. *Behavior Therapy, 16,* 181–194.

Roll, J.M. (2005). The feasibility of using contingency management to modify cigarette smoking by adolescents, *Journal of Applied Behavior Analysis, 38,* 463–467.

Romance, N. R., & Vitale, M. R. (1992). A curriculum strategy that expands time for in-depth elementary science instruction by using science-based reading strategies: Effects of a yearlong study in grade four. *Journal of Research in Science Teaching, 29,* 545–554.

Romanczyk, R. G., Kent, R. N., Diament, C. & O'Leary, K. D. (1973) Measuring the reliability of observational data: A reactive process. *Journal of Applied Behavior Analysis 6*(1) 175–184.

Romaniuk, C., & Miltenberger, R. G. (2001). The influence of preference and choice of activity on problem behavior, *Journal of Positive Behavior Interventions, 3,* 152–159.

Romaniuk, C., Miltenberger, R., Conyers, C., Jenner, N., Jurgens, M., & Ringenberg, C. (2002). The influence of activity choice on problem behaviors maintained by escape versus attention. *Journal of Applied Behavior Analysis, 35,* 349–362.

Romani, P. W., Donaldson, A. M., Ager, A. J., Peaslee, J. E., Garden, S. M., & Ariefdjohan, M. (2019). Assessment and treatment of aggression during public outings. *Education and Treatment of Children, 42,* 345–360.

Romano, L. M., & St. Peter, C. C. (2017). Omission training results in more resurgence than alternative reinforcement. *The Psychological Record, 67,* 315–324. doi.org/10.1007/s40732-016-0214-z

Romeo, F. (1998). The negative effects of using a group contingency system of classroom management. *Journal of Instructional Psychology, 25,* 130–133.

Rortvedt, A. K., & Miltenberger, R. G. (1994). Analysis of a high probability instructional sequence and time-out in the treatment of child noncompliance. *Journal of Applied Behavior Analysis, 27,* 327–300.

Rosales, R., & Rehfeldt, R. A. (2007). Contriving transitive conditioned establishing operations to establish derived manding skills in adults with severe developmental disabilities. *Journal of Applied Behavior Analysis, 40,* 105–121.

Rosales,-Ruiz, J., & Baer, D.M. (1997). Behavioral CUSPS: A developmental and pragmatic concept for behavior analysis. *Journal of Applied Behavior Analysis, 30,* 533–544.

Roscoe, E. M., Fisher, W. W., Glover, A. C., & Volkert, V. M. (2006). Evaluating the relative effects of feedback and contingent money for staff training of stimulus preference assessments. *Journal of Applied Behavior Analysis, 39,* 63–77.

Roscoe, E. M., Iwata, B. A., & Goh, H. (1998). A comparison of noncontingent reinforcement and sensory extinction as treatments for self-injurious behavior. *Journal of Applied Behavior Analysis, 31,* 635–646.

Roscoe, E. M., Iwata, B. A., & Rand, M. S. (2003). Effects of reinforcer consumption and magnitude on response rates during noncontingent reinforcement. *Journal of Applied Behavior Analysis, 36,* 525–539.

Rose, D. J., & Church, R. J. (1998). Learning to teach: The acquisition and maintenance of teaching skills. *Journal of Behavioral Education, 8,* 5–35.

Rose, H.M. & Ludwig, T.D. (2009). Swimming pool hygiene: Self monitoring, task clarification, and performance feedback increase lifeguard cleaning behaviors. *Journal of Organizational Behavior Management, 29,* 69–79.

Rosen, H. S., & Rosen, L. A. (1983). Eliminating stealing: Use of stimulus control with an elementary student. *Behavior Modification, 7,* 56–63.

Rosenbaum, M. E., Chalmers, D. K., & Horne, W. C. (1962). Effects of success and failure and the competence of the model on the acquisition and rehearsal of matching behavior. *Journal of Psychology, 54,* 251–258.

Rosenfield, S. (1991). The relationship variable in behavioral consultation. *Journal of Behavioral Consulting, 1,* 329–336.

Rosenthal, T. L., & Bandura, A. (1978). Psychological modeling: Theory and practice. In S. L. Garfield & A. E. Bergin (Eds.), *Handbook of psychotherapy and behavior change* (pp. 621–658). New York: Wiley.

Rosenthal, T. L., & Downs, A. (1985). Cognitive aids in teaching and treating. *Advances in Behaviour Research and Therapy, 7,* 1–53.

Ross, S. W., & Horner, R. H. (2009). Bully prevention in positive behavior support. *Journal of Applied Behavior Analysis, 42,* 747–759.

Rossi, M. R., Vladescu, J. C., Reeve, K. F., & Gross, A. C. (2017). Teaching safety responding to children with autism spectrum disorder. *Education and Treatment of Children, 40,* 187–208.

Roswal, G. M., & Mims, A. A. (1995). Effects of collaborative peer tutoring on urban seventh graders. *Journal of Educational Research, 88,* 275–279.

Rothbaum, B.O., Hodges, L., Smith, S. Lee, J.H., & Price, L. (2000). A controlled study of virtual reality exposure therapy for the fear of flying. *Journal of Consulting and Clinical Psychology, 68,* 1020–1026.

Rowe, D. A., Mazzotti, V. L., Ingram, A., & Lee, Saunghee. (2017). Effects of goal-setting instruction on academic engagement for students at risk. *Career Development and Transition for Exceptional Individuals, 48,* 25–35. doi: 10.1177/2165143416678175

Rubow, C. C., Noel,C. R., & Wehby, J. H. (2019). Effects of noncontingent attention on behavior of students with emotional/behavioral disorders and staff in alternative settings. *Education and Treatment of Children, 42,* 201–224.

Rubow, C. C., Vollmer, T. R., & Joslyn, P. R. (2018). Effects of the Good Behavior Game on student and teacher behavior in an alternative school. *Journal of Applied Behavior Analysis, 51,* 382–392. doi: 10.1002/jaba.455

Ruskin, R. S., & Maley, R. F. (1972). Item preference in a token economy ward store. *Journal of Applied Behavior Analysis, 5,* 373–378.

Russell, B. (1955). Science and human life. In J. R. Newman (Ed.), *What is science?* (pp. 6–17). New York: Simon and Schuster.

Russell, D., Ingvarsson, E. T., Haggar, J. L., & Jessel, J. (2018). Using progressive ratio schedules to evaluate tokens as generalized conditioned reinforcers. *Journal of Applied Behavior Analysis, 51*(1), 40–52. https://doi-org.mimas.calstatela.edu/10.1002/jaba.424

Rothbaum, B.O., Hodge, L., Smith, S. Lee, J.H., & Price, L.(2000). A controlled study of virtual reality exposure therapy for the fear of flying. *Journal of Consulting and Clinical Psychology, 68*(6), 1020–1026.

Rozalski, M., Yell, M., & Boreson, L. (2006). Using seclusion timeout and physical restraint, an analysis of state policy, research, and the law. *Journal of Special Education Leadership, 19*(2), 13–29.

Ryan J. B., & Peterson, R. L. (2004). Physical restraint in school. *Behavioral Disorders, 29(2),* 154–168.

Ryan, J. B., Peterson, R. L., & Rozalski, M. (2007). State policies concerning the use of seclusion timeout in schools. *Education and Treatment of Children, 30*(4), 215–239.

Ryan, J. B., Sanders, S., Katsiyannis, A., & Yell, M. L. (2007). Using time-out effectively in the classroom. *Teaching Exceptional Children, 39*(4), 60–67.

*Sabin v. Greenville Public Schools*, 31 IDELR 161 (W.D. Mich. 1999).

Sackett, D.L., Rosenberg, W., Gray, J.A., Haynes, R.B., & Richardson, W.S. (1996). Evidence-based medicine: What it is and what it isn't. *British Medical Journal, 312,* (*7023*) 71–72.

Sackett, D.L. (1996). Randomized trials in individual patients. *Research in Complementary Medicine, 3*(3), 140–147.

Sackett, G. P. (1979). The lag sequential analysis of contingency and cyclicity in behavioral intervention research. In J. D. Osofsky (Ed.), *Handbook of infant development* (pp. 623–649). New York: Wiley.

Sadler, O.W., & Montgomery, G.M. (1982). The application of positive practice overcorrection to the use of hearing protection. *American Industrial Hygiene Association Journal, 43*(6), 451–454.

Sagvolden, T., Johansen, E. B., Aase, H., & Russell, V. A. (2005). A dynamic developmental theory of attention-deficit/hyperactivity disorder (ADHD) predominantly hyperactive/impulsive and combined subtypes. *Behavioral and Brain Sciences, 28,* 446–450.

Saini, V., Fisher, W. W., & Pisman, M. D. (2017). Persistence during and resurgence following non contingent reinforcement implemented with and without extinction. *Journal of Applied Behavior Analysis, 50,* 377–392. doi: 10.1002/jaba.380

Saini, V., Greer, B. D., Fisher, W. W., Lichtblau, K. R., DeSouza, A. A., & Mitteer, D. R. (2016). Individual and combined effects of non contingent reinforcement and response locking on automatically reinforced problem behavior. *Journal of Applied Behavior Analysis, 49,* 693–698. doi: 10.1002/jaba.306

Sailor, W., Dunlap, G.,Sugai, G., & Horner, R. (Eds.). *Handbook of positive behavior supports.* New York: Springer.

Salend, S., & Gordon, B. D. (1987). A group oriented timeout ribbon procedure. *Behavioral Disorders, 12,* 131–136.

Salend, S., & Maragulla, D. (1983). The timeout ribbon: A procedure for the least restrictive environment. *The Journal of Special Education, 20,* 9–15.

Salend, S. J., & Sonnenschein, P. (1989). Validating the effectiveness of a cooperative learning strategy through direct observation. *Journal of School Psychology, 27,* 47–58.

Sanford, K. S., & Horner, R. H. (2013). Effects of matching instruction difficulty to reading level for students with escape-maintained problem behavior. *Journal of Positive Behavior Interventions, 15,* 79–89.

Sanok, R. L., & Striefel, S. (1979). Elective mutism: Generalization of verbal responding across people and settings. *Behavior Therapy, 10,* 357–371.

Sansosti, F. J., & Powell-Smith, K. A. (2006). Using social stories to improve the social behavior of children with Asperger Syndrome. *Journal of Positive Behavior Interventions, 8,* 43–57.

Sansosti, F. J., & Powell-Smith, K. A. (2008). Using computer-presented social stories and video models to increase the social communication skills of children with high-functioning autism spectrum disorders. *Journal of Positive Behavior Interventions, 10,* 162–178.

Sara, Y. A. (2017). Effectiveness of response cost and time out in decreasing lateness among senior secondary school students in Jigawa State, Nigeria. *Journal of Teaching and Teacher Education, 5*(2), 75–81. http://dx.doi.org/10.12785/jtte/050205

Sarokoff, R. A., & Sturmey, P. (2004). The effects of behavioral skills training on staff implementation of discrete-trail teaching. *Journal of Applied Behavior Analysis, 37,* 535–538.

Sasaki, S., Omori, Y., Sagimura, S., Mogamiya, T., Tada, M., Nakamura, E., & Omiya, K. (2016). Effects of physical guidance on wheelchair-driving: Patient with severe hemiplegia and cognitive disorder. *Japanese Journal of Behavior Analysis, 30,* 137-144.

Sasson, J. R., & Austin, J. (2004). The effects of training, feedback, and participant involvement in behavioral safety observations on office ergonomic behavior. *Journal of Organizational Behavior Management, 24* (4), 1–30.

Satake, E. B., Jagaroo, V., & Maxwell, D. L. (2008). *Handbook of statistical methods: Single subject design.* San Diego: Plural Publishing.

Saundergas, R. W., Madsen, C. H., & Scott, J. W. (1977). Differential effects of fixed- and variable-time on production rates of elementary school children. *Journal of Applied Behavior Analysis, 10,* 673–678.

Saunders, M. D., Saunders, R. R., & Marquis, J. G. (1998). Comparison of reinforcement schedules in the reduction of stereotypy with supported routines. *Research in Developmental Disabilities, 19,* 99–122.

Saunders, R. R., McEntee, J. E., & Saunders, M. D. (2005). Interaction of reinforcement schedules, a behavioral prosthesis, and work-related behavior in adults with mental retardation. *Journal of Applied Behavior Analysis, 38,* 163–176.

Saunders, R. R., & Saunders, M. D. (2000). An analysis of contingency learning in the treatment of aberrant behavior. *Journal on Developmental Disabilities, 7,* 54–83.

Sawin, D. G., & Parke, R. D. (1979). Inconsistent discipline of aggression in young boys. *Journal of Experimental Child Psychology, 28,* 525–538.

Scattone, D. (2002). Increasing appropriate social interactions of children with autistic spectrum disorders using social stories. *Dissertation Abstracts International, 63,* (10–B) (UMI No. 3067247).

Scattone, D., Tingstrom, D. H., & Wilczynski, S. M. (2006). Increasing appropriate social interaction of children with autism spectrum disorders using social stories. *Focus on Autism and Other Developmental Disabilities, 21*(4), 211–221.

Schaeffer, R. W. (1979). Human preferences for time-dependent and response-dependent reinforcement schedules. *Bulletin of the Psychonomic Society, 14,* 293–296.

Scheirer, M. A., & Kraut, R. E. (1979). Increasing educational achievement via self-concept change. *Review of Educational Research, 49,* 131–150.

Schepis, M.M., Reid, D.H., & Behrman, M.M. (1996). Acquisition and functional use of voice output communication by persons with profound multiple disabilities. *Behavior Modification, 20,* 451–468.

Scherrer, M. D., & Wilder, D. A. (2008). Training to increase safe tray carrying among cocktail servers. *Journal of Applied Behavior Analysis, 41,* 131–135.

Schieltz, K. M., & Wacker, D. P. (2020). Functional assessment and function-based treatment delivered via telehealth: A brief summary. *Journal of Applied Behavior Analysis, 53,* 1–17.

Schilling, D. L., & Schwartz, I. S. (2004). Alternative seating for young children with autism spectrum disorder: Effects on classroom behavior. *Journal of Autism and Developmental Disorders, 34,* 423–432.

Schilmoeller, J. J., & Etzel, B. C. (1977). An experimental analysis of criterion and non-criterion-related cues in "errorless" stimulus control procedures. In B. C. Etzel, J. M. LeBlanc, & D. M. Baer (Eds.), *New developments in behavioral research: Theory, method and application.* Hinsdale, NJ: Lawrence Erlbaum Associates.

Schlinger, H. D., Jr. (1993). Separating discriminative and function-altering effects of verbal stimuli. *The Behavior Analyst, 16,* 9–23.

Schlinger, H.D., Derenne, A. & Baron, A. (2008). What 50 years of research tell us about pausing under schedules of reinforcement. *The Behavior Analyst, 31,* 39–60.

Schmandt-Besserat, D. (1979). An archaic recording system in the Uruk-Jemdet Nasr period. *American Journal of Archaeology, 83*(1), 19–48.

Schmidt, A. C., Hanley, G. P., & Layer, S. A. (2009). A further analysis of the value of choice: Controlling for illusory discriminative stimuli and evaluating the effects of less preferred items. *Journal of Applied Behavior Analysis, 42,* 711–716.

Schmidt, C.R., Ollendick, T.H., & Stanowicz, L.B. (1988). Developmental changes in the influence of assigned goals on cooperation and competition. *Developmental Psychology, 24,* 574–579.

Schmidt, G. W., & Ulrich, K. E. (1969). Effect of group contingent events upon classroom noise. *Journal of Applied Behavior Analysis, 2,* 171–179.

Schmitt, D. R., (1987). Interpersonal contingencies: Performance differences and cost-effectiveness. *Journal of the Experimental Analysis of Behavior, 48,* 226–234.

Schnake, M. E. (1986). Vicarious punishment in a work setting. *Journal of Applied Psychology, 71,* 343–345.

Schneider, B., & Leroux, J. (1994). Educational environments for the pupil with behavioral disorders. A "best evidence" synthesis. *Behavioral Disorders, 19,* 192–204.

Schoen, S. F. (1986). Assistance procedures to facilitate the transfer of stimulus control: Review and analysis. *Education and Training of the Mentally Retarded, 21,* 62–74.

Schonwetter, S. W., Miltenberger, R., & Oliver, J. R. (2014). An evaluation of self-monitoring to improve swimming performance. *Behavioral Interventions, 29,* 213–224. doi: 10.1002/bin.1387

Schreibman, L., Koegel, R. L., & Craig, M. S. (1977). Reducing stimulus overselectivity in autistic children, *Journal of Abnormal Child Psychology, 5,* 425–436.

Schreibman, L., Koegel, R. L., Mills, J. I., & Burke, J. C. (1981). Social validation of behavior therapy with autistic children. *Behavior Therapy, 12,* 610–624.

Schultz, W. (2000). Multiple reward signals in the brain. *Nature Reviews: Neuroscience, 1,* 199–207.

Schumate, E. D., & Wills, H. P. (2010). Classroom-based functional analysis and intervention for disruptive and off-task behaviors. *Education and Treatment of Children, 33*(1), 23–48.

Schunk, D. H. (1987). Peer models and children's behavioral change. *Review of Educational Research, 57,* 149–174.

Schunk, D., & Rice, J. M. (1993). Strategy fading and progress feedback: Effects on self-efficacy and comprehension among students receiving remedial reading services. *Journal of Special Education, 27,* 257–276.

Schuster J. W., Gast, D. L., Wolery, M., & Guiltinan, S. (1988). The effectiveness of a constant time-delay procedure to teach chained resonses to adolescents with mental retardation. *Journal of Applied Behavior Analysis, 21,* 169–178.

Schuster, J. W., Griffen, A. K., & Wolery, M. (1992). Comparison of simultaneous prompting and constant time delay procedures in teaching sight words to elementary students with moderate mental retardation. *Journal of Behavioral Education, 7,* 305–325.

Schwartz, B. (1982). Reinforcement-induced behavioral stereotypy: How not to teach people to discover rules. *Journal of Experimental Psychology, 111,* 23–59.

Schwartz, I.S., Garfinkle, A.N. & Bauer, J. (1998). The Picture Exchange Communication System: Communicative outcomes for young children with disabilities. *Topics in Early Childhood Special Education, 18,* 144–159.

Schweitzer, J. B., & Sulzer-Azaroff, B. (1988). Self-control: Teaching tolerance for delay in impulsive children. *Journal of the Experimental Analysis of Behavior, 50,* 173–186.

Schweitzer, J. B., & Sulzer-Azaroff, B. (1995). Impulsive choice in boys with attention-deficit hyperactivity disorder: Effects of distracters and time. *Journal of Child Psychology & Psychiatry and Allied Disciplines. 36,* 671–686

Scott, D., Scott, L. M., & Goldwater, B. (1977). A performance improvement program for an international-level track and field athlete. *Journal of Applied Behavior Analysis, 30,* 573–575.

Scotti, J. R., Evans, I. M., Meyer, L. H., & Walker, P. (1991). A meta-analysis of intervention research with problem behavior: Treatment validity and standards of practice. *American Journal of Mental Retardation, 96,* 233–256.

Scruggs, T. E., & Mastropieri, M. A. (2000). The effectiveness of mnemonic instruction for students with learning and behavior problems: An update and research synthesis. *Journal of Behavioral Education, 10,* 163–173.

Seaver, J. L., & Boudrret, J. C. (2014). An evaluation of response prompts for teaching behavior chains. *Journal of Applied Behavior Analysis, 47,* 777–792. doi: 10.1002/jaba.159

Secan, K. E., & Egel, A. L. (1986). The effects of a negative practice procedure on the self-stimulatory behavior of developmentally disabled students. *Education and Treatment of Children, 9,* 30–99.

Seeman, H. (1994). *Preventing classroom discipline problems: A guide for educators (second edition).* Lancaster, PA: Technomic Publishing Co.

Seligman, M. E. P. (1975). *Helplessness: On depression development and death.* San Francisco: Freeman.

Selinski, J. E., Greer, R. D., & Lodhi, S. (1991). A functional analysis of the comprehensive application of behavior analysis to schooling. *Journal of Applied Behavior Analysis, 24,* 107–117.

Sellers, T. R., Valentino, A. L., Landon, T J., & Aiello, S. (2019). Board certified behavior analysts' supervisory practices of trainees: Survey results and recommendation. *Behavior Analysis in Practice, 12,* 536–546. doi: org/10.1007/s40617-019-00367-0

Serketich, W. J., & Dumas, J. E. (1996). The effectiveness of behavioral parent training to modify antisocial behavior in children: A meta-analysis. *Behavior Therapy, 27*(2), 171–186.

Sewell, T.J., Collins, B.C., Hemmeter, M.L., & Schuster, J.W. (1998). Using simultaneous prompting within an activity-based format to teach dressing skills to preschoolers with developmental delay. *Journal of Early Intervention, 21*(2), 132–145.

Sexton, C. W. (1989). Effectiveness of the DISTAR reading I program in developing first graders' language skills. *The Journal of Educational Research, 82,* 289–293.

Shabani, D. B., & Fisher, W. W. (2006). Stimulus fading and differential reinforcement for the treatment of needle phobia in a youth with autism. *Journal of Applied Behavior Analysis, 39,* 449–452.

Shabani, D. B., Katz, R. C., Wilder, D. A., Beauchamp, K., Taylor, C. R., & Fisher, K. J. (2002). Increasing social initiations in children with autism: Effects of a tactile prompt. *Journal of Applied Behavior Analysis, 35,* 79–83.

Shadish, W.R., Cook, D.T. & Campbell, J.M. (2002). Experimental and quasi-experimental designs for generalized causal Inference. Boston, Houghton Mifflin College Division.

Shafer, E. (1993). Teaching topography-based and selection-based verbal behavior to developmentally disabled individuals: Some considerations. *Analysis of Verbal Behavior, 11,* 117–133.

Shahan, T. A., & Sweeney, M. M. (2011). A model of resurgence based on behavioral momentum theory. *Journal of the Experimental Analysis of Behavior, 95,* 91–108. doi: 10.1901/jeab.2011.95-91

Shahrestani, E., Symon, J. B. G., & Campbell, R. (2009, March). *Teaching initiations and generalizing skills: Reaching levels comparable to typical peers.* Poster session presented at the annual conference of the California Association for Behavior Analysis, San Francisco, CA.

Shapiro, E. S., & Klein, R. D. (1980). Self-management of classroom behavior with retarded/disturbed children. *Behavior Modification, 4,* 83–97.

Shapiro, E. S., & Shapiro, S. (1985). Behavioral coaching in the development of skills in track. *Behavior Modification, 9,* 211–224.

Sharan, S. (1980). Cooperative learning in small groups: Recent methods and effects on achievement attitudes and ethnic relations. *Review of Educational Research, 50*, 241–271.

Sharp, R. A., Mudford, O. C., & Elliffe, D. (2015). Represesntativeness of direct observations selected using a work-sampling equation. *Journal of Applied Behavior Analysis, 48*, 153–166. doi: 10.1002/jaba.193

Shavelson, R.J., & Towne, L. (2002). Scientific research in education. Washington, D.C.: National Academy Press.

Shepley, C., Lane, J. D., & Ault, M J. (2019). A review and critical examination of the system of least prompts. *Remedial and Special Education, 40*, 313–327. doi.org/101177/07441932517751213

Sheridan, S. M. (1995). *The tough kid social skills book*. Longmont, Colo.: Sopris West.

Sherrill, J. R., O'Leary, S. G., Albertson-Kelly, J. A., & Kendziora, K. T. (1996). When reprimand consistency may and may not matter. *Behavior Modification, 20*, 226–236.

Shevin, M., & Klein, N. (2004). The importance of choice-making skills for students with severe disabilities. *Research and Practice for Persons with Severe Disabilities, 29*, 161–168.

Shih, I. H., Jai, T. M., Chen, H. S., & Blum, S. (2019). Greetins from Emily! The effects of personalized greeting cards on tipping of hotel room attendants. *International Journal of Contemporary Hospitality Management, 31*, 3058–3076. doi.org/10.1108/ijCHM-05-2018-0398

Shillingsburg, A., Marya, V., Bartlett, B., Thompson, T., & Walters, D. (2019). Teaching children with autism spectrum disorder to report past behavior with the use of a speech-generating device. *The Analysis of Verbal Behavior, 35*(2), 258–269. https://doi.org/10.1007/s40616-019-00112-2

Shillingsburg, M.A., Cariveau, T., Talmadge, B., & Frampton, S. (2017). A preliminary analysis of procedures to teach children with autism to report past behavior. *Analysis of Verbal Behavior*, doe:10.1007/s40616-017-0085-7.

Shillingsburg, M. A., Lomas, J. E., & Bradley, D. (2012). Treatment of vocal stereotypy in an analogue and classroom setting. *Behavioral Interventions, 27*, 151–163. doi: 10.1002/bin.1340

Shimabukuro, S. M., Prater, M. A., Jenkins, A., & Edelen-Smith, P. (1999). The effects of self-monitoring of academic performance on students with learning disabilities and ADD/ADHD. *Education and Treatment of Children, 22*, 398–414.

Shimoff, E., & Catania, A. C. (1995). Using computers to teach behavior analysis. *The Behavior Analyst, 18*, 307–316.

Shimp, C. P. (1966). Probabilistically reinforced choice behavior in pigeons. *Journal of the Experimental Analysis of Behavior, 9*, 443–455.

Shipley-Benamou, R., Lutzker, J. R., & Taubman, M. (2002). Teaching daily living skills to children with autism through instructional video modeling. *Journal of Positive Behavior Interventions, 4*, 165–175, 188.

Shirley, M. J., Iwata, B. A., & Kahng, S. (1999). False positive maintenance of self-injurious behavior by access to tangible reinforcement. *Journal of Applied Behavior Analysis, 32*, 201–204.

Shook, G.L. (2005). An examination of the integrity and future of the behavior analyst certification board® credentials. *Behavior Modification, 29*, 562–574.

Shore, B. A., Babbitt, R. L., Williams, K. E., Coe, D. A., & Snyder, A. (1998). Use of texture fading in the treatment of food selectivity. *Journal of Applied Behavior Analysis, 31*, 621–633.

Shrestha, A., Anderson, A., & Moore, D. (2013). Using point-of-view video modeling and forward chaining to teach a functional self-help skill to a child with autism. *Journal of Behavior Education, 22*, 157–167. http://doi-org.mimas.calstatela.edu/10.1007/s10864-012-9165-x

Shull, R. L., & Grimes, J. A. (2006). Resistance to extinction following variable-interval reinforcement: Reinforcer rate and amount. *Journal of the Experimental Analysis of Behavior, 85*, 23–39.

Shumate, E. D., & Wills, H. P. (2010). Classroom-based functional analysis and intervention for disruptive and off-task behaviors. *Education and Treatment of Children, 33*, 23–48.

Sidener, T.M., Shabani, D.B., & Carr, J.E. (2004). A review of the behavioral evaluation strategy and taxonomy (Best$^R$ software application) *Behavioral Interventions, 19*, 275–285.

Sidman, M. (1953). Avoidance conditioning with brief shock and no exteroceptive warning signal. *Science, 118*, 157–158.

Sidman, M. (1960). *Tactics of scientific research*. New York: Basic Books.

Sidman, M. (1969). Generalized gradients and stimulus control in delayed matching to sample. *Journal of the Experimental Analysis of Behavior, 12*, 745–757.

Sidman, M. (1971). The behavioral analysis of aphasia. *Journal of Psychiatric Research, 8*, 413–422.

Sidman, M. (1977). Teaching some basic prerequisites for reading. In P. Mittler (Ed.), *Research to practice in mental retardation: Vol. 2. Education and training* (pp. 353–360). Baltimore, MD: University Park Press.

Sidman, M. (1986). Functional analysis of emergent verbal classes. In T. Thompson & M. D. Zeiler (Eds.), *Analysis and integration of behavioral units* (pp. 213–245). Hillsdale, NJ. Erlbaum.

Sidman, M. (1989). *Coercion and its fallout*. Boston: Authors Cooperative, Inc.

Sidman, M. (1994). *Equivalence relations and behavior: A research story*. Boston: Authors Cooperative.

Sidman, M. (2000). Equivalence relations and the reinforcement contingency. *Journal of the Experimental Analysis of Behavior, 74*, 127–146.

Sidman, M. (2001). *Coercion and its fallout. Revised edition*. Boston: Authors Cooperative Inc.

Sidman, M. (2006). The distinction between positive and negative reinforcement: Some additional considerations. *The Behavior Analyst, 29*, 135–139.

Sidman, M., & Cresson, O. Jr. (1973). Reading and cross-modal transfer of stimulus equivalences in severe retardation. *American Journal of Mental Deficiency, 77*, 513–523.

Sidman, M., Cresson, O. Jr., & Willson-Morris, M. (1974). Acquisition of matching to sample via mediated transfer. *Journal of the Experimental Analysis of Behavior, 22*, 261–273.

Sidman, M., Kirk, B., & Willson-Morris, M. (1985). Six-member stimulus classes generated by conditional-discrimination procedures. *Journal of the Experimental Analysis of Behavior, 43*, 21–42.

Sidman, M., Rauzin, R., Lazar, R., Cunnigham, S., Tailby, W., & Carngan, P. (1982). A search for symmetry in the conditional discriminations of rhesus monkeys, baboons, and children. *Journal of the Experimental Analysis of Behavior, 37*, 23–44.

Sidman, M., & Stoddard, L. T. (1967). The effectiveness of fading in programming a simultaneous form discrimination for retarded children. *Journal of the Experimental Analysis of Behavior, 10*, 3–16.

Sidman, M., & Tailby, W. (1982). Conditional discrimination vs. matching to sample: An expansion of the testing paradigm. *Journal of the Experimental Analysis of Behavior, 37*, 5–22.

Sidman, M., Wynne, C., K., Maguire, R. W., & Barnes, T. (1989). Functional classes and equivalence relations. *Journal of the Experimental Analysis of Behavior, 52*, 261–274.

Siegel, G. M., Lenske, J., & Broen, P. (1969). Suppression of normal speech disfluencies through response cost. *Journal of Applied Behavior Analysis, 2*, 265–276.

Sigafoos, J. (1998). Choice making and personal selection strategies. In J. K. Luiselli, & M. J. Cameron (Eds.), *Antecedent control: Innovative approaches to behavioral support* (pp. 187–221). Baltimore: Brookes.

Sigafoos, J., Couzens, D., Pennell, D., Shaw, D., & Dudfield, G. (1995). Discrimination of picture requests for missing items among young children with developmental disabilities. *Journal of Behavioral Education, 5*, 295–317.

Sigafoos, J., Kerr, M., Roberts, D., & Couzens, D. (1994). Increasing opportunities for requesting in classrooms serving children with developmental disabilities. *Journal of Autism and Developmental Disorders, 24*, 631–645.

Silbaugh, B. C., & Falcomata, T. S. (2019). Effects of a lag schedule with progressive time delay on sign mand variability in a boy with autism. *Behavior Analysis in Practice, 12*, 124–132. doi.org/10.1007/s40617-018-00273-x

Silbaugh, B. C., Falcomata, T. S., & Ferguson, R. H. (2017). Effects of a lag schedule of reinforcement with progressive time delay on topographical mand variability in children with autism. *Developmental Neurorehabilitation*. Advance online publication. https://doi.org/10.1080/17518423.2017.1369190.

Simon, S. J., Ayllon, T., & Milan, M. A. (1982). Behavioral compensation: Contrast-like effects in the classroom. *Behavior Modification, 6*, 407–420.

Simons, L.G., Burt, C.H., & Simons, R.L. (2008). A test of explanations for the effect of harsh parenting on the perpetration of dating violence and sexual coercion among college males. *Violence and Victims, 23*(1) 66–82.

Simonsen, B., MacSuga, A. S., Fallon, L. M., & Sugai, G. (2013). The effects of self-monitoring on teachers' use of specific praise. *Journal of Positive Behavior Interventions, 15*, 5–15.

Simpson, C. (2006). Active prompting to decrease cell phone use and increase seat belt use while driving. *Journal of Applied Behavior Analysis, 39*, 341–349.

Singer, G. S., & Irvin, L. D. (1987). Human rights review of intrusive behavioral treatments for students with severe handicaps. *Exceptional Children, 54*, 46–52.

Singer-Dudek, J., & Oblak, M. (2013). Peer presence and the emergence of conditional reinforcement from observation. *Journal of Applied Behavior Analysis, 46*, 592–602.

Singer-Dudek, J., Oblak, M., & Greer, R. D. (2011). Establishing Books as Conditioned Reinforcers for Preschool Children as a Function of an Observational Intervention. *Journal of Applied Behavior Analysis, 44*(3), 421–434. https://doi-org.mimas.calstatela.edu/10.1901/jaba.2011.44-421

Singh, N. N. (1980). The effects of facial screening on infant self-injury. *Journal of Behavior Therapy and Experimental Psychiatry, 11*, 131–134.

Singh, N. N. (1987). Overcorrection of oral reading errors. A comparison of individual and group-training formats. *Behavior Modification, 11*, 165–181.

Singh, N. N., & Millichamp, C. J. (1987). Independent and social play among profoundly mentally retarded adults: Training, maintenance, generalization, and long-term follow-up. *Journal of Applied Behavior Analysis, 20, 23–34.*

Singh, N. N., & Singh, J. (1986). Increasing oral reading proficiency. A comparative analysis of drill and positive practice overcorrection procedures. *Behavior Modification, 10*, 115–130.

Singh, N. N., & Solman, R. T. (1990). A stimulus control analysis of the picture-word problem in children who are mentally retarded: The blocking effect. *Journal of Applied Behavior Analysis, 23*, 525–532.

Singh, N. N., Watson, J. E., & Winton, A. S. W. (1986). Treating self-injury: Water mist spray versus facial screening or forced arm exercise. *Journal of Applied Behavior Analysis, 19*, 403–410.

Singh, N. N., Winton, A. S., & Dawson, J. J. (1982). The suppression of antisocial behavior by facial screening using multiple baseline and alaternating treatment design. *Behavior Therapy, 13*, 511–520.

Skinner, B.F. (1938). *The behavior of organisms.* New York: Appleton-Century-Crofts.

Skinner, B. F. (1945). The operational analysis of psychological terms. *Psychological Review, 52*, 270–277.

Skinner, B.F. (1953). *Science and human behavior.* New York: The Macmillan Company.

Skinner, B. F. (1957). *Verbal behavior.* New York: Appleton-Century-Crofts.

Skinner, B. F. (1958a). Teaching machines. *Science, 128*, 969–977.

Skinner, B.F. (1958b). Reinforcement today. *American Psychologist, 13*, 94–99.

Skinner, B. F. (1969). An operant analysis of problem solving. In B. F. Skinner, *Contingencies of reinforcement* (pp. 133–157). New York: Appleton-Century-Crofts.

Skinner, B. F. (1971). *Beyond freedom and dignity.* New York: Knopf.

Skinner, B. F. (1974). *About behaviorism.* New York: Knoph.

Skinner, B. F., & Krakower, S. A. (1968). *Handwritting with write and see.* Chicago: Lyons & Carnahan.

Skinner, B. F.. (1981). Selection by consequences. *Science, 213*, 501–504.

Skinner, C. (2002). An empirical analysis of interspersal research: Evidence, implications and the application of the discrete task completion hypothesis. *Journal of School Psychology, 40*, 347–368.

Skinner, C. H., Cashwell, C. S., & Dunn, M. S. (1996). Independent and interdependent group contingencies: Smoothing the rough waters. *Special Services in the Schools, 12*(1/2), 61–78.

Skinner, C. H., Cashwell, T. H., & Skinner, A. L. (2000). Increasing tootling: The effects of a peer-monitored group contingency program on students' reports of peers' prosocial behaviors. *Psychology in the Schools, 37*, 263–270.

Skinner, C. H., Skinner, A. L., & Armstrong, K. J. (2000). Analysis of a client-staff-development shaping program designed to enhance reading persistence in an adult diagnosed with schizophrenia. *Psychiatric Rehabilitation Journal, 24*, 52–58.

Skinner, C. H., Williams, R.L., & Neddenriep, C. E. (2004). Using interdependent group-oriented reinforcement to enhance academic performance in general education classrooms. *School Psychology Review, 3*, 383–397.

Slavin, R. E. (1983). When does cooperative learning increase student achievement? *Psychological Bulletin, 94*, 429–445.

Slavin, R. E. (1991). Cooperative learning and group contingencies. *Journal of Behavioral Education, 1*, 105–115.

Slifer, K. J., Koontz, K. L., & Cataldo, M. F. (2002). Operant-contingency-based preparation of children for functional magnetic resonance imaging. *Journal of Applied Behavior Analysis, 35*, 191–194.

Slocum S. K., Grauerholz-Fisher, E., Peters, K. P., & Volymer, T. R., (2018). A multi-component approach to thinning reinforcer delivery during noncontingent reinforcement schedules. *Journal of Applied Behavior Analysis, 51*, 61–69. doi: 10.1002/jaba.437

Slocum, S. K., Vollmer, T. R., Donaldson, J. M. (2019). Effects of delayed time-out on problem behavior of preschool children. *Journal of Applied Behavior Analysis, 52*, 994–1004. doi: 10.1002/jaba.640

Slocum, T. A. (2003). Evaluation of direct instruction implementations. *Journal of Direct Instruction, 3*, 111–137.

Sloman, K. N., Reyes, J. R., & Vollmer, T. R. (2016). Effects of an independent group contingency special activity program on inappropriate behavior in a residential setting. *Behavioral Interventions, 29*, 186–199. doi: 10.1002/bin.1383.

Smith, B. W., & Sugai, G. (2000). A self-management functional assessment-based behavior support plan for a middle school student with EBD. *Journal of Positive Behavior Interventions, 2*, 208–217.

Smith, D. E. (1981). Is isolation room time-out a punisher? *Behavioral Disorders, 6*, 247–256.

Smith, L. K. C., & Fowler, S. A. (1984). Positive peer pressure: The effects of peer monitoring on children's disruptive behavior. *Journal of Applied Behavior Analysis, 17*, 213–227.

Smith, R. B., Russo, L., & Le, D. D. (1999). Distinguishing between extinction and punishment effects of response blocking: A replication. *Journal of Applied Behavior Analysis, 32*, 367–370.

Smith, R. G., Churchill, R. M. (2002). Identification of environmental determinants of behavior disorders through functional analysis of precursor behaviors. *Journal of Applied Behavior Analysis, 35*, 125–136.

Smith, R. G., & Iwata, B. A. (1997). Antecedent influences on behavior disorders. *Journal of Applied Behavior Analysis, 30*, 343–375.

Smith, R. G., Iwata, B. A., Goh, H., & Shore, B. A. (1995). Analysis of establishing operations for self-injury maintained by escape. *Journal of Applied Behavior Analysis, 28*, 515–535.

Smith, R., Michael, J., & Sundberg, M. L. (1996). Automatic reinforcement and automatic punishment in infant vocal behavior. *The Analysis of Verbal Behavior, 13*, 39–48.

Smith, S., & Farrell, D. (1993). Level system use in special education: Classroom intervention with prima facie appeal. *Behavioral Disorders, 18*, 251–264.

Smith, T. (2001). Discrete trial training in the treatment of autism. *Focus on Autism and Other Developmental disabilities, 16*, 86–92.

Smokowski, P. R., Mann, E. A., Reynolds, A. J., & Fraser, M. W. (2004). Childhood risk and protective factors and late adolescent in inner city minority youth. *Children and Youth Services Review, 26*, 63–91.

Snell, M. E. (1982). Teaching bedmaking to severely retarded adults through time delay. *Analysis of Intervention in Developmental Disabilities, 2*, 139–155.

Snyder, G. (1989). "How do you reinforce a neurosurgeon?" Performance managing the medical profession. *Performance Management Magazine, 7*, 17–25.

Snyder, G. (2013). Morningside academy: a learning guarantee. *Performance Management Magazine*.

Socolar, R. R. S., & Stein, R. E. K. (1996). Maternal discipline of young children: Context, belief, and practice. *Journal of Developmental and Behavioral Pediatrics, 17*(1), 1–8.

Solnick, J.V., & Baer, D.M. (1984). Using multiple exemplars for teaching number-numeral correspondence: Some structural aspects. *Analysis and intervention in Developmental Disabilities, 4*, 47–63.

Solnick, J. V., Rincover, A., & Peterson, C. R. (1977). Some determinates of the reinforcing and punishing effects of timeout. *Journal of Applied Behavior Analysis, 10*, 415–424.

Solomon, R. L. (1964). Punishment. *American Psychologist, 19*, 239–253.

Solomon, R. W., & Wahler, R. G. (1973). Peer reinforcement control of classroom problem behavior. *Journal of Applied Behavior Analysis, 6*, 49–56.

Song, H., & Schwarz, N. (2008). If it's hard to read, it's hard to do: Processing fluency affects effort prediction and motivation. *Psychological Science: Research, Theory, & Application in Psychology and Related Sciences, 19*, 986–988.

Soucy, D. S., Pardi, J. R., Kaye, A. D., & Sulzer-Azaroff, B. (2016). Promoting cooperation with routine dental procedures among children with autism. Unpublished manuscript.

Sparrow, S. S., Cicchetti, D. V., & Saulnier, C, (2016). *Vineland Adaptive Behavior Scales*, Third Edition (Vineland-3). San Antonio, TX: Pearson.

Speidel, G. R., & Tharp, R. G. (1980). What does self-reinforcement reinforce: An empirical analysis of the contingencies in self-determined reinforcement. *Child Behavior Therapy, 2*, 1–22.

Speltz, M. L., Shimamura, J. W., & McReynolds, W. T. (1982). Procedural variations in group contingencies: Effects on children's academic and social behaviors. *Journal of Applied Behavior Analysis, 15*, 533–544.

Spieler, C., & Miltengerger, R. (2017). Using awareness training to decrease nervous habits during public speaking. *Journal of Applied Behavior Analysis, 50*, 38–47. doi: 10.1002/jaba.362.

Spooner, F., Weber, L. H., & Spooner, D. (1983). The effects of backward chaining and total task presentation in the acquisition of complex tasks by severely retarded adolescents and adults. *Education and Treatment of Children, 6*, 401–420.

Spradlin, J. E., & Dixon, M. H. (1976). Establishing conditional discriminations without direct training. *American Journal of Mental Deficiency, 80*, 555–561.

Sprague, J. R., & Horner, R. H. (1992). Covariation within functional response classes: implications for treatment of severe problem behavior. *Journal of Applied Behavior Analysis, 25*, 735–745.

Sprague, J., Sugai, G., & Walker, H. (1998). Antisocial behavior in schools. In H. Watson & F. Gresham (Eds.), *Handbook of child behavior therapy* (pp. 451–474). New York: Plenum Press.

Sprague, J., Walker, H., Golly, A., White, K., Myers, D., & Shannon, T. (2001). Translating research into effective practice: The effects of a universal staff and student intervention on indicators of discipline and school safety. *Education and Treatment of Children, 24*, 495–511.

Springer, C. R., & Pear, J. J. (2008). Performance measures in courses using computer-aided personalized system of instruction. *Computers & Education, 51*, 829–835.

Squires, J., Wilder, D. A., Fixsen, A., Hess, E., Rost, K., Curran, R., & Zonneveld, K. (2007). The effects of task clarification, visual prompts, and graphic feedback on customer greeting and up-selling in a restaurant. *Journal of Organizational Behavior Management, 27*(3), 1–13.

Staddon, J. (2001). *The new behaviorism: Mind, mechanism, and society*. Philadelphia, PA: Psychology Press.

Stage, S. A., Cheney, D., Walker, B., & LaRocque, M. (2002). A preliminary discriminant and convergent validity study of the teacher functional behavioral assessment checklist. *School Psychology Review, 31*, 71–93.

Staley, M. J. (2002). An investigation of social-story effectiveness using reversal and multiple-baseline designs (Doctoral Dissertation, University of Kansas). *Dissertation Abstracts International, 62*, 4770.

Stamps, L.W. (1973). The effect of intervention techniques on children's fear of failure behavior. *Journal of Genetic Psychology, 123*, 85–89.

Stark, L. J., Allen, K. D., Hurst, M., Nash, D. A., Rigney, B., & Stokes, T. F. (1989). Distraction: Its utilization and efficacy with children undergoing dental treatment. *Journal of Applied Behavior Analysis, 22*, 297–307.

Staubitz, J. L., Lloyd, B. P., & Reed, D. D. (2020). Effects of self-control training for elementary students with emotional and behavioral disorders. *Journal of Applied Behavior Analysis, 53*, 857–874. doi: 10.1002/jaba.634.

Statland, E., Zander, A., & Natsoulas, T. (1961). The generalization of interpersonal similarity. *Journal of Abnormal and Social Psychology, 62*, 250–256.

Stauch, T. A., Plavnick, J. B., Sandra, S., & Gallagher, A. C. (2018). Teaching social perception skills to adolescents with autism and intellectual disabilities using video-based group instruction. *Journal of Applied Behavior Analysis, 51*, 647–666. doi: 10.1002/jaba.473

Stebbins, W. C., & Lanson, R. N. (1962). Response latency as a function of reinforcement schedule. *Journal of the Experimental Analysis of Behavior, 5*, 299–304.

Steed, S.E., & Lutzker, J.R. (1997). Using picture prompts to teach an adult with developmental disabilities to independently complete vocational tasks. *Journal of Developmental and Physical Disabilities, 9*(2) 117–133.

Steege, M. W., Wacker, D. P., & McMahon, C. M. (1987). Evaluation of the effectiveness and efficiency of two stimulus prompt strategies with severely handicapped students. *Journal of Applied Behavior Analysis, 20*, 293–299.

Steinhilber, J., & Johnson, C. (2007). The effects of brief and extended stimulus availability on preference. *Journal of Applied Behavior Analysis, 40*, 767–772.

Stenhoff, D. M., Davey, B. J., & Lignugaris/Kraft, B. (2008). The effects of choice on assignment completion and percent correct by a high school student. *Education and Treatment of Children, 31*, 203–211.

Stephens, C. E., Pear, J. J., Wray, L. D., & Jackson, G. C. (1975). Some effects of reinforcement schedules in teaching picture names to retarded children. *Journal of Applied Behavior Analysis, 8*, 435–447.

Stephenson, A., McDonough, S. M., Murphy, M.S., Nugent, C. D., & Mair, J. L. (2017). Using computer, mobile and wearable technology enhanced interventions to reduce sedentary behavior: a systematic review and meta-analysis. *International Journal of Behavioral Nutrition and Physical Acctivity, 12*, 105. http://doi.org/10.1186/s12966-017-0561-4

Sterling, R, Barbetta, P. M., Heward, W. L., & Heron, T.E. (1997). A comparison of active student response and on-task instruction on the acquisition and maintenance of health facts by students with learning disabilities. *Journal of Behavioral Education, 7*, 151–166.

Sterling-Turner, H. E., Watson, T. S., & Moore, J. W. (2002). The effects of direct training and treatment integrity on treatment outcomes in school consultation. *School Psychology Quarterly, 17*, 47–77.

Sterling-Turner, H. E., Watson, T. S., Wildmon, M., Watkins, C., & Little, E. (2001). Investigating the relationship between training type and treatment integrity. *School Psychology Quarterly, 16*, 56–67.

Stevenson, H. C., & Fantuzzo, J. R. (1984). Application of the "Generalization Map" to a self-control intervention with school-aged children. *Journal of Applied Behavior Analysis, 17*, 203–212.

Stewart, C. A., & Singh, N. N. (1986). Overcorrection of spelling deficits in mentally retarded persons. *Behavior Modification, 10*, 355–365.

Stewart, N. R. (1969). Exploring and processing information about educational and vocational opportunities in groups. In J. D.. Krumboltz & C. E. Thoresen (Ed.), *Behavioral counseling cases and techniques* (pp. 213–234). New York: Holt, Rinehart & Winston.

Stewart, P.W., Sargent, D.M., Reihman, J.. Gump. B.B., Lonky, T.D., Hicks, H. & Pagano, J. (2006). Response inhibition during Differential Reinforcement of Low Rates (DRL) schedules may be sensitive to low-level polychlorinated biphenyl, methylmercury, and lead exposure in children. *Environmental Health Perspectives, 114*(12) 1923–1929.

Stocco, C. S., Thompson, R. H., Hart, J.M., & Soriano, H. L. (2017). Improving the interview skills of college students using behavioral skills training. *Journal of Applied Behavior Analysis, 50,* 495–510. doi: 10.1002/jaba.385

Stokes, J. V., Cameron, J. J., Dorsey, M. F., & Fleming, E. (2004). Task analysis, correspondence training, and general case instruction for teaching personal hygiene skills. *Behavioral Interventions, 19,* 121–135.

Stokes, T. F., & Baer, D. M. (1977). An implicit technology of generalization. *Journal of Applied Behavior Analysis, 10,* 349–367.

Stokes, T. F., & Kennedy, S. H. (1980). Reducing child uncooperative behavior during dental treatment through modeling and reinforcement. *Journal of Applied Behavior Analysis, 13,* 41–49.

Stokes, T. F., & Osnes, P. G. (1989). An operant pursuit of generalization. *Behavior Therapy, 20,* 337–355.

Stone, W. L., Ousley, O. Y., & Littleford, C. D. (1997). Motor imitation in young children with autism: What's the object? *Journal of Abnormal Child Psychology, 25,* 475–485.

Stoneman, K. G., & Dickinson, A. M. (1989). Individual performance as a function of group contingencies and group size. *Journal of Organizational Behavior Management, 10*(1), 131–150.

Stoops, W. (2008). Reinforcing effects of stimulants in humans: Sensitivity of progressive-ratio schedules. *Experimental and Clinical Psychopharmacology, 16,* 503–512.

Storey, c., McDowell, C., & Leslie, J. C., (2017). Evaluating the efficacy of the Headsprout©reading program with children who have spent time in care. *Behavioral Interventions, 32,* 285–293. doi: 10.1002/bin.1476

Stouthamer-Loeber, M., & Peters, R. D. (1984). A prior classification system of observation data: The eye of the beholder. *Behavioral Assessment, 6,* 275–282.

Strain, P. S. (1981). Modification of sociometric status and social interactions with mainstreamed mild developmentally disabled children. *Analysis and Intervention in Developmental Disabilities, 1,* 157–169.

Strain, P. S., Cooke, T. P., & Apolloni, T. (1976). *Teaching exceptional children: Assessing and modifying social behavior.* New York: Academic.

Strain, P.S., Kerr, M.M., & Ragland, E.U. (1981). Effects of peer-mediated social initiations and prompting/reinforcement procedures on the social behavior of autistic children. *Journal of Autism and Developmental Disorders. 9*(1), 41–54.

Strain, P. S., & Schwartz, I. (2001). ABA and the development of meaningful social relations for young children with autism. *Focus on Autism and Other Developmental Disabilities, 16,* 120–128.

Strand-Cary, M., & Klahr, D. (2008). Developing elementary science skills: Instructional effectiveness and path independence. *Cognitive Development, 23,* 488–511.

Striefel, S., Bryan, K. S., & Aikins, D. A. (1974) Transfer of stimulus control from motor to verbal stimuli. *Jounal of Applied Behavior Analysis 7*(1), 123–135.

Striefel, S., & Owens, C. R. (1980). Transfer of stimulus control procedures: Applications to language acquisition training with the developmentally handicapped. *Behavior Research of Severe Developmental Disabilities, 1,* 307–331.

Striefel, S., & Wetherby, B. (1973). Instruction-following behavior of a retarded child and its controlling stimuli. *Journal of Applied Behavior Analysis, 6,* 663–670.

Stromer, R., Mackay, H. A., McVay, A. A., & Fowler, T. (1998). Written lists as mediating stimuli in the matching-to-sample performances of individuals with mental retardation. *Journal of Applied Behavior Analysis, 31,* 1–19.

Stromer, R., Mackay, H. A., & Stoddard, L. T. (1992). Classroom applications of stimulus equivalence technology. *Journal of Behavioral Education, 2,* 225–256.

Stromer, R., McComas, J., & Rehfeldt, R. A. (2000). Designing interventions that include delayed reinforcement: Implications of recent laboratory research. *Journal of Applied Behavior Analysis, 33,* 359–371.

Stuesser, H. A, Roscoe, E. M. (2020). An evaluation of differential reinforcement with stimulus fading an intervention for medical compliance. *Journal of Applied Behavior Analysis, 53,* 1606–1621. doi: 10.1002/jaba.685

Sugai, G., & Horner, R. H. (1999). Discipline and behavioral support: Preferred processes and practices. *Effective School Practices, 17*(4), 10–22.

Sugai, G., & Horner, R. R. (2006). A promising approach for expanding and sustaining school-wide positive behavior support. *School Psychology Review, 35,* 245–259.

Sugai, G., Horner, R. H., Dunlap, G., Hineman, M., Lewis, T. J., Nelson, C. M., et al. (2000). Applying positive behavior support and functional behavioral assessment in schools. *Journal of Positive Behavioral Intervention, 2,* 131–143.

Sullivan, W. E., Sainni, V., DeRosa, N. M., Craig, A. R., Ringdahl, J. E., & Roane, H. S. (2020). Measurement of non-targeted problem behavior during investigations of resurgence. *Journal of Applied Behavior Analysis, 53,* 249–264. doi: 10.1002/jaba.589

Sulzer-Azaroff, B. (1978). Behavioral ecology and accident prevention. *Journal of Organizational Behavior Management, 2,* 11–44.

Sulzer-Azaroff, B. (1997). Why should I talk to my baby? A review of meaningful differences in the everyday experience of young American children by Hart and Risley. *Journal of Applied Behavior Analysis, 30,* 599–600.

Sulzer-Azaroff, B. (1998, March). Behavioral safety programs reduce workplace injuries. *Safety First.* Greater New York Safety Council, 2, 1.

Sulzer-Azaroff, B. (2000). Of eagles and worms: Changing behavior in a complex world. *Journal of Organizational Behavior Management, 20*(3/4), 139–163.

Sulzer-Azaroff, B. (2004). The shaping of behaviorists: B.F. Skinner's influential paper on teaching machines, *European Journal of Behavior Analysis, 2*(5), 129–135.

Sulzer-Azaroff, B. (2007). *Effective performance management and support systems: We are all managers.* Unpublished paper.

Sulzer-Azaroff, B., & Associates (2008). *Applying behavior analysis across the autism spectrum: A field guide for practitioners.* Cornwall-on-Hudson: Sloane Publishing.

Sulzer-Azaroff, B., Dyer, K., Dupont, S. & Soucy, D. (2012). *Applying behavior* analysis across the autism spectrum: A field guide for new practitioners, 2nd. Ed., Cornwall-on-Hudson, NY: Sloan Pubishing.

Sulzer-Azaroff, B., & Austin, J. (2000, July). Does behavior-based safety work to reduce injuries? A survey of the evidence. *Professional Safety*, 19–24.

Sulzer-Azaroff, B., & Fellner, D. (1984). Searching for performance targets in the behavior analysis of occupational safety: An assessment strategy. *Journal of Organizational Behavior Management, 6*, 53-65.

Sulzer-Azaroff, B., Fleming, R., Tupa, M., Bass, R., & Hamad, C. (2008). Choosing objectives for a distance learning behavioral intervention in autism curriculum. *Focus on Autism and Other Developmental Disabilities, 23*(1), 29–36.

Sulzer-Azaroff, B., & Harshbarger, D. (1995) Putting fear to flight: While enhancing quality of performance. *Quality Progress, 28*(12), 61–65.

Sulzer-Azaroff, B., Hoffman, A., Horton, C., Bondy, A. S., & Frost, L.A.. (2009). The Picture Exchange Communication System: What do the data say? *Focus on Autism and Other Developmental Disabilities, 24*, 89–103.

Sulzer-Azaroff, B., Loafman, B., Merante, R. J., & Hlavacek, A. C. (1990). Improving occupational safety in a large industrial plant: A systematic replication. *Journal of Organizational Behavior Management, 11*, 99–120.

Sulzer-Azaroff, B., & Mayer, G. R. (1986). *Achieving educational excellence using behavioral strategies.* New York: Holt, Rinehart & Winston.

Sulzer-Azaroff, B., & Mayer, G. R. (1991). *Behavior analysis for lasting change.* Fort Worth: Harcourt Brace College Publishers.

Sulzer-Azaroff, B., & Mayer, G. R. (1994). *Achieving educational excellence: Behavior analysis of achieving classroom and schoolwide behavior change.* San Marcos, CA.: Western Image.

Sulzer-Azaroff, B., Pollack, M.J., Hamad, C., & Howley, T. (1998) Promoting widespread, durable service quality via interlocking contingencies. *Research in Developmental Disabilities, 19*, 39–61.

Sulzer-Azaroff, B., & Reese, E. P. (1982). *Applying behavior analysis: A program for developing professional competence.* New York: Holt, Rinehart & Winston.

Sulzer-Azaroff, B., Thaw, J., & Thomas, C. (1975). Behavioral competencies for the evaluation of behavior modifiers. In S. Wood (Ed.), *Issues in evaluating behavior modification* (pp. 47–98). Champaign, IL: Research Press.

Sulzer, B., Hunt, S., Ashby, E., Koniarski, C., & Krams, M. (1971). Increasing rate and percentage correct in reading and spelling in a class of slow readers by means of a token system. In E. A. Ramp & B. L. Hopkins (Eds.), *New directions in education: Behavior analysis* (pp. 5–28). Lawrence: University of Kansas, Department of Human Development.

Sulzer, E. S. (1962). Reinforcement and the therapeutic contract. *Journal of Counseling Psychology, 9*, 271–276.

Summers, J., Tarbox, J., Findel-Pyles, R. S., Wilke, A. E., Bergstrom, R., & Williams, W. L. (2011). Teaching two household safety skills to children with autism. *Research in Autism Spectrum Disorders, 5*, 629–632. doi: 10.1016/j.rasd.2010.07.008

Sundberg, M. L. (1983). Language. In J. L. Matson & S. E. Breuning (Eds.), *Assessing the mentally retarded* (pp. 285–310). New York, N. Y.: Grune and Stratton.

Sundberg, M. L. (1993a). The application of establishing operations. *The Behavior Analyst, 16*, 211–214.

Sundberg, M. L. (1993b). Selecting a response form for nonverbal persons: Facilitated communication, pointing system, or sign language? *Analysis of Verbal Behavior, 11*, 99–116.

Sundberg, M. L. (2008). *VB-MAPP: Verbal behavior mile-stones assessment and placement program.* Concord, CA: AVB Press.

Sundberg, M. L., Endicott, K., & Eigenheer, P. (2000). Using intraverbal prompts to establish tacts for children with autism. *The Analysis of Verbal Behavior, 17*, 89–104.

Sundberg, M. L., Loeb, M., Hale, L., & Eigenheer, P. (2002). Contriving establishing operations to teach mands for information. *The Analysis of Verbal Behavior, 18*, 14–28.

Sundberg, M. L., & Michael, J. (2001). The benefits of Skinner's analysis of verbal behavior for children with autism. *Behavior Modification, 25*, 698–724.

Sundberg, M. L., Michael, J., Partington, J. W., & Sundberg, C. A. (1996). The role of automatic reinforcement in early language acquisition. *The Analysis of Verbal Behavior, 13*, 21–37.

Sundberg, M. L., & Partington, J. W. (1998). *Teaching language to children with autism or other developmental disabilities.* Pleasant Hill, CA: Behavior Analysts, Inc.

Sundberg, M. L., & Partington, J. W. (1996). The need for both discrete trial and natural environment training for children with autism. In P. M. Ghezzi, W. L. Williams, & J. E. Carr (Eds.), *Autism: Behavior analytic perspectives* (pp. 139–156). Reno, Nev: Context Press.

Sundberg, M. L., San Juan, B., Dawdy, M., & Arguelles, M. (1990). The acquisition of tacts, mands, and intraverbals by individuals with traumatic brain injury. *The Analysis of Verbal Behavior, 13*, 1–19.

Suzuki, K., Kutsuzawa, T., Takita, K., Ito, M., Sakamoto, T., Hirayama, A., et al. (1987). Clinico-epidemiologic study of stroke in Akita, Japan. *Stroke, 18*, 402–406.

Swaggart, B. L., Gagnon, E., Bock, S. J., Earles, T. L., et al. (1995). Using social stories to teach social and behavioral skills to children with autism. *Focus on Autism and Other Developmental Disabilities, 10*, 1–16.

Swain, R., Lane, J. D., & Gast, D. L. (2015). Comparison of constant time delay and simultaneous prompting procedures: Teaching functional sight words to students with intellectual disabilities and autism spectrum disorder. *Journal of Behavioral Education, 24*, 210–229. doi: 10.1007/310664-014-9209-5

Sweeney, E., Barton, E. E., & Ledford, J. R. (2018). Using progressive time delay to increase levels of peer imitation during sculpting play. *Journal of Autism and Developmental Disorders, 48*, doi.org/10.1007/s10803-018-3638-2

Sweigart, C. A., Collins, L. W., Evanovich, L. L., & Cook, S. C. (2016). An evaluation of the evidence base for performance feedback to improve teacher praise using CEC's quality indicators. *Education and Treatment of Children, 39*, 419–444.

Sweigart, C. A., Landrum, T. J., & Pennington, R. C. (2015). The effects of real-time visual performance feedback on teacher feedback: A preliminary investigation. *Education and Treatment of Children, 38,* 429–450.

Swiezy, N. B., Matson, J.L., & Box, P. (1992). The Good Behavior Game: A Token Reinforcement System for Preschoolers. *Child and Family Behavior Therapy, 14*(3), 21–32.

Switzer, E. B., Deal, T. E., & Bailey, J. S. (1977). The reduction of staling in second graders using a group contingency. *Journal of Applied Behavior Analysis, 10,* 267–272.

Sy, J. R., Donaldson, J. M., Vollmer, T. R., & Pizarro, E. (2014). An evaluation of factors that influience children"s instruction following. *Journal of Applied Behavior Analysis, 47,* 101–112.

Sy, J. R., & Vollmer, T. R. (2012). Discrimination acquisition in children with developmental disabilities under immediate and delayed reinforcement. *Journal of Applied Behavior Analysis, 45,* 667–684.

Taber, T. A., Lambright, N., & Luiselli, J. K. (2017). Video modeling training effects on types of attention delivered by educational care-providers. *Behavior Analysis in Practice, 10,* 189–194.

Tai, S. S., & Miltenberger, R. G. (2017). Evaluating behavioral skills training to teach safe tackling skills to youth football players. *Journal of Applied Behavior Analysis, 50,* 849–855. doi: 10.1002/jaba.412

Tailby, R. & Haslam, C. (2003). An investigation of errorless learning in memory-impaired patients: improve the technique and clarifying the theory. *Neuropsychologia, 41,* 1230-1240.

Tarbox, J., Madrid, W., Aguilar, B., Jacobo, W., & Schiff, A. (2009). Use of chaining to increase complexity of echoics in children with autism. *Journal of Applied Behavior Analysis, 42,* 901–906.

Tarbox, J., & Hayes, L.P. (2005). Verbal behavior and behavioral contrast in human subjects. *Psychological Record, 55,* 419–437.

Tarbox, J., Wallace, M. D., & Tarbox, R. S. F. (2002). Successful generalized parent training and failed schedule thinning of response blocking for automatically maintained object mouthing. *Behavioral Interventions, 17,* 169–178.

Tarbox, J., Wallace, M D., Tarbox, R. S. F., Landaburn, H. J., & Williams, W. L. (2004). Functional analysis and treatment of low rate problem behavior in individuals with developmental disabilities. *Behavior Interventions, 19,* 187–204. doi: 10.1002/bin.158

Tarbox, R. S. F., Ghezzi, P. M., & Wilson, G. (2006). The effects of token reinforcement on attending in a young child with autism. *Behavioral Interventions, 21,* 155–164. doi:org/10.1002/bin.213

Tarbox, R. S. F., & Najdowski, A. C. (2008). Discrete trial training as a teaching paradigm. In J. K. Luiselli, D. C. Russo, W. P. Christian, & S. M. Wilczynski (Eds.), *Effective practices for children with autism* (pp. 181–194). NY: Oxford.

Tarbox, R. S. F., Tarbox, J., Ghezzi, P. M., Wallace, M. D., & Yoo, J. H. (2007). The effects of blocking mouthing of leisure items on their effectiveness as reinforcers. *Journal of Applied Behavior Analysis, 40,* 761–765.

Tarbox, R. S. F., Wallace, M. D., Penrod, B., & Tarbox, J. (2007). Effects of three-step prompting on compliance with caregiver requests. *Journal of Applied Behavior Analysis, 40,* 703–706.

Tarbox, R. S. F., Williams, W. L., Friman, P. C. (2004). Extended diaper wearing: Effects on continence in and out of the diaper. *Journal of Applied Behavior Analysis, 37,* 97–100.

Tasky, K. K., Rudrud, E. H., Schulze, K. A., & Rapp, J. T. (2008). Using choice to increase on-task behavior in individual with traumatic brain injury. *Journal of Applied Behavior Analysis, 41,* 261–265.

Taylor, B. A., Hughes, C. E., Richards, E., Hoch, H., & Coello, A. R. (2004). Teaching teenagers with autism to seek assistance when lost. *Journal of Applied Behavior Analysis, 37,* 79–82.

Taylor, B. A., & Levin, L. (1998). Teaching a student with autism to make verbal initiations: Effects of a "tactile prompt." *Journal of Applied Behavior Analysis, 31,* 651–654.

Taylor, C. A., Manganello, J. A., Lee, S. J., & Rice J. C. (2010). Mothers' spanking of 3–year-old children and subsequent risk of children's aggressive behavior. *Pediatrics, 125,* 1057–1065.

Taylor, I., & O'Reilly, M. F. (1997). Toward a functional analysis of private verbal self-regulation. *Journal of Applied Behavior Analysis, 30,* 43–58.

Taylor, J., & Miller, M. (1997). When timeout works some of the time: The importance of treatment integrity and functional assessment. *School Psychology Quarterly, 12*(1), 4–22.

Taylor, J. C., & Hill, D. (2017). Using daily behavior report cards during extended school year services for young students with intellectual and developmental disabilities. *Education and Treatment of Children, 40,* 525–546.

Taylor, S. A., & Mudford, O. C. (2012). Improving behavior in a residential service for youth in drug and alcohol rehabilitation. *Behavioral Interventions, 27,* 109–128. doi: 10.1002/bin.1342

Taylor, T. (2020). Assessment and treatment of pica within the home setting in Australia. *Behavioral Development, 25*(1), 40–51. doi.org/10.1037/bdb0000094

Teichner, G., Golden, C.J., & Giannaris, W.J. (1999). A multimodal approach to treatment of aggression in a severely brain injured adolescent. *Rehabilitation Nursing, 24*(5), 207–211.

Terrace, H. S. (1963). Discriminative learning with and without errors. *Journal of the Experimental Analysis of Behavior, 6,* 1–27.

Terrace, H. S. (1966). Stimulus control. In W. K. Honig (Ed.), *Operant behavior: Areas of research and application* (pp. 271–344). New York: Appleton.

Test, D. W., Spooner, F., Keul, P. K., & Grossi, T. (1990). Teaching adolescents with severe disability to use the public telephone. *Behavior Modification, 14,* 157–171.

Theobald, D. E., & Paul, G. I. (1976). Reinforcing value of praise for chronic mental patients as a function of historical pairing with tangible reinforcers. *Behavior Therapy, 7,* 192–197.

Thiemann, K. S., & Goldstein, H. (2001). Social stories, written text cues, and video feedback: Effects on social communication of children with autism. *Journal of Applied Behavior Analysis, 34,* 425–446.

Thiemann-Boudrque, K., Brady, N., McGuff, S., Stump, K., & Naylor, A. (2016). Picture exchange communication system and pals. A peer-mediated augmentative and alternative communication intervention for minimally verbal preschoolers with autism. *Journal of Speech, Language, and Hearing Research, 59*, 113–114 doi: 10.1044/2016 JSLHR-L-15-03135

Thomas, C. M., Sulzer-Azaroff, B., Lukeris, S., & Palmer, M. (1977). Teaching daily self-help skills for "long-term" maintenance. In B. Etzel, J. LeBlanc, & D. Baer, (Eds.), *New developments in behavioral research: Theory, method and application*. Hillsdale, NJ: Erlbaum Associates.

Thomas, E.M., DeBar, R. M., Viadescu, J. C., & Buffington, D. (2020). A comparison of video modeling and video prompting by adolescents with ASD. *Behavior Analysis in Practice, 12*, 40–52. https://doe.org/10.1007/s40617-019-00402-0

Thomas, J. D. (1976). Accuracy of self-assessment of on-task behavior by elementary school children. *Journal of Applied Behavior Analysis, 9*, 209–210.

Thomas, J. H., Due, K. M., & Wigger, D. M. (1987). Effects of the competence and sex of peer models on children's imitative behavior. *Journal of Genetic Psychology, 148*, 325–332.

Thomason-Sassi, J. L., Iwata, B. A., Neidert, P. L... & Roscoe, E. M. (2011). Response latency as an index of response strength during functional analyses of problem behavior. *Journal of Applied Behavior Analysis, 44*, 51–67. doi:10.1901/jaba.2011.44-51

Thompson, R. H., Cotnoir-Bichelman, N. M., McKerchar, P. M., Tate, T. L., & Dancho, K. A. (2007). Enhancing early communication through infant sign training. *Journal of Applied Behavior Analysis, 40*, 15–23.

Thompson, R. H., Iwata, B. A., Conners, J., & Roscoe, E. M. (1999). Effects of reinforcement for alternative behavior during punishment of self-injury. *Journal of Applied Behavior Analysis, 32*, 317–328.

Thompson, R. H., Iwata, B.A., Hanley, G. P., Dozier, C. L., & Samaha, A. L. (2003). The effects of extinction, noncontingent reinforcement, and differential reinforcement of other behavior as control procedures. *Journal of Applied Behavior Analysis, 36*, 221–238.

Thompson, R. H., McKerchar, P. M., & Duncho, K. A. (2004). The effects of delayed physical prompts and reinforcement on infant sign language acquisition. *Journal of Applied Behavior Analysis, 37*, 379–383.

Thompson, T. J., Braam, S. J., & Fuqua, R. W. (1982). Training and generalization of laundry skills: A multiple probe evaluation with handicapped persons. *Journal of Applied Behavior Analysis, 15*, 177–182.

Thorne, S., & Kamps, D. (2008). The effects of group contingency intervention on academic engagement and problem behavior of at-risk students. *Behavior Analysis in Practice, 2*(2), 12–18.

Thoresen, C. E., & Mahoney, J. J. (1974). *Behavioral self-control*. New York: Holt, Rinehart & Winston.

Thyer, B. A., & Geller, E. S. (1987). The "buckle-up" dash-board sticker: An effective environmental intervention for safety belt promotion. *Environment & Behavior, 19*, 484–494.

Tiger, J. H., Fisher, W. W., & Bouxsein, K. J. (2009). Therapist- and self-monitored DRO contingencies as a treatment for the self-injurious skin picking of a young man with Asperger syndrome. *Journal of Applied Behavior Analysis, 42*, 315–319.

Tiger, J. H., Hanley, G. P., & Hernandez, E. (2006). An evaluation of the value of choice with preschool children. *Journal of Applied Behavior Analysis, 39*, 1–16.

Tiger, J. H., Wierzba, B. C., Fisher, W. W., & Benitez, B. B. (2017). Developing and demonstrating inhibitory stimulus control over repetitive behavior. *Behavioral Interventions, 32*, 160-174. doi: 10.1002/bin.1472

Timberlake, W. (1980). A molar equilibrium theory of learned performance. *Psychology of Learning and Motivation. 14*, 1–58. https://doi.org/10.1016/S0079-7421(08)60158-9.]

Timberlake, W., & Allison, J. (1974). Response deprivation: An empirical approach to instrumental performance. *Psychological Review, 81*, 146–164.

Tincani, M., Crozier, S., & Alazeta, L. (2006). The picture exchange communication system: Effects on manding and speech for school-aged children with autism. *Education and Training in Developmental Disabilities, 42*, 179–184.

Todd, A. W., Horner, R. H., & Sugai, G. (1999). Self-monitoring and self-recruited praise: Effects on problem behavior, academic engagement, and work completion in a typical classroom. *Journal of Positive Behavior Interventions, 1*, 66–76.

Todd, A., Haugen, L., Anderson, K., & Spriggs, M. (2002). Teaching recess: Low-cost efforts producing effective results. *Journal of Positive Behavior Interventions, 4*, 46–52.

Todd, J. T., Morris, E. K., & Fenza, K. M. (1989). Temporal organization of extinction-induced responding in preschool children. *The Psychological Record, 39*, 117–130.

Tolan, P. H., & Guerra, N. G. (1992). *A developmental perspective on adolescent antisocial behavior*. Unpublished manuscript, University of Illinois at Chicago.

Toper-Korkmaz, O., Lerman, D. C., & Tsami, L. (2018). Effects of toy removal and number of demands on vocal stereotypy during response interruption and redirection. *Journal of Applied Behavior Analysis, 51*, 757–768.

Torelli, J. N., Lloyd, B. P., Diekman, C. A., & Wehby, J. H. (2017). Teaching stimulus control via class-wide multiple schedules of reinforcement in public elementary school classrooms. *Journal of Positive Behavior Interventions, 19*, 14–25. doi: 10.1177/1098300716632878

Touchette, P. E. (1971). Transfer of stimulus control: Measuring the moment of transfer. *Journal of the Experimental Analysis of Behavior, 15*, 347–354.

Touchette, P. E., & Howard, J. S. (1984). Errorless learning: Reinforcement contingencies and stimulus control transfer in delayed prompting. *Journal of Applied Behavior Analysis, 17*, 175–188.

Touchette, P. E., MacDonald, R. F., & Langer, S. N. (1985). A scatter plot for identifying stimulus control of problem behavior. *Journal of Applied Behavior Analysis, 18*, 343–351.

Toussaint, K. A., Kodak, T., & Vladescu, J. C. (2016). An evaluation of choice on instructional efficacy and individual preferences among children with autism. *Journal of Applied Behavior Analysis, 49*, 170–175. dos: 10.1002/jaba.263

Trammel, D.L., Schloss, P.J., & Alper, S. (1994). Using self-recording, evaluation, and graphing to increase completion of homework assignments. *Journal of Learning Disabilities, 27,* 75–81.

Trent, J. T. (1983). Role of reinforcement and response cost in discrimination learning. *Psychological Reports, 53,* 207–211.

Trosclair-Lasserre, N. M., Lerman, D. C., Call, N. A., Addison, L. R., & Kodak, T. (2008). Reinforcement magnitude: An evaluation of preference and reinforcer efficacy. *Journal of Applied Behavior Analysis, 41,* 203–220.

Trott, M.C., Maechtlen, A.D. (1986). The use of overcorrection as a means to control drooling. *American Journal of Occupational Therapy, 40,* 702–704.

Trotter, J. R. (1957). The timing of bar-pressing behavior. *Quarterly Journal of Experimental Psychology, 9,* 78–87.

Truchlicka, M., McLaughlin, T. F., & Swain, J. C. (1998). Effects of token reinforcement and response cost on the accuracy of spelling performance with middle-school special education students with behavior disorders. *Behavioral Interventions, 13,* 131–10

Trudel, G., Boisvert, J., Maruca, T., & Loroux, P. (1974). Un-programmed reinforcement of patients' behaviors in wards with and without token economy. *Behavior Therapy and Experimental Psychiatry, 5,* 147–149.

Trump, C. E., Herrod, J. L., Ayres, K. M., Ringdahl, J E., & Best, L. (2020). Behavior momentum theory and humans: A review of the literature. *Psychological Record* https://doi.org/10.1007/s40732-020-00430-1

Tryon, W. W. (1982). A simplified time-series analysis for evaluating treatment interventions. *Journal of Applied Behavior Analysis, 15,* 423–429.

Tsai, S. (2006). *Using social stories to teach children with autism pro-social skills.* Unpublished master's thesis, California State University, Los Angeles.

Tsai, Y., Symon, J. B. G., Campbell, R. V., & Menzies, H. (2009, March). *Effects of antecedent interventions on behaviors for children with autism.* Poster session presented at the annual conference of the California Association for Behavior Analysis, San Francisco, CA.

Tsou, Y.-T., Li, B., Kret, M. E., Sabino da Costa, I., & Rieffe, C. (2020). Reading emotional faces in deaf and hard-of-hearing and typically hearing children. *Emotion.* https://doi-org.mimas.calstatela.edu/10.1037/emo0000863.supp (Supplemental)

Tucci, V., Hursh, D. E., & Laitinen, R. E. (2004). The Competent Learner Model (CLM): A merging of applied Behavior Analysis, Direct Instruction, and Precision Teaching. In D. J. Moran & R. Malott (Eds.), *Evidence-based educational methods* (pp. 109–123). San Diego, CA: Elsevier.

Tucci, V., Hursh, D., Laitinen, R., & Lambe, A. (2005). Competent Learner Model for individuals with autism/PDD. *Exceptionality, 13*(1), 55–63.

Tucci, V., & Johnson, K. (2017). *Fluency FlashCards Application* (i.e., browser-based). Tucci Learning solutions, Inc.

Tudor, R. M. (1995). Isolating the effects of active responding in computer-based instruction. *Journal of Applied Behavior Analysis, 28,* 343–344.

Tung, S. B., Donaldson, J. M., & Kahng, S.W. (2017). The effects of preference assessment type on problem behavior. *Journal of Applied Behavior Analysis, 50,* 861–866. doi: 10.1002/jaba.414

Turley, L.W. & Milliman, R.E. (2000). Atmospheric effects on shopping behavior: A review of the experimental evidence. *Journal of Business Research, 49, 2,* 193–211.

Tustin, R D. (1994). Preference for reinforcers under varying schedule arrangements: A behavioral economic analysis. *Journal of Applied Behavior Analysis, 27,* 597–606.

Twohig, M. P. & Woods, D. W. (2001a). Habit reversal as a treatment for chronic skin picking in typical developing adult male siblings. *Journal of Applied Behavior Analysis, 34,* 217–220.

Twohig, M. P., & Woods, D. W. (2001b). Evaluating the duration of the competing response in habit reversal: A parametric analysis. *Journal of Applied Behavior Analysis, 34,* 517–520.

Twohig, M. P., Woods, D. W., Marcks, B. A., & Teng, E. J. (2003). Evaluating the efficacy of habit reversal: Comparison with a placebo control. *Journal of Clinical Psychiatry, 64,* 40–48.

Twyman, J. S., & Heward, W. L. (2018). How to improve student learning in every class-room now. International *Journal of Educational Research, 87,* 78–90. doi.org/10.1016/j.ijer.2016.05.007

Twyman, J. S., Layng, T. V. J., Stikeleather, G., & Hobbins, K. A. (2005). A non-linear approach to curriculum design: The role of behavior analysis in building an effective reading program. In W. L. Heward, T. E. Heron, N. A. Neef, S. M. Peterson, D. M. Sainato, G. Cartledge, R. Gardner III, L. D. Peterson, S. B. Hersh, & J. C. Dardig (Eds.), *Focus on behavior analysis in education: Achievements, challenges, and opportunities* (pp. 55–68). Upper Saddle River, NJ: Prentice Hall/Merrill.

Tyron, W. W. (1984). Principles and methods of mechanically measuring motor activity. *Behavioral Assessment, 6,* 129–139.

Ulman, J. D., & Sulzer-Azaroff, B. (1975). Multielement baseline design in educational research. In E. Ramp & G. Semb (Eds.), *Behavior analysis: Areas of research and application* (pp. 177–391). Englewood Cliffs, NJ: Prentice-Hall.

Ulrich, R. E., & Azrin, N. H. (1962). Reflexive fighting in response to aversive stimulation. *Journal of the Experimental Analysis of Behavior, 5,* 233–237.

Umbreit, J., Lane, K. L., & Dejud, C. (2004). Improving classroom behavior by modifying task difficulty: Effects of increasing the difficulty of too-easy tasks. *Journal of Positive Behavior Interventions, 6,* 13–20.

U.S. Dept. of Education (2012). *Restraint and seclusion resource document,* Washington, D. C.

United States Department of Education, Public Law 107–110, January 8, 2002 – ("No Child Left Behind")

U. S. Department of Education. (2000). *Effective alternative strategies: Grant competition to reduce student suspensions and expulsions and ensure educational progress of suspended and expelled students.* Washington, D. C.: Safe and drug-free schools program. OMB# 1810–0551.

Utley, C. A., Reddy, S. S., Delquadri, J. C., Greenwood, C. R., Mortweet, S. L., & Bowman, V. (2001). Classwide peer tutoring: An effective teaching procedure for facilitating the acquisition of health education and safety facts with students with developmental disabilities. *Education and Treatment of Children, 24,* 1–27.

Valbuena, D., Miller, B. G., Samah, A. L., & Miltenberger, R. B. (2017). Data presentation options to manage variability in physical activity research. *Journal of Applied Behavior Analysis, 50,* 622–640.

Valleley, R.J., & Shriver, M.D. (2003). An examination of the effects of repeated readings with secondary students. *Journal of Behavioral Education, 12,* 55–76.

Van Acker, R., Boreson, L., Gable, R. A., & Potterton, T. (2005). Are we on the right course? Lessons learned about current FBA/BIP practices in schools. *Journal of Behavioral Education, 14,* 35–56.

Van Acker, R., Grant, S. H., & Henry, D. (1996). Teacher and student behavior as a function of risk for aggression. *Education and Treatment of Children, 19,* 316–334.

Van Camp, C. M., Lerman, D. C., Kelley, M. E., Contrucci, S. A., & Vorndran, C. M. (2000). Variable-time reinforcement schedules in the treatment of socially maintained problem behavior. *Journal of Applied Behavior Analysis, 33,* 545–557.

Van der Burg, J.J.W., Didden, R., Jongerius, P.H., & Rotteveel, J.J. (2007). Behavioral treatment of drooling. A methodological critique of the literature with clinical guidelines and suggestions for future research. *Behavior Modification, 31,* 573–594.

Van Houten, R. (1987). Comparing treatment techniques: A cautionary note. *Journal of Applied Behavior Analysis, 20,* 109–110.

Van Houten, R., (1988). The effects of advance stop lines and sign prompts on pedestrian safety in crosswalks on a multilane highway. *Journal of Applied Behavior Analysis, 21,* 1988.

Van Houten, R., Axelrod, S., Bailey, J. S., Favell, J. E., Foxx, R. M., Iwata, B. A., & Lovaas, O. I. (1988). The right to effective behavioral treatment. *Journal of Applied Behavior Analysis, 21,* 381–384.

Van Houten, R., & Doleys, D. M. (1983). Are social reprimands effective? I. S. Axelrod & J. Apsche (Eds.), *The effects of punishment in human behavior* (pp. 45–70). New York: Academic Press.

Van Houten, R., & Malenfant, L. (1992). The Influence of signs prompting motorists to yield 50 ft (15.5 m) before marked crosswalks on motor vehicle-pedestrian conflicts at crosswalks with pedestrian activated flashing lights. *Accident Analysis and Prevention, 24,* 217–225.

Van Houten, R., & Malenfant, J.E.L. (2004). Effects to a driver enforcement program on yielding to pedestrians. *Journal of Applied Behavior Analysis, 37,* 351–363.

Van Houten, R. J., & Malenfant, J.E.L. (2007). Impact of a comprehensive safety program on bicycle helmet use among middle-school children. *Journal of Applied Behavior Analysis, 40,* 239–247.

Van Houten, R., & Nau, P. A. (1980). A comparison of the effects of fixed and variable ratio schedules of reinforcement on the behavior of deaf children. *Journal of Applied Behavior Analysis, 13,* 13–21.

Van Houten, R., Nau, P. A., MacKenzie-Keating, S. E., Sameoto, D., & Colavecchia, B. (1982). An analysis of some variable influencing the effectiveness of reprimands. *Journal of Applied Behavior Analysis, 15,* 65–83.

Van Houten, R., & Rolider, A. (1984). The use of response prevention to eliminate nocturnal thumbsucking. *Journal of Applied Behavior Analysis, 17,* 509–520.

Van Houten, R., & Rolider, A. (1988). Recreating the scene: An effective way to provide delayed punishment for inappropriate motor behavior. *Journal of Applied Behavior Analysis, 21,* 187–192.

Van Houten, R., & Van Houten, J. (1977). The performance feedback system in a special education classroom: An analysis of public posting and peer comments: *Behavior Therapy, 8,* 366–376.

Van Houten, R., Van Houten, J., & Malenfant, J. E. (2007). Impact of a comprehensive safety program on bicycle helmet use among middle-school children. *Journal of Applied Behavior Analysis, 40,* 239–247.

Vanselow, N. R., & Hanley, G. P. (2014). An evaluation of computerized behavioral skills training to teach safety skills to young children. *Journal of Applied Behavior Analysis, 47,* 51–69.

Vansteenwegen, D., Francken, G., Vervliet, B., Hermans, D., Beckers, T., Baeyens, F., & Eelen, P. (2006). Stronger renewal in human fear conditioning when tested with an acquisition retrieval cue than with an extinction retrieval cue. *Behaviour Research and Therapy, 44,* 1717–1725.

VanWormer, J. J. (2004). Pedometers and brief e-counseling: Increasing physical activity for overweight adults. *Journal of Applied Behavior Analysis, 37,* 421–425.

Vargas, E. A., & Vargas, J. S. (1991). Programmed instruction: What it is and how to do it. *Journal of Behavioral Education, 1,* 235–251.

Van Der Koy, D., & Webster, C D. (1975). A rapidly effective behavior modification program for an electively mute child. *Journal of Behavior Therapy and Experimental Psychiatry, 6,* 149–152.

Vargo, K., & Becknell, K. (2019). An application of the group-oriented concurrent-chains arrangement. *Behavior Analysis in Practice, 12,* 310–319. doi: org/10.1007/s40617-018-00286-6

Vaughn, B. J., Wilson, D., & Dunlap, G. (2002). Family-centered intervention to resolve problem behaviors in a fast-food restaurant. *Journal of Positive Behavior Interventions, 4,* 38–45.

Vaughan, M. E. (1985). Repeated acquisition in the analysis of rule-governed behavior. *Journal of the Experimental Analysis of Behavior, 44,* 175–184.

Vazquez-Moreno, A., Gonzalez-Garrido, A. A., & Ramos-Loyo, J. (2019). Delayed response improves inhibitory control in low- and high-impulsivity adolescents: Effects of emotional contexts. *International Journal of Psychological Studies, 11,* 42–53. doi.10.5539/ijps.v11n2p42

Veerkamp, M. B., Kamps, D. M., & Cooper, L. (2007). The effects of classwide peer tutoring on the reading achievement of urban middle school students. *Education and Treatment of Children, 30*(2), 21–51.

Verguson, C. M., & Gravina, N. E. (2020). Using a guest- and confederate-delivered to-ken economy to increase employee-guest interactions at a zoo. *Journal of Applied Behavior Analysis, 53,* 422–430. doi: 10.1002/jaba.599

Verriden, A. L. & Roscoe, E. M. (2019). An evaluation of a punisher assessment for decreasing automatically reinforced problem behavior. *Journal of Applied Behavior Analysis, 52,* 205–226. doi: 10.1002/jaba.509

Vintere, P., Hemmes, N. S., Brown, B. L., & Poulson, C. L. (2004). Gross-motor skill acquisition by preschool dance students under self-instruction procedures. *Journal of Applied Behavior Analysis, 37,* 305–322.

Virues-Ortega, J. (2010). Applied behavior analytic intervention for autism in early childhood: Meta analysis, meta-regression and dos-response meta-analysis of multiple outcomes. *Clinical Psychology Review, 30,* 387–399.

Vitaro, F., Tremblay, R. E., Kerr, M., Pagani, L., & Bukowski, W. M. (1997). Disruptiveness, friends' characteristics, and delinquency in early adolescence: A test of two competing models of development. *Child Development, 68,* 676–689.

Vladescu, J. C., Day-Watkins, J., Schnell, L. K., & Carrow, J. N. (2020). Safe to sleep: Community-based caregiver training. *Journal of Applied Behavior Analysis, 53,* 1922–1934. doi: 10.1002/jaba.777

Voeltz, L. M., & Evans, I. M. (1983). Educational validity: Procedures to evaluate outcomes in programs for severely handicapped learners. *TASH Journal, 8,* 3–14.

Volkert, V. M., Lerman, D. C., Call, N. A., & Trosclair-Lasserre, N. (2009). An evaluation of resurgence during treatment with functional communication training. *Journal of Applied Behavior Analysis, 42,* 145–160.

Volkmar, F. R., Lord, C., Bailey, A., Schultz, R. T., & Klin, A. (2004). Autism and pervasive developmental disorders. *Journal of Child Psychology and Psychiatry, 45,* 135–170.

Vollmer, T. R. (1999). Noncontingent reinforcement: Some additional comments. *Journal of Applied Behavior Analysis, 32,* 239–240.

Vollmer, T. R. (2002). Punishment happens: Some comments on Lerman and Vorndran's review. *Journal of Applied Behavior Analysis, 35,* 469–473.

Vollmer, T. R., & Iwata, B. A. (1991). Establishing operations and reinforcement effects. *Journal of Applied Behavior Analysis 24,* 279–291.

Vollmer, T. R., & Iwata, B. A. (1992). Differential reinforcement as treatment for behavior disorders: Procedural and functional variation. *Research in Developmental Disabilities, 13,* 393–417.

Vollmer, T. R., Marcus, B. A., & LeBlanc, L. (1994). Treatment of self-injury and hand mouthing following inconclusive functional analyses. *Journal of Applied Behavior Analyses, 27,* 331–344.

Vollmer, T. R., Marcus, B. A., Ringdahl, J. E., & Roane, H. S. (1995). Progressing from brief assessments to extended experimental analyses in the evaluation of aberrant behavior. *Journal of Applied Behavior Analysis, 28,* 561–576.

Vollmer, T. R., Peters, K. P., Kronfli, F. R., Lloveras, L. A. & Ibanez, V. F. (2020). On the definition of differential reinforcement of alternative behavior. *Journal of Applied Behavior Analysis, 53,* 1299–1303. doi: 10.1002/jaba.701

Vollmer, T. R., Progar, P. R., Lalli, J. S., Van Camp, C. M., Sierp, B. J., Wright, C. S., et al. (1998). Fixed-time schedules attenuate extinction-induced phenomena in the treatment of severe aberrant behavior. *Journal of Applied Behavior Analysis, 31,* 529–542.

Vollmer, T. R., Ringdahl, J. E., Roane, H. S., & Marcus, B. A. (1997). Negative side effects of noncontingent reinforcement. *Journal of Applied Behavior Analysis, 30,* 161–164.

Vollmer, T. R., Roane, H. S., Ringdahl, J. E., & Marcus, B. A. (1999). Evaluating treatment challenges with differential reinforcement of alternative behavior. *Journal of Applied Behavior Analysis, 32,* 9–23.

Volpe, J. S., King, G. R., & Logue, A. W. (1988). *Choice in a self-control paradigm with human subjects: Effects of a distractor.* Paper presented at the Fourteenth Annual Convention of the Association for Behavior Analysis, Philadelphia, PA.

Von Brock, M. B., & Elliott, S. N. (1987). Influence of treatment effectiveness information on the acceptability of classroom interventions. *Journal of School Psychology, 25,* 131–144.

Vorndran, C.M., & Lerman, D.C. (2006) Establishing and maintaining treatment effects with less intrusive consequences via a pairing procedure. *Journal of Applied Behavior Analysis, 39,* 35–48.

Voulgarakis, H., & Forte, S. (2015). Escape extinction and negative reinforcement in the treatment of pediatric feeding disorders: A single case analysis. *Behavior Analysis in Practice, 8,* 212–214. doi: 10.1007/s40617-051-0086-8

Vyse, S. A., & Mulick, J. A. (1990). A correlational approach to ecobehavioral assessment. In S. R. Schroeder (Ed.), *Echobehavioral analysis and developmental disabilities* (pp. 64–81). New York: Springer-Verlag.

Wack, S. R., Crosland, K. A., & Miltenberger, R. G. (2014). Using goal setting and feedback to increase weekly running distance. *Journal of Applied Behavior Analysis, 47,* 181–185.

Wacker, D. P., Berg, W. K., Perrie, P., & Swatta, P. (1985). Generalization and maintenance of complex skills by severely handicapped adolescents following picture prompt training. *Journal of Applied Behavior Analysis, 18,* 329–336.

Wacker, D. P., Harding, J. W., Berg, W. K., Lee, J. F., Schieltz, K. M., Padilla,…. Sjahan, T. A. (2011). An evaluation of persistence of treatment effect during long-term treatment of destructive behavior. *Journal of the Experimental Analysis of Behavior, 96,* 261–282.

Wacker, K. P., Schieltz, K. M., Berg, W. K., Harding, J. W. Padilla, D., & Lee, J. F. (2017). The long-term effects of functional communication training conducted in young children's home settings. *Education and Treatment of Children, 40,* 43–56.

Wadden, T. A., Butryn, M. L., & Byrne, K. J. (2004). Efficacy of lifestyle modification for long-term weight control. *Obesity Research, 12,* 151–162.

Wagaman, J. R., Miltenberger, R. G., & Arndorfer, R. E. (1993). Analysis of a simplified treatment for stuttering in children. *Journal of Applied Behavior Analysis, 26,* 53–61.

Wageman, R. (1995). Interdependence and group effectiveness. *Administrative Science Quarterly, 40*(1), 145–180.

Wagenaar, A.C., & Maldonado-Molina, M.M. (2007). Effects of drivers' license suspension policies on alcohol-related crash involvement: Long-term follow-up in 46 states. *Alcoholism: Clinical and Experimental Research, 31*(8), 1–8.

Wahler, R. G. (1975). Some structural aspects of deviant child behavior. *Journal of Applied Behavior Analysis, 8,* 27–42.

Wahler, R. G., & Fox, J. J. (1981). Setting events in applied behavior analysis: Toward a conceptual and methodological expansion. *Journal of Applied Behavior Analysis, 14,* 327–338.

Wahler, R. G., Vigilante, V. A., & Strand, P. S. (2004). Generalization in a child's oppositional behavior across home and school settings. *Journal of Applied Behavior Analysis, 37,* 43–52.

Walker, C. E., Hedberg, A. G., Clement, P. W., & Wright, L. (1981). *Clinical procedures for behavior therapy.* Upper Saddle River, NJ: Prentice Hall.

Walker, G. (2008). Constant and progressive time delay procedures for teaching children with autism: A literature review. *Journal of Autism and Developmental Disorders, 38,* 261–275.

Walker, H. M., & Buckley, N. K. (1972). Programming generalization and maintenance of treatment effects across time and settings. *Journal of Applied Behavior Analysis, 5,* 209–224.

Walker, H. M., & Hops, H. (1979). The CLASS program for acting out children: R & D procedures, program outcomes and implementation issues. *School Psychology Digest, 8,* 370–381.

Walker, H. M., Hops, H., & Johnson, S. M. (1975). Generalization and maintenance of classroom treatment effects. *Behavior Therapy, 6,* 188–200.

Walker, H. M., Ramsey, E., & Gresham, F. M. (2004). *Antisocial behavior in school: Evidence based practices* (2nd Ed.). Belmont, CA: Wadsworth/Thomson Learning.

Walker, H. M., Retana, G. F., & Gersten, R. (1988). Replication of the CLASS program in Costa Rica. *Behavior Modification, 12,* 133–154.

Walker, S. G., Mattson, S. L. & Sellers, T. P. (2020). Increasing accuracy of rock-climbing techniques in movie athletes using expert modeling and video feedback. *Journal of Applied Behavior Analysis, 53,* 2260–2270. doi.org.10.1002/jaba.694

Wall, M.E., & Gast, D.L. (1999). Acquisition of incidental information during instruction for a response -chain skill. *Research in Developmental Disabilities, 20,* 31–50.

Wallace, M. A., Cox, E. A., & Skinner, C. H. (2003). Increasing independent seatwork: Breaking large assignments into smaller assignments and teaching a student with retardation to recruit reinforcement. *School Psychology Review, 32,* 132–142.

Wallace, M. D., Iwata, B. A., & Hanley, G. P. (2006). Establishment of mands following tact training as a function of reinforcer strength. *Journal of Applied Behavior Analysis, 39,* 17–24.

Wallace, M. D., Iwata, B.A., Hanley, G. P., Thompson, R. H., & Roscoe, E. M. (2012). Noncontingent reinforcement: A further examination of schedule effects during treatment. *Journal of Applied Behavior Analysis, 45,* 709–719.

Wallace, M. D., & Mayer, G. R. (2022). *Principles of applied behavior analysis for behavior technicians and other practitioners, 3rd Ed..* Cornwall on Hudson, NY: Sloan Publishing.

Wallace, M. D., Stevenson, M., Ellsworth, C., & MacAleese, A. (2007). *On the Assessment and Treatment of Children with Attention Deficit Hyperactivity Disorder.* Invited Address presented at the Nevada Association for Behavior Analysis, Reno, NV.

Wallach, M. A., Kogan, N., & Burt, R. B. (1967). Group risk taking and field dependence-independence of group members. *Sociometry, 30,* 323–338.

Walls, R. T., Ellis, W. D., Zane, T., & VanderPoel, S. J. (1979). Tactile, auditory, and visual prompting in reaching complex assembly tasks. *Education and Training of the Mentally Retarded, 14,* 120–130.

Walls, R. T., Haught, P., & Dowler, D. L. (1982). Moments of transfer of stimulus control in practical assembly tasks. *American Journal of Mental Deficiency, 87,* 309–315.

Walls, R. T., Zane, T., & Thvedt, J. E. (1980). Trainer's personal methods compared to two structured training strategies. *American Journal of Mental Deficiency, 84,* 495–507.

Walls, R. T., Zane, T., & Ellis, W. D. (1981). Forward and backward chaining, and whole task methods. *Behavior Modification, 5,* 61–74.

Walpole, C. W., Roscoe, E. M., & Dube, W. V. (2007). Use of a differential observing response to expand restricted stimulus control. *Journal of Applied Behavior Analysis, 40,* 707–712.

Walz, G. R., & Johnson, J. A. (1963). Counselors look at themselves on videotape. *Journal of Counseling Psychology, 10,* 232–236.

Warash, B., Curtis, R., Hursh, D., & Tucci, V. (2008). Skinner meets Piaget on the Reggio playground: Practical synthesis of applied behavior analysis and developmental appropriate practice orientations. *Journal of Research in Childhood Education, 22,* 441–453.

Ward, P., & Carnes, M. (2002). Effects of posting self-set goals on collegiate football players' skill execution during practice and games. *Journal of Applied Behavior Analysis, 35,* 1–12.

Ward, P., Johnson, M., & Konukman, F. (1998). Directed rehearsal and preservice teachers' performance of instructional behaviors. *Journal of Behavioral Education, 8,* 369–380.

Ward, R. D., & Higbee, T. S. (2008). Noncontingent reinforcement as treatment for tub-standing in a toddler. *Education and Treatment of Children, 31,* 213–222.

Ward, S., Parker, A. & Perdikaris, A. (2017). Task as reinforcer: a reactive alternative to traditional forms of escape extinction. *Behavior Analysis in Practice, 10,* 22–34.

Ward-Horner, J. C., Muehlberger, A. O., Vedora, J., & Ross, R. K. (2017). Effects of reinforcer magnitude and quality on preference for response-reinforcer arrangements in young children with autism. *Behavior Analysis in Practice, 10,* 183–188.

Warner, R. W., & Swisher, J. D. (1976). Drug-abuse prevention: Reinforcement of alternatives. In J. D. Krumboltz & C. E. Thoresen (Eds.), *Counseling methods.* New York: Holt, Rinehart and Winston. Pp. 510–517.

Warnes, E., & Allen, K. D. (2005). Biofeedback treatment of paradoxical vocal fold motion and respiratory distress in an adolescent girl. *Journal of Applied Behavior Analysis, 38,* 529–532.

*Washougal (WA) School District* 4 ECLPR 131 (OCR 1999).

Watkins, C. L., Pack-Teixteira, L., & Howard, J. S. (1989). Teaching intraverbal behavior to severely retarded children. *The Analysis of Verbal Behavior, 7,* 69–81.

Watkins, C. L., & Slocum, T. A. (2003). The components of Direct Instruction. *Journal of Direct Instruction, 3,* 75–110.

Waters, M.B., Lerman, D.C., & Hovanetz, A.N. (2009). Separate and combined effects of visual schedules and extinction plus differential reinforcement on problem behavior occasioned by transitions. *Journal of Applied Behavior Analysis, 42,* 309–313.

Watson, D. L., & Tharp, R. G. (2007). *Self-directed behavior: Self-modifica-*

tion for personal adjustment. 9th Edition. Brooks/Cole: Pacific Grove, CA.

Watson, J. B. (1924). Behaviorism. New York: W. W. Norton.

Watson, J. B., & Rayner, R. (1920). Conditioned emotional reactions. Journal of Experimental Psychology, 3, 1–14.

Watson, T.S. (1993). Effectiveness of arousal and arousal plus overcorrection to reduce nocturnal bruxism. Journal of Behavior Therapy and Experimental Psychiatry, 24(2), 181–185.

Watt, M. E., Watt, A. (1987). A tape-based system of interactive video for computerized self-instruction. Medical Teacher, 9, 309–315.

Watts, A. C., Wilder, D. A., Gregory, M. K., Leon, Y., & Ditzian, K. (2013). The effect of rules on differential reinforcement of other behavior. Journal of Applied Behavior Analysis, 46, 680–684.

Watts, Z. B., Stenhoff, D. M. (2021). Creating multiple-baseline graphs with phase change lines in Microsoft Excel for windows and macOS. Behavior Analysis in Practice, 14, 996–1009. doi.org/10.1007/s40617-021-00552-0

Wattenberg, W. W., & Clifford, C. (1964). Relation of self-concepts to beginning achievement in reading. Child Development, 35, 461–467.

Wearden, J.H., & Shimp, C.P. (1985). Local temporal pattering of operant behavior in humans. Journal of the Experimental Analysis of Behavior, 44, 315–324.

Webb, T. (2000, June/July). The talking goes on—The Picture Exchange Communication System. Special Children, 130, 30–34.

Webster, D., & Azrin, N. H. (1973). Required relaxation: A method of inhibiting agitative-disruptive behavior of retardates. Behavior Research and Therapy, 11, 67–78.

Webster, R. E. (1976). A timeout procedure in a public school setting. Psychology in the Schools, 13(1), 72–76.

Weeks, M., & Gaylord-Ross, R. (1981). Task difficulty and aberrant behavior in severely handicapped students. Journal of Applied Behavior Analysis, 14, 449–463.

Weems, C. F. (1998). The evaluation of heart rate biofeedback using a multi-element design. Journal of Behavior Therapy and Experimental Psychiatry, 29(2), 157–162.

Wehby, J. H., & Hollahan, M. S. (2000). Effects of high-probability requests on the latency to initiate academic tasks. Journal of Applied Behavior Analysis, 33, 259–262.

Wehby, J. H., Symons, F. J., & Shores, R. E. (1995). A descriptive analysis of aggressive behavior in classrooms for children with emotional and behavioral disorders. Behavioral Disorders, 20, 87–105.

Weiner, H. (1962). Some effects of response cost upon human operant behavior. Journal of Experimental Analysis of Behavior, 5, 201–208.

Weiner, H. (1964a). Conditioning history and fixed-interval performance. Journal of the Experimental Analysis of Behavior, 7, 383–385.

Weiner, H. (1964b). Response cost effects during extinction following fixed interval reinforcement with humans. Journal of the Experimental Analysis of Behavior, 7, 333–335.

Weiner, H. (1969). Controlling human fixed-interval's performance. Journal of the Experimental Analysis of Behavior, 12, 349–373.

Weiner, H. (1980). Response rates and choices of schizophrenics under fixed-ratio schedules of reinforcement. Perceptual and Motor Skills, 51, 1239–1243.

Weiner, H. (1981a). Effects of schedule information on the slowed fixed ratio responding of schizophrenics. Perceptual and Motor Skills, 52, 452–454.

Weiner, H. (1981b). Increasing slowed operant responding of schizophrenics under a fixed-ratio schedule of reinforcement. Perceptual and Motor Skills, 53, 579–582.

Weiner, H. (1982). Histories of response omission and human operant behavior under a fixed-ratio schedule of reinforcement. The Psychological Record, 32, 409–434.

Weiner, H. (1983). Some thoughts on discrepant human-animal performances under schedules of reinforcement. The Psychological Record, 33, 521–532.

Weinger, M. B., Herndon, O.W., Zornow, M. H., Paulus, M. P., Gaba, D. M., & Dallen, L. T. (1994). An objective methodology for task analysis and workload assessment in anesthesia providers. Anesthesiology, 80, 77–92.

Weinstein, N. D., Grubb, P. D., & Vautier, J. S. (1986). Increasing automobile seat belt use: An intervention emphasizing resk susceptibility. Journal of Applied Behavior Analysis, 71, 285–290.

Weisberg, P. (1983–1984). Reading instruction for poverty-level pre-schoolers: A seven year progress report. Direct Instruction News, 3, 16–18, 21.

Weisberg, P., & Waldrop, B. B. (1972). Fixed interval work habits of Congress. Journal of the Experimental Analysis of Behavior, 5, 93–97.

Weiseler, N. A., Hanson, R. H., Chamberlain, T. P., & Thompson, T. (1985). Functional taxonomy of stereotypic and self-injurious behavior. Mental Retardation, 23, 230–234.

Weissman, M. D., Sulzer-Azaroff, B., Fleming, R., Hamad, C., & Crockett, J. L. (2004). Behavioral Intervention in Autism (BIA) Paper presented at the Annual Conference of the American Educational Research Association, San Diego, CA. April. (Retrieved from: http://rockman.com/projects/130.umass.bia/aera_paper_final.pdf)

Weist, M.D., Ollendick, T.H., & Finney, J.W. (1991). Toward the empirical validation of treatment targets in children. Clinical Psychology Review, 11, 515–538.

Wells, K. C., Forehand, R., Hickey, K., & Green, K. D. (1977). Effects of a procedure derived from the overcorrection principle on manipulated and nonmanipulated behaviors. Journal of Applied Behavior Analysis, 10, 679–687.

Welsch v. Likins, 373 F. Supp. 487 (D. Minn., 1974).

Welsh, D. H. B., Luthans, F., & Sommer, S. M. (1993). Organizational behavior modification goes to Russia: Replicating an experimental analysis across cultures and tasks. Journal of Organizational Behavior Management, 13(2), 15–35.

Werts, M. G., Caldwell, N. K., & Wolery, M. (1996). Peer modeling of response chains: Observational learning by students with disabilities. Journal of Applied Behavior Analysis, 29, 53–66.

Wesp, R. (1986). Reducing procrastination through required course involvement. Teaching of Psychology, 13 (3), 128–130.

West, R. P., Taylor, M. J., Wheatley, R. K., & West, J. H. (2007, February). Indicators of behavior support: Relationships to academic achievemenet and school safety. Poster session presented at the annual meeting of the California Association for Behavior Analysis, San Francisco, CA.

West, R. R., & Sloane, H. N. (1986). Teacher presentation rate and point delivery rate: Effects on classroom disruption, performance accuracy, and response rate. *Behavior Modification, 10,* 267–286.

Westling, D. L., Cooper-Duffy, K., Prohn, K., Ray, M., & Herzog, M. J. (2005). Building a teacher support program. *Teaching Exceptional Children, 37,* 8–13.

Wetterneck, C. T., & Woods, D. W. (2006). An evaluation of the effectiveness of exposure and response prevention on repetitive behaviors associated with Tourette's syndrome. *Journal of Applied Behavior Analysis, 39,* 441–444.

Wexley, K. N., & Yukl, G. A. (1984). *Organizational behavior and personnel psychology* (rev. ed.). Homewood, IL: Richard D. Irwin, Inc.

Weyman, J. R., & Sy, J. R. (2018). Effects of neutral and enthusiastic praise on the rate of discrimination acquisition. *Journal of Applied Behavior Analysis, 51,* 335–344. doi: 10.1002/jaba.440

Wheatley, R. K., West, R., P., Charlton, C. T., Sanders, R. B., Smith, T. G., & Taylor, M. J. (2009). Improving behavior through differential reinforcement: A praise note system for elementary school students. *Education and Treatment of children, 32,* 551–571.

Wheeler, A. J., & Sulzer, B. (1970). Operant training and generalization of a verbal response form in a speech-deficient child. *Journal of Applied Behavior Analysis,* 3, 139–147. Also reprinted in O. I. Lovaas and B. D. Bucher (Eds*.), Perspectives in behavior modification with deviant children* (pp. 193–205). Englewood Cliffs, N.J.: Prentice Hall, Inc.

Whitaker, S. D. (2000). Mentoring beginning special education teachers and the relationship to attrition. *Exceptional Children, 66,* 546–566.

White, G. D., Nielsen, G., & Johnson, S. M. (1972). Timeout duration and the suppression of deviant behavior in children. *Journal of Applied Behavior Analysis, 5,* 111–120.

White, M.A. (1975). Natural rates of teacher approval and disapproval in the classroom. *Journal of Applied Behavior Analysis, 8,* 367–372.

White, O. R. (1971). *A glossary of behavioral terminology.* Champaign, IL: Research Press.

White, O.R. (1986). Precision teaching—Precision learning. *Exceptional Children, 52,* 522–534.

White, O.R., & Neely, M. (2004). *The Chart Book: An Overview of Standard Celeration Chart Conventions and Practices,* an on-line tutorial hosted by the University of Washington. http://courses.washington.edu/edspe510/Downloads/ChartBook_W05.pdf

Whorton, D., Walker, D., Locke, P., Delquadri, J., & Hall, R. V. (1987). *A comparison of one-to-one instruction by peers, one-to-one instruction by adults, and small group instruction with children with autism.* Juniper Gardens Children's Project, Bureau of Child Research, University of Kansas: Kansas City, KS.

Wilder, D. A., Atwell, J. & Wine, B. (2006). The effects of varying levels of treatment integrity on child compliance during treatment with a three-step prompting procedure. *Journal of Applied Behavior Analysis* 39(3) pp. 369–373.

Wilder, D. A., Cymbal, D., & Villacorta, J. (2010). The performance diagnostic checklist-human services: A brief review. J*ournal of Applied Behavior Analysis, 53,* 1170–1176. doi: 10.1002/jaba.676

Wilder, D. A., Fischetti, A. T., Myers, K., Leon-Enriquez, Y., & Majdalany, L. (2013). The effect of response effort on compliance in young children. *Behavioral Interventions, 28,* 241–250.

Wilder, D. A., Maidalany, L., Sturkie, L., & Smeltz, L. (2015). Further evaluation of the high-probability instructional sequence with and without programmed reinforcement. *Journal of Applied Behavior Analysis, 48,* 511–522. doi: 10.1002/jaba.218

Wilder, D. A., Masuda, A., O'Connor, C., & Baham, M. (2001). Brief functional analysis and treatment of bizarre vocalizations in an adult with schizophrenia. *Journal of Applied Behavior Analysis, 34,* 65–68.

Wilder, D. A., Normand, M., & Atwell, J. (2005). Noncontingent reinforcement as treatment for food refusal and associated self-injury. Journal of Applied Behavior Analysis, 38, 549–553.

Wilcox, J., Sbardellati, E., & Nevin, A. (1987).Cooperative learning groups aid integration. *Teaching Exceptional Children, 20,* 61–63.

Wilczenski, F. L., Sulzer-Azaroff, B., Feldman, R. S., & Fajardo, D. E. (1987). Feedback to teachers on student performance as a tool for effective mainstreaming. *Professional School Psychology, 2,* 161–172.

Wilder, D., A., Atwell, J., & Wine, B. (2006). The effects of varying levels of treatment integrity on child compliance during treatment with a three-step prompting procedures. *Journal of Applied Behavior Analysis, 39,* 369–373.

Wilhelm, S., Deckersbach, T., Coffey, B. J., Bohne, R., Peterson, A. L., & Baer, L. (2003). Habit reversal versus supportive psychotherapy for Tourette's Disorder: A randomized controlled trial. *Behaviour Research and Therapy, 44,* 639–656.

Williams, B. (1997). Varieties of contrast: A review of "incentive relativity" by Charles F. Flaherty. *Journal of the Experimental Analysis of Behavior, 68,* 133–141.

Williamson, D. A., Williamson, S. H., Watkins, P. C., & Hughes, H. H. (1992). Increasing cooperation among children using dependent group-oriented reinforcement contingencies. *Behavior Modification, 16,* 414–425.

Willis, S. E., & Nelson, R. O. (1982). The effects of valence and nature of target behavior on the accuracy and reactivity of self-monitoring. *Behavioral Assessment, 4,* 401–412.

Wilson, A.N., Glassford,, T. S., & Koerkenmeier, S. M. (2016). Effects of response effort on resurgence. *Behavior Analysis in Practice, 9,* 174–178. doi: 10.1007/s40617-016-0122-3

Wilson, A N., & Gratz, O. H. (2016). Using a progressive ratio schedule of reinforcement as an assessment tool to inform treatment. *Behavior Analysis in Practice, 9,* 257–260. https://doe.org/10.1007/s40617-016-0107-2

Wilson, E. R., Wine, B., & Fitlerer, K. (2017). An investigation of the matrix training approach to teach social play skills. *Behavioral Interventions, 32,* 278–281.

Wilson, C., Boni, N., & Hogg, A. (1997). The effectiveness of task clarification, positive reinforcement and corrective feedback in changing courtesy among police staff. *Journal of Organizational Behavior Management, 17*(1), 65–99.

Wilson, G. R., & O'Leary, K. D. (1980). *Principles of behavior therapy.* Englewood Cliffs, NJ: Prentice-Hall.

Wilson. K.G. & Hayes, S.G. (1996). Resurgence of derived stimulus relations. *Journal of the Experimental Analysis of Behavior, 66,* 267–281

Wilson, P. G., Reid, D. H., Phillips, J. G., & Burgio, L. D. (1984). Normalization of institutional mealtimes for profoundly retarded persons: Effects and noneffects of teaching family-style dining. *Journal of Applied Behavior Analysis, 17,* 189–201.

Winborn-Kemmerer, L., Ringdahl, J. E., Wacker, D. P., & Kitsukawa, K. (2009). A demonstration of individual preference for novel mands during functional communication training. *Journal of Applied Behavior Analysis, 42,* 185–189.

Winett, R. A., & Winkler, R. C. (1972). Current behavior modification in the classroom: Be still, be quiet, be docile. *Journal of Applied Behavior Analysis, 5,* 499–504.

Winkler, R. C. (1970). Management of chronic psychiatric patients by a token reinforcement system. *Journal of Applied Behavior Analysis, 3,* 47–55.

Winkler, R. C. (1971). Reinforcement schedules of individual patients in a token economy. *Behavior Therapy, 2,* 534–537.

Wiskow, K. M., & Donaldson, J. M. (2016). Evaluation of lag schedule of reinforcement in a group contingency to promote varied naming of categories items with children. *Journal of Applied Behavior Analysis, 49,* 472–484. doi: 10.1002/jaba.307

Winn, S. O., Skinner, C. H., Allin, J. D., & Hawkins, J. A. (2004). School consultants can empirically validate interventions. *Journal of Applied School psychology, 20*(2), 109–128.

Winston, A. S., Singh, N. N., & Dawson, M. J. (1984). Effects of facial screening and blindfold on self-injurious behavior. *Applied Research in Mental Retardation, 5,* 29–42.

Wiskow, K. M., Matter, A. L., & Donaldson, J. M. (2019). The Good Behavior Game in preschool classrooms an evaluation of feedback. *Journal of Applied Behavior Analysis, 52,* 105–115. doi: 10.1002/jaba.500

Wisocki, P. A. (1973). A covert reinforcement program for the treatment of test anxiety: Brief report. *Behavior Therapy, 4,* 264–266.

Witt, J. C., & Elliott, S. N. (1983). Acceptability of classroom intervention strategies. In T. Kratochwill (Ed.). *Advances in school psychology* (Vol. 4, pp. 251–288). Hillsdale, New Jersey: Lawrence Erlbaum Associates.

Witt, J. C., Moe, G., Gutkin, T. B., & Andrews, L. (1984). The effect of saying the same thing in different ways. The problem of language and jargon in school-based consultation. *Journal of School Psychology, 22,* 361–367.

Wolf, M. M. (1978). Social validity: The case for subjective measurement or how applied behavior analysis is finding its heart. *Journal of Applied Behavior Analysis, 11,* 203–214.

Wolf, M.M., Braukmann, C. J., & Ramp, K.A. (1987). Serious delinquent behavior as part of a significantly handicapping condition: Cures and supportive environments. *Journal of Applied Behavior Analysis, 20,* 347–359.

Wolf, M. M., Giles, K. K., & Hall. V. H. (1968). Experiments with token reinforcement in remedial classroom. *Behavior Research and Therapy, 6,* 305–312.

Wolf, M. M., Risley, T. R., Johnson, J., Harris, F., & Allen, E. (1967). Application of operant conditioning procedures to the behavior problems of an autistic child, a follow-up extension. *Behavior Research and Therapy, 5,* 103–102.

Wof, M. M., Risley, T. R., & Mees, H. (1964). Application of operant conditioning procedures to the behavior problems of an autistic child. *Behavior Research and Therapy, 1,* 305–312.

Wolfe, J. A., Fantuzzo, J., & Wolter, C. (1984). Student-administered group-oriented contingencies: A method of combining group-oriented contingencies and self-directed behavior to increase academic productivity. *Child & Family Behavior Therapy, 6,* 45–60.

Wolfe, L. H., Heron, T. E., & Goddard, Y. L. (2000). Effects of self-monitoring on the on-task behavior and written language performance of elementary students with learning disabilities. *Journal of Behavioral Education, 10,* 29–73.

Wolko, K. L., Hrycaiko, D. W., & Martin, G. L. (1993). A comparison of two self-management packages to standard coaching for improving practice performance of gymnasts. *Behavior Modification, 17,* 209–223.

Wood, S. J., Murdock, J. Y., & Cronin, M. E. (2002). Self-monitoring and at-risk middle school students: Academic performance improves, maintains, and generalizes. *Behavior Modification, 26,* 605–279.

Wood, S. J., Murdock, J. Y., Cronin, M. E., Dawson, N. M., & Kirby, P. C. (1998). Effects of self-monitoring on on-task behaviors of at-risk middle school students. *Journal of Behavioral Education, 8,* 263–279.

Woods, D. W., & Himle, M. B. (2004). Creating tic suppression: Comparing the effects of verbal instruction to differential reinforcement. *Journal of Applied Behavior Analysis, 37,* 417–420.

Woods, D. W., Miltenberger, R. G., & Lumley, V. A. (1996). Sequestional application of major habit-reversal components to treat motor tics in children. *Journal of Applied Behavior Analysis, 29,* 483–493.

Woods, J., & Poulson, C. L. (2006). The use of scripts to increase the verbal initiations of children with developmental disabilities to typically developing peers. *Education and Treatment of Children, 29,* 437–457.

Woods, J. N., & Borrero, C. S. W. (2019). Examining extinction bursts in the treatment of pediatric food refusal. *Behavioral Interventions, 34,* 307–322. https://doi.org/10.1002/bin.1672

Woods, D. W., Wetterneck, C. T., & Flessner, C. A. (2005). A controlled evaluation of acceptance and commitment therapy plus habit reversal for trichotillomania. *Behaviour Research and Therapy, 44,* 639–656.

Woodward, J., Carnine, D., & Gersten, R. (1988). Teaching problem solving through computer simulations. *American Educational Research Journal, 25,* 72–86.

Woodward, J., Carnine, D., Gersten, R., Moore, L., & Golden, N. (1987). Using computer networking for feedback. *Journal of Special Education, Technology, 8*(4), 28–35.

Woodward, J., & Noell, J. (1991). Science instruction at the secondary level: Duplications for students with leaning disabilities. *Journal of Learning Disabilities, 24,* 277–284.

Worsdell, A. S., Iwata, B. A., Hanley, G. P., Thompson, R. H., & Kahng, S. (2000). Effects of continuous and intermittent reinforcement of problem behavior during functional communication training. *Journal of Applied Behavior Analysis, 33,* 167–179.

Worsdell, A., S., Iwata, B. A., & Wallace, M. D. (2002). Duration-based measures of preference of vocational task. *Journal of Applied Behavior Analysis, 35,* 287–290.

Wright, C. S., & Vollmer, T. R. (2002). Evaluation of a treatment package to reduce rapid eating. *Journal of Applied Behavior Analysis, 35,* 89–93.

Wulfert, E., & Hayes, S. C. (1988). The transfer of conditional control through conditional equivalence classes. *Journal of the Experimental Analysis of Behavior, 50,* 125–144.

Wunderlich, K. L., Vollmer, T. R., & Zabala, K. A. (2017). Assessment and treatment of automatically reinforced self-induced emesis. *Journal of Applied Behavior Analysis, 50,* 418–423. doi: 10.1002/jaba.371

Wyatt v. Stickney. (1972). 344 F. Supp. 373 F. Supp. 387 (M.D. Alabama).

Yang, K. H., Chu, H. C., & Chiang, L. Y. (2018). Effects of a progressive prompting-based educational game on second graders' mathematics learning performance and behavioral patterns. *Educational Technology & Society, 21,* 322–334. Retrieved November 25, 2020, from http://www.jstor.org/stable/26388410

Yates, B. T. (1985). Cost-effectiveness analysis and cost-benefit analysis: An introduction. *Behavioral Assessment, 7,* 207–234.

Yeager, C., & McLaughlin, T. F. (1995). The use of a timeout ribbon and precision requests to improve child compliance in the classroom: A case study. *Child & Family Behavior Therapy, 17*(4), 1–9.

Yi, L. J. (2000). *Effects of the expectation game in a primary classroom.* Unpublished master's thesis, California State University, Los Angeles.

Yoon, S., & Bennett, G. M. (2000). Effects of a stimulus-stimulus pairing procedure on conditioning vocal sounds as reinforcers. *The Analysis of Verbal Behavior, 17,* 75–88.

Yoon, S., & Feliciano, G. M. (2007). Stimulus-stimulus pairing and subsequent mand acquisition of children with various levels of verbal repertoires. *Analysis of Verbal Behavior, 23,* 3–16.

Young, J. A., & Wincze, J. P. (1974). The effects of the reinforcement of compatible and incompatible alternative behaviors on the self-injurious and related behaviors of a profoundly retarded female adult. *Behavior Therapy, 5,* 614–623.

Young, K. R., West, R. P., Howard, V. F., & Whitney, R. (1986). Acquisition, fluency training, generalization, and maintenance of dressing skills of two developmentally disabled children. *Education & Treatment of Children, 9,* 16–29.

Yukl, G. A., & Latham, G. P. (1975). Consequences of reinforcement schedules and incentive magnitudes for employee performance: Problems encountered in an industrial setting. *Journal of Applied Psychology, 60,* 294–298.

Yukl, G., A., Latham, G. P., & Pursell, E. D., (1976). The effectiveness of performance incentives under continuous and variable ratio schedules of reinforcement. *Personnel Psychology, 29,* 221–231.

Yukl, G. A., Wexley, K. N., & Seymour, J. D. (1972). The effectiveness of pay incentives under variable ratio and continuous reinforcement schedules. *Journal of Applied Psychology, 56,* 19–23.

Yurick, A. L., Robinson, P. D., Cartledge, G., Lo, Y., & Evans, T. L. (2006). Using peer-mediated repeated readings as a fluency-building activity for urban learners. *Education and Treatment of Children, 29,* 469–506.

Ysseldyke, J., Dawson, P., Lehr, C., Reschly, D., Reynolds, M., & Telzrow, C. (1997). *School psychology: A blueprint for training and practice II.* Bethesda, MD: National Association of School Psychologists.

Zagrabska, S. P., Mulhern, T., Ming, S., Stewart, I., & McElwee, J. (2020). Training class inclusion responding in individuals with autism: Further investigation. *Journal of Applied Behavior Analysis, 53*(4), 2067–2080. https://doi-org.mimas.calstatela.edu/10.1002/jaba.712

Zane, T., Walls, R. T., & Thvedt, J. E. (1981). Prompting and fading guidance procedures: Their effect on chaining and whole task teaching strategies. *Education and Training of the Mentally Retarded, 16,* 125–135.

Zanolli, K., & Daggett, J. (1998). The effects of reinforcement rate on the spontaneous social initiations of socially withdrawn preschoolers. *The Journal of Applied Behavior Analysis, 31,* 117–125.

Zarcone, J. R., Iwata, B. A., Hughes, C. E., & Vollmer, T. R. (1993). Momentum versus extinction effects in the treatment of self-injurious escape behavior. *Journal of Applied Behavior Analysis, 26,* 135–136.

Zarcone, J. R., Iwata, B. A., Mazaleski, J. L., & Smith, R. G. (1994). Momentum and extinction effects on self-injurious escape behavior and noncompliance. *Journal of Applied Behavior Analysis, 27,* 649–658.

Zarcone, J. R., Napolitano, D., & Valdovinos, M. (2008). Measurement of problem behaviour during medication evaluations. *Journal of Intellectual Disability, 52,* 1015–1028.

Zarcone, J. R., Rodgers, T. A., Iwata, B. A., Rourke, D., & Dorsey, M. F. (1991). Reliability analysis of the Motivation Assessment Scale: A failure to replicate. *Research in Developmental Disabilities, 12,* 349–360.

Zegiob, L. E., Alford, G. S., & House, A. (1978). Response suppressive and generalization effects of facial screening on multiple self-injurious behavior in a retarded boy. *Behavior Therapy, 9,* 688.

Zegiob, L. E., Jenkins, J., Becker, J., & Bristow, A. (1976). Facial screening: Effects on appropriate and inappropriate behaviors. *Journal of Behavior Therapy and Experimental Psychiatry, 7,* 355–357.

Zeilberger, J., Sampen, S. E., & Sloane, H. N., Jr. (1968). Modification of a child's problem behaviors in the home with the mother as therapist. *Journal of Applied Behavior Analysis, 1,* 47–53.

Zerger, H. M., Miller, B. G., Valbuena, D., & Miltenberger, R. G. (2017). Effects of student pairing and public review on physical activity during school recess. *Journal of Applied Behavior Analysis, 50,* 529–537. doi: 10.1002/jaba.389

Zerger, H. M., Normand, M. P., Boga, V., & Patel, R.R. (2016). Adult attention and interaction can increase moderate-to-vigorous physical activity in young children. *Journal of Applied Behavior Analysis, 49*, 449–459. doi: 10.1002/jaba.307

Zhang, R. C., Lai, H. M., Cheng, P. W., & Chen, C. P. (2017). Longitudinal effect of computer-based graduated prompting assessment on students' academic performance. *Computer & Education, 110*, 181–194.

Zhu, J., Bruhn, A., Yuan C., & Wang, L. (2021). Comparing the effect of videoconference and email feedback on treatment integrity. *Journal of Applied Behavior Analysis, 54*, 618–63. doi: 10.1002/jaba.810

Zimmerman, J., & Baydan, N. T. (1963). Punishment of S$^\Delta$ responding of humans in conditional matching-to-sample by timeout. *Journal of the Experimental Analysis of Behavior, 6*, 589–597.

Zimmerman, J., & Ferster, C. B. (1963). Intermittent punishment of S$^\Delta$ responding in matching-to-sample. *Journal of the Experimental Analysis of Behavior, 6*, 349–356.

Zimmerman, B. J., & Rosenthal, T. L. (1974). Observational learning of rule-governed behavior by children. *Psychological Bulletin, 81*, 29–42.

Zohar, D., Cohen, A., & Azar, N. (1980). Promoting increased use of ear protectors in noise through information feedback. *Human Factors, 22*, 69–79.

Zohar, D., & Fussfeld, N. (1981). Modifying earplug wearing behavior by behavior modification techniques: An empirical evaluation. *The Journal of Organizational Behavior Management, 3*(2), 41–52.

# Name Index

In this index, page references followed by a "*b*" refer to material in boxes; by an "*f*," material in figures; by an "*n*," to material in notes; and by a "*t*," to material in tables.

**A**

Aase, H., 355
Abby, L., 648
Abel, D. M., 550
Abramowitz, A. J., 733
Abreu, A., 311$t$, 319
Acker, M. M., 730, 732
Acquisto, J., 717
Adami, S., 518
Adamo, E. K., 239
Adams, A., 408
Adams, C. D., 659
Adams, G. L., 52, 404
Adams, H. E., 52, 407
Adams, M. J., 410
Adamy, P. H., 692
Addington, J., 439
Addison, I., 62
Addison, L., 314, 322, 334, 474
Addison, L. R., 526, 527
Adelinis, J. D., 465, 628, 629, 630
Adelman, B. E., 243
Adshead, V., 467, 469
Agar, G., 597, 636
Ager, A. J., 658
Agran, M., 255, 256
Aguiar, M. J., 433
Aguilar, B., 322
Aguilar, L. N., 392
Ahearn, W. H., 186, 187, 212, 217, 388, 409, 412, 505, 592, 629, 630, 631, 645
Ahlers, A. A., 251
Aiello, S., 247
Aikins, D. A., 443
Ainslie, G., 529
Ainsman, L., 66, 194, 256
Akers, B., 157
Akers, J. S., 444, 630, 633

Akintomide, H., 635
Al-hinai, M. A., 639
al-Nasser, T., 448
Ala'i, S., 764
Alavosius, M. P., 238, 316, 317, 349, 481, 523, 600
Alazeta, L., 446
Alber, S., 368, 458
Alber, S. R., 499, 560
Alberto, P., 689
Alberto, P. A., 399, 534
Albertson-Kelly, J. A., 733
Albin, R. W., 46, 211$t$, 226, 643
Albright, L., 366
Alderman, N., 674
Aldhalaan, H. M., 405
Aleardi, M., 355
Alessi, C., 311$t$
Alevizos, K. J., 704
Alevizos, P. N., 704
Alford, B. A., 46
Alford, G. S., 690
Alhaqbani, O. A., 405
Aljaser, S. M., 405
Allday, R. A., 140, 354, 376, 634
Allen, C., 279
Allen, E., 405
Allen, K. D., 48, 51, 52, 96, 140, 311$t$, 628, 635, 643
Allen, L. C., 664
Allin, J. D., 197
Allison, A. G., 692
Allison, J., 118
Allyon, T., 120
Alnemary, F., 197, 198$f$
Alper, S., 155, 255
AlSaud, A. N., 405
Alter, P. J., 44

Altman, K., 735
Alvarado, M., 329
Alvero, A. M., 129, 141, 523, 553, 555
Aman, M. G., 237
Amari, A., 108
Amari, D., 325
Anders, B. M., 242
Anderson, A., 252, 322
Anderson, C. A., 376, 415
Anderson, C. M., 215$t$, 628, 643, 644
Anderson, D. C., 48, 278, 280, 376, 550
Anderson, D. S., 60
Anderson, J. L., 226, 643
Anderson, K., 65, 354, 551, 623, 628, 641
Anderson, K. B., 60
Anderson, M. M., 720$n$
Anderson, R. C., 471
Anderson, S. R., 408
Andre, J. C., 509
Andreatos, M., 487
Andrews, D., 689
Andrews, D. W., 540
Andrews, L., 49
Anger, W. K., 693
Anthony, J. C., 678
Antonitis, J. J., 611
Antonucci, M., 610
Apolloni, T., 414
Ardoin, S. P., 463
Argott, P. J., 330
Arguelles, M., 440
Ariefdjohan, M., 658
Arkhipov, V., 609$n$
Armendariz, F., 641
Armitage, C. J., 557
Armstrong, K. J., 577
Armstrong, N., 407, 410, 416

889

Armstrong, P. M., 117
Arndorfer, R. E., 156
Arnold, C., 607
Arrington, R. E., 139, 144
Artman-Meeker, K., 548
Asfahani, S. M., 405
Ashby, E., 281, 299, 300*f*
Atak, J. R., 644
Athens, E. S., 138, 464, 686
Atkinson, R. K., 462
Atwell, J., 43, 635
Ault, M., 215*t*
Ault, M. H., 213
Ault, M. J., 388
Austin, J., 135, 250, 251, 479, 523, 532, 548, 549, 553, 557, 558, 602, 644, 678, 679
Austin, J. E., 237
Austin, J. L., 134, 597, 636
Avery, S., 630
Axelrod, S., 203, 559, 622, 670, 727, 737
Ayala, J. M., 346
Ayllon, T., 7, 70, 279, 298, 692
Ayres, K. M., 243, 412, 635
Azar, N., 537
Azrin, N. H., 6, 7, 117, 120, 139, 279, 298, 355, 376, 465, 466, 506, 507, 611, 622, 628, 641, 685, 692, 702, 706, 711, 713, 714, 715, 717, 718, 720, 722, 724, 728, 730, 732, 735, 736
Azulay, R. L., 149

**B**
Babbitt, R. L., 463
Babcock, R. A., 43, 134
Bacher, M., 499
Bachmeyer, M. H., 617, 648
Bacon, D. L., 51, 65
Bacotti, J. K., 716
Badgett, N., 548
Baer, A. M., 705
Baer, D. M., 6, 7, 9, 10, 14, 70, 80, 131, 190, 252, 286, 328, 387, 406, 410, 415, 418, 434, 448, 459, 479, 481, 482, 483, 486, 493, 494, 496, 518, 581, 591, 593, 597, 599, 687, 691, 699, 705, 755
Baer, R. A., 491
Baeyens, F., 609
Bagne, A. G., 316
Bagshaw, M., 525, 527, 535
Baham, M., 656
Baier, P. S., 536
Bailey, A., 651
Bailey, J., 446
Bailey, J. B., 707
Bailey, J. S., 49, 52, 129, 211*t*, 255, 257, 355, 358, 402, 426, 440, 441, 550, 561, 592, 611, 628, 685, 689, 693, 694, 737
Bailey, S. R., 669

Bailin, D., 255, 637
Baillargeon, L., 402
Bakeman, R., 213
Baker, J. N., 691
Baker, S. D., 411
Bakker, A. B., 253
Balcazar, F., 250, 279, 380, 553, 555
Baldes, J. J., 72
Ballard, K. D., 155, 255, 721
Ballard, T., 721
Balleweg, B. J., 509
Balsam, P. D., 98, 511, 540
Bambara, L. M., 40
Bamford, C., 98
Bancroft, S., 388
Banda, D. R., 437, 463, 636
Bandura, A., 49, 327, 407, 413, 414, 415, 416, 417, 617, 719, 723, 724
Banko, K. M., 100
Barbaranelli, C., 327
Barbera, M. L., 437
Barbetta, P. M., 138, 640, 663
Barker, M. R., 402
Barlow, D., 584
Barlow, D. H., 288, 590, 598
Barnard-Brak, L., 648
Barnard, J. C., 304
Barnard, J. K., 735
Barnes, C. S., 444
Barnes, D., 370, 524, 527
Barnes-Holmes, D., 427, 446, 447
Barnes-Holmes, Y., 427, 448
Barnes, T., 369
Baron, A., 95, 504, 517, 536, 551
Barone, V. J., 48, 693, 701
Barrera, F., 688, 702
Barrera, R. D., 410, 419
Barreras, R. B., 331
Barrett, R. P., 690
Barretto, A., 225, 612, 643
Barrish, H. H., 538, 677
Barry, L., 430
Barry, L. M., 311*t*
Barry, N. J., 413, 414
Bartlett, B., 439
Barton, E. E., 239, 457
Barton, E. J., 415, 418, 716
Barton, L. E., 667, 705
Bass, R., 303
Batsche, C., 411
Bauer, A., 640
Bauer, J., 607
Bauman, K. E., 90, 203, 614
Baumeister, A. A., 376, 628, 641
Baxter, E. L., 504, 541
Baydan, N. T., 703, 704
Beaman, A. L., 508
Beastay, A., 527
Beauchamp, K., 628
Beaulieu, L., 560

Bechtel, D. R., 666, 716, 735, 736
Becirevic, A., 49, 50
Becker, J., 690
Becker, W. C., 403, 404, 461, 476
Beckers, T., 609
Becraft, J. L., 120, 674
Beesley, T., 473
Behavior Analyst Certification Board (BACB), 8, 48, 49, 77, 117, 128, 606, 701, 727, 734, 736, 754
Behrman, M. M., 466
Beilby, J. M., 693
Belfiore, P., 215*t*, 636
Belfiore, P. J., 636
Belisle, J., 447, 448
Bell, L. K., 90
Bellack, B., 174
Ben-Tall, A., 406
Benavidas, C., 446
Benchaaban, D., 466
BenitaezSantiago, A., 412
Benitez, B. B., 351
Bennett, C. M., 705
Bennett, G. M., 429
Bennett, M. K., 386
Benoit, B., 321
Benoit, R. B., 706
Bentall, R. P., 527, 536
Berberich, J. P., 410, 430
Berens, N. M., 197, 200*f*, 448
Berg, W. K., 138, 142, 225, 386, 484
Bergarmann, S. C., 44, 132
Berger, S. M., 551
Bergman, J., 541
Bergmann, S., 405
Bergstrom, M. K., 40, 562
Bergstrom, R., 329, 407
Berkler, M. S., 142
Berkowitz, L., 622, 721
Bernal, M. E., 157
Bernhardt, A. J., 238, 724, 733
Bernstein, H., 505
Berotti, D., 637
Berquist, K.L., 386
Berzins, L. G., 311*t*
Besalel, V. A., 715
Best, L., 635
Bethke, S. A., 591
Bethke, S. D., 617, 648
Betz, A. M., 518, 630
Bevan, P., 720
Bevirt, J., 415
Bicard, D. E., 524
Bicard, D. F., 237
Bickel, W. K., 591*n*
Bicklin, D., 760
Biederman, J., 355
Biggs, J., 538
Biglan, A., 257, 562, 623, 634
Bijou, S., 698

Bijou, S. W., 6, 7, 213, 215*t*, 405, 505
Billington, E., 539
Binder, C., 49, 393, 404
Binder, L. M., 49, 237
Binkoff, J. A., 90, 287, 705, 721
Binnendyk, L., 46, 47, 287, 298
Bird, F. L., 652
Birnbrauer, J. S., 7, 694
Bisen-Hersh, E. B., 304
Bishop, J. R., 690
Bittle, R., 584
Bittle, R. G., 666
Black, L. I., 428
Black, S., 473
Blair, B. J., 366
Blampied, N. M., 311*t*, 716
Blanton, R. L., 511
Blew, P. A., 416
Blick, D. W., 155
Block, B. L., 415
Blom, D. E., 328
Bloom, L., 75
Bloom, S. E., 91, 225, 240, 242
Blum, S., 634
Blume, Arthur W., 93
Blumenfeld, G. T., 528, 529*f*
Bocher, J., 189
Bocian, K., 327
Bock, S. J., 651
Boe, E. E., 732
Boehlecke, B., 311*t*
Boelema, T., 411
Boettcher, W., 89
Boga, V., 649
Bogart, L. C., 690
Boggs, S. R., 659
Boivin, M., 650
Boles, S., 157
Bolivar, H. A., 108
Bolton, D. M., 554
Bond, J., 98
Bondy, A., 69*n*, 194, 285*b*, 366, 427, 434, 437, 445, 484, 605, 607
Bondy, A. S., 43, 52, 98, 244, 511, 540
Bonfiglio, C. M., 490
Boni, N., 48
Boren, J., 506
Boren, J. J., 695
Boreson, L., 231, 699
Borgmeier, C. J., 52
Boring, E. G., 6
Borlase, M. A., 335
Bornstein, P. H., 509
Borrego, J., Jr., 695
Borrero, C. S. W., 610
Borrero, J., 355
Borrero, J. C., 512, 540, 672, 674, 728
Bosch, A., 648
Bosch, J. D., 472
Bosch, S., 66

Bostow, D. E., 301, 304, 528, 529*f*, 707
Bothyune, S., 408
Boudreau, J., 413
Bourgeois, B., 607
Bourgeois, B. C., 409
Bourret, J., 287, 388
Bourret, J. C., 212, 217, 474
Bouton, M. E., 609
Bouxsein, K. J., 349, 494, 666
Bovi, G. M. D., 112
Bowman, L. G., 108, 112, 433, 527
Box, P., 677
Boyajian, A. E., 636
Boyajian, L. G., 509
Boyce, T. E., 122, 479, 554, 555, 559
Boyer, E., 411
Boylan, S., 664
Boyle, J. R., 252, 254, 257
Boyle, M., 37
Boyle, M. A., 240, 242
Braam, S. J., 440, 582, 583*f*
Bradley, D., 686
Bradley-Johnson, S., 70, 457, 458
Bradley, L., 600
Bradshaw, C. M., 720
Bradshaw, M. F., 472
Brady, M., 579, 580, 636
Brady, M. P., 416, 462, 636
Brakman, C., 700*b*
Brandt, J. A. A., 3
Brantner, J. P., 698, 700*b*
Braukmann, C. J., 281, 416
Brechner, K. C., 131
Breevaart, K., 253
Bremner, R., 37
Brence, J., 278, 280
Brewer, A. T., 675
Breyer, N. L., 279
Briesch, A. M., 252
Briesch, J. M., 252
Briggs, A. M., 351, 518, 613
Brigham, T. A., 279, 628
Bright, C. N., 630
Brigman, J. L., 119
Brissett, E., 677
Bristow, A., 690
Britner, P. A., 245
Britten, K., 392
Brobst, B., 194, 195*f*, 251
Brockman, M. P., 677
Broden, M., 155, 257
Brodhead, M., 764
Brodhead, M. T., 436, 633, 765, 766
Brody, G. H., 407
Brody, J. A., 407
Broen, P., 694
Brooks, B. D., 245
Brosh, C. R., 637
Brothers, K. J., 485, 639
Brougher, J., 253

Broussard, C., 122, 279
Brouwer, R., 416
Browder, D. M., 457
Brown, B. L., 313, 323, 407
Brown, C. S., 43, 137, 236, 354, 376, 479, 634
Brown, D., 211*t*, 253
Brown, E. M., 557
Brown, J. A., 52
Brown, K., 142, 242, 592
Brown, K. A., 616*n*
Brown, K. E., 389
Brown, M. A., 556
Brown, R., 407, 649
Brown, S. M., 720*n*
Brown, T. M., 311*t*
Brown, T. W., 348
Brown, W. H., 407
Browning-Wright, D., 230, 231
Brulle, A. R., 667
Brunner, J., 559
Brunsting, N. C., 561
Bruzek, J. L., 116
Bryan, K. S., 443
Bryan, L., 466
Buchanan, J. A., 635
Bucher, B., 696
Bucher, B. D., 715, 716, 736
Buckhold, D., 73
Buckley, J., 288
Buckley, N. K., 488
Buckley, S. D., 91, 446, 666
Bucklin, A., 212
Bucklin, B. R., 505, 510, 523, 553
Budd, A., 389, 461
Budd, C. M., 607
Budd, K., 691
Budley, A. J., 253
Buffington, D., 411
Buggey, R., 413
Bugle, C., 298
Bukala, M., 251
Bukowski, W. M., 650
Bulla, A. J., 640
Bullet, J., 485
Bunaciu, L., 136
Bunuan, R. L., 677
Burch, M. R., 129
Burchard, J. D., 670, 688, 702
Burchard, S. N., 670
Burg, M. M., 51
Burgio, L. D., 319, 550, 703, 730
Burke, J. C., 600
Burke, M. M., 407
Burke, R. V., 51
Burlew, S. B., 311*t*
Burnett, J., 388
Burns, M. K., 392
Burt, C. H., 723
Burt, R. B., 382

Busch, A. B., 660, 691
Bush, M. N., 634
Bushell, D., Jr., 279, 628
Bushman, B. J., 376, 415
Buskist, W., 302
Buskist, W. F., 523, 527, 536, 538
Butryn, M. L., 311*t*
Butterworth, T., 355, 633, 721
Buzzella, B., 136
Byra, K. L., 462
Byrne, B., 413, 415
Byrne, K. J., 311*t*

### C

Cagliani, R. R., 243
Cairns, B. D., 650
Cairns, R. B., 650
Caldarella, P., 726
Caldwell, N. K., 323, 456
Call, N. A., 526, 527, 612
Camarata, S., 406
Camare, M., 288, 294
Cameron, J., 100
Cameron, J. J., 311*t*, 462
Cameron, M. J., 286, 294, 298
Cammilleri, A. P., 147
Campbel, V., 402
Campbell, A., 304
Campbell, D. T., 574, 575
Campbell, E., 641
Campbell, J. M., 598, 693
Campbell, N., 499
Campbell, R., 651
Campbell, S., 279
Campbell, S. L., 730
Campbell, V., 405, 642
Campos, B. A., 409
Canale, J., 142
Cannella, H., 612, 643
Cappello, M. J., 286, 294, 298
Caprara, G. V., 327
Cardon, T., 414
Carek, D. J., 666
Carey, R. G., 715, 716, 736
Cariveau, T., 350, 368, 402, 405
Carlile, K. A., 412
Carlson, J. D., 462
Carlson, J. I., 622, 637
Carlson, J. K., 311*t*, 332, 333
Carmignani, K., 288, 642
Carnes, M., 638
Carngan, P., 370
Carnine, D. W., 402, 403, 404
Carpenter, M., 435, 443, 607
Carples, S., 414
Carr, A., 668
Carr, D., 493
Carr, E. G., 18, 45–46, 48, 49–50, 65, 72, 90, 180, 203, 226, 287, 376, 435, 607, 622, 628, 641, 643, 705, 716, 720, 721
Carr, J. E., 51, 136, 144, 157, 335, 368, 429, 440, 442, 556, 592, 654, 716
Carreau, A. B., 225
Carroll, R. A., 43, 112, 405, 429
Carrow, J. N., 418
Carsky, M., 325
Cartelli, L. M., 695
Carter, C. M., 66, 243, 354, 637
Carter, M., 311*t*
Carton, J. S., 280
Casey, S. D., 513, 628
Caspi, A., 327
Castillo, M., 674
Catagnus, R., 764
Catagnus, R. M., 348
Cataldo, M., 717
Cataldo, M. F., 65, 146, 512, 622, 657
Catania, A. C., 23, 24, 28, 128*n*, 236, 304, 305, 322, 355, 478, 510, 515, 516, 521*n*, 524, 527, 536, 539, 541, 592, 597, 609*n*, 637, 644, 684, 712
Cates, G. L., 539, 639
Cautela, J. R., 420
Cautilli, J., 559
Cavalier, A. R., 676
Cavin, M., 255
Cengher, M., 389, 461, 474
Center, D. B., 243, 705
Cerro, N., 459
Cerveti, M., 413
Chafouleas, S. M., 244, 245
Chalmers, D. K., 414
Chamberlain, P., 559
Chan, J. M., 207, 642
Chan, P. E., 288, 295
Chandler, L. K., 327, 483, 488
Chang, S., 136
Chappell, L. R., 506, 510
Chard, D., 404
Charlop-Christy, M. H., 410, 411, 412, 435, 443, 607
Charlop, M., 386
Charlop, M. H., 457, 651, 703, 730
Charlton, C. T., 657
Charman, T., 600
Chase, P. N., 95, 304, 427, 456
Cheatham, J. M., 405
Chee, M. W. L., 715
Cheiken, M., 134
Chen, C. P., 460
Chen, H. S., 634
Cheney, C. D., 26, 521*n*
Cheney, D., 211*t*
Cheng, P. W., 460
Cheung, K., 718
Chiang, L. Y., 460
Child, A., 330
Childs, K. E., 155, 156, 211*t*
Chockalingam, A., 499
Choi, H. Y., 612, 643
Christensen, A., 209*b*, 211*t*
Christian, W. P., 472
Christoph, N. L., 532
Christophersen, E. R., 693, 701, 735
Christy, P. R., 99
Chronis, A. M., 690, 693
Chu, H. C., 460
Chung, B. I., 186, 187, 629, 645
Church, R. J., 52, 553, 555
Church, R. M., 711, 732
Churchill, R. M., 225
Cicchetti, D. V., 60
Cicero, F. R., 466
Cihak, D., 399, 412, 534
Cihelkova, D., 304
Cihon, J. H., 277, 360
Cihoon, J. H., 332
Cipollone, R., 717
Cirelli, C. A., 631
Cividini-Motta, C., 631
Clare, L., 467
Clark, E., 413
Clark, H. B., 705
Clark, K. A., 388
Clark, K. M., 186, 187, 389, 629, 645
Clark, R. J., 554
Clarke, L. S., 640
Clarke, M., 278, 280
Clarke, S., 155, 156, 211*t*, 243, 402, 419, 625
Clayton, M., 386
Clegg, J. C., 129
Clement, P. W., 28, 108
Clements, J. E., 510
Cleveland, J., 119, 121, 225, 335
Clifford, C., 724
Coatee, A.M., 412
Cochran, S. T., 721
Codding, R. S., 51–52, 52, 156, 549, 600, 641
Coe, D. A., 463
Coello, A. R., 628
Cohen, A., 537
Cohen, I. L., 598
Cohen, L. L., 693
Cohrs, C. M., 51
Colavecchia, B., 719, 733
Cole, G. A., 715
Coleman, J., 311*t*
Collier-Meek, M. A., 44
Collins, B. C., 315*t*, 322, 323, 466
Collins, L. W., 554
Collins, S., 214, 411
Collins, T., 592
Colman, A. D., 695
Colombo, R. A., 762
Colón, C. L., 592, 625, 630
Colvin, G., 625
Combs, J. L., 407

Conine, D. E., 108
Connell, D. W., 550
Connell, J. E., 304, 370, 492, 600
Conner, R., 717
Conners, J., 110, 112, 585, 588, 719, 728, 729f
Connolly, J. F., 692
Conroy, M. A., 61, 212
Constantine, B., 391
Contreras, B. P., 518, 633
Contrucci, S. A., 64, 315t, 376, 643, 644
Conyers, C., 243, 412
Cook, C. R., 43, 44, 51, 52, 156, 230, 231, 328, 331, 634, 641
Cook, D. T., 574
Cook, J. L., 630, 665
Cook, K. E., 607
Cook, R., 614
Cook, S. C., 554
Cook, T. D., 575
Cooke, S. A., 414
Cooke, T. P., 414
Cooper-Duffy, K., 39
Cooper, L. J., 242, 592
Coppage, S., 699
Copsey, C. J., 51
Corbin-Newsome, J., 607
Corbin, S., 686, 693, 695
Cordisco, L., 690
Corralejo, S. M., 703
Correa, V. I., 459
Corrigan, P. W., 46, 559, 560
Corsaut, S., 490
Cosgrove, D., 721
Cossairt, A., 251, 553, 555, 561
Costello, M. S., 182
Cote, C. A., 109
Cotnoir-Bichelman, N. M., 457
Cotton, J. L., 46, 626, 638
Courtney, W. T., 633
Couzens, D., 311t, 457
Cowdery, G. E., 65, 408
Cox, D. J., 765
Coyle, J. A., 587
Coyne, A., 400, 704
Craft, M. A., 500, 560
Crafton, D., 640
Craig, A. R., 598, 613
Craig, M. S., 392, 511
Craighead, W. E., 174
Creel, J., 279
Creel, L., 279
Creer, T. L., 315, 322, 326
Cresson, O., Jr., 366, 369, 446
Crews, S. D., 230, 231, 328
Crimmins, D. B., 211t
Crisolo, S. S., 540
Critchfield, T. S., 48, 49, 50, 256, 365
Crockett, J. L., 157, 527
Cronbach, L.J., 128n

Crone, D., 211t
Crone, D. A., 40, 562
Crone, R. M., 487
Crone-Todd, D. E., 302, 303
Croner, M. D., 414
Cronin, J., 51
Cronin, K. A., 325
Cronin, M. E., 252, 255
Crosbie, J., 343, 712, 720n
Crosland, K., 643
Crosland, K. A., 288, 295, 384
Crossett, S. E., 705
Crowell, C. R., 48, 118, 278, 280, 538, 550
Crozier, S., 446, 527
Culig, K., 523
Cummings, A., 238, 719
Cummings, C., 368
Cunnigham, S., 370
Cunningham, T. R., 37, 557, 558
Curtis, R., 303–304
Cush, D., 302
Cuvo, A. G., 325
Cuvo, A. J., 316, 446
Cymbal, D., 556

## D

Daar, J. H., 447
Daggett, J., 623, 641
Dailey, D., 418
Dallery, J., 134, 157
Dally, E. J.,, III, 136
Dalrymple, A. J., 466
Dalton, T., 252
Daly, E. J., 490
Danaher, B. G., 157
Dancho, K. A., 457
Daneshvar, S., 411, 651
Danforth, J. S., 427
Danielle, S., 707n
Daniels, A., 24, 40, 381
Daniels, A. C., 3, 68, 89, 116, 234, 250, 284, 396, 512, 618, 767
Daniels, J., 40
Darcheville, J. C., 523, 524
Dart, E. H., 518
Darwin, C., 4
Davenport, K., 407
Davey, B. J., 376, 637
Davey, G. C. L., 701
Davidson, N. A., 505, 514, 529
Davis, B., 674
Davis, C. A., 376, 635, 636
Davis, D. R., 301
Davis, P. A., 705
Davis, T. N., 434, 504, 630, 642
Dawdy, M., 440
Dawson, G., 408
Dawson, G. R., 609n
Dawson, M. J., 690

Dawson, N. M., 252
Dawson, P., 639
Day, H. M., 446, 589, 638, 642
Day-Watkins, J., 418, 492
De Castro, B. O., 472, 491
De Ceulaer, A., 609
De Luca, R. V., 505, 510
De Rose, J. C., 365, 446
De Souza, D. G., 365
De Souza, D. V., 365
de Wijk, R. A., 376
Deal, T. E., 685, 693
DeBar, R. M., 112, 411, 412
DeBaryshe, B. D., 354, 633
DeCasper, A. J., 429, 443
Decker, P. J., 386
Deckner, C. S., 511
Deckner, P. O., 511
DeGrandpre, R. J., 302
DeHaven, F., 666
Deitz, S. M., 461, 674, 676
Dejud, C., 72, 640
Delano, M., 413, 651
Delano, M. E., 155
DeLeon, I. G., 100, 110, 112, 139, 239, 242, 251, 527, 644, 648, 662, 667, 683
Deliperi, P., 411
Delprato, D. J., 406
Delquadri, J., 138, 715
Delulio, D. W., 388
Demchak, M., 469
Demerouti, E., 253
Demers, M., 402
Demetral, F. D., 690
Deneshvar, S., 412
Dengerink, K., 52, 551
Deochand, N., 182
DePalma, V., 492
dePerczel, M., 243
DeQuinzio, J. A., 298, 409, 410
Derby, K. M., 628, 643
Derenne, A., 504
DeRicco, D. A., 415
DeRosa, N. M., 613, 630, 690
Deschaine, E., 627
DeSouza, A. A., 444, 446, 636
Detweiler, D. D., 716
Devany, J. M., 372
Diament, C., 134
Dibley, S., 142
Dicesare, A., 118
Dickes, N., 236
Dickes, N. R., 441
Dickinson, A. M., 89, 242, 505, 510, 523, 554
Dickman, S. E., 630
Dickson, C. A., 412
Dickson, S., 404
Didden, R., 252, 716
Diekman, C. A., 351

DiGennaro, F. D., 43, 44, 52, 215t, 296, 297, 553, 555, 556
Dingman, L. A., 410
Dinsmoor, J. A., 730
Dishion, J. J., 633
Dishion, T. J., 327, 354, 540, 633, 634, 650
Dittlinger, L. H., 462
Ditzian, K., 672
Dixon, J. A., 717
Dixon, L. S., 471
Dixon, M., 157, 372, 447
Dixon, M. H., 370
Dixon, M. R., 237, 238, 448, 530
Dobson, N., 414
Dodson, K. G., 484, 488
Dogan, R. K., 418
Doggett, R. A., 211t
Doherty, M. A., 698, 700b
Doke, L. A., 64, 715
Dolan, L. J., 677
Doleys, D. M., 695, 711, 724, 733
Dolezal, D., 138
Domen, M., 550
Dominguez, A., 718
Donahoe, J. W., 376, 609n
Donaldson, A. M., 658
Donaldson, J. M., 112, 401, 518, 592, 678, 679, 699, 706
Donaldson, T., 408, 537
Doney, J. K., 657
Donnellan, A. L., 426
Donnelly, D. R., 674
Donnelly, M. G., 43, 325
Donnerstein, E., 376
Donny, E. C., 728n
Dooley, P., 631
Doorn, J. V., 689
Dore-Boyce, K., 155, 156
Dorsey, B. L., 133
Dorsey, M. F., 90, 203, 212, 311t, 366, 376, 614, 628, 641, 705
Doshi, J., 635
Dossett, D. L., 505
Dotson, V. A., 149
Doty, D. W., 695, 706
Dougan, J. D., 527
Dougher, M. J., 464
Dougherty, B. S., 662, 700
Doughty, A. H., 644
Doughty, S. S., 628, 643
Douglas, T. J., 506
Dove, D., 413
Dowdy, A., 656
Dowler, D. L., 457
Downs, A. F. K., 415
Dowrick, P. W., 413
Dozier, C., 678
Dozier, C. L., 188, 335, 351, 518, 607, 608, 644

Drabman, R., 95
Drabman, R. S., 486
Dracobly, J. D., 351, 518
Draper, A., 715
Drasgow, E., 43, 485
Drew, J., 242
Drifke, M. A., 237, 251, 460, 532, 660
Driscoll, M., 686, 693, 695
Drover, A., 499
Drysdale, H., 411
DuBard, M., 554
Dube, W. V., 350, 368, 370, 391, 467, 471, 645
Dubois, D. L., 327
Ducharme, D. E., 490, 628
Ducharme, J. M., 463
Dudfield, G., 457
Due, K. M., 414, 415
Dufour, M.-M., 666
Dufrene, B. A., 211t
Duggan, L. M., 118
Duhon, G. J., 484, 488
Duker, P. C., 719
Dukes, C., 416
Dumas, J. E., 253
Duncan, D. V., 690
Dunkel-Jackson, S. M., 237
Dunlap, G., 47, 60, 155, 156, 211t, 226, 243, 376, 402, 494, 625, 635, 637, 640, 643, 719, 730
Dunlap, K. D., 239
Dunn, E. K., 52, 600
Dupont, S., 40n
Durand, V. M., 72, 90, 203, 211t, 352, 435, 484, 607, 728
Durica, K., 304
Dustin, R., 40
Duyile, L., 660
Dwyer, K., 623
Dyer, K., 40n, 75, 90, 108, 112, 239, 243, 402, 472, 637
Dyer, R., 167, 168

E
Eachus, H. T., 407
Earles, T. L., 651
East, A., 554
Eccles, M., 98
Eckert, T. L., 636
Ecott, C. L., 592
Eddy, J. M., 678
Edelen-Smith, P., 252, 253
Edmunds, S. R., 157
Edrisinha, C., 610, 612, 643
Edwards, G. I., 376
Edwards, G. L., 110, 111
Edwards, K. A., 376, 634
Edwards, L., 155, 253, 498
Edwards, L. J., 157
Edwards, M., 559

Edwards, R. P., 239
Edwards, T. L., 32, 351, 353
Egel, A. L., 120, 414, 512, 716
Egemo-Helm, K., 316, 492
Egervari, G., 95
Eid, A. M., 405
Eigenheer, P., 432, 437
Eikeseth, S., 326, 406, 493
Eisner, H., 720
Elkins, B., 631
Elliffe, D., 142, 144
Ellingson, S. A., 690, 693
Elliott, K. M., 472
Elliott, S. N., 49, 694, 725
Ellis, J., 706
Ellis, W. D., 319, 321, 474
Ellsworth, C., 225, 335, 355
Emara, E., 639
Embree, M. C., 721
Embry, D. D., 677, 678, 679
Endicott, K., 437
Endo, S., 237, 466
Engel, B. T., 550
Engelmann, S., 403, 404, 461, 476, 625
Ennis, B. J., 697
Ennis, R. P., 239
Epperly, A. C., 640
Epstein, L. H., 215t, 676, 715
Epstein, R., 155, 408, 609, 612, 618, 732
Epton, T., 557
Erickson, L. M., 347
Eron, L. D., 721, 723
Ersner-Hershfield, R., 707
Ervin, R., 661
Ervin, R. A., 335
Esch, B. E., 429
Esch, J. W., 444
Esveldt-Dawson, K., 588, 716
Etscheidt, S., 43, 229, 607
Etzel, B. C., 346, 470
Evanovich, L. L., 554
Evans, G. W., 376
Evans, I. M., 316, 599, 718
Evans, L. D., 694
Everett, G. E., 239
Everett, P. B., 506
Ewell, M. D., 52
Eyberg, S. M., 659

F
Fabiano, G. A., 690, 693
Fadiman, A., 36n
Fahmie, T. A., 61, 73, 170, 172, 225, 329, 582, 641
Fahrenkrog, C., 412
Fairbank, J. A., 122
Fajardo, D. E., 65
Falcomata, R. S., 686, 693, 694, 696
Falcomata, T., 407
Falcomata, T. S., 518

Falk, G. D., 155, 156
Fallang, B., 38
Fallon, L. M., 44, 253
Faloon, B. J., 498
Fanino, E., 637
Fantuzzo, J. R., 253, 486
Farber, H., 51
Farmer-Dougan, V., 116
Farmer, V. A., 527
Farone, S. V., 355
Farrar, M. J., 690
Farrell, D., 280
Farrell, D. A., 325
Farrell, N., 389, 461
Farrimond, S. J., 136, 386
Farris, H. E., 118, 539
Fauke, J., 388
Favell, J., 718, 719
Favell, J. E., 376, 628, 641, 683, 705, 729, 737
Fee, V. E., 689
Feeley, K. M., 489
Feinberg, A. B., 52, 600
Felce, D., 705
Felde, A., 439, 639
Feldman, E. K., 89
Feldman, M. A., 466
Feldman, R., 499, 537$n$
Feldman, R. A., 650
Feldman, R. S., 65
Feliciano, G. M., 429
Fellner, D., 146
Fellner, D. J., 36, 46, 553, 557, 626, 638
Fenlons, S., 660
Fenza, K. M., 612
Ferguson, 277
Ferguson, D. L., 289$b$, 293, 534
Ferguson, J. L., 277, 332, 360
Ferguson, R. H., 518
Ferguson, R. J., 666
Ferguson, S., 661
Fernald, P. S., 301
Fernandez, N., 100
Ferraro, F. R., 527
Ferreri, S., 407, 410, 416
Ferreri, S. J., 194, 195$f$, 196, 237, 586, 587$f$
Ferretti, R. P., 676
Ferritor, D. E., 73
Ferster, C. B., 24, 503$n$, 504, 517, 527, 529, 530, 674, 687$n$, 703
Fetrow, R. A., 678
Fetzer, J. L., 335
Fiat, A., 156, 634, 641
Field, D. P., 505
Field, S., 764
Fields, L., 518
Fienup, D. M., 79, 89, 251, 385, 389, 427, 461, 506
Fifer, W. P., 429

Finkel, A. S., 441
Firestone, P. B., 719
Fischer, S. M., 214
Fischetti, A. T., 418, 639
Fish, L. M., 631
Fishbein, J. E., 678
Fisher, J., 715
Fisher, J. E., 635
Fisher, K. J., 628
Fisher, L. B., 637
Fisher, M. H., 407, 491
Fisher, P. A., 420
Fisher, W., 717
Fisher, W. W., 43, 108, 109, 110, 111, 112, 236, 239, 315$t$, 348, 349, 351, 388, 389, 390, 391, 411, 413, 433, 444, 541, 598, 607, 611, 613, 644, 648, 666, 669, 717, 727, 728
Fisk, K. E., 43
Fitlerer, K., 332
Fitterling, J. M., 298
Fixsen, D., 280, 693
Fixsen, D. L., 155, 257, 416
Flaherty, C. F., 538$n$
Flanagan, S., 52, 407
Flanders, N. A., 724
Flannery, K. B., 46
Fleming, E., 311$t$
Fleming, R., 43, 157, 303
Fleming, R. K., 52, 324, 554
Flessner, C., 482, 492
Fletcher, V. I., 418
Flood, W. A., 110, 665, 673
Flores, M., 607
Flores, M. M., 409
Flower, A., 677
Flye, B., 139
Fogel, V., 411
Fogel, V. A., 288, 295
Foley, E. A., 678
Fong, E. H., 36, 764
Fonger, A. M., 285, 286
Fonseca, M., 365, 446
Foodman, G. S., 720
Forehand, R., 52, 238, 376, 407, 628, 641, 707, 716, 724, 733
Forlizzi, J. L., 120, 637
Forman, S. G., 693, 702
Forte, S., 91
Fowler, S. A., 252, 327, 387, 483, 662, 700
Fowler, T., 368
Fox, A. E., 669
Fox, C. J., 52, 122, 734
Fox, D. K., 693
Fox, E. J., 393
Fox, J. J., 212, 351$n$
Fox, L., 226, 626, 643
Foxx, C. L., 706, 707
Foxx, R. M., 49, 50, 465, 660, 666, 689,
690, 694, 706, 707, 715, 716, 722, 725, 735, 736, 737
Frampton, S., 350
Frampton, S. E., 404, 432
France, K. G., 311$t$
Francisco, M. T., 512, 540
Frank, A. R., 253
Frank-Crawford, M. A., 100
Frank, J. L., 557, 623
Franklin, D. E., 693
Frankowsky, R. J., 538
Frantino, E. P., 311$t$, 320
Fraser, M. W., 327
Frazer, T. J., 630
Frea, W., 607
Frea, W. D., 253, 327, 457
Fredericks, D. W., 93
Fredrick, L. D., 399, 534
Freeland, J. T., 496
Freeland, M., 686, 693, 695
Freeman, K. A., 215$t$, 461, 463, 592, 610, 617, 660
Freitag, G., 611
Fremouw, W., 414
French, D. C., 650
French, D. D., 691
Frentz, C., 694
Freud, S., 3
Fricchione, G., 420
Friedman, P., 698
Friedman, P. R., 697
Friman, P., 638
Friman, P. C., 358, 693, 701
Frisch, M. B., 133
Fritz, J. N., 225, 319, 418, 637
Froggatt, A. L., 46, 626, 638
Frost, L., 194, 285$b$, 366, 427, 434, 437, 445, 484, 607
Frost, L. A., 43, 52, 244
Frying, M. J., 43
Fryling, M., 405
Fuerst, J., 155
Fujita, Y., 155
Fullen, J. A., 330
Fuller, E. J., 670
Fuller, J. L., 79, 385, 506
Fullerton, E. K., 628
Fulton, B. J., 51, 65
Funk, D. M., 388, 403
Funk, M., 403
Fuqua, R. W., 66, 182, 253, 311$t$, 507, 582, 583$f$
Fusilier, I., 117, 355
Fussfeld, N., 280
Futtersak, M. W., 733

**G**

Gable, R. A., 52, 231
Gadaire, D. M., 677
Gage, N. A., 100, 720

Gagnon, E., 651
Gaither, G. A., 517
Gajar, A. H., 64
Galbraith, L. A., 678
Gale, B., 230, 231
Galensky, T. L., 690
Galiatsatos, G. T., 110
Galizio, M., 95, 517, 536
Galjour, M., 592
Gallagher, A. C., 411
Gallagher, M. M., 689
Gallessich, J., 561
Gallimore, R., 550
Galvin, G. A., 694
Gansle, K. A., 43
Ganz, J. B., 311t, 409, 607
Garand, J., 651
Garcia-Albea, E., 485, 492
Garcia, E. E., 485, 666
Garden, S. M., 658
Gardenier, N. C., 645
Gardiner, M., 252
Gardner, P., 413
Gardner, R.,, III, 641
Gardner, W., 598
Garfinkle, A. N., 408, 414, 487, 607
Garito, J., 690
Garlinghouse, M., 690
Gary, A. L., 349
Gasior, M., 541
Gassaway, L. J., 315t, 322, 323
Gast, D. L., 325, 327, 372, 457, 466, 704
Gates, B., 562
Gatheridge, B., 482, 492
Gaucher, M., 517, 674
Gaul, K., 459
Gauthier, K. A., 630
Gaylord-Ross, R., 90
Geer, B. D., 613
Gelfand, D. L., 408
Gelfand, D. M., 723
Geller, E. S., 122, 358, 478, 479, 538, 554, 555, 559
Geren, M. A., 391
Gerencser, K. R., 633
Gerow, S., 630
Gershaw, N. J., 61
Gershoff, E. T., 717, 720, 726
Gersten, R., 404, 602
Getch, Y. Q., 643
Gettinger, M., 138
Gharapetian, L., 197, 198f
Ghezzi, P. M., 189, 237, 280, 385, 393, 406, 657
Giannakakos, A. R., 516
Giannaris, W. J., 666
Gibbs, A. R., 631
Gibson, D. M., 157
Gibson, L., 110
Giles, A., 391, 630, 633

Giles, A. F., 467, 469
Gillat, A., 43, 52, 557, 561, 626
Gillund, B., 527
Gilroy, D., 473
Girolami, K. M., 516
Girolami, P. A., 516
Glassanbury, M., 252
Glassford, T. S., 613
Glenn, I. M., 134
Glenn, S. S., 155
Glover, A. C., 110
Glover, J., 349
Glynn, T., 155, 255
Gnagy, E. M., 690, 693
Goddard, Y. L., 252
Goes, L. A., 630
Goetz, E. M., 284, 298, 346, 518, 733
Goh, A. E., 40, 611
Goh, H., 228, 586f
Goh, H. L., 645, 648, 662
Goings, K., 51
Gold, M., 639
Gold, M. J., 611
Golden, C. J., 666
Goldiamond, I., 6, 7, 18, 72
Goldsmith, T. R., 440, 441
Goldstein, A. P., 61, 328
Goldstein, H., 407, 652
Goldstein, R. S., 328, 699
Goldwater, B., 286
Golly, A., 623
Gonzalez-Garrido, A. A., 472
Good, W., 212
Goodkin, K., 518
Gordon, B. D., 689
Gordon, J. S., 157
Gordon, R. K., 600
Gorget, J., 517, 674
Gorski, J. A. B., 577
Gorthmaker, V. J., 136
Gotestam, K. G., 376
Gotjen, D. L., 239, 648
Gottman, J. M., 213, 598
Gottselig, M., 664
Gouboth, D., 189
Gover, H. C., 641
Goza, A. B., 735
Grace, R. C., 167
Grady, E. A., 156, 641
Graff, R. B., 110
Graham, D. P., 70
Graham, S., 252
Granger, R. G., 532
Grant, S. H., 354, 724
Gratz, O. H., 513
Graubard, P. S., 499, 560
Grauerholz-Fisher, E., 644
Gravey, C., 695
Gravina, N., 523, 549
Gravina, N. E., 250, 251

Gray, C., 651
Gray, J. A., 755
Gray, K., 492
Gray, T. W., 358
Greathouse, A. D., 703
Green, C. W., 251, 489
Green, D., 99, 100
Green, D. R., 332
Green, G., 344, 359, 364, 367, 369, 370, 385, 389, 443, 467, 468, 471
Green, K. D., 716
Green, L., 541
Green, M. F., 467
Green, V. A., 355, 411
Greene, B. F., 73
Greene, D., 97
Greenwald, A. E., 656
Greenway, D. E., 464
Greer, B. D., 612
Greer, D. G., 393
Greer, R. D., 106, 315t, 437, 443, 462
Gregg, G., 609n
Gregory, M. K., 672
Gresham, F. M., 43, 44, 231, 327, 328, 331, 335, 464, 600, 628, 630, 688, 694
Grey, I., 577, 578f
Griffen, A. K., 456
Griffin, J. C., 735
Griffin, M. M., 407
Griffith, K., 139
Griffitt, W., 413, 415
Grimes, J. A., 531, 609
Grindle, A. C., 89
Groden, J., 420
Groman, S. M., 119
Groskreutz, M. P., 91
Groskreutz, N. C., 91
Gross, A. C., 419
Gross, A. M., 690
Gross, C. M., 155
Gross, D., 695
Gross, E. J., 690
Grosser, J. W., 335
Grossi, T. A., 641
Groves, E. A., 678, 679
Grow, L. L., 368, 443, 618
Grskovic, J. A., 386
Grubb, L., 648
Grubb, P. D., 358
Gruber, B., 319, 320
Gruber, D., 466
Grunsell, J., 311t
Grusec, J., 724
Grusec, J. E., 723
Guardino, C., 628
Guerra, N. G., 354, 633
Guess, D., 425, 717
Guevremont, D., 412n
Guevremont, D. C., 494
Guilhardi, P., 639

Guiltinan, S., 325
Gulotta, C. S., 138
Gunning, C., 430
Gustafson, C., 325
Gutkin, T. B., 49
Gutshall, K. A., 617, 648

**H**

Haas, A., 414
Hackenberg, T. D., 279, 280
Haggar, J. L., 107, 504
Haggerty, K., 633, 639
Hagiwara, T., 651, 652
Hagopian, L., 156
Hagopian, L. P., 110, 112, 280, 311$t$, 325, 464, 513, 527, 532, 612, 628, 629, 630, 643, 644, 648, 672, 717, 718
Hains, A., 591
Hake, D. F., 408, 537, 584
Hake, D. G., 622, 720
Hake, D. J., 611, 724
Hale, L., 432
Halfon, N., 696
Hall, E. G., 669
Hall, R. V., 155, 251, 257, 548, 553, 577, 578, 579$f$, 628, 715
Hall, S., 335
Halle, J., 180
Halle, J. W., 361, 459, 485
Hamad, C., 52, 157, 303
Hamblin, R. L., 73
Hamilton, R., 636
Hammer, D., 486
Handen, B. L., 456, 459, 694
Hangen, M. M., 670
Hanley, E. M., 692
Hanley, G. P., 64, 106, 109, 112, 118, 119, 136, 147, 170, 172, 188, 211$t$, 225, 243, 301, 303, 304, 315$t$, 327, 407, 416, 433, 437, 477, 503, 560, 585, 602, 607, 608, 610, 637, 642, 643, 644, 648, 649, 671, 717, 727
Hanna, E. S., 365, 446
Hanratty, L. A., 225
Hansen, B., 435, 636
Hansen, B. D., 252, 254, 384
Hansen, D. J., 135
Hansen, G. D., 462
Hanton, S., 638
Hantula, D. A., 28, 538, 558
Haq, S., 405
Harcourt, S., 411
Hardiman, S. A., 284, 298
Harding, J., 142, 225
Harding, J. W., 484
Haring, T. G., 410, 492, 500
Harmatz, M. G., 694
Harmon, T. M., 155
Harper, J., 225
Harper, J. M., 288

Harrell, R., 717
Harrington, H., 327
Harris, D. A., 445
Harris, F., 405
Harris, F. R., 286
Harris, J. W., 510
Harris, K. R., 252
Harris, R. E., 419
Harris, S. L., 666, 705, 707
Harris, V. W., 677
Harrison, A. M., 295
Harshbarger, D., 43, 52, 53$b$, 65, 134, 154, 296, 382, 383$f$, 499, 555, 628, 638, 705$n$
Hart, B., 287$n$, 429, 433, 494, 724
Hart, J. M., 418
Hart, S. L., 463
Hartmann, D. P., 578, 584, 598, 723
Harvey, M. T., 413, 419
Harzem, P., 525, 527, 535
Hasegawa, Y., 155
Hasiam, C., 473
Haskett, G. J., 403, 407
Haslam, C., 467
Hatfield, V. L., 346
Haug, N. A., 511
Haugen, L., 65, 354, 551, 623, 628, 641
Haught, P., 457
Haupt, E. J., 464
Hausman, N. L., 249
Hawken, L. S., 40, 562
Hawkins, A. M., 550
Hawkins, J., 579, 580, 696
Hawkins, J. A., 197
Hawkins, R. P., 45, 71, 72, 73, 74–75, 149
Haydon, R., 640
Haydon, T., 61
Hayes, D., 577, 578$f$
Hayes, L. B., 638
Hayes, L. J., 237, 372, 427, 433
Hayes, S., 609
Hayes, S. C., 129, 133, 155, 197, 200$f$, 256, 370, 372, 427, 433, 446, 448, 598
Hayes, S. G., 609, 612, 616$n$
Haynes, R. B., 755
Haynes, S. N., 130, 131
Hays, T., 556
Hays, V. L., 131
Heal, N. A., 112, 407, 416
Healy, O., 577, 578$f$
Heard, K., 666
Heatherton, T. F., 415
Heckaman, K. A., 368, 458
Hedberg, A. G., 28
Hedquist, O. B., 672
Heekes, S., 719
Heffer, R. W., 695
Hefferman, T., 253, 665
Heflin, L. J., 689

Hegel, M. T., 666
Heimisson, F. T., 301
Heinicke, M. R., 51
Helbig, K. A., 518
Heller, M., 689
Hellman, S. G., 467
Helms, B., 386
Helmstetter, E., 717
Helsel, W. J., 717
Hemmes, N. S., 313, 323, 407, 549
Hemmeter, M. L., 466
Hendrickson, J. M., 252
Henington, C., 211$t$
Hennesy, C. L., 693
Henry, D., 354, 724
Hepburn, S. L., 408
Herbert-Jackson, E., 689
Hergenrada, M., 136
Hermans, D., 609
Hernandez, E., 243
Hernmeter, J. L., 239
Heron, T. E., 252, 640, 663
Herrnstein, R. J., 511, 540, 541
Herrod, J. L., 635
Hersen, M., 288, 584, 590
Herzog, M. J., 39
Hesse, K. D., 404
Heward, W. L., 368, 407, 458, 499, 560, 640, 641, 663
Hewett, A. E., 715
Heyman, G. M., 355
Hickey, K., 716
Hieneman, M., 47
Hienz, R. D., 9
Higbee, T. S., 311$t$, 411, 631, 633, 644
Higgins, J. W., 280
Higgins, R. L., 133
Higgins, S. T., 253
Higgins, T., 659
Hilker, K. A., 516
Hill, D., 245
Hill, M., 252, 253
Hill, S. M., 690
Hillery, J., 252
Hilt, A., 243, 254, 255, 257, 637
Himle, M. B., 136, 140, 482, 490, 665
Hineline, P., 559
Hineline, P. N., 92, 348, 505
Hinshaw, S. P., 327
Hirayama, A., 311$t$
Hirsch, S., 720
Hirst, E. S. J., 237
Hively, W., 461
Hlavacek, A. C., 47, 380, 581
Hobbins, K. A., 393
Hobbs, S. A., 695, 707
Hobson, R. P., 408
Hoch, H., 628
Hockersmith, I., 492
Hodges, A., 504

Hodges, A. E., 676
Hodges, L., 412n, 714
Hoffman, A., 43
Hoffman, H. J., 428
Hoffman, K., 518
Hoffmann, A. N., 240, 242
Hofmeister, A., 404
Hogan, E., 504
Hogan, S., 253
Hogan, W. A., 278, 695, 703
Hogg, A., 48
Hoko, J. A., 471
Holborn, S. W., 490, 505, 510
Holden, B., 550
Holden, G. W., 720
Hollahan, M. S., 138
Holland, J. G., 6, 7, 610
Hollingsworth, P., 633
Holloway, J., 430
Holmes, A., 119
Holt, B., 361
Holth, P., 492
Holtz, W. C., 120
Holz, W. C., 622, 685, 702, 711, 713, 714, 717, 720, 728, 732
Homan, C. I., 692
Homer, A. L., 669
Hood, S. A., 418, 659
Hoogeveen, F. R., 387
Hooper, S., 368, 458
Hopkins, B., 489
Hopkins, B. L., 45, 250, 251, 380, 528, 529f, 553, 693
Hops, H., 488, 601
Horn, W. F., 130, 131
Horne, P., 524
Horne, P. J., 347, 370, 445, 506, 535
Horne, W. C., 414
Horner, K., 140
Horner, R, 60
Horner, R. D., 190, 315, 581, 643
Horner, R. H., 45, 46, 65, 180, 203, 211t, 226, 257, 372, 446, 492, 547, 554, 589, 607, 615, 617, 627, 638, 639, 640, 642, 643, 683, 716
Horner, R. R., 40
Horr, J. A. M., 648
Horton, C., 43
Horton, S. B., 690
Hosford, R. E., 155, 413
Hotte, E., 325
Houchins, N., 209b, 211t, 479
Houlihan, D., 579
House, A., 690
Houvouras, A. J., 419
Hovanetz, A. N., 197, 633, 686, 693, 694
Howard, A. J., 592
Howard, G. S., 550
Howard, J., 610

Howard, J. S., 385, 440, 457, 458
Howard, V. F., 253, 407, 506
Howie, P. M., 288
Howley, T., 52
Howlin, P., 52, 600
Hoyt, R., 376
Hranchuk, K., 437
Hrycaiko, D. W., 252
Hu, M. Y., 251
Hua, Y., 636
Huberman, W. L., 553
Hudson, M. E., 438
Huesmann, L. R., 723
Hughes, C., 255
Hughes, C. A., 252, 254, 257
Hughes, C. E., 628, 636
Hughes, M. W., 466
Hume, A. E., 561
Hummel, T., 376
Hundert, J., 489
Hunkin, N. M., 473
Hunt, G. M., 507
Hunt, J. C., 418
Hunt, K. H., 368
Hunt, P., 488
Hunt, S., 281, 299, 300f, 550
Hurl, K. E., 225
Hurley, C., 253
Hursh, D., 303–304
Hursh, D. E., 303
Hursh, S. R., 541
Hurst, M., 635
Hurwitz, H. M. B., 611
Hutchins, H., 539
Hutchins, T. L., 651
Hutchinson, J. M., 689, 693
Hutchinson, R. R., 506, 507, 611, 622, 720, 721, 724, 726
Hyten, C., 408, 537, 550

**I**

Iannaccone, J. A., 643, 672
Ibanez, E. S., 695
Ibanez, L. V., 157
Ibanez, V. F., 614, 656
Iennaco, F. M., 467
Ingram, A., 381
Ingvarsson, E. T., 107, 119, 147, 249, 301, 303, 304, 407, 416, 477, 504
Inkelas, M., 696
Irvin, L. D., 698, 700b
Isquierdo, A., 119
Israel, A. C., 491
Ito, M., 311t
Ivancic, M. T., 110, 111, 255, 593, 594f, 703, 707, 730
Iwabucki, K., 668
Iwata, B. A., 65, 90, 95, 106, 110, 111, 112, 118, 119, 138, 139, 147, 157, 172, 188, 203, 211t, 212, 213, 214, 218, 222, 225, 228, 248, 335, 375, 376, 433, 437, 503, 513, 585, 586f, 602, 607, 608, 609, 610, 611, 612, 613, 614, 615, 617, 618, 636, 642, 643, 645, 648, 649, 660, 662, 667, 669, 683, 693, 694, 703, 705, 719, 728, 729f, 730, 735, 737

**J**

Jackson, D., 548, 628
Jackson, G. C., 507, 512
Jackson, J., 157
Jackson, L. M., 319, 637
Jackson, Y., 720
Jacobo, W., 322
Jacobs, E. A., 530
Jacobs, K. W., 45
Jacobsen, N. K., 142, 146
Jacobson, J. W., 761
Jagaroo, V., 598
Jai, T. M., 634
James, L., 386
Jarrett, R. B., 129
Jason, L., 376
Jason, L. A., 686, 693, 695
Javed, N., 672
Jeffers, J., 704
Jefferson, G., 717
Jenkins, A., 252, 253, 579, 580
Jenkins, J., 690
Jenner, N., 243
Jennings, K. R., 46, 626, 638
Jensen, J. M., 43
Jensen, S. A., 703
Jenson, W. R., 413
Jerome, J., 311t, 320, 471
Jessel, J., 107, 504
Jessup, P. A., 553
Jimenez-Gomez, C., 633
Jin, C. S., 225
Jin, S., 582, 641
Jitendra, A. K., 457
Johansen, E. B., 355
Johns, G. A., 376, 639
Johnson, B. M., 492
Johnson, C., 112, 367, 627
Johnson, C. M., 70, 458
Johnson, D. P., 278, 695, 703
Johnson, J., 405, 730
Johnson, J. A., 155
Johnson, J. W., 467
Johnson, K., 393
Johnson, K. A., 116
Johnson, K. R., 170, 302, 393, 394, 506, 676
Johnson, L., 136
Johnson, M., 52
Johnson, M. R., 118
Johnson, M. W., 591n
Johnson, P. E., 627
Johnson, R. G., 417

Johnson, S., 407, 649
Johnson, S. M., 488, 702
Johnson, T. A., 628, 643
Johnston, J. M., 24, 179, 212, 593, 693*n*
Johnston, R., 376, 634
Johnstone, E. C., 467
Jolivette, K., 142, 637
Jones, E., 554
Jones, E. A., 489
Jones, F. H., 414
Jones, J., 487
Jones, J. R., 706, 707, 716
Jones, M. L., 659, 729
Jones, R. J., 139
Jones, R. R., 598
Jones, R. T., 254, 414, 593
Jones, S. H., 175
Jongerius, P. H., 716
Jordan, E. A., 301
Joslyn, P. R., 678
Jostad, C. M., 368, 419, 492, 600
Juanico, J. F., 351, 518
Juanito, J. F., 237
Jung, C., 4
Jung, M. E., 386
Jung, S., 407, 410, 416
Jurgens, M., 243
Jusczyk, A. M., 429

**K**
Kabela, E., 237
Kagan, N., 155
Kagel, J., 279
Kagohara, D. M., 434
Kahan, E., 716
Kahlow, T. A., 432
Kahng, S., 112, 136, 139, 157, 214, 222, 516, 610, 645, 648
Kahng, S. W., 513, 585, 667, 685, 693, 696
Kahnt, T., 478
Kalsher, M. J., 65
Kameenui, E. J., 404
Kamps, D., 61, 331, 499
Kamps, D. M., 138, 252, 254
Kanareff, V., 414
Kane, M., 600
Kanowitz, J., 134
Karaszewski, R., 638
Karlson, T., 304
Karlsson, T., 456
Karn, E. A., 157
Karsh, K. G., 467, 492
Karsten, A. M., 43, 325, 441, 654
Kartal, M. S., 252
Kass, R. E., 95
Kassorla, I. C., 611
Kastak, D., 366
Kates, K., 628
Katsiyannis, A., 690

Katslyannis, A., 720
Katz, R. C., 628
Kaufman, A., 551
Kaufman, K. F., 95
Kaye, A. D., 96
Kazdin, A. E., 155, 179, 254, 257, 321, 347, 413, 414, 584, 598, 660, 694, 695, 699, 718, 720, 725, 733
Kee, M., 690, 693
Keenan, M., 524, 527
Keeney, K. M., 648
Keilitz, I., 315
Kellam, S. G., 678
Keller, F., 6, 426
Keller, F. S., 190, 302, 362
Keller, K. J., 322
Kellet, K., 435, 607
Kelley, M. E., 64, 111, 376, 463, 554, 591, 612, 618, 644, 720
Kelley, M. L., 686, 693, 694, 695, 696
Kellogg, W. N., 345
Kelly, H., 412
Kelly, J. F., 610, 611
Kelly, K., 70
Kelly, M. L., 463
Kelly, S., 367
Kelly, S. Q., 525
Kelso, P., 419, 600
Kelso, P. D., 316
Kemmerer, L., 138
Kemper, E., 404
Kendall, P. C., 704
Kendziora, K. T., 733
Kennedy, C., 637
Kennedy, C. H., 132, 208, 216, 217, 355, 376, 410, 456
Kennedy, S. H., 407
Kent, R. N., 134
Kenyon, C. A. P., 166
Kercood, S., 386
Kerkhop, I., 609
Kern-Dunlap, L., 625
Kern, L., 138, 155, 156, 211*t*, 243, 254, 255, 257, 328, 637
Kern, R. S., 467
Kerr, M., 311*t*, 650
Kerr, M. M., 483
Kerwin, M. E., 694
Kestner, K. M., 701
Kettering, T. L., 686, 693, 694
Kheloufi, Y., 516
Kheterpal, S., 386
Kidder, J. D., 694
Kiely, D., 706, 707
Kieta, A. R., 394
Kilanowski, C. K., 676
Killeen, P. R., 45
Killu, K., 636
Kilwein, M., 490
Kimball, R. T., 613

Kime, D., 447
Kinder, D., 403, 404
King, B., 413
King, C. R., 666
King, G. R., 237
King, M. L., 418
Kirby, F., 511, 512
Kirby, K. C., 662
Kirby, P. C., 252
Kirk, B., 370
Kirsch, I., 287
Kisamore, A., 111
Kisamore, A. N., 335, 368, 432, 441
Kishi, G., 607
Kissell, R., 659
Kitsukawa, K., 445
Klahr, D., 404
Klatt, K. P., 118, 429
Kledaras, J. B., 467
Klein-Hessling, J., 420
Klein, L., 579
Klein, N., 315*t*
Klein, P., 61
Klein, R. D., 252
Kleinmann, A. E., 52, 296, 297, 553, 556
Klin, A., 651
Knight, C., 674
Kniveton, B. H., 723
Knoll, M. C., 429
Knowlton, S., 717
Knudson, P., 419, 600
Knutson, L. N., 287
Kobari-Wright, V. V., 436
Kobylecky, A., 642
Koch, R. M., 715
Kodak, T., 43, 90, 111, 116, 243, 368, 388, 389, 390, 391, 400, 402, 405, 441, 526, 527, 637, 666, 704
Kodak, T. M., 44, 132
Koedinger, K., 120, 637
Koegel, L. K., 66, 226, 252, 253, 406, 494, 499, 643
Koegel, R., 405
Koegel, R. L., 66, 90, 226, 253, 390, 392, 402, 406, 469, 487, 494, 499, 510, 600, 643, 719
Koegel, R. L. J., 252
Koerkenmeier, S. M., 613
Koffarnus, M., 118
Kogan, N., 382
Kohler, F. W., 662
Kohn, A., 100
Kohn, C. S., 277
Kollins, S. H., 531, 541
Komaki, J., 155, 156
Kommana, S., 559
Konarski, E. A., Jr., 118
Koniarski, C., 281, 299, 300*f*
Konukman, F., 52
Koontz, K. L., 657

Koops, W., 472
Korn, Z., 256
Kornhaber, R., 413
Kosch, T., 403
Kotses, H., 315
Kowal, B. P., 377
Kraemer, B., 231
Kraemer, V. R., 230, 231
Krajcik, J., 462
Kramme, K. W., 719
Krams, M., 281, 299, 300$f$
Krantz, P. J., 323, 368, 386, 443, 463, 466, 469, 494, 628, 631$n$, 639
Kratochwill, T. R., 155, 693
Kraut, R. E., 73
Krebs, C. A., 675
Kret, M. E., 366
Kristie, L., 60
Kritch, K. M., 301, 304
Kronfli, F. R., 614, 656
Krug, M. A., 335
Kruger, C. B., 719
Krumboltz, H. G., 97, 455, 473, 730
Krumboltz, J. D., 97, 417, 455, 473, 730
Krumhus, K. M., 52
Kubany, E. S., 156
Kubina, R. M., 437, 490, 636
Kudrtz, P. F., 643
Kuhl, S., 638
Kuhn, A. C., 513
Kuhn, B. R., 48
Kuhn, D. E., 348
Kuhn, S. A., 62, 474
Kuhn, S. A. C., 48, 146, 314, 322, 334, 591
Kuhn, S. C., 311$t$
Kulp, S., 142
Kumar, P., 582
Kupers, C. J., 417
Kurtz-Nelson, E., 405
Kurtz, P. F., 239, 648
Kutsuzawa, T., 311$t$
Kuttler, S., 311$t$, 332, 333
Kymissis, E., 487

**L**

Lacey, C., 252
Ladouceur, R., 402
Lafleur, N. K., 417
LaFleur, T., 550
LaFrance, J. J., 244
Lahey, B. B., 407, 693
Lai, H. M., 460
Laitinen, R., 392
Laitinen, R. E., 303
Lake, C. M., 418
Lalli, J. S., 250, 513, 617, 628, 644
Lamal, P. A., 506
Lamb, A. D., 723
Lambe, A., 303

Lambert, N. K., 70$n$
Lambright, N., 548, 660
Lamont, S., 98
Lancaster, B. M., 412
Lancioni, G., 207, 216, 252, 610, 612, 643
Lancioni, G. E., 387, 434
Landa, R. K., 432, 435
Landaburn, H. J., 225
Landaburu, H., 209$b$, 211$t$
Landon, T. J., 247
Landrum, T. J., 550
Landry, L., 136
Lane, J. D., 72, 388, 457
Lane, K. L., 72, 239, 327, 640
Lane, S. D., 365
Lanford, A., 550
Lang, R., 207, 252, 407, 411
Langer, S., 367
Langer, S. N., 214, 215$t$, 360$f$, 361
Lanovaz, M., 516
Lanovaz, M. J., 643, 661, 666
Lanson, R. N., 611
Lantka, A. L., 46
Lanza, R. P., 408
Lanzetta, J. T., 414
Lapuc, P., 694
Laraway, S., 343, 351, 352
LaRocque, M., 211$t$
Larsen, R. A. A., 726
Larson, M., 156, 634, 641
Laschinger, H. S., 420
Latham, G. I., 51
Latham, G. P., 72, 505
Lattal, A. D., 3, 68, 89, 116, 234, 250, 284, 396, 618, 767
Lattal, K. A., 506, 527, 668, 720$n$
Lattimore, J., 51
Lattimore, L. P., 466, 487
Lauterback, W., 211$t$
LaVigna, G. W., 144, 145
Law, S., 448
Lawrence, A. J., 641
Lawrence, J. B., 517
Lawrie, S. M., 467
Laws, D. R., 537
Laws, O. R., 528, 529$f$
Layer, S. A., 138, 617, 637, 648
Layng, T. V. J., 170, 295, 300, 393, 506, 676
Lazar, R., 370
Le, D. D., 335
Le, L., 435, 607
Leader, G., 577, 578$f$
Leaf, J. B., 277, 332, 360, 389
Leaf, R., 277, 332, 360
LeBel, T. J., 245
LeBlanc, B., 405
LeBlanc, B. A., 44, 132
LeBlanc, J. M., 284, 298, 375, 403, 471

LeBlanc, L., 643
LeBlanc, L. A., 144, 280, 335, 412, 435, 440, 441, 607, 648, 716, 717, 764
Lechago, S., 487
Lecomte, T., 108
Ledbetter-Cho, K., 407
Ledford, J. R., 239, 457
Lee, A., 407, 408
Lee, C., 252, 253
Lee, D. L., 636
Lee, J., 225, 400, 704
Lee, J. F., 484
Lee, J. H., 412$n$, 714
Lee, N., 402
Lee, R., 251, 518
Lee, S., 381
Lee, S. J., 721
Lee, Y., 65, 639, 640
Legacy, S. M., 644, 648
Lehr, C., 639
Leibowitz, J. M., 506, 510, 677
Leigland, S., 427
Leinenweber, A., 504$n$
Leitenberg, H., 584, 670
Leland, L. S., Jr., 136, 386
LeLaurin, K., 146
Lenfestey, W., 403, 407
Lengnick-Hall, M. L., 46, 626, 638
Lennox, D. B., 674
Lensbower, J., 492
Lenske, J., 694
Lenz, M., 715
Leon-Enriquez, Y., 639
Leon, Y., 672, 675
Leonard, B. R., 138
Leonard, I. J., 256
Leonard, M. A., 89
Lepper, M. R., 97, 99, 100
Lepper, T. L., 429
Lequia, J., 53
Lerman, D. C., 62, 64, 197, 213, 228, 314, 322, 334, 335, 376, 462, 474, 487, 496, 513, 526, 527, 591, 609, 610, 611, 612, 613, 617, 618, 630, 633, 637, 644, 660, 663, 683, 684, 703, 704, 717, 718, 719, 720, 724, 730, 731, 733
Leroux, J., 488
LeSage, M. G., 132
Leslie, J. C., 301, 459, 609$n$
Lessor, A. L., 678
Lester, S. N., 719
Levin, L., 386, 628
Levy, A., 100
Levy, E. A., 417
Lewin, A. B., 110
Lewis-Palmer, T., 211$t$
Lewis, T. J., 122, 211$t$
Li, B., 366
Li, Y., 157
Libby, M. E., 388, 474

Liber, D. B., 327, 457
Liberman, R. P., 108, 467
Lichstein, K. L., 415
Lieving, G. A., 612
Lifter, K., 75, 408
Light, P., 402, 419
Lignugaris/Kraft, B., 376, 637
Lillie, M. A., 237, 251, 366, 532, 660
Lim, J., 715
Lim, L., 243
Limebeer, C. L., 616, 618
Lin, L. R., 490
Lindauer, S. E., 648
Lindberg, J. S., 66, 106, 118, 643, 644, 648, 667
Lindblad, T. L., 630
Linder, D. E., 131
Lindsley, O. R., 49, 49–50, 136, 170, 393, 506
Lindstrom-Hazel, D., 523
Linehan, C., 668
Liner, D., 690
Ling, P. A., 723
Linscheid, T. R., 721, 735
Lipinski, P., 130
Lippman, L. G., 527
Lipschultz, J., 636
Little, E., 52
Little, N., 626
Littleford, C. D., 408
Livanis, A., 549
Livesay, J., 716, 725
Livesay, J. R., 666
Lizotte, D. J., 462
Lloveras, L. A., 614, 656
Lloyd, B. P., 237, 351
Lloyd, J. L., 467
Loafman, B., 46–47, 380, 581
Lobato-Barrera, D., 410
Lochner, D. G., 525
Locke, S. R., 386
Lodhi, S., 315$t$
Loeb, M., 432
Loeber, R., 354, 633
Logan, F. A., 732
Logan, P., 639
Logue, A. W., 61, 237
Lohaus, A., 420
Loman, S. L., 554
Lomas, I. D., 120, 637
Lomas, J. E., 686
Long, A. C., 156, 641
Long, E. R., 505, 672
Long, E. S., 110, 386, 513, 612, 690, 693, 696
Long, J. S., 405
Longano, J., 437
Lopez, A. R., 386
Lopez, C., 327
Lorah, E. R., 304

Lord, C., 651
Lorimer, P. A., 311$t$, 651
Losinski, M., 636
Lotfizadeh, A. D., 32, 351, 353
Lovaas, O. I., 390, 405, 410, 419, 430, 443, 600, 611, 683, 705, 737
Lovascz, C., 446
Lowe, C. F., 347, 370, 445, 506, 525, 527, 534, 536
Lowe, C. R., 524
Lowery, C. T., 59
Lowitz, G. H., 673
Loyd, B. H., 583
Lozy, E. D., 592
LRP Publications, 698
Lubeck, R. C., 327, 483
Luce, S. C., 75, 416, 443, 472, 715
Luciano, M. C., 440
Lucker, K. D., 592
Lucyshyn, J. M., 46, 47, 287, 298
Luczynski, K. C., 61, 327, 329, 418, 659
Ludwig, D. J., 619, 724
Ludwig, T. D., 358, 499, 538, 551
Luiselli, J. K., 245, 288, 294, 548, 554, 637, 652, 660, 666, 692, 736
Luiten, L., 628, 643
Luke, J., 138
Luke, M. M., 136
Lukeris, S., 298, 466
Lumley, V. A., 156
Lund, D., 548, 628
Luselli, J. K., 288
Luthans, F., 550
Lutzker, J. R., 323, 411, 466, 666, 690, 716
Luyben, P. D., 388
Lynch, D. C., 446
Lyons, G., 53, 665
Lysaght, T. V., 670

## M

McAdam, D. B., 118, 518, 716
McAfee, J. K., 463
MacAleese, A., 225, 335, 355
McCallum, E., 582
McCandless, B. R., 468
McCann, K. B., 129, 257, 483, 628
McClannahan, L. E., 323, 368, 386, 443, 463, 466, 469, 494, 628, 631$n$, 639
McClellan, C. B., 693
McClinton, B. S., 417
McClung, T. S., 694
McClure, G. Y., 517$n$
McComas, J., 136, 140, 142, 237, 661
McComas, J. J., 242, 446, 592
McConnachie, G., 45–46
McCord, B. E., 225, 335, 586, 587$f$, 602
McCord, M., 368
McCormick, N., 609$n$
McCormick, S., 349

McCosh, K. C., 376
McCoy, J. F., 215$t$
McCracken, S. G., 559
McCullagh, P., 415
McCurdy, B., 510, 525, 540
McCurdy, M., 136, 539, 639
MacDonald, G., 550
MacDonald, J., 66$n$, 409
MacDonald, J. M., 366
MacDonald, R., 367
MacDonald, R. F., 214, 215$t$, 360$f$, 361
MacDonald, R. P. F., 186, 187, 404, 409, 412, 629
MacDonald, S., 335
MacDonald, W. S., 550
McDonnell, J. J., 457
McDonough, E. M., 728
McDougall, D., 252, 462, 579, 580
McDowell, C., 301, 459
McDuff, E., 311$t$, 516
MacDuff, G. S., 323, 368, 469
MacDuff, M. T., 386
Mace, F., 215$t$, 636
Mace, F. C., 155, 243, 255, 479, 504$n$, 505, 506, 510, 511, 525, 526, 540, 541, 593, 594$f$, 636, 661, 689, 707
McEachin, J., 332, 360, 443, 602
McEachin, J. J., 277, 600
McElrath, K., 304
McElwee, J. D., 133
McEntee, J. E., 506
McEvoy, M. A., 636
McFall, R. M., 670
McFarland, M. C., 491
McGee, G., 180, 215$t$
McGee, G. G., 116, 443, 494
McGhan, A. C., 663
McGill, P., 354
McGimsey, J. F., 729
McGinnis, E., 61, 328
McGonigle, J. J., 690
McGookin, R. B., 49, 50, 558
McGreevy, P., 136
Machalicek, W., 53, 207, 610, 642
McHugh, C., 665
McHugh, L., 427
McIlvane, W. J., 350, 370, 467, 471
McInnis, T., 695
McIntosh, C. K., 52
McIntosh, K., 557, 561, 623
McIntyre, L. L., 44, 155, 411
MacIver, M. A., 404
Mackay, H. A., 368, 370, 372, 391, 471, 591
McKelvey, J. L., 466
McKenna, J. W., 677
MacKenzie-Keating, S. E., 719, 733
McKeown, C. A., 641
McKerchar, P., 109
McKerchar, P. M., 457

Mclain, L., 207
McLaughlin, T. F., 154, 253, 280, 514, 689, 693, 701
McLaughlin, T. W., 45
McLellarn, R. W., 509
McMahon, C. M., 460
McMaster, K., 140
McMillan, D. E., 517*n*
MacMillan, D. L., 327, 600
McMorrow, M. J., 660
McNamara, C., 60
McNees, M. C., 693
McNees, M. P., 693
McNeill, K. L., 462
McNeill, S. L., 539, 639
MacPherson, M. M., 386
McReynolds, L. V., 702
McReynolds, W. T., 279
MacSuga, A. S., 253
MacSuga-Gage, A. S., 720
McSweeney, F. K., 377, 527, 538
McSweeny, A. J., 693
McVay, A. A., 368
Maden, T., 691
Madrid, W., 322
Madsen, C. H., 52
Madzharova, M., 554
Maechtlen, A. D., 716
Maehr, M. L., 619, 724
Magdol, L., 327
Magee, S. K., 706
Mager, R. F., 78
Maggs, A., 403
Maglieri, K. A., 280, 607, 717, 727
Maguire, R. W., 369
Mahan, M. A., 723
Mahon, J., 405
Mahoney, G., 66*n*
Mahoney, J. J., 155, 156
Maidalany, L., 636
Maier, S. F., 722
Majdalany, L., 438, 556, 639
Malaby, J. E., 154, 514
Maldonado-Molina, M. M., 730
Malenfant, J. E., 170, 171, 174
Malenfant, L., 64, 717
Maley, R. F., 279
Malmberg, D. B., 386, 651
Malone, J., 539
Malone, J. C., 4
Malone, L. W., 461
Maloney, D., 416
Malott, R. W., 40, 51, 52, 65, 199, 285, 286, 301, 557
Manal, H., 386
Mancil, G. R., 61
Mancina, C., 314, 499
Mandelker, A. B., 279, 628
Mandell, C., 644
Manganello, J. A., 721

Mangiapanello, K. A., 549
Manikam, R., 689
Mann, C. C., 441
Mann, D. W., 639
Mann, E. A., 327
Mann, K. R., 665
Mann, P. H., 414
Manne, S., 716
Manos, M. J., 690, 693
Mantegna, M. E., 255, 637
Manteiga, R. D., 609*n*
Manthey, S., 237
Maragulla, D., 689
March, R., 70*n*, 211*t*
Marchand-Martella, N., 419
Marchand-Martella, N. E., 252, 256
Marckel, J., 237, 407, 410, 416
Marckel, J. M., 194, 195*f*, 196
Marcus, A., 413
Marcus, B. A., 43, 111, 207, 643, 644, 645
Markham, V. A., 467, 468, 469, 633
Markowski, A., 637
Marley, J., 530
Marmolejo, E. K., 600
Marquis, J. G., 506
Marr, M. J., 13
Marshall, A. M., 346
Marshall, G., 677
Martella, R. C., 252, 256, 419
Martens, B. K., 52, 215*t*, 296, 297, 463, 490, 504, 525, 541, 553, 556
Martin, G. L., 252, 302, 303
Martin, J. A., 720, 724
Martin, J. E., 386
Martin, T. L., 302, 303
Martindale, A., 142
Martineau, M., 412
Martinez, C. J., 656
Martinez, C. K., 100, 630
Martinez, K. L., 60
Martner, S. G., 157
Marx, R. W., 462
Marx, T. A., 691
Marya, V., 439
Masataka, W., 457
Mash, E. J., 133
Mason, S. A., 116
Massar, M., 628
Massar, S. S. A., 715
Massey, G., 142
Masuda, A., 656
Matese, M., 735
Mathews, B. A., 693, 701
Mathews, S., 557, 561, 623
Mathews, T. L., 418
Mathisen, D., 556
Matos, R., 89
Matson, J. L., 211*t*, 212, 588, 677, 689, 716, 717, 718, 719, 725

Mattaini, M. A., 59
Matter, A. L., 678
Matthews, B. A., 510, 527
Matthews, K., 156
Matthews, R. W., 376
Mattson, S. L., 311*t*, 316, 631
Maurice, C., 405*n*, 443
Mauro, B. C., 250, 506, 636, 661
Mausner, B., 408, 415
Mawhinney, V. T., 528, 529*f*
Maxwell, D. L., 598
May, C., 98
May, J. G., 698
May, R. J., 467, 469
May, S. L., 557, 623
Maydak, M., 591
Mayer, G. R., 35, 40, 41, 47, 49, 50, 51, 52, 55*n*, 66, 97, 146, 154, 163, 194, 230, 231, 239, 254, 257, 288, 330, 335, 354, 355, 413, 415, 459, 462, 464, 498, 550, 551, 553, 554, 558, 622, 623, 626, 628, 633, 634, 641, 676, 706, 721, 722, 764
Mayer-Johnson, R., 651
Maynard, C. S., 468
Mazaleski, J. L., 636
Mazur, J. E., 541
Mazzotti, V. L., 381
Meadows, N., 488
Medres-Smith, A. E., 674
Meehl, P. E., 128*n*
Mees, H., 405
Mehta, S. S., 487
Meindl, J. N., 699
Melchiori, L. E., 365
Melekoglu, M. A., 392
Melin, L., 376
Mellalieu, S. D., 638
Mellor, J. R., 444
Melvin, K. D., 279
Menlove, F., 724
Menzies, R. G., 490
Merante, R. J., 47, 380, 581
Merbaum, M., 722
Merbitz, C. T., 136
Merbitz, N. H., 136
Mercatoris, M., 154
Merrill, M. M., 462
Merry, K. J., 386
Mesches, G. A., 701
Mesmer, E. M., 484, 488
Mestel, R., 354, 723
Methot, L. L., 132
Metoyer, C. N., 418
Metzler, C. W., 623, 634
Meunier, G. F., 659
Mews, J., 138
Meyer, K. A., 208, 216, 217, 355
Meyer, L. H., 718
Meyer, M. E., 527

Meyerson, L., 131
Mezhoudi, N., 93
Michael, A. V., 648
Michael, J., 95, 243, 334, 343, 345, 351, 352, 353, 354, 428, 429, 430, 439, 440, 444, 599, 718, 730
Miguel, C. F., 429, 436, 440, 442, 630
Mihalic, S. F., 44
Milad, M. R., 616
Milan, M. A., 715
Miles, N. I., 479
Millenson, J. R., 120, 611
Miller, A. J., 693
Miller, B. G., 89, 174
Miller, D. L., 716
Miller, H. L., 523, 536
Miller, M., 705
Miller, M. B., 499, 560
Miller, M. L., 301
Miller-Perrin, C. L., 720
Miller, S. R., 253
Millichamp, C. J., 466
Milliman, R. E., 376
Mills, J. I., 600
Milne, B. J., 277, 327
Milne, C. M., 360
Milstein, J. P., 410
Miltenberger, R., 243, 254, 256, 311$t$, 319
Miltenberger, R. B., 174
Miltenberger, R. G., 89, 90, 156, 253, 311$t$, 316, 354, 384, 385, 411, 412, 418, 419, 482, 484, 486, 492, 507, 600, 637, 666, 674, 690, 693, 696
Minkin, B. L., 328, 699
Minkin, N., 328, 699
Minor, L., 554
Mintz, J., 467
Miranda, P., 389
Mirenda, P. M., 426
Mischel, W., 723
Mitchem, K., 499
Mitteer, D. R., 659
Mittelstadt, P. A., 689
Mitts, B., 155, 257
Moe, G., 49
Moffett, K., 693
Moffitt, T. E., 327
Mohtasib, R. S., 405
Moise-Titus, J., 723
Monro, D. W., 640
Montegar, C. A., 52
Montgomery, D. H., 630
Montgomery, G. M., 717
Montgomery, R. W., 715
Moore, A., 692
Moore, B., 358
Moore, D., 322
Moore, D. W., 252
Moore, J., 637

Moore, J. W., 117, 154, 388, 389, 390, 391, 411, 413, 591
Moore, K., 631
Moore, M., 407
Moore, P. S., 652
Morgan, A. B., 538
Morgan, C. A., 287$n$, 418
Morgan, D., 527
Morgan, J. K., 388
Morgan, T. A., 613
Morgenthaler, T. I., 311$t$
Morin, D., 516
Morley, A. J., 630
Morrell, G., 155
Morren, J., 203, 622, 727
Morris, C., 412
Morris, E. K., 149, 612, 720
Morris, J. P., 611
Morrison, J. Q., 592
Morrison, R. S., 466
Mortenson, B. P., 52
Moss, R. E., 155
Mouzakitis, A., 51–52
Mozingo, D. B., 52, 550, 561
Mudford, O. C., 142, 144, 280
Muehlberger, A. O., 251
Mueller, M. M., 117, 463, 468, 591
Muething, C. S., 518, 677
Mulick, J., 376
Mulick, J. A., 213, 761
Mullane, M. P., 504, 541
Mullins, J., 541
Munger, G. F., 583
Munk, D. K., 352
Munt, E. D., 256
Murdock, J. Y., 252, 255
Murph, D., 349
Murphy, E. S., 377
Murphy, G., 335
Murphy, H. A., 355, 685, 689, 693
Murphy, R. J., 690, 705
Murray, L. K., 531, 541
Murray, R., 492
Murray, R. G., 707
Murzynski, N. T., 388
Myers, D., 623
Myers, K., 639
Myerson, J., 541
Myles, B. S., 311$t$, 333, 651, 652

**N**

Nafpaktitis, M., 355, 633, 721
Nagatomi, K., 155
Nagle, R. J., 328
Nail, G. L., 376, 639
Najdowski, A. C., 64, 119, 121, 225, 329, 330, 335, 406, 407, 444, 657
Napolitano, D., 208
Napolitano, D. A., 518, 716
Narozanick, T., 311$t$, 319

Nash, D. A., 635
Nation, J. R., 509
National Alliance for the Mentally Ill, 690
Natsoulas, T., 413
Nau, P. A., 508, 719, 733
Nava, C. E., 582
Nay, W. R., 704
Naylor, A. S., 331
Neal, A., 721
Neef, J. A., 524
Neef, N. A., 194, 195$f$, 196, 237, 243, 407, 410, 416, 492, 506, 512, 526, 527, 586, 587$f$, 591, 668
Neel, R., 488
Neely, M., 43
Neely, M. D., 395$f$
Nehs, R., 715
Neidert, P. L., 225, 242
Nelson, B., 243
Nelson, C. M., 129, 466, 689, 704
Nelson, R., 130, 372
Nelson, R. E., 254, 414
Nelson, R. O., 129, 133, 155, 598
Nesbitt, R. E., 99, 100
Nesset, R., 326, 493
Neuringer, A., 516
Nevin, J. A., 167, 479, 518, 641, 644, 645, 661
Newchok, D. K., 91, 446, 666
Newland, M. C., 726
Newman, D. L., 327
Newsom, C., 718
Newsom, C. D., 65, 90, 287, 705, 721, 722
Nicholson, K., 439
Nicol, N., 558
Niedelman, M., 404
Nielsen, G., 702
Niemann, J. E., 415
Nietupski, J., 459
Nigam, M., 404
Nihira, K., 70, 70$n$
Nikopoulos, C. K., 600
Nikopoulou-Smyrni, P. G., 600
Ninness, H. A. C., 155, 499
Nipe, T., 656
Nissen, J. A., 496, 637
Nist, L., 407, 410, 416
Nix, L. D., 631
Nock, M. K., 288, 590
Noel, C. R., 643, 644
Noell, G. H., 43, 52, 404, 496
Noldus, L. P., 157
Noll, M. B., 692
Nordyke, N. S., 387
Normand, M., 635
Normand, M. P., 277, 429, 649, 678
Northup, J., 109, 122, 173, 174, 279, 355, 400, 704

Nosik, M. R., 136
Novak, M. D., 630
Nunes, D. L., 690, 705
Nuzzolo-Gomez, R., 89

O
Oblak, M., 106, 227
O'Brien, F., 298
O'Brien, M., 638
O'Brien, R. M., 553
O'Brien, S., 255, 593, 594f, 707
O'Callaghan, P. M., 52, 140, 628, 644
O'Carroll, R. E., 467
Ochsner, C. A., 463
O'Connor, C., 656
O'Connor, J., 612
O'Connor, J. T., 239, 648
O'Dell, M. C., 494
O'Dell, S. L., 135
Odom, S., 180
O'Donnell, J., 343, 712
O'Donnell, J. O., 343, 345, 347
Oien, I., 38
Okouchi, H., 533, 537
O'Leary, K. D., 71, 95, 134, 491
O'Leary, S. B., 733
O'Leary, S. G., 718, 730, 732, 733
Oliva, D., 387
Olive, M., 445
Oliver, C., 335
Oliver, J. R., 254, 554
Ollendick, T. H., 418, 588, 593, 716
Olmi, D. J., 239
Olsen, A. E., 418
Olsen, R., 253
Olson, R. L., 693
O'Neil, P. M., 666
O'Neill, R. E., 211t, 413
O'Neill, S. J., 459
O'Niell, R. E., 589
Ono, K., 668
Onslow, M., 490, 689, 693
Onyango, A. N., 690, 693
Oppenheimer, M., 389
O'Reilly, G., 668
O'Reilly, M., 207, 252, 407, 411, 610
O'Reilly, M. F., 208, 216, 315t, 355, 434, 612, 643
Orlando, R., 505
Orr, S. M., 693
Orr, S. P., 616
Ortega, J. V., 225
Ortega, R., 89
Ortiz, E., 89
Osborn, J. G., 716
Osborne, J. G., 505, 514, 529
Osher, D., 239, 623
Osnes, P. G., 483, 491, 494
Ostensjo, S., 38
Ostrosky, M. M., 485

Otalvaro, K. A., 675
Ousley, O. Y., 408
Overman, P. B., 311t, 414
Owens, C. R., 459
Owens, J., 311t
Owens, J. C., 112
Owsiany, J., 405
Ozkan, S. Y., 252

P
Pace, D. M., 702
Pace, G., 251
Pace, G. M., 52, 65, 110, 111, 376, 549, 600
Pack-Teixteira, L., 440
Packard, D., 614
Packman, A., 490, 689
Paclawskyj, T. R., 212, 311t
Paden, A. R., 236
Padilla-Mainor, K., 504
Pagani, L., 650
Pagano, C., 355
Page, S., 516
Page, S.V., 139
Page, T. G., 147
Page, T. J., 110, 111, 214, 255, 593, 594f, 707
Paine, S. C., 700
Pakurar, K., 140, 354, 376, 634
Palevsky, S., 716
Palkovic, C. M., 468
Palmer, D. C., 376, 427, 609n
Palmer, M., 298, 466
Paluch, R. A., 676
Panacek, L., 640
Panahon, C., 579
Pardi, J. R., 96
Park, K. L., 52
Park, M. N., 252
Parke, R. D., 732
Parker, A., 688
Parker, G., 488
Parker, L., 215t
Parker, L. A., 616, 618
Parkin, A. J., 473
Parnell, S., 404
Paronis, C. A., 541
Parrish, J. M., 512, 694
Parrott, K. A., 315t, 322, 323
Parsons, J., 701
Parsons, M. B., 43, 466, 487, 547
Partington, J. W., 406, 429, 440, 441
Pasco, G., 600
Passante, S. C., 251, 489
Pastorelli, C., 327
Patel, M. R., 138, 463, 617, 648, 656
Patel, N., 120, 637
Patel, R. R., 277, 649
Patterson, D. P., 637
Patterson, G. R., 300, 327, 354, 540, 559, 633, 650
Patwa, S. S., 244
Paul, G. I., 591
Paul, G. L., 695
Paul, S. C., 723
Paulus, P. B., 376
Pawich, T. L., 236
Payne, S. W., 237
Pear, J. J., 302, 303, 507, 512
Pearlman, A., 136
Peaslee, J. E., 658
Peck, S., 142
Peck, S. M., 242
Pelham, W. E., 690, 693
Pelios, L., 203, 622, 661n, 727
Pellecchia, M., 600
Pellegerino, R., 376
Pemberton, J. R., 695
Pena-Correal, T. E., 237
Pence, S., 212, 217, 433
Pendergrass, V. E., 697
Pennell, D., 457
Penney, A., 548
Pennington, R. C., 550
Pennypacker, H. S., 24, 136, 179, 212, 348, 593, 693n
Penrod, B., 119, 121, 139, 167, 168, 325
Peoples, A., 614
Perdikaris, A., 688
Perelman, P. G., 692
Perez, B. C., 716
Perkins, D. R., 464
Perloff, B. F., 410, 430
Perri, M. G., 253
Perrie, P., 386
Perrin, C. J., 627
Persampieri, M. J., 136
Persicke, A., 330
Pesses, D. I., 157
Peters, K. P., 614, 644, 656, 716
Peters, R. D., 132
Peters, T. J., 532
Peterson, A. L., 692
Peterson, C., 496, 637
Peterson, C. R., 701
Peterson, G. B., 285
Peterson, L., 669
Peterson, L. D., 252, 253
Peterson, R., 694
Peterson, R. F., 213, 215t, 410
Peterson, R. L., 688, 689
Petscher, E. S., 52, 255, 257, 611, 628
Petty, M. M., 550
Petursdottir, A., 140, 436, 489
Petursdottir, A. I., 429, 440, 442
Pfadt, A., 466, 598
Pfiffner, L. J., 718
Phaneuf, L., 155, 411
Phillips, C. L., 643
Phillips, E. A., 280, 693

Phillips, E. L., 155, 257, 280, 416, 426, 693
Phillips, J. G., 319
Piacentini, J. C., 136, 140
Piazza, C., 717
Piazza, C. C., 108, 112, 138, 208, 315t, 335, 433, 461, 463, 591, 607, 611, 616n, 617, 648, 656, 717, 727
Pierce, W., 100
Pierce, W. D., 26, 521n
Piersel, W. C., 690
Piles, D A., 295
Pinkelman, S., 631, 642
Pinter, E. B., 554
Pipkin, C. C. P., 138, 464
Pisman, M. D., 613
Pitman, R. K., 616
Pitts-Conway, V., 410
Pizarro, E., 401
Platt, J. S., 510
Plaud, J. J., 517, 527
Plavnick, J. B., 411
Poche, C., 416, 492
Podolski, C., 723
Podsakoff, P. M., 118
Pokorny, S. B., 686, 693, 695
Poling, A., 32, 132, 343, 351, 352, 353, 440, 638
Pollack, M. J., 52
Polvinale, R. A., 666, 716
Poonwala, N., 120, 637
Porter, B. E., 60
Porter, J. H., 532
Posadzinska, I., 638
Poterfield, J. K., 689
Potterton, T., 231
Poulson, C. L., 298, 313, 323, 330, 407, 410, 411, 459, 466, 487, 628
Powell, J., 142
Powell, S., 96, 140, 243, 628
Powell-Smith, K. A., 651, 652
Powell, T. E., 467
Power, J., 635
Powers, L. A., 335
Powers, M. A., 388
Prados, J., 609n
Prater, M. A., 252, 253
Preast, J. L., 392
Predy, L. K., 561
Prelock, P. A., 651
Premack, D., 118
Price, L., 412n, 714
Priehs, J. C., 631
Prior, T., 411
Progar, P. R., 617, 661
Prohn, K., 39
Pronovost, P. J., 52, 65
Prue, D. M., 122
Pruett, A., 463, 591
Pryor, K., 289, 293n, 481

Pursell, E. D., 505
Putnam, R. F., 245
Putri, T. R., 439
Pyles, D. A. M., 211t, 295

**Q**
Quattrochi-Tubin, S., 376
Querim, A. C., 225
Quigley, E. A., 510, 525, 540, 765
Quinn, L., 630
Quinn, M., 311t, 319

**R**
Rabinowitz, F. M., 417
Rachlin, H., 703
Radke, A. K., 119
Radley, K. C., 413, 518
Raetz, P. B., 144
Ragland, E. U., 483
Raia, C. P., 536
Rajagopal, S., 439
Ramdoss, S., 434
Ramos-Loyo, J., 472
Ramp, K. A., 281
Ramsey, E., 335, 354, 464, 628, 630, 633
Ramsey, M. L., 637
Rand, M. S., 648
Randle, F. A., 418
Randolph, J. J., 641
Rantz, W. G., 554
Rapp, J. T., 287, 335, 630, 637, 643, 661, 665, 690
Rappaport, E., 129, 141
Rapport, L. J., 245
Rapport, M. D., 355, 685, 693
Rasmussen, E. B., 726
Rauch, S. L., 616
Rauer, S. A., 414
Rauzin, R., 370
Ray, K. P., 636
Ray, M., 39
Rayner, R., 721
Raynor, H. A., 676
Reardon, K., 736
Reber, R. A., 558
Redd, W. H., 720
Redford, P. M., 335
Redmon, W. K., 118, 539
Reed, D. D., 44, 49, 149, 215t, 237
Reed, G. K., 617, 648
Reed, H. K., 203, 716
Reed, P., 389, 613
Reese, E. P., 245, 246, 253, 468, 610, 687n
Reeser, R., 319, 320
Reeve, K. F., 411, 412, 419, 432, 485, 487, 631
Reeve, L., 487
Reeve, S., 411
Reeve, S. A., 335, 411, 412, 485, 631

Regalado, M., 696
Rehfeldt, R. A., 237, 366, 370, 372, 444, 447, 448, 499
Rehg, J. M., 157
Rehm, R., 390
Reichenbach, H., 721, 735
Reichle, J. E., 376, 635
Reid, D. H., 43, 51, 52, 73, 251, 319, 320, 466, 487, 489, 547, 705
Reid, J. B., 327, 678
Reid, R., 252, 253, 254
Reinert, K. S., 631
Reisman, J., 666
Reiss, M. L., 550, 561
Remington, B., 370, 372, 402, 419
Renkl, A., 462
Renne, C. M., 322, 326
Renshaw, R., 156, 641
Repp, A. C., 142, 352, 467, 492, 667, 674, 676, 705
Repp, C. F., 142
Reppucci, N. D., 47, 49
Reschly, D., 639
Retana, G. F., 602
Reuter, K. E., 284, 298
Rey, C., 718
Reyes, J. R., 676
Reynolds, A. J., 327
Reynolds, B., 530, 531, 534
Reynolds, D. S., 609n
Reynolds, G., 389
Reynolds, G. S., 249, 508, 613, 671
Reynolds, L. K., 686, 693, 695, 696
Reynolds, M., 639
Rhymer, K. N., 539, 639
Ricciardi, J. N., 2, 288, 294, 736
Rice, A., 549
Rice, J. C., 721
Rice, J. M., 465
Richards, C. S., 156, 253, 255
Richards, E., 628
Richardson, A. R., 319, 637
Richardson, W. K., 313
Richardson, W. S., 755
Richman, D., 142
Richman, D. M., 643, 648
Richman, G. S., 90, 203, 614
Rick, G., 484
Rickard, H. C., 279
Ricketts, R. W., 735
Riddell, P. M., 472
Rieffe, C., 366
Rieland, W. A., 540
Rieth, S. R., 390
Rigney, B., 635
Riley, G. A., 467
Riley-Tillman, C., 559
Riley-Tillman, R. C., 244
Rilling, M., 461
Rimell, P., 52

Rimmer, B., 715
Rincover, A., 469, 487, 541, 600, 614, 718, 719
Ringdahl, J. E., 43, 111, 138, 207, 243, 254, 257, 445, 613, 635, 644, 645, 662
Ringenberg, C., 243
Riodan, M. R., 550, 561
Risley, T., 287n, 724
Risley, T. R., 6, 9, 10, 64, 70, 80, 116, 131, 146, 405, 429, 433, 448, 494, 593, 598, 599, 689, 698, 722, 755
Rispoli, M., 207
Rivera, C., 639
Rivera, C. J., 438
Rivera, C. M., 89
Riviere, V., 523
Rizvi, S. L., 498
Roane, H., 355
Roane, H. S., 43, 111, 207, 208, 612, 613, 618, 630, 644, 645, 686, 690, 693, 694, 728
Robbins, F. R., 625
Robbins, J. K., 394
Roberson, A. A., 560
Roberts, D., 311t
Roberts, D. M., 142
Roberts-Gwinn, M. M., 628, 643
Roberts, M. S., 693
Roberts, M. W., 689, 695, 707
Robertson, J., 587
Robinson, J. D., 404
Robinson, K. E., 245
Robinson, L., 98
Robinson, N., 726
Robinson, P. W., 467
Robinson, S., 622, 720
Rocco, F. I., 467
Roche, B., 446
Roche, L., 411
Rock, M. L., 255
Roderique-Davis, G., 467, 469
Rodgers, T. A., 212
Rodriguez, B. J., 554
Rodriguez-Catter, V., 242, 648
Rodríguez, M. L., 237
Rodriguez, W. A., 732
Roeyers, H., 408
Rogalski, J. P., 93
Rogers, J. S., 358
Rogers, R. W., 358
Rogers, S. J., 408
Rogers-Warren, A. K., 215t, 415, 418
Rohen, T. H., 415
Rohena, E. I., 457, 458
Rojahn, J., 376, 717
Rolider, A., 211t, 464, 692, 719, 731
Rolider, N. U., 120
Roll, J. M., 89
Rollyson, J. H., 251, 489
Roman, K. M., 498

Romanczyk, R. G., 134, 598
Romani, P. W., 556, 658
Romaniuk, C., 90, 243, 354, 637, 666
Romano, L. M., 669, 701
Romick, K., 209b, 211t
Rooker, G. W., 643
Root, S., 366
Rortvedt, A. K., 696
Rosales, R., 370, 372, 446
Rosales-Ruiz, J., 289b, 293, 406, 534
Roscoe, E. M., 93, 106, 110, 119, 212, 217, 225, 368, 391, 463, 586f, 642, 643, 644, 648, 649, 672, 717, 719, 728, 729f
Rose, D. J., 52, 553, 555
Rose, H. M., 499
Rosen, H. S., 149, 672
Rosen, L. A., 672
Rosenbaum, M. E., 414
Rosenbaum, M. S., 486
Rosenberg, H., 499, 560
Rosenberg, N., 548
Rosenberg, W., 755
Rosenberger, P., 610
Rosenfarb, I., 256
Rosenfield, S., 49
Rosenthal, B. D., 215t
Rosenthal, T. L., 414, 415, 416
Ross, D., 415
Ross, L. V., 693, 701
Ross, N. A., 540
Ross, R. K., 251, 639
Ross, S., 415
Ross, S. W., 615, 617
Rossi, M., 538
Rossi, M. R., 419
Rothbaum, B. O., 412n, 714
Rotteveel, J. J., 716
Rourke, D., 212
Rowbury, T., 705
Rowbury, T. G., 387
Rowe, D. A., 381
Rowell, A., 358
Rowsey, K. E., 447
Royer, D. J., 239
Rozalski, M., 688, 689, 692, 699
Rozga, A., 157
Rubow, C. C., 644, 678
Ruckle, M. M., 175
Rudebeck, P. H., 119
Rudrud, E., 332
Rudrud, E. H., 637, 638
Ruggles, T. R., 375, 403
Runkle, W., 358
Ruprecht, M., 690
Ruprecht, M. L., 705
Rusby, J. D., 623, 634
Rusch, F. R., 386
Rush, K. S., 110, 212, 513, 643
Ruskin, R. S., 279, 302

Russell, B., 4–5
Russell, D., 107, 504
Russell, H. H., 467
Russell, V. A., 355
Russo, L., 335
Russo, S. R., 366
Rust, F. P., 485
Rutherford, R., 155
Rutherford, R. B., 689
Rutterford, N. A., 674
Ryan, J. B., 688, 689, 690, 692
Ryan, V., 554

**S**

Sabino da Costa, I., 366
Sackett, D. L., 755
Sackett, G. P., 213
Sadler, O. W., 717
Saecker, L., 582
Sagvolden, R., 322, 541
Sagvolden, T., 355, 637
Sailor, W., 60, 226, 643
Sainato, D. M., 466
Saini, V., 613, 648, 660
Sainni, V., 613
St. Clair, M., 330
St. Peter, C., 433, 662
St. Peter, C. C., 175, 669, 701, 726
Sajwaj, T. E., 715
Sakamoto, T., 311t
Salama, F., 96, 140, 628
Salant, V., 253
Salend, S., 689
Salil Kumar Dutt, A., 138
Salmonson, M. M., 733
Salo, A., 627
Salzberg, C. L., 252, 253, 411, 459
Samah, A. L., 174
Samaha, A. L., 188, 240, 242, 607, 608
Sameoto, D., 719, 733
Sampen, S. E., 548n, 628
San Juan, B., 440
Sanders, R. B., 657
Sanders, V., 690
Sanderson, M., 43, 134
Sandra, S., 411
Sanetti, L. M., 44
Sanford, K. S., 639
Sanok, R. L., 703
Sansa, J., 609n
Sansosti, F. J., 651, 652
Santana, C. M., 463, 656
Santarcangelo, S., 75
Sara, Y. A., 693
Sareen, H., 696
Sargent, J. D., 415
Sarokoff, R. A., 112, 251
Sasaki, S., 420
Sasmita, K., 715
Sasson, J. R., 548

Sassu, K. A., 244
Satake, E. B., 598
Saulnier, C., 60
Saunders, J. T., 49
Saunders, K. J., 343, 368, 712
Saunders, M., 538
Saunders, M. D., 506
Saunders, R. R., 389, 506
Sautter, R. A., 440, 441
Sawin, D. G., 732
Scalzo, R., 642
Scattone, D., 628, 651
Schaeffer, B., 410, 430
Schaeffer, R. W., 404, 514
Schartz, M., 252, 253, 254
Scheeler, M. C., 636
Scheirer, M. A., 73
Schepis, M. M., 466
Scherrer, M. D., 192, 193f
Schichenmehyer, K. J., 225
Schieltz, K. M., 225
Schiff, A., 322
Schilmoeller, J. J., 470
Schlinger, H. D., 504, 505, 507
Schlosnagle, L., 304
Schloss, C. N., 64
Schloss, P. J., 64, 155
Schmidt, A., 403
Schmidt, A. C., 637
Schmitt, D. R., 538
Schnake, M. E., 696
Schneider, B., 488
Schnell, L. K., 418
Schoen, S. F., 375, 455, 459
Schoenfeld, W. N., 190, 362
Schonwetter, S. W., 254
Schreibman, L., 390, 392, 510, 600
Schrieber, S. R., 518
Schroeder, H., 413
Schroeder, S., 376
Schultheis, K. R., 253
Schultz, R. T., 651
Schultz, W., 18
Schulze, K., 332
Schulze, K. A., 637, 638
Schunk, D., 414, 465
Schuster, J. W., 315t, 322, 323, 325, 456, 466
Schusterman, R. J., 366
Schwartz, A. A., 761
Schwartz, B., 611
Schwartz, I. S., 408, 414, 416, 487, 607
Schwarz, N., 402, 490
Schweitzer, J. B., 237, 280, 529, 530, 532
Scibak, J., 43, 134
Scott, C., 488
Scott, D., 286
Scott, J., 416
Scott, L. M., 286

Scott, T. M., 52, 211t
Scotti, J. R., 215t, 718
Seaver, J. L., 474
Secan, K. E., 716
Seeman, H., 97
Seligman, M. E. P., 619, 722
Selinski, J. E., 315t
Sellers, T. P., 144, 311t, 316, 764
Sellers, T. R., 247
Semantik, P., 405
Seniuk, H. A., 656
Sergio, J. P., 550
Serketich, W. J., 253
Serna, R. W., 370
Serrett, K., 173, 174
Severson, J. H., 157
Sewell, D. K., 721
Sewell, T. J., 466
Sexton, C. W., 404
Sexton, J. B., 52, 65
Seymour, J. D., 505
Seys, D. M., 719
Shabani, D. B., 157, 446, 628, 666, 669
Shade, D., 243, 506, 526
Shadish, W. R., 574n
Shaeffer, R. M., 466
Shafer, E., 446
Shafer, M. S., 512
Shahan, T. A., 612
Shahrestani, E., 651, 652
Shannon, T., 623
Shapiro, E. S., 252, 407, 418, 588, 694, 716
Shapiro, S., 407
Shapiro, S. T., 689, 694
Sharp, R. A., 142, 144
Shaw, D., 457, 609n
Shawler, L. A., 366
Shea, M. C., 243
Sheldon, J. B., 389, 716
Shepley, C., 388, 457
Sheridan, S. M., 328
Sherman, J. A., 389, 410, 677, 716
Sherrill, J. R., 733
Shevin, M., 315t
Shields, F., 511, 512
Shih, I. H., 634
Shillingford, S. W., 536
Shillingsburg, A., 439
Shillingsburg, M. A., 350, 404, 432, 435, 618, 636, 686
Shimabukuro, S. M., 252, 253
Shimamura, J. W., 279
Shimoff, E., 304, 305, 510, 527
Shimp, C. P., 516
Shinske, F. K., 593
Shipley-Benamou, R., 323, 411
Shirley, M. J., 222
Shlesinger, A., 288
Shodhan, S., 120, 637

Shook, G. L., 698
Shore, B. A., 228, 463, 513, 683
Shore, M. F., 691
Shores, R. E., 354
Shourbagi, S. E., 639
Shrestha, A., 322
Shriver, M. D., 51, 490
Shull, R. L., 531, 609
Shumate, E. D., 673
Shupska, U., 638
Sidener, T. M., 116, 157, 432, 622, 631
Sidman, M., 95, 363, 367, 369, 370, 372, 391, 446, 468, 471, 601, 622n, 723n, 730
Siegel, G. M., 689, 694
Sierp, B. J., 617
Sigafoos, J., 311t, 457, 610, 612, 637, 642, 643
Sigman, C., 237
Sigurdsson, S. O., 100
Silbaugh, B. C., 518
Silkowski, E. L., 690
Silva, P. A., 327
Silverman, N. A., 733
Simeone, P. J., 404
Simmons, D. C., 404
Simmons, J. Q., 405
Simon, S. J., 457
Simons, L. G., 723
Simons, R. L., 723
Simonsen, B., 245, 253
Simpson, C., 358, 386, 627
Simpson, R. L., 311t, 692
Sinclair, G. A., 554
Sinclair, T., 255
Sinding, C., 376
Singer-Dudek, J., 106, 227
Singer, G. S., 698, 700b
Singh, J., 716
Singh, N. N., 386, 465, 466, 690, 715, 716
Singleton, B., 550
Siroky, L. M., 48
Sittler, J. L., 733
Skinner, A. L., 577
Skinner, B. F., 2, 4, 5, 6, 7, 22, 24, 38, 59, 68, 84, 95, 127, 284, 289, 405, 408, 426, 427, 430, 436, 438, 439, 441, 444, 478, 487, 503n, 504, 506, 517, 521n, 527, 530, 536, 609, 610, 612, 674, 687n, 764, 766
Skinner, C., 527, 539
Skinner, C. H., 197, 279, 376, 539, 577, 582, 636, 639
Slack, D. J., 142
Sladeczek, I. E., 643
Slater, B. R., 689
Sleiman, A. A., 639
Slevin, I., 112
Slifer, K. J., 90, 203, 614, 657

Sloane, H. N., 402
Sloane, H. N., Jr., 548n, 628
Slocum, S. K., 644, 699
Slocum, T. A., 91, 404
Slocumb, P. R., 666, 692
Sloggett, B. B., 156
Slolberg, K., 118
Sloman, K. N., 464, 676, 686
Slomke, J., 616, 618
Slyman, A., 637
Smalls, Y., 212
Smart, E., 411
Smeets, P. M., 387
Smeltz, L., 636
Smith, B. W., 252, 254
Smith, C., 412
Smith, C. L., 723
Smith, D. E., 692
Smith, D. M., 557
Smith, J., 639
Smith, L., 73
Smith-Myles, B., 311t, 332
Smith, R., 636
Smith, R. B., 335
Smith, R. G., 214, 225, 228, 375, 636
Smith, S., 280, 412n, 714
Smith, S. D., 414
Smith, T., 406, 518, 550, 561, 600
Smith, T. G., 657
Smokowski, P. R., 327
Snell, M. E., 313, 322, 325, 457, 583, 651
Snycerski, S., 343, 351, 352
Snyder, A., 463
Snyder, G., 340, 394
Snyder, M. K., 45
Socolar, R. R. S., 695
Soeda, J. M., 597, 644
Solman, R. T., 386, 465, 466
Solnick, J. V., 311t, 496, 600, 705
Solomon, R. L., 711, 722
Sommer, S. M., 550
Song, H., 402, 490
Sorensen, J. L., 511
Soriano, H. L., 418
Sorrell, S., 715
Soto, P. L., 679
Soucy, D., 40n
Soucy, D. S., 96
Southard, K. L., 376, 635
Sparrow, S. S., 60
Speckman, J. M., 443
Speelman, R. C., 447
Speidel, G. R., 257
Speltz, M. L., 279
Spencer, T., 355
Spendlove, S. J., 695
Spiegler, M. D., 412n
Spieler, C., 256
Spink, A. J., 157
Sponsel, S. S., 48, 278, 280

Spooner, D., 321
Spooner, F., 321
Spracklen, K. M., 540
Spradlin, J. E., 370, 372, 389, 459
Sprafkin, R. P., 61
Sprague, J., 492, 623
Sprague, J. R., 211t, 372, 623, 634
Spriggs, M., 65, 354, 551, 623, 628, 641
Springer, C. R., 302
Squires, E. J., 473
Squires, J., 48
Sreckovic, M. A., 561
Stackhouse, T., 408
Staddon, J., 478
Stage, S. A., 211t
Stahelski, A. J., 553
Stahmer, A. C., 390
Staley, M. J., 652
Stanley, C., 448
Stanley, C. R., 447
Stanton, W. R., 327
Stark, L. J., 635
Statland, E., 413
Stauber, K. A., 551
Staubitz, J. L., 237
Stauch, T. A., 411
Stausbaugh, E., 304
Stebbins, W. C., 611
Steed, S. E., 466
Steege, M. W., 460
Steifman, J. S., 675
Stein, R. E. K., 695
Steinhilber, J., 112
Stenhoff, D. M., 376, 637
Stephens, C. E., 507, 512
Stephenson, J., 640
Stephenson, K. M., 477
Sterling, R., 640
Sterling-Turner, H. E., 52, 254, 257
Stevenson, H. C., 253, 486
Stevenson, M., 355
Stewart, C. A., 716
Stewart, N. R., 417
Stewart, P. W., 517n
Stiefler, N. A., 319, 637
Stikeleather, G., 393
Stocco, C. S., 418
Stocker, S., 689
Stoddard, L. T., 370, 468, 471, 591
Stoffer, G. R., 508
Stoffer, J. E., 508
Stokes, J. V., 311t
Stokes, T., 494
Stokes, T. F., 96, 407, 434, 479, 481, 482, 483, 486, 491, 493, 494, 635
Stolz, S. B., 252
Stone, W. L., 157, 408
Stoolmiller, M., 678
Storey, C., 301
Storey, K., 211t

Storm, R. H., 467
Stouthamer-Loeber, M., 132
Strain, L. A., 556
Strain, P. S., 203, 483, 716
Strand-Cary, M., 404
Strand, P. S., 613
Street, E. M., 394
Stricker, J., 138, 690
Striefel, S., 419, 443, 459, 703
Strikeleather, G., 295, 300
Stromer, R., 237, 368, 370, 391, 591
Strosahl, K., 448
Struss, K., 129, 141
Stuart, A. L., 636
Studer, R. G., 506
Stuesser, H. A., 463
Sturkie, L., 636
Sturm, C. A., 509
Sturmey, P., 251, 298, 311t, 320, 410, 505, 518, 554
Suarez, Y., 250, 380, 553
Sudhalter, V., 598
Sugai, G., 40, 41, 60, 65, 122, 211t, 239, 252, 253, 254, 257, 547, 627, 639, 640
Suhrheinrich, J., 390
Suib, M. R., 673
Sullivan, M. T., 717
Sullivan, W. E., 613
Sulzer-Azaroff, B., 36, 40n, 43, 46–47, 52, 53b, 65, 69n, 96, 122, 129, 134, 135, 137, 146, 154, 157, 204, 236, 237, 238, 243, 245, 246, 253, 254, 257, 279, 289, 296, 298, 303, 316, 317, 324, 330, 349, 354, 355, 376, 380, 382, 383f, 408, 410, 413, 419, 437, 445, 466, 479, 481, 483, 487, 490, 499, 523, 529, 530, 532, 538, 550, 553, 555, 557, 558, 561, 581, 585, 590, 600, 602, 605, 622, 626, 628, 634, 638, 705n, 721, 734
Sulzer, B., 166n, 281, 299, 300f, 388, 426, 685, 693
Sulzer, E. S., 76, 247
Summers, J., 419
Sundberg, C. A., 429
Sundberg, M. L., 406, 429, 432, 437, 439, 440, 444, 446
Sunderland, M., 245
Sunderman, P., 458
Suskin, L. L., 692
Suzuki, K., 311t
Swaggart, B. L., 651, 652
Swain, J. C., 701
Swain, R., 457
Swain, S., 630
Swan, L. J., 674
Swanson, V., 355
Swatta, P., 386
Swearingen, M., 416
Sweeney, E., 457
Sweigart, C. A., 550, 554

Swiezy, N. B., 677
Swisher, J. D., 650
Switzer, E. B., 685, 693
Swope, B. W., 304
Sy, J. R., 236, 239, 401, 512
Symon, J. B. G., 327, 651
Symons, F. J., 136, 354
Szabadi, E., 720
Szczech, F. M., 215*t*
Szekely, S., 237

**T**
Taber, T. A., 548, 660
Tague, C., 694
Tai, S. S., 418
Tailby, R., 467
Tailby, W., 363, 370
Takacs, J., 489
Takita, K., 311*t*
Tallon, R. J., 52
Talmadge, B., 350
Tamiaki, G., 467, 469
Tankersley, M., 499
Taras, M. E., 717, 718, 719, 725
Tarbox, J., 189, 209*b*, 211*t*, 225, 322, 325, 329, 330, 366, 385, 407, 685, 693, 731
Tarbox, R., 209*b*, 211*t*
Tarbox, R. S. F., 189, 225, 280, 325, 358, 385, 406, 731
Tasky, K. K., 637
Tate, T. L., 457
Taubman, M., 323, 411
Taylor, B., 661
Taylor, B. A., 386, 409, 628
Taylor, C. A., 721
Taylor, C. N., 392
Taylor, C. R., 628
Taylor, I., 315*t*
Taylor, J., 705
Taylor, J. C., 245, 622, 720
Taylor, M. J., 641, 657
Taylor, R., 762
Taylor, S. A., 280
Taylor, T., 630
Tegelenbosch, R. A. J., 157
Teichner, G., 666
Telzrow, C., 639
Temple, M., 462
Terrace, H. S., 468, 471, 473
Terraciano, T. E., 464
Terrill, S., 736
Tesch, D., 203, 622, 727
Test, D. W., 155, 637
Tharp, R. G., 257
Thaw, J., 154
Thaxton, J. R., 633
Theobald, D. E., 591
Thiemann-Bourque, K., 434
Thiemann, K. S., 652

Thomas, C., 154
Thomas, C. M., 298, 466
Thomas, D. R., 404, 461, 476, 723
Thomas, E. M., 411
Thomas, J. D., 155
Thomas, J. H., 414, 415
Thomas, R., 631
Thomason-Sassi, J. L., 225
Thompson, A., 136
Thompson, C. K., 64
Thompson, R. H., 106, 109, 116, 118, 136, 188, 348, 418, 433, 457, 503, 585, 607, 608, 610, 642, 648, 649, 719, 728, 729*f*
Thompson, T., 439
Thompson, T. J., 582, 583*f*
Thomson, R. J., 225
Thoresen, C. E., 155, 156, 417
Thrush, N., 554
Thvedt, J. E., 375
Thyer, B. A., 358
Tibbetts, P. A., 530
Ticknor, N., 634
Tidy, J. A., 473
Tiernan, R., 252
Tiger, J. H., 147, 237, 243, 251, 349, 351, 366, 407, 416, 460, 478, 532, 660, 666, 671
Tilley, K., 372
Timberlake, W., 118
Timbers, G. D., 426
Tincani, M., 446, 527, 656
Tindal, G. A., 252, 253
Tingstrom, D. H., 239, 628
Tisdelle, D. A., 135
Titchener, E. B., 3
Tobler, P. N., 478
Todd, A., 65, 354, 551, 623, 628, 641
Todd, A. W., 203, 211*t*, 257, 716
Todd, J. T., 612
Tolan, P. H., 354, 632
Tonneau, F., 505
Toombs, K., 413
Topcuoglu, B., 62
Toper-Korkmaz, O., 630
Torelli, J. N., 351
Torem, C., 631
Torres, N., 332
Touchette, P. E., 214, 215*t*, 360*f*, 361, 385, 457, 458
Toussaint, K., 236
Toussaint, K. A., 243, 637
Townsend, D. B., 298, 330, 410, 411
Trahant, D., 117
Trammel, D. L., 155, 498
Treadwell, K. R. H., 214
Tremblay, R. E., 650
Trent, J. T., 694
Trestman, R. L., 311*t*
Trosclair-Lasserre, N., 612

Trosclair-Lasserre, N. M., 526, 527
Trott, M. C., 716
Trotter, J. R., 611
Trout, A. L., 252, 253, 254
Trtol, K. A., 386
Truchlicka, M., 701
Trump, C. E., 635
Tryon, G., 51–52
Tryon, W. W., 598
Tsai, S., 651, 652
Tsami, L., 630
Tsou, Y.-T., 366
Tu, Q., 540
Tucci, V., 303, 303–304, 393
Tudor, R. M., 301
Tullis, C. A., 631
Tung, S. B., 112
Tupa, M., 303
Turley, L. W., 376
Turnbull, A. P., 226, 643
Turnbull, H. R., 717
Turner, H., 582
Turner, P. L., 686, 693, 695
Turri, M. G., 561
Tustin, R D., 242
Twardosz, S., 698
Twohig, M. P., 156, 592
Twyman, J. S., 122, 295, 300, 506, 640

**U**
Ulman, J. D., 279, 584, 585, 590
Ulrich, R. E., 355
Umbreit, J., 65, 72, 640, 641
United States Department of Education, 693
Upreti, G., 561

**V**
Vaca, L., 549
Vahratian, A., 428
Valbuena, D., 89, 174
Valdovinos, M., 208
Valentino, A. L., 247
Valleley, R. J., 490
Van Acker, R., 231, 354, 724
Van Biervliet, A., 372
Van Camp, C., 706
Van Camp, C. M., 64, 376, 612, 617, 638, 644, 720
Van der Burg, J. J. W., 716
van der Meer, J., 715
van der Meer, L., 434
Van Houten, J., 170, 174
Van Houten, R., 64, 170, 171, 174, 211*t*, 386, 464, 508, 554, 669, 692, 711, 717, 719, 724, 731, 733, 737
Van Kirk, M. J., 464
Van, M. V., 331
Van Oost, P., 408
van Stone, M., 527

VanderPoel, S. J., 474
VanLaarhoven, T., 467, 492
Vannest, K., 414
Vanselow, N. R., 225, 407
Vansteenwegen, D., 609, 609*n*
VanWormer, J. J., 403
Vargas, E. A., 299
Vargas, J. S., 299
Vaughan, M. E., 527
Vaughn, B. J., 376, 635
Vaught, R., 598
Vautier, J. S., 358
Vazquez-Moreno, A., 472
Vedora, J., 251
Veerman, J. W., 472
Vega, R., Jr., 677
Ver Steeg, D., 504, 541
Vera, A., 640
Verriden, A. L., 717
Viadescu, J. C., 411
Vigilante, V. A., 613
Villacorta, J., 556
Vincent, J., 579
Vinquist, K., 138
Vintere, P., 313, 323, 407
Virues-Ortega, J., 52
Vitaro, F., 650
Vittimberga, G., 607
Vladescu, J. C., 112, 116, 243, 335, 418, 419, 637
Voeltz, L. M., 316, 599
Volkert, V. M., 110, 612, 656
Volkmar, F. R., 651
Vollmer, R. R., 706
Vollmer, T. R., 43, 108, 111, 119, 138, 173, 174, 207, 211*t*, 212, 228, 236, 287, 335, 401, 464, 540, 614, 617, 636, 643, 644, 645, 656, 669, 674, 676, 678, 683, 686, 699, 716, 728, 737
Vollrath, D. A., 46, 626, 638
Volpe, J. S., 237
Volymer, T. R., 644
Von Brock, M. B., 725
Vona, J., 516
Vorndran, C., 62, 683
Vorndran, C. M., 64, 243, 255, 314, 322, 334, 376, 474, 591, 637, 644, 684, 703, 704, 717, 718, 719, 720, 724, 732, 733
Voulgarakis, H., 91
Vyse, S. A., 213

## W

Wack, S. R., 384
Wacker, D. P., 138, 142, 225, 242, 386, 445, 460, 484, 592, 661
Wadden, T. A., 311*t*
Waddington, H., 411
Wade, A., 600
Wade, J. A., 304

Wagaman, J. R., 156
Wagenaar, A. C., 730
Wagner, S., 538
Wahler, R. G., 215*t*, 351*n*, 613
Walker, B., 211*t*
Walker, C. E., 28
Walker, G., 456, 459
Walker, H., 623
Walker, H. M., 335, 464, 488, 601, 628, 630
Walker, L., 634
Walker, P., 718
Walker, S. G., 311*t*, 316
Walkup, J. T., 140
Wall, M.E., 327
Wallace, C. J., 108, 467
Wallace, D. P., 643
Wallace, M., 197, 198*f*, 762
Wallace, M. D., 18, 43, 55*n*, 110, 112, 119, 121, 138, 139, 154, 163, 167, 168, 189, 209*b*, 211*t*, 225, 325, 335, 355, 385, 433, 437, 498, 550, 553, 559, 611, 642, 644, 648, 649, 657, 731, 764
Wallach, M. A., 382
Wallin, J. A., 558
Walls, R. T., 319, 321, 375, 457, 474
Walpole, C. W., 368, 391
Walsh, A. D., 392
Walsh, M. E., 457
Walters, D., 439
Walters, R. H., 617, 723
Walz, G. R., 155
Wangasgard, N., 414
Warash, B., 303–304
Ward, C. L., 719
Ward-Horner, J. C., 251
Ward, P., 52, 194, 195*f*, 251, 638
Ward, R. D., 644
Ward, S., 688
Ware, M. E., 518
Warner, R. W., 650
Warren, S. F., 415, 418
Warzak, W. J., 313, 418
Wascom, A. M., 705
Wasik, B. H., 678
Waters, M. A., 316
Waters, M. B., 197, 633
Watkins, C., 52
Watkins, C. E., 539, 639
Watkins, C. L., 404, 440
Watkins, L., 407
Watson, J. B., 4, 721
Watson, R. S., 636
Watson, T. S., 52, 211*t*, 666, 716
Watt, A., 304
Watt, M. E., 304
Watt, S. J., 472
Wattenberg, W. W., 724
Watts, A. C., 672
Wearden, J. H., 516, 523

Weatherly, N. L., 250, 251
Webb, T., 487, 607
Weber, K., 628, 643
Weber, L. H., 321
Webster, D., 692
Weeks, M., 90
Weems, C. F., 587
Wehby, J. H., 138, 142, 351, 354, 644, 726
Wehmeyer, M., 255
Wehner, E., 408
Weil, T. M., 592
Weiner, H., 506, 510, 515, 527, 533, 536, 684, 693
Weinger, M. B., 315*t*
Weinstein, N. D., 358
Weisberg, P., 404
Weiss, J. J., 656
Weiss, J. S., 388
Weiss, S. L., 438
Weissman, M. D., 157
Weist, M. D., 690
Welch, C., 118
Welfenbach, B., 630
Wells, K. C., 695, 716
Welsh, D. H. B., 550
Welsh, J. L., 45
Wemura, H., 155
Wertalik, J. L., 640
Werts, M. G., 323, 456
Wesolowski, M. D., 466, 706
Wesp, R., 534
West, J. H., 641
West, R., 657
West, R. P., 252, 253, 407, 506, 641, 657
West, R. R., 402
Westbrook, A. C., 577
Westling, D. L., 39
Weston, R., 504
Wetherby, B., 419
Wetterneck, C. T., 136
Wexler, D., 698
Wexley, K. N., 313, 314, 505
Weyman, J. R., 239
Wheatley, R. K., 641, 657
Wheeler, A. J., 426
Wheller, D. J., 598
Whitaker, S. D., 560
White, D., 367
White, G. D., 702
White, J. L., 666
White, K., 623
White, M. A., 724
White, O. R., 395*f*
White, R., 243, 640
White, S., 462
Whiteside, E., 243
Whitley, A. D., 415
Whitman, T. L., 118
Whitney, R., 407, 506

Wiediger, R. S., 377
Wierzba, B. C., 351, 460
Wigal, J. K., 315
Wigger, D. M., 414, 415
Wilcox, B., 492
Wilczenski, F. L., 65, 147, 631
Wilczynski, S. M., 117, 628
Wilder, D., 636
Wilder, D. A., 43, 110, 189, 192, 193*f*, 413, 479, 554, 556, 600, 628, 635, 636, 639, 656, 665, 672, 673, 718
Wildmon, M., 52
Wilke, A. E., 685, 693
Wilkinson, C., 635
William, O. B., 559
Williams, A. M., 720*n*
Williams, B., 538
Williams, D. C., 343, 712
Williams, D. E., 157, 214, 735
Williams, J., 494
Williams, J. A., 491
Williams, K. E., 463
Williams, L., 726
Williams, R., 636
Williams, R. E., 636
Williams, R. L., 280, 441
Williams, W. L., 225, 358, 656
Willis, R. G., 414
Willis, S. E., 155
Willis, T. J., 144, 145
Wills, H., 331
Wills, H. P., 252, 254, 384, 673, 726
Willson-Morris, M., 369, 370
Wilson, A. N., 513, 613
Wilson, C., 48
Wilson, C. C., 130
Wilson, C. L., 416
Wilson, D., 243, 376, 635, 640
Wilson, D. W., 376
Wilson, E. R., 332
Wilson, G., 280
Wilson, G. L., 509
Wilson, G. R., 71
Wilson, K. G., 448, 479, 609, 612, 616*n*
Wilson, K. M., 715
Wilson, P. G., 319
Wimberly, B. S., 319, 637
Winborn-Kemmerer, L., 445

Winchester, J., 253
Wincze, J. P., 661
Wine, B., 43, 332, 418
Winett, R. A., 72
Winkler, R., 279
Winkler, R. C., 72, 687, 693
Winn, S. O., 197
Winston, A. S., 690
Winterling, V., 243, 637
Wiseman, N., 636
Wiskow, K. M., 386, 518, 678, 679
Wisocki, P. A., 619
Wissow, L. S., 696
Witt, J. C., 49, 52, 304, 370, 694
Witts, B. N., 638
Wojcicki, C. A., 691
Wolchik, S. A., 666, 705
Wolery, M., 180, 239, 323, 325, 456
Wolf, M., 735
Wolf, M. M., 6, 7, 9, 10, 70, 80, 131, 155, 257, 280, 281, 286, 405, 426, 448, 538, 593, 599, 693, 694, 755
Wolfe, L. A., 463
Wolfe, L. H., 252
Wolkin, J. R., 417
Wolko, K. L., 252
Wolpin, M., 287
Womack, L. M., 467
Wood, C. L., 637
Wood, S. J., 252, 255
Woods, A., 508
Woods, C. L., 288
Woods, D. W., 136, 140, 156, 253, 311*t*, 592, 665
Woods, J., 628
Woods, J. N., 610
Woodward, J., 404
Woonsocket, D., 412*n*
Worling, D. E., 463, 628
Worsdell, A. S., 110, 136, 138, 513, 585, 610, 643, 644, 648
Wray, L. D., 507, 512
Wright, C. S., 617, 674, 728
Wright, L., 28
Wright, S., 243
Wu, A. W., 52, 65
Wu, J., 239
Wulfert, E., 256, 372

Wunderlich, K. L., 335
Wundt, W., 3
Wynne, C. K., 369

**Y**

Yakich, T. M., 706
Yang, K. H., 460
Yang, N., 460, 548
Yassine, J., 197, 198*f*
Yassine, J. N., 43
Yates, B. T., 601
Ybarra, W. J., 35, 41, 239, 633
Yeager, C., 689, 693
Yell, M., 699
Yell, M. L., 43, 690
Yi, L. J., 658
Yoo, J. H., 189, 385
Yoon, S., 429
Young, A. E., 490
Young, H., 392
Young, J. A., 661
Young, K. R., 252, 253, 407, 499, 506
Ysseldyke, J., 639
Yukl, G. A., 313, 314, 505
Yurich, K., 304

**Z**

Zabala, K. A., 335
Zambone, A., 438
Zander, A., 413
Zane, T., 319, 321, 375, 456, 459, 474
Zangrillo, A. N., 661
Zanolli, K., 623, 641
Zarcone, J. R., 208, 212, 228, 518, 636, 672
Zdanowski, D. M., 237
Zegiob, L. E., 690
Zeilberger, J., 548*n*, 628, 693
Zerger, H. M., 89, 649
Zettle, R. D., 256
Zhang, R. C., 460
Zimbardo, P. G., 327
Zimmerman, B. J., 328, 416
Zimmerman, J., 703, 704
Zohar, D., 280, 537
Zorzos, C., 660

# Subject Index

In this index, page locators followed by a "*b*" indicate material in boxes; by an "*f*," material in figures; by an "*n*," material in notes; and by a "*t*," material in tables.

## A

A-B-C analysis. *See also* Three-term contingency
    illustrated, 213*f*, 214*f*
ABAB design. *See* Withdrawal (return-to-baseline) design
Ablative effect, defined and illustrated, 351–352
Abolishing operations (AOs), defined and illustrated, 351–352
Abscissa, in graphing, 161–163
Abulia
    defined and illustrated, 620
    positive punishment and, 721
Acceptance and Commitment Training or Therapy (ACT), verbal behavior and, 448
Accountability. *See also* Evidence-based practices
    defined, 179
Accuracy, defined, 80*t*
*Achieving Educational Excellence Using Behavioral Strategies* (Sulzer-Azaroff & Mayer), xxvi
Across-behaviors multiple-baseline design, illustrated, 194–195, 196*f*
Across-individuals (subjects) multiple-baseline design, illustrated, 193*f*, 194
Across-settings (subjects) multiple-baseline design, illustrated, 195–196
ACT (Acceptance and Commitment Training or Therapy), verbal behavior and, 448
Activity reinforcers, defined, 107
Activity schedules
    defined and illustrated, 630, 632–633
    summary table, 740*t*
Activity tables, use of, 657–658
Adaptation
    data validity and, 130–131, 157
    habituation versus, 377
    reinforcement and, 240–243
ADHD
    activity schedule use, 532–533
    medication responses, 355
    program support, 53
    punishment with, 725
    reinforcement and, 237
    self-management with, 254
Adjusting FR schedules. *See* Progressive ratio (PR) schedules
Adult learners, shaping and, 289–290
Advocate/advocacy, goal selection and, 76
Age, goal selection and, 75
Aggressive behaviors
    antecedent conditions and, 607–608
    extinction and, 611–613, 617–618
    noncontingent reinforcement and, 644–645
    punishment and, 694–695, 720, 722, 725
    ratio strain and, 508
    reducing, 607–608, 641–642, 688, 689
Alternating-treatment (multi-element) design
    advantages and disadvantages, 590–592
    defined and illustrated, 585–588
    effective use of, 588–590
    summary table, 597*t*
Alternative goals, illustrated, 73
Analysis
    defined, 10
    in practice, 603–604
    statistical, 182, 183
Animals
    limited hold use, 536
    noncontingent reinforcement with, 643
    shaping used, 288–289
Antecedent control strategies, defined and illustrated, 624–625
Antecedents
    defined and illustrated, 26, 26*f*, 31–32
    in functional analysis assessment, 222–224
    in problematic behavior, 633–634
    and three-term contingency, 24
Antisocial behaviors
    motivating operations and, 354–355
    reinforcement and, 641–642
Applied Behavior Analysis (ABA). *See also* Ethical issues; Professional requirements
    analysis in, 603–604
    BACB task list, 769–775
    contemporary practice, 13–14, 15*t*
    defined, 6–7, 8*b*
    ethical values summary, 765–766
    evolution of, xxv–xxvi, 6–8
    factors in decision to use, 63–68, 69*f*
    features of approach, 9–13, 755
    organizations, 20*t*
    philosophical concepts, 7, 8*b*
    professionalism of, 13
    as technology of behavior change, 750
    typical analysis process, 14, 16–20, 33
Applied behavior analysts
    BACB task list, 769–775
    professional requirements, 753–759
    professional roles, 12–13
Applied research, defined, 9
*Applying Behavior Analysis Across the Autism Spectrum, Second Edition* (Sulzer-Azaroff & Associates), xxix
*Applying Behavior Analysis Procedures*

913

*with Children and Youth* (Sulzer-Azaroff & Mayer), xxvi
Arbitrary reinforcers, defined, 108
Artificial reinforcers, in token systems, 271, 278
Assessment
   behavioral assessment. *See* Behavioral assessment
   for contextual fit, 45–46
   ethical issues, 117
   in reinforcer selection, 108–109
Association for Behavior Analysis International (ABAI)
   ethical standards, 13, 86
   on seclusion procedures, 690
Augmentative/alternative verbal communication (AAC) methods, use of, 445–446
Autism
   ABA effectiveness in, 12
   chaining with, 319
   delayed prompting with, 457, 458*f*
   distraction techniques, 635
   DTT use with, 404–406
   early intervention effectiveness, 601
   evidence-based practices, 760
   modeling with, 408–411
   peer-mediated interventions, 269
   program support, 53
   shaping in, 285–286
   social skills in, 418, 629
   stereotypy illustration, 186–188
   stimulus control and, 350–351
   stimulus generalization training, 490
   verbal behavior training, 429–430, 432, 439, 601–602
*Autism Social Skills Profile (ASSP)* (Bellini & Hopf), 329
Autoclitic behavior, defined and illustrated, 439–440
Automated recording systems, options of, 156–157
Automatic reinforcers
   defined and illustrated, 107
   extinction and, 615
   in functional analysis, 222–224
Aversive stimuli
   defined and illustrated, 90–91, 710–713
   habituation to, 723–724
   positive punishment and, 727–729
   primary and secondary, 104–106
   in program implementation, 729–731
   as reinforcers, 94
Avoidance behavior
   defined and illustrated, 91–92, 93*f*, 105
   and phobias, 288
   and ratio strain, 508
   timeout and, 704–705

Ayllon, Theodore, as behavior analysis pioneer, 7
Azrin, Nathan, as behavior analysis pioneer, 6, 7

**B**

Backup reinforcers, in token systems, 271, 275, 278
Backward chaining, defined and illustrated, 319–322
Baer, Donald, as behavior analysis pioneer, 6, 7
Bar graphs, illustrated, 163–164, 165*f*
Baseline phase, importance of, 184–185
Baselines
   defined, 153
   graphing of, 161–162
   *See also specific design*
Basic research, defined, 9
Behavior
   ABA perspective, 22–23
   defined, 9, 22
Behavior Analysis Certification Board (BACB)
   ABA definition, 8*b*
   requirements of, xxix, 13
   role of, 751–752
   Task List, 769–775
*Behavior Analysis for Lasting Change* (Sulzer-Azaroff & Mayer), xxvi
Behavior chains
   classes and components, 313–314
   defined, 307
   linking, 310–312
Behavior intervention/improvement plans (BIPs), legal aspects of, 43, 229–231
*Behavior Modification Procedures for School Personnel* (Sulzer & Mayer), xxv
Behavior-reinforcer contingencies, societal uses, 85
Behavior Support Plan–Quality Evaluation Guide (BSP-QE), and BIP quality, 231
Behavioral assessment
   definition and levels of, 60–62, 128
   importance of, 290–291
   measuring. *See* Measurement
   recording. *See* Recording data
*Behavioral Assessment* (journal), 600
*Behavioral Consulting: Improving Client and Consultee Learning and Behavior* (Mayer & Wallace), xxix, 47
Behavioral contracts
   goal selection and, 76
   purposes and uses, 245–247
Behavioral contrast
   with DRO, 669–670
   extinction and, 614–615

   response rates and, 539–540, 721–722
Behavioral cusps, illustrated, 66–67
Behavioral dimensions
   defined, 78
   in objectives selection, 78–80
Behavioral economics, choice and, 733
Behavioral functions, verbal. *See* Verbal behavior
Behavioral functions. *See* Functions
Behavioral goals. *See* Goals
Behavioral links. *See* Links
Behavioral momentum
   defined, 519
   in reducing behaviors, 635–637
   summary table, 737*t*
Behavioral objectives
   collaborative selection of, 38, 607
   defined, 78
   determination of, 78–80
   goal setting and, 58–59, 382
   illustrated, 80–81
Behavioral packages, defined, 547
Behavioral principles, defined, 25
Behavioral procedures
   defined, 25
   reinforcement as, 84, 85
Behavioral repertoires, defined, 86–87
Behavioral skills training (BST)
   illustrated, 418–419
   summary table, 422*t*–423*t*
Behaviorally-anchored rating scale (BARS), defined, 146
Behaviorism, history of, 2–5
Best-fit lines. *See* Trendlines
*Beyond Freedom and Dignity* (Skinner), 765
Bias, observational, 134
Bijou, Sidney, as behavior analysis pioneer, 6, 7
Birnbrauer, Jay, as behavior analysis pioneer, 7
Board Certified Assistant Behavior Analysts (BCaBAs)
   data collection by, 154
   defined, 14*t*
Board Certified Associate Behavior Analysts (BCaBAs), professional requirements, 752
Board Certified Behavior Analysts (BCBAs)
   defined, 14*t*
   professional requirements, 752
Bonus contingencies, use of, 672
Bonus reinforcers, use of, 672
Bonus response cost systems, defined and illustrated, 685–686
Boring, Edwin G., *History of Experimental Psychology*, 6
Break and run responses, in fixed ratio

SUBJECT INDEX • 915

schedules, 506
Breaking point, defined, 505
Bug-in-ear method, program integrity and, 549
Bullying, extinction procedure, 616

**C**

CAPSI (computer-aided PSI). *See* Computer-aided PSI (CAPSI)
Carryover effects
 in alternating-treatment design, 591–592
 defined and illustrated, 585
Catch'em Being Good Game, use of, 657–658
Celeration charts. *See* Standard celeration charts
Chaining
 backward chaining, 319–322
 classes and components, 313–314
 current repertoires in, 316–318
 defined and illustrated, 307–312
 evaluating progress, 582
 everyday terms for, 50*t*
 fading combined with, 326
 forward chaining, 319
 pairs instruction, 326–327
 shaping combined with, 325–326, 338*t*
 social skills teaching, 327–332
 summary of practices and procedures, 337*t*, 338*t*
 supplementary discriminative stimuli, 322–325
 supplementary reinforcers with, 322
 task analysis in, 315–316, 316*f*, 318*b*
 total task method, 319
 unchaining, 334–335
 unwanted chains, 332–335
Challenging behavior, positive interventions for. *See* Positive behavioral interventions (PBI)
Change in level, graphing and analyzing, 170–175
Changing-criterion design
 advantages and disadvantages, 578–579
 defined and illustrated, 578
 summary table, 597*t*
 use and control in, 579–582
Checklists
 in chaining, 323–324
 for program support, 566
 as prompts, 51–52
Choice
 in behavior reduction, 637–638
 behavioral economics and, 733
Choral responding
 defined, 640
 use of, 640–641

CLASS (Contingencies for Learning Academic and Social Skills) program, 602–603
Class-wide peer tutoring (CWPT), benefits of, 268–269
Classical conditioning. *See* Respondent behavior/conditioning
Client rights
 to effective treatment, 735–736
 protection of, 762–763
Clients
 defined, 35
 as reinforcement sources, 561
 reinforcer choices, 243–244
 self-recording by, 155–156
Clinical significance, defined and illustrated, 600
*CLM Course of Study*, features of, 304
Coercion. *See also* Punishment
 voluntariness versus, 77–78
Cognitive behavior strategies, in generalization promotion, 499
Communication skills. *See also* Verbal behavior
 aggression reduction and, 608
 critical skills, 448–449
 shaping and, 287–288
 and treatment integrity, 48–50
Comparative analyses, of intervention effectiveness, 585
Competence, professional, 754–755
The Competent Learner Model
 fluency flashcards, 393
 shaping in, 303–304
Competing contingencies, handling, 247–248
Competing reinforcers, with non-contingent reinforcement, 647–648
Competition, in reinforcement schedules, 539
Complex behavior, alternating-treatment design for, 590–591
Compliance training, fading with, 463–464
Component analysis, defined and illustrated, 592–593
Computer-aided PSI (CAPSI), shaping and, 302–305
Computer-assisted instruction (CAI), shaping and, 303–305
Computerized voice-operated communication device, 445
Conceptual analysis of behavior, 10–11
Concurrent multiple-baseline design, illustrated, 196–197
Concurrent schedules. *See also* Alternating-treatment (multi-element) design
 defined, 506
Concurrent teaching method, chaining

use of, 319
Conditional discrimination, defined and illustrated, 377–378
Conditioned motivating operations (CMOs), illustrated, 352
Conditioned stimuli (CSs)
 aversive. *See* Aversive stimuli
 in respondent conditioning, 27–28, 29*f*
Confidentiality, protection of, 758–759, 761
Conflict, in goal setting, 75–78
Confounding variables, and experimental design, 179
Consent
 informed. *See* Informed consent
 for token economies, 274
Consequences, selecting for intervention, 228
Constant delayed prompting, defined and illustrated, 456–459
Constant time-delayed prompting, defined and illustrated, 456–459
Constructional approach
 DRA as, 658
 goal-setting in, 18, 72–73
 usefulness of, 607–609
Contact desensitization, illustrated, 288
Context
 discriminative learning and, 239–240
 with extinction, 616–617
 in setting objectives, 78
Contextual fit, in program selection, 45–52
Contextually inappropriate behavior (CIB), defined and illustrated, 606
Contingency contracts, goal selection and, 76
Contingency managers
 behavior recording by, 156
 defined, 41
 in generalization support, 498–500
 peers as. *See* Peer-mediated strategies
 performance feedback, 52–54
 in program development and selection, 45–52
 in program maintenance. *See* Program maintenance
Contingency-shaped behavior, defined and illustrated, 400–402
Contingent delay, timeout and, 706
Contingent effort (exercise/exertion)
 defined and illustrated, 713–714
 use of, 734–735
Contingent observation, defined and illustrated, 688
Continuous behaviors, defined, 139
Continuous reinforcement (CRF)
 defined and illustrated, 249–250

and extinction, 510
and problem behaviors, 514
summary table, 545*t*
Contrived reinforcers, 97
Control conditions, in functional assessments, 222–224
Control variables, defined and illustrated, 576*b*
Coping Cat FEAR protocol, in generalization promotion, 499
Coping models, defined, 414
Core values, of BACB, 752
Corporal punishment, prevalence and effects, 718–719, 725
Corrective procedures, in reducing behaviors, 662
Correspondence training, for generalization promotion, 491–492
Cost effectiveness
in program evaluation, 602
of punishment procedures, 724
Criteria. *See also* Changing-criterion design
defined, 78
in objective selection, 78, 79*t*
Culture
in environment preparation, 36–37
organizational, 59–60
in procedure choice, 694
in relationship building, 762–763
Cumulative records, method and uses, 164–168

**D**

Daily report cards, illustrated, 244–245
Dangerous behaviors
DRA with punishment, 655
DRL schedules with, 673
extinction with, 617–618, 655
punishment with, 716–717
seclusion procedures, 690–692
Data
defined, 153
interpreting, 172–175
Data collection
in analysis process, 16*t*, 18–19
during punishment procedures, 733
Dead Man's Test
definition of, 620
DRO tested, 669
Delay discounting, impulsivity and, 531*n*
Delayed cuing. *See* Delayed prompting
Delayed prompting
advantages and disadvantages, 458–459
with chaining, 326–327
defined and illustrated, 456–458
effective use of, 459
summary table, 567*t*

Delayed reinforcement, DRA and, 659
Demographic variables, reporting, 175
Dependent group contingencies
advantages and disadvantages, 265–266
illustrated, 264–265
Dependent variables, defined and illustrated, 177–178, 180–182, 576*b*
Deprivation
defined, 117
extinction and, 611, 619–620
response deprivation hypothesis, 117–118
Descriptive assessments
advantages and disadvantages, 216–217
defined, 212–213
formats, 212–216
hypothesis development, 217–218
illustrated, 61
Desensitization treatment, aversive stimuli and, 713
Determinism
behaviorism and, 4
defined, 8*b*
Developmentally disabled clients
avoiding abulia, 620
errorless learning, 468–471
multiple-probe design case, 583–584
prompting with, 407–408
punishment with, 717–718, 727–728*f*
ratio schedules with, 508
shaping with, 286–287
Differential observing responses (DOR)
method, use of, 391–392
Differential reinforcement (DR)
in behavior reduction, 607–609, 636–637
effective use of, 348–350
with extinction, 620
in goal-setting, 384–385
imitation and, 408–409
reductive procedures summary, 679*t*
in stimulus control, 345–346, 348–350, 421*t*
Differential reinforcement of alternative behavior (DRA)
advantages and disadvantages, 658–660
in combination, 645, 646, 658, 661–662, 671–672, 716, 726–727
defined and illustrated, 585–586, 654–658
DRI versus, 656
DRO versus, 662, 663*f*
effective use of, 660–662, 677–678
extinction with, 618–619
group management programs, 657–658
NCR and, 645, 646, 658

with punishment procedures, 726–727
in reducing behaviors, 533, 612, 618–619, 659
in reversal design, 188
social skills training, 331
summary table, 679*t*, 744*t*
Differential reinforcement of diminishing rates (DRD)
advantages and disadvantages, 674–676
defined and illustrated, 673–674
DRL versus, 673–674
effective use of, 676
Good Behavior Game package, 676–678
summary table, 679*t*, 745*t*
Differential reinforcement of high rates (DRH)
defined and illustrated, 516, 517, 534
in high response promotion, 536
summary table, 545*t*, 571*t*
Differential reinforcement of incompatible behavior (DRI)
in combination, 662, 671–672
defined and illustrated, 552, 656–657
Differential reinforcement of low rates (DRL)
advantages and disadvantages, 674–676
defined and illustrated, 516, 518–519, 672–673
DRD versus, 673–674
effective use of, 676
in ratio schedules, 512
summary table, 545*t*, 572*t*, 679*t*, 745*t*
Differential reinforcement of other behavior (DRO)
advantages and disadvantages, 668–670
in combination, 671–672
defined and illustrated, 662
DRA versus, 662, 663*f*
effective use of, 670–672
momentary DRO, 663–667
progressive DRO (DROP), 667
in reducing behaviors, 609–610, 663–667
in reversal design, 188
summary table, 545*t*, 744*t*–745*t*
whole-interval DRO, 663–667
Differential reinforcement of paced responding (DRP)
defined and illustrated, 516, 517–518
summary table, 545*t*, 572*t*
Differential reinforcement of rate schedules, illustration and use of, 516–519
Differential reinforcement of spaced responding. *See* Differential

reinforcement of low rates (DRL)
Differential reinforcement of zero occurrences. *See* Differential reinforcement of other behavior (DRO)
Differentially reinforcement of diminishing rates (DRD)
   defined, 516–517
   illustrated, 512, 519
Direct approach, advantages of, 73
Direct Instruction (DI), features and uses, 403–404
Direct replication, and generalization, 602–603
Discrete trial training (DTT)
   features and uses, 404–405
   for listener behavior, 443
Discrete trials, defined, 404
Discriminated operants
   defined, 341, 405
   free operants versus, 405–406
   discrimination, stimulus generalization versus, 477
Discriminative control. *See* Stimulus control
Discriminative learning
   contextual factors in, 239–240
   defined, 239
   differential reinforcement in, 348–350
   punishment procedures and, 693
Discriminative stimuli
   in alternating-treatment design, 585–586, 588–589
   in generalization, 477–479
   instructions as, 402
   with interval schedules, 536–538
   modeling and, 408–409
   motivating operations (MOs) versus, 352–353
   in positive behavior intervention, 624–625
Discriminative stimuli for extinction (S$^{\text{De}}$s), defined and illustrated, 31–32, 342
Discriminative stimuli for punishment (S$^{\text{Dp}}$s)
   as antecedent control strategy, 624–625
   defined and illustrated, 342–343
Discriminative stimuli for reinforcement (S$^{\text{Dr}}$s), defined, 342
Discriminative stimuli (S$^{\text{D}}$s)
   in behavior chaining, 310–312, 322–325
   classes of, 342–344, 345$t$
   defined, 311
   in operant learning, 31–32
   in shaping, 294–295
Distraction
   in delay of gratification, 237–238
   in reducing behaviors, 634–635
   summary table, 737$t$
Diversity, equity, and inclusion (DEI), professional development, 763
Do Not Conduct lists, checking, 608
Doctoral level BCBA (BCBA-D), 14$t$
Documentation, ethical issues, 755–756, 760–761
Duplics
   defined, 428
   in verbal behavior, 428–430
Duration
   defined, 135
   illustrated, 576$b$
   IOA calculation, 148
   measuring and recording, 137–138, 148, 151$t$
Duration-based assessment, in reinforcer selection, 111
Duration recording, scheduling of, 158

## E

*Early Echoic Skills Assessment*, 444
Earthquake effect, defined, 191
Echoics
   defined, 428
   in verbal behavior, 429–430
Ecobehavioral assessment, features, 214–216
Edible reinforcers, defined, 107
Educational significance, defined and illustrated, 600
Effectiveness, of program. *See* Program evaluation
Electronic devices
   and activity schedules, 633
   pagers as prompts, 629
Emitted behavior, defined, 87$n$
Emotional and behavioral disorders (EBD), punishment with, 725
Empiricism, defined, 8$b$
Environment
   in assessment for change, 64–65
   defined, 25
   in reducing behaviors, 619–620
   in stimulus generalization training, 488–491
   stimulus versus, 25–27
Environment preparation
   change methods design and selection, 39–41
   client and setting familiarization, 35–39
   contextual fit and, 45–52
   performance feedback and, 52–54
   program development and selection, 42–45
Episodic severity (ES), assessment of, 144–146
Errorless learning
   defined and illustrated, 467–468
   disadvantages of, 472–473
   extra-stimulus prompting in, 471–472
   fading in, 468–471
Escape behavior
   choice and, 638
   defined and illustrated, 91–93
   noncontingent reinforcement for, 644
   punishment and, 694–695, 729
   reducing, 607–608
   timeout and, 704–705
Escape extinction, defined and illustrated, 612, 655
Establishing operations (EOs). *See also* Motivating operations (MOs)
   defined and illustrated, 351–352
   in punishment, 732–733
Ethical issues
   of assessment, 117
   of aversive stimuli use, 711
   BACB guidelines, 86, 751–752
   of behavioral assessment, 226–227, 229–231, 753–754
   behavioral contracts, 245–247
   of client cultural values, 762–763
   confidentiality, 758–759, 761
   consent. *See* Consent
   of data collection, 159$b$, 175
   of documentation, 755–756, 760–761
   of experimental design, 183$n$, 190–191, 753–754
   human values in ABA, 751–752
   in organizational culture, 59–60, 764–765
   of physical guidance, 419
   of professional competence, 754–755
   of program design, 19, 67–68
   of program selection and monitoring, 759–764
   of punishment, 695–696, 706, 724, 726–727, 735–736, 757–758
   of reducing behaviors, 673
   of reinforcement scheduling, 537–538
   of response cost use, 683, 695–696
   of response generalization, 482
   of supervision, 763–764
   of termination of services, 761–762
   of timeout use, 687–692, 695–696, 706
*Ethics Code for Behavior Analysts* (BACB)
   on appropriate services, 759–764
   on assessments and interventions, 753–754
   on clients' best interests, 757–758

on confidentiality, 758–759
on conflicts of interest, 756–757
contents of, 13, 753
on language, 49
on professional competence, 754–755
on punishment, 735–736
on service termination, 77
on stakeholder involvement, 48
on truthful documentation, 755–756
Event recording, IOA calculation, 147–148, 151*t*
Every Student Succeeds Act, guidelines of, 608, 624
Evidence-based practices
ethics of, 753–754, 760
method selection and, 39, 760
in program design, 178–180
Evocative effect, defined and illustrated, 351–352
Exchangeable reinforcers, in token systems, 271
Exclusionary timeout, defined and illustrated, 688–690
Exemplars
defined, 492
in generalization promotion, 492–494
Experimental analysis of behavior
evidence-based, 753–754
terminology, 576*b*
validity concerns, 127
Experimental control
in changing-criterion design, 579–582
demonstrating, 180–182, 184
importance of, 178–179
Experimental design. *See also* Multiple-baseline design
combination illustrated, 594, 595*f*
myths about, 177–179
novel, 753–754
purposes of, 179
single-subject design. *See* Single-subject experimental design
Experimental relations. *See* Functional relations
Experimental significance, determining, 599–600
Experimental variables, defined and illustrated, 576*b*
External validity
defined, 576–577
in single-subject design, 598–601
Extinction
in combined procedures, 614, 615, 617–618, 618–619, 646–647
defined and illustrated, 30, 609–610
effective use of, 615–620
everyday terms for, 50*t*

group contingencies and, 266–268
interval schedules and, 531–532
with positive punishment, 731–732
properties of, 610–615
ratio schedules and, 509–510
summary table, 545*t*, 743*t*–744*t*
Extinction bursts
defined and illustrated, 611–613
handling, 618
Extinction-induced aggression, defined, 612
Extraneous variables, and experimental design, 179
Extrinsic aversive stimuli, defined and illustrated, 712

**F**

Facial screening, defined and illustrated, 689–690
Fading. *See* Stimulus fading
*Families* (Patterson), 300
Feedback
combined with other methods, 278–279, 554–557
for contingency managers, 52–54, 53*b*
defined, 550
effective use of, 250, 550–557
in organizational systems, 500, 550–557
video modeling, 411–412
Feeding disorders, fading with, 463
Fidelity of implementation. *See also* Treatment integrity
analysis of, 593–594
defined, 43
feedback and, 555
measuring, 44–45, 132–134
with reductive procedures, 705
Fixed-interval (FI) schedules
advantages and disadvantages, 532–533
consistency in, 528–530, 532
defined and illustrated, 523–524
extinction with, 531–532, 610–611
fixed-time versus, 523–524
response rates in, 525–527
summary table, 545*t*, 570*t*
Fixed-ratio (FR) schedules
consistency in, 508–509
defined and illustrated, 504–505
extinction with, 610–611
high-rate promotion, 516
response rates, 506–508, 525
summary table, 545*t*, 569*t*
Fixed-time schedules
fixed-interval versus, 523–524
for noncontingent reinforcement, 645–646
summary table, 545*t*

Fluency. *See* Response fluency
Fluency flashcards, use of, 393
Food acceptance
chaining and, 309
reinforcement procedures, 655, 656
response cost use, 684
Form discrimination, prompting with, 387–388
Forward chaining, defined and illustrated, 319, 322–323
Foundational skills, importance of, 73–74
Frames, in programmed instruction, 299–302
Free and appropriate public education (FAPE), 43
Free operants
defined, 405
discriminated operants versus, 405–406
Free reinforcement. *See* Noncontingent reinforcement (NCR)
Frequency
defined, 135
illustrated, 576*b*
Frequency recording. *See* Event recording
Full-session DRL. *See* Differential reinforcement of diminishing rates (DRD)
Functional analysis assessments
advantages and disadvantages, 221–222, 224
determining function, 222–224
illustrated, 224*b*
purposes and uses, 205*t*, 221
variations, 225
Functional behavior assessments (FBAs)
before punishment procedures, 726
biological factors in, 208–209
defined, 203, 205
descriptive assessments, 212–218
ethical issues, 226–227, 229–231, 607
functional analysis in, 221–225
indirect (anecdotal) assessments, 209–212
purposes and uses, 61–62, 203–204, 206, 290–291, 607
self-management and, 254–255
Structured ABC Assessment, 218–221
telehealth service, 225–226
terminology, 205*t*
treatment development and, 226–229, 232*t*
Functional communication training (FCT)
defined and illustrated, 435
NCR combined with, 645

reinforcement schedules in, 514
topography and, 445–446
Functional consequences, defined and
illustrated, 204–205
Functional equivalence. *See also*
Reducing behaviors
extinction and, 611
Functional goals, illustrated, 73
Functional reinforcers, defined, 108
Functional relations
correlation and, 216*b*, 217
defined, 10, 179
demonstrating, 180–182, 184
illustrated, 185–188
Functional utility, defined, 430
Functions
of behavior, 206–208
defined and illustrated, 204–205
Functions/functional, determining,
222–224

## G

Generalization. *See* Stimulus
generalization
Generalization promotion, resurgence
and, 660–661
Generalized imitation
increasing, 410
as response class, 409
Generalized reinforcers
defined, 107
development of, 106–107
in reinforcement procedures, 240–243, 244–247
Generative learning
programmed instruction (PI) and, 300–302
for social skills, 332
Goal selection
behavioral assessments in, 60–62
behavioral objectives and, 78–81
decision to apply ABA, 63–68, 69*f*
defining behaviorally, 68–70
factors in, 62–63
general considerations, 58–60, 71–75
goal conflict management, 75–78
legal aspects, 63, 76
in program development, 16*t*, 18
refining, 70–71
in strategic planning, 60
Goal-setting
in behavior reduction, 638
defined and illustrated, 379–380, 553*b*
effective, 382–385
feedback and, 552, 554
instructions combined with, 403
as motivating operations (MOs), 380–382, 422*t*
participative, 558–560

prompting and, 422*t*
in self-management, 253–254
in shaping, 295–296
Goals
defined, 62
mastery levels and maintenance, 385
in program development, 16*t*, 18
in program maintenance, 558–560
Goldiamond, Israel, as behavior analysis pioneer, 6, 7
Good Behavior Game, effective use of, 539, 593, 676–678
Goodbye Teacher (Keller), 302
Goodness-of-fit assessments, 46
Graduated guidance, defined and illustrated, 465–466, 633
Graduated prompting
defined and illustrated, 459–460
summary table, 567*t*
Graduated time-delayed prompting, defined and illustrated, 456–459
Graphing data
bar graphs, 163–164, 165*f*
cumulative records, 164–168
functional relations determination, 180–182, 599
in generalization promotion, 500
guidelines for, 161
importance of, 153–154
monitoring behavior changes, 170–172
purposes of, 159–161
standard ABA format, 161–163, 162*f*, 164*f*
standard celeration charts, 169–170
Gratification, delay of, 236–238
Greetings, in reducing behaviors, 634
Group contingencies
advantages and disadvantages, 265–266
defined, 262
extinction and, 266–268
Good Behavior Game, 676–678
illustrated, 684
peer-mediated strategies, 268–271
token systems and. *See* Token systems
types of, 262–266
Guidance, for rules learning, 703

## H

Habituation
to aversive stimuli, 723–724
reinforcement and, 240–243
stimulus change and, 376–377
*Handwriting Without Tears*, 299
*Headsprout Reading Basics Program*
goal-setting, 295
shaping in, 300
High-probability requests, in momentum

promotion, 635–637, 695
Hippocrates, ethics of, 751
*History of Experimental Psychology*
(Boring), 6
Holland, James, as behavior analysis
pioneer, 6, 7
*How U. S. Torture Left a Legacy of
Damaged Minds* (New York Times), 725
Human values, in ABA, 751–752
Humane animal training, shaping in, 288–289

## I

Imitation. *See also* Modeling
defined, 407
modeling and, 407–409
reinforcement and, 417–418
Imitative responses, defined and
illustrated, 428
Impulsivity, management of, 530–531
In-vivo contact desensitization, defined and illustrated, 412
Incidental teaching (IT)
for listener behavior, 443–444
for manding, 433–434
prompting in, 406
verbal behavior and, 429
Inclusion timeout, defined and
illustrated, 687–688
Incremental practice, use of, 392
Independent group contingencies,
illustrated, 262–263
Independent variables, defined and
illustrated, 178, 180–182
Indirect (anecdotal) assessments
illustrated, 60–61, 203*b*, 209*b*, 211*t*
purposes and uses, 209–212
Indiscriminable contingencies, in
generalization promotion, 496–497
Individual education plans (IEPs), legal aspects of, 43
Individuals with Disabilities Education Act (IDEA), guidelines of, 63, 229, 624
Individuals with Disabilities Education Improvement Act (IDEIA), guidelines of, 63, 229, 624
Informed consent
for behavioral contracts, 234–235, 245–247
for punishment procedures, 726
for reinforcement schedules, 505*n*–506*n*
written documentation, 760–761
Instructional demand
defined and illustrated, 133, 400–401
effects on validity, 133
Instructional programs
direct instruction (DI) methods,

402–403
discrete trial training (DTT), 404–405
Instructions
  in behavior reduction procedures, 626–628
  effective use of, 516
  with interval schedules, 526–528
  with modeling, 416
  prompting by. *See* Telling
  rules versus, 537
Intensity, defined, 135
Intensive behavioral intervention, defined and illustrated, 601, 603
Interdependent group contingencies
  advantages and disadvantages, 265–266
  illustrated, 263–264
Intermittent reinforcement
  defined and illustrated, 250–251
  interval schedules. *See* Interval schedules
Internal validity, defined, 575–576
Interobserver agreement (IOA), calculation methods, 132, 147–149
Interpretation of data, 172–175
Interreinforcement intervals, interval schedules and, 533
Interresponse time (IRT)
  defined, 135
  IOA calculation, 148
  measuring and recording, 139, 151*t*
Interspersal techniques, in reducing behaviors, 639–641
Interval schedules
  advantages and disadvantages, 532–533
  after ratio schedules, 527–528
  behavioral contrast with, 539–540
  characteristics of, 524–532
  competition and, 539
  consistency of response, 528–530, 532
  defined and illustrated, 522–524
  discrimination stimuli use, 536–538
  error patterns, 530
  extinction and responses, 531–532
  impulsivity management, 530–531
  interspersing tasks, 540–541
  limited hold (LH) use, 534–536
  matching law and, 541–543
  planning considerations, 533–534
  preferred response rates promotion, 533–541
  rates of response, 525–528
  ratio schedules versus, 515
  schedule interactions, 543–544
Interval time-sampling systems
  defined and illustrated, 139, 140–141, 142–143

IOA calculation, 148–149
methods and selection, 139–140, 141–144
Interventions. *See also* Program development and selection
  defined, 153
  selecting, 227–229*b*, 232*t*
Intraverbals
  defined and illustrated, 438–440
  intraverbal training, 440–441, 442*f*
Intrinsic aversive stimuli, defined and illustrated, 712
Intrinsic motivation, rewards and, 99–100
Ipsative data
  defined, 179
  in evidence-based practice, 179

**J**

*Journal of Applied Behavior Analysis*, 6, 66
  treatment integrity data, 44
Journal resources, xxxviii

**K**

Keller, Fred, as behavior analysis pioneer, 6

**L**

Labeled praise, illustrated, 238–239
Lag schedules
  defined, 517
  illustrated, 519
  summary table, 545*t*, 572*t*
Language, clarity of tasks, 48–50
Language development
  delayed prompting with, 457–458
  shaping in, 287–288
Latency
  defined, 135
  illustrated, 576*b*
  measuring and recording, 138, 151*t*
Latency FA, 225
Learned (conditioned) reinforcers, defined and illustrated, 104–105
Learned helplessness
  defined and illustrated, 620
  positive punishment and, 721
Learning, defined, 23
Least restrictive environment, Florida guidelines, 697
Least-to-most prompting, use of, 388–391
Legal issues. *See also* Ethical issues
  of behavior reduction methods, 726–727
  in education, 43, 179–180, 229–231, 624
  of goal selection, 63, 76

of seclusion procedures, 691–692
of timeout, 696–698
of token systems, 274–275
*Let me hear your voice* (Maurice), 405*n*
Level changes, and data interpretation, 180–182
*The Life of the Bee* (Maeterlinck), 426
Limited hold (LH)
  defined and illustrated, 534–536
  summary table, 545*t*, 571*t*
Line graphs
  defined, 161
  features of, 161–162, 162*f*, 164*f*
Links
  choosing, 309–310
  defined, 307
  parameters of, 308–309
Listening behavior, in verbal behavior, 441–444
Logistical changes, and goal selection, 64
Low-Rate Functional Analysis, 225

**M**

Magnitude size
  defined, 135
  in interval schedules, 527
  in negative punishment, 701–702
Maintenance. *See* Program maintenance
Malpractice, avoiding, 751–752
Mand frames, defined and illustrated, 440
Mands
  defined, 430–432
  mand training, 432–436
  shaping in, 287–288
Masochism, development of, 713, 732
Masturbation, public, 644, 659
Matching law
  interval schedules and, 536, 540, 541–543
  ratio schedules and, 512
Matching-to-sample (MTS), in errorless learning, 468–469
Maximum-to-minimum prompting
  in errorless learning, 467–468
  use of, 388–389
Measurement
  characteristics of good system, 128–130
  process of, 134–135
  selection of measures, 130–134
  in shaping, 291
  of treatment integrity, 44–45, 132–134
  treatment utility, 129
Measurement complexity
  defined, 133
  effects on validity, 133
Methylphenidate (MPH), responses to,

355, 532, 542
Minimum-to-maximum prompting, use of, 388–391
Mission
  of BACB, 752
  and goal selection, 58–59
Mnemonics, defined and illustrated, 641
Modeling
  advantages and disadvantages, 649–650
  in antecedent control strategy, 624–625
  contingency management, 415–419
  defined and illustrated, 406–408
  DRA combined with, 657–658, 662
  everyday terms for, 50*t*
  fading in, 467
  as imitative prompt, 408–409, 410
  instructions combined with, 403
  of positive punishment, 722
  problematic behavior and, 648–650, 739*t*–740*t*
  selection of model, 413–415
  shaping combined with, 287–288, 409–410
  for social skills, 410–411
  video modeling, 410–413
Modified Incidental Teaching Sessions (MITS), use of, 443–444
Momentary DRO
  defined and illustrated, 662–665
  summary table, 679*t*
  whole-interval DRO versus, 666–667
Momentary time sampling
  defined, 140
  selection of, 141–144, 151*t*
Monitoring behavior change
  during punishment procedures, 705, 733
  professional role in, 759–764
Morningside Model of Generative Instruction, student reading performance, 394, 396*f*
Motivating operations (MOs)
  as antecedent control strategy, 624–625
  defined and illustrated, 32, 351–355
  discriminative stimuli versus, 352–353
  in functional analysis assessment, 222–224
  goals as, 380–382
  in mand training, 432–436
  in problematic behavior, 633–634
  in punishment, 732–733
  in reinforcer selection, 117–119
  in stimulus control, 351–355
  subclasses defined, 353–355
Motivating stimuli ($S^M$)
  defined and illustrated, 353

in verbal behavior, 432–433
Multi-element design. *See* Alternating-treatment (multi-element) design
Multiple-baseline design
  advantages and disadvantages, 197–201
  defined and illustrated, 191–193
  planning and implementing, 197
  selection and use of, 191–193
  summary table, 596*t*–597*t*
  variations of, 193–197
Multiple-probe design
  defined and illustrated, 582, 583–585
  ethical issues, 190–191
  summary table, 597*t*
Multiple schedules. *See* Alternating-treatment (multi-element) design
Multiple-Stimulus Assessment, in reinforcer selection, 112, 113–116
Multiple-Stimulus Assessment with Replacement and without Replacement, 112–114
Multiple-treatment interference, defined and illustrated, 585

**N**
Narratives, in descriptive assessments, 213*n*, 218*b*
National Autism Center, evidence-based practices, 754, 760
Natural language paradigm (NLP), training loosely for, 496
Natural reinforcement, in token systems, 278
Negative behavioral contrast, defined and illustrated, 540
Negative discriminative stimuli ($S^{Dp}s$), 31–32
Negative practice
  defined and illustrated, 715–716
  summary table, 747*t*
Negative punishment
  advantages and disadvantages, 692–698
  in behavior reduction, 608–609
  in combination, 699–700
  defined and illustrated, 30–31, 682–683
  effective use of, 698–706
  minimizing outbursts, 705–706
  misuse of, 694, 695–696
  response cost. *See* Response cost
  safeguards for, 698, 699*b*
  timeout. *See* Timeout
Negative reinforcement
  advisability of use, 95–96
  defined and illustrated, 29–30, 31*f*, 90–91, 92*t*
  differentiation from positive, 95
  escape as, 93

  increasing behavior with, 260*t*
  punishment comparison, 94–95, 709–710
Negative reinforcement procedures, defined and illustrated, 90–91
Negative reinforcers
  defined and illustrated, 90–91
  differentiation from positive, 94–95
*No Child Left Behind Act (NCLB)*, and seclusion procedures, 690
Nonconcurrent multiple-baseline design, illustrated, 196–197
Noncontingent reinforcement (NCR)
  advantages and disadvantages, 645–647
  in behavior reduction, 607–609, 646–647
  in combination, 646, 716
  defined and illustrated, 642–645
  effective use of, 533, 647–648
  extinction and, 614, 617–619, 646–647
  illustrated, 585–586
  summary table, 679*t*, 738*t*–739*t*

**O**
Objective measures, defined, 128
Observation
  recording products. *See* Recording data
  of social skills, 329–330
Observational bias, effects on validity, 134
Observer awareness of being assessed, effects on validity, 134
Observer drift, correcting, 149
Obtain data (O), experimental control and, 180–182
Omission training. *See* Differential reinforcement of other behavior (DRO)
Ontogeny, defined, 4
Operant behavior/learning
  antecedents in, 31–32
  consequences in, 29–31
  three-term contingency in, 28–29
Operant classes
  in ABA process, 24
  defined, 24, 199
Operational definitions, defined, 155*b*
Operationally defined behaviors, defined, 70
Operations, defined, 70
Ordinates, in graphing, 161–163
Organizational behavior management
  compliance in, 628
  feedback in, 500, 550–557
  goal-setting in, 382–385
  group contingencies and, 267–268
  implementation assessments, 557

negative reinforcement in, 557
program generalization, 563–564
program maintenance, 558–564
reinforcement schedules in, 513
social facilitation in, 538
Organizational culture
  ethics evaluation, 764–765
  goal selection and, 59–60
Outcome recording. *See* Permanent product recording
Outcomes, goal selection and, 71
Overcorrection
  in behavior reduction, 608–609
  defined and illustrated, 714–715
  summary table, 747*t*
  use of, 734–735
Overgeneralization, generalization and, 477–479
Overjustification effect, 99–100
Overselectivity
  avoiding, 389
  training loosely and, 495–496

**P**

Pacing schedules, defined and illustrated, 517–518
Paired-Stimulus Assessment, in reinforcer selection, 112, 113*f*
Parameters, defined, 86
Parametric analysis
  alternating-treatment design, 591
  defined and illustrated, 593–594
Parents, in program maintenance, 560–561
Parsimony, defined, 8*b*
Partial-interval time sampling
  defined, 140
  selection of, 141–144, 151*t*
Participative goal setting
  in behavior reduction, 638
  in program maintenance, 558–560
Partner learning, benefits of, 268–269
*A Passion for Excellence* (Peters and Austin), 533
Pavlov, Ivan, respondent conditioning, 27–28, 33
PEAK *(Promoting the Emergence of Advanced Knowledge) Rational Training System*, 444
PECC. *See Professional and Ethical Compliance Code for Behavior Analysts* (BACB)
Peer-mediated strategies. *See also* Group contingencies
  defining and applying, 268–271
  for generalization promotion, 492
Peers
  as models, 413–414
  in motivating operations, 227
  as reinforcement sources, 561, 563

Percentage of opportunities, in event recording, 137
Performance Diagnostic Checklist-Human Services (PPC-HS), use of, 557
*Performance Management: Changing Behavior that Drives Organizational Effectiveness* (Daniels and Daniels), 40
Permanent product recording
  defined, 134
  selection of, 134–135, 151*t*
Permanent products of behavior
  IOA calculation, 147
  measuring, 134
Personalized system of instruction (PSI), mastery in, 515
Phase labels, in graphing, 162
Phobias, shaping and, 288, 295–296
Phylogeny, defined, 4
Physical guidance
  chaining and, 325
  defined and illustrated, 419
  effective use of, 419–420, 423*t*
  shaping and, 298
Picture Exchange Communication System (PECS)
  features and use of, 445
  generalization and, 488
  for manding, 434
  prompting in, 406
  support requirements, 52–53
  for tacting, 437
  treatment integrity and, 43–44
  use of, 61, 386, 601
Pivotal behaviors, illustrated, 66–67
PLA-Check (Planned Activity Check), illustrated, 146–147
Planned ignoring, defined and illustrated, 687–688
Planning process. *See* Program development and selection
Play, choice in, 637
Positive Behavior Support Team (PBST), function and role, 40–41
Positive behavioral contrast, defined and illustrated, 539–540
Positive behavioral interventions (PBI)
  advantages of, 623–624
  defined, 623
  punishment versus, 623
Positive behavioral support (PBS), defined, 18, 18*n*
*The Positive Classroom: Improving Student Learning and Behavior* (Mayer), xxix
Positive discriminative stimuli (S$^{Dr}$s), 31–32
Positive practice, defined and illustrated, 589–590, 714–715

Positive punishment
  advantages of, 716–718
  aversive stimuli in, 710–713
  in behavior reduction, 608–609
  behavioral packages, 713–716
  in combination, 716, 726–727, 731–732
  defined and illustrated, 30–31, 709–710
  disadvantages of, 718–726
  effective use of. *See* Punishment procedures
  extinction with, 731–732
  summary table, 747*t*–748*t*
Positive reinforcement
  defined, 29, 709
  differentiation from negative, 95
  illustrated, 10, 25, 29–30, 31*f*, 89–90, 92*t*
  increasing behavior with, 259*t*, 552, 554*b*
  punishment comparison, 709–710
Positive reinforcers
  defined and illustrated, 89–90
  differentiation from negative, 94–95
POVs (Predication/Obtain data/Verify)
  in changing-criterion design, 578–582
  functional relations and, 180–182
  in multi-element design, 590
PPC-HS, use of, 557
Pragmatism, defined, 8*b*
Praise, as reinforcer, 238–239
Precision teaching
  celeration charts in, 393–395
  defined, 393
  features and examples, 393–396
  graphing, 170
Precursor Functional Analysis, 225
Precursors, defined, 335
Predication (P), experimental control and, 180–182
Premack principle, and reinforcer selection, 118–119
Primary aversive stimuli, defined and illustrated, 104, 711
Primary prevention, illustrated, 41
Primary reinforcers, defined and illustrated, 87–88, 103–104
*Principles of Applied Behavior Analysis for Behavior Technicians and Other Practitioners, Third Edition* (Wallace & Mayer), xxix
Problematic behavior
  common environmental factors, 633–634
  differential reinforcement in. *See* specific differential reinforcement procedure
  importance of environment, 641–642

modeling and, 648–650
noncontingent reinforcement (NCR) for, 642–648
positive behavior interventions for. *See* Positive behavioral interventions (PBI)
prompting strategies, 626–633
punishment. *See* Negative punishment; Positive punishment
reductive procedures summary, 679*t*
reinforcement operations, 633–641
social stories and, 650–651
stimulus change procedures, 625–626
summary table, 737*t*–748*t*
Procedural fidelity. *See* Treatment integrity
*Professional and Ethical Compliance Code for Behavior Analysts* (BACB), 38, 86, 128*n*, 607, 697–698
Professional requirements. *See also* Ethical issues; *Ethics Code for Behavior Analysts* (BACB)
  of ABA practitioners, 13–14, 750–753, 755
  professional development, 753, 755, 763
Program development and selection
  in behavior analysis path, 16–20
  for generalized change, 42–43
  treatment integrity, 43–45
Program evaluation
  alternating-treatment design. *See* Alternating-treatment (multi-element) design
  analysis for function, 575–577
  changing-criterion design, 578–582
  component analysis, 592–593
  cost effectiveness, 602
  generality and change persistence, 19–20, 602–603
  large group applicability, 601–602
  multiple-probe design, 582–585
  parametric analysis, 593–594
  professional role in, 759–764
  single-subject design, 594–601, 609–610
  validation in, 575–577
Program generalization, in organizational settings, 563–564
Program implementation
  effective prompt use, 549
  negative reinforcement in, 557
  providing feedback, 550–557
  support in, 547–549
Program maintenance
  checklist, 566
  fading of prompts in, 558
  goal-setting in, 558–560
  in punishment procedures, 733

reinforcement sources in, 560–563
summary table, 567*t*–572*t*
Program selection. *See* Program development and selection
Programmed instruction (PI), shaping and, 299–302
Progressive delayed prompting, defined and illustrated, 456–459
Progressive DRO (DROP), defined and illustrated, 667
Progressive ratio (PR) schedules, defined and illustrated, 505, 512–514
Progressive time delay. *See* Progressive delayed prompting
Prompt dependence
  avoiding, 389–392
  defined, 389
  stimulus control transfer, 455–456, 464–465
Prompting
  in behavior reduction, 628–629
  defined and illustrated, 385
  delayed. *See* Delayed prompting
  direct instruction. *See* Direct Instruction (DI)
  effective use of, 398, 549
  fading in, 51–52, 558
  imitative. *See* Modeling
  physical guidance, 419–420
  prompt complexity, 387–388
  selection of, 385–389
  selectivity and dependence, 389–392
  in shaping, 294–295
  and stimulus generalization, 485–486
  summary table, 421*t*–423*t*, 567*t*
  by telling, 398–403
Proprioceptive cues, defined, 420
*Publication Manual of the American Psychological Association* (APA), 754
Punishers. *See* Aversive stimuli
Punishment
  advantages of, 692–694, 716–718
  cautions in using, 682
  disadvantages of, 694–698, 718–726
  ethical issues, 757–758
  negative. *See* Negative punishment
  overuse of, 723
  positive . *See* Positive punishment
  reinforcement versus, 90, 94–95
  stimulus control and, 379
  summary table, 747*t*–748*t*
Punishment procedures
  alternative behavior reinforcement, 726–727
  aversive stimuli choice, 727–729
  contextual factors, 732–733
  contingent effort use, 734–735
  defined, 683
  ethical issues, 757–758
  generalization and maintenance, 733

illustrated, 729–732, 733–734
implementation, 729–732
preliminary steps, 726
summary table, 747*t*–748*t*

**R**

Radical behaviorism, behavior change in, 5–6
Random ratio, defined, 505
Range-bound changing-criterion design, illustrated, 581
Rate of behavior
  illustrated, 576*b*
  interval schedules and, 525–527
  and mastery, 393–396
  reporting of, 137
Rate of criterion level, in objectives selection, 78–79
Rating scales, for social skills, 330–331
Ratio schedules
  advantages of, 510–511
  defined and illustrated, 504–505
  differential reinforcement of rates, 516–519
  disadvantages of, 514–515
  effective use of, 511–514
  extinction in, 509–510
  performance characteristics, 505–510
Ratio strain
  avoidance of, 513–514
  defined and illustrated, 505
  and performance quality, 514–515
Reactivity, data validity effects, 130–131, 157
Recording data
  in generalization promotion, 500
  implementing systems, 154–157
  scheduling, 157–159
  self-recording, 155–156, 555
  transitory behavior, 136–147
Records
  in punishment procedures, 733
  in token systems, 275
Redirection
  defined and illustrated, 630–632
  summary table, 737*t*
Reducing behaviors
  antecedent methods. *See* Antecedent control strategies
  common environmental factors, 633–634
  differential reinforcement in. *See specific differential reinforcement procedure*
  extinction in. *See* Extinction
  importance of environment, 641–642
  modeling and social stories in, 648–651
  noncontingent reinforcement (NCR) for, 642–648

prompting in, 626–633
punishment. *See* Negative punishment; Positive punishment
reinforcement schedules in, 514
reinforcing environment in, 633–641
summary table, 679*t*, 737*t*–748*t*
targeting and analyzing, 606–609
Reflexes, conditioning and, 27–28
Reflexive motivating operations, defined and illustrated, 353–354
Registered Behavior Technicians (RBTs)
as contingency managers, 41
defined, 14*t*
professional requirements, 752
as recorders, 154–155
Regression
defined, 613*n*
during extinction, 610
Reinforcement
in behavior chaining, 335–336
in behavior maintenance, 473, 560–563
concerns and disadvantages, 97–100
defined, 84–86
everyday terms for, 50*t*
extinction and, 615–620
feedback combined with, 554–556
and functions of behavior, 206–208
illustrated, 85*t*, 86*t*
in imitation, 417–418
importance of, 641–642
natural vs. planned, 84–86
negative. *See* Negative reinforcement
positive. *See* Positive reinforcement
positive and negative comparison, 29–30
as procedure. *See* Reinforcement procedures
in program maintenance, 473, 560–563
punishment versus, 94–95
in reducing behaviors, 633–641
Reinforcement procedures
client choice in, 243–244
competing contingencies, 247–248
defined and illustrated, 86–87, 88
delay of gratification, 236–238
discriminative learning in, 239–240
generalization support, 244–247
praise in, 238–239
reinforcement schedules use, 51
reinforcer magnitude and quantity, 240–243
reinforcers versus, 88
selecting effective, 235
self-management. *See* Self-management
summary tables, 259*t*–260*t*
supplementary reinforcers, 238
targeted behaviors and, 248–249

timing of delivery, 235–236
Reinforcement schedules
defined and illustrated, 249–251
interval. *See* Interval schedules
ratio schedules. *See* Ratio schedules
summary table, 545, 569*t*–572*t*
using NCR with, 645–648
*Reinforcer Assessment for Individuals with Severe Disabilities*, 108
Reinforcer menus, in reinforcer selection, 110
Reinforcer preference assessments (RPAs)
duration-based assessment, 111
Multiple-Stimulus Assessment, 112, 113–116
Paired-Stimulus Assessment, 112, 113*f*
Single-Stimulus Assessment, 111–112
Reinforcer selection
ethical considerations, 117
general considerations, 235
illustrated, 234*b*, 251*b*
motivating operations in, 117
observation in, 109–110
preference assessments, 109–110
in reducing behaviors, 643–644
sampling, 120–122
surveys and reports, 108–109
variety and novelty in, 119–121
Reinforcers
classes of, 107
contrived, 97
defined, 87
in extinction, 619–620
identification of. *See* Functional behavior assessments (FBAs)
primary, 103–104
reinforcement procedures versus, 88
response rate factors, 527
secondary. *See* Secondary reinforcers
selection of. *See* Reinforcer selection
supplementary, 238
in timeout, 700–701
Relational Frame of Coordination, 447
Relational Frame Theory
for social skills, 332
verbal behavior approach, 447–449
Relaxation training, for special-needs clients, 420
Reliable measures
defined, 128
selection of, 131–132
Replacement behaviors, selecting, 226–227, 229*b*
Replication, experimental control and, 180–182, 602–603
Reporting, reliability data, 149
Required relaxation, defined and

illustrated, 691
Research, applied vs. basic, 9
Respondent behavior/conditioning, characteristics of, 27–28, 29*f*
Response cards strategy
defined, 641
use of, 640–641
Response classes. *See* Operant classes
Response cost
advantages and disadvantages, 692–696
in behavior reduction, 608–609, 631
bonus response cost, 685–686
in combination, 699–700
defined and illustrated, 683–685
effective use of, 698–706
everyday terms for, 50*t*
minimizing outbursts, 705
summary table, 746*t*
Response delay, defined and illustrated, 472
Response deprivation hypothesis (RDH), and reinforcer selection, 117–118
Response effort
extinction and, 610, 614
in reducing behaviors, 638–639
summary table, 738*t*
Response fluency
defined, 392
promotion of, 491
in ratio schedules, 507
Response generalization
advantages and disadvantages, 481–482
defined, 479
stimulus generalization versus, 479–480
Response interruption and redirection (RIRD), use of, 631–632
Response prompts, defined, 385
Response suppression, from punishment, 719–720
Restitution, defined and illustrated, 714–715, 734–735
Restrained timeout, defined and illustrated, 691–692
Restrictive stimulus control. *See* Stimulus overselectivity
Resurgence
defined, 613
with differential reinforcement, 660–661, 668
during extinction, 610, 613–614, 619
with positive punishment, 721
Return-to-baseline design. *See* Withdrawal (return-to-baseline) design
Reversal design. *See also* Withdrawal (return-to-baseline) design
defined and illustrated, 188
in intervention evaluation, 585

summary table, 596*t*
Rewards
    defined, 87
    overjustification effect, 99–100
    reinforcers versus, 87
RIRD. *See* Response interruption and redirection (RIRD)
Risley, T. R., as behavior analysis pioneer, 6, 7
Role playing
    modeling and, 407
    for rules learning, 627, 703
    in self-management, 253
Rule-governed behavior. *See* Verbally-governed behavior
Rules
    in antecedent control strategy, 624–625, 626*b*
    in behavior reduction procedures, 626–628, 703
    instructions versus, 537
    with interval schedules, 526–528
    with modeling, 416
Rumination, facial screening with, 689

**S**

S-delta, defined, 342, 347
Safety programs, BDT in, 418–419
Sampling, for progress analysis, 197
Satiation
    everyday terms for, 50*t*
    extinction and, 611
    interval schedules and, 532
    reinforcement and, 240–243
Scallops, fixed-interval, 528–530
Scatter Plot analysis, uses, 214, 215*t*
Schedule history, in schedule planning, 534, 611
Scheduling, everyday terms for, 50*t*
School environment
    activity schedules, 632–633
    behavior support teams, 40–41
    differential reinforcement methods, 350, 656–657
    feedback in, 551–552
    functional behavior assessments and, 205–206, 229–231
    generalization training and, 488–491
    goal-setting examples, 253–254, 559*b*
    group contingencies and, 263–265, 279, 281
    improved reinforcement in, 251
    legal mandates, 624
    peer-mediated interventions, 269–271
    ratio schedules in, 513–514
    reducing behaviors, 615–616, 633–641
    self-management in, 253–254, 255–256
    stimulus control in, 350
    Structured ABC Assessment, 218–221
*School Wide Positive Behavior Support program*, goals of, 60
*Science and Human Behavior* (Skinner), 284
Scientific method
    ABA approach, 9–11, 753–754
    defined, 8*b*
Scope of practice, ethics of, 754–755
Seclusion timeout, defined and illustrated, 690–692
Secondary aversive stimuli, defined and illustrated, 105, 711
Secondary prevention, illustrated, 41
Secondary reinforcers
    in chaining, 310–311
    defined and illustrated, 104–105
    development of, 105–107
    feedback as, 552, 554*b*
Selectionism, defined, 4, 8*b*
Self-control, delayed gratification, 236–238
Self-esteem, punishment and, 722–723
Self-injurious behavior inhibiting system (SIBIS), use of, 733–734
Self-injurious behavior (SIB)
    alternating-treatment design for, 587, 590
    chain blocking and, 335
    DRO methods with, 665–666
    extinction with, 612, 613
    facial screening with, 689–690
    illustrated, 185–186
    punishment procedures and, 727–728*f*
    reinforcement role in, 90–91
    self-injurious behavior inhibiting system (SIBIS), 733–734
    stimulus change with, 376
    timeout with, 704–705
Self-management
    defined and illustrated, 252–254
    effective methods, 254–257
Self-monitoring
    context and, 240
    in self-management, 51, 255–257
Self-recording
    considerations of, 155–156
    for feedback, 555
    in generalization promotion, 498–499
Sensitive measures, defined, 128
Separation anxiety disorder, whole-interval DRO with, 666–667
Sequence effects
    in alternating-treatment design, 591–592
    defined and illustrated, 585
    with single-subject designs, 594, 595
Setting events (SEs). *See* Motivating operations (MOs)
Shaping
    adult learners, 289–290
    in animal training, 288–289
    chaining combined with, 325–326, 338*t*
    combined with other methods, 298–299, 325–326, 338*t*
    computer-aided instruction (CAI) and, 302–305
    current repertoires assessment, 290–291
    defined and illustrated, 284–290
    discriminative stimuli use, 294–295
    evaluating progress, 582
    everyday terms for, 50*t*
    goal selection and setting, 291, 295–298
    measurement system choice, 291
    modeling combined with, 287–288, 409–410
    origin of theory, 285, 285*b*
    personalized system of instruction (PSI) and, 302
    programmed instruction (PI) and, 299–302
    setting parameters and criteria, 291–294
    verbal behaviors and, 429–430
Sign language, delayed prompting with, 457–458
Significance
    experimental, 598–601
    non-experimental forms, 600–601
Significant others, and reinforcer selection, 109
Similarity, in modeling, 413–414, 415
Simple correction, defined and illustrated, 714
Simultaneous prompting, use of, 389
Simultaneous treatment. *See* Alternating-treatment (multi-element) design
Single-Stimulus Assessment, in reinforcer selection, 111–112
Single-subject experimental design
    advantages of, 179–182
    considerations with, 594–600
    defined, 178
    extinction in, 609–610
    multiple-baseline design. *See* Multiple-baseline design
    requirements for, 183
    selection of, 594
    significance considerations in, 598–601
    summary table, 596*t*–597*t*
    withdrawal design. *See* Withdrawal

(return-to-baseline) design
Skill cards, in chaining, 328
Skinner, B. F.
    as behavior analysis pioneer, 6–7, 33
    on behavioral conformity, 59
    on change focus, 54–55
    on freedom, 765
    on shaping, 285*b*
    on verbal behavior, 426–428
Social comparison strategy, illustrated, 64
Social facilitation, response rates and, 538
Social reinforcers
    defined, 107
    in functional analysis, 222–224
Social skills
    chaining for, 327–332
    DRD and, 676
    identifying deficits, 328–331
    modeling for, 410–411
    prompting for, 386
    summary table, 742*t*
    task analysis, 328
Social stories
    chaining and, 332, 333
    in reducing behaviors, 650–651
    summary table, 741*t*
Social validity, defined and illustrated, 600–601
Socially-mediated reinforcers, illustrated, 107, 257
Software. *See* Computer-assisted instruction (CAI)
Specific praise, illustrated, 238–239
Spontaneous recovery, defined, 613
Standard celeration charts
    methods and uses, 169–170
    in precision teaching, 393–396
Standardized tests, as assessment tools, 70
Stereotypy
    defined, 89
    generalization and, 499–500
    illustrated, 89, 186–188
    response cost with, 684–685
    RIRD use, 631–632
Stimulus
    defined, 26
    environment versus, 25–27
    summary of terms and abbreviations, 345*t*
Stimulus change
    advantages and disadvantages, 378
    defined and illustrated, 375–379
    everyday terms for, 50*t*
    failure of, 379
    prompting and, 422*t*
    in reducing behaviors, 625–626
Stimulus classes, defined and illustrated, 26–27
Stimulus control
    complex behavior and, 350–351
    conditions of, 340–344
    control levels described, 375
    defined, 31, 340, 343
    differential reinforcement use, 345–346, 348–350, 421*t*
    establishing, 344
    fluency and precision training, 392–396
    illustrated, 31–32, 342*t*, 344–348
    importance of, 340
    maintaining, 473
    motivating operations (MOs) in, 351–355
    prompting in. *See* Prompting
    summary table, 567*t*–572*t*
Stimulus control transfer
    benefits of, 455–456
    delayed prompting, 456–459
    errorless learning in, 467–473
    graduated prompting, 459–460
    stimulus fading in, 460–467
    summary table, 567*t*–568*t*
Stimulus equalization, in errorless learning, 471
Stimulus equivalence, Relational Frame Theory and, 446–447
Stimulus fading
    chaining and, 326
    defined and illustrated, 460–464
    effective use of, 464–467
    in errorless learning, 467, 468–471
    everyday terms for, 50*t*
    shaping and, 298–299
    summary table, 567*t*
    as temporary measure, 51–52
Stimulus generalization
    advantages and disadvantages, 480–483
    assessment for, 482–483
    defined, 477
    discrimination versus, 477, 479*t*
    evaluating for, 19–20, 603, 604
    everyday terms for, 50*t*
    inappropriate, 720–721
    in organizational settings, 563–564
    and overgeneralization, 477–479
    planning for, 42–43
    response generalization versus, 479–480
    summary table, 578*t*
    training. *See* Stimulus generalization training
    of verbal behavior, 441
Stimulus generalization training
    carry-over strategies, 491–492
    contingency managers in, 498–500
    continuing training, 497–498
    exemplars, 492–494
    fluency promotion, 491
    generalization maps, 487–488
    importance of, 483–484
    incorporating common stimuli, 488–491
    prompting in, 485–486
    recording and graphing, 500
    requesting generalization, 484–485
    in sequential environments, 486–487
    training loosely, 495–496
    using indiscriminable contingencies, 496–497
Stimulus overselectivity, handling, 389–392
Stimulus prompts
    defined, 385
    illustrated, 387
Stimulus/stimuli, summary of terms and abbreviations, 345*t*
Stimulus-stimulus pairing, verbal behavior and, 429–430
Strategic planning, defined and illustrated, 60
Structuralism, history of, 3–4
Structured ABC Assessment, use of, 218–221
Student Success Team (SST), function and role, 41
Sub-goals, in goal-setting, 380
Subjective measures, defined, 128
Successive approximations
    defined, 284
    illustrated, 287–288, 299–302
Supervision
    program support and, 573
    as reinforcement sources, 561–563
Supplementary reinforcers
    in chaining, 322
    defined, 238
Support for program, goal selection and, 67
Surrogate motivating operations, defined and illustrated, 354
Surveillance, accuracy and, 256–257
Surveys, in reinforcer selection, 108–109
Symptom substitution, defined, 613*n*
Synthesized FA, 225
Systematic replication, and generalization, 602–603

**T**

Tact frames, illustrated, 437–438
Tacts
    defined, 436–437
    tact training, 437–438
Tangible reinforcers, defined, 107
Target behaviors, illustrated, 68–70
Task analyses
    in behavior chaining, 308, 315–316,

316f, 318b
  for social skills, 328
Teaching, defined, 23
Teaching interaction procedure, for social skills, 332
Teaching machine, programmed instruction, 299
Team approach, organizing and managing, 40–41
Technological features
  of ABA, 10, 11–12
  defined, 10
Telehealth service delivery (TSD) model, and functional behavior assessments, 225–226
Telling
  defined and illustrated, 398–399
  effective use of, 399–403
Termination of services, ethical issues, 761–762
Terminology
  avoiding jargon, 49–50
  everyday terms for ABA, 50t
Tertiary prevention, illustrated, 41
Therapeutic contracts, goal selection and, 76
Thinning of reinforcers
  extinction and, 614
  fading versus, 512n
  in ratio scheduling, 512–514
Three-term contingency
  defined, 24
  illustrated, 24, 213f, 214f
Tiered economies, use of, 280–281
Time-delayed prompting. See Delayed prompting
Time-series statistical analysis, significance and, 599
Timeout
  advantages and disadvantages, 692–698
  in behavior reduction, 608–609
  in combination, 699–700
  defined, 685
  effective use of, 698–706
  everyday terms for, 50t
  extinction versus, 686–687
  legal issues, 696–698
  minimizing outbursts, 705–706
  response cost versus, 686–687
  safeguards for, 698, 699b
  summary table, 746t
  variations of, 687–692
Timeout ribbon, defined and illustrated, 688
Token systems
  advantages and disadvantages, 272–274
  effective implementation, 274, 277–279
  illustrated, 629, 684, 705
  maintaining performance, 280–281
  preliminary steps, 274–277
  reducing behaviors with, 279–280
  response costs, 693
Tokens, selection of, 275–276
Topography
  defined, 135, 425
  illustrated, 80–81, 576b
Torture, effects of, 725–726
Total communication format, use of, 402
Total task teaching method, chaining use of, 319, 323
*Training for the Special Child* (Reese), 468
Transition FA, 225
Transitive conditioned motivating operations (CMO-Ts), defined and illustrated, 353
Transitory behaviors
  duration recording, 137–138
  episodic severity or intensity, 144–146
  event recording, 136–137
  group situations, 146–147
  interresponse time (IRT) recording, 139
  interval time-sampling recording, 139–144
  latency recording, 138
  measuring, 135, 141–144
Treasure Box, reinforcer choice and, 244, 244b
Treatment drift
  avoiding, 45
  handling of, 133
Treatment integrity
  ensuring, 42, 43–44
  measuring, 132–134
Treatment utility of assessment, consideration of, 129
Trendlines, illustrated, 173, 181–182
Trends, graphing and analyzing, 170–175, 180–182, 599
Trial-based FA, 225
Trials to criterion, defined, 137
"True" reversal design, selection and use of, 188
Typical analysis process, 14, 16–20

## U

Unchaining, defined and illustrated, 334–335
Unconditioned motivating operations (UMOs), illustrated, 352
Unconditioned reinforcers. *See* Primary reinforcers
Unconditioned responses (URs), in respondent conditioning, 27–28, 29f
Unconditioned stimuli (USs)
  aversive. *See* Aversive stimuli
  in respondent conditioning, 27–28, 29f
Unit of analysis, for behavior recording, 158–159
United States Department of Education
  on evidence-based practices, 179–180
  on FBAs, 206
  on goal mandates, 63n
  on problematic behavior, 639
  on restraint procedures, 692, 694
  on seclusion procedures, 690
Unrelated variables, and experimental design, 179

## V

Valid measures
  defined, 128–129
  selection of, 130–131
Validity
  factors influencing, 133–134
  in program design, 575–577
  scheduling and, 157
Variability, graphing and analyzing, 170–175, 180–182
Variable-interval (VI) schedules
  advantages and disadvantages, 532–533
  consistency in, 529–530, 532
  defined and illustrated, 524
  extinction with, 531–532, 610–611
  matching law and, 541
  response rates in, 525–527
  summary table, 545t, 571t
Variable ratio (VR) schedules
  consistency in, 508–509
  defined and illustrated, 504–505
  extinction with, 610–611
  response rates, 506–508
  summary table, 545t, 569t
Variable time schedules
  for noncontingent reinforcement, 645–646
  summary table, 545t
Variables, defined and illustrated, 576b
Varied practice, defined, 392–393
Verbal behavior
  augmentative strategies, 444–446
  B. F. Skinner's analysis of, 426–428
  critical skills, 448–449
  defined, 425
  duplics in, 428–430
  intraverbals in, 438–442
  listener behavior, 441–444
  manding, 430–436
  Relational Frame Theory, 446–449
  tacting, 436–438

teaching summary table, 449t–453t
*Verbal Behavior Milestones Assessment and Placement Program (VB-MAPP)*, 61, 444
*Verbal Behavior* (Skinner), 426
Verbal operants, defined and illustrated, 426–428
Verbal relating, defined and illustrated, 447
Verbally-governed behavior, defined and illustrated, 399–401
Verification (V), experimental control and, 180–182
Vertical-phase change lines, in graphing, 162, 171f
Video modeling
  confidentiality and, 759, 761
  in generalization promotion, 493
  in reducing behaviors, 650
  use of, 410–413
Video self-modeling, defined and illustrated, 412–413
*The Vineland Adaptive Behavior Scales: Third Edition*, 60
Virginia Strategic Plan for Pedestrian Safety (2005–2010), 60
Vision, of BACB, 752
Voluntariness, defined, 77

## W

*Wëlsch v. Likins* (1974), 696–697
*Who Killed My Daddy: A Behavioral Safety Fable* (Sulzer-Azaroff), xxix
Whole-interval DRO
  defined and illustrated, 662–665
  momentary DRO versus, 666–667
  summary table, 679t
Whole-interval time sampling
  defined, 140
  selection of, 141–144, 151t
Whole-task teaching method, chaining use of, 319, 323
Withdrawal of materials, defined and illustrated, 687
Withdrawal of treatment condition, in withdrawal design, 184
Withdrawal (return-to-baseline) design
  advantages and disadvantages, 190–191
  illustrated, 183, 185–188
  selecting and using, 183–186
  summary table, 596t
  variations, 188–190
Within-stimulus prompts, defined and illustrated, 468–471
Wolf, Montrose, as behavior analysis pioneer, 6, 7
Wyatt vs. Stickney (1972), 274, 696, 757

## X

X-axis, in graphing, 161–163

## Y

Y-axis, in graphing, 161–163

## Z

Zone system, illustrated, 146